THE ROUGH GUIDE TO
ANDALUCÍA

This tenth edition written and researched by
Marc Di Duca and Tim Hannigan

ROUGH
GUIDES

Contents

A NOTE TO READERS

At Rough Guides, we always strive to bring you the most up-to-date information. This book was produced during a period of continuing uncertainty caused by the Covid-19 pandemic, so please note that content is more subject to change than usual. We recommend checking the latest restrictions and official guidance.

Introduction to
Andalucía

Andalucía is the southernmost territory of Spain and the part of the Iberian Peninsula that is most quintessentially Spanish. The popular image of Spain as a land of bullfights, flamenco, sherry and ruined castles derives from this spectacularly beautiful region. The influences that have washed over Andalucía since the first paintings were etched on cave walls here more than 25,000 years ago are many – Phoenicians, Carthaginians, Greeks, Romans, Visigoths and Vandals all came and left their mark. And the most influential invaders of all, the Moors, who ruled the region for seven centuries and named it *al-Andalus*, have left an enduring imprint on Andalucían culture and customs.

The heartland of Andalucía is the fertile valley of the mighty **Río Guadalquivir**, flowing across the region from its source in the Cazorla mountains in the northeast through the magnificent cities of Córdoba and Seville, before draining into the marshes and wetlands of the Coto de Doñana National Park and the Gulf of Cádiz. North of this great artery rise the undulating hills of the **Sierra Morena**, from where was gouged the mineral wealth – silver, lead and tin – sought by successive waves of invaders from Phoenicians to Romans. The **Moors**, who arrived in the eighth century, were more interested in harvesting Andalucía's natural wealth and turned the region into an orchard rich in olives, citrus fruits, almonds, saffron, figs and vines – still the major products of the land today. In 1492 the Christian Reconquista, after centuries of struggle, finally succeeded in wresting Spain from its Moorish occupiers, the victors symbolically planting their flags on the towers of the Alhambra, the emblematic monument of Andalucía.

The **Moorish legacy** is the most striking feature of Andalucía today, not only in the dazzling historical monuments such as those of Seville, Córdoba and Granada, but also in the whitewashed houses of many of its smaller medieval towns such as Ronda or the flat-roofed villages of Las Alpujarras. The Moorish love of water is to be seen in the pleasure gardens of the Alhambra, and the typical Andalucían patio – tiled, plant-bedecked courtyards, often with a central fountain – is another Arab legacy, as are the ubiquitous wrought-iron window grilles which lend character to any village street. The dances and music of **flamenco**, while probably not of Moorish origin, display the soul of Andalucía and can be an electrifying spectacle when dancers in brilliantly coloured dresses drill their heels into the floorboards in a frenzy of emotion or, in *cante jondo* (deep song), turn the art form into a blues-style lament. The Muslim influence on speech and vocabulary, a stoical fatalism in the face of adversity and an obsession with the drama of death – publicly displayed in the spectacle of the bullfight – are also facets of the modern Andalucían character. Contrastingly, the *andaluzes* also love nothing more than a party, and the colour and sheer energy of the region's countless and legendary fiestas – always in proudly worn traditional flamenco costume – make them among the most exciting in the world. The **romerías**, wild and semireligious pilgrimages to honour local saints at country shrines, are yet another excuse for a celebration.

Despite the region's abundant natural wealth, poverty is widespread, a legacy of the repressive **latifundia** landholding system of large estates with absentee landlords. The Christian monarchs who ousted the Moorish farmers doled out the conquered land to the Church, the military orders and individual nobles. These new proprietors often had little interest in the land or personal contact with those who worked their estates,

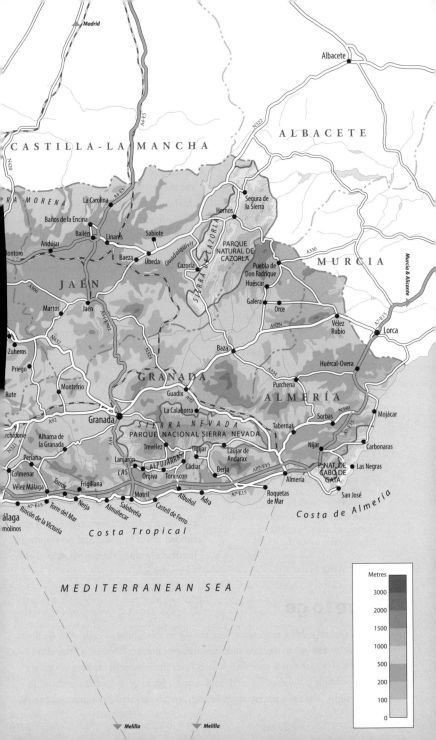

often leaving an overseer in charge, and an atmosphere of resentment built up towards the wretched pay and miserable conditions that this system entailed.

It is perhaps not surprising that many inhabitants emigrated to find work in northern Spain or abroad, or that anarchism found many converts among the desperate *braceros* (farmhands) of Andalucía before the Spanish Civil War. Two percent of the landowners still possess sixty percent of the land today, and in the 1960s alone a million Andalucíans left their native region to seek a better life elsewhere.

While life for many in the countryside remains hard, new industries, particularly tourism, have had a major impact on the region's **economy**. Apart from the petrochemical industry around Algeciras, mining in Huelva and aircraft manufacture in Seville, Andalucía has little heavy industry and those not employed in agriculture are usually working in fishing or tourism. One growth industry these days is the servicing of the population of mainly northern European emigrants who have come to the south of Spain to live, retire or do business. Now numbering close to a million, these expatriates have funded much building and development, particularly along the coastal strip of the Costa del Sol.

Where to go

Andalucía's manageable size makes it easy to take in something of each of its elements – inland cities, extensive coastline and mountainous sierras – even on a brief visit. The region's eight provinces take their names from the **provincial capitals**, which are both compellingly individual cultural centres and vibrant cosmopolitan beehives in their own right. The most important is **Seville**, Andalucía's stylishly exuberant capital

city, home of *Carmen* and all the clichés of the Spanish south with beautiful *barrios* (quarters), major Christian and Moorish monuments, fine museums and extraordina **festivals** at Easter and at the April *feria*. Close behind comes **Granada**, whose Alhamb palace has a fair claim to being the most sensual building in Europe, while in **Córdob** the exquisite Mezquita – a former mosque – is another breathtakingly beautiful building left behind by the Moors. Coastal **Málaga** boasts a fine Moorish fort as well a clutch of splendid art museums including an outstanding one dedicated to its most famous son, **Picasso**, and further down the coast sea-locked **Cádiz** is one of the most atmospheric cities of the south and Andalucía's seafood capital. While they do not always attract the attention lavished on their more immediately appealing neighbours, the cities of **Huelva**, **Jaén** and **Almería** all have sights well worthy of a visit. Inland, small-scale towns and villages, once grand, now hardly significant, are an Andalucían speciality. **Baeza** and **Úbeda** in Jaén are remarkable treasure houses of Renaissance architecture, while **Ronda** and the **pueblos blancos** (White Towns) to the west are among the most picturesque hill villages in Spain.

Not that Andalucía is predominantly about cities and monuments. Few places in the world can boast such a wealth of **natural wonders** in so compact an area. The 400km-long Río Guadalquivir, which crosses and irrigates the region, reaches the sea at the dune-fringed beaches and *marismas* (wetlands/marshes) of the **Coto de Doñana National Park**, Europe's largest and most important wildlife sanctuary. To the east and

ANCIENT ANDALUCÍA

Andalucía's rich and varied history has resulted in a great number of ancient sites, many unique in Europe. The dolmens at **Antequera** and the third-millennium BC settlement at **Los Millares** in Almería are remarkable vestiges from the prehistoric age. Roman sites are scattered across the region, but the excavated towns at **Baelo Claudia** near Tarifa and **Itálica** near Seville, plus a fascinating necropolis at **Carmona**, are worth making a special effort to get to. Two sites in superb locations are the Roman town of **Turóbriga** near Aroche in the Sierra de Aracena, and **Ocuri**, another township atop a bluff to the north of Ubrique in Cádiz, while one sensational discovery of recent years is the Roman villa at **Almedinilla**, complete with a spectacular cascade feature in its dining room.

towering above Granada are the peaks of the **Sierra Nevada National Park**, snowcapped for most of the year, and only thirty or so kilometres from the sweltering coastal beaches. Nestling in the folds of the same mountains are the valleys of the **Alpujarras**, a wildly picturesque region dotted with dozens of mountain villages, many of them little changed since Moorish times. Further east come the gulch-ridden badlands and lunar landscapes of Almería's **deserts**, sought out by film-makers and by astronomers for the clearest skies in Europe.

Andalucía's rural areas are a paradise for hikers and naturalists. The Sierra Nevada and Las Alpujarras are excellent places for **trekking**, as are the densely wooded hills of the **Sierra de Cazorla** and the **Sierra Morena** – including the latter's less well-known offshoot, the **Sierra de Aracena**, to the north of Huelva. The region also has a score of other *parques naturales* (natural parks), all located in areas of great natural beauty and detailed throughout the Guide.

On the **coast** it can be easy to despair. Extending to the west of **Málaga** is the **Costa del Sol**, Europe's most developed coastline, with its beaches hidden behind a remorseless density of concrete hotels and apartment complexes. This is Andalucía's summer playground, famous for its in-your-face brashness and the unlimited nightlife on offer at every resort. Despite the fact that many places such as **Torremolinos** have given themselves a thorough makeover with new theme parks and improved facilities, the Costa del Sol's appeal is not to everyone's taste. Thankfully though, even here a more authentic Andalucía is still to be found if you're prepared to seek it out: go a few kilometres inland and you'll encounter the timeless Spain of high sierras, white village and country fiestas.

Alternatively, travel further both east and west along the coast and you'll find some of the best beaches in all of Spain: the **Costa de la Luz** to the west, where Atlantic breakers wash the white-sand strands of **Tarifa**, **Conil de la Frontera** and **Isla Cristina**; in the centre at the less frenzied resorts of **Nerja** and **Almuñecar** on the **Costa Tropical**; and to the east along the **Costa de Almería** where appealing resorts like **San José**, **Agua Amarga** and **Mojácar** all hark back to a pre-Costa del Sol tranquillity.

Wherever you go in Andalucía you can't fail to notice the *andaluzes'* infectious enthusiasm for life. This is always ebulliently evident in the countless celebrations, **ferias** and **fiestas** that happen almost daily at one town or village or another throughout the summer months. But at other times too, and even in the smallest towns, there will always be good food, drink and a surprising range of nightlife and entertainment to be enjoyed. And there are few greater pleasures than joining the regulars at a local bar to wind down over a glass of **fino** (dry sherry from Jerez) while nibbling **tapas** – one of Andalucía's great inventions.

When to go

In terms of climate the question is mainly one of how much heat you can take. During the **summer** months of July and August temperatures of over 40°C (104°F) on the coast are normal and inland they can rise even higher in cities such as Seville, generally reckoned to be the hottest in Spain. The solution here is to follow the natives and get about in the relative cool of the mornings and late afternoons, finding somewhere shady to rest up as the city roasts in the midday furnace. The major resorts are busy in July and packed in August (the Spanish holiday month) when prices also are at their highest.

Better times to visit are the **spring** months of April, May and early June when lower temperatures combine with a greener landscape awash with wild flowers. **Autumn** is good, too, although by late October much of the coastal landscape looks parched and the resorts have begun to wind down; in hilly and mountainous areas, however, such as the sierras of Cazorla, Nevada and Aracena and the high valleys of Las Alpujarras, the splendours of autumn can be especially scenic. The **winter** months – particularly December and January – can often be dismal and wet as well as cold at high altitude. However, after the extended drought of the 1990s was followed by some unusually wet winters in the first decade of the new century, normal weather patterns have tended to be thrown into some confusion. The winter, of course, is a good time to visit the museums and monuments of Seville, Málaga, Córdoba and Granada when they are far less crowded and – should you be lucky with the weather – the cities themselves can look wonderful, too. The desert province of Almería sees only one day of rain a year on average and in winter has many days of perfectly clear visibility.

uthor picks

r hard-travelling authors have visited every
ner of Andalucía, from the cool mountains of
e Sierra Nevada and the lush Coto de Doñana
tional Park to the sweltering deserts of Almería.
ese are some of their favourite personal
ndalucían experiences.

me for tapas Andalucía's tapas bars are
e best in Spain. Top-notch bars include *Casa
lbino* (see page 171), *Bar Maestro* (see page
30), *Sociedad Plateros* (see page 368) and *Casa
uga* (see page 499).

Moorish magic The Moors left Andalucía with
wealth of fabulous monuments ranging from
Córdoba's Mezquita (see page 353) and Jaén's
emarkable baths complex (see page 399), to the
astonishing Alhambra (see page 432) in Granada.

Gorgeous gardens Another hangover from
Moorish times, Andalucía has some of the most
delightful gardens in Spain. Málaga's Jardín
Botánico La Concepción (see page 72),
Córdoba's Jardín Botánico (see page 360) and
the Alhambra's Generalife (see page 437) are
sublime sanctuaries away from the city sprawl.

Great hikes Andalucía's stunning natural parks
are just the place to put those boots to work.
Three of the best are Sierra de Grazalema (see
page 214), Sierra de Aracena (see page 331)
and Cazorla (see page 418).

Fresh from the sea Feasting on fish and
crustaceans in sight of the sea is a top treat.
Three of the best places to do it are *La Ola* (see
page 510), *Casa Bigote* (see page 171) and *La
Escollera* (see page 117).

Going underground Los Refugios, Almería's
civil war air raid shelters (see page 497), the
Paleolithic Cueva de los Murciélagos (see page
383) and Cueva de la Pileta (see page 132) are
three sights that make leaving the light of day
behind more than worthwhile.

Deserted beaches Among scores of candidates
our votes go to Playa Cuesta de Maneli (see page
319), Playa Camarinal (see page 193) and the
Cala d'En Medio (see page 512).

> Our author recommendations don't end
> here. We've flagged up our favourite places
> – a perfectly sited hotel, an atmospheric
> café, a special restaurant – throughout the
> Guide, highlighted with the ★ symbol.

TAPAS

JARDÍN BOTÁNICO LA CONCEPCIÓN, MALAGA

25

things not to miss

It's not possible to see everything Andalucía has to offer in one trip – and we don't suggest you try. What follows, in no particular order, is a selection of the region's highlights, including outstanding monuments and natural wonders, vibrant festivals and delicious food. All entries are colour-coded by chapter and have a page reference to take you straight into the Guide, where you can find out more.

1 ALCÁZAR, SEVILLE
Page 251
This fabulous Mudéjar palace, with enchanting gardens and dazzling *artesonado* ceilings, tiles and stuccowork, is one of the glories of the city.

2 RONDA
Page 124
Ringed by mountains and perched astride the yawning El Tajo gorge, irresistible Ronda is one of the most dramatically sited towns in Andalucía.

3 HIKING
Pages 88 & 465
Andalucía is prime hiking territory. There are great walks to be had in the Sierra Nevada National Park and in the region's 24 natural parks, including El Torcal in Málaga province.

4 MINI HOLLYWOOD
Page 520
Clint Eastwood, Yul Brynner and Steve McQueen all faced gunfighters on the streets of Mini Hollywood in the Almerian desert, where the film sets of many famous Westerns are preserved.

5 GIBRALTAR
Page 206
Beneath a towering rock, this colonial hangover with its pubs, sterling currency and Barbary apes makes a bizarre contrast with the rest of the region.

6 FLAMENCO
Page 547
The soul of Andalucía, flamenco dance, music and song express the *alegría y dolor* (happiness and pain) of *andaluz* life.

7 ENCIERRO
Page 231
No village fiesta is complete without an *encierro* (bull run), when a fierce *toro bravo* roams the streets looking for an encounter with anyone who's brave enough – though every year bulls and people get hurt, or even killed.

8 ALHAMBRA, GRANADA
Page 432
One of the most sensual palaces ever built, the magical Alhambra is the pinnacle of Moorish architectural splendour in Spain.

9 MEZQUITA, CÓRDOBA
Page 353
Nothing can prepare you for the beauty of Córdoba's medieval mosque, one of the greatest Islamic buildings of all time.

10 PARQUE NACIONAL DE COTO DE DOÑANA
Page 313
The vast wilderness of Spain's biggest wildlife reserve is home to exotic flamingos, imperial eagles and the endangered Spanish lynx.

11 CABO DE GATA, ALMERÍA
Page 506
The Cabo de Gata Natural Park is famous for its rugged coastline, salt marshes and birdlife including storks, egrets and magnificent pink flamingos.

12 SEVILLE CATHEDRAL
Page 243
The world's largest Gothic church is a treasure house full of artistic riches. Its astonishingly beautiful Moorish minaret, the Giralda, is now its bell tower, and can be climbed for a stunning view.

13 THE ALBAICÍN, GRANADA
Page 441
Granada's atmospheric old Moorish quarter stands on the Sacromonte hill. Its sinuous alleys and cobblestoned streets are a delight to explore.

14 LAS ALPUJARRAS
Page 466
Ancient cobble-streeted villages are situated in a dramatically beautiful area of woodland and gushing mountain streams.

15 TAPAS BARS
Page 38
Dine Andalucían style, sampling plates of delicious tapas in a variety of atmospheric bars.

16 SIERRA DE GRAZALEMA
The pretty white village of Grazalema lends its name to the surrounding *parque natural*, where soaring limestone peaks are swathed in forests of oak and fir.

17 MUSEO BELLAS ARTES, SEVILLE
An eighteenth-century former convent provides a magnificent setting for Seville's fine arts museum, filled with major works.

18 CÁDIZ
Steeped in history, sea-locked Cádiz is one of the great cities of the Spanish south and serves up the best seafood in Andalucía.

19 CAZORLA NATURAL PARK
Andalucía's largest natural park is a vast area of soaring peaks and forested valleys inhabited by an abundance of wildlife. Hilltop Segura de la Sierra is its most dramatically sited village.

20 EL ROCÍO
On the edge of the Doñana National Park and surrounded by wetlands, this village's church holds a venerated image of the Virgin, the focus for one of the most extraordinary pilgrimages in Spain.

21 MEDINA AZAHARA
Page 369
The ruins of Caliph Abd ar-Rahman III's palace-city, named after his favourite wife, az-Zahra, evoke the splendour of the Cordoban caliphate.

22 PLAZA DE VÁZQUEZ DE MOLINA, ÚBEDA
Page 409
Along with nearby Baeza, Úbeda has a cornucopia of ravishing Renaissance buildings and this square, at its heart, is one of the most beautiful in Andalucía.

23 SEMANA SANTA
Page 44
Nowhere does Semana Santa quite like the big cities such as Seville and Málaga, but small-town affairs like those at Arcos de la Frontera have their own charm.

24 PRIEGO DE CÓRDOBA
Page 384
A jewel of Córdoba province, Priego has a collection of spectacular Baroque churches and a flower-bedecked old Moorish quarter, the Barrio de la Villa.

25 MUSEO PICASSO, MÁLAGA
Page 68
Málaga's most famous son has a spectacular museum in the city's old quarter displaying hundreds of his works.

Itineraries

Whether you want to take in a few of the major high points, feast on Andalucía's best culinary treats or focus your trip on some truly special places to stay, these itineraries – each of which also takes you through some of the region's most dramatic scenery – will lead the way. You'll need a couple of weeks to cover each route in detail, but it's possible to do part of one in a week or so, perhaps mixing and matching it with sections of the others.

THE BEST OF ANDALUCÍA

❶ **Málaga** As a major transport hub, Málaga is the obvious place to start, but it's also worth lingering to enjoy this vibrant coastal city. See page 60

❷ **Ronda** Sited astride a towering gorge is the queen of Andalucía's white towns, with a magnificent eighteenth-century bridge and old town. See page 124

❸ **Seville** The essence of all things *andaluz*, with a stunning cathedral, Moorish Alcázar and atmospheric old quarter. See page 242

❹ **Córdoba** A must-see destination, featuring one of the world's greatest Moorish buildings, the Mezquita, at its heart. See page 348

❺ **Baeza and Úbeda** These twin Renaissance architectural jewels are filled with a wealth of monuments sculpted out of honey-tinted stone. See pages 402 & 407

❻ **Cazorla Natural Park** A stunning array of wildlife inhabits the rugged mountains, gorges and forested valleys of Cazorla. See page 416

❼ **Granada** Overlooked by the seductive Alhambra, the historic city of Granada is one of Spain's most compelling attractions. See page 428

❽ **Almuñécar** The Costa Tropical's main resort has great beaches and plenty of places to eat, drink and dance the night away. See page 502

A TASTE OF ANDALUCÍA

❶ **Villaluenga del Rosario** This Cádiz mountain village is famous for its prize-winning goat's cheese. See page 223

❷ **Jerez** The home of fino and brandy, where you can stop off to visit a bodega, taste their blends and buy some to take home. See page 172

❸ **Jabugo** The sensational and incomparable taste of *jamón de bellota* can be sampled at producers' outlets in the village. See page 338

❹ **Rute** This pleasant country town is famed throughout Spain for its anís (aniseed liqueur); sample it at *Bodega Machequito*. See page 379

Create your own itinerary with Rough Guides. Whether you're after adventure or a family-friendly holiday, we have a trip for you, with all the activities you enjoy doing and the sights you want to see. All our trips are devised by local experts who get the most out of the destination. Visit **www.roughguides.com/trips** to chat with one of our travel agents.

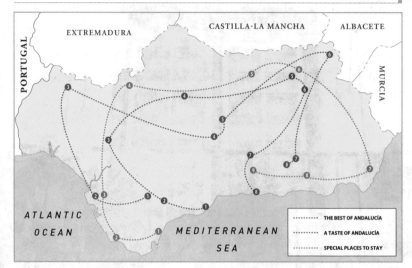

❺ Baena Córdoba province's olive oil has been prized since Roman times – you can see why by tasting it at the Núñez de Prado mill. See page 381

❻ Segura de la Sierra The Sierra de Cazorla's most stunningly sited village, clinging to a hilltop, produces another famed olive oil with its own *denominación de origen*. See page 418

❼ Trevélez Tucked away in the mountains, the highest village in Spain is the home of Granada province's famed *jamón de Trevélez*. See page 474

❽ Lanjarón The mineral springs here have attracted cure seekers since ancient times – at the village's spa you can taste the waters straight from the mountain. See page 468

SPECIAL PLACES TO STAY

❶ Convento la Almoraima, Castellar de la Frontera Just above the Bay of Algeciras, this is a magical hotel housed inside a seventeenth-century convent with a stunning patio and imposing Florentine tower. See page 204

❷ La Casa del Califa, Vejer de la Frontera Reflecting the town's Moorish origins, the enchanting *Califa* occupies a partly Moorish house and has magnificent views towards the coast far below. See page 188

❸ La Casa Grande, Arcos de la Frontera Perched on a clifftop, this former *casa señorial* has a spectacular columned patio and sensational views across the *vega* from a terrace bar. See page 234

❹ Hospedería La Cartuja, Cazalla de la Sierra The gatehouse of a former Carthusian monastery has been transformed into a charming hotel, while the evocative ruin of the fifteenth-century monastery behind contains an art gallery. See page 343

❺ Los Pinos, Andújar Secreted away in the densely wooded Parque Natural Sierra de Andújar – home to the threatened Iberian lynx – this is a very pleasant *hotel rural* with villas arranged around a pool and plenty of good hiking nearby. See page 394

❻ Palacio de la Rambla, Ubeda This elegant Renaissance *casa palacio* is the last word in understated taste, furnished with artworks and featuring a dreamy patio. See page 412

❼ Hotel Rodalquilar, Rodalquilar In a former gold-mining village in Almería's desert, this modern spa-inn is focused on a sunken courtyard with lofty palms and makes a great base to explore a dramatic gulch-riven landscape. See page 511

❽ Alquería de Morayma, Cadiar The *cortijo* (farmhouse) of an extensive estate is now a superb hotel. Watch its organic farm in action, producing the wine, cheese and olive oil served in its restaurant. See page 479

❾ La Seguiriya, Alhama de Granada The amiable proprietors – he a former flamenco singer, she a wonderful chef – make a stay in this charming hotel-restaurant very special and the perfect end to any Andalucía trip. See page 463

TRADITIONAL FLAMENCO DRESSES

Basics

Getting there

Flying is the quickest way of getting to Andalucía, with by far the widest choice of routes being from the UK and Ireland. Málaga is Andalucía's busiest airport, though the summer holiday trade to the areas beyond the costas, and the rapid growth of European budget airlines, has opened up regional airports right across Andalucía from Seville and Jerez in the west, to Granada and Almería in the east. It's also possible to take the (indirect) train from the UK to Andalucía, and should you want to drive (a bit more of an adventure) there are several routes.

Air, **train and ferry fares** are seasonal, at their highest in summer (June to end September) and around Christmas/New Year and Easter week. You should always book as far in advance as possible to get the best deals.

towards the summer holiday season, but flights depart on a regular basis from regional airports all around the UK.

The widest range of **scheduled flights** is with the merged services from Iberia (wiberia.com) and British Airways (wba.com), direct from London Gatwick or Heathrow to Málaga and Seville. You'll also be able to arrange add-on connections to London from regional English airports such as Manchester or Newcastle, or from Scotland. Special offers mean prices start at a reasonable level, though again a typical late-booking summer rate will cost you considerably more.

From Ireland, you can fly with Iberia from Dublin to Madrid, or with Aer Lingus (waerlingus.com) from Dublin or Cork to up to eight Spanish airports (including Málaga). Ryanair also connects Dublin and Shannon with Málaga, plus Seville and Almería. Prices are highly flexible, though these rise sharply for last-minute bookings or to popular summer destinations.

Flights from the UK and Ireland

Flight time to Andalucía is two to three hours, depending on the route, and usually the cheapest flights are with the no-frills **budget airlines** such as easyJet (weasyjet.com) and Ryanair (wryanair. com), who between them fly from over twenty regional airports across the UK, including Northern Ireland, direct to destinations all over Andalucía. London flights tend to depart from Stansted or Luton; other budget airlines, including Jet2 (from Leeds/ Bradford, Manchester, Newcastle, and Edinburgh; wjet2.com). **Fares** for flights on all routes start low – sometimes passengers essentially only pay the airport taxes. However, book last minute in the summer and you can expect to pay considerably more,.

For flights to the **Costa del Sol**, you can also check the websites of holiday and charter companies such as First Choice (wfirstchoice.co.uk), Thomas Cook (wflythomascook.com) and TUI (wtui.co.uk/flight). You might not get the rock-bottom deals of the budget airlines, as schedules and prices are geared

Flights from the US and Canada

The widest choice of scheduled flights **from the United States** to Spain is with Iberia (wiberia. com), which flies direct, nonstop from New York to Madrid or Barcelona, and from Miami and Chicago to Madrid. Journey time (typically overnight) is between 7hr 10min and 8hr 30min, depending on the route. The advantage of flying with Iberia is that it offers connecting flights to six airports throughout Andalucía, which can be very good value if booked with your transatlantic flight. Other airlines offering Spanish routes (some on a code-share basis with Iberia or other airlines), include American Airlines (waa.com) and United (wunited.com).

You can also fly to Spain with airlines such as Air France, British Airways, KLM, Lufthansa or TAP Air Portugal, which tend to fly via their respective European hubs – in which case, you can add three to four hours to your total travel time, depending on the connection.

At the time of writing flights from Canada were still at a post-Covid low, with no direct flights from any

---

A BETTER KIND OF TRAVEL

At Rough Guides we are passionately committed to travel. We believe it helps us understand the world we live in and the people we share it with – and of course tourism is vital to many developing economies. But the scale of modern tourism has also damaged some places irreparably, and climate change is accelerated by most forms of transport, especially flying. We encourage all our authors to consider the carbon footprint of the journeys they make in the course of researching our guides.

Canadian airport. If this continues to be the case, flying with Air Canada (Ⓦ aircanada.com) or other international airlines to another European destination, then taking a connecting flight to Spain will be your only option.

Flights from Australia, New Zealand and South Africa

There are no direct flights to Spain **from Australia or New Zealand**, but many airlines offer through-tickets with their partners via their European or Asian hubs. Flights via Asia are generally the cheaper option, but fares don't vary as much between airlines as you might think, and in the end you'll be basing your choice on things like flight timings, routes and possible stop-offs on the way. If you're seeing Spain as part of a wider European trip, you might want to aim first for the UK, since there's a good choice of cheap flights to Spain once you are there. Or consider a Round-the-World fare, with most basic options able to offer Madrid or Barcelona as standard stopovers.

Package holidays, tours and city breaks

The basic, mass-market **package holidays** to the traditional resorts on the Costa del Sol and elsewhere are not to everyone's taste, but bargains can be found online or at any UK high street travel agent, starting with very cheap seven-night flight-and-hotel package deals. There are often really good deals for families, either in hotels or in self-catering apartments, although the time of year you visit can increase prices significantly (notoriously, school holidays are always most expensive). The vast majority of tour operators to Spain seem to have survived the Covid-19 hiatus, something of a miracle when you look at some other European destinations.

A huge number of **specialist tour operators** offer a wider range of **activity holidays** or tours, from hiking in the Alpujarras to touring the artistic highlights of Andalucía. We've given a flavour of what's available in the reviews at the end of this section, but the options are almost endless. Prices vary wildly depending on the quality of accommodation offered and whether the tours are fully inclusive or not. Many cycle or hiking tours, for example, can either be guided or done on a more independent (and cheaper) self-guided basis. Spanish-based tour operators offer some of the more interesting, off-the-beaten-track options (but for these you'll usually have to arrange your own flights to Spain), while some foreign-based operators also tend to quote for their holidays exclusive of airfares.

Popular Andalucían **city break** destinations include Seville, Córdoba and Granada. The cheapest deals start with three-day (two-night) breaks including return flights, airport transfers and B&B in a centrally located one-, two- or three-star hotel. Adding extra nights or upgrading your hotel is possible, too, usually at a fairly reasonable cost. The bigger US operators, such as American Express and Delta Vacations, can also easily organize short city breaks to Spain on a flight-and-hotel basis.

Other package deals worth considering are **fly-drive** offers, where you'll get a flight, accommodation and car rental arranged through your tour operator. Some companies specialize in villas and apartments, or off-the-beaten-track farmhouses and the like, while on other holiday packages you can tour the country's historic *paradores*, with car rental included.

Specialist tour operators

BACKPACKER TRAVEL

Busabout UK Ⓦ busabout.com. The European backpacker bus service offers a seven-day Spain/Portugal bus tour (basically Andalucía and the Portuguese Algarve); prices include hostel accommodation, guides, transport, surf lessons and the like, all aimed at a young party crowd.

BIRDWATCHING

Limosa Holidays Ⓦ limosaholidays.co.uk. Birdwatching tours to the Straits of Gibraltar with some trips following migrating birds into Morocco. See the great spring and autumn migrations accompanied by knowledgeable guides.

Spainbirds Ⓦ spainbirds.com. This Madrid-based birdwatching tour company don't run any scheduled tours to Andalucía, but can organise private trips anywhere in Spain.

CYCLING

Bravobike Ⓦ bravobike.com. A variety of cycle tours across the region, including a guided eight-day trip taking in Seville, Córdoba and Granada, staying at four-star hotels.

Easy Rider Tours US Ⓦ easyridertours.com. Guided cycling and sightseeing tours in Andalucía (and elsewhere). One week-long trip takes in the White Towns. Tours are all-inclusive (except airfares) and are fully supported.

Explore! UK Ⓦ explore.co.uk. Walking and cycling holidays in the Sierra de Aracena, the zone around Gibraltar and Tarifa, plus elsewhere.

Iberocycle Ⓦ iberocycle.com. An English-run, Spain-based company specializing in supported or self-guided cycling tours, offering White Towns, Moorish villages and tours in the provinces of Córdoba and Granada.

Switchbacks Ⓦ switch-backs.com Expertly guided, partially uplifted mountain bike holidays based out of Malaga in the winter, and Bubion up in Las Alpujarras through the summer, both on an excellent range of enduro-style downhill trails. Accommodation and transfers included.

DANCE

Escuela de Carmen Cuevas Granada Ⓦ carmencuevas.com. Reputable dance school teaching beginners and advanced courses in flamenco. They can assist with finding accommodation, but you will need to sort out your own flights.

Flamenco Dance Courses in Seville. Book through the rather ironically named Not In The Guidebooks (Ⓦ notintheguidebooks. com) for flamenco dance and guitar courses that can also be linked to language courses (120min per day technique/dance). They can help with accommodation (not included), but you'll need to arrange your own flights.

FOOD AND DRINK

A Taste of Spain Ⓦ atasteofspain.com. Gourmet Iberian culinary tours, with a six night, all-inclusive Andalucía option focusing on fino in Jerez, *jamón serrano* in Jabugo and olive oil in the provinces of Córdoba and Jaén, with tastings, meals and cookery lessons.

Arblaster & Clarke UK Ⓦ arblasterandclarke.com. The most notable wine-tour specialist, with quality all-inclusive trips to all of Spain's wine-producing regions, including a tour of bodegas in the sherry triangle.

HISTORY, ART AND CULTURE

Abercrombie and Kent UK & US Ⓦ abercrombiekent.co.uk. Pricey, upmarket independent or fully escorted tours, taking in cities like Córdoba, Granada and Seville, including luxury hotels and a private guide for monument visits.

Kirker Travel UK Ⓦ kirkerholidays.com. Short breaks and holiday packages in Andalucían towns and cities. Their seven-night tour of Moorish Seville, Córdoba and Granada comes particularly well recommended

Martin Randall Travel UK Ⓦ martinrandall.com. Small-group cultural tours to Seville, Granada, Córdoba and elsewhere, led by experts on art, archeology or music. Several departures a year on various trips and themes. About as far away from the classic Spain beach holiday as you'll get

HORSERIDING

Fantasia Adventure Holidays Ⓦ fantasiaadventureholidays. com. British-run company offering riding breaks on the Costa de la Luz, from full-board weekends to week-long holidays. Prices don't include flights to Spain.

Sierra Trails Ⓦ spain-horse-riding.com. Reliable Alpujarras-based company specializing in horse trekking holidays. Prices include transfers, but not flights.

PAINTING

Andrew John Studio Ⓦ paintingholidays.com. Watercolour painting courses run by professional British expatriate artist. Based

in a small village in the Axarquía, with all-inclusive seven-night holidays including transfers, but excluding flights.

Paint-Andalucía Spain Ⓦ paint-andalucia.com. British-run (with Spanish and German tutors) painting courses based in Grazalema, Cabo de Gata and Torrox. Eight-day courses include accommodation, food and airport transfers, but flights are extra.

SURFING

Nomadsurfers Ⓦ nomadsurfers.com. This long-established, international surf tour organiser runs popular surf camps across Spain and on the Canary Islands, and provides a great way to get into the sport under the watchful eye of experienced tutors.

Oceano Surf School Ⓦ www.surf-school-spain.com. Surf camps and short-break surfing-course holidays based at El Palmar and Conil on the Costa de la Luz. Prices include accommodation and tuition, but exclude flights.

WALKING, CYCLING AND ADVENTURE

Walk Andalucia Ⓦ walk-andalucia. Locally-based, expert hiking company with scheduled guided walks year round. Can also arrange accommodation and transfers but not flights.

Exodus Travels UK, Ⓦ exodus.co.uk. Walking and cycling in Andalucía, as well as cultural and sightseeing trips. There's a wide range of options at all prices.

Inntravel UK Ⓦ inntravel.co.uk. Experienced and reliable company offering self-guided cycling tours and walking tours (Sierras de Aracena and Grazalema, White Towns, Las Alpujarras, Cabo de Gata and more) on which your baggage is moved to the next destination.

Naturaventura Spain, Ⓦ natur-aventura.com. Based in the white village of Villaluenga in the Sierra de Grazalema this outfit offers a range of activities from caving and canyoning to kayaking. Insurance and expert guides included.

Ramblers Worldwide Holidays UK Ⓦ ramblersholidays.co.uk. Long-established tour operator, offering all-inclusive walking and hiking holidays throughout Spain, including Andalucía. Prices usually include flights and half-board at all accommodation.

Walkers' Britain UK Ⓦ walkersbritain.co.uk. Despite the recently changed name (previously Sherpa Expeditions), this tour operator actually offers self-guided trekking in the Sierra de Nevada, the Alpujarras and the Sierra de Aracena. Prices include B&B, but exclude flights.

Wildside Holidays Ⓦ wildsideholidays.com. Guided explorations of the Sierra de Grazalema. Seven-day guided holidays with expert guides including accommodation, breakfast and picnics, with transfers included, but no flights.

Trains

Travelling **by train from the UK to Andalucía** is just about a viable option, although not particularly popular. With a total journey time from London of around thirteen hours to Madrid, plus an extra two hours (the following day) on the superlative high-speed AVE to Seville or Málaga. You can do the main journey in one (admittedly very long) day if you take the 9.15am Eurostar (𝕎 eurostar.com) from London St Pancras International to Paris and change there for the double-decker TGV Duplex, which arrives in Barcelona (via Figueres and Girona) at about 8.40pm. From Barcelona, you can catch a high-speed AVE train, which will get you to Madrid (via Zaragoza) at around midnight. You will not be able to take the AVE from Madrid to Málaga (or Seville) until the following morning, so you have the option of breaking the journey with an overnight stop in Barcelona or Madrid. You'll have to book well in advance on all services to get the lowest prices. There are alternative daytime services through France and Spain, though they don't save you any money.

The best first stop for information about train travel to Spain is the excellent 𝕎 seat61.com, which provides full route, ticket, timetable and contact information. You can book the whole journey **online** with Rail Europe (𝕎 raileurope.com), or contact a specialist **rail agent** such as Ffestiniog Travel (𝕎 ffestiniogtravel. co.uk) or the Spanish Rail Service (𝕎 renfe.com). As well as selling tickets, Rail Europe can also advise about **rail passes** (principally InterRail and Eurail).

Buses

You can reach most major cities in Andalucía **by bus** from the UK with **Eurolines** services (𝕎 eurolines. com). The main routes are from London (though add-on fares are available from any British city) to Barcelona (25hr), Madrid (27hr) and Valencia (30hr), with connections to Andalucía adding an additional five to six hours, so it's a long time to spend cooped up in a bus. There are advance deals and special offers and it's always cheapest to book online.

Driving to Spain

Provided you're not in a hurry, **driving to Spain** from the UK is an interesting way to get there, but with fuel, toll and overnight costs it doesn't compare in terms of price with flying or taking the train. It's about 2500km from London to Málaga, for example, which, not including stops, takes almost two full days to drive.

Many people use the conventional **cross-Channel ferry links**, principally Dover–Calais, though services to Brittany or Normandy might be more convenient depending on where you live (and they cut out the trek around Paris). However, the quickest way of crossing the Channel is to use the **Eurotunnel** (𝕎 eurotunnel.com), which operates drive-on-drive-off shuttle trains between Folkestone and

Calais/Coquelles. The 24-hour service runs every twenty minutes throughout the day; though you can just turn up, booking is advised, especially at weekends and in the summer holidays, or if you want the best deals.

The best way to cut driving time is to use either of the direct **UK–Spain ferry crossings**. Brittany Ferries (𝕎 brittany-ferries.co.uk) operates a car and passenger ferry from **Portsmouth** and **Plymouth to Santander** in Cantabria (2 weekly; 20–24hr) or **Bilbao** in the Basque country (2 weekly; 31–36hr). Fares can be significantly higher in summer, particularly in August – it's cheaper for foot passengers, although everyone has to book some form of seating or cabin accommodation. From the Basque country to the northern border of Andalucía is a journey of around 650km – or a day's drive.

Any ferry company or travel agent can supply up-to-date schedules and ticket information, or you can consult the encyclopedic 𝕎 directferries.com, which has details about, and links to, every European ferry service.

Getting around

Most of Andalucía is well covered by public transport. The rail network reaches all the provincial capitals and the main towns along the intercity lines, and high-speed trains connect the cities of Málaga and Seville with Madrid. Intercity bus services are often more frequent, cheaper and just as fast as the regular trains, and will usually take you closer to your destination, as some train stations are a few kilometres from the town or village they serve. Driving, meanwhile, will give you the freedom to head away from the major tourist routes and take in some of the spectacular scenery at your own pace.

One important point to remember is that all public transport, and the bus service especially, is drastically reduced on **Sundays and public holidays** – don't even consider travelling to out-of-the-way places on these days. The words to look out for on timetables are *diario* (daily), *laborables* (workdays, including Saturday), and *domingos y festivos* (Sunday and public holidays).

By train

Andalucía's trains, operated by **RENFE** (𝕎 renfe.com), tend to be efficient and comfortable, and nearly always run on time. There's a confusing array of services, though the website has a useful English-language version on which you can check timetables and buy tickets to show on your mobile phone (or printing them out before you travel).

Cercanías are local commuter trains in and around the major cities, while **media distancia** (regional) and **larga distancia** (long-distance) trains go under a bewildering number of names, including Intercity (IC), Regionales and Talgo services. These trains differ in terms of speed, service and number of stops, and you'll always pay more on the quickest routes (sometimes quite a lot more). The premier services are the high-speed trains, such as the expanding **AVE** (Alta Velocidad Española) network from Madrid to Seville and Málaga. The AVE trains have cut travelling times dramatically, with Madrid to Seville, for example, taking two hours thirty minutes compared with six to nine hours on the slower trains. One great feature of Andalucía's train network is that it still takes in a wide variety of inviting rural destinations including the Sierra de Aracena, the Sierra Norte, the Serranía de Ronda and the Parque Natural de los Alcornocales with many small rural stations set in the midst of scenic countryside.

Tickets and fares

Although you can just turn up at the station for short hops, **advance booking** is advisable for longer journeys between, say, Seville and Granada or Almería, and especially at weekends in summer or Spanish public holidays. Advance tickets can be bought at the stations between sixty days and five minutes before departure, but don't leave it to the last minute, as there are usually long queues (and often separate windows for the different types of train). Automatic **ticket machines** at main stations take some of the hassle out of queueing, or you can buy tickets at **travel agents** that display the RENFE sign – the cost is the same as at the station.

Actual fares vary wildly, with the best deals available **online** on the RENFE website, where "Web" and "Estrella" fares offer discounts of up to sixty percent on the full fares. Otherwise, **return fares** (*ida y vuelta*) are discounted by ten to twenty percent, depending on the service – you can buy a single, and so long as you show it when you buy the return, you'll still get the discount. For the high-speed AVE services, there are no discounts for buying a return ticket. There's also a whole range of other **discounted fares** of between 25 and 40 percent for those over 60 or under 26 years, the disabled, and children aged 4 to 11 years.

Rail passes

The major pan-European **rail passes** (InterRail and Eurail) are only worth considering if you're visiting Spain as part of a wider European tour. Both schemes also have single-country rail passes available, which might be better value depending on your Spanish itinerary. The **InterRail Spain Pass** (Ⓦinterrailnet.com) is only available to European residents and allows three, four, six or eight days' train travel within one month, with under-26, second- and first-class versions available. Again, these really only become cost-effective if you're combining your stay in Andalucía with journeys to other parts of Spain. For anyone else, **Eurail** (Ⓦraileurope.com) has various Spain passes available, typically offering three days' travel in two months, again in various classes. You can check current prices on the websites, but bear in mind that it often works out cheaper to buy individual tickets in Spain as you need them, and it's certainly more convenient to be free to choose long-distance buses on some routes. All passes have to be bought before you leave home, and you'll still be liable for supplements and seat reservations on long-distance and high-speed trains.

By bus

Buses will probably meet most of your transport needs, especially if you're venturing away from the larger towns and cities. Many smaller villages and rural areas are only accessible by bus, almost always originating in the capital of their province. Services are pretty reliable, whether it's the two-buses-a-day school or market run, or the regular services between major cities (the latter often far more conveniently scheduled than the equivalent train services). **Fares** are very reasonable, too. On intercity runs, you'll usually be assigned a seat when you buy your ticket. Some destinations are served by more than one **bus company**, but main bus stations have posted timetables for all services and you can check timetables on the company websites; Alsa (Ⓦalsa.es) is one of the main companies with nationwide services, and has an English-language version of its website.

There are only a few cities in Andalucía (Seville and Granada, for example) where you'll need to use the **local bus** network. You'll also sometimes need to take a local bus out to a campsite or distant museum or monastery. Fares are very cheap – rarely more than €1.50.

By car

Andalucía's roads and highways are generally toll free but exceptions are the toll **autopista** (motorway) between Seville and Cádiz and the *Autopista del Sol*, which passes all the major Costa del Sol resorts between Málaga and Estepona. The second-grade

THE SPANISH DRIVING EXPERIENCE

If it's your first time out on a Spanish road, especially in one of the bigger cities, you could be forgiven for thinking you've stumbled upon the local chapter of *Mad Max* devotees, out for a burn-up. In fact, those wild-eyed, dangerously speeding, non-signalling, bumper-hogging, mobile-talking, horn-sounding road warriors are normal law-abiding Spanish citizens on their way to work. **Traffic lights** and **pedestrian crossings** in particular present a difficult conceptual challenge – if you are going to stop at either, make sure you give plenty of warning to avoid another vehicle running into the back of you, and keep an eye out for cars crossing your path who have jumped the lights. **Signposting** is universally poor (yes, *that* was the turn you wanted), even on main roads and highways, while joining and exiting **autopistas/autovías** can be particularly dangerous, as it's almost a point of honour not to let anyone in or out. Many of the worst **accidents** are on the N roads, which have only a single carriageway in each direction, so take particular care on these. Major roads are generally in good **condition**, though some minor and mountain roads can be rather hairy and are little more than dirt tracks in the more remote regions. Sheep, goats and cattle are also regular hazards. Having said all this, things are (slowly) improving and drivers are a bit more careful these days because of increased use of radar and speed controls and the introduction of a points system for infractions which (if you accumulate too many) can lead to a driving ban. The police are also setting up more **drink-driving** controls than before, though you have to remember that this is a country where it's considered a good idea to have bars in motorway service stations.

roads, **autovías**, often follow similar routes and in many respects resemble motorways, but their speed limits are lower. Locals tend to shy away from the toll routes, which are relatively expensive by local standards, but the lighter traffic encountered perhaps makes it a price worth paying for the visitor. You can usually pay with a credit card, although it would be wise to carry enough cash just in case. Toll roads are usually designated by an "AP" or "R" or the word "*peaje*".

You can pay by credit card (with proof of identity) at most petrol stations for **fuel** (*gasolina*), the main companies being Cepsa and Repsol. Unleaded petrol (*sin plomo*) comes in normal (95 octane) and super (98 octane) grades and diesel is referred to as *diesel* or *gasóleo*. Pumps are colour coded to avoid error: green for unleaded; yellow and black for diesel.

Rules and regulations

An EU or UK **driver's licence** is sufficient if you want to drive in Spain. US, Canadian, Australian and New Zealand licences should also be enough, though you may want to get an International Driver's Licence as well, just to be on the safe side. If you are bringing your own car, you will need your vehicle registration and insurance papers – and check with your insurers that you are covered to drive the car abroad. It's also **compulsory** to carry two hazard triangles, reflective jackets in case of accident or breakdown, an official first-aid kit and a set of spare bulbs. Rear seatbelts are also compulsory, as are child seats for infants.

The Spanish **drive on the right**, and **speed limits** are enforced throughout the country. On most *autopistas* it is 120km/h (130km/h on clearly signed sections), on the *autovía* 120km/h, on minor roads 70km/h or 90km/h (where there is a hard shoulder of 1.5m or more), and in towns and villages 50km/h (often lowered to 20km/h or 30km/h – pay attention to signs). Police have the power to fine drivers on the spot for speeding or any other transgressions (such as using a hand-held mobile phone while driving), and if you don't have any cash, they will escort you to the nearest cash machine and issue you with a receipt there and then. Failure to pay will result in your car being impounded until you do.

Parking

Parking can be a major pain in the neck, especially in big cities and old-town areas. Finding on-street parking spaces is often impossible, although if you can time your arrival with the start of the siesta (around 2pm, when everyone rushes home for lunch) you stand a better chance. Metered parking zones usually have stays limited to a couple of hours, though parking between 8pm and 8am, on Saturday afternoons and all day Sundays tends to be free. It's always worth double-checking street signs, or asking the locals, whether you're allowed to park where you've just left your car, as any illegally parked vehicle will be promptly removed in the bigger cities. If your car disappears off the street, it is best to assume that it has been towed to the local pound, and enquiries in any hotel, government office or police station should produce the address. In cities it's probably best to pay extra for a hotel with parking or use a pay car park, for which you'll need to budget anything from €12 to €20 a day. In rural hotels and *hostales* parking is usually free. There's usually no problem finding on-street parking in villages, although even here things are more difficult than they used to be.

Car rental

Car rental is often cheapest arranged in advance through one of the large multinational agencies (Avis, Budget, Europcar or Hertz, for example).Local Spanish companies (such as Pepecar; Ⓦ pepecar. com) can sometimes offer better value for money, as can the online rental outfits easyCar (Ⓦ easycar. com) and Holiday Autos (Ⓦ holidayautos.com), with high-season prices starting from around €40 per day for renting a small car in Andalucía. Reliable and competitive **Andalucía-based companies** include the long-established Málaga Car Hire (with pick-up and drop-off points throughout the region; Ⓦ malagacarhire.com) and MalagaCar (Ⓦ malagacar. com). Car hire costs have been greatly affected by the Covid-19 hiatus and you will certainly pay more per day than you did a few years ago. Out of high season rates fall substantially. Brokers are also a way of comparing prices across a spectrum of rental companies and two worth a look are Rentspain (Ⓦ rentspain.com) and Auto Europe (Ⓦ autoeurope. com); be sure to check out the terms and conditions though, as what may seem initially to be the cheapest deals often insist on things like you buying a full tank from the rental company (at premium prices compared to pump stations) and often don't include wing mirrors, windows, windscreen, tyres and suchlike in the insurance (meaning you are charged the full cost of repair should they need replacing).

You'll need to be 21 or over (and have been driving for at least a year) to rent a car in Spain. It's essential to check that you have adequate **insurance cover** for your rental car, and that all visible damage on a car you're picking up is duly marked on the rental sheet. It's definitely worth considering paying the extra charge to reduce the "excess" payment levied for any damage, but these waiver charges (by the day) soon add up. However, you can avoid all **excess charges** in the event of damage by taking out an annual insurance policy with Ⓦ insurance4carhire. com, which also covers windscreen and tyre damage.

By bike

Cycling is a great way to see parts of the region that might otherwise pass you by, though bear in mind that peninsular Spain is one of the most mountainous countries in Europe and Andalucía contains its two

---

ANDALUCÍA'S FIVE BEST DRIVES

Colmenar to Málaga This 35km/45min drive from the Axarquía village of Colmenar (see page 95), known for its honey, descends through the Montes de Málaga natural park offering, in its latter stages, magnificent views over the Costa del Sol. Route: A7000.

Grazalema to Vejer A dramatic 130km/3hr drive from the gorgeous White Town of Grazalema (see page 214) through the spectacular Sierra de Grazalema and Alocornocales natural parks, the latter with Europe's largest cork oak forest, to the atmospheric Moorish hilltop town of Vejer (see page 186). Route: A2304 and A2228.

Valverde del Camino to Aracena One of the most striking drives in Andalucía is this 77km/1hr 15min journey from the small town of Valverde del Camino (see page 323) along the N435, turning off along the A461 to traverse the strange, forbidding landscape of the Río Tinto mining zone. This mineral-rich panorama with fissured crags and glinting rivulets of ochre, rust and cadmium has been mined for five millennia. Route: N435 and A461.

Cazorla to Segura de la Sierra Starting out in the charming town of Cazorla (see page 413), this 90km/2hr 30min route through the densely forested Cazorla Natural Park – Andalucia's biggest – takes in the source of the Río Guadalquivir and finally climbs dizzily to the hilltop village of Segura de la Sierra (see page 418) with its impressive Moorish fort. Route: A319 and JA9118.

Lanjarón to Yegen Traversing the delightful wooded foothills of the Sierra Nevada mountain range, this 75km/2hr route visits many of the rustic villages of Las Alpujarras, starting at Lanjarón (see page 468) and ending up at the most famous of them all, Yegen (see page 480), the inspiration for Gerald Brenan's *South from Granada*. Route: A4132 and A4130.

highest peaks. Added to punishing climbs, there are often searing high-summer temperatures with which to contend. However, don't be put off; pacing yourself and using the cooler hours of the day (after dawn and before dusk) can make for a highly enjoyable trip.

For serious cycle touring, you'll need your own bike and to be properly equipped. **Bike rental** is not common, except in resort areas or in tourist-oriented cities such as Seville, Córdoba or Granada, where you can expect to pay up to €25 a day – or around €40 for a half-day bike tour. In Seville tourists can also use the excellent Sevici bike rental scheme, which is run by the city government. Although the Spanish themselves are keen sport cyclists, other facilities are practically nonexistent, although things are changing. As part of the 2014–2020 Cycle Plan, the Junta de Andalucía (Andalucía's regional government) constructed a network of cycle paths in all towns and cities with a population above 100,000. With the aid of EU funding, towns and cities such as Seville, Córdoba, Cádiz, Jerez, Granada, Huelva and Almería have already started work on making urban cycling safe by laying down cycle lanes and installing bike rental schemes. However, pedestrians are still not accustomed to the idea, and casually stroll along designated cycle lanes while many cyclists infuriate locals by careering along pavements and pedestrianized streets.

Most airlines are happy to take bikes as ordinary **baggage**, though it's essential to check first, especially if you're flying with a budget airline, when extra charges may apply. Spanish bus drivers are reasonably amenable, and (space permitting) should let you throw your bicycle in with the baggage. Trains are more problematic, as there are specific trains, times and routes on which bikes are not allowed. As a rule, local trains are fine but high-speed trains are out, unless your bike is boxed up or you're travelling by overnight sleeper.

You should have no trouble finding bike shops in cities and larger towns, and parts can often be found at auto repair shops or garages. On the road, cars tend to hoot before they pass, which can be alarming at first, but is useful once you're used to it.

Be especially aware of **road safety** when cycling. On busier roads you should never ride two abreast as Spanish drivers (unused to cyclists) have frequently caused accidents and even fatalities when colliding with the cyclist on the outside. In recent years there have been a number of horrific accidents by drivers (often drunk or drugged) ploughing into a group of cyclists from behind. Make sure you are clearly visible by wearing a **hi-vis fluorescent vest**, and avoid cycling during the hours of darkness. Finally, try not to leave your bike on the street overnight (especially in

cities), even with a secure lock, as thieves view them as easy pickings. Most hotels and *hostales* will usually be able to provide a secure place to store it. See Specialist tour operators (see page 28) or "Specialist Guides" (see page 555) if you are planning a cycle trip.

Accommodation

There's a great variety of accommodation in Andalucía, ranging from humble family-run pensiones and hostales to five-star luxury hotels, often in dramatic historic buildings. The mainstay of the coastal resort is the typical beachfront holiday hotel, though renting an apartment or a villa gives you more freedom, while farm stays, village guesthouses and mountain inns are all increasingly popular options.

In almost any town, you'll be able to get a no-frills double room in a *pensión* or *hostal* (both words are used to describe the equivalent of a one- or two-star hotel) for around €50, sometimes even less, especially if it's out in the sticks. As a rule, you can expect to pay upwards of €100 for a three-star city hotel in high season (less in small towns and country areas), around €140 for four-star and boutique places, and €200 upwards for five-star hotels and historic *paradores*. However, the trend is bucked by Seville and Granada, in particular, and some coastal and resort areas, where hotel (but not *hostal*) rooms are often appreciably more expensive.

If you want to guarantee a room at a particular place, **advance reservations** are essential in major cities and resort areas at peak holiday, festival or convention times. Local festivals and annual events also tend to fill all available accommodation weeks in advance. Unlike most countries, you don't always pay more for a central location; indeed, the newer three- and four-star properties tend to be located more on the outskirts. **Families** will find that most places have rooms with three or even four beds at not a great deal more than the price for a double room; also extra beds for children can often be added to double rooms for little extra cost. However, **single travellers** often get a comparatively bad deal, and can end up paying sixty to eighty percent of the price of a double room. Accommodation prices are **seasonal**, but minimum and maximum rates should be displayed at reception. In high season on the coast (usually the month of August), some hotels only take bookings for a minimum of a week, while others also require at least a half-board stay.

Note, however that high season isn't always summer – in the ski resorts of the Sierra Nevada for example – and that inland cities such as Seville, Córdoba and Granada tend to have cheaper prices in August, when everyone heads for the coast. Be aware, too, that the Spanish love to build *puentes* (bridges) between a national or regional holiday that occurs on say, a Thursday or a Tuesday, and the weekend that follows or precedes it. The hotel trade treats these dates as "high season" and not only are prices higher, but accommodation in many places becomes tight.

Where possible, **website bookings** nearly always offer the best deals, especially with the larger hotel groups that have made big inroads into Spain – it's always worth checking *NH Hoteles* (Ⓦnh-hotels.com), *Accor/Ibis* (Ⓦaccorhotels.com) and *Meliá* (Ⓦmelia. com) for current deals. Most hotels now also use **specialist sites** to fill their rooms, especially in low season, and often you can find some real bargains: in addition to Ⓦbooking.com (always referred to by the hotel trade in Spain as "Booking") two of the best Spanish sites are Ⓦatrapalo.com and Ⓦrumbo.es; they are in Spanish only, but are fairly easy to use. For accommodation in the province of Cádiz check out Ⓦdestinia.com. Many of these sites quote prices up to thirty percent below the official rates. A useful tip: if you are travelling with a smartphone or tablet and you do not wish to enter your credit card details via a (possibly insecure) wi-fi connection, you can consult the booking services mentioned above to obtain a price. If you then ring the hotel and quote the price on the site they will usually let you make a same-day booking for the same price, stipulating that the room will be held for you until a specific time.

Rooms

The cheapest beds are usually in **private rooms**, in someone's house or above a bar or restaurant. The signs to look for are *habitaciones* (rooms) or *camas*

WI-FI IN HOTELS AND HOSTALES

It is only in very rare cases that hotels and *hostales* in Andalucía don't provide wi-fi ("wee-fee" in Spanish) throughout. However, dated routers and thick walls can make connection patchy. The closer you are to the router, the better. Again, the vast majority of places make no charge for this service. Thus, we only state in the Guide when an accommodation recommendation has no wi-fi or charges for the service.

(beds), both becoming less obvious in Andalucía, especially now that the tax authorities are clamping down on the "grey economy" or undeclared income. They might be touted at resort bus and train stations in high summer as you arrive. The rooms should be clean, but might well be very simple and timeworn; you'll probably share a communal bathroom.

Pensiones, hostales and hotels

Official places to stay are generally classified as *pensiones*, *hostales* or **hotels**, though that's just the start of it, as several other names are used to describe accommodation throughout the region.

Pensiones

Of the official guesthouses and hotels, at the budget end of the scale are *pensiones* (marked P, classified by a two-star system), where straightforward rooms often have shared bathroom facilities (there's usually a washbasin in the room). Other variants are *fondas* (F), which traditionally had a restaurant or dining room attached, and *casas de huéspedes* (CH), literally an old-fashioned "guesthouse". In some such *pensiones*,

ACCOMMODATION PRICE CODES

Throughout this guide we have given a price code to each accommodation review. The codes are based on the cost of a standard double room (or in campsites, a standard camping pitch for two) for one night in peak season. Prices in most hotels will include breakfast; private rooms and apartments will not. Outside these times rates can drop considerably, sometimes as much as 50 percent, so check establishments' websites and booking sites for the best current rates.

€̲	under €65
€€̲	€65–€100
€€€̲	€100–€150
€€€€̲	over €150

facilities are likely to be minimal and comforts rationed; things like heating, furniture (other than bed, chair and desk) and even external windows might be too much to hope for. On the other hand, some *pensiones* are lovingly cared for and very good value.

Hostales

Next step up from the *pensiones*, and far more common, are **hostal-residencias** (HsR) and **hostales** (Hs), classified with one to three stars. These are not hostels, in any sense, but budget hotels, generally offering good, if just functional, rooms, usually with private bathrooms, TV and – in the better places – probably heating and air-conditioning. Many also have cheaper rooms available without private bathrooms. Some *hostales* really are excellent, with good service and up-to-date furnishings and facilities, including wi-fi or internet access.

Hotels

Fully fledged **hotels** are graded from one to five stars, with star-rating dependent on things like room size, staffing levels and whether or not there's a lift, rather than being based any intrinsic attraction. There's often not much difference in price between a one-star hotel and a three-star *hostal*, for example, and the *hostal* might be nicer. At three and four stars, prices start to increase and you can expect soundproofing, a lift, an English-language channel on the TV and a buffet breakfast spread (if included, which it may not be). At five stars, you're in the luxury class, with pools, gyms, jacuzzis and prices to match. The excellent Rusticae (ⓦ rusticae.es) highlights stylish **rural and urban hotels** across the country.

Paradores

Spain has over ninety superior hotels in a class of their own, called **paradores** (ⓦ parador.es), spectacular lodgings often converted from castles, monasteries and other Spanish monuments (although some are purpose-built). They can be really special places to stay, sited in the most beautiful parts of the country, and in some of the most historic cities, and prices are very good when compared with the five-star hotels with which they often compete.

Paradores are banded into five categories, depending on location and popularity, with high-season rates starting at around €140 a night, though €200–300 is more typical. That said, a whole host of special offers and web deals (through the official website) offer rooms from as little as €100, and there are special deals too, for people aged over 60, for 20 to 30 year-olds, or for multi-night stays. Three-night and five-night packages, where you stay in a different *parador* every night, start at around €200 per person (based on two sharing, car rental not included). All the details are on the website, or contact the official *parador* **agents**, Keytel in the UK (ⓦ keytel.co.uk) or Petrabax in the US (ⓦ petrabax.com).

Villas, apartments and rural tourism

Most UK and European tour operators can find you a self-catering **villa** or **apartment**, usually (but not exclusively) on the coast or in one of the many sierras. They are rented by the week, and range from simple town-centre apartments to luxury coastal villas with private pools, and prices vary wildly. The best deals are often packages, including flights and car rental, offered by numerous companies like TUI (ⓦ tui.co.uk/ holidays/villas) and James Villa Holidays (ⓦ james-villas.co.uk).

Casas rurales (rural houses) are where many Spanish holiday-makers stay. These cover a broad range, from cave dwellings to restored manor houses, many with pools and gardens, plus all mod cons. You can rent by the room, or by the property, sometimes

---

ANDALUCÍA'S TOP FIVE PARADORES

Mazagón A modern *parador* made very special by its isolated location on one of the best beaches in Andalucía, reached via steps from the hotel's extensive gardens. See page 319.

Jaén Housed in a Moorish fortress atop a crag high above the city of Jaén, this is the most spectacularly sited *parador* in Andalucía, if not Spain. See page 401.

Úbeda On arguably the most beautiful square in Andalucía, this *parador* occupies a stunning sixteenth-century Renaissance mansion. See page 412.

Cazorla Natural Park Another modern *parador*, but its setting deep inside the lushly wooded Cazorla Natural Park makes for a memorable hotel. See page 420.

Granada One of the world's top hotels, in a fifteenth-century monastery inside the Alhambra grounds, this offers a heady combination of opulence and history. See page 452.

on a B&B basis and sometimes self-catering. Many of the *casas* also come with opportunities to take part in outdoor activities such as horseriding, walking, fishing and cycling. They offer excellent value for money, starting at around €40 per person, even cheaper if you're in a group or staying for longer than a night or two.

ASETUR (Ⓦ ecoturismorural.com), the association for rural tourism in Spain, is a website where you can search properties by region; the Spanish site Ⓦ milan-uncios.com is another resource and can be navigated with minimal Spanish. Many of Andalucía's tourist-office websites also carry information on *casas rurales*. You could also contact **agencies** like Vrbo (Ⓦ vrbo. com), which has many properties in Andalucía, and Andalucía-based agencies such as Rustic Blue (Ⓦ rusticblue.com) or the comprehensive Escapada Rural a Spanish site, which is easy to navigate (Ⓦ esca-padarural.com).

Youth hostels

There are twenty official youth hostels (*albergues juveniles*) in Andalucía under the umbrella of the **Red Española de Albergues Juveniles** (REAJ; Ⓦ reaj. com), the Spanish youth hostel association that is affiliated to the international organization, Hostelling International (HI; Ⓦ hihostels.com). Partly funded by the Junta de Andalucía, the network in Andalucía is administered by **Inturjoven** (Ⓦ inturjoven.com). There are full details of each hostel on the Inturjoven website (English-language version available), and we've included some of the best in the Guide.

Andalucía has some of the most modern youth hostels in the country – including a stunning one in **Jaén with a full-blown spa** (see page 399) – many with two- or four-bed en-suite rooms, and a handful of options in stunning **rural locations**. Bear in mind, though, that in some cities hostels may be inconveniently located and at school holiday periods can be block-booked by school/youth groups. You'll also need an HI membership card, though you can buy one at most hostels on your first night. And at over €30 per person a night in high season (less for under 26s, and out of season), they can end up no cheaper than a basic double room in a *hostal* or *pensión*. That said, hostels are also good places for cheap meals and meeting other travellers.

Camping

There are hundreds of authorized **campsites** in Spain, mostly on the coast and in holiday areas. They work out at about €5–8 per person plus the same again for a tent, and a similar amount for each car or caravan. The best-located sites, or the ones with top-range facilities (restaurant, swimming pool, bar, supermarket), are significantly more expensive. If you plan to camp extensively, buy the annual *Guía de Campings*, which you can find in large bookshops, or visit Ⓦ vayacamping.net.

In most cases, camping outside campsites is legal – but there are certain restrictions. You're not allowed to camp "in urban areas, areas prohibited for military or touristic reasons, or within 1km of an official campsite". Whenever possible, ask locally first.

Food and drink

The rich and varied cuisine of Andalucía is a reflection of its dramatic history. One of its signature dishes, gazpacho, was introduced by the Romans in the first millennium BC, and didn't reach its final version until peppers and tomatoes arrived in Spain following the voyages of Columbus. Another great influence came from the Moors who changed the face of southern Spain forever with the planting of orange, olive and almond trees. They also introduced spices such as cumin, cinnamon, nutmeg and saffron plus vegetables and fruits like aubergine, spinach, quince and pomegranate.

The cooking of modern Andalucía falls into mountain and coastal food. Five of Andalucía's eight provinces have access to a coastline, and in this region **fish** and **seafood** is king. Inland, rich stews, *jamones* (cured hams) and game are preferred. In recent years there has been a revival of interest in developing the region's cuisine in a more creative direction, and a reflection of this is evident in the number of very good restaurants around, with several chefs sporting one or even two Michelin stars. Of course, not every restaurant in Andalucía is a gourmet experience and not every dish is a classic of its kind. Tourist resorts can be disappointing, especially those aimed at a foreign clientele, and a week on the Costa del Sol can just as easily convince you that the Spanish national diet is egg and chips, sangria, pizza and Guinness. However, even here you'll always find good restaurants and tapas bars where the locals eat, and few places in Europe are still as good value, especially if you order the *menú del día*, the bargain fixed-price lunch (and often dinner) that's a fixture across the region. There's a useful **menu reader** in our Spanish section (see page 558).

EATING OUT PRICE CODES

The price codes used throughout this guide are as follows, and generally refer to two courses, plus one drink and service, for one person:

€̲	under €25
€€̲	€25–50
€€€̲	€50–80
€€€€̲	over €80

Breakfast, snacks and sandwiches

The traditional *andaluz* **breakfast** (*desayuno*) is *chocolate con churros* – long, extruded tubular doughnuts served with thick drinking chocolate or coffee. Some places specialize in these but many city bars and cafés also serve cakes and pastries (*bollos* or *pasteles*), croissants (*cruasán*) and toast (*pan tostada*), or crusty sandwiches (*bocadillos*) with a choice of fillings (try one with omelette, *tortilla*). A "sandwich", incidentally, is usually a less appetizing ham or cheese sandwich in white processed bread. Other good places for snacks are **cake shops** (*pastelerías* or *confiterías*) or the local bakery (*panadería*), where they might also have savoury pasties and turnovers.

Bars, tapas and raciónes

One of Spain's and Andalucía's glories is the phenomenon of **tapas** – the little portions of food that traditionally used to be served up free with a drink in a bar. The origins are disputed but the word is from *tapar*, "to cover", suggesting a cover for drinks' glasses, perhaps to keep the flies off in the baking sun. Tapas can be anything – a handful of olives, a slice or two of cured ham, a little dish of meatballs or chorizo, spicy fried potatoes or battered squid. They will often be laid out in a glass-fronted chill-cabinet on the counter, so you can see what's available, or there might be a blackboard menu. Occasionally the *dueño* (boss) or barman carries the list around in his head to be verbally rattled off to each new customer – an exacting test of your Spanish. Most bars have a speciality; indeed, Spaniards will commonly move from bar to bar, having just the one dish that they consider each bar does well. Conversely, if you're in a bar with just some pre-fried potatoes and day-old Russian salad on display, and a prominent microwave, go somewhere else to eat.

Aside from a few olives or crisps sometimes handed out with a drink, you generally pay for tapas these days (the eastern end of Andalucía, particularly the city of Granada, is an honourable exception here) – usually around €2–5 a portion in normal bars and slightly more in the recently arrived "gastrobars."

Raciónes (around €7–15) are simply bigger plates of tapas, perfect for sharing or enough for a meal – you're sometimes asked if you want a *tapa* or a *ración* of whatever it is you've chosen. And in the evenings many bars give up serving the cheaper tapas, and serve only the more profitable *raciones* when you'll be told "*solo hay raciones*". Seville, as the city that claims to have invented tapas, is one of the best places to sample this culinary art, but you'll find many other outstanding bars throughout Andalucía.

Most cafés and bars have some kind of tapas available, while you'll also find a decent display in **bodegas**, **tabernas**, **mesónes** (various kinds of taverns) and **cervecerías** (beer-houses). It's always cheapest to stand at the bar to eat; you'll pay more to sit at tables and more again to sit outside on a terrace.

Restaurants

The simplest kind of restaurant is the highway **venta**, or inn, dotted along the main roads between towns and cities. These have been serving Spanish wayfarers for centuries – some of them quite literally – and the best places are immediately picked out by the line of cars and trucks outside. Proper restaurants, **restaurantes**, come in a myriad of guises, from rustic village *comedores* to stylish Michelin-starred eateries; **asadores** specialize in grilled meats, **marisquerías** in shellfish and seafood.

Almost every *venta* and *restaurante* serves a weekday, fixed-price lunchtime meal, the **menú del día**. For this you generally get three courses including a beer or glass of wine for €8–15 depending on where you are (you might also see the words *menú de la casa*); this is obviously a terrific deal. The *menú del dia* is only sporadically available at night, and in Andalucía it's generally not available at all at weekends, the time traditionally when families eat out together. The very cheapest places are unlikely to have a written menu, and the waiter will tell you what the day's dishes are. In smarter restaurants in bigger cities and resorts, there will still be a *menú del dia*, though it might be a shadow of the usual à la carte menu, and drinks may be excluded. Even so, it's a way of eating at a restaurant that might normally cost you three or four times as much. Top city restaurants often also feature an upmarket *menú* called a **menú de degustación** (tasting menu), which again can be excellent value, allowing you to try out some of the country's finest cooking for anything from €30 to €60 a head; some even throw in a bottle of decent wine.

Otherwise, in bars and so-called *cafeterías*, meals often come in the form of a **plato combinado** – literally a combined dish – which will be a one-plate meal of something like steak, egg and chips, or *calamares* and salad, occasionally with bread and a drink included. This will generally cost in the region of €5–15.

If you want a menu in a restaurant, ask for **la carta**; *menú* refers only to the fixed-price meal. In all but the most rock-bottom establishments it is customary to leave a small **tip** (*propina*), though five percent of the bill is considered sufficient and service is normally included in a *menú del día*. IVA, the ten-percent **tax**, is also charged, but it should say on the menu if this is included in the price or not.

Spaniards generally eat very late and *andaluzes* eat later still, with **lunch** served from around 1pm (you'll generally be the first person there at this time) until 4pm, and **dinner** from 8.30pm or 9pm to midnight. In rural areas people dine slightly earlier, but making a dinner reservation for 10.30pm or even later is considered perfectly normal in Andalucía and it's not uncommon to see a group of diners being ushered to a table with midnight approaching. Most restaurants **close one day a week**, usually Sunday or Monday.

What to eat

If you like **fish and seafood** you'll be in heaven in Andalucía, as it forms the basis of a vast variety of tapas and is fresh and excellent everywhere. It's not cheap, unfortunately, so rarely forms part of the lowest priced *menús* (though they might feature the most common fish – cod, often salted, and hake – or squid) but you really should make the most of what's on offer. Fish **stews** (*zarzuelas*) and rice-based paellas (which also contain meat, usually rabbit or chicken) are often memorable in seafood restaurants. Paella comes originally from Valencia and is still best there, but you'll find **arroz marinero**, the Andalucían version, to be very good. The coastal strip is great for seafood, of course, although Cádiz and the nearby "sherry triangle" of Sanlúcar, El Puerto de Santa María and Jerez deserve top billing for sheer volume and variety. Be aware when ordering fish in restaurants that the price quoted is usually per kilo or (sometimes) per 100g, and an average white-fish portion will be around 200–300g. The letters S/M next to the name of the fish on the menu means *según mercado* – that day's market price, which means that the waiter will tell you if you ask. And don't be afraid to ask the waiter for a price quote when ordering or to select a fish before it's weighed. If you leave it to him, you're guaranteed to get the biggest. You may need to go to the kitchen to do this – often an adventure in itself. Sometimes restaurants will try to fob you off with a big fish as being all they have: it's worth remembering that a single large fish 500–600g is enough for two to share ("*para compartir*" in Spanish). Most fish restaurants will do the filleting for you when your plate arrives at the table.

Meat is most often grilled and served with a few fried potatoes and a couple of salad leaves, or cured or dried and served as a starter or in sandwiches. *Jamón serrano* is superb, makes a wonderful starter

---

ANDALUCÍA'S TOP TEN RESTAURANTS

Andalucía has some of the best restaurants in Spain, and quite a few places where you could blow a pretty big hole in your credit card account. While many recommended restaurants in the Guide may score higher in terms of cuisine alone, at any of the places below we feel the welcome, ambience, location and excellent food all contribute to creating a truly memorable experience.

Bar-Restaurante La Ola La Isleta del Moro. See page 510
Casa Bigote Sanlúcar de Barrameda. See page 171
El Chaleco Almuñécar. See page 505
José Vicente Aracena. See page 330
La Escollera Estepona. See page 117
Mesón Arrieros Linares de la Sierra. See page 332
Parador de Málaga-Gibralfaro Málaga. See page 75
Restaurante Venta Esteban Jerez. See page 181
Santiago Marbella. See page 113
Taberna del Alabardero Seville. See page 279

CERDO IBÉRICO

One special meat that you will come across in Andalucía and not many other areas of Spain is **cerdo ibérico** – meat from the Iberian black pig. Thought to be of eastern Mediterranean origin (where they interbred with wild boars) the animals were probably introduced to the peninsula by the Phoenicians. Although Spain produces an astonishing forty million hams a year, only a fraction of this is true *ibérico*. This is due to the fact that Iberian pigs need acorns to eat and these are limited to the **dehesas**, an ecosystem in the provinces of Extremadura and western Andalucía close to the border with Portugal, where prairie-like grazing land is dotted with *encinas* (holm oaks). This is where the *cerdo ibérico* thrives as it snuffles over the dusty ground in its search for acorns. Because of its high price, the production of *cerdo ibérico* is strictly regulated and the very best pigs (those fed solely on acorns for the final four months of their lives) are mainly used in the making of **jamón ibérico de bellota** (acorn-fed cured ham). Other pigs fed on *recebo* (acorns and grain) or *cebo* (grain) during this period can be classed as "*ibérico*" but not "*de bellota*". One bonus of eating a tasty *solomillo ibérico* sirloin (or other cuts called *presa, secreto, pluma* or *carillada*) is that it's a healthier option: because of their genetic make-up and their unique diet, much of the fat produced in an Iberian pig's meat is mono-unsaturated – as healthy as olive oil. One farmer joked that all their *bellota*-scoffing transformed his pigs into four-legged amphoras of olive oil.

and is consumed with a passion in Andalucía. The finest varieties, though, produced from *cerdos ibéricos* (Iberian black pigs) at Jabugo in the Sierra de Aracena (see page 338) and Trevélez in the Sierra Nevada (see page 474), are extremely expensive. If you're tempted, they are best appreciated with a glass of *fino* (see page 43). More meat is eaten in inland provinces than on the coast and Córdoba's **rabo de toro** (stewed bull's tail) is renowned. The Sierra de Aracena is also a good place for *setas* (mushrooms) and cooked pork dishes, with **solomillo de cerdo** (pork loin) usually outstanding. In country areas bordering the slopes of the Sierra Morena and in the province of Jaén, game is very much a speciality – venison, partridge, hare and wild boar all feature on menus in these parts, as well as fresh trout.

Vegetables

Vegetables rarely amount to more than a few fries or boiled potatoes with the main dish (though you can often order a side dish à la carte). The provinces of Córdoba and Jaén are again the exceptions, and the latter's **pipirrana jaenera** (salad with green peppers and hard-boiled eggs) is just one of a number of hearty vegetable-based dishes to be found in these parts. It's more usual, though, to start your meal with a simple salad or with Andalucía's most famous dish, chilled **gazpacho**. Made from puréed bread and garlic with added peppers, cucumbers and tomatoes, regional variations of gazpacho include Córdoba's *salmorejo* (tomato based) and Málaga's *ajoblanco* (garlic and crushed almonds) and *porra antequerana* (a thicker tomato base hailing originally from Antequera).

Cheese

Cheese (*queso*) is always eaten as a *tapa* rather than after a meal in Andalucía. The cheeses of the region don't usually travel beyond their immediate area of production, which offers you the chance to make some interesting discoveries, especially in areas such as Las Alpujarras. The best-known region-wide brand is Córdoba Province's sheep's-milk cheese from Pedroches, although the hard, salty Manchego from neighbouring La Mancha is also common. One cheese worth knowing about from the Sierra de Grazalema is cured goat's-and sheep's-milk cheeses made by prizewinning cheesemaker Payoyo.

Desserts

Dessert (*postre*) in Andalucía tends to be sweet and sticky – another hangover from the region's long Moorish period. The cheaper places will usually offer little variety: nearly always fresh fruit or *flan*, the Spanish crème caramel, often replaced on Andalucían menus by the similar *tocino de cielo* ("heavenly lard") or *natillas* (custard). *Arroz con leche* (cold rice pudding), *crema catalana* (crème brûlée) and *helado* (ice cream) often make an appearance in the more mundane places. Keep an eye out in upmarket restaurants for delicious **regional specialities** such as *peras al vino* (pears baked in wine with cinnamon) from Málaga, *piononos* (liqueur-soaked cakes) from Granada and *crema de Jerez* (sherry pudding) from Cádiz, as well as *brazo de gitano* (rolled pastry filled with cream), an Andalucía-wide dessert. In smarter places the desserts will always be made in house or by a reputable local artisan (or even convent), but in cheaper and out-of-the-way places they often cut corners by offering factory-produced desserts, anathema to most *andaluz* diners; "*es casero?*" ("is it home-made?") is the question to ask.

Vegetarians & Vegans

Vegetarians and vegans generally have a harder time of it in Andalucía than in other Western European destinations, though there's an increasing number of veggie and veggie-friendly restaurants in the bigger cities. In more rural areas, there's usually something to eat, but you may get weary of eggs and omelettes. It's worth noting that many **tapas** favourites are vegetarian dishes: *espinacas con garbanzos* (spinach with chickpeas), *tortilla* (potato omelette with or without onions, *cebollas*), *berenjenas fritas* (fried aubergine) and *patatas bravas* (potatoes in spicy sauce) are to be found throughout Andalucía. Otherwise, superb fresh fruit and veg, and excellent cheese, is always available in the markets and shops.

In restaurants, you're faced with the extra problem that pieces of meat – especially ham, which the Spanish don't regard as real meat – and tuna are often added to vegetable dishes and salads to "spice them up". You'll also find chunks of chorizo and sausage turning up in otherwise veg-friendly soups or bean stews. The phrases to get to know are "*Soy vegetariano/a. Como sólo verduras. Hay algo sin carne?*" ("I'm a vegetarian. I only eat vegetables. Is there anything without meat?"); you may have to add "*y sin marisco*" ("and without seafood") and "*y sin jamón*" ("and without ham") to be really safe.

Some salads and vegetable dishes are strictly **vegan**, but they're few and far between. Fruit and nuts are widely available; nuts are sold by street vendors everywhere and stocked in larger supermarkets.

Coffee, tea and soft drinks

Café (coffee) is invariably an espresso (*café solo*); for a large cup of weaker, black coffee, ask for an *americano*.

A *café cortado* is a *café solo* with a drop of milk; a *café con leche* is made with lots of hot milk. Coffee is also frequently mixed with brandy (*coñac*) or *whisky* (pronounced "whicky"), all such concoctions being called a *carajillo*. Iced coffee is *café con hielo* (you'll be served a coffee and a separate glass of ice cubes – you pour the former over the latter to make a great summer refresher). **Chocolate** (hot chocolate) is a popular breakfast drink, or for after a long night on the town, but it's usually incredibly thick and sweet. For a thinner, cocoa-style drink, ask for a brand name, like Cola Cao.

Spaniards usually drink **té** (tea) black, so if you want milk it's safest to ask for it afterwards, since ordering *té con leche* might well get you a glass of warm milk with a tea bag floating on top. Herbal teas (*infusiones*) are widely available, like *manzanilla* (camomile), *poleo* (mint tea) and *hierba luisa* (lemon verbena).

Local soft drinks include **granizado** (slush) or **horchata** (a milky drink made from tiger nuts or almonds), available from summer street stalls, and from milk bars and ice-cream parlours (*heladerías*). Although you can drink the **water** almost everywhere, it tastes revolting in some cities and coastal areas – inexpensive *agua mineral* comes either sparkling (*con gas*) or still (*sin gas*).

Wine, beer and spirits

Wine (*vino*), either *tinto* (red), *blanco* (white) or *rosado/clarete* (rosé), is the invariable accompaniment to every meal and is, as a rule, extremely inexpensive. Andalucía's wine-making genius is mainly concerned with sherry (see page 43) and so most table wines are imported from outside the region (see page 42). One thing worth knowing about Spanish wine is the terms related to the **ageing process** which defines the best wines: *crianza* wines must have a minimum of two years ageing before sale; red *reserva* wines at least two years, of which one must be in oak barrels; red *gran reserva* must have at least two years in oak

---

CONVENTO DULCES

Many convents throughout Andalucía and Spain are in the business of supporting their orders by making **dulces de convento**: cakes and pastries that they can sell to the community. Many recipes date back to the Arabs, who used rich combinations of eggs, almonds, sugar and honey to concoct their Moorish goodies. Each convent guards its recipes jealously, and many are so good that they supply local restaurants. The **sherry manufacturers** also had an influence on the development of *convento dulces*, since they traditionally used egg-whites to clarify their wines and donated the leftover yolks to the nuns. This is the origin of many egg-yolk-based creations such as *tocino de cielo* (Andalucía's richest flan) and *yemas* (sweet cakes), two of the region's most popular confections.

WINING AND DINING

One of the great pleasures of eating out in Andalucía is the chance to sample some of Spain's excellent wines. Restaurant **wine prices** compare very favourably with other parts of Europe and in most restaurants and *ventas* you'll often be able to find a decent bottle for €10–15. Most establishments usually have an economical house wine too for around half this price (ask for *caserío* or *vino de la casa*) and sometimes this will be served straight from the barrel in a half-litre or litre carafe (*jarra*). This can be great or it can be lousy, but at least it will be distinctively local.

The most common bottled red wine in Andalucía is **Valdepeñas**, a good standard wine from the central plains of New Castile (Los Llanos, Viña Albali and Señorío de Guadianeja are good labels). **Rioja**, from the area round Logroño in the north, is one of Spain's classic wines but a lot more expensive (Cune, Faustino, Coto de Imaz, Muga, Beronia, Marqués de Cáceres, Bordón, Viña Ardanza, Marqués de Riscal and Izadi are some names to look out for). Another top-drawer, and currently fashionable, region is **Ribera del Duero** in Castilla-León. This produces Spain's most expensive wine, Vega Sicilia, along with outstanding whites (Belondrade y Lurtón) and reds (Pesquera, Viña Pedrosa, Protos and Señorio de Nava). There are also scores of other excellent wines from regions such as Catalunya (Bach, Raimat, Torres) which also produces the champagne-like Cava (Codorníu, Freixenet) and the new and pricey Priorat reds which have a high reputation (Clos Mogador, Alvaro Palacios). Galicia, known for its fragrant whites (Fefiñanes, Fin de Siglo and San Trocado), Navarra (Gran Feudo, Señorio de Sarría, Ochoa) and Valencia (Murviedro, Gandía) are others, and even the once unpromising La Mancha (Santa Rita, Casa Gualda, Estola) has in recent years been making a name for itself as a producer of quality wines.

Andalucía's solitary table-wine area of any volume is the **Condado de Huelva**, which turns out reasonable dry whites that go well with seafood. Red wines have also made some headway in a region long thought to be too hot to produce quality vintages: in 2007 US wine guru Robert Parker caused a sensation when he awarded 95 points (out of a hundred) to Arcos de la Frontera bodega Huerta de Albalá's Taberner no. 1, comparing it to "the best of the northern Rhones". Across the border from here in Málaga, there has been a mushrooming of *micro-bodegas* around **Ronda** and many of these are now producing excellent vintages. Local wines are also made in the country districts, with some, such as the **costa** wine of the western Alpujarras, and the **Laujar de Andarax** wines of the eastern Alpujarras, always worth trying.

and three in the bottle. *Vino de Mesa* and *Vino de la Tierra* are the equivalent of France's Vin de Table, and DO (*Denominación de Origen*) is Spain's version of the French Appellation Contrôlée regulating grape varieties and region of origin.

Dining out away from the larger towns and cities your choice of wine (especially in remote *ventas*) will be severely limited. Busier *ventas* and restaurants with a healthy reputation, however, usually have well-stocked cellars and will only be too pleased to let you peruse their *carta de vinos*. In Andalucía you will often be asked in restaurants – especially at lunchtime in summer – if you would like your wine *"con Casera"*. *La Casera* is a brand of lemonade that many *andaluzes* use to dilute the wine, turning it into a "spritzer". This combination also forms a legitimate bar drink called *tinto de verano* where red wine is mixed with soda or lemonade and makes a great summer refresher. Equally refreshing, though often deceptively strong, is **sangría**, a wine-and-fruit punch that you'll come across at fiestas and in tourist bars.

In a bar, a small glass of wine will generally cost around €1.50–3 depending on location (rural bars are usually much cheaper than city places) and whether it's a quality wine (eg Rioja) or the local plonk. Often a *menú del día* (set meal) will include wine, but these days, in times of paring costs to the bone, many establishments are tending to cut the "free" wine from their *menús*, or offering at best a single glass.

Beer

Beer (*cerveza*) is nearly always lager-style, though some Spanish breweries also now make stout-style brews, wheat beers and other types. It comes in 300ml bottles (*botellines*) or, for about the same price, on tap – a *caña* of draught beer is a small glass, a *caña doble* larger, and asking for *un tubo* (a tubular glass) gets you about half a pint. Mahou, Cruz Campo (now produced by Heineken), San Miguel, Damm, Estrella de Galicia and Alhambra are all decent beers. A **shandy** is a *clara*, either with fizzy lemon (*con limón*) or lemonade (*con casera*).

Spirits

In mid-afternoon – or, let's face it, even at breakfast – Spaniards take a *copa* of liqueur with their coffee, such as *anís* (similar to Pernod) or *coñac*, the local **brandy**, which has a distinct vanilla flavour. Most brandies are produced by the great sherry houses in Jerez and the best – such as Carlos 1 or Lepanto – compare favourably with any top Cognac. Other classy non-*jerezano* brands include the Armagnac-like Mascaró and Torres, both from Catalunya. Instead of brandy, at the end of a meal many places serve **chupitos** – little shot glasses of flavoured schnapps or local firewater, such as *pacharán* (a sloes and anis combination).

You should order **spirits** by brand name, since there are generally less expensive Spanish equivalents for standard imports, or simply specify *nacional*. Larios gin from Málaga, for instance, is about half the price of Gordon's. Measures are staggeringly generous – bar staff generally pour from the bottle until you suggest they stop. Long drinks include the universal *Gin-Tónic* and *Cuba Libre* (rum and Coke), and there are often Spanish Caribbean rums (*ron*) such as Cacique from Venezuela or Havana Club from Cuba.

Sherry

The classic Andalucían wine is **sherry** – *vino de jerez* or *fino* as it's popularly known – which is excellent, widely available and consumed with gusto by *andaluzes*. Served chilled or at bodega temperature – a perfect drink to wash down tapas – like everything Spanish, it comes in a perplexing variety of forms. The main distinctions are between *fino* or *jerez seco* (dry sherry), *amontillado* (medium) and *oloroso* (full-bodied) or *jerez dulce* (sweet), and these are the terms you should use to order. Similar in the way they are made – though not identical in flavour – are Montilla and Manzanilla, which are not fortified with alcohol as is the case with other finos. The first of these dry, sherry-like wines comes from the province of Córdoba, and the latter from Sanlúcar de Barrameda, part of the "sherry triangle" along with Jerez and El Puerto de Santa María.

The media

The ubiquitous Spanish newspaper kiosk is your first stop for regional and national newspapers and magazines, though **hotels and bars nearly always have a few lying around for customers. The bigger cities, tourist towns and resorts will also have foreign newspapers available (some of which are actually published in Spain), generally on the day of issue or perhaps a day late. Television is all-pervasive in bars, cafés and restaurants; most pensión and hotel rooms have a TV, too, though only in the fancier places will you get any English-language programming, and then probably only BBC World, CNN or Eurosport satellite channels.**

Newspapers and magazines

Andalucíans, in line with the Spanish generally, are not great devourers of newsprint and none of the Spanish **national newspapers** has a circulation above 400,000. The best of these are the Madrid-based centre-left *El País* (Ⓦelpais.es) and the centre-right *El Mundo* (Ⓦelmundo.es), both of which have good arts and foreign news coverage, and include Andalucía **regional supplements** with news and "what's on" listings. Other national papers include the solidly old-order *ABC* with a hard moral line against divorce and abortion, and Barcelona's centrist *La Vanguardia* (also available in Andalucía). Andalucía's **regional press** is generally run by local magnates and predominantly right of centre, but often provides an entertaining read. The best of Andalucía's regional **dailies** are *Sur* from Málaga, *Diario de Cádiz*, *Córdoba* and Granada's *Ideal*. The paper with the highest circulation is *Marca* (Ⓦmarca.com), the country's top **sports daily**, mainly football-dominated; there's also *As* (Ⓦas.com), *El Mundo Deportivo* (Ⓦelmundodeportivo.es) and *Sport* (Ⓦsport.es). The main cities such as Seville, Málaga and Granada are also awash with **free newspapers**, which are handed out at bus stops and train stations.

There's a bewildering variety of **magazines** specializing in celebrity gossip (known collectively as *la prensa rosa*), ranging from the more traditional *Hola* to the sensationalist *QMD!* (*Que me Dices*). *El Jueves* is the Spanish equivalent to the British comic *Viz*, while the online daily *El Confidencial* (Ⓦelconfidencial.com) gives the inside track on serious economic and political stories. There are also various **English-language magazines** and papers produced by or for the huge expatriate community now resident in Andalucía. Málaga's *Sur* newspaper produces the free weekly *Sur in English* (Ⓦsurinenglish.com) which has a news digest and popular classified columns. Another decent production is the monthly **online** Ⓦandalucia.com, but the best of the bunch is the *Olive Press* (⦿theolivepress.es), a fortnightly paper which frequently campaigns on local and regional issues.

Radio

There are hundreds of local radio channels (almost every major town in Andalucía has its local radio station), broadcasting alongside a handful of national ones. The state-run **RNE** (⦿rtve.es/radio) network covers five stations: RNE 1, a general news and information channel; Radio Clásica, broadcasting mainly classical music and related programmes; the popular music channel RNE 3; RNE 4, in Catalan; and the rolling news and sports channel RNE 5. Radio Exterior is RNE's international shortwave service. Other **popular channels** include Cadena Ser and Onda Cero (news, talk, sports and culture), the rightist Catholic Church-run COPE, 40 Principales (for the latest hits, Spanish and otherwise) and Cadena 100 (music and cultural programming). Radio Marca (dedicated sports radio) is also very popular. Full listings, local stations and frequencies can be found in *El País* and the local press.

Television

RTV (⦿rtve.es) provides the main, state-run channels, namely TVE1, a general entertainment and news channel, and its sister La 2 (ie "Dos"), given over to sports and culture. Although the state channels no longer carry advertising following a change in the law in 2009, they still compete aggressively (particularly TVE 1) for audience share with the private stations, which largely results in a tedious mix of game, reality and celebrity scandal shows, sport, films and *telenovelas* (soaps) across the board. **Private national stations** are Antena 3, Cuatro (ie Four), Telecinco (Five) and La Sexta (Sixth); the latter adopts a more critical stance towards the political scene and frequently produces hard-hitting documentaries. Andalucía's Canal Sur is funded by the Junta de Andalucía (regional government) and puts out local programming and regional news. The main **satellite** channel is Canal+.

Festivals

The fiesta or feria is a crucial part of Spanish life. Even the smallest village or most modern city suburb devotes at least a couple of days a year to partying, and taking in such an event can be huge fun, propelling you right into the heart of Spanish culture. It's hard to beat the experience of arriving in some tiny hamlet, expecting no more than a bed for the night, to discover the streets decked out with flags and streamers, spectacular fireworks lighting up the sky, a band playing in the plaza and the entire population out celebrating the local fiesta.

Festivals usually mark the local saint's day, but there are celebrations, too, of harvests, of deliverance from the Moors, of safe return from the sea – any excuse will do.

Each festival has its own particular characteristics but there are facets common to them all. Horses, **flamenco**, fireworks and the guitar are essential parts of any celebration, usually accompanied by the downing of oceans of **fino** – which is probably why the sherry companies seem to provide most of the bunting. And along with the music there is always **dancing** – usually *sevillanas* (see box, page 547) in traditional flamenco costume and an immense spirit of enjoyment. The main event of most fiestas is a **parade**, either behind a revered holy image, or a more celebratory affair with fancy costumes and *gigantones*, grotesque giant carnival figures which are both celebrated and feared by children.

Although these festivals take place throughout the year – and it is often the obscure and unexpected event that proves to be most fun – there are certain occasions that stand out. Easter Week (**Semana Santa**) and **Corpus Christi** (in early June) are celebrated throughout Andalucía with magnificent religious processions. Easter, particularly, is worth trying to coincide with – head for Seville, Málaga, Granada or Córdoba, where huge *pasos*, floats of wildly theatrical religious scenes, are carried down the streets, accompanied by weirdly hooded penitents atoning for the year's misdeeds. And just as moving in their own more intimate way are the countless small town and village observances of Semana Santa with smaller processions, traditional customs and sometimes a Passion play. Outsiders are always welcome, the one problem being that during any of the most popular (though usually not at the small town and village affairs) you'll find it difficult and expensive to find a bed. If you're likely to be visiting somewhere at festival time, try and book your accommodation well in advance.

Among the biggest and best-known of Andalucía's **other popular festivals** are the Cádiz Carnaval (mid-February); Seville's enormous April Feria (a week at the end of the month); Jerez's Feria del Caballo (Horse Fair, April/May); the Romería del

Roció, an extraordinary pilgrimage to El Roció near Huelva (arriving there on Whit Sunday); and Málaga's boisterous and good-humoured Feria (mid-August).

Listed below are some of Andalucía's main fiestas, all worth trying to get to if you're going to be in the area around the time; more are described with the relevant locations covered in the Guide section. Note that saints' day festivals – indeed all Spanish celebrations – can vary in date, and are often observed over the weekend closest to the dates given here.

The list is potentially endless. In addition to our selection (see below), check the Junta de Andalucía's annual **Ferias y Fiestas de Andalucía** guide, available from local tourist offices, and see ⓦ fiestas-deandalucia.com.

A festival calendar

JANUARY

1–2: Día de la Toma. Celebration of the 1492 entry of the Reyes Católicos into the city – at Granada.
5: Cabalgata de los Reyes Magos. Epiphany parade at Málaga.
6: Romería de la Virgen del Mar. Pilgrimage procession from Almería.
17: Romería del Ermita del Santo. Pilgrimage procession at Guadix.

FEBRUARY

1: San Cecilio. Fiesta in Granada's traditionally *gitano* (gypsy) quarter of Sacromonte.
Mid-month: Carnaval. Extravagant week-long event (leading up to Lent) in all the Andalucian cities. Cádiz, above all, celebrates with fancy dress, flamenco, spectacular parades and street-singers' competitions.

MARCH

5–15: El Puerto de Santa María (Cádiz) Carnaval. Spain's most important and wittiest carnival celebrations.
March/April: Semana Santa (Holy Week). Following Palm Sunday, this has its most elaborate and dramatic celebrations in Andalucía. You'll find moving and memorable processions of floats and penitents at (in descending order of importance) Seville, Málaga, Granada and Córdoba, and to a lesser extent in smaller towns such as Almería, Jerez, Arcos, Baeza and Úbeda. All culminate with the full drama of the Passion on Good Friday, with Easter Day itself more of a family occasion.

APRIL

Last week: Feria de Abril (two weeks after Easter, usually in April, occasionally May; check with the tourist office). Week-long Feria de Abril in Seville: the largest fair in Spain, a little refined, in the way of the city, but an extraordinary event nonetheless. A small April fair – featuring bull-running – is held in Vejer.

Last Sunday: Romería de Nuestra Señora de la Cabeza. Three days of celebrations in Andujar (Jaén) culminate in a huge procession to the Sanctuary of the Virgin in the Sierra Morena.

MAY

1–2: Romería de Nuestra Señora de la Estrella. At Navas de San Juan. Jaén province's most important pilgrimage.
3: "Moors and Christians" Carnival. At Pampaneira (Alpujarras).
First two weeks: Cruces de Mayo (Festival of the Patios). Córdoba celebrates the Holy Cross; includes a competition for the prettiest patio and numerous events and concerts organized by the local city council.
Early May (usually the week after Seville's fair): Horse Fair. Somewhat aristocratic Horse Fair at Jerez de la Frontera.
17: San Isidro Romería. At Setenil (Cádiz).
Pentecost (seven weeks after Easter): Romería del Rocío. Spain's biggest *romería*: a million often inebriated pilgrims in horse-drawn carriages and processions converge on El Rocío (Huelva) from all over the south.
Thurs after Trinity (Variable): Corpus Christi. Bullfights and festivities at Granada, Seville, Ronda, Vejer and Zahara de la Sierra. At Seville, Los Seises (Six Choirboys) perform a dance before the altar of the cathedral.
Third weekend: Romería de Santa Eulalia. Pilgrimage, fireworks, parades and fandangos at Almonaster La Real in the Sierra de Aracena in honour of the village's patron saint.
Last week: Feria de la Manzanilla. Prolonged binge in Sanlúcar de Barrameda to celebrate the town's major product. The sherry is used to wash down huge quantities of seafood while watching flamenco and sporting events from beachfront *casetas* (party tents).

JUNE

Second week: Feria de San Bernabé. Marbella's fair is often spectacular, since this is the richest town in Andalucía.
13–14: Fiestas Patronales de San Antonio. At Trevélez (Alpujarras); includes mock battles between Moors and Christians.
23–24: Candelas de San Juan. Bonfires and effigies at Vejer and all along the coast as crowds party all night while waiting to celebrate the dawn.
23–26: Feria de Alhaurín de la Torre. Processions, giants and an important flamenco competition in Málaga.
30: Conil (Cádiz) feria.
End June/early July: International Festival of Music and Dance. Major dance groups, chamber orchestras and flamenco artistes perform in Granada's Alhambra palace, Generalife and Carlos V palace.

JULY

Early July: International Guitar Festival. Brings together top international acts in Córdoba from classical, flamenco and Latin American music.
9–14: Feast of San Francisco Solano. Montilla (Córdoba) celebrates its annual *feria*.

End of July: Virgen del Mar summer fiesta. Parades, horseriding events and usually a handful of major jazz and rock concerts in Almería's Plaza Vieja.

AUGUST

First week: Berja fiesta. Annual fiesta in Almería in honour of the Virgin of Gádor.

3: Huelva fiesta. Colombinas celebrate Columbus's voyages of discovery with a fiesta.

5: Trevélez (Granadan Alpujarras) romería. A midnight *romería* to Mulhacén.

13–21: Feria de Málaga. One of Andalucía's most enjoyable fiestas for visitors, who are heartily welcomed by the ebullient *malagueños*.

15: Ascension of the Virgin. Fair with *casetas* at Vejer and throughout Andalucía.

15: Noche del Vino. A riotous wine festival at Competa (Málaga) with dancing, singing and endless drinking.

17–20: The first cycle of horse races along Sanlúcar de Barrameda's beach. Heavy official and unofficial betting; the second tournament takes place exactly a week later.

19–21: Vendimia. Grape harvest fiesta at Montilla (Córdoba).

Third week: Algeciras fair and fiesta.

Third weekend: Fiesta de San Mamés. At Aroche (Huelva) in the extremities of the Sierra de Aracena, this is unpretentious and great fun, everything a village fiesta should be.

22–25: Feria de Grazalema (Cádiz).

23–25: Guadalquivir festival. Bullfights and an important flamenco competition at Sanlúcar de Barrameda.

25–30: Fiestas Patronales. In honour of San Agustín at Mojácar (Almería).

SEPTEMBER

6: Fiesta de Cascamorras. Annual *feria* at Baza (Granada) where the Cascamorras or interloper from nearby Guadix attempts to make off with their Virgen and is doused in dirty oil for his pains.

7: Romería del Cristo de la Yedra. Singing and dancing in the streets at Baeza (Jaén).

6–13: Celebration of the Virgen de la Luz. Street processions and horseriding in Tarifa.

7–14: Feria de la Moscatel/Feria de Nuestra Señora de Regla. At Chipiona (Cádiz): includes bull-running, flamenco tournaments and much wine-swilling to acclaim the sweet sherry grape grown hereabouts.

8: Romería de Nuestra Señora de los Ángeles. Colourful event at Alajar (Huelva), with horse races to the peak sanctuary of Arias Montano.

8–9: Fiesta de la Virgen de la Cabeza. At Almuñécar (Granada).

First/second week: Vendimia. Celebration of the vintage at Jerez. Starts with the blessing of the new grapes, after which everyone gets sozzled on the old.

First two weeks: Ronda feria. Ronda bursts into life with a *feria*, flamenco contests and the Corrida Goyesca, bullfights in eighteenth-century dress.

24–25: Día del Señor (Lord's Day). Celebrated at Orgiva (Granada) with impressive fireworks and processions.

29: Fiesta de San Miguel. A fair and *casetas* at Úbeda (Jaén).

OCTOBER

1: Fiesta de San Miguel. Held in Granada's Albaicín quarter and dozens of other towns, including Torremolinos.

6–12: Feria del Rosario. Fuengirola horseriding events and flamenco.

15–23: Feria de San Lucas. Jaén's major fiesta, dating back to the fifteenth century.

NOVEMBER

1: Todos Los Santos (All Saints' Day). Celebrated throughout Andalucía with church services and processions to graveyards.

DECEMBER

28: Fiesta de los Verdiales/Santos Inocentes. Various towns and villages of Málaga's mountain districts celebrate Spain's equivalent of April Fool's Day with dances, pulsating Moorish-inspired music and outlandish headdress. Good places to see it include Comares, Almogía, Casabermeja in the Axarquía to the east of Málaga and the Venta de San Cayetano, Puerto de la Torre, slightly to the northwest.

Bullfighting

Bullfights are an integral part of many Spanish festivals. In Andalucía especially, any village that can afford it will put on a corrida for an afternoon, while in big cities like Seville, the main festivals are accompanied by a week-long (or more) season of prestige fights attended by a veritable who's who of the great and the good. It is no coincidence that the fighting bull is the country's national symbol or that a province like Cádiz – where many bulls are bred – is devoted to the whole culture of taurinismo and treats its matadores like gods.

Los Toros (or *La Lidia*), as Spaniards refer to bullfighting, is big business. Each year an estimated 24,000 bulls are killed before a live audience of over thirty million (with many more watching on television). It is said that 150,000 people are involved, in some way, in the industry, and the top performers, the *matadores*, are major earners, on a par with the country's biggest pop stars.

In recent years opposition has been growing to the "*fiesta nacional*" and there have been frequent protests at festivals such as Pamplona's San Fermín and the Feria de San Isidro in Madrid, the major event in the bullfighting calendar. Reflecting this change in public attitude the city of Barcelona outlawed bullfighting, as did the Canary Islands. The bullfighters' federation have argued for respect for the "traditional culture of Spain," but there is evidence that the tide may be slowly turning against them.

Whether you attend a *corrida*, obviously, is down to your own feelings and ethics. If you spend any time at all in Spain during the **season** (which runs from March to October), you will encounter *Los Toros*, at least on a bar TV, and that will as likely as not make up your mind. If you decide to go, try to attend the biggest and most prestigious that is on, in a major city, where star performers are likely to dispatch the bulls with "*arte*" and a successful, "clean" kill.

The matadores

Top **matadores** include the current idol of the rings, the moody, quixotic and media-shy José Tomás, who nearly died after a goring in Mexico in 2010 only to return in triumph to the *corrida* a year later; the world's top-paid matador, he earns a minimum of €150,000 to dispatch each bull and attracts huge crowds. Other established and popular *matadores* include the veteran Enrique Ponce, El Fandi, Juan José Padilla, El Cid and Julian "El Juli" López who learned his trade in Mexico as an underage teenager before he was legally able to fight in Spain. Since the eighteenth century women have also fought bulls and the now retired Cristina Sánchez became the first woman to have been carried shoulder-high through the *puerta grande* of Las Ventas, the prestigious Madrid ring – a distinction awarded to few of her male peers. Currently the top female *matador* (now into her forties) is Mari Paz Vegá from Málaga.

Perhaps the most exciting and skilful performances of all are by mounted *matadores*, or **rejoneadores** as they are known (from *rejón*, "lance"). This is the oldest form of *corrida*, developed in Ronda in the seventeenth century, in which supremely skilful riders manoeuvre their steeds away from the bull's lethal horns to plant the *banderillas* and then make the kill – all while mounted.

The corrida

The **corrida** begins with a procession, to the accompaniment of a *paso doble* by the band. Leading the procession are two *alguacilillos* or "constables", on horseback and in traditional costume, followed by the three *matadores*, who will each fight two bulls, and their *cuadrillas*, their personal "team" of assistants (*bandilleros*). The ensuing *corrida* takes the form of a

> ## ANTI-BULLFIGHT ORGANIZATIONS
>
> **ADDA (Asociación para la Defensa de los Derechos del Animal)** Ⓦ addaong.org. Coordinates Spain's national opposition to bullfighting.
>
> **ASANDA (Asociación Andaluza para la Defensa de los Animales)** Ⓦ asanda.org. Andalucía's anti-bullfighting pressure group.
>
> **World Animal Protection** Ⓦ worldanimalprotection.org. uk. The website has links to affiliates in Australia, Canada and the US.

drama in three acts or stages (called *suertes*) presided over by a **presidente** who is there to see that a multitude of regulations are adhered to, and award trophies if a matador's performance has merited them.

Once the ring is empty, the first bull (weighing 500–600kg) appears – a moment of great physical beauty – to be "tested" by the matador or their *banderilleros* using pink and gold capes. These preliminaries conducted (and they can be short, if the bull is ferocious), the **suerte de picar** ensues, in which mounted **picadores** drive a short-pointed lance into the bull's neck, while it tries to toss their padded and blindfolded (on the right eye) horse. The whole purpose here is to tire and weaken the bull's powerful neck and shoulder muscles, thus forcing him to lower his head – without which it would be impossibly dangerous to fight and kill on foot. This is for most neutral spectators the least acceptable and most squalid stage of the proceedings, and it is clearly not a pleasant experience for the horses, their ears stuffed with rags to shut out the noise of the bull and spectators, and their vocal cords cut to prevent any terrified cries from alarming the crowd.

The next stage, the **suerte de banderillas**, involves the placing of three sets of *banderillas* (barbed darts mounted on coloured shafts) into the bull's shoulders. Each of the three **banderilleros** delivers these in turn, attracting the bull's attention with the movement of their own body rather than a cape, and deftly placing the *banderillas* while both they and the bull are running towards each other.

Once the *banderillas* have been placed, the **suerte de matar** begins, and the **matador** enters the ring alone, having exchanged the pink and gold cape for the red *muleta*. The matador salutes the president and then dedicates the bull either to an individual, to whom they give their hat, or to the audience, by placing the hat in the centre of the ring. It is in this part of the *corrida* that judgements are made and the performance is focused, as the matador displays their skills on the (injured and by now exhausted) bull. They use the movements of the cape to attract the bull, while their body remains still. If they do well, the band will start to play, while the crowd *"olé"* each pass. This stage lasts around ten minutes and ends with the kill.

Tickets

Tickets for *corridas* in the major city *plazas de toros* start at around €15 for a *sol* seat, rising to €100 and above for the prime seats at prestigious fights in rings such as Seville's Maestranza. Seats are divided into *sol* (sun), *sombra* (shade) and *sol y sombra* (shaded after a while), though these distinctions have become less relevant as more bullfights start later in the day, at 6pm or 7pm, rather than the traditional 5pm. The *sombra* seats are more expensive – not so much for the spectators' personal comfort but because most of the action takes place in the shade. Tickets for *novilladas* (novice fights with young bulls) are much cheaper, costing €10–40, and are often given away free by bars or agents outside the bullring prior to the *corrida* if there hasn't been much demand (which is often the case).

Football

The nation threw a huge party when finally, at the 2008 European Champion-ships, the Spanish national football team shook off decades of habitual underper-formance and actually won something, beating Germany to become European champions in some style. They threw an even bigger party when this football-crazy nation added the World Cup to the trophy cabinet in 2010. However, in 2014 and 2018 the national team had miserable tournaments, causing a massive cloud of disappointment to descend over the nation.

Spain's success had been a good while coming – although **fútbol** has long been the most popular sport in Spain, it's only recently that Spanish football has made much of an international splash, possibly because many of Spain's better players went abroad to hone their skills. In the English Premier League alone there have been countless Spanish professionals of whom Juan Mata, Fernando Torres, David de Gea, Santi Cazorla and David Silva are the best known. The Spanish domestic top flight has been weakened as a result, but still remains one of the most competitive in Europe. Certainly, if you want the excitement of a genuinely Spanish event, watching a Sunday-evening game in La Liga (**W**lfp.es) usually produces as much passion as anything you'll find in the Plaza de Toros.

For decades, the country's two dominant teams have been Real Madrid and F.C. Barcelona. Since the early years of the new millennium, the big two have faced a bit more opposition than usual from clubs like Atletico de Madrid (2021 La Liga champions), Valencia and Sevilla, but on any weekend, the big football story will be if either of the two giants fails to win by a convincing score. And should either lose, the inquest goes on for days.

Andaluz teams

Sevilla are the main team in Andalucía, closely followed in recent seasons by their fierce city rivals **Real Betis**. Other *andaluz* clubs in the top flight include yo-yo team **Málaga** who fluctuate between the top flight and the second division. Others of note are **Recreativo de Huelva**, Spain's oldest club (now in Division Three), and the remarkable U.D. (Unión Deportivo) **Almería** who reached the Primera División less than twenty years after being founded in 1989. The most amazing *andaluz* story, though, belongs to plucky little CF Granada who nearly went out of business due to financial difficulties in July 2009 when in the Third Division; they dramatically turned things around and following successive promotions attained the dizzy heights of the First Division where they last played in the 1970s. They managed to hang on to their place in the top flight for a remarkable six seasons before being relegated in 2017. Another minnow, **Córdoba C.F.**, produced more heroics at the end of the 2013–14 season; despite finishing seventh in the Second Division table, they performed valiantly in the play-offs to gain a place in the Primera División – where they played against the likes of Barça and Real. The dream lasted only for one season, however, and they were relegated in 2015.

Seeing a game

The league **season** runs from late August until mid-May or early June, and most games kick off at 5pm or 7pm on Sundays, though live TV demands that one key game kicks off at 9pm or 10pm on Saturday and Sunday.

With the exception of a few important games – such as when either of the big two plays Sevilla or the two Seville teams play their derbys – match tickets are pretty easy to get; they start at around €30 for average First Division games, but get close to double this when Real or Barça are in town. Trouble is very rare: English fans, in particular, will be amazed at the easy-going family atmosphere and mixed-sex crowds. August is a surprisingly good time to catch games since there's a glut of warm-up matches for the new season, often involving top foreign clubs.

If you don't go to a game, the atmosphere can be pretty good watching on TV in a local bar, especially in a city whose team is playing away. Many bars advertise the matches they screen, which, if they have satellite connections, can include Sunday afternoon English League and Cup games. ⓦ soccer-spain.com is a very good English-language website where you'll find comprehensive news and articles.

Travelling with children

Spain is a good country to travel with children of any age; they will be well received everywhere, and babies and toddlers, in particular, will be the centre of attention. You will probably have to change your usual routine, since young children stay up late in Spain, especially in the summer. It's very common for them to be running around pavement cafés and public squares well after 10pm or 11pm, and yours will no doubt enjoy doing likewise. It's expected that families dine out with their children, too, and it's not unusual to see up to four generations of the same family eating tapas in a bar.

Holidays

Many holiday hotels and self-contained club-style resorts offer things like kids' clubs, babysitting, sports and entertainment. The only caveat is that, of course, you're unlikely to see much of Spain on these family-oriented holidays. The two best cities to take children to, hands down, are **Seville** and **Granada**, which have loads of child-friendly attractions. Otherwise, the region also has various theme parks and leisure activities specifically aimed at kids, most notably the **Isla Mágica** in Seville (see page 271), **Tivoli World** near Benalmádena on the Costa del Sol (see page 103) and the Western film set of **Mini Hollywood** in Almería (see page 520), while Andalucía's long coastline has a bunch of popular **water parks**.

Museums, galleries and sights throughout Andalucía either offer **discounts** or **free entry** for children (places are often free for under-4s or even under-7s),

and it's the same on trains, sightseeing tours, boat trips and most other usual tourist attractions.

Accommodation

If you're travelling independently, finding **child-friendly accommodation** shouldn't be a problem, as *hostales* and *pensiones* generally offer rooms with three or four beds. Bear in mind, though, that much budget accommodation in towns and cities is located on the upper floors of buildings, often without lifts. It's also worth noting that some older-style *hostales* don't have efficient heating systems (very occasionally none at all) – and it can get very cold in winter. If you want a cot provided, or baby-listening or **baby-sitting** services, you'll usually have to stay in a more expensive hotel – and even then, never assume that these facilities are provided, and always check in advance. **Self-catering accommodation** offers the most flexibility, and there's plenty of it throughout the region, from seaside apartments to country houses; even in major cities, it's easy to rent an apartment by the night or week and enjoy living like a local with your family.

Travel essentials

Addresses

Addresses are written as: C/Picasso 2, 4° izda. – which means Picasso Street (*calle*) no. 2, fourth floor, left- (*izquierda*) hand flat or office; dcha. (*derecha*) is right; cto. (*centro*) centre; s/n (*sin número*) means the building has no number; *bajo* signifies ground floor.

Climate

Overall, spring, early summer and autumn are ideal times for a trip to Andalucía – though the weather does vary significantly from region to region: the Sierra de Grazalema records Spain's highest **rainfall**, while the province of Almería has the most hours of **sun**. Note that our chart (see box) shows average temperatures – and while Seville, the hottest city in Spain, can soar up into the high 30s at mid-afternoon in summer, it is a fairly comfortable 23–27°C (75–80°F) through much of the morning and early evening. Temperatures in mountain regions, in the Sierra Nevada or the Sierra de Cazorla for example, can approach freezing at night in winter, but remain refreshingly cool throughout the hottest summers – a boon for hikers and anyone uncomfortable with blistering heat.

AVERAGE DAILY TEMPERATURES

	Feb	Apr	Jun	Aug	Oct	Dec
ALMERÍA						
Max/min (°C)	16/8	20/12	26/18	29/22	23/16	17/9
Max/min (°F)	61/46	68/54	79/64	84/72	73/61	63/48
GRANADA						
Max/min (°C)	14/2	20/7	30/14	34/17	22/9	12/2
Max/min (°F)	57/36	68/45	86/57	93/63	72/48	54/36
JAÉN						
Max/min (°C)	14/5	20/10	30/17	34/21	22/13	12/5
Max/min (°F)	57/41	68/50	86/63	93/70	72/55	54/41
MÁLAGA						
Max/min (°C)	17/8	21/11	28/17	30/20	24/15	17/9
Max/min (°F)	63/46	70/52	82/63	86/68	75/59	63/48
SEVILLE						
Max/min (°C)	17/6	23/11	32/17	36/20	26/14	16/7
Max/min (°F)	63/43	73/52	90/63	97/68	79/57	61/45
TARIFA						
Max/min (°C)	17/11	20/13	24/17	27/20	23/17	17/11
Max/min (°F)	63/52	68/55	75/63	80/68	73/63	63/52

Complaints

By law, all establishments (including hotels and restaurants) must keep a *libro de reclamaciones* (**complaints book**) and bring it out for regular inspection by the authorities. If you think you've been overcharged, or have any other problems, you can usually produce an immediate resolution by asking for the book. Most establishments prefer to keep them empty, thus attracting no unwelcome attention from officialdom, which, of course, works in your favour. If you do make an entry, English is acceptable, but write clearly and simply; add your home address, too, as you are entitled to be informed of any action, including – but don't count on it – compensation. You can also take your complaint to any local Turismo, which should attempt to resolve the matter while you wait.

Costs

Prices in Andalucía and Spain have increased considerably over the last decade or so, but there are still few places in Europe where you'll get a better deal on the cost of simple meals and drinks. Public transport, too, remains very good value. Big cities and tourist resorts are invariably more expensive than remoter areas, and prices are hiked to take advantage of special events, so for example you'd be lucky to find a room in Seville during Semana Santa (Holy Week) or the Feria de Abril at less than a third above the usual rate.

It's difficult to come up with a **daily budget** for the region, as your €1.50 glass of wine and €40 *pensión* room in rural Andalucía might be €3 and €70, respectively, in Seville or Granada. However, as a very rough guide, if you always share a room in the cheapest *pensiones* and hotels, use public transport and stick to local restaurants and bars, you could get by on between €70 and €100 a day per person. Stay somewhere a bit more stylish or comfortable, eat in fancier restaurants, and go out on the town, and you'll need more like €100–150 a day. And if you're holidaying in Spain's magnificent *paradores* or five-star hotels, that figure will hardly cover your room. There's more detailed information about prices in the "Accommodation" (see page 35), "Getting around" (see page 30) and "Food and drink" (see page 38) sections.

Visiting museums, galleries, churches and monasteries soon adds up – if you visited every sight we cover in Granada alone, for example, you'd be out of pocket by over €60. Accordingly, it pays to take along any **student/youth** or **senior citizen cards** you may be entitled to, such as the International Student ID Card (ISIC; Ⓦisic.org), as most attractions offer discounts (and make sure you carry your passport or ID card, although most places will accept a reasonably clear photocopy of these). Children (as well as seniors) usually get a discount, and younger kids are often free. Some museums and attractions are **free** on a certain day of the week or month (though note that this is sometimes limited to EU citizens only, and you'll need to show your passport).

Crime and personal safety

The **Guardia Civil**, in green uniforms, is a national police force, formerly a military organization, and has responsibility for national crime, as well as roads, borders and guarding public buildings. There's also the blue-uniformed **Policía Nacional**, mainly seen in cities, who deal with crime, drugs, crowd control, identity and immigration matters and the like. Locally, most policing is carried out by the **Policía Local** or **Municipal**, who wear blue-and-white uniforms, and these tend to be the most approachable in the first instance if you're reporting a crime. There's obviously a certain overlap between regional and municipal forces, and you may be passed from one to another, depending on what you're reporting.

In the unlikely event that you're mugged or otherwise robbed, go straight to the police, where you'll need to make an official statement known as a **denuncia**, not least because your insurance company will require a police report. Expect it to be a time-consuming and laborious business – you can do the bulk of it by phone, or even online (Ⓦpolicia.es), but you'll still have to go into the station to sign it. If you have your passport stolen, contact your nearest embassy or consulate; to find this visit a site such as Ⓦprojectvisa.com or Ⓦspainexpat.com, who have complete lists with contact numbers. Alternatively, see the "Directory" sections in Málaga (see page 78) and Seville (see page 287) for consulates in Andalucía.

Avoiding trouble

Petty crime – pickpocketing and bag-snatching – is, unfortunately, a fact of life in Spanish cities and tourist resorts, though no more so than anywhere else in Europe. The usual sensible **precautions** include: carrying bags slung across your neck, not over your shoulder; not putting wallets or phones in your back pocket; leaving passport and travel tickets in the hotel room's safe (or your hotel's safe); and keeping a photocopy of your passport, plus notes of your credit card number helplines and so on. Take special care on public transport, and don't leave **bags** unattended anywhere, even if you're looking at rooms upstairs in a *hostal*; know where your belongings are at all times.

Drivers shouldn't leave anything in view in a **parked car**, particularly in Málaga or Seville, and especially so at night; take the satnav and (if detachable) the radio/CD player, with you. **On the road**, be cautious about accepting help from anyone other than a uniformed police officer – some roadside thieves pose as "good Samaritans" to people experiencing car and tyre problems, some of which, such as slashed tyres, may have been inflicted at rest stops or service stations in advance. The thieves typically attempt to divert your attention by pointing out a problem and then steal items from the vehicle while you are looking elsewhere.

Incidentally, if you are stopped by a proper police officer for a **driving offence**, being foreign just won't wash as an excuse. They'll fine you on the spot, cash or card.

Sexual harassment

Spain's macho image has faded dramatically, and these days there are relatively few parts of the country where **women travelling alone** are likely to feel intimidated or attract unwanted attention. There is little of the pestering that you have to contend with in, say, the larger Italian cities, and the outdoor culture of *terrazas* (terrace bars) and the tendency of Spaniards to move around in large, mixed crowds, help to make you feel less exposed. "*Déjame en paz*" ("leave me in peace") is a fairly standard rebuff and if you are in any doubt, taking a taxi is always the safest way to travel late at night.

The major **resorts** of the *costas* have their own artificial holiday culture, where any problems are most likely to be caused by other alcohol-fuelled holiday-makers. You are actually more vulnerable in isolated, **rural regions**, where you can walk for hours without coming across an inhabited farm or house, though it's rare that this poses a threat – help and hospitality are much more the norm. Many single women happily tramp the long-distance footpaths, from Tarifa to the Sierra Nevada, though you are always best advised to stay in rooms and *hostales* rather than camp wild.

EMERGENCY NUMBERS

- ☎**112** All emergency services
- ☎**061** Ambulance
- ☎**080** Fire service
- ☎**062** Guardia Civil
- ☎**091** Policía Nacional

Electricity

The current in most of Spain is 220v – bring an adaptor (and transformer) to use UK and US laptops, mobile phone chargers and the like.

Entry requirements

EU citizens (and those of Norway, Iceland, Liechtenstein and Switzerland) need only a valid national identity card or passport to enter Spain. Other Europeans, including those from the UK, and citizens of the **US**, **Canada**, **Australia** and **New Zealand** require a passport but no visa, and can stay as a tourist for up to ninety days. Other nationalities (including South Africans) will need to get a visa from a Spanish embassy or consulate before departure. Visa requirements do change, and it's always advisable to check the current situation before leaving home.

Most EU citizens who want to stay in Spain for longer than three months, rather than just visit as a tourist, need to register at a provincial **Oficina de Extranjeros** (Foreigners' Office), where they'll be issued with a residence certificate; you'll find a list of offices (eventually) on the Ministry of Interior website (ⓦ www.interior.gob.es). Note this no longer applies to UK citizens who are not covered by the Withdrawal Agreement (those were already provably resident in Spain when the UK left the EU in 2020). UK visitors may have to prove they have sufficient funds for their stay in Spain. In 2022 this was €100 a day. From 2023, UK citizens (and all other non-EU citizens) arriving in Spain will have to pay a €7 visa waiver fee.

US citizens can apply for one ninety-day extension, showing proof of funds, but this must be done from outside Spain. Other nationalities wishing to extend their stay will need to get a special visa from a Spanish embassy or consulate before departure.

UK citizens are entitled to free or reduced cost medical treatment on production of a GHIC (Global Health Insurance Card; apply for it online at ⓦ nhs.uk). UK citizens in possession of a pre-Brexit EHIC still within its validity date can carry on using it until it expires. Nationals of other countries should check whether their government has a reciprocal health agreement, and/or ensure that they have adequate insurance cover.

Health

The **European Health Insurance Card** (EHIC; available online in Ireland from whse.ie) gives EU citizens access to Spanish state public health services under reciprocal agreements. While this will provide free or reduced-cost medical care in the event of minor injuries and emergencies, it won't cover every eventuality – and it only applies to those in possession of the card – so travel insurance (see page 53) is essential.

UK residents are entitled to free or reduced cost medical treatment on production of a GHIC (Global Health Insurance Card; apply for it online at ⓦ nhs.uk). Holders of a pre-Brexit EHIC still within its validity date can carry on using it until it expires.

No **inoculations** are required for Spain, and the worst that's likely to happen to you is that you might fall victim to an upset stomach. To be safe, wash fruit and avoid tapas dishes that look as if they were prepared last week – ensalada rusa (Russian salad, sometimes referred to as ensaladilla) is one of the main culprits here. Water at public fountains is fine, unless there's a sign saying "agua no potable", in which case don't drink it.

For minor complaints, go to a **farmacia** – they're easy to find, and pharmacists are highly trained, willing to give advice (often in English) and able to dispense many drugs that would be available only on prescription in other countries. They keep usual shop hours (Mon–Fri 9am–1.30pm & 5–8pm or 9pm), but some open late and at weekends, while a rota system keeps at least one open 24 hours in every town. The rota is displayed in the window of every pharmacy, or you can check the list in the local newspaper. The Farmacia Caffarena (see page 78) in the city of Málaga is open 24 hours all year long.

Treatment at **hospitals** for EHIC or GHIC card holders is free; otherwise, you'll be charged at private hospital rates, which can be very expensive.

In emergencies, dial ☎112 for an ambulance.

Mosquitos

Mosquitos in Spain carry nothing worse than their bite, but can be infuriating. The most widespread solution is the small plug-in electrical device that vaporizes a semi-odourless insecticide tablet; many hotels and hostales provide them routinely. Liquid insect repellents are available from most supermarkets and pharmacies. If you are camping, use insect repellent, lotion, wrist or ankle bands or pyrethrin coils. And make sure your tent has a screen that lets the air in but keeps the mozzies out. One worrying new arrival from Asia is the mosquito tigre (tiger mosquito) which is more aggressive than the usual variety, attacks in the daytime and is armed with a proboscis that can penetrate clothing. The tiger mosquito can also transmit major diseases (including nile fever and dengue) although so far no cases have been found in Spain. The repellents mentioned above seem to be effective in dealing with the new threat.

Insurance

You should take out a comprehensive **insurance policy** before travelling to Spain, to cover against loss, theft, illness or injury. A typical policy will provide cover for loss of baggage, tickets and – up to a certain limit – cash or travellers' cheques, as well as cancellation or curtailment of your journey. When securing baggage cover, make sure that the per-article limit will cover your most valuable possessions (if it doesn't as in the case of cameras or laptops you'll need to insure these separately). Most policies exclude so-called **dangerous sports** unless an extra premium is paid: in Spain, this can mean most watersports are excluded (plus rafting, canyoning, horseriding etc), though probably not things like bike tours or hiking.

If you need to make a claim, you should keep receipts for medicines and medical treatment, and in the event you have anything stolen, you must obtain an official statement from the police (see page 51).

Internet

Wireless internet access (wi-fi, pronounced "wee-fee" in Spain) is now widespread in cafés, bars and supermarkets as well as hotels and *hostales*. In the Guide's "Accommodation" listings, unless stated otherwise, the hotel or *hostal* provides **free wi-fi**. This is usually in all rooms, although in a few places access may be restricted to a part of the hotel (eg reception). However, these days, most visitors use their smartphone data plan to access the internet. If you are from the EU, you can use your phone as though you were at home. Visitors from the UK and other countries should look into rates for using your phone while roaming with their provider before you leave home. For more information on this, see Phones.

LGBTQ+ travellers

Same-sex marriages were made legal in Spain in 2005, giving same-sex couples the same rights as hetero-sexual couples, including the right to adopt, and the age of consent is 16 – the same as for heterosexual couples.

There's a thriving **gay scene** in most of Andalucía's main cities, most notably, of course, in Seville and Cádiz. The latter is long famous for its liberal traditions and its **Carnaval** is a wonderfully hedonistic time to visit, while **Torremolinos** (voted best Spanish gay destination by one LGBTQ+ website) is another popular holiday location. The Spanish term for the gay scene is "*el ambiente*" ("the atmosphere"), while another useful expression is "*entiendo*", literally, "I understand", but meaning "I'm gay".

USEFUL CONTACTS

Ⓦ **andalucia.com/living/gay.htm**
Ⓦ **fundaciontriangulo.org**
Ⓦ **gayiberia.com**

Mail

Post offices (Correos; Ⓦ correos.es) are normally open weekdays from 8am to 2pm and again from 5pm to 7.30pm, though branches in bigger places may have longer hours, may not close at noon and may open on Saturday mornings. In smaller towns and villages, many offices have cut the Saturday service altogether, and some the evening service too. Often, where there is no evening service, morning hours will be extended to 2.30pm. The office-finder on the website gives exact opening hours and contact details for each post office in Spain. As you can also pay bills and buy phonecards in post offices, queues can be long – it's often easier to buy **stamps** at tobacconists (look for the brown and yellow *estanco* sign).

Outbound mail is reasonably reliable, with letters or cards taking around three days to a week to the UK and the rest of Europe, a week to ten days to North America, New Zealand and Australia, although it can be more erratic in the summer. There's also a whole host of express mail services (ask for *urgente* or *exprés*).

ROUGH GUIDES TRAVEL INSURANCE

Rough Guides has teamed up with WorldNomads.com to offer great travel insurance deals. Policies are available to residents of over 150 countries, with cover for a wide range of adventure sports, 24hr emergency assistance, high levels of medical and evacuation cover and a stream of travel safety information. Roughguides.com users can take advantage of their policies online 24/7, from anywhere in the world – even if you're already travelling. And since plans often change when you're on the road, you can extend your policy and even claim online. Roughguides.com users who buy travel insurance with WorldNomads.com can also leave a positive footprint and donate to a community development project. For more information go to Ⓦ roughguides.com/travel-insurance.

Maps

In addition to the maps in this Guide, you'll probably want a reasonable **road map**. These can be bought in Spain from most bookshops (*librerías*), and at street kiosks and petrol stations. The best single map for Andalucía is the regularly updated *Michelin Andalucía* (1:400,000), which includes a plan to get you in and out of Seville, the region's only serious traffic headache. It's widely available from bookshops in Spain and abroad. This has been complemented by the equally excellent, larger scale *Michelin Costa del Sol* (1:200,000) covering not only the coast between Algeciras and Almería but a considerable way inland too, taking in significant chunks of the provinces of Cádiz, Málaga, Granada and Almería. An alternative is the rip-proof/waterproof *Rough Guide Andalucía Map* (1:650,000/1:150,000).

Any good book or travel shop in your own country should be able to provide a decent range of maps, or buy online from specialist stores such as ⓦ stanfords. co.uk. For hiking and trekking maps, specialist map/ travel shops – and the **CNIG** (National Geographical Information Centre; ⓦ ign.es with English option) in each of Andalucía's provincial capitals – will stock the **topographical maps** issued by two government agencies, the Instituto Geográfico Nacional and the Servicio Geográfico del Ejército. These are available at scales of 1:200,000, 1:100,000, 1:50,000 and even occasionally 1:25,000. The various SGE series are considered to be more up to date, although neither agency is hugely reliable.

A Catalunya-based company, *Editorial Alpina* (ⓦ editorialalpina.com) produces useful 1:40,000 or 1:25,000 map/booklet sets for many of the **mountain and foothill hiking areas** in Andalucía, and these are also on sale in many bookshops.

When it comes to electronic navigation, Google Maps does a reasonable job, but you could also try the excellent ⓦ mapy.cz, which provides an unsurpassed level of detail and can be downloaded pre-departure for offline use.

Money

Spain's currency is the **euro** (€), with notes issued in denominations of 5, 10, 20, 50, 100 and 200 euros, and coins in denominations of 1, 2, 5, 10, 20 and 50 cents, and 1 and 2 euros. It's worth noting that many shops and businesses refuse to accept the larger €200 notes, due to counterfeiting incidents in recent years. Up-to-the-minute currency **exchange rates** are posted on ⓦ oanda.com.

By far the easiest way to get money is to use your bank debit card to withdraw cash from an **ATM**, found in villages, towns and cities all over Spain, as well as on arrival at the airports and major train stations. You can usually withdraw up to €300 a day, and instructions are offered in English once you insert your card. Make sure you have a personal identification number (PIN) that's designed to work overseas, and take a note of your bank's emergency contact number in case the machine swallows your card. This can be a major hassle and it's worth drawing money from the ATM while the bank is open; should you lose your card there's then a reasonable chance the bank can retrieve it for you. It is now normal to pay by card for everything you can, but note a fee will be charged on payments in foreign currency, and these can add up. This usually costs a little less to take out cash and pay with that (especially where that is the only option), but the convenience and security of not carrying cash and paying by card or phone is usually best.

Spanish **bancos** (banks) and **cajas de ahorros** (savings banks, on the way out after recent scandals) have branches in all but the smallest villages. **Banking hours** are usually Monday to Friday 8.30am to 2pm, with some city branches open Saturday 8.30am to 1pm (except June–September when all banks close on Saturday), although times can vary from bank to bank. Outside these times, it's usually possible to change cash at larger hotels (generally with bad rates and high commission) or with travel agents – useful for small amounts in a hurry. One place that doesn't charge a hefty commission on exchange is the department store El Corte Inglés, with branches in all Andalucía's provincial capitals and many large towns.

In tourist areas, you'll also find specialist **casas de cambio**, with more convenient hours (though rates vary), while some major tourist offices and larger train stations also have exchange facilities open throughout business hours.

Opening hours

Almost everything in Andalucía – shops, museums, churches, tourist offices – closes for a **siesta** of at least three hours in the middle part of the day. There's a lot of variation, with many major supermarkets now tending to stay open all day, but you'll get far less aggravated if you accept that the early afternoon is best spent asleep, in a bar, or both.

Basic **working hours** are Monday to Friday 9.30am to 2pm and 5pm to 8pm. Many **shops** open slightly later on a Saturday (at 10am) and close for the day at 2pm, though you'll still find plenty of places open in cities, and there are regional variations. Moreover, department and chain stores, and shopping malls, tend to open a straight Monday to Saturday 10am to 9pm or 10pm.

Museums and galleries, with very few exceptions (Granada's Alhambra is one), also have a break between 1pm or 2pm and 4pm. On Sundays, most open mornings only, and on Mondays the majority close all day. Opening hours vary from year to year, though normally not by more than half an hour or so. Some are also seasonal, and usually in Andalucía "summer" means from Easter until September and "winter" from October until Easter. However, some museums and tourist offices and hotels regard summer as referring to the high summer months of July and August.

The most important **cathedrals, churches and monasteries** operate in much the same way as museums, with regular visiting hours and admission charges. Other churches, though, are kept locked, opening only for worship in the early morning and/or the evening (usually between 6pm and 9pm).

Phones

Spanish **telephone numbers** have nine digits; mobile numbers begin with a "6" or "7", freephone numbers begin "900" and other "90 +" and "80 +" numbers are nationwide standard rate or special rate services. To **call Spain from abroad**, you dial your country's international access code + 34 (Spain's country code) + the nine-digit Spanish number. With most Spaniards owning a smartphone, public phones are essentially a thing of the past, though some rusty booths do linger in the odd spot.

Most European **mobile phones** will work in Spain, though it's worth checking with your provider whether you need to get international access switched on and whether there are any extra charges involved. For visitors from the UK – since leaving the EU – and other non-EU nationalities, you'll need to check with your provider whether there are roaming fees for using your phone abroad (including texts and data services), or you could go home to a very hefty bill. Another option is to buy a cheap SIM card on arrival that includes a data package for your time here.

Public holidays

Alongside the Spanish **national public holidays** (see page 55) there are scores of regional holidays and local fiestas (often marking the local saint's day), any of which will mean that everything except hotels, bars and restaurants will lock its doors.

In addition, **August** is traditionally Spain's holiday month, when many of the big cities – especially Seville and Córdoba – are semi-deserted, with many of the shops and restaurants closed for the duration. In contrast, it can prove nearly impossible to find a room in the more popular coastal and mountain resorts at these times; similarly, seats on planes, trains and buses in August should be booked in advance, if possible.

Shopping

Shopping in Andalucía can range from digging around in local **flea markets** to browsing the **designer boutiques** in Seville and Granada. In the larger towns and cities, most high streets will feature Spanish clothing favourites such as Mango and Zara, along with Camper, the country's most famous shoe brand. For food, **supermarkets** are easy to locate, while **street markets** (*mercadillos*) are held virtually everywhere, and are a great place to pick up fresh produce. The main department store found in most major towns and cities is El Corte Inglés, where you can buy almost anything.

The region is also well known for its local crafts. **Leatherwork**, such as belts, bags, purses and even saddles are best sought out in Córdoba or the medieval leather town of Ubrique (Cádiz), while Seville is where you'll be able to pick up the most authentic **flamenco** accessories such as dresses, fans, shawls and lace. Córdoba is also the place for stylish handmade **hats**, which are sold at bargain prices. **Ceramics** are widely available, but are especially good in Úbeda (where there's a thriving ancient pottery tradition), Níjar and Sorbas (both in Almería). Handwoven **carpets** and **ponchos** are to be found in Las Alpujarras and the Sierra de Grazalema, and Níjar is also famed for its *jarapas* (carpets made from rags).

SPANISH AND ANDALUCÍAN PUBLIC HOLIDAYS

January 1 *Año Nuevo* New Year's Day
January 6 *Epifanía* Epiphany (referred to as "Los Reyes" – the Kings)
February 28 *Día de Andalucía* Andalucía Day
March/April *Jueves Santo/Viernes Santo* Maundy Thursday/Good Friday
May 1 *Fiesta del Trabajo* May Day
August 15 *La Asunción* Assumption of the Virgin
October 12 *Día de la Hispanidad* National Day
November 1 *Todos los Santos* All Saints'
December 6 *Día de la Constitución* Constitution Day
December 8 *Inmaculada Concepción*
December 25 *Navidad* Christmas Day

Jerez is, of course the place for buying **sherry**, and nearby Sanlúcar de Barrameda's *manzanilla* variety shouldn't be overlooked either. **Olive oil** makes a great gift to take home and Andalucía has some of the finest producers in the world in places like Baena and Zuheros (Córdoba) and Segura de la Sierra (Jaén). The region is also the home of the acoustic **guitar** and some of the finest (and most beautiful) instruments are made by the craftsmen in Granada.

Smoking

Since 2006 **smoking in public places** in Spain has been regulated by law, and tougher restrictions introduced in 2011 mean that it's now forbidden to smoke in all public buildings and transport facilities, plus bars, restaurants, clubs and cafés – and you'll find that the ban is generally observed. The law allows smoking on bar and restaurant terraces "that are not completely enclosed" which means in practice that they can have a roof but must be open on at least two sides. Where bars have installed plastic curtains (against the wind), this is regarded as a room when they enclose a terrace on four sides, and therefore smoking is not allowed.

Taxes

Sales tax – **IVA** (pronounced "eeba") – often comes as an unexpected surprise when you pay the bill for food or accommodation. It's not always specified, and is ten percent for hotels and restaurants and 21 percent for other goods and services (though most other prices are quoted inclusive of IVA). **Non-EU residents** are able to claim back the sales tax on purchases that come to over €90. To do this, make sure the shop you're buying from fills out the correct paperwork, and present this to customs before you check in at the airport for your return flight.

Time

Spain is one hour ahead of the UK, six hours ahead of Eastern Standard Time, nine hours ahead of Pacific Standard Time, eight hours behind Australia, ten hours behind New Zealand, and the same time as South Africa. Clocks go forward in the last week in March and back again in the last week in October. It's worth noting, if you're planning to cross the border, that Portugal is an hour behind Spain throughout the year.

Tipping

Tipping is common in Spain, although not always expected. And restaurants in Andalucía (or Spain) never impose a "discretionary" ten to fifteen percent service charge "tip" on the bill as happens at many restaurants in the UK. And should you tip at the US level of fifteen to twenty percent, you'll get little respect from a waiter who – behind the grateful smile – will dismiss you as a high roller with more money than sense. Locals are frugal tippers and twenty cents on a bar table or five percent in a restaurant is usually enough, although many Spaniards would add "only if the service merits it". It is also common practice to tip taxi drivers, hotel porters and the like in small change.

Toilets

Public **toilets** are generally reasonably clean, but don't always have paper. They can very occasionally, in rural locations, still be squat-style, although these are now dying out. They are most commonly referred to and labelled *Los Servicios* (which is what you should ask for), though signs may point you to *baños* or *aseos*. *Damas* or *Señoras* (Ladies, often signed with a "D" or "S") and *Caballeros* (Gentlemen, often marked simply "C") are the usual distinguishing signs for gender.

Tourist information

The Spanish national tourist office, **Turespaña** (Ⓦ spain.info), is an excellent source of information when planning your trip. The website is full of ideas, information and searchable databases, and there are links to similar websites of Turespaña offices in your own country. In Andalucía, you'll find Junta de Andalucía (regional government) **Turismos** (tourist offices) in every provincial capital and many reasonably sized towns. These are typically open Monday to Friday 9am to 2pm & 4pm to 7pm, Saturday and Sunday 10am to 2pm, but hours do vary from place to place. In major cities and coastal resorts the offices tend to remain open all day Saturday and on Sunday morning between April and September. In addition to the Junta's offices many towns and cities also provide their own **municipal tourist offices** which are frequently excellent and usually less busy than the Junta's outlets.

Travellers with disabilities

The classic tourist images of Andalucía – the medieval old towns, winding lanes, castles and monasteries – don't exactly fill you with confidence if you're in a wheelchair. However, Spain is changing and facilities are improving rapidly, especially in the more go-ahead, contemporary cities. There are accessible rooms and hotels in all major Spanish cities and resorts and, by law, all new public buildings (including revamped museums and galleries) are required to be fully accessible. Public transport is the main problem, since most local buses and trains are virtually impossible for wheelchairs, though again there are pockets of excellence throughout the region. The AVE high-speed train service, for example, is fully accessible, as is every city bus in Málaga and Seville, which has also designed a number of city tours that can be done by wheelchair. In most towns and cities, acoustic traffic-light signals and dropped kerbs are common.

Some organizations at home may be able to advise you further about travel to Spain, like the very useful UK-based **Tourism For All** (ⓦ tourismforall.org.uk). **Access Travel** (ⓦ accesstravel.co.uk) can arrange flights, transfers and accommodation in Andalucía, and at the very least, local tourist offices in Spain should also be able to recommend a suitable hotel or taxi company.

Accessible Travel (ⓦ accessibletravel.co.uk) specialises in holidays for disabled travellers and offers a range of destinations in Andalucía.

Málaga
province

EL CAMINITO DEL REY, MALAGA

1

Málaga province

The Andalucian sun starts singing a fire song, and all creation trembles at the sound.

Federico García Lorca

The smallest of Andalucía's eight provinces, Málaga is also its most populous, swelling to bursting point with the sheer weight of visitors in high summer. Although primarily known as the gateway to the Costa del Sol and its unashamedly commercial resorts such as Torremolinos and Marbella, the province has much more to offer than just its coastline. To most incoming tourists the provincial capital of Málaga is merely "the place by the airport", but it's also a vibrant city in its own right, with an atmospheric centre and plenty of exciting nightlife and places to eat, as well as a collection of outstanding art galleries.

In the west of Málaga's provincial heartland lies the **Serranía de Ronda**, a series of small mountain ranges sprinkled with gleaming, whitewashed *pueblos blancos* (White Towns), of which **Ronda**, located astride the stunningly beautiful El Tajo gorge, is justly the most famous. To the north lies the appealing market town of **Antequera** with its remarkable prehistoric dolmens and sumptuous Baroque churches, and from here it's a quick hop south to the natural wonders of **El Torcal**, where vast limestone outcrops have been eroded into a landscape of weird natural sculptures. Another possible trip from Antequera is to the spectacular **El Chorro Gorge**, which, along with the Embalse de Guadalhorce, is a major climbing and camping centre. Nearby, the saline **Laguna de Fuente de Piedra** is Europe's only inland breeding ground for the greater flamingo, whose flocks make a spectacular sight in summer.

The far eastern section of Málaga province is the **Axarquía** region, which sees comparatively few tourists. An area of rugged natural beauty, it was once the haunt of mountain bandits. Now the domain of the Spanish ibex, a distinctive Iberian long-horned goat, the area's magnificent scenery and earthy villages contrast starkly with the crowded **beaches** to the south.

Málaga

For many visitors, **MÁLAGA** is little more than an airport and a gateway to the Costa del Sol, but break through the industrial outskirts and you'll find yourself in one of the most atmospheric cities in Spain. A large and bustling seaport with a population passing half a million, it's the second city of Andalucía (after Seville), yet the historic central area remains colourful and well-preserved. Lorca described Málaga as his favourite town and, given a chance, it remains an attractive place and a good base for explorations further afield, an impression boosted by the ebullient and big-hearted *malagueños*, among the friendliest people in Andalucía.

Overlooking the town and port, the wonderfully preserved fourteenth-century citadels of the **Alcazaba** and **Gibralfaro** bear witness to the city's Moorish past, while a **Roman theatre** below predates them by over a millennium. The city also has a plethora of outstanding art galleries, including the spectacular **Museo Picasso**, housing a major collection of work by Picasso (who was born in Málaga), the **Centre Pompidou Málaga** – a branch of the famous contemporary art museum in Paris – and the **Museo de Málaga**, housing an impressive archeological and art collection. And if on sultrier days

Highlights

❶ **Málaga** A vibrant city crammed with bars, cafés, museums and a fabulous Moorish fortress. See page 60

❷ **Museo Picasso** With over 280 artworks by Málaga's most famous son, this remarkable museum shouldn't be missed. See page 68

❸ **El Caminito del Rey** One of Europe's most spectacular gorge walks along a recently restored 1920s walkway in El Chorro. See page 79

❹ **Parque Natural El Torcal** El Torcal is famous for its almost lunar landscape and surreal limestone formations. See page 87

❺ **Laguna de Fuente de Piedra** The largest natural lake in Andalucía and a major breeding ground for the greater flamingo. See page 88

❻ **Costa del Sol** Despite its downmarket image, there are individual resorts – Nerja, Marbella and Estepona – with plenty of style. See page 103

❼ **Marbella** Lively resort with bags of glitz and glamour, plus a vibrant nightlife and great tapas bars and restaurants. See page 109

❽ **Ronda** Beautiful hill town set astride a yawning gorge with sensational views over the Serranía de Ronda. See page 122

❾ **Serranía de Ronda** This mountainous country south of Ronda is some of the wildest and most spectacular in Andalucía. See page 132

HIGHLIGHTS ARE MARKED ON THE MAP ON PAGE 62

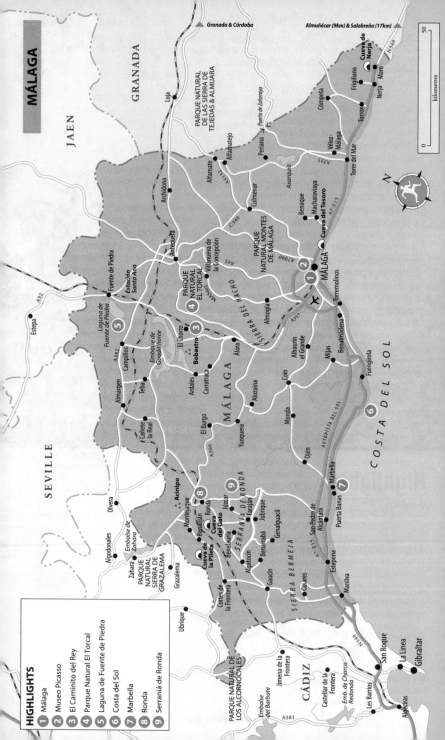

you want to escape from the crowds and heat, the nineteenth-century **Jardín Botánico de la Concepción** (botanical garden) is tailor-made, with a fine collection of plants and trees from all over the world. Further afield, the traditional fishing villages of **El Palo** and **Pedregalejo**, now absorbed into the suburbs, are home to a series of small beaches and a *paseo* lined with some of the best fish and seafood cafés in the province.

Málaga is bisected by the seasonal **Guadalmedina river**, which is due for redevelopment following unsuccessful landscaping in the 1990s at colossal cost, with dismal walkways and reluctant grass. All the major sights lie to the east of this and below the Alcazaba. From the **Alameda**, the city's main thoroughfare, the cathedral, Museo Picasso, Carmen Thyssen and modern art museums, and a clutch of interesting churches, all lie within a few minutes' walk. The city government has done an impressive job in recent decades of tidying up the monumental zone and the *casco antiguo* (old quarter), making it a wonderful place to wander through streets and squares filled with animated bars and cafés as well as craft and fashion shops. The centrepiece of this scheme is the marble-laid Calle Marqués de Larios – the city's most fashionable shopping street – and the focal Plaza de la Constitución. The modernised port district, known as **El Palmeral** and **Muelle Uno**, is also an attractive area, breezy and open in contrast to the narrow streets of the old quarter, and featuring a spectacular pergola stretched along one side of a marina lined with shops, bars and restaurants. The Soho district, between the port and **CAC Málaga**, is the art neighbourhood, decked with murals and home to some of the city's most innovative places to eat.

Brief history

The **Phoenicians** founded the settlement they called Malaka in the eighth century BC, building a fortress on the summit of the hill that is today dominated by the Alcazaba. Later incorporated into the Roman province of Baetica in the wake of Rome's victory over Carthage, Málaga prospered as a **trading port** exporting iron, copper and lead from mines in the hills near Ronda, as well as olive oil, wine and *garum*, a relish made from pickled fish to which the Romans were particularly partial. After falling to the **Moors** early in the eighth century, Málaga was soon flourishing again as the main port for the city of Granada. Although in the fourteenth century the ruler Yusuf I constructed the Gibralfaro as defence, in 1487 Málaga was taken by Christian forces following a bitter siege, after which the large Moorish population was persecuted and its property confiscated on a grand scale; the city's main mosque was also transformed into a cathedral, and a further twenty into churches. Málaga then entered a period of decline only exacerbated by a revolt of the Moors in 1568 that resulted in their complete expulsion. It was not until the nineteenth century that real prosperity returned – and then only briefly. Middle-class families arriving from the north invested in textile factories, sugar refineries and shipyards, and gave their names to city streets such as Larios and Heredia, while Málaga **dessert wine** became the favourite tipple of Victorian ladies. Then, in the early part of the twentieth century, the bottom fell out of the boom as the new industries succumbed to foreign competition and the phylloxera

FESTIVALS IN MÁLAGA

While *sevillanos* loudly proclaim that there is only one **Semana Santa** worthy of the name, *malagueños* furiously disagree. The Holy Week processions are celebrated here with great fervour and with much larger floats (*tronos*, or "thrones" as they're called here) than those in Seville, carried by up to two hundred sober-suited males or robed penitents. In mid-August, at the peak of the tourist season, the town lets rip in its **Feria de Málaga** – one of the wildest and most spectacular in Andalucía. Málaga celebrates a Bienal de flamenco with performances in the city and provincial towns throughout the year. The annual Jazz Festival, takes place in November.

1

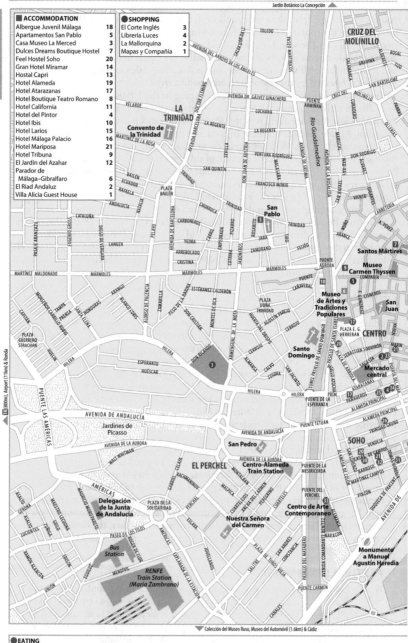

■ **ACCOMMODATION**

Albergue Juvenil Málaga	18
Apartamentos San Pablo	5
Casa Museo La Merced	3
Dulces Dreams Boutique Hostel	7
Feel Hostel Soho	20
Gran Hotel Miramar	14
Hostal Capri	13
Hotel Alameda	19
Hotel Atarazanas	17
Hotel Boutique Teatro Romano	8
Hotel California	11
Hotel del Pintor	4
Hotel Ibis	10
Hotel Larios	15
Hotel Málaga Palacio	16
Hotel Mariposa	21
Hotel Tribuna	9
El Jardín del Azahar	12
Parador de Málaga–Gibralfaro	6
El Riad Andaluz	2
Villa Alicia Guest House	1

● **SHOPPING**

El Corte Inglés	3
Librería Luces	4
La Mallorquina	2
Mapas y Compañía	1

● **EATING**

Alexso	1	Café Lepanto	22	Jose Carlos García Restaurante	27
Antigua Casa Guardia	25	Cañadu	4	Mamuchis	30
La Antxoeta	31	Casa Aranda	23	El Mesón de Cervantes	2
Araboka	14	Casa Mira	18	Mesón Mariano	7
La Bella Julieta	24	La Cosmopolita	10	Mixtúrate	28
Bodegas Quitapeñas	21	El Gastronauta	13	El Mortal	17
				Óleo	33
				Parador de Málaga-Gibralfaro	5
				Los Patios de Beatas	6
				Picnic Soho	32
				El Pimpi	8
				El Refectorium Catedral	19

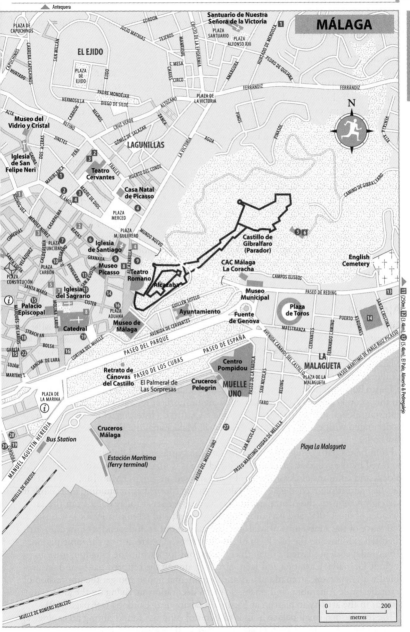

MÁLAGA

1

bug got to work wiping out the vines. A number of radical revolts leading up to the Civil War also brought the city an unhealthy reputation.

The Civil War to today

Given its volatile nature it was inevitable that Málaga would be staunchly Republican during the **Civil War**. In the turbulent years leading up to the war and during the conflict itself churches and convents were burned, while in 1937 Italian planes bombed the city, destroying much of its ancient central core, and mass executions of "reds and anarchists" by the conquering Franco forces left enduring emotional scars. This period is vividly described in a contemporaneous account, *Malaga Burning*, by Gamel Woolsey (see page 554).

The 1960s finally brought an economic lifeline in the form of **mass tourism** and the exploitation of the Costa del Sol, though the major coastal developments barely touched the heart of Málaga. The opening of the Picasso Museum in 2003 raised the city's profile, and was followed by the arrival of a clutch of further high-profile galleries. In recent decades, local authorities have worked to redevelop the less attractive parts of the city, and it has built a reputation as a cultural centre, particularly of art, and has rebranded itself as the "City of Museums", of which it has more than thirty. Visitor figures have risen dramatically and Málaga now ranks among the most-visited cities in Spain. It has, however, preserved its unique character and remains relatively untarred by the brush of mass tourism.

Alcazaba

Main entrance at Pza de la Aduana; alternatively, there's a lift (not in operation on Mondays) on C/Guillen Sotelo, directly behind the Ayuntamiento • **Alcazaba** Daily: April–Oct 9am–8pm; Nov–March 9am–6pm • Charge (combined ticket with Gibralfaro available); free entry Sun after 2pm • **Centro de Interpretación** Tues–Sat 10am–6pm, Sun 10am–4pm • Free • ⓦ alcazabaygibralfaro.malaga.eu

Málaga's magnificent **Alcazaba** – along with the Gibralfaro (see page 66) – is an exuberant contrast to the dour fortresses of Castile. At the Alcazaba's entrance stands a **Teatro Romano**, unearthed in 1951 during building works. The theatre, constructed in the second century BC, is now used as an auditorium for various outdoor entertainments. Access to the theatre is via a Centro de Interpretación, whose exterior is decorated with extracts from the Lex Flavia Malacitana, the Roman city's municipal law code.

From here a path winds upwards, lined by the cypresses and flower-encircled arbours so loved by the sybaritic Moors. The citadel too is Roman in origin, with recycled blocks and columns of classical marble interspersed among the Moorish brick of the double- and triple-arched gateways. Although the Moors began building on the hill in the eighth century, the Alcazaba with its palace as we see it today dates from the early decades of the 1100s, and was substantially restored and rebuilt in 1930. It was the residence of the Arab emirs of Málaga, who carved out an independent kingdom for themselves following the break-up of the Western Caliphate during the same period. Their independence lasted a mere thirty years, but for a while the kingdom grew to include Granada, Carmona and Jaén. Strolling among the restored patios and terraces lined with cypresses, aromatic plants and ornamental pools, you get the impression of a smaller-scale Alhambra, and traces of stucco decoration surviving on the arches are similar to the artistry to be seen at Medina Azahara near Córdoba (see page 369).

The refurbished small **palace** houses displays of ceramics found during archeological excavations. Many more are housed in the **Museo de Málaga** (see page 67).

Castillo de Gibralfaro

Monte de Gibralfaro • Daily April–Oct 9am–8pm; Nov–March 9am–6pm • Charge (combined ticket with Alcazaba available); free entry Sun after 2pm • ⓦ alcazabaygibralfaro.malaga.eu• Bus #35 from the Alameda in the city centre will drop you by the castle entrance

1

Rising to the northeast of the Alcazaba (and connected to it by a long double wall – the *coracha*), is the **Castillo de Gibralfaro**. It's reached by climbing a steep, twisting path for 800m from the Alcazaba that skirts the southern walls, passing bougainvillea-draped ramparts and sentry-box-shaped Moorish wells. You can also approach from the town side, as the tourist coaches do, using the Subida al Gibralfaro (accessed from C/Mundo Nuevo), but this is a lengthy, rather unattractive walk.

Built by Yusuf I of Granada in the fourteenth century and last used in 1936 during the Civil War, the castle, with its formidable walls and turrets, has, like the Alcazaba, been wonderfully restored and now houses an interesting **museum** dealing with the Gibralfaro's history. Among a collection of military exhibits from all periods there is a splendid scale model letting you see how the city and Alcazaba complex would have looked in Moorish times. There's also a display of seventeenth-century playing cards that were made in the factory in nearby Macharaviaya (see page 90). A walk around the castle's **ramparts** affords terrific views over the city, the *coracha* and the complex fortifications of the Alcazaba.

The Gibralfaro has its own **bar**, but while you're up here, a pleasant place for a **meal** or a **drink** is the nearby *Parador de Málaga – Gibralfaro* (see page 75), with its terrace overlooking the city. It's reached by following the road leading out of the castle's car park for 100m and turning right into the *parador*'s grounds. Next to the *parador*'s entrance is a **mirador** with a stunning **view** over the harbour, city and Plaza de Toros.

Museo de Málaga

Plz de la Aduana • Tues–Sat 9am–9pm, Sun 9am–3pm • Charge • ⓦ museosdeandalucia.es

Housed in the old customs building adjacent to the **Alcazaba** the **Museo de Málaga** is the largest museum in Andalucía and the fifth biggest in Spain. The early eighteenth-century Neoclassical building underwent a multi-million-euro refurbishment, and since its opening in 2016 is home to the city's huge archeological and fine art collection, one of the most significant in the country. It's divided into two sections: archeology (on the third floor) where two thousand of the fifteen thousand pieces are on display, and fine art (on the second floor) showing a tenth of the total two thousand in store. The archeology is easily the most interesting section for non-locals and its exceptionally well-curated spaces include several fine pieces such as a Neolithic cheese-maker from the Cueva de la Pileta cave near Ronda; Roman marble figures collected by the Loring family and originally on display at the **Jardín Botánico La Concepción**; and a sixth-century BC bronze Corinthian mask excavated in the city centre. Roman mosaics and Moorish ceramics also form part of the display. Downstairs, the fine art section has a predominance of Málaga artists, mostly from the nineteenth century when the city's art school reached its heyday. Must-sees here include the sixteenth-century ceiling corbels, some fine Picasso sketches and Simonet's painting "And she had a heart!", a romantic vision of an autopsy and one of the city's best-known art works. Don't miss the magnificent main stairwell, the central courtyard with perhaps the tallest palms in Andalucía and the roof whose six thousand aluminium tiles carry engravings of Málaga.

Catedral and Iglesia del Sagrario

C/Molino Lario • **Cathedral and Iglesia del Sagrario** Mon–Fri 10am–8pm, Sat 10am–6pm, Sun 2pm–6pm • **Roof** Guided visits (advance tickets online) Mon–Sat 11am–6pm, Sun 4pm–6pm • Charge • ⓦ malagacatedral.com

The city's most conspicuous edifice seen from the heights of the Gibralfaro is the peculiar, unfinished **Catedral**. Constructed between the sixteenth and eighteenth centuries, it still lacks a tower on the west front because a radical *malagueño* bishop donated the earmarked money to the American War of Independence against the British. Unfortunately – and despite its huge scale – it also lacks any real inspiration

1

and is distinguished only by an intricately carved seventeenth-century *sillería* (choir stall) by noted sculptor Pedro de Mena. However, the **Iglesia del Sagrario**, on the Catedral's northern flank, is worth a look, if only for its fine Gothic portal, dating from an earlier, uncompleted Isabelline church. Inside, a restored and magnificent gilded Plateresque **retablo**, which is brilliantly illuminated during services, is the work of Juan de Balmaseda. Equally worthwhile is the climb (two hundred steps) up to the **Catedral's** restored terracotta domed rooftops for a guided tour (English available – ask when you buy your tickets) round the perimeter from where you get sweeping views of the city centre.

Museo Picasso Málaga

C/San Agustín • July & Aug 10am–8pm; Sept, Oct & March–June 10am–7pm; Nov–Feb 10am–6pm • Charge; combined tickets including temporary exhibitions available; audio guide included with admission fee; free entry last two hours on Sunday • ⓦ museopicassomalaga. org

Just around the corner from the Catedral is the **Museo Picasso Málaga**, housed in the elegant sixteenth-century mansion of the counts of Buenavista. It was opened by the king and queen in 2003, 112 years after Picasso left Málaga at the age of 10 and to where he returned only once for an unhappy, fleeting visit in his late teens. In later life, he toyed with the idea of sending "two lorries full of paintings" to set up a museum in Málaga but vowed never to set foot in Spain while the ruling General Franco – who described the artist's work as "degenerate" – was still alive. Picasso died in 1973 and was outlived by the dictator by two years.

The **permanent collection** is refreshed every few years, and consists of around 120 works (paintings, sculptures and ceramics), displayed thematically and donated or loaned by the foundation belonging to Bernard Ruiz-Picasso, the artist's grandson. The **temporary collection** comprises loaned works and special exhibitions (usually connected with Picasso). Though not on a par with the Picasso museums in Paris and Barcelona, the museum does allow you to see some of the lesser-known works that Picasso kept for himself or gave away to his lovers, family and friends – rather harshly described as the "less saleable stuff" by one critic.

Among the highlights on display are a portrait of Picasso's cousin Lola, painted when he was just a teenager; Restaurante, a piece of canvas painted in 1914 and stuck on glass; Las Tres Gracias, a take on the Grecian Three Graces and one of his largest paintings; Siesta, whose distorted sleeping figure is unmistakably Picassian; and the Cabeza de Toro, where Picasso used a bike handlebars and saddle to recreate a bull's head. The beguiling yet tragic Dora Maar and Picasso's second wife, Jacqueline Roque also feature in several works. The collection is rotated and thus not all the works mentioned above may be on show at any one time.

Don't miss the basement containing **archeological remains** revealed during the building's refurbishment. These include substantial chunks of a Phoenician city wall and tower dating from the seventh century BC, parts of a Roman *salazones* factory used to produce the famous *garum* and vestiges of the **Palacio de Buenavista** cellar. The museum also has an excellent book store and gift shop as well as a *cafetería* with a pleasant courtyard.

Casa Natal de Picasso

Pza de la Merced 15 • Daily 9.30am–8pm • Charge • ⓦ fundacionpicasso.es

Picasso was born in 1881 in the Plaza de la Merced, where the **Casa Natal de Picasso** is home to the Fundación Picasso, a centre for scholars researching the painter's life and work. An exhibition space displays lithographs, etchings and washes by Picasso – mainly with women as the subject matter – plus temporary exhibitions centred around the artist's work. Upstairs are photos of the artist at various stages in his long life and a reconstructed reception room, furnished as it might have looked when Picasso was growing up here at the end of the late nineteenth century. Items on display include some embroidered bed linen by the artist's mother, a canvas by his art-teacher father and the infant Picasso's christening robe used in the ceremony at the nearby Iglesia de Santiago.

Paseo del Parque

South of the cathedral, the **Paseo del Parque** is an elegant, palm-shaded avenue laid out at the beginning of the twentieth century on land reclaimed from the sea – an ideal place for a stroll, especially on summer evenings when the air has cooled. Along its length are a number of architectural delights as well as a remarkable **botanical garden** containing hundreds of exotic plants and flowers and many varieties of fig, bamboo, jacaranda and yucca trees. Discreet plaques placed at intervals along the esplanade identify the different species.

Among the buildings of note are the Neoclassical **Aduana**, the former customs house, now home to the city's Museo de Málaga (see page 67), started in 1788, with an austerely impressive patio. Further west lies **El Rectorado de la Universidad de Málaga**, the university headquarters that houses good temporary exhibitions and some exceptional medieval walls in the basement, followed a little further on by the paseo's star turn, the exuberant **Ayuntamiento**, a delightful cream-and-brown Art Nouveau pile, constructed to coincide with the opening of the esplanade.

In the adjacent rose gardens stand the first two of *malagueño* Jaime Pimentel's trio of evocative bronzes, which are among Málaga's best-loved sculptures: **El Biznaguero** (*The Jasmine Seller*) celebrates the men who sell trays of their blooms throughout the city, while the nearby **El Verdialero** pays tribute to the colourful and frenetic Verdiales musicians from the mountains of Málaga to the northeast of the city. The third bronze, **El Cenachero** (*The Fish Seller*), commemorating men who, with their baskets of fish dangling from a yoke, used to be a common sight on the city's streets, is behind the municipal tourist office on Plaza de la Marina.

El Palmeral de las Sorpresas

Cross through the **Paseo del Parque** to reach **El Palmeral de las Sorpresas**, palm tree gardens flanked by a stunning pergola structure that undulates 450m along the north side of the port. Designed by architects Jerónimo Junquera and Liliana Oba, the pergola has become one of the city's icons and most pleasant places to stroll. You get the best views of the pergola with the city's monuments behind it from **Muelle Uno**, the continuation of the marina.

Fuente de Genova

Pza del General Torrijos

At the Paseo del Parque's eastern end you'll come to the **Fuente de Genova**, or Genoa Fountain, on a roundabout almost constantly encircled by traffic and difficult to appreciate. An extremely fine Italian Renaissance work, it was captured by pirates during the reign of Carlos V while being transported to its Spanish buyer; when it was finally retrieved, the king awarded it to the city by royal edict.

Cementerio Inglés de Málaga (English Cemetery)

Avda de Pries 1 • Tues–Sun 9am–2pm • Charge • ⓦ cementerioinglesmalaga.org

Flanked by carved stone rampant lions, the **Cementerio Inglés de Málaga (English Cemetery)** is the oldest Protestant cemetery in mainland Spain. For centuries following

1

the *Reconquista*, Spanish authorities followed a custom of denying Christian burial to all "infidels" unlucky enough to die on Iberian turf. British Protestants – who were included in this grouping – suffered the indignity after death of "burial upright in the sand till their necks, below the tide line". Málaga's expatriate population, which increased during the early nineteenth century, was, understandably, not amused when some of these "shore burials" were washed up on the beach or even seen bobbing on the waves. Thus in 1830 the British consul, William Mark, finally persuaded the authorities to let him found the English Cemetery. In the early days, and to get the place established, it seems that Mark pursued corpses with the zeal of a body snatcher, hardly waiting for the deceased to expire before carting them off to the new graveyard. Traveller Richard Ford, whose wife's frailty was his original reason for coming to Spain, became alarmed when Mark began to make overtures. "Hearing of my wife's ill health, he tried all in his power to get me to Málaga to have a pretty female specimen in his sepulchral museum", he wrote to a friend.

The site

The cemetery itself, once an isolated site overlooking the sea but now enveloped by urban sprawl, is still nevertheless a leafy and tranquil oasis. Follow the path from the Paseo de Reding up to the modest red stone **church of St George** where, just before it, stands the sepulchre of William Mark. Further up the hill you'll see the original **walled cemetery** containing the oldest graves, among them a number studded with seashells (an ancient symbol of immortality), marking the passing of infant victims of fever and consumption, the scourge of that age.

Alongside the old cemetery's eastern wall the tombstone of **Gamel Woolsey**, poet and wife of Gerald Brenan, and author of *Malaga Burning* (see page 554), is inscribed with a poignant message from Shakespeare's *Cymbeline*: "Fear no more the heat o' the sun". In 2001 the remains of her husband (who died in 1987) were finally placed in a grave alongside hers. The writer's epitaph is eloquently laconic: "RIP Gerald Brenan, Escritor Inglés, Amigo de España". Many of the other tombstones dotted around the cemetery with their dedications to wives, loyal servants and men of military zeal, most of them in English, make fascinating reading.

Museo Carmen Thyssen

C/Compañia 10 • Tues–Sun 10am–8pm • Charge (includes audio guide and guided tours when available); free Sunday from 4pm • ⓦ carmenthyssenmalaga.org

Just off the west side of Plaza de la Constitución and housed in the refurbished sixteenth-century Palacio de Villalón is the **Museo Carmen Thyssen**, named after the spouse of the late baron whose collection forms the core of the Thyssen-Bornemisza museum in Madrid. The museum comprises 230 loaned works from Thyssen's personal collection of Spanish nineteenth-century art. Displayed on three floors (the fourth floor houses temporary exhibitions which have featured Monet, Hopper, Matisse, Miró and Van Gogh) and divided into sections titled "Romantic", "Naturalist Landscape" and "Fin-de-siècle", the works are perhaps most interesting for the glimpses they give of Spanish and *andaluz* life and times, rather than intrinsic artistic merit or originality. The museum also has a *cafetería* with a good *menú del día* as well as a shop selling gifts and books on, and reproductions of, the artworks.

Centro de Arte Contemporaneo

C/Alemania s/n • July–Sept Tues–Sun 9am–2pm & 5–9.30pm; Oct–June Tues–Sun 9am–9.30pm • Free • ⓦ cacmalaga.eu

The superb **Centro de Arte Contemporaneo (CAC Málaga)** sits on the east bank of the Río Guadalmedina, housed in a former market building. The tone for this modern art museum is set by an amusing sculpture at the entrance, *Man Moving*, by German artist Stephan Balkenhol, while inside the permanent collection displays works by international artists Louise Bourgeois, Cindy Sherman, Damien Hirst and Tony Cragg. Frequent temporary exhibitions display the best of the world's contemporary art scene – check out the centre's website for information. There is a second branch, CAC Málaga La Coracha, in the neighbourhood immediately south of the Castillo de Gibralfaro.

Pasaje de Chinitas

Tucked behind the Plaza de la Constitución, is one of Málaga's most evocative corners, the **Pasaje de Chinitas**. In the first half of the last century, when Málaga was a thriving industrial town, this narrow white-walled street was filled with *tascas*, or bars, where businessmen would meet to discuss deals over fine wines before slinking off to the *Café de Chinitas* to hear some of the best flamenco in town. In the 1920s and 1930s the fame of this flamenco shrine, now a mundane textile store, grew as it became a noted meeting place of artists and writers, bullfighters and singers. Lorca loved the place and composed a poem in its honour, part of which appears on a plaque fixed to the former café, at the junction with Calle Sánchez Pastor:

In the Café de Chinitas
Said Paquiro to his brother:
"I'm more valiant than you,
more brave and more gitano."

Centro Pompidou

Pasaje Dr Carrillo Casaux • Wed–Mon 9.30am–8pm • Charge; free Sun from 4pm • ⓦ centrepompidou-malaga.eu

Occupying the corner of **Muelle Uno**, Málaga's branch of Pompidou Centre, known as El Cubo after its large multi-coloured glass cube decorated by the French artist Daniel Buren and now one of the city icons, the **Centro Pompidou** houses modern art works on loan from its Parisian big sister. As its central theme, the main exhibition takes the human body, whole, in bits or in metamorphosis, and includes works by artists such as Bacon, Magritte, Giacometti and Léger. Highlights include portraits by Chagall, Kahlo and Picasso; Landau's *Barbed Hula*; Attia's rows of aluminium foil *Ghosts*; and sculptures by Brancusi, Miró and Schütte. Several temporary exhibitions take place every year, also of works on loan from Paris and with a strong French focus. Artists on show have included Miró, Starck and Buren as well as Dada cinema and modern French architects. The Centro Pompidou also showcases the performing arts with concerts, dance performances and films throughout the year. Check the website for details.

Mercado Central

C/Atarazanas, just north of the Alameda • Mon–Sat 8am–3pm

Lying at the heart of an area that bustles with life, the nineteenth-century wrought-iron, Mudéjar-style **Mercado Central** (officially the Mercado Central de Atarazanas) incorporates a little-known architectural gem, largely unnoticed by the daily shoppers. This, a remarkable fourteenth-century **Moorish arch** on its southern facade, was built for Yusuf I of Granada – the ruler also responsible for that other great gateway, the Puerta de la Justicia in the Alhambra – when Málaga was part of the Nasrid kingdom. In those days it formed the entrance to the Moorish arsenal, and the original building's purpose is preserved in the market's present name: Atarazanas in Arabic translates as "the house that guards the arsenal". Note the two coats of arms in the upper corners inscribed in Arabic with the confident proclamation, "There is no Conqueror but Allah. All Praise to Him".

Museo del Vidrio y Cristal

Pza Santísimo Cristo de la Sangre 2 • Tues–Sun guided visits 11am–7pm • Charge • ⓦ museovidrioycristalmalaga.com

Housed in an eighteenth-century inn in the historic artisans' quarter, the **Museo del Vidrio y Cristal** contains one of the largest glass collections in Europe. Over 3000 pieces encompass the history of glass-making from the Phoenicians to Lalique and Whitefriars in the mid-twentieth-century via the Romans, Persians and Venetians. The museum also showcases stained glass windows and antique furniture and paintings.

Colección del Museo Ruso

Av. Sor Teresa del Prat 15, to the west of the city centre on bus #15 • Tues–Sun 9.30am–8pm • Charge; free Sunday from 4pm • ⓦ coleccionmuseoruso.es

The restored tobacco factory (La Tabacalera, built in the 1930s and modelled on the Antigua Fábrica de Tabacos in Seville) usually houses works of the Colección del Museo Ruso loaned from the Russian State Museum in St Petersburg, but at the time of writing had changed to display other works from its own extensive municipal collection or loaned from elsewhere. The main exhibition changes annually in February – themes have included Russian icons, the four seasons and the Romanov dynasty – and the smaller exhibitions (two a year) focus on a particular artist such as Chagall, Filonov and Kandinsky or a Russian theme such as the Knave of Diamonds movement in the 1910s or Soviet pop art. While many of the artists are relatively unknown in western Europe, their work offers an interesting insight into Russian culture and history. The museum has also provided online access to the entire Russian State Museum collection and hosted Russian-themed concerts and conferences. See the website for details of what's on. The shop has gifts, a collection of books and reproductions of paintings that are on show, plus a small *cafetería* serving snacks and tapas.

Museo del Automóvil

Av. Sor Teresa del Prat 15, to the west of the city centre on bus #15 • Daily 10am–2.30pm & 4pm–7pm • Charge • ⓦ museoautomovilmalaga.com

Next door to the Museo Ruso and probably the best of its kind in Spain, the **Museo del Automóvil** takes in the entire history of cars from the first models such as a 1912 Barron Acoryd to a 2010 hydrogen-powered prototype. Expect to see plenty of signature designs – the collection of Rolls-Royce and Italian cars is particularly large – as well as more unusual makes such as the Czech Tatra. Mannequins dressed in appropriate period costume accompany each car and there's also an impressive fashion display.

Santuario de Nuestra Señora de la Victoria

Pza del Santuario s/n • Mon–Fri 10am–1pm • Charge • ⓦ bit.ly/SantuarioDeNuestra

Northeast of the city centre and sited on the spot where Fernando and Isabel pitched their tent during the 1487 siege of Málaga, **Santuario de Nuestra Señora de la Victoria** is, after the cathedral, Málaga's most prestigious church, where the city's Virgin patron is venerated. The fifteenth-century building was substantially rebuilt in the seventeenth century by the Count of Buenavista, whose remains, along with those of his descendants, lie in an eerie **crypt** decorated with symbolic stucco skeletons and skulls. Above the main altar's centrepiece is an image of the Virgin in a *camarín* attributed to Pedro de Mena.

Jardín Botánico La Concepción

5km north of Málaga and signposted off the A45 *autovía* • Tues–Sun: April–Sept 9.30am–8.30pm; Oct–March 9.30am–5.30pm • Charge; free Sun after 4.30pm in summer and after 2pm in winter • ⓦ laconcepcion.malaga.eu • By car, take the A45 north out of Málaga, turn off at km166, and follow signs for the Jardín Botánico, otherwise take bus #2

1

A pleasant trip out of town if you want to escape the centre for a few hours is to the remarkable **Jardín Botánico La Concepción**, the city's botanical garden. Among the finest in Spain, the gardens were originally designed in the 1850s by Amalia Loring, granddaughter of the British consul, and only purchased in 1990 by Málaga city council, since when they have been converted into the present tropical gardens. Beneath the thirty species of soaring palms, waving pines and lofty eucalyptus, you'll find yellow-flowering acacia, violet-blooming jacaranda and all kinds of exotic shrubs and grasses. There are trees of all shapes and continents, such as the Australian banyan with its serpentine aerial roots, giant sequoias and a variety of bamboos.

ARRIVAL AND DEPARTURE   MÁLAGA

BY PLANE

Málaga Airport (☎ 902 404 704, bit.ly/MalagaCostaAirport) is 11km west of the city centre. From there the electric train (cercanías; every 20min, 6.44am–0.24pm; charge) provides the easiest and cheapest way into town. From the arrivals hall or baggage carousels go to the exit and cross the forecourt to the train station marked "Aeropuerto". Buy a ticket from the machine for the C1 Cercanías line to the "Centro-Alameda" stop (12min). The train also makes a stop en route at the Málaga train station (María Zambrano), which is also convenient for the bus station next door. Leave the Centro-Alameda station via the Alameda exit, effectively the town centre.

Taxis leave from the rank in front of the El Corte Inglés department store just north of Centro-Alameda station. Alternatively, city bus Línea A leaves from outside the Terminal 3 arrivals hall (roughly hourly, 7am–midnight; charge), stopping at the train and bus stations en route to the centre and the Paseo del Parque near the port. A taxi into town from the rank outside the arrivals hall takes roughly 15min, depending on traffic and time of day.

BY TRAIN

The city's impressive RENFE train station (María Zambrano) lies southwest of the centre and is linked by the high-speed AVE with Córdoba and Madrid. There is also a high-speed route to Granada. Bus #3 runs from here to the centre (every 10min or so; ⓦ renfe.es). For current timetables and ticket information, see the website.

Destinations Algeciras (1 daily; change at Bobadilla; 3hr 30min); Córdoba (6 daily; 1hr 5min; 13 AVE daily; 55min); El Chorro (1 daily; 45min); Fuengirola (every 20min; 35min); Ronda (1 daily; 1hr 50min); Seville (13 daily; 2hr 30min); Torremolinos (every 20min; 25min).

BY BUS

Most buses from and to destinations outside Málaga (run by a number of different companies) operate from the bus station on Paseo de los Tilos a little northwest of the RENFE station. Bus timetables can be checked at ⓦ estabus. emtsam.es. Buses to Benalmádena, Fuengirola, the Axarquía and Vélez-Málaga leave from Muelle de Heredia near the port behind Turismo on Pza de la Marina.

Destinations Algeciras (7 daily; 2hr); Almería (3 daily; 3hr 15min); Antequera (15 daily; 55min); Cádiz (4 daily; 4hr); Córdoba (4 daily; 2hr 30min); Estepona (13 daily; 1hr 20min); Fuengirola (2 daily; 45min); Gibraltar (stops at La Línea border; 4 daily; 3hr); Granada (hourly; 1hr 45min); Jaén (3 daily; 3hr 15min); Jerez (1 daily; 4hr 35min); Marbella (up to 23 daily; 50min); Motril (8 daily; 2hr); Nerja (26 daily; 1hr); Osuna (2 daily; 2hr 25min); Riogordo (Mon–Fri 7 a day, Sat & Sun 3 a day; 1hr); Ronda (3 daily; 2hr); Seville (5 daily; 2hr 45min); Tarifa (2 daily; 2hr 30min); Torremolinos (hourly; 20min); Vejer (1 daily; 4hr 45min); Vélez-Málaga (hourly; 1hr 20min).

BY FERRY

Trasmediterranea (ⓦ trasmediterranea.es) and Balearia (ⓦ balearia.com) run regular ferries from the Estación Marítima to the Spanish enclave of Melilla in Morocco (6.5hr). If you're heading for Fes and eastern Morocco, this is a useful connection, particularly for taking a car over.

BY CAR

There's very little street parking available in Málaga, and the many signed car parks around the centre are extremely expensive; it's best to use a garage connected to your accommodation (for which you will still need to pay €12–25, although many hotels offer discounts). Theft from cars is commonplace; never leave anything valuable on view in a street-parked vehicle, especially overnight.

INFORMATION AND TOURS

Turismo Pza de la Constitución (Mon–Fri 9am–7.30pm, Sat & Sun 9.30am–3pm; ☎ 951 308 911). This central office can provide information on cultural events and has a detailed map of the city. There's also a Turismo Municipal on Pza de la Marina (daily: June–Sept 9am–8pm; Oct–

March 9am–6pm; ☎ 951 926 020), with other branches outside the Alcazaba, at the bus station and in the airport arrivals hall.

Websites ⓦ malagaturismo.com, ⓦ andalucia.org.

Guide to Malaga ⓦ guidetomalaga.com. Tourist

1

information online and via an app; written by one of the authors of this guidebook.

Bus tour A hop-on hop-off service from the bus station is operated by City Sightseeing (every 30min, 10am–8pm; ⓦcity-sightseeing-spain.com; charge; tickets valid 24hr); there are two lines, red and green, and the many stops

include the cathedral, Alcazaba, Gibralfaro and Santuario de Nuestra Señora de la Victoria.

Guided trips Numerous companies offer boat trips around the Bahía de Málaga from Muelle Uno. Segway and bike tours are also available. Pick up a leaflet from Turismo or look out for them in Soho and around Muelle Uno.

ACCOMMODATION

SEE MAP PAGE 64

Although Málaga boasts plenty of **accommodation**, much of which is good-value, the recent rise in visitors has made getting a hotel room at short notice something of a challenge, and practically impossible during Semana Santa and the August *feria* (when prices are also hiked) unless you book well in advance. Málaga's **high season** is July and August; outside this period there are some real bargains to be had even in central hotels. There's also a wide choice of Airbnb options and self-catering apartments. Málaga has no **campsite**: the nearest facilities are at Torremolinos to the west (see page 104) and Torre del Mar (see page 91) to the east.

HOTELS AND HOSTALES

SOHO

Feel Hostel Soho C/Vendeja 25; ⓦfeelhostels.com. Part of a chain of hostels targeted at younger travellers, with accommodation as double en-suite rooms or four- to eight-person dorms. The facilities are well maintained and include a *cafetería*, bar and laundry. Also offers bike rental and guided visits to Málaga nightlife. One of two branches in Málaga (see website for other). €

Hotel Alameda C/Córdoba 11; ⓦhotelalamedamalaga. com. Pleasant small hotel in a high-rise block (which lessens traffic noise). Rooms are adequately furnished and come with a/c and TV. €€

Hotel Mariposa C/Casas de Campos 17; ⓦmariposahm. es. Designer-chic boutique hotel where rooms come with flat-screen TV, DVD player, minibar and safe. Also has own bar-restaurant and garage. €€€

NORTH OF THE ALAMEDA

Apartamentos San Pablo C/Trinidad 39; ⓦapartamentossanpablomalaga.com. Excellent new apartments and studios (sleeping 2–6) in a building alongside the church of San Pablo on the west bank of the Río Guadalmedina. All come with well-equipped kitchen, plasma TV and lounge area. Just the place for a longer stay (offering the best value) with welcoming owners and (relatively) easy street parking nearby. €€

Casa Museo La Merced C/Hinestrosa 16; ⓦcasamuseolamerced.com. An attractive apartment hotel on a quiet residential alley; the seven apartments here are quiet and comfortable with stylish tilework and individual kitchens. Best prices are for extended stays. €€€

Dulces Dreams Boutique Hostel Pza de los Martires 6; ⓦdulcesdreamshostel.com. With individually styled rooms above a laidback café-art gallery facing the church of the Santos Mártires, this enterprise run by friendly young proprietors offers en-suite rooms with a/c and extras, and simpler rooms sharing a bath. There's also a roof terrace with comfortable sofas for chilling out. Doubles €, en suites €€

Hotel Atarazanas C/Atarazanas 19; ⓦhotel-atarazanas-malaga.com. Pleasant three-star hotel near the market with well-appointed a/c rooms featuring room safe, minibar and satellite TV. Also offers reduced rate parking. Frequent special offers on website. €€€

Hotel Boutique Teatro Romano C/Alcazabilla 7; ⓦhotelteatroromano.com. Overlooking the Teatro Romano, this boutique hotel has an excellent central location and crisp modern decor. €€€

Hotel del Pintor C/Álamos 27; ⓦhoteldelpintor.com. Small, arty hotel with decor and furnishings designed by *malagueño* painter Pepe Bornoy. The colour scheme is red and white and each of the soundproofed minimalist rooms is decorated with his art. Features include TV and safe. Breakfast is included. €€

Hotel Ibis Paseo Guimbarda 5; ⓦibishotel.com. On the west bank of the Guadalmedina, this is part of the international chain, offering functional rooms at good prices with frequent online offers. Can arrange parking. €€

Hotel Larios C/Marqués de Larios 2; ⓦroom-matehotels.com. Modern, upmarket four-star property on an elegant pedestrianized shopping street. The hotel has been reconstructed inside the shell of an original Art Deco edifice; satellite TV, room safes and a panoramic rooftop bar are among the features. Frequent special offers online. €€€€

Hotel Málaga Palacio Cortina del Muelle 1; ⓦmarriott. com. This four-star luxury option near the Paseo del Parque has sea-view rooms with minibar and bathrobes. Facilities include rooftop pool and gym. See website for special offers. €€€€

Hotel Tribuna C/Carretería 6; ⓦsercotelhoteles. com. Elegant hotel offering rooms with satellite TV, room safe and minibar. Has its own café-bar next door and can arrange parking. €€€

El Riad Andaluz C/Hinestrosa 24; ⓦelriadandaluz. com. En-suite doubles in friendly townhouse near Pza de la Merced. Decoration comes riad style. Attractive interior patio. Can help with parking. €€

OUT OF THE CENTRE

Albergue Juvenil Málaga Pza de Pio XII; ⓦinterjoven. com. Modern youth hostel on the western outskirts of town, with double and single rooms, disabled facilities, sun terrace and restaurant. Tends to fill up in season, so book ahead. Bus #18 heading west across the river from the Alameda will drop you nearby. Singles €, doubles €€

★**Gran Hotel Miramar** Paseo de Reding 22; ⓦgranhotelmiramarmalaga.com. Built in 1926 as a holiday residence, the huge white palace has been restored to its former glory, but with all the luxury extras you'd expect including butler service, pool, spa and pleasant gardens on the seafront. Large en-suite rooms and suites. Own car park. Check the website for special offers. €€€€

Hostal Capri Av. de Pries 8; ⓦhostalcaprimalaga.com. Near the bullring, this is one of the best budget places to have the beach on its doorstep. Cosy a/c en-suite doubles and friendly owners. €

Hotel California Paseo de Sancha 17; ⓦhotelcaliforniamalaga.com. Charming small hotel near the beach with a flower-bedecked entrance. The well-appointed rooms come with a/c and safes, and the hotel has its own garage. Minimum stay five nights in Aug. Buses #3,

#11, #34 and #35 from the Alameda stop outside. €€€

El Jardín del Azahar C/San Mateo 6; ☎722 259 135. In the Pedregalejo district on buses #3 and #11 routes, this restored 1920s mansion has attractive en-suite rooms and apartments furnished with antiques and a/c, set around a quiet garden just a 10min walk from the beach. Bikes and beach towels included. Free parking available nearby. Three-night minimum stay in July and August. Rooms/ apartments €€

Parador de Málaga-Gibralfaro Monte de Gibralfaro; ⓦparador.es. You won't get a better panoramic view of the coast than from this eagle's nest on top of the Gibralfaro hill. Comfortable, spacious rooms have balcony views and come with satellite TV and, although it's quite small for a *parador*, it does have a pool. Well worth calling in for a drink or a meal (see page 76). €€€€

★**Villa Alicia Guest House** Conde de Ureña 12; ⓦguesthousealicia.com. In the elevated residential district above the city centre, this charming boutique guesthouse has good views from its terraces, and quirky, comfortable rooms. The cheaper ones, with shared bathrooms, are excellent value in the off-season. €–€€

EATING SEE MAP PAGE 64

Málaga has a justified reputation for its splendid signature seafood platter, **fritura malagueña** (fried mixed fish). You'll find many fish restaurants grouped around the Alameda and the focal Plaza de la Constitución. Some of the earthier, more typically *malagueño* places are in the eastern seafront suburbs of Pedregalejo and El Palo, served by buses #3 and #11 from the Paseo del Parque. Málaga has a variety of bustling breakfast cafés for *churros* and coffee, the best of which are clustered around the Mercado Central and in Soho.

CAFÉS AND TEAHOUSES

La Bella Julieta C/Puerta del Mar 10; ⓦlabellajulieta. com. Nice spot for breakfast coffee and afternoon tea. Delicious array of bagels, *pasteles* and fresh juices. €

Café Lepanto C/Marqués de Larios 7; ⓦcateringlepanto.com. This smart central café with an outdoor terrace is the perfect place for afternoon tea or coffee and they cook up a magnificent array of tempting *pasteles* to accompany the beverages. €

★**Casa Aranda** C/Herrería del Rey; ⓦcasa-aranda. net. One of the best of the market cafés, renowned for its excellent *churros*, served at outside tables. There are actually two bars here, one each side of the alley, but owned by the same family and operating as one. €

Casa Mira C/ Marqués de Larios 5; ⓦdimasmiraehijos. com. This is the place where *malagueños* flock on summer nights for the best ice creams in town. Besides ices, house specialities include *horchata* (tiger nut drink) and *granizada* (sorbet). €

Picnic Soho C/Barroso 10 in Soho; ⓦpicnicsoho.com. Relaxed café with a food truck theme and nice outside terrace. Excellent coffee, home-made cakes, burgers and salads, plus cocktails and craft beers. Live music on Friday evenings in the winter. €€

Santa Coffee C/Tomás Heredia 5; ⓦsantacoffee. es. Combining hipster coffeeshop vibes with traditional pavement café, this is an excellent spot for a caffeine hit in Soho. Good cakes, pastries and light meals are available. €

★**La Tetería** C/San Agustín 9; ⓦla-teteria.com. Cosy Moroccan tearoom with terrace almost opposite the Museo Picasso, serving a wide range of teas, infusions, fresh juices and milkshakes. They also offer a wonderful range of north African *pasteles* (pastries) and cakes. €

RESTAURANTS

PLAZA MERCED AND CATHEDRAL AREA

★**Alexso** C/Mariblanca 10; ⓦrestaurantealexso.es. Small restaurant serving some of the most creative food in town, the best of which you can try from the two tasting menus. Sharing plates is another good way to sample the Málaga *salchichón* sausage éclair, the *lubina con salsa de zanahoria* (sea bass with carrot sauce) or *cochinillo con chutney de manzana* (suckling pig with apple chutney). €€€

Cañadu Pza de la Merced 21; ⓦcanadu.es. A vegetarian option with a creative touch serving a good selection of salads, couscous and pasta-based dishes, accompanied by organic wines and beers. They also serve a wide range of

1

teas and there's a fixed-price lunch *menú*. €€

Araboka C/Pedro de Toledo 4; ⓦ arabokarestaurante. com. Wine and gastrobar where the menu varies according to what chef Antonio Fernández finds in the market. The concept here is a fine dining twist on heritage, passed down from generation to generation. Excellent wine list and the maître d' offers good advice on suitable pairing. €€€

El Mesón de Cervantes C/Alamos 11; ⓦ elmesondecervantes.com. The offshoot of the tapas bar of the same name nearby (see page 77) which, although serving tapas, also has *raciones*, enabling you to make a square meal of it. Among the tempting plates on offer you could try *chipirones a la sartén* (fried baby squid) or *secreto ibérico con calabaza asada* (pork with roast squash). Numerous vegetarian options, plus a dessert menu and fairly priced wine list. €€

Mesón Mariano C/Granados 2; ⓦ restaurantemesonmariano.es. One of the longest standing traditional restaurants serving well-prepared local dishes such as *ensalada malagueña* (salad with cod and oranges) and *chivo malagueño* (kid goat). The house speciality is artichokes, particularly good with ham. €€

Los Patios de Beatas C/Beatas 43; ⓦ lospatiosdebeatas. com. One of the best wine restaurants in the city with over six hundred wines by the bottle (on display) and over fifty by the glass, serving excellent fusion tapas and main dishes. Located in two historic houses, the central patio has a stunning stained-glass cupola as well as the original nineteenth-century iron pillars. House specials include *cochinillo paletilla* (leg of suckling pig) and *salmón al gin con remolacha* (salmon with gin and beetroot). Wine tasting sessions and classes available. Enquire via the website for details. €€€

Siete Semillas Pza Arriola 1 T645 935 796. The only 100% organic restaurant in Málaga. Meat, vegetarian and vegan options available on the well-priced daily menu, plus cakes, pastries and fresh juice. €€€€

El Vegetariano de la Alcazabilla C/Pozo del Rey 5, off C/Alcazabilla; ☎ 952 214 858. Good vegetarian and vegan restaurant serving soup, cheese, salads and pasta-based dishes in a cosy atmosphere. €€€€

SOHO

La Antxoeta C/Barroso 7; ⓦ antxoeta.com. The very modern and open kitchen sets the scene for the fusion cooking created by Catalan chef Pablo Caballero. The menu changes frequently depending on the local produce available, but usually includes signature dishes such as *tartar de navaja con aire de limón* (razor shell tartare) and *cordero con hummus de berenjenas* (lamb with aubergine hummus). Good-value lunch time menu. €€€€

Mamuchis C/Casas de Campo 27; ☎ 664 722 369. The small dining room comes packed with memorabilia and ornaments, and the kitchen serves an eclectic menu from round the world. Asia and South America feature heavily, but France, Holland

and Spain all put in appearances. The menu changes almost daily, but staples include dim sum and tacos. €€

Mixtúrate C/Casas de Campo 4; ☎ 951 330 806. Brazil meets Asia via Spain at this upmarket fusion restaurant serving some of the most visually spectacular dishes In Málaga. The decor is fresh and modern to match a menu that includes *babó de langostinos* (shrimp stew) and *pato tucupí* (duck with maracuya and pak choy). Desserts are served in kilner jars and you take your pick from the tray. Excellent value weekday lunch menu. €€€

Óleo C/Alemania, next to CAC Málaga; ⓦ oleorestaurante.es. Mediterranean cooking gets a modern twist here, at one of the best-value restaurants in town. Try the *chivo malagueño* (local kid goat) in Vietnamese rolls or the *atún rojo con tomate seco* (red tuna with dried tomatoes). They also do a long sushi menu and excellent cocktails to sip on the outdoor terrace next to the river. €€€€

PLAZA DE TOROS AND LA MALAGUETA

José Carlos García Restaurante Pza de la Capilla, on Muelle Uno 8; ⓦ restaurantejcg.com. Offers *cocina malagueña* at its creative best, under the direction of Michelin-starred chef José Carlos García, originally at the helm at Café de París. Dining à la carte doesn't come cheap nor do the *menús de degustación*, but you do get what you pay for. €€€€

OUT OF THE CENTRE

★**Parador de Málaga-Gibralfaro** Monte de Gibralfaro; ⓦ parador.es. Superior terrace dining with spectacular views over the coast and town from this parador (see page 75) next to Gibralfaro (see page 66), specializing in *malagueño* fish and meat dishes. À la carte is affordable and wine prices are reasonable, or you could also try the excellent-value *menú*. Also offers a vegetarian *menú*. Book ahead if you want a table with a view. If you can't face the climb, take a taxi or bus #35 east along Paseo del Parque. €€–€€€

El Tintero Playa del Dedo s/n, El Palo; ☎ 952 206 826. Right at the far eastern end of the seafront, just before the *Club Náutico* (bus #11; ask for "Tintero"), this is a huge beach restaurant where the waiters charge round with plates of fish and you shout for, or grab, anything you like the look of. Beware of the larger platters, or *bandejas*, which can cost significantly more. The fish to go for are, above all, *mero* (a kind of gastronomically evolved cod) and *rosada* (dogfish and catfish), plus Andalucian regulars such as *boquerones* (fresh anchovies), gambas (prawns) and *sepia* (cuttlefish). Haute cuisine it certainly ain't, but for sheer entertainment it's a must. €€

TAPAS BARS

★**Antigua Casa Guardia** Corner of C/Pastora, on

the Alameda; ⓦantiguacasadeguardia.net. Great old nineteenth-century spit-and-sawdust bar (which opened its doors in 1840). Picasso was a devotee of their wines, and a photo on the wall shows him toting one of the bar's *jarras*. Some of the new and incredibly sweet Málaga wine – served from huge vats – is overpowering; Seco Añejo, which has matured for a year, is much more palatable. For a *tapa*, try the house *mejillones* (mussels) or *cola de langosta* (lobster's tail). €€

Bodegas Quitapeñas (aka La Manchega) C/Marín García 4; ⓦquitapenas.es. Another fine old drinking den with its own off-site bodega (which can be visited). House specials include *tortita de camarones* (shrimp fritters) and *jibias guisadas* (stewed cuttlefish) – and you can wash them down with Málaga's traditional Moscatel and Sierras de Málaga wines. €€

La Cosmopolita C/Jose Denis Belgrano 3; ⓦlacosmopolita.es. This welcoming restaurant north of the Plaza de la Constitución serves sophisticated Mediterranean cuisine in a low-key setting. There are pavement tables for outdoor dining and an airy interior. Seafood is a speciality, with excellent prawn and oyster dishes. €€€€

El Gastronauta C/Echegaray 3, off C/Granada; ⓦelgastronauta.es. Small tapas venue decorated with artwork, and an even smaller outside terrace. Innovative tapas with good choice of vegan and vegetarian options such as the aubergine timbale or kofta. Paellas and steaks are also good. €€

El Mortal Pza García Herrera 18, just north of Atarazanas; ☏951 243 506. Friendly venue with a lovely terrace on the peaceful square serving hearty breakfasts and *tablas* (boards) of cheeses and cold cuts from around Spain. You could try the *tosta de sardina* (sardine toast) or the *tabla andaluza*. Local vermouth on tap, as well as craft beers and a good range of wines. €€

★ **El Pimpi** C/Granada 62; ⓦelpimpi.com. Cavernous and hugely popular bodega-style bar and *malagueño* institution serving up (among other concoctions) tasty vino dulce by the glass or bottle. There are tapas and *raciones* to go with the drinks and you can do a bit of celebrity-spotting on their wall of photos – including one of a young Antonio Banderas. The frequent live events include flamenco. Don't miss the superb terrace (with Alcazaba view) out the back. €€

El Refectorium Catedral C/Postigo de los Abades 4, near the cathedral; ⓦelrefectorium.net. Stylish bar (and restaurant) with a spacious bar and excellent (if pricier than the norm) tapas range. Try the *revuelto de erizo* (sea urchin) or the *ensaladilla rusa* (potato salad), reputedly one of the best in the city. €€€

El Rincón del Cervecero C/Casas del Campo 5, Soho; ⓦelrincondelcervecero.com. Craft beer shop and bar with a long list of local and international beers. Serves platters of cold cuts and cheese, and organizes tasting and beer-making classes. €€

★ **El Tapeo de Cervantes** C/Carcer 8; ⓦeltapeodecervantes.com. Excellent, if Lilliputian, tapas bar with a cosy and welcoming ambience and some creative tapas. Try the *atún rojo en salsa coliflor* (tuna in a cauliflower sauce) or *envuelta de jamón* with cheese and rocket. Also has excellent wines sold by the glass. Book if you want to get one of a handful of tables. When full, you can try their equally good *mesón* around the corner (see page 76). €€

Uvedoble C/Cister 15; ⓦuvedobletaberna.com. Chic little bar offering "designer" tapas in a minimalist setting, with a small but interesting tapas and *raciones* menu. Try their *croquetas caseras ibéricos* (croquettes with jamón) or *fideúa con chipirón de Málaga* (black noodles with squid). Lengthy wine list. €€

Wendy Gamba C/Fresca 10; ☏952 223 024. Diminutive backstreet bar devoted to the *gamba* (prawn) in all its variations. House specials include *gambas con garbanzos* and they even serve *gamba churros*. €€

DRINKING AND NIGHTLIFE

SEE MAP PAGE 64

The city has a good range of atmospheric **bars** where you can while away an evening. You'll find most of Málaga's **nightlife** north of the cathedral around Plaza de Uncibay and Plaza del Siglo plus *calles* Granada and Beatas, Plaza de la Merced and the tiny Plaza Marqués Vado del Maestre, which is filled with drinking bars and plenty of night-time action. In the summer months there's also a scene in **Malagueta**, south of the bullring. At weekends and holidays dozens of youth-oriented *discotecas* fill the crowded streets in these areas, and over the summer – though it's dead out of season – the scene spreads out along the seafront to the suburb of **Pedregalejo**. Here the streets just behind the beach host most of the action, and dozens of discos and smaller music bars lie along and off the main street, Juan Sebastián Elcano. *Más Málaga*

(ⓦmmalaga.es) is an online publication covering events and entertainment in the city. *Sur in English*, published on Fridays free (ⓦsurinenglish.com), is a weekly version of Málaga's main daily *Sur* with lots of gen on nightlife, concerts and other events.

BARS, DISCOTECAS AND CLUBS

Batik C/Alcazabilla 12; ⓦhotelalcazabapremium.com. One of the roof terraces in town serving food in the restaurant and drinks with views of the Alcazaba.

Clarence Jazz Club C/Cañón 5; ⓦclarencejazzclub.com. Málaga's main venue for live jazz with year-round concerts by local and international artists, and jam sessions (usually Thursday); see the website for details. Entrance includes a drink.

1

Morrissey's Irish Pub C/Mendez Nuñez 5; ⓦ morrisseysirishpub.es. Irish-style pub – and a pretty good imitation of a varnished Dublin bar – that occasionally stages live gigs. Popular with a foreign crowd, and the Guinness isn't bad.

Puerta Oscura C/Molina Lario 5, near the cathedral; ⓦ puertaoscuramalaga.com. Slightly incongruous classical-music venue-cum-cafetería – sometimes with live performers – which also mounts art exhibitions. Serves cocktails, ices and baguettes. T-shirts are definitely a no-no here.

Sala Premier C/Molina Lario 2; ⓦ salapremier.com. Busy venue with Wild West memorabilia downstairs and a Hobbit themed upstairs, packed with locals and tourists who come here to watch sport and play board games.

ZZ Pub C/Tejon y Rodríguez 6; ⓦ zzpub.es. Popular club that's been around for a while, featuring jazz, funk, soul, rock and salsa sounds. Live gigs most nights starting around midnight.

FLAMENCO

Genuine flamenco in Málaga is now easier to come by and the venues below often approach the real thing. Many flamenco events happen in and around the town throughout the year – several are held at the Museo Picasso (see page 68) and during the Bienal de Flamenco (see page 63). The Turismo Municipal (see page 73) is the best source of information on these.

Kelipe C/Muro de Puerta Nueva 10; ⓦ kelipe.net. This flamenco centre puts on shows with a good atmosphere, and the price includes two drinks. Tickets should be reserved online in advance. Shows Thurs–Sun 8pm.

Peña Juan Breva C/Ramón Franquelo 4; ⓦ peñajuanbreva.eu. Founded in 1958, this is one of Málaga's most authentic and welcoming *peñas*, with weekly concerts. Their excellent museum (free, but contributions welcome; Mon–Sat 10am–2pm) showcases a fascinating collection of flamenco costumes, posters and antique phonographs, plus a range of musical instruments and guitars including one that belonged to Federico García Lorca. Shows on Friday at 9.30pm; occasionally on other nights.

SHOPPING
SEE MAP PAGE 64

El Corte Inglés Avda de Andalucía 4; Welcorteingles. es. A great department store with a basement supermarket that sells a terrific selection of the nation's wines and spirits, and gourmet store on the top floor.

Librería Luces Alameda Principal 16; ⓦ librerialuces. com. The town's most central general bookshop stocks a selection of titles in English and often stages literary events with readings by popular authors.

La Mallorquina Pza Felix Saenz (near the market); ☎ 952 213 352. A good place to pick up *malagueño* cheese, wines, almonds and dried fruit.

Mapas y Compañía C/Compañia 33; ⓦ mapasycia. es. Málaga's best travel bookshop sells IGN walking maps, as well as 1:50,000 *Mapas Cartografía Militar* (military maps).

DIRECTORY

Banks and exchange There are numerous ATMs all over town, especially along C/Marqués de Larios and on and around the Plaza de la Constitución. El Corte Inglés (see above) will also change currency free of charge.

Basketball The Málaga team Unicaja regularly achieve high rankings in the Spanish ACB league. Matches take place at the Martín Carpena Stadium, to the west of the city centre (bus #16 from the Alameda Principal or metro Line 2) and tickets can be purchased online (ⓦ unicajabaloncesto.com).

Consulates UK, Edificio Eurocom, C/Mauricio Moro Pareto 2 (☎ 952 352 300); US, Avda Juan Gómez 8, Fuengirola (☎ 952 474 891); Republic of Ireland, Avda de los Boliches 15, Fuengirola (☎ 952 475 108).

Football C.F. Málaga isn't one of the country's top-flight teams, and it tends to move back and forth between La Liga and the Second Division, but it still inspires passionate local support. Games are at La Rosaleda stadium, Paseo de Martiricos s/n, at the northern end of the Río Guadalmedina. Tickets can be purchased from the stadium (ⓦ malagacf.es).

Hospital Hospital Carlos Haya, Avda Carlos Haya, 2km west of the city centre (☎ 951 290 000).

Pharmacy The handy Farmacia Caffarena (24hr) is located at Alameda 2, near the junction with C/Marqués de Larios. (☎ 952 212 858, ⓦ farmaciacaffarena.net).

Police Policía Local, Avda de la Rosaleda 19 (☎ 952 126 500); in emergencies dial ☎ 092 (local police) or ☎ 091 (national).

Post office C/Santa Lucía 7, slightly north of Pza de la Constitución (Mon–Fri 8.30am–8.30pm, Sat 9.30am–1pm).

El Chorro Gorge and around

Some 50km northwest of Málaga is the **El Chorro Gorge (Garganta del Chorro)**: an immense cleft cut through a vast limestone massif by the Río Guadalhorce, with daunting walls of rock as high as 400m along its 3km length. But the gorge's most stunning feature is a concrete catwalk, **El Caminito del Rey**, which threads the length of the gorge hanging precipitously halfway up its side. Built in the 1920s as part of a burgeoning hydroelectric scheme, the Caminito was opened by King Alfonso XIII, who walked its whole length and gave it its name. It quickly became a major tourist attraction, but for decades it received little maintenance work, and by the early 2000s the Caminito had fallen into a dangerous state of disrepair.

After many false starts and multi-million-euro investment, the provincial authorities carried out spectacular and ambitious restoration work (helicopters were used to put some of the structure in place) and in 2015 reopened a new catwalk that mostly runs 1m above the line of the old one.

El Caminito del Rey

Tues–Sun: 10am–5pm • Charge (includes bus fare) • ℗ caminitodelrey.info

Although sometimes still billed as one of the world's most dangerous walkways, the current version of **El Caminito del Rey** is actually very safe (helmets are compulsory and the entire walkway is fenced and has a steel cable to hold on to) and now ranks among the most popular attractions in the province. You do need a reasonable head for heights – the suspension bridge at the end can be a challenge – and allow at least a half-day for the 7.7km trail (4.4km on the catwalk itself). Book well in advance via the website, wear stout walking shoes and take plenty of water, especially in the summer months, when temperatures in the gorge can easily surpass 35ºC. The website provides full details on the visit including how to get to the start point and return.

If you have no head for heights it's still possible to explore the rest of the gorge, however, and get a view of the Caminito on a walk (see page 79). It's also possible to get a glimpse of both gorge and Caminito from any of the non-AVE trains going north from Málaga – the line, slipping in and out of tunnels, follows the river for quite a distance along the gorge, before plunging into a last long tunnel just before its head.

El Chorro and the Embalse del Guadalhorce

If you want to explore more of the gorge, head for **EL CHORRO**, which is reachable by train from Málaga. Not much more than a cluster of houses, bars and hotels around the railway station, it has nevertheless turned itself into one of Spain's major centres for rock climbing.

A DIFFERENT VIEW OF THE CAMINITO DEL REY

An alternative (and free) way to view the **Caminito del Rey** and the **Garganta del Chorro** on your own – and easily accessed by car or a fine **walk** in itself – is to follow the road from El Chorro train station, signposted "Pantano de Guadalhorce", reached by crossing over the dam and turning right, then following the road north along the lake towards the hydroelectric plant. After 8km turn right at a junction to reach – after 2km – the bar-restaurant *El Mirador*, poised above a road tunnel and overlooking the various lakes and reservoirs of the Guadalhorce scheme. From the bar (where you should leave any transport), a dirt track on the right (signed "Gaitanejo"), just south of the tunnel entrance, heads towards the gorge. Follow this and take the first track on the right after about 700m. This climbs for some 2km to where it splits into two small trails. The trail to the left leads you to a magnificent viewpoint over the gorge from where you can see the Caminito del Rey clinging to the rock face. The right-hand track climbs to an obvious peak, the Pico de Almochon, with more **spectacular views**, this time over the lakes of the Embalse del Guadalhorce (see page 79). On both walks you'll need to return the way you came.

1

From the train station it's about 12km to some attractive lakes and reservoirs, such as the **Embalse del Guadalhorce**, part of the huge Embalse Guadalhorce-Guadalteba reservoir and hydroelectric scheme constructed in the early part of the twentieth century. In dry years water levels fall, making the area a great deal less attractive, but the lakes still generally offer sufficient water to swim in, and there are also kayaks for rent (see Finca La Campana on page 80). You can camp along the rocky shores; alternatively, the village of Ardales (see page 81), 4km beyond the lake, has shops, bars, accommodation and buses to and from Ronda (roughly every two hours from 9.30am to 10pm). Just beyond the *El Mirador* restaurant (see page 79) you are able to view the impressive dam at the junction of the two great Guadalteba and Guadalhorce reservoirs, with the marble table and throne where Alfonso XIII signed off the completed works on May 21, 1921.

ARRIVAL AND DEPARTURE
EL CHORRO

By train and bus El Chorro is served by two daily direct trains (40min) from Málaga. There are also regular buses to El Chorro from nearby Álora (40min), which itself is served by several daily trains from Málaga (30min).

By car To get there with your own transport, take the

A357 heading west from Málaga towards Pizarra, turning here along the A343 to Álora. Continue beyond Álora for 15km and turn west at Valle de Abdalajís along the minor MA4401, a journey of around 65km in total.

ACCOMMODATION AND EATING

Bar-Restaurante Garganta del Chorro ⓦlagarganta. com. Restaurant-and-rooms complex which also rents pleasant apartments and suites, many with terraces and views, inside a converted mill and overlooking a pool. Their restaurant (€€) is the one of the best places to eat in the village. **€€€**

★ **Finca La Campana** ⓦfincalacampana.com. Signs from the station will direct you 2km to this farmhouse set in rural surroundings with a bunkhouse and a cluster of attractive cottages (with fully equipped kitchen) sharing a pool. Run by qualified Swiss climber Jean Hofer, the place also offers courses in rock climbing and caving, rents out mountain bikes, can arrange kayaks on the nearby lake/ reservoir, and does hiking excursions, as well as organizing

tickets for the Caminito del Rey. For longer stays (two nights plus) transfers can be arranged from Álora or Málaga airport and camping is also possible. **€**

The Olive Branch El Chorro ⓦolivebranchelchorro. com. In a picturesque setting above the village, this friendly places has both dorms and simple en-suite rooms, and a small campsite. There are cooking facilities and a small swimming pool. **€**

La Posada del Conde Pantano del Chorro 16; ⓦhoteldelconde.com. Attractive small three-star hotel close to the *El Mirador* restaurant (see box, page 79). Rooms come with TV and a/c and some have balcony views overlooking the lake. **€€**

Bobastro

A few kilometres southwest of El Chorro • Hourly guided tours on the hour: July–Sept Tues–Sun 10am–2pm; Oct–June Tues–Fri 10am– 6pm, Sat & Sun 10am–7pm • Charge • Cross the dam from El Chorro train station and turn right along the road to El Mirador (see box, page 79); after 4km a signed turn-off for the site indicates a twisting 3km route to a ticket booth, where you should leave your vehicle

Amid some of the wildest scenery in the province lies **BOBASTRO**, the mountaintop remains of a Mozarabic fortified settlement. Famous as the isolated eyrie of colourful ninth-century rebel **Ibn Hafsun** (see box, page 81), the castle was said to be the most impregnable in all Andalucía, but only a ruined **church**, carved into an enormous boulder, remains of the once-great fortress. At the start of the tour, the guardian will open the entry gate and lead you along a path for 400m through the pinewoods to the site of the church and other remains. Situated outside the original fortified area, and below some cave dwellings of uncertain date, the church is typically Mozarabic in style, its nave and two aisles separated by horseshoe-arched arcades. The transept, and a deep apse chapel flanked by two side chapels, can clearly be seen, making the edifice one of the few identifiable traces of building from the period. Nearby and to the west is the **Cueva de Doña Trinidad** with paleolithic cave paintings; guided visits to see them are organized by the museum at Ardales (see page 81). After your visit, it's worth

IBN HAFSUN

Born near Ronda around 860, **Ibn Hafsun** was a *muwallad* (of mixed Christian-Arab parentage) who, after killing a man, fell out with the Umayyad caliphate at Córdoba and resorted to a life of brigandage. Gathering around him a formidable army, he built his stronghold at Bobastro, and from 880–917 scored a number of spectacular victories over the many Umayyad forces sent to defeat him. At the height of his power Hafsun controlled an area between the straits of Gibraltar in the west and Jaén in the east. His defence of the poor against excessive Umayyad taxation and forced labour further served to increase the popularity of this Robin Hood-style figure, especially among his fellow *muwalladin* who believed they were getting a raw deal from their pure-blooded Arab rulers. After he converted to Christianity in 899, the church at Bobastro was constructed to receive his remains, which were duly interred there upon his death in 917. When Abd ar-Rahman III finally conquered Bobastro in 927, he exhumed the body of Hafsun and hung it on a gibbet along with a dog and a pig outside the Alcázar in Córdoba as a "salutary warning to imitators and a pleasant spectacle to believers (true Muslims)".

continuing 3km along the road, which climbs to the elevated and isolated hill top with spectacular views over the Garganta del Chorro and the Guadalhorce valley.

Ardales

At the southern point of the reservoirs that comprise the Guadalhorce-Guadalteba scheme, the compact, snow-white farming village of **ARDALES** tumbles down the hill below La Peña, a rocky outcrop topped by remains of the Iberian settlement of Turóbriga, as well as a Roman fort and ruined Moorish *alcázar*. From the main square, the wide and animated Plaza San Isidro around which most of the activity in Ardales revolves, a steep street climbs to the summit.

Iglesia de la Virgen de los Remedios

Open occasionally with no fixed timetable • Free

On the way up the hill, look out for the fifteenth-century Mudéjar **Iglesia de la Virgen de los Remedios** with its distinctive, partly tiled, tower. When you get closer, it becomes clear that the tower was once the minaret of the former mosque it replaced. The interior also has Moorish arches dividing the nave and side aisles, the right of which has the mosque's original *mihrab*, oriented towards Mecca.

Museo de la Prehistoria

Mid-June to mid-Sept Tues–Sun 10am–2pm; mid-Sept to mid-June Tues–Sun 10am–2.30pm • Charge • ☎ 609 207 239

Doubling as a tourist information centre, the **Museo de la Prehistoria**, facing the bridge as you enter the village, has Roman and Moorish archeological finds as well as a virtual visit of the nearby paleolithic Cueva de Doña Trinidad and copies of its rock paintings.

Cueva de Doña Trinidad

Guided tours (bookable in advance with the Museo de la Prehistoria) Tues–Sun 10.30am, Fri & Sat also 4pm; 1hr 30min • Charge • 🌐 bit. ly/CuevaDeDona

The **Cueva de Doña Trinidad**, 1.5km deep, was discovered in 1918 and is one of the most important in Andalucía – traces were found of human occupation dating back to the later Stone Age, making it contemporaneous with the Cueva de la Pileta near Ronda (see page 132). Among some remarkable paintings and engravings dating from between ten and thirty thousand years ago are images of deer, horses, goats, bulls, fish, snakes and what is thought to be the first artistic representation of a human hand. The discovery of human remains in the cave suggests also that it may

1

have had some form of funerary purpose in its latter period. The museum curator can also advise on visiting other caves in the area as well as some recently discovered trenches from the Civil War.

ACCOMMODATION   ARDALES

★ **Apartamentos Ardales** C/El Burgo 7, just off the main square; ⓦapartamentosardales.com. The best accommodation option, this charming aparthotel has seventeen apartments ranged around a tranquil patio. All the modern and distinctively decorated a/c apartments come with a kitchen and balcony or terrace, while the communal rooftop terrace has fine views plus a plunge pool and jacuzzi. The proprietors can provide information on a number of great walks in the surrounding sierra and get tickets for Caminito del Rey if you book directly. See website for special offers. €€–€€€

Camping Parque Ardales 6km east of Ardales along the MA5403; ⓦparqueardales.com. Scenic "lakeside" (although it's actually the reservoir) campsite, which also rents out apartments sleeping up to four and offers a variety of activities including rock climbing, archery and canoeing on the lake. There's no bus to the campsite, but a taxi from Ardales will cost about €20 (any of the bars should be able to arrange this for you). Camping €, apartments €€

Hostal-Restaurante El Cruce ⓦardaleselcruce.com. Sited at the junction before the bridge across the Río Turón, this is a decent option, with simple a/c en-suite rooms above a restaurant (€). There's also a pool. €

EATING AND DRINKING

Bar Millan Pza San Isidro 1; ☎652 072 542. One of a couple of popular bars on the main square, this offers an excellent choice of tapas (over forty make up the menu) including *bacalao frito con alioli de miel* (fried cod with honey alioli) and *col llenada de carne* (stuffed cabbage). €̄

Restaurante Juan Vera C/Andrades Navarrete 9; ☎952 458 249. With a pleasant terrace fronting the Ayuntamiento, this is an excellent place for economical *comida casera* – they hand you the soup tureen and you

help yourself. Specialities include carrillada (pork cheeks), croquetas and ajo blanco (cold almond soup). €€

La Tienda del Turista C/Fray Juan 4; ☎952 458 443. Just downhill from the main square, this is an Aladdin's cave of a shop selling products of the region – wines, cheeses, olive oil – as well as Ardales's renowned *tortas de almendras* (almond cakes) made from traditional family recipes. Also a café serving breakfasts, ice creams and home-made cakes. €€

Carratraca

Five kilometres south of Ardales, and reached via a turn-off from the A357 Málaga road, lies the village of **CARRATRACA**, once famous throughout Europe for its **sulphur spa**, now extensively refurbished as part of the *Villa Padierna* hotel. Although the baths date back to the days of the Greeks and Romans, it wasn't until the nineteenth century that Carratraca became one of the foremost spas in Europe, and a gathering point for the continent's aristocracy. During its heyday the *balneario* (spa) attracted kings, princesses and literary bigwigs such as Lord Byron, Alexandre Dumas and Rainer Maria Rilke. The three *casinos*, where these socialites used to while away their time between plunges in the stinking, sulphurous waters which gush from the rocks, are long gone. However, two wonderfully elegant, eighteenth-century open-air (now glassed-in) pools circled by classical Tuscan columns have survived intact, forming the refurbished spa's centrepiece. You can use the spa without staying at the hotel. A basic twenty-minute soak will set you back about €40, although other treatments (including various types of massage, detox and thermal circuits) are much pricier.

Ayuntamiento and bullring

Carratraca's sights include a Regency-style **Ayuntamiento**, on the edge of the village, formerly the residence of Doña Trinidad Grund, a local benefactor who donated funds for the excavation of the cave near Bobastro that bears her name. She also provided the backing for the curious **bullring** nearby, hacked out of solid rock and scene of an impressive village Passion play – with villagers in costume – during Semana Santa.

ACCOMMODATION AND EATING

CARRATRACA

Casa Pepa C/Los Baños 18, ⓦ labocacha.com. Just along from the spa, this friendly *fonda* – run by its eponymous proprietor – offers clean and simple rooms with or without bath. Pepa also makes hearty meals (€€) – the aromas emerging from the kitchen are usually very tempting. €
Venta El Trillo C/Álora–Carratraca s/n; ☏ 952 458 199.

The last in a line of three *ventas* on the road out of the village, offering tapas, *raciones*, *combinados* and a weekday *menú*. House specials include roast lamb and grilled meats. They also let some simple, clean chalets (€) with en suite and some with a/c. Wi-fi only in communal areas, where there's a pool. €–€€

Antequera and around

Sitting on two low hills in the valley of the Río Guadalhorce, **ANTEQUERA** is an attractive market town with some important ancient monuments and a clutch of fine churches. On the main train line from Málaga to Granada and Seville, at the junction of roads heading inland to Córdoba, Granada and Seville, it's easy to get to, and makes a good day-trip from Málaga, which lies 40km to the south. Travelling from Málaga, the bus takes you along the fast but largely uninteresting A45 *autovía*. If you're driving, it's far nicer to take the older, more picturesque road (MA3402) that meanders through **Almogía**, a small hill town with tortuously narrow streets.

Antequera has a modern appearance that belies its history. In Roman times Anticaria ("ancient city") is thought to have had a substantial population; much later, in 1410, the town was the first in Andalucía to fall to the Christian forces in the *Reconquista*. It's now a bustling agricultural centre where farmers from the surrounding *vega* come to stock up on everything from tractor tyres to seeding attachments.

The town divides into two zones: a **monumental quarter** situated at the foot of the hill dominated by the **Alcazaba**, and the mainly nineteenth-century **commercial sector** concentrated around the Alameda de Andalucía. This end of town is where modern Antequera works and plays, and there's not much in the way of sights, though the nineteenth-century bullring is worth a look. Probably the most famous sights, however, are the prehistoric **dolmen caves**, on the northern edge of town, declared UNESCO World Heritage Sites in 2016. A couple of enjoyable trips further afield are to the vast **Parque Natural El Torcal**, with its weathered limestone rock formations, and the important flamingo breeding grounds of **Fuente de Piedra**.

Antequera has its spring *feria* at the end of May, but the annual *feria* happens during the third week in August, taking the form of a harvest fiesta (*recolección*) with *corridas*, dancing and parades.

Museo de la Ciudad de Antequera

Pza Coso Viejo s/n • June–Sept Tues–Fri 10am–2pm & 7–9pm, Sat 9.30am–2pm & 6–9pm, Sun 10am–2pm; Oct–May Tues–Fri 10am–2pm & 4.30–6.30pm, Sat 9.30am–2pm & 4.30–6.30pm, Sun 9.30am–2pm • Charge, free on Sun • ⓦ museoantequera.wordpress.com

At the heart of the monumental quarter, the **Museo de la Ciudad de Antequera** is located in a striking eighteenth-century ducal palace. It's just as well that the palace is worth visiting for itself, because the exhibits do little justice to the setting. The collection is, however, distinguished by two works of sculpture: a fine first-century AD **Roman bronze** of a youth known as the *Efebo de Antequera*, and an eerily lifelike carving in wood of **St Francis of Assisi** by the seventeenth-century *andaluz* sculptor Pedro de Mena.

More fragments of ancient statuary and tombstones are dotted around the courtyard, and a room on the ground floor devotes itself to the artwork of modern realism painter **Cristóbal Toral**, who was born near Antequera and whose work is interesting and often controversial. In 2014 he caused a storm of protest when, in an installation at an exhibition in Madrid, he depicted a framed image of the newly abdicated King Juan Carlos tossed on to a pile of junk in a full-size builder's skip.

1

▲ Train Station (150m)
Granada, Dolmens, Málaga, Córdoba & 🔟 ▲

ANTEQUERA

■ ACCOMMODATION	
Hospedería Arte de Cozina	4
Hostal Colón	6
Hotel Coso Viejo	5
Hotel Los Dólmenes	1
Número Uno	3
Parador de Antequera	2

● EATING	
Abrasador Bodegas Triana	8
La Antequerana	2
Bar-Cafetería A La Fuerza	5
Café del Centro	4
El Hacebuche	6
Mesón Adarve	1
Restaurante Arte de Cozina	3
Restaurante Mar De Gloria	7
El Rincón de Lola	9

Convento de la Carmelitas Descalzas

Pza de las Descalzas • Tues–Fri 10am–1.30pm & 5–7pm, Sat 9am–12pm & 5–6.30pm, Sun 9am–12pm • Charge • ⓦ museoconventualantequera.com

The eighteenth-century **Convento de la Carmelitas Descalzas** (Carmelite nunnery of San José) is noted for its convent *dulces* (see box, page 41), sold via a *torno* in the mornings only (afternoon hours are for access to the convent's museum). The entrance is behind the small fountain. Inside, asking for a *surtido* (selection) gets you a bit of everything. You won't see the nun who serves you, but, in a sign of changing times, she may ask you to pay first.

Iglesia del Carmen

Pza del Carmen • Tues–Fri 11am–1.30pm & 4.30–5.45pm, Sat & Sun 11am–2pm • Charge • ☎ 952 702 505

Cuesta de los Rojas climbs steeply to the Postigo de la Estrella, an old postern gate. To the east of this – and not to be missed – lies the seventeenth-century Mudéjar church of **Iglesia del Carmen**, whose plain facade little prepares you for the eighteenth-century interior, painstakingly restored to its former glory. The main altar's sensational 13m-high **retablo** – one of the finest in Andalucía – is a masterly late-Baroque extravaganza of carved wood by Antonio Primo and Diego Márquez, its centrepiece a Virgin in a *camarín* flanked by a bevy of polychrome saints and soaring angels.

Alcazaba

Pza Alta • Mon–Sun 10am–6pm • Charge (includes access to Colegiata de Santa María), free Tues 2–6pm • ☎ 951 700 737

Beyond Nuestra Señora del Carmen on Cuesta de las Rojas lies the refurbished medieval **Alcazaba**, with its thirteenth-century Islamic fortification, the **Torre del Homenaje**. The first fortress to fall to the Christians during the *Reconquista* of the kingdom of Granada, the ruined Alcazaba now encloses a municipal garden, giving fine views over the town towards the curiously anthropoid **Peña de los Enamorados** (Lovers' Rock), resembling the profiled head of a sleeping giant. The outcrop acquired its name from two lovers (a Christian girl and a Muslim youth) during the Moorish period, who are said to have thrown themselves from the top when their parents forbade their marriage.

Adjoining the Alcazaba, the sixteenth-century **Arco de los Gigantes** preserves stones and inscriptions embedded in its walls that were rescued by antiquaries from the destruction of the Roman town in the same period.

Real Colegiata de Santa María la Mayor

Pza Alta • Mon–Sun 10am–6pm • Charge, free Tues 2–6pm or with Alcazaba ticket

East of the Alcazaba, the sixteenth-century collegiate church of **Real Santa María la Mayor** boasts a great Plateresque facade inspired by a Roman triumphal arch. Inside the triple-naved church – which now serves as a concert hall – you'll also see a superb Mudéjar coffered ceiling.

Iglesia de San Sebastián and around

Pza San Sebastián • Daily 8.30am–1pm & 6–8pm • Free

The seventeenth-century church of **San Sebastián**, in the elegant plaza of the same name, possesses a striking brick steeple that dominates the town. Note the carved angels and the tower's weather vane, El Angelote, which has the remains of Antequera's patron saint, Santa Euphemia, in a reliquary hung around its neck. The interior contains some beautifully carved choir stalls, as does the nearby eighteenth-century **San Agustín**, at the start of Calle Infante Fernando.

Iglesia de San Juan de Dios

C/Infante Fernando • Tues–Sat 10am–2pm & 4–6pm, Sun 9.30am–2.30pm • Charge, free Sat noon–2pm & Sun

At the western end of Calle Infante Fernando lies the Renaissance church of **San Juan de Dios**, constructed (or so Richard Ford maintained) in the late sixteenth and early seventeenth centuries almost entirely with stone taken from the demolition of what was a perfectly preserved Roman theatre.

Santa María de Jesús

Pza del Portichuelo 14 • Tues–Sun 11am–1pm • Free

The white-walled Baroque chapel of **Santa María de Jesús**, with storks' nests in its belfry, is also worth a look. From a *mirador* behind the churches there are great **views** towards the Alcazaba and the surrounding hills.

Plaza de Toros

Pza de la Constitución s/n

The western end of town has little in the way of sights, though the nineteenth-century **Plaza de Toros**, on the Alameda de Andalucía, is well worth a look – access is usually available to the ring during the day. This bullring staged its first *corrida* on August 20, 1848, and whatever your views on bullfighting, it's difficult not to pick up on the

1

atmosphere that the old place generates, especially when you view the amphitheatre from the matador's position in the centre of the arena.

Dolmens

Ctra Antequera–Archidona s/n • April to mid-June Tues–Sat 9am–8pm, Sun 9am–3pm; mid-June to mid-Sept Tues–Sun 9am–3pm; mid-Sept–March Tues–Sat 9am–6pm, Sun 9am–3pm • Free

On the town's northern outskirts – an easy 1km walk along the Granada road – lies a group of three **prehistoric dolmens**, which rank among the most important in Spain, now enclosed in a "dolmen park". It houses the Centro Solar sculpture marking the cardinal points and the solstices, built in honour of Michael Hoskin, the British archeoastronomer, whose work included a study of the Antequera dolmens, a visitor centre with small shop and car park. The two major dolmens are remarkable constructions, while the third lies further away and is best reached with your own transport or a taxi.

Cueva de Menga

The grandest of Antequera's megalithic monuments is the **Cueva de Menga**, its roof formed by massive stone slabs, among them a 180-tonne monolith. Dating from around 2500 BC, the columned gallery leading to an oval burial chamber was probably the final resting place of an important chieftain. On the last stone slab of the left wall (nearest the entrance) you'll see some engraved – and probably symbolic – forms; the star, however, is a later addition. A recently discovered **well** in the rear of the chamber probably dates from the Roman period. If you stand just inside the entrance to the Menga dolmen you will be able to see the Lovers' Rock, precisely framed in the portal – something that cannot have been accidental and suggests that the rock may have had some religious or ritual significance. This is underlined by the fact that the sun rises behind the "head" of the rock at the summer solstice and penetrates the burial chamber.

Cueva de Viera

The **Cueva de Viera**, dating from a century or two later than the Cueva de Menga, has better-cut stones, forming a long, narrow tunnel leading to a smaller burial chamber. The roof consisted of seven stones of which only four remain. To the west it's possible to make out the quarry on the peak of a nearby hill (topped by a rather incongruous school) from where the stone used to construct the dolmens was hewn before being hauled across the intervening valley.

El Romeral

The third dolmen, **El Romeral**, is a further 2km down the road on the left behind an old sugar factory (easily identified by its chimney), reached by following signs from a roundabout (direction Córdoba). Built more than half a millennium later than Cueva de Menga and Cueva de Viera and containing dual chambers roofed with splendid corbel vaulting, El Romeral has something of an eastern Mediterranean feel, and bears an uncanny resemblance to the *tholos* tombs constructed in Crete at around the same time.

ARRIVAL AND INFORMATION   ANTEQUERA

By train Regular trains run from Málaga run throughout the day (30min), and there are onward routes to Madrid (2hr 30min) and Córdoba (40min).

By bus Málaga buses (14 daily; 1hr) terminate at the station near the bullring. From here the Alameda de Andalucía and its continuation C/Infante Don Fernando, the effective centre of town, are in easy walking distance.

Turismo Municipal Pza San Sebastián, alongside the church of the same name (June–Sept Mon–Sat 9.30am–7pm, Sun 10am–2pm; ☎ 952 702 505; ⓦ turismo. antequera.es). Very helpful office with info about the town tapas tour in February plus details of magical night-time "Luz de Luna" guided visits (summer) to the Alcazaba, dolmen caves and El Torcal.

Sendero Sur C/Cuesta Zapateros 4, 70m from the tourist office (Mon–Fri 10am–2pm & 5–8.30pm, Sat 10am–2pm; Aug mornings only; ☎ 635 378 824; ⓦ senderosur.es). This centre for "turismo activo" offers guided tours of Antequera

(Tues–Sun, charge) and to El Torcal (charge) as well as caving, hang gliding, rock climbing and more. Their shop stocks a range of outdoor gear.

ACCOMMODATION
SEE MAP PAGE 84

★ **Hospedería Arte de Cozina** C/Calzada 25; ⓦ artedecozina.com. Comfortable and good-value en-suite rooms with a/c, TV, plus a friendly welcome, make this a winner. Free breakfast for stays of two nights plus. €-€€

Hostal Colón C/Infante Don Fernando 29; ⓦ hostal-colonantequera.com. This pleasant central *hostal* is another reliable choice for competitively priced rooms with balcony and fridge (some), a/c and satellite TV. €

Hotel Coso Viejo C/Encarnación 9; ☎ 952 705 045. Three-star hotel housed in a striking eighteenth-century *casa palacio* with a beautiful patio. Rooms are elegantly furnished and some have views towards the Alcazaba. €€

Hotel Los Dólmenes Cruce del Romeral; ⓦ hotellosdolmenes.com. Pleasant three-star hotel close to the dolmen caves offering spacious, comfortable rooms with terrace balcony and views. Ideal if you have a vehicle, as their ample car park is free. €€

Número Uno C/Lucena 40; ⓦ hotelnumerouno.com. Small hotel with welcoming proprietors and pleasant if sparsely furnished a/c en-suite rooms. There's a roof terrace solarium above and a very good bar-restaurant below; parking can be arranged. €

Parador de Antequera Paseo García del Olmo s/n; ⓦ parador.es. A strikingly modern *parador*, to the north of the Plaza de Toros, with well-appointed and equipped rooms, plus pleasant gardens and pool. €€€€

EATING
SEE MAP PAGE 84

RESTAURANTS

Abrasador Bodegas Triana C/Infante Don Fernando 20; ⓦ abrasador.com. Just off the Plaza San Sebastián, this sleek, modern grill restaurant specializes in meat dishes, with steaks, gourmet burgers and more. €€€

El Hacebuche Pza Coso Viejo s/n; ☎ 952 846 574. Sited on the elegant square fronting the museum, this is a decent restaurant with an attractive terrace. Specials include *flamenquín de ibérico* (pork roll) and *boquerones rellenados* (stuffed anchovies). €€

Mesón Adarve C/Merecillas 10; ☎ 661 563 658. Little restaurant preparing home-made *antequerana* specialities including *croquetas de rabo* de *toro* (oxtail croquettes) and *timbal de alcachofas y jamón ibérico* (artichoke timbal with ham). €€

Restaurante Arte de Cozina C/Calzada 25; ⓦ artedecozina.com. Located inside the hotel of the same name, this is a very good restaurant offering typical dishes of the region in a seasonal menu – try the *porrilla de espinacas con huevo* (spinach stew with egg), the *choto malagueño* (goat in a spicy sauce) or any of the mouthwatering desserts. Their *Arte de Tapas* tapas bar next door is also excellent and has a range of tasty tapas including *torilla rellena* (omelette stuffed with tomato, lettuce and tuna) and *lomo con ajo frito* (pork with garlic). €€-€€€

Restaurante Mar De Gloria C/ Infante Don Fernando 68; ⓦ mardegloria.es. A stylish but informal restaurant, serving an impressive range of meat and fish dishes, plus pasta and lighter lunch dishes. It's also a good spot for coffee and desert during the day. €€€

CAFÉS AND TAPAS BARS

★ **La Antequerana** C/Merecillas 16; ⓦ laantequerana.com. Wonderful bar-café in a refurbished *fabrica de manticados* (cake factory), founded in 1888 with much of the original machinery still in place and functioning (their confectionery is now made elsewhere). Does breakfasts and pizzas as well as teas and their celebrated pastries, cocktails and liqueurs are on offer in the early evening. €€

Bar-Cafetería A La Fuerza C/Alameda de Andalucía 32; ⓦ restaurantealafuerza.com. This excellent bar near the bullring makes a good breakfast stop and is noted for its *churros*. There are tapas and the main menu includes *paté de perdiz* (partridge paté) and *cochinillo segoviano* (Segovian-style suckling pig). €€€

★ **Café del Centro** C/Cantareros 3, slightly north of the main street; ☎ 952 845 919. A good and atmospheric breakfast bar, where the walls are decorated with photos from Antequera's past and all the daily press is stocked. Later in the day it gets into its stride with a good tapas and *raciones* selection – try the paella. €€

El Rincon de Lola C/Encarnación 8; ☎ 625 040 997. Great tapas and *raciones* bar with a creative slant. Specialities include *pastel de conejo* (rabbit terrine), *chivo lechal* (kid goat) and *tomato relleño* (stuffed toms). See the *pizzara* (blackboard) for daily specials. There's also a pleasant terrace on the nearby Plaza del Coso Viejo. €€

Parque Natural El Torcal

Parque Natural El Torcal, 13km south of Antequera and 32km north of Málaga, is the most geologically arresting of Andalucía's natural parks. A massive high plateau

1

of eroded grey limestone dating from the Jurassic period, tempered by a lush growth of hawthorn, ivy, wild rose and thirty species of orchid, it's quite easily explored using the **walking routes** that radiate from the centre of the park where the road ends. Try to leave your explorations until the more peaceful late afternoon, when the setting sun throws the natural rock sculptures into sharp relief.

Trails

The best-designed and most exciting **trails** are the yellow and red routes, the former climaxing with suitable drama on a cliff edge with magnificent views over a valley. The latter gives fantastic vantage points of the looming limestone outcrops, eroded into vast, surreal sculptures. Because of the need to protect flora and fauna, the red route is in a restricted zone and can only be visited with a **guide** – information on this is available from the Centro de Recepción (see page 88). The **green** and **yellow routes** (waymarked) can be walked without a guide. The green route is the shortest at 1.5km (about 40min if you don't dawdle) while the yellow route takes about two hours. In late spring on the popular green route you may find yourself competing with gangs of schoolkids, who arrive en masse on vaguely educational trips, excitedly trying to spot La Copa (the wineglass), El Lagarto (the lizard) and La Loba (the she-wolf) as well as other celebrated rock sculptures. Keep an eye on the skies while you're here for Griffon vultures, frequent visitors whose huge wingspans make a spectacular sight as they glide overhead.

ARRIVAL AND INFORMATION

PARQUE NATURAL EL TORCAL

By car There's no public transport to El Torcal. From Antequera it's a 13km hike or drive; the park is reached by following the A7075 towards Villanueva de la Concepción and heading down the second signed turning on the right to El Torcal.

By taxi You can arrange a taxi through the Turismo or by ringing ☎952 845 530 (Spanish only). If you decide to take the taxi one way, you can also use this number for your return journey. Make sure to agree a price with the *taxista* before starting out.

Group visits Sendero Sur (see page 86) offers guided group visits to the park.

Centro de Recepción The centre (daily: April–Oct 10am–7pm; Nov–March 10am–5pm; ☎952 243 324; ⓦtorcaldeantequera.com) gives out maps and general information on the park and its walks, has audiovisual presentations covering geology, flora and fauna and operates a restaurante/cafetería with a terrace overlooking the park.

ACCOMMODATION

Camping rough is not allowed inside the park. The Turismo at Antequera can provide information regarding some attractive *casas rurales* to rent in the area.

Camping Torcal Just off the A7075, 6km south of

Antequera, ⓦcampingeltorcal.com. Rural campsite with plenty of shade, plus a restaurant, supermarket and pool. Also has en-suite *cabañas*. April–Sept. €

Laguna de Fuente de Piedra

About 20km northwest of Antequera lies **Laguna de Fuente de Piedra**, the largest natural lake in Andalucía and a celebrated site for observing birdlife. The shallow water level and high saline content of the lake, and the crustaceans that these conditions encourage, attract a glorious flock of **greater flamingo** each spring, making this Europe's only inland breeding ground for the species. The number of birds each year fluctuates depending on water levels in the lake, but at least 11,000 populate the area during breeding season.

Besides supporting a variety of waders at all times of the year, in winter the lake is often a haven for **cranes**, and the surrounding marshes provide a habitat for numerous amphibians and reptiles. Remember that because this is a sanctuary, the beaches are strictly out of bounds (ruling out swimming) and because many sections are privately owned, limiting access, it's not possible to make a complete circuit of the lake. You're also at a distinct advantage if you come here with your own transport, as species such as flamingo often gather at the far end of the lake, up to 7km away, although **mountain bikes** can be rented from the visitor centre (see page 89).

ARRIVAL AND INFORMATION

LAGUNA DE FUENTE DE PIEDRA

By bus Three buses on weekdays, two on Sat, one on Sun from Antequera (30min) or Málaga (changing at Antequera; 1hr 30min).

By train The nearest station to the lagoon is Antequera Santa Ana, 11km south of the village on the AVE high-speed line between Málaga and Córdoba. There are no buses linking the station with the village, although a taxi is a possibility. You'll need to ring one of two companies: Santa Ana–Fuente de Piedra: Taxista Cebrian (☎659 000 242); Fuente de Piedra–Santa Ana: Taxista Roman (☎687 366 334).

By car Take the A45 north from Antequera/Málaga to join the A92 *autovía* (direction Sevilla), and continue along this for 14km until the signed turn-off.

Centro de Visitantes Over the bridge beyond the train station (April–June Mon–Fri 10am–2pm & 5–7pm, Sat & Sun 10am–7pm; July–Sept daily 10am–2pm & 5–7pm; Oct–March daily 10am–2pm & 4–6pm; ☎952 712 554; ⓦvisitasfuentepiedra.es). Has displays on the flora and fauna of the lake, and rents out binoculars and multilanguage audio guides which cover both the centre's displays and observation points around the lake.

ACCOMMODATION

Camping Fuente Piedra C/Campillos 88 ⓦcamping-rural.com. The most attractive place to stay is the campsite, close to the village and overlooking the lake. Accommodation is in a/c double rooms or fully equipped wood cabins, sleeping up to four people. There's also a swimming pool and a decent restaurant (€) with an economical *menu*. Camping €, doubles €, cabins €€

Málaga to Torre del Mar

The dreary eastern stretch of the **Costa del Sol** – the beaches within easy distance of Málaga – is a largely unbroken landscape of urbanization and unlovely holiday towns, packed to the gunwales in summer with day-tripping *malagueños*. There are enough places of interest, however, to warrant stopping off en route, before arriving at the unremarkable resort of **Torre del Mar**. With your own transport it's possible to avoid the Málaga suburbs by using the M20 *circunvalación* (ring road) – picked up on the northern edge of town – which becomes the A7 *autovía* linking Málaga with Nerja. To follow the coastal route described below, leave the *autovía* at the Rincón de la Victoria exit (see page 90). Otherwise, the road heading out of Málaga along the Paseo de Reding (passing the north side of the bullring) traverses the suburbs of Pedragalejo and El Palo, where for most of the summer the beaches are covered with a forest of parasols, before arriving at the small resort of La Cala de Moral.

Cueva del Tesoro

Guided visits daily: mid-June to mid-Sept 10.30am–1pm & 4.30–7pm; mid-Sept to mid-June 10am–1pm & 3–5pm • Charge • ⓦ cuevasturisticas.es

Just beyond Cala del Moral, a signed road on the left indicates the **CUEVA DEL TESORO**, a spectacular network of underground marine caves less commercialized than those at Nerja (see page 98). A series of seven chambers leads to the eighth, the **Sala de los Lagos**, a Gaudí-esque rock cathedral with natural underground pools. Paleolithic cave paintings were discovered here in 1918 (presently not on view) as well as other prehistoric remains indicating almost continual human habitation. The cave's name (*tesoro* means treasure) derives from the legend that five fleeing Moorish kings took refuge in its depths and stashed a large quantity of gold here (now long gone).

1

Macharaviaya

Beyond the Cueva del Tesoro, **Rincón de la Victoria** is a no-nonsense, untidy sort of place, and a popular resort for *malagueño* families. A seafood speciality here is *coquinas*, tasty small clams. To break the monotony along this strip of coast you could follow a small road heading inland at the featureless suburb of Torre de Benagalbón that winds up into the hills and approaches the attractive hamlet of **MACHARAVIAYA** (from the Moorish Arabic Machar Ibn Yahya, or "lands of the son of Yahya"). Surrounded by slopes covered with olive and almond trees, the village was expanded in the eighteenth century by the Gálvez family, one of Andalucía's great imperial dynasties. Count Bernardo de Gálvez – a statue of whom stands before the Ayuntamiento – became governor general of Spanish North America and gave his name to Galveston in Texas after laying siege to the town in 1777. Today, even taking into account its impressive Baroque church (a Gálvez construction), it's hard to believe that this tiny, cobble-paved village was once known as "little Madrid". It was a wealthy place, benefiting from the extensive Gálvez family vineyards as well as a playing-card factory that had a monopoly on supplying cards to the Americas. This was all to end, however, when the phylloxera plague of the 1870s wiped out the vines, the card monopoly lapsed and the Gálvez line died out. The family title died with them, and the last Vizconde de Galveston is buried in the church crypt among the tombs and alabaster statues of his ancestors.

San Jacinto

Guided visits, which include the museum, church and house of Salvador Rueda in Benaque (see page 90) Tues–Thurs 11am–2pm, Sat & Sun 11am–3pm) • Free

At the entrance to the village is a rather proprietorial whitewashed brick temple erected by the Gálvez family in 1786 and, at its centre, the once crumbling exterior of the outsized church of **San Jacinto**, somewhat over-restored as part of the Expo '92 celebrations. Inside the single-nave church, altars dedicated to various Gálvez family members are decorated with fine marble, and inscriptions express the ultimately vain hope that Mass would be said on certain days for their souls *in perpetuum*. Don't miss the eerie crypt (open 24hr) behind the church, where a remarkable collection of sombre **alabaster family busts** face each other around an alcove and seem about to start up a gloomy conversation. The great marble tomb of Don José Gálvez, Marquis of Sonora and Minister for the Indias during the eighteenth-century reign of Carlos III, stands nearby.

Museo de los Gálvez

Avda de los Gálvez 13, 200m east of the Ayuntamiento • Tues–Thurs 11am–2pm, Sat & Sun 11am–3pm • Free

The small **Museo de los Gálvez** is dedicated to explaining the history of Macharaviaya and its connection with the Gálvez family. There are many documents, weapons and artefacts to peruse as well as three entertaining audiovisual displays which tell the story through the mouths of historical characters. Connections between the village and the southern Florida colonies remain strong and delegations from the village and the US travel frequently in both directions.

Benaque

Two kilometres north of Macharaviaya – and approached via a side road to the left at the entrance to the village – the village of **BENAQUE** has a Mudéjar church, **Nuestra Señora del Rosario**, its tower formed out of the minaret of the mosque it replaced. The building has recently been sensitively restored.

House of Salvador Rueda

Key available from Señor José (Pepe) Cabrera, C/Salvador Rueda 19, just before the bus shelter to the left as you arrive; the museum can also be seen on guided visits from Macharaviaya (see page 90) • Free, but donations welcome

Just before the church, a house on the right was the birthplace of Benaque's most famous son, the modernist poet **Salvador Rueda** (1857–1933). Now converted into a **museum**, the disarmingly simple interior has been sensitively preserved more or less as it was when the poet lived here, offering a glimpse into life in bygone times.

Torre del Mar

On the main coast road, the chain of localities with "torre" in their names refers to the numerous *atalayas*, or watchtowers, which have been used to guard this coast since Roman and Moorish times, many strikingly visible on the headlands. There's little to detain you between Torre de Benagalbón and Almayate, from where it's only a couple of kilometres to **TORRE DEL MAR**. A line of concrete tower blocks on a grey, pebble beach, this is Torremolinos without the money or bluster. It's a fairly easy-going place with a good beach, although you'll find much more to detain you in nearby Vélez-Málaga (see page 91).

ACCOMMODATION AND EATING · TORRE DEL MAR

La Bella Julieta Avda de Andalucía s/n, at the north end of Paseo de Larios; ⓦ labellajulieta.com. Excellent spot for breakfast, morning coffee, afternoon tea or a quick bite. The home-made bread and cakes are the best in town and the filled bagels and fresh juices delicious. Pleasant outside terrace. €€

Camping Laguna Playa Paseo Maritimo s/n; ⓦ lagunaplaya.com. West of the centre of Torre del Mar and close to the sea, this is a reasonable site with shade; although it fills to the gunwales in high season. €

★ **Chinchin Puerto** Puerto de Caleta de Vélez, 2-5km east of Torre del Mar and a pleasant stroll along the beach; ☎ 952 030 443. On the marina and one of the best places to eat fresh fish and seafood in the province. Chef Lourdes Villalobos creates dishes based on the catch of the day in the Caleta de Vélez fish market, just a few metres away. Staples on the menu include *delicia de raya* (spring rolls with skate) and *pastel de salmonete con ensalada de col* (red mullet terrine with white cabbage salad), but your best bet are the daily specials. €€

Hotel Miraya C/Patrón Veneno 6; ⓦ hotelmiraya.com. This pleasant seafront hotel offers en-suite rooms with a/c, small fridge and room safe. €

SHOPPING

Pasa Tiempo C/Infantes 30; ☎ 952 543 703. Bookshop facing Plaza de la Paz selling new and used books in English, as well as the British press and hiking maps.

The Central Axarquía

The **Axarquía** makes a refreshing change from the sun-bed culture of the Costa del Sol. Bounded by the coast, the Sierra de Alhama to the north and, on its eastern flank, the mountainous edge of the province of Granada, this rugged territory offers excellent walking country with an abundance of wildlife and a host of attractive mountain villages, not to mention the interesting market town of Vélez-Málaga which is worth a visit. Long a breeding ground for *bandoleros* who preyed on traders carrying produce from the coast to Granada, during the Civil War the Axarquía was also a notorious guerrilla encampment whose members fought on against Franco's Guardia Civil until the early 1950s.

The main villages of the **Eastern Axarquía** – Cómpeta, Archez and Salares – are covered in the "Torre del Mar to Nerja" section (see page 96).

Vélez-Málaga

In the fertile valley of the Río Vélez and 4km inland from Torre del Mar lies **VÉLEZ-MÁLAGA** (often simply referred to as Vélez), the capital of the Axarquía and a bustling market town and supply centre for the region's farmers. It was important in both

1

Roman times – under the name of Menoba – and Moorish, when as Ballix-Malaca ("Fortress of Málaga") it had an important role in subduing what has always been a turbulent zone. A number of Phoenician cemeteries and tombs discovered nearby testify to an older pedigree still. Fernando's conquest of the town in 1487 drove a wedge through the kingdom of Granada, dividing it in two and paving the way for the fall of the Nasrid city five years later.

Castillo

C/de la Fortaleza • Daily during daylight hours • Free

The town climbs up a slope from the main streets, Calle Canalejas and its continuation Calle Cristo, towards the **castillo**, as good a place as any to start a tour of the sights. What's left of the settlement founded by the Moors and successively rebuilt and restored after the *Reconquista* clings to a rocky outcrop, which from its dominant position above the white-walled *barrio* of San Sebastián gives some nice views out over

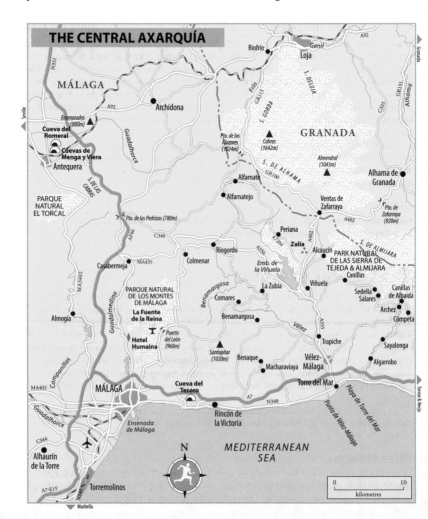

the coast. There isn't a huge amount to see here otherwise as the castle suffered badly during the War of the Spanish Succession, when the English lost to the French here after a bitter struggle in 1704.

Santa María de la Encarnación and San Juan Bautista

Both churches Tues–Sat 10am–1pm & 6–8pm; Santa María also Sun 10am–2pm • Free

Visible from the castle is the sixteenth-century Mudéjar church of **Santa María de la Encarnación**, whose beautiful tower incorporates the minaret of the mosque that preceded it. Inside, Moorish arches separate a triple nave, and there's a fine Mudéjar ceiling. East of Santa María de la Encarnación, the late Gothic **San Juan Bautista**, on Plaza Constitución, is also worth a look, featuring an elegant tower and, inside, a superbly naturalistic sculpture, *Cristo Crucificado*, by Pedro de Mena.

Palacio del Marqués de Beniel

Pza del Palacio 1 • Mon–Fri 9am–3pm • Free

The restored **Palacio del Marqués de Beniel** is an elegant sixteenth-century mansion – formerly the town hall – with a delightful patio. The building now houses an exhibition on the life and work of local philosopher María Zambrano, plus a selection of art including works by Miró.

Centro de Arte Contemporáneo (CAC Vélez-Málaga)

C/Féliz Lomas 26 • Tues–Sat 10am–2pm & 6–9pm, Sun 10am–2pm • Free • ☎ 952 504 349

The town's newest museum plays host to regular exhibitions by local (Spanish and international) artists in light and airy rooms as well as cultural events that take place in the central patio. Live jazz concerts on Wednesdays in July and August.

Ermita de la Virgen de los Remedios

Cerro de San Cristóbal, to the east of the centre • Tues–Sun 9.30am–1.30pm & 3.30–6pm • Free

Perched atop a landscaped hill with plenty of *miradores* from where you can admire the stunning views down to the sea, the whitewashed chapel, home to the town's miracle-working Virgin, dates from the seventeenth century. The fifteenth-century image of the virgin and surrounding retablo are richly decorated and the rest of the church walls are entirely covered in frescoes depicting local scenes and countryside, painted by local artist Evaristo Guerra at the end of the last century.

ARRIVAL AND INFORMATION   **VÉLEZ-MÁLAGA**

By bus Vélez-Málaga's bus station is next to the Parque de Andalucía, south of the centre. Frequent buses from Málaga (every 30-50 minutes; 1hr 15min) and Torre del Mar (every 40 minutes; 10min).

Turismo Housed in the Ayuntamiento on C/Romero Pozo (April–June, Sept & Oct Mon–Sat 10am–2pm & 5–8pm; July & Aug Mon–Sat 10am–2pm; Nov–March Mon–Sat 10am–2pm & 5–8pm, Sun 10am–2pm; ☎ 952 541 104, Ⓦ turismo.velezmalaga.es); the helpful staff can supply

a town map plus details of local events.

Website Ⓦ mivelezmalaga.com, a locally run portal with information in English.

Walking The Axarquía is a great place to do some hiking: *Walk! the Axarquía* by Charles Davis is devoted to hikes in the region; alternatively, *Walking in Andalucía* by Guy Hunter-Watts (see page 556) has half a dozen routes to follow in the western Axarquía.

ACCOMMODATION

Cortijo Bravo Ctra Vélez-Benamocarra km 1.5, a 15min drive west of the town; Ⓦ hotelcortijobravo. com. Delightful hotel set in olive groves with views to the mountains and sea, gardens and large pool. Spacious en-suite rooms with a/c, satellite TV and terrace or balcony. €€€

Dila Hotel Avda Vivar Téllez 3, 200m east of the centre; Ⓦ hoteldila.com. Decent small hotel where a/c rooms

come with satellite TV, safe and minibar. Public areas include sauna and breakfast bar. €

Palacio Blanco C/Feliz Lomas 4, below the Castillo; Ⓦ palacioblanco.com. Stunningly attractive boutique hotel in a restored *casa palacio* with a delightful patio. The beautifully furnished rooms are equipped with shower wet-rooms, plus there's a rooftop pool and bar. €€€

1

FLAMENCO AND EVENTS IN VÉLEZ-MÁLAGA

Vélez-Málaga has a rich **flamenco** history – some of the province's most famous singers such as Juan Breva and José Beltrán Ortega (El Niño de Vélez) hail from the town – and local artists have recently re-established the flamenco scene. The main focus centres around the **Peña Flamenca Niño de Vélez** (C/Tejeda 3, 400m west of CAC Vélez-Málaga, Thurs–Sat 10pm–late) where spontaneous performances often take place. **Flamenco Abierto Axarquía** runs from February to May with weekly performances on Fridays at the Peña. With room for just seventy and no sound systems, the concerts showcase local artists and provide some of the most intimate flamenco experiences in the province. The season continues into the summer with free concerts at venues in both Vélez-Málaga and Torre del Mar. See the Facebook page for details (🅦 bit.ly/AbiertoAxarquia).

A prestigious **annual guitar competition** is held in Veléz-Malaga every July, with free concerts held in the patio of the Palacio del Marqués de Beniel. The Ayuntamiento has details of these and other cultural activities taking place throughout the summer.

EATING AND DRINKING

El Caserío de las Monjas C/Félix Lomas 31; ☎ 952 557 363. On the same street as the Palacio Blanco hotel (see page 93) this is an excellent small tapas and *raciones* bar plus formal dining room and pleasant outdoor terrace. Grilled meats are a speciality plus the weekly gourmet mini-burger. €€

La Gamba Dorada C/Pintor Antonio de Vélez, two blocks west of CAC Vélez-Málaga; 🅦 lagambadorada.com. One of the best places in town for fresh fish and seafood. The decor is stark and neon-lit – sit outside if there's room – and the

restaurant usually packed to capacity, but you're here for the *mejillones* (mussels), *pulpo a la Gallega* (Galician-style octopus) and, of course, the *gambas* (prawns). €€

La Sastrería Pza de la Constitución; 🅦 lasastreriaasador.es. The place to eat if you want views of the historic centre at sunset, this restaurant serves tapas at the bar, mains in the dining room and on the terrace. The menu runs to a good list of salads, cold cuts and stir-fry dishes, but grilled meats are the house specials, along with the home-made ice cream. €€

Comares

A number of good driving **routes** around the Axarquía begin at **Trapiche**, about 3km north of Vélez. One heads northwest from Trapiche along the MA3113 towards Benmargosa and, after taking in a detour to Comares, climbs eventually to Colmenar. Another (the A356) takes the other fork at Trapiche to end up, by way of Periana, at the twin northernmost outposts of the Axarquía – Alfarnate and Alfarnatejo.

Taking the northwesterly route from Trapiche you soon arrive at **Benamargosa**, a village surrounded by citrus orchards and avocado plantations. You could take a look at its sixteenth-century Gothic-style church of La Encarnación before moving on to La Zubía, where a winding road signed on the left climbs dizzily to **COMARES**, an impeccably tidy White Town (or village in this case), spectacularly clinging to the peak of its conical hill. At the highest point of all, beside an attractive cemetery, the ruined Moorish fort – built on Roman foundations – was one of the strongholds of rebel leader Ibn Hafsun (see box, page 81).

In the village is yet another church of **Nuestra Señora de la Encarnación**, this time a sixteenth-century Mudéjar building with a picturesque hexagonal tower, the minaret of the mosque that preceded it. A **mirador** in the focal Plaza del Ayuntamiento gives fine views over the Axarquía. There's a **walking route** around the village's major sights, taking in all the above, plus an ancient Roman path down the mountain and various Moorish architectural remains; it's waymarked by ceramic footprints embedded in the pavement.

A welcome municipal **swimming pool** is sited close to the *Mirador de la Axarquía*.

ACCOMMODATION AND EATING   COMARES

Hotel Restaurante Atalaya ☎ 952 509 208. South of   the main village, this simple, rustic hotel has good value

rooms, some with spectacular views across the rugged hills. The attached restaurant serves hearty meals. €
Mirador de la Axarquía C/Encinilla 4, slightly before the entrance to the village; ☎952 509 209. This

welcoming restaurant has a pleasant terrace with stunning views, serves up regional dishes and specializes in *carnes a la braza* (charcoal-grilled meat') and paella. €€€

Riogordo

Continuing north along the MA3107, beyond La Zubía the road follows the course of the Río Cueva, finally ascending to **RIOGORDO**, a village with Phoenician and Roman origins that was a fortified stronghold during the Moorish period. After the *Reconquista* the Moors were replaced by settlers from Castile. The Semana Santa celebrated here is a particularly vivid affair, when local people – dressed for the part – act out the scenes from the Passion, often with bloodcurdling gusto. The village also boasts an attractive municipal swimming pool.

Colmenar and around

From Riogordo, you have a choice of routes: east to Alfarnate (see page 96) or west, following a stiff climb, to **COLMENAR**, another brilliant-white hill town and the Axarquía's most westerly outpost. A centre of honey production thanks to the rich variety of flowering plants and shrubs growing in the surrounding hills, the village takes its name from *colmena*, Spanish for "beehive".

A wonderful route twists down from here via the Puerto del Léon down to Málaga, through the forests of cork oaks and pines forming the **Parque Natural de los Montes de Málaga**, and offering stunning views over Málaga and the Costa del Sol during its latter stages.

ACCOMMODATION   **COLMENAR AND AROUND**

Hotel Balcón De Los Montés C/Serrania de Ronda; ☎952 730 530. A simple, slightly old-fashioned guesthouse in the village, with simple but well-kept rooms that have attached, modern bathrooms. The restaurant downstairs is also good value. €
Taberna Flores C/Iglesia 11; ☎651 843 062. One of

the best places to eat in the village and its oldest bar, this historic tavern has been restored and now serves modern dishes based on traditional recipes. Try the *chistorra al vino de nuestro bodega* (spicy sausages in the house wine) or the *paletilla de cordero lechal* (roast leg of suckling lamb). €€

Alcaucín

Still following the old road, at the Puente de Don Manuel, a bridge 3km beyond Viñuela, a road cuts off on the right and ascends to the village of **ALCAUCÍN**. On the way up keep an eye to your left where, across a valley, you will be able to make out the ruins of the deserted medieval village of Zalía (see page 95) and, beyond, the Puerto de Zafarraya, a great U-shaped cleavage in the Sierra de Alhama through which the ancient route to Granada passes.

Alcaucín itself, perched on the slopes of the Sierra de Tejeda, is a beautiful little village with wrought-iron balconies ablaze with flowering geraniums and a web of narrow white-walled streets reflecting its Moorish origins. As befits a mountain village, there are numerous spring-fed fountains, among which the five-spouted Fuente San Sebastián has been restored very much in the Moorish style, complete with *azulejos*.

Zalía

Continuing north from the Puente de Don Manuel, the A402 heads on towards Granada, passing en route the dauntingly impressive **Zafarraya Pass**, where 30,000-year-old remains found in a nearby cave in 1983 have now been confirmed as

1

the last-known site in Europe inhabited by Neanderthal man. On the way, the road passes the ruins of the fort and the deserted medieval village of **ZALÍA**. Local legend has it that the Moorish village was attacked by a plague of vipers after Patricio, a *malagueño* church minister, arrived in an attempt to convert the inhabitants to Christianity and they spurned him. The more likely explanation is that the population was put to the sword during the uprisings that followed the *Reconquista*. Throughout most of the Moorish period Zalía's fortress, together with those at Comares and Bentomiz (near Arenas to the south), formed a defensive triangle to control this central sector of the Axarquía region.

Taking a left fork along the A7204 heading northwest from the junction just beyond Viñuela leads to **Periana**, a noted centre of peach-growing and *anís* production. Some 3km beyond here, heading into the Axarquía's more remote extremities, you'll reach a fork; if you don't want to face a tortuous switchback secondary road, ignore the sign labelled "Alfarnate 15km" and continue along the road signed to Riogordo and Colmenar. A further 4km will bring you to a right turn and an easier route to the village of Alfarnatejo and its neighbour Alfarnate.

Alfarnatejo and Alfarnate

The Axarquía's most northerly settlements, **ALFARNATEJO** and **ALFARNATE** lie a mere couple of kilometres apart, but it would be difficult to find two places in Andalucía with less in common. Alfarnatejo, the smaller of the two, is staunchly right-wing, while Alfarnate has always been on the left, and, unable to agree or cooperate on anything, they have built up a strong mutual animosity, which even discourages marriages between the two communities. In truth, neither village would win any beauty prizes, though Alfarnate, set on a plain covered with wheatfields, is worth a visit for its attractive church of **Santa Ana**, a sixteenth-century edifice with a graceful Mudéjar tower.

Alfarnate's real claim to fame is the thirteenth-century **Venta de Alfarnate** on the village's western edge, which maintains – with some justification – that it is the oldest **inn** in Andalucía. Situated in an isolated spot in the midst of brooding hills, it's not hard to see what attracted the various brigands and highwaymen to the place. Indeed, the interior, as well as being a bar-restaurant, is also a **museum** dedicated to keeping alive the memory of such outlaws as Luís Candelas, who spent a night in the *venta's* well-preserved prison cell en route to justice in Málaga. By far the most terrifying *bandolero* of all, however, was El Tempranillo, who arrived unannounced one hot day in the 1820s, and, when there were no spoons for him to eat with, ordered the dining clients to eat their wooden ones at gunpoint, cracking their teeth in the process. The place is more civilized these days and its mid-priced restaurant (see page 96) serves hearty mountain specialities.

Keep your eyes peeled in this area for the amazingly agile *cabra hispánica*, the rare Spanish goat; the long-horned male is a spectacular sight as he effortlessly scales almost vertical cliff faces.

EATING   **ALFARNATE**

Venta de Alfarnate Antigua Ctra Málaga–Granada s/n; ☏ 952 759 388. Wonderfully atmospheric restaurant inside this historic *venta*. House specialities include *huevos a la bestia* (fried eggs with local sausage, ham and black pudding), *cochinillo* (suckling pig) and *cordero asado* (spit-roasted lamb). You can even eat at a table placed in the cell once occupied by Luís Candelas. **€€€**

Torre del Mar to Nerja

The coast east from Torre del Mar is a nondescript stretch of faceless towns and the occasional concrete resort, dotted with more ancient *atalayas* (watchtowers). Inland lie

more tempting villages in the **eastern Axarquía** but along the coast the first town of any
real interest is **Nerja**, with some fine beaches and a relatively slow pace.

Algarrobo and the Phoenician tombs

East of Torre del Mar the coast road climbs slightly to **Algarrobo-Costa**, an
unappealing high-rise beach resort. With your own transport it's worth ignoring this
– and the bleak stretch of coast that follows – to head inland for some delightful
villages in the **eastern Axarquía**, finally rejoining the coastal road 10km east at
Torrox Costa.

From Algarrobo-Costa the A7206 climbs inland towards the village of Algarrobo
proper. Look out for some well-conserved **Phoenician tombs** (signposted on the right)
dating from the eighth century BC. Originally these tombs formed part of an extensive
cemetery, built of stone blocks and roofed in wood.

The older village of **Algarrobo**, 3km inland, which lent its name to the coastal
settlement, is a pleasant enough place, though rapidly being enveloped by urban sprawl
as the developers move inland from the coast.

Cómpeta and around

Beyond Algarrobo, the road toils on upwards as the fruit orchards of the coastal
strip give way to the olive groves and vineyards of the higher slopes. The road then
passes **Sayalonga** 5km further on, a pretty village nestling in the valley of the Río
Algarrobo, and then ascends again, twisting and turning for a further 8km until it
reaches **CÓMPETA**, a huddle of brilliant-white cubes tumbling down a hillside and
surrounded by vineyards. A Moorish settlement in origin, and now discovered by
expats from northern Europe, Cómpeta retains a relaxed atmosphere, and the easy-
going villagers don't seem too worried about being swamped by foreigners. The sweet
– and potent – **wine** made from the area's muscatel grapes is renowned as the best in
the whole province. You can try it for yourself at the **Museo del Vino** on Avenida de la
Constitución close to the charming main square, Plaza de la Almijara (the Jarel brand is
recommended).

Each August 15 beneath the lofty bell tower (a later addition) of the sixteenth-
century church of La Asunción, Cómpeta rolls out the barrels – scores of them –
during its annual **fiesta**, the Noche del Vino. This is when the square fills with revellers
determined to sink as much of the free *vino* as they can hold. Above the plaza to the
left, Calle San Antonio leads to a shrine with a superb **view** over the valley to the west
and the sea beyond.

The road continues for a further 4km north of Cómpeta where it comes to a dead
end at the village of **CANILLAS DE ALBAIDA**, something of a mini-Cómpeta, with a
place to stay and a couple of decent restaurants.

INFORMATION CÓMPETA

Turismo Avda de la Constitución, close to where buses
terminate (Mon–Sat 10am–3pm, Sun 10am–2pm; ☏ 952
553 685).

ACCOMMODATION

Finca El Cerrillo Canillas de Albaida; ⓦ hotelfinca.
com. To the west of neighbouring Canillas de Albaida, this
friendly British-run restored olive mill offers Moorish-style
en-suite rooms (Garden 4 has a private roof terrace) with
views, a pool, several patios and library with an open fire.
Evening meals are available four nights a week (pre-book)
and the owners can advise on walking and birdwatching in

the area. Breakfast is included. €€€
Hotel Balcón de Cómpeta C/San Antonio s/n; ⓦ hotel-
competa.com. Central and comfortable hotel with balcony
rooms overlooking a pool with mountain views beyond;
facilities include a tennis court. They also rent fully equipped
wooden bungalows sleeping two to four people. Breakfast
is included. €€–€€€

EATING AND DRINKING

Bar-Restaurante Perico Pza Almijara s/n; ☎ 952 553 739. This economical bar-restaurant on Cómpeta's main square has a pleasant terrace and makes a good place to eat after the sun has set. Their *pollo al vino de Cómpeta* (chicken cooked in the local wine) is recommended, as are the tapas and paella. €€

El Pilón C/Laberinto s/n, down steps slightly southwest of the main square; ⊕ restaurantelpilon.com. A pleasant small restaurant with eclectic international cuisine, including numerous vegetarian options and salads. €€

Restaurante María C/San Antonio 75; ⊕ hotel-competa.com. The restaurant of the *Hotel Balcón de Cómpeta* is another possibility and has a terrace. A speciality here is *pollo al Balcón* (chicken with guacamole and cheese). €€

La Taberna de Óscar Pza Pantaleón Romero 2, at the back of the church; ☎ 952 553 722. Pleasant bar serving slightly larger than tapas serving plates. Expect traditional dishes such as gazpacho and croquettes, as well as more innovative ones like *paté de moscatel con hummus* (muscatel pate). Plenty of vegetarian options and a lively outdoor terrace. €€

SHOPPING

Marco Polo C/José Antonio 3, ☎ 651 884 484. This friendly English-run bookshop, just off the main square, stocks walking books, maps and equipment.

Archez

To penetrate further into the Axarquía from Cómpeta you'll need to double back for 2km to the turning north to **ARCHEZ**. Nestling in the foothills of the Sierra Almijara, it's an attractive village with strong Moorish roots.

This influence is vividly in evidence at the church of **Nuestra Señora de la Encarnación** (open during service times), whose remarkable fourteenth-century tower is the minaret of an earlier mosque, one of the best examples from this period – the *sebka* brickwork and blind arches above are particularly fine.

Salares

From Archez, the road climbs for another 5km to the brilliant white village of **SALARES**, a centre of olive oil and wine production and one of the most picturesque villages of the Axarquía. Its charms are enhanced by the banning of traffic from its narrow streets, where colourful potted geraniums line the walls and dogs lie prostrate in the afternoon heat. There's a car park at the top of the village. From here head downhill along Calle Iglesias to reach the church of **Santa Ana**. Just as the church at Archez, this one retains a fine **minaret** from the mosque it replaced. Inside, a simple interior holds the image of Santa Ana, *patrona* of the village.

INFORMATION   SALARES

Turismo The Ayuntamiento, C/Iglesia 2, next door to the church of Santa Ana (Mon–Fri 9am–3pm), can provide a small map and information about the village.

Nerja

Although **NERJA**, 20km along the coast from Torre del Mar, cannot claim to have been bypassed by the tidal wave of post-1960s tourist development, this attractive resort has, nevertheless, held out against Torremolinos-type tower blocks, and its mainly villa and *urbanizaciones* construction has been more in keeping with its origins. Its setting, too, is spectacular, nestling among the foothills of the Almijara range and flanked by some good beaches, including the attractive **Playa Burriana**, an easily walkable kilometre east of the centre – while there's also a series of coves also within walking distance if you want to escape the crowds.

Nerja's **old town** fans out to the north of the **Balcón de Europa**, a striking, palm-lined seafront **belvedere** which offers magnificent views over the rocky coastline. The tangle of pretty, narrow streets is crowded with visitors all summer long, but the brash shops that service them have yet to suffocate the town's easy-going tranquillity. Nerja's obvious charm has attracted the inevitable colony of migrants – in this case the English – who make their presence felt in the numerous foreign-owned shops and bars. Sights, as such, are few, and once you have taken in the museum, strolled along the Balcón and taken a look at the nearby seventeenth-century whitewashed **El Salvador** church (open service times) – which has a fine *dolorosa* – you should head for the beach or make a short excursion out of town.

An entertaining **market** takes place on Tuesday (main market) and Sunday (flea market) mornings in the Urbanización Flamingo to the northeast of the centre near the Ciudad Deportivo sports stadium. The resort's major summer event is the annual **Festival Internacional de Música** (June–July), with many big names; the Turismo can provide details.

Museo de Historia de Nerja

Pza de España 4 • Tues–Sun: July & Aug 10am–6.30pm; Sept–June 10am–4pm • Charge

The Museo de Historia de Nerja has information and artefacts (some are copies) from the Cueva (see page 102) although plainly speaking, these hardly justify the entry fee. The building's other three floors are devoted to mildly interesting sections on Nerja today (including the arrival of the tourist boom) and the history of local fishing as

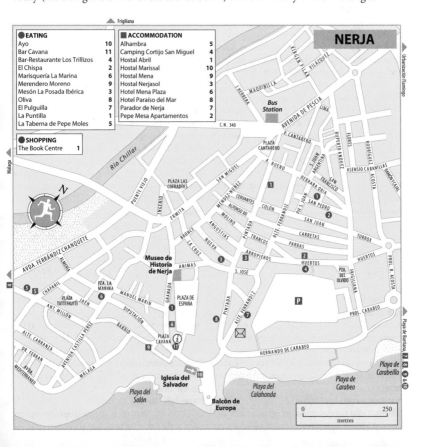

●EATING		■ACCOMMODATION	
Ayo	10	Alhambra	5
Bar Cavana	11	Camping Cortijo San Miguel	4
Bar-Restaurante Los Trillizos	4	Hostal Abril	1
El Chispa	2	Hostal Marissal	10
Marisquería La Marina	6	Hostal Mena	9
Merendero Moreno	9	Hostal Nerjasol	3
Mesón La Posada Ibérica	3	Hotel Mena Plaza	6
Oliva	8	Hotel Paraíso del Mar	8
El Pulguilla	7	Parador de Nerja	7
La Puntilla	1	Pepe Mesa Apartamentos	2
La Taberna de Pepe Moles	5		

●SHOPPING	
The Book Centre	1

NERJA

1

well as an entertaining 360° audiovisual gizmo that takes you on a quick tour of local landmarks.

ARRIVAL AND INFORMATION   NERJA

By bus The bus station is on Avda Pescia s/n, at the north end of town close to Pza Cantarero (☎ 902 422 242).

Destinations Almuñécar (12 daily; 30min); Granada (5 daily; 2hr 15min); Málaga (over 20 daily; 1hr–1hr 30min).

Turismo C/Carmen 1, 50m west of the church of El Salvador and next door to the Ayuntamiento (Mon–Fri 10am–2pm & 4.30–8.30pm, Sat & Sun 10am–1.45pm; ☎ 952 521 531; ⓦ nerja.es).

Website A good locally produced website with lots of insider info is ⓦ nerjatoday.com.

Walking The Turismo has its own leaflets (in English), while the English bookshop W.H. Smiffs, a few doors along from the post office on C/Almirante Ferrandiz, sells individual leaflets detailing walks in the area by Mancunian local resident and hiker Elma Thompson.

ACCOMMODATION   SEE MAP PAGE 99

Alhambra C/Antonio Millón s/n, ⓦ hostalalhambra.es. Pleasant *hostal* a little west of the centre offering a friendly welcome and immaculate en suites, some with sea-facing balcony. €€

Camping Cortijo San Miguel Ctra N340, km340; ⓦ campingcortijosanmiguel.com. Nerja's nearest campsite lies 2km west of the town. It's an attractive site with clean facilities and plenty of shade amongst the exotic plants. €

Hostal Abril C/Pintada 124, ⓦ hostalabril.com. Sparkling *hostal* with excellent en-suite a/c rooms, lots of cool marble and a friendly proprietor. Also has apartments and studios sleeping up to four. €

Hostal Marissal Paseo Balcón de Europa 3; ⓦ hostalmarissal.com. Bang in the centre of the action, this *hostal* offers attractive a/c en-suite rooms, many with sea view (try for rooms 102–5 or 204–5). Also rents apartments in same location. €€–€€€

Hostal Mena C/El Barrio 15; ⓦ hostalmena.es. Welcoming *hostal* with central a/c en-suite rooms, some with terrace and sea views. There's also a delightful garden at the rear. €€

Hostal Nerjasol C/Pintada 54; ⓦ hostalnerjasol.com. On a quiet street, with spotless a/c en-suite rooms equipped with safe, fridge and TV. There's also a rooftop solarium and mini-gym. €€

Hotel Mena Plaza Pza España 2; ⓦ hotelmenaplaza. es. Attractive modern two-star hotel in the heart of the old town from the proprietors of the *Hostal Mena*. Elegant and well-equipped a/c rooms come with fridge and (many) sea views and terraces. Public areas include a bar, rooftop solarium and pool. Minimum three-night stay in high season. €€€

Hotel Paraíso del Mar C/Prolongación de Carabeo 22, almost next door to the parador; ⓦ hotelparaisodelmar. es. Pleasant upmarket alternative to the *Parador de Nerja*. All rooms come with jacuzzi and many come with sea-view balcony; there's also a pool, gardens, sauna dug out of the cliff face, and stairway access to the beach. Breakfast is included. €€€€

Parador de Nerja C/Almuñécar 8; ⓦ parador.es. Modern *parador* which, despite an exterior resembling an open prison, has spacious, comfortable rooms, a pleasant, plant-filled garden and patio, a small park with bar (worth a visit) overlooking the sea, plus an elevator (guests only) down the cliff to Burriana, one of Nerja's most popular beaches. The restaurant serves a good-value *menú*. Breakfast is included. €€€€

Pepe Mesa Apartamentos C/Los Huertos 33; ⓦ pepemesa.com. Good-value apartments and studios with kitchenette and satellite TV, plus rooftop pool. €€

EATING   SEE MAP PAGE 99

RESTAURANTS

Ayo Burriana beach (central zone); ⓦ ayonerja.com. A reliable and very reasonably priced (for this location) beachfront lunchtime *chiringuito*. A *fritura de pescado* with a salad will easily serve two. Their giant open-air paella fry-up served everyday throughout the day is a Burriana institution. No table reservations taken. Reasonable wine prices. €€

Bar-Restaurante Los Trillizos C/Los Huertos 38; ☎ 952 520 998. Cheap and cheerful budget restaurant with well-prepared fish and meat standards and *platos combinados*,

and an attractive terrace at the back. Their *menú* is the best value in town. €

★ **Marisquería La Marina** Pza la Marina s/n; ☎ 952 521 299. *Marisquerías* don't come any better than this, which is why it's so popular. Enjoy superb tapas at the bar or mouthwateringly fresh fish (with some great wines) at their restaurant tables or terrace. Tapas and full meals are excellent value. €€

Merendero Moreno Burriana beach (western end); ☎ 952 525 480. Nicest out of a cluster of economical eating places at this end of the beach; one of the chefs cooks the fish barbecue-style (in an old boat) outside on the terrace. The fried *sardinas* and paella are pretty good. €€

★ **Oliva** C/Pintada 7; ⓦrestauranteoliva.com. Treat yourself at one of the finest dining venues in town with a well-earned reputation for excellence. The dining room is intimate, as is the small terrace. The menu is essentially Mediterranean with a creative twist. Dishes change with the seasons and may include *bacalao gratinado* (cod gratin) or Torta del Cásar cheese coulant. The lengthy wine list runs to over fifty labels including several Malaga wines. €€€€

★ **El Pulguilla** C/Almirante Ferrandiz 26; ⓦelpulguilla.com. Outstanding, long-established seafood tapas and *raciones* bar-restaurant. Everything sold is straight from the sea – *cangrejo* (crab), *calamares*, *sardinas*, you name it – and beyond the bar lies a huge and superb terrace restaurant with more of the same. It's worth noting that drinks in the bar come with a free *tapa* (but not in the restaurant). *Raciones* of grilled fresh fish on offer here include superb *rosada* (rockfish), *dorada* (sea bream) and *boquerones fritos* (fried anchovies). €€

La Taberna de Pepe Moles C/Antonio Millón s/n; ⓣ952 966 200. Excellent restaurant where the amiable owner-chef (Pepe) serves tapas at the bar only at lunchtime (try the excellent *morcilla* – black pudding) and the restaurant has a small terrace. Specials include *berenjenas de la casa*

(aubergine with a leek and prawn sauce) and *carrillada al vino de Málaga* (pork cheek in Malaga wine). €€€

TAPAS BARS

Bar Cavana Pza Cavana 12; ⓣ952 520 741. One of the oldest and most comfortable bars in Nerja and just the spot for a lazy breakfast on its outdoor terrace. Later in the day it serves a limited range of tapas and it's also a nice place in the evening to share a bottle of wine or go for one of their cocktails. €

El Chispa C/San Pedro 12, northeast of the centre; ⓣ952 523 697. Friendly neighbourhood tapas bar specializing in fried fish and octopus (cooked in a variety of ways). Try the *jibia con ajo y peregil* (cuttlefish) or superb *almejas* (clams). €€

★ **Mesón La Posada Ibérica** C/Nueva 1 ⓣ952 526 286. Pleasantly cosy and rustic little bar serving a range of tapas and *tostas* (slice of bread with topping). Try the cured meats, salads and fiery *patatas bravas*. Mon–Sat 7pm–midnight. €

La Puntilla C/Bolivia 1, close to El Chispa; ⓣ952 528 951. Lively *barrio* tapas bar specializing in fish and *mariscos*, and also does *raciones*. Try their *puntillitas* (fried baby squid) from which it takes its name or *gambas pil-pil* (spicy prawns). There's an outside terrace in warmer weather. €€

SHOPPING   SEE MAP PAGE 99

The Book Centre C/Granada 32; ⓦnerjabookcentre. com. One of the best secondhand bookshops on the coast

for books in English and many European languages. They also take books in part exchange.

A WALK NEAR FRIGILIANA

A circular 8km walk covers the **hill country** to the northwest of Frigiliana. Follow the road north out of the village towards the pleasant refreshment stop of *Venta de Frigiliana* (summer only; daily 11am–4pm), which you'll reach after 3km. Turn left down the dirt track just beyond the entrance, which leads down the ridge, passing some old cottages and villas.

Ten minutes or so further on you'll pass the gates of the Peñones and the Cortijo del Peñon farmhouses on the right. Continue down this track between pinewoods and crags until you reach a crossroads, with a walled villa on the far side. Fork sharply left at this point, passing some more old cottages on the right. One of these has a single palm tree, the ancient Moorish sign of welcome. At the first fork, below a large villa, continue left, uphill. The road winds round the villa wall, swings right and crosses the lower Pedregal valley, from where it climbs up the hill to the col on the Loma de la Cruz. Just below the crest of the ridge, where a *carril* (track) comes up from the right, keep straight on up, passing a villa.

In front of this villa, a water-cover stamped "SAT no. 7196 Monte Ariza" will confirm that you're on the right road. At the col, go straight across at the cross-tracks marked with red paint and follow the track down and round, keeping left of the fork on the next ridge. This will bring you down past the Casa del Valle, on the left. A little further on, round the bend, you'll see some tumbledown houses on the right; the first of these contains an old olive or wine press which is worth a look. The *carril* now passes through open country, then through *huertas*, rejoining the Torrox road at Casa Fernando. A right and then a left turn will take you to the upper car park on the edge of Frigiliana.

Frigiliana

A popular excursion from Nerja is the 6km trip north to **FRIGILIANA**, a pretty Moorish hill village clinging to the lower slopes of Monte El Fuerte. After the *Reconquista*, Frigiliana became a Morisco settlement where only those Moors who had converted to Christianity were allowed to live. Although a little of the atmosphere of this period survives in the steep, narrow streets, the place is prettified today by the addition of geranium pots and historical plaques.

ARRIVAL AND INFORMATION
FRIGILIANA

By bus Buses leave for Frigiliana from the bus station in Nerja (Mon–Fri at least 9 daily, 7.20am–8.30pm; Sat 7 daily), the earliest of which gives you enough time to take a walk in the surrounding hills and catch the last bus back at 9pm.

Turismo Cuesta de Apero 10, 50m from the bus terminus (July to mid-Sept Mon–Sat 10am–2.30pm & 5.30–9pm; mid-Sept to June Mon–Fri 10am–6pm, Sat 10am–2pm & 4–8pm, Sun 10am–2pm; ☎ 952 534 261, ⓦ turismofrigiliana.es). The tourist office houses an absorbing archeological museum (same hours) and can provide lists of apartments to rent around the village as well as a useful map. They also have hiking pamphlets for this area.

ACCOMMODATION

Hospedería El Caravansar Callejón de la Ermita s/n; ⓦ bit.ly/Hospederia. A *casa rural* with nine compact but comfortable a/c en-suite rooms in a charming converted village house. €

Hotel Las Chinas Pza Doña Amparo Guerrero 14; ☎ 952 533 073. This hospitable hotel, next to the *Restaurante Las Chinas* (see page 102), is a good bet for light and airy a/c balcony rooms (ask for a room at the rear to avoid street noise). Also has its own garage. €

Hotel Villa Frigiliana C/San Sebastián s/n, near the bus halt; ⓦ hotelvillafrigiliana.com. The village's three-star option offers pleasant rooms with balcony views (some with terraces) and manages to squeeze in a small pool. Breakfast is included. €€€

EATING AND DRINKING

★**La Bodeguilla** C/Chorruelo s/n, just above Pza de la Iglesia (main square); ⓦ labodeguillafrigiliana. com. An excellent and economical village restaurant now into its fourth decade, is an all-female operation run by the founder Rosario and her four daughters. The food is honest and simple, and *malagueño* specialities such as *ajo blanco*, *choto con papas a lo pobre* (kid goat with potatoes) and *fritura* (fried fish) are all competently done. There's a wonderful terrace with vistas at the back. €€

Restaurante Las Chinas Pza Doña Amparo Guerrero 14; ☎ 636 401 664. Close to the southern entrance to the village, this is another good-quality place to eat with well-priced *menús*. House specials include *paletillo de cordero asado* (roast lamb) and *chuletón de ternera* (beef chop) and there's also a *menú vegetariano*. €€

Taberna del Sacristán Pza de la Iglesia 12; ☎ 952 533 009. On the main square, fronting the church of San Antonio, with an attractive terrace, this is the upmarket place to eat in the village. The cooking is good and *chuletas de cordero con tomillo y ajo* (lamb chops with thyme and garlic) and the *brocheta de rape* (grilled monkfish) are house specials; there are also some vegetarian options. €€€

Cueva de Nerja

Ctra de Maro s/n • Daily: July & Aug 9am–6.30pm; Sept–June 9am–4pm; for more serious explorations (the standard visit allows access to only one third of the caves), there are discovery and night-time tours in English and Spanish (see website for details) • Charge for caves, Centro de Interpretación free • ⓦ cuevadenerja.es

Cynics might find the "accidental" discovery in 1957 of the **CUEVA DE NERJA** – neatly coinciding with the arrival of mass tourism – a little suspect. Immediately they were revealed, the series of enormous caverns, scattered with Paleolithic and Neolithic tools, pottery and cave paintings stretching back thirty thousand years, became a local, then national, sensation. Nowadays, however, the fairy lights, piped muzak and cave theatre – which hosts various shows from rock to ballet and flamenco as well as serving as the venue for Nerja's **International Festival of Music and Dance**, featuring Spanish and international performers and orchestras – can't help but detract from the appreciation of a spectacular natural wonder. Still, if you can block out the razzmatazz the cave is astonishingly huge and the dangling limestone stalactites and soaring stalagmites are certainly impressive. The prehistoric cave paintings are currently not on public view (and possibly never will be). However, you might want to seek out the world's longest known **stalactite** – all 32m of it, and verified by the *Guinness Book of Records* – while you're probing the depths.

Close to the cave entrance, a **Centro de Interpretación** uses dioramas to document the history of the cave and its geology.

ARRIVAL AND DEPARTURE — CUEVA DE NERJA

By bus/taxi Taking a taxi or a bus (running approximately hourly; 15min) from Nerja bus station is a better alternative to the easy but not particularly pleasant 3km walk east along the main coast road.

ACCOMMODATION AND EATING

Hotel-Restaurante Al Andalus C/Siroco 1, 200m downhill from the cave entrance; w hotelalandalusnerja.es. Pleasant hotel with a decent restaurant (and shady terrace) serving an excellent *menú*. The attractive rooms are good value and come with balconies or (some) terrace balconies and most have sea views. There's also a garden pool. Their ample (free) car park out front makes this a good place to stay to avoid overnight parking fees in Nerja. €€€

Maro

East of Nerja, the coastal road zigzags around the foothills of the Sierra Almijara, climbing above a number of tiny coves. The first settlement, the coastal hamlet and former fishing village of **MARO**, is a sparkling cluster of white-walled houses set above an attractive cove beach. Lying close to the ancient Roman settlement of Detunda, the town was revitalized in the eighteenth century by the construction of a sugar factory, now a ruin behind the simple church of Nuestra Señora de las Maravillas, which dates from the same period.

ACCOMMODATION AND EATING — MARO

Balcón de Maro Pza de las Maravillas, near the church; t 952 529 523. Inexpensive sea-view balcony studios – sleeping up to four – in a central location. The bar below serves breakfasts and tapas. €

Casa Maro C/Maravillas s/n; w hotelcasamaro.com. An attractive option, this German-run hotel offers elegant rooms, most with sea-view balcony and kitchenette; there are also some studio apartments. €€

Costa del Sol

West of Málaga, the real **Costa del Sol** gets going. If you've never seen this level of touristic development before, it can be quite a shock, not least when you see how grit-grey the sands are; you have to keep going, around the corner to Tarifa (see page 195), before you reach the golden sands of the tourist brochures. With their faceless 1960s' and 1970s' concrete tower blocks, these are certainly not the kind of resorts you find in Greece or even Portugal. Since the 1980s' boom in time-share apartments and leisure complexes, it's estimated that 300,000 foreigners live on the Costa del Sol, the majority of them retired and British. On the other hand, the cheap package-tour industry – largely responsible for the transformation of the string of poverty-stricken fishing villages that dotted this coast until the 1950s – no longer brings in the numbers it once did, placing the future of purpose-built resorts such as Torremolinos in peril.

Approached in the right kind of spirit, it *is* possible to have fun in **Torremolinos** and, at a price, in **Marbella**. The sea, at least, is reasonably clean, the resorts tend not to be plagued with rampaging foreign drunks in high season (as happens in other parts of Spain) and there's a much stronger family feel to it all. However, if you're looking for a more authentic version of Spain, your best bet is to keep going until at least Estepona.

1

Torremolinos

The approach to **TORREMOLINOS** – easiest on the electric railway from Málaga or the airport – is a depressing trawl through a drab, soulless landscape of apartments. The town itself is certainly an experience: a vast, grotesque parody of a seaside resort with its own kitsch fascination. This bizarre place, lined with sweeping (but crowded) beaches has a thriving LGBTQ+ scene – it's home to the Costa del Sol's only LGBTQ+ hotel (*Hotel Ritual*) and celebrates Torremolinos Pride (first weekend in June) and the Mad Bear Beach Festival (August). In complete contrast, the resort is also Spain's ballroom dancing capital and regularly hosts national and international championships.

In recent years a dynamic town council has been moving heaven and earth to rid the resort of its package tour image, and while they've stopped short of flattening the concrete monsters overlooking the beach, they have smartened up the seafront promenade and pedestrianized the central boulevard. They have ambitious plans to clear the tawdry souvenir shops, remove all tacky signage and restore the resort's cultural heritage, although cumbersome council debt will curtail their efforts.

ARRIVAL AND INFORMATION

TORREMOLINOS

By train The station is on Avda Jesús Santos Rein. The train from Málaga drops you right in the centre of the action, a couple of blocks west of the town's main artery, C/San Miguel.

By bus The bus station is at C/Hoyo 10, a 5min walk away from the centre. All out-of-town buses arrive here.

Turismo The Turismo on Pza de Andalucía 1 (Mon–Fri 9am–2pm; ☎951 954 379; ⦿turismotorremolinos.es),

is supported by a number of two suboffices located on the seafront at Pza de las Comunidades Autónomas, southeast of the centre (mid-June to mid-Sept daily 10am–2pm & 6–8pm; mid-Sept to mid-June Tues–Sun 10am–2pm), and in La Carihuela on the seafront just off Pza del Remo (mid-June to mid-Sept daily 10am–2pm & 6–8pm; mid-Sept to mid-June Mon–Fri 9.30am–2pm). The helpful main office can provide a town map and a "Ruta de Tapas" leaflet.

ACCOMMODATION

Apartamentos Alegría C/Carmen 23, La Carihuela; ⦿lacarihuela.com. Charming, two-person a/c seafront studios with modern kitchens and fittings; minimum stay two nights. The friendly owners offer similar apartments nearby when this one is full. €€

Camping Torremolinos Loma del Paraíso 2; ☎952 382 602. Rather pricey site (in high summer – rates fall substantially outside June to mid-Sept) some 3km east of the centre on the main N340 Málaga–Cádiz highway, near *Hotel Los Alamos* and 500m from the sea. Facilities aren't the best, but there's plenty of shade and it's the only camping option in the area. To get here, take the *cercanías* train (get off at Los Alamos) or go by bus (Línea B) from the central Plaza Costa del Sol. €

Hostal Micaela C/Bajondillo 4; ⦿hostalmicaela.es. Serviceable rooms with bath, close to the beach, some with sea view. Prices fall by almost thirty percent outside

August. €€

★ **Hotel Miami** C/Aladino 14; ⦿residencia-miami.com. One of the most charming hotels on the whole Costa del Sol, this enchanting villa was built by a cousin of Picasso in 1950 and contains many of the original designer furnishings like the stone-built *chimenea* (hearth) and carved wood fittings and beams, along with a walled garden sporting palms and oleanders, and a swimming pool. The simple but comfortable rooms – many with balconies overlooking the garden – come with a/c and TV. Free car park. €€

Hotel Tarik Paseo Marítimo 49; ⦿hoteltarik.com. Attractive refurbished beachfront hotel offering well-equipped a/c rooms with TV and safe, half with sea-view terrace balconies. Public areas include a garden pool, solarium and café-restaurant. €€€

EATING AND DRINKING

Beirut C/Antonio Navajas Ruiz 11; ⦿restaurantebeirut.es. Outstanding Lebanese restaurant with a pleasant terrace down a side street at the eastern end of the seafront. A wide-ranging menu includes falafel and other Middle Eastern favourites. Don't miss the aptly named Katastrof (the chef's selection) which easily feeds two. €€

★ **Bodega La Guerola** C/Las Mercedes 2, at junction with C/San Miguel; ☎952 381 057. A real beehive of a

place that's everything a tapas bar should be. It manages to squeeze in a few tables, but serious *tapeadores* rest one elbow on the bar. Try their delicious *boquerones al limón* (anchovies in lemon) with a glass of sherry on tap. €€

Casa Juan Los Mellizos Pza de San Ginés, one block back from La Carihuela seafront; ⦿losmellizos.net. A La Carihuela favourite and one of the oldest fish restaurants in the resort, Casa Juan fills the entire square. Specials include *bacalao al pil-pil* (spicy cod) and *zarzuela de marisco* (seafood stew), but it's difficult to go wrong with anything on the menu. €€€

★ **Mesón Galego Antoxo** C/Hoyo 5; ⓦ antoxo.com. Oozing class, this is an excellent, if seriously expensive,

Galician restaurant offering dishes and wines from northwestern Spain, including the mandatory tarta de Santiago dessert. Fish is shipped in from Galicia daily, including *merluza a la gallega* (hake) and memorable *zamburriñas* (baby scallops). €€€€

NIGHTLIFE

When night falls, Torremolinos comes into its own, with a vibrant **nightlife** lifting off in high summer at about 10pm and continuing well beyond dawn. Torremolinos also maintains its thriving **gay scene**. C/Casablanca, running west from C/San Miguel, is the centre of gay nightlife, with bars and clubs dotted along here and the streets off it.

Atrévete Avda Salvador Allende 10, opposite the Hotel Pez Espada, La Carihuela; ☎ 609 861 148. Themed music nights at one of the most established nightclubs on the Costa del Sol. The venue has two dance floors and a real party atmosphere after midnight. Five bars keep dancers

fuelled with shots and and mojitos until dawn.

Boomerang Bar Pza Tientos, in central Torremolinos 3; ☎ 665 455 318. Good drinking hole with a warm welcome where the action spills out onto the square on warmer nights. Excellent cocktails and live music or DJs.

Chicago Karaoke C/Danza Invisible 8; ☎ 619 423 065. One of several karaoke clubs in Torremolinos, although this one has perhaps the biggest choice of songs (and in several languages). Good cocktails and fun atmosphere to sing your heart out to.

Benalmádena

Beyond Carihuela to the west of Torremolinos, the built-up coastline merges imperceptibly – after 4km – into the neighbouring resort of **BENALMÁDENA COSTA**, with its Puerto Deportivo, a pseudo-Moorish harbour complex and a seafront lined with bars, restaurants and *chiringuitos*, popular with holidaying families. Some 3km inland lies the hilltop **BENALMÁDENA PUEBLO**, the original Benalmádena and an attractive white village, considerably quieter than Torremolinos and a good base for visiting nearby resorts and villages.

Museo de Arte Precolombino Orlando

Avda Peralta 49 • April–Oct Tues–Sat 9.30am–1.30pm & 6–8pm; Nov–March Tues–Sat 9.30am–1.30pm & 5–7pm • Free

The **Museo de Arte Precolombino**, in Benalmádena Pueblo, is well worth a visit. It houses a unique collection of pre-Columbian artefacts, assembled in the last century by Felipe Orlando García-Murciano. The two upper floors are devoted to the pre-Columbian collection and there are some stunning **ceramics** on display from the Nasca and Inca civilizations in Peru, as well as the Toltec, Aztec and Maya civilizations of Mexico. Other ancient artefacts displayed come from Ecuador, Nicaragua and Costa Rica. The basement is dedicated to finds from Roman Benalmadena, including a 1.5m-high statue of Artemis believed to have been retrieved from a Roman coastal wreck, but which now turns out to be from a nineteenth-century British factory making classical copies – it was en route to a colonial villa in India.

Tivoli World

Avda del Tivoli • July & Aug daily 6pm–1am; March, April, Sept & Oct Sat & Sun noon–7pm; May Thurs–Sun 12.30–7.30pm; June Wed–Sun 5pm–midnight • Charge • ⓦ tivoli.es

A big attraction for most visitors to Benalmádena is **Tivoli World**, the Costa del Sol's biggest amusement park, sited between Benalmádena Pueblo and Benalmádena Costa and easily reached by train from Fuengirola or Torremolinos ("Arroyo de Miel" stop). The park has the usual cocktail of rides – including Tower Drop, which plummets riders from 60m – as well as restaurants and shows featuring flamenco and assorted tribute bands.

Teleférico

Opposite Tivoli World • Daily: July & Aug 10am–midnight; Sept 11am–7pm; Oct & mid-Feb to April 11am–6pm; Nov & Dec 11am–5pm • Charge, online discounts available • ⓦ telefericobenalmadena.com

1

Opposite the Tivoli World entrance the **Teleférico** (cable car) ascends to the peak of Monte Calamorro, from where there are panoramic **views** over the Costa del Sol and – in summer – daily falconry displays. If you choose the one-way fare you have the option of a scenic **walk** back down the mountain along a signed path (a 1hr to 1hr 30min trek).

Sea Life

Puerto Marina s/n • Daily July & Aug 10am–12.30am; Sept–June 10am–8.30pm; feeding times throughout the day (see website) • Charge, online discounts available • ⓦ visitsealife.com

On the seafront and close to the Puerto Deportivo, **Sea Life** is the resort's well-presented aquarium, home to a vast array of sea creatures including rays, crabs, octopuses, jellyfish, tropical exotics and turtles. The highlight is a walk-through glass tunnel devoted to sharks who glide eerily a metre above your head; if you coincide your visit with feeding time, you'll see just what those molars are capable of.

Selwo Marina

Parque de la Paloma • Daily July & Aug 10am–9pm; Sept–June 10am–6pm; feeding times and shows throughout the day (see website) • Charge, online discounts available • ⓦ selwomarina.es

On the west side of the seafront, **Selwo Marina** offers yet more marina animals – the residents here include dolphins, sea lions and penguins, as well as numerous birds and reptiles. The biggest attractions are the dolphin show and feeding time for the penguins.

ARRIVAL AND INFORMATION   BENALMÁDENA

By train The cercanías train station on the Málaga-Fuengirola line is in Arroyo de la Miel on Avda de la Constitución, just east of Tivoli World (see page 105). From here, it's a 30min walk to the Puerto Deportivo. Trains run daily every 20 minutes to Fuengirola (20min), Torremolinos (8min), Málaga Airport (20min) and Málaga (30min).

By bus Buses from Málaga stop at various points along the coast road for Benalmádena Costa (every 30 mins; 35min)

and in the centre of Benalmádena Pueblo (Mon–Sat 4 daily, Sun 3 daily; 1h 5min).

Turismo Main tourist office, Avda Antonio Machado 10, one block from the Puerto Deportivo (daily 9am–3.30pm; ☏ 952 442 494; ⓦ disfrutabenalmadena.com) and the information point, Avda del Sol s/n, next to Castillo Bilbil (daily 9am–3.30pm) provide useful information on attractions and events.

ACCOMMODATION AND EATING

Blankko Paso de Bellavista 7, Benalmádena Costa; ⓦ blankko.es. Down on the coast towards Torrequebrada, this venue has a stunning terrace with sea views and makes a lovely spot for a meal, afternoon tea or an after-dinner drink. The innovative menu includes strawberry gazpacho, several tartars such as salmon and avocado, plus more elaborate dishes such as *as bacalao gratinado con alioli y chutney de piña* (cod gratin with aioli and pineapple chutney). €€€

La Fonda C/Santo Domingo de Guzmán 7; ⓦ lafondabenalmadena.es. Superb hotel with elegant, marble-floored rooms. Public areas include a spa, a pool,

bar and restaurant with a long list of dishes such as *verduras de temporada con perfume de ajo* (seasonal vegetables with garlic essence) and *perdiz estofado con castañas* (stewed partridge with chestnuts). The bar serves tapas on a terrace with spectacular views over the coast. All are open to non-guests. Breakfast is included. €€€€

Hotel Pueblo Avda Juan Luis Peralta, ☏ 952 568 723. Attractive boutique hotel in the central square with a sparkling white facade decked with bright blue flower pots. The en-suite rooms come colourful with a/c and strong box. Superior doubles have good views of the square and village. Free parking nearby. €€

Fuengirola

FUENGIROLA, a thirty-minute train journey west from Torremolinos, or a rapid 21km along the old N340 or the A7 *autovía*, is very slightly less developed and infinitely more staid, middle aged and family-oriented than Torremolinos. You wouldn't think it today, but Fuengirola has a distinguished Phoenician (the town started out as a colony), Roman and Moorish past. A number of sights from these eras remain, although most people are here for the **beach**, a huge strand, 7km long, divided into restaurant-beach strips, each renting out lounge chairs and sunshades.

Castillo de Sohail

C/Tartesios • Mid-Sept to June Wed–Sun 10am–2.30pm • Free

On the road west out of town is the restored but still impressive **Castillo de Sohail**, a tenth-century fortress built by Abd ar-Rahman III of Córdoba as the hub of a string of towers along the coast to defend against piracy. There are fine views from the battlements over the town and out to sea. Concerts featuring international and Spanish names are held during the summer months.

Finca El Secretario

Avda Padre Jesús Cautivo s/n • Daily 10am–9pm • Free • ☎ 952 467 457

An excavated Roman villa, the extensive **Finca El Secretario** lies at the eastern end of town close to the Los Boliches train station on the Fuengirola–Málaga line (whose construction in 1970 first brought the villa to light). It was in use from the first to the fifth century, and excavations have revealed mosaic floors as well as part of the hypocaust system that would have heated the villa's bathhouse. They also unearthed a statue of the Roman goddess Venus, later dubbed the "Venus de Fuengirola", now on display in the **Museo de la Historia** (Pza de España, Tues–Sat 11am–1pm, free). Adjoining the villa, a fish-salting factory was also discovered, no doubt used to make *garum*, a pungent fish sauce.

Bioparc Fuengirola

Avda Camilo José Cela 6 • Daily July & Aug 10am–11pm; Sept–June 10am–6pm • Charge, combined ticket and train deals available, see website • ☎ bioparcfuengirola.com

One of the best zoos in Europe with the emphasis on conservation, Bioparc is divided into different habitats, such as Madagascar, housing an island of free-roaming lemurs, Africa and East-Asia, and home to a wide range of species. Daily shows and talks.

ARRIVAL AND INFORMATION · FUENGIROLA

By train The cercanías train station is on Avda Juan Gómez Juanito s/n, one block north of the bus station (☎ renfe.com). Trains every 20 mins daily to Benalmádena (20min), Torremolinos (30min), Málaga Airport (40min) and Málaga (50min).

By bus The bus station is on Avda Matías Saenz de Tejada s/n, slightly west of the Turismo (☎ 952 475 066). Buses to Málaga (at least 9 daily Mon–Sat, 6 daily Sun; 55min), Marbella (4 direct daily; 35min) and Mijas (at least every hour; 30min).

Turismo The Turismo, Avda Jesús S. Rein 6 (Mon–Fri 9am–6pm, Sat & Sun 10am–2pm; ☎ 952 467 457, ☎ turismo. fuengirola.es) can supply a town map.

ACCOMMODATION

Hostal Cuevas C/Capitán 7; ☎ hostalcuevas.com. Pleasant and central *hostal* offering spotless a/c en-suite rooms with TV, some with balconies overlooking a garden. Can assist with parking if necessary. €

Hostal Italia C/de la Cruz 1; ☎ hostalitalia.com. This friendly *hostal* is the nicest option around the Plaza de la Constitución for a/c en-suite terrace balcony rooms. Garage parking available. €€

Hotel Las Piramides Paseo Marítimo s/n; ☎ hotellaspiramides.com. A luxury option at the western end of the seafront with sea-view rooms, indoor and outdoor pools, gym, sauna and plenty more four-star frills. Check website for special offers. Own garage. €€€€

EATING AND DRINKING

★ **Bar La Paz Garrido** Avda de Mijas 1, just north of the Pza de la Constitución; ☎ lapazgarrido.com. This outstanding and hugely popular bar-restaurant serves up some of the best-value seafood in town – the gazpacho, *boquerones a la plancha* (fried anchovies) and *patatas* *bravas* (spicy sautéed potatoes) are highly recommended. It's worth trying to grab a table and making a meal of it. €€

Freiduría Pulpería El Choco C/Francisco Cano 13, Los Boliches; ☎ 952 468 169. A short walk southeast from Los Boliches train station, this is one of the best places to eat

1

fish and seafood in town. Octopus is the house specials, but the menu also runs to a good list of fried fish, seafood dishes and salads. Arrive first thing to be sure of a table. €€

Mesón Salamanca C/del Capitán 1, just off the Pza de la Constitución, facing Hostal Italia; ☎ 952 478 351. Reliable bar-restaurant with a pleasant dining room offering well-prepared Spanish traditional cuisine (fish and meat). It has a range of good-value *menús del día* (including wine) and has an extensive tapas menu. €€€

Old Swiss House C/Marina 28, one block in from the sea and close to the Hotel Las Piramides; ⓦ oldswisshouse.

com. Small mid-priced restaurant where the Swiss-influenced cooking has a dash of panache – including the Chateaubriand, *Züricher Art* (veal in mushroom sauce) and *crêpes suzette* dessert. Also offers fondue and good-value takeaway menus. €€€

La Plaza Pza de la Constitución; ⓦ barlaplazafuengirola. es. This vibrant bar with a popular terrace on the square opens for breakfast and serves economical tapas, *platos combinados*, snacks and salads throughout the day with many daily specials. In the evening it serves *copas* (alcoholic drinks). €€

Mijas

Often grouped with the more famous White Towns further north (see page 119), the once tranquil hill town of **MIJAS**, a winding 8km climb into the hills above Fuengirola, is a little too close to the Costa del Sol for its own good, making it an obvious target for bus tours in search of the "typical" Andalucian village, although if you visit in the afternoon you'll miss most of them. However, despite a host of tacky gift shops and the numbered *burro* (donkey) taxis that transport visitors around the main square (Plaza Virgen de la Peña), the village retains some of its original character, and there are fine views towards the coast. A **modern art museum** provides an additional focus for visitors. Each Wednesday there's a **crafts market** (11am–2pm) in the main square and in the same location a free flamenco show is staged at noon.

Plaza de Toros and the church of the Inmaculada Concepción

Southeast of the main square the century-old – and curiously rectangular – **Plaza de Toros**, with a museum (Mon–Sat 10am–7pm; Sun 10am–6pm; charge), is worth a look, as is the nearby sixteenth-century **church of the Inmaculada Concepción** (daily 9am–8pm; free) with a Mudéjar tower, and the adjacent ruins of a Moorish fort and a **mirador** with a spectacular view over the coast far below.

Casa Museo Etnográfico

Pza de la Libertad • Daily: July & Aug 10am–3pm & 5–9pm; Sept–June 9am–7pm • Charge

West of the main square, the **Casa Museo Etnográfico** holds an interesting collection of artefacts from Mijas's past as well as a re-creation of the room where Mijas's last socialist mayor, Manuel Cortés Quero, went into hiding in 1936 to avoid the Franco purge. With the aid of his family he stayed hidden in the same underground room for 33 years, to emerge in 1969 when the government announced an amnesty.

Centro de Arte Contemporaneo (CAC)

C/Málaga 28 • Daily 10.30am–2pm • Charge • ⓦ cacmijas.info

Situated 100m or so northeast of the Casa Museo Etnográfico, the **Centro de Arte Contemporaneo (CAC)** is an exciting museum laid out on two floors. The ground floor's permanent collection is devoted to a stunning display of **Picasso ceramics** – the largest on view anywhere in Spain. The second floor is used for temporary exhibitions of work by artists of the same generation and has so far featured a number of Picasso's contemporaries including Braque, Miró, Dalí and Foujita as well as the more modern Yul Hanchas and Piet Peere.

Carromato de Max

Avda de Compás s/n • Daily: Easter–June, Sept & Oct 10am–7pm; July & Aug 10am–10pm; Nov–Easter 10am–6pm • Charge

Above the main square, the ludicrous **Carromato de Max** is a railway wagon full of junk and claims to house "the smallest curiosities in the world". If items such as

Churchill's head sculpted from a stick of chalk, a copy of Leonardo's *Last Supper* painted on a grain of rice, or the shrunken head of a white man retrieved from South American Indians and "certified genuine by the FBI" grab you, then it's well worth the entry fee.

ARRIVAL AND INFORMATION   MIJAS

By bus Frequent daily buses run between Fuengirola and Mijas (30min) stopping on the focal Plaza Virgen de la Peña, the main square. Also buses to Málaga (Mon–Sat 4 daily, Sun 3 daily; 1h 20min).

By car Mijas has transformed itself from one of the most difficult places to park into one of the easiest on the whole Costa del Sol. A huge, multistorey car park descends the cliff behind the Turismo on the main square and is also one of the cheapest to use.

Turismo The very helpful Turismo, on Pza Virgen de la Peña, s/n (July–Sept Mon–Fri 9am–8pm, Sat & Sun 10am–2pm; Oct–June Mon–Fri 9am–7pm, Sat & Sun 10am–2pm; ☎ 952 589 034; ⓦ turismo.mijas.es), can provide a useful village map and gives out a free leaflet detailing a number of walks (2–3hr) in the surrounding hills. They can also provide information on free, twice-weekly guided treks (mid-Sept to mid-June Sat & Sun at 9am; charge).

ACCOMMODATION

★ **Casa El Escudo** C/Trocha de los Pescadores 7; ⓦ el-escudo.com. Off Plaza de la Constitución, the village's second largest square, this is a delightful small hotel with charming a/c rooms equipped with TV, DVD player, minibar and – in rooms 8, 9 and 10 – terraces with fine views. €€
Finca La Tierra Urb. La Alcaparra 5, about half-way up A387 between Mijas and Fuengirola; ☎ 603 311 594. Lovely, quiet B&B set in extensive gardens with fruit trees

and natural pool. Welcoming suites with a/c and terrace. Guests have use of the pool, library and a kitchen. €€
La Posada C/Coín 47; ☎ 952 485 310. A friendly and good-value *hostal* with a range of studio and apartment options. To get there, find your way to Plaza de la Constitución, a small square below the bullring, and ask for directions. €

EATING AND DRINKING

Bar La Gamba C/San Sebastián 19, near the museum; ☎ 952 485 722. A good bar-restaurant serving *platos combinados* as well as *mariscos* and paellas, plus a good-value *menú del día*. €
El Mirlo Blanco Pza de la Constitución 13; ⓦ mirlo-blanco.es. Elaborate meals are on offer at this very good Basque restaurant. House specialities include *bacalao a la vizcaína* (salted cod), *txangurro* (spider crab baked in shell) and a belt-busting soufflé Grand Marnier. €€€

★ **Sollo** Avda del Higuerón 48, near A7 autovía southeast of Mijas; ⓦ sollo.es. Well worth the splurge if you're a serious foodie, Sollo, run by award-winning and Michelin-star chef Diego Gallegos, takes freshwater fish cuisine to another level. The Andalucian sturgeon caviar is as good as the best Iranian or Russian, and the nineteen-course tasting menu will set your taste buds alive; the views of the coast from the restaurant will keep your eyes happy too. Booking is essential. €€€€

Marbella

Undisputedly the "quality resort" of the Costa del Sol, **MARBELLA** stands in considerable contrast to most of what's come before. Sheltered from the winds by the hills of the Sierra Blanca, it has a couple of excellent **beaches** which first brought it to the attention of the 1960s' smart set. However, don't strain your eyes for celebrities nowadays; the only time the mega-rich motor down from their villas in the hills is to attend a private club or put in an appearance at glitzy places like the *Puente Romano Hotel* on the way to San Pedro, where a beluga caviar starter in the restaurant will cost you the price of a good hotel room.

Spared the worst excesses of concrete architecture that have been inflicted upon Torremolinos, Marbella is decidedly tasteful, retaining the greater part of its old town or *casco antiguo*. Slowly, this original quarter is being bought up and turned over to "quaint" clothes boutiques and restaurants, but you can still sit in an ordinary bar in a small old square and look up beyond the whitewashed alleyways to the Sierra Blanca mountains.

1

Brief history

Marbella's image took a nose dive in the 1970s when British crooks and drug barons began setting up home here, bringing their feuds and rivalries with them. In the late 1980s the authorities became even more exercised by the arrival of Russian and Italian Mafia bosses, who controlled their empires from luxury villas and yachts harboured in nearby Puerto Banús. Marbella's notoriety continued throughout the 1990s during the period of rule by the corrupt mayor Jesús Gil y Gil (who avoided a lengthy jail term by dying in 2004) and his GIL political party. In 2005 Spanish police uncovered Europe's biggest-ever money-laundering operation, channelling billions of euros from crime syndicates across Europe through Marbella companies into anonymous "trusts". In the last couple of decades, political life has concentrated on local affairs and on recuperating the vast amounts of public funds lost by previous corrupt councillors. In an ironic twist of history, Marbella is hugely popular with Middle Eastern Arabs,

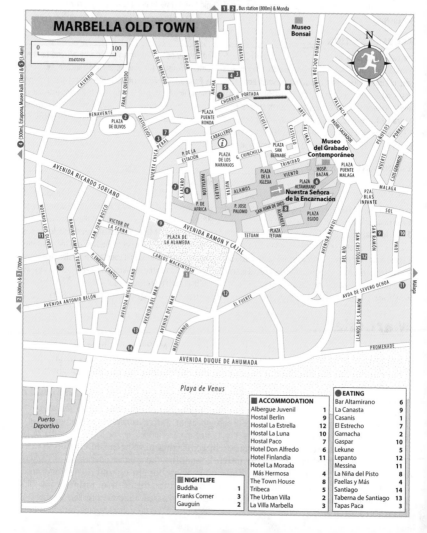

■ ACCOMMODATION		● EATING	
Albergue Juvenil	1	Bar Altamirano	6
Hostal Berlin	9	La Canasta	9
Hostal La Estrella	12	Casanis	1
Hostal La Luna	10	El Estrecho	7
Hostal Paco	7	Garnacha	2
Hotel Don Alfredo	6	Gaspar	10
Hotel Finlandia	11	Lekune	5
Hotel La Morada		Lepanto	12
Más Hermosa	4	Messina	11
The Town House	8	La Niña del Pisto	8
Tribeca	5	Paellas y Más	4
The Urban Villa	2	Santiago	14
La Villa Marbella	3	Taberna de Santiago	13
		Tapas Paca	3

■ NIGHTLIFE	
Buddha	1
Franks Corner	3
Gauguin	2

especially since the late King Fahd of Saudi Arabia built a White House lookalike, complete with adjacent mosque, on the town's western outskirts.

Plaza de los Naranjos

The *casco antiguo*, partially walled, is set back from the sea and hidden from the main road – the Avenida Ramón y Cajal – that slices through the town. The main sights are clustered in the web of streets surrounding the picturesque **Plaza de los Naranjos**, whose charms are somewhat marred by the invasive terraces of the surrounding restaurants that use it as an open-air dining room. On the plaza (next to the Turismo) is the striking sixteenth-century Ayuntamiento, still functioning as such and actually built by Fernando and Isabel following their conquest of the town in 1485. The area now occupied by the plaza was formerly a warren of narrow streets in the Moorish town of Marbil-la, but the monarchs cleared this area of housing to create the open space that Spanish civic life required. On the square's southern flank – and not easy to see for the surrounding clutter – lies a fountain constructed in 1504 by Marbella's first Christian mayor.

Just off the square in the nearby Plaza de la Iglesia is the church of **Nuestra Señora de la Encarnación**. Also built in the sixteenth century, it was later remodelled in the Baroque style and has a fine tower as well as a striking retablo inside.

Museo del Grabado Contemporáneo

C/Hospital Bazán s/n • Mid-June to mid-Sept Mon & Sat 10am–2pm, Tues–Fri 9am–7pm; mid-Sept to mid-June Mon–Fri 9am–7.30pm, Sat 9am–2pm • Charge • Ⓦ mgec.es

A fine Renaissance hospital – founded in the sixteenth century by Alonso Bazán, then mayor of Marbella – now hosts a mildly interesting **Museo del Grabado Contemporáneo**, an engraving museum with works by Miró, Dalí and Picasso.

Museo Ralli

Urb. Coral Beach, N340 km176 • Tues–Sat 10am–3pm • Free • Ⓦ rallimuseums.com • Buses from Marbella to San Pedro de Alcántara or Estepona will drop you outside the museum (ask for "Parada Coral Beach")

Part of the Ralli chain of museums (five worldwide), the **Museo Ralli** is dedicated to displaying the work of contemporary European and Latin American artists with an emphasis on surrealism. Founded with the fortunes of the Ralli Brothers trading and banking empire, the museums are free and non-profit-making. Among works on show in the permanent collection are sculptures by Dalí and Soriano as well as by Mexican sculptors Aguirre and Quiroz. Temporary exhibitions have included work by Beryl Cook, Picasso (notebooks) and Miró.

Beaches

The resort has three main **beaches** stretching from the easternmost Playa de la Bajadilla and Playa de Venus, both located between its twin harbours, and the Playa de la Fontanilla to the west, which gets progressively less crowded the further west you go.

ARRIVAL AND INFORMATION   MARBELLA

By bus The bus station is at the northern of Avda Trapiche, a 20min walk from the centre. Buses from Estepona and San Pedro de Alcántara (every 30 mins, heading east) and Fuengirola (every 30 mins, heading west) also stop in the centre. Otherwise take buses #2 or #7 from the bus station, which will drop you near to the centre of the old town. There are also buses to Málaga (every hour daily; 50min) and Málaga Airport (at least 10 daily; 45min).

By car Signed pay car parks are dotted around the centre and all accommodation (if they don't have their own garage) will advise on possible on-street parking places.

Turismo The Turismo, on the north side of Pza de los Naranjos (mid-June to Sept Mon–Fri 8.30am–9.30pm, Sat & Sun 10am–9.30pm; Oct to mid-June Mon–Fri 8.30am–7.30pm, Sat & Sun 9am–2pm; ☏ 952 768 707; Ⓦ turismo. marbella.es), has detailed town maps. A second office (same hours) is sited on Glorieta Fontanilla, a roundabout at the western end of the seafront near the Puerto Deportivo.

1

ACCOMMODATION

SEE MAP PAGE 110

Albergue Juvenil C/Trapiche 2; ⓦinturjoven.com. A very good hostel, if a little removed from the action (5–10min walk to the centre), with double rooms (some with bath), a big pool and tennis court, plus plenty of activities such as sea angling, mountain biking and watersports. €

Hostal Berlin C/San Ramón 21; ⓦhostalberlin.com. Sparkling and very friendly *hostal*; all rooms come with bath, a/c and satellite TV. Bargain rates outside July and August. €€

Hostal La Estrella C/San Cristóbal 36; ⓦhostallaestrella.es. Nicely located and welcoming option on a pleasant street, offering a/c en-suite rooms with fridge, TV and (some rooms only) balcony. €€

Hostal La Luna C/Luna 7; ⓦhostallaluna.wordpress.com. Delightful, friendly and spotless *pensión* with balconied rooms around a renovated old patio at the rear; all rooms have bath, fridge, a/c and TV. Can assist with parking. €

Hostal Paco C/Peral 16; ⓦhostalpacomarbella.com. Central *hostal* in a traditional town house; all rooms are en suite and come with TV. Can advise on parking. Small discount for stays of two nights or more. €€

Hotel Don Alfredo C/Portada 11; ⓦhoteldonalfredo.com. Very pleasant small two-star hotel facing the walls of a ruined *castillo*. All rooms have a/c, satellite TV and balcony. Street parking is often available nearby – the hotel can advise. €€

Hotel Finlandia C/Notario Luis Oliver 12; ⓦhotelfinlandia.es. Welcoming and comfortable little one-star hotel on a quiet street. Rooms – some with balcony – come with a/c and TV. €€€

★ **Hotel La Morada Más Hermosa** C/Montenebros 16; ☏952 924 467. Taking its name from the first words of Columbus on sighting the New World ("beautiful place"), this is an enchanting small hotel in a refurbished eighteenth-century townhouse with elegant, individually styled a/c rooms (most with terraces) and more expensive suites. €€€

The Town House C/Alderete 7; ⓦtownhousemarbella.com. Attractive en-suite a/c rooms, most with balconies, set in a peaceful square in the heart of the old town. There's also a lovely rooftop terrace. Breakfast is included. €€€€

Tribeca C/Montenebros 5A; ⓦtribecamarbella.com. Welcoming B&B in the heart of the old town with small but well-equipped rooms with en suite and TV. Breakfast is included. €€€

The Urban Villa Hacienda Los Canasteros 5, to the north of the town; ☏952 113 955. A good choice away from the resort, although you need a car to get there. British-run B&B with cosy rooms and suites with views of the coast from the terraces and pool. Communal kitchen and guests may use the piano, bongo and guitar. Breakfast is included with direct bookings. €€€

La Villa Marbella C/Príncipe 10; ⓦwww.lavillamarbella.com. One of the poshest options in the old town offering apartments and rooms in different townhouses near the reception. Decorated in an Asian style, rooms come with lots of extras. Guests have use of the rooftop terrace and pool. Breakfast is included with direct bookings. Doubles €€€, apartments €€€€

EATING

SEE MAP PAGE 110

You're better off heading for Marbella's numerous excellent **tapas bars** rather than the touristy and overpriced **restaurants** around the Plaza de los Naranjos. There are, however, a fair number of good-value spots within a five-minute walk of the square, and in the Fontanilla district to the west of the Alameda. The seafront promenade also has plenty of bars and restaurants.

RESTAURANTS

Casanis C/Ancha 8; ☏952 900 450. Mid-priced bistro with a French-Belgian kitchen and plenty of ambience and style. *Confit de pato con lentejas* (duck confit with lentils) and *pierno de cordero* (leg of lamb) are house specials, and there are also pasta-based dishes and some veggie options. And, it goes without saying, Belgian *frites*. €€€

Garnacha Pza de los Olivos s/n, to the northwest of the old town; ⓦgarnachamarbella.es. A modern restaurant serving excellent-value innovative dishes. The menu changes regularly, but expect to find specials such as ceviche de lubina (seabream) and codorniz con curry (curried grouse). There's a bargain weekday *menú* plus an equally good value menú de degustación. €€€

★ **Gaspar** C/Notario Luis Oliver 19; ⓦtabernagaspar.es. A gem of a restaurant run by Gaspar Fernández and his family from Rioja – which explains the comprehensive wine list. Besides their standard dishes – including the best *tortilla* in town, *cordero asado* (charcoal grilled lamb) and *pastel de berenjenas* (aubergine terrine) you can also order a few plates of *raciones* to share. Lunchtimes they serve up an *arroz marinero* (paella) and a *ración* easily serves two. Should you have to wait for a table you can peruse the books in the restaurant's library, and impromptu flamenco sometimes happens when *cantantes* (singers) drop in for a meal. €€€

★ **Messina** Avda Severo Ochoa 12; ⓦrestaurantemessina.com. Mauricio Giovanini cooks Mediterranean dishes with a modern take. Two tasting menus showcase his signature dishes *raya en amarillo* (skate) and *chivo lechal malagueño* (suckling goat) or you can eat à la carte where innovative dishes such as *erizo micuit* (mi-cuit sea urchin) and Spanish Thai French toast feature. Extensive wine list. €€€€

Paellas y Más C/Hermanos Salom 3, a 10min walk west of the old town; ⓦ restaurantepaellasymas.com. There's not much they don't know about rice here where paellas and fideuas are the absolute stars of the show, in both their traditional versions and with more unusual ingredients. Sharing plates and creative salads are also available. The spacious outdoor terrace makes for very pleasant dining. €€€

★ **Santiago** Avda Duque de Ahumada s/n; ⓦ restaurantesantiago.com. One of Marbella's swankiest restaurants, founded in the 1950s by Santiago Domínguez – who started out with a *chiringuito* on the beach opposite. Now one of Spain's great restaurateurs, Santiago is still the boss and the cuisine is traditional with a creative touch. Signature dishes include *ensalada de bogavante* (lobster salad) and *fritura del Mediterráneo* (fried fish). There's an attractive seafront terrace. €€€

CAFÉS

La Canasta Alameda Gardens, Avda Ramón y Cajal. Founded in 1920 and extensively restored in 2016, this makes a nice place for breakfast or afternoon tea, in the gardens overlooking the main drag with two shady terraces. €

Lepanto Avda Puerta del Mar s/n, southeast corner of the Alameda; ⓦ cateringlepanto.com. Stylish café and *pastelería* just south of the old quarter, which excels in chocolate confectionery creations. €

TAPAS BARS

Bar Altamirano Pza de Altamirano 4, southeast of Pza. del los Naranjos; ⓦ baraltamirano.es. Great place for some of the freshest seafood tapas and *raciones* in town; try their *cigalas plancha* (grilled langoustines) or the *boquerones fritos* (deep-fried anchovies). Has a terrace with tables spread across a small square. €€

El Estrecho C/San Lázaro 12, slightly southwest of Pza de los Naranjos; ⓦ barelestrecho.com. Founded in 1954, this is an excellent and atmospheric little tapas bar with a wide range of possibilities. There's a small dining room off to the side and cool jazz and blues sounds often float in the background. Try their *carne mechada* (larded meat) or *mejillones tigres* (tiger mussels). €€

Lekune Avda La Fontanilla 1; ☎ 952 868 494. Smart bar combining modern art with white plastic chairs. The house special is *pintxos* (Basque tapas on sticks) – try the *bacalao al pil-pil* (spicy cod). Their *tortilla* pairs perfectly with a coffee for breakfast. When the bar hits its evening stride, waitresses circle with trays of tapas. You take what you want and save the sticks (the number of which determines your final bill). Can get busy and crowded after 9pm and at weekends. Has small outdoor terrace. €€

La Niña del Pisto C/Lázaro 2, opposite El Estrecho (see page 113); ☎ 633 320 022. Intimate bar with tables upstairs and down while the Montilla wine flows to accompany the house special, *pisto* (ratatouille) and croquettes. There's a good choice of hot and cold tapas, and *raciones*. €€

Taberna de Santiago Avda del Mar 20; ☎ 952 770 078. Sited on an avenue dotted with Dalí bronzes leading to the sea, this is the tapas and *raciones* bar of the famous nearby *Santiago* restaurant (see page 113). Everything is top quality and the prices are very reasonable. Has a pleasant sea-view terrace. €€

Tapas Paca C/Peral 16, at the western end of Pza de los Naranjos; ⓦ tapaspaca.com. Dishes from the northern region of Asturias comes into their own here washed down with sparkling *sidra* (cider). Try the *fabada* (bean stew), steaks, smaller *tostas* (open sandwiches) with a variety of toppings or the generous salads. Small outside terrace is great for people watching. €€€

NIGHTLIFE SEE MAP PAGE 110

Buddha Avda del Mar 3; ☎ 952 772 891. Central retro *discoteca* and club with themed nights (such as *música Cubana*, salsa and Sixties sounds). You can also dine here in the "Fun Kitchen".

Franks Corner C/Camino José Cela 12; ☎ 952 822 748. A classic on the Marbella live music scene as well as one of the places to play pool and/or watch televised sport.

Gauguin Avda Fontanilla 7; ⓦ facebook.com/GauguinMarbella. Popular lounge and cocktail bar with a long G&T menu and outdoor terrace (heated in winter). In-house DJs play music from the 1980s onwards.

Puerto Banús

Around 7km west of Marbella the A7 coastal road passes the marina and casino complex of **PUERTO BANÚS**, where the jet set park up their yachts. A modern resort devoid of any architectural charm, in summer it presents a bizarre spectacle as crowds of Costa del Sol gawpers come to celebrity-spot, while the bronzed plutocrats attempt to steer their Bentleys and Ferraris through the crush to their vessels.

  If you're determined to see what the fuss is about – or fancy some deisgner shopping at the numerous designer clothes and jewellery emporia – a useful tip when coming in by car is to use the car park of the El Corte Inglés department

1

store and walk the five minutes to the gated harbour zone, which only vehicles with permits may enter.

San Pedro de Alcántara

Six kilometres west of Puerto Banús, and about the only place on the Costa del Sol that isn't purely a holiday resort, is the small town of **SAN PEDRO DE ALCÁNTARA**, a none-too-inspiring place striving to go the way of its neighbour, but hindered by the fact that its centre is set back over 1km from the sea, which lies at the end of the Avenida del Mar Mediterráneo.

In the town proper what activity there is centres on the tranquil, palm-fringed **Plaza de la Iglesia** – at its most lively during the Thursday morning **flea market** – but there's not much else to disturb the calm.

Beach

The seafront area behind the beach has been landscaped with the almost obligatory palm-lined promenade and some holiday *urbanizaciones* have been constructed, but this has done little to raise San Pedro's profile. Despite this lack of seafront pizzazz, the **beach** itself is top-quality blue flag and 5km long, so you'll never have a problem finding somewhere to lay your towel.

INFORMATION
SAN PEDRO DE ALCÁNTARA

Turismo The helpful Turismo is on Avda Marqués del Duero 69, the main street you turn in to when leaving the A7 (Mon–Fri 9am–8pm, Sat 10am–8pm; ☎ 952 768 750). Can supply a map of the town and provide latest information on visiting the three ancient monuments (see page 114).

ACCOMMODATION AND EATING

Hostal Acemar C/19 Octubre 17; ⓦ hostalacemar.com. Not far from the Turismo, this is a budget possibility for basic but clean a/c en-suite rooms with TV. Can assist with finding on-street parking. €

Hotel Doña Catalina Avda Oriental 14; ⓦ hoteldonacatalina.com. Three-star hotel southeast of the church for comfortable a/c balcony rooms with safe and satellite TV. Public areas include a bar and *cafetería*. Breakfast is included. €€€

Restaurante Alfredo Avda Andalucía 8; ☎ 952 786 165. Smoothly professional traditional restaurant offering a good selection of *andaluz* dishes served up in a cool and comfortable dining room, or on a terrace. Everything on the menu – both fish and meat – is carefully prepared and the service is excellent. Try their baked fish or *solomillo ibérico* (pork loin). €€€

Restaurante Casa Fernando Avda Mediterraneo s/n; ⓦ casafernandos.com. About halfway down the main avenue leading to the sea, this is the nearest decent place to eat near the seafront. It specializes in seafood – *bogavante* (lobster) and *urta* (bream) are house specials – and there's a leafy garden terrace to enjoy on summer nights. €€€

SHOPPING

Shakespeare C/Lagasca 69, one block west of the Turismo; ☎ 662 258 642. Useful secondhand bookshop; they will also take any books you wish to offload in part exchange.

Ancient ruins around San Pedro

There are three remarkable **ancient ruins** in the vicinity of San Pedro. Outside the limited opening hours you can get a partial sight of the **Roman villa** and **Visigothic basilica** from behind their fences. The **Roman baths** however, now lie inside a gated *urbanización* and are inaccessible without visiting through a pre-booked guide, although the exterior can be viewed from the beach. There's a possibility that the opening hours may be extended in the future (and entry allowed to the Roman baths); enquire at the San Pedro Turismo for the most up to date news. Unfortunately, there is no public transport to any of the sites so your own transport or the use of a tour guide is pretty much essential.

Roman villa (Villa Romana de Río Verde)

Río Verde, Puerto Banús • July & Aug Fri–Sun 11am–1pm; Sept–June Thurs 11am–1pm • Free

Four kilometres back along the road east to Marbella are the remains of a **Roman villa** at Río Verde. To get here from San Pedro, pass the turn-off for Puerto Banús and, after crossing the river, take a right before the *Puente Romano Hotel* and follow the signs. Constructed in the late first or early second century, the villa has rooms decorated with an unusual series of black and white **mosaics** depicting not classical themes or intricate designs as elsewhere, but everyday kitchen equipment. The kitchen utensils are a delight, and the flipflops portrayed by the door are evidence of the Roman custom of leaving one's footwear outside the *triclinium*, or dining room. One of the mosaic's amphorae is so accurately portrayed that its style has helped to date the villa almost precisely. Note also the hanging fowl and fish, ready for the pot.

Visigothic Christian basilica (Basilica Paleocristiana)

C/Las Flores s/n • July & Aug Fri–Sun 11am–1pm; Sept–June Fri 11am–1pm • Free

The sixth-century **Visigothic Christian basilica** of Vega del Mar lies close to the sea at the bottom of the Avenida del Mediterráneo, the main road from San Pedro towards the coast. Take the last road on the right before the beach and you'll come to the railed-off site in the midst of a stand of eucalyptus trees. It's one of the most important Visigothic monuments on the peninsula; the remains enable you to clearly make out a rectangular basilica with a double apse, unique in Spain. Large boulders cemented with lime-mortar were used in its construction along with still-visible brickwork at the corners. A wonderful **baptismal font** is especially well preserved and was designed to be deep enough for total immersion, the custom of the time.

In and around the basilica is a cemetery of some two hundred tombs (which yielded a wealth of artefacts now in Marbella and Madrid museums), most with the head to the north, the orientation of the church. Note the graves lined with marble, evidence of social stratification even in death.

Roman bathhouse (Termas Romanas)

Playa Linda Vista • July & Aug Fri–Sun 11am–1pm; Sept–June Fri 11am–1pm • Free

The third site, the **Roman bathhouse** of Las Bovedas, lies a little way west of the Visigothic basilica, almost on the beach. Leave any transport at the *chiringuito* and walk the 50m along the beach to the site. The substantial remains belong to an octagonal third-century Roman baths. Seven chambers, which would have served as a series of heated steam rooms, surround the well-preserved central bath (parts of the underfloor hypocaust system are visible). Above the central pool was a skylight surrounded by a roof terrace. Because the complex was constructed with a special lime – which, when mixed with sand and pebbles from the beach, set to a granite-like hardness – the building has defied the elements impressively.

Estepona

West of San Pedro the *autopista* heads inland before turning west, while the coast road is littered with more depressing *urbanizaciones* bearing names such as Picasso or – taking irony to the limit – Paraíso (paradise). Should you feel the urge to stop, **ESTEPONA**, 17km beyond San Pedro, is about the only good bet, a more or less Spanish resort with much of its identity still intact. Lacking the enclosed hills that give Marbella character, it is at least developed on a human scale, while the hotel and apartment blocks which sprawl along the front are restrained in size and free of garish clutter. The seafront too is attractive, with a promenade studded with flowers and palms, and an expansive EU-blue-flagged stretch of sand which is also home to the **Costa Natura**, the Costa del Sol's oldest nudist beach.

1

The town behind the seafront has plenty of character, while the **old quarter** has some charming corners with cobbled alleyways and two delightful squares, the Plaza Las Flores and Plaza Arce plus more than twenty giant murals (ask for a map at the Turismo). Calle Terraza bisects the centre; around here you'll find most of the town's eating and drinking options, especially along the pedestrianized Calle Real. To the west of the centre, the modern **Plaza de Toros** is home to three interesting museums, while on the coast the **Puerto Deportivo** is a daintier version of Marbella's, with its few bars and clubs only becoming really animated at weekends.

The daily **market** – a good place for picnic supplies – is located in Plaza Cañada, to the west of Calle Terraza. A street market is held in the Puerto Deportivo each Sunday morning. The town's **Feria Anual** is held the first week of July and is one of the best on this stretch of coast. Events continue day and night for a week, when whole families of *esteponeros* parade in their flamenco-style finery.

The museums of the Plaza de Toros

2km west along the seafront to the Puerto Deportivo and then turn inland • Tues–Sun 9am–4pm • Free

From May onwards, the town's **bullfighting** season gets under way in the modern **Plaza de Toros** on the west side of town, reminiscent of a Henry Moore sculpture. The building is also home to three museums: the **Museo Etnográfico** (folk museum), **Museo Paleontológico** and the **Museo Taurino** (bullfighting). The folk museum showcases many artefacts from Estepona's agricultural and maritime past; the paleontology museum houses a collection of fossils and seashells millions of years old; and the Taurino museum – whatever your position on bullfighting – gives you some idea of the importance of *taurinismo* in Andalucian culture. There are the usual trophies and photos of past big names as well as (in the centre of the museum itself) the actual *toril* (bull pen) from where the raging bulls are released into the adjoining ring during *corridas*.

Museo Ángel Garó and Archeological Museum

Antigua Casa Consistorial, Pza de las Flores • Mon 9am–3pm, Tues–Fri 9am–8pm, Sat 10am–1.30pm & 4–8.30pm • Free

Housed in the nineteenth-century former Ayuntamiento (the same building as the Turismo), the **Museo Ángel Garó** is a privately assembled art collection by the Spanish actor Ángel Garó and contains eighteenth-century works by Del Piombo and Pedro de Mena, as well as more modern paintings and drawings by Denis Belgrano, García Lorca, Rafael Alberti and Picasso. The same building also contains the town's **Archeological Museum** with finds from the Phoenician, Roman and Moorish periods.

Selwo Adventure Park

6km east from Estepona (signed from A7 and the Autopista del Sol and served by regular buses from all the major Costa del Sol resorts) • July & Aug daily 10am–8pm (see website for rest of year opening times) • Charge, discount tickets frequently available from the Estepona Turismo and the website • Ⓦ selwo.es

East of town, the **Selwo Adventure Park** is a landscaped zoo, home to some two thousand-plus resident animals who are allowed to roam around in semi-liberty, complete with re-creations of African Zulu and Maasai villages (you can even stay overnight here in an expensive "African-style" hut with all mod cons – see the website for details).

ARRIVAL AND INFORMATION
ESTEPONA

By bus The bus station is on Avda de España, west of the centre behind the seafront.
Destinations Cádiz (3 daily; 2h 45min); Málaga (7 daily; 1h 30min); Málaga Airport (6 daily; 1h 15min); Marbella

(7 daily direct; 30min).
Turismo Town and mural maps are available at the Turismo (Mon–Fri 9am–3.30pm, Sat 10am–2pm; ☎ 952 802 002) on the focal Pza de las Flores.

ACCOMMODATION

Camping Parque Tropical 6km east of town on the N340 (km162); Ⓦ campingparquetropical.com. The

nearest campsite to Estepona, set a few hundred metres back from the beach in a former tropical garden with plenty of shade, plus a spectacular conservatory-pool and restaurant. €

Casa de la Borrega C/Correo Viejo 9; ⓦ casalaborrega. com. Functional, clean apartments sleeping two to four and named after the Andalucian provinces in restored sixteenth-century mansion, north of Pza de la Flores. €€€

Costa Natura 4km west of town; ⓦ costanatura.com. Estepona's nudist beach and naturist holiday village is located a short bus ride from the centre in a complex with bars, restaurant, pool and gardens. Accommodation is in studios and apartments. Studios come with sun terrace, a/c, TV and kitchenette, while apartments (sleeping up to four)

are duplex, have a larger terrace and add a *salón*, breakfast bar and kitchen. Studios €€, apartments €€€

Hostal La Malagueña C/Castillo s/n, close to Pza de Las Flores; ⓦ hlmestepona.com. Comfortable, welcoming and reliable pensión, offering a/c en-suite rooms with TV, plus a roof terrace solarium. Own car park. €

Hotel Mediterráneo Avda de España 68, on the seafront to the east of C/Terraza; ⓦ mediterraneo-estepona.com. Functional but good-value seafront hotel, where a/c en-suite rooms come with TV and (most) balcony sea views. Own (pay) car park or can advise on street parking nearby. €€

EATING AND DRINKING

RESTAURANTS

★ **La Escollera** Puerto Pesquero; ☎ 952 806 354. Beneath the lighthouse in the fishing harbour adjoining the Puerto Deportivo, this is a vibrant, very reasonably priced place for excellent sea-fresh fish and mariscos. In addition to a great tapas bar there's also a wonderful sea-view terrace restaurant. It's best to book at weekends. €€€

El Palangre C/Cristóbal Colón 20, slightly east of the Pza de Toros; ⓦ restauranteelpalangre.com. Another top-notch, Michelin-recommended fish restaurant. A house special is *arroz a la marinera con cigalas* (seafood paella with langoustines). Other dishes include a wide range of fish and *mariscos*, plus Galician-style octopus. There's also a pleasant sea-view terrace for warmer days. €€€

Restaurante El Gavilán del Mar C/Correo 1, actually on Pza Arce; ☎ 952 802 856. A decent place for seafood (meat dishes are also on offer), specializing in paella, and with a terrace on this charming square. Try their *sardinas asadas* (grilled sardines) or a *zarzuela* (fish casserole), which is enough for two. €€€

Los Rosales C/Damas, just north of Pza de Las Flores; ☎ 952 792 945. Superb fish restaurant which also has *mariscos*. The fried fish is outstanding, as is the fresh tuna caught off Tarifa in Cádiz. Has a small street terrace. €€

CAFÉS AND TAPAS BARS

La Casa del Rey C/Raphael 7, southwest off Pza de las Flores; ☎ 951 965 414. A good tapas and *raciones* bar with a long wine list (tasting sessions take place weekly Oct–May). €€

La Esquina del Arte C/Villa 8, next to the clock tower to the west of the centre ☎ 951 965 718. Impressive line-up of fifty-odd *pintxos* (tapas on sticks) plus main dishes and paella on Sundays. Staff recommend pairing wines. Mon & Wed–Sun 1pm–midnight. €€

La Palma C/Terraza 57; ⓦ restaurantebarlapalma.com. Busy tapas and *raciones* bar specializing in excellent fresh fish and *mariscos*, though some meat is served too. Try the *gambas pil-pil* (prawns with chilli and garlic) or *boquerones fritos* (fried anchovies). €€€

NIGHTLIFE

Peña Flamenca C/Fuerzas Armadas s/n; ⓦ bit.ly/pena-flam. In the north of town, this place puts on the genuine stuff with both dance and song; sessions are open to all. The Turismo can provide more information or consult the Facebook page. Good tapas bar.

La Pepa Puerto Deportivo 29-30; ☎ 646 136 691. One of the Puerto's busiest bars with an extensive terrace overlooking the port and coast. Good cocktail menu. One of many other bars along this strip.

Casares and around

The greyish coast west of Estepona is punctuated with watchtowers used by peoples as diverse as the Phoenicians, Romans and Arabs to protect themselves from pirate attacks. There's little reason to stop along here, although it's worth detouring to **CASARES**, 18km inland from Estepona. One of the lesser known of Andalucía's White Towns, it's a beautiful place, clinging tenaciously – and spectacularly – to a steep hillside below a castle and attracting its fair share of arty types and expatriates. The village is reputed to take its name from Julius Caesar, who is said to have used the still-functioning sulphurous springs at nearby Manilva (see page 118) to cure a liver complaint. There are also the ruins of an impressive Moorish **Alcázar** (built on Roman foundations) offering spectacular views as far as Gibraltar on clear days. Most *andaluces* know of Casares today as the birthplace of **Blas Infante Pérez de Vargas** (1885–1936), the father of "Andalucian nationalism" and designer of Andalucía's green and white flag, based on historical examples. When Franco's forces took this area early in the Civil War he was summarily executed as a regional autonomist and libertarian socialist, both anathema to the new order. His birthplace now houses the *turismo*.

Apart from an excellent museum, there's little in the way of sights, but it's satisfying enough simply to wander around, losing yourself in the twisting, narrow white-walled streets – another vestige of the Moorish period. Flanked by an eighteenth-century church, the central plaza is a good place to sit and have a drink, cooled by breezes off the sierra. In addition, the surrounding hill country, richly wooded with cork oaks and pine as well as stands of *pinsapo*, the rare Spanish fir, offers a verdant contrast with the arid plains below and is fine **walking** terrain, with plenty of dirt tracks to follow winding through the folds of the Sierra Bermeja. The tourist office (see page 118) gives out a free hiking booklet describing a number of routes (in English and Spanish) between 2km and 14km.

Centro Cultural Blas Infante

C/Villa s/n, to the south of the central Pza de España • Wed–Fri: July & Aug 9.30am–2pm; Sept–June 10.30am–2.30pm & 4–6pm • Charge

At the top of a punishing hill, in one of the gates of the ancient *alcázar* that once stood here, the delightful **Museo de Etnohistoria** (history and folk museum) showcases fascinating displays of Roman artefacts and jewellery found on the site. The folk section of the museum has a wealth of items relating to Casares's agricultural past and cultural traditions, the highlight being a wonderful room dedicated to the role of the cinema in Casares, including the picture house's original projector along with various photos relating to the cinema and its history.

Roman Sulphur Baths of Manilva

Heading west out of the village brings you to a junction on the A377. If you've got your own transport you can turn right here to make the 16km detour to the pretty White Town of Gaucín (see page 119). Alternatively, turning left (south) along the same road takes you to the remarkably well-preserved **Roman sulphur baths** (open access). To get here, follow the signs for 3km from Manilva where the road passes beneath a spectacular viaduct carrying the latest extension of the Autopista del Sol. Park your vehicle here and take the path under the viaduct signed "Venta Los Alamos – Charca de la Mina." Following this path, on your right you'll soon pass the *venta*, reached by a bridge over the river. Continuing along the same path for a further 150m, at the top of a rise, the small chapel of San Adolfo comes into view. It's normally locked, but if you happen to arrive on the last weekend in May it will be the focus of a huge *romería* and beanfeast, when the village of Manilva turns out en masse to honour its patron saint.

In quieter times you'll need to keep ahead beyond the chapel to where, some 300m further, a flight of steps descends right to the baths – now under a whitewashed concrete canopy. Here you'll need to don a bathing suit – or perhaps not if there's no one around – and plunge inside to see the original Roman stonework. One dubious souvenir you'll take away from the place is a sulphurous stench, which is guaranteed to cling to your swimwear for weeks.

ARRIVAL AND INFORMATION

CASARES AND AROUND

By bus Twice-daily buses (Mon–Sat) leave for Casares from Estepona at 1pm (2pm Sat) & 6.45pm (7.30pm Sat); return 7.45am & 4pm (8.30am & 4.30pm Sat); 55min; Ⓦ avanzabus.com. So if you're without transport, you'll have a very brief visit or an overnight stay.

Turismo The Turismo, downhill from Pza de España at C/ Carrera 51 (July & Aug daily 9.30am–2pm; Sept–June Mon– Fri 10.30am–2.30pm & 4–6pm, Sat & Sun 10am–2.30pm;

☎ 952 895 521), can provide a village map and information about activities such as walking and horse riding; it also has a list of *casas rurales* to rent for longer stays.

ACCOMMODATION

Las Casitas de Mi Abuela C/Barrio Bajo 58, close to the tourist office; ☎ 658 544 810. Two excellent apartments with all mod cons including heating, wood-burning stove and fully-equipped kitchen, sleeping up to four; ideal for longer stays. €€

Hotel Casares C/Coperas 52, signed from the main square, Pza de España; ☎ 952 895 211. Currently the village's only hotel accommodation, this is a welcoming place to stay and offers a/c rooms with TV, balcony and views. Breakfast is included. €€

EATING AND DRINKING

La Bodeguita del Medio Pza de España s/n; ☎ 952 894 036. Sited on the main square this is the village's most serious bar, offering a combination of *andaluz* and Mediterranean cuisine as well as *casareño* specialities. They have a delightful roof terrace overlooking the square. €€

The Forge Restaurant 3km out of Casares on the Estepona road; ☎ 952 895 120. Charming and high-quality restaurant in a nineteenth-century farmhouse run by British proprietors (the Forges). You can eat in a homely dining room or on a leafy terrace, and an eclectic menu includes *ajo blanco* (almond soup), *kleftiko*, vegetarian *papoutsaki* (stuffed

aubergine) and Morrocan-style chicken. €€€

Mesón Los Claveles C/Arrabal 1, by the church; ☎ 952 894 095. Very friendly, family-run bar and restaurant offering economical *platos combinados*, *tortilla*, salads, and in summer, a delicious gazpacho *casareño* soup. Also good for breakfasts of local bread and *tortas fritas con miel* (local cakes with honey). €€

Venta El Mirador On the exit road in the direction of Gaucín; ☎ 610 345 182. Very good *venta*, with a good choice of local dishes and a pleasant location with great views of the village and coast. House specials are *morcilla de chivo* (black pudding) and *venado en salsa* (venison). €€

The White Towns

Though Andalucía boasts many pretty *pueblos blancos*, the best known are the group of **White Towns** (see map on page 215) – unfeasibly picturesque places, each with its own plaza, church and tavern – set in the roughly triangular area between Málaga, Algeciras (see page 202) and Seville (see page 242). At their centre, in a region of wild mountainous beauty, is spectacular **Ronda**, very much the transportation hub and a great attraction in its own right. From Ronda, almost any route north or west is rewarding, taking you past a whole series of lovely little villages, among cherry orchards and vines, many of them fortified since the days of the Beconquist – hence the mass of "de la Frontera" suffixes. Of these, Arcos de la Frontera (see page 231), a truly spectacular White Town perched on a high limestone spur, comes close to Ronda as the best place to spend a few days in the region, one of several white towns in Cádiz province (see page 138).

ARRIVAL AND DEPARTURE   THE WHITE TOWNS

By bus and train There are several possible approaches to Ronda from the coast. From Málaga, most of the buses to Ronda follow a rather bleak route, heading along the coast to San Pedro de Alcántara before turning into the mountains along the A397. The train ride up from Málaga is better, although only one of the two daily services is direct (1hr 50min). Easily the most rewarding approach, however,

is the route up from Algeciras (see page 202) via Gaucín by train (5 daily; 1hr 30min).

On foot If you've time and energy, the Algeciras via Gaucín route is feasible as a four- or five-day walk – worth going out of your way to experience. En route, you're always within reach of a river and there's a series of hill towns, each one visible from the next, to provide targets for the day.

Gaucín

Beyond Jimena the A405-A369 climbs for 23km through cork oak woods and olive groves to reach **GAUCÍN**, just beyond the Málaga border. Almost a mountain village and perched on a ridge below yet another Moorish fort, Gaucín commands tremendous

1

views and makes a fine place to stay. The village has a prosperous air sustained by a long-standing community of British and other European emigrants, many of whom are artists. Art Gaucín with exhibitions and open studios takes place at weekends in May and June (⌨ artgaucin.com).

The station serving Gaucín is actually 13km away at **El Colmenar** on the Algeciras–Ronda line. This village – in reality a hamlet – consists of little more than a couple of rows of houses, bars and restaurants each side of the railway line and station.

Castillo del Aguila

C/de Gaucín s/n • Wed–Sun: April–Oct 10.30am–1.30pm & 6–8pm; Nov–March 10.30am–1.30pm & 4–6pm • Free

The village's only attraction of any note is the **Castillo del Aguila**, a Moorish castle reached by a track at the eastern end of the village. From the battlements there are great views across terrain studded with olive, oak and chestnut trees to Gibraltar and even the Moroccan coast beyond on a very clear day. Easter Sunday is always celebrated here with a fiesta and *encierro* (bull run), when beefy fighting bulls career through the streets looking for partying inebriates to get their horns into.

ARRIVAL AND DEPARTURE   GAUCÍN

By bus You can reach Gaucín by bus on weekdays with Transportes Comes (☎ 952 871 992; ⌨ tgcomes.es) from Algeciras (Mon–Fri 6am & 1pm).

By train The nearest train station is at El Colmenar, 13km distant, on the line between Algeciras and Ronda (3 trains daily in each direction; 45min). It's a 2–3hr uphill walk from here to Gaucín (there's no bus service). Alternatively, a taxi can be arranged outside the station at Bar Flores (☎ 952 153 026) or, when closed, from the *taxista* (☎ 630 226 657).

ACCOMMODATION

GAUCÍN

Hostal Moncada Next to the filling station as you come into the village from Jimena; ☎ 952 151 156. Decent en-suite rooms above a restaurant; get a room at the back for less noise plus a view of the Serranía de Ronda – now somewhat obscured by a recent housing development. €̄

Hotel Rural Fructuosa C/Convento 67; ⌨ lafructuosa. com. Near the centre, this is a charming upmarket option owned by the restaurant of the same name (see page 120). All the attractive individually styled (and differently priced) rooms come with a/c, minibar and TV, and most enjoy spectacular views. They produce their own walks leaflets and also rent out a couple of equally attractive houses in the village for longer stays (see website). Breakfast is included. €̄€̄

EL COLMENAR

★ **Ahora Casa Rural** Bda. El Colmenar, 500m downhill from the train station; ⌨ casaruralahora.com. A friendly little oasis near the train station with en-suite cabin-style rooms. There's a communal room with *chimenea* (stove), library, games and a wellbeing centre offering all kinds of alternative therapies, plus a sauna and jacuzzi. Also has its own restaurant (weekends only, with an organic *menú*, vegetarian and vegan options) and there are reductions for stays of two nights plus. €̄€̄

EATING AND DRINKING

GAUCÍN

El Ático C/Barrio Alto s/n, close to the entrance to the village coming from Jimena; ⌨ elaticogaucin.com. Pleasant restaurant with a compact international menu featuring curries as well as creative takes on Spanish and Mediterranean cuisine. Also has vegetarian options and can cater (with notice) for vegans and coeliacs. Economical snacks are on offer at lunchtime and there's a terrace with spectacular view towards Morocco and Gibraltar. Best to book. €̄€̄

Bar Paco-Pepe C/de los Bancos 3, off C/San Juan de Díos; ☎ 952 151 182. Excellent tapas and *platos combinados* are served at this homely bar with a pleasant outdoor terrace on a plazuela with spluttering fountain. Try the *croquetas* (croquettes) or equally tasty *jamón serrano*. €̄€̄

Bonissim C/Luís Armiñán 54, opposite the Hotel Rural Fructuosa; ☎ 952 151 270. Superb English-run delicatessen/shop/café that bakes breads, pastries and pies, and squeezes its own juices. Tapas are on offer too, as well as lasagne, pasta, tagines and a range of salads, all to eat in or take away. €̄€̄

La Fructuosa C/Convento 67; ☎ 617 692 784. In the same building as the *Hotel Rural Fructuosa* (see page 120), this mid-priced restaurant offers delicious traditional cooking with a Mediterranean slant. *Bombón de rabo de toro* (bull's tail stew) is a house special and the kitchen uses local *setas* (wild mushrooms) and goat's cheese in many of its dishes. €€

EL COLMENAR

Café-Bar España Avda de Santiago 44 (the main street fronting the station); ☎ 952 153 060. A friendly and good place to eat, with *platos combinados*, tapas, *raciones* and a *menú*. Also has a pleasant terrace. €€

Mesón Las Flores Opposite the station; ☎ 952 153 026.

Colmenar's main bar-restaurant is a lively place specializing in *venado* (venison) and *jabalí* (wild boar), and offering a cheap weekday *menú*. €€

Rincón del Cani C/Ruiz Zorrilla 2, behind Bar Las Flores; ☎ 952 153 179. Very good bar-restaurant, popular with locals and serving up *carnes a la brasa* (grilled meats) and a range of sierra specialities including – in season – *setas* (wild mushrooms), *alcachofas con jamón* (artichokes), *carillada* (pork cheeks) and a mean gazpacho. There's an economical weekday *menú* and they also offer a pleasant apartment, sleeping up to 4. €

Benarrabá, Algatocín and Jubrique

Five kilometres beyond Gaucín a turn-off from the Ronda road leads to the village of **BENARRABÁ**, sited amid glorious wooded hill country. If you are using this as a staging post on a hiking route to Ronda, there's useful accommodation at Jimera de Libar (see box on page 134), from where you're within striking distance of Ronda.

A couple of kilometres from Benarrabá, the village of **ALGATOCÍN** (take the road on the left – the A373 – 2km along the A369 beyond the Benarrabá turn-off) offers another possible base, while 2km further along the A369 and then right along the MA8301, **JUBRIQUE** is another attractive hill village sited on the slopes of the Río Genal valley in the heart of more picturesque *serranía* walking country. Guy Hunter-Watts's book *Walking in Andalucía* (see page 556) has an 11km circular walk from the *Hotel Rural Banu Rabbah* (see page 121), which takes in the picturesque "artists' village" of **GENALGUIACIL**, whose streets are lined with sculptures crafted from wood, iron, clay and stone.

ACCOMMODATION AND EATING   BENARRABÁ, ALGATOCÍN AND JUBRIQUE

BENARRABÁ

Bar Barroso C/Posito 16, near the Ayuntamiento; ☎ 646 849 631. In the village proper, so it's a nice way to stretch your legs if you're staying at *Hotel Rural Banu Rabbah*, this cosy bar is noted for its tapas and in particular the *cerdo ibérico* (pork) and locally cured *jamón serrano*. €€

Hotel Rural Banu Rabbah C/Sierra Bermeja s/n; ⓦ hbenarraba.com. Adopting the village's original

Moorish name, this very pleasant hotel has comfortable a/c balcony rooms with TV and stunning views, a pool and a good restaurant serving innovative and traditional dishes. Specials include *cordero al curry con couscous* (curried lamb) and *ensalada de aguacate y naranja con mostaza* (avocado and orange salad with mustard). Organic and vegetarian dishes. €€

Algatocín

ART IN GENALGUACIL

In early August Genalguacil celebrates a **cultural festival** (ⓦ genalguacil.es), whose name and format alternate every year, although its main focus always lies in a temporary exhibition of works by invited artists (Spanish and international) in the streets and on façades around the village. *Encuentros del Arte* lasts for a fortnight and centres mostly on art with a smattering of music and dance performances. *Arte Vivo* lasts for a week and includes cinema, song and workshops as well as art.

The **Museo del Arte Contemporáneo** (C/Lomilla 9; Nov–March Wed–Sun 11am–2pm & 4–9pm; April–July, Sept & Oct Fri–Sun 11am–2pm & 4–8.30pm; Aug daily 11am–2pm & 4–8.30pm; ⓦ macgenalguacil.com; charge) was created in 2004 to house art works that can't be displayed outside and to offer exhibitions all year-round. The three-storey modern museum holds a permanent collection of art works displayed during the art festivals plus regular temporary exhibitions of work by contemporary artists.

1

Complejo Turístico Salitre ⓦturismosalitre.com. Attractive complex of hotel, cabins and campsite in wooded surroundings, offering all kinds of outdoor activities as well as a full-blown rooftop observatory for use by guests. Breakfast is included in hotel. Camping €̄, cabins €̄, doubles €€

Venta Valdivia Ctra A-373 s/n, ☎952 117 067. Almost next door to *Complejo Turístico Salitre*, this leafy *venta* is renowned for its *conejo asado* (grilled rabbit) and is a hugely popular Sunday lunch venue. Also has a terrace next to the mill run. €€€

Jubrique

Camping Genal Ctra Algatocín–Jubrique km6; ⓦcampingenal.com. Efficient campsite next to the river with a very good (and inexpensive) restaurant attached.

Campsite is shaded and it also offers fully equipped bungalows in leafy surroundings. Proprietors can also give directions to the best swimming places on the river – a 10min walk. Camping €̄, bungalows €̄

Posada Mirador de Jubrique C/Algatocín s/n; ⓦposadamiradordejubrique.com. This friendly hotel offers simple rooms with ceiling fans, heating, TV and balcony views, and is another potential base for exploring the area. Also has its own bar-restaurant. They can provide information on hiking and other outdoor activities in the Genal valley and rent out mountain bikes. The proprietors will also give directions to reach the river, where there are wonderful pools deep enough to swim – and you can do a delightful "river walk" (swim shoes required) between them. €€

Ronda

Rising amid a ring of dark, angular mountains, the full natural drama of **RONDA** is best appreciated as you enter the town. Built on an isolated ridge of the sierra, it's split in half by a gaping river gorge (El Tajo, though the river itself is the Guadalevín) that drops sheer for 130m on three sides. Still more spectacular, the gorge is spanned by a stupendous eighteenth-century arched bridge, the **Puente Nuevo**, while tall, white-washed houses lean perilously from its precipitous edges.

This extraordinary setting was bound to be a magnet when mass tourism hit the nearby Costa del Sol, but the town has taken this in its stride, sacrificing little of its enchanting character to the flow of day-trippers that frequently fills the central areas to bursting point. And to escape the crowds (who anyway tend to return to the coast at sundown) there are always quieter corners to be found throughout the old Moorish quarter or, by expending a little more energy, simply walking down by the river, following one of the donkey tracks through the rich green valley.

The town divides into three parts: on the northwest side of the gorge is the largely modern **Mercadillo** quarter, while across the bridge is the old, maze-like Moorish town, **La Ciudad**, and the **Barrio de San Francisco** quarter. The astonishing El Tajo and its magnificent bridge apart, Ronda has a wealth of other sights and museums that can easily fill a couple of days. In the Mercadillo quarter stands the eighteenth-century

---

PEDRO ROMERO: FATHER OF THE CORRIDA

Born in Ronda in 1754, **Pedro Romero** is the father of the modern **bullfight**; previously bulls had been killed only on horseback with a *rejón* or spear, as a patrician pastime. However, Romero was not the first to fight bulls on foot: legend has it that this accolade goes to his grandfather Francisco Romero, who leapt into the ring when an aristocrat had been dismounted by a bull and began to distract it with his hat, delighting the crowd in the process. The hat was changed for the red *muleta*, or cape, and the bullfight was born. Once the *corrida* had been created, however, it was Pedro Romero who laid down the pattern for all future contests with his passes and moves, many still in use today, along with the invention of the almost mystical *arte* – the union of animal and man in a form of ballet. In the newly constructed Ronda ring, Romero killed over five thousand bulls and fought into his 80s, passing on to his students his soberly classical Ronda style, which is markedly different from the more flamboyant styles of Seville and Córdoba. A statue honouring Romero stands in the Alameda del Tajo.

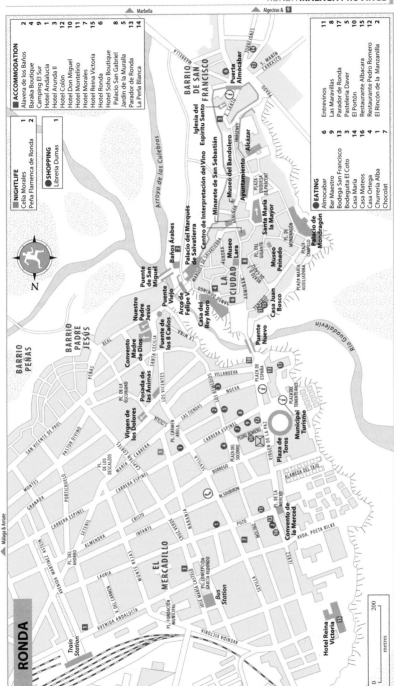

RONDA

▲ Marbella   ▲ Algeciras & 9

ACCOMMODATION
Alavera de los Baños 4
Baraka Boutique 9
Camping El Sur 1
Hotel Andalucía 3
Hotel Arunda II 12
Hotel Colón 10
Hotel Don Miguel 11
Hotel Montelirio 7
Hotel Morales 15
Hotel Reina Victoria 6
Hotel Ronda 8
Hotel Soho Boutique
  Palacio San Gabriel 5
Jardín de la Muralla 13
Parador de Ronda 14
La Perla Blanca

NIGHTLIFE
Celia Morales 1
Peña Flamenca de Ronda 2

● **SHOPPING**
Librería Dumas 1

● **EATING**
Almocabar 6
Bar Maestro 9
Bodega San Francisco 13
Bodeguita El Coto 3
Casa María 14
Casa Mateos 16
Casa Ortega 4
Churrería Alba 1
Chocolat 7
Entrevinos 11
Las Maravillas 8
Parador de Ronda 17
Pastelería Daver 5
El Portón 10
Restaurante Albacara 15
Restaurante Pedro Romero 12
El Rincón de la Manzanilla 2

1

Plaza de Toros that played a major role in the development of bullfighting, while in the *barrio* of La Ciudad stands the **Iglesia de Santa María La Mayor**, built on the site of a former mosque. Nearby, the **Palacio de Mondragón** contains some impressive remnants of Islamic artistry. From the same epoch date the remarkable **Baños Arabes**, a Moorish *hammam* or public bathhouse, one of the best preserved in Spain. Among a clutch of galleries and museums the pick is perhaps the **Museo Lara**, a fascinating and eclectic collection put together by its eponymous owner, while the **Museo del Bandolero** chronicles the history of the brigands who once roamed the surrounding sierra.

Brief history

Not surprisingly, this dramatic and dominant location attracted not only the early Celts, who named it Arunda, but Phoenicians and Greeks as well. Under Rome it became an important military bastion referred to by Pliny the Elder as Arunda Laus ("the glorious"). When the Moors later came to rule the roost here, Medina Runda was transformed and enlarged into the provincial capital of the Tarakuna district. Embellished with lavish mosques and palaces, the town ruled an independent and isolated **Moorish kingdom** until annexed by Seville in the mid-eleventh century. It then passed successively through the hands of the Almoravids, Almohads and Merinid Emirate of Morocco before ending up as a fief of Nasrid Granada in 1349. Only after a long and bitter struggle did the town finally fall to Fernando and Isabel in 1485.

Ronda is also notable for having been the birthplace of the **Maestranza**, an order of knights who laid down the rules for early bullfights performed on horseback. During the nineteenth century the town became an increasingly popular destination for Romantic travellers, epitomized by author Richard Ford, who describes being awestruck when gazing down from the bridge into El Tajo, able only to proclaim: "Well done, rock and water, by Heavens!"

La Ciudad

Ronda's oldest quarter, **La Ciudad** retains much of its Moorish street plan and a great many of its original houses, interspersed with a number of fine Renaissance mansions – an intricate maze tumbling down to the eighteenth-century **Puente Nuevo**, suspended between walls of limestone rock high above the yawning El Tajo and the Río Guadalvín far below. Spanning the river further East are the **Puente Viejo** of 1616 and the fourteenth-century single-span Moorish **Puente de San Miguel**.

Puente Nuevo

The late eighteenth-century **Puente Nuevo** bridge spans the gorge between the Mercadillo quarter and La Ciudad, allowing you the chance to peer down the walls of limestone rock into the gorge, with the river – a mere brown sliver – far away in its depths. The bridge has its own **Centro de Información** (April–Sept Mon–Fri 10am–7pm, Sat & Sun 10am–3pm; Oct–March Mon–Fri 10am–6pm, Sat & Sun 10am–3pm; charge), housed in a former prison above the central arch, with exhibits documenting the story of its construction and history. Hemingway, in *For Whom the Bell Tolls*, recorded how prisoners were thrown from the bridge to their deaths. Today the bridge and the gorge provide a much needed habitat for a large flock of choughs (members of the crow family) who glide around the rock cliffs seeking

---

RONDA EVENTS

The **Feria Goyesca** takes place in the first week in September when *corridas* are staged in the bullring with matadors wearing eighteenth-century costumes. **Semana Santa** (Holy Week) is also a wonderful spectacle in Ronda.

perches. Birdwatchers should look out for the lesser kestrels, nesting in and launching themselves from beneath the bridge and the nearby Alameda park, while, lower down, crag martins can be spotted.

Palacio del Marqués de Salvatierra

C/Marqués de Parada

Crossing the Puente Nuevo into La Ciudad and following Calle Santo Domingo will eventually take you to the **Palacio del Marqués de Salvatierra**, a splendid Renaissance mansion with an oddly primitive, half-grotesque frieze of Adam and Eve on its portal together with the colonial images of four Peruvian Indians; the house is still used by the family and so isn't open to the public.

Baños Árabes

Cuesta de Santo Domingo s/n · Mon–Fri: April–Oct 10am–7pm; Nov–March 10am–6pm; all year Sat & Sun 10am–3pm · Charge, free on Tues from 3pm · ☎ 656 950 937

Close to Puente de San Miguel on the southeast bank of the river, are the distinctive hump-shaped cupolas and bizarre glass roof-windows of the wonderfully preserved thirteenth-century **Baños Árabes** (public bathhouse), with remarkable star-shaped windows set in a barrel-vaulted ceiling and beautiful octagonal brick columns supporting horseshoe arches. An aqueduct carried water from the nearby river to the bathhouse complex, which was formerly surrounded by plant-filled gardens. One room shows a film on the history of the baths every fifteen minutes.

Minarete de San Sebastián

Heading uphill from the Baños Arabes, following Calle Marqués de Salvatierra, brings you to the **Minarete de San Sebastián**, a surviving tower from a fourteenth-century mosque which was razed to make way for the church of San Sebastián. This also fell into disrepair and was demolished, leaving the minaret standing alone.

Museo del Bandolero

C/Armiñán 65 · Mon–Fri & Sun 11am–7.30pm, Sat 11am–8pm · Charge · ⊕ museobandolero.com

The **Museo del Bandolero** is largely devoted to celebrating the Serranía's illustrious, mainly nineteenth-century bandits who preyed on richer travellers and merchants and were greatly feared. The museum includes displays of their weapons and possessions as well as tableaux and audiovisual presentations.

Museo Lara

C/Armiñán 29 · Daily 11am–7pm · Charge · ⊕ museolara.org

On the main street which bisects La Ciudad, the interesting **Museo Lara**, contains the eclectic lifetime collection of *rondeño* Juan Antonio Lara, a member of the family who own and run the local bus company of the same name. An avid collector since childhood, Señor Lara has filled the extensive museum with a fascinating collection of antique clocks, scientific instruments, pistols and armaments, musical instruments and archeological finds, as well as early cameras and cinematographic equipment, all superbly displayed.

Santa María La Mayor

Pza Duquesa de Parcent · Mon–Sat: April–Sept 10am–8pm; Oct–March 10am–6pm; Sun 10am–12.30pm & 2–8pm (until 6pm Oct–March) · Charge · ☎ 952 874 048

At the centre of La Ciudad in Ronda's most picturesque square stands the cathedral church of **Santa María La Mayor**, originally the town's Friday Mosque. Externally it's a graceful combination of Moorish, Gothic and Renaissance styles, with a double gallery overlooking the square and the belfry built on top of the old minaret. Climb this to reach the rooftop walkway from where you get magnificent views of the town

1

and countryside. Inside, the church itself is sombre and dull but you can see an arch covered with Arabic calligraphy, and, in front of the current street door, a part of the old Arab *mihrab*, or prayer niche.

Museo Joaquín Peinado

Pza del Gigante • Mon–Fri 10am–5pm, Sat 10am–3pm • Charge • Ⓦ museojoaquinpeinado.com

To the rear of the cathedral, the **Museo Joaquín Peinado** displays the works – influenced by Cézanne and Picasso – of *rondeño* artist Joaquín Peinado (1898–1975), a Paris contemporary and close friend of Picasso in the 1920s. The museum's seven rooms display a varied selection of his output, with room 6 ("Nudes and Erotica") featuring paintings in a similar style to Picasso, particularly the ink wash entitled *Desnudo acostado*. The museum is housed in the Palacio de Moctezuma, a former aristocratic mansion with two fine patios.

Palacio de Mondragón

Pza de Mondragón • Mon–Fri: April–Sept 10am–7pm; Oct–March 10am–6pm; Sat & Sun (all year) 10am–3pm • Charge • ☎ 952 870 818

A short distance west from Santa María La Mayor is the most important of Ronda's palaces, the fourteenth-century **Palacio de Mondragón**. Probably the royal palace of the Moorish kings, following the *Reconquista* it was much altered in order to accommodate Fernando and Isabel. Inside, three of the patios preserve original stuccowork and mosaics and there's a magnificent carved wood ceiling; the palace also houses a **museum** covering local archeology and aspects of Moorish Ronda, in particular burial practices relating to the recently discovered cemetery outside the walls (see page 126). From a restored Mudéjar courtyard there's a fine **view** over the Tajo towards the Serranía de Ronda.

Alcázar

On Calle Armiñan, near the southern end of La Ciudad, are the ruins of the **Alcázar**, once impregnable until razed by the French in 1809 and now partially occupied by a school.

Iglesia del Espíritu Santo

Mon–Sat 10am–2pm & 4–7pm • Charge • ☎ 952 872 246

If you walk downhill along Calle Armiñán, close to the Barrio de San Francisco you'll pass the sixteenth-century **Iglesia del Espíritu Santo**, a fine sandstone church with an elegant vaulted interior, constructed at the behest of King Fernando in 1485 and finished twenty years later.

Puerta de Almocábar

Beyond the Iglesia del Espíritu Santo lies the town's principal Moorish gate, the magnificent **Puerta de Almocábar**, leading into the Barrio San Francisco. Deriving from the Arabic *al maqabir* (cemetery) it would have led to the burial grounds which – following the Roman practice – were always located outside the walls. In 1485, the Christian conquerors, led by Fernando, passed through this gate to claim the town. The adjoining arch of **Puerta de Carlos V** was constructed during the reign of Fernando's successor, the Habsburg emperor.

El Mercadillo

When Ronda was retaken from the Moors in 1485, the impoverished governors imposed such heavy taxes on all goods and foodstuffs entering it that the merchants set up their own quarter outside La Ciudad to avoid paying them. This area, **El Mercadillo**, has effectively become the centre of the modern town, and the buildings around the focal Plaza de España include a stylish *parador* (see page 129) – the

1

former Ayuntamiento – overlooking the Tajo. A path, the **Paseo Blas Infante** (and its continuations the Paseo O. Welles and Paseo E. Hemingway) at the rear of the *parador*, can be followed along the edge of the Tajo northwards to the Alameda del Tajo park (see page 127) and the *Hotel Reina Victoria* (see page 129) and offers fine **views** towards the Serranía de Ronda.

Plaza de Toros

Bullring and museum open daily: April–Sept 10am–8pm; Oct–March 10am–6pm • Charge • ☎ 952 874 132

El Mercadillo's major monument is the **Plaza de Toros**, the oldest, one of the largest and certainly the most venerated bullring in Spain. Opened in 1785, it became the stage upon which the father of the modern bullfight, Pedro Romero, laid down the rules of fighting bulls on foot (see box, page 122). Once you've passed through the elaborate Baroque doorway, it's possible to wander around the arena with its unusual stone barriers and an elegant double tier of seats supported by stone columns.

The artist Goya made a number of paintings here of the *matadores* in action, and each September in a tribute to Goya and Romero the *corrida goyesca* is staged, with fighters garbed in eighteenth-century-style gear similar to those in the paintings.

La Bola and Plaza del Socorro

A short distance along the pedestrianized **Carrera Espinel** (known colloquially as "**La Bola**" by *rondeños*), the Mercadillo *barrio*'s main thoroughfare and shopping street, the picturesque **Plaza del Socorro** opens to the left. The pedestrianized square is a favourite spot with *rondeños*, especially on summer nights, when they gather to chat on the terraces of the numerous bars and restaurants. The northern end is overlooked by the **Círculo de Artistas**, a fine eighteenth-century *casa señorial* mansion, now superbly restored as the town's *casino*. The doorman usually won't object to you stepping inside to have a look at the building's delightful patio.

Alameda del Tajo

To the north of the Plaza de Toros lies the **Alameda del Tajo**, a pleasant public park completed in the early nineteenth century with views towards the Serranía de Ronda. The garden – filled with mature plane trees offering welcome shade in summer – is said to have been laid out at no cost to the local council, the funds raised by fines on those using "obscene language in public, thereby causing a scandal".

Convento de la Merced

Pza de la Merced • Church Daily 10.15am–1.15pm & 5–6.45pm; the same opening times apply to view the hand of Santa Teresa and purchase dulces • Free • ☎ 952 872 965

Slightly north of the Alameda lies the elegant Renaissance Carmelite **Convento de la Merced**, its main door flanked by two great palms. Beyond lies an impressively large triple-naved church built in sandstone. The convent (closed to visitors) is home to the **hand of Santa Teresa**, one of Spain's most venerated saints. When Teresa died her incorrupt remains (confirming sainthood) were distributed among the Carmelite order (which she had reformed) and Ronda got the left hand. At the end of the Civil War, General Franco, a devoted admirer of the saint, seized the hand and slept with it by his bedside until he died in 1975, after which it was returned to the convent in 1976.

Beyond a doorway at the end of the short street to the left of the church, the nuns sell their *dulces* via a *turno* (dumb waiter): *pan rondeño* and *magdalenas* are specialities. British chef Jamie Oliver visited the shop in one of his TV programmes in 2010 and raved about the quality of the convent's cakes and buns, which he described as "little drops of heaven".

Centro de Interpretación del Vino

C/González Campos 2-8 • Mon–Thurs & Sat 10.30am–7pm, Fri 11am–6pm, Sun 11am–3.30pm • Charge • ⊛ museodelvinoderonda.com

1

In the heart of La Ciudad Nueva, the **Centro de Interpretacíon del Vino** chronicles the history of wine-making in Ronda (currently enjoying a revival). It offers a tasting session and occupies a restored Ronda townhouse, once part of a Moorish palace, with a fine patio and remains from the Romans and Moors, including the wine cellar. There's also a shop selling local wines.

Hotel Reina Victoria
C/Jerez 25

From the Convento de la Merced, it's a short walk to the **Hotel Reina Victoria**, built by an English company in the first decade of the last century to house British visitors, many of whom came from the military base at Gibraltar. The Austrian poet Rainer Maria Rilke put up here in 1913, and as a mark of honour his room (no. 208) was left exactly as when he departed, including his hotel bill. Times have changed, however, and a century later the hotel's new proprietors decided to bring the room back into service. Various pieces of Rilkiana once displayed in the room "museum" are now to be seen in a glass case at the entry to the hotel's basement spa. The hotel's bar has a terrace – great for afternoon tea – with stunning views down the Guadiaro river valley to the distant Serranía. It's an interesting place to stay too (see page 129).

Virgen de los Dolores
C/Virgen de los Dolores s/n

A couple of minutes east from the Plaza de España lies the eighteenth-century **Virgen de los Dolores**. Though the chapel is permanently closed it has a curious porch projecting into the street. Carved on the porch's pillars are some weird, bird-like creatures, as well as others that are part beast and part human, with ropes fastened around their necks. The site of the church was formerly a gallows for condemned prisoners and this strange imagery may be a representation of these unfortunates.

ARRIVAL AND DEPARTURE
RONDA

By bus The bus station – used by all companies – is on Pza Concepción García Redondo s/n, to the north of the centre. Destinations Arcos (3 daily; 2hr 15min); Cádiz (3 daily; 3hr 15min); Jerez (3 daily; 2hr 30min); Málaga (10 daily; 1hr 45min); Marbella (6 daily; 1hr 15min); Olvera (1 daily Mon–Fri; 1hr 30min); San Pedro de Alcántara (6 daily; 1hr 5min); Setenil (1 daily Mon–Fri; 1hr 5min); Seville (7 daily; 2hr or 2hr 30min); Ubrique (2 daily; 1hr 30min); Zahara de la Sierra (2 daily Mon–Fri; 45min).

By train The train station is at Avda de la Victoria 31, off Avda de Andalucía.
Destinations Algeciras (5 daily; 1hr 40min); Málaga (1 daily; 1hr 15min).

By car For street parking your best bet is to park as far out as possible (near the train station is usually feasible) and walk to the centre, or head straight for one of the pay car parks (clearly signed). There is a large pay car park on the square facing the bus station.

INFORMATION AND ACTIVITIES

Turismo Paseo de Blas Infante s/n, facing the south side of the Pza de Toros (April–Sept Mon–Fri 10am–7pm, Sat 10am–2pm & 3–5pm, Sun 10am–2.30pm; Oct–March Mon–Fri 10am–6pm, Sat 10am–2pm & 3–5pm, Sun 10am–2.30pm; ☏ 952 187 119, ⓦ turismoderonda.es). This combined regional and municipal tourist office can provide a detailed town map with information on both Ronda and the Serranía.

Wine tours Several companies organize tours round Ronda bodegas including ⓦ ruta-vinos-ronda.com and ⓦ milamoresronda.com.

Outdoor activities Sierraventura Ronda, C/Sevilla 16 (ⓦ sierraventuraronda.com) offers all kinds of outdoor activities in and around Ronda, including guided hiking, climbing, mountain biking, canoeing, canyoning and caving. Horse riding is available with Rejertilla (ⓦ rejertilla. com). Birdwatching trips in the Serranía for beginners and experienced birders are offered by Spanish Nature (ⓦ spanishnature.com).

Post office Virgen de la Paz 20, near the Pza de Toros (Mon–Sat 8.30am–2.30pm). The town has no post boxes.

ACCOMMODATION
SEE MAP PAGE 123

★ **Alavera de los Baños** C/San Miguel s/n; ⓦ alaveradelosbanos.com. Enchanting small hotel next to the Moorish baths, with compact but elegant a/c rooms, garden and pool. Rooms at the rear (with terraces) have fine views towards grazing sheep on the hill across the river. Breakfast is included. €€€

Baraka Boutique C/Ruedo Doña Elvira 16; ⓦ barakaronda.com. Lovely Moorish-style accommodation in historic mansion on a quiet street. Welcoming en-suite rooms with access to terrace with stunning views and courtyard. €€

Camping El Sur Ctra Ronda–Algeciras km2.8; ⓦ campingelsur.com. Sited 2km out of town along the road to Algeciras, Ronda's campsite is well equipped with swimming pool, bar and a decent restaurant. You can rent bungalows here, too. It's not served by bus, so if you don't fancy the walk, take a taxi. Camping €, bungalows €€

Hotel Andalucía C/Martínez Astein 19; ⓦ hotel-andalucia.net. Functional but comfortable and good value a/c en-suite rooms (some more spacious than others) in leafy surroundings opposite the train station. €

Hotel Arunda II C/José María Castelló Madrid 10; hotelarunda2.es. Close to both train and bus stations, this is a good bet for a/c rooms with satellite TV. Plenty of parking space in own garage. €

Hotel Colón C/Pozo 1; ⓦ hcolon.es. Charming, friendly small hotel with sparkling a/c en-suite facilities and – in rooms 301 and 302 (extra charge) – your own spacious roof terrace. Breakfast is included. €

Hotel Don Miguel C/Villanueva 8; ⓦ dmiguel.com. Pleasant hotel with comfortable rooms offering spectacular views over the Tajo. Facilities include room safe, minibar, satellite TV and solarium. Own garage. €€

Hotel Montelirio C/Tenorio 8; ⓦ hotelmontelirio.com. Spectacularly sited on the edge of the Tajo, this luxury four-star hotel occupies a tastefully renovated *casa palacio* where most of the well-equipped a/c rooms have stunning views. It also manages to squeeze in a small pool and a very good restaurant, the *Albacara*. €€€

Hotel Morales C/Sevilla 51; ⓦ hotelmorales.es.

Welcoming small hotel where (small) en-suite rooms come with TV and a/c. The exterior-facing rooms have more light, the interior-facing rooms less noise. €

★ **Hotel Reina Victoria** C/Jerez 25; ⓦ cataloniahotels.com. Nineteenth-century retreat for British military visitors from Gibraltar which, although recently refurbished, has a lingering air of decaying grandeur. Ask for one of the corner rooms with a spectacular view over the Serranía de Ronda. Facilities include a pool, gardens and parking (charge). Website special offers can make this a real bargain. €€€

★ **Hotel Ronda** Ruedo Doña Elvira 12; ⓦ hotelronda.net. Charming flower-bedecked five-room (all exterior-facing) hotel in a quiet street only minutes from the Tajo bridge. The welcome is warm and the rooms are light and airy, with a/c and TV. €€

★ **Hotel Soho Boutique Palacio San Gabriel** C/José Holgado 19; ⓦ sohohoteles.com. Stunning restoration of an eighteenth-century mansion, with beautifully furnished a/c rooms, plus a wonderful five-seater cinema with tip-up seats (for guests) and a collection of classic films on DVD. Friendly proprietors. See website for excellent special offers. €€€€

Jardín de la Muralla C/Espíritu Santo 13; ☎ 952 872 764. Charming hotel in La Ciudad situated in a wonderful eighteenth-century *casa palacio* with classically furnished rooms, many overlooking a delightful leafy garden with pool. €€

Parador de Ronda Pza de España; ⓦ paradores.es. This imposing *parador* teetering on the edge of the Tajo is Ronda's flagship hotel, a superb and tasteful building (the former *Ayuntamiento*) with luxurious accommodation, pool, terrace bar, restaurant and garage. €€€€

La Perla Blanca Fuente la Higuera 11, northwest of Ronda off the A-374; ⓦ la-perlablanca.com. A couples-only B&B set in its own vineyards and gardens with pool. The seven rooms come with all sorts of luxury touches and the King Suite has a hot tub and private garden. Private free parking. €€€

EATING

SEE MAP PAGE 123

RESTAURANTS

★ **Almocabar** C/Ruedo Alameda 27, Barrio San Francisco; ☎ 952 875 977. Excellent tapas bar with an equally good mid-priced restaurant behind. Creative variations on regional dishes are served in the restaurant along with a range of salads such as the *ensalada almocabar*, including figs, cheese, pear and honey. Specials include *pâté de perdiz* (partridge) and *cochinillo* (suckling pig). Has a pleasant terrace on this square. Reservations advised. €€€

Casa María C/Ruedo Alameda 27, Barrio San Francisco; ☎ 951 083 663. Chef Elías Vega's little restaurant doesn't have a menu – he cooks whatever inspires him on the day. Excellent fish and meat dishes and – as he's a wine

aficionado – one of the best cellars in Ronda. Also offers excellent and reasonably priced tapas at lunchtime and early evening. Open for three weeks every month (the week of closure varies; phone ahead to book). €€€€

Casa Ortega Pza del Socorro 17; ⓦ restauranteortega.es. Popular restaurant run by a local family whose specials include *ensalada de tomate* (they grow their own variety: marvel at the size of them piled on the counter) and home-reared roast kid goat. €€

Las Maravillas Carrera Espinel 12; ☎ 666 219 462. Restaurant serving Mediterranean tapas, generous salads and mains on the busy outside terrace or inside in the dining area decorated with Ronda-themed art and quotes or quieter patio. Try the *salmorejo con helado de mascarpone* (thick tomato soup with mascarpone ice cream) or the *carpaccio de champiñón* (mushroom carpaccio). €€

★**Parador de Ronda** Pza de España; ⓦparadores. es. The *parador's* restaurant has an excellent choice of local and regional dishes such as *ajo blanco* (almond gazpacho), *ensalada malagueña* (Málaga fish salad) and *cochinillo asado* (suckling pig), many of them appearing on a good-value *menú*. €€€

Restaurante Albacara Hotel Montelirio, C/Tenorio 8; ⓦhotelmontelirio.com. Excellent, albeit expensive, restaurant with one of the best terraces in town enjoying a stupendous view towards the Serranía de Ronda. The top-notch kitchen puts the emphasis on Mediterranean cuisine such as *salmón relleno* de *jamón y langostinos* (salmon stuffed with ham and prawns) and *confit de pato con setas y nueces al oporto* (duck with mushrooms and walnuts). €€€

Restaurante Pedro Romero C/Virgen de la Paz 18, opposite the Pza de Toros; ⓦrpedroromero.com. Excellent restaurant with an attractive main room, serving signature dishes like *rabo de toro* (stewed bull's tail) and *magret de pato al con pera asado* (duck breast with baked pear); there's also a moderately priced *menú*. In the winter locals dine in the interior room surrounded by bullfighting memorabilia. €€€

CAFÉS

Churrería Alba Carrera Espinel 44; ☎952 871 009. Popular place serving up piping hot *churros* and delicious breakfast coffee (or chocolate) on a street terrace. Later in the day also serves tapas. €

Chocolat Carrera Espinel 9; ☎952 876 984. This chocoholic's heaven has 32 different flavours of handmade chocolate in addition to dozens of different teas and seven kinds of coffee in its café. Delicious home-made cakes and tarts, too. €€

Pastelería Daver C/Los Remedios 6; ☎952 877 163. Great *pastelería* and café with some tempting confections to go with a tea or coffee – try their *millefeuille* and *yemas* (sweet made with egg yolk and sugar). €

TAPAS BARS

Bar Maestro C/Espinel 7; ☎952 871 017. One of Ronda's oldest tapas venues, this great hole-in-the-wall establishment offers a tempting menu recited verbally by proprietor Rafael Peña. It's also a *bar taurino*, so the photos of past *torero* greats plus Ernest and Orson (all one-time customers) gaze down from the walls. Try their *pintxos de gambas* (prawns), *costillas* (ribs) or paella. €€

Bodega San Francisco C/Ruedo Alameda 32, close to the Puerta de Carlos V in the Barrio San Francisco; ☎952 878 162. A highly popular tapas bar in this atmospheric *barrio*. The tapas are excellent and there's a long list of raciones and carnes a la brasa (grilled meats). They also have a pleasant terrace under the trees on this attractive square. €€

Bodeguita El Coto C/Nueva 6; ☎606 661 538. Excellent and popular tapas bar with very cheap food and drinks. Try their *tortilla* or *rabo de toro* (braised oxtail). Has some tables outdoors on this pedestrianized street. €

Casa Mateos C/Jerez 6; ☎670 679 762. Efficient tapas bar with plenty of meat possibilities as well as good *queso*. House specials include *hamburguesa ibérica* (Iberian pork burger) and *pinchito de chivo* (kid goat kebab). €€

★**Entrevinos** C/del Pozo 2; ☎658 582 976. Tiny venue with bar stools only, but the best place in town to try Ronda wines paired with tapas. The wine list runs to nearly a hundred and there's a good choice of tapas including *fideos negros* (black noodles) and mini-burgers. Local craft beers also available. €€

El Portón C/Pedro Romero 7, off the west side of Pza del Socorro; ☎952 877 420. Favourite haunt of bullfighting aficionados; try their *rabo de toro* (oxtail) or fried fish dishes. €€

El Rincón de la Manzanilla C/Remedios 13; ☎633 611 411. Busy bar packed to the hilt with locals sampling the tempting tapas (all cold) such as *ensaladilla rusa* (potato salad) and *pastel de cabracho* (rockfish terrine). The manzanilla and sherries on tap come direct from Sanlúcar de Barrameda. €€€

NIGHTLIFE SEE MAP PAGE 123

Ronda is a good place to catch some **flamenco** and the places we review try to keep to the line of authenticity. Several flamenco events take place annually (details from the Turismo).

Celia Morales C/Calvo Asencio 8, off Carrera Espinel; ⓦceliamorales.es. Flamenco guitar concerts (charge, 1hr) by Celia, one of the Andalucia's most talented guitar players (and teachers). Mon–Sat 7.30pm.

Peña Flamenca de Ronda C/Dolores Ibarruri 8; ⓦpflamencaronda.es.tl. Regular performances and annual competitions take place at Ronda's longest-established *peña*, a block north of the bus station. Check the website for details of events.

SHOPPING SEE MAP PAGE 123

Librería Dumas C/Jerez 8, north of the Pza de la Merced; ☎952 161 133. Hiking maps of the Serranía de Ronda and Grazalema.

Around Ronda

Ronda makes an excellent base for exploring the superb countryside in the immediate vicinity, or for visiting more of the White Towns, including the unusual **Setenil de las Bodegas**, 15km away, with its curious cave-like streets. If you're attracted by ancient ruins and prehistoric caves don't miss Ronda's Roman predecessor **Acinipo** or the **Cueva de la Pileta**, whose remarkable Stone Age cave paintings are unique on the Iberian peninsula. To the west are the temptingly scenic villages of **Benaoján** and **Montejaque**, ringed by rugged limestone heights that hold numerous underground caverns such as the Cueva del Gato, a magnet for cavers.

Acinipo

Some 12km northwest of Ronda are the ruins of **ACINIPO** (also known as Ronda la Vieja), a first-century Roman town, set in the midst of beautiful hill country. Stone from the ruins of Acinipo was carted away to build up the town of medieval Ronda.

The ruins

Opening hours changes monthly, but usually open Sat & Sun 9am–2pm (check with the tourist office in Ronda in advance; English spoken) • Free • No bus services to Acinipo

The **ruins** are reached by leaving Ronda on the Arcos–Seville road (A374). After 6km turn right at a signed turn-off ("Acinipo, Ronda la Vieja") along the MA7402, following this, and its continuation the MA8406, for 16km to reach the site. Upon arrival you might have to wake the guardian up, and in return will receive a free site plan (in Spanish).

Based on Neolithic foundations, Acinipo served as a Phoenician outpost but reached its zenith in the first century AD as a Roman town. The piles of stones interspersed with small fragments of glittering marble strewn across the hillside once constituted the forum, baths, temples and other edifices of this prosperous agricultural centre (its coins depicted grapes, a major economic asset), which also had access to iron ore, marble, good building stone and fine potters' clay in close proximity.

Today only an impressive **Roman theatre** – of which just the stage backdrop and some seating survives – alludes to the importance of Acinipo. Immediately west of the theatre, the ground falls away in a startlingly steep escarpment and from here there are fine **views** towards the hill village of Olvera to the north (see page 221). For reasons not entirely clear, Acinipo declined in the third century and, in the fourth, ceded its power in the area to nearby Arunda (modern Ronda). On your way out take a look at the foundations of some recently discovered prehistoric stone huts beside the farmhouse. From here a track leads off towards Setenil de las Bodegas.

Cueva de la Pileta

Daily 10.30am–6pm; hourly guided tours (1hr) in Spanish (guide may speak some English); final tour leaves at 6pm (5pm Nov–March); advance booking through the website is essential • Charge • Ⓦ cuevadelapileta.es

Perhaps the most interesting trip out from Ronda is westwards to the prehistoric **Cueva de la Pileta**, set in a deep valley and surrounded by a spectacular wall of white rock. These caverns, with their remarkable Paleolithic paintings, were discovered by a local farmer in 1905 when hunting for guano fertilizer for his fields, and are still supervised by the same family, the Bullóns, one of whom will be your guide.

After the usual jokes, as various "cauliflowers", "castles" and a "Venus de Milo" are pointed out among the stalactites and stalagmites en route, the paintings in the depths of the caves, when you reach them, are genuinely awe-inspiring, particularly those in the central chamber. Etched in charcoal and red and yellow ochres, they depict an abundance of wildlife including fish, the *cabra hispánica* and a pregnant mare, all painted on walls which bear the scorch marks of ancient fires. Other abstract signs and symbols have been interpreted as having some magical or ritual purpose. The

1

PAINT IT (SMURF) BLUE

The Spanish tourist board has invested a lot of time and resources in attracting visitors to the sparkling White Towns and villages of the Serranía de Ronda. But in 2011 the village of **Júzcar** sensationally opted out of this conformity and painted itself **bright blue** – Smurf blue. The idea was launched by Sony Pictures when seeking a way to promote its film *The Smurfs* (*Los Pitufos* in Spanish). When Sony put the idea to the village (including the cost of the painting) almost everyone agreed – including the church and hotels. Sony contracted to return the village to its original white once the campaign was over. But in the year following the film's release some eighty thousand Smurf fans visited "Smurf Village", spending money in the bars and hotels. When Sony contacted the mayor, whose nickname is "Papa Pitufo", with the aim of restoring Júzcar to its former snow-white glory, the villagers' representative said they'd prefer to stay blue. A referendum confirmed this and the village has enthusiastically embraced its new fame with Smurf fairs, Smurf fun runs and even Smurf-themed weddings. In August 2017, however, in the light of demands from the heirs of Smurf creator Pierre Culliford for royalties, Júzcar decided to rid the village of all Smurf motifs and murals, although the façades remain bright blue. Aptly, for the Smurfs are famed for their mushroom craving, Júzcar has a long **mycology tradition** and each autumn villagers head for the surrounding hills in search of delicious fungi.

occupation of the caves, and the earliest red paintings, date from about 25,000 BC, thus predating the more famous caves at Altamira in northern Spain, through to the end of the Bronze Age. The section of the caves (and paintings) open to view is only a small part of a more massive **subterranean labyrinth**, and archeologists will be kept busy for many years to come documenting this Paleolithic art gallery. Note that no photography is allowed inside the cave, and bring a sweater as it can get chilly. Drivers leaving their vehicles at the car park should remove any valuables not locked in a secure boot.

ARRIVAL AND DEPARTURE
CUEVA DE LA PILETA

By car Take the A374 Arcos/Seville road northwest from Ronda, turning left after 14km along the MA8403 to Montejaque; the caves are a further 12km from the turn-off, beyond Benaoján.

By bus The bus from Ronda drops you in Benaoján. There's a bar at the train station where you can stock up on refreshments before the 90min (6km) walk to the caves. Follow the farm track from the right bank of the river until you reach the farmhouse (approximately 30min). From here

a track goes straight uphill to the main road just before the signposted turning for the caves.

By train Take an Algeciras-bound local train (4 daily; 20min) to the Estación Benaoján-Montejaque. From the station follow the route described in the "By bus" section above.

By taxi A taxi from Ronda costs around €50 return – get the Turismo to arrange the fare – though renting a car for a day could work out cheaper.

Serranía de Ronda

Starkly beautiful and offering some of the best walking terrain in Andalucía, the **Serranía de Ronda** is a region of great natural diversity where wooded ravines, awesome crags and vast forests of cork oaks provide abundant habitats for a rich variety of flora and fauna. The remote hamlets are reachable by road, albeit often with difficulty, but the ideal way to travel this region is with a backpack and compass, from which perspective the landscape – with whitewashed villages set among cherry orchards and vines – becomes an enchanting adventure. The Ronda tourist office (see page 128) should have details on the villages and the limited accommodation available.

ARRIVAL AND INFORMATION
SERRANÍA DE RONDA

By bus The heart of the Serranía can be reached by a daily bus (currently Mon, Wed & Fri 10.30am & 1.30pm; the

return service is on the same days in the morning) from Ronda, run by Autobuses Lara (☎ 952 872 260), passing

Parauta, Cartajima, Júzcar, Igualeja, Pujerra, Farajan and Alpandeire.

Maps The best maps of the Serranía are the 1:200,000 IGN Mapa Provincial de Málaga, complemented by the 1:50,000 IGN sheet 1065.

ACCOMMODATION AND EATING

Hotel Bandolero Avda Havaral 43, Júzcar; ⓦ hotelbandolero.es. A pleasant country hotel – Smurf blue rather than white (see box, page 132) – offering comfortable a/c rooms, with terrace and *chimenea* (wood-burning fire). It has its own bar and decent restaurant on the ground floor serving the house special, *cochinillo* (suckling pig) and other dishes such as *solomillo de venado* (venison steak) and *potaje de garbanzos con espinacas y castañas* (chickpea stew with spinach and chestnuts). Breakfast is included. €€

Hotel Casa Grande C/Barranco 76, Alpandeire; ⓦ hotelcasagrande.es. Charming hotel in a refurbished eighteenth-century mansion. The individually styled rooms come with a/c, heating and satellite TV. Breakfast is included. €€

Hotel Los Castaños C/Iglesia 40, Cartajima; ⓦ loscastanos.com. A lovely, welcoming hotel in the centre of one of the prettiest white villages. Comfortable a/c rooms (the best have views over the valley) with lots of luxury touches. The upstairs terrace has superb vistas of the chestnut forests and downstairs, there's a library, small patio and open fire. Dinner and tapas are available. Owners Di and John are extremely knowledgeable about the area and can give lots of advice about walks. Breakfast is included. €€€

Benaoján

North of the Cueva de la Pileta, **BENAOJÁN** takes its name from the Berber tribal chieftan Ojan (the village's name means "sons of Ojan"). The village was a Moorish stronghold well into Christian times, but its history goes much further back than that and evidence has been found of early human occupation hereabouts dating back some 250,000 years. Neanderthal man also tramped through this sierra landscape, while *homo sapiens* left behind the cave paintings in nearby Cueva de la Pileta (see page 131).

There are in fact two villages here: the old village around the church and a smaller hamlet clustered around the train station a good kilometre below. The old village is a pleasant enough place, gathered around its sixteenth-century church of Nuesta Señora del Rosario in Plaza San Marcos, itself built on the site of an earlier mosque.

ACCOMMODATION AND EATING   BENAOJÁN

Molino del Santo Bda Estación, near the train station, 1km below the village on the Ronda road; ⓦ molinodelsanto.com. This upmarket option is a British-run haven in a converted olive-mill with elegantly furnished rooms – many with terraces and balconies – surrounded by lush gardens and a pool. Hosts occasional art exhibitions. Breakfast is included. The mid-priced restaurant serves up very good food on a terrace beside the tumbling falls that once turned the *molino* (watermill) itself. The cuisine is a mix of *andaluz* and international, with meat, fish and vegetable dishes. Hotel and restaurant closed Nov–Feb. €€€

★ **Restaurante El Muelle** Train station; ⓦ asadorelmuelle.com. One place definitely worth seeking out is this friendly *asador*, actually on the platform at the train station in a converted *muelle* (warehouse). Its speciality is *carnes al horno de leña* (charcoal-grilled meats) including game, but fish is also served and comes up fresh on the train from Algeciras. Generous *raciones*. €€

Montejaque

Some 3km northeast of Benaoján lies the attractive *pueblo blanco* of **MONTEJAQUE**, cradled between two rocky crags. At its heart it possesses a typically Spanish square – the Plaza de la Constitución – surrounded by bars and overlooked by an elegant Ayuntamiento and the sparkling white church of Santiago. Built in the sixteenth century, with a few later modifications, this is yet another church constructed on the site of a mosque. The narrow, winding streets are a further legacy of the settlement's Moorish roots – the village's name derives from the Arabic *monte-xaquez* ("lost mountain"), probably referring to the nearby 1000m peak of El Hacho.

1

A WALK FROM BENAOJÁN TO JIMERA DE LIBAR

There's a fine, none-too-taxing **walk** from Benaoján to the attractive village of Jimera de Libar, 9km down the railway line linking the two communities. When you've reached Jimera you could take in a well-earned lunch at the *Hotel Rural Inz-Almaraz* (booking advised; see below) and return to Benaoján on the afternoon train – currently leaving Jimera station at 4.19pm (daily). Confirm current times with the Ronda tourist office or the *Hotel Rural Inz-Almaraz* or Renfe (⊛ renfe.com). The station is on the Algeciras–Granada line. It's useful to take a **map** with you (50:000 IGN sheets 1050 and 1064); alternatively, the walk is described with its own map in Guy Hunter-Watts' *Walking in Andalucía* (see page 556).

The walk begins from the *Molino del Santo* hotel (see page 133). Turn left from the hotel and head downhill until you come to a stop sign at a level crossing. Turn left along the railway line, cross over a river, and at a second level crossing turn right and cross over the railway track. The road drops before crossing the Río Guadiaro and leads up to a sign marking the official start of the walk. The route from here is fairly straightforward except for a fork just beyond a ruined farm (after 3km), where you should veer left, away from the river. At a second fork at a telegraph pole just before Jimera bear right (*not* towards Camino de Huertas Nuevas) to follow the path down to the train station of Jimera de Libar. You could stay overnight at the village's *hotel rural* or its campsite.

ACCOMMODATION AND EATING

Camping Jimera de Libar ⊛ rural-jimera.com. Located near the train station, this leafy campsite also rents out fully equipped en-suite log cabins and has a pool. Camping €, cabins €€

Hotel Rural Inz-Almaraz C/Mártires de Igueriben 18; ☎ 951 100 572. A very pleasant small hotel in the village offering comfortable rooms with TV. It also has its own decent restaurant. The proprietor will pick up guests from and return them to the train station if you ring. Breakfast is included. €

INFORMATION

Turismo Avda de Andalucía 45, the entry road into the village (Mon–Fri 10am–2pm & 5–8pm, Sat 10am–2pm; ☎ 651 304 141; ⊛ montexaquez.org). This private and well-organized tourist office has bags of information on activities in and around the village, including hiking, rock climbing and caving. They also rent out paddle tennis racquets for

MONTEJACQUE

use on the village's court. Also has a small shop where you can buy village produce including cheeses and cured meats.

App A useful app (in Spanish but self-explanatory), called simply Montejaque, for Android and iOS listing accommodation and bars in the village as well as activities and walking routes.

ACCOMMODATION

Casas de Montejaque C/Manuel Ortega 16; ☎ 952 168 120. A similar operation to the *Casitas de la Sierra*, with a range of village houses for rent. €€

Casitas de la Sierra Avda Andalucía 1; ⊛ bit.ly/ CasitasSierra. Fully equipped village houses with a minimum stay of two nights, assuming there's a property available. Also has an excellent restaurant (see page 135). €€

EATING AND DRINKING

Montejaque has more than its fair share of **tapas bars**. An annual *Ruta de Tapas* competition is held during the second week of September. Maps of competing venues are available free from the tourist office or participating bars.

El Altillo Avda Andalucía s/n; ☎ 952 167 281. On the road heading towards the main square, this is a very good tapas bar and restaurant. Try the *solomillo ibérico* or their hearty *plato de la sierra* with *pimientos* (peppers), *lomo* (pork steak), eggs and *patatas*. Also does a good value weekday *menú*. €€

Bar El Rincón Pza de la Constitución 1. In the corner of

the main square (hence the name), this is a friendly bar for tapas and *raciones*. House specials include *ensaladilla de patatas* (potato salad), *boquerones en vinagre* (anchovies) and a tasty *tortilla*. €€

Bar La Cuesta C/Pablo Ruiz Picasso 2B, round the corner from the Guardia Civil; ☎ 654 537 869. Friendly little bar with some of the cheapest tapas in town that range from simple such as *boquerones fritos* (fried anchovies) and *melva con tomate* (tuna with tomato) to more unusual like *lengua en salsa* (ox tongue). Eat in the tiny bar or outside on the pleasant terrace. €

Las Campanitas Bda Santiago 42; ☎678 535 996. Excellent little bar on the entry road coming in from Ronda. Has a pleasant patio and a lengthy tapas menu. The *croquetas caseras* (croquettes) or *chipirones a la plancha* (fried squid) are worth a try. Tues–Sun 10am–midnight. €

La Casita C/Herrera Oria 5 in the Casitas de la Sierra complex (see page 134); ⓦlacasitademontejaque.es.

This international-flavoured restaurant run by chef Max Chieppa is excellent. He collects the fish daily from Málaga harbour and serves produce such as buffalo mozzarella from Campania. The pasta is home-made as are the pizzas. House specials include salmon with samphire, onion and crispy cassava and lamb in Thai sauce. €€€

Cueva del Gato

Ctra Ronda–Benaoján • Open access

Returning to Ronda along the direct road from Benaoján (MA7401), the road follows the course of the Río Guadiaro and, after 2km, you'll pass the *Venta Cueva del Gato* (see page 135) on the left, while a short distance beyond the *venta* a signed road on the left leads down to the *Hotel Cueva del Gato* (see page 135), where you should park any vehicle.

From just beyond here a path leads to a footbridge across the Río Guadiaro and a tunnel beneath the rail line to arrive at the gaping mouth of the **Cueva del Gato**, a cave fronted by an oleander-fringed lagoon (a popular bathing spot). Continue ahead to a viewing platform overlooking a spectacular waterfall gushing out of the cave. Given the close proximity of the Cueva de la Pileta (see page 131) it seems likely that this cave, too, may well have been occupied by early humans, but no paintings have so far been discovered. The cave is open, but for those without caving experience, entry beyond the first 50m is only by permit (obtained in advance) from the authorities. For information on this contact Jean Hofer at El Chorro (see page 78).

ACCOMMODATION AND EATING	**CUEVA DEL GATO**

Hotel Cueva del Gato Ctra Ronda–Benaoján km3; ⓦhotelcuevadelgato.com. Comfortable individually styled a/c balcony rooms with TV in a stone building facing the cave; also has its own bar and restaurant. Can provide information on horse riding, caving and hiking in the Guadiaro valley. April–Oct two nights minimum stay. Breakfast is included. €€

Venta Cueva del Gato Ctra Ronda–Benaoján s/n; ⓦcuevadelgato.com. A couple of kilometres outside the village of Benaoján towards Ronda and close to the cave mouth, this locally celebrated roadside *venta* is famed for its superb *conejo casero* (grilled rabbit). They also do excellent paella and rice dishes as well as hearty mountain specials like asparagus and vegetable soups. €€€

Cádiz
province

CATEDRAL NUEVA, CÁDIZ

Cádiz province

Cádiz province is the most southerly in Andalucía, with a 200km coastline fronting both the Atlantic and the Mediterranean. Inevitably, the sea has played a large part in the area's history, and most of the dozen or so major settlements are within easy distance of a beach. The mountainous interior, dotted with numerous picturesque villages, contrasts sharply with the coast and holds two of Andalucía's largest natural parks.

Founded by the Phoenicians over three millennia ago, the provincial capital, **Cádiz**, makes up for in sheer elegance, atmosphere and sea-girthed location what it lacks in the way of irresistible sights. To the north and south of the city stretch the broad white beaches of the **Costa de la Luz**, large swathes of which have so far survived the developers' attentions and are often deserted. Resorts such as **Conil**, **Chipiona** and **Sanlúcar de Barrameda** possess a low-key charm, while at the southern tip of the coast **Tarifa** has developed into a major windsurfing and kitesurfing centre. A short distance to the east lies **Algeciras**, Andalucía's main port for sailings to Morocco, while across the Bay of Algeciras the British colony of **Gibraltar** sits beneath its daunting mountain of rock, regarded uneasily by Spaniards and as a strange, hybrid curiosity to almost everyone else.

Inland, the province offers a fascinating variety of towns and landscapes. Immediately north of Cádiz lies the famous **sherry triangle** between **Jerez**, a fine town in its own right, **El Puerto de Santa María** and **Sanlúcar de Barrameda**, with the oldest vineyards in Europe spread across thousands of acres of dazzling white chalk soil. To the east of the city stretches a landscape of rolling hills covered with clumps of walnut trees, pines and Spanish firs, while *toros bravos* – ominous black fighting bulls – graze in the shade of cork oaks at ranches around **Medina Sidonia**.

Further inland still, the northeastern corner of the province is dotted with hilltop White Towns such as **Zahara**, **Olvera** and **Arcos de la Frontera**, while the green oasis of **Grazalema**, the wettest point in Spain, is surrounded by a fine natural park, a paradise for walkers and naturalists. There's further excellent hiking south of here in the vast, rugged **Parque Natural de los Alcornocales**, home to one of the largest cork oak forests in the world.

Cádiz

Sited on a tongue of land enclosing a bay and a perfect natural harbour, with some fine beaches besides, **CÁDIZ** has – you would think – all the elements that make for an appealing place to visit. But despite an atmospheric old town and some fine museums, oddly enough the place seems unable to shake off a brooding lethargy when it comes to entertaining visitors, and the world of mass tourism has largely passed it by. Once you've got through the tedious modern suburbs on its eastern flank (now possible to avoid, by arriving via a spectacular bridge), inner Cádiz, built on a peninsula-island entered via the **Puertas de Tierra** (Land Gates) – a substantial remnant of the eighteenth-century walls – looks much as it must have done in the great days of the empire, with grand open squares, sailors' alleyways and high, turreted houses. Literally crumbling from the effect of the sea air on its soft limestone, it has a tremendous atmosphere – slightly seedy, definitely in decline, but still full of mystique. Above all, Cádiz is a city that knows how to enjoy itself. It has always been noted for its vibrant fiestas: the ancient Roman poet Martial was among the many who commented on the sensuous and swirling dances of the townswomen ("they click their Tartessian castanets

JEREZ SHERRY AND IBERIAN CURED HAM

Highlights

❶ **Cádiz** A beguiling air of genteel decay
pervades this old seaside town, definitely one of
the great cities to visit of the Spanish south. See
page 138

❷ **Jerez** Visit a sherry bodega and sample the
legendary *aperitivo*, then head to one of the
town's numerous excxellent tapas bars. See
page 172

❸ **Gibraltar** This colonial hangover with
its vast rock, sterling currency and Barbary
apes makes a bizarre contrast with the rest of
Andalucía. See page 206

❹ **Costa de la Luz** The "Coast of Light"
stretching from Tarifa to the Portuguese border

has some of the finest – and emptiest – beaches
in Spain. See page 182

❺ **Tarifa** One of the world's top windsurfing
destinations and also home to a wonderfully
atmospheric old Moorish town. See page 195

❻ **Pueblos blancos** Cádiz province's White
Towns are picturesque settlements set amid
spectacular scenery: Zahara de la Sierra, clinging
to a rocky hill below its castle, is one of the
loveliest. See page 214

❼ **Parques naturales** Get away from it all in
the natural parks of Sierra de Grazalema and
Los Alcornocales, site of Europe's largest cork
oak forest. See pages 216 & 227

HIGHLIGHTS ARE MARKED ON THE MAP ON PAGE 140

2

with a deft hand"), implying a pre-Moorish origin for flamenco. Although settled after the *Reconquista* with immigrants from the northern city of Santander, Cádiz maintains its Roman reputation for joviality with an **annual carnival** in February, universally acknowledged to be the best – and wildest – in all of Spain and a must-visit for anyone in town at this time of year.

Unlike most ports of its size, Cádiz seems immediately relaxed, easy-going, and not at all threatening, even at night. Perhaps this is due to its reassuring compactness, the presence of the sea making it impossible to get lost for more than a few blocks. Although there are plenty of sights to make a beeline for, including an excellent **museum**, a Baroque **cathedral** and some memorable church art, Cádiz is actually most interesting as a destination simply for its general convivial ambience with its inviting cafés and unassuming but excellent tapas bars, as well as for its **vernacular architecture** – elegant *mirador*-fronted facades painted in pretty pastel shades, blind alleys and ancient *barrio* backstreets, often seemingly imprisoned behind formidable fortifications.

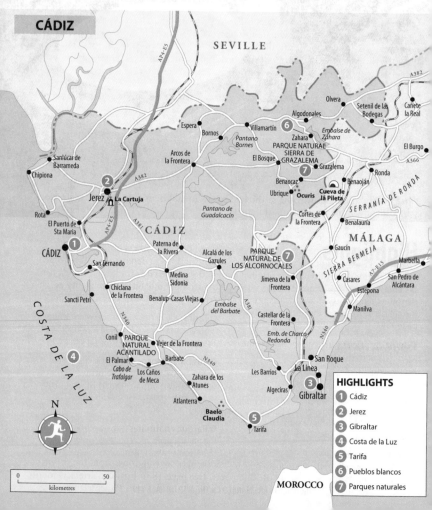

CÁDIZ

HIGHLIGHTS

1. Cádiz
2. Jerez
3. Gibraltar
4. Costa de la Luz
5. Tarifa
6. Pueblos blancos
7. Parques naturales

Brief history

Founded about 1100 BC by the Phoenicians as Gadir, a transit depot for minerals carried from the mining areas of the Río Tinto to the north, Cádiz has been one of Spain's principal ports ever since, and lays claim to being the oldest city in Europe.

Historically Cádiz served as an important base for the navies of Carthage, Rome and – following a long decline under the Moors – imperial Spain. Because of its strategic importance, Cádiz was prone to attack and the city's nose was bloodied on numerous occasions, especially by the English. Drake's "singeing of the king of Spain's beard" occurred here in 1587, followed not long after by Essex's ransacking of the port in 1596 and Nelson's bombardment in 1797.

The city's greatest period, however, and the era from which much of **inner Cádiz** dates, was the eighteenth century. Then, with the silting up of the river to Seville, the port enjoyed a virtual monopoly on the Spanish-American trade in gold and silver: on its proceeds were built the **cathedral**, public halls and offices, broad streets and elegant squares, as well as a clutch of smaller churches. This wealth spawned Spain's first modern middle class which, from early on, was free-thinking and liberal, demanding such novelties as a free press and open debate. One historian has claimed that political dialogue in Spain originated along the Calle Ancha, Cádiz's elegant central thoroughfare, where politicians met informally.

In the early nineteenth century the city made arguably its greatest contribution to the development of modern Spain, when a group of radicals set up the short-lived Spanish parliament or **Cortes** in 1812 during the Peninsular Wars. The Cortes drew up a Constitution (popularly known as "La Pepa") that upheld the sovereignty of the people against the throne and set down a blueprint for a liberal Spain that would take a further century and a half to emerge. Major celebrations throughout 2012 commemorated the bicentenary of these events and a magnificent road bridge, Spain's longest, linking the city with Puerto Real across the bay was constructed as the city's enduring tribute to its illustrious forebears. Named the "Puente de la Pepa", it was designed by Javier Manterola and is almost 4km in length with a central span hovering 70m above the water.

Loyal to its traditions, the city relentlessly opposed General Franco during the **Civil War**, even though this was one of the first towns to fall to his forces, and was the port through which the Nationalist armies launched their invasion. Later, when Franco often referred in power to the forces of "Anti Spain" he had in mind the sentiments expressed in the Cádiz Constitution of 1812, ramming home his disapproval by renaming the city's major plazas after himself and other members of the Falangist pantheon. Left-wing Cádiz merely bided its time and when democracy was restored, these landmarks regained their original designations. The city's tradition of liberalism and tolerance is epitomized by the way *gaditanos* (as the inhabitants of the city are known) have always breezily accepted a substantial **gay** community here, who are much in evidence at the city's brilliant Carnaval festivities.

Museo de Cádiz

Pza de la Mina 5 • June–Sept Tues–Sat 9am–9pm, Sun 9am–3pm; Oct–May Tues–Sat 9am–8pm, Sun 9am–3pm • Charge, free with EU passport • ⓦ bit.ly/MuseoCadiz

The **Museo de Cádiz**, housed in an imaginatively restored and extended nineteenth-century Neoclassical building (originally the Museo de Bellas Artes) on an elegant square, is an ideal place to start a tour of the city.

Archeological collection

The ground-floor **archeological collection** (information in Spanish only) includes some fine Phoenician jewellery excavated in the city and bronze figurines from the shrine of the god Melkaart on the island of Sancti Petri (see page 183). Etruscan artefacts found at the same site hint at sophisticated early trading links. Another Phoenician temple

2

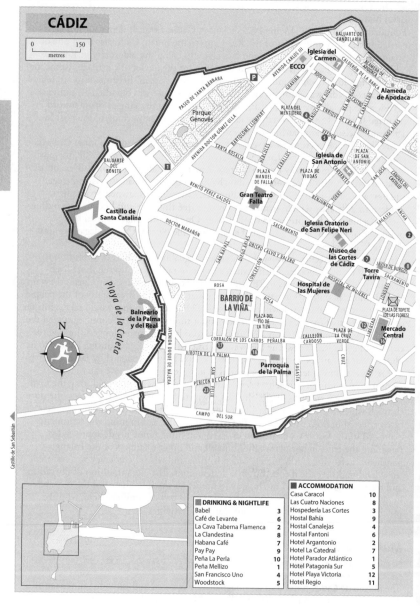

CÁDIZ

0 ————— 150
metres

BALUARTE DE
CANDELARIA

Iglesia del
Carmen

ECCO

Alameda
de Apodaca

PASEO DE SANTA BÁRBARA

AVENIDA CARLOS III

GRAVINA

BENDICIÓN DE DIOS

ADOLFO DE

VEA MURGUÍA

BUENOS AIRES

ALAMEDA DE APODACA

CALDERÓN DE LA BARCA

Parque
Genovés

PLAZA DEL
MENTIDERO

ENRIQUE DE LAS MARINAS

AVENIDA DOCTOR GÓMEZ ULLA

SANTA ROSALÍA

BARTOLOMÉ LLOMPART

HÉRCULES

CEBALLOS

VEEDOR

Iglesia de
San Antonio

PLAZA
DE SAN
ANTONIO

SAN JOSÉ

CÁNOVAS DEL CASTILLO

BALUARTE
DEL
BONETE

PLAZA
MANUEL
DE FALLA

PLAZA DE
VIUDAS

CERVANTES

BENITO PÉREZ GALDÓS

Gran Teatro
Falla

BENJUMEDA

TORRE

SAGASTA

ANCHA

Castillo de
Santa Catalina

DOCTOR MARAÑÓN

SACRAMENTO

Iglesia Oratorio
de San Felipe Neri

2

SAN RAFAEL

DIEGO ARIAS

OBISPO CALVO Y VALERO

CONCEPCIÓN

Museo de
las Cortes
de Cádiz

7

JAVIER DE BURGOS

6

Torre
Tavira

SACRAMENTO

ROSA

Hospital de
las Mujeres

HOSPITAL DE MUJERES

LONDRES

BARRIO DE
LA VIÑA

ROSA

PLAZA DE TOPETE
(DE LAS FLORES)

12

playa de la Caleta

Balneario
de la Palma
y del Real

N

PLAZA DEL
TÍO DE
LA TIZA

AVENIDA DUQUE DE NÁJERA

CORRALÓN DE LOS CARROS   PEÑALBA

CALLEJÓN
CARDOSO

PLAZA DE
LA CRUZ
VERDE

LIBERTAD

Mercado
Central

10

VIROTEN DE LA PALMA

18

SAN FÉLIX

CRUZ

Parroquia
de la Palma

SAGASTA

ABREU

PERICÓN DE CÁDIZ

23

CAMPO   DEL SUR

Castillo de San Sebastián

DRINKING & NIGHTLIFE	
Babel	3
Café de Levante	6
La Cava Taberna Flamenca	2
La Clandestina	8
Habana Café	7
Pay Pay	9
Peña La Perla	10
Peña Mellizo	1
San Francisco Uno	4
Woodstock	5

ACCOMMODATION	
Casa Caracol	10
Las Cuatro Naciones	8
Hospedería Las Cortes	3
Hostal Bahía	9
Hostal Canalejas	4
Hostal Fantoni	6
Hotel Argantonio	2
Hotel La Catedral	7
Hotel Parador Atlántico	1
Hotel Patagonia Sur	5
Hotel Playa Victoria	12
Hotel Regio	11

to Astarte/Venus on the site of the modern Bastion of Santa Catalina yielded incense burners (*quemaperfumes* – the only ones found in Spain) with Egyptian decoration and a terracotta head with striking negroid features. Two remarkable fifth-century BC **Phoenician carved sarcophagi** in white marble (one male, the other female) are also unique to the western Mediterranean. It's interesting to observe the fusion of influences here: Egyptian for the sarcophagus, Greek for the depiction of the sculpted images.

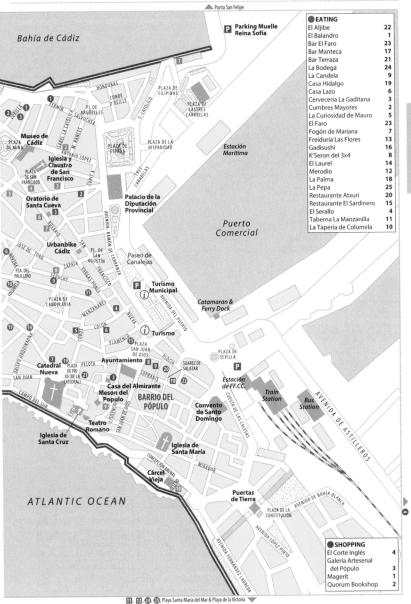

In the same section there's a display of ancient glassware – some of it of a very high standard – from the Phoenician, Greek and Roman periods.

Roman section

In the Roman section a **reconstructed boat wreck** displays various amphorae exported from Cádiz to other parts of the empire; they contained *garum* (fish sauce), *salazones*

2

CARNAVAL IN CÁDIZ

Claiming to be saltier than the carnivals of Havana and Río de Janeiro rolled into one, each February Cádiz launches into its riotous **Carnaval**, the most important and wittiest in Spain. Largely a disorganized series of fiestas in origin, it was given its present shape in the late nineteenth century by Antonio Rodríguez Martínez, now known by his nickname El Tío de la Tiza ("Chalky", after the chalk or *tiza* he used in his job) who was improbably employed as a Customs official in the port. He organized the *murgas* or bands – a major feature of Carnaval – into four categories:

Coros Groups of about thirty (formerly all male, now mixed) who tour the city on flamboyantly decorated floats singing to the accompaniment of guitars, lutes and mandolins.
Comparsas Groups of around fifteen people who parade on foot with guitars and drums.
Chirigotas Arguably the most popular with *gaditanos*, these are groups of around ten people accompanied on a reed whistle or *pito*, who tour the bars singing hilarious satirical songs about people and events in the public eye.
Trios, Cuartetos, Quintetos These smaller groups not only sing, but also act out parodies and satirical sketches based upon current events as they tour the town in costume.
Illegales Given the city's innate anarchy these bands do not compete officially (see below), but take to the streets for the sheer hell of it with whatever instruments they can lay their hands on. They include whole families, groups of friends and even collections of drunks, staggering about as they attempt to make music.

The above groups provide only the focus, however, for the real Carnaval, which takes place on the streets with everyone dressed up in costume and apparently drunk for ten whole days. The "legal" groups compete before judges in the Teatro Falla in between sessions on the streets and are symbolically awarded a *pelotazo* (good shot) for a bitingly witty composition and a *cajonazo* (a box drum) for a bomb. The various groups work at their repertoire for months before road-testing their compositions during the two weekends prior to Carnaval (but not in costume, which is regarded as bad form) at the warm-up shindigs of the Erizada (sea urchin party) or the Ostionada (oyster party), great street fiestas which feature sea-urchin and oyster tasting.

ATTENDING CARNAVAL

During Carnaval there are **no rooms** to be had in town at all unless you've made reservations well in advance. One way round this is to see it on **day-trips from El Puerto de Santa María** (a 40min ferry ride across the bay) or Seville, catching an evening train (a couple of hours' journey) and returning with the first train the next day, around 5.30am. These trains are a riotous party in themselves and, packed as they are with costumed carnival-goers from Seville, you'd be well advised to get dressed up yourself if you don't want to stand out like a sore thumb. The opening and final weekends are the high points of the whole show.

(cured meat and fish), wine and olive oil, and the ship also carried minerals such as copper and lead – all demonstrating the great part played by Spain in making Rome rich. Two enormous anchors nearby, attest to the size of vessels that were used. Notable among the Roman statuary is a giant marble sculpture of the second-century emperor Trajan, which prior to excavation stood in the forum of Roman Baelo Claudia (see page 194) near Tarifa.

Museo de Bellas Artes

The second-floor **Museo de Bellas Artes** (fine art museum) is one of the best in Andalucía. The kernel of the collection is a group of 21 canvases by **Zurbarán** in Room 2, including a quite exceptional series of saints brought here from La Cartuja, the Carthusian monastery at Jerez, and one of only three such sets in the country preserved intact, or nearly so (the others are at Seville and Guadalupe). With their sharply defined shadows and intense, introspective air, Zurbarán's saints are powerful and very Spanish, even the English figures such as Hugh of Lincoln, or the Carthusian John Houghton, martyred by Henry VIII, whom he refused to accept as head of the English Church. Perhaps this is not surprising, for the artist spent much of his life travelling round the Carthusian monasteries of Spain and many of his saints are in fact portraits of the monks he met.

Highlights of the many other works on display include, in Room 3, Murillo's *Ecce Homo* and *San Pedro y San Paulo*, as well as his final work, the *Mystic Marriage of Santa Catalina* – during the painting of which he fell from a scaffold to his death – and a *Sagrada Familia* by Rubens. The same room also contains *The Vision of San Félix Cantalicio*, a canvas displaying tenebrist influences by seventeenth-century sculptor, painter, architect and all-round genius, *sevillano* Alonso Cano.

An interesting section here houses a collection of **modern art** featuring, among others, works by Miró, Rafael Albertí and noted Tarifa artist Guillermo Perez Villalta.

Third floor

The museum's third floor has an interesting **ethnological collection** divided into two rooms; the first has examples of traditional *artesanía* including ceramics, basketwork, leatherwork and textiles. The second room contains some wonderful **antique marionettes**, part of a section covering the long tradition of Tía Norica, or satirical marionette theatre, in Cádiz (see box, page 145).

Iglesia y claustro de San Francisco

Pza de San Francisco • Mon–Sat 11am–7.30pm, Sun noon–7.30pm • Free

Immediately behind the Museo de Cádiz, the **Iglesia y claustro de San Francisco** lies on a tiny square of the same name – the square is the site of the church's former orchard. Dating from the eighteenth century, the former convent church has a wonderful cloister with a colonnade supported by Tuscan pillars. In the church itself, the high altar's retablo is a magnificent work by Gonzalo Pomar with a central *hornacina* (shrine) holding an image of the Virgen de los Remedios. The flying angels on each side of the retablo are attributed to *sevillano* sculptor Pedro Roldán, while in the church's *sacristia* are two sculptures, one of San Diego and the other of San Francisco de Assisi, attributed to the *andaluz* master Martínez Montañés.

Oratorio de Santa Cueva

C/Rosario • July & Aug Tues–Fri 10am–2pm & 5.30–8.30pm, Sat 10am–2pm, Sun 10am–1pm; rest of year Tues–Fri 10am–2pm & 5–7pm, Sat 10am–2pm, Sun 10am–1pm • Charge • ☎ 956 222 262

A short walk southeast from the Museo de Cádiz, the eighteenth-century **Oratorio de Santa Cueva** houses three fine Goya frescoes. The church is divided into two

---

TÍA NORICA PUPPET THEATRE

Tía Norica, or satirical marionette theatre, has been used for more than two centuries to pillory the city's rulers and dignitaries, through the "mouths" of its characters taken from the streets – travelling salesmen, waiters, sailors, fishermen, *toreros*, drunks – often in times when overt political activity was dangerous. The fascinating puppets can be seen behind glass on the third floor of the Museo de Cádiz (see page 145), where there's also a video presentation of a Tía Norica show from the 1980s (you may need to ask for it to be played). However, the puppets are truly brought to life in a live show – the **Teatro de Títere** (C/San Miguel 15, near the Torre Tavira) stages performances each summer and Cádiz still holds an annual marionette theatre **festival** in June or July (details on both from either Turismo).

dramatically contrasting parts; in the elliptical **upper oratory** beneath an elegant dome are the three frescoes representing the *Miracle of the Loaves and Fishes*, the *Bridal Feast* (either side of the main altar) and the *Last Supper* (above the entrance), an unexpected depiction of Christ and the disciples dining sprawled on the floor, Roman style. The other works here are depictions of biblical scenes by minor artists.

In sharp contrast to the chapel above is the **subterranean chapel**, containing a sculpture of the Crucifixion whose manifest pathos adds a sombre note. An eighteenth-century work of the Genoa school, the image is said to have inspired visiting composer Joseph Haydn to write his *Seven Last Words* (of Christ) oratorio. Each Good Friday a sermon on the theme of Christ's last words is preached in the chapel, following which Haydn's work is performed. The chapel used to be maintained in a state of unilluminated gloom which is probably how Haydn saw it. Somewhat breaking with tradition, spotlights have been added and a formerly blacked-out lunette has been cleaned, flooding the chapel with light – which inevitably lessens the sculpture's dramatic impact. A small museum has been added between the two chapels, giving background information – including a display of Haydn's original score – on the building's history.

Catedral Nueva

Pza de la Catedral s/n • **Cathedral** July & Aug Mon–Sat 10am–9pm, April–June, Sept & Oct Mon–Sat 10am–8pm, Nov–Mar Mon–Sat 10am–6.30pm; Sun (all year) 2–6.30pm • Charge • **Torre del Reloj** Guided visits daily: June–Sept 10am–9pm, Sun from noon; Oct–May 10am–6pm • Charge • ⓦ catedraldecadiz.com

The huge **Catedral Nueva**, so titled because it replaced the former cathedral, Santa Cruz, is one of the largest churches in Spain. Begun in 1722, it took 110 years to finish, and even then, the towers – shortened when the money ran out – were completed only in 1853 in an unsympathetic white limestone whose patchwork effect jars with the original sandstone. The time lapse also led to a curious architectural potpourri, strikingly visible on the main facade, where the exuberance of the earlier Baroque below was topped off in a contrastingly sober Neoclassical style. What is more, on closer inspection you'll see that the distinctive "gilded" dome, which appears so impressive from afar, is in fact made from glazed yellow tiles. Sadly, in the latter half of the twentieth century the building fell into an advanced state of decay – caused by sea air calcifying the stone – as chunks of the ceiling started falling on the congregation below. A costly programme of restoration in the last decade or so has slowly restored the building to its former grandeur.

Interior

Even if you don't normally go for High Baroque, it's hard to resist the attraction of the austere **interior**. From inside, the soaring 52m-high dome is illuminated by a powdery violet light, the whole perfectly proportioned building decorated entirely in stone with no gold or white in sight. **Artworks** include a sculpture of San Bruno by Martínez Montañés in the chapel of San Sebastián and some other polychrome sculptures including an *Ecce Homo* attributed to Luisa Roldán ("La Roldana"), the daughter of Pedro Roldán. Also worth a look are the wonderful **choir stalls** dating from 1702 (the work of Roldán disciple Agustín Perea) which were originally in the Cartuja of Seville and moved here upon the latter's Disentailment in 1835. In the crypt is buried Manuel de Falla, the great *gaditano* composer of such Andalucía-inspired works as *Nights in the Gardens of Spain* and *El amor brujo*.

The cathedral's **museum** holds some dubiously attributed paintings as well as a rather tedious collection of ecclesiastical silver enlivened only by a monstrance – an eighteenth-century bejewelled custodial nicknamed the *Millón* (million), a reference to the number of precious gems and pearls set into the work.

For a magnificent view over the city you can also climb the **Torre del Reloj**, one of the cathedral's twin towers; entrance to the tower is close to the main entrance.

Plaza San Juan de Dios

Dominated by the delightful wedding-cake Neoclassical facade of the Ayuntamiento, the **Plaza San Juan de Dios** is the city's main square and, dating from the sixteenth century, also its oldest. Completed in 1799, the Ayuntamiento is the work of Torcuato Benjumeda and its bells sound the hour with notes from *gaditano* composer de Falla's *El amor brujo*. The revamped and pedestrianized square has substituted fountains for the traffic lanes that used to cross it, and with its stately palms and inviting café terraces has been transformed into one of the city's most attractive places to sit out. As in former days, the northeast end of the square opens on to the port and it is quite a visual shock to see the profile of giant cruise ships moored so close to the city centre. The heart of the square has a 15m-high column and statue dedicated to Cádiz-born Segismondo Moret, who served as Spain's prime minister in the early years of the last century.

Barrio del Pópulo

The best view of the cathedral is from the waterfront behind, where the golden dome is perfectly set off by the pastel-tinted facades of the adjacent houses along Calle Campo del Sur. To the east of the Plaza de la Catedral fronting the cathedral lies the **Barrio del Pópulo**, a once poor and run-down area of narrow alleyways and decaying tenements, which was substantially refurbished in the last decade, and now provides one of the city's nightlife zones.

The *barrio* is a surviving remnant of the thirteenth-century medieval city and many of its streets are graced by the odd crumbling *palacio*, formerly residences of merchants made wealthy by empire trade, and now split up into residential blocks. One of these, the **Casa del Almirante** on Calle Posadilla, is a splendid Baroque pile with an ebullient facade featuring barley-sugar and Tuscan columns in rose-tinted Italian marble. There are long-standing plans to turn this into a luxury hotel. An ancient, seventeenth-century inn, the **Mesón del Pópulo** at C/Mesón Nuevo 11 – at the crook in the street – has the typical layout of these travellers' hostelries with stables below and living quarters above. It now the serves as the entrance to the Teatro Romano (see page 147). Calles Sopranis and Santa María – with the Palacio Lasquetty (no. 11) and the church of Santa María – are other good places to sample the typical atmosphere of this quarter.

Iglesia de Santa Cruz

Pza Fray Félix s/n • Tues–Fri 9.45am–12.45pm & 5.30–7pm, Sat 9.45am–12.45pm & 5.30–6.30pm, Sun 10am–noon & 6–7.30pm • Charge, Fri–Sun free • ☎ 956 287 704

Just east of the Catedral Nueva stands the "Old" Cathedral, the **Iglesia de Santa Cruz**. Originally a thirteenth-century church built on top of a mosque, it was almost destroyed by the Earl of Essex during the English assault on Cádiz in 1596, and is effectively a seventeenth-century rebuild with only occasional vestiges such as the entrance arch surviving from the earlier Gothic structure. The sober grey stone interior contrasts with the magnificent seventeenth-century gilded retablo, a beautiful work with sculptures by Martínez Montañés. Don't miss the Capilla de los Genoveses, with its own stunning retablo of red, white and black Italian marble now wonderfully restored.

Teatro Romano

Avda Campo del Sur s/n • Entry from Mesón del Populo, C/Mesón Nuevo 12 • April–Sept Mon–Sat 11am–5pm, Sun 10am–2pm; Oct–March Mon–Sat 10am–4.30pm, Sun 10am–2pm; closed first Mon of every month • Free • ☎ 956 982 945

Just behind the church of Santa Cruz is the **Teatro Romano** (Roman theatre), dating from the first century BC. Discovered in 1980, it is partly cut into by a corner of the Iglesia de Santa Cruz and was built over by a later Moorish *alcazaba*. It was one of the earliest and largest theatres constructed by the Romans in Spain with a *cavea* (semicircular auditorium) more than 120m in diameter and capable of seating an audience of twenty thousand. It merited a mention in the letters of the orator Cicero who relates that one actor was knighted following a memorable performance here, while another was sent for execution after an abysmal flop. The theatre fell into disuse in the late third century and the building was used as a stone quarry by the builders of the Moorish and medieval periods. A number of the remaining banks of seats have been restored.

The **centro de interpretación** documents the theatre's history and displays artefacts found during the excavations. Further excavations have revealed an impressive gallery (vomitorium) running beneath the seating area which allows access to viewing points.

Plaza de las Flores and Mercado Central

Heading west from the cathedral, it's a couple of blocks to the **Plaza de las Flores** (aka Plaza Topete), one of the city's most emblematic squares. Fronted by the striking early twentieth-century Correos, the square is a riot of colour most days due to the many flower sellers that have their stalls here. There are a couple of elegant mansions, too: **no. 1** with a portal decorated with pilasters in the Cádiz Baroque style dates from 1746 and, around the corner in Calle Libertad, numbers **15** and **16** are a couple more eighteenth-century mansions with *torres-miradores* (lookout towers).

Fronting these two, the whole of Plaza de la Libertad is taken up by the early nineteenth-century **Mercado Central**, an elegant Neoclassical construction with a colonnade of Doric pillars enclosing the central area. A five-year refurbishment restored the building to its former glory with – in addition to the usual fruit, veg, meat and fish sellers – a kaleidoscopic multitude of stalls selling everything from herbs and spices to exotic teas and world beers, along with takeaway food stalls selling French, Italian as well as Spanish regional cuisine – there's even a fish and chip stall. Monday to Saturday mornings it's a vibrant beehive of activity and not to be missed.

Hospital de Mujeres

C/Hospital de Mujeres • Mon–Fri 10am–1.30pm & 5.30–8pm • Charge (ask the porter for admission) • ☎ 956 807 018

Northwest of the Mercado Central lies the Hospital Misericordia, known now as the **Hospital de Mujeres**, on the street of the same name. One of the finest Baroque buildings in the city, it was built as a hospital for women arriving in the port – many seeking a passage on boats to the Americas – who got sick and frequently died in the doorways and colonnades of public buildings.

The hospital's main **chapel**, dedicated to San Francisco, is an exuberant Baroque extravaganza and displays a brilliant El Greco, *St Francis in Ecstasy*. It's one of the Cretan artist's finest portrayals of the saint, albeit a rather sombre study using copious shades of grey. Don't miss also the hospital's two elegant patios linked by an unusual double-sided staircase.

Oratorio de San Felipe Neri

C/San José • Tues–Fri 10am–2pm & 5–7pm, Sat 10.30am–2pm, Sun 10am–2pm • Charge • ☎ 662 642 233

The eighteenth-century **Oratorio de San Felipe Neri**, to the northwest of Plaza de las Flores, is one of the most important historical buildings in Spain, evidenced by the number of commemorative plaques from countries as far apart as Chile and the Philippines attached to the exterior. It was here, on March 29, 1812, that a group of patriotic radicals defied the Napoleonic blockade and set up the Cortes, or parliament, which drew up a liberal constitution (popularly known as "La Pepa") enshrining the principles of universal male suffrage, freedom of the press and land reform.

The church itself, an elegant oval structure, has a double tier of balconies that would once have echoed with the roar of fierce debate, and above which eight *ventanillas* in the dome allow the brilliant light to illuminate the sky-blue decor and the central nave, punctuated by seven chapels. The high altar's retablo is crowned with a fine *Inmaculada* by Murillo.

Museo de las Cortes de Cádiz

C/Santa Inés 9 • Tues–Fri 9am–2.30pm • Free • ☎ 956 221 788

Next door to the oratory, the **Museo de las Cortes de Cádiz** was set up in 1912 to commemorate the first centenary of the 1812 Constitution. The highlights of the museum are a large Romantic-style mural depicting the events of 1812, together with a number of the original documents of the Cortes and an enormous eighteenth-century scale model of the city – almost filling a room – made of mahogany and ivory at the behest of King Carlos III.

Plaza de España

Four hundred metres northeast of the museum, the **Plaza de España** is dominated by a rather pompous **monument to the Constitution**, set up in 1912 and now crowned with the rather impertinent addition of a crane's nest. *Gaditanos* like to claim that it's the only monument in the world honouring and topped by a book – a representation of the 1812 Constitution.

Torre Tavira and Calle Ancha

C/Marqués del Real Tesoro 10 • Daily: June–Sept 10am–8pm; Oct–May 10am–6pm • Charge

Just southeast of the Museo de las Cortes de Cádiz, the **Torre Tavira** is an eighteenth-century mansion with the tallest tower in the old city, which you can climb to get a great view over the white roofs below and the sea beyond. Many houses had these towers added so that shipowners and merchants could see ships arriving in the port. The tower also holds a camera obscura, which gives equally dramatic views, and the rooms below contain historical displays covering Cádiz and its past.

A couple of blocks north, the **Calle Ancha** – an historic thoroughfare (see page 141) that is today an attractive pedestrianized shopping street – makes a pleasant place for a stroll.

Barrio de la Viña

Squeezed between Calle Campo del Sur and the Playa de la Caleta on the west side of the centre lies the **Barrio de la Viña**, the old fishermen's quarter, typically *gaditano* and traditionally renowned for the spirited and sarcastic humour of its inhabitants. Its main street is the **Calle Virgen de la Palma**, close to the eastern end of which lies the tiny Plaza Tío de la Tiza, a charming square (filled with terraces for seafood tapas and *raciones* in summer) named after the man who, in the late nineteenth century, gave the famous Carnaval the form it has today (see box, page 144).

Playa de la Caleta

The western flank of the Barrio de la Viña faces the **Playa de la Caleta**, an over-popular – and often none too clean – beach in a small bay sandwiched between the most impressive of Cádiz's eighteenth-century sea fortifications, the **Castillo de Santa Catalina** and the **Castillo de San Sebastián**, the latter constructed on an islet and reached by a causeway. This is believed to be the site of the ancient Phoenician harbour

2

where, tradition has it, there once stood an impressive temple to the Phoenician god Melkaart.

A walk along the seafront here can be wonderfully bracing day or night (when cooling breezes blow in off the Atlantic and many of the monuments are floodlit), with the possibility of a stroll through the Parque Genovés (April–Sept 8am–10.30pm), planted with palms and cypresses as far as the bastion of Candelaria, or onwards to the Alameda Apodaca, another waterfront garden, beyond.

Ecco (Espacio de Cultura Contemporanea)

Paseo Carlos III 5 • Mon–Sat 11am–9pm, Sun 11am–3pm • Free • ⓦ eccocadiz.com

Close to the northern tip of Cádiz's peninsula, **ECCO (Espacio de Cultura Contemporanea)** is an exhibition and performance space within a revamped eighteenth-century military barracks. It has a small permanent collection of modern artworks by local artists, but mainly functions as a space for modern art exhibitions as well as performance arts (contemporary dance and music). The latter take place in a superbly designed wooden floored-patio space at the heart of the complex. Check their website for the events calendar.

Beaches south of the centre

On the southern side of the city centre, the **Playa Santa María del Mar** is the old town's main beach, lying some 500m east of the cathedral. However, the city's main beach, and the one with all the action – including restaurants and *chiringuitos* – is the **Playa de la Victoria**, 2km of excellent sand, cleaner and usually less crowded than the two old town beaches. Getting here is an easy thirty-minute walk from the old town – just find the seafront on the south side of the peninsula and head east, or take public transport (see opposite). The **Playa Cortadura** begins where the Playa de la Victoria ends and it's an altogether less commercialized affair – in fact there are no bars or *chiringuitos* at all.

ARRIVAL AND DEPARTURE   CÁDIZ

By train The train station is on Pza Sevilla at the periphery of the old town, close to the Pza San Juan de Dios, busiest of the city's many squares.

Destinations Córdoba (10 daily; 3hr 29min; AVE 10 daily 2hr 50min); El Puerto de Santa María (16 daily; 34min); Granada (1 daily, change at Seville; 5hr); Jerez de la Frontera (16 daily; 45min); Seville (12 daily; 1hr 40min)

By bus The city's impressive new bus station is on the east (or harbour) side of the train station on C/Astilleros.

Destinations Alcalá de los Gazules (4 daily; 2hr); Algeciras (8 daily; 2hr); Arcos de la Frontera (9 daily; 1hr 30min); Córdoba (6 daily; 4hr); El Puerto de Santa María (15 daily; 35min); Granada (4 daily; 5hr 45min); Jerez de la Frontera (15 daily; 1hr); Los Caños de Meca (1 daily, Sat & Sun 3 daily; 1hr 30min); Málaga (6 daily; 4hr); Ronda (Mon–Fri 4 daily, Sat & Sun 1 daily; 3hr 25min); Seville (9 daily; 1hr 45min).

By car Coming in by car you're best off taking accommodation with a garage (all the hotels will assist with

parking) or heading for a car park rather than looking for street parking. Parking Paseo de Canalejas near the harbour is a convenient central car park inside the city walls (but also one of the most expensive). The car parks are privately run and vary between €12 and €25 a day. Two of the cheapest are Santa Catalina (near the *parador*) and the very cheap Muelle Reina Sofía on the northern side of the harbour. Both tourist offices keep a list of car parks and their rates.

By boat Local ferries sail across the bay to El Puerto de Santa María and the beach resort of Rota (see page 161), leaving from the dock on the south side of the Puerto Comercial. There are eight departures daily to Rota (50min) plus more frequent departures to El Puerto de Santa María by catamaran (Mon–Fri every 30min 7.45am–10pm, Sat & Sun reduced sailings ending at 8.30pm; 40min; information/timetables in Spanish only ⓦ cmtbc.es). Check Wdirectferries.co.uk for ferries to the Canary Islands, as the service was in a state of flux at the time of writing.

INFORMATION

Turismo Avda Ramón de Carranza s/n (Mon–Fri 9am–7pm, Sat & Sun 10am–2pm; ☎ 956 203 191), just north of Pza San Juan de Dios. This office hands out current transport

and ferry timetables as well as general information, a detailed street map and a useful *Ruta de Tapas* leaflet.

Turismo Municipal Paseo de Canalejas (July–Sept Mon–

Fri 9am–7pm, Sat & Sun 9am–5pm; Oct–June Mon–Fri 8.30am–6.30pm, Sat & Sun 9am–5pm; ☎ 956 241 001). Just 70m from the Turismo, this is another useful office for maps and information. They also produce their own *Ruta de Tapas* leaflet and self-guided themed walking-tour leaflets.

Listings *El Diario de Cádiz* (✆ diariodecadiz.es) is the city's daily paper – good for local information, upcoming flamenco concerts and entertainment details.

Useful websites Information on the city is available at ✆ cadiz.es, ✆ cadizturismo.com and ✆ andalucia.org. For information on Cádiz province see ✆ cadiznet.com.

TOURS AND ACTIVITIES

Open-top bus tour One way to get to grips with the city is to do an open-top bus tour – especially good if you're pressed for time. City Sightseeing Cádiz (daily 10am–6.30pm; charge; ✆ city-sightseeing.com) runs a hop-on hop-off clockwise service around the peninsula, with stops at or near Pza San Juan de Dios, the cathedral, the Parque Genovés, the Playa de la Victoria, and places in between.

Football C.F. Cádiz, nicknamed Submarino Amarillo ("Yellow Submarine" – they play in canary shirts), is the city's team, currently playing in La Liga (Spain's top flight league). Their ground is the Estadio Ramón Carranza, Pza Madrid, behind the Playa de la Victoria (✆ cadizcf.com). Tickets can be purchased at the ground.

GETTING AROUND

By bus These offer a handy way of getting around and a route map is available from the Turismo. A ten-trip Bonobus travelcard – from *estancos* (tobacconists), bus kiosks and many newspaper stands – gives you a healthy discount compared to buying single-journey tickets.

Destinations The #7 bus goes to Playa de la Victoria from Parque Genovés, following the coast as far as the *Hotel Playa Victoria*; walk east from here to reach Playa Cortadura.

No buses risk traversing the labyrinthine streets of the old town, but bus #2 goes around the periphery of the peninsula (in both directions) between the train station and the cathedral.

By train There are stops at Segunda Aguada (for Playa de la Victoria) and Cortaduras, from where the Playa de la Cortadura is a short walk (every 20min; 5min).

ACCOMMODATION SEE MAP PAGE 142

In tune with the city itself, much of Cádiz's budget accommodation has seen better days, and although things are slowly improving there's still a shortage of good-quality accommodation in all categories. Except during the Carnaval, and in July and August, **finding a place to stay** shouldn't be a problem. Again it's worth noting that outside high season (used for the price codes included) rates fall considerably. All places listed below can advise on parking.

AROUND PLAZA SAN JUAN DE DIOS (EAST SIDE)

★ **Casa Caracol** C/Suárez de Salazar 4; ✆ hostel-casacaracol.com. Friendly backpackers' place with dorm beds, some double rooms sharing bath and pricier en-suite rooms in a *hostal* nearby. Rates include breakfast and use of a kitchen. €

Las Cuatro Naciones C/Plocia 3; ☎ 956 255 539. Centrally located close to Pza San Juan de Dios, a clean and unpretentious place with low-priced rooms sharing bath. €

Hostal Bahía C/Plocia 5; ✆ hostalbahiacadiz.com. Reasonable-value and conveniently located *hostal* offering en-suite rooms with a/c and TV. Ask for one of the more attractive exterior balcony rooms. €‾

AROUND PLAZA SAN JUAN DE DIOS (WEST SIDE)

Hostal Canalejas C/Cristóbal Colón 5;

✆ hostalcanalejas.com. Pleasant two-star *hostal* in completely restored townhouse. The en-suite rooms come with a/c and TV, and there's a pay car park nearby. Avoid the windowless interior rooms, though. €‾€‾

Hostal Fantoni C/Flamenco 5; ✆ hostalfantoni.es. Pleasant en-suite rooms with a/c and TV in a charming renovated eighteenth-century house filled with *azulejos* and cool marble. €‾€‾

★ **Hotel La Catedral** Pza de la Catedral 9; ✆ hotellacatedral.com. Charming small hotel 50m from the cathedral's front door. Comfortable rooms are well equipped and many have balconies (extra charge) where you can feast your eyes on the cathedral's imposing facade. Add an infinity rooftop pool – where you seem to swim almost within touching distance of the cathedral's bell tower – and you have the perfect place to stay. Ring reception for the best available rate. Breakfast is included. €‾€‾€‾

Hotel Patagonia Sur C/Cobos 11; ✆ hotelpatagoniasur. es. Stylish hotel in a renovated townhouse. The well-equipped a/c rooms come with minibar, safe and plasma TV. Either of the attic suites (penthouses) is worth the few euros extra – no. 52 has its own expansive sun terrace with loungers and cathedral view. Breakfast is included. €‾€‾

AROUND PLAZA DE SAN FRANCISCO

★ **Hospedería Las Cortes** C/San Francisco 9;

hotellascortes.com. Splendid three-star hotel in a stylishly restored *casa señorial*. The attractive rooms come with a/c and minibar, while public facilities include a sauna, gym, *cafetería* and restaurant. Own car park. High-season price Aug only, and good value at any time of the year. Breakfast is included. €€€

Hotel Argantonio C/Argantonio 3; hotelargantonio. com. Very pleasant hotel housed in an elegant nineteenth-century townhouse and decorated throughout with Moroccan furnishings and fittings (many of them for sale). All rooms come with plasma TV and minibar. The top-floor, outward-facing rooms are the ones to go for. Breakfast is included. €€€

OUT OF THE CENTRE

Hotel Parador Atlántico Parque Genovés 9; parador.es. This state-of-the-art rectilinear construction fronting the sea opened its doors in 2012 and replaced the old *parador*, which was razed to make way for it. Beyond an austere stone, wood and steel exterior lie 124 rooms and suites filled with five-star comforts, all with terrace balcony and sea view. Features include full-sized infinity rooftop pool, spa, solarium, bars, restaurant, gardens and its own underground garage. €€€€

Hotel Playa Victoria Glorieta Ingeniero La Cierva 4; palafoxhoteles.com. Perfect if you're after a beachfront location, this giant four-star hotel fronting the Playa de la Victoria has well-appointed rooms with terraces and sea views (especially from rooms 609–11), while facilities include a pool, solarium, restaurant, bars, own underground parking and beach hammocks. €€€

Hotel Regio Avda Ana de Viya 11; hotelregiocadiz. com. Catering mainly to the corporate sector, this modern three-star sited outside the walls is nevertheless convenient and comfortable, with parking nearby and a bus stop (for transport into the centre – a 5min ride) almost outside. €€€

EATING
SEE MAP PAGE 142

Cádiz's best **cafés**, **tapas bars** and **restaurants** tend to be clustered around its many grand squares, especially Plaza San Juan de Dios and the leafy Plaza de la Mina. Across the old town there are more places to hunt down in and around the adjoining Plaza de las Flores and Plaza de la Libertad, the latter containing the **market**. West of here, the old seamen's quarter, the Barrio de la Viña, is where *gaditanos* make for on warmer nights to scoff fried fish and *mariscos* at economical *marisquerías* in the narrow streets around Plaza Tío de la Tiza and along C/Virgen de la Palma. The city's summer playground, the Paseo Marítimo – the long boulevard fronting the Playa de la Victoria – is lively and fun all season, with tapas bars, restaurants and beach *chiringuitos* all doing a roaring trade.

RESTAURANTS

El Aljibe C/Plocia 25; 956 266 656. First-rate restaurant serving up a range of traditional *andaluz* and Mediterranean dishes. Dining is on a terrace out front or in an elegant beamed dining room upstairs. Also serves very good tapas in its bar, and the *menú de degustación*, including wine. The downstairs bar also serves tapas, with a very reasonably priced three *tapa menu* including a drink. €€

★ **El Balandro** C/Apodaca 22; restaurantebalandro. com. Highly popular venue that offers a range of excellent seafood tapas (try the *papas aliñados con bacalao* – marinated potatoes with cod) served at the bar, and *raciones* and fresh fish and meat dishes in the ground floor restaurant. A window table will enable you to watch the sunset over the Bay of Cádiz. They offer a range of fresh pasta too, plus various *arrozes* (paella-style dishes) and some delicious desserts. Extensive and fair-priced wine list. €€

La Bodega Paseo Marítimo 23, on the Playa de la Victoria seafront and close to Cádiz's football stadium; restaurantelabodega.com. Excellent mid-priced restaurant and *marisquería* tapas bar with a wide range of meat and fish dishes. Just the place if you're looking for somewhere to eat while at the beach. €€€

La Curiosidad de Mauro C/Veedor 10; 956 992 288. Michelin-starred chef Mauro Barreiro has opened the city's first "cocina de autor" (creative kitchen). Behind a small tapas bar lies an 8-table restaurant serving interesting fusions of flavours and textures. Typical is the *tartar de atún rojo de almadraba* (bluefin tuna tartar with a Peruvian spicy sauce). Perhaps the best deal is the 8-course *viaje gastrónomico* which gives you an overview of what the place is all about. €€€€

★ **El Faro** C/San Félix 15; elfarodecadiz.com. In the heart of the Barrio de la Viña, this is one of Andalucía's best fish restaurants. Specialities include *pulpo* (octopus), *merluza* (hake), *urta* (sea bream) and a delicious *arroz marinero* (Andalucian paella). There's a *menú de degustación* (excluding wine, Sept–June only). Their tapas bar next door (see page 153) is also well worth a visit. €€€

Fogón de Mariana C/Sacramento 39; fogondemariana.com. Good economical place for carnivores in this fish-crazy city. The lamb dishes, especially, are excellent, and they are famous for their quality *jamón ibérico* and *hamburguesa montanera* (hefty hamburger). The *ensalada montanera* (cheese and pepper salad) is also recommended, and don't forget to check out the dish of the day. €€

★ **Freiduría Las Flores** Pza de las Flores 4; 678 082 012. One of the best *freidurías* in town. You can get an economical takeaway and eat it at the terrace tables of the nearby bar *La Marina* (facing the post office), who don't seem to mind, as long as you buy a drink; alternatively, you can eat at *Las Flores* itself in their café-restaurant. €

La Palma C/Virgen de la Palma 7; ☎ 679 678 160. In the heart of the Barrio de la Viña fishermen's quarter, on a street lined with seafood restaurants, this vibrant place has a lively outdoor terrace and the house special is a *frito gaditano* (mixed fried fish). €€

La Pepa Paseo Marítimo 14, on the seafront beyond the Hotel Playa Victoria; ⓦ arrocerialapepa.com. Excellent family-run terrace restaurant at the eastern end of the Paseo Marítimo, serving fish and their speciality rice dishes as well as fresh pasta. Try their paella *mixta gaditana* (with meat and *mariscos*). Also serves "half-plates" plus tapas in the bar. €€

★ **Restaurante Atxuri** C/Plocia 7; ⓦ atxuri.es. This outstanding and popular (booking advisable) mid-priced Basque fish restaurant is one of the city's top tables. The kitchen – where head chef Pedro Ladrón de Guevara has been running the show for four decades – turns out a fusion of *andaluz* and Basque dishes served in a spacious white-walled dining room, beyond a small (and very good) *raciones* bar at the entrance with a pleasant street terrace. Try the *almejas a la marinera* (clams) or *bacalao al pil-pil* (salted cod casserole). €€€

Restaurante El Sardinero Pza San Juan de Dios 4; ☎ 956 265 926. Traditional *gaditano* fish restaurant offering good-quality fish dishes served on a shaded terrace. House special is *frito variado* (assorted fried fish). Also does meat dishes and salads. €€

TAPAS BARS

★ **Bar El Faro** C/San Félix 15; ☎ 956 211 068. Tapas bar of the renowned restaurant (see page 152), and probably the best in town. A stand-up place where the finos and manzanillas are first rate, the service is slick and the seafood tapas are mouthwateringly delicious. House specials include *tortillitas de camarones* (shrimp fritters) and *tostaditas de pan con bacalao* (cod). €

Bar Manteca Corralón de los Carros 66, near C/San Félix; ☎ 956 213 603. Great old place in the Barrio de la Viña run by a retired *torero* and decorated with bullfighting memorabilia. Excellent fino and *oloroso*. House specials include *chicharrones* (pork crackling), *lomo* (cured pork loin) and *salchichón ibérico* (salami) all served up on a square of greaseproof paper. Impromptu flamenco often takes place here too. €

Bar Terraza Pza de la Catedral 3; ☎ 956 265 391. Facing the cathedral and founded in 1952, despite a touristy location this is a good tapas bar and fish restaurant with a popular terrace on the most scenic square in town (which is why the prices are slightly higher than elsewhere). €€€

★ **La Candela** C/Feduchy 3; ⓦ lacandelatapasbar. com. Endearingly slovenly *barrio* bar with a great buzzing vibe and outstanding (and reasonably priced) tapas and *raciones*, many with a creative edge. The house *croquetas*

(croquettes), *pulpo* (octopus) and *ravioli de pato* (duck ravioli) are all delicious. It's highly popular and you'd be advised to book to be sure of a table. €€

Cervecería La Gaditana C/Zorilla 3; ☎ 956 221 031. Fine bar where the tasty *montaditos* (tapas on bread) are wonderful; try also the *boquerones fritos* (fried anchovies) and their *bombita* (baby bomb, a ball of potato with onion and tuna fish). €

Cumbres Mayores C/Zorilla 4; ⓦ cumbresmayores. com. Excellent lively restaurant and tapas bar located in a century-old former brewery where *carnes ibericas* (particularly Huelva *jamón*) is king. The tapas bar has daily specials and in winter serves up a delicious *berza* – a chickpea- and *morcilla* (blood sausage)-based broth. The restaurant comprises a group of cosy dining rooms at the rear. €€€

★ **Gadisushi** Mercado Central, southeast corner; ⓦ gadisushi.com. Actually a stall inside the central market (with tables in the plaza), this highly original Japanese-style sushi bar is the brainwave of a *gaditano* restaurateur who spent a few years in Japan. The portions – of sushi, sashimi and uramaki (rice roll) – are tapas-sized and not particularly expensive. You can wash them down with Japanese beers or Cádiz's local brew, Maier. €

K'Seron del 3x4 C/Barrie 29; ☎ 956 115 259. Great and welcoming *gaditano* bar, which celebrates Carnaval all year long. The walls are covered with photos of great carnival moments and there are frequent live concerts featuring flamenco artistes as well as local musical groups. They also serve good tapas: try the *salchichón de bellota* (top-quality salami). €

El Laurel C/Obispo Urquinaona 3, slightly east of Pza de las Flores; ☎ 956 225 824. Popular neighbourhood tapas bar with a loyal clientele. What it lacks in elegance it certainly makes up for with the quality of its tapas – listed on a blackboard behind the bar. The *boquerones fritos* (fried anchovies), *rabo de toro* (stewed bull's tail) and *garbanzos con langostinos* (chickpeas with prawns) are all worth a try, and their hearty winter *berza* soup with pork, *morcilla* and chickpeas is a meal in itself. €

Merodio Pza Libertad 4, fronting the market; ☎ 626 83 13 14. One of the city's best-loved old bars. Don't be fooled by the rather dingy exterior – with its simple tiled walls, this is a great place inside, and there's an inviting little terrace at the rear. Things tend to get riotous here during Carnaval and the place really hums on market days and Sunday lunchtimes. Specializes in *erizos de mar* (sea urchins) in season, as well as shellfish. €

El Serallo Pza del Mentidero 1; ☎ 956 225 188. One of a number of tapas bars with inviting terraces circling an elegant fountain on one of Cadiz's most delightful (and least-known) squares, dotted with jacaranda trees. There's a decent tapas selection – try the *mejillones al vapor* (mussels) – and most days they serve *arroz* (paella). €€

2

Taberna La Manzanilla C/Feduchy 18, north of Pza Candelaria; ❶956 285 401. Wonderful, atmospheric eighteenth-century bodega serving the odd *tapa* in addition to excellent manzanilla decanted from huge butts. If you ask, the proprietor will show you his cellar with some classic vintages. €

La Tapería de Columela C/Columela; ⓦlataperiadecolumela.es. Another outstanding (and thus highly popular) tapas place. A long, narrow bar leads to an area with few tables at the back. From a lengthy tapas menu you could try *salteado de alcachofas* (artichokes with octopus) or *bacalao al pil-pil* (cod in garlic sauce). €

CAFÉS AND SNACKS

Casa Hidalgo Pza Catedral 8; ⓦcasa-hidalgo.com. A great snack at any time of the day are *empanadas gallegas* (fish or meat pasties), obtained from the only Galician bakery in town, opposite the cathedral. €

★ **Casa Lazo** C/Barrié 17, northeast of the Torre Tavira; ❶956 229 499. Charming little shop/bar with marble-topped tables and a tasty tapas selection. Try their *jamón*, *brochetas de pulpo* (octopus) or *croquetas caseras* (croquettes). They also do full meals – the urta a la roteña (bream) and arroz de la casa (paella) are excellent – and they open for breakfast. The delicatessen sells fine *jamón*, cheeses and regional wines. €

DRINKING AND NIGHTLIFE

SEE MAP PAGE 142

Outside carnival and fiesta times, nightlife in Cádiz centres on the areas around the **Plaza de la Miña** and **Plaza de España**, while a nightlife *copas* (drinks) zone has opened up in the **Barrio del Pópulo** centred on *calles* Mesón Nuevo and Silencio (filled with late-night bars and clubs such as *La Favorita*, *El Malagueño* and *Mesón de la Posadilla*), and **Plazuela San Martín**. In summer much of the nightlife scene migrates to the **Paseo Marítimo**, behind the beaches to the east of the centre (C/Muñoz Arenillas, behind the *Hotel Playa Victoria*, is the focus), where you'll find most of the bars and clubs. In winter revellers flock to the **Punta de San Felipe** (there's a less frenetic scene here in summer, too), known locally as La Punta, the peninsula beyond the harbour to the northeast of Plaza de España.

CLUBS AND BARS

Babel C/Manuel Rancés 2, just west of Pza de España. A relaxed and friendly late-night *copas* cocktails and music bar (aka *BD8*) open until the small hours, and which tends to fill up on weekends. There are quite a few other lively places in this street.

Café de Levante C/Rosario 35, near Pza de San Agustín; ⓦcafedelevante.com. Relaxed bar with a cultural ambience, often staging literary events, live music and even flamenco.

La Clandestina C/José de Toro 23; ❶956 221 210. Compact, friendly literary café-bar serving tea, coffee, snacks and pastries, and beer – besides selling the books on shelves that line the walls. If your Spanish is up to it, it's worth attending the occasional literary presentations with authors giving readings.

Habana Café C/Rosario 21, near Pza San Francisco. Atmospheric bar for late-night drinking. The house speciality is cocktails and they claim to make the best mojitos and daiquiris in town.

Pay Pay C/Silencio 1, Barrio del Pópulo; ⓦcafeteatropaypay.com. Large café-bar with a long history as a former sailors' hangout. Now renamed and revamped, it stages live music, theatre and poetry readings

and there are noticeboards with information on cultural events around the city.

San Francisco Uno Pza San Francisco 1; ❶956 21 25 97. Wine bar with an inviting terrace on this delightful square is good for breakfast coffee and perfect for late-night liqueurs or even a wine from their extensive list. They also serve tapas and *raciones*.

Woodstock C/Canovas del Castillo, old town, at the corner with C/Sagasta; ❶956 212 163. Popular music bar serving up eighty-plus of the world's top beers to the accompaniment of rock, blues, jazz and the occasional blast of Celtic pipes.

FLAMENCO

Flamenco is an irregular feature at private *peñas* or clubs, and isn't always that easy to find. We've listed a few places below, but check with the Turismo for more, as well as for details of "barrio flamenco" staged by bars and restaurants across the city; these are amateur shindigs, but often hugely enjoyable. The Turismo will also have details of special concerts and festivals at venues such as the Teatro Falla and the Diputación (regional government building) on Plaza de España. The *Baluarte de Candelaria* on the northern tip of the peninsula is the venue for some wonderfully authentic open-air flamenco concerts organized by the Peña Flamenco Enrique Mellizo or the Fundacion Cajasol, staged every Thursday evening from mid-July to late August. It gets going about 10pm and there's food and drink. Information regarding concerts and advance tickets is available from the Ayuntamiento's tourist section (❶956 241 001, English spoken) or either tourist office.

La Cava Taberna Flamenca C/Antonio Lopez 16, near the Pza de la Mina; ⓦflamencolacava.com. Tourist-oriented place where the performers are reasonably serious. Entry includes a drink. For times, see the website which also offers an online booking facility.

Peña La Perla C/Carlos Ollera s/n; ⓦlaperladecadiz. es. Down a tiny street behind the Cárcel Vieja (Old Prison), to the east of the cathedral, this wonderfully atmospheric old *peña* (where many "greats" have performed) is open to visitors and is somewhere that flamenco can happen spontaneously on any night of the week, with a regular performance on Fri at 10pm (not July or August). Enquire in their bar, give them a ring, or alternatively, check with the Turismo.

Peña Mellizo Paseo de San Felipe s/n, close to the Punto de San Felipe. Very friendly bar (open daily) and flamenco theatre. Outside July and August there are performances of flamenco here on Fridays (formal concert) and Saturdays (informal open house) at 10pm; both are free. Details are available on ☎ 956 221 985 or from either tourist office.

SHOPPING
SEE MAP PAGE 142

For the latest designer fashions head for C/Columela running between C/San Francisco and Plaza Flores, where many of the national and international clothes store chains have their outlets.

El Corte Inglés Avda de las Cortes de Cádiz s/n, 1.5km east of the train station; buses #5 or #8 from the eastern end of Avda del Puerto (close to the train station); ☎ 956 205 122. Cádiz's branch of the well-known department store.

Galería Artesenal del Pópulo C/San Antonio Abad 14, south of Pza San Juan de Dios; ☎ 671 474 263.

This venture comprises the studios of six craftspeople working in leather, ceramics, paintings and engravings, who sell their inventive wares under one roof.

Magerit C/Fermín Salvochea 2 west of Pza de España; ⓦ vinosmagerit.com. Excellent wine shop selling a wide range of national and Cádiz province wines and finos. The engaging female proprietor is a Spanish Master of Wine and also conducts tasting courses (see website for details).

Quorum Bookshop C/Ancha 27; ☎ 956 807 026. The city's best bookshop stocks a decent selection of books in English.

DIRECTORY

Banks There are ATMs throughout the city centre, with several banks around Pza San Juan de Dios and Avda Ramón de Carranza (facing the port).

Hospital For urgent medical treatment go to the *urgencias* (emergency) department of the Residencia Sanitaria Hospital, Avda Ana de Viya 21, near the *Hotel Playa Victoria* (☎ 956 002 100).

Police In emergencies dial ☎ 091 for the Policía Nacional

(serious crimes) and ☎ 092 for the Policía Local (theft and petty crime). Both police forces have their headquarters in the Playa de la Victoria zone: the national police are located on Avda de Andalucía and the local police are on the Avda José León de Carranza, next to the football stadium.

Post office Pza de las Flores, near the market (Mon–Fri 8.30am–8.30pm, Sat 9.30am–1pm).

The Sherry Triangle

The northwest corner of Cádiz province is sherry country, a dramatic landscape of low, rolling hills and extensive vineyards. The famous triangle of **sherry** towns – **Jerez de la Frontera**, **El Puerto de Santa María** and **Sanlúcar de Barrameda** – are the main production centres, but smaller places like **Chipiona** and even tiny **Rota** manage to muscle in on the action.

Besides their bodegas, many of which can be visited, all the sherry towns make interesting places for a stopover in themselves. Jerez and El Puerto de Santa María both have sufficient churches, museums and architectural sights to take up at least a couple of days, while coastal Sanlúcar has a castle and also offers the chance to take a boat trip into the wilderness of the **Doñana National Park**, Spain's largest. Sanlúcar is also home to some of the finest seafood bars and restaurants in Andalucía, while the town's golden sands – the setting for some exciting horse races in summer – are another attraction, as are the further string of magnificent **beaches** which stretch along the 40km stretch of coastline between here and El Puerto de Santa María. In fact, when Cádiz's city beaches are full you might want to take a thirty-minute trip by catamaran across the bay to El Puerto, where you'll find superb beaches with space to breathe all summer long.

El Puerto de Santa María

Just 10km across the bay from Cádiz, **EL PUERTO DE SANTA MARÍA** is the obvious choice for a day-trip from the provincial capital. It's a traditional family resort for both

2

gaditanos and *sevillanos* – many of whom have built villas and chalets along the fine **Playa Puntilla**, which you'll pass as the boat comes in to dock at the Muelle del Vapor in the estuary of the Río Guadalete. The town itself, some distance from the beach, has an easy-going air and, despite some ugly modern development on its periphery, is surprisingly picturesque, with many narrow, white-walled streets and plant-filled balconies, plus an impressive medieval castle, imposing *casas palacios*, some fine churches and Spain's third most prestigious bullring. On the cultural front, El Puerto will always be associated with one of the major Spanish poets of the twentieth century, **Rafael Alberti** (1902–99); his birthplace at C/Santo Domingo 25 is now a museum (see page 157). The town stages a cultural festival each summer (July and August) with concerts (mainly classical) taking place on Thursday evenings in the Castillo San Marcos; you can get details from the Turismo.

Today one of the three centres of **wine** production (along with Jerez and Sanlúcar) that make up the sherry triangle, El Puerto de Santa María came to prominence in the eighteenth century as a botanical garden where plants brought from the New World were cultivated for seed. This and other trading enterprises helped increase local prosperity, as demonstrated by the numerous mansions around the town, which was once known as the *ciudad de los cien palacios* (city of a hundred palaces).

EL PUERTO DE SANTA MARÍA

ACCOMMODATION
Camping Playa Las Dunas	9
Casa de Huéspedes Santa María	8
Casa de los Leones	4
Casa No. 6	5
Duques de Medinaceli	1
Hostal Loreto	3
Hotel Santa María	7
Monasterio San Miguel	2
Palacio San Bartolomé	6

EATING
Aponiente	2
Bar Apolo	7
Bar Vicente	4
Bodega Jerezana	11
Las Capuchinas	3
La Dorada	10
El Faro de El Puerto	1
Los Portales	6
Romerijo	8
La Taberna	5
Toro Tapas	9

DRINKING & NIGHTLIFE
La Cristalera	2
Guateque	4
Milwaukee	3
Trocadero	1

El Fuente de las Galeras

Arriving by ferry, close to the landing quay, the Muelle del Vapor, you'll immediately spot the fine six-spouted eighteenth-century fountain, **El Fuente de las Galeras**, constructed, as the Latin inscription on it tells you, to provide galleys leaving for the Americas with water. Voyages from here in the years following the discovery of the Americas in 1492 charted much of the New World's coastline and in 1500 El Puerto resident and sea captain Juan de la Cosa produced his famous **mappa mundi**, the first map to include the continent of America and show Cuba surrounded by water (Columbus never believed that it was an island).

2

Castillo de San Marcos and Antigua Lonja

Pza de Alfonso El Sabio • July–Aug Tours (lasting 90min & including wine tasting) Mon 10am, 11.30 (English), 1pm, 6pm, 7.30pm (English) and 9pm. Tues 7pm, 8pm (English) & 9pm. Wed–Sat 10.30am, 11.30am (English), 12:30pm, 1.30pm, 7pm, 8pm (English) & 9pm. Sun 10am, 11.30am (English), 1pm. Free visits (excluding wine tasting) Tues 11.30am (English), 12.30pm & 1.30pm (must be booked by phone or 🖂 servicios.turisticos@caballero.es). Rest of year, phone (or check with Turismo) to confirm times • Charge • ☎ 627 569 335

West of El Fuente is the **Castillo de San Marcos**, a thirteenth-century fort built by Alfonso X on the site of a Moorish watchtower and mosque. The towers of the castle bear the stirring (restored) proclamations of devotion to the Virgin, a symbol of the victory over the vanquished Moors. So besotted was the king with her that he sang the Virgin's praises in a surviving poetic work, *Las Cantigas*, and renamed El Puerto after her. Inside the fort – today owned by the Luis Caballero bodega – Alfonso also constructed a triple-naved Mudéjar church, in which the mosque's ancient *mihrab* can still be identified. The current proprietors have long used one of the castle's halls as a sherry bodega, stacked with butts. You can take a full tour of the castle, leaving via the bodega, where you'll be invited to taste (and buy) their finos.

Slightly southwest of here, the elegant eighteenth-century **Antigua Lonja** (aka El Resbaladero) on Calle Micaela Aramburu served for two centuries as the town's fish market – note the piscatorial reliefs decorating its exterior.

Iglesia Mayor Prioral

Pza Mayor • Mon–Fri 10am–1pm & 6–8pm, Sat 10am–1pm & 6.30–8.30pm, Sun 8.30am–1.45pm & 6.30–8.30pm • Charge

Following the pedestrianized Calle Luna west into town from the ferry quay will bring you to El Puerto's **Plaza Mayor** (officially the Plaza de España), fronted by the **Iglesia Mayor Prioral**. A thirteenth-century Gothic edifice, it has suffered much rebuilding and the shell is now largely Baroque, but don't miss its superb Plateresque south portal. Inside, a richly gilded retablo in the Capilla de la Virgen de los Milagros holds La Patrona, a thirteenth-century image of the Virgin formerly housed in the castle of San Marcos and to which the town is devoted. Note also some fine choir stalls richly carved in walnut and cedar.

Museo Municipal

C/Pagador 1 • Tues–Fri 10am–2pm, Sat & Sun 11am–2pm • Free • ☎ 956 542 705

Across the Plaza Mayor from the church lies the **Museo Municipal**, housed in an elegant eighteenth-century palacio, the **Casa de la Marquesa de Candia**. The museum contains archeological finds from the surrounding area plus a selection of indifferent artworks only relieved by a couple of paintings by Alberti (see page 157).

Fundación Rafael Alberti

C/Santo Domingo 25 • Tues–Fri 10am–2pm Sat & Sun 11am–2pm • Charge • ☎ 956 850 711

Around the corner from the Museo Municipal lies the **Fundación Rafael Alberti**, an excellent museum dedicated to El Puerto's great poet and artist, Rafael Alberti, who was born here. A communist and supporter of the Republic, Alberti fled abroad following the victory of Franco in 1939 and spent time in Argentina, Paris and Rome

2

before returning to Spain in 1977 after the dictator's death. Aged 76, shortly after his return he was elected deputy for Cádiz in the new Spanish parliament. He died here in 1999, in the same house where he was born 97 years earlier. Many of his vibrant engravings decorate the walls and a fascinating photographic biography illustrates his life, contacts and friendships with many of Spain's twentieth-century literary and artistic giants, including Lorca and Picasso.

Plaza de Toros

Pza Elías Ahuja s/n • Guided visits Mon–Fri 10am–2pm & 6–9pm, Sat & Sun 10am–2pm • Charge • ☎ 956 861 188

A few blocks south of the Plaza Mayor (Plaza de España), the **Plaza de Toros** is one of the largest in Spain (third only to Madrid and Seville) and among the most celebrated by aficionados. Opened in 1880 with a capacity of fifteen thousand, the bullring has hosted all the great names. A mosaic inside the entrance records the words of the legendary *sevillano* bullfighter Joselito, who fought here: "He who has not seen bulls in El Puerto does not know what bullfighting is."

The palacios

Scattered all over town are the **palacios** left behind by the great eighteenth-century families of El Puerto and decorated with their shields. The Turismo's town map marks them all, but three of the most outstanding are **Casa de Vizarrón** (aka Casa de las Cadenas) on Plaza del Polovorista, near the El Resbaldero market, with an elegant escutcheoned doorway; the **Casa de los Leones**, now the *Casa de los Leones* hotel (see page 159), with a fine facade and patio; and **Palacio de Aranibar**, with another elegant portal fronting the Castillo de San Marcos, and which now houses the Turismo (see page 158).

The beaches

The closest beaches, **Playa La Puntilla** and **Playa Valdelagrana**, are some distance from town (15min walk or local buses from the ferry dock at Plaza Las Galeras: #1 and #2 for La Puntilla or #3 for Valdelagrana) and are pleasant places to while away an afternoon with lots of lively *marisquerías* and beach bars. For fewer crowds you're better off on the **Playa Santa Catalina** to the west of Playa La Puntilla; bus #3 (direction Fuenterrabía) from Calle Micaela Aramburu near the ferry dock will take you there.

ARRIVAL AND DEPARTURE | EL PUERTO DE SANTA MARÍA

By train The train station is on Pza de la Estación s/n, on the northern periphery of the old town. Exit the station and turn left along C/Albareda to reach the centre.
Destinations Cádiz (13 daily; 28min); Jerez (at least 15 daily; 10min); Seville (10 daily; 1hr 15min).

By bus Arriving by bus you'll be dropped by the Pza de Toros – the "bus station" here is little more than a couple of bus stands.
Destinations Arcos (4 daily; 50min); Cádiz (14 daily; 30min); Chipiona (14 daily; 50min); Jerez (2 daily; 20min); Sanlúcar (14 daily; 35min); Seville (2 daily; 1hr 40min).

By car El Puerto has the usual problem of too many cars and too few parking spaces. A good tip is to head for the riverfront facing the *Hotel Santa María* where there are three large car parks (the furthest south is currently the cheapest).

By boat Opposite the *Hotel Santa María* is the catamaran ferry dock for sailings to Cádiz (40min); the service is roughly hourly on weekdays between 7am and 9pm, with a reduced service at weekends. The last sailing back from Cádiz is currently 10.35pm (weekdays) and 10.40pm (weekends). Phone ☎ 955 038 665 for information.

INFORMATION

Turismo The Turismo, at Palacio Reinoso Mendoza, Pza del Polvorista 2 (daily: May–Sept 9am–2pm & 6–8pm; Oct–April 10am–2pm & 5.30–7.30pm; ☎ 956 483 714; ⓦ turismoelpuerto.com), is handily sited for picking up a detailed street map as well as a *Ruta del Tapeo* leaflet to help find the best tapas bars. Many of the main sights (including the Castillo San Marcos) are covered in a two-hour guided tour leaving from the Turismo (July–Sept Tues & Sat 10.30am; April–June & Oct Sat 11am; free).

ACCOMMODATION   SEE MAP PAGE 156

Many visitors come to El Puerto for the day, but should you be tempted to stay – and it makes a great break from Cádiz – you'll find plenty of **rooms** within easy walking distance of the ferry. Bear in mind that things get tight during August, when it's worth ringing ahead. If you have problems, ask at the Turismo for assistance; they also keep a list of **apartments** for longer stays.

Camping Playa Las Dunas Paseo Marítimo, Playa La Puntilla; ☎ 956 872 210. Just behind the Playa La Puntilla, this site has modern facilities and plenty of shade. Take bus #2 from Pza de Galeras by the ferry dock. €

★ **Casa de Huéspedes Santa María** C/Pedro Múñoz Seco 38; ⓦ casadehuespedessantamaria.com. Very welcoming refurbished family *pensión*, for spotless rooms with bath, run by an ebullient *dueña andaluza* (female proprietor) and her son. Rooms come with a/c and fans. There's a guests' kitchen and if you want to practise your Spanish, here's the place to stay. €

Casa de los Leones La Placilla 2; ⓦ casadelosleones. com. Enchanting eighteenth-century *casa palacio* – with a fabulous exterior – converted into an elegant aparthotel with a/c apartments featuring bedroom and sitting room plus kitchen equipped with washing machine, fridge and microwave. Higher apartments have more light. €€

Casa No. 6 C/San Bartolemé 14; ⓦ casano6.com. Rooms in a delightful *casa palacio* lovingly restored by an Anglo-Spanish couple; the en-suite rooms above a gorgeous patio (with a bar) are well furnished and come with ceiling fans or a/c, and there are also two fully equipped rooftop apartments with terraces. Doubles €€, apartments €€€

Duques de Medinaceli Pza de los Jazmines 2; ☎ 956 860 777. A palatial five-star hotel housed in the former mansion of the Irish sherry family, Terry, this eighteenth-century edifice has been restored to its former glory with stunning patio, opulent furnishings and rooms decorated with original artworks. Elegant public areas include a (medium-sized) pool, bar-restaurant plus a magnificent botanical garden in the hotel's grounds. Own garage. €€€

Hostal Loreto C/Ganado 17; ⓦ pensionloreto.com. Pleasant *hostal* with a delightful patio. Rooms come with or without bath; en suites have ceiling fans, fridge and TV. €

Hotel Santa María Avda Bajamar s/n; ⓦ hotelsantamaria.es. Good-value three-star riverfront hotel in an eighteenth-century *palacio* beginning to show its age. Has attractive a/c balcony rooms (many with river view). Some have fridges; specify at check-in if you need

THE SHERRY BODEGAS OF EL PUERTO DE SANTA MARÍA

The long, whitewashed warehouses flanking the streets and the banks of the Río Guadalete belong to the big **sherry bodegas**: Luís Caballero, Terry, Osborne and Duff Gordon, the last three founded in the eighteenth and nineteenth centuries by Irish and English families. Osborne (pronounced "Osbornay" in Spanish) and Duff Gordon are now co-owned after a takeover by Osborne, although separate production is maintained and the Duff Gordon brand is sold only outside Spain. Osborne is also the largest producer of Spanish brandy, and its black bull logo – long used as a billboard perched on hills throughout Spain – has become a familiar part of the country's landscape.

In sherry circles, El Puerto is noted for a lighter, more aromatic fino with more *flor* aroma (see box, page 172) imparted due to its humid geographical location, close to the sea.

VISITING THE BODEGAS

It's easy enough to visit the bodegas; many welcome visitors for tours and tastings, although you'll need to call Osborne and Caballero in advance to book a place. Other bodegas also do visits and the Turismo can supply a full list with opening hours.

Bodega Obregón C/Zarza 51; ☎ 956 856 329. A small bodega, founded in 1935. Their bar claims to be the oldest in El Puerto. On Sundays visitors are treated to a free flamenco concert.

Caballero Castillo de San Marcos; ⓦ caballero. es. Another old wine family, the Caballeros have been making wine in El Puerto since the late eighteenth century and their bodega is yet another "wine cathedral" with thousands of sleeping vats. Visits to the bodega are combined with visits to the Castillo de San Marcos (see page 157), which the bodega owns.

Gutiérrez Colosía Avda de Bajamar 40, near the Hotel Santa María; ⓦ gutierrez-colosia.com. Highly rated small producer with a wonderfully atmospheric old bodega founded in the early nineteenth century. Tours in English include tasting of six wines.

Osborne and Duff Gordon C/Los Moros 7; ⓦ osborne.es. The biggest of El Puerto's sherry producers. The beautiful old bodega dates from 1837, while its vinification plant is one of the most modern. Tours daily in English & Spanish; including tasting of wines and brandy.

one. Public areas include restaurant, bar and rooftop pool. Own garage, and there's a pay car park by the river. €€

Monasterio San Miguel C/Larga 27; ⓦ hotelmonasteriodesanmiguel.es. One of the best accommodation options in town, this sixteenth-century monastery has been converted into a luxurious four-star hotel complete with patios, pool and rooftop solarium. Try for a balcony room on the interior patio overlooking

the pool, as street-facing rooms get some noise. See website for offers. Own garage. €€€

Palacio San Bartolomé C/San Bartolomé 21; ⓦ palaciosanbartolome.com. A beautifully converted eighteenth-century *casa palacio* with eleven elegant, individually styled and well-equipped rooms and five suites. The basement also has a gym, spa, sauna and pool for use of guests. €€

EATING

SEE MAP PAGE 156

The best areas in town for places to eat are the **Ribera del Marisco**, a street upstream from the ferry dock lined with a variety of seafood restaurants and bars serving tapas and *raciones*, and the nearby **Plaza de la Herrería**. You should also try the **beaches** of La Puntilla and Valdelagrana for their cluster of friendly bars.

RESTAURANTS AND CAFÉS

Aponiente C/Francisco Cossi Ochoa s/n; ⓦ aponiente. com. Celebrity chef Ángel León's twin-starred Michelin restaurant is located in an old tide mill on the marshes behind the train station, where the inner sanctum dining room may only be visited with a reservation (two sittings at lunch and dinner). Each sitting has a set menu of nineteen courses (3 are desserts) and the food itself is almost exclusively fish and shellfish (plankton features strongly). See the website for menu prices which hardly dip under €200). €€€€

Bodega Jerezana Avda de la Paz, Valdelagrana seafront; ⓦ bodegajerezana.es. Briny tapas bar and traditional restaurant offering a wide range of well-prepared tapas in its bar and more elaborate seafood dishes in the restaurant. Pleasant terrace. €€

Las Capuchinas Monasterio San Miguel, C/Larga 27; ☎ 956 540 525. The *Monasterio* hotel's pleasant *cafetería* serves up good-value tapas and *platos combinados* and a *menú*. €

El Faro de El Puerto 0.5km along the Rota road; ⓦ elfarodelpuerto.com. Outstanding seafood and meat dishes produced under the direction of top chef Fernando Córdoba in this stylish establishment (the twin of the restaurant of the same name in Cádiz). Widely regarded as having the best wine cellar in the province, there's also a pleasant garden terrace, a *menú de degustación,* and a tapas bar. €€€

Los Portales Ribera del Marisco 7; ⓦ restaurantelosportales.com. Long-established, predominantly fish and *mariscos* restaurant, although meat does feature. The dishes are well presented and the kitchen has a creative edge. There's a *menú de degustación* and an extensive wine list. €€€

★ **Romerijo** Ribera del Marisco; ⓦ romerijo.com. This enormous, economical and justifiably popular seafood bar dominates the strip. You can get a takeaway of *mariscos*

in a *cartucho* (paper funnel) from their shop and eat it at outdoor tables where waiters serve beer, and buckets are provided for debris; the *cóctel de mariscos* (seafood cocktail) or any of the six types of *langostinos* are delicious. The same firm's *freiduría* restaurant over the road is equally excellent, where a generous *pescado frito variado* (assorted fried fish) easily serves two. €€

La Taberna C/Puerto Escondido 6; ⓦ latabernadelchefdelmar.com. The original *Aponiente* (see page 160) has been transformed into a more affordable seafood offshoot of Ángel León's culinary empire. The colours are pastel and the atmosphere is refreshingly more relaxed than at León's new venue. However, the influence of the master is visible throughout and a house special is *arroz con plankton*. €€€

TAPAS BARS

Bar Apolo C/Palacios 44; ☎ 956 542 265. Superb neighbourhood bar with a decent tapas and *raciones* range. Specialities include *tortilla* and *pulpo a la gallega* (octopus). €

★ **Bar Vicente** C/Abastos 7; ☎ 956 854 608. This wonderful bar first opened its doors over a century ago and is now part of El Puerto folklore. Show an interest and the latest Vicente (in a long line) will tell you its story and show you an atmospheric photo of the bar in its early days (the wall tiles are originals). Serves delicious tapas and *raciones*; a house special is *atun encebollado* (tuna in onion sauce). €

La Dorada Avda Bajamar 26, 150m south of Pza de las Galeras Reales; ⓦ ladoradarestaurantes.com. Part of a local chain, this vibrant seafood bar offers inexpensive tapas and meal-sized *raciones* with a terrace overlooking the river. The *pescado frito* is superb, and house specials include *choco a la plancha* (cuttlefish) and *boquerones fritos* (fresh anchovies). €

Toro Tapas C/Los Moros 7; ☎ 956 905 020. Spectacular tapas and raciones bar inside a former Osborne wine bodega. The elegant stone arches and brickwork have been scrubbed and a spacious, airy feel is added to by the lightwood furnishings. Recommended options include *pavía de merluza* (hake fingers), *tataki de presa* ibérica (black-pig pork Japanese style) and *chips de berenjenas con tres salsas* (fried aubergine slices with sauces). Also has an inviting patio terrace. €€

DRINKING AND NIGHTLIFE

SEE MAP PAGE 156

Nightlife in El Puerto means just that – in summer many places don't even open until around 11pm. The action centres on the **bars** around the eighteenth-century former fishmarket (El Resbalero) and the focal Plaza Herrería, nearby C/Jesús de los Milagros and the river area.

La Cristalera Pza de las Galeras s/n; ☏ 686 928 738. On the river near the ferry dock, this glass-walled bar – just to the north of the Galeras fountain – is a laidback late-night music venue for the summer months only.

Guateque C/Bajada del Castillo 1; ☏ 647 845 447. From June through to September this is a popular club featuring funk, reggae, latin and blues sounds.

Milwaukee Avda de Bajamar 10; ⓦ www.mkjazz.com. Cavernous riverfront bar with frequent live performances by local and national rock and jazz bands.

Trocadero Pza de la Herrería s/n; ☏ 954 230 344. A roomy place that features lots of dancing to Top40 hits plus frequent live gigs, especially at weekends.

Rota

Much of the 15km between El Puerto and the town of **ROTA** is occupied by one of the three major **US military bases** in Spain. Installed in the 1950s as part of a deal in which Franco exchanged strips of Spanish sovereign territory for economic aid and international "respectability", the base is surrounded by a seemingly endless barbed-wire fence bristling with military gadgetry. Behind the wire it's possible to glimpse farms and whole villages linked by their own bus service along a road system where signs are in English. Huge Ford trucks trundle to and from Rota's harbour, from where the base services and supplies the US Sixth Fleet – including nuclear submarines. In 2011 the Spanish and US governments announced that the base was to be expanded as part of NATO's anti-ballistic missile defence system. In 2014 the first missile-loaded destroyers arrived at the base's harbour and the number of US military personnel and families doubled in size to six thousand, while mammoth works started on extending the harbour facilities. This expansion continues to provide much-needed jobs for the economically down-at-heel town of Rota.

The US military population tends to keep to itself, however, and Rota exudes an affable character very much its own, with an attractive *casco antiguo* and some excellent tapas bars. In season, the resort fairly bounces with life, its magnificent **beach**, the Playa de la Costilla, being the main attraction for the crowds who flock here in August. The town's sights can be seen in under an hour, but Rota's big festival is the early-August **Fiesta de la Urta**, when all the restaurants in town compete to win the prize for the best *urta*-based dish (see page 162).

Castillo de Luna

C/Cuña 2 • June–Sept guided visits Sat & Sun 10am & 8pm; Oct–May Sat & Sun 1pm & 5pm • Charge • ☏ 956 846 345

Highlights in the old quarter include a thirteenth-century castle now housing the Ayuntamiento – the frequently remodelled and much-restored **Castillo de Luna**, with a stunning fifteenth-century patio. Built on the ruins of a Moorish fort, it passed into the hands of two of Spain's great dynastic families, the Guzmáns and the Ponce de Leóns (their arms appear throughout the building), who used it until the middle of the eighteenth century. It then fell into a ruinous state and changed hands numerous times. The Ayuntamiento subsequently took it over in 1987 and spent a fortune restoring the building to the rather too-perfect-looking edifice you see today.

Nuestra Señora de la Expectación

Pza Padre Eugenio s/n • Daily 9am–1pm & 6.30–7.30pm • Free

Also worth a look is the sixteenth-century Gothic church, **Nuestra Señora de la Expectación** (known locally as Nuestra Señora de la O). Behind a box-like exterior lies a fine single-naved church with elegant vaulting, magnificent choir stalls depicting the twelve Apostles by Diego Roldán and – in the chapel of Jesús Nazareno – a delightful eighteenth-century image of the Last Supper crafted in *azulejos* from Triana in Seville province (the barely surviving image of Judas has received some rough treatment over the years).

Capilla de San Juan Bautista

Pza Andalucía • Mon–Fri 10am–1pm & 6.30–8.30pm, Sat 10am–1pm • Free

Worth a visit is the **Capilla de San Juan Bautista** (aka Capilla de la Caridad), near the Turismo, with a spectacular Baroque *altar mayor* (high altar) by Diego Roldán, one of the finest in the province.

ARRIVAL AND DEPARTURE

By bus The bus station is at C/Zoilo Ruíz Mateos s/n, just off Pza del Triunfo, a 10min walk or an easy bus ride south to the centre along C/Calvario.

Destinations Cadiz (5 daily; 1hr 15min); Chipiona (4 daily; 25min); El Puerto de Santa María (11 daily; 35min); Jerez (6 daily; 25min); Sanlúcar (2 daily; 15min); Seville (2 daily; 1hr 30min).

By car Parking in the centre is almost impossible and car parks tend to fill up quickly in high season. Make your

ROTA

way to the seafront – the *Hotel Duque de Najera* is a good place to aim for (see page 162) – where there are street parking spaces along Avda San Juan de Puerto Rico and its continuation Paseo Marítimo Cruz del Rompidillo.

By boat There's a useful and enjoyable catamaran service across the Bay of Cádiz linking Rota to Cádiz (eight services daily between 7am and 9pm from a quay in the Puerto Deportivo; 25min). Services are reduced at weekends.

INFORMATION

Turismo The very helpful Turismo is located in the Torre de la Merced, 2min walk northeast from the focal Pza de España (June–Sept Mon–Fri 9.30am–1.30pm & 6–8.30pm, Sat & Sun 10am–2pm & 6–9pm; Oct–May Mon–Fri 9.30am– 1.30pm & 5–7.30pm, Sat & Sun 11am–2pm; ☎ 956 846 345, ⓦ descubrerota.com). They can provide a useful town map.

ACCOMMODATION

Camping Playa Aguadulce 7km from Rota along the A491 to Chipiona; ⓦ playaaguadulce.com. Fronting a magnificent beach, this is the nearest campsite to Rota with decent services and plenty of shade. €

Duque de Najera C/Gravina 2; ⓦ hotelduquedenajera. com. The town's highly-rated four-star flagship hotel, with sea-view rooms overlooking the harbour. Facilities include a pool, two restaurants, bar, gym and sauna plus there's secure parking on site. See website for offers. €€€

★ **Hostal El Torito** C/Constitución 1, near the Pza de España in the old town; ⓦ eltoritoderota.com. This stunningly minimalist *hostal* has to rank as one of Andalucía's most original, with individually styled a/c rooms (and bathrooms) decorated with cutting-edge furnishings

and artworks with large-lettered Zen quotes running across the walls. Room 5, with its own terrace, is a gem. Facilities include a shared guests' kitchen. €

Hostal Macavi C/Écija 11, off the main Avda Sevilla; ⓦ hostalmacavi.es. Excellent and friendly *hostal* offering a/c en-suite rooms with TV, a mere 50m from the beach, plus a decent restaurant. Breakfast is included. Parking can be tricky in high summer – call ahead for advice. €€

Hostal Sixto Pza Barroso 6; ⓦ hostalsixto.com. Enchanting small *hostal* in a restored townhouse in the heart of the old quarter, with attractive a/c rooms with TV, set around a pretty patio in the house or above their nearby (and good) restaurant a few metres away. Breakfast is included. €€

EATING AND DRINKING

The modern town fans out from the central Plaza Jesús Nazareno fronting the beach, and it's here that you'll find most of the bars, restaurants and nightlife. Look out for the town's very own speciality, the outstandingly tasty *urta a la roteña* (sea bream in a caramelized onion and tomato sauce). Note also that the *urta* season lasts from June to September, outside which many restaurants revert to *mero a la roteña* (grouper). Rota's **tapas bars** tend to be better value than the restaurants, many of which are overpriced and bland. For tapas head down atmospheric C/La Mina, a little northwest of the Castillo de Luna, where a number of

bars line the pedestrianized street.

Bar Torito C/Italia 2; ☎ 605 796 320. A stone's throw from the proprietor's chic *hostal* of the same name (see page 162); less cutting-edge than the *hostal*, but a cosy place with tapas, *raciones* and some cool sounds. Try their *tortilla española*. Also does breakfasts. €

La Callejuela C/San Clemente 2, north of the Castillo; ☎ 605 385 620. Excellent compact fish restaurant with an attractive shaded terrace on the *callejuela* (small street). House specials include *coquinas a la marinera* (clams) as well as fresh fish, *mariscos* and *arroces* (various rice dishes). €€

La Mina C/Mina 27; ☎618 426 009. Fine little tapas bar with a good selection of meat and fish tapas – house specials include *angulas* (baby eels) and *tortillas de camarones* (shrimp fritters). €̄

Mesón Alicantino Avda Sevilla 39, near the Hostal Macaví; ☎688 21 61 70. Friendly and excellent bar-restaurant with a street terrace. Serves good local fish and seafood and does a variation on the town's signature dish with *corvina a la roteña* (meagre). Also paella and some meat dishes *a la plancha*. €̄

Restaurante Tuscania Hostal Sixto, Pza Barroso 6; ☎956 846 310. Located on the ground floor of a *hostal*, this is an authentic Italian family restaurant offering a range of meat and fish dishes and home-made pasta. Has a pleasant (pedestrian) street terrace. €̄€̄

2

Chipiona

From Rota the road north winds inland behind a coast lined with further golden sand beaches to **CHIPIONA**, 18km away, on a point at the edge of the estuary of the Guadalquivir. The town is famed for the Faro de Chipiona – Spain's tallest lighthouse.

Presenting itself as a modest, straightforward seaside resort crammed with family *pensiones* and small hotels, Chipiona is a great place to spend a few days, and has some magnificent beaches. The town has a charming **old quarter** on its northern flank, cut through by sinuous, white-walled alleyways. The major thoroughfare here is the pedestrianized Calle Isaac Peral (and its continuation C/Miguel Cervantes), lined with shops, bars and some elegant buildings and hotels. It's perhaps best avoided in August, however, when the town's charms are all but submerged beneath an onslaught of mainly Spanish visitors.

Nuestra Señora de Regla

Avda Nuestra Señora de la Regla s/n • Daily 8am–noon & 5–8.30pm • Free

Older tourists come to Chipiona for the spa waters, channelled into a fountain at the fourteenth-century church of **Nuestra Señora de Regla**, which incorporates a delightful *claustro gótico* (Gothic cloister) adorned with seventeenth-century Triana *azulejos* – although it's kept shut (try to find a priest or church warden to open it for you).

The main altar displays the **Virgen de la Regla**, the town's iconic patroness. This curious black Virgin is said to have been the image to which St Augustine prayed when the Vandals were about to attack his city, Hippo in North Africa, in the fifth century. He died and, so the story goes, his Virgin was carried off to Spain and safety by his disciple St Cyprian. She was venerated for three centuries in Chipiona prior to the Moorish invasions when Augustinian monks hid her in an underground cistern where she remained for five hundred years. After the *Reconquista* she was retrieved and – following numerous miracles – the shrine was built which finally grew into the church we see today.

Faro de Chipiona

Pza de las Americas • Visits May–Sept; same hours as Turismo (see page 164), where you will need to call first and they will open it for you • Charge • ☎956 929 065

Constructed in 1863–67 over the remains of its Roman predecessor, the giant 72m-high **Faro de Chipiona** is the tallest lighthouse in Spain, the third highest in Europe and the fifth loftiest in the world. There has been a lighthouse on this site since the first century BC, when the Roman consul, Quinto Servilius Caepion, ordered the construction of a beacon to help shipping navigate the hazardous offshore rocks and currents. The lighthouse became known as Caepionis Turris, which lent its name to the settlement as well. An image of the Roman lighthouse and its Latin name now comprise the town's coat of arms. It's a gruelling 344-step climb to the top – from where there are fine **views** along the coast.

Beaches

For most visitors to Chipiona it is the 12km of beaches that are the lure. Stretching south of the town beyond the lighthouse is the long **Playa de la Regla** and its

2

continuation **Playa Camarón**, both best avoided in August, although for much of the year it's possible to leave the crowds behind. In the opposite direction lie **Playa de las Canteras, Playa Cruz del Mar** and – beyond the Puerto Deportivo – the tranquil **Playa Micaela**. Northeast of here, towards Sanlúcar, are sand bars and rocks with fine views towards the Marismas de Doñana and the Guadalquivir estuary.

ARRIVAL AND DEPARTURE   CHIPIONA

By bus The bus station is at the junction of Avda de Almería and Avda de Andalucía at the eastern end of town. To reach the centre (a 10min walk, or take a taxi), follow Avda de Andalucía and its continuation Avda del Ejército until you reach the junction with C/Isaac Peral, the old quarter's main pedestrianized artery.

Destinations Cádiz (13 daily; 1hr 30min); El Puerto de Santa María (13 daily; 1hr 5min); Rota (4 daily; 25min); Sanlúcar (19 daily; 15min); Seville (12 daily; 2hr 30min).
By car Outside August, coming into Chipiona by car shouldn't present any great problems and street parking is plentiful and easy to find.

INFORMATION

Turismo C/Castillo 5, in the restored castle on the seafront (June–Sept daily 10am–2pm & 5–7pm; Oct–May Mon–Fri 10am–2pm & 5–7pm, Sat & Sun 10am–2pm; ☎ 956 929 065, ⓦ turismochipiona.es). A well-organized Turismo, it can help with maps, information and accommodation and has a list of tapas bars. A museum (entered via the Turismo)

in the same building mounts an exhibition entitled "Cádiz y El Nuevo Mundo" (Cádiz and the New World) documenting Cádiz's role in the history of the Americas from Columbus to the decline of the Spanish empire (Tues–Sun 10am–2pm; charge).

ACCOMMODATION

Hostal Andalucía C/Larga 14, close to the seaward end of C/Isaac Peral; ⓦ hostal-andalucia.com. Welcoming, central *hostal* with refurbished and spotless a/c en-suite rooms. There's also a pleasant patio and a rooftop solarium. €

★ **Hostal Gran Capitán** C/Fray Baldomero González 3, close to the seaward end of C/Isaac Peral; ⓦ hostalgrancapitan.com. Very attractive and friendly *hostal* housed in a venerable *casa antigua* now owned and run by one of the descendants of Spain's fifteenth-century military commander Gran Capitán Gonzalo de Córdoba. The simple but attractive a/c en-suite rooms come with TV and the proprietor also rents out bicycles. €

Hostal San Miguel Avda de la Regla 79; ☎ 956 372 976. Comfortable en-suite rooms in a charming Art Nouveau mansion close to the church of Nuestra Señora de Regla. The friendly proprietors also rent some apartments nearby sleeping up to four. June–Sept. Doubles €, apartments €€

Hotel La Española C/Isaac Peral 4; ⓦ hotellaespanola. com. Superbly renovated and good-value old hotel – the front door is a mere 20m from the waves and many rooms have sea views. There's parking in an underground garage, but get staff to park your vehicle as the entry is tortuously crooked. €

EATING AND DRINKING

Chipiona has a gratifying range of restaurants, all excelling in **seafood**. For tapas and bars – some with music – take a stroll along the pedestrianized C/Isaac Peral. The bars also serve up Chipiona's excellent **moscatel wine** made in numerous small bodegas around the town.

★ **Bar Peña Bética** C/Larga 46 at the junction with C/Isaac Peral; ☎ 956 374 344. Highly popular and wonderfully atmospheric *gaditano* bar. It matters little that it's the Chipiona branch of the Real Betis supporters' club (one of Seville's two big football teams), the fried fish is excellent and the welcome ebullient. Try the *chipirones en salsa verde* (small squid). €

★ **Las Canteras** Playa de las Canteras s/n; ⓦ barlascanteras.es. A superb seafront fish and *mariscos* restaurant with a shady terrace and fine sea views at the end of the tiny Playa de Las Canteras close to the lighthouse.

Everything is fresh from the sea and the *urta* and *dorada* are especially recommended, as are the *boquerones fritos* (anchovies) – and they do pretty good *patatas fritas* (chips) too. €€

★ **Los Corrales** Playa de las Canteras s/n; ☎ 956 375 129. Next to *Las Canteras* at the northern end of this small beach cove, and just as good as its rival (although slightly pricier), with its own great seafront terrace. House specials include *arroz de mariscos* (shellfish paella), *salmonetes fritos* (red mullet) and wonderful *langostinos de Chipiona* (deepwater prawns). €€

La Pañoleta C/Isaac Peral 5; ⓦ hotellaespanola.com. Belonging to (and in the same building as) the *Hotel La Española*, this restaurant offers a varied menu of fish (try the *urta a la roteña*) and meat dishes. €€

Sanlúcar de Barrameda

Like El Puerto de Santa María, **SANLÚCAR DE BARRAMEDA**, 8km beyond Chipiona, is a major sherry town. A substantial place with an attractive old quarter set at the mouth of the Guadalquivir, it is the main depot for **manzanilla** wine – a pale dry fino variety with a salty tang – highly regarded by connoisseurs and much in evidence in the bars round here. Sanlúcar is also one of the best places in Andalucía for **seafood**, for which manzanilla is the perfect accompaniment.

The fiesta of the Virgen de la Caridad takes place on August 15, honouring the town's patron, the Virgin of Charity; the central Calle Ancha is the site of a colourful spectacle, laid end to end with a carpet of colourful "flowers" – actually tinted sawdust. The town's other big knees-up is the Feria de la Manzanilla at the end of May, an excuse to celebrate Sanlúcar's famous wine, with much drinking and dancing.

The town is split into three distinct quarters, the older and formerly walled **Barrio Alto** on the hill, the **Barrio Bajo** below and the town's former port – the **Bajo de Guía** – 1km away on the river. Many of the monuments are in the Barrio Alto, where a good number of bodegas and their warehouses are also to be found, emitting a pleasant hint of sherry into the air.

Brief history

Although there was a small settlement here in Roman times and the Moors built a fort to guard the vital Guadalquivir estuary from sea raiders, it was only after the recapture of the town in 1264 by Alfonso X that Sanlúcar grew to become one of sixteenth-century Spain's leading ports. **Columbus** sailed from here on his third voyage to the Americas and it was also from here in 1519 that Magellan set out to circumnavigate the globe. Decline in the eighteenth century, however, was exacerbated by the War of Independence and the town was revived only in the mid-nineteenth century when the duke of Montpensier built a summer palace here. Since then Sanlúcar has grown into the popular resort it is today.

Plaza del Cabildo and around

The **Plaza del Cabildo**, a charming, palm-fringed square ringed with bars and sporting a splendid fountain, is a good place to start your explorations. Directly southwest of

---

VISITING THE COTO DE DOÑANA NATIONAL PARK

Access to the vast, marshy expanse of the **Coto de Doñana National Park** (see page 313), on the shore opposite Sanlúcar, is strictly controlled in order to protect Europe's largest wildlife sanctuary and a vital wetland for a variety of migrating birds. However, a three-hour **boat cruise** aboard the *Real Fernando* allows visitors to access the park, giving a wonderful introduction to this remarkable area. The boat – which has a *cafetería* on board – leaves from the Bajo de Guía (Wvisitasdonana.com) The trips allow two short guided walks led by wildlife experts inside the park, where you'll visit a hamlet of *chozas* (traditional Doñana huts) and should see *jabalí* (wild boar), wild horses, flamingos and a profusion of birdlife including buzzards, herons, kites, cranes and eagles, as well as stunning wild flowers, depending on your luck and the season. In summer it's best to book as early as you can, since the trips are limited to 94 passengers; binoculars (essential) can be rented on board.

Collect your tickets (at least 30min in advance of the sailing) from the Fábrica de Hielo, Bajo de Guía s/n (daily 9am–8pm), virtually opposite the *Real Fernando*'s jetty. This extravagant exhibition centre in Sanlúcar's old ice factory was created by the National Park authority and contains stunningly unimaginative displays of the park's flora and fauna. Viajes Doñana, C/San Juan 20 (❶956 362 540), also do all-terrain **vehicle-based trips** into the park and covering about 70km in four hours. The Turismo has details of other companies offering specialist tours for birdwatching and flora and fauna.

2

the square Plaza de San Roque adjoins the **morning market**, which is one of the town's great shows when it's in full swing – Saturday mornings are best, when burly *señoras* give no quarter while attempting to get their hands on the best fish.

Iglesia de San Jorge

C/San Jorge • Mon–Sat 10am–1pm • Free

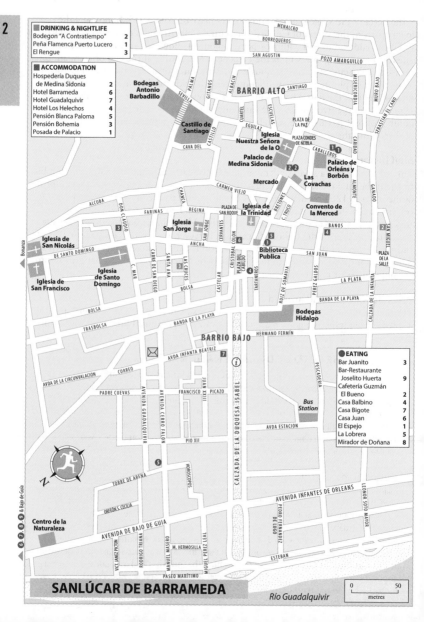

DRINKING & NIGHTLIFE
Bodegon "A Contratiempo" — 2
Peña Flamenca Puerto Lucero — 1
El Rengue — 3

ACCOMMODATION
Hospedería Duques
  de Medina Sidonia — 2
Hotel Barrameda — 6
Hotel Guadalquivir — 7
Hotel Los Helechos — 4
Pensión Blanca Paloma — 5
Pensión Bohemia — 3
Posada de Palacio — 1

EATING
Bar Juanito — 3
Bar-Restaurante
  Joselito Huerta — 9
Cafetería Guzmán
  El Bueno — 2
Casa Balbino — 4
Casa Bigote — 7
Casa Juan — 6
El Espejo — 1
La Lobrera — 5
Mirador de Doñana — 8

SANLÚCAR DE BARRAMEDA — *Río Guadalquivir*

0 — 50 metres

The sixteenth-century **Iglesia de San Jorge** was constructed by English sherry merchants with special permission from the duke of Medina Sidonia, who was keen to encourage their lucrative trade. Henry VIII of England allowed the merchants to levy the substantial English community for funds to build the church, but soon after its completion in 1517 it became embroiled in Henry's struggles with Rome. A document dated 1591 records that Sanlúcar's English community – the majority still loyal to Rome – decided to hand over the church to some Irish monks who themselves had been chased out of England by Henry's daughter, Elizabeth I. After serving as a church and a hospital for the poor, the church was rebuilt in the eighteenth century in the Baroque style, funded by the duke of Medina Sidonia and the town council. Inside, a magnificent retablo by Juan González de Herrera is topped off by a mounted San Jorge (St George) slaying the dragon.

2

Iglesia de Santo Domingo
C/Ancha • Open 30min before services, which are held Mon–Fri 9.30am & 8pm, Sat 8pm, Sun 10.30am, noon & 7.30pm • Free

Sanlúcar's only church built entirely of stone, the sixteenth-century **Iglesia de Santo Domingo** was formerly the church of a Dominican monastery to which it was attached. Inside, there are a couple of fine retablos and the interesting tombs of a seventeenth-century duke and duchess of Niebla on either side of the main altar.

Las Covachas
C/Bretones

The Barrio Alto is reached by following Calle Bretones uphill from the Plaza San Roque. To the left, beyond the market you pass the remarkable fifteenth-century **Las Covachas** (market stalls) with an elegantly carved, if worn, Gothic frontage. Built at the behest of the second duke of Medina Sidonia, next to the *alcaicería* or silk market, this was Sanlúcar's first shopping centre, comprising ten (now glassed-in) ogival arches separated by pillars decorated with serpents. Soon established as the town's commercial district, with the construction of the adjoining market in the eighteenth century so it has remained.

Convento de la Merced
C/Bretones • Enquire at the Turismo about visits • Free

Continuing uphill from Las Covachas from the way bends left, passing the seventeenth-century **Convento de la Merced**. The religious order abandoned the ruinous convent in 1960, after which it fell into a dilapidated state. The then owner, the Duchess of Medina Sidonia (see box, page 168), finally ceded ownership to the Ayuntamiento of Sanlúcar, who restored the building as a concert hall, the function it serves today. Designed by Juan de Oviedo and Alonso de Vandelvira, son of the more famous Andrés (see page 348), the interior has fabulous stone vaulting, while a rather plain white-walled facade on Calle Bretones has a soberly worked entrance portal with tympanum flanked by six stone porthole windows.

Palacio de Orleáns y Borbón and gardens
C/Bretones • Mon–Fri 8.30am–2.30pm • Free (no visits when the Ayuntamiento is being used for an official function); gardens open Mon–Fri 8.30am–1.30pm

Beyond the Covento de la Merced stands the neo-Mudéjar **Palacio de Orleáns y Borbón**, a flamboyantly decorated nineteenth-century summer palace of the dukes of Montpensier, now occupied by the Ayuntamiento. You are allowed to step inside the building's entrance to take a look at an impressive patio but the building's other rooms – decorated in a potpourri of neo-Mudéjar, Rococo and ancient Egyptian styles – are off limits outside guided visits. The palace's true glory, however, are the magnificent **gardens** behind (access via the Ayuntamiento), filled with palms, follies and fountains as well as offering magnificent views over the town and river.

2

THE RED DUCHESS

In 2008, Sanlúcar mourned the passing of **Luisa Isabel Álvarez de Toledo**, more formally known in the town as the Duchess of Medina Sidonia or by her nickname "La Duquesa Roja" (the Red Duchess). The great ducal family of Medina Sidonia – Spain's oldest dynasty, founded in 1455 – has had a hand in most of the country's great historic events from the *Reconquista* to the launching of the Spanish Armada – which was commanded by the seventh Duke of Medina Sidonia.

A freethinker from her earliest days, she was expelled from numerous convent schools due to her tomboyish and nonconformist behaviour. Upon the death of her father in 1955 Isabel inherited the title of the ducal house and moved into the palace in Sanlúcar. She joined the then illegal Socialist Workers Party (PSOE) and displayed contempt for Franco and his regime at every opportunity. One of her anti-Franco activities – supporting farmers in Almería who had been affected by the nuclear incident at Palomares in 1966 (see box, page 515) – landed her in jail for eight months in 1969. The Franco government – embarrassed when the story hit the world headlines – offered her a pardon providing she repented. Typically she refused and served out the full sentence. She then wrote a devastating indictment of prison conditions, shaming the government into a programme of reforms. A fervent believer in land reform, she gave away vast tracts of her estates to form rural cooperatives, until only the Palace of Medina Sidonia remained in her hands. As a historian, she spent most of her time organizing the massive and important historical archive of the ducal family and set up the foundation that now continues the work.

She died as she had lived, controversial to the end. On her deathbed – thanks to Spain's new law permitting same-sex marriages – she married her secretary and long-time companion Liliana Dahlmann who, as its president, now runs the Fundación Casa Medina Sidonia. Her memory is much cherished here, and in 2009 the town honoured the duchess by renaming one of its major thoroughfares after her. The former Calzada del Ejército (Boulevard of the Army), an avenue leading down to the river, now bears the name Calzada de la Duquesa Isabel. As a pacifist, she would no doubt have approved.

Nuestra Señora de la O

Pza de los Condes de Niebla • Fri & Sat 11am–1pm (also open for daily Mass Mon–Sat 8pm, Sun noon & 8pm) • Free

Taking a left at the top of Calle Bretones into Calle Caballero will bring you to – on the right – **Plaza de la Paz**, a delightful small square, and, almost opposite, the church of **Nuestra Señora de la O**, Sanlúcar's oldest. Founded in the thirteenth century by the family of Guzmán El Bueno (see page 197) but much altered since, the exterior has an exquisite Gothic-Mudéjar portal with archivolt moulding above which are depicted lions bearing the coats of arms of the Guzmans. Inside there's an impressive *artesonado* ceiling.

Palacio de los Duques de Medina Sidonia

Pza de las Condes de Niebla • **Palace** Tours Wed, Thurs & Fri at noon, Sun 11.30am & noon • Charge **Gardens** Daily 9am–1pm • Charge • ⓦ fcmedinasidonia.com

Nuestra Señora de la O is connected to the **Palacio de los Duques de Medina Sidonia**, whose sixteenth- to eighteenth-century interior houses the family's important historical archive and has wonderful views over the Coto de Doñana. Until her death in 2008 the duchess of Medina Sidonia (see box, page 168) lived here. The guided tour of the palace and its beautiful gardens takes an hour and proceeds through impressive rooms stuffed with works by Spanish masters such as Roelas, Morales and Goya.

Castillo de Santiago

C/Sevilla • June–Sept Mon–Tues audio-guided visits 10.15am–2.30pm & 7–10pm; Wed–Sun 10.15am–10pm; consult Turismo or website for visits Oct–May • Charge • ⓦ castillodesantiago.com

Heading northeast from the palace brings you to the fifteenth-century **Castillo de Santiago**, where audio-guided visits and tours enable you to see the castle's barbicans, Plaza de Armas and towers with stunning views. Besides information on the castle's history, a museum also has an exhibition of clothing styles from the eighteenth to the twentieth centuries.

A flight of steps beside the castle leads back down to the Barrio Bajo.

Bajo de Guía

Bus #3 from the Calzada de la Duquesa Isabel, taxi from Pza del Cabildo or a 15min walk

A kilometre north of the centre, the **Bajo de Guía** used to be Sanlúcar's fishing port, with boats moored along a wharf and pier – both long gone. In 1947 the Fábrica de Hielo (ice factory, and now the Doñana park's exhibition centre) was built to provide ice for the preservation of the catches of fish and shellfish. When, in 1967 it was decided that the upstream port of Bonanza (see page 169) was more suited to the demands of a modern fishing industry, the Bajo de Guía metamorphosed into the tranquil backwater it is today. It has not given up on its piscatorial past, however, and now makes its money from a line of fish restaurants widely regarded as among the best in the country.

Fronting the restaurants, the shell-encrusted **river beach** – unfortunately marred by a lengthy and rather ugly concrete esplanade – is nevertheless a nice place to while away some time, and is usually quite deserted. In early and late August, the beach is the setting for some exciting horse races, a tradition dating from 1845, accompanied by lots of betting and riotous partying by revellers filling the bars and restaurants along the Bajo de Guía riverfront.

Coto de Doñana beaches

Ferry to Coto de Doñana runs daily 8am to 9pm

From April to September, a *barcaza* (ferry barge) carries passengers to the **Coto de Doñana's beaches** on the opposite bank of the Guadalquivir. It leaves from a quay at the Bajo de Guía, near the *Real Fernando* jetty (see box, page 165) and is operated by the same company. The Doñana's beaches suffer from pollution, but do provide a change of scene and some birdwatching possibilities. There are absolutely no facilities, so be sure to take along food and drink, and perhaps a parasol. And remember that no incursions into the national park are allowed; wardens are on patrol and tend to be severe with those who flout the regulations.

Bonanza

By taxi from the Pza del Cabildo, or by bus #1 from the top of the Calzada de la Duquesa Isabel

Four kilometres upstream from Sanlúcar, the small port of **Bonanza** is where the town's sizeable fishing fleet is based, their catch sold at entertaining auctions (Mon–Sat at 5pm) on the harbourside. This is also the very spot from where Columbus and Magellan set sail on their epic voyages.

ARRIVAL AND DEPARTURE   SANLÚCAR DE BARRAMEDA

By bus The bus station is at Avda Guzmán El Bueno, between the river and the centre, to the west of the main avenue Calzada de la Duquesa Isabel. Services are run by Amarillos (☎ 956 385 060) and Linesur (☎ 956 341 063). Destinations Cádiz (12 daily; 1hr 15min); Chipiona (19 daily; 15min); El Puerto de Santa María (3 daily; 40min);

Jerez (10 daily; 40min).

By car It's best to avoid the congested central zone and find a parking place along the Calzada de la Duquesa Isabel. When this is full, there's a subterranean pay car park at this avenue's southern end (nearest the centre).

INFORMATION AND ACTIVITIES

Turismo At Calzada de la Duquesa Isabel s/n (July & Aug Mon–Sat 10am–2pm & 6–8pm, Sat & Sun 10am– 2pm; March–June & Sept–Nov Mon–Fri 10am–2pm & 4–6pm, Sat & Sun 10am–2pm; Dec–Feb Mon–Sat

2

SANLÚCAR'S MANZANILLA BODEGAS

The delicate taste of Sanlúcar's distinctive **manzanilla** is created by the seaside environment in which the wine is matured, and by the fact that it's not fortified with alcohol (as happens in Jerez and El Puerto). The humid microclimate necessary for the growth of the dense *flor* (yeast) inside the wine butts is added to by the moist *poniente* (westerly) wind that blows across the Coto de Doñana, imparting the characteristic saltiness to this driest of all sherries.

Sanlúcar is less aggressive than Jerez in its public relations (despite manzanilla recently overtaking fino sales on the peninsula for the first time), and only a few of Sanlúcar's **bodegas** are open for visits and tastings. We have quoted the bodega's guided tours in English; visit their websites for visits in Spanish and other languages.

VISITING THE BODEGAS

Antonio Barbadillo C/Sevilla 25, near the castle; ⓦ barbadillo.com. The town's major producer, founded in 1821, is responsible for seventy percent of all manzanilla, and also makes *manzanilla pasada*, an exceptional 15-year-old wine (as against the normal four for standard fino), as well as one of Andalucía's best white table wines (Castillo de San Diego) from the same Palomino grape. The bodega's Museo de Manzanilla (daily 10am–3pm; free) is located slightly east of the castle and has a shop attached where you can buy their produce.

Bodegas Herederos de Argüeso C/Mar 8; ⓦ argueso.es. Founded in 1822, this is another old established firm, makers of San León manzanilla, another highly popular brand. Phone to reserve a tour.

Bodegas Hidalgo C/Banda Playa 24; ⓦ lagitana. es. Founded at the end of the eighteenth century, this bodega produces the La Gitana brand, one of Spain's most popular manzanillas. To visit, first go to the Hidalgo shop, located almost opposite the Turismo on the Calzada de la Duquesa Isabel (which also sells the bodega's wines). The bodega is a short walk away around the corner. Reserve in advance by phone or at the shop.

Bodegas La Cigarrera Pza Madre de Dios s/n, near the Hotel Los Helechos; ⓦ bodegaslacigarrera.com. Another family-controlled bodega, La Cigarrera (the name means "cigarette seller", whose image appears on their bottles) dates from the eighteenth century. Their leading brand is the La Cigarrera manzanilla, although they also produce *oloroso* and amontillado wines.

10am–2pm & 4–6pm, Sun 10am–2pm; ☎ 956 366 110, ⓦ sanlucarturismo.com or ⓦ sanlucardebarrameda.es). Staff can provide a detailed street map, a tapas guide and details of weekend guided tours (free) of the town throughout the summer.

Horseriding A number of companies run guided tours in the Río Guadalquivir area. The reliable Club Equestre La Arboleda (ⓦ clubecuestrelaarboleda.com) is one; the Turismo can provide details of others.

ACCOMMODATION

SEE MAP PAGE 166

There's a shortage of budget accommodation in Sanlúcar, and in August you'll be pushed to find anything at all. This is when a number of *casas particulares* open to mop up the overflow.

★ **Hospedería Duques de Medina Sidonia** Pza Condes de Niebla 1; ⓦ ruralduquesmedinasidonia. com. The best address in town, in the palace of the dukes of Medina Sidonia, one of Spain's most blue-blooded dynasties. The *hospedería* has nine excellent-value beamed rooms and suites with original features and tasteful furnishings surrounding a charming patio – suites also come with private terrace. Breakfast is included. Doubles €€, suites €€€

Hotel Barrameda C/Ancha 10; ⓦ hotelbarrameda. com. Built just over a decade ago, this central two-star hotel offers light and airy a/c rooms with large TVs, some with a terrace balcony. Also has a pleasant patio, a solarium roof terrace and garage. €€

Hotel Guadalquivir Calzada de la Duquesa Isabel 20; ⓦ hotelguadalquivir.com. Modern three-star hotel towering over the thoroughfare leading to the river. The functional rooms come with a/c, while some also have balcony, and there are good views from higher ones. See website for offers. €€€

Hotel Los Helechos Pza Madre de Dios 9, ⓦ hotelloshelechos.com. Smart, very reasonably priced three-star central hotel in converted former bodega with attractively furnished rooms around two charming patios and lots of traditional features such as fountains and tiled patios. Also has a pool and garage. €€

Pensión Blanca Paloma Pza de San Roque; ☎ 956 380 981. Good-value and friendly *pensión* in a central position, offering simple but acceptable rooms sharing bath. €

Pensión Bohemia C/Don Claudio 5; ☎ 956 369 599.

Comfortable en-suite a/c rooms with TV – albeit slightly dark due to windows facing an internal corridor – on a quiet street. €

★ **Posada de Palacio** C/Caballeros 11;

EATING

SEE MAP PAGE 166

Sanlúcar is renowned for the quality of its **seafood**, and the place to head for is the Bajo de Guía, the old fishing district upstream from where the Calzada de la Duquesa Isabel meets the river. Numerous bars and restaurants lining the waterfront have terrace views towards the Coto de Doñana and serve excellent seafood, washed down with manzanilla. In the Barrio Bajo, the Plaza del Cabildo has a number of good **tapas and breakfast bars**.

RESTAURANTS

Bar-Restaurante Joselito Huerta Bajo de Guía s/n, at the upstream end of the strip; ⓦ joselitohuerta.com. Friendly seafood restaurant, slightly less expensive than its neighbours and with a popular river terrace. The *pescaíto frito* (fried fish), *almejas* (clams), *cazón con tomate* (shark) and *acedías* (baby sole) are all excellent, and they also serve good tapas at the bar. €€

★ **Casa Bigote** Bajo de Guía 10; ⓦ restaurantecasabigote.com. Celebrated establishment and one of the "big two" on the waterfront – which has edged ahead of its neighbour. Excellent tapas in their lively bar or more formal dining in the restaurant, with outstanding fish and *arroz de marisco* (seafood paella). Don't miss the succulent local *langostinos* (prawns), either. An upstairs dining room offers panoramic views across the river. Reservations advised. €€€

Casa Juan Bajo de Guía 26; ⓦ restaurantecasajuanorozco.com. Another Bajo de Guía favourite with a great river-view terrace and house specials including *arroz a la marinera*, *rape al cerco* (monkfish) plus excellent *langostinos* (deepwater prawns) and *coquinas* (clams). €€

Mirador de Doñana Bajo de Guía s/n; ⓦ miradordonana.com. The second of the Bajo de Guía's "big two" is in new hands and has had a makeover with redesigned tapas bar below and river-view restaurant above. There's also a pleasant outdoor terrace. Thirty-plus brands of manzanilla (in addition to a wide range of mariscos) are on offer in the bar, while corvina a la plancha

ⓦ posadadepalacio.com. Elegantly converted eighteenth-century *casa palacio* with a delightful patio and tastefully furnished rooms with character. Rooftop terraces, bar and an intimate atmosphere make it rather special. €€

(meagre) and urta a la roteña (Cádiz bream) are specialities of the restaurant. €€

TAPAS BARS AND CAFÉS

Bar Juanito Pza San Roque 18; ☎ 956 368 137. Reliable local tapas venue, noted for its seafood (try the *almejas*) and *chacinas* (cured pork meats), with a terrace on this lively square. €

Cafetería Guzmán El Bueno Pza Condes de Niebla 1; ☎ 956 360 161. With its chintz furnishings, antiques display cabinets and suits of medieval armour, the cafetería of the *Hospedería Duques de Medina Sidonia* hotel makes an elegant venue for breakfast or afternoon tea. Pastries, bread and preserves come from their own kitchen and there's an enchanting patio garden. €

★ **Casa Balbino** Pza del Cabildo; ⓦ casabalbino.es. Behind an unassuming facade lies one of the best tapas bars in Andalucía. Long established, its walls are hung with faded photos and the obligatory bulls' heads, and the smoothly efficient bar staff will guide you through a daunting tapas menu. The manzanillas are outstanding and their *tortillita de camarones* (shrimp fritter) is justly famous and has been lauded by a visiting Ferran Adriá. There is a (self-service) terrace on the square. €€

El Espejo C/Caballeros 11; ⓦ elespejo-sanlucar.es. Entertaining *raciones* gastro-bar with a bright, white and modern interior. Seating is on bar-stools at high tables and the dishes have a creative edge. There's also a patio terrace at the rear. Try the *atún de cuatro texturas* (tuna tempura), *tartar de atun con ajo blanco (tuna with white gazpacho)* or one of their interesting salads. €€

★ **La Lobrera** Avda Cerro Falón 32; ⓦ restaurantelalobera.com. Outstanding and highly popular tapas and *raciones* bar with a "*toque creativo*" and a lively terrace. Recommended dishes include *risotto de vieras y pulpo* (scallops & octopus), *mini hamburguesa de bacalao* (cod "hamburger") and *croquetas de mariscos* (shellfish croquettes). €

DRINKING AND NIGHTLIFE

SEE MAP PAGE 166

Bodegón "A Contratiempo" C/San Miguel 5; ☎ 653 071 099. Flamenco performances between June and August in an atmospheric small theatre with professional singers and dancers. Seats must be reserved in advance (when you should also confirm show times).

Peña Flamenca Puerto Lucero C/de la Zorra 1 (near junction with C/Palomar) in the Barrio Alto; ☎ 666 70 49 23. Wonderful old flamenco *peña* with walls lined

with photos. The bar is open daily, but performances are irregular; phone (Spanish only) or enquire at the Turismo.

El Rengue C/Las Luces s/n at the junction with C/Benegil (off the north side of C/Ancha); ☎ 610 063 968. Late-night *rociero* bar with a great atmosphere. Often stages impromptu flamenco, especially at weekends, usually on Saturdays.

2

Jerez de la Frontera

Encircled by vines planted in the chalky, *albariza* soil, **JEREZ DE LA FRONTERA**, 22km inland from Sanlúcar and 35km from Cádiz, is the home and heartland of sherry (itself an English corruption of the town's Moorish name, Xerez) and also, less known but equally important, of Spanish brandy. Once you've penetrated some architecturally bleak suburbs, you'll find a town centre that possesses a charming *casco antiguo* and a number of elegant, palm-fringed squares, as well as a handful of notable Renaissance and Baroque churches and palaces.

Jerez's biggest attractions are indisputably the great **sherry bodegas** located in the heart of the town. The sherry dynasties that own these companies (or used to own them, as many have been taken over by international conglomerates) are renowned as some of the biggest snobs in Spain, and take a haughty pride in aping the traits and customs of the English upper-middle class – their strutting around on polo horses,

---

SHERRY – JEREZ'S LIQUID GOLD

It's believed that the Phoenicians brought the vine to this area early in the first millennium BC. The Romans shipped wine from here to all parts of their empire, and the Roman settlement of Asido Caesaris may well be the town from which Jerez derives its name, later corrupted to **Xerez** (pronounced "Sherrish") by the Moors.

British merchants were attracted here in the fourteenth century and, following the expulsions of Moors and Jews in the wake of the *Reconquista*, they established firms that first traded, and later produced, Falstaff's "sack" (probably derived from the Spanish *sacar* – to draw out – referring to the *solera* system). Some of the bodegas, or cellars, were founded by British Catholic refugees, barred from careers at home by the sixteenth-century Supremacy Act. The names of the great sherry firms today testify to the continuing love affair of the British with this wine: Britain, along with the Netherlands, still consumes up to seventy percent of all exports.

It's a particular combination of climate, soil and grape variety that gives **sherry wine** its distinctive style. The chalky, white *albariza* soil of the region is the natural habitat for the Palomino sherry grape, and though the resulting wine is fairly ordinary stuff, it's what happens inside the bodegas that transforms it into sherry. Here the wine is transferred to oak butts with loose stoppers to let in air. Then the **flor** – a puffy layer of scum (actually yeast) – magically appears on the surface of the wine, not only preventing oxidization but feeding on it too, in the process adding a special flavour and bouquet. It is the subtle nature of the *flor*, the ingredient that cannot be duplicated by competitors, that imparts a different flavour to the sherries of Jerez, El Puerto de Santa María and especially Sanlúcar, where it absorbs the salty breezes off the sea, producing the most delicate fino of all, manzanilla. The bodegas of Jerez, unlike in other wine-producing areas, are situated above ground in order to maintain the humid conditions necessary for the growth of this *flor* – helped by sprinkling the sand-covered floors with water.

The final stage in the creation of sherry – but not manzanilla – is the fortification of the wine with alcohol (up to fifteen percent in the case of fino sherry) before it enters the **solera** system. Because sherry is not a vintage, or yearly, wine, it is always blended with older wines through the *soleras* and *criaderas*, as many as six rows of butts placed on top of each other from which the wine is gradually transferred from the topmost to the bottommost over a period of time. This process, mixing the new, younger, wine with the greater quantity of mature, older, wine, "educates" it to assume its character. The wine drawn off at the end for bottling has an even consistency year after year, conveniently with none of the problems of "good" and "bad" years. The classic sherry is the bone-dry fino, but variations on the theme include amontillado (where the *flor* is allowed to "die" in the butt, imparting a nutty flavour), oloroso (produced as fino but minus the *flor*) and cream – pronounced "cray-am" in Andalucía – a purely British concoction where sweet grapes are blended with oloroso.

wearing tweeds and speaking Spanish with an affected accent has earned them the nickname of *señoritos*, or "toffs".

Sherry bodegas apart, the town has many other worthwhile sights, not least the **Barrio de Santiago**, a fascinating and authentic white-walled *gitano* (gypsy) quarter to the north of the cathedral. Conveniently, all the major sights and most of the bodegas are within just a few minutes' walk of the central, elegant and palm-fringed **Plaza del Arenal**, dominated by a bronze statue of the 1920s dictator Primo de Rivera, who was born here.

Brief history

The area around Jerez has been inhabited since Neolithic times. In the first millennium BC the settlement here may have been founded by – or had trading links with – the lost city of Tartessus (see page 526), while the Phoenicians were active in the area around the same time. It was later, however, under the Romans that the city – now known as Asta Regia – grew to prominence. The vine is inextricably linked with Jerez's fortunes and the conquering legions discovered a town already producing **wine** (the Greek geographer Strabo states that the Phoenicians first planted the grape here). Under Roman tutelage, production methods were improved and it was soon being exported to Rome where the "Vinum Ceretensis" acquired a healthy reputation. The Moorish occupation did nothing to dampen the region's wine industry – despite the Koran's prohibition – and it seems the production of raisins and the drinking of alcohol for medical purposes served as pretexts to maintain the city's wine output. Briefly in the eleventh century the city became an independent *taifa* state before passing under the control of Arcos and later Seville.

In 1264 the city fell to the conquering Christian forces under Alfonso X, a great sherry aficionado who purchased vineyards here. Later, the city prospered through its trading connections with the newly discovered Americas (wine was allocated one third of the cargo space on all merchant vessels bound for the New World) as well as European markets, particularly Britain and the Low Countries. This prosperity continued throughout the seventeenth and eighteenth centuries and created a flourishing aristocracy and bourgeoisie. They were responsible for the arrival of the railway, a water supply and gas-powered street lighting by the mid-nineteenth century, and electricity and the telephone before 1900. It was only in the latter half of the twentieth century that the **sherry industry** began to show signs of flagging and in the 1980s alone exports fell by fifty percent.

This trend has caused serious employment problems in a city with few other sources of jobs. The post-Covid economic turmoil has further exacerbated matters, but it's a fairly safe bet that a wine loved by Chaucer, Shakespeare, Pepys, Columbus, Magellan, Pérez Gáldos and Hemingway will bounce back once again, as it has done so many times before in its three-millennia history.

Alcázar

C/M. María González • Jan–June & Oct–Dec daily 9.30am–2.30pm; July–Sept Mon–Fri 9.30am–5.30pm, Sat & Sun 9.30am–2.30pm • Charge • ☎ 956 149 955 • July–Sept there are also nighttime visits to the monument, with actors recreating events from its history (in Spanish only); Tues & Thurs at 9pm, but reservations should be booked on ☎ 627 578 362; Charge

Constructed in the twelfth century by the Almohads, though much altered since, Jerez's substantial **Alcázar** has been extensively excavated since the millennium. The **gardens** have received particular attention: the plants and arrangements have been modelled as closely as possible – using historical research – on the original. The interior contains a well-preserved mosque complete with *mihrab* from the original structure, now sensitively restored to its original state after having been used as a church for many centuries.

There's also a **bathhouse** modelled, by the Almohads, on those of the earlier Romans with cold and hot plunges, which contains wonderfully preserved *bóvedas* (vaults).

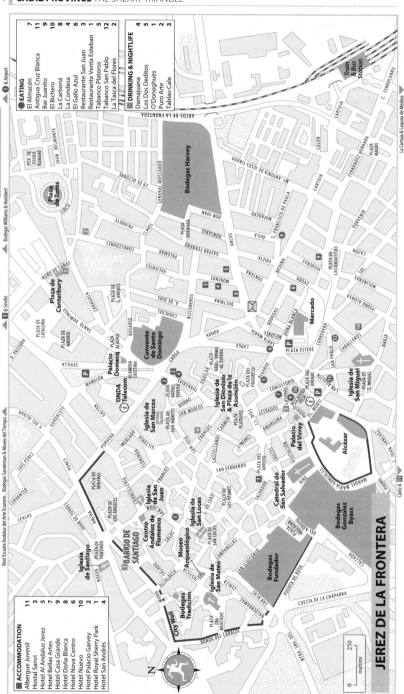

JEREZ DE LA FRONTERA

ACCOMMODATION
Albergue Juvenil	11
Hostal Sanvi	3
Hotel Al Andalus Jerez	5
Hotel Bellas Artes	7
Hotel Casa Grande	9
Hotel Doña Blanca	8
Hotel Nova Centro	10
Hotel Nuevo	6
Hotel Palacio Garvey	2
Hotel Royal Sherry Park	1
Hotel San Andrés	4

EATING
El Almacén	7
Antigua Cruz Blanca	11
Bar Juanito	9
El Bichero	10
La Carboná	8
La Condesa	4
El Gallo Azul	6
Restaurante San Juan	3
Restaurante Venta Esteban	1
Tabanco Plateros	5
Tabanco San Pablo	12
La Tasca del Flores	2

DRINKING & NIGHTLIFE
Damajuana	4
Los Dos Deditos	5
O'Donoghues	1
Puro Arte	2
Tablao Cale	3

The complex is surrounded by impressive walls and eighteen towers on the site's outer perimeter. The eighteenth-century **Palacio de Villavicencio** constructed on the west side of the Alcázar's Patio de las Armas (parade ground) houses a **camera obscura** offering views of the major landmarks of the town, as well as the sherry vineyards and the sea beyond.

Catedral de San Salvador

Pza del Arroyo s/n • Mon–Sat 10am–8pm, Sun from 1pm • Charge, free Sun 10.30–11.30am • W catedraldejerez.es

Immediately north of the Alcázar, the eighteenth-century **Catedral de San Salvador** was rather harshly dismissed by Richard Ford as "vile Churrigueresque" because of its mixture of Gothic and Renaissance styles, but an elegant facade – largely the work of Vincente Acero – is not without merit. Inside, over-obvious pointing gives the building an unfinished, breeze-block aspect, while in the sacristy museum, there's a fine, little-known painting by Zurbarán, *The Sleeping Girl*. On the left aisle is an interesting eighteenth-century retablo by Diego Roldán. Titled *Las animas de San Francisco*, it vividly depicts the saint hauling souls from the flames of hell.

The most exciting time to be here is September, when the wine harvest celebrations begin with the crushing of grapes on the broad cathedral steps below the freestanding bell tower – actually part of an earlier, fifteenth-century Mudéjar castle.

Palacio del Virrey

C/Pozuelo 8 behind the Turismo • Tues–Sat 10am–2pm & 4–7pm, Sun 11am–2pm • Charge • W palaciodelvirreylaserna.com

Also on the north side of the Alcázar and the home of Spain's last viceroy (*virrey*) of Peru, the **Palacio del Virrey** dates from the fourteenth century. It is stuffed with artefacts and paintings collected by the Laserna family over three centuries. A family member will give you a guided tour; the enchanting gardens often stage flamenco concerts in summer (details from the Turismo).

Iglesia de San Miguel

Pza San Miguel 1 • Mon–Fri 9.30am–1.30pm • Charge

South of the Alcázar is another church worth a visit – the fifteenth-century Gothic **Iglesia de San Miguel**. An ornate classical facade added in the eighteenth century climbs dizzily to a pretty bell tower adorned with blue and white *azulejos*. The Gothic interior exhibits some fine vaulting, and the main altar has a magnificent retablo by Juan Martínez Montañés, one of Andalucía's greatest sculptors.

Plaza de la Asunción

The town's most charming square, the **Plaza de la Asunción** (known as Plaza San Dionisio to *jerezanos*), has a sixteenth-century former **Ayuntamiento** which features – on its elegant Plateresque facade – ornamental statues of Hercules and Julius Caesar. It's flanked by the fifteenth-century Gothic-Mudéjar **Iglesía de San Dionisio** (visits at service times June–Aug 8pm, Sept–May 7pm; free) with a graceful bell tower and a triple-naved interior with three Baroque retablos and a fine *artesonado* ceiling.

Barrio de Santiago

Jerez's ancient *gitano* quarter, the **Barrio de Santiago**, stretches uphill from the cathedral in a maze of narrow lanes and alleys to the church of Santiago on its northern boundary. On the small square opposite the church stands a bronze bust dedicated to Fernando Terremoto, one of many legendary **flamenco artists** the *barrio* has produced. You'll come across others dotted around this quarter (including one of Tio José de Paula behind the church), all testifying to the *barrio*'s great pride in its contribution to Andalucía's musical heritage.

Also part of the attraction of visiting the *barrio* is its many fascinating churches. The sixteenth-century Gothic **Iglesía de San Mateo** (Mon 5–9pm, Sat 7.30–9pm, also open for Mass Mon–Sat 8.30pm; free), with a fine retablo and superb vaulting over the chapels, is one of a quartet of churches dotted around the *barrio* dedicated to the four Evangelists: the other three, dedicated to saints Marcos, Lucas and Juan, all to the east of San Mateo, are also worth seeking out. All three have similar visiting and Mass times as San Mateo.

Iglesia de Santiago

Pza de Santiago s/n • Mon–Fri 10.30am–2.30pm • Charge

To the north of the Iglesía de San Mateo, Calle Muro is flanked by a substantial chunk of the original Moorish **city wall**. You can follow this north to another Gothic church, the fifteenth-century **Iglesia de Santiago**, from which the *barrio* takes its name. The exterior has wonderfully florid Plateresque portals, while inside there's some beautiful Gothic vaulting and a celebrated sixteenth-century sculpture of the *Prendimiento* – or arrest of Christ – attributed to La Roldana, the sculptor daughter of Pedro Roldán. This image forms the centrepiece of Jerez's Semana Santa processions when it's carried through the streets on a float.

Centro Andaluz de Flamenco

Pza de San Juan 1 • Mon–Fri 9am–2pm • Free • ⓦ centroandaluzdeflamenco.es

Housed in the elegant eighteenth-century Palacio de Pemartín, the **Centro Andaluz de Flamenco** is home to a library of *flamencología* (plus sound and vision archive) dedicated to preserving the works and performances of past greats, while a dance

---

THE BODEGAS OF JEREZ

The tours of the sherry and brandy **bodegas** in Jerez provide a fascinating insight into the mysteries of sherry production, although sampling – nowadays restricted to a couple of tots at the end of a tour – is hardly as much fun as when Richard Ford was here in the nineteenth century and saw visitors emerging "stupefied by drink". There are a great many bodegas to choose from and, with the exception of August when all but a few firms close down, most welcome visitors throughout the year. Some companies insist that you book at least a day in advance. The following bodegas offer tours throughout the whole or part of August; should you wish to visit some of the smaller establishments, get hold of a complete list from the Turismo. Details of many of these, together with visiting times, maps and contact details appear on the Turismo's site at ⓦ turismojerez.com. Visiting hours frequently change so it's worth confirming these in advance with the bodega or getting an updated list from the Turismo.

Each bodega has its celebrity barrels signed by famous visitors – Dr Martin Luther King, Orson Welles, Queen Victoria, Cole Porter and Franco (protected by a glass screen) are some of the big names in the González collection, while in 1965 Williams & Humbert fortuitously managed to get the Beatles to sign a barrel each. All the bodegas also have a transparent butt that allows you to see the action of the magical *flor* on the sherry.

BRANDY

Many of Jerez's bodegas are today as renowned for their **brandies** as their finos – some are as good as any in the world. As with sherry, the *solera* system is used here too, with the spirit being transferred from one vat to another, creating Jerez brandy's unique character. The barrels themselves are also old sherry vats and impart an oaky subtlety, a further distinctive feature. As with wine and sherry, brandy has its own *consejo regulador* (regulatory body) and the brandies are ranked into three grades of quality: *solera*, *solera reserva* and *solera gran reserva*, the last of which must spend at least three years in the barrel. The inexpensive mass-market *solera* brands – which tend to give Spanish brandies a "cheap and cheerful, but not much else" reputation – do not have the same cachet as Jerez's more sophisticated labels, where great care is taken over grape quality and production methods. These are worth seeking out and we mention a few below.

room on the top floor is used to teach students from all over the world. The staff are welcoming and anyone is free to use the video archive to see performances by flamenco masters past and present – just give them a name and they'll do the rest. There's also a good audiovisual presentation, *El Arte Flamenco* (hourly, on the half-hour, in Spanish and English), which – if you know little about flamenco – will give you a grasp of the basics and an understanding of why it is so important to *andaluzes*.

Museo Arqueológico

Pza del Mercado • Tues–Sat 9am–3pm• Charge • ☎ 956 149 560

2

Located inside a renovated eighteenth-century mansion close to San Mateo is the delightful **Museo Arqueológico**. A plant-filled patio leads to the early rooms dealing with prehistory: note a 3500-year-old, remarkably well-preserved decorated ceramic vessel from Benaocaz in the Sierra de Grazalema. Upstairs, Room 3 has some curious **Chalcolithic** (early second millennium BC) cylinder-shaped idols with starburst eyes from Cerro de las Vacas, 20km to the north of the town. Room 4 has a wonderfully preserved **Greek** military helmet dating from the seventh century BC, which was found on the banks of the nearby Río Guadalete. This was a time when the early Greeks were colonizing sites all around the Mediterranean, and they evidently expected to meet resistance from the Iberian tribes. Also in Room 4 are finds from the ancient town of **Asta Regia**, as Pliny, Strabo and Ptolemy referred to Jerez in Roman times. A wide

VISITING THE BODEGAS

Bodegas Fundador C/San Ildefonso 3; ⓦ grupoemperadorspain.com. Now incorporating Jerez's oldest sherry producer, Domecq, founded in the eighteenth century by an Irish immigrant who married into a French immigrant family called Domecq. Pedro Domecq took over the business in 1816 and dramatically expanded the firm with the help of a brilliant British agent, John Ruskin, the father of the Victorian art critic. Fundador have also taken over production of the Harveys brand range of *finos*, one of which won the "best wine in the world" category at the 2016 International Wine Challenge. Visits available with wine tasting, or with tasting of prizewinning wines.

González Byass (aka Bodegas Tío Pepe) C/Manuel González s/n, behind the Alcázar; ⓦ bodegastiopepe.com. The city's most central bodega and for well over a century one of the giants of Jerez. Established in 1835 by Manuel María González, the bodega's buildings now form almost a small town in their own right. The González cellars are perhaps the oldest in Jerez and, though no longer used, preserve an old circular chamber, La Concha, designed by Eiffel (of Eiffel Tower fame). Among their brands are the most famous fino of all, Tío Pepe ("Uncle Joe", named after the founder's uncle), and an exceptional Lepanto brandy. Visits in English available with wine tasting, or tapas and wine tasting.

Sandeman C/Pizarro 10; ⓦ sandeman.com. Founded by Scottish grandee George Sandeman in the late eighteenth century, the bodega is famous for its trademark depicting the don in the black cape. The seventh generation of Sandemans are still involved in running the company, which makes the less well-known but excellent amontillado brand Royal Esmerelda and the Capa Negra brandy. See website for timetable of tours in English; reservations not necessary, but turn up 10min before starting time.

Tradición Pza Cordobeses 3; ⓦ bodegastradicion. es. An interesting newcomer, this bodega was created in 1998 by three members of old Jerez families who bought a derelict bodega in the old quarter of the city and completely renovated it. They then filled it with very old wines purchased from bodegas that had ceased trading, and so founded their own top-notch *soleras*. Their wines have been critically acclaimed: the Tradición Oloroso is one of their best finos while their Gold brandy is also top quality. The visit includes a tasting of four wines (including old rare sherries) and two brandies as well as a tour of their *pinacoteca* (art gallery) displaying works by Goya, Velázquez, Zurbarán, Sorolla and Solana among many others. Reservations for tours required.

Williams & Humbert Ctra Nacional IV km641, the Seville road; ⓦ williams-humbert.com. Alexander Williams married Amy Humbert and, with backing from his father-in-law, founded W&H in 1877. It went on to become one of the great sherry houses with the largest wine cellar in Europe. Its best-known fino is Dry Sack (formerly Pando) and it also produces Gran Duque de Alba brandy. Reservations required for tours. See website for details.

range of amphorae, funerary stones and sculptures are evidence of Asta's importance. More Roman amphorae – some stamped with the maker's name – appear in Room 5, once used for the shipping of *garum* (see page 194), olive oil and other products around the Mediterranean. Room 6 has items from the **Visigothic** period, displaying ceramics and metalwork in addition to an intriguing seventh-century sarcophagus from La Peñuela carved with curious vegetal, animal and human symbols.

Room 7 houses the **Moorish** collection, with some fine ceramics, including a tenth-century Caliphal bottle vase with Kufic script, found near Jerez. This section concludes with displays relating to Moorish daily life. Upstairs again, on the third floor, rooms 8 to 10 deal with **medieval** and **Christian** Jerez. This section includes an outstanding alabaster relief, *La Resurrección*, carved in England in the fifteenth century and depicting Christ emerging from the tomb. It had been placed in the keystone position in the entrance arch of a Jerez almshouse. The fact that it comes from England and is one of many similar works found in Jerez underlines the importance of trade – not only in wine – between the town and the British Isles in the late Middle Ages.

Before leaving, take a look at the exterior patio, where there's a reconstruction of an eighteenth-century *almazara* (oil mill) and, next to the ticket office, a numismatic section with an interesting chronological display of coins found around Jerez. One coin bears a good image of the Roman emperor Tiberius (no. 44) and is followed by dirhams of rulers Al-Hakam and Abd Ar-Rahman (no. 84) from the period of the Cordoban emirate.

Convento de Santo Domingo

C/Larga • Tues–Fri 10am–2pm & 6–9pm, Sat & Sun 10am–2pm • Charge

The northern end of the pedestrianized **Calle Larga** is dominated by the august frontage of the **Convento de Santo Domingo**. Although badly damaged by fire in the Civil War, it has been diligently restored and, in common with many of the town's other religious buildings, has a curious mixture of styles: in this case Mudéjar, Romanesque and Gothic. The church's seventeenth-century retablo *mayor* is an orgy of gilded wood, with the Virgen de la Consolación – the city's patroness, carved in Italian marble – as its centrepiece. The fifteenth-century cloisters have been restored and display fine vaulting as well as gargoyles and delicate tracery in the windows.

South from here, at the junction with Calle Santa María, stands the old **Café Cena Cirullo** (now the *El Gallo Azul* café), a fine Modernist building which used to be the great meeting place of Jerez's salon society.

Palacio Domecq

Alameda Cristina s/n • Tue-Sat 10am-7pm • Charge • ☎ 673 92 36 40

Just to the north of the Convento de Santo Domingo stands the eighteenth-century **Palacio Domecq**, a grand pile until recently owned by the Domecq sherry family. The palace was built in 1778 by the Marqués de Montana, and typifies the opulent mansions being constructed at the time by Jerez's wealthy farmers and winemakers. However, the Marqués and his family lived here for only seven years prior to his death in 1785. The house then lay empty until it was purchased in 1855 by Juan Pedro Domecq and became the sherry dynasty's home. Beyond an entrance flanked by barley-sugar pillars and topped by an ornate balcony, visits take in an exquisite marble-floored and porticoed Baroque patio as well as rooms richly decorated with period furniture, artworks, carpets, tapestries, clocks and countless other objets d'art assembled by the Domecq family.

Museo del Tiempo

C/Cervantes 3 • Tours Mon–Fri 9.30am–12.30pm • Charge • ☎ 956 182 100 • 10–15min walk from the centre along *calles* Guadalete and Pozo de Olivar

At the northern end of town, the **Museo del Tiempo** (aka Museo de Relojes) claims to have the largest collection of fully functioning antique clocks and watches in Europe, all chiming on the hour. It is situated inside an elegant eighteenth-century mansion and the bonus of a visit here is a tour of the extensive gardens.

Real Escuela Andaluz del Arte Ecuestre

Avda Duque de Abrantes s/n • **Performances, stable visits and rehearsals** See website for exact times and tickets • Charge • ⓦ realescuela.org • 10–15min walk from the centre along *calles* Guadalete and Pozo de Olivar, turning from C/Pozo de Olivar into Avda Duque de Abrantes

North of the Barrio de Santiago and close to the Museo del Tiempo, the nineteenth-century Palacio de las Cadenas, the former seat of the Duques de Abrantes, is home to the famous **Real Escuela Andaluz del Arte Ecuestre** (Royal Andalucian School of Equestrian Art). Here you can see teams of horses performing to music: a mesmerizing spectacle that has been described as "an authentic equestrian ballet". It doesn't come cheap, however, and it's more affordable and it's almost as interesting to watch training and rehearsals (without music), which includes a visit to the stables and museum.

La Cartuja de Santa María de la Defensión

4km out of town on the road to Medina Sidonia • Daily 7.30am–6pm (gardens and patio); Mass Mon & Sun 5.30pm, Tues–Sat 8.15pm; vespers Tues–Sat 6pm, Sun 5pm • Free

The remarkable Carthusian monastery of **La Cartuja de Santa María de la Defensión** lies 4km southeast of town in the midst of lush countryside and surrounded in summer by a sea of sunflowers. The monastery was founded in 1477 and, following great destruction by billeted French troops in 1810, was abolished in 1835 during the liberal backlash against the church and male religious orders.

After serving as a military barracks for almost a century, La Cartuja was restored to the Carthusians in 1949, since when the handful of monks here have dedicated themselves to restoring and maintaining this beautiful building. The Baroque **facade** you see today – added in the 1660s – is one of Spain's most spectacular. Unfortunately, access is restricted to the building's exterior (with a magnificent main doorway), gardens, central patio and (occasionally) cloister; currently the impressive church and its artworks may be seen only by those attending mass or vespers (confirm times with the Turismo).

ARRIVAL AND DEPARTURE

JEREZ DE LA FRONTERA

By plane Jerez Airport lies 7km northeast of the centre on the NIV *autovía*, with domestic connections to Madrid, Barcelona and other Spanish airports, as well as international flights to Britain and Germany. A meagre bus service (three buses on weekdays, one daily at weekends) links the airport with the town (details from airport information desk). There is also a train station (on the opposite side of the airport car park) with connections to Jerez central station running roughly hourly between 7.30am and 7.15pm. If you arrive outside these times you'll need to take a taxi.

By bus The bus station is at Pza Estación s/n, 1km east of Pza del Arenal. To reach the centre, take the #10 urban bus from a stop outside the train station (next to *Bar El Andén*). Destinations Algeciras (2 daily; 1hr 15min); Arcos de la

---

FESTIVALS IN JEREZ

The city's big festival is the **Feria del Caballo** (horse fair) in the first half of May, perhaps the most refined or (depending on your viewpoint) snooty of Andalucian *ferias*. Held at the Recinto Ferial (fairground) to the northeast of the centre, this is a huge knees-up with exhibitions of horsemanship and dressage along with singing and dancing in the couple of hundred *casetas* (marquees) open to all. The **Festival de Jerez** is a two-week flamenco-fest held at the end of February or the start of March, featuring many big-name flamenco artists at various venues around the town. You can get details from the Turismo or their website. The annual **Fiesta de la Vendimia**, held during September (details from the Turismo), celebrates the end of the grape harvest with concerts of flamenco, bullfights, equestrian events and a procession of the Virgin, Nuestra Señora de la Merced.

2

Frontera (14 daily; 35min); Cádiz (3 daily direct, 6 daily via El Puerto; 45min); Chipiona (6 daily; 40min); Córdoba (5 daily; 2hr 40min); El Puerto de Santa María (10 daily; 30min); Málaga (3 daily; 4hr); Ronda (2 daily; 2hr 30min); Sanlúcar de Barrameda (10 daily; 30min); Seville (12 daily; 1hr 30min); Vejer de la Frontera (1 daily via Cádiz; 1hr 30min).

By train The train station is at Pza de Estación s/n, 1km east of Pza del Arenal. To reach the centre, take the #10

urban bus (see "By bus" above) from outside the station. Destinations Cádiz (14 daily; 40min); Córdoba (15 daily; 2hr 30min); Seville (13 daily; 1hr 5min).

By car Street parking is at a premium and you'd be advised to use the car park at your hotel or *hostal* if it has one (and for which you'll pay extra), or one of the pay car parks signed in the centre. A huge car park lies under the focal Pza del Arenal and there's another handy one beneath Pza Mamelón, near the Convento de Santo Domingo.

INFORMATION

Turismo The office on Pza del Arenal s/n, on the north side of the town's main square (June–Sept Mon–Fri 9am–3pm & 5–7pm, Sat & Sun 9.30am–2.30pm; Oct–May Mon–Fri 9am–3pm & 4.30–6.30pm, Sat & Sun 9.30am–2.30pm; 📞 956 341 711; 🌐 turismojerez.com) is well stocked with lots of information about the town and the staff there can supply a detailed map.

ACCOMMODATION
SEE MAP PAGE 174

There's usually no problem finding **rooms** in Jerez, except during the period from March to May when Semana Santa, the Festival de Jerez, the World Motorcycle Championship (held at the town's Formula 1 racing circuit) and the Feria del Caballo come one after the other and fill the town to bursting point; make sure to book ahead if you are planning to visit at this time.

CENTRAL ZONE

Hostal Sanvi C/Morenos 10; 🌐 hostalsanvi.com. Sparklingly clean *hostal* with lots of *azulejos* and friendly proprietors offering economical, a/c en-suite rooms with TV. Garage parking available. €̄

Hotel Al Andalus Jerez C/Arcos 29; 🌐 hotelalandalusjerez.es. Comfortable hotel with two pretty patios. Refurbished rooms – the better ones are off the inner patio – come equipped with a/c and TV. Can advise on parking. €̄

Hotel Bellas Artes Pza del Arroyo 45, facing the Catedral; 🌐 hotelbellasartes.net. Charming and good-value small hotel inside a refurbished casa palacio on the cathedral square. Individually styled rooms are well equipped with minibar and plasma TV and the public areas include a library and roof terrace (with loungers) for having breakfast or enjoying a fine view of the Catedral and surrounding town. Also has a couple of suites. €̄

Hotel Nova Centro C/Arcos 13; 🌐 hotelnovacentro. com. Pleasant and very central small hotel offering rooms with a/c, satellite TV and room safe. Request a higher room to avoid street noise. Parking available for a small charge per night. €̄

★ **Hotel Palacio Garvey** C/Tornería 24; 🌐 hotelpalaciogarvey.com. Beautiful sixteen-room four-star in the former mansion of the Garvey family, one of the great sherry dynasties of nineteenth-century Jerez. The elegant and spacious rooms have modern designer furnishings and large beds and come with minibar and TVs

from this millennium. €̄

★ **Hotel San Andrés** C/Morenos 12 & 14; 🌐 hotelypensionsanandres.com. Great-value hotel and *hostal* side by side. The friendly *hostal* has en-suite rooms (with a/c and TV) and others sharing bath, plus an attractive, plant-filled patio. The hotel's rooms are slightly more comfortable. Can advise on parking places nearby, but don't have any of their own. Hostal €̄, hotel €̄

SOUTH CENTRAL ZONE

Hotel Casa Grande Pza de las Angustias 3; 🌐 hotelcasagrandejerez.com. Beautifully presented three-star in a restored nineteenth-century *casa señorial*. Marble-floored rooms are bright and comfortable, and public areas include a library and a delightful roof terrace where you can take breakfast (extra). Own parking for a small charge. €̄€̄

Hotel Doña Blanca C/Bodegas 11; 🌐 hoteldonablanca. com. In a quiet street, this is one of the most central and intimate of the upper-range places with light, well-equipped a/c balcony rooms with minibar and satellite TV, plus your car can spend a comfortable night here for a small charge. €̄€̄

Hotel Nuevo C/Caballeros 23; 🌐 nuevohotel.com. Attractive and excellent-value hotel set in a lovely nineteenth-century *casa palacio*; rooms – some with original faux-Moorish tiles and plasterwork – come with a/c and TV. See website for offers. €̄€̄

OUT OF THE CENTRE

Albergue Juvenil Avda Blas Infante 30, bus #9 from by the bus station or Pza de las Angustias; 🌐 inturjoven. com. Jerez's modern youth hostel has a fine pool, but lies out in the suburbs; all rooms are en-suite doubles with a/c. €̄

Hotel Royal Sherry Park Avda Alvaro Domecq 11; 🌐 hipotels.com. One of the nearest of the peripheral

FLAMENCO IN JEREZ

Given Jerez's great **flamenco** traditions, it's worth trying to hear some of the real stuff at one of the many *peñas* (clubs) concentrated in the old *gitano* quarter of Santiago, north of the cathedral (though be careful in this area after dark). The ones listed below are some of the best; turning up at around 10pm at weekends (although they're open at other times, too) should provide an opportunity to hear some authentic performances. Otherwise consult the Turismo, who also publish a sheet listing all of Jerez's *peñas*; the Centro Andaluz de Flamenco (see below), who also have details of the special flamenco festivals held in town over the summer; or the local paper *El Diario de Jerez*, which has a special flamenco listings page on Fridays.

PEÑAS

Centro Andaluz de Flamenco Pza San Juan 1, Santiago ☎956 349 265.
Peña Antonio Chacón C/Salas 2, Santiago ☎605 858 371.
Peña La Buena Gente Pza San Lucas 9, Santiago ☎690 281 627.
Peña Los Cernícalos C/Sancho Vizcaíno 25, south of the church of San Miguel ☎956 333 871.
Peña Tío José de Paula C/La Merced 11, Santiago ☎956 320 196.

luxury hotels to the centre; notwithstanding its four-star rating, this is a rather bland and modern affair with sober rooms furnished for the corporate market, although it has an attractive pool and gardens, plus car park. €€

EATING

SEE MAP PAGE 174

Jerez's sherry trade ensures that the town's **restaurants** are kept busy, and a few of these are very good indeed. Befitting the capital of sherry production Jerez also has a range of great **bars** where *fino* – the perfect partner for tapas – can be sampled on its own turf. In recent years there has been a revival of the *tabancos*, a combination of bar and wine store, serving food. Many old ones with character have been rediscovered and new ones have opened. The Turismo can provide a list.

RESTAURANTS AND CAFÉS

★ **El Bichero** C/Pescadería la Vieja 4; ⊕ elbichero.com. Taking its name from the fisherman's gaff, this is a bar-restaurant specializing in *mariscos* and seafood and their claim is that they sell the freshest *langostinos de Sanlúcar* (deep sea prawns) in town. Other worthwhile options on the menu include *almejas Gallegas* (clams), an *arroz marinero* (seafood paella) plus the daily array of fresh fish. Add in an extensive (and fair-priced) wine list, an attractive (and well-lit in the evening) terrace and you have the makings of a memorable repast. €€

La Carboná C/San Francisco de Paula 2; ⊕ lacarbona. com. Cavernous but wonderfully atmospheric Michelin-recommended restaurant inside an old beamed *bodega*. The kitchen specializes in charcoal-grilled fish and meat dishes (the house favourite is Cantabrian beef T-bone steaks) and – in season – fresh tuna. Their *maridaje con vinos de jerez* presents five courses, each accompanied by the appropriate Jerez wine. €€€

La Condesa Pza Rafael Rivero, C/Tornería 24; ☎956 326 700. The Michelin-recommended restaurant of the *Hotel Palacio Garvey* is an excellent place for a meal, especially on the attractive terrace facing the ancient city wall. A three-course lunch *menú* is a good deal and often features *solomillo en salsa oloroso* (pork loin in sherry sauce). Specials include a tasty *gazpacho con mango* and *setas estofadas con oloroso* (mushrooms in sherry sauce). €€€

Restaurante San Juan Pza Malgarejo 2; ☎956 326 471. Excellent Italian restaurant in a beautiful old bodega fronting the church of San Juan in the Barrio de Santiago. Offers a wide range of meat and fish courses as well as salads and authentic pasta and pizzas. There are also tables on an internal patio. €€€

★ **Restaurante Venta Esteban** Colonia de Caulina, off the Arcos de la Frontera road; ⊕ restauranteventaesteban.es. Arguably Jerez's best-value restaurant, this is a little way out of town near the airport, with four attractive dining rooms and a wonderful terrace. Both the welcome and the cooking are top notch and everything is done with panache, presenting traditional *andaluz* and *gaditano* cuisine at its best. Try the outstanding *urta a la roteña* (sea bream in onion sauce), their celebrated *alcachofas de la casa* (artichokes), any of the meat dishes or a whole *bogavante* (lobster) if you feel like pushing the boat out. Extensive wine list. Easy on-site parking for diners. €€€

TAPAS BARS, TABANCOS AND MARISQUERIAS

El Almacén C/La Torre 2; ☎680 448 232. Atmospheric tapas bar installed in an old grocery shop (*almacén*).

Tapas and raciones include *patatas bravas* (potatoes with spicy sauce) as well as *tablas* (boards of cheese and cured meats to share) plus various vegetarian options. Make sure not to miss out on the *tarta de manzana templada con helado* (warm apple tart with ice cream) which can only be described as paradise on a plate. €€

Antigua Cruz Blanca Pza del Arenal s/n; ☎956 321 388. In the southern corner of the city's main square, this busy *cervecería* sports a minimalist interior featuring stripped wood tables, chairs and stools. The tapas are mainly *mariscos* with what's on offer chalked up on a big board inside. Try the *langostinos* (prawns), *cañaillas* (whelks), *mejillones* (mussels), *pimientos asados* (roasted peppers) or *salmorejo* (Córdoba-style gazpacho). €

★ **Bar Juanito** C/Pescadería Vieja 8; ⓦbar-juanito.com. In a small passage off the west side of Plaza del Arenal, this is one of the best and most celebrated tapas-bar-*marisquerías* in town, with a menu as endless as the number of excellent finos on offer. Specials include *boquerones fritos* (fried fresh anchovies) and their wonderful *alcachofas* (artichokes). There's also a restaurant which offers a good-value lunchtime menú on its terrace. €€

El Gallo Azul C/Larga 2; ⓦelgalloazuljerez.com. Iconic building from noted architect Aníbal González constructed by the Domecq family at the time of the 1929 World Fair in Seville. Once the city's most fashionable meeting place, today it's a "gastrobar" serving decent raciones (try the *carillada ibérica* – pork cheek), with the town's best terrace

for people-watching. €

Tabanco Plateros C/Algarve 35; ☎956 104 458. One of the wave of *tabancos* to open over the last decade, this is a highly popular place slightly northeast of the Plaza del Arenal. There's a good and extensive wine list (including the classics of Jerez) or excellent tapped beer to accompany a lengthy tapas menu. Standouts are *salchichón* (salami), *sardinas ahumadas* (smoked sardines), *alcachofas con anchoas* (artichokes with anchovies). €

★ **Tabanco San Pablo** C/San Pablo 12, an alleyway downhill from the Iglesia de San Miguel; ☎655 993 090. One of Jerez's oldest *tabancos*, the wonderful San Pablo opened its doors in 1934. The walls of its spacious beamed interior are decorated with farm implements, antique clocks and old fino posters, while behind the bar huge vats stand ready to dole out fino, *oloroso* and *amontillado* wines. Tapas on offer are chalked up behind the bar and include a tasty *tortilla* as well as *carne mechada* (larded pork) and *anchoas* (anchovies): "*¡todo exquisito!*" as the blackboard informs you. There's also a street terrace. €

La Tasca del Flores Pza Rafael Rivera, facing the Hotel Palacio Garvey; ☎667 887 734. This diminutive tapas bar sits on a delightful plaza where a handful of other bars also spread their terraces. Just the place to sit out during Jerez's sultry summer nights, the bar serves a range of tapas including *chicharones* (crackling), *tortilla de bacalao* (Spanish tortilla with cod) and a tasty *carne retinto* hamburger made with prized red cattle beef. €

DRINKING AND NIGHTLIFE

SEE MAP PAGE 174

Much of Jerez's nightlife centres around the **bars and clubs** near the bullring and the zone around the Avda de Mexico to the northeast. One place which is very popular with younger *jerezanos* is Plaza de Canterbury, C/Nuño de Cañas s/n, a renovated plaza pulsing with numerous bars and *discotecas* where live music is frequently staged. The local paper *El Diario de Jerez* is a good place to find out about upcoming concerts and festivals.

★ **Damajuana** C/Francos 18; ☎956 320 464. Delightful café-bar in a fabulous seventeenth-century mansion with two charming patios. The music varies from flamenco and blues to rock and soul and there are frequent live concerts of flamenco and jazz on the patios. Also has a gallery featuring shows by contemporary artists and photographers.

Los Dos Deditos Pza Vargas 1 off the end of C/Pescadería Vieja s/n, off Pza del Arenal; ☎956 325 462. Relaxed *copas* (drinks and music) bar – serving more than

eighty world beers. Popular with over 30s.

O'Donoghues C/Nuño de Cañas 16, next door to the Pza de Canterbury; ☎956 326 246. Music bar that packs them in after midnight, especially at weekends – but stays serious enough to stock a good supply of Hibernian whiskies plus decent Guinness in pint glasses.

Puro Arte C/Conocedores 28, near the Pza de Toros; ⓦpuroarteflamencojerez.com. Commercial flamenco theatre featuring the very good Raul Ortega company of professional performers (song and dance) who, in the hour-long show, get pretty close to the real thing. Daily show at 10pm.

Tablao Cale C/Muro 14; ☎649 383 978. Slightly west of the Iglesia de Santiago, this is a commercial flamenco bar-restaurant offering shows by professional artistes. The performers are enthusiastic and if you're new to flamenco you won't be disappointed.

Costa de la Luz (Cádiz)

Cadiz province's 120km stretch of the **Costa de la Luz** – the "Coast of Light" – between the cities of Cádiz and Algeciras is far less developed than the Costa del Sol with a succession of broad, golden-sand beaches washed by Atlantic breakers backed by rolling pastures and a chain of green hills. There are good beaches at Sancti Petri and even better ones at Conil, Los Caños de Meca, Zahara de los Atunes and Tarifa. The latter's beaches are a magnet for surfers attracted by the often ferocious *levante* (east) and *poniente* (west) winds which vie continuously, it seems, for the upper hand. There's also a variety of coastal settlements to choose from including the low-key resorts like **Conil** and **Zahara de los Atunes** or, for a little more action, chilled-out **Los Caños de Meca** or bustling **Tarifa**, Spain's most southerly town where the mountains of Morocco loom across the straits. Inland, the haunting Moorish hilltown of **Vejer de la Frontera** beckons, while set back from the sea at Bolonia is the ancient Roman settlement of **Baelo Claudia**.

2

San Fernando and around

Heading south from Cádiz along the CA33 *autovía* you soon skirt the town of **SAN FERNANDO** – once an elegant place (and still so, at its centre) but now being swallowed up by industrial and commercial suburbs. Beyond San Fernando you emerge into a weird landscape of marshes, dotted with drying salt pyramids, an industry begun by the Phoenicians, and later an essential element in the fish salting industry of the Romans.

Sancti Petri

The road west from the rather unexciting town of **Chiclana de la Frontera** first hits the new town of Novo Sancti Petri, one of a dismal chain of overspill *urbanizaciones* for the sealocked city of Cádiz. Following signs for the Puerto Deportivo will lead you, after a couple of kilometres, to the isolated fishing village of **SANCTI PETRI**, surrounded by marshes and sand bars and now a popular **watersports** centre.

When you reach it, at the end of a causeway, the village itself is a place under threat from encroaching urban development to the south; its future remains uncertain. The harbour now contains more weekend yachts than fishing vessels and, since the tuna-canning factory closed down, there are few jobs. The focus of the tiny cluster of dwellings is the *Club Náutico de Sancti Petri* where the few remaining fishermen meet up. On Sunday mornings they sell their catch outside the club, offering some of the freshest oysters and *cañaillas* (murex sea snails) you've ever had, for ridiculously low prices. They're best washed down with a beer from the *Náutico*'s bar (they'll also lend you a plate) at a table overlooking the harbour. The restaurant is very popular with seafood aficionados, especially at weekends.

Castillo de Sancti Petri

A kilometre offshore lies an islet occupied by the **Castillo de Sancti Petri**, whose silhouette rises above the horizon. This was once a ruined thirteenth-century castle on

---

WATERSPORTS AT SANCTI PETRI

There's a small but nice enough beach to the south of the Puerto Deportivo, where a number of **watersports centres** rent out equipment.

Cruceros Sancti Petri ⓦ albarco.com. With a kiosk on the Puerto Deportivo waterfront, this company offers tourist boat excursions to see dolphins and whales, as well as trips to the Castillo de Sancti Petri.

Escuela de Vela Zaida ⓦ escueladevelazaida. es. Nearer to the Club Náutico, offering sailing and windsurfing courses for all ages.

Novo Jet ⓦ novojet.net. This long-established centre rents out windsurf boards, kayaks and catamarans and offers scuba diving courses and guided canoe expeditions to the Castillo de Sancti Petri and around the marshes (*marismas*) and watercourses of the Parque Natural de la Bahía de Cádiz to the north.

Sancti Petri Kayak ⓦ sanctipetrikayak.net. Kayak courses and rental. Guided tours include trips around the marshes and to the Castillo de Sancti Petri.

2

an offshore island, but as part of the bicentenary celebration of the Cádiz Córtes (see page 141) it has been partially restored at great cost and can now be visited by boat or kayak (see box, page 183). The castle's gaunt tower – once used as a lighthouse – dominates the horizon as you approach and despite the renovations, which many critics say have destroyed the romance of the ruins, there's not a great deal to see when you get there. An exhibition centre inside the castle relates its history. Apart from the fortress, however, the site has a much more ancient and distinguished past. The Phoenicians built an important first millennium BC temple to their god Melkaart here which the Romans later turned into a major shrine to Hercules. Hannibal was a visitor to the former, hoping to enlist Melkaart's aid in his projected conquest of Italy, and Julius Caesar to the latter, who while here is said to have had a prophetic dream that he would conquer the world. Archeological finds from both temples are now on display in the Museo de Cádiz (see page 141).

EATING AND DRINKING   SANCTI PETRI

Club Nautico de Sancti Petri Poblado de Sancti Petri; 956 495 428. The club's earthy bar is just the place for a *tapa* of *boquerones fritos* (fresh anchovies) or *chocos* (cuttlefish). Their restaurant has a cosy dining room for when the wind is up and on balmier days you can eat on the pleasant terrace overlooking the harbour. Depending on the day's catch the *lubina* (sea bass) is usually excellent, as is the local speciality *urta* (bream). €€

Conil

Heading south from Sancti Petri along a road (not marked on many maps) that hugs the coast and traverses more overspill *urbanizaciones* brings you, after 15km, to the increasingly popular resort of **CONIL**. Though this former fishing village appears entirely modern when viewed from the beach, it has a distinguished history dating back to ancient times. Founded by the Phoenicians (who were responsible for inventing the *almadraba* method of catching tuna along this coast) it was later a supply base for the Roman navy. Sacked successively by the Vandals, Visigoths and Byzantines, little was heard of the settlement again until, after the *Reconquista*, it once more became a centre of tuna fishing. If you take a stroll around the town you'll see plenty of older buildings that have survived from earlier days. Today, tourism is an important part of the economy too, with the resort's mainly domestic visitors creating a fun, family-oriented, atmosphere. During the second week in June Conil celebrates the **Semana del Atún de Almadraba** (tuna-catch week) when the first half of the tuna season reaches its peak (see box, page 193) and the town's restaurants participate in a *ruta gastronómica* offering different dishes prepared with the fish at discount prices (details from the Turismo).

Beaches

Conil's **beaches** are its *raison d'être:* the central Playa de Los Bateles and Playa la Fontanilla to the north, which appear as a wide bay of brilliant yellow stretching for kilometres to either side of town, lapped by an amazingly gentle Atlantic. The area immediately in front of town is the family beach: up to the northwest you can walk to some more sheltered coves; across the river to the southeast is a topless and nudist area. The beach here is virtually unbroken until it reaches the Cabo de Trafalgar, off which Lord Nelson achieved victory, but lost his life on October 21, 1805. When the winds are blowing, this is one of the most sheltered beaches in the area. You can get there by road, save for the last 400m across the sands to the rock.

ARRIVAL AND DEPARTURE   CONIL

By bus Most buses drop passengers off at the Transportes Comes station at C/Carretera s/n, just north of the Turismo. Destinations Atlanterra (3 daily; 1hr); Cádiz (9 daily; 1hr); El Palmar (2 daily; 15min); Los Caños de Meca (2 daily; 30min); Vejer de la Frontera (9 daily; 20min); Zahara de los Atunes (3 daily; 55min).

By car The older part of the town is now mostly pedestrianized and parking spaces elsewhere are usually taken (especially in high season). Your best bet arriving by car is to head for the seafront Paseo de Atlántico, where there's a kilometre of (free) parking spaces stretching west from the junction with Avda de la Playa.

INFORMATION

Turismo C/Carretera 1, on the northern edge of the old town, at the junction of C/Carretera and C/Menéndez Pidal (June–Sept Mon–Fri 9am–2pm & 6–9pm, Sat & Sun 9.30am–2pm; Oct–May daily 8.30am–2.30pm; ☎ 956 440 501; ⦿ turismo.conil.org). The very helpful staff here can provide a useful town map as well as lots of information on the town and nearby coast. Their handy booklet *Conil en su Bolsillo* details all the town's tapas bars, restaurants and much more. A summer office is located in the focal Torre de Guzmán, an ancient tower in the old town (June–Sept Wed–Sat noon–2pm & 6–9pm).

ACCOMMODATION

Conil has numerous hotels and *hostales* – most within easy walking distance of the focal Plaza de España, the old quarter's main square. August is the only time when you'll struggle to find a bed, and is also when rates peak.

HOTELS AND HOSTALES

Camping Fuente del Gallo Fuente del Gallo s/n; ⦿ campingfuentedelgallo.com. The nearest campsite to the town lies a stiff 3km walk (or easy taxi ride) north of the centre and is sited 400m inland from the superb Playa de la Fontanilla, with good facilities, bar-restaurant and pool. €

★ **Casa Alborada** C/G. Gabino Aranda 5, slightly west of Pza España; ⦿ alboradaconil.com. Delightful small boutique hotel with flamboyantly decorated and individually styled bedrooms and bathrooms – the bathroom of room 10 gets the star prize. Also has a stunning roof terrace/solarium with loungers and sofas offering spectacular views of the coast. Own car park. Outside July and August rates can be halved, making this a real bargain. €€

★ **Hipotels Flamenco** Playa Fuente del Gallo; ⦿ hipotels.com. Set in a tranquil location fronting the Fuente del Gallo beach, this elegant and completely refurbished hundred-room four-star is one of the resort's established luxury addresses. Well-appointed rooms have balcony terraces and sea views and there's a bar-restaurant, two garden pools, tennis courts and steps down to a fine beach. The same group has a four-star hotel nearby, *Hipotels Gran Conil*, with similar facilities. Breakfast is included. €€€

Hostal La Posada C/Quevedo s/n, just northeast of Pza de España; ⦿ laposadadeconil.com. Dapper and welcoming *hostal* that has clean and tidy en-suite a/c rooms with TV – many with sea views (extra) – above a good restaurant. There's also a charming garden pool. High season is August only, outside which rates halve. Breakfast is included. €

Hostal La Villa Pza de España 6; ☎ 670 242 731. Economical en-suite rooms with TV above a bar-restaurant on the old quarter's main square. May–Oct. €

Hostal Torre de Guzmán C/Hospital 5, southwest of Pza de España; ⦿ hostaltorredeguzman.com. Attractive and comfortable en-suite a/c rooms with TV in a beautifully refurbished eighteenth-century mansion close to the Torre de Guzmán. The friendly proprietors also rent out studios with kitchenette and fridge and there's a decent restaurant with patio terrace below. Breakfast is included. Outside high season (July & August) rates fall by forty percent; see website for special offers. €€

Hotel Almadraba C/Señores Curas 4, slightly south of Pza de España; ⦿ hotelalmadrabaconil.com. A pleasant three-star hotel in yet another modernized eighteenth-century townhouse. Elegantly furnished, beamed and well-equipped rooms are ranged around a charming patio and come with minibar and safe, and the public areas include a jacuzzi and plunge pool. The hotel also has its own bar-*cafetería* and parking facilities. Breakfast is included. €€

Hotel Diufain Cañada del Rosal s/n, Fuente del Gallo, 3km north of the centre behind the Playa la Fontanilla; ⦿ hoteldiufain.com. Appealing three-star hotel in its own grounds with large garden pool and a/c sea-view terrace balcony rooms with satellite TV. Free parking. €€

El Roqueo Apartamentos Urbanización Las Palmeras s/n, at the northern end of the Fuente del Gallo beach; ☎ 956 443 280. Very good apartments at the north end of the beach with the bonus of a great fish restaurant next door. Apartments come with *salón*, kitchen and satellite TV, but a sea-view terrace costs extra. Free parking. €

EATING

La Almazara C/Laguna 5; ☎ 670 018 251. Excellent tapas and *raciones* bar a couple of hundred metres north of Plaza de España with one of the best (tree shaded) terraces in town. Among a tempting range of dishes, standouts are *carillada en salsa de vino* (pork cheeks) and any of their tuna specials once the season begins. Also offers a selection of tasty salads including *ensalada de bogavante y manzana* (lobster & apple) and there's an extensive and fairly priced wine list. €

★ **La Azotea de la Mejorana** C/Cádiz 10, northwest

of the Torre de Guzmán; ☎629 380 150. This is an outstanding restaurant and arguably the best place to eat in the old town. The dining rooms are compact but cosy and on summer nights there's also a wonderful roof terrace (*azotea*). Highlights from the *carta* include *bacalao al vapor con bambú y jengibre* (steamed cod with bamboo shoots and ginger) and *albondigas con cuscús* (meat balls). €€€

★ **La Fontanilla** Playa de la Fontanilla, next door to Francisco; ⊛lafontanilla.com. The second of the town's top-rated fish restaurants – whether you're eating in the beamed dining room or on the terrace, you won't be disappointed. House specials here include *arroz con bogavante* (lobster in rice), *gambas con espinacas* (prawns with spinach) and, their pride and joy, *urta a la fontanilla* (Cádiz bream). €€€

★ **Francisco la Fontanilla** Playa de la Fontanilla s/n; ⊛franciscofontanilla.com. One of Conil's three outstanding seafood restaurants, with a terrace on the beach, this is a great place to spend a summer afternoon

if you can get a table – not an easy task in high summer. Everything is fresh from the sea whether it be *bogavante* (lobster), *urta* (bream) or one of the house specials such as *lubina al horno* (oven-baked sea bass) or *atún de almadraba* (fresh-landed tuna). €€

★ **Restaurante Mirador El Roqueo** Urbanización Las Palmeras s/n, at the northern end of the Fuente del Gallo beach, 1km beyond the Hotel Diufain (see page 185); ⊛elroqueo.com. An excellent fish restaurant worth making an effort to get to, this is perhaps the best of the three (by a catfish's whisker). It fronts the beach of El Roqueo and comprises two restaurants in one: the more formal dining room "El Roqueo" sits on the street behind the seafront "Mirador" (aka "Chiringuito"), which is more relaxed and slightly cheaper with a great terrace overlooking the shore below. House specials include *carpaccio de pulpo* (octopus), *ijada de atún a la sal* (tuna baked in salt) and an outstanding *salmonete a la plancha* (red mullet). The restaurant also has a *menú de degustación*. €€€€

Vejer de la Frontera

While you're on this stretch of the Costa de la Luz, be sure to take time to head inland and visit **VEJER DE LA FRONTERA**, a classically white, Moorish-looking hill town set in a cleft between great protective hills that rear high above the road from Tarifa to Cádiz. Sited off the main A48 *autovía* some 15km southeast of Conil via a dizzily climbing road, this ancient town is encircled by fifteenth-century walls. In what maybe a hangover from Moorish times, until relatively recently the women of Vejer wore long, dark cloaks that veiled their faces like nuns' habits; however, this custom is now virtually extinct outside fiestas.

Maintaining a brooding detachment from the world below for most of its history, Vejer has a remoteness and a Moorish feel as potent as anywhere in Spain. Almost certainly a prehistoric hilltop Iberian citadel, Vejer was utilized as a fortress during the **Phoenician** and **Carthaginian** epochs of the first millennium BC to protect coastal factories and fishing grounds from the warlike Iberians of the interior. Dubbed Besipo by the later **Romans**, it was as the **Moorish** town of Bekkeh that Vejer rose to prominence as an important agricultural centre on the western frontier of the kingdom of Granada. Taken by Fernando III in 1250, it was immediately handed over to Alonso Pérez de Guzmán, founder of the ducal house of Medina Sidonia and later hero of Tarifa.

Vejer is best savoured by randomly exploring the brilliant-white, labyrinthine alleyways, wandering past iron-grilled windows, balconies and patios, and slipping into one of numerous bars.

Castillo

C/Ramón y Cajal s/n • Mon–Sat: June–Sept 10am–2pm & 5.30–9.30pm; Oct–May 10am–2pm & 4–6pm • Free

The **castillo**, in the heart of the old quarter, is Moorish in origin but underwent substantial rebuilding in the fifteenth century when it was used by the dukes of Medina Sidonia as a summer retreat. The main things to see are a splendid horseshoe arch and some Moorish plasterwork, as well as great views from the terrace. A small **museum** displays ancient and more recent finds discovered in and around the town.

Divino Salvador and around

Pza. Padre Angel s/n • June–Sept daily 5–7pm; Oct–May service times Mon–Fri 7.30pm, Sat 8pm • Free

To the northwest of the castle, the church of **Divino Salvador** is a sixteenth-century rebuild of an earlier mosque whose minaret now serves as the tower. The interior is a curious mix of mainly Gothic and Mudéjar styles.

From here, Calle Castrillón descends to the **Plaza de España**, the lovely palm-fringed main square, overlooked by a white-walled Ayuntamiento, and centred on a delightful fountain decorated with nineteenth-century Triana tiles from Seville. North of here, the **Paseo de la Corredera** offers spectacular views over the countryside to the nearby hill towns of Medina Sidonia and Alcalá de los Gazules. The **Torre de la Corredera** halfway along here was a watchtower used for communicating with those towns.

NMAC modern art museum

5km southeast of the town along the N340 in the grounds of the Dehesa Montenmedio • July–Sept Tues–Sun 10am–2pm & 5–9pm; Oct–June Tues–Sun 10am–2.30 & 4–6pm (confirm hours with website) • Charge • Ⓦ fundacionnmac.org • Allow 90 min to complete the itinerary • No public transport; a taxi from Vejer (for up to four) costs around €15 (one way)

One visit well worth making outside Vejer is to the impressive open-air **NMAC modern art museum**. Featuring major works by renowned international artists, the collection consists of installations – Fernando Sánchez Castillo's *Pacto de Madrid*, a half-buried equestrian bronze of dictator Franco, is a showstopper – sited throughout a beautiful park. Other highlights include *Human Nest* by Marina Abramovic – with "nest holes"

2

bored into the walls of an old quarry – and *Secondwind* by James Turrell, a labyrinth of optical illusion on the themes of light and sky. *Hamman* by Huang Yong Ping has transformed a former military barracks into a Turkish bath. Other indoor exhibition areas display sculpture and photography. The route around the artworks passes through stunning parkland and forest replete with birdlife – and (in season) nesting storks – and makes the perfect place for a picnic.

ARRIVAL AND DEPARTURE

VEJER DE LA FRONTERA

By bus Buses drop off passengers at the Parque de Los Remedios just to the side of the Turismo, from where you'll need to ascend Avda Los Remedios to reach La Plazuela, the effective centre of town.

Destinations Algeciras (8 daily; 1hr 30min); Cádiz (6 daily; 1hr 30min); Conil (6 daily; 25min); Jerez (1 daily; 1hr 35min); Seville (1 daily; 3hr 10min); Zahara de los Atunes (1 daily; 35min).

By car It's best to park in the car park at the entrance to town near the foot of Avda Los Remedios, as the old town's streets are narrow and convoluted. If you must park further in, head for the new multistorey car park on the Paseo de Corredera.

INFORMATION

Turismo Next to the car park as you enter Vejer, at Avda Los Remedios 2 (April–Sept Mon–Sat 10am–2pm & 5–7pm, Sun 10am–2pm; Oct–March Mon–Sat 10am–2pm & 4–6pm, Sun 10am–2pm; ☎ 956 45 17 36; ⊕ turismovejer.

es). Staff here hand out an excellent free town map (also available from the *Hotel Convento* when the Turismo is closed).

ACCOMMODATION

SEE MAP PAGE 187

Camping Vejer Ctra N340 km39.5, Santa Lucía; ⊕ campingvejer.es. Good campsite with plenty of shade plus a pool, *cafetería* and supermarket. It lies 2km east of town on the main N340 road, close to the roadside *El Valenciano* restaurant. €

★ **La Casa del Califa** Pza de España 16; ⊕ califavejer. com. Stunning hotel created inside a refurbished, part-Moorish house, featuring individually styled rooms decorated with Moroccan lamps and fittings. Guests have use of two patios, a terrace with views and a library. *Rough Guide* readers with this Guide are entitled to a ten percent discount, which should be claimed at check-in. Breakfast is included. €€

★ **El Cobijo de Vejer** C/La Viña 7; ⊕ elcobijo.com. Excellent-value and welcoming *hostal* inside an enchanting traditional house with a delightful vine-shaded, flower-filled patio and individually styled rooms on various levels. The slightly higher-priced apartment-style rooms *Zahara* and *Xauen* (the latter with a fabulous terrace), with own kitchens, are the ones to go for. All rooms are a/c and come with fridges and satellite TV. €€

Hostal La Janda C/Antonio Machado 10, signposted up a side road on the way in; ⊕ hostallajanda.com. Excellent *hostal* with light and airy en-suite rooms with a/c and TV. Three-night minimum stay in Aug. €

Hotel Convento de San Francisco La Plazuela s/n; ⊕ tugasa.com. Housed in a converted seventeenth-century convent on the smaller of the town's two main squares, this very pleasant and reasonably priced hotel has transformed the austere former cells – with exposed stone walls – into attractive a/c rooms with TV. Also has its own *cafetería* housed in the convent's former refectory with surviving wall paintings. Breakfast is included. €€

Las Palmeras del Califa Pza de España; ⊕ califavejer. com. The *casa rural* of the adjacent *La Casa del Califa* (see page 188), set in a restored, partly Moorish house with elegantly furnished rooms ringed around an inviting pool (most with private terrace), offering fine views. Guests have use of a shared kitchen and there's easy parking behind. *Rough Guide* readers with this Guide are entitled to a ten percent discount, which should be claimed at check-in. €€€

EATING

SEE MAP PAGE 187

Bar Peneque Pza de España 27; ☎ 956 450 209. Traditional local bar built into a cave with tables at the back for munching *raciones* should you not feel like joining in the domino games favoured by regulars. €

Casa Varo C/Nuestra Señora de la Oliva 9; ⊕ casavaro. com. Stylish *raciones* and *media raciones* restaurante-gastrobar with a pleasant outdoor terrace facing the church. The kitchen produces traditional Mediterranean dishes

– meat and fish – with a creative edge, plus ultrafresh *mariscos*. Try the *cañaillas* (sort of whelk) or any of their tuna offerings including (in season) *carpaccio de atún de almadraba*. €€

★ **Castillería** Barrio de Santa Lucía s/n; ⊕ restaurantecastilleria.com. Wonderful and highly popular mid-priced garden restaurant in this rural *barrio* below the town. They hang their own meat and specialize in *carnes a la brasa* (charcoal-grilled meats) and excellent salads. Try the *solomillo de vaca retinta* (red cattle beefsteak) or the *magret de pato* (duck). Chef/owner Julian Valdés insists on personally cooking every piece of meat that leaves his kitchen, which can add to waiting times when the place is busy (especially at weekends, when booking is advisable), but it's worth it. €€€

Cuatro Estaciones C/Juan Relinque 3, almost opposite the market; ⦿ 4estacionesvejer.com. Stylish restaurant offering fusions of tastes and styles from Asia, Latin America and the Middle East. Two dishes that typify their philosophy are *albondigas de atún en sofrito campero con curry verde* (fresh tuna meatballs in a curry sauce) and *ceviche de vieras y pulpo* (marinaded scallops with octopus). Their salads and desserts are equally adventurous and there's a small street terrace. €€

El Jardín del Califa Pza de España 16; ⦿ califavejer. com. The mid-priced and Michelin-recommended restaurant attached to the hotel of the same name has a Moroccan chef and serves up a variety of Moroccan and Middle Eastern-inspired dishes on a tree-shaded courtyard terrace. Specialities include tagines and spicy Moroccan fish dishes, as well as couscous and barbecued meats. There's also a stylish bar-*tetería* with stunning views from its roof terrace. €€€

Mercado de Abastos C/San Francisco behind La Plazuela. An innovative project has transformed Vejer's old marketplace and hall into a highly popular gastro-emporium where up to a dozen stalls sell or produce various offerings ranging from *almadraba* tuna sushi to *jamones* (cured ham), cheeses, *tortillas de camarones* (shrimp fritters) authentic pizzas and lots more. Prices are reasonable, a couple of stalls sell wines and beers and there

are tables outside where you can turn your purchases into a feast.

Mesón Pepe Julián C/Juan Relinque 7, just off La Plazuela; ⦿ 956 451 098. Popular local bar with *azulejo*-lined walls serving up decent tapas – specials include *atun almadraba* (tuna), *chorizo ibérico* and *calamares* (squid) and there's a good wine list. €€

La Oficina C/Juan Bueno s/n, outside the old walls below the castle; ⦿ 655 099 911. Enchanting tiny restaurant and tapas bar, with tables inside or on the white-walled street fronting it. The venture is the brainchild of ebullient proprietor, former lawyer and now artist Candido Carballo whose paintings (for sale) are usually hanging on the walls outside (if the wind's not up). The kitchen has a creative slant – you could try the *tataky de presa ibérica* which fusions Japanese and Iberian styles or there's a *retinto* (local beef) burger or *champi-chocos* (mushrooms with cuttlefish). €€

Trafalgar Pza de España 31; ⦿ 956 447 638. Adventurous *tapería-restaurante* with a great terrace on this charming square. The tapas bar (below) and restaurant (above) do things with a creative twist and the *atún rojo en escabeche* (tuna) in the former and *presa ibérico teriyaki* (pork loin with a soy-sherry sauce) in the latter are both worth a try. €€

★ **Venta Pinto** La Barca de Vejer s/n; ⦿ ventapinto. com. Down below the town at the road junction with the N340, this is an outstanding mid-priced restaurant with a great range of seafood, fish and game dishes. House specials include *jabalí al horno* (oven-baked wild boar) and *rape con azafrán y langostinos* (monkfish with saffron and prawns) and the star *tapa* in the bar is a mouthwatering *lomos de sardinas en vinagre* (marinaded sardines). The delightful rooftop terrace is the place to head in the evenings. €€€

DRINKING AND NIGHTLIFE
SEE MAP PAGE 187

Café-Bar La Bodeguita C/Marqués de Tamarón 9, uphill from La Plazuela; ⦿ 956 451 582. Entertaining late-night *copas* bar with a street terrace and an often lively

crowd; also does tapas – house specials include *atún de almadraba* (fresh tuna) and *salchichón* (salami). Weekends in summer often stages live music (blues and jazz).

SHOPPING
SEE MAP PAGE 187

Bodegas Gallardo Ctra N340, km1; ⦿ bodegasgallardo. com. Sited just below the town, close to the junction of the N340 with the A314, Vejer's century-old wine bodega

produces a range of finos and even adds a liqueur made with oranges. All are available for tasting at the bodega and can be purchased in their shop.

El Palmar

On the coast below Vejer, some 15km distant, lies the sleepy and isolated seafront settlement of **EL PALMAR**, with a waterfront dotted with holiday apartments, bars and restaurants. The narrow, 2km-long blue-flag beach here is popular with surfers, but – Sundays and the month of August excepted – it never gets overcrowded and this all adds up to about as peaceful a place as you could wish.

ACCOMMODATION AND EATING
EL PALMAR

Camping El Palmar Playa de El Palmar, southern end; ⦿ campingelpalmar.es. Set 1km back from the beach, this

2

is a very good campsite with a great pool, plenty of shade, restaurant, bar and supermarket, and lots of activities on offer, including trekking, scuba diving and horseriding. €̄
Hostal-Restaurant Casa Francisco Playa de El Palmar s/n, southern end; ⓦcasafranciscoeldesiempre.com. Twenty-five metres from the beach, this slightly upmarket *hostal* has pleasant en-suite rooms with TV, terrace and some with sea-views (extra charge). Rates drop by a third outside Aug. Breakfast is included. €€
La Torre Playa de El Palmar, near the old atalaya (watch tower) at the north end of the seafront; ⓦlatorredelpalmar.com. Laidback restaurant and *copas* bar with easy sounds and cocktails after sundown.

Breakfasts, snack food and salads are the menu's mainstay and they offer a seafood paella for two. €€
★ **Restaurant Casa Francisco** Playa de El Palmar s/n; ⓦcasafranciscoeldesiempre.com. This seafood restaurant belonging to the *hostal* of the same name (see page 190) is El Palmar's best place to eat and has even made it into the Michelin guide. Recommended dishes include *caribineros con arroz* (scarlet prawns with rice), *tataki de atún rojo* (red tuna Japanese-style) and *alcachofas con vieiras* (artichokes with scallops). The bar offers mouthwatering tapas such as *mini tartar de atún con guacamole y cilantro* and *tosta de sardina ahumada con tomate natural y aceite* (smoked sardine). There's also an attractive sea-view terrace. €€€

Los Caños de Meca

Reached via the coast road from El Palmar or the A2230 from Vejer, **LOS CAÑOS DE MECA** (served by sporadic buses from Conil to Barbate) is another modest resort with bags of easy-going charm. A small village surrounded by pine groves and a favourite summer escape for *sevillanos*, Los Caños has a long, beautiful beach lined with rocky coves and freshwater springs (*caños*), marred only by some unfortunate hotel and housing developments on its southern flank. At the western end of the seafront, a side road off Avenida Trafalgar – the main road running behind the beach – leads to a landmark lighthouse (traffic blocked after 150m but you can walk the kilometre to reach it) and the historically famous Cabo (or cape) de Trafalgar (see page 184). Be careful if you plan to swim here as there are rip tides on the west side of the lighthouse peninsula and dangerous currents off the southern tip. The eastern side is usually safe. Los Caños used to be home to a hippy colony and, although this crowd has now gone, some of the laidback atmosphere lingers, especially among the groups of nudists who swim out to the more secluded coves along the coast.

ACCOMMODATION   **LOS CAÑOS DE MECA**

HOTELS AND HOSTALES
★ **Casas Karen** Camino del Monte 6, down a signed track 500m east of the turning for the lighthouse; ⓦcasaskaren.com. Very friendly place run by the eponymous Dutch proprietor with various styles of rooms and apartments (including traditional *chozo* huts) in a wonderful garden setting. High season applies August only; see website for special offers. €€
Hostal Mar de Frente Avda Trafalgar 3, 100m beyond the Hotel Fortuna (see page 190); ☎956 437 025. In a brilliant white mansion overlooking the sea and with its own access to the beach, all rooms are en suite with TVs, and many have a terrace and sea view (supplement). Breakfast is included. €€
Hotel Fortuna Avda Trafalgar 34, at the eastern end of the seafront; ⓦhostalfortuna.com. This friendly family-run hotel has cosy en-suite rooms with balcony (most have sea view), safe and TV. They also have some attractive seafront chalets nearby, sleeping up to four. Free parking. Doubles €€, chalets €€€
Hotel Madreselva Avda Trafalgar 102; ☎956 437 255.

A welcoming, compact hotel offering comfortable rooms with terraces surrounding a central plant-filled patio. There's a good-sized pool in the grounds and the beach is just a stone's throw away. The proprietors can advise on horseriding and mountain bike rental and also run surfing and kitesurfing courses with discounts for guests. *Rough Guide* readers with this guide receive a ten percent discount which should be claimed at check-in. Free parking. Breakfast is included. €€

CAMPING
Camping Camaleón Ctra de Trafalgar s/n; ⓦcampingcamaleon.com. This central campsite is a decent option with plenty of shade and its own bar-restaurant. €
Camping Caños de Meca Ctra Vejer a Los Caños, km10, just west of the village; ⓦcampingcm.com. The better of Los Caños's two campsites, this is a family-oriented site 600m from the beach, with plenty of shade provided by pines and eucalyptus. There is also disabled access. March–Oct. €

EATING

There are plenty of places to eat in the resort, although the more obvious places are not always the best value. **Zahora**, the village's next door neighbour to the west, has become a culinary hotspot with a clutch of new restaurants and bars.

Arohaz Zahora, near the Caños de Meca campsite; ☎ 956 437 005. Of course, you realized that it's the village's name spelt backwards. That's where the jokes end, though, as this is a serious Michelin-recommended restaurant/ gastrobar where head chef and owner Alberto Reyes puts together fusion dishes influenced by his travels – Japan, the Maghreb and Latin America. Standouts are an *ensalada de langostinos con mango* and *tataky de atún*. Also offers a variety of *arroces* (rice dishes). €€€

La Bruma Playa de Zahora, reached via the road to the Zahora beach; ☎ 650 587 300. Excellent little terrace restaurant and bar run by a female duo, both named Patricia. The dishes are creatively presented and there are plenty of vegetarian options. Try the *tortillitas de camarones con jengimbre* (shrimp fritters with ginger) or Thai-style vegetarian noodles. And don't miss the star dessert: *tiramisu con whiskey irlandés*. After your meal, a stroll along the beach to the *Amarna* cocktail bar would make the perfect place for a sundowner, usually accompanied by a stupendous sunset. €€

La Laja Avda Trafalgar 146, close to the road to the lighthouse; ⊛ la-laja.com. High-end restaurant on the main avenue with a swish all-white interior and shaded terrace. The food is good and *corvina a la naranja* (meagre) or *perdiz al oloroso* (partridge with sherry sauce) are typical main courses. Also does tapas – try the *mejillones a la cava* (mussels). €€€€

Venta Curro C/Zahora s/n; ☎ 956 437 064. Near the *Caños de Meca* campsite, this is perhaps the best-value place to eat in the resort. They do both fish and meat – try the *solomillo ibérico* (pork loin) – dishes well, and all the seafood is caught locally. There's also an economical *menú* offering regional specialities. €€

DRINKING AND NIGHTLIFE

Las Dunas Ctra del Cabo de Trafalgar; ⊛ barlasdunas. es. On the road leading to the lighthouse, this cavernous, stone-built bar with a thatched roof serves breakfasts and juices as well as tapas and *raciones*. In summer they also operate a barbecue for grilling *carnes ibéricos* (black pig pork). As dusk falls it metamorphoses into a *copas* and music bar and in summer there are frequent concerts (jazz, blues, flamenco).

La Jaima Avda de Trafalgar s/n; ⊛ jaimameccarola. com. Popular *discoteca* with dance floor inside an exotically decorated Bedouin tent that attracts quite a crowd in summer. All kinds of drinks are served; the house special is a stiff mojito.

Parque Natural de Acantilado

From Los Caños the route southeast towards Barbate first ascends into the **Parque Natural de Acantilado** (aka Parque Natural La Breña) and then follows a rolling, scenic road through the park's verdant pinewoods. Some 4km into the park a signed turn on the left leads to the wonderful *El Palomar de la Breña* (see page 192), a superb *hotel rural* with a remarkable eighteenth-century dovecote of immense proportions authenticated by the *Guinness Book of Records* as the largest in the world. No longer in use, the dovecote's eight thousand nesting places once produced birds for the Spanish Indies fleet who used them to communicate with Spain while out in the Atlantic. Doves no longer nest here and their places have been taken by three pairs of kestrels as well as little owls and barn owls, all serious discouragements should the original occupants try to reclaim their former home.

The *parque natural* is Andalucía's smallest, but holds a rich variety of habitats including an umbrella pine forest, wetlands, mobile dunes and sea cliffs. The proprietors of the *El Palomar de la Breña* hotel can advise on hikes in the park as well as the Sendero de los Acantilados clifftop walk with spectacular views. A linear route of 7km, this heads off west from the beach car park at the Playa Yerbabuena on the west side of Barbate and continues through stands of umbrella pine and junipers before passing a number of ancient watchtowers – including the sixteenth-century Torre del Tajo – once used for spotting invading pirates. The route along the cliffs has great views out to sea, and is followed by a final descent into Los Caños de Meca (see page 190). Details of the route (in English) plus a map may be downloaded at ⊛ bit.ly/barbate-walk.

The Palomar hotel can also provide details of a 4km walk to the remarkable Visigothic church of San Ambrosio, tucked away in woods to the west of the hotel.

Constructed in the seventh century with its dome still intact, this is a stunning vestige from almost 1400 years ago. Believed to have been constructed over the remains of a Roman villa, girders are now supporting what remains of the nave and sadly vandals have broken through the fence, damaged brickwork and column capitals, and daubed the walls with graffiti. Hopefully this unique vestige of Andalucía's history will soon receive the protection it merits.

ACCOMMODATION
PARQUE NATURAL DE ACANTILADO

El Palomar de la Breña Off the A2233, 5km out of Barbate or Los Caños, check the website for details: ⓦalomardelabrena.com. This eighteenth-century *cortijo* has been transformed into a charming fifteen-room *hotel rural* in the middle of the park. The en-suite rooms are simple but perfectly adequate and come with TV, fridge and a terrace to sit out, plus a pool – and the beaches of Trafalgar are only 5km distant. The hotel has its own restaurant and the proprietors can advise on many activities in the park including hiking, horseriding, mountain biking and birdwatching. Outside of the August rate, prices fall by fifty percent. Breakfast is included. €€

Barbate

BARBATE, 10km southeast of Los Caños, is the next town along the coast and linked by a frequent daily **bus** service with Vejer de la Frontera. It's an unkempt and rather featureless little place dominated by its harbour and canning industry which processes the tuna caught along this stretch of coast. As the major fishing port in these parts Barbate has some excellent **tapas bars** and **fish restaurants** along its seafront, many serving up the town's celebrated dish *atún encebollado* (tuna in onion sauce), but that's about the limit of its appeal.

Zahara de los Atunes

A further 10km southeast of Barbate lies the ancient fishing village of **ZAHARA DE LOS ATUNES**, long involved (as its name tells you) in the catching of tuna – now an industry in decline. Linked by an infrequent **bus** service with Barbate (see page 192), Zahara is now beginning to show signs of development, but outside of high summer it remains a slow-moving resort with good tapas bars, hospitable locals and a fabulous 8km-long **beach**.

ARRIVAL AND DEPARTURE
ZAHARA DE LOS ATUNES

By bus Zahara has good links to larger towns. Destinations Algeciras (1 daily; 1hr 10min); Cádiz (2 daily; 2hr 10min); Conil (2 daily; 1hr); El Palmar (1 daily; 45min); Los Caños de Meca (1 daily; 30min); Vejer (2 daily; 20min).

ACCOMMODATION

Camping Bahía de la Plata 1.5km out of town on the road towards Atlanterra; ⓦcampingbahiadelaplata.com. Efficient, refurbished campsite with reasonable shade plus a pool, supermarket and restaurant. It also rents out bungalows and studios, both with cooking facilities. Camping €, bungalows €€, studios €€€

Gran Sol Avda de la Playa 20; ⓦgransolhotel.com. Excellent three-star seafront hotel (sea-view rooms cost extra) with comfortable a/c traditional rooms and an extension overlooking a garden pool. Their restaurant is also good and has a daily *menú*. Free on-street parking. Breakfast is included. €€

Hostal Monte Mar C/Peñón 12; ⓦhostalmontemarzahara.com. A decent budget place bang on the seashore offering simple en-suite rooms with balconies. The service can occasionally be a bit hit and miss, but the owners are friendly and usually get there in the end. More of a bargain in spring and autumn than high summer. They have a seafood restaurant with great sea views, on the terrace above, which is worth a visit. To reach the *hostal* turn right once over the bridge into the village, and keep ahead for 150m. €

Hotel Antonio C/Atlanterra km1; ⓦantoniohoteles.com. Pleasant two-star seafront hotel on the road out towards Atlanterra. In addition to the hotel's decent-value rooms, they have added more luxurious accommodation in an adjoining four-star extension. Most rooms have terraces and sea views (extra charge) and there's a solarium and a large pool. Breakfast is included. €€€

2

COSTA DE LA LUZ AND THE BLUEFIN TUNA

The catch of the **bluefin tuna** is a ritual that has gone on along the Costa de la Luz since ancient times and today still employs many of the age-old methods. The bluefin is the largest of the tuna family, weighing in at around 200kg, and the season lasts from April to June as the fish migrate towards the warmer waters of Mediterranean (*el derecho*) to reproduce, and from early July to mid-August when they return to the high seas (*el revés*). Fishing communities dotted along this stretch of Andalucian coast have been taking advantage of this annual abundance of tuna since the Phoenician period and probably long back into prehistory. The methods used to catch the tuna are still referred to by the Moorish name *almadraba* ("place for hitting"), which involved dragging the giant fish ashore in great nets and clubbing them to death.

Today the fish are caught at sea by herding and corralling them in a huge net stretched between a circle of boats where they are gaffed – their blood turning the sea crimson – before the weakened fish are then hauled aboard. The biggest market is Japan, and Japanese factory ships can often be spotted waiting offshore in season ready to buy up as much of the catch as they can. Once the tuna are on board, the fish are rapidly gutted, washed, filleted and frozen ready to cross another ocean to be eaten raw as sushi. Tuna numbers have been declining and the season shortening – probably the result of overfishing – much to the concern of the people of Barbate, Conil de la Frontera and Zahara de los Atunes, for whom the catch represents an important source of income for fishermen and a provider of employment in the canning factories nearby.

EATING AND DRINKING

A Los Cuatro Vientos La Zarzuela village, 3km inland from Zahara; ⓦ restaurantealoscuatrovientos.es. Easy to reach with your own transport (but also possible with a taxi), this modernized country *venta* is well worth a visit. A beamed white-walled dining room has plain wooden chairs and tables and the kitchen is excellent, turning out a range of fish and meat dishes. They also do tasty pizzas and there's tapas on offer in the bar. €

Almadraba Hotel Almadraba & Almadrabeta, C/María Luisa 13; ☎ 956 439 274. This popular hotel restaurant is an excellent place for seafood. Everything is as fresh as can be and the speciality here, not surprisingly, is tuna – *almadraba* refers to netting the tuna catch (see box, page 193). They also do a special seafood *arroz* for two. €€

★ **Antonio** Hotel Antonio, C/Atlanterra km1; ☎ 956 439 542. Excellent mid-priced fish restaurant almost on the beach, with fine sea views. This establishment oozes quality and the fish and *mariscos* are outstanding. Signature dishes include *atún al horno* (baked tuna) and *dorada a la sal* (sea bream baked in sea salt). €€€

Bar Casa Juanito (aka El Costero) C/Alcalde Ruíz Cana

7; ☎ 956 439 211. The outstanding tapas and *raciones* bar of the restaurant of the same name (see page 193) with a light and modern interior featuring a long, marble-topped bar and slick service. Among a wide tapas selection (check out the daily specials on a blackboard) featuring fish and *mariscos*, their *tapa de mejillones* (mussels) makes a perfect partner for a *copa* of manzanilla. €

La Botica C/Real 13 & C/Duquesa de Medina Sidonia 14; ☎ 956 439 183. A superb bar-restaurant for fish and meat dishes. The bar (in C/Real) does fried fish tapas and *raciones* (a generous *frito variado* easily feeds two) as well as great *jamón* and *salchichón*. Their restaurant (C/Duquesa de Medina Sidonia, around the corner) offers a variety of fish and meat dishes with the emphasis on tuna. Try the *pescado a la roteña* (white fish in onion sauce). €€

★ **Casa Juanito** C/Alcalde Ruíz Cana 7; ⓦ casajuanito. com. One of the oldest (founded 1948) and the best tapas bars and restaurants on this stretch of coast, serving up deliciously fresh seafood. Try the delectable *tataki de atún rojo* (red tuna Japanese-style). €€€

Atlanterra

South from Zahara a road winds down for 4km to the settlement of **ATLANTERRA**, another hamlet seized upon by developers and, a few kilometres beyond this, to a wonderful beach, the **Playa Camarinal**. Atlanterra itself is rapidly being transformed into a warren of holiday apartments ringed around the bland *Hotel Melia*, part of the luxury hotel chain. Just 100m out of this settlement, however, lies the delightful boutique hotel *El Cortijo de Zahara* (see page 194). Beyond here the road continues for a further 4km passing a few secluded villas (owned by many of Spain's rich and famous) circled by lofty palms before coming to a dead end at the Playa Camarinal and, a bit further on, the Faro del Punta Camarinal lighthouse. It's a stunning beach, but there are no facilities whatsoever. With a day to spare you could walk the 5km from the lighthouse to the Roman ruins at Baelo Claudia (see page 194), but take a map and plenty of water in high summer.

ACCOMMODATION   ATLANTERRA

★ **El Cortijo de Zahara** Avda de Atlanterra; ⓦ elcortijodezahara.com. Stunning beach hotel, partly housed in a converted nineteenth-century military barracks (although it has been extended) and surrounded by gardens filled with palms, cactus and hibiscus and a pool. The individually and elegantly styled rooms and suites are equipped to four-star standard and most have a sea view (rooms 7, 9, 106 and 119 are the ones to go for). There's also a bar, *cafetería* and restaurant. See website for offers. **€€€**

Bolonia and Baelo Claudia

Ensenada de Bolonia s/n • April–Sept Tues–Sat 9am–8pm, Sun 9am–3pm; Oct–Mar Tues–Sat 9am–6pm, Sun 9am–3pm • Charge, free with EU passport • ☎ 956 106 796

The next beach settlement of note, the scattered coastal village of **BOLONIA,** lies a mere 4km to the south of Atlanterra, but the lack of a road means a hefty 33km dogleg along the A2227 and the N340 to reach it. A side road (the CA8202) off this to the right, a couple of kilometres beyond the village of Facinas, winds for 7km through the Sierra de la Plata – where *retinto* long-horned cattle graze – to reach the coast. Your first view of Bolonia will be its magnificent windswept beach with golden, powder-sand stretching for a kilometre to the west until it meets the Duna de Bolonia, a spectacular 30m high sand dune.

Next to the village, and almost on the magnificent beach at Bolonia Cove are the extensive ruins of the Roman town of **BAELO CLAUDIA**. The site is entered via a concrete bunker with a car park and visitor centre where there's a small museum with finds from the site, historical reconstructions and a photo history of the excavations. Established in the second century BC, the Roman town – rather like modern Zahara and Barbate nearby – became prosperous with the exploitation of tuna and mackerel to make the fish sauce **garum**, of which the Romans were passionately fond. The town reached the peak of its prosperity during the first century AD when it was raised to the status of a municipium or self-governing township by Emperor Claudius, and the buildings you see today date from this period. In the mid-second century BC the town declined, probably the result of a major earthquake.

Puerta de Carteia and fish factory

Following the numbered information boards detailed on the leaflet you receive with your ticket, a tour of the site starts by crossing a footbridge over the stream of La Chorrera where you can see the remains of the Punta Paloma **aqueduct**, the longest of the three that formerly supplied the town, bringing water from springs at Punta Paloma, 8km southeast. The route then tracks the remains of the town wall as far as the substantial bastions of what must have been an impressive entry gate – the **Puerta de Carteia** – in the town's eastern wall. You enter the town via this gate as most ancient visitors to Baelo would have done.

The route then follows the decumanus maximus (main street) to the first intersection, where it detours left to take in what are probably the most interesting series of buildings, actually on the beach. Here has been revealed a **fish factory** which produced *garum*, and you can still clearly make out the great stone vats used to make this concoction – always located as near to the sea and as far away from the town as possible because of the stench. The process involved removing the heads, entrails, eggs, soft roes and blood of the fish, layering these in the vats with salt and brine, and leaving them for weeks to "mature".

The resulting mixture was then slopped into amphorae and shipped all over the empire, particularly to Rome, where the poet Martial droolingly described it as "made of the first blood of a mackerel breathing still, an expensive gift". The mackerel sauce was the Roman equivalent of beluga and they paid the earth for small quantities of it; the tuna-based variety produced here, however, was less of a luxury and much cheaper.

Forum and around

Continue to the well-preserved rectangular **forum**, best viewed from the platform at the northern end supporting a row of **three temples** to Jupiter, Juno and Minerva, the great gods of imperial Rome. Just west of here is a smaller temple dedicated to the Egyptian goddess Isis, and directly ahead, occupying the whole south side of the forum, are the remains of the **basilica**, or law court. At the eastern end of this building stood a colossal white marble statue of the second-century emperor Trajan, the head of which is now preserved in the museum at Cádiz (see page 141). A replica of the statue now occupies the site. On the forum's eastern flank stood a line of tabernae (shops), which seem to have been superseded by the later **macellum** (market), built to the west of the basilica.

Walk west along the main street and then turn north at the town's western gate, the Puerta de Gades (Cádiz), to take in a baths complex en route to the newly restored **theatre**, built into the hillside to take advantage of the slope. The route then crosses the forum's northern end to lead you back to the visitor centre.

ARRIVAL AND DEPARTURE

By bus In July and Aug there are three buses daily in each direction (confirm times with Turismo) from Tarifa bus station to Baelo. The last bus returns in the late afternoon, allowing you to combine a visit to the site with some time on the wonderful beach fronting it. Outside high summer there is no public transport and a taxi (one way) for up to four costs around €30.

By car Baelo is a 23km trip from Tarifa via the N340

BOLONIA AND BAELO CLAUDIA

Tarifa–Cádiz road, with a turn-off down a small side road (signed "Bolonia"), on the left at the *San José del Vallé* hotel-restaurant.

On foot You can walk to Bolonia along the coast from either Punta Paloma west of Tarifa or, coming from the opposite direction, Zahara de los Atunes (both a 3–4hr hike). Be sure to take water with you in summer.

ACCOMMODATION

Hostal Bellavista Near the turn-off into the village of Bolonia; ⓦ hostalbellavista.es. Decent en-suite rooms with a/c above a restaurant – it's worth paying a few euros more to get one with a terrace. Also rents out some studios and apartments nearby. €̄

★ **Hostal La Hormiga Voladora** C/El Lentiscal 15, at the eastern end of Bolonia; ⓦ lahormigavoladora. com. Delightful garden retreat with individually styled

en-suite garden rooms and apartments that are simple but charming. A couple of more expensive rooms (7 and 16) have sea views and there are plenty of nooks for lazing around. Breakfast is not provided, but if you buy in your own vittles (from the bakery next door or the nearby bar) you can dine on an enchanting patio shaded by a prodigious mulberry tree. Rooms €̄, apartments €̄€̄

EATING AND DRINKING

There are a couple of beach *chiringuitos* actually on the beach serving grilled fish – try the *Bahía de Bolonia* – otherwise most of the places to eat are in the small village of Bolonia itself.

Hostal Bellavista Near the turn-off into the village of Bolonia; ⓦ hostalbellavista.es. This *hostal* restaurant isn't bad, and serves standard *venta* food with an

economical *menú*. €̄€̄

Las Rejas Close to the Hostal La Hormiga Voladora; ☏ 956 688 546. This is perhaps Bolonia's best restaurant. All the fish and mariscos are fresh – as is of course the tuna in season – and they can rustle up a decent paella for two if you're looking for a beach snack. There's a reasonably priced wine list and a terrace. €̄€̄

Tarifa

Some 15km southeast from the Bolonia turnoff, along the N340, you reach the breezy town of **TARIFA**, spilling out beyond its Moorish walls. Until the mid-1980s it was a

2

quiet village, known in Spain, if at all, as the southernmost point on the European landmass and for its abnormally high suicide rate – attributed to the unremitting winds that blow across the town and its environs. Occupying the site of previous Carthaginian and Roman cities, Tarifa takes its name from Tarif Ibn Malik, leader of the first band of Moors to cross the straits in 710, a sortie that tested the waters for the following year's all-out assault on the peninsula. In the 1990s Tarifa – and its winds – were discovered by **windsurfing** enthusiasts and, over the couple of decades since, the resort has become an international centre for windsurfing and kiteboarding.

San Mateo and around

C/Sancho IV El Bravo s/n • Mon–Sat 8.45am–1pm & 5.30–8pm, Sun 10am–1pm & 6.15–8.30pm • Free

There's great appeal in wandering the crumbling ramparts of Tarifa's old walls, gazing out to sea or down into the network of lanes that surround the fifteenth-century church of **San Mateo**. Don't be fooled by the crumbling Baroque exterior here, fine

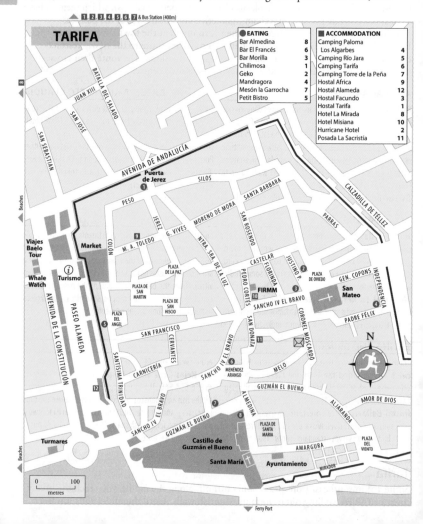

TARIFA

1, **2**, **3**, **4**, **5**, **6**, **7** & Bus Station (400m)

● EATING	
Bar Almedina	8
Bar El Francés	6
Bar Morilla	3
Chilimosa	1
Geko	2
Mandragora	4
Mesón la Garrocha	7
Petit Bistro	5

■ ACCOMMODATION	
Camping Paloma	
Los Algarbes	4
Camping Río Jara	5
Camping Tarifa	6
Camping Torre de la Peña	7
Hostal Africa	9
Hostal Alameda	12
Hostal Facundo	3
Hostal Tarifa	1
Hotel La Mirada	8
Hotel Misiana	10
Hurricane Hotel	2
Posada La Sacristía	11

ANDALUCÍA'S BIRD MIGRATIONS

While Andalucía's birdlife is fascinating throughout the year, the region also plays host to one of the remarkable spectacles of the natural world, the great **spring and autumn migrations**, attracting an audience of birdwatchers from far and wide. Many birds spend the winter in warmer African climes, a journey that involves a sea crossing – a major challenge for many large birds such as eagles, vultures and storks, who rely on the warm air that rises from the earth to keep them aloft. With no thermals over the sea it's essential that they seek out the shortest possible crossing point: the Strait of Gibraltar.

The main "flight path" across the Strait hits land between Gibraltar and Tarifa. Gibraltar (there's an ornithological information centre on the Upper Rock) and the Punta del Carnero (south of Algeciras) are particularly worth a visit when the wind is in the west, and anywhere along the main Algeciras–Tarifa road is good when there's an easterly breeze. The birds tend to cross in waves so there will inevitably be times when little is visible, and few birds will attempt the crossing in gales or heavy rain. The variety you are likely to see changes from month to month, but storks return from Africa in the first months of the New Year. Many black kites, short-toed eagles and other raptors cross the Strait in February and March, but April is the "rush hour" month when huge numbers of honey buzzards are often to be seen aloft and you may even be lucky enough to spot the rare and beautiful black stork.

though it is; this was added in the eighteenth century and hides, inside, a beautiful late-Gothic church with elegant rib-vaulting in the nave and some interesting modern stained-glass windows. A very helpful leaflet in English will guide you around the church's many features, including a fine crucified Christ by the great eighteenth-century sculptor Pedro de Mena, situated along the right aisle. Nearby, a small seventh-century tombstone confirms that there was a Christian presence here before the Moorish invasion of 711. Further along, the *sagrario* (shrine) is a stunning Baroque extravaganza in pink and violet, with an enchanting cupola. The church's stirring finale is at the top of the left aisle, where a copy of the original (and now lost) retablo contains the early seventeenth-century image of San Mateo by Juan Martínez Montañés, Spain's greatest exponent of wood sculpture.

Castillo de Guzmán el Bueno

Entrance from C/Guzmán El Bueno • Wed–Sun 10am–4pm • Charge, free on Sun from 2pm • ⓦ castilloguzmanelbueno.com

The restored **Castillo de Guzmán el Bueno** has great views from its towers and battlements, both over the town and across the water towards Morocco. In origin a tenth-century Moorish *alcázar* constructed by the great Abd ar-Rahman III, ruler of Córdoba, on the ruins of a Roman fort, the building underwent many later alterations. It was also the site of many a struggle as a strategic foothold into Spain, and its name now refers to **Guzmán El Bueno** (the Good), Tarifa's infamous commander during the Moorish siege of 1292, who earned this tag for his role in a superlative piece of tragic drama. Guzmán's 9-year-old son had been taken hostage by a Spanish traitor – surrender of the garrison was demanded as the price of the boy's life. Choosing "honour without a son, to a son with dishonour", Guzmán threw down his own dagger for the execution. The story, a famous piece of heroic resistance in Spain, had echoes in the Civil War siege of the Alcázar at Toledo in 1936, when the Nationalist commander refused similar threats – an echo much exploited for propaganda purposes.

Plaza de Santa María

Worth a look is the charming **Plaza de Santa María**, behind the castle, with a tranquil central garden and neatly trimmed hedges overlooked by lofty palms. Here you'll find the Ayuntamiento and, just to the west of this behind railings, the ancient church of **Santa María** (part of the castle visit). Tarifa's oldest church, it was founded in the fourteenth century and built over a former mosque in the Gothic-Mudéjar style. A **mirador** off the east side of the square offers more spectacular **views** (weather permitting) of the African coast.

Puerta de Jerez

At the northern end of the walled town lies the **Puerta de Jerez**, the only survivor of the four thirteenth-century gates which once led into Tarifa. Sandwiched between two crenellated towers the gate has survived the intervening centuries impressively. A plaque affixed to the wall above its arch records the capture of the town by Sancho El Bravo in 1292. Displayed in a glassed-in alcove inside the arch is a large painting of *El Cristo de los Vientos* (Christ of the Winds) by Tarifa's most famous son, the renowned modern artist Guillermo Pérez Villalta.

A little way beyond the gate to the right into the walled town stands the daily covered **market** (Mon–Sat mornings) with Moorish-style arches – a colourful beehive of activity when in full swing, and with numerous bars in the vicinity and inside the market itself doing a roaring trade.

Beaches

The town **beaches**, separated by a causeway leading to the Isla de las Palomas (not open to the public), include the small, popular and sheltered **Playa Chica** on the Mediterranean side and the **Playa de los Lances** (aka Playa Grande) facing the Atlantic.

Heading **northwest from Tarifa**, towards the Punta Paloma, you'll find some of the loveliest beaches along the whole Costa de la Luz: wide stretches of yellow or silvery-white sand, washed by some magical rollers.

One of these, **Tarifa Beach** arcs around a little bay 9km from town, where there are restaurants and campsites at the base of a tree-tufted bluff. A number of exclusive hotels also overlook the strand here. The same winds that have created such perfect conditions for windsurfing can, however, be a problem for more casual enjoyment, sandblasting those attempting to relax on towels or mats and whipping the water into whitecaps.

ARRIVAL AND DEPARTURE   TARIFA

By bus The bus station is at C/Batalla del Salado 13 in the north of town close to the main Algeciras–Cádiz road. From here it's a 5–10min walk along C/Batalla del Salado to the walled old town. Buses operated by the Comes company

---

THE STRAITS OF DEATH

In Tarifa's cemetery above the town, lines of nameless headstones mark where the dead lie three deep, mostly the remains of unknown sub-Saharan Africans washed up on the beach. The trickle of "wetbacks" eager for a share of European prosperity has turned into a flood, as gangs operating in Tangier offer to get **illegal immigrants** into Spain by evading the Spanish helicopters and coastal patrols. The usual method of transport is *pateras*, flimsy, easily capsized, flat-bottomed fishing boats designed to carry six people. Often packed with as many as thirty – who pay thousands of euros each – these fragile craft set out to cross one of the most treacherous stretches of water in the world. Crooked skippers often tip unfortunates into the water too far out from shore and many non swimmers drown. More often though, the boats themselves don't make it and the toll of bodies washed up along Spanish beaches has risen to alarming levels in recent years. Of those that do get safely across the straits, many are picked up by the authorities and held in a detention centre on the sealed-off island, Isla de las Palomas, near the harbour, pending extradition. The few that wriggle through the police net face life as noncitizens without papers, drifting between illegal and low-paid jobs or street-selling. The high death toll seems to have no effect on the numbers willing to take their chances on the open seas and the temptation to migrate seems to be getting ever stronger.

(⊛ tgcomes.es) run up and down the coast.

Destinations Algeciras (daily every 30min until 9.15pm; July–Aug until 2.45am; 45min); Cádiz (8 daily; 1hr 30min); Conil (5 daily; 1hr 15min); Jerez (1 daily; 2hr 30min); La Línea (4 daily; 1hr); Málaga (4 daily; 3hr 30min); Seville (4 daily; 3hr 45min); Vejer (4 daily; 45min).

TO MOROCCO

Day-trips Tangier can be visited as a day-trip by boat from Tarifa using the catamaran fast ferry, which takes 35min to cross from Spain to Morocco. Tarifa is now the only port in Spain with direct passenger sailings to Tangier port. There are eight sailings in each direction in summer between 8am and 11pm, with reduced sailings in winter. The last sailing

back from Tangier runs at 11pm (local time – which is 2hr behind Spanish time in summer, 1hr in winter). You can check current timetables at the Turismo. If you're planning a day-trip, book a few days in advance as groups sometimes make block bookings.

Package tours One- or two-day package tours to Tangier are also available, starting at €70 for the one-day excursion, which includes a sightseeing tour, lunch and all transport. The two-day version (€100) adds in breakfast and a night in a three-star hotel. Details from Viajes Baelo Tour.

Ticket agent FRS in the Estación Marítimo building in the harbour (Ferrys Rápido del Sur; ⊛ frs.es), plus travel agents along C/Batalla del Salado.

2

INFORMATION

Turismo Staff at Paseo de la Alameda s/n (Mon–Fri 10am–2pm & 4–8pm, ⊛ tarifaturismo.com) can provide a useful

town map – also available from many hotels and *hostales*.

ACTIVITIES

Whale- and dolphin-spotting Dolphin- and whale-watching boat trips are run by a non-profit-making organization called FIRMM (Foundation for Information and Research on Marine Mammals; ⊛ firmm.org), C/Pedro Cortés 3, slightly west of the church of San Mateo. You need to book in advance (two days' notice is preferable). Trips last about 3hr and if you don't see any dolphins or whales you get a free trip on the next sailing. A commercial

operation, Turmares, Alcalde Nuñez 3, at an office on the beach road near the foot of the Paseo de la Alameda (⊛ turmares.com), runs whale-spotting trips with a glass-bottomed boat.

Birdwatching The area around Tarifa and the Campo de Gibraltar is prime birding territory, particularly during the annual migrations (see box, page 197). Birding Tarifa (⊛ birdingtarifa.es) offers guided birdwatching trips.

ACCOMMODATION
SEE MAP PAGE 196

Tarifa has plenty of places to stay, although due to its popularity prices tend to be higher than other places along this coast. It's wise to **book ahead** throughout the year, and especially in August or whenever there are windsurfing tournaments. As elsewhere, room prices fall sharply (by up to fifty percent) outside July and August. Tarifa's **campsites** are served by a frequent bus service in July and August from Avda Andalucía, just to the north of the Turismo.

HOTELS AND HOSTALES

Hostal Africa C/María Antonia Toledo 12; ⊛ hostalafrica.com. Charming small *hostal* with clean and simple rooms, with and without bath, and spectacular sea views from a communal terrace. Rooms 5 and 6, with individual balconies, are the ones to go for. €

Hostal Alameda Paseo de la Alameda 4; ⊛ hostalalameda.com. Central *hostal-restaurante* on the Alameda with en-suite rooms with TV and sea views (from some). Outside August, prices fall significantly. €€

Hostal Facundo C/Batalla del Salado 47; ⊛ pensionfacundo.com. Reliable and friendly family *hostal* on the main road into town just outside the walls, offering rooms sharing bath and en-suite rooms with TV (same price for both). €

Hostal Tarifa C/Batalla del Salado 40; ⊛ hostaltarifa. com. This impressive *hostal* belonging to the proprietors of *Hostal Facundo* (sited opposite), is a three-star hotel in all but name. Pristine rooms come with all facilities, a/c, TV and sparkling bathrooms, and most have sit-out balconies. The welcome is warm and the price for July and August halves for the rest of the year. Own garage. €€

Hotel La Mirada C/San Sebastián 41; ⊛ hotel-lamirada.com. Comfortable hotel outside the walls, but only 3min from the beach. Rooms come with balcony and sea view, satellite TV, a/c and safe. Breakfast is included. €€

Hotel Misiana C/Sancho IV El Bravo 18; ⊛ misianahotel. com. Stylish hotel above a chic bar offering rooms with arty decor and a mishmash of colour schemes, fabrics and furnishings, some Moroccan. €€€

Hurricane Hotel Ctra Cádiz s/n; ⊛ hotelhurricane.com. Set in dense gardens 7km west of Tarifa at the ocean's edge, this luxurious California-style hotel has tastefully decorated a/c rooms (not all with TV) and suites, fully equipped gym, two pools, stables, windsurfing school and its own restaurant. Price guide is given for rooms with inland view. Breakfast is included. €€€

Posada La Sacristía C/San Donato 8, off C/Sancho IV El Bravo; ⊛ lasacristia.net. Stylish boutique hotel in a

2

WATERSPORTS ON THE GULF OF CÁDIZ

The stretch of Atlantic coast around Tarifa provides some of the best conditions in the world for **windsurfing** and **kitesurfing** – according to windsurfing aficionados, Tarifa now ranks alongside Diamond Head in Hawaii and Fuerteventura in the Canaries as one of the top three windsurfing beaches in the world. Equipment rental shops line the main street, and in peak season crowds of windsurfers pack out every available bar and *hostal*. Even in winter, there are windsurfers to be seen, drawn by regular competitions held year-round. Kitesurf novices are advised to get some instruction (especially regarding potential hazards) before striking out on their own. Details of some of the main beaches are given below, while more information as well as details of courses and companies renting out equipment is available at ⓦ bit.ly/TarifaSurf.

Board surfing is currently less popular due to the often difficult conditions, but on the right day you can still have some great rides. Courses in all watersports are available in Tarifa and equipment can be rented at numerous shops along Calle Batalla del Salado (the Turismo can also supply information).

The Turismo has an extensive list of companies offering watersports and diving **courses**. One company offering **diving** courses in English is Yellow Submarine Tarifa, a fully PADI authorized outfit based in the harbour (ⓦ divingtarifa.com). Surfing and kitesurfing courses (in English) are offered by Dragon Kite School (ⓦ dragontarifa.com) and Hot Stick Kite School (ⓦ hotsticktarifa.com).

BEACHES

Barbate Sheltered town beach protected by harbour wall. Good option when winds are strong and everywhere else is blown out.

Yerba Buena West-facing beach just beyond Barbate, with 200m right-breaking wave off point. Generally needs 2m of swell. North/northeast winds are best. Experienced surfers only.

Caños de Meca South-facing bay approached via pine forest on road from Vejer de la Frontera. Right-breaking wave from point and left-breaking reef breaks. Works on northwest winds. Low tide. Experienced surfers only.

El Palmar West-facing beach with waves from both right and left. Best at mid-to-low tide when waves can reach heights of up to 3m (but is best on 1.5–2m swells).

Conil Good town beach but only works on pushing and dropping tide.

Cabo de Roche (northwest of Conil) Protection from strong east winds. Very fast hollow waves that have tendency to snap boards with no mercy.

La Barrosa (near Sancti Petri) Extensive beach breaks working on same conditions as El Palmar.

---

seventeenth-century townhouse with elegantly furnished rooms ranged around a central patio. Also has a decent restaurant with sushi and tempura often featuring on the menu. Can organize activities for guests from horseriding to windsurfing and rock climbing. €€€

CAMPING

Camping Paloma Los Algarbes 10km northwest of town; ⓦ campingpaloma.com. Not quite as close to the beach as some others, but the magnificent Playa de Valdevaqueros is only 500m away. There's plenty of shade, plus a restaurant, pool and supermarket on site. €̄

Camping Río Jara On the N340 road 4km northwest of town; ⓦ campingriojara.com. The nearest campsite to the town, with plenty of shade and access for disabled campers. €̄

Camping Tarifa On the N340 6km northwest of town; ⓦ campingtarifa.es. Pleasant site in a pine wood with plenty of shade and its own pool, 100m from the beach. €̄

Camping Torre de la Peña On the N340 7km northwest of town; ⓦ campingtp.com. Reliable campsite close to the sea with plenty of shade, pool and a decent restaurant. €̄

EATING

SEE MAP PAGE 196

Tarifa has a wide range of places to eat, divided between the old town inside the walls and the new town beyond.

TAPAS BARS AND BARS

Bar Almedina C/Almedina s/n; ☎ 956 680 474. Popular

food and tapas bar in a twelfth-century gatehouse with a battered piano to one side as you enter, and some equally battered-looking regulars propping up the bar. There's a great ambience when it fills up in the evening with the *copas* and cocktails crowd. They also stage live events and flamenco takes place year-round on Thursday around 10pm. €€

★ **Bar El Francés** C/Sancho IV El Bravo 21; ☎ 685 857 005. A highly popular French-owned tapas and *raciones* bar adding a subtly Gallic touch to such staples as *calamares*, *pulpo braseado* and *tortilla de camarones*. Don't miss their *cous cous con pollo y verduras* (chicken & vegetable) or the mouthwatering *tarta de zanahoria* (carrot cake). Also has a lively street terrace. €€

Geko Pza de Oviedo 1; ☎ 673 447 220. Fronting the church of San Mateo, this pleasant little terrace bar with an Italian kitchen serves a variety of economical salads, *tablas de queso* (cheese boards), *fajitas* and pasta dishes, as well as *bocadillos* and plenty of vegetarian options. A house special is their *carpaccio, rucula and parmigiano* wrap. €

Mesón La Garrocha C/Guzmán El Bueno 22; ☎ 647 023 327. Very good tapas bar with tables inside to sample their more elaborate fare including the house-produced *jamón ibérico*. Try the *chuleta de vaca retinto* (local high-quality beef) or (in season) the house special *atun de almadraba* (fresh bluefin tuna). €€

RESTAURANTS

Bar Morilla C/Sancho IV El Bravo 2; ☎ 956 681 757. Central bar where *tarifeños* gather to breakfast or munch early-evening tapas while contemplating the ancient stones of nearby San Mateo. Later, cloths are thrown over the tables as the restaurant hits its stride serving very good fish – *urta a la plancha* (sea bream) is a house special – and meat dishes. Also does pasta and vegetarian options. €€€

Chilimosa C/Peso 6, just by the Puerto de Jerez; Ⓦ chilimosa.com. Lilliputian vegetarian (and vegan) diner with only a few tables, but they also do takeaways. Daily specials feature samosas, *empanadas* (pasties), falafel, quiche, salads and curries. Also makes its own tasty *dulces* and serves organic wine, beer, teas and soft drinks. €

★ **Mandragora** C/Independencia 3; ☎ 956 681 291. Located behind the church of San Mateo, this is one of Tarifa's best restaurants, and offers dishes from both sides of the straits: in addition to Moroccan couscous and *berenjenas bereber* ("Berber-style" aubergine), it does excellent *raciones*, including *boquerones rellenos* (stuffed anchovies) and fish plus quite a few vegetarian options. Generous portions mean that a *cous cous cordero* (lamb) will easily serve two. There's an attractive outdoor terrace and on cooler days the dining room – decorated with ferns and plants – also does justice to the cuisine. €€

Petit Bistro Paseo Alameda s/n, with entry also at C/ Santísima Trinidad 19; Ⓦ petitbistrotarifa.com. Excellent mid-priced French-run bistro with a terrace on the Alameda. They serve up a range of fish and meat dishes – *magret de pato a l'orange* (duck) is a house special – accompanied by great (French) wines. Their crêpes are mouthwateringly authentic. €€

NIGHTLIFE

There's little in the way of **entertainment** outside of some of the bars we've listed, but Tarifa's main summer nightlife scene happens when the town council erects *carpas* (disco tents) on the **Playa de los Lances beach** at the eastern end of town.

Campo de Gibraltar

The **Campo de Gibraltar** (a county of the province of Cádiz) is the area surrounding the British colony of **Gibraltar** and was given this name by Spain prior to its seizure by the British in 1704, when it was a Spanish municipality. To the north and west of the controversial colony, which sits on a headland dominated by its famous Rock, lie the other towns of the region of which by far the largest is **Algeciras**. A major port and industrial centre, it has few charms, but provides the easiest ferry crossing for a visit to Morocco.

More charming are the White Towns of **Castellar de la Frontera** and **Jimena de la Frontera**, both within the huge green mass of Alcornocales natural park (see page 227). **San Roque** and **La Línea** owe their existence to the dispute over the Rock, with the former providing the original refuge for those fleeing Gibraltar during the British siege, and the latter becoming "the line" (*la línea*) or boundary between the colony and Spain. San Roque has little in the way of sights, but La Línea has a lively central zone and provides a range of places to stay that are more attractive as well as cheaper than those in Gibraltar.

Algeciras

ALGECIRAS occupies the far side of the bay from Gibraltar, spewing out smoke and pollution in its direction. The last town of the Spanish Mediterranean, it was once an elegant resort; today it's unabashedly a port and industrial centre, its suburbs sprawling out on all sides. When Franco closed the border with Gibraltar at La Línea it was Algeciras that he decided to develop to absorb the Spanish workers formerly employed in the British naval dockyards, thus breaking the area's dependence on the Rock.

Most travellers are scathing about the city's ugliness, and unless you're waiting for a bus or train, or heading for Morocco, there's admittedly little reason to stop. However, Algeciras has a real port atmosphere, and even if you're just passing through it's hard to resist the urge to get on a boat south. This is the main port for Moroccan migrant workers, who travel home every year during their holidays from the factories, farms and mines of northern Europe. In summer, the port bustles with groups of Moroccans in transit, dressed in flowing *djelabas* and yellow slippers, and lugging unbelievable amounts of possessions. Half a million cross Spain each year, and at the major Islamic festival periods huge queues build up at the port as the ferries struggle to cope.

Plaza Alta

Once you start to explore, you'll discover that the old town has some very attractive corners that seem barely to have changed in fifty years, especially around the **Plaza Alta**. This leafy square, arguably the town's only sight of any note, lies a five-minute walk from the bus station/port area, and if you're killing time, provides a much more pleasant place to sit out than around the port. On the square, the eighteenth-century church of Nuestra Señora de la Palma and the Baroque chapel of Nuestra Señora de Europa – with a fine facade – are worth a look.

Hotel Reina Cristina

Paseo de la Conferencia s/n

Near the port, where impressive but now crumbling edifices echo faded glories, the romantic **Hotel Reina Cristina** is a wonderful throwback to the days of the Grand Tour and steam trains, built in the nineteenth century in British colonial style and set in a park on a rise south of the harbour. Call in for a drink in their terrace bar and take a look at the plaques behind the reception desk bearing the signatures of famous guests, such as Sir Arthur Conan Doyle, W.B. Yeats, Cole Porter and Federico García Lorca.

ARRIVAL AND DEPARTURE

ALGECIRAS

By bus The bus station is at C/San Bernardo, 1.2km behind the port.

Destinations Cádiz (9 daily; 2hr); Estepona (11 daily; 1hr); Fuengirola (9 daily; 2hr); Granada (4 daily; 5hr 30min); Jerez de la Frontera (Mon–Fri 8 daily; 1hr 30min); La Línea, for Gibraltar (every 30min from 7am–10.30pm; 30min); Málaga (14 daily; 3hr 15min or 1hr 45min direct); Marbella (14 daily; 1hr 30min or 1hr direct); Seville (8 daily; 2hr 45min); Tarifa (every 30min; 45min).

By train The train station is just beyond the bus station at Avda Gesto por la Paz s/n. From here the line heads to Ronda and the Bobadilla Junction, where there are connections with Seville, Málaga, Córdoba and Granada. The stunningly scenic route to Ronda is one of the best journeys in Andalucía.

Destinations Córdoba (5 daily; 3hr 15min); Granada (3 daily; 4hr 15min); Málaga (2 daily, change at Bobadilla; 4hr); Ronda (5 daily; 1hr 30min–1hr 45min); Seville (5 daily; 4hr 15min).

TO MOROCCO

Morocco is easily visited from Algeciras: in summer, there are crossings to Tangier and to the Spanish *presidio* of Ceuta, little more than a Spanish Gibraltar with a brisk business in duty-free goods, but a relatively painless way to enter Morocco. Tickets to Tangier or Ceuta (depending on the company) are sold at scores of travel agents along the waterfront and on most approach roads. For up-to-date information on hydrofoils and fast-ferries, check with the *Turismo* or with the ferry companies based in Estación Marítima inside the harbour terminal: Trasmediterránea (ⓦ trasmediterranea.es), FRS (ⓦ frs.es) or Viajes Transafric (ⓦ viajestransafric.com).

FRS do a daily all-inclusive day-trip to Tangier by fast-ferry, which includes a guided tour, lunch and time for shopping. They also offer a two-day excursion adding a night in a three-star hotel. Wait till Tangier – or if you're going via Ceuta, Tetouan – before buying any Moroccan currency; rates in the embarkation building kiosks are very poor. Check the date and time on your ferry ticket, and beware the ticket sellers who congregate near the dock entrance wearing official Ceuta/Tangier badges: they add a whopping "commission" charge. A useful site for checking the latest ferry schedules is ⓦ directferries.co.uk.

To Ceuta At least twenty departures daily in summer to the Spanish *presidio* of Ceuta (fast ferry 55min), little more than a Spanish Gibraltar with a brisk business in duty-free goods, but a relatively painless way to enter Morocco.

To Tangier Hourly departures in summer (fast ferry 45min, normal ferry 2hr 30min). Note that all ferries from Spain to Tangier (except for sailings from Tarifa) now dock at the new Tanger-Med port some 40km east of the town itself. The road connections are good but it adds some 30–45min to the journey in both directions.

INFORMATION

Turismo The helpful Turismo at C/Juan de la Cierva s/n, a pedestrianized avenue near the port (Mon–Fri 9am–7.30pm, Sat & Sun 9.30am–3pm; ☎ 670 948 731), can provide a town map and copious information on the Campo de Gibraltar and has ferry schedules.

ACCOMMODATION

Albergue Juvenil Ctra Nacional 340, 8km west of town on the Tarifa road; ⓦ inturjoven.com. Algeciras's luxurious youth hostel has a fine pool, tennis courts, en-suite doubles and a car park. Buses heading for Tarifa will drop you outside on request. €

Hostal Lisboa C/Juan Morrison 46; ⓦ pensionlisboa. com. A couple of minutes' walk from the Turismo, this simple but welcoming *hostal* offers spotless en-suite rooms with TV (most also have balconies), plus use of a communal guests' kitchen and a washing machine. Also has a couple of roomier studios that add a kitchenette. €

Hostal Nuestra Señora de la Palma Pza Ntra Sra de la Palma 12; ⓦ hostalnuestrasenoradelapalma.es. Very spruce place on the market square offering neat and tidy en-suite rooms with a/c and TV. €

Hotel Don Manuel C/Segismundo Moret 4; ☎ 956 634 606. Reliable two-star hotel opposite the Turismo, offering functional, a/c rooms with TV, good for a night if waiting for a ferry, but probably no longer. Can advise on parking. €

Hotel Reina Cristina Paseo de la Conferencia s/n; ⓦ reinacristina.es. This grand, historic four-star hotel (see page 202) has affordable and attractive well-equipped rooms with minibar, safe and satellite TV. Facilities include superb indoor and outdoor pools, gardens and car park. Breakfast is included. €

Marina Victoria Avda de la Marina 7: ⓦ hotelmarinavictoria.es. A very pleasant hotel close to the waterfront with a/c balcony rooms overlooking the port and bay with great views towards Gibraltar. €

EATING AND DRINKING

The huge number of people passing through the town guarantees virtually limitless possibilities for **food and drink**, especially around the port/harbour area. There are also **tapas bars** worth checking out around Plaza Alta (C/Sevilla has quite a few), as well as the main market, on Plaza Nuestra Señora de la Palma down by the port, a riot of colour on Saturday mornings.

Bar La Casita C/Tarifa 16, slightly west of the market; ☎ 956 632 886. A typical little *barrio* tapas bar in business for over forty years that gives service with a smile and great-value tapas and *raciones*. Try the paella or *pollo al limón* (chicken with lemon). Puts out tables on the pedestrianized street. €

La Posada de Millan C/Sevilla 43, two blocks west of the Pza Alta; ☎ 856 222 075. Traditional restaurant with plenty of space and a Moorish-style fountain in the rear patio. Offers a wide range of well-prepared fish and meat dishes. Also opens for breakfast. €€

Castellar de la Frontera

Heading north out of Algeciras along the A405, after 24km a signed turn-off on the left leads to **CASTELLAR DE LA FRONTERA**, a bizarre hill village within a thirteenth-century Moorish castle, whose population was moved downriver in 1971 to a "new" town on the edge of nearby La Almoraima. A few locals subsequently moved back to their houses in the old village, but many of the vacated dwellings were taken over by retired hippies (mainly affluent Germans). Perhaps not surprisingly, the result wasn't totally successful, and the two groups didn't gel – reflecting this tension, the place today has a brooding, claustrophobic atmosphere.

★**Convento La Almoraima** Ctra Algeciras–Ronda s/n, just before the turn-off for Castellar; ⓦ laalmoraimahotel.com. Following the turning on the left signed "Casa Convento" leads you through expansive woodlands to this enchanting hotel located inside a renovated seventeenth-century convent with a fine Florentine tower and a restaurant in the former cloister. The rooms are elegantly furnished to four-star standard and there's a pool and tennis court. The hotel is surrounded by vast tracts of wooded walking country in the Parque Natural de los Alcornocales (see page 227), making it hard to imagine a more serene stopover. €€€

Hotel-Casas Rurales de Castellar C/Rosario 3; ⓦ tugasa.com. Well-equipped rooms (some with outstanding views) built into the castle walls, along with further *casas rurales* accommodation in a number of renovated and well-equipped dwellings. The hotel also runs the decent and adjacent *Restaurante Aljibe*, offering a range of fish and meat dishes. Breakfast is included (in hotel). €

Jimena de la Frontera

JIMENA DE LA FRONTERA, 20km further north along the A405, is another hill town, far larger and more open than Castellar, rising to a grand if ruined thirteenth-century Moorish **castle** with a triple-gateway entrance and round keep. The town is home to a considerable contingent of British expats, attracted by its proximity to Gibraltar. Jimena is also a gateway to the **Parque Natural de los Alcornocales** (see page 227), a vast expanse of verdant hill country stretching south to the sea and north to El Bosque and covered with cork oaks (*alcornocales*) – a haven for large numbers of birds and insects. It's a lovely drive from Jimena to Gaucín (see page 119), just over the border in Málaga.

Bar Ventorrillero C/Sevilla s/n; ☎ 956 640 997. At the foot of C/Sevilla, this friendly bar-restaurant serves good-value tapas and *raciones* as well as local mountain specialities such as *jabalí al tomillo con trompetas negras* (wild boar with thyme and wild mushrooms), and there's a cheap weekday lunchtime *menu*. €

Camping Los Alcornocales On the north side of town (follow C/Sevilla to its end); ⓦ campinglosalcornocales. com. In a superb location with great views; also rents out en-suite wood cabins and has its own restaurant. €

Restaurante Bar Cuenca Avda de los Deportes 31; ☎ 956 640 152. Serving locals and visitors for over a century, this is a decent bar-restaurant for typical meat and fish dishes. A speciality here in season is *setas* (wild mushrooms) which is evident in one of its autumn signature dishes *pluma de cerdo ibérico con boletus* (Iberian pork loin with boletus mushrooms). It also has a pretty terrace patio at the rear. €

San Roque and around

Now a rather undistinguished small industrial town, **SAN ROQUE**, 35km south of Jimena and close to the frontier with Gibraltar, was founded in 1704 by Gibraltar's original inhabitants fleeing the British, who had captured the Rock and looted their homes and churches. They expected to return within months, since the troops had taken the garrison in the name of Archduke Carlos of Austria, whose rights Britain had been promoting in the War of the Spanish Succession, but it was the British flag that was raised on the conquered territory – and so it has remained (the Ayuntamiento's council chamber, on the central Plaza de la Iglesia, has a **banner** given to the earlier, Spanish, Gibraltar by Fernando and Isabel). On the same square, the eighteenth-century church of **Santa María Coronada** – built over the ancient hermitage of San Roque – has a fine image of the Virgin, also rescued from the Rock in the flight from the British invaders.

If you're looking for a place to stay, a far better place to overnight is **LOS BARRIOS**, 10km to the west, a tidy and tranquil place away from the somewhat depressing nature of this industrial area.

Los Barrios is a more attractive proposition for **accommodation** than San Roque, with a couple of pleasant places to stay. Both hotels below have restaurants and there are numerous places to eat along C/Pablo Picasso, Los Barrios' main thoroughfare.

LOS BARRIOS

Hotel Montera Pza Avda Carlos Cano s/n, on the west side of Los Barrios near the A381 autovía and opposite the Pza de Toros; ⊕hotelmontera.com. Don't be put off by first impressions: behind a fairly humdrum exterior, this excellent-value four-star hotel has smart, well-equipped rooms, many with terrace balcony and views. Add in a good restaurant, gardens, pool, free car park and friendly staff

and you have a bargain. €̲

Hotel Real C/Pablo Picasso 7; ☎956 620 024. Central, pleasant hotel on this elegant palm-lined avenue (the town's main street) offering a/c balcony rooms with TV. Also has its own decent bar-restaurant and can advise on parking nearby. €̲

SAN ROQUE

Camping La Casita San Roque, on the N340 (km126.2) highway 8km northeast of San Roque; ☎956 780 031. Occupying a site with plenty of shade; facilities include a pool and bar-restaurant. €̲

La Línea

The **Spanish–British frontier** is 8km south of San Roque at **LA LÍNEA** ("the line"). When Franco closed the frontier in 1969, it was La Línea that suffered most, as workers lost their jobs on the Rock overnight and the town's population dropped by 35 percent. After sixteen years of Spanish-imposed isolation, the gates were reopened in February 1985, and the five-minute crossing between here and Gibraltar is now routine – except for the odd flare-up when petulant disputes impose long delays on those waiting to cross. La Línea remains in a largely depressed state, a fact that has pushed many of its people into assisting the Rock's smugglers by warehousing contraband tobacco prior to its distribution throughout Spain. Post-millennium, there was also an explosion of drugs trafficking here with criminal gangs working with their counterparts in Gibraltar and Morocco to bring shipments into mainland Europe. There are no sights as such; it's just a fishing village that has exploded in size due to the employment opportunities in Gibraltar and the industrialized zone around the Bay of Algeciras.

ARRIVAL AND DEPARTURE
LA LÍNEA

By train The closest mainline train station is San Roque-La Línea, 11km west of town, from where you can pick up a train to Ronda (5 daily; 1hr 25min) and beyond.

By bus The bus station is on Pza de Europa, 250m from the frontier with Gibraltar.

Destinations Algeciras (daily; every 30min 7.30am–

10.30pm; 30min); Cádiz (2 daily; 2hr 30min); Conil (6 daily; 1hr 45min); Estepona (11 daily; 1hr 30min); Málaga (4 daily; 3hr); Marbella (4 daily; 1hr 30min); San Roque (23 daily; 20min); Tarifa (6 daily; 1hr); Vejer (2 daily 1hr 35min).

By car There's an expensive underground car park beneath the central Pza. de la Constitución.

INFORMATION

Turismo Avda 20 Abril, south of the main Pza de la Constitución, a large modern square at the heart of La Línea (Mon–Wed 9.30am–7.30pm, Thurs & Fri 9am–3pm, Sat &

Sun 9.30am–3pm; ☎956 784 135). A very helpful office. Their Campo de Gibraltar leaflet has street maps of both La Línea and Algeciras.

ACCOMMODATION

Although La Línea's greater number of **hotels** make it a better overnight bet than Gibraltar, many of its *hostales* are depressingly grim (we've listed a couple of honourable exceptions). Budget accommodation is concentrated around the focal Plaza de la Constitución, while both hotels listed below offer much better value than anything of the same standard in Gibraltar.

La Campana C/Carboneras 3, off Pza de la Constitución; ⊕hostalcampana.es. A very friendly refurbished *hostal* offering attractive en-suite rooms with a/c, heating and TV. €̲

Hostal-Restaurante Carlos C/Carboneras 6; ⊕hostalcarlos.es. Almost opposite *La Campana*, this is a fractionally cheaper option, with light, a/c, en-suite balcony rooms, with similar facilities. The restaurant here is good and has a cheap *menu*. €̲

Hotel AC La Línea C/Caireles 2; ⊕marriott.com. Good value four-star option close to the Bay of Algeciras seafront, and a 10min walk from the Gibraltar border. It offers well-appointed rooms (many have Gibraltar views) with minibar and facilities include pool, gym and garage. €̲

Ohtel Campo de Gibraltar Avda Príncipe de Asturias

2

s/n, on the seafront; ⓦ ohtelscampodegibraltar.es. A 5min walk from the Gibraltar border, this is an attractive four-star hotel with spacious executive-style terrace balcony rooms with sea view, safe and minibar. Also has a very nice pool and large underground (pay) car park. See website for special offers. Breakfast is included. €€

EATING AND DRINKING

La Línea has lots of **eating and drinking** options. Close to the focal Plaza de la Constitución lies C/Real, the town's main pedestrianized shopping street, offering plenty of reasonably priced bars, cafés and restaurants (while you're here, it's worth having a look at the elegant Casino Mercantil at no. 25, dating from 1925). For picnic supplies, head for the market, north of C/Real.

★ **Café Modelo** C/Real 30; ⓦ cafemodelo.es. Wonderful mid-twentieth-century café boasting a glorious interior full of antique fittings and fixtures and one of La Línea's most fashionable terraces. The kitchen serves up all kinds of tasty snacks from *bocadillos de bacón* to *platos combinados*, or you can take afternoon tea (over twenty different varieties) with pastries. €

Gibraltar

GIBRALTAR's interest is essentially its novelty: the genuine appeal of the strange, looming physical presence of its rock, and the increasingly dubious one of its preservation as one of Britain's last remaining colonies; a bizarre mixture of southern Spain and British seaside resort, with bobbies on the beat, pubs and the gentle tolling of church bells redolent of the Home Counties. This enormous hunk of limestone, 5km long, 2km wide and 450m high – a land area smaller than the city of Algeciras across the water – has fascinated and attracted the people of the Mediterranean basin since Neanderthal times, confirmed by the finds of skulls and artefacts in a number of the Rock's many caves.

The Rock (as it is colloquially known) is opening to mass tourism from the Costa del Sol and this threatens both to destroy Gibraltar's highly individual society and at the same time to make it much more British, after the fashion of the expat communities and huge resorts up the coast. The frontier opening has benefited most people: Gibraltarians can buy cheaper goods in Spain, a place ironically where thirty percent of them now have second homes, while expats living on the Costas can shop in familiar British stores like Morrisons and Marks & Spencer. Despite a healthy economy based on tourism, offshore banking and its role as a major bunkering port, the colony has reached yet another crossroads in its tortuous history, and the likely future – whether its population agrees to this or not – is almost certain to involve closer ties with Spain. Brexit has been a huge issue here since 2016 - only 4% of Gibraltarians voted to leave the EU, but the colony was dragged out by default when the UK finally left in January 2020. The Rock has been the subject of special negotiations between the Spanish and UK governments ever since, but as of summer 2022 many things were still to be decided.

The Rock

Cable car Daily: 9.30am–7.15pm, last trip down 7.15pm • Charge • **All sites** Daily: summer 9.30am–7.15pm; winter 9.30am–6.15pm • Small charge for **nature reserve,** or an inclusive ticket for St Michael's Cave, Moorish castle, siege tunnels and exhibition (but excluding O'Hara's Battery)

Near the end of Main Street you can hop on the expensive **cable car**, which will carry you up to the summit – the **Top of the Rock** as it's logically known. A way to avoid paying the return fare is to walk back down via the Mediterranean Steps (see page 208).

The cable car ascends via the **Apes' Den** halfway up, a fairly reliable viewing point to see the tailless monkeys (Barbary apes) who live here and to hear the guides explain their legend. The story goes that the British will keep the rock only so long as the apes remain too; Winston Churchill was superstitious enough to augment their numbers during World War II when they started to decline. Be aware that the warning notices are there for a reason: cute as they seem, the monkeys are wild animals and love nothing more than to make off with cameras, hats, purses and sunglasses and have given many a visitor a painful bite. The Top of the Rock gives fantastic views over to the Atlas mountains in Morocco and the town far below, as well as an elaborate water catchment system cut into the side of the rock. This is also an ideal spot for observing bird migrations between Africa and the Spanish peninsula.

Upper Rock Nature Reserve

Much of the area of the upper Rock has now been grandly designated the **Upper Rock Nature Reserve**, which the resident colony of Barbary apes and a few rare plant species hardly justifies. To enter this area you will need to pay the pedestrian fee, while you'll also need to pay again to view attractions inside the reserve.

Tower of Homage

On the upper Rock's northern flank, this remnant of Gibraltar's Moorish alcázar can be reached from the cable car station by following Signal Station Road north, eventually turning left into Willis's Road where – after 100m or so – you will see the tower to the right. When you reach it, what remains is little more than a collection of ruins, gatehouses and fortified walls of which the fourteenth-century **Tower of Homage** is the most visible survivor from Gibraltar's original Moorish castle. The interior is now filled with wax dummies of British soldiers hacking at the stone and doing battle with the Spanish.

Gibraltar: City Under Siege

Near the Tower of Homage, in an eighteenth-century former ammunition store on Willis's Road, the **Gibraltar: City Under Siege** exhibition uses tableaux to document the history of the Great Siege and the hardships suffered by both the military and the local population.

Upper Galleries

Further up the same road you'll find the **Upper Galleries** (aka the Great Siege Tunnels), blasted out of the rock during the Great Siege of 1779–82 when the Spanish forces and their French allies attempted to reclaim Gibraltar while the British were distracted by the American War of Independence. The opening of the galleries and the boring of holes in the Rock's north face allowed gun emplacements to point down at the Spanish lines.

St Michael's Cave

From the Top of the Rock cable-car station a leafy path leads some 500m south to **St Michael's Cave**, an immense natural cavern that led ancient people to believe the Rock was hollow and gave rise to its old name of Mons Calpe (Hollow Mountain). Used during World War II as a bomb-proof military hospital, the cave nowadays hosts occasional concerts. You can arrange at the tourist office for a guided visit to **Lower Saint Michael's Cave**, a series of chambers going deeper down and ending in an underground lake.

O'Hara's Battery

Charge; not covered by inclusive Rock ticket

Built in 1890, O'Hara's Battery was one of a series of gun batteries aimed at protecting the Rock from Spanish incursions. The gun emplacements and turntables on which they were mounted have been privately restored and are now opened to the public. The nine-inch gun was used in World War II and was last fired during training exercises in 1976.

2

Mediterranean Steps

Close to St Michael's Cave at the end of O'Hara's Road, the **Mediterranean Steps** offer one possible route if you want to walk down from the Top of the Rock (it'll take you about twenty minutes) rather than taking the cable car. They're not very well signposted and you'll need a good head for heights. To get to the steps you need to pass through O'Hara's Battery (see page 207) where the steps begin, with a very steep descent most of the way down the east side, before turning the southern corner of the Rock. You'll eventually pass through the **Jews' Gate** and into Engineer Road, from where the return to town is through the Alameda Gardens, complete with a statue of Molly Bloom, James Joyce's Gibraltar-born heroine in the epic *Ulysses*.

The Town

The town has a necessarily simple layout, as it's shoehorned into the narrow stretch of land on the peninsula's western edge in the shadow of the towering Rock. **Main Street** (La Calle Real) runs for most of the town's length, a couple of blocks back from the port. On and around Main Street are most of the shops, together with many of the British-style pubs and hotels.

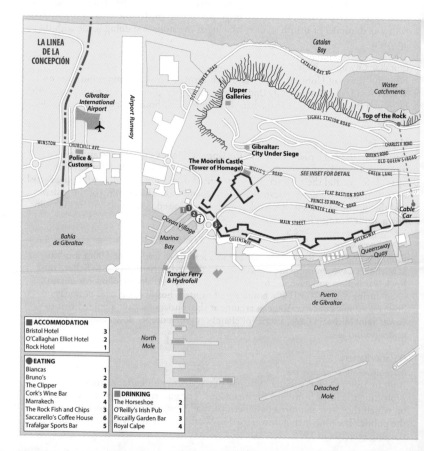

■ ACCOMMODATION	
Bristol Hotel	3
O'Callaghan Elliot Hotel	2
Rock Hotel	1

● EATING	
Biancas	1
Bruno's	2
The Clipper	8
Cork's Wine Bar	7
Marrakech	4
The Rock Fish and Chips	3
Saccarello's Coffee House	6
Trafalgar Sports Bar	5

■ DRINKING	
The Horseshoe	2
O'Reilly's Irish Pub	1
Piccailly Garden Bar	3
Royal Calpe	4

Trafalgar Cemetery

Prince Edward's Rd • Daily 9am–sunset

To the south of the town centre, beyond the city walls, lies the evocative **Trafalgar Cemetery**, where some of those who perished at the Battle of Trafalgar are buried. A memorial to the battle stands in the cemetery grounds and number of graves display a good line in imperial epitaphs.

Gibraltar Museum

Bomb House Lane • Mon–Fri 10am–6pm, Sat 10am–2pm • Charge • ⓦ gibmuseum.gi

Perhaps the most interesting item in the **Gibraltar Museum** are two beautiful, well-preserved fourteenth-century **Moorish Baths**. Resembling the ancient Roman model, the baths had a cold room and hot rooms heated by a hypocaust. Note the star-shaped skylights, and the pillars used in the construction: one Roman, two Visigothic and four Moorish. Otherwise, the museum's collection is an odd assortment, including an incongruous Egyptian mummy washed up in the bay, a natural history display of stuffed birds in glass cases and a rather dreary military section documenting how the British came to rule the roost here.

The museum's star exhibit should be a female skull, dating from around 100,000 years ago and unearthed in 1848 on the Rock's north face. Ironically, because the

2

GIBRALTAR'S SOVEREIGNTY

Sovereignty over the Rock will doubtless eventually return to Spain, but at present neither side is in much of a hurry. For Britain it's a question of precedent – Gibraltar is in too similar a situation to the Falklands/Malvinas, a conflict that pushed the Spanish into postponing an initial frontier-opening date in 1982. For Spain, too, there are unsettling parallels with the *presidios* (Spanish enclaves) on the Moroccan coast at Ceuta and Melilla. Nonetheless, the British presence is in practice waning, and the British Foreign Office clearly wants to steer Gibraltar towards a new, harmonious relationship with Spain, despite the problems caused by Brexit. To this end they are running down the significance of the military base, and now only a token force remains – most of these working in a top-secret hi-tech bunker buried deep inside the Rock from where the Royal Navy monitors the sea traffic through the straits (accounting for a quarter of the world movement of all shipping). In financial terms this has cut the British government's contribution to Gibraltar's GDP from 65 percent in the early 1980s to less than seven percent today, and the figure is still falling.

The majority of the 30,000 Gibraltarians see all these issues as irrelevant in light of their firmly stated **opposition** to a return to **Spanish control** over the Rock. In 1967, before Franco closed the border in the hope of forcing a quick agreement, the colony voted on the issue – rejecting it by 12,138 votes to 44 (a poll not recognized, incidentally, by the UN). Most people would probably sympathize with that vote – against a Spain that was then still a dictatorship – but half a century has gone by, Spanish democracy is now secure and the arguments are becoming increasingly tenuous.

AN UNCERTAIN FUTURE

The UK's 2016 Brexit referendum on leaving or remaining in the EU also had major implications for Gibraltar's future. Whereas in Britain the vote was narrowly in favour of leave, in Gibraltar (which was included in the poll) the vote to remain was an overwhelming 96 percent. Negotiations between the UK and the EU have begun, but Spain won an early concession from the EU guaranteeing it an important role in deciding Gibraltar's post-Brexit status. The EU has informed the UK government that it must reach an agreement with Spain

find was then stored away, it was the later discovery of a skull in Germany's Neander Valley that gave its name to the era we know as Neanderthal, which could just as easily have been termed "Gibraltarian". The museum now retains only a copy, the original having been removed to the research collection of the Natural History Museum in London.

King's Chapel
Daily 9am–7pm • Free

Not far away from the Gibraltar Museum, and next door to the Governor's Residence, is the sixteenth-century **King's Chapel**, harking back to precolonial days – the seventeenth-century remains of the wife of the last Spanish governor are buried here. It's a fine old church – now rather marred by the military flags, regalia and wall plaques of Empire – and was formerly the chapel attached to the Convent of Franciscan friars (now the Governor's Residence). This should, of course, have been titled "Friary", but a mistranslation by early British settlers fixed the erroneous name and this was confirmed as its title in the 1940s by order of King George VI.

Nelson's Anchorage
Rosia Rd • Mon–Sat 9.30am–6.45pm • Charge, or covered by inclusive Rock ticket

At **Nelson's Anchorage**, to the south of the harbour, a monstrous **100-ton Victorian gun** marks the site where Nelson's body was brought ashore – preserved in a rum barrel – from HMS *Victory* after the Battle of Trafalgar in 1805.

regarding Gibraltar's future or risk exposing its citizens to "economic peril" by pushing the Rock outside any EU–UK trade deal. This caused alarm bells to ring in the colony and the usual "Gibraltar will never be Spanish!" slogans were wheeled out once again by the Rock's politicians.

What most outsiders don't realize about the political situation is that the Gibraltarians feel very vulnerable: caught between the interests of two big states, they are well aware that both governments' concerns have little to do with their own personal wishes. Until very recently people were sent over from Britain to fill all the top civil service and Ministry of Defence jobs, a practice which, to a lesser degree, still continues.

The general election of December 2011 saw a change in the trend of internal politics, with the defeat of Caruana's **Social Democratic administration** that had won victories in 2000, 2004 and 2007. Apparently weary of Caruana's arrogant manner, the electorate (in the Rock's highest-ever turnout) gave a narrow victory to a Labour-Liberal coalition, which made Oxford-educated Labour leader Fabian Picardo chief minister. Picardo won the last election held in 2015 and still remains in power.

Locals – particularly on the Spanish side of the border – also vigorously protest about the Royal Navy nuclear-powered and armed submarines that dock regularly at the naval base. Secrecy equally surrounds the issue of whether nuclear warheads and/or chemical and biological weapons are stored in the arsenal, probably deep inside the Rock itself, which is honeycombed with 51km of tunnels.

In tune with their rejection of most things Spanish (although 7000 of the Rock's citizenry own second homes on the Spanish side of the frontier, including Chief Minister Fabian Picardo) Gibraltarians stubbornly cling to British status, and all their institutions are modelled on British lines. Contrary to popular belief, however, they are of neither mainly Spanish nor British blood, but an ethnic mix descended from Genoese, Portuguese, Spanish, Menorcan, Jewish, Maltese and British forebears. **English** is the official language, but more commonly spoken is what sounds to an outsider like perfect Andalucian Spanish. It is, in fact, llanito, an Andalucian dialect with odd borrowed English and foreign words reflecting its diverse origins – only a Spaniard from the south can tell a Gibraltarian from an Andalucian.

Europa Point

Reached by bus #2, which runs along Line Wall Rd and Europa Rd – its continuation

If you have the time to spare you can take a bus south to the tip of the peninsula at **Europa Point**. On clear days you get fine views across the strait towards the mountains of Morocco and the sight of the odd leaping dolphin, but there's little else here but a lighthouse, souvenir shop, bus terminal and, interestingly, an impressive mosque donated in the 1990s by King Fahd of Saudi Arabia for the benefit of Muslim immigrants working in Gibraltar.

Catalan Bay

Bus #4 or #8 from Line Wall Rd (every 15min) stops here and at the other eastern beaches

Gibraltar's best **beach** is at the tiny fishing village of **Catalan Bay**, a characterless stretch of seafront reminiscent of a humdrum British holiday resort whose inhabitants like to think of themselves as distinct from the townies on the other side of the Rock.

ARRIVAL AND DEPARTURE

GIBRALTAR

By car If you have a car, don't attempt to bring it to Gibraltar – the queues at the border to get in (and out) are often atrocious, and parking on the Rock is limited. Use the underground car parks in La Línea instead (there's one in the focal Pza de la Constitución) and walk across. If you're determined to take your car in, ring ☎ 2004 2777 for the latest information on waiting times at the border.

By bus From the frontier at La Línea, where passport checking is a formality, it's a short bus ride (#5, every 15min; charge) or a 10min walk across part of the airport's runway

2

GIBRALTAR'S WEALTH

With a per capita income of almost €100,000 and an unemployment rate of under two percent Gibraltar is one of the richest territories on the planet. In contrast, over the border in the neighbouring province of Cádiz the per capita income is less than €7000 and the level of unemployment over thirty percent (the EU's highest). A third of the Rock's income comes from tobacco sales while an astonishing 25 percent comes from online gaming. Over sixty percent of UK companies trading in online gambling are based (for tax reasons) in Gibraltar – a market with a turnover of half a billion pounds annually. Incidentally, some of the World War II tunnels bored in the rock now house the servers powering these betting behemoths' websites. Added to this, Gibraltar is an important financial centre with over 60,000 registered companies. In the absence of a fiscal agreement between the Hacienda (Spain's Treasury Department) and Gibraltar there is a big question as to the role many of these companies play in assisting Spanish citizens to avoid tax duties on their wealth. Gibraltar states that it answers all requests for information from Spain regarding tax matters while the Madrid government (who maintain the colony on their blacklist of offshore tax havens) insists that up to now it has received no data of any relevance from the colony.

---

to Main St (La Calle Real), which runs for most of the town's length a couple of blocks back from the port. Services run to La Línea from Algeciras (on the hour and half-hour; 30min).

By taxi Be on your guard at the frontier for touting taxi drivers who offer "tours of the Rock" – they're generally overpriced and very rushed. If you wish to take a taxi tour that includes the Upper Rock Nature Reserve (excluding entry to the attractions), book with the Gibraltar Taxi Association on ☏ 2007 0052.

By plane Blands Travel (see page 212) can assist with booking easyJet (2 daily) flights to London.

By boat to Morocco A catamaran service, sails weekly to Tangier Med taking 1hr. Tickets, current timetables and rates are available from the agent Turner & Co, 65/67 Irish Town (Mon–Fri 9am–1pm & 2–5pm; ⓦ turnershipping. com).

INFORMATION

Tourist office 13 John Mackintosh Square (Mon–Fri 9am–4.30pm, Sat 9am–3.30pm, Sun 10am–1pm; ⓦ visitgibraltar.gi); there's a sub-branch in the customs and immigration building at the border (Mon–Fri 9am–4.30pm).

Phoning Gibraltar From Spain, the UK or anywhere in Europe dial 00 + 350 then number; from North America dial 011 + 350 then number.

Travel agents Blands Travel, Cloister Building, Irish Town (ⓦ blandstravel.com), is the leading travel agent in Gibraltar and sells twice-weekly day-trips to Tangier in Morocco on Wed and Sat, which include a guided tour and lunch. The sailing is from Tarifa, to where you are bussed.

Opening hours Much of Gibraltar, including restaurants and cafés (but with the exception of the cheap booze shops), closes down on Saturday, but the tourist sights remain open, and this can often be a quiet time to visit. Virtually everything is closed on Sunday.

ACCOMMODATION SEE MAP PAGE 208

Shortage of space on the Rock means that **accommodation** is at a premium, especially in summer. In addition, most of it isn't overly inviting and (compared to Spain) is expensive too. It's really not worth your while searching out a good place to stay unless you have to, and accept the fact that you're going to have to pay standard British hotel prices.

NEANDERTHAL MAN

Discoveries in a cave on the southeast tip of the Rock (not open to the public) suggest that Gibraltar was one of the last habitats of Neanderthal man who may have lived here some 24,000 years ago – much later than previously thought. Earlier finds of flint tools and evidence of campfires and cooked meals are regarded as one of the most important **prehistoric** finds in modern times. The cave appears to have been inhabited by both Neanderthals and *Homo sapiens*, and it's hoped that further excavations will provide vital evidence as to the extinction or amalgamation of our species with the earlier race.

Your best bet is to visit on day-trips from Algeciras or La Línea. No **camping** is allowed on the peninsula, and if you're caught sleeping rough or in abandoned bunkers, you're likely to be arrested and fined.

Bristol Hotel Cathedral Square; ⓦ bristolhotel.gi. Long-established, if rather staid, three-star place with refurbished rooms and a pool. The price code is for the cheapest interior-facing double, but you'll pay a supplement for a sea view. €€

O'Callaghan Elliot Hotel Governor's Parade; ⓦ ocallaghanhotels.com. Attractive four-star hotel where well-equipped rooms – some with sea view – come with safe, bathrobes and trouser press. Public areas include a pool, bar and restaurant. See website for offers. €€€€

Rock Hotel 3 Europa Rd; ⓦ rockhotelgibraltar.com. Gibraltar's flagship hotel, immediately below the Apes' Den, trades on its Empire connections, with photos of the great and good who have stayed here during the days when Gibraltar was an important staging post on the route to and from the imperial east. Rooms are decorated in "colonial style" and come with ceiling fans and a trouser press, and there's also a garden pool, restaurant and hairdresser. Free parking. €€€

EATING

SEE MAP PAGE 208

Eating – with a few honourable exceptions – is a bit of a sad affair in Gibraltar: relatively expensive by Spanish standards, with pub grub or fish and chips as the norm and bottled wine prices to make your eyes water. Main St is crowded with dismal touristy places and fast-food outlets but there are some more inviting places with waterfront terraces in **Marina Bay** and its continuation **Ocean Village**, or on the east side of the Rock at **Catalan Bay**.

Biancas Marina Bay; ⓦ biancas.gi. Popular and friendly all-day local restaurant which kicks off with a giant "English breakfast" (served from 9am) before moving on to pizzas, snacks and sandwiches – served in the bar – or more elaborate steak and fish dishes (as well as salads and veggie options) in the restaurant. Reasonable wine prices and a terrace overlooking the waterfront. €€

Bruno's The Boardwalk, Ocean Village; ☎ 2006 4211. Chic waterside bar-restaurant with glitzy decor not always matched by the food and service. The menu is Mediterranean and there are jacket potatoes, salads and seafood pasta dishes. €€

The Clipper 76 Irish Town; ⓦ theclipper.gi. British-style pub grub – a house special is steak and ale pie – served up in a lounge decorated with naval memorabilia. Serves a variety of UK beers on draught. €€

Corks Wine Bar 79 Irish Town; ⓦ corks.gi. A relatively tranquil venue offering a variety of salads and pasta dishes as well as pub-style favourites such as steak and Guinness pie. €€

Marrakech 9 Governor's Parade; ☎ 5600 0281. Very good Moroccan restaurant with a welcome outdoor terrace, which does lamb, chicken and vegetarian couscous, along with tagines and other Maghrebi dishes. €€

The Rock Fish & Chips 1 Casemates Square; ☎ 2005 1218. Chip shop on the main square, serving up the British national dish (eat in or takeaway). Does the "heart-attack-on-a-plate" full English breakfast, too – all day. Outdoor terrace. €

Saccarello's Coffee House 57 Irish Town; ⓦ saccarellosgibraltar.com. A local institution founded in 1888 by a Genoese immigrant and still in the hands of the same family, this has a rather select ambience and makes a great place for afternoon tea or coffee (they roast their own) and home-made confectionery. They also serve lunches including pies, pasta, quiche and salads. €

Trafalgar Sports Bar La Rosia Rd, near the Trafalgar Cemetery; ⓦ bit.ly/TrafalgarSportsBar. Unless you're a sports nut this is probably not the place to eat when there's a big match on TV (numerous huge screens). Not a bad diner at other times though, serving up decent pub grub, Sunday roast and – of course – fish and chips. Small outdoor terrace. €

SHOPPING AND SMUGGLING IN GIBRALTAR

Spain's tobacco and alcoholic drinks are among the cheapest in Europe, but Gibraltar – which avoids **excise duty** as it's not part of the European Economic Zone – can do it even more cheaply, thus explaining the crowds of plastic-bag-toting individuals passing through the Spanish customs border post at all hours of the day and night. Remember though that this means you are only allowed to take normal duty-free limits back into Spain (two hundred cigarettes and one litre of spirits per adult), and which also explains why you may be approached by locals asking you to carry a pack of cigarettes over the border into Spain. Think twice about doing so, however, as what may seem to be a simple carton of cigs could contain drugs (this is a major supply route from North Africa) and – if searched – you, and not they, will suffer the consequences.

Most of Gibraltar's duty-free booze and tobacco shops, along with outlets of major UK stores such as Marks Spencer, BHS, The Body Shop, Next and Mothercare are located on Main Street, while Morrisons supermarket lies northwest of Main Street near the harbour.

DRINKING   **SEE MAP PAGE 208**

Gibraltar's pubs mimic traditional English styles (and prices), but are often rowdy, full of soldiers and visiting sailors.

The Horseshoe 193 Main St; ☎ 2007 7444. Serves a range of British and international beers along with hearty pub grub; also has an outdoor pavement terrace.

O'Reilly's Irish Pub Ocean Village; ☎ 2006 7888. Vibrant Irish pub in the harbour zone with live (often Irish) music (Wed & Fri) and a traditional Sunday brunch, which you can wash down with a wide selection of international beers as well as the house staple, Guinness.

Piccadilly Garden Bar 3 Rosia Rd, just beyond the Referendum Gates (aka South Port); ☎ 2007 5758.

A garden bar serving breakfasts (full British blowout or Spanish with churros) as well as meat and fish *raciones*. A Spanish kitchen ensures the food is more authentic than most places – try the *sardines a la plancha*. Also has reasonable wine prices and later in the evening it transmutes into a drinks bar.

Royal Calpe 176 Main St; ☎ 2007 5890. Pub with outdoor terrace (and another at the rear) and pub grub: the house special is chicken and mushroom pie, while they also do quiches and salads, backed up by a wide selection of beers. Both kitchen and pub are known to close early when trade is slack.

DIRECTORY

Banks ATMs can be found along Main St along with bureaux de change (which stay open longer).

Money exchange The official currency is the Gibraltar pound (same value as the British pound, but different notes and coins – although you'll often find British coins mixed in with your change); ask for your change in euros if you are on a brief day-trip and note that Gibraltar pounds can be hard to change in Spain or anywhere else. Euros are accepted without problems all over Gibraltar, although you generally fork out about five percent more if you pay using them.

Sierra de Grazalema and the White Towns

The green lung at the heart of Cádiz's province, the **SIERRA DE GRAZALEMA** was one of the first *parques naturales* (natural parks) to be established in Andalucía. Covering around 550 square kilometres, it has been a UNESCO biosphere reserve since 1984 and contains a wealth of some 1300 plant species including a large number of orchids. The park is also home to many of the celebrated *pueblos blancos* or **White Towns** – more often villages (there are also several in Málaga province; see page 119). Among these, the sparkling whitewashed town of **Grazalema** itself, **El Bosque** and the enchanting village of **Zahara de la Sierra** stand out. Other villages well worth a visit include the province's highest, **Villaluenga del Rosario**, and **Benaocaz**, from where the outstanding hilltop Roman site of **Ocuri** is nearby. Below Ocuri, the major conurbation of **Ubrique** is attractively set in a valley beneath steep crags and has been noted since medieval times for its leatherwork. On the natural park's northern flank the villages of **Benamahoma**, **Algodonales** and **Olvera**, the latter with a spectacular biking and walking route along a disused railway line, are more *pueblos blancos* with plenty to offer.

All the places mentioned have places to stay, plus bars and restaurants to try out sierra specialities such as goat's cheese, *trucha con jamón* (trout with serrano ham) and *sopa de grazalema*, a hearty mountain soup with chorizo, eggs, *jamón* and herbs. The Sierra de Grazalema is also a walkers' paradise, with plenty of fine hikes to be had among the craggy limestone peaks cloaked in forests of oak and *pinsapo*, the rare Spanish fir, which grows nowhere else. Many of the villages have tourist or information offices ready to provide advice and even leaflets on hiking in the park. *Walking in Andalucía* by Guy Hunter-Watts (see page 556) also details half a dozen walks in the park.

Grazalema

Some 18km west of Ronda as the crow flies lies **GRAZALEMA**, the central point of the Sierra de Grazalema, and its natural park. A pretty white village beneath the craggy peak of San Cristóbal, with lots of sloping narrow streets and window boxes full of blooms in summer, it makes an ideal base for delving into the park. This is also the spot with the country's highest rainfall – and there's often quite a bit of snow in winter, too – which explains the lush vegetation covering the surrounding area, home to a spectacular variety of flora and fauna. Quite apart from the attractions of the park, the village has its own charms, and often fills up in summer with hikers and climbers and in winter with more sedentary Spanish tourists.

If the weather's warm enough, you could try out the communal **swimming pool**, which is spectacularly sited on the Arcos/Benamahoma road at the eastern edge of the village.

Brief history

The earliest traces of the village are connected with the remains of a Roman settlement named Lacidulia which traveller Richard Ford described as "plastered like a martlet-nest on the rocky hill". In the Moorish period the area was populated by Berbers who gave the town the name of Raisa lami Suli, which eventually passed down to Ben-salama "son of Zulema" who was often referred to in Spanish as Gran Zulema. Following the *Reconquista* the town was assigned to the estates of the Duke of Arcos – whose crest still forms the town's coat of arms today – and the name was changed to Zagrazalema, soon shortened to its current form.

In the seventeenth century the woollen industry became an important activity and the town grew rapidly as the fame of Grazalema shawls, blankets and cloaks spread. Attacks by Napoleonic troops in the War of Independence caused extensive damage but the town soon recovered and grew in size to almost ten thousand inhabitants by 1850 (compared with today's couple of thousand). The prosperity was so impressive that its name was often appended with the tag "Cádiz Chico" (Little Cádiz), favourably comparing its affluence with that of the provincial capital. However, the industrial revolution that reached Spain in the later nineteenth century decimated the town's cottage industry as large factories in Catalunya began to produce blankets and textiles much more cheaply. The industry went into decline and today only a couple of producers make the once-renowned Grazalema shawls. It is only with the creation of the Parque Natural – and with it the development of rural tourism – that some measure of prosperity has returned.

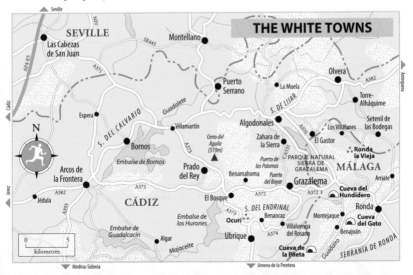

Plaza de España

The simple main square, the **Plaza de España**, is the hub of activity here, as it has been for a couple of centuries. At the southern end stands the eighteenth-century church of **Nuestra Señora de la Aurora** with a sober, unadorned facade topped off by a trio of belfries. Facing it at the elongated square's northern end lies the elegant and porticoed **Ayuntamiento**, with a four-spouted eighteenth-century fountain nearby. On the western side lies the early twentieth-century **Casino**, a tranquil place (open to visitors) where (mainly) male members of the community gather to play dominoes, cards, read the papers and down the odd *carajillo* (or two).

2

ARRIVAL AND INFORMATION
GRAZALEMA

By bus There is no bus station; buses pull up and leave from outside the Ayuntamiento on the main square, Pza de España.
Destinations El Bosque (1 daily; 45min); Málaga (2 daily; 3hr 40min change in Ronda); Ronda (2 daily; 1hr); Ubrique (3 daily; 35min).
Turismo Grazalema's tourist office, Pza Asomaderos 3, just

east of the main square (Tues–Sat 9am–3pm; ☎ 956 132 052), sells walking maps and can provide information about the park and activities such as horseriding.
Useful website Lots of useful background information (in Spanish) on the sierra's towns and villages and their histories as well as the natural park's flora and fauna is available on ⓦ sierradecadiz.com.

EXPLORING THE PARQUE NATURAL SIERRA DE GRAZALEMA

Bounded by the towns of Grazalema, Ubrique, El Bosque and Zahara, plus Algodonales and Olvera to the north, the **Parque Natural Sierra de Grazalema** is an important mountain wilderness, unique to Andalucía. The limestone mass of the sierra was formed in the Jurassic and Triassic periods and the close proximity of the range to the sea – which traps many of the clouds drifting in from the Atlantic – has produced a microclimate where numerous botanical species dating from before the Ice Age have survived. The most famous of these is the rare **pinsapo**, or Spanish fir, native only to this area of Europe, which grows at an altitude of between 1000m and 1700m. The high rainfall here, plus the wet, cool summers, are essential to its survival. The sierra also supports a wealth of **birdlife**: eagles (Bonelli's, booted and golden), vultures (griffon and Egyptian), as well as various owls and woodpeckers are all common. The streams and riverbanks are the domain of water voles and otters, the latter not popular with a number of fish farms in the area. On the sierra's higher reaches the magnificent Spanish ibex has been reintroduced to a craggy habitat, and its numbers are increasing.

The best way to appreciate the park is by **walking**, but to protect wildlife and nesting birds, access is restricted to different sections at certain times, and in June, July and August many routes are closed due to the high fire risk.

INFORMATION

The natural park's main **information office** (Centro de Visitantes; daily 10am–2pm; ☎ 956 709 733) is at El Bosque, C/Federico García Lorca s/n, next to the Plaza de Toros, and there is a smaller branch in Zahara de la Sierra. The main office issues access *permisos* (permits; free) and takes bookings for the Itinerario del Pinsapar (closed June–Sept), guided walks through the major stands of the *pinsapo* Spanish fir. If you contact them, they may be able to fax the permit free of charge to your hotel in Grazalema (see page 214) and/or the natural park office in Zahara de la Sierra (see page 219) to save you a journey. The office also stocks park maps with walking routes.

Horizon, at C/Las Piedras 1 in Grazalema (ⓦ horizonaventura.com), organizes a broad range of **outdoor activities** in the park, including hiking (with English-speaking guides), mountain bike tours, Land Rover trips and much more. They also conduct a variety of wildlife and birdwatching excursions and can even arrange accommodation for you. Wildside Holidays, C/Lajuneta s/n (ⓦ wildsideholidays.co.uk) is another Grazalema-based outfit that offers self-guided and guided walks with experienced and knowledgable guides. It's also possible to join a day walk at short notice.

LOCAL CRAFTS IN GRAZALEMA

Grazalema has long been a centre of **wool production** and famous for its woven cloaks and blankets. One of the two factories carrying on the tradition, Artesanía Textil de Grazalema (Ctra de Ronda s/n; Mon–Thurs 8am–2pm & 3–8.30pm, Fri 8am–2pm; closed Aug; ☎ 956 132 008) can be visited and their products, including blankets, scarves and ponchos, are on sale in the factory shop. As you approach the village from Ronda the factory is up a signed turning on the right just after the petrol station.

Leatherwork has also been a strong tradition here since medieval times and although the sierra's main centre of production is in Ubrique (see page 226), there are quality craftworkers here too. La Tienda Chica, at C/Agua 25 (Mon, Tues & Thurs–Sun 10am–2.30pm & 4–7pm; ☎ 674 278 195) close to the main square, turns out creative work by Fernando García including bags, belts, wallets and accessories made from the finest Ubrique leather.

The goat and sheep **cheeses** produced in the sierra are also highly prized and Finca La Huzuelas, a cheese factory making the famous Payoyo brand of cheese, can be visited (daily 10am–2pm & 3–7pm; ☎ 956 234 018). The factory is below the village on the right as you enter from Ronda and its cheeses can be purchased from their shop.

ACCOMMODATION

HOTELS AND HOSTALES

Camping Tajo Rodillo 400m above the village at the end of C/Las Piedras; ⓦ campingtajorodillo.es. Grazalema's campsite is pleasantly shady and rents out fully equipped cabins in addition to the usual facilities. There's a pool and restaurant and its office has literature on the park and can provide information about walks and horse-treks in the sierra. They also rent out mountain bikes. €

Casa de las Piedras C/Las Piedras 32; ⓦ casadelaspiedras.es. Sited above the main square, this *hostal* is the village's only budget option, offering rooms with and without bath. They also rent out two-person apartments. The proprietors can provide information on trekking in the area and arrange transport to the start of walks. €

Hotel Fuerte Baldío de los Alamillos; ⓦ fuertehoteles. com. Four kilometres out of the village at the start of the Ronda road, this huge modern four-star caters to the mainly Spanish winter trade, offering well-equipped rooms with fine views plus pool, tennis courts, restaurant and large car park. Activities such as horseriding are on offer. Two-night minimum stay in July and Aug. €€

Hotel Peñon Grande Pza Pequeña 7; ⓦ hotelgrazalema.com. Pleasant and central two-star hotel close to the main square with clean, light and airy a/c rooms. €

Hotel Villa de Grazalema Finca El Olivar s/n; ⓦ villasdeandalucia.com. This refurbished three-star hotel lies on the village's northern edge (3min walk) and has comfortable rooms with terrace balconies and fine views. It also rents out cottages (sleeping up to four). Facilities include a restaurant and bar, pool and free parking. Doubles €€, cottages €€€

★ **La Mejorana** C/Santa Clara 6; ⓦ lamejorana. net. Perhaps the most attractive place to stay, housed in an elegant *casa señorial* reached by following C/Mateos Gago 300m uphill from Pza de España. With welcoming proprietors, individually decorated and charming en-suite balcony rooms (some with great views – try for "Mejorana") plus a pool, this is a winner. Street parking possible nearby (ring ahead for advice). €

EATING AND DRINKING

The bars and restaurants on the focal Plaza de España have terraces and are reasonably priced for tapas and *raciones*, while the nearby C/Agua off the square's east side has another cluster of bars and restaurants.

Bar Zulema C/Agua 44; ☎ 956 132 402. A decent tapas and *raciones* bar with good-value tapas, *raciones* and *platos combinados*. Also offers an economical lunchtime *menú* and has an outdoor terrace. €

Cádiz El Chico Pza de España 8; ☎ 956 13 20 67. Located on the main square, this is one of the town's better restaurants and specializes in dishes of the sierra – *cordero al horno de leña* (lamb baked in a wood-fired oven) is a signature dish. Also does good tapas in its bar. There's an inexpensive lunchtime weekday *menú*. €€

Casa de las Piedras C/Las Piedras 32; ☎ 956 132 014. The *hostal*'s mid-priced restaurant serves local dishes with a creative edge. House specials include gazpacho *verde* (green gazpacho made with avocado) and *asado de cerdo con setas* (charcoal-grilled pork with wild mushrooms). There's a vine-covered patio for alfresco dining. €€

2

LUNES DE TORO CUERDO

One of Grazalema's major events is the **Lunes de Toro Cuerdo** festival, held on a Monday during the third week in July, when a full-size *toro bravo* (fighting bull) is released in the streets of the village. It's the oldest such event in Spain, dating back to the eighteenth century, and the town fills up with thousands who line the streets to taunt the animal, but attempt to get out of the way when he charges. Not always successfully, however; one spectator was seriously gored in 2011.

Torreón C/Agua 44; ☎ 956 132 313. Reliable, traditional restaurant for dishes of the sierra, including game and venison. The *sopa de grazalema* is the region's hearty mountain soup, and there are also fish dishes and salads. The wine list is fairly priced and you can eat in the cosy dining room upstairs or, in better weather, on a street terrace below. €€

El Bosque and around

Located on the park's western flank, the village of **EL BOSQUE**, surrounded by slopes of planted pine, is easily reached from Grazalema via a delightfully wooded drive along the A372, which bisects the park. It provides an alternative to Grazalema as a base for visiting the park.

When travel writer Richard Ford passed through here in the 1830s he described it as a robbers' lair and counted "fifteen monumental crosses in the space of fifty yards" – victims of the ruthless bandits who preyed on travellers. He advised his readers to make sure they carried a watch to buy off these brigands, preferably one with a gaudy gilt chain, "the lack of which the bandit considered an unjustifiable attempt to defraud him of his right." Today the village is a far more peaceful place, bisected by the Río Majaceite, with few sights as such, but plenty of places to tame a thirst and grab a *tapa* or two. The major annual event here is the Feria Gastronómica (normally held the first or second week of October) featuring much sampling of the products of the sierra – *chacinas* (cured meats) and the celebrated local goat's cheeses. El Bosque's tranquillity is also interrupted in August when nearby summer camps increase the two thousand-odd population threefold.

A walk along the Río Majaceite

The nearby settlement of **Benamahoma**, another picturesque sierra village some 4km east of El Bosque, provides the starting point for a particularly scenic **walk** along the **Río Majaceite** back to El Bosque (the walk is more easily tackled starting from Benamahoma rather than El Bosque). Starting from the *El Bujío* bar (a taxi will drop you there if you don't fancy the walk from El Bosque), make for some green gates at the end of the car park. Step through a small stand of eucalyptus to the right of the gates and keep ahead along the left bank of the river. As you follow the river back to El Bosque, there are plenty of opportunities for birdwatching and picnicking.

ARRIVAL AND DEPARTURE   EL BOSQUE AND AROUND

By bus El Bosque's bus station (call Ubrique on ☎ 956 468 011 for information) is on the Ctra Benamahoma–Grazalema s/n, the main road running through the village

Destinations Cádiz (3 daily; 1hr 45min); Grazalema (1 daily; 45min); Jerez (6 daily; 1hr 30min); Ubrique (12 daily; 20min).

ACCOMMODATION

EL BOSQUE
Hotel Enrique Calvillo Avda Diputación 5; ⊕ hotelenriquecalvillo.com. Decent *hotel rural* with comfortable modern rooms with a/c and TV in the centre of the village. Also has a pool and restaurant. Breakfast is included. €

Hotel Las Truchas Avda Diputación 1; ⏺tugasa.com. Named after the village's local speciality, trout (El Bosque has Europe's southernmost trout river – the Río Majaceite), this is a pleasant enough place with attractive and spacious terrace balcony rooms with a/c and TV. Public areas include a decent restaurant and there's also a pool. Own car park (free). €

Posada San Antonio C/Huelva 14; ⏺posadasanantonio. es. In the heart of the village close to the *Ayuntamiento*, this is a very pleasant hotel and restaurant offering spacious newly decorated en-suite rooms with a/c, heating and TV. €

BENAMAHOMA

Camping Los Linares C/Nacimiento s/n; ☎661 70 46 80. Sited above the village with plenty of shade, a superb pool and its own restaurant. Also rents out some attractive fully equipped wood cabin apartments. €

2

EATING AND DRINKING

EL BOSQUE

La Divina Avda Diputación 11, on the main street facing the church; ☎956 727 025. Stylish new restaurant aiming to give the sierra a taste of contemporary creative cuisine. The spacious dining room is uncluttered and bright while the kitchen brings a *toque creativo* to old favourites such as *solomillo de retinto* (red cattle beef) and *codillos de cerdo al horno* (ham knuckle). There are also pizzas and tapas and the wine list is confined to the wines of the region. €€

Hotel Las Truchas Avda Diputación 1; ⏺bit.ly/HotelLasTruchas. The hotel's restaurant specializes in sierra and *andaluz* cuisine, both fish and meat; given its name it's

no surprise that fresh trout from the nearby river features strongly on the menu, often with a slice of *jamón serrano* tucked inside. €€

Mesón Majaceite Reached by following the road to the Albergue El Bosque that climbs behind the Hotel Las Truchas; ☎666 360 519. Opposite the *piscifactoría acuario* (fish farm), this *venta* does the freshest trout you can get as part of a lunchtime *menú*. €

Venta Julian Avda Diputación 11; ☎956 716 006. Near the bus station, this is a reliable place for *platos combinados*, tapas and *raciones*. Also has an economical *menu*, plus a pleasant terrace that's popular on warmer evenings. €

Zahara de la Sierra

It's worth going back to Grazalema from El Bosque to take the spectacular CA9104 road, which climbs to the Puerto de las Palomas (Pass of the Doves, at 1350m the second highest pass in Andalucía). A little before the pass you'll see on the left an entrance to the forest of the *pinsapo* Spanish fir – this is the start of the Itinerario del Pinsapar walking route (see box, page 216).

Once over the pass the road embarks on a dramatic descent to **ZAHARA DE LA SIERRA** (or *de los Membrillos* – "of the Quinces"), surrounded by olive groves. This is perhaps the most perfect of Andalucía's fortified hill *pueblos*, a landmark for kilometres around, its red-tiled houses huddled round a church beneath a ruined castle on a stark outcrop of rock. It was once an important Moorish town, and its capture by the Christians in 1483 opened the way for the conquest of Ronda – and ultimately Granada.

PUERTO DE LAS PALOMAS WALK

From the car park at the Puerto de las Palomas *mirador* there is a fine circular 5km (45min) **walk** offering spectacular views over the whole sierra. The walk has plenty of nooks to spot wild flowers and in the skies griffon vultures are frequent visitors. If you're very lucky you may even see the nimble Spanish ibex (*cabra montés*), the scimitar-horned wild goat which is relatively common at this altitude. The hike begins from an opening in the fence at the left (northwest) side of the car park. The well-defined path heads uphill and circles the Cerro Coros peak (1327m) taking in stirring views of the village of Zahara de la Sierra and its lake (reservoir) and castle and, further away, the white splashes denoting the villages of Algodonales and Olvera, topped by its twin-towered church. After a couple of kilometres the path climbs and winds around the north side of the mountain before turning south along its eastern flank. Another ascent follows as fine views open up over the Sierra de Gaidovar and its river valley. The track then slowly descends to the Puerto de las Palomas where, beyond a gate, you enter the opposite side of the car park from where you started out.

2

The heart of the village, which was declared a national monument in 1983, is an orange tree-fringed main street connecting the churches of San Juan and the eighteenth-century Baroque church of **Santa María de la Mesa**, which has a vermilion painted exterior and tower. Inside, there's a fine retablo with a sixteenth-century image of the Virgin. The surviving tower of the twelfth-century Moorish **castle** (daily; free) – constructed over a previous Roman one – looms over the village and incorporates the remains of an early church.

Embalse de Zahara y El Gastor reservoir

The terrain near the village has changed dramatically over recent years due to the creation of the **Embalse de Zahara y El Gastor reservoir**, the waters of which now lap the foot of its hill on the northern and eastern flanks. The Río Guadalete, once crossed by a Roman bridge, was dammed in the late 1980s and the valley took six years to flood, creating the immense lake-like dam that dominates the landscape today. It was controversial when built, but now provides vital water for irrigation and livestock and is today a great attraction for fishermen and kayakers, and even boasts its own artificial beach known locally as "La Playita".

ARRIVAL AND INFORMATION
ZAHARA DE LA SIERRA

By bus There is no bus station; buses park up and leave from a stop near the entrance to the village close to the Guardia Civil barracks.
Destinations Algodonales (Mon–Fri 1 daily; 15min; from here there are onward connections to Jerez, Cádiz, Málaga and Seville); Ronda (Mon–Fri 1 daily; 55min; from where there are connections to Málaga, Cádiz and Jerez).
Information centre At the eastern end of the main

street, C/San Juan, and fronting the church of Santa María (daily 10am–2pm; ✆ 956 123 114), the centre can provide information on the village and the natural park. The office also serves as a base for Naturaventura (🌐 naturaventura.com) offering a range of park-based activities from caving, kayaking and canyoning to climbing, paintball and hiking.

ACCOMMODATION

Al Lago C/Félix Rodríguez de la Fuente 11, on the edge of the village going towards Grazalema; 🌐 al-lago.es. This boutique hotel (also featuring a good restaurant, see page 220) has six elegant a/c rooms with walk-in wet rooms and plasma TV. Public areas include a solarium, and staff can arrange horseriding excursions and kayaking on the reservoir. €€
Hostal Marqués de Zahara C/San Juan 3; 🌐 marquesdezahara.com. An attractive small *hostal* on the village's main street offering en-suite a/c balcony rooms above a shady patio with TV. Breakfast is included. €

Hotel Arco de la Villa Camino Nazarí s/n🌐 tugasa. com. On the road leading up to the castle, this stylish three-star has decent a/c rooms with spectacular views over the nearby reservoir, along with its own restaurant and bar. €
★ **Hotel Rural Los Tadeos** Paseo de la Fuente s/n; 🌐 alojamientoruralcadiz.com. Towards the village swimming pool on the eastern edge of the village, this is a welcoming, modernized *hotel rural* with comfortable a/c rooms, many with terrace balcony views; all come with wet rooms (a couple have jacuzzis) and there's a restaurant and infinity pool. €

EATING AND DRINKING

For tapas and *raciones* there is a cluster of bars around the church of Santa María. Both the *Hotel Arco de la Villa* and the *Hotel Rural Los Tadeos* have decent restaurants of their own.
Al Lago C/Félix Rodríguez de la Fuente 11, on the edge of the village going towards Grazalema; 🌐 al-lago.es. Interesting mid-priced restaurant belonging to the hotel

of the same name (see page 220) with the village's most attractive terrace overlooking the lake/reservoir. The cuisine is slanted towards Mediterranean-influenced dishes (with numerous vegetarian options) including salads and paella, as well as creative takes on sierra standards. €€€

Algodonales

Enclosed by the folds of the Sierra de Líjar, **ALGODONALES**, 6km north of Zahara, is an unassuming farming settlement with a long, central plaza dominated by the lofty tower of the eighteenth-century Neoclassical church of Santa Ana. Although lying a couple of kilometres beyond the park boundary, the village is endeavouring to make itself an activity centre for the park particularly as a centre for **parapente** (paragliding); Zero Gravity (Avda. de la Constitución 44; ⓦzerogravity.es) is one company offering courses with a shop on the main square, while another, Flyspain (ⓦflyspain.co.uk) lies slightly out of the village; phone for directions.

Valeriano Bernal's guitar workshop

C/Ubrique 8 • Mon–Fri 10am–1.30pm & 5–8pm, Sat 10am–1.30pm • ⓦ guitarrasvalerianobernal.com

One place worth a visit in Algodonales is the workshop of renowned guitar maker **Valeriano Bernal**, whose beautiful instruments are sought after by many of the leading classical and flamenco guitarists in Spain. His modest workshop is a two-minute walk from *Hostal Sierra de Líjar*, whose proprietor can provide directions. Prices range from €500 for a student's model to €5000-plus for a virtuoso instrument.

2

ARRIVAL AND DEPARTURE	**ALGODONALES**

By bus The village's proximity to the main A382 *autovía* means that it has frequent bus connections.

Destinations Cádiz (2 daily; 2hr 30min); Jerez (3 daily; 1hr 15min); Málaga (3 daily; 2hr 50min); Ronda (2 daily;

50min); Seville (1 daily; 2hr 15min); Zahara de la Sierra (1 daily; 15min).

By taxi A taxi from Algodonales to Zahara will cost you about €20 one way.

ACCOMMODATION AND EATING

Hostal Sierra de Líjar C/Ronda 5; ☎ 956 137 065. Just below the main square, this welcoming, family-run *hostal* has tidy en-suite a/c rooms with TV, a free garage, and a

very good restaurant serving tapas and *raciones*, with a bargain-priced *menú*. Breakfast is included. **€**

Olvera

OLVERA, 18km beyond Algodonales in an area thick with olives (from which the town's name may derive), couldn't look more dramatic: a great splash of whitewashed houses tumbling down a hill below the twin towers of its giant church and fine Moorish castle. You can ascend the hill along the town's long main street, the aptly named Calle Calvario and its continuation Calle Llana, to reach the church, **Nuestra Señora de la Encarnación** (Tues–Sun 11am–1pm). However, up close it's a somewhat uninspiring nineteenth-century edifice built on the site of a fifteenth-century Gothic-Mudéjar church, thought too small for the town's growing population, which was cleared to make way for it.

Moorish castle

Entered via Turismo on the Pza de la Iglesia • Tues–Sun 10.30am–2pm & 4–7pm (Oct–March closes 6pm) • Charge

More interesting than Olvera's church is the somewhat over-restored twelfth-century **Moorish castle**, which formed part of Nasrid Granada's line of defence against the Christian lands – communication between these forts was apparently carried out by means of reflecting light with mirrors. Inside, you can appreciate how the castle has been built into the triangular shape of the huge rock on which it sits, and a vertiginous spiral staircase in the tower leads to the summit from where there are great **views** over the town and to the surrounding hill villages.

Museo de la Frontera

Tues–Sun 10.30am–2pm & 4–7pm • Charge (same ticket as castle)

The castle's **Museo de la Frontera**, also entered via the Turismo (see page 222), uses tableaux and information boards to explain the fortress's history and its evolving role between the eighth and fifteenth centuries as a military outpost on the frontier with Christian Castile. Separate sections have details on daily life in the castle as well as in the town during the same period.

2

THE VÍA VERDE

An imaginative development in Olvera is the transformation of a disused rail line – running 34km east to Puerto Serrano through rolling, wooded hill country – into a track for cyclists and walkers. Known as the **Vía Verde** (⬥ fundacionviaverdedelasierra.com), the track has stations along the route transformed into hotels and *ventas*. Whether you cycle or walk, some kind of flashlight is useful as some of the lengthier tunnels are very dark and the automatic lighting doesn't always function. The Turismo at Olvera can also provide a detailed map of the Vía Verde, which will enable you to locate accommodation, places providing food and drink and the sites of some remarkable vulture colonies – particularly the one at the Zaframagón crag – along the route.

BIKE RENTAL

Hostal Estación Verde (see page 222). Bikes (including electric bikes, kids' bikes and tandems) can be rented for trips along the Vía Verde. The proprietors will provide you with a route map and phone ahead to book rooms at your next stop. If you don't want to do the return journey you can deposit the bike in Puerto Serrano.

ARRIVAL AND INFORMATION

OLVERA

By bus Olvera's bus station is on C/Bellavista, slightly northeast of the focal Pza de la Concordia in the lower town. Destinations Cádiz (Mon–Fri 1 daily; 3hr 50min); Jerez (4 daily; 55min); Málaga (3 daily; 2hr 15min); Ronda (2 daily; 1hr 30min); Seville (2 daily; 2hr).

Turismo The Turismo (Tues–Sun 10.30am–2pm & 4–6pm, closes 7pm April–Sept; ⬥ olvera.es), at Pza de la Iglesia s/n, facing the Encarnación church, can provide a town map and information on nearby birdwatching sanctuaries where you can see such species as vultures, eagles, owls and falcons.

ACCOMMODATION

Hostal Estación Via Verde C/Estacion s/n; ⬥ hotelviaverdedelasierra.es. This pleasant *hostal* has a/c en-suite rooms with TV in the old train station along with new and delightful fully equipped apartments inside converted railway wagons in the sidings next door. It also has its own bar-restaurant and rents bikes for the Vía Verde (see box, page 222; fifty percent discount for guests). €̄

Hotel Sierra y Cal Avda Nuestra Señora de los Remedios 2; ⬥ tugasa.com. Slightly out of the centre, this comfortable hotel offers attractive a/c rooms and public areas include a pool and bar-restaurant. €̄

Number 31 B&B C/Maestro Arnado 31; ⬥ no31olvera. com. Just south of the Encarnación church and castle this is a homely B&B with three en-suite rooms run by a Canadian couple. €̄

EATING

Bodeguita Mi Pueblo Pza de Andalucía, C/Cañada Real 2, three blocks east of the Hotel Sierra y Cal; T956 131 105. Olvera has dozens of tapas bars and this is one of the best. Tapas chef Paco Medina runs the kitchen and searches out the tapas of bygone days to present to his clientele. He'll also sell you his book on the topic (La Tapa Antigua). Try the *langostinos a la plancha* (fried prawns) or *croquetas rabo de toro* (oxtail croquettes). There are half a dozen other tapas bars nearby (along C/Julian Besteiro) should you want to make a night of it. €̄

Sierra y Cal Avda Nuestra Señora de los Remedios 2; ☎ 956 130 542. The bar-restaurant of the *Sierra y Cal* hotel has a decent kitchen and serves tapas in its bar and more elaborate fare in the restaurant. Inexpensive weekday *menú*. €̄

Taberna Juanito Gómez C/Bellavista s/n, just off the upper end of C/Calvario; ☎ 956 130 160. Another of Olvera's popular tapas haunts with a good selection of reasonably priced tapas and *raciones* and a lively street terrace. €̄

Restaurante Vía Verde C/Estacion s/n; ☎ 661 463 207 The remodelled restaurant of the *Hostal Estación Via Verde* is another dining possibility. As well as a dining area in the old station waiting room there is an attractive terrace on what would have been the station platform. The carta has also been revamped and besides tapas such as *carpaccio de langostinos* (deep water prawns), the main menu has *cordero al horno* (oven baked lamb) and a selection of salads. €̄€̄

Setenil de las Bodegas

Fourteen kilometres southeast of Olvera **SETENIL DE LAS BODEGAS** is the strangest of all the White Towns, its cave-like streets formed from the overhanging ledge of a gorge carved through the tufa rock by the Río Trejo. Many of the houses – sometimes two or three storeys high – have natural roofs in the rock that, in places, blocks out the sky completely. This was once a major wine-producing centre, since the caves made good wine cellars (*bodegas*); hence the latter part of the town's name. The phylloxera plague of the nineteenth century destroyed the vines, however, and brought economic ruin in its wake, from which Setenil has only just recovered.

From Setenil it's possible to walk the 6km to the ruins of Ronda La Vieja via the hamlets of Campiña and Venta de Leche.

La Encarnación and the Castillo

C/Villa 23 • Tues–Fri 10am–1pm, Sun noon (for service) • Free • ☎ 956 134 455

The village's most impressive monument is the Gothic-Mudéjar church of **La Encarnación**, built over the site of the mosque that stood here in Moorish times. If you can gain access you'll see a fine, twelve-panelled sixteenth-century Flemish painting that survived Civil War devastation. The ruins of the nearby Moorish **castillo** are worth a look, too.

ARRIVAL AND INFORMATION
SETENIL DE LAS BODEGAS

By bus There is a regular bus service from Ronda to Setenil (Mon–Sat 1 daily).

By car Setenil's sinous and narrow streets are a hazard for visiting drivers. Try to park near the main road (CA 4223) and walk into the village.

By train Setenil train station is 8km east of the village. There is a single daily train in each direction between Ronda and the village.

Turismo Setenil's Turismo (Tues–Sun 10am–2pm; June–Aug also 4–6pm; ☎ 956 134 261; ⊕ turismodesetenil.com) is housed in the former Ayuntamiento (see box, page 223).

Market Every Friday 8am–2pm, C/Cuevas del Sol. This colourful mercadillo snakes along the Río Trejo gorge beneath the dramatic overhanging rock cliffs and sells everything from plants and pots to flamenco dresses and antiques, while the bars do a roaring trade.

ACCOMMODATION AND EATING

El Almendral Ctra Setenil s/n; ⊕ tugasa.com. On the road just outside town, with comfortable, refurbished rooms, an Olympic-size pool and a good restaurant downstairs. Breakfast is included. €

Bar-Restaurante Domínguez Pza de Andalucía s/n; ☎ 956 134 331. This long-established bar-restaurant at the heart of the village is a solid country hostelry serving up *carnes de caza* (game) in its restaurant, and tapas and *raciones* in the bar. There's an attractive terrace on the square. €

Bar-Restaurante Las Flores Avda del Carmen 24 (near the river at the opposite end of the town from the church); ☎ 956 124 044. This welcoming bar with some fine views from its dining room serves tapas, *raciones* and *platos combinados* and there are three economical *menús*. €

Hotel Villa de Setenil C/Callejón 10; ⊕ setenil.com. Attractive new hotel belonging to El *Mirador* restaurant. Stylish rooms come with slick designer furnishings and some have terraces and views. €

El Mirador C/Callejón 10; ☎ 956 134 044. Reached through an arch uphill from the tourist office, this modern restaurant in the *Hotel Villa de Setenil* offers regional meat and fish dishes, as well as *jamón* and *salchichón* and a variety of salads. The weekday *menú* is commendably inexpensive. €€

Villaluenga del Rosario

Some 13km southwest of Grazalema, the tiny village of **VILLALUENGA DEL ROSARIO** is the highest in Cádiz province. Tucked beneath a great crag, it's a simple place, with

SEPTEM NIHIL

Setenil's former Ayuntamiento (now housing the Turismo), at C/Villa 2, has a superb Mudéjar *artesonado* ceiling with an inscription dating from September 21, 1484 – the day Isabel and Fernando captured the town. They achieved this triumph only after seven previous attempts (*septem nihil* – seven times nothing) had failed, giving origin to the first half of **Setenil's name** today.

2

narrow streets, flower-filled balconies and pantiled roofs, frequently enveloped by mountain mists.

In the twilight years of the Nasrid Emirate of Granada and after Ronda had fallen to the Christians in 1485, an unprotected Villaluenga was conquered and repopulated with settlers from Arcos de la Frontera and Villamartín. Some impressive brick-built ancient Moorish wells can be seen in the fields along the roadside to the left as you approach. Research suggests that these wells were part of a much more sophisticated water supply system and were linked to create a form of subterranean aqueduct.

The twentieth-century Civil War was also bitterly fought here when one of the village's two churches was torched: its gutted ruin, located at the top of the village, now serves as the cemetery. Villaluenga's ancient and curious **Plaza de Toros**, partly hacked out of the rock, is also worth a look and sees action once a year during the annual *feria* (first week of September) with top *toreros* performing. The festival honours the village's *patrona*, the Virgen del Rosario, when performances of flamenco and other cultural events take place.

Villaluenga is also famous for goat's **cheese**, which can be purchased at the multi-award-winning Payoyo cheesemaker's factory on the south side of the main road running through the village.

ARRIVAL AND DEPARTURE
VILLALUENGA DEL ROSARIO

By bus Buses stop on the main road, close to the Payoyo cheesemaker's factory.
Destinations Grazalema (3 daily; 20min); Málaga (2 daily;

3hr 45min, change in Ronda); Ronda (2 daily; 1hr); Ubrique (3 daily; 20min).

ACCOMMODATION, EATING AND DRINKING

Bar Alameda Pza Alameda 2; ☎956 460 049. On the main square, the village's liveliest (and friendliest) bar fills up for major football matches and *corridas*, but at other times is an inviting place for a drink and a *tapa* or raciones. Try the *carillada en salsa* (pork cheeks). You have a choice of two terraces: one at the back of the bar with a fine view across the valley or another out front on Villaluenga's picturesque main square. €̲

Hotel La Posada C/Torre 1; ⊗tugasa.com. The village's only place to stay, the charming *Hotel La Posada* lies in the upper village near the ruined church, housed in a beautifully renovated stone-built *casa señorial*. Not all the rooms have views, so it's worth requesting one that does (try for room 4). The hotel also has a bar-restaurant and rents out some pleasant apartments nearby. €̲

Benaocaz

From Villaluenga the A2302 road descends through a spectacular pass, La Manga de Villaluenga, an area that has yielded many prehistoric artefacts and dolmens and is traversed by the remains of a medieval road. This road was laid on top of an ancient Roman road that connected Ocuri (see page 225) to Lacidulia (Grazalema) and Arunda (Ronda). Once through the pass, the road turns north to the farming settlement of **BENAOCAZ**, another ancient village founded by the Moors in the eighth century. A series of wall plaques dotted around the Barrio Nazarí – with substantial Moorish ruins and cobbled streets – in the upper village provides information (in Spanish) on buildings and locations from this period. The village's main Baroque church of San Pedro has more vestiges of Moorish days and is built over the former mosque, part of whose minaret was used to make its tower. The annual *feria* takes place in the middle of August to coincide with the feast of the Ascension (of the Virgin). There are numerous concerts and other events over the three days.

Museo Histórico

C/Jabonería 7, near the Ayuntamiento • Mon–Fri 9am–1.30pm (enquire at the Ayuntamiento during these times and they will open it for you) • Free

The village's very well-presented **Museo Histórico** includes background on life in the sierra ranging from the times of the prehistoric cave-dwellers through to the colourful *bandoleros* who preyed on travellers in these parts until well into the twentieth century. There are also sections devoted to the nearby Cueva de la Pileta (see page 132) and displays focusing on the village's Roman and Moorish periods, with interesting ceramic displays from both.

Roman road

If you want to stretch your legs, there's a fine 6km downhill walk from Benaocaz to Ubrique along a remarkably preserved **Roman road** complete with a bridge and culverts to protect it from flooding. The start of the route (marked by an information board) is across the road from the bus stop on the main road below the village. If you time your arrival to coincide with the afternoon bus from Ubrique to Benaocaz (currently running at 3.30pm), this will save you the hike back up the hill. The route is picturesque and shaded in parts with likely places for a picnic. Allow ninety minutes to complete the walk. Information on the walk is available at ⊛bit.ly/benaocaz-walk.

2

ARRIVAL AND INFORMATION   BENAOCAZ

By bus Buses stop on the main road below the village. Destinations Grazalema (3 daily; 20min); Málaga (2 daily; 3hr 45min, change in Ronda); Ronda (2 daily; 1hr 20min); Ubrique (3 daily; 10min).
Tourist information Staff in Benaocaz's elegant

eighteenth-century Ayuntamiento on the main square, Pza de las Libertades 1 (Mon–Fri 9am–2pm; ☎956 125 500), can provide a village map as well as tourist information on the village and the surrounding area.

ACCOMMODATION

Benaocaz makes a pleasant place to stop over, with a few attractive places to stay. The Ayuntamiento (see page 225) can also provide a list of apartments to rent around the village.
Los Chozos Sendero Ojo del Moro s/n; ⊛loschozos.com. Just outside the village on the Ubrique road, *Los Chozos* rents out *chozos* (modern versions of traditional circular thatched-roofed dwellings) sleeping two or more, in a scenic location with pool. April–Sept. Two night minimum stay during July and August. €€

Hostal El Refugio Pza de San Antón 5; ☎608 558 223. Pleasant, fully equipped two- and four-person apartments with *chimenea* (wood-burning stove) for the winter months; some have fine views. Also rents two fully equipped village houses nearby. €̄
El Parral Laderas del Parral 1; ☎956 12 55 65. At the village's western edge beyond the *Hostal San Antón*, this *hostal-rural* has simple en-suite rooms sharing an outdoor terrace and small pool, with a bar-restaurant below. €̄

EATING AND DRINKING

Bar Las Vegas Pza de las Libertades 5, opposite the Ayuntamiento; ☎608 817 140. The village's main bar is a good breakfast stop and offers sierra standards with a more elaborate menu at weekends when *jabalí al horno* (oven baked wild boar) is a good bet. €̄
Mesón El Refugio Pza San Anton 5, in the same

building as Hostal El Refugio; ☎608 558 223. Another good bar-restaurant, where the house speciality is *carnes a la brasa* (charcoal-grilled meats) including both *ibérico* (pork) and *retinto* (Spanish Dehesa beef) meats. Has a shaded terrace with fine views. Salads, tapas and *raciones* are also available. €€

Ocuri

Tues–Sat guided visits at 10am, noon & 4pm, Sun 10am & noon. Places should be booked in advance on ☎954 464 900 • Charge

Four kilometres west of Benaocaz, close to the junction with the A373, a small road (signed) on the left leads to the spectacularly situated Roman site of **OCURI**. The road is easy to miss and if you reach the petrol station at the junction beyond it you will need to turn around. Leave any transport at the *Venta Ocuris* fronting the site entrance.

Beyond the entry gate a paved path climbs into the woods for a good kilometre to the site of the former Roman town, located on the crest of the hill above. Just before you arrive at the ruins, to the left stands a well-preserved (although partly restored) first-century AD **columbarium** tomb with wall niches for burial urns. This is followed by some impressive Cyclopean dry-stone **walls** that date from the site's origin as an

Iberian *oppidum*, or tribal settlement, in the pre-Roman era – the Romans would have had to overcome defences like these during the subjugation of the peninsula in the first and second centuries BC.

Once through the walls, you enter the heart of the Roman settlement where the substantial remains of **dwellings**, **baths** and huge **cisterns**, with their mortar linings still intact, surround the ancient **forum**. Archeologists are still busy excavating here and it will be some time before the remains are entirely revealed and understood. On all sides of the site the hill falls sharply away and there are wonderful **views** over the sierra and the town of Ubrique, far below.

Ubrique

From Benaocaz the road corkscrews down from the mountainous sierra until the snow-white vista of **Ubrique** comes into view below, spreading along the valley of the Río Ubrique with the daunting knife-edged crag of the Cruz de Tajo rearing up behind. Despite this stunning first appearance, on closer contact it's a rather large and dull industrial centre, but the town's bustling prosperity ensures a good variety of places to eat and drink on and around Avenida Dr Solis Pascual, the tree-lined main artery.

A place that has always bred tenacious guerrilla fighters and which fought against the French in the War of Independence (actually defeating a contingent of the Imperial Guard near Gaucín), Ubrique is a natural mountain fortress which was one of the last Republican strongholds in the Civil War. Today, it's a relatively wealthy if unexciting town, surviving largely on its medieval guild craft of **leather manufacturing**, the products of which are sold in numerous shops lining the main street, where most of the bars and restaurants are also gathered. Although cheap leather imports from Asia have caused a downturn in the town's fortunes in recent decades, the most highly skilled of Ubrique's leather workers keep busy working for many of the big designer names like Loewe, Louis Vuitton and Gucci.

ARRIVAL AND INFORMATION
UBRIQUE

By bus The bus station is at northern end of town at Avda Manuel de Falla s/n.
Destinations Benaocaz (3 daily; 10min); Cádiz (3 daily; 2hr); Grazalema (3 daily; 30min); Jerez (6 daily; 2hr 15min); Málaga (2 daily; 3hr 55min, change in Ronda); Ronda (2 daily; 1hr 30min); Seville (3 daily; 1hr 45min); Villaluenga del Rosario (3 daily; 20min).

Turismo The Turismo on Moreno de Mora 19, the continuation of Avda Dr Solis Pascual (Mon–Sat 10am–2pm & 4–7pm, Sun 11am–2pm; ☎ 956 464 900), can provide a town map and has information on the town and local area including Ocuri.

ACCOMMODATION

Hotel Ocurris Avda Dr Solis Pascual 49, close to the main junction and roundabout as you enter the town from the north; ⓦ hotelocurris.com. Bright and modern two-star hotel on the main street offering serviceable enough en-suite rooms with TVs, and its own bar and restaurant. €

Hotel Sierra de Ubrique Avda Sierra de Ubrique 1; ⓦ hotelsierradeubrique.com. On the road leading out of town towards Alcalá, this is an attractive three-star hotel with well-equipped rooms, plus a restaurant and bar, pool, solarium and parking. €

EATING AND DRINKING

★**Juande en la Peña Betica** Pza de los Ejércitos 9, 200m south of the tourist office; ☎ 687 527 730. Located inside the Peña Betica club and run by chef Juande Gómez, this is probably Ubrique's best tapas and *raciones* bar. There's a charming garden terrace and among a range of house specials *higaditos de pollo* (sautéed chicken livers), *brocheta de pez espada y langostinos* (swordfish and prawn kebab) and *carne mechada* (larded pork) are all excellent. Also sells reasonably priced bottled wine giving you an excuse to make a meal of it. €€

El Laurel de Miguel C/San Juan Bautista 7, just behind the main street (Avda Dr Solis Pascual); ⓦ ellaureldemiguel.com. Good tapas and *raciones* bar with a decent range of tapas and wines plus a street terrace. Try the *pluma ibérica* (pork loin) or *magret de pato* (duck breast). €

From Ubrique towards Cádiz

From Ubrique the mountain route towards Cádiz passes through the northern flank of one of the world's largest cork oak (*alcornoque*) forests, the huge **Alcornocales natural park**, and ascends to the Puerto de Galis Pass with its lonely *venta*, at the junction of the CA8201. From the pass the A2304 heads west to join the valley of the Río Barbate for the final descent into the White Town of **Alcalá de los Gazules**, the geographical centre of the province of Cádiz. To the northwest of Alcalá lies the charming town of **Medina Sidonia**, perched on its conical hill and with plenty to see.

2

Parque Natural de los Alcornocales

Ten kilometres south of Ubrique along the A373, the road enters the **Parque Natural de los Alcornocales**, with magnificently rugged but sparsely populated mountain scenery. There are a number of fine **walking routes** in the park starting close to the *Venta del Puerto de Galis* (see page 228), where the friendly proprietors are happy to provide information. One 12km hike begins at La Sauceda (4km south of the Puerto de Galis and marked on the Andalucía *Michelin* map) taking you to the park's highest peak, El Aljibe. There's an information board (with map) at the starting point. Another wonderful walk, La Garganta de Puerto Oscuro, leaves the A2304 (the Alcalá road) some 8km west of the Puerto de Galis at a recreation area called El Picacho, which has a car park. The waymarked walk is described (with

---

THE CORK OAK STRIPPERS

Whether a supermarket bottle of wine is stopped with a **cork** or with a screw-top cap may be a matter of indifference to most wine buyers, but it's a hot topic in and around the forest of **Los Alcornocales**. Each summer *tiradores* (cork strippers) head deep into the forest with their mules to strip the cork bark from the *alcornoques* (cork oak trees) that are ready. They use long pointed lances called *burjas* and special axes to split and strip the outer bark leaving a bright orange inner layer – the *casca* – which gives a stand of freshly stripped trees a rather surreal stark-naked appearance.

It's tough work for these gangs of men who toil far from any road or track, which is where the mules come in. The mule drivers load up their beasts with the *panos* (square chunks of bark about half the size of a door) and take them to the patio where they are weighed – the *tiradores* are paid by weight collected. Then they are carried to a point where a truck can access the forest edge. These vehicles' trailers, loaded with thousands of neatly stacked *panos*, are a common sight on the roads of Cádiz all summer long. The *tiradores* camp out in the forest during the cutting season and drinking and singing around their campfires is a long tradition.

However, the wine industry is in a state of revolution as cork is abandoned for more economical means of bottle closure. A wine cork costs about five times what a plastic cork or a cap does, and there lies the rub. The Australians now bottle only fifty percent of their wine with cork, many wine-producing countries are following them, and this has got the *tiradores* worried for their future. Perhaps just in time, the naturalists have now taken up their cause. Reports by bodies such as the WWF (World Wide Fund for Nature) and RSPB (Royal Society for the Protection of Birds) argue that cork oak forests like Los Alcornocales are unique **ecosystems** vital to a whole food chain of insects, flora and fauna which in turn support species such as Bonelli's eagle, the Iberian lynx, the spectacular azure-winged magpie, otters, mouflon, wild boar, roe deer, the Egyptian mongoose and many more. The cork oak forests are protected, but if the trees lose their economic value there will be sustained pressure to make other use of the land. Which is why, next time you buy a bottle of wine, you may just decide to take the one with the cork.

a map) on an information board next to the gate where the trail begins. It takes in some stunning woodland and the lagoon of El Picacho where, in spring and autumn when there is sufficient moisture, amphibians such as frogs, toads, newts and salamanders are numerous.

Tourist offices in the area usually stock a *Junta de Andalucía* booklet in straightforward Spanish detailing eight trails of between 2km and 7km in various parts of the park. *Walking in Andalucía* by Guy Hunter-Watts also describes half a dozen walks, two of which start in Jimena de la Frontera (see page 204).

ACCOMMODATION AND EATING   PARQUE NATURAL DE LOS ALCORNOCALES

The hill town of **Jimena de la Frontera** is a good place to base yourself for trips into the park as it is surrounded by beautiful countryside and has a good selection of hotels and restaurants.

★ **Venta del Puerto de Galis** Junction of A373 and CA8201 **☎** 956 231 486. Isolated but excellent lunch stop in the Alcornocales park, popular with local hunters, and often featuring game on its menu. There's an inviting shaded terrace with views and house specials include a succulent *carne mechada* (larded pork), *solomillo ibérico* (pork loin) and *ciervo* (venison). **€€**

Alcalá de los Gazules

Some 22km southwest of the Puerto de Galis, the town of **ALCALÁ DE LOS GAZULES** is a cascade of white dwellings gathered beneath its ruined *alcázar*. It's a sleepy little place today, and apart from the winding, narrow streets, little remains of the later Moorish settlement founded by a Berber family, the Gazules, who gave their name to the town in the twelfth century when this was a *taifa* state of the kingdom of Granada.

In the Plaza Alta in the upper town stands the fifteenth-century Gothic church of **San Jorge**, built over the mosque that was razed to make way for it. It has an imposing tower (probably the mosque's minaret) and, inside, a beautifully carved choir and an effigy attributed to Martínez Montañés, but not much else.

Alongside the church is the sixteenth-century **Casa del Cabildo**, which until the last century served as Alcalá's Ayuntamiento. In the lower town the **Plaza de Toros** has been turned into a *discoteca*, somewhat sacreligiously given the surrounding bull-breeding country.

TOROS BRAVOS

This part of Cádiz province is **bull country**, and the roads around the towns of Álcala de los Gazules and Medina Sidonia are lined with the ranches of the breeders of fighting bulls destined for bullrings all over Spain. Behind warning signs posted on roadside fences it's often possible to catch a view of the mean, black *toros bravos*, or fighting bulls used in the *corridas*. These magnificent beasts, weighing 500 to 600kg, the descendants of the *bos taurus ibericus* of ancient times, graze on pastures shaded by olives and holm oaks, and are tended by mounted *vaqueros* who guard them while noting their potential for valour. This is eventually tested in the *tienta* or trial ring, an important first step in deciding whether the bull will die in the *corrida* or the abattoir. The *vaqueros* are always on the lookout for the exceptional bull displaying outstanding bravery and physical construction and these are separated from the herd to be used exclusively at stud, to improve the breed. The bulls that leave these ranches to fight in the ring usually die there, although very occasionally bulls displaying exceptional bravery and spirit will receive the *indulto*, or pardon, to be returned to their ranch of origin for stud.

If you'd like to see a bull-breeding ranch, **A Campo Abierto** (**☎** 956 304 312; **ⓦ** acampoabierto.com) offers visits to the renowned Domecq ranch to the west of Medina Sidonia. The visit includes displays of herding the *toros bravos* as well as riding by the *vaqueros*. Get details from the Turismo in Medina or from their website.

2

Brief history

When the Romans were conquering this area early in the second century BC, they tried to divide and rule the Iberian tribes by granting the status of *colonia* to selected settlements – a crucial first step on the way to full Roman citizenship and all the privileges such status could bestow. One such settlement so rewarded was the Iberian Turris Lascutana, as Alcalá then was, and this was an attempt by Rome to win its allegiance away from the Turditanian tribal capital at Asta Regia near Jerez. A unique bronze plaque (in the national archeological museum in Madrid) records the decree of the Roman governor, Lucius Aemelius Paullus, in 189 BC, which granted Turris possession of the fields and town that they had formerly held as a fief of Asta.

ARRIVAL AND DEPARTURE · ALCALÁ DE LOS GAZULES

By bus Services arrive and depart from the central Avda Alcornocales.

Destinations Cádiz (4 daily; 1hr 45min); Jerez (3 daily; 1hr); Medina Sidonia (4 daily; 45min).

ACCOMMODATION AND EATING

Hotel San Jorge C/Antonio Alzaga 51; ⓦ hotelsanjorgelosgazules.com. Uphill from *Restaurante Pizarro*, which is owned by the same people, this two-star hotel has light, well-equipped rooms with a/c and TV, plus bar and free car park. €̄

Restaurante Pizarro Paseo de la Playa 9; ☎ 676 60 70 13. Decent mid-priced restaurant on the main street serving up typical dishes of the sierra. *Carne de caza* (game and venison) is a speciality here, and they also serve a cheap weekday lunchtime *menú*. €̄€̄

Medina Sidonia

Some 25km west of Alcalá lies the ancient town of **MEDINA SIDONIA**, sited on a low hill and huddled below the tower of its ancient church. Legend has it that the town's Phoenician founders (from Sidon) gave it the latter part of its name while the Moors added Medina. Following its reconquest by Alfonso X in 1264, Medina became one of Spain's most prestigious ducal seats, supplying the admiral who led the Armada against England. The title of Duque de Medina Sidonia was bestowed upon the family of Guzmán El Bueno for his valiant role in battles against the Moors, a line which continues, and was led by the firebrand socialist duchess of Medina Sidonia up to her death in 2008 (see box, page 168). Today Medina is an atmospheric little town where tidy narrow cobbled streets lined with *reja*-fronted houses circle the lower slopes of a peak dominated by the striking church of Santa María.

Plaza de España

A good place to begin a look around is the elegant **Plaza de España**, dominated at its southern end by the wonderful porticoed facade of the seventeenth-century Ayuntamiento. The facade reflects the history of its construction: the columned ground floor is seventeenth-century Baroque while the second floor – added later – is Neoclassical with pediments above the windows. The third floor, finished in the nineteenth century, has square windows placed to each side of a central clock. At the plaza's northern end lies the **Mercado de Abastos**, or market, dating from 1871. Part of the building now houses the tourist office.

Santa María la Coronada

Pza de la Iglesia Mayor · Daily 11am–2pm & 6–8.30pm · Charge (free Sat 6–8.30pm)

To the rear of the Ayuntamiento, at the top of a steeply climbing road (Calle Arrieros), is the **Plaza Iglesia Mayor**, dominated by the tower and portal of **Santa María la Coronada** church, built over an earlier mosque. Inside, beneath some beautiful vaulting, is an enormous and exquisite **retablo** depicting scenes from the life of Christ – a stunning sixteenth-century work of craftsmanship in polychrome wood by the *sevillano*

2

school. There's also an imposing sculpted image of *Cristo del Perdón* attributed to Luisa Roldán ("La Roldana") and a fine wood sculpture of *San Francisco de Asís* by Juan Martínez Montañés. On the church's eastern aisle are two sixteenth-century benches used by the Inquisition.

Roman sewers

C/Ortega 10 • April–Sept daily 10am–2pm & 6–9pm; Oct–March hours vary • Charge

Medina's importance in Roman times, when it was known as Asido Caesarina, is evidenced by some remarkable **Roman sewers** ("Cloacas Romanas") buried beneath the town's northern flank. Dating from the first century AD, the extensive stone-built sewers stand more than 2m in height and are a tribute to Roman engineering skills. On the same site is a small **museum** displaying sculptures, mosaics, coins and amphorae unearthed in various excavations around the town.

The same ticket covers entry beneath another building nearby to see a remarkably well-preserved stretch of paved **Roman road** – complete with guttering, sewers and pavement – lying directly below the town's main street, Calle San Juan. Don't miss the child's game etched into one of the paving stones, which adds a wonderfully human touch.

Moorish gates

Medina Sidonia also boasts three **Moorish gates** – all shown on the Turismo map – of which the tenth-century Arco de la Pastora, close to the Jerez road, is the best preserved. The others, the twelfth-century Arco de Belén and the Puerta del Sol, are also worth a look.

ARRIVAL AND INFORMATION
MEDINA SIDONIA

By bus The bus station is on Avda del Mar, a few minutes' walk north of the focal Pza de España.

Destinations Alcalá de los Gazules (3 daily; 45min); Cádiz (4 daily; 1hr 30min); Jerez (3 daily; 1hr).

Turismo C/San Juan s/n, effectively inside the old Mercado de Abastos on Pza de España (daily: April–Sept 10.30am–2pm & 5.30–7.30pm; Oct–March 10.30am–2pm & 4.30–6.30pm; ⓦturismomedinasidonia.es). Staff can provide a useful town map, plus the latest information on visiting the nearby and remarkable Tajo de las Figuras caves and *abrigos* (rock shelters) with prehistoric paintings. This important site is currently closed during works to protect it.

ACCOMMODATION

★**La Casa de Abú** C/Espíritu Santo 6, west of Pza de España; ☏661 55 54 22. Delightful *casa rural* in a beautifully restored nineteenth-century flour mill with five apartments ranged around a leafy patio with a mature banana tree. The a/c apartments come with state-of-the-art kitchens and bathrooms plus satellite TV. Most have terraces to sit out and there's a solarium. €€

★**Hotel El Castillo** C/Ducado de Medina 3 1; ⓦwww. hotelrestauranteelcastillo.com. High on the hill, and just behind the church of Santa María la Coronada, this is an excellent little family-run hotel with modern, well-equipped rooms all with balcony terraces and views to take your breath away. Add in a wonderful *comida casera* restaurant – run by "Mamá" Manuela – where all ingredients used are locally sourced – and you have a superb deal. Easily reached by car and free parking. €

★**Posada Alegria** C/Manso 1; ⓦposadaalegria.com. Just around the corner from the main square (Pza España) this is another charming option inside an eighteenth-century *casa palacio* with a delightful patio. The house is divided into beautifully presented rooms and apartments, some on two levels and most with a terrace and all with a/c and plasma TV. Apartments come with fully equipped kitchen. €

EATING AND DRINKING

Bar-Restaurante Ortega Pza de España 10; ☏956 410 157. On the main square – and with fewer pretensions than the neighbouring *Restaurante Cádiz* – this is a popular tapas and *raciones* place with a terrace on the square. Also does fish and meat *platos combinados* and there's an inexpensive *menú*. €€

Restaurante Cádiz Pza de España 13; ☏956 410 250. The best restaurant in town comes with a Michelin recommendation. A wide choice of local dishes are on offer – including *venado* (venison), *jabalí* (wild boar) and *solomillo de cerdo* (pork loin) – plus an interesting selection of wines (local and national) and some tasty desserts. Their

tapas bar – with a terrace on the square – is also good. €€€
Sobrina de las Trejas Pza España 7; ☎ 956 411 577.
Medina was noted in Moorish times for its sweets and
pastries, a tradition continued here – the *alfajores* (sugary
tubes containing honey, almonds and dried fruit) are
delicious.

★**Venta la Duquesa** Ctra Medina–Vejer km3;
ⓦ ventaladuquesa.com.   Excellent   restaurant
masquerading as a humble *venta* in the countryside
just outside Medina. But there's nothing humble about

the kitchen – under the direction of head chef Miriam
Rodríguez Prieto – which pushes out a variety of traditional
gaditano specialities from the sierra and the sea. Any of the
meat dishes are recommended (particularly the lamb) and
venado con niscalos (venison with wild mushrooms) and
rabo de toro (stewed bull's tail) are signature dishes. They
also offer a variety of salads (all vegetables come from their
own *huerta*) and there's a tapas bar and attractive terrace.
€€€

Arcos de la Frontera

Some 35km northeast of Medina Sidonia, the ancient hill town of **ARCOS DE LA
FRONTERA** straddles the notional border between the Sierra de Cádiz to the east,
and the parched, wine-growing flatlands of Jerez de la Frontera to the west. From
whichever direction you approach it, your first view of Arcos – the westernmost
of the White Towns – will be fabulous, with the towers of its castle and numerous
churches silhouetted against the sky. In full sun the town shimmers magnificently
on its great double crag of limestone high above the Río Guadalete. This dramatic
location, enhanced by low, white houses and fine sandstone churches, gives the town
a similar feel and appearance to Ronda – except Arcos is rather poorer and, quite
unjustifiably, far less visited. By far the best thing to do here is take a stroll around the
tangle of narrow streets, lined with a mix of Moorish and Renaissance buildings. Most
of Arcos's monuments are located in the higher old town – where you'll be spending
much of your time. The new town has spilled out to the west and east of here at the
foot of the crag.

Brief history
Dating from Iberian times and known as Arco Briga to the Romans, Arcos came to
prominence as the Moorish town of Arkos within the Cordoban caliphate. When
Córdoba's rule collapsed in the eleventh century, Arcos existed as a petty *taifa* state
until its annexation by al-Mu'tamid of Seville in 1103. The seizure of Arcos by
Christian forces under Alfonso El Sabio (the Wise) in 1264 was a real feat against
what must have been a wretchedly impregnable fortress. In the following three
centuries most of Arcos's churches were built and, in a less warlike age, the town
expanded beyond its walls for the first time when the "new town" of La Corredera
was created. In the nineteenth century an outbreak of yellow fever decimated the
population while the Napoleonic invasions caused extensive damage to much of the
town, including the castle and many churches. The town only really recovered in the
latter part of the last century with the arrival of mass tourism, from which Arcos gains
most of its income today.

FERIA DE SAN MIGUEL AND THE ALELUYA TORO

Each September 29 (and the two days before and after), Arcos celebrates the **Feria de San
Miguel**, honouring the town's patron saint, with parades, concerts of music and flamenco
and wine tasting. Since the eighteenth century each Easter Sunday Arcos has celebrated
Christ's resurrection with the **Aleluya Toro** (Hallelujah Bull), when a fighting bull is released.
During this *encierro*, the town's narrow streets echo to the screams of hundreds of children
who lift themselves clear of the rampaging *toro*'s horns by grabbing an overhanging balcony.
It's a truly nail-biting sight, yet remarkably few seem to get injured.

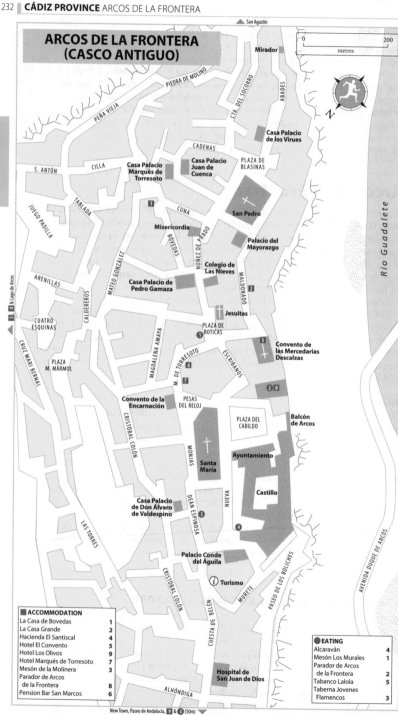

ARCOS DE LA FRONTERA (CASCO ANTIGUO)

San Agustín

Mirador

Casa Palacio de los Virues

Casa Palacio Juan de Cuenca

PLAZA DE BLASINAS

Casa Palacio Marqués de Torresoto

PIEDRA DE MOLINO

CTA. DEL SOCORRO

ABADES

PEÑA VIEJA

CADENAS

CILLA

S. ANTÓN

CUNA

San Pedro

Misericordia

TABLADA

JUEGO PADILLA

Palacio del Mayorazgo

BÓVEDAS

NÚÑEZ DE PRADO

Colegio de Las Nieves

MATEO GONZÁLEZ

Casa Palacio de Pedro Gamaza

ARENILLAS

CALDEREROS

MALDONADO

Jesuitas

CUATRO ESQUINAS

PLAZA DE BOTICAS

MAGDALENA AMAYA

Convento de las Mercedarias Descalzas

CRUZ MARI BERNAL

PLAZA M. MÁRMOL

M. DE TORRESOTO

ESCRIBANOS

Convento de la Encarnación

PESAS DEL RELOJ

PLAZA DEL CABILDO

Balcón de Arcos

CRISTÓBAL COLÓN

MONJAS

Santa María

Ayuntamiento

Castillo

Casa Palacio de Don Álvaro de Valdespino

DEÁN ESPINOSA

NUEVA

LAS TORRES

Palacio Conde del Águila

ⓘ Turismo

CRISTÓBAL COLÓN

CUESTA DE BELÉN

MURETE

PASEO DE LOS BOLICHES

AVENIDA DUQUE DE ARCOS

Río Guadalete

Hospital de San Juan de Dios

ALHÓNDIGA

0 — 200
metres

& Lago de Arcos

ACCOMMODATION

La Casa de Bovedas	1
La Casa Grande	2
Hacienda El Santiscal	4
Hotel El Convento	5
Hotel Los Olivos	9
Hotel Marqués de Torresoto	7
Mesón de la Molinera	3
Parador de Arcos de la Frontera	8
Pension Bar San Marcos	6

EATING

Alcaraván	4
Mesón Los Murales	1
Parador de Arcos de la Frontera	2
Tabanco Lalola	5
Taberna Jovenes Flamencos	3

Plaza del Cabildo

At the heart of the *casco antiguo* or monumental quarter is the **Plaza del Cabildo**, easily reached by following the signs for the *parador*. Flanking another two sides are (behind the Ayuntamiento) the castle walls and towers (the castle is privately owned and off limits) and the large fifteenth-century Gothic-Mudéjar church of Santa María de la Asunción, built over an earlier mosque; one side is left open, offering spectacular plunging views to the river valley and the *vega*.

2

Santa María de la Asunción

Mon–Fri 10am–12.45pm & 4–7pm, Sat 10am–1.30pm, Sun 8.30am for Mass • Charge

The Plateresque south facade of **Santa María de la Asunción**, with later additions, is a stunning work, although an unfinished bell tower unbalances the whole – the original was destroyed by the Lisbon earthquake of 1755 and the plan was to raise this new one to 58m, second in height only to Seville's Giralda. Three years later, however, the money ran out and the tower was left at 37m. The church's gloomy interior has fine Gothic vaulting, a stunning retablo, exquisitely carved choir stalls by Pedro Roldán, and a treasury with the usual collection of church silver and some dubiously attributed artworks.

San Pedro

C/Núñez de Prado • Mon–Fri 10am–12.45pm & 3.30–6.15pm, Sat 10am–1.30pm • Charge

At the northeastern end of the old town, the Gothic church of **San Pedro**, perched precariously on the cliff edge, was rebuilt in the sixteenth century over an original Moorish fort. The later imposing Baroque exterior and tower are in strong contrast to the interior, where a fine sixteenth-century retablo (the oldest in the province) documents the life of San Pedro and San Jerónimo. To each side of this are paintings of *San Ignacio* and *La Dolorosa* by Pachecho, the tutor of Velázquez. There's also the rather grisly undecomposed body of San Victor (thankfully behind glass) and an image of the Virgin attributed to Luisa Roldán ("La Roldana"), the sculptor daughter of Pedro Roldán. You can climb the tower, but you'll need a good head for heights, as there are few guardrails on the top to prevent a fall.

San Agustín

Mon & Wed–Sun 10.30am–1.30pm & 3.30–6.30pm • Free

A few minutes' walk to the north of San Pedro lies the convent of **San Agustín**, on the narrow neck of the spur, whose church contains a fine seventeenth-century carved wood retablo and the town's most venerated image of Jesús Nazareno (Christ bearing the Cross).

River beaches and Lago de Arcos

Buses for the lake and its beaches leave from the Pza de España, below the old town (11 daily in each direction, with reduced service Sat; Sun service only July & Aug)

East of town, the A372 road to Ronda leads down to a couple of sandy **beaches** on the riverbank, while to the north of here the **Lago de Arcos** (actually a reservoir) is a good spot for swimming; bring insect repellent if you plan to stay overnight.

ARRIVAL AND DEPARTURE	ARCOS DE LA FRONTERA

By bus The bus station is in the new town on C/Corregidores below and to the south of the Paseo de Andalucía. It is served by the Comes and Amarillo companies. Destinations Algodonales (4 daily; 50min); Cádiz (4 daily;

1hr 5min); Jerez (14 daily; 30min); Málaga (1 daily; 3hr 15min).

By car Parking in the narrow streets of the old town is tricky (although all the hotels have their own arrangements) and

2

DOLPHIN TOURS

A number of companies run rather pricey daily **dolphin-spotting boat trips** and trips around the bay. Most leave from Marina Bay – ring first to book places or ask the tourist office to do it for you. Operators include Dolphin Safari (Ⓦdolphinsafari.gi) and Dolphin Adventure (Ⓦdolphin.gi). You can also book online with both companies, which works out 20 percent cheaper.

you'd be much better off trying to find space on the Paseo de Andalucía or using a pay car park (there's one beneath the Paseo itself).

INFORMATION, TOURS AND GETTING AROUND

Turismo The Turismo at Cuesta de Belén 5 (Mon–Sat 10am–1.30pm & 4–6pm, Sun 11am–2pm; Ⓦturismoarcos. com), can provide a detailed map, which you'll need to find your way around the new town. Also has details of daily guided morning tours of the old town (free, but excluding monument entry charges); there is also a nocturnal tour (charge) which includes a drink at a typical tapas bar. The same building houses a Centro de Interpretación (same hours as Turismo; free) covering the town's history.

Minibus A useful minibus service (Mon–Sat every 30min until 9pm) runs back and forth between Pza de España and the Paseo de Andalucía in the new town and Pza del Cabildo in the *casco antiguo* – saving you a climb.

ACCOMMODATION SEE MAP PAGE 232

Outside the *feria* periods (early May and late September) there is usually no problem in finding accommodation in Arcos, and outside high season prices can fall by up to fifty percent. In addition to the in-town options there is also the possibility of staying a little out of town at the Lago de Arcos (see page 234), where there's a *hostal* and a couple of inviting hotels.

ARCOS DE LA FRONTERA

La Casa de Bovedas C/Bovedas 9; Ⓦlacasadebovedas. com. Friendly little upmarket *hostal* close to the church of San Pedro offering rooms around a delightful patio in a renovated historic house. The rooms are individually styled and come with a/c, heating and TV and most have a balcony or terrace with spectacular views. Breakfast (extra) is served on the plant-filled patio. €€

★ **La Casa Grande** C/Maldonado 10; Ⓦlacasagrande. net. Perched along the same clifftop as the *parador*, this elegant hotel has beautiful individually styled rooms (and more expensive suites) – some with terrace – inside a restored *casa señorial* with a columned inner patio and a sensational view from the bar terrace across the river valley. €€

★ **Hotel El Convento** C/Maldonado 2; Ⓦhotelelconvento.es. Stunning hotel in a seventeenth-century former convent whose comfortable a/c rooms – 8 and 9 are recommended – have spectacular views over the *vega*. Breakfast (extra) is served in a charming courtyard. April to May is high season here, when the rate is thirty percent higher. €€

Hotel Los Olivos C/San Miguel 2, in the new town; Ⓦhotel-losolivos.es. Charming and friendly little hotel near the Paseo de Andalucía gardens, in a superbly restored *casa antigua*. Some of the light a/c rooms have fine views and there's a plant-filled interior patio and further views from a rooftop terrace. Also offers parking for a small charge per night. Breakfast is included. €€

Hotel Marqués de Torresoto C/Marqués de Torresoto 4; Ⓦhotel-marques-de-torresoto.webnode.es. Attractive, good-value a/c rooms with minibar and satellite TV in a converted seventeenth-century mansion, the former seat of the *marqueses* de Torresoto. The delightful colonnaded patio – complete with Baroque chapel – now serves as the hotel restaurant (open to the public). Has rooftop terrace with views. €

Pension Bar San Marcos C/Marqués de Torresoto 6; Ⓦpensionsanmarcosdearcos.es. Excellent small guesthouse in the old town offering pleasant a/c en-suite rooms with TV. Also has its own bar-restaurant below, and breakfast included there makes it a great deal. €

ON LAGO DE ARCOS

Hacienda El Santiscal 3km out of town on the lakeside; Ⓦsantiscal.com. Small country hotel in a beautifully converted hacienda, partly dating from the sixteenth century, with individually styled and furnished a/c rooms (with ceiling fans). Public areas include bar and restaurant and a pool in the grounds. Horseriding available. See website for special offers. €€

Mesón de la Molinera Lago de Arcos; Ⓦmesondelamolinera.com. Tranquil hotel-*hostal* on the waterfront with stunning views across the lake towards Arcos on its hilltop. Comfortable balcony rooms with minibar and safe are offered in the hotel (where breakfast is included), while chalet-style bungalows comprise the *hostal*. Facilities include a sun terrace, great pool and easy parking. Also has its own bar and restaurant. €€

★**Parador de Arcos de la Frontera** Pza del Cabildo; ⓦparador.es. One of the region's smaller and more intimate *paradores*, occupying the former Casa del Corregidor (house of the king's magistrate) with parts dating from the sixteenth century. The striking building is perched on a rock pedestal with reassuringly reinforced foundations to prevent it from sliding over the cliff and elegant balconied rooms from which to enjoy the view. There's also a delightful patio (open to the public for drinks and afternoon tea), a restaurant (see page 235), and the *cafetería*'s "crow's nest" terrace has the best views in town. Parking on the square outside. €€€

EATING

SEE MAP PAGE 232

Alcaraván C/Nueva 1, close to the castle walls; ☎956 703 397. This atmospheric cave restaurant serves tapas and *platos asados* (roasted meats) as well as a variety of salads. €

Mesón Los Murales Pza de Boticas 1; ☎685 809 661. One of the best low-price options in the old town, near the church of San Pedro, serving tapas, *raciones*, *platos combinados* and *montaditos* (tapas on bread) plus salads. Has an economical *menú* and a street terrace. €€

★**Parador de Arcos de la Frontera** Pza del Cabildo; ⓦparador.es. The *parador*'s restaurant – in a beamed and pastel-tinted dining room – has a recommended *menú* that includes local specialities. On the à la carte menu *salmorejo de aguacate* (avocado gazpacho), *corvina a la roteña* (meagre) and *conejo de Serranía de Cádiz* (rabbit with honey) are signature dishes. Also offers vegetarian and diabetic menus. €€€

Tabanco Lalola C/Corredera 11; ☎622 84 27 46. Vibrant bar-shop (*tabanco*) near the Turismo with wooden furnishings and lots of exposed brick and stonework. There's a decent tapas and *raciones* selection and *gazpacho* and *carne mechada* (larded pork) are house specials. €€

Taberna Jovenes Flamencos C/Dean Espinosa 11, near the Pza del Cabildo; ☎657 133 552. Lively and popular flamenco-themed bar with a terrace, offering well-prepared *raciones* and *media-raciones*. Dishes include *pulpo a la gallega* (octopus) and *secreto ibérico* (iberian pork loin), and there are plenty of vegetarian options. Sometimes stages flamenco concerts. €€

Seville and Huelva

PLAYA DE CUESTA MANELI, COSTA DE LA LUZ

Seville and Huelva

The irresistible city of Seville, Andalucía's capital, has many of the region's most beautiful monuments: the Giralda tower, a magnificent Gothic cathedral and a fabulous Mudéjar Alcázar are just the highlights. Add to these the stunning Museo de Bellas Artes, the nearby Roman site of Itálica and a number of remarkable Renaissance mansions – not to mention the atmospheric *barrios*, each with its own strong character and traditions – and you're looking at a stay of at least two days. Beyond Seville, the central and western regions of Andalucía are little visited – a great pity, as the city's province and its neighbour Huelva can spring a variety of surprises, both scenic and cultural, on visitors who wander off the beaten track to find them.

3

East of Seville, a clutch of smaller towns on the way to Córdoba includes Moorish **Carmona**, which possesses a remarkable Roman cemetery, and Baroque **Écija**, with its striking churches and mansions. Also in Seville's Campiña – the name given to this broad and fertile agricultural plain watered by the Guadalquivir – are the towns of **Osuna** and **Estepa**, both with their own Renaissance architectural gems. To the north, the wooded hills of the **Sierra Morena** offer welcome respite from the intense summer heat, with charming small towns making excellent base camps for hiking.

The **province of Huelva**, which stretches from Seville to the Portuguese border, hardly deserves to be the least-visited province of Andalucía. The area boasts the huge **Parque Nacional de Doñana** spreading back from the Guadalquivir estuary in vast expanses of *marismas* – sand dunes, salt flats and marshes. The largest roadless area in western Europe, the park is vital to scores of migratory birds and to endangered mammals including the Iberian lynx, and is also home to Andalucía's rumbustious Whitsuntide pilgrimage and fair, the Romería del Rocío. **Huelva**, the provincial capital, although scarred by its industrial surrounds, tries its best to be welcoming and does have a number of things to see; it also makes a convenient base for trips to local sites associated with the voyages of Columbus, which set out from here. It was at the nearby monastery of **La Rábida** that the explorer's 1492 expedition was planned and from the tiny port of **Palos de la Frontera** that he eventually set sail to discover a new route to the Indies. The province of Huelva was also the site of ancient Tartessus, a legendary kingdom rich in minerals that attracted the Minoans, Phoenicians and Greeks in ancient times, and is mentioned in the Bible. Minerals are still extracted from the hills to the north of Huelva – the awesome **Minas de Ríotinto** display evidence of the human quest for minerals stretching back over five thousand years.

Some of the most beautiful and neglected parts of this region are even further north, in the dark, ilex-covered hills and sturdy rural villages of the **Sierra de Aracena**. Perfect walking country, with its network of streams and reservoirs between modest peaks, this is a botanist's dream, brilliant with a mass of spring flowers. You also find here some of the finest *jamón* in Spain, produced from acorn-eating *cerdos ibéricos* (black pigs).

While the landlocked province of Seville takes its relaxation along the banks of the Guadalquivir, Huelva has a sea coast that harks back to pre-Costa del Sol tranquillity. This section of the **Costa de la Luz** has some of the finest beaches in Andalucía, with long stretches of luminous white sand and gloriously little sign of mass hotel development.

ALCÁZAR, SEVILLE

Highlights

❶ The Cathedral and La Giralda, Seville The city's landmark building and the world's largest Gothic church, whose soaring minaret – now the bell tower – is one of the most beautiful of all Moorish monuments. See page 243 & 248

❷ Alcázar, Seville A Moorish fortress-palace adorned with breathtakingly beautiful stuccowork, tiles and coffered ceilings within, and serene gardens for relaxing outside. See page 251

❸ Tapas bars, Seville The city that invented tapas has some of Spain's very best bars to sample them – two not to miss are *Bar Giralda* and *El Rinconcillo*. See page 280

❹ Semana Santa, Seville The solemn pomp and pagan ecstasy of the Holy Week processions are the most impressive and moving in Spain. See page 284

❺ Coto de Doñana National Park Europe's largest and most important wildlife sanctuary. See page 313

❻ Costa de la Luz Huelva's stretch of the Atlantic has a string of nice resorts and some of the finest beaches in Andalucía. See page 319

❼ Sierra de Aracena A landscape of wooded hills, babbling streams and attractive villages which produce the best cured ham in Spain. See page 331

HIGHLIGHTS ARE MARKED ON THE MAP ON PAGE 240

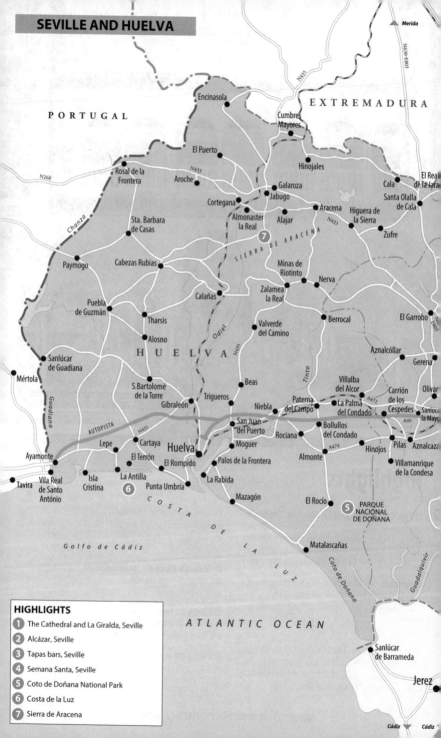

SEVILLE AND HUELVA

Merida

PORTUGAL

EXTREMADURA

N630-E803

N835

Encinasola

Cumbres
Mayores

El Puerto

N433

Hinojales

Cala

El Real
de la Jafa

N260

Rosal de la
Frontera

Aroche

Galaroza

Santa Olalla
de Cala

Cortegana

Jabugo

Aracena

Higuera de
la Sierra

Almonaster
la Real

Alajar

N433

Zufre

Sta. Barbara
de Casas

7

SIERRA DE ARACENA

Paymogo

Cabezas Rubias

Minas de
Riotinto

Nerva

El Garrobo

Puebla
de Guzmán

Calañas

Zalamea
la Real

Tharsis

Odiel

Valverde
del Camino

Berrocal

Alosno

H U E L V A

N435

Tinto

Aznalcóllar

Gerena

Mértola

Sanlúcar
de Guadiana

Beas

Villalba
del Alcor

Olivar

Guadiana

S.Bartolomé
de la Torre

Trigueros

Niebla

Paterna
del Campo

Carrión
de los
Cespedes

Sanlúca
la Mayo

A49

Gibraleón

La Palma
del Condado

A472

AUTOPISTA

N431

San Juan
del Puerto

Bollullos
del Condado

Aznalcáza

Lepe

Cartaya

Huelva

Moguer

Rociana

A474

Pilas

Ayamonte

El Terrón

El Rompido

Palos de la Frontera

Almonte

Hinojos

Villamanrique
de la Condesa

Tavira

Vila Real
de Santo
António

Isla
Cristina

La Antilla

6

Punta Umbría

La Rabida

Mazagón

El Rocío

5

PARQUE
NACIONAL
DE DOÑANA

COSTA   DE   LA   LUZ

Matalascañas

Coto de Doñana

Guadalquivir

Golfo de Cádiz

ATLANTIC   OCEAN

Sanlúcar
de Barrameda

Jerez

HIGHLIGHTS

1 The Cathedral and La Giralda, Seville

2 Alcázar, Seville

3 Tapas bars, Seville

4 Semana Santa, Seville

5 Coto de Doñana National Park

6 Costa de la Luz

7 Sierra de Aracena

Cádiz   Cádiz

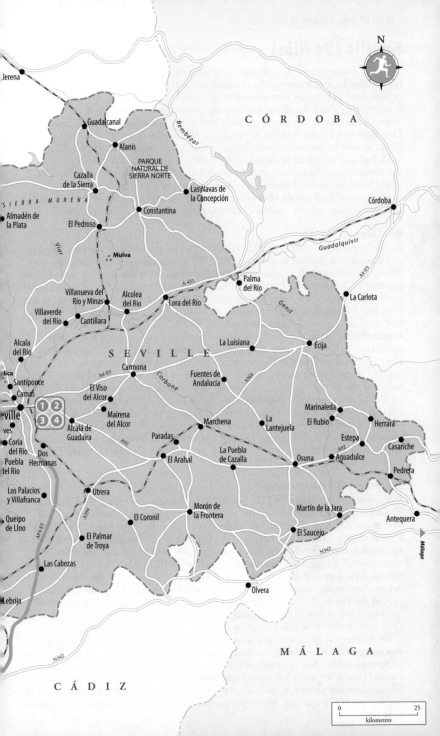

Seville (Sevilla)

"Seville," wrote Byron, "is a pleasant city, famous for oranges and women." And for its heat, he might perhaps have added, since **SEVILLE** is one of the hottest cities in mainland Europe. Its summers are intense and they start early, in May. What is captivating about Seville, as much as the monuments and works of art, is its essential romantic quality – the greatest city of the Spanish south, of Carmen, Don Juan and Figaro, and the archetype of Andalucían promise. *Sevillanos* are world leaders in the art of street theatre, too. During **Semana Santa**, for example, sandalled and helmeted Roman soldiers sombrely escort the *paso*, or effigy, of the condemned Christ through the crowded but silent streets, while a couple of weeks later the mood changes dramatically when the city launches into the wild exuberance of the **Feria de Abril** (which also inaugurates the start of the bullfighting season – second only to Madrid's in importance – another *sevillano* passion).

Brief history

Seville began when ancient Iberian tribes settled on the banks of the Guadalquivir perhaps early in the first millennium BC. The settlement grew into the town now known as **El Carambolo**, whose great wealth derived from the minerals mined in the mountains to the north. The demand for copper, silver and gold lured in the Greeks and Phoenicians, who traded their own ceramics, jewellery and ivory goods. It was the same Phoenicians, or perhaps their successors the Carthaginians, who attacked and then conquered the settlement around 500 BC, subsequently renaming it **Hispalis**, meaning "flat land". When the **Romans** finally wrested Spain from Carthage the Roman general Scipio founded **Itálica** in 206 on a hill overlooking the river. The final conquest of the peninsula cost the Romans a further two hundred years of dogged campaigning against the ferocious Iberian tribes and in the latter stages of this struggle, during the Roman civil war, Julius Caesar captured Hispalis in 45 BC and renamed it **Julia Romula** ("Little Rome"). As a leading centre of the Roman province of Baetica (roughly corresponding to modern Andalucía) the city flourished and nearby Itálica provided Rome with two of its greatest second-century emperors, Trajan and Hadrian. The city later fell to the **Visigoths**, whose Christian archbishop San Isidro made sixth-century Seville into a forward-thinking European centre of learning.

The Moors and the Reconquista

Conquered by the **Moors** in 712, Seville briefly became the capital of al-Andalus. The Moors left an indelible imprint on the city, not only in its architecture, but also in the Arabic-influenced local dialect, renaming the River Baetis Wadi El Kabir ("great river"), a title it still retains as the Guadalquivir. The Almohad dynasty of the twelfth and thirteenth centuries brought great prosperity, and when Seville was captured during the **Reconquista** by Fernando III in 1248 the city became a favoured residence of the Spanish monarchy, in particular Pedro the Cruel, who was responsible for the construction of the outstanding Alcázar. Religious intolerance racked the city in the wake of the Reconquista, however, and in 1391 the Jewish quarter in the Barrio Santa Cruz was sacked – a harbinger of the banishment of all Jews from Spain to be proclaimed by Fernando and Isabel a century later.

The fifteenth century also saw, as well as the construction of the cathedral, the **discovery of the New World** – an event that would catapult the city to the forefront of Spanish affairs. Seville's navigable river, with access to the Atlantic, made it a natural choice for the main port of commerce with the Americas. In the 1500s, as fabulous wealth poured in from the empire, Seville was transformed into one of the great cities of Europe and, with a population of over 150,000, one of the largest at that time.

Decline and revival

The **silting up of the Guadalquivir** in the 1680s deprived Seville of its port and with it the monopoly of trade with the Americas. The merchant fleet was transferred to Cádiz and the city went into a decline exacerbated by the great earthquake of 1755 which, although centred on Lisbon, caused much destruction. The city was further ravaged by the **Napoleonic occupation** of 1810–12 and was largely bypassed by the industrial revolution which permeated slowly from the north. It was only in the later nineteenth century that Seville was rediscovered by travellers such as Richard Ford, who declared it to be "the marvel of Andalucía".

While wealthy European travellers flocked to the city in the wake of Ford and other writers, life in the early twentieth century for the majority of *sevillanos* was harsh. The huge Spanish Americas Fair of 1929 (see page 260) was intended to launch the city into an economic revival but – coming at the time of a world recession – instead bankrupted it. In 1936 Seville was the first major city to fall to Franco's Nationalist forces at the start of the Civil War and the infamous General Queipo de Llano then subjected the city to a murderous repression in order to root out "villainous Marxists" in the working-class *barrios*. The long years of poverty that followed were only alleviated with the return of democracy and the election of a *sevillano* prime minister, Felipe González, in 1982. During his years in power he pumped significant funds into his native city, culminating with the AVE high-speed train connection to Madrid and a massive investment in infrastructure connected with the staging of **Expo 92**, a world fair to mark the quincentenary of Columbus's voyage to the Americas. In what was almost a re-run of the 1929 event, this once again left the city with colossal debts. Seville today projects a prosperous air despite many serious social, and not always visible, problems.

Seville Cathedral

Mon–Sat 10.30am–7.30pm, Sun 2.30–7.30pm; ticket valid for Catedral and the Giralda • Charge; tickets available online (recommended), or at cathedral entrance • ⓦ catedraldesevilla.es

After the reconquest of Seville by Fernando III (1248), the Almohad mosque was consecrated to the Virgin Mary (the church's full name is La Catedral de Santa María de la Sede) and kept in use as the Christian cathedral. As such it survived until 1402, when the cathedral chapter dreamed up plans for a new and unrivalled monument

---

SEVILLE ORIENTATION

The **old city**, where you'll be spending most of your time, takes up the east bank of the Guadalquivir. At its heart, side by side, stand the three great monuments: the **Giralda** tower, the **Cathedral** and the **Alcázar**, with the cramped alleyways of the **Barrio Santa Cruz**, the medieval Jewish quarter and now the heart of tourist life, extending east of them. North and west of the *barrio* is the main shopping and commercial district, **El Centro**, its most obvious landmarks the **Plaza Nueva** and **Plaza Duque de la Victoria**, and the smart pedestrianized **Calle Sierpes** which runs between them. To the north lies the gritty **Macarena** quarter, from whose church the *paso* of the bejewelled Virgin of Macarena – the most revered in Seville – sails forth on the Maundy Thursday of Semana Santa to enormous popular acclaim. Just beyond the walls here in the converted sixteenth-century **Hospital de las Cinco Llagas** ("Five Wounds of Christ") is the permanent seat of the Andalucían parliament.

Across the river is the earthier district of **Triana**, traditionally home to the city's artist community. It's flanked to the south by **Los Remedios**, the former business zone and now an upmarket residential quarter. Adjoining this to the south lie the grounds where Seville's Feria de Abril is held, and also on this bank, to the north of Triana, lie the remains of the **Expo 92 exhibition ground**, at Isla de la Cartuja.

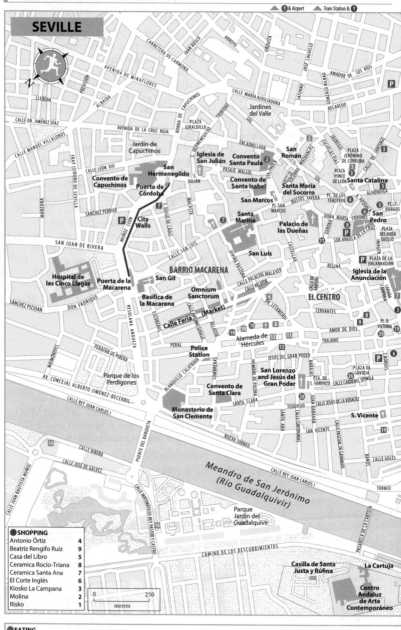

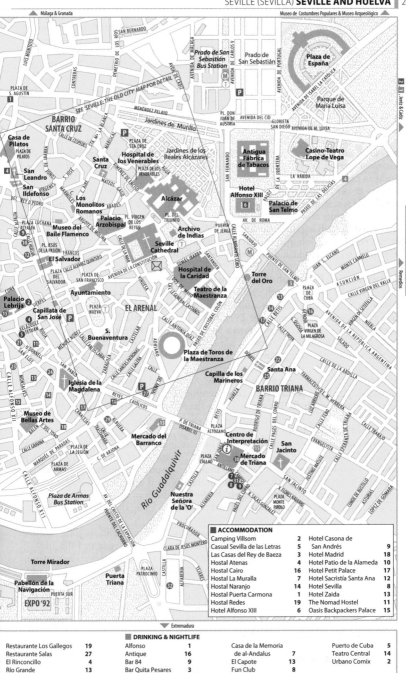

△ Málaga & Granada

Museo de Costumbres Populares & Museo Arqueológico △

▽ Extremadura

ACCOMMODATION		Hotel Casona de	
Camping Villsom	2	San Andrés	9
Casual Sevilla de las Letras	5	Hotel Madrid	18
Las Casas del Rey de Baeza	3	Hotel Patio de la Alameda	10
Hostal Atenas	4	Hotel Petit Palace	17
Hostal Cairo	16	Hotel Sacristía Santa Ana	12
Hostal La Muralla	7	Hotel Sevilla	8
Hostal Naranjo	14	Hotel Zaida	13
Hostal Puerta Carmona	1	The Nomad Hostel	11
Hostal Redes	19	Oasis Backpackers Palace	15
Hotel Alfonso XIII	6		

DRINKING & NIGHTLIFE							
Restaurante Los Gallegos	19	Alfonso	1	Casa de la Memoria		Puerto de Cuba	5
Restaurante Salas	27	Antique	16	de al-Andalus	7	Teatro Central	14
El Rinconcillo	4	Bar 84	9	El Capote	13	Urbano Comix	2
Río Grande	13	Bar Quita Pesares	3	Fun Club	8		
Sal Gorda	9	La Bicileteria	6	Gigante Bar	12		
Taberna Coloniales	5	Café Central	10	Java	15		
El Viajero Sedentario	18	Café Jazz Naima	11	Muelle New York	4		

to Christian glory: "a building on so magnificent a scale that posterity will believe we were mad". To this end the Almohad mosque (see box, page 250) was almost entirely demolished, and the largest Gothic church in the world, **Seville Cathedral**, was completed, extraordinarily, in just over a century (1402–1506). As Norman Lewis said, "it expresses conquest and domination in architectural terms of sheer mass". Built upon the huge, rectangular base-plan of the old mosque whose minaret, the **Giralda**, now serves as the bell tower, it was given the extra dimension of height by the Christian architects, probably under the direction of the French master architect of Rouen Cathedral. It was previously reckoned to be the third largest church in the world – after St Paul's in London and St Peter's in Rome – but new calculations based on cubic measurements have now placed it in the number one position, a claim upheld by the *Guinness Book of Records*, a copy of whose certificate is proudly displayed in the church (next to the Capilla Real).

Entry to the cathedral is through the **Puerta de San Cristóbal**, on the building's south side where, beyond a reception area displaying minor artworks by Murillo and Zurbarán among others, you enter the church to the west of the portal itself. If you're interested in studying the abundant artworks dotted around the various chapels en route, visit the bookshop at the entrance to obtain a copy of the official *Guide to the Cathedral of Seville*, which deals with them in detail.

Mausoleum of Christopher Columbus

The enormous late nineteenth-century **Mausoleum of Christopher Columbus** (Cristóbal Colón in Spanish), by *sevillano* sculptor Arturo Mélida, may or may not house the navigator's remains (see box, page 249). It was originally intended to be erected in the Cuban cathedral of Havana, then a Spanish colony, where it would have become a sepulchre for Columbus's remains, but the Spanish-American War – and Cuba's subsequent independence – intervened. As a result the plans were changed and the work was placed here. The mariner's coffin is held aloft by four huge allegorical figures, representing the kingdoms of León, Castile, Aragón and Navarra; the lance of Castile should be piercing a pomegranate (now inexplicably missing), the symbol of Granada (and the word for the fruit in Spanish), the last Moorish kingdom to be reconquered.

Nave and Capilla Mayor

In the **nave**, first impressions are of the sheer size and grandeur of the place, but as you grow accustomed to the gloom, two other qualities stand out: the rhythmic balance and interplay between the parts, and an impressive overall simplicity and restraint in decoration. Successive ages have left monuments of their own, but these have been limited to the two rows of side chapels. In the main body of the cathedral only the great box-like structure of the **coro** (choir) stands out, filling the central portion of the nave.

The **Capilla Mayor** (main chapel) is dominated by a vast and fabulous gilded Gothic retablo composed of 45 carved scenes from the life of Christ. Begun in 1482 and the lifetime's work of a single craftsman, Fleming Pieter Dancart, this is the supreme masterpiece of the cathedral – the largest and richest altarpiece in the world and one of the finest examples of Gothic woodcarving. The guides provide staggering statistics on the amount of gold involved in the gilding. Above the central tabernacle, the *Virgen de la Sede* (Virgin of the Chair) is a stunning thirteenth-century Gothic figure of silver-plated cedar. Just to the right, a panel depicts an image of the Giralda as it appeared prior to any Renaissance additions.

Sacristía de los Cálices

In the church's southeast corner is the **Sacristía de los Cálices**, where many of the cathedral's main art treasures are displayed. Among some outstanding works are a masterly *Santas Justa y Rufina* by Goya, depicting Seville's patron saints who were put

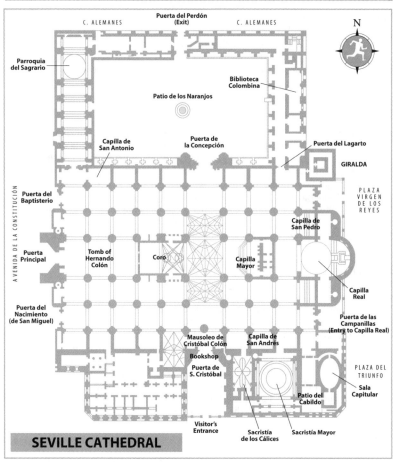

SEVILLE CATHEDRAL

to death in 287 during the Roman emperor Diocletian's persecution of the Christians, and a powerful *Cristo Crucificado* by Zurbarán.

Sacristía Mayor

Behind the **Capilla de San Andrés**, which has an exceptional polychrome image of the crucified Christ by Juan Martínez Montañés, lies the grandiose sixteenth-century **Sacristía Mayor** designed in 1528 by Diego de Riaño. It's a prime example of the rich Plateresque style, and Riaño was one of the foremost exponents of this predominantly decorative architecture of the late Spanish Renaissance. Forming a veritable church-within-a-church it induced Philip II to remark to the members of the chapter: "Your sacristy is finer than my Chapel Royal." The sacristy houses more paintings, including a poignant *Santa Teresa* by Zurbarán, and the **treasury**, a dull collection of silver reliquaries and monstrances. Also here are the keys presented to Fernando III by the Jewish and Moorish communities on the surrender of the city in 1248; sculpted into the Moor's key in stylized Arabic script are the words "May Allah render eternal the dominion of Islam in this city". Nearby is a polychrome image of Fernando by Pedro Roldán, one of Andalucía's great eighteenth-century sculptors.

Sala Capitular

Passing through a small antechamber beyond the diminutive Patio del Cabildo brings you into the remarkable oval-shaped **Sala Capitular** (Chapter House), whose elaborate domed ceiling is mirrored in the outstanding geometric marble decoration of the floor. The stone benches provide seats for the members of the chapter. It contains a number of paintings by Murillo, a native of Seville, the finest of which, a flowing *Concepción Inmaculada*, occupies a place of honour high above the bishop's throne.

Capilla de San Antonio

On the southwest side of the cathedral is the **Puerta del Nacimiento**, the door through which pass all the *pasos* and penitents who take part in the Semana Santa processions; from here, turning right (north) along the west wall, passing the **Puerta Principal**, takes you to the northwest corner. Here the **Capilla de San Antonio** contains the *Vision of St Anthony*, a magnificent work by Murillo, depicting the saint in ecstatic pose before an infant Christ emerging from a luminous golden cloud. Try and spot where the restorers joined San Antonio back into place after he had been crudely hacked out of the picture by thieves in the nineteenth century. He was eventually discovered in New York and returned to the cathedral. The *Baptism of Jesus* above this is another fine work by the same artist.

Capilla Real

Entry from Pza Virgen de los Reyes • Mon–Sat 8am–2pm & 4–7pm, Sun for services between 8.30am & 6pm • Free • As the chapel is used for services and private prayer, no photography or conversation is allowed

The nave's north side leads to the **Puerta de la Concepción**, where an altar on the left side has a fine portrayal of the Virgen de Belén painted in 1635 by *granadino* artist Alonso Cano. Before exiting here, head for the northeast corner to view the domed Renaissance **Capilla Real**, built on the site of the original royal burial chapel and containing the body of Fernando III (El Santo) in a suitably rich, Baroque silver sepulchre before the altar. The large tombs on either side of the chapel are those of Fernando's wife, Beatrice of Swabia, and his son, Alfonso the Wise. The entrance to the chapel from the cathedral is normally closed, meaning that to view the interior you'll need to use the street entrance in the Plaza Virgen de los Reyes.

Capilla de San Pedro

To the north of the Capilla Real, the **Capilla de San Pedro** has a fine seventeenth-century retablo by Diego López Bueno with nine Zurbarán scenes depicting the life of St Peter (except for the image of God, which is a later replacement). Also here is the **Puerta del Lagarto** (Door of the Alligator), so named in commemoration of a stuffed reptile given to Alfonso X by the sultan of Egypt in 1260. A wooden replica now hangs in place of the perished original.

La Giralda

Unquestionably the most beautiful building in Seville is the square-sided tower known as La Giralda, which was named after the sixteenth-century *giraldillo* – or weather vane – on its summit. The Giralda dominates the skyline and, with its perfect synthesis of form and decoration, is one of the most important examples of Islamic architecture in the world.

Formerly the minaret of the mosque that once stood here, the Giralda was the culmination of **Almohad architecture** and served as a model for those at the imperial capitals of Rabat and Marrakesh. Said to be built on a foundation of destroyed Roman statuary, it was designed by the architect of the original mosque, Ahmed ibn Baso, and was used by the Moors both for calling the faithful to prayer and as an observatory. They so worshipped the building that they planned to destroy it before the Christian conquest of Seville, but were prevented from doing so by the threat of Alfonso

WHERE LIES CHRISTOPHER COLUMBUS?

The dispute about Christopher Columbus's birthplace – claimed by both Italy and Spain – is matched by the labyrinthine controversy surrounding the **whereabouts of his remains**. After his death in **Valladolid** in 1506, Columbus was originally buried there, but three years later his remains were removed to **Seville** and interred at the monastery of Santa María de las Cuevas, across the river on La Cartuja island, to be joined shortly afterwards by those of his son Diego. But Diego's widow was determined to have both bodies interred in **Hispaniola** (modern Haiti and the Dominican Republic), the site of Columbus's first landfall in 1492, the capital of Spanish America and where Diego had served as governor. Following an intervention by the emperor Carlos V supporting her wishes, in 1544 the remains of both bodies were packed into lead coffins and shipped to the island, where they were placed in the cathedral. The remains of Columbus's grandson, Luís, were interred in the same cathedral in 1783.

Later, during repairs to the cathedral in Hispaniola, it seems that the coffins were mislaid, then opened, and the names mixed up. It did not take the authorities long to resolve the dilemma of which was which, by having all three sets of remains placed in one coffin. Shortly after, in 1795, when Spain was forced to cede Santo Domingo to the French, the remains were moved to Cuba and the cathedral in **Havana**, still Spanish territory. When Cuba was lost in 1898 the remains were transported back across the Atlantic and placed in the tomb in Seville. The lingering uncertainty lies in the accidental discovery in 1879 of another lead coffin in the cathedral in **Santo Domingo** bearing a silver plate inscribed with Columbus's name. This box of remains then disappeared, and despite the government of the Dominican Republic's claim to have recovered them (now enshrined in a national monument), numerous coffins of bones claiming to be the same have made frequent appearances at auction houses ever since.

Were the correct remains dispatched from Santo Domingo to Havana in 1795? Was the discovery of 1879 a fraud? Are the remains in the tomb today really those of Christopher, Diego and Luís? The only certainty in the story is that one member of the Columbus family, at least, was buried in Seville's cathedral and has stayed here – Christopher's bookish son **Hernando**, who wrote a biography of his father and donated his large library to what became the cathedral's Biblioteca Colombina. His tombstone lies in the centre of the pavement towards the main west door, the Puerta Principal, and is decorated with the arms of the cathedral flanked by sailing vessels.

In 2002, science was called on to try to resolve the mystery and a plan was drawn up to subject all the known remains of Columbus family members to **DNA testing** in the hope that a common genetic code could be established. Initial reports on samples taken from the Seville tomb by scientists at Granada university were inconclusive due to the poor condition of the remains, although the tests did indicate that there were matches with other members of the family. A request was then made to test the remains in Santo Domingo which – if this proved negative – would go some way to confirming the authenticity of those in Seville. After initially agreeing to this request the government of the Dominican Republic had second thoughts. An announcement by scientists that the Santo Domingo remains are not those of Columbus would be hugely embarrassing for a country where the navigator is a national hero. Thus in early 2005 the republic's government stated that it didn't have sufficient confidence in the reliability of DNA testing to allow the research to go ahead. When the Spanish ambassador announced that Spain would not make an issue of the matter the outcome of this tortuously tangled tale was, for the time being, put on hold, leaving the location of Columbus's remains a mystery for at least a few more years yet.

Some experts are convinced that Columbus's remains may lie in both the Dominican Republic and Seville, as the remains found in the cathedral tomb do not make up a complete skeleton. When the Dominican Republic eventually allows access to their remains it could well be proven that the navigator's bones lie on both sides of the Atlantic: a messy but probably apt ending to the story.

3

MOORISH SEVILLE

Seville was one of the earliest **Moorish conquests** (in 712 AD) and, as part of the caliphate of Córdoba, became the second city of al-Andalus. When the caliphate broke up in the early eleventh century it was by far the most powerful of the independent states (or *taifas*) to emerge, extending its power over the Algarve and eventually over Jaén, Murcia and Córdoba itself. This period, under a series of three Arabic rulers from the **Abbadid** dynasty (1023–91), was something of a golden age. The city's court was unrivalled in wealth, luxury and sophistication, developing a strong chivalric element and a flair for poetry – one of the most skilled exponents was the last ruler, al Mu'tamid, the "poet-king". But with sophistication came decadence, and in 1091 Abbadid rule was usurped by a new force, the **Almoravids**, a tribe of fanatical Berber Muslims from North Africa, to whom the Andalucíans had appealed for help against the threat from the northern Christian kingdoms.

Despite initial military successes, the Almoravids failed to consolidate their gains in al-Andalus and attempted to rule through military governors from Marrakesh. In the middle of the twelfth century they were in turn supplanted by a new Berber incursion, the **Almohads**, who by about 1170 had recaptured virtually all the former territories. Seville accepted Almohad rule in 1147 and became the capital of this last real empire of the Moors in Spain. Almohad power was sustained until their disastrous defeat in 1212 by the combined Christian armies of the north, at Las Navas de Tolosa in Jaén. Within this brief and precarious period Seville underwent a renaissance of public building, characterized by a new vigour and fluidity of style. The Almohads rebuilt the Alcázar, enlarged the principal mosque and erected a new and brilliant minaret, a tower over 100m tall, topped with four copper spheres that could be seen from far and wide: the Giralda.

(later King Alfonso X) that "if they removed a single stone, they would all be put to the sword". Instead the Giralda went on to become the bell tower of the Christian cathedral. The Patio de los Naranjos (see page 250), the old entrance to the mosque, also survives intact.

The structure took twelve years to build (1184–96) and derives its firm, simple beauty from the shadows formed by blocks of brick trelliswork or *ajaracas*, different on each side, and relieved by a succession of arched niches and windows. The original harmony has been somewhat blemished by the Renaissance-era addition of balconies and, to a still greater extent, by the four diminishing storeys of the belfry – added, along with the Italian-sculpted bronze figure of Faith which surmounts them, in 1560–68, following the demolition by an earthquake of the original copper spheres. The fact that a weather vane blown by the four winds should epitomize the ideal of constant faith, or that this female figure should possess a masculine name ("Giraldillo"), has never seemed to trouble whimsical *sevillanos*.

From inside the cathedral you can **climb to the bell chamber** for a remarkable view of the city – and, equally remarkable, a glimpse of the Gothic details of the cathedral's buttresses and statuary. Keep an eye out, too, for the colony of kestrels that has long nested in the tower – the descendants no doubt of the "twittering, careering hawks" seen by Ford when he climbed up here in the 1830s. Most impressive is the tower's inner construction, a series of 35 gently inclined ramps wide enough for two mounted guards to pass.

Patio de los Naranjos

The **Patio de los Naranjos** takes its name from the orange trees that now shade the former mosque's entrance courtyard where ritual ablutions were performed prior to worship. In the centre of the patio a Moorish fountain incorporates a sixth-century carved marble font, a surviving remnant of the earlier Visigothic cathedral which was itself levelled to make way for the mosque. Cross to the patio's northern side and the **Puerta del Perdón**, the mosque's original entrance. Although sadly marred by Renaissance embellishments, there remains some exquisite Almohad plasterwork and the original great doors made from larchwood faced with bronze. Minute Kufic script inside the lozenges proclaims that "the empire is Allah's". The pierced bronze door-knockers are copies of the beautiful hand-crafted twelfth-century originals now preserved inside the church (not currently on view).

Archivo de Indias

Mon–Sat 9.30am–4.30pm, Sun 10am–1.30pm • Free

If you've been inspired by the Columbus saga after seeing his monument in the cathedral, visit the **Casa Lonja**, opposite the cathedral. Built in the severe and uncompromising style of El Escorial near Madrid, and designed by the same architect, Juan de Herrera, it was the former merchants' commodity exchange (*lonja*), adapted in the eighteenth century to house the remarkable **Archivo de Indias**, a monumental storehouse of the archives of the Spanish empire. Following a three-year restoration programme the archive (holding around 38,000 documents and files covering four centuries of Spanish rule) has been moved around the corner to the Cilla Cabildo on Calle Tormes, revealing Herrera's masterpiece in all its splendour. The exterior is defined by four identical facades, with corner pyramids supporting weather vanes. Inside, the sumptuous marble floors, bookcases in Cuban wood, arcaded central patio and grand staircase in pink and black marble are a visual feast. The upper floor houses temporary exhibitions of interesting documents from the archive; these frequently include items such as Columbus's log and a letter from Cervantes (pre-*Don Quixote*) petitioning the king for a position in the Americas – fortunately for world literature, he was turned down.

Alcázar

Daily: April–Sept 9.30am–7pm; Oct–March 9.30am–5pm • Charge, buy tickets online through the website to avoid long queues and arrive 15mins before scheduled time of visit • ⓦ alcazarsevilla.org

Rulers of Seville occupied the site of the **Alcázar** from the time of the Romans. The fortified palace was probably founded in the eighth century on the ruins of a Roman barracks, with the surrounding walls being added in the ninth. In the eleventh century it was expanded to become the great court of the **Abbadid** dynasty, who turned the wealth gained from the production of olive oil, sugar cane and dyes into a palace worthy of their hubris. This regime reached a peak of sophistication and decadence under the ruthless al Mu'tamid, a ruler who further enlarged the Alcázar in order

---

WHO WILL BUY MY BEAUTIFUL ORANGES?

Sevillanos love to tell each other stories of seeing tourists picking oranges from trees in the streets of Seville only to spit out their first mouthful. These oranges, which are actually very bitter in taste, were originally planted there by the Arabs. Because of the lack of carbon fuel in the area, the skins of these fruits were ground down for powder and used as **explosives**. Notoriously cheeky, the Sevillians purportedly sold a boatload of these oranges to the British, who thinking they were sweet, dug in on the journey home. Though they found to have been tricked by the Spanish, the bitter orange (*Citrus aurantium*) cured the scurvy of the seamen on board. And so **marmalade** was born. Each year workers from the Seville town hall harvest 150,000 tonnes of fruit from the city's forty thousand trees, the best of which is then shipped off to British marmalade factories. In recent years though, the amount exported has fallen due to contamination of the fruit by the city's traffic fumes and changing tastes in Britain. Increasingly, the unsold, inferior and contaminated oranges are turned into fertilizer.

to house a harem of eight hundred women, and decorated the terraces with flowers planted in the skulls of his decapitated enemies. Later, in the twelfth and thirteenth centuries under the **Almohads**, the complex was turned into a citadel, forming the heart of the town's fortifications. Its extent was enormous, stretching to the Torre del Oro on the bank of the Guadalquivir. Parts of the Almohad walls survive, but the present structure dates almost entirely from the Christian period following the fall of the city in 1248.

Seville was a favoured residence of the Spanish kings for some four centuries after the *Reconquista* – most particularly of **Pedro the Cruel** (Pedro I, 1350–69) who, with his mistress María de Padilla, lived in and ruled from the Alcázar. Pedro embarked upon a complete rebuilding of the palace, utilizing fragments of earlier Moorish buildings in Seville, Córdoba and Valencia. Pedro's works form the nucleus of the Alcázar as it is today and, despite numerous restorations necessitated by fires and earth tremors, offer some of the best surviving examples of Mudéjar architecture – the style developed by Moors working under Christian rule.

Later monarchs have also left many traces and additions. In the **fifteenth century** Isabel built a new wing in which to organize expeditions to the Americas and control the new territories; in the sixteenth century Carlos V married a Portuguese princess in the palace, adding huge apartments for the occasion; and under Felipe IV (c.1624) extensive renovations were carried out to the existing rooms. On a more mundane level, kitchens were installed to provide for General Franco, who stayed in the royal apartments whenever he visited Seville.

ESSENTIALS ALCÁZAR

Visiting the Alcázar The pressure of visitors to the Alcázar has resulted in the introduction of a flow-control system whereby 750 people are allowed in every 20–30min. It's still advisable, however, to visit in the early morning or late afternoon to savour the experience in relative calm.

Guidebooks An official guidebook to the complex is

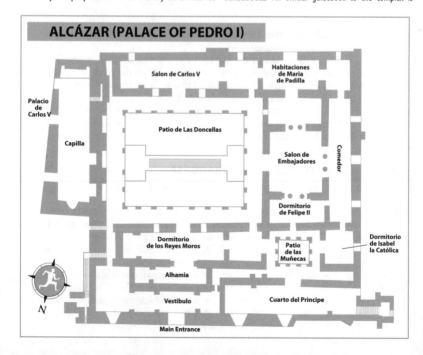

ALCÁZAR (PALACE OF PEDRO I)

Palacio de Carlos V

Salon de Carlos V

Habitaciones de Maria de Padilla

Capilla

Patio de Las Doncellas

Salon de Embajadores

Comedor

Dormitorio de Felipe II

Dormitorio de los Reyes Moros

Patio de las Muñecas

Dormitorio de Isabel la Católica

Alhamia

Cuarto del Principe

Vestibulo

N

Main Entrance

on sale at the gift shop in the Apeadero (see page 256) near the exit (there's a short cut to it from the Patio de la Montería – ask a guardian) or a smaller shop opposite the ticket office at the entrance; the guide has detailed maps of the palaces and information on the gardens beyond.

Patio del León

The Alcázar is entered from the Plaza del Triunfo, adjacent to the cathedral, through the **Puerta del León**, which bears a heraldic image of a lion in fourteenth-century glazed tiles above the lintel. The gateway, flanked by original Almohad walls, opens onto a courtyard – the **Patio del León** – where Pedro (who was known as "the Just" as well as "the Cruel", depending on one's fortunes) used to give judgement; to the left is the Sala de Justicia built by Alfonso XI in the 1340s with exquisite *yesería* (plasterwork) in the Grenadine style and a beautiful *artesonado* ceiling. Beyond, the restored **Patio del Yeso** is the only visible surviving remnant of the Almohads' *alcázar*, with more fine plasterwork.

Patio de la Montería

The main facade of Pedro's palace stands at the end of the **Patio de la Montería**, or "hunting patio", where the royal hunt gathered; on either side are galleried buildings erected by Isabel. This principal facade is pure fourteenth-century Mudéjar and, with its delicate, marble-columned windows, stalactite frieze and overhanging roof, is one of the finest features of the whole Alcázar. The castles, lions and other heraldic devices were intended to emphasize the king's power over both Christians and Muslims, but Kufic lettering still proclaims that "There is no God but Allah".

Salón del Almirante

It's a good idea to look round the **Salón del Almirante** (or Casa de la Contratación de Indias), the sixteenth-century building on the right, before entering the main palace. Founded by Isabel in 1503 as an office where personnel could be hired to man expeditions to the New World, this gives you a standard against which to assess the Moorish forms. Many of the early voyages were planned in the first room, the Cuarto del Almirante, a name that commemorates Columbus's appointment as Gran Almirante (Senior Admiral), although he probably never used it. Balboa, who discovered the Pacific, Vincente Pinzón, who discovered the Amazon, and many other *conquistadors* all spread their maps across tables here and planned the plunder of the Americas. Most of the rooms seem too heavy, their decoration ceasing to be an integral part of the design, and much of the time many of them are closed to public view – as is the whole of the upper floor (except for periodic visits), which provides the residence of the royal family when staying in Seville.

The only notable exception, architecturally speaking, is the **Sala de Audiencias** (or Capilla de los Navigantes), with its magnificent *artesonado* ceiling inlaid with golden rosettes. Within is a fine early sixteenth-century retablo by Alejo Fernández depicting the Virgin of the Navigators spreading her protective mantle over the *conquistadors* and their ships – which are so well portrayed that they have been of great assistance to naval historians. Columbus (dressed in gold) is flanked by the Pinzón brothers, who sailed with him on his first voyage to the New World, while Carlos V (in a red cloak) shelters beneath the Virgin. In the rear to the left are the kneeling figures of the Indians to whom the dubious blessings of Christianity had been brought by the Spanish conquest. The painting synthesizes the sense of a divine mission – given to Spain by God – prevalent at the time. Slightly further along the patio to the right lies the entrance to the **Sala de los Azulejos**, containing a display of relatively modern tilework and, beyond, a couple of delightfully serene patios.

3

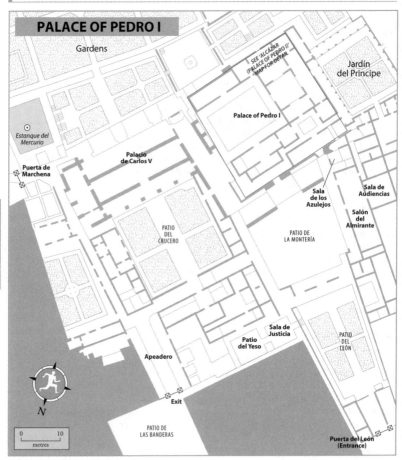

Palacio Real Alto

Daily 10am–1.30pm; 30min guided tours (charge) take place every 30min

The royal apartments, known as the **Palacio Real Alto**, are open for visits when not in use and shouldn't be missed. Tours take in the **royal chapel**, with an exquisite early sixteenth-century retablo consisting of painted *azulejos* (tiles) by Nicola Pisano, the so-called bedroom of Pedro I, with fine early Mudéjar plasterwork and *artesonado* ceiling, and the equally splendid Sala de Audiencias – with more stunning plaster and tile decoration – which is still used by the royal family when receiving visitors in Seville.

Palace of Pedro I

As you enter the main **Palace of Pedro I**, the "domestic" nature of Moorish and Mudéjar architecture is immediately striking. This involves no loss of grandeur but simply a shift in scale: the apartments are remarkably small, shaped to human needs, and take their beauty from the exuberance of the decoration and the imaginative use of space and light. There is, too, a deliberate disorientation in the layout of the rooms, which makes the palace seem infinitely larger and more open than it really is.

Patio de las Doncellas

From the entrance court a narrow passage leads beyond the **Vestíbulo**, where visitors removed their outer clothing, straight into the central courtyard, the **Patio de las Doncellas** (Patio of the Maidens), its name recalling the Christians' tribute of one hundred virgins presented annually to the Moorish kings. The heart of the patio has been restored to its original fourteenth-century state after being buried under a tiled pavement for four centuries. Archeologists have replanted the six orange trees that once grew in sunken gardens to either side of a central pool, filled with goldfish – as it was in the time of Pedro I – a medieval method of eliminating mosquitoes in summer. The court's plaster frieze and dado composed of polychrome *azulejos* and doors are all of the highest Granada craftsmanship, and are the finest in the palace. Interestingly, it's also the one location where Renaissance restorations are successfully fused – the double columns and upper storey were added by Carlos V, whose *Plus Ultra* ("Yet still further") motto recurs in the decorations here and elsewhere.

Salón de Embajadores

Beyond the **Salón de Carlos V**, distinguished by a truly magnificent *artesonado* ceiling, are three rooms from the original fourteenth-century design built for María de Padilla (who was popularly thought to use magic in order to maintain her hold over Pedro – and perhaps over other gallants at court, too, who used to drink her bath water). These open onto the **Salón de Embajadores** (Salon of the Ambassadors), the most brilliant room of the Alcázar, with a stupendous wooden dome of red, green and gold cells, and horseshoe arcades inspired by the great palace of Medina Azahara outside Córdoba. An inscription in Arabic states that it was constructed by craftsmen from Toledo and completed in 1366. Although restored, for the worse, by Carlos V – who added balconies and an incongruous frieze of royal portraits to commemorate his marriage to Isabel of Portugal here – the salon stands comparison with the great rooms of Granada's Alhambra. Note also the original Mudéjar tiles, with their Moorish geometric patterns expressing artistically the fundamental Islamic tenet of the harmony of creation. Adjoining are a long dining hall (*comedor*) and a small apartment installed in the late sixteenth century for Felipe II.

Patio de las Muñecas

Beyond the Salón de Embajadores is the last great room of the palace, the **Patio de las Muñecas** (Patio of the Dolls), which takes its curious name from two tiny faces decorating the inner and outer surfaces of one of the smaller arches. The elegant columns in the tenth-century Caliphate style are believed to have come from the ruins of Medina Azahara near Córdoba. Thought to be the site of the harem in the original palace, it was here that Pedro is reputed to have murdered his brother Don Fadrique in 1358; another of his royal guests, Abu Said of Granada, was murdered here for his jewels, one of which – an immense spinel which Pedro later gave to Edward, England's "Black Prince" – now figures in the British Crown Jewels. The upper storey of the court is a much later, nineteenth-century restoration. On the other sides of the patio are the bedrooms of Isabel and of her son Don Juan, and the arbitrarily named Dormitorio de los Reyes Moros (Bedroom of the Moorish Kings).

Palacio de Carlos V

To the northeast of the main palace (and reached via a stairway out of the southeast corner of the Patio de las Doncellas) loom the large and soulless apartments of the **Palacio de Carlos V**. With its many tapestries (eighteenth-century copies of the sixteenth-century originals now in Madrid) and pink-orange or yellow paintwork, the apartments' classical style asserts a different and inferior mood to the main palace.

3

Alcázar gardens

The beautiful and relaxing **Alcázar gardens** are the rambling but enticing product of several eras. Here are the vaulted **baths** in which María de Padilla was supposed to have bathed (actually an auxiliary water supply for the palace), and the **Estanque del Mercurio**, a pool with a bronze figure of the messenger of the gods at its centre, specially built for Felipe V (1733), who whiled away two solitary years at the Alcázar fishing here and preparing himself for death through religious flagellation. In the gardens proper – and close to an unusual maze of myrtle bushes – lies the pavilion (*pabellón*) of Carlos V, the only survivor of several he built in the gardens. This one, designed by Juan Hernández, was completed in 1543 and has the king's motto, *Plus Ultra*, displayed on the tiles of the steps leading to the pavilion's entrance.

The gardens are a spacious and tranquil haven – filled with birdsong and the cries of resident peacocks – to escape the crowds; particularly the **Jardín Inglés** on the southwest side, which would make an ideal place for a picnic. A *cafetería* can be reached via the Puerta de Marchena, to the left of the Estanque del Mercurio, which has a pleasant terrace overlooking the gardens.

The way out is via the **Apeadero**, a large coach hall built for Philip V in the eighteenth century, which housed not only the coaches used by the royals, but also legions of servants who slept on the floor. Beyond lies the impressive **Patio de las Banderas** (Patio of the Flags) edged with orange trees and until fairly recently the parade ground of the military barracks surrounding it, now luxury apartments. The flags of the various regiments were assembled here and reviewed by the king prior to battle. Exit from this square to the street, where you emerge on the edge of the Barrio Santa Cruz.

Plaza de San Francisco

North of the cathedral, the **Plaza de San Francisco** takes its name from the great monastery that once covered much of this square and Plaza Nueva to the west. During the Semana Santa processions the plaza forms part of the part of the official route leading to the cathedral, and huge temporary grandstands fill the square providing prime vantage points for the city's dignitaries and their families and friends. The pointed *capirote* hoods worn by the penitent brotherhoods are eerily identical to those worn by the inquisitors of the Spanish Inquisition who, between the fifteenth and eighteenth centuries, sentenced an untold number of "heretics" to death by burning in public *autos-da-fé*, or trials, held in this same square.

Ayuntamiento

Pza de San Francisco • Guided visits Mon–Thurs 5pm & 7.30pm, Sat 10am; closed Aug • Charge • ☎ 902 559 386

The sixteenth-century **Ayuntamiento** is well worth a visit, with a richly ornamented Plateresque facade by Diego de Riaño, one of the finest in Spain. Substantially enlarged early in the nineteenth century, the building's western exterior, facing Plaza Nueva, dates entirely from this time and forgoes the exuberant decoration of the original. The interior – decorated with numerous artworks including canvases by Zurbarán and Murillo – features Riaño's star-vaulted *vestíbulo* (entrance hall), the elaborately ornate Sala de Consistorio (council chamber) and an upper Sala de Consistorio above it, with a ravishing gilded coffered ceiling dating from the time of Philip II.

Barrio Santa Cruz

The city's Jewish quarter until the Alhambra Decree of 1492, the **Barrio Santa Cruz** is very much in character with Seville's romantic image. Its streets are narrow and tortuous to keep out the sun, the houses brilliantly whitewashed and festooned with flowering plants. Many of the windows are barricaded with *rejas* (iron grilles), behind

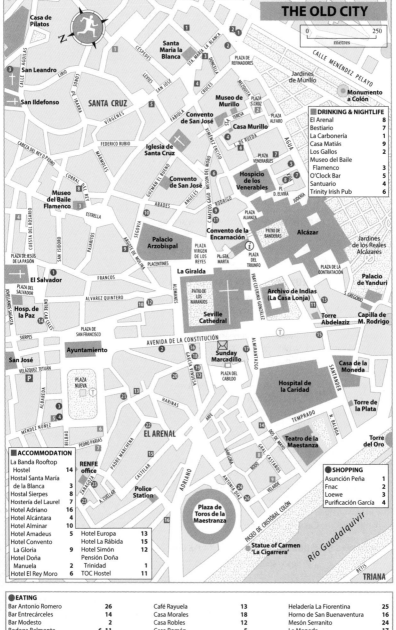

THE OLD CITY

0 — 250 metres

DRINKING & NIGHTLIFE

El Arenal	8
Bestiario	7
La Carbonería	1
Casa Matías	9
Los Gallos	2
Museo del Baile Flamenco	3
O'Clock Bar	5
Santuario	4
Trinity Irish Pub	6

ACCOMMODATION

La Banda Rooftop Hostel	14
Hostal Santa María de la Blanca	3
Hostal Sierpes	8
Hostería del Laurel	7
Hotel Adriano	16
Hotel Alcántara	4
Hotel Alminar	10
Hotel Amadeus	5
Hotel Convento La Gloria	9
Hotel Doña Manuela	2
Hotel El Rey Moro	6
Hotel Europa	13
Hotel La Rábida	15
Hotel Simón	12
Pensión Doña Trinidad	1
TOC Hostel	11

SHOPPING

Asunción Peña	1
Fnac	2
Loewe	3
Purificación García	4

EATING

Bar Antonio Romero	26	Café Rayuela	13	Heladería La Fiorentina	25
Bar Entrecárceles	14	Casa Morales	18	Horno de San Buenaventura	16
Bar Modesto	2	Casa Robles	12	Mesón Serranito	24
Bodega Belmonte	6, 11	Casa Román	5	La Moneda	17
Bodega de Juan García Aviles	9	Cervecería Internacional	21	Puerta de la Carne	1
Bodega Paco Gongora	22	Convento de San Leandro	3	Taberna Coloniales II	20
Bodega Santa Cruz (aka Las Columnas)	8	Corral del Agua	7	Taberna del Alabardero	23
Bodeguita Casablanca	15	Duplex	10	Las Teresas	4
		Freiduría La Isla	19		

A WALK AROUND THE BARRIO SANTA CRUZ

The Barrio Santa Cruz is a great place for a stroll. Starting out from **Plaza Virgen de los Reyes**, behind the cathedral, the **Palacio Arzobispal** (free access to the patio if open) conceals, behind a Baroque facade, a remarkable staircase made entirely of jasper. Along Calle Mateos Gago, **Bar Giralda** at no. 2 incorporates part of a Moorish *hammam* (steam baths), while over the road and up a bit, at no. 20, is one of Seville's institutions, the hole-in-the-wall **bodega of Juan García Aviles** (see page 281) with its prized gleaming bar counter of Spanish mahogany, well over a century old and one of the few remaining in the city.

When you've downed a *manzanilla*, continue east and turn right into Calle Mesón del Moro where *San Marco* at no.6 is a popular fine dining restaurant operating inside a Moorish bathhouse. Further up Mateos Gago, a left turn will bring you into Calle Guzmán El Bueno where, at no. 10, the charming sisters at the **Convento de San José** will allow you to view (outside siesta period; free, but a small contribution is appreciated) some stunning Mudéjar plaster decoration (on a par with the Alcázar) in what was the salon, and is now the chapel, of this former fourteenth-century palace. There are some lovely **patios** – take a look at no. 4, with its plants, *azulejos*, wall-mounted bulls' heads and Roman statuary.

Retracing your steps and following Calle Mesón del Moro will bring you – via Calle Ximénez de Enciso (a left and then a right) – to Calle Santa Teresa where, at no. 8, is **Casa Murillo**. Located in the artist's seventeenth-century home, this museum is furnished with contemporaneous art, craftsmanship and furniture, but, sadly, none of his original paintings.

PLAZA SANTA CRUZ AND SANTA MARÍA LA BLANCA

Continuing along Calle Santa Teresa – note the old grindstones sunk into the wall on the left – will bring you to the delightful **Plaza Santa Cruz** where, until the French burned it down in 1810, stood the church which gave the square (and the *barrio*) its name and in which Murillo was buried. The French consulate appears to see no irony in occupying a building directly overlooking the scene of Napoleonic devastation. The attractive seventeenth-century **cross**, circled by rose bushes, marks the centre of the original church and was placed here when the plaza was created in 1918.

Heading east along *calles* Mezquita and Doncellas brings you to the ancient Gothic-Baroque church of **Santa María la Blanca** (Mon–Fri 10am–1pm & 6–8pm; free), on the street of the same name, which has, built into its south wall in Calle de los Archeros, the entrance to the original synagogue, the only surviving architectural remnant of the Jewish quarter. The church's main portal is flanked by Visigothic columns probably from a church predating both the synagogue and the Moorish period, while the interior has lots of *azulejos* from Triana as well as an extravagant filigree stucco ceiling and two artistic gems: a moving *piedad* (pietà) by the sixteenth-century artist Luís de Vargas, and a fine Santa Cena (*Last Supper*) by Murillo, the latter a rare tenebrist work. For reasons of security, both works are displayed in the nearby church of San Nicolás, 250m north along the same street.

In the next street along from the church on the right heading north, tiny Callejon Dos Hermanas has, at no. 7, the **Casas de la Judería** hotel – a restored *casa señorial*, with a fine patio and bar.

JARDINES DE MURILLO AND THE PLAZA DE LOS VENERABLES

An alternative route heads south from Plaza de Santa Cruz to the **Jardines de Murillo**, a peaceful oasis to get your breath back among shady arbours decorated with Triana tiles.

You could also head west from the plaza along Callejón del Agua back towards the town centre. here you'll find **Corral del Agua** restaurant (at No.6) on charming **Calle Pimienta**. Turn right onto Calle Gloria to reach the **Plaza de los Venerables** where, if you don't want see the artworks inside the Hospital de los Venerables (see page 259) you could stop at tapas bars: **Hostería del Laurel** and **Casa Román**. Otherwise, heading north and then west along Calle Jamerdana and the Pasaje Vila returns you to Calle Mateos Gago, just before which (on tiny Calle Rodrigo Caro) there's the **Bodega Santa Cruz**, another tapas institution.

which girls once kept chaste evening rendezvous with their *novios* who were forced to *comer hierro* ("eat iron") as passion mounted. Almost all of the houses have patios, often surprisingly large, which in summer become the principal family living room. Most of the time they can be admired from the street beyond the wrought-iron screen inside the doorway, something the residents don't appear to mind.

Hospital de los Venerables

Pza de los Venerables 8 • Mon–Sat 9am–3pm; guided visits every 30min • Charge • ⓦ hospitalvenerables.es

One of the most beautiful patios is within the Baroque **Hospital de los Venerables**, on the northeast side of the Alcázar, originally a home for infirm clerics. Built around the patio, the hospice and church now house an outstanding gallery including sculptures by Martínez Montañés, Pedro and Luisa Roldán, a painting of the *Last Supper* by Lucás Valdés and some wonderfully restored frescoes by the same artist and his son Valdés Leal. The museum is also home to the **Centro Velázquez** which, besides works by the master – including an image of Santa Rufina and a spectacular *Inmaculada Concepción* – displays canvases by Pacheco, Murillo and Zurbarán.

3

South of the cathedral

South of the cathedral stand a number of buildings of note: the **Hotel Alfonso XIII**, the **Palacio de San Telmo** and the **Fábrica de Tabacos**, the city's old tobacco factory and the setting for Bizet's *Carmen*. Further south, but still just ten minutes from the Giralda, lies the **Plaza de España** and adjoining **Parque de María Luisa** – laid out in 1929 for a gargantuan "Fair of the Americas", these are among the most impressive public spaces in Spain. Within the park the **Museo Arqueológico** houses Andalucía's most important archeological collection.

Hotel Alfonso XIII

C/San Fernando 2 • Daily • Free

The **Hotel Alfonso XIII**, Seville's grandest, is worth a look inside – no one minds as long as you aren't dressed too outrageously. Named after the ill-starred monarch Alfonso XIII who was forced to abdicate soon afterwards, it was built to house important guests attending the 1929 exhibition, and an elegant neo-Baroque facade conceals one of the city's most beautiful patios, best enjoyed over a beer or afternoon tea.

Palacio de San Telmo

Avda de Roma s/n • Tours Thurs, Sat & Sun (must be booked in advance) • Free • ☎ 955 001010

Slightly west of the *Hotel Alfonso XIII*, the **Palacio de San Telmo**, built as a marine training academy for the Indies fleet and completed in 1734, is another expression of Seville's full-tilt Baroque period. During the mid-nineteenth century, it was purchased by the dukes of Montpensier, a member of whose family – the dowager duchess María Luisa – in 1893 presented part of the palace's vast grounds to the city, which became the park now named after her. The palace's main facade overlooks Avenida de Roma and has a marvellous Churrigueresque entrance arch topped – in a central niche – by San Telmo (of St Elmo's fire fame), patron saint of navigators. The building fell into a ruinous state in the latter part of the twentieth century and a five-year refurbishment was completed in 2010. The building now houses the office of the President of the Junta de Andalucía (the region's autonomous government) and other regional government departments. Inside, highlights include two beautiful pillared patios, marble staircases and a church with an exquisite painted cupola.

Santa María de Jesús

Puerta de Jerez s/n • Open service times Mon–Sat 7pm, Sun 11.30am • Free

CARMEN

Completed in 1875, Bizet's opera **Carmen** was a worldwide success in the first quarter of the last century when it was performed on both sides of the Atlantic. The opera tells the story of a beautiful and sensual *gitana* (gypsy), who falls in love with Don José, a corporal, who deserts his regiment to join her band of smugglers. When Carmen tires of him and transfers her affections to the *toreador* Escamillo, an insanely jealous Don José stabs her to death outside the bullring where a statue of "Carmen" now stands. Though a fictional story, legions of foreign travellers later made pilgrimages to Seville in search of their own Carmen. The disillusion of the 1930s Irish traveller Walter Starkie was typical: he said that he had never seen "an uglier collection of women in my life", and was then hounded out of the workshops with a chorus of obscene abuse.

Near the Palacio de San Telmo, on the northeast side of the Puerta de Jerez road junction – a name referring to its former importance as one of the twenty gates in the city's ancient walls – on the corner of Calle San Gregorio, lies the small former mosque and now chapel of **Santa María de Jesús**. Converted into a Christian church in 1248, it was frequently visited by Columbus on his trips to the city. The interior contains some elegant Gothic vaulting, an impressive *artesonado* ceiling and an outstanding early sixteenth-century retablo by Alejo Fernández.

Antigua Fábrica de Tabacos

Sept–June Mon–Sat 8am–9pm & Sat 8am–2pm • Free

The **Antigua Fábrica de Tabacos**, or Old Tobacco Factory, just behind the *Hotel Alfonso XIII* along Avenida San Fernando, was where Carmen – in the nineteenth-century story by Mérimée, made into an opera by Bizet – worked as a cigar maker (see box, page 260).

Now part of the university and only open during term time, this massive structure – 250m long by 180m wide – was built in the 1750s and still retains its position as the largest building in Spain after El Escorial in Madrid. Above the main entrance – facing Calle San Fernando – perches a marble angel, a trumpet to its lips, which malicious popular legend had it would only sound when a virgin entered the factory for the first time. The entrance arch below aptly incorporates medallion busts of Columbus (discoverer of the tobacco lands) and Cortés (reputedly Europe's first smoker) – in effect the factory's founding fathers.

The building was divided into residential quarters below with the work areas on the upper – and lighter – level. The entrance leads through a vestibule into the Clock Patio (with fountain), off which is a cafetería. At its peak in the nineteenth century the factory was also the country's largest single employer, with a workforce of some ten thousand women *cigarreras* (cigarette makers) – "a class in themselves" according to Richard Ford and forced to undergo "an ingeniously minute search on leaving their work, for they sometimes carry off the filthy weed in a manner her most Catholic majesty never dreamt of". Production of cigars, cigarettes and snuff – originally ground by two hundred donkey-driven rolling mills – continued here until 1965 when its operations were moved to a new factory across the river close to the Puente de Los Remedios.

Plaza de España

The **Plaza de España** lies beyond the Avenida del Cid – the latter, incidentally, the site of the Inquisition's *quemadero*, or burning platform, where for three hundred years convicted heretics were put to death; the last "witch" was burned here in 1781.

The vast semicircular complex was designed as the centrepiece of the Spanish Americas Fair, which was somewhat scuppered by the Wall Street Crash abroad and political upheavals at home. Designed by Anibal González with theatrical towers, sprinkling fountains, majestic stairways and masses of brick and tile work, its flamboyance would seem strange in most Spanish cities but here it looks entirely natural, carrying on the great tradition of civic display. At the fair, the Plaza de España was used for the Spanish exhibit of industry and crafts, and around the crescent are *azulejo* scenes and maps of each of the provinces: an interesting record of the country at the tail-end of a moneyed era. After falling into disrepair in the latter part of the twentieth century, an expensive renovation has made it once more one of the city's major architectural sights. Locals and tourists alike again come out to the plaza to sit on the many benches or potter about in the little boats rented out on its tiny strip of canal.

Parque de María Luisa
Avda de la Palmera s/n • Daily 8am–midnight • Free

The **Parque de María Luisa**, which adjoins the Plaza de España, is a favourite haven for *sevillanos*. With its tree-shaded avenues, ornamental pools and decorative bridges and follies, it is just the place to linger for an hour or two to escape the heat of the city's summer afternoons. The park is designed, like the plaza, in a mix of 1920s Art Deco and mock-Mudéjar. Scattered about, and round its edge, are more buildings from the fair, some of them amazingly opulent, built in the last months before the Wall Street Crash undercut the scheme's impetus.

3

Museo Arqueológico
Pza de América s/n • June–Sept Tues–Sat 9am–3pm; Oct–May Tues–Sat 9am–8pm, Sun 9am–3pm • Charge • ☎ 955 120 632

Towards the southern end of Parque de María Luisa, the grandest mansions from the Spanish Americas Fair have been adapted into museums, of which the **Museo Arqueológico** is the most important of its kind in Andalucía. The collection's wide remit, divided among 27 rooms on three floors, spans the period from prehistory to the end of the Moorish age. At the time of writing it was closed for renovation, but without a clear date set to reopen. Check online for current status before going.

Basement and ground floor
Starting in the basement with the prehistoric sections, Room 4 displays a collection of funerary stelae from the Iberian period. The rooms on the ground floor contain the substance of the **Roman collection**, with an interesting display of kitchen equipment in Room 13. The same room also has a fine third-century mosaic from Écija depicting the god Bacchus being transported on a chariot drawn by tigers. In Room 17 there's a sensitive, second-century sculpture of Venus from Itálica, which was imported from Greece.

There's yet more statuary in rooms 19 and 20, as well as portrait busts of the emperors Augustus and Nero and local boys Trajan and Hadrian, the latter particularly striking. In a small room off Room 19 you'll find a number of remarkable **bronze plaques** inscribed with the "Lex Irnitana", a rare set of laws illustrating how the Romans – the inventors of jurisprudence – went about ruling their empire. The laws make a fascinating read but are sadly translated only into Spanish. Rubric 72 of the code deals with the freeing of public slaves while number 82 relates to the upkeep of roads, tracks, irrigation channels, drains and sewers, all vital to the Roman way of life. The laws are sanctioned by the despotic emperor Domitian, whose name appears at the end of the document dated April 10, 91 AD. A portrait bust of Domitian is displayed in Room 20.

Finally, rooms 26 and 27 display **post-Roman finds** including early Christian tombstones and Mudéjar ceramic works, among which a fifteenth-century green-glazed baptismal font stands out.

Upper floor

A lift to the upper floor brings you to the new Sala de Carambolo, dedicated to displaying the stunning **Carambolo Treasures** discovered in the Seville suburb of Camas in 1958. This remarkable hoard of gold jewellery dating from the eighth century BC was at first thought to have originated in Tartessus and fuelled the debate surrounding the whereabouts and existence of the ancient land of Tartessus, known to the Greeks and mentioned in the Bible as Tarshish. However, new research in addition to the discovery at the site of an eighth-century BC bronze statuette of **Astarte-Tanit** (also displayed here), the Phoenician fertility goddess, has led scholars to believe that the jewellery belonged to a Phoenician sanctuary. Information boards give background on the legendary mineral wealth of Tartessus, the trading relationships of the Tartessians with the Phoenicians and later Greeks, and the likely whereabouts of this land. Current knowledge indicates a location in the area between Seville and the mineral-rich hills of Huelva, but despite investigations by archeologists for most of the last hundred or so years it has never been found.

Museo de Costumbres Populares

Pza de América s/n • June–Sept Tues–Sat 9am–3pm; Oct–May Tues–Sat 9am–8pm, Sun 9am–3pm • Charge • ☎ 955 035 325

Opposite the archeological museum is the fabulous-looking **Museo de Costumbres Populares** (Popular Arts Museum) with, inside, an equally fine patio, which despite displays of costumes, implements, furniture, textiles, photos and posters describing life in eighteenth- and nineteenth-century Andalucía, feels a bit lifeless. The basement ceramics displays are the highlight, illustrating the regional developments of this craft inherited from the Moors. In spring there are also special exhibitions devoted to Semana Santa and the April *feria*.

Río Guadalquivir east bank

The **Río Guadalquivir** is Seville's historic artery, and a number of important monuments and museums are to be found along or close to its banks, including the Moorish **Torre del Oro** and the **Maestranza** bullring, second in prestige only to Madrid's Las Ventas. Very few swim in this river, as its slow current means it verges closer to being a stagnant than clean body of water, but you can take in the riverside sights on a scenic **boat tour** (see page 275) or by renting your own pedalo or kayak.

Torre del Oro and the naval museum

Paseo de Cristóbal Colón s/n • **Naval museum** Mon–Fri 9.30am–6.45pm, Sat & Sun 10.30am–6.45pm • Charge, free on Mon • ☎ 954 222 419

On the Río Guadalquivir to the west of the Alcázar, the main riverside landmark is the twelve-sided **Torre del Oro** (Tower of Gold), built by the Almohads in 1220 as part of the Alcázar fortifications. It was connected to another small fort across the river by a chain which had to be broken by the Castilian fleet before their conquest of the city in 1248. The tower later saw use as a repository for the gold brought back to Seville from the Americas; hence its name. It now houses a small **naval museum**, which exhibits charts and engravings of the port in its prime.

Hospital de la Caridad

Entrance on C/Temprado 3 • Daily 10.30am–7.30pm • Charge, includes audio guide • ⓦ santa-caridad.es

One block east of the Torre del Oro is the **Hospital de la Caridad**, founded in 1674 by Don Miguel de Mañara, who may well have been the inspiration for Byron's Don Juan. According to the testimony of one of Don Miguel's friends, "there was no folly which he did not commit, no youthful indulgence into which he did not plunge ... (until) what occurred to him in the street of the coffin". What occurred was that Don Miguel, returning from a wild orgy, had a vision in which he was confronted by a funeral procession carrying his own corpse. He repented his past life, joined the Brotherhood of Charity (whose task was to bury the bodies of vagrants and criminals), and later set up this hospital for the relief of the dying and destitute, for which it is still used. Touchingly, whenever a patient dies here, the chapel is closed on the day of the funeral.

Between 1670 and 1674 Don Miguel commissioned a series of eleven paintings by Murillo for the chapel, seven of which remain after Marshal Soult looted four of them during the Napoleonic occupation. Murillo always created pictures "made to measure" for the available light, and it's a real treat to see the pictures in the place they were originally intended to hang. Among the surviving works are a colossal *Loaves and Fishes* depicting Christ feeding the Five Thousand, and "a *San Juan de Dios* equal to Rembrandt" as Richard Ford, a fervent Murillo fan, described it. Mañara himself posed as the model for the saint. Alongside them hang two *Triumph of Death*s by Valdés Leal. One, portraying the fleeting nature of life, features a skeletal image of Death pointing to the message *in ictu oculi* ("in the blink of an eye"), while the other depicts a decomposing bishop being eaten by worms (beneath the scales of justice labelled *Ni más, Ni menos* – "No More, No Less"). Murillo found this so repulsive that he declared "you have to hold your nose to look at it". The mood of both works may owe a lot to the vivid memory of the 1649 plague that killed almost half the population of the city. The main altar's retablo features a superlative *Burial of Christ* carved by Pedro Roldán, and the steps to the left of this descend to a crypt where Mañara is buried.

As you're leaving the Caridad, step inside the private car park and look across to the **Torre de la Plata** (Tower of Silver), a castellated Moorish watchtower, at C/Santander 13. It probably got its name to correspond with the nearby Torre del Oro, although there is no evidence to suggest that it was once coated with silver tiles or was ever a silver store, as local legends have it.

Plaza de Toros de la Maestranza and around

Paseo de Cristóbal Colón 12 • Tours daily: 9.30am–9.30pm; fight days 9.30am–3.30pm • Charge, entrance by guided tour only (available in English) • ⓦ realmaestranza.com

The **Plaza de Toros de la Maestranza** is the most famous and, for aficionados, the most beautiful bullring in the world. It was completed in the latter half of the eighteenth century to provide a home for the Real Maestranza de Caballería (Royal Equestrian Society). Subsequently altered, it is still one of the finest in Spain and has featured in numerous novels, poems and films – and most enduringly in Bizet's *Carmen*. Once inside the arena, you will see a metal frame in the roof holding a furled canvas. On fight days this is unfurled – not to give spectators more shade but to temper the wind, which often whips over the river causing the capes of the *matadores* to behave in unpredictable and possibly dangerous ways. The Maestranza's museum has the usual posters, prints, photographs and memorabilia. A monument to "Carmen" (see box, page 260) stands opposite the entrance to the bullring, across the road near the river.

Three blocks downriver – with a dome that's hard to miss – is the **Teatro de la Maestranza** concert hall and opera house. Built as part of the Expo 92 improvements, it incorporates the remains of the Artillería ammunition works that previously occupied the site. The rather dominating and uninspired design caused much controversy when it was unveiled because of its detrimental effect on the magnificent view of the city from across the river.

Museo de Bellas Artes

Pza del Museo 9 • June–Sept Tues–Sun 9am–3pm; Oct–May Tues–Sat 9am–8pm, Sun 9am–3pm • Charge

A ten-minute walk north of the Maestranza bullring, and fronted by a formidable bronze statue of Murillo, lies the **Museo de Bellas Artes**. Housed in modernized galleries in a startlingly beautiful former convent, the Convento de la Merced, it ranks second in Spain only to the Prado in Madrid. Founded in the thirteenth century by Fernando III after Seville had been taken from the Moors, the convent was subsequently remodelled and reached its present form in the eighteenth century, although it lost most of its own commissioned paintings during the nineteenth-century Disentailment when it was secularized, and it opened as a museum in 1838. Be aware that the museum has a policy of rotating its collection and not all the works mentioned here may be exhibited. A Sunday morning **art market** (8am–12pm) takes place in the plaza fronting the museum, where local artists and craftspeople sell their work.

Downstairs galleries

Among the highlights of an outstanding collection is a wonderful late fifteenth-century painted terracotta sculpture in Room 1, *Lamentation over the Dead Christ*, by the *andaluz* **Pedro Millán**, founding father of the Seville school of sculpture. A marriage of Gothic and expressive naturalism, this style was the starting point for the outstanding seventeenth-century period of religious iconography in Seville – a later example, in Room 2, is a magnificent *San Jerónimo* by the Italian **Pietro Torrigiano**, who spent the latter years of his life in Seville. Ever his own man, Torrigiano once broke the nose of his contemporary Michelangelo in a quarrel and eventually died at the hands of the Inquisition in Seville, condemned for impiety after he had smashed his own sculpture of the Virgin when the duke of Arcos refused to pay the price asked. His *Virgen de Belén* here is another powerful work. This room also has **El Greco**'s portrait of his son, Jorge Manuel Theotokopoulos.

Room 3 has a retablo of the *Redemption*, c.1562, with fine woodcarving by **Juan Giralte**. Originally made for the Convento de Santa Catalina in Aracena, tableaux 6 (the crowning with thorns) and 10 (Mark writing his gospel) are especially fine. Here also is displayed the grisly terracotta sculpture of the severed head of John the Baptist by **Núñez Delgado**, not something you want to see too soon after lunch. Dated 1591, this work is a prototype of the Baroque images later carried on the *pasos* during Semana Santa.

Room 4 has works by **Pacheco**, one of the protagonists of both the Naturalist and Mannerist school and the father-in-law and tutor of Velázquez. His series of canvases for the Convento de la Merced is represented here by images of San Pedro and San Ramón Nonato. There are also two **Velázquez** works here, produced in his teens: a portrait of Don Cristóbal Suarez de Ribera and *Cabeza del apóstol* (thought to be an image of St Paul). Both betray sure signs of the master's touch as well as an unparalleled ability to illuminate his figures from within.

Beyond a serene patio and cloister containing more Pachecos, Room 5 is located in the monastery's former church. The restored paintings on the vault and dome by the eighteenth-century *sevillano* **Domingo Martínez** are spectacular. Here also is the nucleus of the collection: a monumental *Last Supper* by **Alonso Vásquez** painted for the monastery of La Cartuja and **Zurbarán**'s *Apotheosis of St Thomas Aquinas* stand out, as well as a clutch of **Murillos** in the apse crowned by the great *Immaculate Conception* – known as "*la colosal*" to distinguish it from the other work here with the same name. Below this is the same artist's stunning *Virgin and Child*. Popularly known as *La Servilleta* because it was said to have been painted on a dinner napkin, the work is one of Murillo's greatest. In the same room are more Murillos and also works by the early seventeenth-century *sevillano* **Roelas**, including a magnificent *Martirio de San Andrés*.

Upstairs galleries

Room 6 displays works from the Baroque period, among which a stark *Crucifixión* by Zurbarán stands out. The same artist's luminous *Virgen del Rosario* is also outstanding. Room 7 is devoted to Murillo and his school and has a superb *San Agustín y la Trinidad* by the master. In Room 8, eighteenth-century *sevillano* **Valdés Leal** symbolizes the city's enduring fascination with agony and mortality: his depiction of Fray Juan de Ledesma wrestling with the devil disguised as a serpent has the brooding intensity of much of his work.

MURILLO IN ALL HIS GLORY

Born in Seville in 1618 and orphaned ten years later, **Bartolomé Estebán Murillo** grew up in the home of his brother-in-law. After enrolling as a student under Juan de Castillo he came to the attention of another *sevillano*, Velázquez, who was by then established in Madrid. Murillo studied with Velázquez for three not very happy years in the capital, where he found the social scene oppressive, but was apparently much impressed by the works of the Flemish and Italian schools he saw in the royal collections there.

Once back in his native city Murillo started work in earnest, often using poor *sevillanos* from districts such as La Macarena as his models. In 1682, still at the height of his artistic powers he was painting an altarpiece for the Capuchin church in Cádiz when he fell from the scaffold, suffering serious injury. He was brought back to Seville where he died in the Convent of San José near to his home in the Barrio Santa Cruz.

Downgraded by critics in the nineteenth century for his sentimentalism – a view largely based on the genre paintings of rosy-faced urchins that had found their way across Europe – Murillo's reputation has since been restored. A greater familiarity with the powerful works that remained in Seville, such as those in the Caridad, substantiates Richard Ford's proclamation: "At Sevilla Murillo is to be seen in all his glory ... a giant on his native soil."

Room 9 contains works from the European Baroque, among which there's an outstanding La Adoración de los Pastores (Adoration of the Shepherds) by the Flemish painter Pieter Van Lint and a striking San Sebastian by Ribera – Spain's master of tenebrismo (darkness penetrated by light). In Room 10, there are sculptures by the sixteenth-century genius Martínez Montañés, whose early Saint Dominic in Penitence and San Bruno from his mature period display mastery of technique. Also here are imposing canvases by Zurbarán: San Hugo visiting the Carthusian monks at supper (San Hugo in the Refectory), The Visit of San Bruno to Pope Urban II and the Virgen de los Cartujos were all painted for the monastery of La Cartuja across the river. There's also another almost sculptural crucifixion to compare with his earlier one in Room 6 as well as Niño de la Espina, a portrait of the infant Christ.

The collection ends with works from the Romantic and Modern eras where an austere late work by **Goya**, in Room 11, of the octogenarian *Don José Duaso* compensates for some not terribly inspiring works accompanying it. In Room 13 there's a portrait of the incompetent and indolent ruler Alfonso XIII painted in 1929 by Gonzalo Bilbao, which tells you all you need to know about this monarchical disaster. The same artist has more works in Room 12 – his *Las Cigarreras* is a vivid portrayal of the wretched life of women in the tobacco factory during the early years of the last century. In the same room a monumental canvas by José Villegas Cordero, *La Muerte del Maestro*, depicts the death of a *torero*. Room 13 has an evocative image of *Sevilla en Fiestas* dated 1915 by Gustavo Bacarisas. Finally, in Room 14 there's *Juan Centeño y su cuadrilla* by Huelvan artist Daniel Vásquez Díaz, who worked in Paris and was a friend of Picasso. This stirring image of the *torero* and his team provides an appropriately *andaluz* conclusion to a memorable museum.

El Centro

El Centro, the central zone, lies north of the cathedral at the geographical heart of the city. It contains the main shopping areas, including **Calle Sierpes**, the city's most fashionable street, as well as the Museo de Baile flamenco. Here, too, you'll find many of Seville's finest churches, displaying a fascinating variety of architectural styles. Several are converted mosques with belfries built over their minarets, others range through Mudéjar and Gothic (sometimes in combination), Renaissance and Baroque. Most are kept locked except early in the morning, or in the evenings from about

7 until 10pm – a promising time for a church crawl, especially as they're regularly interspersed with tapas bars.

Casa de Pilatos

Pza de Pilatos 1 • Daily 9am–6pm • Charge • ☎ 954 225 298

Of Seville's numerous mansions, by far the finest is the **Casa de Pilatos** on the Plaza de Pilatos, close to northern edge of the Barrio Santa Cruz. Built by the Marqués de Tarifa of the Ribera family on his return from a pilgrimage to Jerusalem in 1519, the house was popularly – and erroneously – thought to have been an imitation of the house of Pontius Pilate, supposedly seen by the duke on his travels. In fact it's a harmonious mixture of Mudéjar, Gothic and Renaissance styles, featuring brilliant *azulejos*, a tremendous sixteenth-century stairway and the best domestic patios in the city. After the Civil War the dukes of Medinaceli returned to live here and inaugurated a programme of restoration that has gradually brought the house back to its original splendour.

The lower floors

Entering by the **Apeadero**, where the old carriages were boarded, and which for most of the year is a riot of magenta bougainvillea, brings you to a gateway leading into the wonderful **Patio Principal**. Here, Muslim elements such as the irregular arches, plasterwork and glazed tiles combine with Gothic tracery on the upper balustrades and an Italian Renaissance fountain and columns below. The imposing statues in each corner of the patio are classical originals, of which the Athene (bearing a spear) is attributed to the fifth-century BC school of the Greek master, Phidias; the others are Roman. Antique Italian busts of Roman emperors and men of letters such as Trajan, Hadrian and Cicero occupy niches in the arcades.

The **Salón Pretorio** is notable for its coffered ceiling, incorporating the Ribera family's coat of arms. The Roman sculptures – collected in Italy by the sixteenth-century duke of Alcalá – in the nearby Zaquizamí corridor are extremely fine, especially the slumbering Venus and a marble relief fragment, depicting weapons, above. Passing the Jardín Chico (Small Garden), the Chapel of the Flagellation (its central column is supposed to represent the one at which Christ was scourged) and Pilate's "study", you reach the **Jardín Grande**, a verdant oasis with palms, pavilions and a bower, not to mention a wonderful abundance of orange trees. A tradition associated with this garden relates that the first duke of Alcalá obtained from Pope Pius V the ashes of the emperor Trajan (born in nearby Itálica), which were then displayed in a vase in the library. Later, a servant is supposed to have dumped them in the garden thinking the urn to be full of dust. The legend grew that an orange tree sprouted up wherever the ashes had fallen.

The upper floors

The **upper floors** (still partly inhabited by the Medinaceli family) are reached from the Patio Principal via the fine, tiled staircase with a gilded, sixteenth-century semicircular dome, but can be seen only by guided tour (frequent, on an informal basis). The rooms are decorated with various frescoes, canvases by Goya (a tiny bullfighting scene), Ribera and Jordáns and objets d'art collected by the family. Outstanding here is the **Salón de Pacheco** with the *Apotheosis of Hercules* painted on the ceiling in 1603 by the *sevillano* artist after whom the room is named.

San Ildefonso

C/Rodríguez de Marín 4 • Open service times Mon–Sat 7pm, Sun 10am–noon • Free

San Ildefonso is a fourteenth-century church later rebuilt in the classical style. Inside, behind the altar on the north aisle, there's a fresco of the Virgin dating from the original building. The church also has some seventeenth-century wood sculptures by Roldán and a bas-relief, *The Trinity* by Martínez Montañés, dated 1609.

Museo del Baile Flamenco

C/Manuel Rojas Marcos 3 • Daily 11am–6pm • Charge • ⓦ museoflamenco.com

A few minutes' walk to the west of the Casa de Pilatos lies the **Museo del Baile Flamenco**, an innovative and entertaining museum dedicated to the history and evolution of this emblematic *andaluz* art form. Set up in collaboration with celebrated flamenco dancer Cristina Hoyos, the museum is interactive (and multilingual), employing the latest sound and image technology to illustrate the origins of flamenco and the range of dance styles (*palos*). The final section of the museum displays photos of, as well as costumes used by, some flamenco greats. The museum also stages hour-long concerts of flamenco (charge), which bring the art form to life, at a high standard.

Not far away, and heading in a more or less westerly direction, Calle Boteros will bring you to **Plaza Alfalfa**, the site of the forum of Roman Hispalis and a good place for tapas bars.

Los Monolitos Romanos

A couple of blocks south of Plaza Alfalfa are three enormous columns, known as **Los Monolitos Romanos,** which once belonged to what must have been a gigantic Roman temple dating from the second century. There were originally five surviving pillars here but in the nineteenth century two were transferred to the Alameda de Hércules where they now act as plinths for statues of Julius Caesar (who granted the city its first urban statute) and Hercules (mythical creator of Hispalis), the city's "founding fathers".

Plaza del Buen Suceso

Heading north from Plaza Alfalfa, along *calles* Sales y Ferré and Padre Llop will lead you to the **Plaza del Buen Suceso** on which lies the **convent** of the same name. Inside, there's a marvellous sculpture of St Anne with the Virgin by Martínez Montañés.

San Pedro and around

North from Plaza del Buen Suceso, Calle Velilla leads to the Gothic church of **San Pedro**, with a Mudéjar tower modelled on the Giralda, and where a marble tablet records Velázquez's baptism. Just behind the church on Calle Dueñas, the splendid **Palacio de las Dueñas** was the birthplace (marked by a plaque) of another *andaluz* genius, the poet Antonio Machado.

Palacio Lebrija

C/Cuna 8 • July & Aug Mon–Fri 9am–3pm, Sat 10am–2pm; Sept–June Mon–Fri 10.30am–7.30pm, Sat 10am–2pm & 4–6pm, Sun 10am–2pm • Charge • ⓦ palaciodelebrija.com

A stroll west from San Pedro along Calle Imagen passes the Renaissance Iglesia de la Anunciación on Calle Laraña, leading to Calle Cuna on the left. Here at no. 8, stands the sixteenth-century **Palacio Lebrija**, housing a vast collection of Iberian and Roman antiquities gathered by the Condesa (countess) de Lebrija who acquired the house in 1900. She transformed the interior to incorporate some fine Roman mosaics – particularly that of the deity Pan – from the Roman site at Itálica. As well as the antiquities carted away from Itálica – before there were laws to prevent this – there are marbles plundered from the Moorish site at Medina Azahara as well as various exhibits purchased on her travels and a number of artworks.

Alameda de Hércules

A route directly north from the Palacio Lebrija brings you to the tree-lined **Alameda de Hércules**, once a swamp and converted in the sixteenth century into a promenade. The southern end has two pillars taken from a Roman temple on Calle Mármoles – hence the promenade's name. King Alfonso X believed that only Hercules (the city's mythical founder) could have raised these pillars and it was later alleged (without evidence) that the Roman temple had been dedicated to the Greek god and thus, via this convoluted thought process, the Alameda acquired its name. Once fashionable, in the latter part of the last century the area went to seed and became the city's red-light district. However, since the millennium a costly makeover has transformed it, attracting numerous new bars and hotels and the Alameda is re-emerging as a vibrant centre of *sevillano* life.

Jesús del Gran Poder

Pza de San Lorenzo 13 • Mon–Fri 10am–1.30pm & 5–9pm • Free

West of the Alameda lies the church of **San Lorenzo** and, next to it, the modern church of **Jesús del Gran Poder**. In the latter's retablo is displayed the much-venerated figure of *Jesús del Gran Poder* (Christ bearing his cross) by Juan de Mesa, carved in 1620. This image is borne in procession in the small hours of Good Friday morning.

Calle Sierpes

Leading out of Plaza de San Francisco is the true heart of Seville, **Calle Sierpes**, where, according to Cervantes – who spent some time in prison here serving a sentence for his tax debts – "all the social classes of the city come together". This narrow pedestrianized street, today lined with souvenir stores, private clubs and smart *pastelerías* (confectioners), is a wonderful place to stroll. It's particularly dramatic – though quite uncharacteristic – during Semana Santa, when the brotherhood of El Silencio passes through in total silence in the early hours of Good Friday, watched by an equally hushed crowd lining the route.

Look out for Seville's most famous *pastelería*, **La Campana**, at no. 1 (the northern end). At no. 65 a wall plaque indicates the site of the **Cárcel Real**, or royal prison, where Cervantes was incarcerated and where – according to legend – he scribbled the first notes that were eventually to be transformed into *Don Quijote*. A short way down on the left, on Calle Jovellanos, lies the small **Capillata de San José**, one of the best examples of full-blown Baroque in the city, with a beautiful gilded retablo.

Otherwise, just behind Calle Sierpes in the parallel Calle Tetuán, a detour will lead you to a wonderful old tiled **billboard** advertising a 1924 Studebaker Special Six convertible. The Triana tiles are hand-painted and the work of noted ceramicist Enrique Orce Mármol (who did much of the tile work on the Plaza de España), and it prompts the question of just how long the company (now out of business for fifty years) expected the model to remain in production. It's sited opposite the C&A department store.

El Salvador

Pza del Salvador • July & Aug Mon–Sat 10am–5pm, Sun 3–7pm; Sept–June Mon–Sat 11am–5.30pm, Sun 3–7pm (also service times 7.30–9pm) • Charge

To the east of Calle Sierpes, the collegiate church of **El Salvador** was built on the site of a ninth-century – and the city's first – Friday mosque. Most of what you see today dates from the seventeenth century, with remnants of the mosque preserved in its tower, formerly the minaret, and its patio, originally the ablutions courtyard. Inside, there's a magnificent Churrigueresque retablo as well as a number of sculptures, among them the renowned *Jesús del Pasión* by the great master of wood sculpture, Juan Martínez Montañés, who also embellished the church's exterior and whose bronze monument stands in the plaza outside.

Plaza de la Encarnación

A couple of blocks north of Plaza del Salvador lies another of the city's major squares, **Plaza de la Encarnación**, created in 1819 after Napoleon's invading forces demolished the convent of the same name that stood on the spot. Long criticized for its bleakness – its main function throughout the twentieth century was to serve as a market and then bus terminal — at the start of the new millennium the city government decided to spectacularly raise its profile with a breathtaking piece of modern architecture.

Las Setas (Metropol Parasol)

Pza de la Encarnación • Mirador and rooftop walkway Sun–Thurs 10–10.30am, Fri–Sat 10am–11am • Charge • Museum Tues–Sat 10am–8pm, Sun 10am–2pm • Charge • Ⓦ setasdesevilla.com

Seven years under construction, **Las Setas** is a 30m-high, 150m-long structure comprising a series of undulating, wood-waffle flat-topped mushroom structures on giant concrete pillars. Claimed by its German architect, Jürgen Mayer, to be the world's largest timber construction, it incorporates a market, shopping mall, restaurant and a basement museum displaying the ruins of Roman Hispalis – complete with mosaics – discovered in the preliminary excavations. The structure's high point (in all senses) is a spectacular undulating pedestrian walkway winding across the roof to a sky deck with stunning views over the city.

Typically, the structure's official name, **Metropol Parasol**, did not last more than a couple of days after the unveiling. *Sevillano* wags took one look and tagged it Las Setas (the mushrooms), the name everyone uses today when debating how long it'll stay standing. Many critics argue that the work has no place in a square surrounded by Baroque edifices, while supporters claim it has launched the city into the new millennium with a flourish.

Barrio Triana

The **Barrio Triana**, an endearingly scruffy, lively and not at all touristy neighbourhood, across the river from the old town, is generally believed to have taken its name from the Roman emperor Trajan who was born at nearby Itálica. This was once the heart of the city's *gitano* (gypsy) community and, more specifically, home of the great flamenco dynasties of Seville. The *gitanos*, belonging to the Romani ethnic group, lived in extended families in tiny, immaculate communal houses called *corrales* around courtyards ablaze with flowers. Today only a handful remain intact.

Triana is still the starting point for the **annual pilgrimage to El Rocío** (at the end of May), when myriad painted wagons leave town, drawn by elephantine oxen. And one of the great moments of **Semana Santa** occurs here in the early hours of Good Friday when the candlelit *paso* of the Virgin Esperanza de Triana is carried back over the Puente de Triana (Isabel II) to be given a rapturous welcome home by the whole *barrio* assembled on the other side.

Plaza de la Virgen de la Milagrosa

In the centre of **Plaza de la Virgen de la Milagrosa** is a modern statue to **Rodrigo de Triana**, a sailor on Columbus's initial voyage who was the first to set eyes on the New World. In spite of his name, however, more recent research suggests that he hailed not from Triana, but Lepe, in the neighbouring province of Huelva. Determined not to be put off by this academic meddling with their history, the *barrio* erected the sculpture anyway with the laconic "Tierra" ("Land") inscribed on its base, the word an unidentified Rodrigo is presumably yelling as he clings to the mast.

Calle Gonzalo Segovia

Calle Gonzalo Segovia was the site of the **former gunpowder factory** that supplied the vessels of the Indies fleet. An enormous explosion here in 1579 not only destroyed half of Triana, but also blew the stained-glass windows out of the cathedral across the river. In Roman times, clay was collected from this riverbank to make the amphorae used to transport cereals, wine, oil and pickled fish to the imperial capital – much of the broken pottery piled up in ancient Rome's towering rubbish dump at Monte Testaccio has now been identified as coming from Triana. The same clay also made the bricks for the Giralda and many more of the city's houses and monuments.

Church of Santa Ana

C/Pureza 84 • Mon–Sat 11am–1pm & 6.30–8.30pm, Sun 9.30am–1pm & 6.30–8pm • Free

Triana's main church, the **Church of Santa Ana**, is the oldest parish church in Seville. Built for Alfonso X in the thirteenth century, it includes many later additions: note, for example, the Mudéjar tower with blocked lobed windows topped by a Renaissance belfry. Inside, look out for the fine sixteenth-century retablo of the Virgen de la Rosa and the church's baptismal font – Pila de los Gitanos – from which, according to tradition, the gifts of flamenco singing and dancing are bestowed on the newborn infants of the *barrio*.

Capilla de los Marineros

C/Pureza 5 • Mon–Sat 10am–1.30pm & 6–9pm, Sun 10am–2pm & 5.30–8.30pm • Free

The eighteenth-century chapel of **Capilla de los Marineros** is now seat of the Cofradía de Jesús de las Tres Caídas y Nuestra Señora de la Esperanza (Brotherhood of Jesus of the Three Falls and Our Lady of Hope), one of the major brotherhoods who march in the Semana Santa processions. The chapel's Baroque retablo incorporates the figure of the Virgin known as the Esperanza de Triana to which the *barrio* is devoted.

From the Capilla de los Marineros to the Puente de Triana

Triana has long been a centre of glazed-tile production, and you'll see plenty of examples of this fine ceramic work as you stroll around the streets. A walk from the Capilla de los Marineros – perhaps taking a detour to the **Casa Anselma** (fronting C/Pages), a great old tiled place with occasional impromptu flamenco (see page 283) – will bring you to sixteenth-century **church of Nuestra Señora de la "O"** at C/Castilla 30, with its splendid tiled tower. The interior, as well as holding some fine ceramics, contains a seventeenth-century sculpture of Jesús Nazareno by Pedro Roldán. Heading south, with the river to your left, a small alley bears the name Callejón de la Inquisición; this was the site of the northern flank of the former **Castillo de Triana** (see below). Almost opposite, *Cervecería Casa Cuesta* is a welcoming bar with tiled interior serving good tapas. Continuing around the corner you'll come to the spectacular tiled facade of **Cerámica Santa Ana** at Plaza Callao 12. The city's oldest working ceramics factory, over a century old, this is a good place to buy hand-painted Triana pots and tiles. South of here is **Plaza Altozano**, where there are monuments to the *barrio*'s great flamenco traditions and another to Triana's famous *torero*, Juan Belmonte. The latter sculpture by Venancio Blanco nestles against the **Puente de Triana** – designed by Gustave Eiffel of "tower" fame.

La Cartuja

C/Américo Vespucio 2 • Tues–Sat 11am–9pm, Sun 11am–3pm • Charge for entrance and temporary exhibitions; another ticket includes entry to Centro Andaluz de Arte Contemporáneo (see page 272) • Buses #C1 or #C2 from the Prado de San Sebastián bus station or the Puente de los Remedios, or on foot via the Pasarela de la Cartuja pedestrian bridge

Across the river from El Centro is **La Cartuja**, a former Carthusian monastery. Founded in 1399 on the site where there had been an apparition of the Virgin in some pottery workshops (*cuevas*) installed here during the Almohad era, the monastery of Santa María de las Cuevas was expanded by the Carthusians in the fifteenth and sixteenth centuries with donations from Seville's leading families.

This was where Columbus lodged on his visits to Seville, where he planned his second voyage to the New World, and where he was buried for a few years. The core of the monastery suffered eighteenth-century Baroque additions and was made

---

EXPO 92

The staging of **Expo 92** secured a year of publicity and prosperity for Seville during which the sybaritic *sevillanos* started to believe their own hype, billing it as the "event of the century". After the fuss died down and the visitors departed, the city was left with a staggering debt of sixty billion pesetas (€360 million), financial scandals, endless recriminations and a dilapidated site which no one knew what to do with. Plans to turn it into a science park came to nothing and the western side of the complex has now been split between the University of Seville and a technological/industrial park.

Expo's artificial lake on the east side of the site has been revamped as the focus of the **Isla Mágica** amusement and theme park (April–Nov daily 11am–7.30pm; closes 11pm July & Aug; charge, extra to enter Aquapark; ⓦislamagica.es) based on the theme of the sixteenth-century Spanish empire.

The remains of the Expo site lying beyond this and to the south of La Cartuja are mostly a hotchpotch of desolate and overgrown structures, but one has been rehabilitated to become the **Pabellón de la Navegación** (May–Oct Tues–Sat 11am–8.30pm, Sun 11am–3pm; Nov–April 10am–7.30pm; charge; ⓦpabellondelanavegacion.es) an exhibition space dedicated to the history of Spanish navigation and discovery with lots of interactive gadgetry. Your entry ticket also allows you to ascend the 65m-high **Schindler Torre Mirador** (taking its name from the Swiss company who built it), another Expo leftover, from where there are stunning views over the river and the old city.

---

the headquarters of the notorious Marshal Soult's garrison during the Napoleonic occupation of 1810–12, when the monks were driven out and fled to Portugal. A final indignity was visited on the place when, after Disentailment in 1836, it was purchased by a Liverpudlian, Charles Pickman, and turned into a ceramics factory, which it remained until 1982. The whole complex – including the towering brick kilns and chimney that can be glimpsed from outside the site, and which are now regarded as industrial history – was restored for **Expo 92** at enormous cost.

Capilla de Afuera and the monastery church

The visit begins at the **Capilla de Afuera** where the chapel's gilded Baroque retablo has lost its central effigy of the Virgen de las Cuevas, a carved work in cedar and once the monastery's most venerated image. In the chapels of **Santa Catalina** and **San Bruno** (the founder of the Carthusian order) there are fine Triana tiles; Felipe II used the latter as his oratory when he visited Seville in 1570.

Apart from a few surviving architectural fragments, the monastery's **church** is now bare, but maintains a serene dignity after its use as a workshop in the ceramics factory. Off it, the chapel of Santa Ana contains the **tomb of Christopher Columbus** where the navigator's bones rested for 27 years prior to beginning their travels (see box, page 249). Also here in wall niches are the remains of some fine polychrome tile panels depicting San Juan Evangelista and San Mateo.

Cloister, chapter house and refectory

Also off the church are the elegant Mudéjar **cloister**, the centre of Carthusian community life and home to more tile work, and the **Capítulo de Monjes** (chapter house), with the sixteenth-century tombs of the Ribeira family and finely sculpted retablos made in Italy. Finally, the **refectory**, with more partially tiled walls and a tiled pulpit, retains a beautiful *artesonado* ceiling which was used by the French for target practice. The visit ends with a chance to view Pickman's enormous bottle-shaped kilns close up en route to the *huerta* (market garden) of the former monastery, which has been transformed once again into a tranquil oasis of shade-giving trees.

3

Casilla de Santa Justa y Rufina

Along the garden's northwest wall you can see the pumps which once drew water from the river to irrigate the garden, while from a *mirador* in the reconstructed **Casilla de Santa Justa y Rufina** there is a great view over the whole complex to the west, the river and city to the east and, to the north, the rather forlorn and weed-festooned site of Expo 92.

Centro Andaluz de Arte Contemporáneo

C/Américo Vespucio 2 • Tues–Sat 11am–9pm, Sun 10am–3.30pm • Charge, also includes entry to La Cartuja • ⓦ caac.es

A separate building within the La Cartuja complex houses the **Centro Andaluz de Arte Contemporáneo**, one gallery of which displays changing selections from a large and interesting collection of contemporary work by *andaluz* artists including canvases by Joaquín Peinado, José Guerrero and Daniel Vásquez Díaz. Two other galleries stage temporary exhibitions by international artists and photographers. The art doesn't stop at the bounds of the gallery's walls, though. Among the outdoor displays, Cristina Lucas' installation is a striking expression of female suppression. *Alicia* depicts Carroll's overgrown Alice, attempting to reach beyond the confines of the home in which she's trapped.

Barrio Macarena

"The Macarena, now as it always was, is the abode of ragged poverty, which never could or can for a certainty reckon on one or any meal a day." Things have changed considerably for the better since Ford was in the **barrio Macarena** in the middle of the nineteenth century, and since Murillo used the *barrio*'s beggars and urchins as models for his paintings. Northwest of the Centro and enclosed by the best surviving stretch of the city's ancient walls, Macarena's very unfashionability, along with its solid working-class traditions, have helped prevent its wholesale dismemberment at the hands of developers. The result today is an area full of character, with many attractive cobbled streets, and quite a few jewels to show off in the way of churches and convents. The Macarena's pride was further increased when it was decided that the *barrio* would become the home of the newly autonomous Andalucían parliament in the converted Renaissance hospital of the Cinco Llagas.

A good place to start a tour around La Macarena is the **Plaza de los Terceros**, some 250m to the north of the Casa de Pilatos (see page 266); on the corner with Calle Gerona lies one of Seville's great institutions, the bar *El Rinconcillo* (see page 283), founded in 1670 and believed to be the oldest in the city.

Santa Catalina

Pza de los Terceros • Access is difficult, but try service times 6.30–7.30pm

The fourteenth-century Mudéjar church of **Santa Catalina** has a tower modelled on the Giralda and topped off with Renaissance embellishments. The interior has some interesting Mudéjar features including an elegant panelled ceiling as well as – in the Cristo de la Exaltación chapel (the most easterly on the south side) – a fine sculpture of Christ by Roldán.

Convento de Santa Paula

Pza Santa Paula • Daily 9.30am–1.30pm & 5.30–6.45pm • Charge

Following Calle Sol out of the Plaza Terceros will bring you to **Plaza San Román**, where another fourteenth-century Gothic-Mudéjar church, **San Román**, has a fine coffered ceiling. North of the church is the fifteenth-century **Convento de Santa Paula**, renowned for its beautiful belfry and church. It's entered through an imposing fifteenth-century Gothic doorway built with Mudéjar brickwork and decorated with Renaissance *azulejos* by Pedro Millán, with ceramic decoration by Niculoso Pisano.

Inside there's a sumptuously gilded San Juan Evangelista retablo by Alonso Cano with a magnificent central figure of St John by Martínez Montañés dated 1637.

The **convent museum**, crammed with treasures, is entered through a small patio to the left of the church entrance. Guided tours (in Spanish) are led by one of the convent's 48 nuns, who has been given a special dispensation to break the order's vow of silence. The first room has a painting of *San Jerónimo* by Ribera, and, almost as beautiful, a view out onto a seventeenth-century patio cloister. In Room 2 there's a fascinating maquette made by Torrigiano before starting on his full-size masterpiece of *San Jerónimo Penitente*, which is now in the Museo de Bellas Artes (see page 263). Room 3 holds two outstanding, though damaged, painted sculptures by Pedro de Mena, a *Virgin* and an *Ecce Homo*. Immediately before the exit there is also a *Crucifixión* by Zurbarán. The hard-working sisters are famous for their *dulces* and *mermaladas* (including a tomato jam), which you can buy from their small shop.

City wall

The **Puerta de Córdoba** (Córdoba Gate), with its horseshoe arch, is the best surviving section of the **city wall**. The Almoravids constructed the wall in the early twelfth century, possibly on Roman foundations, and it was further strengthened by the later Almohads as wars against the Christians intensified. This stretch of the fortification – which once spanned twelve gates and 166 towers – owes its survival to the poverty of the *barrio* during the nineteenth century when, elsewhere in the city, the wall was pulled down to allow expansion.

Basílica de la Macarena

Puerta de la Macarena • Daily 9am–2pm & 6–9.30pm (Sun opens 30min later) • Church free; charge for treasury museum

Just beyond the **Puerta de la Macarena** (a city gate reconstructed in the eighteenth century and the only one to retain its pre-Christian name), stands the **Basílica de la Macarena** which, despite an apparently Baroque facade, dates from the 1940s. The basilica's importance, however, derives from the revered image of the Virgen de la Esperanza Macarena it was constructed to house. Inside the church, to the left, is the solid silver *paso* used to carry the image around the city during the Semana Santa processions. To the right is a second *paso* (the brotherhoods normally carry them in pairs), Jesús de la Sentencia, depicting Pilate washing his hands with a fine, but now modestly cloaked, Christ, by the seventeenth-century sculptor, Felipe Morales. The retablo of the main altar is dominated by a seventeenth-century image of La Macarena, as the Virgin is popularly called by this city of fanatical devotees. Depicted in the trauma of the Passion when her son has been condemned, the work is attributed to La Roldana – largely based on the *sevillano* sentiment that only a woman could have portrayed the suffering of a mother with such intensity. La Macarena's elaborate costume is often decorated with five diamond and emerald brooches bestowed on her by Joselito el Gallo, a famous *gitano torero* of the early part of the last century, and on which he spent a considerable fortune. She didn't return the favours though – he died in the ring in 1920. Despite this mishap, the Virgin is still regarded as the patron of the profession and all matadors offer prayers to her before stepping out to do business in the Maestranza. The basilica's **treasury museum** features a rather gaudy display of the Virgin's other jewels and regalia.

Hospital de las Cinco Llagas

C/San Juan de Ribera • Free afternoon guided tours Sept–June twice weekly; must be booked in advance; closed from July–first week of Sept • ☎ 954 595 929

The sixteenth-century **Hospital de las Cinco Llagas** (aptly, of the Five Wounds of Christ), was one of the first true hospitals of its time and the largest in Europe. Sited outside the walls because hospitals then were places of pestilence and contagion, the restored building is now the seat of Andalucía's autonomous government (and

THE FORGOTTEN BROTHERHOOD

The Macarena church of Santa Marina is home to the **Cofradía del Resucitado** (Brotherhood of the Resurrection), the newest of all the brotherhoods who march in the Semana Santa processions. Founded in 1969, it has never been taken to its heart by a citizenry whose apparent lack of interest in this celebration of the Redeemer's return is in marked contrast with the grisly enthusiasm they show for each act in the Passion leading up to his death. However, this apathy is the visitor's opportunity, for when El Resucitado leaves Santa Marina at 4.30am in the early dawn of Easter Sunday you'll get a perfect view of the intricate manoeuvres performed by the *costaleros* (porters) to negotiate the two *pasos* – the Risen Christ and the aptly titled Vírgen de la Aurora (Virgin of the Dawn) – through the church's doors, which are normally obscured by vast crowds elsewhere. And as there are no seats lining the atmospheric Calle Sierpes, which is almost impossible to get near during the other processions, you will be able to accompany the *pasos*, the band and the masked, candle-bearing *nazarenos* (penitents) in their all-white tunics along here as the dawn breaks – calling in at nearby bars for a *café* and maybe a *churro* or two.

The procession then passes through a sombre Plaza de San Francisco where the normally packed grandstands are eerily empty. Security is also lax at the cathedral, and with a bit of nimble footwork you should be able to follow the *pasos* through the church and past the enormous monstrance inside to emerge in a sunlit Plaza Vírgen de los Reyes beneath the Giralda tower, where a few *sevillanos* have usually gathered to pay their respects. If you wanted to follow El Resucitado back to Santa Marina it's a great (if slow) meander until they arrive home at about 2pm.

many *sevillano* wags drily comment that nothing's changed). The enormous edifice, once capable of holding a thousand beds, is noted for a fine Mannerist facade with a Baroque central doorway of white marble. The interior – including the hospital's impressive former church, now the debating chamber – is open for public view when parliament is not sitting.

Santa Marina

C/San Luis s/n • Mon–Fri 7pm–9pm, Sun 11am–1pm • Free

Founded in the thirteenth century, the Gothic-Mudéjar church of **Santa Marina** is set back from the road in a *plazuela*. The oldest feature here must be the doorway, dating from around 1300, which has Gothic archivolts, or arch mouldings, with Mudéjar star decoration on the outer band. Another church badly damaged in the Civil War, Santa Marina was in ruins for decades, and only spruced up for Expo 92 when the interior was entirely restored. It is now home to the Cofradía del Resucitado, the Brotherhood of the Resurrection (see box, page 274).

San Luís

C/San Luis s/n • Not usually open to the public

The church of **San Luís** is a glorious eighteenth-century structure, preserved in 1995 from demolition after the city government had said they couldn't afford to save it. Public outcry forced a change of heart and the riot of a Churrigueresque facade, topped by glazed-tile domes, has now been restored, along with the interior, which features a fine fresco by Lucas Valdés on the central dome. The church is also floodlit at night to spectacular effect.

San Marcos

Pza San Marcos

The fourteenth-century **San Marcos** sits in the plaza of the same name. A fine Macarena church built on the site of an earlier mosque, it has a Mudéjar tower – note the

Giralda-style *sebka* brickwork – and a superb Gothic-Mudéjar entrance. Although gutted by fire during the Civil War and since restored, its interior uniquely preserves the original Mudéjar horseshoe arches dividing nave and aisles. At the head of the north aisle there's a seventeenth-century sculpture in painted wood of San Marcos, by Juan de Mesa. Cervantes used to climb San Marcos's tower to view the plant-filled and peaceful patio of the convent of Santa Isabel just behind the church. You can see why.

ARRIVAL AND DEPARTURE
SEVILLE (SEVILLA)

By plane Seville's airport (ⓦaena.es) lies 12km northeast of town along the A4 (NIV) *autovía* towards Córdoba. The airport bus (daily; roughly hourly between 5am–1am), takes 45min to the centre and terminates at the central Pza de Armas bus station, stopping at the train station en route. A taxi from the airport will cost €25–30 when taken from the taxi rank just in front of the terminal. There are companies, such as Book Taxi Sevilla (ⓦbooktaxisevilla. com), with whom you can pre-arrange a pick up and pay in advanced; the mark-up on these fares tends to be about twenty percent.

By train Points of arrival are straightforward, through the train station, Santa Justa, 5km out northeast on Avda Kansas City, the airport road. Bus #32 will take you from here to Pza del Duque, from where all sights are within easy walking distance; alternatively, bus #C1 will take you to the Prado de San Sebastián bus station. For timetables and ticket information, consult RENFE (ⓦrenfe.es). Alternatively, there's a RENFE office on C/Zaragoza, where you can buy advanced tickets in person.

Destinations Algeciras (7 daily, change at Antequera or Bobadilla; 3hr 30min); Almería (4 daily; 5hr 40min); Barcelona (2 daily; 5hr 30min); Cádiz (16 daily; 1hr 45min); Córdoba (AVE 19 daily, 45min; 5 *cercanías* daily, 1hr 20min); Granada (4 daily; 3hr 15min); Huelva (5 daily; 1hr 35min); Madrid (AVE 16 daily; 3hr 20min); Málaga (12 daily; 2hr 30min); Osuna (3 daily; 1hr).

By bus The city has two bus stations, from which several private companies operate. From Pza de Armas; located on the square of the same name by the Puente del Cachorro

on the river) the buses you're most likely to take are run by Alsa (ⓦalsa.es), who cover long-distance national and international destinations, and Damas (ⓦdamas-sa.es), who are the most prominent provider for longer routes within Andalucía. It's easy to book Alsa/Damas tickets online or via their apps, which have the most up-to-date schedule. For the majority of coaches, you'll have an allocated seat. Prado de San Sebastián, the city's subsidiary bus station, is on Avda Carlos V, which runs along the north edge of the San Sebastián park. Both Alsa and Damas buses call here.

Pza de Armas destinations Almería (3 daily; 3hr 30min); Aracena (2 daily; 1hr 20min); Ayamonte (6 daily; 2hr 45min); Córdoba (7 daily; 1hr 45min); El Rocío (2 daily; 1hr 30min); Faro (5 daily; 2hr 45min); Granada (8 daily; 3hr); Huelva (every 30min; 1hr 15min); Madrid (9 daily; 6hr); Málaga (7 daily; 2hr 45min); Matalascañas (7 daily; 2hr); Mérida (4 daily; 2hr 15min).

Prado de San Sebastián destinations Albufeira (3 daily; 3hr 15min); Algeciras (4 daily; 3hr 50min); Cádiz (10 daily; 1hr 45min); Carmona (hourly; 45min); Écija (9 daily; 1hr 15min); Jerez de la Frontera (7 daily; 1hr 15min); Mérida (5 daily; 1hr 15min); Ronda (7 daily; 2hr 30min).

By car Driving in Seville is an ordeal, especially in the narrow streets of *barrios* such as Santa Cruz, which was supposed to remain pedestrianized. As on-street parking spaces are almost impossible to find, your best bet for parking is to find a pay car park (they are signed all around the central zone), or to choose accommodation with a garage (for which you will be charged extra).

INFORMATION

Turismo Pza del Triunfo 1, close to the exit from the Alcázar (Mon–Fri 9am–7.30pm; Sat & Sun 9.30am–7.30pm; ☎954 210 005). This office tends to be overwhelmed in peak periods.
Municipal tourist office Less chaotic, and therefore much more helpful, this office is at Paseo Alcalde Marqués de Contadero s/n (Mon–Fri 9.30am–1.30pm & 3.30–7.30pm, Sat & Sun 10am–1.30pm; ☎955 471 232; ⓦvisitasevilla. es). There are City Expert information points dotted around

the city, noticeable by their orange glow: the most helpful being at Santa Justa train station, Avda de la Constitución and inside the Mercado del Barranco (daily 9.30am–8pm).
Newspapers Seville's best all-round daily paper is *El Diario de Sevilla*, although the older *El Correo* also sells well; both are good for entertainment listings and local news.
Useful **websites** See ⓦvisitasevilla.es and ⓦexploreseville.com.

TOURS AND ACTIVITIES

Boat tours Cruceros Turísticos (ⓦcrucerostorredeloro. com) have a quayside office below the Torre del Oro and run an hour-long cruise (daily every 30min 11am–9pm) which

takes in all the major riverside sights, including a view of the Expo 92 site. On Saturdays (May–Oct) they also run a scenic downriver cruise from Sanlúcar's Bajo de Guía to Sanlúcar

CYCLING SEVILLE

Though public transport is plentiful, the best way to get around the city is as the locals do: by bike. Thanks to the efforts of enterprising cyclist Manuel Calvo, Seville has since 2007 been home to an ambitious network of **cycle lanes**. The lanes, which run along almost 120km of road, are easily recognized, with green strips of road segregated from traffic by either barriers or a curb. So Sevillians tend to cycle with no high-vis or helmets. Around 70,000 cycle trips are made daily in the city, making Seville the only Spanish city to rival the likes of Scandinavia and the Netherlands in sustainable transport.

Plenty of companies offer a variety of **city tours and rentals**. The most established of these is Sevilla Bike Tour (☎ 954 562 625; C/Arjona 8, next to the Triana bridge), who run daily tours in the morning and for sunset (3 hours) along the river to the Plaza de España and through the narrow, winding streets of Santa Cruz. Most tours avoid the heat of the day, but still make sure to bring a hat and an extra bottle of water. If you're staying in the city for a few days, it might be worth registering with **SEVici** (🌐 sevici.es) – the municipal bike rental system; a weekly pass (charge) allows unlimited journeys under 30mins.

de Barrameda, leaving the Torre del Oro at 8.30am. For a self-powered boat trip, kayak tours can be booked from a City Expert office.

Bus tours Sevilla Tour offers hop-on hop-off open-top bus tours (with earphone commentary), stopping at or near the main sights (every 30min from the riverside Torre del Oro, summer 10am–10pm; 24hr ticket €18; ☎ 902 101 081).

Football Seville has two major teams: Sevilla CF (🌐 sevillafc.es) play at the Sánchez Pizjuán stadium and Real Betis (🌐 realbetisbalompie.es) use the Manuel Ruiz de Lopera stadium, in the southern suburbs. Match schedules are in the local or national press, and tickets are surprisingly easy to get hold of for many matches (check the stadium or *turismos*).

Pedalo To see the river under your own steam, pedalos can be rented from Pedalquivir (Mon–Fri 12–9pm, Sat–Sun 11am–10pm; ☎ 659 29 91 83), on the east bank of the river near the Torre del Oro.

GETTING AROUND

The *Guía Verde Callejero* street guide, available from kioskos and bookshops, is an invaluable aid to finding your way around the city's more convoluted corners.

By bus All inner-city bus journeys have a flat fare single tickets. Seville's bus & tram company, Tussam (🌐 tussam. es), also sells one-day or three-day *tarjetas turísticas* for unlimited journeys. These are available from the Tussam offices at Prado San Sebastián, Plaza Ponce de León station, Avda Andalucía 11 (one of the two local bus hubs with Puerta de Jerez), or at the Santa Justa train station. If you're staying for longer, it's worth buying a *Tarjeta Multiviaje* rechargeable card from a kiosk (also good for trams). A bus map detailing routes is available from the *turismo*.

By tram Confusingly called Centro-Metro, the city tram runs from Plaza Nueva to San Bernando bus station, stopping at Archivo de Indias, San Fernando and Prado de San Sebastian along the way. You buy tickets at the stops (you can also use the *Tarjeta Multiviaje* rechargeable card on board).

By metro Seville currently has just one, 18km long metro line (three more are planned), connecting the suburbs beyond Triana with Montequinto to the east. It's efficient and well-air conditioned – convenient if you arrive to San Bernardo in the heat of the day and are staying close to or over the river.

By open-top bus tour Good if you're pressed for time, this hop-on, hop-off service is operated by City Sightseeing Sevilla (🌐 city-sightseeing.com); buses leave half-hourly from the riverside Torre del Oro, stopping at or near the main sites. Information is provided by earphone commentary in sixteen languages.

By taxi The main central ranks are in Pza Nueva, the Alameda de Hércules and the Pza de Armas and Prado de San Sebastián bus stations. The basic charge for a short journey is around €5, but rates rise at night and weekends. For a reliable taxi pickup, try Radio Taxi (☎ 954 580 000).

By bike Seville is famous for its cyclists and the city is very accommodating to those who decide to discover it upon two wheels. There are **SEVici** (🌐 sevici.es) bike depots dotted throughout the city. Alternatively, lots of private companies do rentals.

ACCOMMODATION

SEE MAPS PAGES 244 AND 257

Seville has some of the finest **hotels** in Andalucía. The most attractive area to stay is undoubtedly the **Barrio Santa Cruz**, though this is reflected in the prices, particularly during high season (April–June). Slightly farther out, another promising area is to the north of the Plaza Nueva, and especially over towards the river and the Plaza de Armas bus station. If you're arriving during any of the major **festivals**, particularly Semana Santa or the Feria de Abril (April fair), you're strongly advised to book ahead – be aware also that this is when hotel rates rise above the high season rates quoted by the price guides below. Many hotels have **garages** or can assist with parking (usually €15–20/day).

BARRIO SANTA CRUZ AND CATHEDRAL AREA

★**La Banda Rooftop** Hostel C/Dos de Mio 16; ⓦlabandahostel.com. An artistic place that fosters community. There are shared "family" dinners up on the rooftop that overlooks the cathedral, where they also host live music and DJs. The dorms (sleeping 4–8) are clean & comfortable; the kitchen is well equipped; 24hr reception. Dorms €

★**Las Casas del Rey de Baeza** Pza Jesús de la Redención 2; ⓦhospes.com. Wonderful hotel with rooms arranged around an eighteenth-century *sevillano corral*. Stylishly furnished pastel-shaded rooms come with traditional exterior *esparto* blinds; the restaurant's just as special and there's a rooftop pool to cool off in – a surprisingly rare find in Seville. €€€

Casual Sevilla de las Letras C/Alhondiga 24; ⓦcasualhoteles.com. Cool hotel with literature-inspired decor and an elegant shaded patio. All rooms come with a/c, comfy beds and individual murals. €€€

Hostal Atenas C/Caballerizas 1; ⓦhostalatenas.com. A pretty, plant-festooned passage leads to a charming two-star *pensión* decorated with *azulejos*; the proprietors are welcoming and all rooms are en suite and have a/c. €

Hostal Puerta Carmona Pza de San Agustín 5; ☎954 988 310. Very pleasant *hostal* with good-value modern en-suite rooms with a/c and TV; they will advise (solely in Spanish) on where to park nearby. €

Hostal Santa María de la Blanca C/Santa María la Blanca; ☎954 421 174. Friendly small *hostal* close to the church of the same name. Its basic rooms are above a shop, through which you gain entry. Some are en suite and have the benefit of light, while others have very little. €€

Hostal Sierpes Corral del Rey 22; ☎954 224 948. Welcoming *hostal* with traditional Andalucían decor. The light-filled en-suite a/c rooms (104 and 306 are particularly spacious) are arranged around a central patio. Boasts its own tapas bar and garage. €

Hostería del Laurel Pza de los Venerables 5; ⓦhosteriadellaurel.com. With 21 comfortable a/c en-suite rooms above a very good restaurant and tapas bar, this has a superb location, although it can get a bit overrun with visitors in high season. Breakfast is included. €€

Hotel Adriano C/Adriano 12; ⓦadrianohotel.com.

Close to the bullring, this stylish two-star hotel has elegantly furnished a/c rooms with satellite TV (half are no-smoking). There's also a roof terrace, compact gym/spa and a garage. €€

Hotel Alcántara C/Ximénez de Enciso 28; ⓦhotelalcantara.net. Smart, compact and good-value two-star hotel close to Plaza Santa Cruz, with light, tastefully furnished a/c rooms (including some singles). There's a pleasant breakfast patio where you can talk to staff about discounted flamenco tickets. €

Hotel Alfonso XIII C/San Fernando 2; ⓦlartisien.com. A monument in its own right (see page 259), this five-star establishment has a fair claim to being Seville's best hotel. The public rooms and patio are stunning, but unless you like the idea of sleeping in a museum, a visit just to the bar might be better bet. €€€€

Hotel Alminar C/Álvarez Quintero 52; ☎954 293 913. Tasteful, small hotel inside a former textile workshop, 50m from the Giralda. Elegantly furnished exterior balcony rooms are equipped with a/c, writing desks and minibar. Up top are two pricier superior rooms with terrace, both with armchair views of the cathedral. Check website for offers, including breakfast. €€

★**Hotel Amadeus** C/Farnesio 6; ⓦhotelamadeussevilla.com. Welcoming hotel housed in an eighteenth-century *casa señorial* where there's a *sala de música*, a grand piano on the patio and you can loan a variety of musical instruments. Thoughtfully, the stylish rooms are also soundproofed and come with a/c, satellite TV, and their own laptops, which you're free to take and use anywhere in the hotel. It's topped off with a stunning roof terrace (with telescope and jacuzzi) for breakfasting, which is available as late as till 2pm. €€

★**Hotel Convento La Gloria** C/Argote de Molina 26; ⓦhotelconventolagloria.es. Charming three-star hotel inside a former convent with many features – such as painted ceilings, *azulejos* and patios – surviving from its former incarnation. The rooms are comfortable and well equipped, with safe and a/c; six have views of the Giralda and cathedral. Public garage nearby. Breakfast is included. €€

★**Hotel Doña Manuela** Paseo de Catalina de Ribera 2; ☎954 546 400. Good-value two-star in a great location, with rooms on the west side overlooking the Jardines de Murillo. Rooms come with a/c, satellite TV and safe, and there's a roof terrace with sunloungers (the three top-floor suites have their own terraces). Offers rare parking facilities. €€

★**Hotel El Rey Moro** C/Lope de Rueda 14; ⓦelreymoro.com. Attractive boutique hotel with beautifully furnished rooms and bathrooms overlooking two patios. Ask for a room (any of nos. 10–25) on the quieter "interior" patio – the others get noise from the hotel's restaurant. Free cycle rental for guests. Garage nearby. €€

3

★ **Hotel La Rábida** C/Castelar 24; ⓦ vinccihoteles. com. Refurbished traditional four-star hotel inside a *casa palacio* with a nice patio, lots of marble and good facilities. Rooms in the older part have more character, but all come well equipped and there's a library, tapas bar and parking. See website for offers. **€€€**

★ **Hotel Simón** C/García de Vinuesa 19; ⓦ hotelsimonsevilla.com. Well-restored mansion in an excellent position across from the cathedral with parking nearby. All rooms are en suite and a/c, and this can be a bargain out of high season. Public parking nearby. **€€€**

★ **Pensión Doña Trinidad** C/Archeros 7 ☎ 954 541 906. Sparkling *hostal* with simple but pleasant a/c en-suite rooms (some single) with TV around a central patio. Public parking nearby. **€**

★ **TOC Hostel** C/Miguel Mañara 18-22; ⓦ tochostels. com. So close to the cathedral that it almost sits in its shadow, *TOC* is a forward-looking place. They have the efficiency of a hotel coupled with the open atmosphere of a hostel. The brilliance is also in the detail: environmentally friendly automatic lighting and a fingerprint entry system. Dorms €, suites **€€**

PLAZA NUEVA, REYES CATÓLICOS AND MUSEO DE BELLAS ARTES

Hostal Naranjo C/San Roque 11; ⓦ bandbsevilla.com. Welcoming and competitively priced *hostal*, a stone's throw from the Museo Bellas Artes. Offers decent a/c en-suite rooms with TV. Breakfast is included. **€**

Hostal Redes C/Redes 28; ☎ 954 901 946. Clean and comfortable budget *hostal* offering en-suite rooms with a/c. Wifi restricted to some areas. Breakfast is included. **€**

★ **Hotel Europa** C/Jimios 5; ⓦ hoteleuropasevilla. com. Elegant, traditional and welcoming hotel in an eighteenth-century mansion offering comfortable if soberly furnished rooms. Have their own garage, but there's a hefty charge per night for leaving your car there. **€€€**

Hotel Madrid C/San Pedro Mártir 22; ⓦ hotelmadridsevilla.es. Pleasant, refurbished family-run hotel in a vibrant part of the city offering functional a/c balcony rooms with TV. There's also a café attached for a cheap breakfast. **€**

★ **Hotel Petit Palace** C/Canalejas 2; ⓦ petitpalace. com. With an impressive Neoclassical facade – the work of Aníbal González, architect of the Plaza de España – this refurbished hotel has compact but well-equipped rooms, complete with TV and computers. The hotel also has free bikes for guests to use. **€€€**

Hotel Zaida C/San Roque 26; ⓦ hotelzaida.com. Charming and intimate hotel in an eighteenth-century

neo-Mudéjar mansion with a fine exterior and an interior replete with plasterwork and *azulejos*. The comfortable rooms come with bath, TV and a/c, although some single rooms lack light. **€**

The Nomad Hostel C/Itálica 1⊠ ⓦ thenomadhostel. com. A clean, 21st-century hostel with well-considered communal areas. From the lounge with books and instruments to the roof terrace with bar, travellers settle in quickly. Fully equipped kitchen with energy saving focus. Dorms (with balcony) **€**

Oasis Backpackers Palace C/Almirante Ulloa 1; ⓦ oasisseville.com. One of two of its kind in the city, young travellers flock here for clean, spacious dorm rooms and a rooftop pool. Complimentary sangrías get the night started. **€**

SANTA CATALINA, SAN PEDRO, ALAMEDA DE HÉRCULES

Hostal Cairo C/Reyes Católicos 13; ☎ 954 563 448. Clean, simple option close to the Plaza de Armas bus station. All rooms come with a/c and en suite; most have large windows. There's a restaurant next door that's open almost around the clock. **€**

Hotel Casona de San Andrés C/Daóiz 7⊠ ⓦ casonadesanandres.com. Former nineteenth-century *casa palacio* transformed into a pleasant hotel, with attractive en-suite rooms facing either a pedestrianized square or two interior patios. Some rooms come with private terrace. Singles available. **€€**

Hotel Patio de la Alameda Alameda de Hércules 56; ⓦ patiodelaalameda.com. Partly sixteenth-century *casa palacio* revamped into an elegant three-star with light and airy balcony rooms plus a 'chill-out terrace', *cafetería* and own garage. **€€€**

★ **Hotel Sacristía de Santa Ana** Alameda de Hércules 22; ⓦ hotelsacristia.com. Beautiful boutique hotel inside a seventeenth-century *casa señorial* with delightful rooms; the external ones have Alameda views. Facilities include minibar, room safe and plasma TV. **€€**

Hotel Sevilla C/Daóiz 5; ⓦ hotelsevillaweb.es. Refurbished old hotel a 5min walk to C/Cuna, with spacious if gaudy rooms, some of which offer balcony views onto a pleasant *plazuela*. **€€**

LA MACARENA

Hostal La Muralla C/Fray Diego de Cádiz 39; ☎ 954 371 049. Pleasant if basic little *hostal* overlooking the medieval walls. En-suite rooms with tasteful wood panelling, traditional tiles and flat-screen TVs. Own car park with low rates. **€**

EATING

SEE MAPS PAGES 244 AND 257

Seville is tremendously atmospheric in the evening, packed with lively and enjoyable bars and clubs. The fact that the

city has never been particularly noted for its restaurants may have a lot to do with its strong **tapas** tradition (see page 280). Great though this is, even the most enthusiastic *tapeadores* eventually tire of "plate-pecking" and seek out a place to sit down for a more conventional meal.

RESTAURANTS

To eat well without breaking the bank, you generally have to steer clear of the restaurants around the major sights and in the Barrio Santa Cruz. However, there are some reasonable options: the streets around the *barrio*'s northern edge (framed by *calles* Menéndez Pelayo and Santa María la Blanca) are a good hunting ground.

BARRIO SANTA CRUZ AND CATHEDRAL AREA

Bar Modesto C/Cano y Cueto 5; w modestorestaurantes. com. At the north end of Santa Cruz, *Modesto* built its reputation on its tapas, and has now opened a separate tapas bar opposite the restaurant. House specials include *brochetas:* one of *solomillo ibérico* (pork sirloin), and another of monkfish. If one of their *menú gustacións* is out of budget, you can opt for the cheap daily *menú*, which includes wine, and if you get there early, can be eaten on an attractive terrace. In both venues the kitchen continues throughout the day. €€

Café Rayuela C/Miguel de Mañara 9, near the Alcázar; ☎954 225 762. Pleasant lunchtime venue serving economically priced *raciones* (and *media raciones*), *montaditos* (*tapa* on bread) and salads at outdoor tables in a pedestrianized street. €

Corral del Agua Callejón del Agua 6; w corraldelagua. es. You won't mind paying a little more for this *cocina andaluz* as the patio here is one of the most romantic spots in the city. For lunch, there's a great traditional paella and in the evening try the *lubina al Tio Pepe* (sea bass with sherry sauce). Perfectly located for a pre-flamenco meal. €€

Duplex C/Don Remondo 1; ☎954 225 762. Cosy and friendly little diner, typical of many now opening up across the city, with a nonstop kitchen serving up a well-priced two-course *menu*, plus a range of *platos combinados*, curries and a dozen varieties of salad. €

THE RÍO GUADALQUIVIR AND TRIANA

Across the river, Triana offers some excellent restaurants. Along C/Betis close to the water's edge are a number of restaurants with terraces looking out over the city, and around C/García Vinuesa to the west of the cathedral there's an abundance of reasonable *bocadillo* bars and delis for picnic food.

Bar-Restaurante Casa Manolo C/San Jorge 16; w donfadrique.net. Buzzing Triana bar-restaurant with tapas and *raciones* (or breakfast) in the bar or economical *platos combinados* in a dining room just off it. Their fish arrives fresh daily from Isla Cristina and their *menu* is a good price. €€

Bodeguita Casablanca C/Adolfo Rodríguez Jurado 12; w bodeguitacasablanca.com. Smart, mid-priced restaurant and tapas bar with one of the best locations in the city (their patio overlooks the cathedral). It's noted for its excellent fish dishes – including *atún al vinagre de frambuesa* (tuna with strawberry vinegar) – but also does meat dishes. €€

Mesón Serranito C/Antonia Díaz 11; ☎954 211 243. Twin restaurant of the one near El Corte Inglés (see page 286) and with similar dishes and economical *platos combinados* and – due to the location – a line of bulls' heads gazing down from the walls. Only *raciones* are available on the outdoor terrace. €€

La Primera del Puente C/Betis 66; w laprimeradelpuente.es. The riverside terrace of the restaurant over the road has one of the city's best vistas; soft-talk a waiter to get a frontline table. You can enjoy generous *raciones* or *media raciones* of fish, meat and seafood. Paella is a daily special and there's a reasonably priced wine list. €€

Restaurante Salas C/Almansa 15; w hosteriasalas. com. The impeccable table linen and elegant scoured brick and tiled interior denote quality, and the food follows suit. The specialities of the house include grilled fish and meat dishes. There's a bar area serving tapas and two spacious dining rooms with efficient service. €€€

Río Grande C/Betis 70; w riogrande-sevilla.com. One of the best upscale places for a lunchtime feast of traditional meat and fish dishes. Whether you're seated behind the panoramic windows or on the terrace, the view across the river to the Torre del Oro and Giralda, illuminated at night, is stunning. Their next-door tapas bar – with the same terrace view – is worth a visit too. €€€

★**Taberna del Alabardero** C/Zaragoza 20; w tabernadelalabardero.es. Elegant nineteenth-century *casa-palacio sevillana* with attractive decor and an upmarket clientele. Pricey – and outstanding – cutting-edge restaurant upstairs where you can experience seven-course and five-course tasting menus. However, a daily bargain lunchtime menu (more expensive on Sat & Sun) in the patio bar below comes from the same kitchen. They also offer a tapas menu in the bar. €€€€

EL CENTRO, LA MACARENA, ALAMEDA AND SANTA JUSTA

Many parts of El Centro still possess a seedy charm, especially in its southern reaches and the remoter bits of La Macarena. This is where *sevillanos* tend to do their eating and drinking, away from the tourist sights, and you'll have no trouble finding low-priced *comidas* in and around streets such as C/San Eloy, which runs into Plaza Duque de la Victoria, as well as all the main arteries of La Macarena. The Alameda de Hércules is a formerly dubious area now heading upmarket with new places opening all the time.

Bar Dueñas C/Dueñas 1, on the junction of three

streets; ☎954 215 941. Ancient and atmospheric *barrio* bar and just the place for a good lunch with delicious home cooking and a very inexpensive *menú*. Their long-standing tapas specials are *riñones al jerez* (kidneys in sherry) and *menudo de ternera* (tripe stew). €

★**Contenedor** C/San Luís 50; ⓦrestaurantecontenedor.com. Lively, colourful slow-food restaurant whose founders are so proud of the veg they serve that they even decorate the tables with it. Always fresh, and local where possible, the ever-changing menu features dishes such as *pappardelle con setas y alchachofas* (pasta with mushrooms and artichokes) and *arroz negro crudiente de calamar* (crunchy, black rice with squid). Booking is recommended for the evenings, especially on Tuesday when there's live music. €€

Mesón Serranito Alfonso XII 9; ⓦmesonserranito.com. Cosy little restaurant beyond a lively tapas bar out front, with excellent fish and meat dishes – *rosada a la vasca* (rockfish) and *rabo de toro* (stewed bull's tail) – are house specials and there's a *menú* for a handful of euros. The kitchen is nonstop and it also does breakfasts. €€

Pando C/San Eloy 47; ⓦpandorestaurantes.com. An ideal lunch stop as most *raciones* are available in tapas form. There's a wide range of meat and fish on offer – try their *ortiguillas de Chipiona* (Atlantic anemone) – and they also serve interesting rice dishes. €

Restaurante Las Piletas C/Marqués de Paradas 28; ⓦlaspiletasrestaurante.com. Diminutive, atmospheric (bulls' heads and framed photos) and typically *sevillano* mid-priced restaurant with tapas bar (listing fifty possibilities) and small outdoor terrace attached. Specialities include fish and *mariscos* as well as *cola de toro* (stewed bull's tail) which is heaved over from the nearby Maestranza ring. €€

Restaurante Los Gallegos C/Capataz Franco 1; ☎954 214 011. Friendly and inexpensive restaurant in a tiny alley off C/Martín Villa, serving *Galician* specialities – try the excellent *pulpo gallego* (spicy boiled octopus). Finish off the mid-priced *menú* with a traditional *tarta de Santiago*. €€

TAPAS BARS AND CAFÉS

A popular saying here is *En Sevilla no se come sino que se tapea* ("In Seville you don't eat, you *tapear*"). As the city that claims to have invented tapas, Seville knocks spots off the competition. There is simply nowhere else in Andalucía – or even Spain – with such a variety of places to indulge this culinary art. *El tapeo* means eating "on the go" and *sevillanos* do it on their feet, moving from bar to bar where they stand with a manzanilla or beer – leaving the seats to tourists – while wolfing back fistfuls of whatever tapas take their fancy. Locals tend to drink the cold, dry fino with their tapas, especially *gambas* (prawns), but often change to beer in high summer. Another popular tapas partner is a *tinto de verano* – the local version of sangría – consisting of wine mixed with lemonade, ice and fresh lemon.

BARRIO SANTA CRUZ AND THE CATHEDRAL AREA

Bar Entrecárceles C/Manuel Cortina s/n; ⓦrestaurante-entrecarceles.es. Tiny, 150-year-old

---

SWEET-TOOTH SEVILLE

Many of Seville's *conventos de clausura*, or enclosed orders of nuns, earn money to support themselves by turning out **dulces** (confectionery), and supply many of the city's leading restaurants with their desserts. Other good places to head for cakes and pastries are the *pastelerías* along Calle Sierpes, or in the heat of high summer, search out some of the best *helado* (ice cream) in Spain.

La Campana C/Sierpes 1; ☎954 450 810. The most celebrated *pastelería* in town.

Convento de San Leandro Pza Ildefonso 1. Renowned for its *yemas*, a sugar, syrup and egg-yolk concoction.

Convento de Santa Inés C/Doña María Coronel 5, near the church of San Pedro. The speciality here are *bollitos* (sweet buns) and *tortas almendradas* (almond cakes).

Convento Santa Paula In the heart of Macarena. Famous for its nineteen varieties of jams and marmalades, this convent also gets into the *dulces* business with Andalucía's signature dessert, the egg-yolk confection *tocino de cielo* (translated, very inadequately, as "heavenly lard").

★**Heladería La Fiorentina** C/Zaragoza 16; ☎954 221 550. Seville's most delicious and creative ices. Flavours such as *lima y albahaca* (lime and basil) and *sandía y romero* (watermelon and rosemary) have been lauded by Spanish super-chefs Ferran Adrià (of *El Bullí*) and Dani García and adopted by the likes of Rick Stein.

Heladería Rayas C/Almirante Apodaca 1 (near the church of San Pedro); ☎954 221 746. To cool down in Seville's intense summer heat, head for one of the city's favourite ice-cream makers, which has a terrace to sit out.

★**Horno de San Buenaventura** C/García de Vinuesa 10, on the cathedral's doorstep; ☎954 221 819. Two-floor confectionery shop and *cafetería* where *sevillanos* love to indulge themselves with creamy pastries and *andaluz* classics such as *polvorones* (almond and cinnamon cookies).

Dickensian-style bar on the site of the prison that once housed Cervantes. Specials include *tataki de atún* (fresh tuna) and *melva con pimientos* (tuna with peppers). To create more space they've expanded into an adjoining *raciones* bar, *Los Corrales*, serving a range of fish and meat dishes. €€

★ **Bar Europa** Junction of C/Alcaicería de Loza and C/Siete Revueltas; ☎954 217 908. Approaching its centenary, this is a fine old watering hole with lots of cool tiled walls, plus excellent *manzanilla* and a variety of inventive tapas served on marble-topped tables. Their deliciously sweet and velvety *croquetas de jamón iberico* (*jamón* croquettes) are a must-try. Has a large terrace and also does breakfasts. €

Bodega Belmonte C/Mateos Gago 24; ⓦ tabernabelmonte.com. Named after bullfighting legend Juan Belmonte, the menu at this bar–restaurant is just as brave. If you sit on the romantic terrace out back, the waiter/waitress will give you both a tapas and restaurant menu, from which the *alcachofas a la plancha* (grilled artichokes) and *pan de ajo con carne* (garlic bread with larded meat) are top picks. €

Bodega de Juan García Aviles C/Mateos Gago 20. Officially renamed *Bar Álvaro Peregil* when Juan García passed away, this ancient and renowned bathroom-sized spit-and-sawdust place serves top-notch manzanilla and a range of tapas – arrive early to catch the *tomate aliñado* (marinated tomatoes) or *mojama en aceite* (tuna in olive oil) – as well as *jamón*, olives and manchego cheese. An interesting house speciality is *vino de naranja* (orange-flavoured wine). €

Bodega Santa Cruz (aka Las Columnas) C/Rodrigo Caro 1; ☎954 218 618. Close to the Hospital de los Venerables, this is another local favourite, with long-in-the-tooth waiters who will chalk your bill up on the counter in front of you. Serves up generous tapas portions and house specials include a very good *ensaladilla* (potato salad with crab) and *langritos de pollo* (chicken nibbles). €

★ **Casa Morales** C/García de Vinuesa 11; ☎954 221 242. Earthy, traditional bar (founded 1850) with wine barrels from bygone days now looming empty around the cosy dining area. House staples are *tablas* (tapas served on wooden boards) of regional meat and cheeses, including *morcilla* (blood pudding). What's for daily special tends to be a riff on one of their delicious stews; if the *arroz con carilla* is on, go for that. €

Casa Robles C/Álvarez Quintero 58; ⓦ casarobles. es. Fronting the cathedral, with an inevitably tourist-dominated clientele, this remains a first-rate tapas venue with an equally fine mid-priced restaurant. House specials include *ortiguillas* (sea anemones), *bacalao con garbanzos* (cod with chickpeas) and a very tasty *alcachofas con salmón* (artichokes with salmon). €

Casa Román Pza de los Venerables 1;

ⓦ casaromansevilla.com. Ancient and renowned tapas institution specializing in *jamón serrano*, eaten at the bar or around the elf-sized tables outside. Other signature plates include *carillada* (stewed pork cheek) and *chorizo de Jabugo* plus there's a seasonal *menú*. €€

Cervecería Internacional C/Gamazo 3; ⓦ cerveceriainternacional.com. High-ceilinged beer bar with fifteen world beers on draught and many more by the bottle. Offers perfect beer accompaniments: a large selection of motaditos, such as *pan con jabalí* (wild boar on bread), and cured fish. €

Freiduría La Isla C/García de Vinuesa 13; ☎954 228 355. Founded in 1935, this is a great little *freiduría* serving up a wide variety of mouthwatering fried fish. Once you've paid for your *cartucho* (paper funnel) of fish, you're welcome to use their dining room. All servings come with a delicious tomato salsa. €

La Moneda C/Almirantazgo 4. Lively, upscale place with prices to match, serving up superb – if not over-generous – tapas and excellent manzanilla. Specials include *langostinos con bacon* (prawns wrapped in bacon) and *tortillas de camarones* (fried shrimp tortillas). €€

Puerta de la Carne C/Santa María la Blanca 36; ☎954 411 159. Not strictly a tapas bar, but a *freiduría* where you can buy a *cartucho* of delicious fried fish by weight and – with a beer from the bar – eat it out of the paper on a very pleasant terrace. Tasty things to order include *puntillitas* (small squid) and *gambas fritas* (fried prawns). €

Las Teresas C/Santa Teresa 2; ⓦ lasteresas.es. Good beer and sherry are served in this atmospheric L-shaped bar with hanging cured hams and tiled walls lined with faded *corrida* photos. It's also worth stopping here for breakfast the morning after. Try the *pulpo al la gallega* (Galician octopus) and their traditional *arroz dominical* ("Sunday rice") served only on the Sabbath. €

Sal Gorda C/Alcaicería de la Loza 17; ☎955 385 972. Gourmet tapas in hip corner bar. It's a popular place and there's not much space, so make sure you reserve. Try the steak tartare and *risotto de boletus y langostinos* (risotto with mushrooms and langoustines). €

Taberna Coloniales II C/Fernández y González 36; ⓦ tabernacoloniales.es. Offspring of the similarly named establishment in Plaza Cristo de Burgos, this is up to the same high standard. Tapas are served at the bar, but cornering a table (not always easy) will allow you to feast on a wide range including *solomillo al whisky* (pork loin in grog) and *papas a la brava* (potatoes in a spicy sauce); the *raciones* are meal-sized portions, so why bother with a restaurant? €€

THE RÍO GUADALQUIVIR AND TRIANA

The streets near the river surrounding the Maestranza bullring have always been a prime spot for tapas bars, no doubt to serve the gargantuan appetites of fight fans.

3

FLAMENCO FESTIVALS AND FREE SHOWS

Various **festivals**, such as the Bienal de Flamenco, A Palo Seco (Cante Jondo) and Un Verano de Flamenco, as well as concerts staged by the various *barrios*, take place throughout the summer, offering a good chance of hearing something special – and you're guaranteed to hear authentic flamenco at the Triana *barrio*'s annual festival **Velá de Santa Ana** in the final week in July. There are flamenco performances (free) every night starting around 10 or 11pm in the **Plaza del Altozano** and along the waterfront **Calle Betis**. Performances by top artistes are also staged at the **Museo del Baile Flamenco** (see page 267). All festivals and shows are widely advertised, and the Turismo and local press should have details.

Triana is another excellent tapas hunting ground, both on the riverfront along C/Betis, and further into the *barrio*.

Bar Antonio Romero C/Antonia Díaz 19; ⓦ bodeguitasantonioromero.com. A real *tapeador*'s bar that is much visited by the Maestranza crowd before and after *corridas*. Specials are *muslo de pato* (duck) and *salmón ahumado con alcaparras* (smoked salmon with capers). The *anchoas en salazón* (anchovies in olive oil) is a delicious mini-feast. They have another bar slightly east of here at C/Gamazo 16. €

★ **Bar Bistec** C/Pelay y Correa 34; ☎ 954 274 759. Excellent, ancient and hearty Triana hostelry, with a sparkling Triana-tiled interior and outdoor tables in summer fronting the church of Santa Ana. Specials include *cabrillas en salsa* (spicy snails) and *tortillas de bacalao* (cod tortilla). They also do *raciones* and sell excellent wine by the bottle, tempting you to make a meal of it. €

Bar Sol y Sombra C/Castilla 151; ⓦ tabernasolysombra.com. At the northern end of Triana, this is another favourite with bullfight fans, and an atmospheric bar pleasingly lost in time. House specials include *cola de toro* (oxtail), *almejas* (clams) and *cazuela Tío Pepe* (stew with fino). €

Bodega Paco Gongora C/Padre Marchena 1; ☎ 954 214 139. Wonderful and atmospheric tapas bar in another ancient house. Polish off a wide range of fish and meat tapas and *raciones* with house special – *vino de chocolate* (chocolate wine) and see the nearby Plaza de Espana with new eyes. €

Bodega Siglo XVIII C/Pelay y Correa 32; ☎ 954 274 113. The neighbour of Bar Bistec and another great Triana bar. House specialities include *cordero en salsa de frutos secos* (lamb in dried fruit sauce). If you want to try a well-curated selection, opt for the six-tapas tasting menu. €€

★ **Las Golondrinas** Antillano Campos 26; ☎ 954 338 235. Outstanding bar on two floors filled with Triana *azulejos* and serving quality tapas. Specials include *punta de solomillo* (sirloin steak), *alcachofas aliñados* (artichokes), *chuletitas de cordero* (lamb chops) and *rabanillos* (radishes). €

Kiosko de las Flores C/Betis s/n; ☎ 954 274 576. Wonderful riverside location for this mid-priced restaurant specializing in fish and seafood. Their terrace has great views over the river to the Torre del Oro. Tapas are served at the bar and there's a decent *menú*. €€

Mariscos Emilio (aka Cervecería La Mar) C/Génova 1; ☎ 697 108 049. Excellent and long-established bar specializing in quality, if slightly overpriced, seafood tapas. House specials include *almejas* (clams), *ostras* (oysters) and *cañaíllas* (murex shellfish). Also has an intimate restaurant off the bar serving more elaborate dishes. Equally good Triana offshoots of the same bar are to be found at C/López de Gomara 18 (with a terrace) and C/San Jacinto 39 (corner with C/San Romero). €

EL CENTRO, ALAMEDA DE HÉRCULES AND LA MACARENA

El Centro is the bustling heart of Seville in a culinary as well as geographical sense. The areas surrounding four of the *barrio*'s focal landmarks – the Museo de las Bellas Artes, the bustling C/Sierpes, Plaza Alfalfa and the Iglesia de Santa Catalina – provide rewarding hunting grounds for the *tapeador*, while the rejuvenated Alameda de Hércules is also now a vibrant area for tapas bars and nightlife.

Bar Dos de Mayo Pza de la Gavidia s/n; ⓦ bodegadosdemayo.com. Neighbourhood bar popular with a younger crowd. There's a nice tiled floor, relaxed ambience and a terrace on the square, plus very good tapas including *tortillitas de bacalao* (cod fritters), *pastel de berenjena* (aubergine terrine) and a tasty paella. €

★ **Bar Eslava** C/Eslava 3, facing the Iglesia de San Lorenzo; ⓦ espacioeslava.com. Excellent, modern tapas venue with low prices and a great atmosphere. House specials include *costillas a la miel* (ribs with honey), *strudel de verduras* (pastry with veggie filling) and *boquerones rellenos* (stuffed anchovies). Shares a kitchen with the equally good small restaurant next door. €€

Casa Antonio – Los Caracoles C/Pérez Galdos; ☎ 954 213 172. Classic tapas bar in the vibrant Alfalfa *barrio* just off its main square. There's a spacious bar for winter dining, but in summer everyone sits out on the terrace. House specials include (you've guessed it) *caracoles (snails)* as well as *bacalao a la Bilbaina* (cod in chilli sauce), and there's a good value *menú*. €

Lizarrán C/Javier Lasso de la Vega 14; ⓦ lizarran.es.

Cheap, cheerful and busy bar serving Basque-style *pintxos* (snacks on sticks). There's a wide variety to choose from and when you want to pay, the barman/woman counts up the number of sticks on your plate (no cheating). Look for daily deals on *raciones*, too. €

Patio San Eloy C/San Eloy 9; ☎954 501 070. Have fun making yourselves heard over the crashing plates and hurrahs of this youthful bar. There's a giant tiled "bleachers staircase" at the back where everyone sits to eat their generously-filled *bocadillos*; other options include *chicharones* (pork crackling) and *montaditos* (titbits on bread). €

★ **El Rinconcillo** C/Gerona 32; ⊕elrinconcillo.es. Seville's oldest bar (founded in 1670) does a fair tapas selection as well as providing a hang-out for the city's literati. Now with a more contemporary wing around the corner, it's renowned for *espinacas con garbanzos* (spinach with chickpeas), one of the city's most popular tapas; you could also try a tasty *bacalao en costra y crema de piquilllos* (encrusted cod with a chilli cream). Its dining rooms function as a very good mid-priced restaurant. €

★ **Taberna Coloniales** Pza Cristo de Burgos 19; ⊕tabernacoloniales.es. Typical ancient *sevillano* tavern decorated with mementos from the town's bygone days, serving up outstanding, generous and fair-priced tapas. House specials include *rulo de queso de cabra y espinica* (roulade of goat's cheese with spinach), *Roquefort dulce con moras* (scooped Roquefort cheese with raisins) and *pluma ibérica* (pork shoulder). Has a very pleasant terrace that you'll need to queue for in summer (add your name to the blackboard inside). €€

El Viajero Sedentario Alameda de Hércules 77; ☎677 535 512. Do as the name suggests and be a "sedentary traveller" for the afternoon, and journey with your mind at this delightful little café and book exchange just off the Alameda. €

DRINKING AND NIGHTLIFE   SEE MAPS PAGES 244 AND 257

Seville has plenty to offer in the way of nightlife, from expensive, touristy **flamenco** shows to atmospheric, tucked-out-of-the-way drinking holes. On summer evenings bar terraces by the river (see page 286) often put on live musical entertainment. Major **concerts** take place in one of the football stadiums or in the Auditorio de La Cartuja across the river. Throughout the summer the Alcázar, the Prado de San Sebastián gardens and other squares host occasional free concerts. The Turismo, the local press and the *El Giraldillo* listings magazine have **information** on nightlife; La Teatral, C/Velázquez 12, near Plaza Duque de la Victoria (⊕teatralentradas.com), is the official ticket agent for many concerts.

FLAMENCO

Flamenco music and dance – now strutting more proudly than ever after being recognized as an intangible world heritage art form by UNESCO in 2010 – is on offer at dozens of places around the city, some of them extremely tacky and overpriced. Finding flamenco *puro* isn't easy, possibly because of – like good blues or improvised jazz, with which flamenco shares an affinity – its spontaneous nature. Visitor demand for this romantic Spanish art form has resulted in a form of "theatre flamenco", where you can pay to see two shows a night – a far cry from the time when the *gitanos* sang in their *juergas* (shindigs) for as long and as often as the mood took them.

El Arenal C/Rodo 7; ⊕tablaoelarenal.com. Most palatable of the pricey tourist flamenco spots, and run by a former dancer who sees to it that the spectacle doesn't veer too far into burlesque. Tickets for shows can be rather steep (including one drink), almost double with tapas and drinks and more for show and dinner. If they're not too busy, after the first show you can stay to see the second for free.

Bar Quita Pesares Pza Jerónimo de Córdoba, near the church of Santa Catalina; ☎954 229 385. Owned and run by a flamenco singer, this is a chaotic place where there's often impromptu music, especially at weekends (Fri–Sat), when things get lively around midnight.

La Carbonería C/Levies 18 ☎954 563 749. An excellent bar that often has spontaneous flamenco (try Thurs after 10pm). It used to be the coal merchants' building (hence the name) and is a rambling and welcoming place. They also do tapas and *raciones*. Tricky to find, but well worth the effort.

Casa de la Memoria de al-Andalus C/Jiménez de Enciso 28; ⊕casadelamemoria.es. This cultural centre is dedicated to promoting the art of flamenco and features up-and-coming talent – many flamenco luminaries made their first appearances here – staging nightly flamenco performances. Space is limited and tickets must be booked in advance – in person or by phone or email. Check the website for schedules and tickets.

Los Gallos Pza Santa Cruz; ⊕tablaolosgallos.com. Professional *cantantes* do their best to create some *duende* (magic) and succeed when mesmerising guitarists are granted solos and performers actually meet their cues. It's pricey, but the ticket includes a drink, which is brought to you at your seat; and with the longest running time of those listed, a real tableau of flamenco is able to form.

★ **Museo del Baile Flamenco** ⊕museodelbaileflamenco.com. Nightly concerts are staged in-a-round at the *museo's* atmospheric courtyard (see page 267). Visit their website for details and to reserve tickets, which is necessary in the summer months.

Teatro Central C/José de Gálvez 6, Isla de la Cartuja; ☎955 542 155. It's worth checking on this venue in the local press or with the Turismo, as they often stage festivals featuring up-and-coming flamenco talents as well as

SEMANA SANTA AND THE FERIA DE ABRIL

Seville boasts two of the largest festival celebrations in Spain. The first, **Semana Santa** (Holy Week), always spectacular in Andalucía, is here at its peak with extraordinary processions of masked penitents and lavish floats. The second, the **Feria de Abril**, is unique to the city – a one-time market festival, now a week-long party of drink, food and flamenco. The *feria* follows hard on the heels of Semana Santa so if you have the energy, experience both.

SEMANA SANTA

Semana Santa may be a religious festival, but for most of the week solemnity isn't the keynote – there's lots of carousing and frivolity, and bars are full day and night. In essence, it involves the marching in procession of **brotherhoods** of the church (*cofradías*) and **penitents**, followed by *pasos*, elaborate **floats** on which sit seventeenth-century images of the Virgin or of Christ. For weeks beforehand, the city's fifty-plus *cofradías* painstakingly adorn the hundred or so *pasos* (each brotherhood normally carries two; Christ and a Virgin), spending as much as €350,000 on flowers, costumes, candles, bands and precious stones. The **bearers** (*costaleros*, from the padded *costal* or bag protecting their shoulders) walk in time to traditional dirges and drumbeats from the bands, which are often punctuated by impromptu street-corner **saetas** – short, fervent, flamenco-style hymns about the Passion and the Virgin's sorrows.

Each procession leaves its district of the city on a different day and time during Holy Week and finally ends up joining the official route at La Campana (off Plaza Duque de la Victoria) to proceed along Calle Sierpes, through the cathedral and around the Giralda and the Bishop's Palace. **Good Friday** morning is the climax, when the *pasos* leave the churches at midnight and move through the town for much of the night. The highlights then are the procession of El Silencio – the oldest *cofradía* of all, established in 1340 – in total silence, and the arrival at the cathedral of La Esperanza Macarena, an image of the patron Virgin of bullfighters, and by extension of Seville itself.

On **Maundy Thursday** women dress in black and it's considered respectful for tourists not to dress in shorts or T-shirts. Triana is a good place to be on this day when, in the early afternoon, Las Cigarreras (the *cofradía* attached to the chapel of the new tobacco factory) starts out for the cathedral with much *gitano* enthusiasm.

To see the climax of all the processions – save that of the Cofradía del Resucitado (Resurrection) on Easter Sunday – there's always a crush of spectators outside the cathedral and along Calle Sierpes. However, without a **seat** (the best of which are rented by the hour

established performers.

DISCOTECAS AND LIVE MUSIC

Earlier on in the evening, Seville's *discotecas* attract a young crowd of 17- to 20-year-olds, but the serious action starts after midnight and often lasts till well beyond dawn. For live music the bars around Plaza Alfalfa and Alameda de Hércules tend to have the best of what's on offer. In summer as the town heats up, much of the action switches to the terrace bars along the river to the north of the Puente de Triana as far as the Puente de la Barqueta.

Antique Avda Matemáticos Rey Pastor y Castro s/n; ⓦantiquetheatro.com. Popular with Seville's fancier dancers, this place comes with a transparent dancefloor, a summer terrace ("Rosso"), and sounds that range from Latin pop to heavier stuff.

Bestiario C/Zaragoza 33, at the Pza Nueva end; ☎954 213 475. Disco-bar throbbing with manic techno and house sounds, usually attracting an over-30s crowd.

Sunday is the big day/night of the week here.

★ **La Bicileteria** C/Feria 36; ☎608 734 806. The nucleus for Seville's alternative scene, this mysterious bar/club operates on a discretionary basis: who to let in, which laws to abide by and when to close. You'll have to knock on the door for entry (look for the bicycle frame above).

Fun Club Alameda de Hércules 86; ⓦfunclubsevilla. com. Popular weekends-only music and dance bar – favouring rock, reggae, hip-hop and salsa – with live bands.

O'Clock Bar C/Mendez Nuñez 17; ⓦbaroclock.com. Situated in the historic city centre, this elegant bar is a popular over-30s venue where you can sip a G&T (the house speciality) or a designer cocktail listening to the latest chart hits.

Santuario Cuesta del Rosario s/n; ☎667 796 972. Attractive and upmarket smaller club playing techno, funk, soul and hip-hop to a predominantly over-30s clientele. Sometimes hosts live bands.

and booked up weeks in advance; contact the Turismo for details) or an invitation to share someone's balcony, viewing spots near the cathedral are almost impossible to find. A good **place to stand** is beneath the Giralda, where the processions exit into Plaza de la Virgen de los Reyes, but even here it gets chaotic. The best way of all to see the processions is to pick them up on the way from and to their *barrios*, which is where you'll see the true *teatro de la calle* – the theatre of the streets.

During Semana Santa the population of the central district increases from 400,000 to 1.5 million people, and the pattern of events changes daily. While newsstands stock the official programme – **Programa de la Semana Santa** – they quickly sell out. A daily detailed timetable is issued with local papers (*El Correo* and *Diario de Sevilla* both do coloured route maps) and is essential if you want to know which processions are where. The ultra-Catholic *ABC* paper has the best background information, and the Turismo's *El Giraldillo* listings magazine prints a brief programme, while the banks and bigger hotels tend to produce their own guides. The national *El País* and *El Mundo* newspapers also carry excellent daily supplements with all the routes and *cofradías* tunics listed in colour.

THE FERIA DE ABRIL

The nonstop, week-long Feria de Abril takes place in the second half of the month when a vast area on the west bank of the river, the **Real de la Feria**, is taken over by rows of *casetas*, canvas pavilions and tents of varying sizes. Some of these belong to eminent *sevillano* families, some to groups of friends, others to clubs, trade associations or political parties. Each one resounds with flamenco singing and dancing from around 9pm until perhaps 6am or 7am the following morning. Many of the men and virtually all the women wear traditional costume, the latter in an astonishing array of brilliantly coloured, flounced gypsy dresses.

The sheer size of this spectacle makes it extraordinary, and the dancing, with its intense and knowing sexuality, is a revelation. But most infectious of all is the universal spontaneity of enjoyment; after wandering around staring, you wind up a part of it, drinking and dancing in one of the "open" *casetas* which have commercial bars. Earlier in the day, from 1pm until 5pm, *sevillana* society parades around the fairground in carriages or on horseback in an incredible extravaganza of display and voyeurism with subtle but distinct gradations of dress and style. Each day, too, there are **bullfights** (at around 5.30pm; very expensive tickets in advance from the ring), generally reckoned to be the best of the season.

COPAS AND MUSIC BARS

Copas bars (drinking bars) are scattered all over the centre. Clusters of good ones are to be found in the Alameda de Hércules and Plaza Alfalfa zones in El Centro, with more gathered to the north of the Maestranza bullring – where there's also a gay scene – and along C/Betis in Triana.

Café Central Alameda de Hércules s/n; ☎ 954 370 999. As it's always the last bar to close on the Alameda, this bar attracts an eclectic, international crowd. The atmosphere is laidback and conversational – just the place to chill out with new friends.

Café Jazz Naima C/Conde de Barajas 2; ☎ 653 753 976. There's quality jazz on a nightly basis at this cosy bar on the corner. Drinks are slightly pricier than average, but you don't have to pay for entry, just contribute to a tip jar that's passed around between songs.

Casa Matiás C/Arfe 11. Bottles of ancient liquor gather dust on the wooden beams of this delightfully pokey *peña de flamenco* (flamenco clubhouse). Come in small groups

and, after ordering a *canita*, ask the bar man if he'll show you the room upstairs – dedicated to the national dance.

Gigante Bar Pza Alameda de Hercules 17; ☎ 955 294 529. Cosy, fun café-come-bar on the Alameda. Perfect place for a post-dinner drink and dessert; try the pina colada and *tarta queso platano* (banana cheesecake).

Java C/San Jacinto 31; ☎ 954 001 140. Cross over the Triana bridge to savour this bar's relaxed atmosphere in this vibrant pedestrianized street. Good place for people-watching while nursing an afternoon tea or coffee on its terrace.

Trinity Irish Pub C/Madrid s/n, just off Pza Nueva; ☎ 954 224 970. For those with a fondness for Guinness, this is Seville's nearest approximation to a Dublin hostelry, with plenty of nooks to converse and ruminate.

Urbano Comix C/Matahacas 5; ☎ 954 210 387. Popular student bar – with hippy overtones – featuring zany urban decor. Sounds include grunge metal, rock, punk and R&B, often with live bands. Open 365 days per year.

> ## SEVILLE MARKETS
>
> Entertaining Sunday markets (*mercadillos*; roughly 10am–2pm depending on weather) take place on the **Plaza del Cabildo** opposite the cathedral (stamps, coins, ancient artefacts) and the **Plaza del Museo** fronting the Museo de las Bellas Artes (local art, tiles and woodcarvings). Calle Feria's long-standing **El Jueves** (Thursday) market near the Alameda de Hércules, with secondhand articles and antiques, is another good one. An excellent *artesanía* market, **El Postigo**, C/Arfe s/n, just west of the cathedral, displays a range of fans, glassware, ceramics, silverware and jewellery with innovative designs made by local craftspeople. The Mercado de Triana (Mon–Sat 9am–2pm) is the *barrio* Triana's central market, built over the site of the Castillo de Triana (visible through a glass floor).

SUMMER TERRACE BARS

On sultry summer nights it's worth doing what *sevillanos* do and making a beeline for these riverside oases, which are the only place to stay really cool in July and August (and often in June and September too). Note that these bars open June–Sept only and some only for a season, opening up the next year under different names and owners, but usually in the same location.

Alfonso Avda de la Palmera, Parque de María Luisa; ☎ 954 233 735. Popular terrace bar in the park for cooling off over a long drink. The neighbouring *Bilindo* and *Libano* opposite are similarly relaxing places.

Bar 84 Alameda de Hércules 84; ☎ 954 904 099. The terrace of this gay-friendly bar is the perfect spot for a tinto verano, or four.

El Capote Next to the Puente de Triana (aka Isabel II); ☎ 954 216 890. Highly popular riverside bar with outdoor terrace which has DJs spinning cool sounds and often stages live bands in summer.

Muelle New York Paseo de las Delicias s/n; ⓦ muellenewyork.com. Popular upscale riverside cocktail bar and a good place to smoke a shisha on a summer's evening. Wednesday evening features live flamenco artists accompanied by guitar or piano.

Puerto de Cuba C/Betis s/n; ☎ 667 796 972. Tucked beneath the San Telmo bridge this dual-level club is frequented by the city's smart set. The upper level is mellow with a nautical theme, while the ground floor overlooking the river reverberates with pop dance hits and eternal favourites.

SHOPPING

SEE MAPS PAGES 244 AND 257

Seville is a great place to **shop**, offering everything from regional crafts and ceramics to chic designer fashions and accessories. Seville's main shopping area is in the streets surrounding C/Sierpes. Shops – except for the larger department stores such as El Corte Inglés – generally close during the afternoon siesta (roughly 1.30–5.30pm) and stay open until 8 or 9pm.

BOOKS AND NEWSPAPERS

Casa del Libro C/Velázquez 8; ☎ 954 222 496. Central bookshop that stocks a range of books in English (and other languages) as well as maps.

El Corte Inglés Pza Duque de la Victoria; ⓣ elcorteingles.es. Seville's branch of Spain's major department store chain has designer fashions as well as an excellent supermarket, bookstore and travel agent. It also stocks the international press.

Fnac Avda de la Constitución 8; ⓦ fnac.es. An electronics, music and literature store with a small but well-curated English language section of mostly fiction titles.

Kiosko La Campana La Campana s/n. The city's best news kiosk with a comprehensive range of international newspapers. It's located in front of the *pastelería La Campana* at the northern end of C/Sierpes.

Risko Avda Kansas City 26, close to Santa Justa train station; ⓦ risko.es. Stocks maps and a range of outdoor clothing and equipment.

DESIGNER FASHIONS

Antonio Ortíz C/Velázquez 5; ☎ 954 212 059. For those in search of quality (and quirky) footwear.

Loewe Pza Nueva 12; ⓦ loewe.com. Pretty but pricey clothes and bags.

Purificación García Pza Nueva 8; ⓦ purificaciongarcia. com. One of Spain's most celebrated designers, noted for her simple and stylish lines.

FLAMENCO DRESSES

Asunción Peña C/Lineros 7; ☎ 954 229 952. Traditional flamenco dresses and accessories.

Molina C/Sierpes 11; ⓦ molinaflamenca.es. Exuberant dresses and shoes and chic accessories.

POTS AND TILES

Beatriz Rengifo Ruiz C/Antillano Campos 10. Interesting potter whose pottery shop has a wonderfully ebullient nineteenth-century exterior. Mixes traditional styles with more modern designs.

Cerámica Rocío-Triana C/Antillano Campos 8. Displaying work by Rafael Muñiz, a creative potter producing pieces with a modern slant. He can also create customized painted tile images (any size) to take home or have sent.

Cerámica Santa Ana C/San Jorge 31, near the Puente de Triana; ☎ 954 340 908. Good for typically Andalucían souvenirs, with a wide selection of Triana pots and tiles.

DIRECTORY

Banks and currency exchange Numerous banks around the centre have ATMs, specifically on the Avda de la Constitución and around Plaza Duque de la Victoria. Bureaux de change can be found on Avda Constitución near the cathedral, but banks offer better rates.

Consulates UK, contact the Málaga consulate (see page 78); Ireland, Avda de Jerez 46 (☎ 954 690 689); USA, Plaza Nueva 8 (☎ 954 218 751).

Hospital English-speaking doctors are available at Hospital Universitario Virgen Macarena, C/Dr Marañón s/n (☎ 955 008 000), behind the Andalucía parliament building to the north of the centre. For emergencies, dial ☎ 061.

Left luggage There are coin-operated lockers (ask for the *consigna*) at the Santa Justa train station. The Prado de San Sebastián bus station has a left luggage office (daily 9am–9pm), and there's another *consigna* at the Plaza de Armas bus station (9.30am–1.30pm & 3–6pm) – note that the locker system is slightly confusing so you may need to ask for assistance.

Lost property Oficina de Objetos Perdidos, C/Manuel V. Sagastizábal 3, next to the Prado de San Sebastián bus station (Mon–Fri 9.30am–1.30pm; ☎ 954 420 703).

Pharmacy There's a well-stocked Farmacia at C/Tetuán 4 (Mon–Fri 9am–9pm, Sat 9.30am–9pm).

Police For emergencies dial ☎ 092 (local police; less serious matters) or ☎ 091 (national; violent crime and so on). Central local police stations are at C/Arenal 1 and C/Crédito 11, off the north end of the Alameda de Hércules.

Post office Avda de la Constitución 32, by the cathedral; poste restante (*lista de correos*) is also held here (Mon–Fri 8.30am–8.30pm, Sat 9.30am–1pm).

North of Seville: Itálica and around

The Roman ruins and remarkable mosaics of **Itálica** and the exceptional Gothic monastery of **San Isidoro del Campo** lie some 9km to the north of Seville, just outside the village of **Santiponce**. Both can be easily visited by bus as a day-trip from Seville and there are excellent places to eat near the archeological site.

Itálica

Avda de Extremadura 2 · See website for opening hours · Charge · ⓦ italicasevilla.org

As you survey the dusty, featureless landscape of the site of **Itálica** today, it's hard to believe that this was once the third largest city of the Roman world, surpassed only by Alexandria and Rome itself. Itálica was the birthplace of two emperors (Trajan and Hadrian) and one of the earliest Roman settlements in Spain. Founded in 206 BC by Scipio Africanus after his decisive victory over the Carthaginians at nearby Alcalá del Río, it became a settlement for many of his veterans, who called the place "Italica" to remind them of home. With a thriving port – now beneath Santiponce – the city rose to considerable military importance in the second and third centuries AD, when it was richly endowed during the reign of Hadrian (117–138). Grand buildings dripped with fine marble brought from Italy, Greece, Turkey and Egypt, and the population swelled to half a million. Itálica declined as an urban centre only under the Visigoths, who preferred Hispalis (Seville). Eventually the city was deserted by the Moors after the river changed its course, disrupting the surrounding terrain.

In the Middle Ages the ruins were used as a source of stone and lime extraction for Seville, and, from the eighteenth century onwards, lack of any regulation allowed enthusiastic amateurs to indulge their treasure-hunting whims and carry away or sell whatever they found. The Duke of Wellington spent some time "excavating" here during the Peninsular Wars and later the Countess of Lebrija conducted her own "digs" to fill her palace in Seville with mosaics and artefacts (see page 267).

The site

Somehow, the shell of the enormous **amphitheatre** – the third largest in the Roman world and originally standing outside the city walls – has survived. It is crumbling perilously, but you can clearly detect the rows of seats for an audience of 25,000, the access corridors and the dens for wild beasts.

Beyond, within a rambling and unkempt grid of streets and villas, about twenty **mosaics** have been uncovered in what was originally the northern, richer sector of the city. Look for the outstanding Neptune mosaic in the house of the same name, as well as the colourful bird mosaic in the Casa de los Pájaros depicting 33 different species. Towards the baths, in the Casa del Planetario, is a fascinating representation of the Roman planetary divinities who, in the Roman calendar, gave their names to the days of the week. Also here is the giant, underground oven of the city. Finally, on the site's western edge, the **Hadrianic baths** – named the Termes Mayores to distinguish them from a smaller baths discovered in the village of Santiponce – are divided into those for men to the centre and right, and those for women to the left.

On the site's southern edge, to the rear of the still-functioning walled cemetery of Santiponce – which was here long before excavations began – is the recently unearthed **Traianeum**, a great religious complex constructed by Hadrian and dedicated to the worship of his adoptive father Trajan.

Outside the main site, in the village of **Santiponce** itself – beneath which lies another sizeable chunk of unexcavated Itálica – there's also a well-preserved **Roman theatre** and the **Termes Menores baths** (both usually open at least 8am–3pm, Sun from 10am, closed Monday; free), both a five-minute walk away from the site entrance and signposted from the main road.

Monasterio Isidoro del Campo

C/San Isidoro s/n • Tues–Thurs 10am–3pm, Fri & Sat 10am–7pm, Sun 10am–2.30pm • Charge

A little over 1km south of Santiponce on the road back to Seville lies the impressive former Cistercian **Monasterio Isidoro del Campo**. Founded by the thirteenth-century monarch Guzmán El Bueno of Tarifa fame (see page 197), the monastery is a masterpiece of Gothic architecture which, prior to its confiscation during the nineteenth century Disentailment, was occupied by a number of religious orders. Among these were the *ermitaños jerónimos* (Hieronymites) who, in the fifteenth century, decorated the central cloister and the Patio de los Evangelistas with a remarkable series of **murals** depicting images of the saints – including scenes from the life of San Jerónimo – as well as astonishingly beautiful floral and Mudéjar-influenced geometric designs. In the sixteenth century the monastery was renowned for its library and in 1569 a member of the order, Casiodoro de Reina, made the first translation of the Bible into Castilian Spanish (a copy is on display). But when de Reina and others began to display an over-zealous interest in the Protestant ideas of Martin Luther the community fell foul of the Inquisition and was dissolved, with some monks being executed and others escaping abroad.

The monastery was then assigned to the non-hermitic main order of San Jerónimo which employed the seventeenth-century sculptor Juan Martínez Montañés to create the magnificent **retablo mayor** in the larger of the complex's twin churches. Depicting scenes from the Nativity, the Adoration of the Kings and San Jerónimo himself, this is one of the greatest works by this *andaluz* master of wood sculpture. In wall niches alongside the retablo – and positioned above their tombs – are images of Guzmán El Bueno and his spouse, also by Montañés.

Other highlights of this remarkable building include the **Sala Capitular** (chapter house) with more wall paintings and the **Refectorio** (refectory), with a fine mural of the *Sagrada Cena* (Last Supper) occupying an end wall and displaying more geometric designs worked into the table linen.

ARRIVAL AND INFORMATION

By bus Itálica and Monasterio Isidoro del Campo are easily reached by bus from the Plaza de Armas bus station in Seville (Bus #M-172 from stop 41; Mon–Sat every 30min, on the half-hour; Sun hourly; 20min). The bus will make its way into the village of Santiponce before stopping at the monastery, so don't panic when you go careering past it. It then turns back on itself and heads out of town again where

ITÁLICA AND AROUND

you'll be able to get off at the "Parada Monestario", 200m down from the gates to the Itálica site entrance. Buses return to Seville from this same stop every 30min.

Turismo Santiponce has a Turismo close to the archeological site at C/La Feria s/n (Tues–Sun 8am–3pm; ☎ 955 998 028).

ACCOMMODATION AND EATING

★ **La Caseta de Antonio** C/Rocío Vega 10, Santiponce; ⓦ lacasetadeantonio.com. Fifty metres down a side street behind the *Ventorrillo Canario*, this is undisputably the place to go for fish or an outstanding paella. €€

Hotel Anfiteatro Romano Avda Extremadura 18, facing the Itálica site entrance ⓦ hotelanfiteatroromano.es. Comfortable a/c rooms in a three-star hotel attached to the sprawling *Ventorrillo Canario* restaurant. Breakfast is extra. €

3

East from Seville

The direct route **east from Seville** by train or car, along the valley of the Guadalquivir heading towards Córdoba, is a flat and largely unexciting journey. The more interesting route follows the A4-E5 route just to the south of this (the one used by most buses), via **Carmona** and **Écija**, both ancient towns with plenty to see. To the south of Écija lies the ducal town of **Osuna** and its neighbour **Estepa**, both with compelling architectural delights. With good bus connections to Seville (and trains running from Osuna), these towns are all easily reached on a day-trip – Carmona in particular is an easy 30km journey.

Leaving Seville, the A4-E5 crosses **La Campiña**, a rich and undulating lowland framed between the Guadalquivir to the north and the hills of Penibetic Cordillera to the south. It's a sparsely populated area, its towns thinly spread and far apart – a legacy of post-*Reconquista* days when large, landed estates were doled out to the nobility by the crown. The feudal nature of this system of *latifundia* (great estates where the nobles owned not only the towns but also the inhabitants and the serfs on the land) wrought much bitterness in Andalucía, vividly described in Ronald Fraser's book, *Pueblo*.

Carmona

Sited on a low hill overlooking a fertile plain planted with fields of barley, wheat and sunflowers, **CARMONA** is a small, picturesque town that has burst beyond its ancient walls. Founded by the Carthaginians in the third century BC probably on the site of a Turditani Iberian settlement, they named it Kar-Hammon (City of Baal-Hammon) after their great deity – the origin, via the Roman "Carmo", of its present name. A major Roman town (from which era it preserves a fascinating subterranean necropolis), it was also an important *taifa* state in Moorish times. Following the *Reconquista*, Pedro the Cruel built a palace within its walls, which he used as a "provincial" royal residence – it's now the modern *parador*.

The majority of Carmona's monuments and churches lie inside the ancient walls. The only site involving a bit of effort to get to is the remarkable Necrópolis Romana (Roman cemetery) on the west side of town, a ten-minute walk from the old quarter.

San Pedro

C/San Pedro s/n • Mon, Thurs & Sun 9.30am–3pm • Charge

The fifteenth-century church of **San Pedro**, near the main bus stop, is a good place to start exploring Carmona. With its soaring tower built in imitation of the Giralda

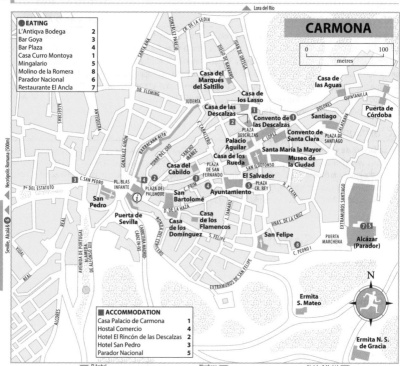

and added a century later, San Pedro evokes a feeling of Seville – entirely appropriate since the two towns share a similar history, and under the Moors Carmona was often governed by a brother of the Sevillian ruler. Inside, the church has a superb Baroque *sagrario* (side chapel) by Figueroa.

Just behind the church at the top of Avenida de Portugal lies a famous fifteen-spouted **fountain** that has figured in many flamenco songs and poems about the town.

Puerta de Sevilla

Pza Blas Infante • Guided tours (organised by the Turismo) July & Aug Daily 10am–3pm; Sept–June Mon–Sat 10am–6pm, Sun 10am–3pm • Charge

The old town – circled by 4km of ancient walls containing substantial Carthaginian, Roman and Moorish elements – is entered by the **Puerta de Sevilla**, an impressive double gateway. Although most of what you see now is of Roman origin there has been a gate of some form here since Iberian times: remains dating back to the late second millennium BC have been found in excavations. Through this gate passed the great Vía Augusta on its way from Hispalis (Seville) to Corduba (Córdoba). During the Moorish period a fortified *alcázar* was added, creating the great bastion that still dominates the town's western flank today.

Plaza de San Fernando

Inside the walls, narrow streets wind upwards past Mudéjar churches and Renaissance mansions. Follow Calle Prim uphill to the **Plaza de San Fernando** (or Plaza Mayor), modest in size but overlooked by splendid Moorish-style buildings, including the Casa del Cabildo (the old Ayuntamiento).

A striking Renaissance facade fronts the town's present **Ayuntamiento** (Mon–Fri 8am–3pm; free) in the square's southeast corner, worth a visit to view a striking geometric-patterned Roman mosaic with a head of Medusa in its patio.

Behind the plaza (reached by taking Calle Sacramento and turning right along Calle Dominguez de Aposanto) there's a bustling **fruit and vegetable** market in an elegant porticoed square.

Santa María La Mayor

Tues–Sat 9.30am–2pm & 6.30–8pm, Sat 7–8.30pm, Sun 10–12pm & 7–8.30pm; closed second half Aug and first half Sept • Charge

Moving east from the Ayuntamiento, you'll reach **Santa María la Mayor**, a fine fifteenth-century Gothic church built over the former Almohad Friday (main) mosque, whose elegant patio it retains, complete with orange trees and horseshoe arches. Like many of Carmona's churches it's capped by a Mudéjar tower, possibly utilizing part of the old minaret. One of the patio's pillars is inscribed with a Visigothic liturgical calendar, said to be the oldest in Spain. The church's high altar has a splendid Renaissance retablo and, in the third chapel to the right, a fifteenth-century triptych by Alejandro Fernández. Off the patio is a museum containing artworks by Zurbarán, Roldan and Bocanegro.

Museo de la Ciudad

Mid-June to Aug Daily 10am–2pm; Sep to mid-Jun Mon 11am–2pm, Tues–Sat 11am–7pm • Charge • ⓦ museociudad.carmona.org

Housed in the elegant eighteenth-century Casa del Marqués de las Torres is the **Museo de la Ciudad**, documenting the history of the town with mildly interesting displays of artefacts from the prehistoric, Iberian, Carthaginian, Roman, Moorish and Christian epochs. The most entertaining feature is a series of interactive screens in a section dedicated to the role of flamenco in Andalucían culture – enabling you to call up a flamenco style of your choice and fill the museum with the sound. There's little in the way of bars in this area so the museum's *cafetería* provides a useful refreshment stop.

Alcázar

Parador bars, restaurants and public areas open to non-guests

Looming above the town's southeastern ridge are the massive ruins of Pedro's **Alcázar**, an Almohad fortress transformed into a lavish residence by the fourteenth-century king – employing the same Mudéjar craftsmen who worked on the Alcázar at Seville – but which was destroyed by an earthquake in 1504. It received further architectural attentions from Fernando (after Isabel's death) but later fell into ruin, until it was renovated to become an extremely tasteful *parador*, entered through an imposing Moorish gate.

Puerta de Córdoba

To the northeast of the Alcázar, beyond and below Pedro's palace, the town comes to an abrupt and romantic halt at the Roman **Puerta de Córdoba**, a second-century gateway with later Moorish and Renaissance additions, from where the old Córdoba road (now a dirt track) drops down to a vast and fertile plain. Following this ancient route for a few kilometres will lead you to a five-arched **Roman bridge**, just visible on the plain below. Near the gate, the **church of Santiago**, at the end of Calle Calatrava, is another impressive fourteenth-century Mudéjar building with an elegant brick tower decorated with *azulejos*.

Convento de Santa Clara and around

C/Torno de Santa Clara • Fri–Mon 11am–2pm & 4–6pm (May–Sept 5–7pm) • Charge

Following Calle Dolores Quintanilla and its continuation, Calle López, from the Puerta de Córdoba back to the centre, you'll pass by more *palacios* and churches, among them the fifteenth-century **Convento de Santa Clara**, with a *mirador* tower on

3

the left and paintings by Valdés Leal in its church, while beyond lie the eighteenth-century **Convento de las Descalzas** and the Baroque **Palacio de los Águilar** (on the right), with a fine facade. A working convent, some of the nuns here will be happy to speak English with you, and you sell their delicious artisanal cakes.

Necrópolis Romana

June to mid-Sept Tues–Sun 9am–3pm; mid-Sept to Dec Tues–Sat 9am–6.30pm, Sun 9am–3pm; Jan–March Tues–Sat 9am–6.30pm, Sun 9am–3pm; April to mid-June Tues–Sat 9am–8.30pm, Sun 9am–3pm • Charge • ☎ 600 143 632

Lying on a low hill outside the walls, as was the Roman custom, Carmona's remarkable **Necrópolis Romana** (Roman cemetery) is one of the most important in Spain. Here, amid the cypress trees, more than nine hundred family tombs dating from the second century BC to the fourth century AD were excavated between 1881 and 1915. Enclosed in subterranean *columbaria* – chambers hewn from the rock – the tombs are often frescoed in the Pompeian style with images of garlands, birds and fruit, and contain a series of niches in which many of the funeral urns remain intact.

Some of the larger tombs, such as the **Tumba del Elefante** (complete with a stone elephant, perhaps symbolic of long life) are enormously elaborate, in preparation for the ceremonies that went with burial and after, when the tomb became a focus for family rituals centred on the dead. Alongside its burial chamber, a bath, pantry and kitchen with chimney as well as stone benches and tables for funeral banquets are wonderfully preserved. Most spectacular is the **Tumba de Servilia**, a huge colonnaded temple with vaulted side chambers and separate *columbaria* for the servants of the family. Information boards provide interesting detail regarding the various types of tombs, together with the cremation pits where the corpse would have been burned while members of the family (and hired mourners if they were rich) threw clothes and food into the flames for use in the afterlife. The paths between the tombs were also used in Roman times, and it doesn't take a lot of imagination to visualize a slow procession of grieving relatives and mourners preceded by flute players or trumpeters making their way to the family vault.

The site also has a small **museum** with finds from the tombs including gravestones, mosaics and vases. Opposite is a partly excavated second-century amphitheatre.

ARRIVAL AND INFORMATION   CARMONA

By bus Buses arriving from Seville and other destinations will drop you on the Paseo del Estatuto in sight of the Moorish Puerta de Sevilla, a grand and ancient fortified gateway to the old town.

Destinations Córdoba (3 daily; 1hr 20min); Écija (3 daily; 35min); Seville (16 daily, 6 Sat & Sun; 30min).

By car The subterranean car park beneath the Paseo del Estatuto is central and convenient. Parking places also

become free along the main C/San Pedro during siesta and after 7pm.

Turismo The Puerta de Sevilla also houses an efficient Turismo (July & Aug Mon–Fri 10am–3pm & 4.30–6pm, Sat & Sun 10am–3pm; Sept–June Mon–Sat 10am–6pm, Sun 10am–3pm; ⓦ turismo.carmona.org), which is well stocked with information and can provide a town map.

ACCOMMODATION   SEE MAP PAGE 290

Carmona has a shortage of places to stay, especially in the budget category, and particularly in spring and high summer it's worth ringing ahead. The **cheaper places** lie outside the walls, while a clutch of more **upmarket options** all occupy scenic locations in the old town and have their own restaurants and garages. Prices below are for the *temporada media* (shoulder season), which covers the months of May, September and October. All other periods are low season when (particularly hotel) prices will be significantly cheaper.

Casa Palacio de Carmona Pza de Lasso 1; ⓦ casadecarmona.com. Stylish transformation of a sixteenth-century *casa palacio* into a serene hotel with many original features plus light and spacious individually styled rooms decorated with genuine antiques and artworks. €€

Hostal Comercio C/Torre del Oro 56; ☎ 954 140 018. Built into the Puerta de Sevilla gateway, this is a charming small and friendly family-run *hostal* that has been around since 1914. Offers compact a/c en-suite rooms (without TV)

around a pretty patio, some with views of the church. €
Hotel El Rincón de las Descalzas C/Descalzas 1; ⊛ elrincondelasdescalzas.com. The staff at this cosy two-star will do everything they can to make you feel at home. It's a 2min walk from the city museum; all rooms come with a/c and some have balconies. *Restaurant La Yedra* lies beneath in the ivy-laden patio, serving good Mediterranean cuisine. €
Hotel San Pedro C/San Pedro 3; ⊛ hotelsanpedro.es. Near the church of San Pedro this is a central and pleasant

budget option for a/c en-suite rooms with TVs. Below, a café serves a decent breakfast. €
★ **Parador Nacional** Alcázar Rey Don Pedro; ⊛ www. parador.es. Despite competition at this end of the market, the superb location, patios and swimming pool ensure this is still the nicest – and best value – of the luxury places in town. Pay a few euros extra for a room with a balcony. It's worth calling in for a drink at the bar, to enjoy the fabulous views from the terrace. €€€€

EATING

SEE MAP PAGE 290

There are plenty of places to eat both in the old and new town and you don't need to spend a fortune to dine well. However, a step up in price will allow you to sample some of the best food in the province. In addition to the places below, all the upmarket hotels have their own restaurants, often with a reasonably priced *menú*. Carmona has its fair share of **tapas bars** too – the Turismo produces a free tapas guide and map, *Des Tapa Carmona*.

RESTAURANTS

L'Antiqva Bodega Pza del Palenque. Wine tavern with old barrels hung to the walls and locals sharing *croquetas de merluza* (hake croquettes) and *tortilla al whiskey*. Most tapas available in main sizes. €€
Casa Curro Montoya C/Santa María de Gracia 13l; ☎ 657 903 629. Named after a flamenco *cantante* related to the proprietors, this is a very pleasant and intimate little tapas bar with an upstairs restaurant. Specialities include *ensalada* de *atún fresco* (fresh tuna salad) as well as *carnes ibéricas*. Good tapas range in the bar – try the *morcilla* (black pudding). Has a small street terrace. €€€
★ **Molino de la Romera** C/Pedro s/n; ⊛ molinodelaromera.es. With a great terrace view across the *campiña* and housed in a sixteenth-century Moorish oil mill, this pleasant restaurant serves up regional dishes, has a good-value menu and also does *raciones* (try the pulpo in cream sauce*)*. Its *dulces* are prepared by the nuns of the nearby Convento de Santa Clara. €€
Parador Nacional Alcázar Rey Don Pedro; ⊛ parador.

es. The restaurant of the *parador* is a model of baronial splendour that can be experienced on a *menú del día* that includes many local dishes; they also offer vegetarian and diabetic menus. €€€
Restaurante El Ancla C/Bonifacio IV, about 500m along the Alcalá road; ⊛ elanclarestaurante.es. Out of the centre but well worth the effort, this is a great fish restaurant; meat is also served and there's an excellent tapas bar with a tempting *menú*. Specialities include *riñones de cordero al ajillo* (lamb kidneys with garlic) and there's a pleasant terrace. €€

TAPAS BARS

Bar Goya C/Prim 42; ☎ 954 143 060. This lively tapas bar is housed in a fifteenth-century edifice off the west side of Pza De San Fernando in the old town. There's also a pleasant terrace and cheap house specials include *alboronía* (ratatouille) and *croquetas de merluza* (hake croquettes). €
Bar Plaza Pza de San Fernando s/n; ☎ 954 190 067. Focal tapas bar on the main square and well worth a try. Specials include *carillada* (stewed pork cheeks) and *berenjenas con miel* (aubergine) and they also have a well-priced *menú*. €
Mingalario Pza Cristo del Rey 1; ☎ 954 143 893. In the old town, facing the church of El Salvador, this is another fine old bar with excellent tapas. House specials include *gambas al ajillo* (shrimps in garlic). €

Écija

One of the most distinctive and individual towns of Andalucía, **ÉCIJA** lies almost midway between Seville and Córdoba, in a basin of low sandy hills. The town is known, with no hint of exaggeration, as *la sartenilla de Andalucía* (the frying-pan of Andalucía) and once registered an alarming 52°C on the thermometer. Laurie Lee wrote in *A Rose for Winter* "in summer it is so hot that the very natives fall dead in the street". In mid-August the only way to avoid this heat is to slink from one tiny shaded plaza to another. It's worth the effort, since Écija has eleven superb, decaying church towers, each glistening with brilliantly coloured tiles. The town also has a unique domestic architecture – a flamboyant style of twisted or florid forms, displayed in a number of fine mansions close to the centre.

Brief history

The Romans knew Écija as 'Astigi' (the modern inhabitants are known as *astigitanos*), probably the name of an earlier Iberian settlement. It was an important and prosperous olive-growing town, trading the prized Baetican oil all over the empire during the first and second centuries. In the early Christian era Écija became a bishopric, but in Moorish times (now named Estadja) sank into relative obscurity as part of the caliphate of Córdoba. Conquered by Fernando III in 1240, it was only in the seventeenth and eighteenth centuries that it staged a recovery, when the prosperity brought by the new *latifundia* – harking back to the immense slave-worked Roman estates – encouraged the nobility to build impressive mansions in the town. Following the devastation wrought by the Lisbon earthquake of 1755, Écija's ruined churches were painstakingly restored at great cost, and with some terrific additions; hence the magnificent collection of late Baroque towers that are the glory of the place today.

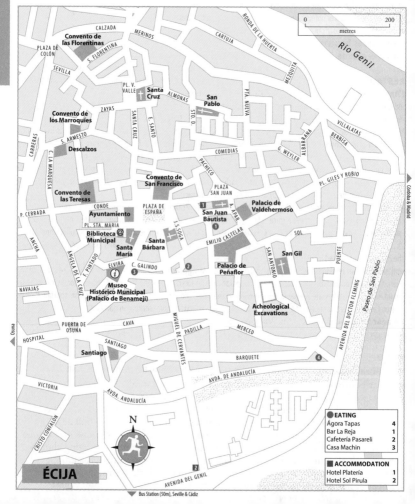

● EATING	
Ágora Tapas	4
Bar La Reja	1
Cafetería Pasareli	2
Casa Machin	3

■ ACCOMMODATION	
Hotel Platería	1
Hotel Sol Pirula	2

ÉCIJA

Plaza de España

Écija's most important churches and palaces are all within a few minutes' stroll of the once delightful arcaded and palm-shaded **Plaza de España** (known locally as the Plaza Mayor), although a controversial revamp to create an underground car park has transformed it into a rather desolate, modernistic space jarring with the Baroque splendours surrounding it. A Roman bath discovered in the course of these works – only one of many archeological discoveries – can now be viewed under a canopy in the plaza's southeast corner.

At the plaza's western end stands the **Ayuntamiento** which contains – in the imposing council chamber – a fine second-century Roman mosaic depicting the mythological Dirce being dragged by a bull as a punishment meted out by the two sons of Antiope, Zethus and Amphion – whose mother she had mistreated. Ask in the reception for permission to view.

Just behind the Ayuntamiento, overlooking the southwest side of Plaza España, stands the lyrically beautiful tower of **Santa María** (daily 9.30am–1.30pm & 5.30–9pm; free) – one of the eighteenth-century rebuilds. Inside, a cloister displays archeological finds from the surrounding area.

Museo Histórico Municipal

Palacio de Benamejí, C/Canovas de Castillo • Opening times change, check the website • Free • Ⓦ museo.ecija.es

Behind Santa María, on Calle Canovas de Castillo, lies the magnificent eighteenth-century Palacio de Benamejí, with a stunning portal in contrasting tints of marble. The palace now houses the Turismo and the **Museo Histórico Municipal**, providing an opportunity to view this imposing mansion and its patio.

Inside the museum, exhibits cover the town's history, from Neolithic hunters and gatherers through the Romans – there's a particularly good section on Astigi's role in the olive oil trade – to the Moorish and medieval epochs. One sensational feature is the **Amazona de Écija**, a stunning, 2m high, almost totally intact first-century-AD Roman statue accidentally discovered in the 2002 excavations to build a car park beneath the main square, Plaza de España (see page 295). Depicting an Amazon resting against a pillar, it is of the highest craftsmanship and still bears traces of ochre paint; it has now become the town's civic icon. The museum has been expanded to include a whole upper floor dedicated to displaying a marvellous collection of **Roman mosaic pavements** which have been unearthed in excavations in and around the town.

Santa Cruz

Pza Nuestra Señora del Valle • Mon–Sat 9am–1pm & 6–9pm, Sun 10am–1pm & 7–9pm • Free

North of Plaza España lies the church of **Santa Cruz**, whose brick tower was once a minaret, with tenth-century Arabic inscriptions recording the setting up of public fountains. Inside are more superb retablos and an early Christian sarcophagus, all beneath a lofty cupola. The charming *plazuela* fronting the church has two fine old iron crosses on a plinth, backed in summer by a wonderful avalanche of crimson bougainvillea down the wall behind.

San Juan Bautista

Pza San Juan • Mon–Sat 10am–1.30pm & 6–9pm, Sun 10.30am–1.30pm

Heading along a narrow street out of the Plaza España's northeast corner you'll soon spot the ornate belfry of **San Juan Bautista**, perhaps the best of all Écija's Baroque towers. In its churchyard are the substantial ruins of the earlier church destroyed in the eighteenth-century earthquake.

Palacio de Peñaflor

Continuing east from San Juan Bautista leads you to the sixteenth-century **Palacio de Valdehermoso**, with a Plateresque facade incorporating Roman pillars and, almost opposite and running along Calle Castellar, the enormous eighteenth-century **Palacio de Peñaflor** (currently closed; enquire at the Turismo), where a magnificent painted curved frontage is complemented by a full-blown Baroque portal topped with twisted barley-sugar columns. Formerly the residence of the marquises of Peñaflor until the line became heirless in 1958, the edifice was sold to the town council for the nominal sum of 50,000ptas (€300). The cost of restoration and maintenance, however, may result in the palace being sold again, it is rumoured, to be converted into a luxury hotel. The interior has a fine staircase with intricate stuccowork and cupola off a twin-tiered arched central patio.

San Gil and around

Pza de San Gil • Wed–Sun 10.30am–1pm, plus Fri 6–9pm • Free

The Gothic-Mudéjar church of **San Gil** is famed for its pencil-slim tower, and has a restored interior with an elegant retablo in its *sagrario*. Just beyond San Gil more **archeological excavations** are in progress and have so far revealed the foundations of enormous Roman buildings, plus some extremely fine mosaics many of which are now displayed in the town museum. The progress of the excavations can be viewed through the surrounding fence.

ARRIVAL AND INFORMATION ÉCIJA

By bus Frequent daily buses to and from Seville and Córdoba stop at the station on Avda Andalucía. Destinations Carmona (2 daily; 35min); Córdoba (5 daily; 1hr); Seville (9 daily; 1hr 15min).

Turismo Located at the Museo Histórico Municipal (see page 295) inside the Palacio de Benamejí (opening times are complex, see the website; ⓦturismoecija.com).

ACCOMMODATION SEE MAP PAGE 294

Hotel Platería C/Garcilópez 1; ⓦhotelplateria.net. Off the east side of the Pza Mayor, this comfortable hotel has modern a/c rooms. Despite what the muted decor might lead you to believe, there's a lot of personality under the surface. The restaurant below serves up fun *pinchos* and *tostadas* including pork loin bites with Roquefort and mini-

hamburgers. They also offer laughter therapy for those inclined (see website for details). €

Hotel Sol Pirula C/Miguel de Cervantes 50; ⓦhotelpirula.com. South of the centre, this three-star modern hotel has decent a/c rooms above its ground-floor restaurant. Own garage. €

EATING SEE MAP PAGE 294

Ágora Tapas C/Barquette 38A; ☎955 317 077. Food cooked with finesse in a light, spacious setting. They have a small, rotating menu which includes their deliciously sticky *milhojas de berenjena y queso de cabra* (aubergines with goat's cheese) and a daily three-course set meal. €€

Bar La Reja C/Garcilopez 1; ⓦbarlareja.es. Next door to the *Hotel Platería*, this bar has a wide choice of delicious tapas and *raciones*. Highlights include the *flamenquin Iberico* (ham and pork loin roulade), and you can't go wrong with any of their fresh *mariscos*. €€

Cafetería Pasareli Pasaje Virgen del Rocío 2; ☎955

904 383. Tucked away in a cul-de-sac off the east side of the Pza de España, this bar-restaurant serves up a range of fish and meat dishes – including *pez espada a la maninera* (swordfish in seafood sauce) in season – and has a budget *menú*. Also has a small terrace. €€

Casa Machin C/Galindo 4; ⓦcasamachin.es. Mid-priced restaurant housed in an elegant *casa señorial* and popular with locals. House specials include *carrillada ibérico* (pork cheeks) and *dorada a la sal* (bream baked in salt). Beautiful terrace open July & Aug. €€

Osuna

Some 34km south of Écija along the A351, **OSUNA** is one of those small Andalucían towns which are great to explore in the early evening: slow and quietly enjoyable, with elegant streets of tiled, whitewashed houses and some of the finest Renaissance mansions in Spain.

Another settlement of obscure Iberian origin, Osuna first came to prominence as the Roman town of Urso, and ten bronze tablets from this period recording the town's statutes are preserved in Madrid's Archeological Museum. In Moorish times the town was of little note and it was during the post-*Reconquista* period, when it became the seat of the dukes of Osuna with enormous territories, that it was embellished with most of the outstanding buildings that make it so attractive today. Osuna's major sights are its collection of stunning **Renaissance mansions** and, on the hill to the east of the centre, the old **university**, the **Collegiata** church and the convent of **La Encarnación**. The town was featured as a filming location in the fifth season of popular series *Game of Thrones*. Since then, Osuna has seen a surge in tourism, dedicating a floor of its museum to the show.

Plaza Mayor

Osuna's main square is the elegant Plaza Mayor in the heart of the town and here it's worth taking a look at the eighteenth-century **Ayuntamiento** and, on the west side, the sixteenth-century **Convento de la Concepción** (open service times), with a fine eighteenth-century retablo.

Don't miss the wonderful **Casino** on the east side of the square, with a 1920s Mudéjar-style decor and the best *boquerones* in town. Despite a very local (and mostly male) clientele, it's open to all visitors and makes an excellent spot for people watching over the square.

Museo de Osuna

C/Sevilla 37 • Tues–Sat 10am–2pm & 5–7pm, Sun 10am–2pm • Charge

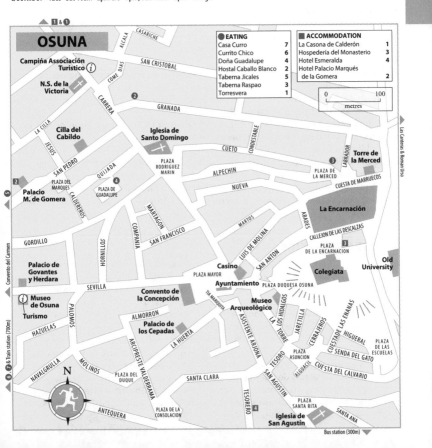

OSUNA

● EATING	
Casa Curro	7
Currito Chico	6
Doña Guadalupe	4
Hostal Caballo Blanco	2
Taberna Jicales	5
Taberna Raspao	3
Torresvera	1

■ ACCOMMODATION	
La Casona de Calderón	1
Hospedería del Monasterio	3
Hotel Esmeralda	4
Hotel Palacio Marqués de la Gomera	2

0 — 100 metres

Directly opposite the Palacio de Govantes y Herdera lies the **Museo de Osuna**, housed in yet another stunning eighteenth-century *casa palacio*, the Palacio de Arjona y Cubas. The museum has information on the history of the *palacios* as well as artworks about the town and its countryside over the last five hundred years. It's also now home to the Salon de Fuego y Hielo, a *Game of Thrones* themed exhibit with signed photographs and props.

Old University

C/Cuesta del Calvarios • Patio and lecture halls open term-time Mon–Fri 9am–7pm; closed July & Aug • Free

On a hilltop overlooking the town, the **Old University**, now part of the Universidad de Sevilla, has an elegant arcaded Renaissance patio. The beautifully preserved beamed lecture halls on the upper floor are decorated with wonderful eighteenth-century religious paintings. Founded in 1548 by one of the predecessors of the dukes of Osuna, the university was later suppressed by the reactionary Fernando VII in 1820 and only recently recovered its academic status. Here you could join the students at the patio's coffeehouse.

Colegiata

May–Sept Tues–Sun 10am–1.30pm & 4–7pm, July & Aug closed Sun pm; Oct–April Tues–Fri 10am–1.30pm & 3.30–6.30pm • Charge

Looming over the town from a hilltop near the Old University is the lavish sixteenth-century **Colegiata** – a fine Renaissance building with a Plateresque west doorway damaged, so the story goes, by French soldiers in the War of Independence who used it for target practice. Inside, a guide will point out a sumptuous gilded retablo and the remarkable seventeenth-century *Expiración de Cristo* (Crucifixion) by Ribera – one of the artist's greatest works. Also in the church some exquisite sculptures include a superb *Crucifixion* by Juan de Mesa, from the same period. More Riberas are to be seen in the *sacristía*, which now holds the church's impressive **art collection**. His *San Jerónimo*, *San Pedro* and a moving *Martirio de San Bartolomé* are all of the highest quality.

The highlight of the visit's latter stages is the descent to the subterranean depths to view the gloomy **pantheon and chapel of the dukes of Osuna**, where these descendants of the kings of León and former "Lords of Andalucía" are buried in niches in the walls. Some of the Renaissance ornamentation and sculpture is extremely fine, especially the polychrome wooden *Santo Entierro* (Burial of Christ), as well as panels from the Flemish school and a fine relief of San Jerónimo. The tour ends with the guide pointing out an antique portable sixteenth-century **organ** – one of few to survive from the period.

OSUNA'S PALACIOS

The best of the mansions erected in Osuna by its aristocrats and wealthy landowners are on the streets off Calle Carrera, running north from the Plaza Mayor, particularly Calle San Pedro. Many have an information board outside. On Calle San Pedro the **Cilla del Cabildo** (no. 16) has a superb geometric relief round a carving of the Giralda. Further along, the eighteenth-century **Palacio Marqués de Gomera** is another Baroque extravaganza with undulating ornamentation, balcony and solomonic columns beneath the family crest; it has now been converted into an upmarket restaurant and hotel (see page 300). Calle de la Huerta, south of the Plaza Mayor, has further interesting buildings, including the **Palacio de los Cepadas** (now the palace of justice) with an elegant patio and staircase, and nearby slightly north, on Calle Sevilla, the **Palacio de Puente Hermoso**. On the same street are more fine *palacios*, with the outstanding – but tragically crumbling – **Palacio de Govantes y Herdara** in urgent need of salvation. More *casa palacios* are to be found on *calles* Gordillo and Compañia (a street off the latter) to the west of the Plaza Mayor.

La Encarnación

Pza de la Encarnación • Tues–Sun: May & June 10am–1.30pm & 4–7pm; July–Sept 10am–1.30pm; Oct–April 10am–1.30pm & 4–6.30pm • Charge

Opposite the entrance to the Colegiata is the Baroque convent of **La Encarnación**, founded in the seventeenth century by a duchess of Osuna. The highlight of the nun-led guided tour is a fine plinth of eighteenth-century Sevillian *azulejos* (from Triana) round its cloister and gallery, depicting curiously secular scenes. Complete your visit by filling up on the tasty convent *dulces* sold here.

Torre de la Merced

From La Encarnación it's a pleasant walk north and then west along Calle Abades and the Cuesta de Marruecos to the **Torre de la Merced**, the tower of the former convent church of the same name, with its stupendously carved late Baroque tower and portal by Alonso Ruiz Florindo.

Roman Urso

3

Las Canteras is the site of **Roman Urso**, Osuna's ancient predecessor. Located to the northeast of La Encarnación convent (and signposted), the site is still in the process of investigation, but you will soon make out the foundations of once significant buildings and here also you'll find a necropolis with tombs quarried from the sandstone, as well as the vague remains of a theatre and fort plus a gigantic quarry – with steps leading down into it – where the Romans obtained the stone to build the city.

Museo Arqueológico

Pza de la Duquesa s/n • Tues–Sun: May & June 10am–1.30pm & 5–7pm; July–Sept 10am–2pm; Oct–April 10am–1.30pm & 3.30–6.30pm • Charge

Sited on the more direct descent to the town from the Colegiata, the **Museo Arqueológico** is housed in the Torre del Agua, a twelfth-century Almohad tower. The small museum displays local finds, none spectacular so far, unfortunately, although this situation is bound to change as excavations of the Roman town (see page 299) progress. Disappointingly, many of the most striking items are copies, with the originals having been sent to Madrid.

ARRIVAL AND DEPARTURE

OSUNA

By train The train station is on Avda de la Estación s/n, on the western edge of town. Osuna lies on the Seville–Granada line and is served by six daily trains from the provincial capital.

By bus The bus station lies southeast of the centre on Avda de la Constitución s/n, with frequent services to Seville and (less frequently) to Málaga and Granada.

INFORMATION AND TOURS

Turismo Housed in the town museum, Museo de Osuna, C/Sevilla 37, west of the main square (July & Aug Tues–Sat 10am–2pm & 5–8pm, Sun 10am–2pm; Sept–June Tues–Sat 10am–2pm & 5–8pm, Sun 10am–2pm; ☎ 954 815 732, ⓦ osuna.es).

Guided tours You can explore Roman (including excavations, caves and quarries) and Baroque (including the *palacios* and churches) Osuna with Campiña Asociación Turistico, C/Carrera 83 (☎ 609 764 818). There is also a free weekly tour of Osuna and its palaces (☎ 954 812 855 for details).

ACCOMMODATION

SEE MAP PAGE 297

Accommodation in Osuna is not plentiful, but outside national holiday periods and the local *feria* (third or fourth week in May) there's usually no great problem finding a place to stay.

★ **La Casona de Calderón** Pza de Cervantes 16; ☎ 954 815 037. Charming hotel in a restored eighteenth-century *casa palacio* with regally furnished and well-equipped beamed rooms, wet-room-style bathrooms and a tranquil patio with trailing plants. It houses a small town museum, complete with a display of cowbells. Also has a pool and its own restaurant. **€€**

★ **Hospedería del Monasterio** Pza de la Encarnación

3; ⓦhospederiadelmonasterio.com. Stunning hotel housed in a refurbished ancient building alongside the Colegiata. Individually styled rooms come with tiled floors, iron bedsteads and elegant furnishings, and there's a wonderful terrace pool outside. Has own bar-restaurant, offering a delicious range of tapas and *raciones* including *solomillo ibérico* (pork loin) and *lubina* (sea bass). €€

Hotel Esmeralda C/Tesorero 7; ⓦhotelesmeralda.es. Welcoming hotel with elegant a/c en-suite rooms. Stunning rooftop terrace with plunge pool and view towards the hilltop Colegiata. Free parking (reserve in advance). €€

★ **Hotel Palacio Marqués de la Gomera** C/San Pedro 20; ⓦhotelpalaciodelmarques.es. The town's four-star option, set inside one of the most beautiful *casa palacios* in the country, is a dream. A national monument in its own right, this eighteenth-century mansion has a breathtakingly beautiful patio with a Baroque chapel just off it and all rooms are tastefully and individually furnished. Room 7 was used by Franco Zeffirelli when here making a film about the life of María Callas and has a spectacular exterior balcony, while the irresistibly romantic Room 10 is situated in the palace's tower. There's a restaurant on-site too. Breakfast is included. €€

EATING

SEE MAP PAGE 297

There are places to eat and drink all over town. Osuna also has some outstanding **tapas bars**: those we've listed below are all top-notch and well worth seeking out.

★ **Casa Curro** Pza Salitre 5; ☎ 955 820 758. The town's best (and liveliest) tapas and *raciones* bar cooks up a tasty range of seafood and meat dishes, many with a creative slant. Choose from the specials chalked up on the numerous blackboards covering the walls. There's a superb restaurant in the back. €€

Currito Chico Pza Salitre 9; ☎ 630 501 768. Just around the corner from *Casa Curro*, the owner's son has set up his own place – *Currito Chico* – that's definitely worth trying for a more informal affair. €

Doña Guadalupe Pza Guadalupe 6; ⓦdona-guadalupe-restaurante.negocio.site. A sound mid-priced restaurant with an elegant dining room that specializes in *cocina andaluza*. *Lomo ibérico en salsa de almendras* (pork loin) is a signature dish and there's a good value *menú*. €€€

Hostal Caballo Blanco C/Granada 1. This *hostal's* Michelin-recommended restaurant is very good for *comida*

casera serving up dishes such as *redondillo guisado* (beef stew) and *gachas de osuna* (local gruel), plus the usual standards. €€

Taberna Jicales C/Esparteros 11; ☎ 954 810 423. Excellent tapas bar with an outdoor terrace. There's a mouthwateringly long tapas *carta*, and house specials include *boquerones al limon* (anchovies), *croquetas pollo bechamel* (chicken croquettes with béchamel sauce). Since the owner won the lottery, they're only open at lunchtime. €

Taberna Raspao Pza de la Merced 7; ☎ 617 537 599. A welcoming neighbourhood restaurant, very good for fish – try their *el revuelto se bacalao* (cod) – or *carnes ibéricas*, tapas and *raciones*. Also has a pleasant terrace on the square. Booking is advised. €€

Torresvera C/Alfonso XII; ☎ 630 467 883. Another of Osuna's brilliant tapas bars, with a wide (and often creative) range of tapas. Try their *croquetas de merluza y gambas* (croquettes with hake and prawns) or *solomillo de cerdo con miel de caña* (pork loin with molasses). Most dishes come in *tapa*, *medio* and *entera* sizes. €

Estepa

Another delightful Baroque town, **ESTEPA**, 24km east of Osuna, resembles a miniature version of its larger neighbour. Originally a Carthaginian settlement, it took the side of the North African state during the Punic Wars with Rome, and when the victorious Romans finally took the city in 208 BC they found that the citizens had burned their possessions and killed themselves rather than surrender. Repopulated, it eventually became the Roman Ostipo and, later, the Moorish Istabba. The town climbs up the slopes of San Cristóbal to its peak, where stands the impressive church of **Santa María** and the ancient **Moorish fort**. In the lower *barrios* – the main focus of life in Estepa today – there are quite a few churches and monuments worth a look. Visit in the run-up to Christmas time and the town smells like a cake factory as local bakers work to meet demands for its famous icing-covered provolone biscuits.

Iglesia de la Santa María de la Asunción

Cerro de San Cristóbal s/n • Open service times or by guided visit (see page 301) • Free

Crowning the hill above the town and reached by following Calle Saladillo, the fifteenth-century **Iglesia de la Santa María de la Asunción** is built on the remains of a tenth-century *mezquita*, and is one of Estepa's oldest churches. The Gothic interior, entered via the tourist office – as well as a museum – has various treasures, many rescued from other churches and monasteries. Look out for a fine sculpture of *San Juan Evangelista* by Juan de Mesa.

Convento de Santa Clara Jesús

Cerro de San Cristóbal s/n • Open service times or by guided visit (see page 301) • Free

Just east of the church of Santa María, the **Iglesia de Santa Clara** is another impressive convent church, dating from the late sixteenth century. Inside, the gilded seventeenth-century Plateresque retablo by Pedro Ruíz Paniagua is one the finest in the province.

Torre de la Victoria

C/Ancha

The spectacular Baroque **Torre de la Victoria** is all that remains of the eighteenth-century convent of the same name. A Civil War casualty, the convent was demolished in 1939 but the 50m-high tower, designated a national monument in 1955, survived to become the town's iconic symbol. Bear left up the Carrill Sta Clara to the Balcón de Andalucía for an excellent view from above.

Iglesia del Carmen

Pza del Carmen s/n • Open service times or by guided visit (see page 301) • Free

From the Torre de la Victoria, heading north and downhill for a couple of blocks along *calles* Toralba and Libertad leads to the Plaza del Carmen and the stunning eighteenth-century **Iglesia del Carmen** with an exuberant Baroque facade in black and white stone and a stunningly ornate, beautifully restored interior.

Palacio de los Marqueses de Cerverales and around

C/Castillejos 16 • Mon–Fri 9am–1pm • Charge

From the Plaza del Carmen, following Calle Mesones (and its continuation, Calle Castillejos) west through the town, you pass another fine church, the **Iglesia de la Asunción**, known locally as Estepa's Sistine Chapel due to a splendid painted ceiling depicting scenes from the life of the Virgin. The church was originally the chapel of one of Estepa's best mansions, the **Palacio de los Marqueses de Cerverales** next door, a superb eighteenth-century palace with barley-sugar columns supporting its balcony and delightful patio within.

ARRIVAL AND INFORMATION · ESTEPA

By bus Estepa's bus station is on the Avda Andalucía close to the *Hostal Balcón de Andalucía* (see page 301). Destinations Córdoba (1 daily; 2hr 15min); Osuna (8 daily; 1hr 10min); Seville (8 daily; 2hr).

Turismo Tourist information is available from the Ayuntamiento, Plaza Carmen 1, near the Iglesia del Carmen (Mon–Fri 8am–3pm; ☎ 955 912 717) and, between Oct–

Dec, from the Torre Ochavada at the Cerro de San Cristóbal (daily 10.30am–2pm & 4–6pm.)

Guided visits Currently the only way to see the churches outside service times is with Visita Estepa (☎ 630 220 839). Their English-speaking guide, Señora José Amador, conducts visits on most days (call for details).

ACCOMMODATION AND EATING

Hostal Balcón de Andalucía Avda de Andalucía 23; ⓦ balcondeandalucia.com. A decent *hostal* offering functional, clean a/c rooms with TV. The lively bar below serves meals and *platos combinados*, specializing in charcoal-grilled meat and fish. Free parking and close to famous cake shop Dolces Olmedo Garcia. €

West from Seville

With your own transport, the fastest – but dullest – way from **Seville west to Huelva** is via the A49 *autovía*. More tranquil and interesting is the A472, which cuts through the area to the west of the city called **El Aljarafe** by the Moors (the "high lands", although they're actually rather flat), planted with olives, vines and orange trees.

La Palma del Condado and around

West of Seville along the A472, in the province of Huelva, is the wine-producing town of **LA PALMA DEL CONDADO**. It's highly probable that this terrain, an area first planted with vines by the Greeks, produced the local wine taken on the voyage to the New World by Columbus when he sailed from nearby Palos. The wine produced here today is the Condado de Huelva, which hardly ranks with Spain's top-drawer vintages, although the dry whites are an excellent partner for seafood. With its impressive eighteenth-century Baroque church of San Juan Bautista towering over a palm-fringed central plaza, this slow-moving, white-walled country town makes a good stopping point for a drink of the local brew at one of the central bars.

Some 6km south of La Palma, **BOLLULLOS DEL CONDADO** is a busy little town filled with bodegas and *ventas* (called *bodegones* here) – big, high-ceilinged places capable of seating more than one hundred diner-imbibers at long trestle tables. A number of them line the main street – *Abuelo Curro*, *Tío Paco* and *El Postigo* are all worth a try for their local wines and great tapas.

The A483 continues south from Bollullos to El Rocío (see page 316) and the Coto de Doñana National Park (see page 313).

Niebla and around

Twelve kilometres west from La Palma along the A472, the salmon-pink ancient walls and towers of **NIEBLA** make a spectacular sight. The approach is wonderful, almost a medieval fairytale come true – this is a real walled town and looks the part. The Roman bridge you cross to reach it – probably built in the second century during the reign of Trajan – is remarkably well preserved and carried traffic for two thousand years until it was blown up during the Civil War (though it's now been meticulously restored). The town's four **gates** are worth seeking out, each with its Moorish horseshoe arch and features, and once you are inside the 2km-long encircling walls, Niebla's tidy streets of whitewashed houses and small squares are a delight to explore, and you'd see none of it by simply taking the road through town.

Brief history

Little is known about a Phoenician settlement here or the possible Iberian village of the Turditanian tribe, which may have preceded it. However, coins found dating from the Roman period gave the town's name as Ilipla, which is probably derived from the Iberian name. Described by the Roman writer Pliny as a fortified city of strategic importance, it was a crucial link in the massive Roman mining operations carried out upriver at the Río Tinto mines. The metals – mostly silver – were moved down the river by barge and then transferred to galleys here for the voyage to Rome and other parts of the empire. A bishopric under the Visigoths, after the Moorish conquest it became successively part of the Almoravid and then Almohad domains until, as an independent *taifa* state, it experienced its greatest period of prosperity during the twelfth century, trading in saffron and raisins. After falling to the Christian forces under Alfonso X in 1262, Niebla was passed around as a fief of various rulers, until in 1369 it came into the hands of the Guzmán dynasty, following which it entered a long period of decline.

Santa María de Granada

Pza Santa María • Open service times: Mon–Sat 7.30–8.30pm, Sun noon–1pm • Free

The Puerta del Socorro leads from the Seville–Huelva road to the Plaza Santa María in the heart of the town, dominated by the church of **Santa María de Granada**. The key is available from the custodian of the Casa de Cultura (itself the former fifteenth-century Hospital de Nuestra Señora de los Ángeles) almost facing the church.

Entered through a splendid Mozarabic eleven-lobed portal, the original tenth-century church is believed to have been constructed over a Visigothic cathedral, and was used by Christians during the Almoravid period. Among the artefacts dotted around the austere and much-restored Mudéjar-Gothic **interior** are a couple of Roman altars and the remarkable, stone-carved Silla Episcopal, the throne of the Visigothic bishops. It was converted into a **mosque** by the Almohads in the thirteenth century: the *mihrab* in the side wall and the elegant tower – the former minaret – both date from this period. The pillars in the second-floor windows of the tower, incidentally, are believed to have come from the original Visigothic church. Outside the entrance, a patio is dotted with remnants of the building's chequered history – various Visigothic, Christian and Moorish stones and pillars.

San Martín

Pza San Martín · Fri 9.30am–noon · Free

Only the apse, bell tower and a chapel survive of the ruined church of **San Martín**, near the town's main gate and sliced through by a plazuela. It was built in the fifteenth century on the site of a former synagogue donated in more tolerant times by Alfonso X as a concession to the Jews of Niebla, and before the Inquisition began its grisly work. The chapel contains a fifteenth-century sculpture of Christ being scourged.

Castillo de Guzmán

C/Niebla 1 · Mon–Fri 10am–3pm, Sat & Sun 10am–6pm · Charge

The **Castillo de Guzmán**, to the east of the main entrance arch into the walled town, has splendid views from its towers. In origin the Moorish *alcázar*, but much added to by Enrique de Guzmán in the fifteenth century, it later fell into decay and was ruined after Marshal Soult used it as a barracks for French troops during the War of Independence. Inside you can see the fort's barracks, stable and church and various tableaux depicting life as it would have been lived in medieval times. Today it stages concerts and theatrical productions as part of Niebla's annual summer festival of theatre and dance.

ARRIVAL AND INFORMATION · NIEBLA

By train Niebla's train station, on the Seville–Huelva line, lies at the end of C/Walabonso, which heads downhill between the Casa de Cultura and the church of Santa María. Destinations Huelva (2 daily; 21min); Jerez (3 daily; 2hr 27min); Seville (2 daily; 1hr 6min).

Turismo You can pick up a map and visitor information at the town's Turismo (daily 10am–2pm & 5–8pm; ☎ 959 362 270; ⓦ turismoniebla.com), inside the Castillo, the Centro de Interpretación del Condado and the Casa de la Cultura.

EATING

Brasería Las Almenas C/Padre Marchena 2; ☎ 959 363 426. Among a number of restaurants, bars and *ventas* lining the main road outside the walls, the best value is perhaps to be had at this *brasería* specializing in charcoal-grilled meat. €

Huelva and around

Sprawling and industrialized, **HUELVA** struggles to present an attractive face to visitors. Still, once you've got past the suburbs with their fish canneries, cement factories and petrochemical refineries, the tidy city centre – perched on a peninsula between the confluence of the Odiel and Tinto river estuaries – comes as a pleasant surprise. Huelva's populace escapes the city in summer to enjoy the Atlantic beaches at the resorts of **Punta Umbría** and **El Rompido** across the Río Odiel estuary to the south and southwest.

Brief history

Huelva was born as **Onuba**, a trading settlement founded by the Phoenicians early in the first millennium BC (modern inhabitants still call themselves *onubenses*). These early merchant traders were attracted by the minerals in the mountainous areas to the north, and by the time the Carthaginians came to dominate the area in the third century BC, Onuba was an established port, conveying these minerals throughout the Mediterranean world. When Spain fell into **Roman** hands the mining operations at Río Tinto were dramatically expanded to satisfy the empire's insatiable demand for metals such as silver and copper and the city prospered even more. Following Rome's demise the **Visigoths** and **Moors** displayed little interest in mineral extraction; the latter concentrated on dominating the seaborne trade with North Africa.

Huelva's maritime prowess gained for the city its crowning glory when **Columbus** set out from across the Río Tinto to find a new sea passage to India in ships manned by hardy Huelvan sailors. The city enjoyed a boom when the Extremadurans to the north of Huelva – the men who conquered the Americas – used the port as a base for their trade with the new territories overseas, but eventually Seville, and later Cádiz, came to dominate the silver and gold routes from the Americas and Huelva was squeezed out. Largely flattened by the Lisbon earthquake of 1755, it is only in the last century that the place has begun to regenerate itself: first as the base for mineral exports from Río Tinto in the early 1900s, when the **British Río Tinto Mining Company** largely ruled the roost here, and later when Franco established a petrochemical industry in the 1950s.

Incidentally, the British workers employed in the mines were also responsible for the importation of **football** into Spain, helping set up Huelva's league club, Recreativo – the oldest in the country – in 1889.

Plaza de las Monjas and around

Many of Huelva's key sights are a short walk from **Plaza de las Monjas**, the city's palm-lined and pedestrianized main square. Just south of the plaza along Calle Vásquez López is the impressive Neoclassical **Gran Teatro**, while south of the square at Calle Rico 26 you'll find the Art Nouveau **Clínica Sanz de Frutos** (now the Conservatorio de Música), one of a number of elegant buildings in the centre.

Museo Provincial and Museo de Bellas Artes

Avda Alameda Sundheim 17 • June–Sept Tues–Sat 9am–3pm, Sun 10am–5pm; Oct–May Tues–Sat 10am–8.30pm, Sun 10am–5pm • Free

The best place to start a tour of the city is at Huelva's **Museo Provincial**, where the interesting archeological collection has exhibits of equipment, tools and oil lamps used by slave miners at Río Tinto in the Roman period as well as information about early mining in the north of the province. The museum's star exhibit (located in a huge glass case next to the entrance) is a magnificent Roman waterwheel – used to drain water from the mineworkings at Río Tinto. On the second floor, the **Museo de Bellas Artes** houses a fairly humdrum collection of works alleviated by a few canvases by Daniel Vásquez Díaz, a Huelvan artist and friend of Picasso.

Casa Colón

Pza del Punto • Mon–Fri 11am–2pm & 6–9pm • Free entry to public areas

Just south of the Museo Provincial lies the elegant salmon-pink and white **Casa Colón**, Huelva's first luxury hotel, which played a large part in the story of "*Huelva*

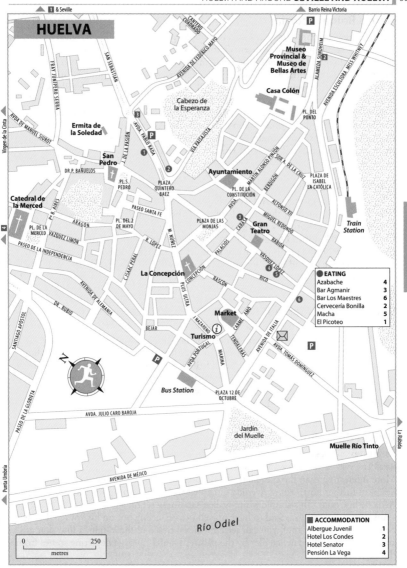

británica", housing many of the Río Tinto Mining Company's visitors and providing a venue for important functions. The hotel was built in the final years of the nineteenth century in a variety of styles around a central courtyard with palms and a fountain, and was subsequently purchased by the mining company (who used it to house guests and families of mining employees) after it ran into financial difficulties. Now owned by the city council, it functions as a conference centre and holds the municipal archive. You are free to take a look at the public areas and view the central court.

Barrio Reina Victoria

One of Huelva's more bizarre features is a whole quarter designed by English architects. The **Barrio Reina Victoria** (or Queen Victoria housing estate), east of the Museo Provincial alongside the Avenida de Guatemala, was constructed by the Río Tinto Mining Company in the early years of the twentieth century to house its British workers. It's a truly weird experience to stroll along the tree-lined avenues flanked by bungalows with rose gardens and semis with dormer windows and mock-Tudor gables – more resembling Acacia Avenue, Essex, than an Andalucían town. Even the street names have a colonial symmetry about them: Calle A, Calle B and so on. Given the drab uniformity it's little wonder that the present occupants have attempted to relieve these humdrum northern exteriors with a few primary colours.

Muelle Río Tinto

A legacy of the British era – and well worth the walk to see – is the **Muelle Río Tinto** (Río Tinto pier), sited on the east side of the harbour, a huge nineteenth-century ironwork structure formerly used to ship out the minerals which arrived by train from the mines to the north. Designed by the British engineer George Barclay Bruce and finished in 1874, the pier is now redundant, its restored ironwork curving gracefully out into the estuary and today serving as a boardwalk for loungers, anglers and courting couples.

Catedral de la Merced

Pza de la Merced • Open for services Tues–Thurs 11am–1pm, Sun 10am–1pm

The **Catedral de la Merced**, north of Plaza de las Monjas, was one of the few buildings to survive the eighteenth-century earthquake, resulting in its upgrading to cathedral status which – apart from a brilliant-white Baroque interior and an interesting salmon-pink colonial facade with elegant belfries – it hardly merits. It's worth looking inside at the image of the *Virgen de la Cinta* (the city's patron) attributed to Martínez Montañés.

Virgen de la Cinta

Avda de la Cinta s/n • Daily 9am–1pm & 4–7pm • Free • #6 bus from the bus station; ask for the "Parada escuela Montessori" on Avda de Manuel Suirot, which will leave you close to the sanctuary

More interesting than the cathedral, the restored fifteenth-century **Virgen de la Cinta** lies 3km further north along Avenida Cristóbal Colón (with a signed turn-off along Avda de la Cinta). This simple white-walled sanctuary set on a low hill overlooking the sea is where Columbus is said to have prayed before setting out on his voyage. Inside, beneath the Mudéjar roof, you can see a medieval fresco of the Virgin, a fine altar grille, and a series of 1920s faïence tiles by the painter Daniel Zuloaga depicting scenes from the explorer's life.

ARRIVAL AND INFORMATION
HUELVA

By train Frequent trains to Seville leave from the splendid neo-Moorish train station, a short distance southeast of the centre on Avda Italia.

Destinations Almonaster (1 daily; 1hr 45min); Jabugo (1 daily; 1hr 55min); Seville (3 daily; 1hr 30min).

By bus Huelva's bus station is at Avda Dr Rubio s/n, west of Plaza de las Monjas. The Autobuses Damas (ⓦ damas-sa.es) timetable lists all services throughout the province – handy if you're going to be using the town as a base.

Destinations Aracena (2 daily; 2hr); Ayamonte/Portuguese border (5 daily; 1hr); Isla Cristina (10 daily; 1hr); La Antilla (5 daily; 45min); Matalascañas (5 daily; 3 on Sat & Sun; 50min); Moguer (14 daily; 40min); Palos de la Frontera (15 daily; 30min); Punta Umbría (13 daily; 30min); Seville (7 daily; 1hr 15min).

By car Finding street parking can often verge on the impossible and the city's new one-way system is tortuously convoluted. The easiest solution is to use a pay car park:

the multistorey one immediately north of the bus station is convenient.

Turismo C/Jesús Nazareno 21, near the bus station (Mon–Fri 9am–7.30pm, Sat & Sun 9.30am–3pm: ☎ 959 650 200).

ACCOMMODATION SEE MAP PAGE 305

Finding a **place to stay** is usually not a problem this far off the tourist trail, although budget options are severely limited. The town's nearest **campsite** is in Punta Umbría, a 15min bus ride away (see page 308).

Albergue Juvenil Avda Marchena Colombo 14, in the northern suburbs (bus #6 from the bus station); ☎ 959 650 010. Modern and well-run hostel with double and triple en-suite rooms and cafetería. €̄

Hotel Los Condes Avda Alameda Sundheim 14; ⊛ hotelfamiliaconde.com. Comfortable hotel near the museum, with serviceable a/c rooms and its own bar-

restaurant, plus parking. €€

Hotel Senator C/Pablo Rada 10; ⊛ hotelesmonte. com. A three-star hotel aimed at the corporate market, but perfectly adequate for a short stay. Light and well-equipped rooms include minibar, satellite TV and safe. Also offers handy parking facilities. €€

Pensión La Vega Avda Alemán 96; ⊛ pensionlavega. es. The city's only budget choice is this pleasant and friendly *hostal* near the cathedral, offering clean and tidy en-suite rooms with TV, some with balcony. €̄

EATING SEE MAP PAGE 305

Named Spain's **gastronomical capital** of 2017, Huelva isn't short of great, inexpensive places to eat.

Azabache C/Vásquez López 22; ⊛ restauranteazabache. com. Excellent tapas and *raciones* bar-restaurant with a modern, tiled interior. Offers fish, *mariscos* and *jamón*-based dishes from as little as a small fillet to a plate of *gambas*. There's also an esteemed house *menú* , which includes steak and wine. €€€

Bar Agmanir C/Carasa 9; ☎ 959 250 479. Great and atmospheric local bar with outdoor tables and friendly, well-turned out waiter. There's a wide tapas range including house specials *mojama de atún* (cured tuna). €̄

Bar Los Maestres Pza Doce de Octubre 1; ⊛ barlosmaestres.com. Busy local favourite with exclusively outdoor seating close to the train station. The house tortilla will set you up for a long journey, but their

huge mussels – served simply with salt and lemon – steal the show. €̄

Cervecería Bonilla C/Pablo Rada s/n; ⊛ cerveceriasbonilla.com. A much livelier alternative to its original, sister restaurant on Avda Martin Alonso Pinzón. Tapas and *raciones* still at low prices, but here bratwurst is the speciality. €̄

Macha C/Vázquez López 22; ☎ 959 100 250. Ultramodern tapas bar with swish furnishings and decor and offering a range of fish and *mariscos* and charcoal-grillled meats. Excellent wine selection by bottle or glass. €€

El Picoteo C/Pablo Rada 5; ☎ 959 802 218. Of the bars that line this busy avenue, *El Picoteco* isn't the most immediately persuasive. But, look past its shabby exterior – the food is fresh and interesting. Try the *ventresca de atún en escabeche de naranja* (tuna belly marinated with orange). €̄

Punta Umbría

PUNTA UMBRÍA, 20km southwest of Huelva and sitting astride a finger of land between the Atlantic and the Tinto-Odiel river estuary, is the city's nearest – and biggest – seaside resort. The mineworking processes used in the nineteenth century by the Río Tinto Mining Company (see box, page 324) in the north of the province involved emitting noxious fumes into the atmosphere and many workers became ill. In the early 1880s the company built a rest and recovery centre at Punta Umbría for its employees. Shortly after this, and attracted by the point's unspoilt beauty, senior management began to build holiday homes here and the tourist resort was born. Quite a few of their dwellings, built in the British colonial style, survived until the 1970s; they have gone now, however, and the only vestige from this era is the *barrio*'s name, Los Ingleses.

Casa Museo de los Ingleses

Avda Ciudad de Huelva s/n, close to the Turismo • June–Aug Tues–Sat 11am–1.30pm & 6–10pm• Free

The resort has paid a belated tribute to its British founders by reconstructing one of the curious British stilted dwellings that the company's architects designed for its senior staff. This now houses the **Casa Museo de los Ingleses**, decorated with typical period furnishings and reconstructed living and cooking areas. There's also a photo history and a fascinating video about the life of the British community in Punta Umbría.

Beaches

Punta Umbría's later growth into a seaside town has produced a resort with magnificent **blue-flag beaches** flanking the north and south sides of its *punta* (point). It makes a great day trip from the city, so if you head there on the weekend, don't be surprised to see truck loads of Huelvans with iceboxes and parasols (both advisable, for the heat is still intense). There are shaded sunbeds to rent if you're without.

ARRIVAL AND INFORMATION   PUNTA UMBRÍA

By bus There are hourly buses from Huelva bus station.
Turismo At the junction of Avda de Andalucía and Avda Ciudad de Huelva near the Ayuntamiento (June–Aug Mon–Sat 9am–2pm & 7–9pm; Sept–May Mon–Fri 9am–2pm, Sat 10am–1pm; ☎ 959 495 160; ⓦ puntaumbria.es); they stock copious amounts of information and a useful street-indexed town map.

Boat trips Turismar (☎ 959 315 526) runs boat trips (June–Sept) around the estuary and nature reserve of Marismas del Odiel from the Muelle Viajeros quay near the fishing harbour.

ACCOMMODATION

Most places to stay are within walking distance of the Turismo behind the beaches on each side of the point. Rates fall significantly outside August.

Albergue Juvenil Avda del Océano 13; ⓦ inturjoven. com. Even during high season, you'll find a room at this very pleasant, substantial youth hostel, with a seafront location and some double en-suite rooms. €

Camping Playa La Bota 6km west of Punta Umbría, near the hamlet of La Bota; ⓦ campingplayalabota. es. Close to the beach with plenty of shade; they also rent *cabañas* (cabins) sleeping up to four. Camping €, cabins €€

Hostal Manuela C/Carmen 8; ⓦ hostalmanuela.es. Near the harbour on the *punta*'s river flank, this welcoming and beautifully renovated *hostal* offers sparkling a/c en-suite rooms with TV. €

Hostal Playa Avda del Océano 95; ⓦ hostalplayapuntaumbria.com. Very pleasant *hostal* on the west side of the point, with light and airy en-suite rooms 50m from the sand. Many rooms come with sea view. €€

Hotel Barceló Mar Avda del Océano s/n; ⓦ barcelo. com. Situated between two nature reserves, this beachfront four-star is one of the resort's top addresses, with luxurious rooms (most with sea view) and a huge garden pool plus bars, restaurant and a spa and wellness centre. €€€

Hotel Emilio C/Ancha 21; ⓦ hotelemilio.es. Close to the Atlantic side of the point, this is a decent small one-star hotel offering a/c rooms with safe and fridge (some also with balcony or terrace and sea views). Also has its own bar-restaurant and parking. €€€

EATING AND DRINKING

For food and drink, *chiringuitos* – open-air bars on the seafront serving snacks – are popular, and the resort is full of the usual *freidurías* and *marisquerías*.

Bar Antonio C/Combes Ponzones 10; ☎ 959 314 132. Popular *freiduría* near the fishing harbour with lots of cool tiles inside and a terrace in the pedestrianized street outside. Serves up the usual favourites including *cazón* (smooth hound shark) and *coquinas* (cockles). €€

Camarón Avda Océano s/n; ⓦ chiringuitocamaron.com. Next to the *Hotel Barceló Mar*, this is a popular beachfront *chiringuito* serving a wide range of fresh fish and *mariscos*. Specially noted for its *bogavantes* (lobster) and *langostas* (crayfish). Has a great seaview terrace with fabulous sunsets. €€€

Chriniguito Oliver Pza del Cantábrico 4; ☎ 959 311 535. A troupe of men in Superman t-shirts serve up delicious paella on this beachfront bar. There's a chilled urn of gazpacho and a variety of cocktails available from a reconstituted fishing boat bar. €€

Miramar C/Miramar 3; ☎ 959 311 243. Welcoming place near the youth hostel with an attractive seafront terrace actually on the beach. They serve *platos combinados* and *fritados variados*, and house specials include *sopa de mariscos* (shellfish soup) and simply grilled fish, charged by the kilo. €€

The Columbus Trail

Huelva's greatest source of pride lies with the momentous expeditions of **Christopher Columbus** to the New World, the first of which sailed from Palos de la Frontera (or simply Palos), across the Tinto estuary from the city. When he was unable to get backing for his voyages, Columbus cooled his heels for many years in and around

Huelva and the La Rábida monastery until he finally managed to obtain a commission from the king and queen in the spring of 1492. At the Punta del Sebo – the tip of land where the Tinto and Odiel rivers meet – stands a **monument to Columbus** dating from the 1920s. Although most Huelvans think the 37m-high monster statue of a cowled figure clutching a huge Tau cross is that of the navigator himself, it actually represents a monk from the nearby Franciscan monastery at La Rábida (the Tau or "T"-form cross is a symbol of the Franciscan order) in recognition of the role the monks played in the Columbus story. A Cubist-inspired work, sculpted by Gertrude Vanderbilt Whitney in 1929, it was donated to the province by the USA.

The main sites connected with Columbus – **La Rábida**, **Palos** and **Moguer** – are all within a 30km round-trip from Huelva. Buses running between Huelva and Moguer call at all three locations.

La Rábida and around

Pza la Rábida, 8km from Huelva • Tue–Sun 10am–6pm • Charge (audio guide extra) • ⓦ monasteriodelarabida.com • Reached by bus (roughly hourly from Huelva) or, with your own transport, by taking the Mazagón road southeast across the Río Tinto road bridge

Situated amid a forest of umbrella pines (which serve to mask the petrochemical refineries across the polluted river estuary), the small whitewashed Franciscan monastery of **La Rábida** is a surprisingly pleasant oasis once you reach it. The monastery lies at the end of Avenida de la América, linking it with Palos and lined with ceramic pavement tiles marking all the countries of the New World. Dating from the fourteenth century, the buildings suffered structural damage during the Lisbon earthquake of 1755 and have been extensively restored.

The tour begins with a room containing stylized modern **frescoes** of the explorer's life by distinguished Huelvan artist Daniel Vásquez Díaz. At the building's heart is a tranquil fifteenth-century Mudéjar **cloister**, opening off the monks' **refectory** where Columbus would have dined during his many stays here. You will also see the **cell** where the abbot, Juan Pérez, and Columbus discussed the explorer's ideas. Beyond the cloister, a fourteenth-century **church** contains an alabaster statue of the *Virgin and Child* to which the mariner and his men prayed before setting sail.

Upstairs, above the refectory, lies the **Sala Capitular** (Chapter House), an impressive, beamed room with heavy period furniture where Fray Pérez, Columbus and the Pinzón brothers discussed the final plans before the first voyage set sail. In other rooms on the same floor you can see models of the three caravels, as well as navigation charts, cases containing various artefacts brought back from the expedition and "team pictures" of the crew.

Don't miss the curious **Sala de Banderas**, or Flag Room, where, beneath flags of the various South American nations of the New World, is a casket of earth donated by each. If some of these caskets look a bit roughed-up it's probably due to visiting South Americans who, after reverentially handling the soil of their fatherland, often treat the caskets of their neighbours with some disrespect. There's a pleasant, if predictably overpriced restaurant next to the monastery that's open for lunch, serving *raciones* typical to the region (also 10am–6pm).

Muelle de la Carabelas

June–Sept Tues–Sun 10am–9pm; Oct–May Tues–Sun 9.30am–8pm • Charge

The reconstructed **Muelle de la Carabelas** (Harbour of the Caravels), on the Río Tinto estuary, has impressive full-size replicas of the three caravels that made the epic voyage to the New World. Realistic displays on board reconstruct the grim realities of life at sea, while the surrounding quays are lined with re-creations of fifteenth-century quayside bars and market stalls. In the adjoining museum are displays illustrating Columbus's life (including facsimiles of some of his geographical books annotated in a surprisingly delicate hand), video presentations on a giant screen and a *cafetería*.

THE VOYAGES OF COLUMBUS

Probably born in Genoa around 1451 to the son of a weaving merchant, Christopher Columbus (in Spanish, Cristóbal Colón) went to sea in his early teens. After years of sailing around the Mediterranean, in 1476 he was shipwrecked off the coast of Portugal and it was in **Lisbon** – then the world leader in navigation – that Columbus learned the skills of map-making. In 1479 he married into a high-ranking Portuguese family and spent the following years on trading voyages to the British Isles and elsewhere, including in 1482 a journey down the coast of **West Africa** to Ghana, a major source of spices, ivory and slaves.

During this time the idea germinated in his mind of attempting to **sail west to reach the Indies and the Far East**, thus shortening the route that Portugal was then exploring around the coast of Africa. He built up an enormous library of ancient and contemporary geographical writings, now preserved in Seville, all heavily annotated in his own hand. By some optimistic interpretations of these works and a misreading of an Arab geographer, Alfraganus, Columbus seriously undercalculated the earth's circumference, believing that Marco Polo's fabulous island of Cipangu (Japan) lay a mere 3900km west of the Canaries instead of an actual 17,000.

Trying to find backers, when the Portuguese monarch, still more interested in the African route, demurred, Columbus turned to Spain. In 1486 at **Córdoba** he presented his plan to reach the gold-rich Orient to Fernando and Isabel, still involved in the protracted and costly war against the Moors. Desirous of the gold to boost their fortunes but wary, after consultations with advisers, of Columbus's calculations, they both refused support. Now desperate, Columbus turned to France and then to Henry VII of England, with no success.

During his earlier journey from Portugal to Córdoba, Columbus had stayed at **La Rábida** Franciscan monastery. It was to here that he returned frustrated and depressed in the autumn of 1491. The explorer's luck turned when **Juan Pérez**, the abbot of La Rábida and a former confessor to Isabel, was moved to write to the queen on Columbus's behalf. It was a timely moment. In January of 1492 Granada had fallen, the treasury was empty, and the promise of gold and glory for a resurgent Spain now attracted the monarchs.

Columbus set out from Palos on **August 3, 1492**, with three small vessels, the *Santa María*, the *Niña* and the *Pinta*, carrying a total of 120 men recruited from Palos and Moguer by the Pinzón brothers. Columbus's discovery of the **Atlantic wind patterns** ranks alongside his other feats; he sailed via the Canaries to take advantage of the trade winds, but the incredible voyage almost ended in mutiny by crews who believed that they would never find a wind to bring them home. This was avoided when, on October 12, Columbus made landfall on **Watling Island** (aka San Salvador) in the Bahamas. Watched silently by the indigenous community, he took the island in the name of Spain and gave thanks to God. After leaving a colony of men on Hispaniola (modern Haiti) he returned to Palos on March 15, 1493, to enormous acclaim.

Successful as a mariner, Columbus was disastrous as a **colonizer**, epitomized by his forcing of the native population of Hispaniola into the gold mines in a brutal process that reduced their numbers from a quarter of a million in 1492 to sixty thousand fifteen years later. In 1500, Columbus was removed from office as governor and sent back to Spain in chains and disgrace. He was eventually released and made his final voyage in 1502 – a last desperate attempt to find a strait leading to India – but ended up stranded in Jamaica for a whole year after losing his ships to sea worms. Columbus died at Valladolid in 1506, still believing that he had reached the East Indies.

ARRIVAL AND INFORMATION

By bus There are frequent buses from Huelva to the monastery. In summer a tourist road train links La Rábida with Palos de la Frontera.

LA RÁBIDA

Information The monastery's gardens contain an information office as well as a pleasant bar-restaurant with terrace tables.

Palos de la Frontera

Four kilometres north of La Rábida along the Río Tinto estuary lies **PALOS DE LA FRONTERA**, a rather featureless village but an important site in the Columbus story. It was from the silted-up bay below the church of San Jorge – then a major harbour and sea port – that Columbus's three caravels, the *Niña*, the *Pinta* and the *Santa María*, set out to reach Asia by crossing the western ocean. The harbour area is now marshland, and it was due to the river's silting up that the decline of Palos set in. In 2014 archeological excavations close to the church revealed much of the **ancient port**, including the quayside from where Columbus sailed, as well as a taverna and seamans' *fonda* (simple hotel) from the same period. Archeologists claim also to have discovered the *alota*, or port administrative building, in which Columbus is known to have interviewed mariners applying to be taken on as crew for the voyage. The aim of the authorities is open up these remains to public view in the near future – get details from the Ayuntamiento in Palos or the Turismos in Moguer (see page 313) or Huelva (see page 307).

San Jorge

C/Fray Juan Pérez 19 • Open for mass at 7pm • Free • ☎ 959 350 758

O Palos, no one can equal your glory.
Not Memphis, nor Thebes nor eternal Rome.
Not Athens nor London.
No city can dispute your historical fame!

This modern poem fixed to the exterior wall of the fifteenth-century parish church of **San Jorge** leaves you in no doubt of how Palos views its role in world history. It was here that Columbus and his crewmen attended Mass before taking on water for their voyage from the nearby **La Fontanilla**, a medieval well tarted up in 1992 as the centrepiece of a dismal park to mark the quincentenary. Near the fountain there's a statue honouring the Pinzón brothers (see page 311).

The church of San Jorge has a simple, bare-brick interior containing some mural fragments as well as a distinctive wrought-iron pulpit – from which the edict was read ordering an initially reluctant Palos to provide ships, crew and provisions for the voyage – and some thirteenth- and sixteenth-century alabaster sculptures of Santa Ana and the Crucifixion.

On that August morning in 1492 Columbus is supposed to have left the church through its southern Mudéjar portal flanked by his captains Martín Alonzo Pinzón and his younger brother Vincente, both from Palos.

Casa Museo Martín Alonso Pinzón

C/Colón 24 • July & Aug Mon–Sat 10am–2pm; Sept–June 10am–2pm & 5–8.30pm (last entrance 8pm) • Charge

South of San Jorge on the main street, the **Casa Museo Martín Alonzo Pinzón** survives, and is well worth a visit. The substantial mansion has been converted into a museum with lots of background information on the Pinzón brothers and their role in the voyages to the New World. It is these native sons that Palos today celebrates, even more than its Columbus connection, claiming that their contribution to the epic voyage has been eclipsed. Indeed, at the time the Pinzón family insisted that Martín – a mariner of great local repute – had planned such a voyage long before Columbus.

ARRIVAL AND INFORMATION

PALOS DE LA FRONTERA

By bus Buses arrive and depart from a stop on Avda América, close to the Ayuntamiento.
Destinations Huelva (9 daily; 30min); La Rábida (9 daily;

10min); Moguer (9 daily; 20min).
Tourist information The Ayuntamiento (Mon–Fri 9am–3pm; ☎ 959 350 100), facing Plaza Mayor on C/Rábida 3,

the main street, along with the Casa Museo and Museo Naval (also worth a visit for its model boats) can provide information and a town map.

ACCOMMODATION AND EATING

Hotel La Pinta C/Rábida 79, Palos; ⓦhotellapinta. com. This pleasant two-star hotel is a good bet for a/c en-suite rooms and there's a decent restaurant downstairs with a cheap *menú*. Breakfast is extra. €

Restaurant El Paraíso Avda America 15, near Hotel La Pinta; ☏ 959 350 003. The village's best restaurant,

offering a wide selection of fish and meat dishes. The *carnes a la brasa* (charcoal-grilled meats) are particularly good; the cooking of which produces a sumptuous woody smell around the lovely stone building. There's an excellent-value weekday *menú* and well-priced desserts. €€

Moguer

Like Palos, the compact and beautiful whitewashed town of **MOGUER**, 8km north, also takes pride in its Columbus connections: many of the crew members were recruited here. Quite apart from this, it's a place with plenty to see, including the Festival de Flamenco (held annually in the middle of September), and it achieved worldwide fame in 1956 as the birthplace of the Nobel prize-winning poet **Juan Ramón Jiménez** (1881–1958).

Plaza del Cabildo

Starting from the **Plaza del Cabildo** in the centre – where there's a bronze statue of Jiménez – it's easy to find your way around. First take a look at the elegant eighteenth-century **Ayuntamiento** (Mon–Fri 8.30am–2pm) on the same square, a quintessentially Andalucían edifice in cream, ochre and terracotta.

Convento de Santa Clara

Hourly guided tours Tues–Sat 10 am–2pm • Charge

Close to Plaza del Cabildo in Plaza de las Monjas lies the Gothic-Mudéjar **Convento de Santa Clara**. Founded in the fourteenth century, this housed nuns from the order of St Clare until 1898, but is now a museum. Inside, a Mudéjar cloister leads into the nuns' former quarters, which include a kitchen, refectory and a large sixteenth-century dormitory. The **church** possesses a fine retablo and some notable alabaster tombs of the Portocarrero family, the convent's founders, as well as – at the entry to the choir – a seventeenth-century diptych of the Sienese school portraying the Immaculate Conception.

Look out for an inscription in the right aisle, which tells of **Columbus's visit** to offer thanksgiving for his safe return. He is reputed to have spent the whole night in prayer here upon returning from his first voyage in March 1493, in fulfilment of a vow he made in the middle of a terrifying storm. Other parts of the tour take in sculptures by La Roldana and Martínez Montañés and many other beautiful if anonymous works from the fourteenth, fifteenth and sixteenth centuries.

San Francisco

Pza de San Francisco s/n • Mon–Fri 11am–2pm • Free

Behind the convent of Santa Clara lies the fifteenth-century monastery of **San Francisco**, with its stunning ochre-tinted Mudéjar brick church from where legions of missionaries were sent out to the New World. The monastery's elegant Mannerist patio/cloister can be viewed by going through the archival museum next door.

Nuestra Señora de la Granada

C/Trasera Iglesia 1 • Mon–Fri 11am–3pm & mass at 7.30pm • Free (donations welcome)

To the east of the centre the eighteenth-century church of **Nuestra Señora de la Granada** was raised over a church of the same name which was flattened in the Lisbon

JUAN RAMÓN JIMÉNEZ IN MOGUER

The work that most Andalucíans remember Jiménez for today is *Platero y yo* ("Platero and I"), the story of a little donkey who is a "friend of the poet and children" based on his own donkey, Platero, in whose company he often toured Moguer's streets. Glazed plaques on walls around town mark streets or buildings that occur in the story and there are a couple of worthwhile sites dedicated to the author.

You can tour the house where Jiménez was born, which has now been restored and opened as **la Jiménez museum** (C/Jiménez 5; hourly Tues–Sat 10.15am–1.15pm & 5.15–7.15pm, Sun 10am–1pm; charge; ☎959 372 148; ⓦfundacion-jrj.es). This interesting place displays various mementoes from the poet's life. Moguer's cemetery (Avda Hermanos Niño, the road leading towards the Seville–Huelva highway) has the **grave of the poet** and his wife, Zenobia. His body was returned to the town he loved for burial in 1958 after twenty years spent in exile in Puerto Rico, to where he had emigrated after Franco came to power.

earthquake of 1755. It boasts a scaled-down, whiter version of Seville's Giralda tower "which from close up looks like Seville's from far away", wrote Jiménez. An impressive triple-naved interior is complemented by some fine vaulting.

ARRIVAL AND INFORMATION

MOGUER

By bus Buses to and from Huelva drop off and leave from Avda de America, just south of the castle.
Destinations Huelva (12 daily; 45min); La Rábida (12 daily; 25min); Palos (12 daily; 15min).

Turismo Moguer's Turismo (Tues–Sat 10am–2pm & 5–7pm; ☎959 371 898; ⓦaytomoguer.es) is inside the Teatro Felipe Godínez, C/Andalucía 17, just west of the Convento de Santa Clara.

ACCOMMODATION

Hotel Plaza Escribano Pza Escribano 5, south of the Pza del Cabildo; ⓦhotelplazaescribano.com. Elegant, gleaming-white small hotel with comfortable a/c rooms equipped with minibar, plasma TV and safe. €̄
Pensión Platero C/Aceña 4 slightly east of Pza del

Cabildo, Moguer 13; ☎959 372 159. This central *hostal* has good-value en-suite rooms with a/c and windows which let in stacks of light. The friendly owner can advise on free parking nearby. €̄

EATING AND DRINKING

Mesón El Lobito C/La Rábida 31; ☎959 370 660. Unique beamed and cavernous bar with decor that belongs in a museum and where there's usually a good atmosphere if you turn up after 10pm. Food is served; specialities include *mariscos* and *jamón ibérico* as well as charcoal-grilled meat and fish. €€

Mesón Restaurante Parrala Pza de las Monjas 22; ☎959 370 452. Opposite the entrance to Santa Clara, this is the best restaurant in town, and serves up excellent regional fish and meat dishes – try the *rape con salsa alemendra* (monkfish with almond sauce), plus tapas and an inexpensive *menú*. €€

Coto de Doñana National Park

Sited at the estuary of the Guadalquivir, the vast roadless area of the **COTO DE DOÑANA NATIONAL PARK** is Spain's largest wildlife reserve, a world-class wetland site for migrating birds and one of Europe's greatest wilderness areas. The seasonal pattern of its delta waters, which flood in winter and then drop in the spring, leaving rich deposits of silt, raised sandbanks and islands, give the Coto de Doñana its special interest. Conditions are perfect in winter for ducks and geese, but spring is the most exciting season, when the exposed mud draws hundreds of flocks of breeding birds. In the marshes and amid the cork oak forests behind you've a good chance of seeing squacco heron, black-winged stilt, whiskered tern, pratincole and sand grouse, as well as flamingos, egrets and vultures. There are, too, occasional sightings of the Spanish imperial eagle, now reduced to a score of breeding pairs. In late summer and early autumn, the swamps – or *marismas* – dry out and support far less birdlife. The park is also home to an estimated 75 Spanish lynx, now in severe peril of extinction, although a captive breeding programme has had some success in reversing the trend.

Inevitably, it seems, the park is under threat from development, and several lynx have been killed by traffic on the road to the beach resort at Matalascañas. Even at current levels the drain on the water supply is severe, and made worse by pollution of the Guadalquivir by farming pesticides, Seville's industry and Huelva's mines. The seemingly inevitable disaster finally occurred in April 1998, when an upriver mining dam used for storing toxic waste burst, unleashing millions of litres of pollutants into the Guadiamar river which flows through the park. The noxious tide was stopped just 2km from the park's boundary, but catastrophic damage was done to the surrounding farmland, with nesting birds decimated and fish poisoned. The mining dams have not been removed (the mines are a major local employer), but merely repaired. Proposals for a huge new tourist centre on the fringes of the park were shelved a decade ago, but the pressure for development remains. Bitter demonstrations organized by locals who saw the prospect of much-needed jobs in the Costa Doñana development have abated into an uneasy truce, further exacerbated by the economic downturn of the last decade. Some experts have proposed that "green tourism", allowing a greater but controlled public access to the park, and thereby providing an income for the local community, is the only way to bring both sides together.

Brief history

This area was known to the Romans as **Ligur**, and in the 1990s archeologists were surprised to discover a Roman quayside 3km into the swamps, showing just how much the area has expanded in the ensuing two millennia. It was Alfonso X, however, who claimed the territory of Las Rocinas as a hunting reserve for the Spanish crown in 1262 during the *Reconquista*. In 1294 his heir, Sancho IV (the Brave), rewarded the "hero" of the siege of Tarifa, Guzmán El Bueno, with the territories of Doñana. The area, still a hunting reserve, remained part of the lands of the dukes of Medina Sidonia – as the Guzmán line became – for the next five centuries, and the park's hunting lodge was named the palace of Dona Aña in honour of the wife of the seventh duke in 1595. The reserve hit a bad patch when it was sold by the Medina Sidonias in 1897 to sherry baron William Garvey, whose company is still operating in Jerez. Garvey turned it into a hunting club and sold off much of the woodland for profit; following his death in 1909, however, people began to realize the unique importance of the area.

In 1957 scientific interest in the park began in earnest and, as a result of concern expressed about proposals to carve a highway across the zone and build tourist developments along its coastline, in 1969 the World Wildlife Fund (Spain) was set up following the parent organization's purchase of seventy square kilometres of Doñana in 1963. Soon after this the fund persuaded the Spanish government to set up the national park. Since then the Coto de Doñana, now under the management of the National Institute for the Conservation of Nature (ICONA), has expanded to 190,000 acres (750 square km). The park's administrators then enlisted divine assistance in safeguarding its future when they diplomatically petitioned the brotherhoods to allow the Virgin of Rocío (see opposite) to become the national park's patron. The brotherhoods graciously acceded to this request.

Hides in the park

If you don't go on a tour (see page 316), you're currently restricted to the **hides** at three access and information centres open to the public. The five hides adjacent to the **Centro Recepción del Acebuche** overlook a lagoon where marbled teal, purple gallinule

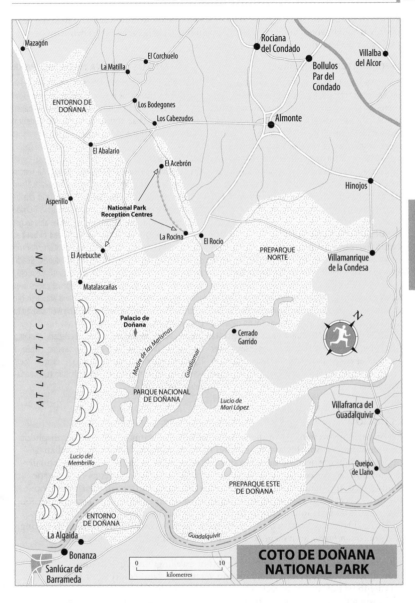

COTO DE DOÑANA NATIONAL PARK

(aka swamphen), various grebes and – around the trees – azure-winged magpies have all been spotted and where, with luck, you may even glimpse the extremely rare Audouin's gull. You'll need to bring your own binoculars or they can be rented from the centre.

Beyond the **La Rocina** information centre, a 4km route called the "Charco de la Boca" leads to five well-concealed hides in marshland, pinewoods and along the riverbank, where you might see Cetti's warbler, the spectacular hoopoe, red-crested pochard and herons as well as – in summer – flamingos and a plethora of singing nightingales. A

1.5km marked route from **El Palacio de Acebrón** threads from the centre, circling a lake mainly through woodland, and offering possibilities to sight the rare hawfinch. It's a great spot for a picnic.

INFORMATION AND TOURS

Visiting the Coto de Doñana involves – understandably – a certain amount of frustration. At present the heart of the reserve is still open only to brief, organized bus **tours**, though you can also take a boat cruise into the park from Sanlúcar de Barrameda (see box, page 165). If you're a serious ornithologist or naturalist you should consider a group booking, which costs a little more than the daily excursion and lets you create your own itinerary (details from the Centro Recepción del Acebuche). It's worth noting that during the Pentecost *romería* (the seventh week after Easter) all three visitor centres are closed.

INFORMATION CENTRES

Centro Recepción del Acebuche The starting point for bus tours into the park, this information office (daily: April–Sept 8am–3pm & 4–9pm; Oct–March 8am–3pm & 4–7pm; ☎ 959 430 432; English spoken), 4km north of Matalascañas towards El Rocío and Almonte, then 1.5km up a signed road on the left, can supply a useful free map and has a bookshop, a natural history exhibition and a *cafetería*.
El Palacio de Acebrón Along a minor road 5km west of La Rocina (daily 9am–3pm & 4–7pm). An impressive former hunting lodge with another information centre housing an ethnographic exhibition dealing with the area's history and development.

COTO DE DOÑANA NATIONAL PARK

La Rocina Nine kilometres north of the Centro Recepción del Acebuche, close to the El Rocío bridge (daily 9am–3pm & 4–7pm; ☎ 959 439 569). Information centre (free maps), car park and a small open-air museum with historical reconstructions of life in the *marismas*.

BUS TOURS

Cooperativa Marismas del Rocío tours All-terrain 24-seater buses tour the park (May–Sept daily 8.30am & 5pm; Oct–April Tues–Sun 8.30am & 3pm) and can be booked at the Centro de Recepción del Acebuche. Outside July, August and holiday periods you should be able to get on to the next day's trip, otherwise you'll need to book at least a week in advance. Tours consist of an 80km, 4hr trip sampling the park's various ecosystems: dunes, beach, *marismas* and woodland, with the guide pointing out only spectacular species such as flamingo, imperial eagle, deer and wild boar. Binoculars are essential, and although the centre has some available for rent, you'd be well advised to bring your own.

Other tour operators Other operators running trips into the park include: Discovering Doñana (ⓦdiscoveringdonana.com), Doñana Bird Tours (ⓦdonanabirdtours.com) and Doñana Nature (ⓦdonana-nature.com).

El Rocío

Set on the northwestern tip of the marshes, **EL ROCÍO** has one of the most atmospheric evening scenes in Andalucía: a tiny cluster of white cottages, sandy streets and an imposing church where the most famous pilgrimage-fair of the south occurs annually at Pentecost. As the cowboy-hatted farmers nonchalantly ride horses along the wide sandy streets and tie up at Wild West-style hitching rails in front of their timber cabins, you half expect Clint Eastwood to emerge from a nearby saloon chewing on a cheroot. Street lights do little to undermine the time-warp quality of an area unchanged for centuries. Daytimes, however, are somewhat overrun by coach-loads of tourists buying overpriced *sombreros*, so it's a good idea to book your Doñana tour in advance and escape the village during those hours.

Beyond the El Rocío's core, ghostly streets of dwellings belonging to the **brotherhoods** – all with hitching rails and verandas – stand empty most of the year waiting to be put to service each May or June in the *romería del Rocío* (see box, page 317), when the ninety or so brotherhoods use them to house their members.

Nuestra Señora del Rocío

C/Ermita s/n • Daily 8.30am–9.30pm • Free

Centre of the town's Pentecost celebrations, the church of **Nuestra Señora del Rocío** was, despite its Baroque appearance, built in the 1960s on the site of a church which collapsed in the eighteenth-century Lisbon earthquake. It holds the venerated image of the **Virgen del Rocío**, a thirteenth-century work in carved wood.

ARRIVAL AND DEPARTURE

EL ROCÍO

By bus There are at least three buses a day to and from Seville en route to Matalascañas, enabling a stop to be made at the La Rocina or El Acebuche National Park visitor centres – make sure to let the driver know you want to be dropped off. Getting to or from Huelva is more complicated, requiring a change at Almonte. It's easy to come slightly off-route when driving from Seville, and though cars pass through these tracks regularly, the ground is loose and undulating. There's parking in El Rocío's central sandy square (charge).

INFORMATION AND TOURS

Turismo C/Muñoz y Pavón 44, the village's main street (daily 8am–5pm; ☎ 959 442 166) close to the *La Posada el Rocío* bar. Staff can supply a village map and lots of information about the national park including a 5km scenic walk along the Raya Real to the Palacio del Rey, northeast of the village, where deer, wild boar and the Spanish lynx have all been spotted.

Tours On the side of the main A483 road through the

THE ROMERÍA DEL ROCÍO

The **Romería del Rocío**, a Whitsun pilgrimage to the sanctuary of the Virgen del Rocío, is one of the most extraordinary spectacles in Europe, with whole village communities and some ninety local "**religious brotherhoods**" from Huelva, Seville, Málaga and even one from Gibraltar converging on the village on horseback and in lavishly decorated ox-carts. The event is part pilgrimage and part jamboree as the intense emotions awakened by the two- to four-day journey (not to mention the drinking) often spill over uncontrollably.

The brotherhoods coming from Sanlúcar de Barrameda have a special dispensation to follow their ancient route across the heart of the Parque de Doñana which takes them three nights and four days, with all the attendant fire risks en route. The army is employed to get pilgrims and their carts over the Guadalquivir safely, and the park's rangers set up campsites for them and provide firewood for their great feasts in the woods. Sadly, the rubbish left behind by these large crowds is the cause of many wildlife fatalities as species such as boar choke on the plastic containers they attempt to devour. Throughout the *romería*, which climaxes on the Saturday evening, everyone parties in fiesta costume, while by the time the carts arrive at El Rocío they've been joined by hundreds of busloads of pilgrims.

What they have all come for – apart from the spectacle itself – is the commemoration of the miracle of **Nuestra Señora del Rocío** (Our Lady of the Dew). The miracle concerns the venerated statue believed to have been found on this spot by a shepherd in the thirteenth century – conveniently after the eviction of the Moors – which, so it is said, resisted all attempts to move it elsewhere. A shrine was built, miraculous healings and events were reported, and El Rocío was suddenly on the map. In the early hours of **Pentecost Sunday** when many of the revellers either are gripped by religious frenzy or lie prostrate in an alcoholic stupor, the image of the Virgin, credited with all kinds of magic and fertility powers, is paraded before the faithful as she visits each one of the brotherhoods' houses (which lie empty for the rest of the year).

In the last few decades the sheer size of the *romería* has begun to worry the authorities, as it has exploded from a few thousand pilgrims in the 1970s to an incredible half a million in the early years of the new century. Despite the whole affair having become a spectacular TV event with arc lamps, amplified music and fireworks, popular enthusiasm is undiminished. The brotherhoods wrestle with each other to carry the Blanca Paloma (the "White Dove", as the Virgin is fondly known) one more time in procession before she's returned to her shrine for another year, and the weary homeward trek begins.

Accompanying one of the brotherhoods on their pilgrimage to El Rocío is a memorable and exhilarating experience. Anyone is entitled to be a pilgrim: just turn up when the processions leave the major villages in the provinces of Seville and Huelva in the days leading up to Pentecost, taking with you a sleeping bag and some food and water. The walking is easy with plenty of stops for dancing and liquid refreshment, and the nightly encampments, when folk songs are sung around campfires, are magical.

village, Doñana Reservas (w donanareservas.com) offers jeep tours into Doñana National Park. They also offer horseriding and landau excursions in and around the park.

ACCOMMODATION AND EATING

El Rocío makes a nice place to **stay** – except during the *romería* at Pentecost when rooms (costing a whopping €200–500 per night) are booked up months, even years, in advance. All the hotels and *hostales* have **restaurants** – note that El Rocío's eating places tend to close earlier than is normal in Andalucía and start shutting down around 10.30–11pm. **Tapas** and *raciones* are cooked to a high standard at many restaurants and bars on and around the village's main street – but to eat out on their terraces after sundown in summer you'll need plenty of mosquito protection.

Camping La Aldea w campinglaaldea.com. El Rocío's campsite lies on the village's northern edge along the Almonte road (A483), and offers good facilities and a reasonable amount of shade. €

Hospedería El Cazadero Real C/Moguer 13; w hospederiareal.es. Part of the *Grupo Hosped'Arte* chain, this spick and span guesthouse has spacious rooms, some

with their own bathrooms, and a terrace with a view of the *marismas*. €

Hostal Cristina C/Real 32; ☎959 406 513. One of El Rocío's oldest budget establishments, this is a welcoming place with en-suite a/c rooms (some with *marismas* views) and its own restaurant. €

Hotel La Malvasia C/Sanlúcar 38; w hotellamalvasia. com. Well-appointed, bird–themed rooms are host to traditional Andalucían tiling, balconies and sensational beds. Request room 13 (the *cigüeña blanca*/white stork) for a view of the *marisma*. €€

★ **Hotel Toruño** Pza Acebuchal 22; w toruno.es. This is the best of the more expensive places, with comfortable rooms overlooking the *marismas*. The best view is from Room 225, but some of the ground-floor rooms (109, 111 & 115) also allow you to spot flamingos, herons, avocets and lots more while lying in bed. B&B, with an excellent restaurant for dinner downstairs. €

BIRDWATCHING AROUND EL ROCÍO

In the spring, El Rocío is probably the best birdwatching base in the area. The *marismas* and pinewoods adjacent to the town itself are teeming with birds, and following tracks east and southeast along the edge of the reserve you'll see many species from white stork, herons and egrets to masked great grey shrike and honking wild geese.

At the water's edge 150m east of the *Hotel Toruño* (see page 318) the **Centro Ornitológico Francisco Bernis** (Tues–Sun 9am–2pm & 4–6pm; w seo.org) has information on the birds to be seen plus a rooftop hide overlooking the *marismas*. The **Boca del Lobo** ("wolf-breath") sewage treatment plant a further 400m east of the centre is an unlikely-sounding birdspotting location, but vultures and storks are frequent visitors there.

El Rocío bridge, on the village's southern edge (carrying the A483), has been described by one naturalist as "the best free birdwatching site in Europe". From this spot, red kite – a common sight here – soaring flocks of whiskered terns, disturbed by the ominous approach of a majestic booted eagle, and migrating greenshank, ruff and sandpiper are all to be seen in season. In high summer, though, the marshes dry out and are grazed by horses while the birdlife is restricted to coot and avocets breeding by the river. The view across the marshes towards the village and church of El Rocío from here is also superb.

With your own transport another great birdwatching location is the **Cerrado Garrido** (aka Centro José Antonio Valverde; June–Sept 10am–8pm; Oct–May 10am–6pm; ☎671 564 145) on the park's northern fringes. To get there from El Rocío follow the signs from the centre of the village, a 30km trip via Villamanrique de la Condesa. Approaching the centre the route traverses the Preparque along unmade tracks and is quite feasible in summer; after heavy rains access may not be possible and you should check with El Acebuche visitor centre (see page 316). Cerrado's visitors' centre has a *cafetería*-bar, as well as telescopes and hides. You'll have plenty of other birdwatching and wildlife-spotting opportunities en route – keep an eye out for purple gallinules (aka swamphen) in the ditches between the paddy fields. The sunrises and sunsets over the *marismas* at Cerrado Garrido are quite spectacular, too.

Beaches south of El Rocío

With your own transport, you can explore many fine, empty dune-backed **beaches** to the northwest of the humdrum resort of Matalascañas, 16km south of El Rocío. These fabulous strands retain their tranquillity thanks to the lack of settlements along the 30km of coastline flanking the A494 west of here. There are a number of access points to beaches such as the signed **Playa Cuesta de Maneli**; here boardwalks cross the pine- and juniper-covered dunes to a magnificent swathe of golden sand, stretching far into the distance in both directions – you will rarely see another soul. The last stop along this coastline before the industrial suburbs of Huelva is the resort of **Mázagon**, an uninspiring place with a decent beach but few other charms.

ACCOMMODATION   **BEACHES SOUTH OF EL ROCÍO**

★ **Parador Cristóbal Colón** Playa de Mazagón, 6km from Mázagon; ⓦ parador.es. This four-star is set above the stunning beach and surrounded by pinewoods. The hotel's tile-floored rooms are attractively furnished, while public areas include spa, restaurant and tapas bar and a solarium for epic sunset viewing. Outside, there are wonderful gardens with superb pools (both indoor and outdoor) and steps leading down to a fabulous strand. Rates drop by fifty percent or more outside August. €€€€

Costa de La Luz (Huelva)

The stretch of coast between the **Guadiana** – which marks the border with Portugal – and **Tinto** rivers is lined with some of the finest **beaches** in Andalucía. Chillier and with a choppier sea than the neighbouring coast, but no less scenic, the resorts here rarely see a foreign tourist. There's no train service, but plenty of buses run along this main route to Spain's westerly edge.

From Huelva the **coast road to Portugal** loops around the Marisma de San Miguel, passing through the dull towns of **Cartaya** and **Lepe**. Geoffrey Chaucer (whose father was a vintner) wrote in the *Pardoner's Tale* that the potent white wine of Lepe "creepeth subtilly … that whan a man hath dronken draughtes three, and weneth he be at hoom in Chepe, He is in Spaigne, right at the toune of Lepe" – an out-of-body experience no doubt familiar to many modern inebriates. Lepe's main claim to fame today is their strawberry production, which averages at two million tonnes per year. A stint of prosperity, however, hasn't changed Lepe's status as the liability of the region. Its inhabitants are still seen as gormless drunkards; many jokes begin "did you hear about the man from Lepe …?"

Playa de la Antilla

The road hits the coast 5km south of Lepe at **PLAYA LA ANTILLA**, a low-key beach resort with a wide, sandy blue-flag beach backed by a palm-lined promenade. The residents here welcome tourists and there are some very good seafood restaurants close to the seafront. Outside high season it's a very peaceful place to stay.

ACCOMMODATION   **PLAYA DE LA ANTILLA**

You won't find a room in Playa de la Antilla in August without prebooking. Places to stay cluster around the junction of Avda Castilla and C/La Parada, which is also where the bus drops you.

★ **Camping Luz** Ctra La Antilla–Isla Cristina s/n; ☎ 959 341 142. Five kilometres west of the resort towards Isla Cristina, this is an excellent campsite with plenty of shade, good facilities and a large pool. €

Hostal Azul La Parada 9; ⓦ hostalazul.com. The nearest to the seafront of a line of places along La Parada, this dapper *hostal* has en-suite balcony rooms with sea views plus an attractive roof terrace with loungers. €€

Hostal El Álamo Avda Castilla 82; ⓦ elalamoplaya. com. Halfway down the main strip, this welcoming *hostal* has distinctively decorated en-suite rooms – from 'Hindu gods' to 'Antarctica'. There's a bar on the premises with lively atmosphere. €

EATING AND DRINKING

There's a good spread of bars and cafés near the seafront plus a scattering of *marisquerías* and restaurants to choose from. Many of these line the main street, Avda Castilla, a couple of blocks in from the sea.

Café-Restaurante Coral C/Estrella del Mar 3; ☎959 481 406. A good stop for breakfast snacks, with sea views and pleasant terrace; from lunchtime onwards it functions as a decent restaurant offering a range of fish and meat dishes served on a seaview terrace. €€

Casa Rodri C/Adelfa s/n, just off Avda Castilla; ☎638 827 078. Excellent fish and shellfish – the *dorada* (bream) and *boquerones fritos* (anchovies) are recommended – and they also serve up an astonishingly good-value *menú*. €

Pastelería Heladería Los Angeles Avda Castilla 34–36; ☎959 481 533. A giant pastelería and heladería with a range of the region's best desserts, including *fresas de Lepe* ice cream (Lepen strawberries) and *tarta de picoles y caramel* (caramel and pine nut tart). €

La Islantilla

On the western edge of Playa La Antilla the coast road passes some pretty awful beach development as well as, a couple of kilometres further, the newly created coastal nightmare of **La Islantilla**, where a clutch of tasteless upmarket hotels and *urbanizaciones* are flanked to the right of the road by a sprawling 25-hole golf course – a misguided joint venture by Lepe and Isla Cristina to attract well-heeled visitors. Beyond the campsites *Luz* (see page 319) and *Taray*, the vista clears to provide a pleasant few kilometres of pinewoods and, behind the dunes, more good beaches.

INFORMATION

Turismo If you're driving, La Islantilla has a conveniently located Turismo (daily: March–Oct 9am–2pm & 5–10pm; Nov–April Mon–Fri 9am–2pm & Sat 9–2; ☎959 646 013), on the left of the through road, with stacks of information. Otherwise, there's an information point just off Avda Castilla, opposite the pharmacy, which is open daily 10am–2pm.

Isla Cristina

ISLA CRISTINA, 8km beyond La Islantilla, was, as its name implies, once an island, but infilling has transformed it into a stunning resort surrounded by *marismas* and tidal estuaries. For most of the year the town's prevailing atmosphere is one of tranquillity, and its residents have an equally relaxed disposition to match. They rise to the party in August, however, when *sevillanos* invade for their annual break, and during Carnaval in February. The commercial centre is concentrated around the **port** which is the second most important in the province and from where shellfish and wet fish are transported overnight on ice to the markets, bars and restaurants of Seville, Córdoba and Madrid.

Life in town revolves around the central **Plaza de las Flores**, from where it's an easy ten-minute walk down Ctra de la Playa, shaded by giant eucalyptus trees, to the town's fine sandy **beach**. Alternatively there's a bus (every 30min May–Sept, except during the siesta) from the bus station close to the same square.

ARRIVAL AND INFORMATION

By bus The bus station is on Avda de Huelva, a couple of blocks east of Plaza de las Flores.
Destinations Ayamonte (at least 5 daily, from 9.30pm); Huelva (6 daily; 1hr 25min); Seville (4 daily; 2hr 45min).
Turismo Slightly northwest of Plaza de las Flores at C/San Francisco 12 (June–Oct Mon–Fri 10am–2pm & 5.30–7.30pm, Sat & Sun 10am–2pm; Nov–May daily 10am–2pm; ☎959 332 694). Multi-lingual staff can provide a town map. There's also an info point on the Playa Central.

ACCOMMODATION

Due to the severe shortage of accommodation, if you want to stay – in August especially – you'll need to book ahead. We use August rates for the price codes; prices tend to fall dramatically outside this period.

Camping Giralda 2km from town on La Antilla road; ⓦcampinggiralda.com. The nearest campsite to the resort, with adequate shade, good services and a pool, plus canoeing and sailing. €

Hotel Brisamar C/Baja 187; ☎959 331 130. The best location in town (signed from the beach and centre) this pleasant, refurbished small hotel offers sparkling, light and airy rooms around a balcony coloured with fauna. All rooms equipped with fridges. Be patient with the hot water. €€

Hotel Paraíso Playa Ctra de la Playa s/n; ⓦhotelparaisoplaya.com. Comfortable, bright hotel, slightly inland from the beach, with attractive balcony rooms with TV, plus pool and car park. Breakfast is included. €€€

Hotel Sol y Mar Paseo Marítimo s/n; ⓦhotelsolymar.org. Right on the beach, this inviting hotel has spacious rooms with terrace balcony and sea views, plus its own car park and a very good bar-restaurant. €€

EATING AND DRINKING

★ **Casa Rufino** Ctra de la Playa; ⓦrestauranterufino.com. Less than 100m from the beach and with an outdoor terrace, this is one of the town's best – and priciest – fish restaurants. Specials include *brochetas de rape* (monkfish) and a superb *arroz negro de marisco* (rice with squid); there's also a good-value *menú* and a "*tonteo*", featuring eight different kinds of fish. €€€

★ **Hermanos Moreno** Avda Padre Miravent 39; ☎959 343 571. You won't get fish any fresher than at this popular and reasonably priced bar-restaurant, a stone's throw from the fishing harbour. Everything served in the tapas bar (and its terrace) below is straight from the sea, while their upstairs restaurant is also outstanding – *atún* (fresh tuna) and *urta* (sea bream) are specialities. €€€

Restaurante La Sal Paseo de Las Flores 13; ☎662 159 386. Popular tapas bar and restaurant just off the Plaza de Flores. House specialities include lightly fried *albóndigas de choco* (cuttlefish meatballs) and *millejos de berenjenas* (sliced aubergine with goats' cheese), though all tapas are served with pride and, if you're lucky, a complimentary *caña*. €€

Ayamonte and around

Although the sprawling, slightly down-at-heel border town of **AYAMONTE** lies just 8km from Isla Cristina, the road has to dogleg 16km around the *marismas* to get there. With Portugal only a few hundred metres away on the opposite bank of the Río Guadiana – and easily visitable – there's a pronounced Portuguese feel to the town. The pleasing labyrinth of the old quarter is home to many quaint restaurants and bars, some of which hold infamously late parties on the weekends.

Old town

The warren of narrow streets behind the main square, **Paseo de la Ribera** (and its continuation Plaza de la Coronación) overlooking the harbour, leads up to the old town. Here, the fourteenth-century **Iglesia de San Francisco** (open Sun and holidays), has a beautiful Mudéjar *artesonado* ceiling; following the same street, Calle San Francisco, further north will bring you to the fifteenth-century **Iglesia de San Salvador** (Mon–Wed & Fri–Sun 6.30–8pm; free) with a striking tower which you can climb for fine views across the river to Portugal.

Beaches

Ayamonte's beaches, the blue-flagged **Playa Isla Canela**, 7km south of town, and its eastward continuation, the **Playa Punta del Moral**, are excellent places for a bit of basking in the sun, although what was once an attractively wild stretch of coast has undergone a mammoth building programme, turning the Punta del Moral into a complex of high-rise holiday apartments and tasteless hotels. Along its asphalted main street, however, are some tapas bars such as *Bar Nuevo Simón* and *La Pamela*, which are famed for their *mariscos*.

Playa Isla Canela

Easily reached by half-hourly bus (April–Sept) from Ayamonte's main bus station or the stop opposite the zoo, **Playa Isla Canela** makes a pleasant day-trip. While its long cove of fine sand with a deceivingly strong current isn't as clean as its blue-flagged neighbours, the beach clubhouse Playa Alta (10am–3am) is the perfect hang out spot – expect extravagant cocktails and live music in the evenings.

ARRIVAL AND INFORMATION

By bus Buses from Huelva and Seville arrive at the bus station (ⓦdamas-sa.es) on Avda de Andalucía, slightly north of the Paseo de la Ribera.

Destinations Huelva (4 daily; 1hr 30min); Punta del Moral and Playa Isla Canela (April–Sept; 15 daily; 30min); Seville (4 daily; 2hr 40min).

By ferry Operated by the Transporte Fluvial del Guadiana (ⓦrioguadiana.net) ferries cross hourly from 9am–6pm (then the last crossing is 7.15pm) to Vila Real de Santo Antonio, the Portuguese town on the opposite bank of the Guadiana. Leaving from the *puerto* just south of the city, it's a 15min crossing, with space for bikes and scooters.

Turismo Plaza de España 1, a contemporary, white building just over the river, next to the zoo (Mon–Fri 9am–8pm; Sat 10am–12pm; ⓦayto-ayamonte.es). Staff can provide a town map and extensive information on local transport.

ACCOMMODATION

Places to stay are limited and rooms can be hard to find, especially in summer when it's worth ringing ahead.

Hostal Los Robles Avda Andalucía 119; ☎959 470 959. This welcoming *hostal* is one of the best-value options in town, with pleasant a/c en-suite rooms with TV. It's opposite the petrol station as you enter Ayamonte from Isla Cristina. €

Hotel Ayamonte Center Avda Ramón y Cajal 2; ⓦayamontecenter.com. Clean, spacious rooms with their own balconies. There's a pleasant lounge area with a coffee machine and microwave. Try for a room on the third floor, overlooking the zoological garden. €€

Parador Costa de la Luz Avda de la Constitución; ⓦwww.parador.es. Overlooking the Río Guadiana and its spectacular bridge, this is the town's luxury address, with elegant, well-equipped rooms, many with river views, plus pretty gardens and a pool. A bar and restaurant (with river views and a quality *menú*) complete the picture. Also boasts its own car park. €€€

EATING AND DRINKING

Cafetería Restaurante Barberi Paseo de la Rivera 13; ☎959 320 229. Worth a try for *platos combinados* and more elaborate dishes in the restaurant, while its café next door has an inexpensive *menú del día*. €

★**La Casona** C/Lusitania 2; ☎959 321 025. It's unanimously agreed this tapas-bar-come-restaurant is the best place to eat in town. The grilled meats and fish are definitely worth the wait, especially given how cosy the restaurant is. The owner recommends *solomillo al Pedro Jiménez* (pork fillet in white wine) with their signature sauce. Most dishes available in tapas, *racciones* and main sizes. €€

Galeria Passage Café Pza de la Laguna 11; ☎959 470 978. The perfect spot for an afternoon *café con leche* and slice of *tarte almedra* (almond tart), among an eccentric collection of clocks and works by local artists. €

★**Ultramarínos Orta** C/Lusitania 8, near La Casona; ☎959 321 172. Founded in 1863, this is a wonderful bar-shop selling wines, cheeses and *jamones* out front, while an atmospheric bar uses barrels for tables and serves tapas in the back. Try the fresh *atún* (tuna), *caballa* (mackerel) or *sardinas* tapas. €

Inland to Río Tinto

Of the potential routes to the mountainous north of the province, the Sierra de Aracena and Sierra de Morena, the westernmost, from near Ayamonte, is the least interesting. Here the road ploughs on endlessly through a dreary landscape dominated by stands of voracious and alien eucalyptus which have sucked the lifeblood from the soil.

Far more attractive is the **N435** heading northeast from Huelva to Aracena which offers – with your own transport – an interesting detour to the mines of **Río Tinto** (see box, page 324). The bus uses the same route to reach Aracena or you could take a train, which will drop you at Almonaster La Real at the Sierra de Aracena's western end.

AÑO DE LOS TIROS

In 1888 the village of Ríotinto was the setting for possibly the first **ecological protest** in modern times. The Río Tinto Mining Company was using a copper processing method (banned many years before in Britain) that polluted the village and surrounding agricultural zone with a "*manta*" (blanket) of toxic fumes. Unable to convince the company or the Spanish governmental authorities (who were very much in awe of the company) to end a practice which was grievously affecting the health of the miners' families and children, the whole community staged a protest demonstration on February 4, 1888 culminating in a march to the Ayuntamiento where miners' representatives had requested a meeting with the mayor, company officials and the provincial governor. The latter had brought with him a regiment of Spanish troops to ensure that order was maintained.

While the meeting was taking place within, the troops outside received an order (it is unclear who gave it) to open fire on the peaceful demonstrators. In what is now infamously known as the **Año de los Tiros** (Year of the Shootings) up to two hundred men, women and children lost their lives. In an attempt to obscure the scale of the tragedy many corpses were disposed of in disused mine shafts, which is why the precise death toll was never known.

For more, read *Corazón de la Tierra* (Heart of the Earth), a novel centred on these events, written by Juan Cobos Wilkins, a native of Río Tinto and the descendant of an English Río Tinto employee. His work in Spanish, *La Huelva Británica* is a fascinating history of the British in Huelva and particularly in the village of Bella Vista.

3

Huelva to Minas de Ríotinto

Once clear of Huelva the N435 climbs steadily towards **Trigueros**, a pleasant agricultural village, and the market town of **Valverde del Camino**, noted more for its leather footwear factories than its charms. A further 10km on, a turn on the right towards the hamlet of El Pozuelo allows you to see three **dolmens** from the third millennium BC. Following this minor road for about 2km brings you to a signed road just before a cemetery on the outskirts of the village. Follow this on foot or by car as it loops around the village for a further 2km to reach a rest area and information board. Leave any transport here and follow the track on the right, which ascends the hill through trees for about 100m to the first dolmen, from where the other two can be seen on hills nearby. The first is the most impressive and has three burial chambers, two with their capstones still in place. The second has four burial chambers, and the last is in ruins. A further six dolmens displayed on the information board are not so easy to spot.

Return to the N435, which soon begins to wind into the wooded hill country of the **Sierra Morena** until – just beyond Zalamea La Real – a right turn along the A461 leads you into the area of the **Río Tinto mines**.

Minas de Ríotinto and around

Set in an area dramatically scarred by open-cast mineworkings, where the exposed faces of mineral-rich rock are streaked with glinting rivulets of ochre, rust and cadmium, the village of **MINAS DE RÍOTINTO**, 6km east of the N435, was created by the Río Tinto Mining Company in the early twentieth century after they had dynamited its predecessor – complete with Baroque church – which had stood in the way of mining operations.

Barrio de Bella Vista

As you approach it from the west, watch out on the left for the **Barrio de Bella Vista**, or what the locals refer to as the "English colony". This estate of Victorian villas, complete with mock-Gothic Presbyterian church and village green, was constructed to house the largely British management and engineering staff when the mines passed into Anglo-German hands in the nineteenth century. The attitude of this elite to the surrounding village – where the mineworkers lived – is indicated by the estate's high perimeter wall and once-guarded entry gates intended rigorously to exclude "the natives", as they were disdainfully described. In a company policy with racist overtones these "colonialists" were forbidden from living in Bella Vista if they dared to marry a Spanish woman, thus deterring any dangerous interbreeding.

The estate now houses local people and no one minds if you wander in for a look around. The former "**Social Club**", membership of which was exclusively male (women were allowed only as guests), is now a bar named *Club Inglés* (Mon–Fri 1–3pm & 7–11pm) with a terrace overlooking the former village green/cricket pitch with a pool (open to patrons of the bar).

Casa No. 21

Daily 4–6.30pm • Same ticket as the mining museum

The mining museum (see page 325) acquired this house in Bella Vista, which has been wonderfully restored in late nineteenth-century style. Known as **Casa No. 21** it

---

THE MINES OF RÍO TINTO

The **Río Tinto** (Red River) takes its name from the oxidized iron minerals that flow down from the fissured crags of this strange, forbidding landscape, turning the river blood-red. Evidence of mineral exploitation here goes back at least five millennia – popular tradition asserts that these were the legendary mines of King Solomon, as seen in place names such as Cerro (or hill) de Saloman and Zalamea La Real. More secure historical evidence shows it was the **Phoenicians** (giving the name Ur-yero – "river of fire" – to the Río Tinto) who encouraged exploitation here early in the first millennium BC, during the age of the fabled kingdom of Tartessus from where they acquired the copper to smelt with the tin of Cornwall to make bronze. It was not copper but silver, however, that attracted the **Romans** in the second century BC. Production was dramatically stepped up during the late republic and early empire using remarkable – if brutal – systems to combat flooding, the perennial hazard in deep mining. This they overcame by means of slave-operated *norias*, or waterwheels; in some workings as many as eight pairs of these wheels were used in relays to raise water from depths of 100m and more. For the shackled slave miners working with primitive tools by the light of small clay lamps in warrens of cramped, dark galleries (now vividly reconstructed in the Río Tinto mining museum), life must have been wretched. The scale of the Roman operations can be judged from the fifty million tonnes of visible slag left behind.

After the Romans had gone, the **Visigoths** worked out the Roman shafts but the mines were then run down during the **Moorish** period – although Niebla built part of its prosperity on its rights of ownership by granting permits. The **Reconquista** brought further decline in its wake as cheap mineral wealth flooded into Spain from the New World. Loss of empire and hard times induced efforts to restart the industry which, in 1873, resulted in the Spanish government selling the mines to a consortium of British and German bankers. Out of this the **Río Tinto Mining Company** was born, bringing numerous northern Europeans to work here. In 1954 control of the company returned into Spanish hands but falling world mineral prices led to it being sold on to a succession of multinational companies before, in 1995, it was purchased by its 523 employees for the nominal price of one peseta. The worker-owned company also ran into difficulties and went bankrupt. After the mines lay dormant for over a decade, the soaring price of copper on world markets led to another multinational, Emed Mining (now Atalaya Mining; ⓦ atalayamining.com), purchasing them in 2010. The mines are operational again, with copper production at full capacity. The scheme promised to create 1500 new jobs. At present, Atalaya Mining employs 350 people in the Río Tinto area.

THE RÍO TINTO AND OUTER SPACE

The almost Martian landscape of much of the Río Tinto area has attracted scientists from Madrid University's Centro de Astrobiologia and the Astrobiological Institute of NASA, who have begun joint research into the remarkable **microbial life** that has developed here in some of the most inhospitable conditions on the planet. The enormous diversity of eukaryotic life forms (organisms with genetic cells) able to prosper in the poisonous and highly acidic waters of the Río Tinto mining zone initially astonished experts, who went on to discover a variety of previously unknown life forms here. Now formally known as the **MARTE Project** (Mars Astrobiology Research and Technology Experiment; ⓦmarte.arc.nasa.gov), it comprises of researchers who hope that the thousands of species of microorganisms that have evolved here over millennia in the toxic depths of the Red River will provide clues as to how life may have developed and evolved in other parts of the universe, including Mars.

---

uses period furnishings, clothing, domestic appliances and fascinating photos of the village and its social life to re-create a bygone age.

3

Museo Minero

Pza del Museo s/n • Daily 10.30am–3pm & 4–7pm • Charge, book online to buy combo train and museum ticket • ⓦ parquemineroderiotinto.es

At the village's western edge on a hill above the Río Tinto company's former offices lies the Río Tinto Foundation's remarkable **Museo Minero**. Housed in the company's former hospital, the museum presents an interesting panorama of mining in the area from prehistoric to modern times. The Roman period is the best represented, with exhibits illustrating their mining methods, daily life and burial practices in addition to a variety of coins and statuary. A section here has a walk-through reconstruction of a Roman mineworking gallery discovered in the nearby mining area. The actual site cannot be visited as it lies within the zone of the modern mineworkings and is thus dangerous, but the museum has done an excellent job in re-creating it. The section includes a functioning reconstruction of a *noria*, or waterwheel, which were worked by slaves and used to drain the mines of flood water. Modern mining is also covered, as well as the geology, flora and fauna of the area. Don't miss the luxurious **wagon of the maharaja**, built in 1892 by the Birmingham Railway Carriage and Wagon Company to be used by Queen Victoria on her proposed visit to India. When this didn't happen it was sold to the Río Tinto company and used for the visit of King Alfonso XIII to the mines.

The museum can also provide information on visits to old underground mineworkings at **Peña de Hierro**, the source of the Río Tinto and the site where NASA and Spanish academics are carrying out their research for the Mars project (see box, page 325). A *cafetería* serves snacks and drinks and its adjoining shop sells a wide variety of souvenirs.

The Río Tinto Foundation also runs ninety-minute **train trips** through the mining area (call ☎959 590 025 or consult ⓦparquemineroderiotinto.com for timetable and prices), aboard century-old restored rolling stock – on the first Sunday of each month they use a 120-year-old steam locomotive. Buy tickets online or from the museum.

ARRIVAL AND DEPARTURE
MINAS DE RÍOTINTO AND AROUND

By bus Minas de Ríotinto is connected by bus with Aracena, Seville and Huelva.

Destinations Aracena (2 daily; 45min); Huelva (2 daily; 1hr 40min); Nerva (2 daily; 10min).

By car To reach the village proper from Barrio de Bella Vista head east along the A461 and turn right following the "*centro urbano*" signs. The road leads to a roundabout with palms on its central island, with the former Río Tinto Mining Company's offices (now the Ayuntamiento) to the left. The village's centre lies to the left (east) from here while the mining museum is reached by taking a right uphill from the roundabout. On foot, from the west side of the same roundabout you can follow a path which ascends through the pine and eucalyptus woods to emerge at the museum.

3

ACCOMMODATION

★ **Cortijo Zalamea** 8km west of Minas de Ríotinto, off the main N435 close to the village of Zalamea La Real; ⊛ cortijozalamea.es. With your own transport, the *Cortijo Zalamea* provides a delightful oasis in leafy surroundings with accommodation in self-contained, fully equipped cottages; there's also a pool, plus horseriding, mountain biking and walking. Breakfast is included. €€

Hostal-Restaurante Atalaya Avda de Esquila 13; ⊛ atalayahostalrestaurante.com. Near the mining museum, this inviting two-star *hostal* offers comfortable en-suite rooms with TV and also has a decent restaurant. Free parking on the weekend. €

EATING AND DRINKING

Minas de Ríotinto has plentiful bars and eating options, in addition to the restaurant of the *Hostal Atalaya* (see page 326).

Bar La Esquila Avda Esquila 3. Slightly down the hill on the far side of the museum, this lively bar serves up a variety of tapas and *platos combinados* as well as a cheap *menu*. €

Restaurante Epoca Paseo de los Caracoles 6; ⊛ restaurante-epoca.com. Heading 150m west downhill from the *Galán* and *Esquila* restaurants, this is another very good place offering sierra cuisine such as *churrasco minero* (grilled pork) and *pollo a la Inglesa* (roast chicken "English style"); also does a range of salads and has a well-priced daily *menú*. €€

Restaurante Galán Avda de la Esquila 10; ☎ 959 590 840. Just around the corner from the museum this reliable bar-restaurant specializes in *carnes a la brasa* (grilled meats), with an inviting terrace and a lunchtime *menú*. €€

Towards La Dehesa

Two kilometres northeast of Minas de Ríotinto, along the A461 as it heads north towards Aracena, you pass two spectacular open-cast mines: the **Corta Atalaya** and, with five thousand years of exploitation, the **Cerro Colorado**, set in an awesome landscape of rock cliffs glittering with iron pyrites, copper, silver and gold. From a viewing platform by the roadside you can see into the giant elliptical basin of the Corta Atalaya, which at 1200m long and 330m deep is one of the biggest open-cast mines in the world – far below, enormous trucks are dwarfed by the immense walls of rock.

Another 2km further on, at **LA DEHESA**, the Río Tinto Company headquarters are backed by a **Roman graveyard** discovered in the 1990s and featuring a number of interesting tombstones. Alarmingly close to the present mining operations which rumble on in the background, the graveyard (signed "Necropolis Romana") can currently only be viewed behind a fence, set slightly back from the road.

Nerva

NERVA, 4km east of Minas de Ríotinto, is a pleasant little place, its pedestrianized main street fringed with orange trees and overlooked by a splendid redbrick Ayuntamiento with a wonderful minaret-inspired octagonal tower. It was completed in in 1885, the same year that the village became a municipality. A mining settlement in origin, Nerva's name was inspired by a copper plaque found a few years earlier in the Roman mineworkings honouring the emperor Nerva.

Centro de Arte Contemporáneo

Opposite the Ayuntamiento • Opening times vary, see website • Free • ⊛ vazquezdiaz.org

The extravagant **Centro de Arte Contemporáneo** honours Daniel Vázquez Díaz (a Paris contemporary and friend of Picasso), who was born in Nerva. In addition to a handful of canvases by Díaz, the museum also displays an indifferent collection of works by other *nerveuses*, plus temporary exhibitions to fill the rather cavernous interior.

ARRIVAL AND DEPARTURE   NERVA

Three **buses** currently run from Nerva to Aracena (Mon–Fri   12.15pm, 3.15pm & 4.45pm; Sat 4.45pm; 45min).

ACCOMMODATION AND EATING

Cervecería Robles Avda de Andalucía 11; ☎ 959 581 192. On the main street almost opposite the Ayuntamiento, this is a popular bar-restaurant for *copas*, tapas and *raciones* – try their *carpaccio presa o paté a la reducción de P. Ximénez*

(paté with regional white wine). €

El Círculo Comercial (aka Círculo Mercantil) Avda de Andalucía s/n; ☎ 959 580 411. Facing the fountain on the main street, the elegant and friendly town *casino* has a grand and spacious interior with plenty of comfortable chairs to sit and eat tapas and *raciones*. Everything is good, and any of the

fried fish or grilled pork dishes is worth a try. €€

Hotel Vázquez Díaz C/Cañadilla 51; ☞ hotelvazquezdiaz.es. Reached by turning first left into the town coming from Minas de Ríotinto, this is a welcoming rural hotel with tidy a/c rooms above a bar-restaurant, and offers karaoke, if you're so inclined. €

Towards Aracena

The easiest way to leave the mining area, heading towards Aracena, is to return to Minas de Río Tinto and take the A461 to **Campofrío**. This tiny village – which claims to have the oldest bullring in Spain – lies some 11km to the north. Beyond here, the landscape softens and the road progresses through verdant forests of cork and holm oaks, chestnut and walnut trees as it climbs into the Sierra de Aracena.

Sierra Morena

The longest of Spain's mountain ranges, the **Sierra Morena** extends almost the whole way across Andalucía from Rosal on the Portuguese frontier to the dramatic pass of Despeñaperros, north of Linares. Its hill towns once marked the northern boundary of the old Moorish caliphate of Córdoba and in many ways the region still signals a break today, with a shift from the climate and mentality of the south to the bleak plains and villages of Extremadura and New Castile. The range is not widely known – with its highest point a mere 1110m, it is not a dramatic sierra – and even Andalucíans can have trouble placing it. All of which, of course, is to your advantage if you like to be alone. Tracks are still more common in these hills than roads, and rural tourism, which the government of Andalucía is keen to encourage, has so far led to little more than a handful of signs pointing out areas of special interest. The wealth of good walking country invites organizing your routes around **hikes** if you want to spend any amount of time here. **Cycling**, too, is an option, though you'll need a sturdy bike with plenty of gears, especially on the winding and muscle-taxing hill roads.

This is also an area rich in **wildlife** – including frogs, turtles, lizards, dragonflies, bees, hares and foxes – while bird fanciers should keep an eye out for imperial and booted eagles, as well as goshawks, peregrine falcons and the rare black vulture. In villages such as Cortegana, Zufre and Santa Olalla del Cala the black stork nests on the church towers. The Sierra de Aracena sector of the sierra has been designated as a ZEPA (Zona de Especial Protección a las Aves) in recognition of its importance as a bird sanctuary. The sierra is also home to one of two surviving populations of Spanish lynx on the peninsula, although, with only thirty or so pairs eking out an existence as their forest habitat is gnawed away, you'll only spot one if you venture to Jaén's stretch of the range and even then it's unlikely. Locals maintain that while the last bears disappeared only a short time ago, there are still a few wolves in remoter parts.

The **climate** is mild – sunny in spring, hot but fresh in summer – but it can get very cold in the evenings and mornings. A good time to visit is between March and June, when the flowers, perhaps the most varied in the country, are at their best. You may get caught in the odd thunderstorm but it's usually bright and hot enough to swim in the reservoirs or splash in the springs and streams, most of which are good to drink from. High season for Sierra Morena falls to the end of September and continues through to November.

GETTING AROUND | **SIERRA MORENA**

By bus East–west transport in the sierra is limited, but with a little planning most places mentioned in our account can be reached on public transport. For the area east of

Aracena, specifically the terrain beyond the main A66-E803 in Seville province, bus services are radial and north–south, with Seville as the hub.

3

Aracena

Clustered beneath its hilltop medieval castle, the attractive town of **ARACENA** is the highest conurbation in the Sierra Morena as well as the gateway to its own **Sierra de Aracena** to the south and west. Sheltered by this offshoot of the larger Morena range, Aracena is blessed by remarkably sharp, clear air – all the more noticeable, and gratifying, if you've arrived from the heat of Seville.

Although traces of Paleolithic occupation of this area have been found, it was only in the Middle Ages that more concrete historical events happened here, namely the passing of this territory into the kingdom of Castile by a treaty of 1267 following a long struggle with Portugal. Once inside the domains of Castile, Alfonso X ceded the zone around Aracena to the **Knights Templars** to maintain and protect the sierra. They constructed the castle, one of many erected in this frontier zone, and ruled the roost here until 1312. Today, the town's main role is as a centre of agriculture and cattle breeding, assisted by the tourist magnet of the **Gruta de las Maravillas** (Cave of Wonders).

Iglesia del Castillo

Pza del Castillo · Daily: April–Sept 10.30am–7pm, Oct–May 10.30am–5pm · Free

The town's southern flank rambles up the side of a hill topped by the **Iglesia del Castillo** – or, more correctly, Nuestra Señora de los Dolores – an impressive thirteenth-century Gothic-Mudéjar church built by the Knights Templar around the remains of a Moorish **castle**. Its tower was formerly the *alminar* (minaret) of the castle's twelfth-century Almohad mosque, destroyed by the Templars. Decorated with some exquisite *sebka* brickwork above two polylobed arches, it is reminiscent of Seville's Giralda. Inside the church there's an unusual and finely made glazed clay tomb of the sixteenth-century prior, Pedro Vásquez de Miguel.

The climb to the **castle** offers good views over the town from the imposing sixteenth-century brick gate, complete with belfry, which gives access to the castle.

Plaza Alta

The track up to the Iglesia del Castillo begins from the **Plaza Alta**, where there's the unfinished church of **Nuestra Señora de la Asunción** (open service times: Mon–Sat 7.30–9pm, Sun noon–1pm; free) with remnants of Renaissance craftsmanship, flanked by a sixteenth-century *cabildo viejo* or old **Ayuntamiento**, the oldest in the province, which now houses the Natural Park information centre (see page 330). The Ayuntamiento's imposing main portal is by Hernán Ruíz II and dates to 1563.

Gruta de las Maravillas

C/Manuel Suirot, southwest of the Mueso del Jamón · Daily 10am–1.30pm & 3–6pm (tours every hour, or every 30min at weekends; 50min) · Charge · ☎ 663 937 876

Aracena's principal attraction is the **Gruta de las Maravillas**, the largest and arguably the most impressive cave in Spain, discovered, so they say, by a local boy in search of a lost pig. Due to the cave being damaged by the overwhelming number of visitors, there's now a maximum of 35 visitors per tour. The best time to visit is before noon; if you're planning an afternoon visit (the time favoured by coach tours) call them to see whether you will be able to gain entry. It can be chilly inside, so bring a sweater.

A guide takes you round the cave and the "marvels" are explained in Spanish only (leaflet in English). Although the garish coloured lighting is more Santa's Grotto than geological wonder, the cave is still astonishingly beautiful, and entertaining too – the last chamber of the tour is known simply as the **Sala de los Culos** (Room of the Buttocks), its walls and ceiling an outrageous, naturally sculpted exhibition, tinged in a pinkish orange light. You might care to ponder why this section of the caves did not appear in the film *Journey to the Centre of the Earth*, much of which was shot here. Taking photos is prohibited, but if you're really keen to get a shot at the *gruta*, there's a

EATING

Bar Joaquinito	5
Casas	6
Casino Arias Montano	1
Confitería Casa Rufino	3
Puerta 20	2
Restaurante José Vicente	4
La Serrana	7

ARACENA

ACCOMMODATION

Finca Valbono	2
Hospedería Reina de los Angeles	5
Hostal Molino del Bombo	1
Hotel Convento de Aracena	6
Hotel de los Castaños	4
Hotel Sierra de Aracena	3

professional photographer capturing everyone as they walk in and selling the prints for an extortionate sum.

In the Plaza de San Pedro outside the *gruta*, a **contemporary sculpture garden** features 34 donated works by many noted artists including *Reconocimiento del Vacío* by the famous Basque sculptor Eduardo Chillida, a graceful cube-like structure, and Carmen Perujo's *Paloma*, near the cave entrance.

Museo del Jamón

Gran Via s/n • Tours (some in English) every 40min daily 10am–1.30pm & 3.30–5.30pm • Charge

A unique attraction is the town's **Museo del Jamón**, dedicated to explaining the story of the Sierra de Aracena's celebrated *jamón ibérico* hams: how they're produced and the importance of the *dehesa* (evergreen parklands with sparse plantations of holm and cork oaks), where the pigs are pastured. The traditional and modern methods of slaughter and subsequent curing of the *jamones* is informatively explained.

A separate (free) section of the museum deals with the sierra's **setas** (wild mushrooms) – almost seven hundred species have been identified here.

ARRIVAL AND DEPARTURE   ARACENA

By bus Aracena's bus station (Avda de Sevilla s/n) lies on   the southeast side of town close to the Parque Municipal.

Buses leave for Seville and Huelva Mon–Fri at 7.45am & 4pm, then Sat & Sun at 10.30am & 6pm. The Damas website (W damas-sa.es) or app have the latest timetables and ticket purchasing if you're short on cash.

INFORMATION AND TOURS

Turismo Beneath the Gruta de las Maravillas ticket office (daily 10am–2pm & 4–6pm; ☎ 663 937 877; W aracena. es); it has information and a town map. Information on the surrounding Parque Natural Sierra de Aracena y Picos de Aroche is obtainable from the information centre in the old Ayuntamiento, Plaza Alta 5 (Tues–Sun: July & Aug 10am–2pm & 6–8pm; Sept–June 10am–2pm & 4–6pm; ☎ 959 129 553).

ACCOMMODATION

SEE MAP PAGE 329

Finca Valbono Ctra Carboneras, km1; W fincavalbono. com. Rural hotel set in thirty acres of scenic woodland, 1km north of town on the road to Carboneras. The rustic-style self-contained *casas rurales* come equipped with *chimeneas* (wood-burning stoves) or there are conventional rooms with minibar, satellite TV, heating and a/c. Facilities include a bar, restaurant and pool, while hiking and horseriding excursions are on offer. €€

Hospedería Reina de los Angeles Avda Reina de los Angeles s/n, near the Gruta de las Maravillas; W hospederiaaracena.com. A rather institutional-looking place that betrays its origins as a former student hostel. However, redecorated and refitted, its ninety en-suite and rather Spartan rooms (some single) are nevertheless clean, bright and good value. Easy street parking. €

Hostal Molino del Bombo C/Ancha 4, close to the bullring in the upper town; W molinodelbombo.com. Charming *hostal rural* in a superbly refurbished townhouse offering attractive, comfortable en-suite rooms. Hydro-massages available as part of room package. €

Hotel Convento de Aracena C/Jesús María 19; W hotelconventoaracena.es. The town's four-star luxury option is located inside a tastefully restored sixteenth-to-eighteenth-century former Dominican convent. Rooms overlook the cloisters and quadrangle now planted with trees and aromatic herbs. Facilities include a spa and pool with a view over the mountains. A former convent herb garden now stands outside the hotel's top-notch restaurant, *Huerto*. See website for offers, which include breakfast. €€

Hotel de los Castaños Avda de Huelva 5; W loscastanoshotel.com. Decent, if rather formally furnished, rooms (aimed at business travellers) with heating, a/c and TV. Facilities include a restaurant with a *menú* and a garage. €

Hotel Sierra de Aracena Gran Vía 21; W hotelsierradearacena.com. This traditional hotel has pleasant, decent-sized rooms (including ten singles), half of which have views of the castle. €€

EATING

SEE MAP PAGE 329

Aracena has plenty of places to eat, some of which are excellent – and many hotels also have their own **restaurants**. As Aracena is at the heart of a prestigious *jamón*-producing area, anything with *cerdo ibérico* (black-pig pork) is highly recommended, as are the delicious wild asparagus (spring to autumn), mushrooms (Sept onwards) and local snails (June–Aug).

RESTAURANTS AND TAPAS BARS

Bar Joaquinito Avda de Andalucía 23; ☎ 627 205 531. Near the *Restaurante José Vicente*, this is an excellent and friendly family-run tapas bar with mouth-watering grilled meats and a large selection of tapas. €

Casas Pozo La Nieve 40; W restaurantecasas.es. One of the town's top three restaurants, this is sited near the Gruta de las Maravillas and is only open lunchtimes. All the pork-based dishes are excellent, as is the *jamón* and *salchichón* (salami), and some interesting hot and cold soups incorporate these ingredients. Wine prices are reasonable and there's a decently priced *menú* (including wine) and an outdoor terrace. €€

Puerta 20 Pza Marqués de Aracena 20; ☎ 959 099 350. A large, friendly restaurant that certainly makes the most of Aracena's local produce. If you're in town between Sept–Dec, be sure to order the *pataje de castañas y setas* (potatoes with chestnuts and mushrooms) and/or the *risotto de boletus con aciete de trufa* (risotto with mushrooms and truffle oil). Both come in *medio* or main-sized portions. €€

★ **Restaurante José Vicente** Avda Andalucía 51; ☎ 959 128 455. For a memorable splurge this is the place to come. Arguably the town's best restaurant, patrons gather to savour the five grades of Jabugo *jamón ibérico* (black-pig ham) under the approving gaze of owner/chef José Vicente Sousa. The menu, which often includes a mouthwatering *solomillo ibérico* (black-pig loin), is recommended. The *costillas de cerdo ibérico* (ribs) are also superb, and the *helado de castañas* (chestnut ice cream) makes a perfect end to a feast. It's essential you reserve a table in the evenings. €€€

La Serrana Pozo de la Nieve s/n; ☎ 959 127 613. The third of the triumvirate of Aracena's best restaurants, and located opposite *Casas* (see page 330), this is another place where sierra cooking is at its best. All the pork dishes are recommended and there's a good *menú* during the week and at weekends (when it costs a little more). There's also a pleasant street terrace. €€€

CAFÉS AND SNACKS

Casino Arias Montano C/Mesones 2; ☎959 128 398. For breakfast or evening drinks, sit with the locals at the outdoor tables of the *casino* above the main square, from where you get a wonderful view towards the castle. This elegant early twentieth-century building is the work of noted architect Aníbal González, who also designed Seville's Plaza de España. €

Confitería Casa Rufino C/Constitución 3; ☎959 128 121. For superb *dulces*, this 125-year-old *confitería* and *pastelería*, just off the main square, is a must; their *tocino de cielo*, *vitorías* (liqueur-soaked, iced cakes) and *sultanas* (filled coconut cakes) are truly memorable. €

Sierra de Aracena

If you have a few days to spare, the rugged villages perched on the **Sierra de Aracena** to the west of Aracena make a fine walking tour. Along the route you'll find a number of good places to stay and plenty of tracks to follow through a rich landscape of orange and lemon orchards and forests of cork oaks, chestnut and gum trees. In spring the profusion of flowers is extraordinary: rosemary, French lavender, peonies and Spanish irises are most common, and you may also be lucky enough to see the rare brown bluebell and members of the orchid family. The hills are one of the last native habitats (outside the Coto de Doñana) of the rarely sighted Spanish lynx, while the skies are home to black vultures and peregrine falcons on patrol and even the occasional imperial eagle, a stirring image as they glide regally above their domain. You might also be lucky enough to see one of the rare black storks that are known to nest in the church towers of Cortegana (see page 335) and Zufre (see page 341).

GETTING AROUND

SIERRA DE ARACENA

By bus Buses run between Aracena and the villages of Alájar, Almonaster, Cortegana and Aroche (2 daily Mon–Sat 1pm & 6pm, the latter terminating at Cortegana) and between Aracena and Galaroza, Jabugo, Cortegana and Aroche (5 daily Mon–Sat 7.10am, 10.30am, 1.15pm terminating at Cortegana, and two at 5.30pm – one via Linares, Alájar and Cortegana; the other travelling via the main N432; also Sun at 10.30am). Similar services return in the reverse direction. All leave from Aracena's bus station on Avda de Sevilla s/n near the Parque Municipal.

By train Sierra Morena's main train station is at Cortegana (see page 335), 30km west of Aracena with infrequent

SIERRA DE ARACENA

connections to Huelva.

Walking guides The useful *Sierra de Aracena* by David and Ros Brawn (see page 555) has clear descriptions of 27 walks in the sierra ranging from 4 to 14km. An accompanying map for the book is sold separately and all walks also have GPS waypoints identifying key locations en route. *Walking in Andalucía* by Guy Hunter-Watts (see page 556) also covers half a dozen walks in the Sierra de Aracena. Alternatively, the Aracena and Huelva *turismos* give out the free *Senderos de la Sierra de Aracena y Picos de Aroche* map listing 23 waymarked routes, and there's the more detailed *Mapa Guía de la Sierra de Aracena y Picos de Aroche* on sale at the Aracena Turismo.

Linares de la Sierra

Leaving Aracena by the minor HU8105, after about 7km a turn-off left leads to the tiny village of **LINARES DE LA SIERRA**, a fairly simple and impoverished place huddled around its eighteenth-century Baroque church, a typical example of the sierra style, and curious bullring plaza. The latter's sandy surface has been paved over but the *barreras*, behind which the *toreros* dodge the fearsome fighting bulls, survive and seem a somewhat eccentric aberration considering that the ring is put to use only a couple of times a year in the village's fiestas.

EATING AND DRINKING   LINARES DE LA SIERRA

Bar Riandero Pza del Pueblo s/n; ☎629 714 073. This rather sleepy rustic bar makes a decent stop for breakfast – which can be taken on their terrace in the bullring/square. Later in the day they serve tapas and *raciones*; *carnes ibéricos* (black-pig pork products) frequently feature on the menu. €

★**Mesón Arrieros** C/Arrieros 2, below the church and off a street to the right; �🌐restaurantearrieros.es.

This outstanding mid-priced restaurant has arguably the sierra's most creative chef, Luis Miguel López. Its main room has a homely, rustic, white-walled interior and any of the *cerdo ibérico* dishes are highly recommended – the house *solomillo ibérico* is a classic; *setas* (wild mushrooms) also feature in season. Make sure to leave some room for the delicious desserts. Also offers a *menú de degustación*. €€€

Alájar

Some 4km beyond Linares de la Sierra, along the HU8105, lined with chestnut orchards and great clumps of oregano, a turning on the left descends to **ALÁJAR**, a delightful, cobble-streeted hamlet at the foot of the Peña de Arias Montano. There's an eighteenth-century Baroque church here – dedicated to San Marcos – with a typical spire, along with plenty of places to eat or have a beer, all clustered around the main square. Each September 7 and 8, the village holds a pilgrimage to the hermitage of the Virgen de los Ángeles on the Peña de Arias Montano hill, 1km above the village. This involves the young men of the village in the *polleo*, a rite of passage in which they race horses along the narrow streets and then up the steep slope to the shrine. The horses are spurred mercilessly and arrive foaming and bleeding at the top of the climb.

ACCOMMODATION & EATING   ALÁJAR

Casa El Padrino C/Miguel Moya 2; ☎959 125 601. Sited to the rear of the church, this is a very good restaurant with a rustic dining room and pleasant patio terrace. Specials include *lomo con castañas* (pork with chestnut sauce) and they're famous for using unusual parts of the pig in their dishes, including *glándulas salivales* (salivary glands). €€

★**Casona del Duende** C/Pintor Antonio Milla 1; ☎959 125 918. Well-kept boutique hotel with the best breakfast in the sierra. All rooms are en suite and come with a delightful mismatch of furniture, some of which is antique. Room 8 has a beautiful view over the garden (with pool) to the mountains in the distance. €€

Peña de Arias Montano

On quieter days the **Peña de Arias Montano**, the rock cliff that towers above the village, is a beautiful leafy spot set among woods of cork oaks, with cold springs surrounding the sixteenth-century **ermita** (hermitage) of the Virgen de los Ángeles. The Sierra Morena is liberally dotted with these buildings, almost always in isolated spots and dedicated to the Virgin. The site here has been hallowed since prehistoric times, and Iberian shamans are reputed to have gained their "second sight" from the hallucinogenic *amanita muscaria* mushroom which grows in the woods here – don't experiment yourself, though, as some species can kill in thirty minutes. The hermitage itself – filled with ex votos from pilgrims and distinguished more by the beauty of its setting than for any architectural qualities – was formerly the retreat of humanist Benito Arias Montano, confessor and librarian to Philip II, who was born nearby in 1527 and gave his name to the site. The belfry to the side of the church dates from the same period and offers glorious views over Alájar beneath and the sierra beyond. A **cavern** below the car park is said to be where magical and religious ceremonies were carried out in ancient times and where Philip II is supposed to have meditated during a visit – giving it the name Sillita del Rey (The King's Chair), a reference to the huge boulder at the cave's mouth.

The true peace of the place is best appreciated by leaving the visitors' area – and its stalls selling honey, garish pots and religious tack – and heading along the track into the woods of cork oaks where there are plenty of likely picnic spots, and more fine views over the sierra. Continuing along the track for a couple of kilometres will bring you to a ferociously steep climb leading to the "true" *peña* (peak) where Arias Montano is said to have done much of his meditating, with a **mirador** at the summit offering fine views.

Santa Ana La Real

Six kilometres west of Alájar the modest but pretty white-walled village of **SANTA ANA LA REAL** – with a crumbling eighteenth-century church at its heart – is worth a detour. Traditionally the village was known for it *arrieros* (mule drivers), who carried the products of the sierra to Seville. In the age of the truck these are long gone, together with countless others who emigrated to find work. The village population today consists of four hundred souls, mostly elderly, and is still shrinking.

A WALK FROM ALÁJAR TO LINARES DE LA SIERRA

A fine walk (6km) from Alájar to Linares de la Sierra takes in the delightful isolated hamlet of Los Madroñeros, whose grassy streets can only otherwise be reached by tractors and off-road vehicles. To find the **start of the walk** take the street left along the north side of Alájar's church to a plazuela (small square) and follow the street downhill to an open area. The path follows the old road, climbing beyond a board (detailing the walk) on the far side. Should you lose the way, ask for the *camino antiguo a Los Madroñeros*.

Once on the track it soon leads away from the village running between dry-stone walls behind which are cork oaks sheltering *pata negra* black pigs, soon to be turned into the region's prized *jamón*. The settlement of **Los Madroñeros** is a tranquil haven: a huddle of traditional white-walled dwellings topped by distinctive chimneypots with green grass all around. You'll be lucky to see any inhabitants as they seem to keep a low profile, unlike their numerous cats who will eye you curiously as they sun themselves on rooftops or any convenient flat stone.

The *camino* (with frequent yellow and white PR – Pequeño Recorrido – waymarks to guide you) leads on eastwards away from the village, gently climbing and falling with only one place which may confuse. Just after crossing a stream, about halfway between Los Madroñeros and Linares, you'll come to a deserted **semi-ruined farmhouse**; the path here isn't immediately clear but you need to go through the gateway of the farmhouse to pick up the track on the other side. Soon after this, you reach Linares. To return to Alájar you can retrace your route or follow the road back (the HU8105). In David and Ros Brawn's book (see page 555) they describe an alternative route back to Alájar with one steep climb. Alternatively you could time your arrival to meet up with Alájar-bound buses (see page 331) passing through about 1.15pm or 5.45pm. Going in the other direction the Aracena bus currently passes through at 4.15pm.

Hostal El Cruce Junction of the HU8105 and the N435; ☏ 959 122 333. Convenient and good-value *hostal* a couple of kilometres beyond Santa Ana, set amid fine scenery. The modern, flower-bedecked building has en-suite rooms (heated in cooler seasons) plus a lively tapas bar and popular restaurant with a pleasant terrace and an economical *menú*. Free parking. €

Almonaster La Real

Continuing west of Santa Ana La Real for another 6km brings you to the main village in this corner of the sierra, the picturesque agricultural centre of **ALMONASTER LA REAL**, huddled in a river valley below the peak of the same name, which at 912m is the sierra's highest summit.

La Mezquita

Daily 9am–8pm • Free

Almonaster has an impressive Moorish past, and an important tenth-century **mezquita**, or **mosque**, still stands on a hill south of town. The mosque may have Roman and Visigothic antecedents and, after it became Christianized in the thirteenth century, was little altered, thus preserving its square minaret, the *mihrab* (said to be the oldest in Spain) and beautiful interior of five naves with brick horseshoe arches supported by what are probably recycled Roman columns. Tacked on to the mosque/church is the village bullring where each August a *corrida* is staged during Almonaster's annual fiesta (see box, page 335). The mosque's tower is a favourite with the kids of the village at this time, as it provides a free (if dangerously precarious, due to a lack of barriers) view of the ring. If you're here during winter, the mosque will light up after the sun goes down.

By train The station lies 3km north of the village (actually nearer to Cortegana), with infrequent services to Huelva. Destinations Huelva (1 daily; 1hr 48min); Jabugo (1 daily; 8min).

WALKS AROUND ALMONASTER

There are some superb **walks** around Almonaster, following the old cobbled mule paths and village tracks (*senderos*). The paths are well preserved, on the whole – though at times you are forced on to the tarmac road – and are waymarked with paint splashes on trees and rocks. You need sharp eyes to spot the beginning of the paths, below the road – if possible, get hold of the *Senderos de la Sierra de Aracena y Picos de Aroche* walks pamphlet, which the *ayuntamientos* in Almonaster, Cortegana or Jabugo should stock. This is easy to follow with minimal Spanish and has route descriptions and an excellent foldout survey map. Cortegana also produces its own leaflet, *Senderos de Pequeño Recorrido en el Entorno de Cortegana*, with a good map and covering much of the same ground, which is usually available from the Ayuntamiento (if they haven't run out). You'd be advised also to take a decent 1:100,000 or 1:50,000 map (CNIG sheets 895 and 916 for the latter), in case you lose the way.

One of the most enjoyable walks, starting from Almonaster, is the **PRA-5** which leads off to the left of the Cortegana road, around 1km out of Almonaster. This takes you through woodland peppered with streams to the hamlets of Arroyo and Veredas (2hr), where there are bars with food, and on to Cortegana (3hr). Alternatively, if it's just a brief country ramble you're after, follow the sign to Acebuches along the **PRA-5-2** path, under an hour from Almonaster, and again endowed with a small bar.

Another fine walk from Almonaster is to head straight up the hillside northeast of the village along the **PRA-5-1**. This is actually a paved Roman track, presumably built for some kind of quarrying. It takes a couple of hours' strenuous walking to get up to the summit, and, if you're making a day of it, you could continue on to Cortegana or Jabugo.

COUNTRY CORRIDAS

Like many country rings, the bullring at Almonaster does not see much action. In fact, the prohibitive cost of mounting a **corrida** with six bulls, three matadors and their retinues often restricts a small village to one *corrida* each year, usually in the middle of its annual fiesta. To see a bullfight at places like Almonaster, however, is to get a fascinating insight into many of the brutal secrets of the *corrida* as, with the ring barely big enough to contain the crowd, bulls and matadors, many of the preparations have to take place outside.

First of all, while the arena is doused from a water tanker, the *picadores* (see page 47) select their 2.5m-long lances from a couple of dozen leaning against the wall of the ring. When they've chosen, a blacksmith attaches one of three lethal-looking steel points, again selected by the *picador*. Meanwhile, below the walls of the mosque, the grooms prepare the horses – whose vocal cords have been severed so as not to alarm the crowd with their terrified shrieks – by fastening the *peto* (heavy padding) protection against the bull's ferocious horns. Next the horses' ears are stuffed with oil-soaked rags and securely tied to block out the sound of the crowd and the bull. Finally, they are blindfolded over the right eye, the side from which the bull will attack.

Fifteen minutes before the *corrida* is due to start the village band marches up the hill playing a lively tune before disappearing into the arena. Once inside, they strike up a *paso doble* for the prefight parade before the grotesque figure of the helmeted and armoured *picador* is pushed through the small doorway into the ring and a great cheer goes up from the crowd inside. They are soon yelling "*fuera!*" (away), however, because they don't want the bull too weakened by the lance to be able to put up a decent fight. A few minutes later the trumpets sound and the door opens to allow the *picador* to exit the arena. With fresh blood dripping from his lance, the image of this warrior is almost medieval. Big-name *toreros* appear in these village *corridas* because the pay is good, but equally the risks are high. The primitive nature of rings such as the one at Almonaster means a long journey to reach a hospital with adequate facilities should the matador be seriously gored, a factor that has in the past proved fatal.

By bus There are frequent bus services that run in sierra (see page 331).

Tourist information The village has no Turismo, but basic information might be available from the Ayuntamiento, Plaza de la Constitución s/n (☎ 959 143 003).

ACCOMMODATION AND EATING

Bar Alamonster C/Jacinto Navas 5. Fun tapas bar with local meat *montaditos* and a smattering of tables in the shaded alley. €

Las Palmeras C/Carretera s/n; ☎ 609 232 078. A string of apartments on one side of the road, and a restaurant on the other, *Las Palmeras* is a promising place to arrive at. In their plant-bedecked terrace, they serve up sierra specialities including *parrillada de carne*. €€

El Rincón de Curro C/Carretera 3, on the Cortegana road; ✆ rincon.de.curro.la-colmena.org. Small family restaurant serving up *platos de la sierra* – *solomillo de cerdo ibérico* (pork loin) is a house special. It's advisable to book at weekends. €€

Vivienda Real C/Urbanización la Real 19; ☎ 616 609 902. Traditional guesthouse close to the village hub. Five spacious bedrooms are all en suite, and there's a shared living room with fireplace and kitchen. €€

Cortegana

Roughly 2km out of Almonaster the road forks left to **CORTEGANA**, a bustling and populous *pueblo* of almost five thousand people spreading along the valley of the Río Carabaña below a heavily restored castle. Cortegana's big annual knees-up is the **Jornadas Medievales** *feria*, held in the first or second week in August with archery contests, falconry, various tournaments and re-enactments of the storming of the castle walls – accompanied by much music, drinking and dancing. Its other main *feria*, **Fiestas Patronales**, occurs in early September with *corridas*, processions and concerts. There's a visitor centre near the castle (daily 10am–2pm & 5–9pm).

Castillo

Pza del Castillo s/n • Officially Tues–Sun: June–Sept 11am–2pm & 5–7pm; Oct–May 11am–2pm & 4–6pm; otherwise enquire at the Ayuntamiento, C/Maura 1, just off the Pza de la Constitución • Charge • ☎ 627 695 801 • Take the Almonaster road – signed from the N433 on the village's eastern edge; after 100m you come to a junction where a driveable road (or a 10min walk) on the left climbs to the castle

Built in the thirteenth century during the frontier disputes with the Portuguese, the heavily restored **Castillo** provided a necessary observation post and today gives fine views from its battlements. It is flanked by the fourteenth- to fifteenth-century *ermita* of **Santa María del Castillo** whose chapel has been refurbished with the addition of some rather tedious modern frescoes.

Iglesia del Divino Salvador

Pza de la Iglesia • Open service times only (7–9pm) • Free

The town's major church, the **Iglesia del Divino Salvador** was started in the late sixteenth century, but has later elements including the bell tower, constructed after the original collapsed in the earthquake of 1755. The interior has a finely worked Baroque pulpit, and the eighteenth-century retablo in the *capilla* (chapel) of Nuestra Señora del Rosario is the only one of the church's original nine to survive the Civil War conflagration when local churches became a part of the ideological battleground.

ACCOMMODATION
CORTEGANA

Pensión Cervantes C/Cervantes 26; ⓦ pensioncervantes2000.com. This welcoming *hostal* lies just up the hill from focal Pza Constitución, offering small but clean and comfy heated en-suite rooms with a/c and TV; try for a room overlooking a peaceful garden at the rear. €

La Posada de Cortegana Ctra El Repilado–La Corte s/n, follow a minor road (signed to the hotel) just east of the village of El Repilado for about 4km; ⓦ posadadecortegana.es. Charming hotel buried deep in the countryside to the north of Cortegana, consisting of log cabins set in woodland with a restaurant and reception housed in the main building nearby. Breakfast is included. €€

EATING AND DRINKING

El Aceitón Avda de Portugal 5, a 5min walk from the centre along C/Talero; ☎ 959 131 356. Reasonably priced and welcoming restaurant close to the Guardia Civil barracks on the main N433. House specials include *solomillo de cerdo con castañas* (pork loin with chestnut sauce). Enquire about their five en-suite double rooms by knocking on the door to the right. €€

Casino Pza de la Constitución s/n; ☎ 959 131 160. The town's elegant *casino* – a stately turn-of-the-twentieth century building with tiled interior – makes a pleasant breakfast or morning-coffee stop, stocks all the daily newspapers and has wifi. €

Aroche and around

Heading west for 14km from Cortegana along the N433 brings you to **AROCHE**, in sight of the border with Portugal. Perched on a hill dominated by its castle with a fertile plain below, it's a neat little place, with white-walled, cobbled streets where – because it gets so few visitors – you can be sure of a hearty reception. Aroche was originally the Roman town of Arruci Vetus, but many more ancient vestiges of habitation have been discovered here, including giant prehistoric single standing stones, or menhirs, erected in the Neolithic period. Arriving with your own transport, take the first – and fully asphalted – entry on the left into the town coming from Aracena; using the other entry road to the east leads up into a warren of steep cobbled backstreets which are difficult to negotiate.

A pleasant walk out of the village starts on the opposite (north) side of the main N433 to the twelfth- to fourteenth-century Gothic-Mudéjar **Ermita de San Mamés** and the impressive remains of Roman **Turóbriga**. The (driveable) track leading to both is signed between the two entry roads to the town.

Castillo

Contact the visitor centre for access (see page 338)

Once you have made it up the hill to the village, the obvious place to aim for is the **Castillo**. Constructed by the Almoravids in the twelfth century, the fort was remodelled after the *Reconquista* – but the most bizarre alteration of all was to make the interior into a full-scale bullring. A curiosity here are the sallyports – narrow openings in the arena's stone wall – used by the *toreros* to dodge the bull, instead of the normal *barrera* (fence).

La Cilla convent and archeological museum

C/Fray J Bross s/n • Fri–Sun: June–Sept 11am–3pm; Oct–April 11am–2pm & 3–5pm; contact the visitor centre for access (see page 338) • Free

In the same building as the Centro de Visitantes (see page 338), the splendid seventeenth-century former convent of **La Cilla** – incorporating an olive-oil pressing room from the original edifice – also houses the town's **archeological museum**. The interesting collection has numerous finds from the Roman and Moorish periods as well as ceramics and other artefacts from Turóbriga, a first-millenium BC Iberian and later important Roman settlement discovered 3km north of the town (see page 337).

Nuestra Señora de la Asunción

Contact the visitor centre for access (see page 338)

Just below the castle, the parish church of **Nuestra Señora de la Asunción** was started in 1483, with a mixture of Mudéjar, Gothic and Renaissance styles being added by the time it was completed 150 years later. Behind a dour, buttressed exterior, the triple-naved church has a trio of retablos: the image of Christ lowered from the cross at the top of the right-hand (or south) nave is by La Roldana; the representation of Christ *nazareno*, bearing his cross, in the retablo at the end of the left aisle is a seventeenth-century work by Alonso Cano. Along the south wall an altar has a small and sensitively worked image of the Virgin perched on an inverted half-moon and coiled serpent, another seventeenth-century work by La Roldana. The church's other treasures (only viewable when the *cura* or priest is available, due to their value) include the fifteenth-century crucifix of Cardenal Mendoza of Seville, the supporter of Isabel, as well as a seventeenth-century Russian icon from St Petersburg.

Museo del Santo Rosario

C/Ordoñez Valdes s/n • Fri–Sun: June–Sept 11am–3pm; Oct–April 11am–2pm & 3–5pm; contact the visitor centre for access (see page 338) • Free

There are some pretty strange museums in Andalucía, but Aroche's **Museo del Santo Rosario** (Museum of the Holy Rosary) has to be one of the most eccentric. Located a little downhill to the east of the Ayuntamiento and near the *correo* (post office), the exhibits consist of well over a thousand rosaries donated by such leading religious luminaries as Pope John XXIII and Mother Teresa, in addition to others from *toreros* and soccer players and one each from John F. Kennedy and King Juan Carlos. Those sent in by Richard Nixon and General Franco betray suspiciously little sign of wear.

Ermita de San Mamés

Tues–Thurs 8am–3pm, Fri–Sun 10am–5pm (May–Sept closes 3pm) • Charge

Following the (driveable) signed track heading north off the N433 between the two entry roads to the town for 2km leads to the **Ermita de San Mamés**. A triple-naved church built on the site – and using the walls – of an important building, perhaps the basilica or law court, adjoining the Roman forum, the church has some remarkable fourteenth-century fresco fragments including a spectacular painting (discovered not long ago beneath centuries of whitewash) of the *Last Supper*.

Turóbriga

3km north of town • Same hours as San Mamés • Free

A WALK FROM EL REPILADO TO LOS ROMEROS

Returning to Aracena from Aroche by the N433 takes you through the village of **El Repilado** from where a picturesque 5km walk heads south along the Río Caliente to the charming village of **Los Romeros**. Leave Repilado by the N433 road towards Cortegana and after crossing the bridge over the river, turn left along the HV-111 going to Los Romeros. Where the road traverses to the east bank of the river, follow the track along the west bank which leads through woods of chestnut and black poplar, and where in spring you'll see a profusion of wild flowers. When the road recrosses the river, use the bridge to gain access to the tiny and picturesque village of Los Romeros, a place devoted to *jamón* production (it takes its name from a major ham family).

Behind the Ermita de San Mamés are the extensive remains of the first-century BC to third-century AD Roman town of **Turóbriga**. Substantial buildings surrounding the forum alongside the *ermita* have been unearthed, including the foundations of temples plus administrative and judicial buildings. The archeological excavations are now uncovering the substantial town that surrounded the forum and various streets with dwellings as well as a bathhouse and exercise gymnasium have come to light. A leaflet (available free from the site guardian) provides more information on the finds.

INFORMATION

AROCHE AND AROUND

Visiting the monuments For access to all the town's sights (except the Ermita de San Mamés and Roman Turóbriga), including the Castillo, you'll need to call at the Centro de Visitantes (Thurs–Sun: May–Sept 11am–3pm; Oct–April 10am–2pm & 3–5pm) at C/Fray J Bross s/n, close to the main square, Plaza Juan Carlos 1. When the office is closed the Ayuntamiento (also on the main square) can usually help out with information and provide a map.

ACCOMMODATION

There is currently no hotel or *hostal* accommodation in Aroche; the visitor centre can provide details of *casas rurales* to rent in and around the town.
Apartamentos Picos de Aroche Ctra Las Peñas s/n; ☎667 756 445. On the west side of the village, this is a possible option for overnighting here. There are six apartments, all well equipped with two bedrooms and sleeping two to five. There is also a bar-restaurant with an inexpensive *menú*. €

EATING AND DRINKING

Cafetería Granizo Pza Juan Carlos I s/n; ☎697 960 151. This popular *cafetería* is a good breakfast stop, and later serves tapas, *raciones* and platos combinados. House specialities include seafood tapas and cured meats of the region, and there's an inviting terrace on the square. €
Centro Cultural Las Peñas C/Real 8; ☎959 140 003. Near the church of La Asunción, a wonderfully atmospheric bar and social centre. Tapas and *raciones* are served at lunchtime and early evening, and the fried fish – try the *pulpo* (octopus) or *chocos* (cuttlefish) – is excellent. €€
Restaurante El Canario Ctra Seville–Lisboa (N433) km127, below the town on the main road; ☎661 100 153. Reliable *venta* offering dishes of the sierra in two spacious *comedores* or on a terrace. Any of the pork or *bacalao* (cod) dishes are recommended and there's a well-priced *menú*. €

Jabugo

The mere mention of the name of **JABUGO** is enough to make any Spanish carnivore's mouth water, and once you've tasted what all the fuss is about it's easy to understand why. As roadside billboards depicting smiling pigs proclaim, *jamón* is king in Jabugo. To get stuck into ham sampling, when you approach the village from the N433, ignore the sign directing you to the *centro urbano* and continue straight on. You'll come to Carretera de San Juan del Puerto, where a clutch of bars and restaurants will all be eager to sell you a *bocadillo* stuffed with *jamón de Jabugo* – or even a whole ham shank, should you feel like splashing out. There are tapas, too, but keep an eye on the prices as the *pata negra* (from acorn-fed black pigs) doesn't come cheap. To try before you buy

De Jabugo la Cañada (daily 10am–2pm & 3–7pm; ☎959 121 207), about halfway along, is a well-stocked shop where you can sample and buy *jamón de Jabugo* and other tasty products of the sierra such as *morcilla* (black pudding) and *salchichón* (salami).

Ham apart, the village of Jabugo is a sleepy place gathered around a charming square, the aptly named **Plaza de Jamón**, with a central fountain overlooked by the village *casino* – a relaxing place for a beer – and the restored Baroque **Iglesia de San Miguel**.

The **villages around Jabugo** – Aguafría, Castaño del Robledo and Fuenteheridos – all make rewarding destinations for walks amid splendid wooded hills, though all are equally ill served by public transport and you may well find yourself in for a walk both ways.

Castaño del Robledo

Four kilometres southeast of Jabugo, but a few kilometres more by road, lies the isolated village of **CASTAÑO DEL ROBLEDO**, which has not one but two outsized churches for its meagre population. Both named Santiago, they attest to a time in the seventeenth and eighteenth centuries when the population here was growing so rapidly that the church of Santiago la Mayor, then under construction, had to be enlarged. However, the population declined as quickly as it had grown and the crumbling, cavernous and now little-used church was left unfinished, while the congregation remained in the older and smaller of the two churches built in the sixteenth century. The larger Neoclassical hulk – containing a rare eighteenth-century organ – today looks down grimly on the surrounding pantiled roofs. Other remnants from more illustrious days are a number of decaying mansions along the village's narrow, cobbled streets.

ACCOMMODATION   **CASTAÑO DEL ROBLEDO**

★ **Posada del Castaño** C/José Sánchez Calvo 33; ⓦposadadelcastano.com. A very pleasant place to stay

---

THE KING OF HAMS

Surrounding Jabugo is a scattering of attractive but economically depressed villages mainly dependent on the *jamón* industry and its curing factory, which is the major local employer. Things were little different when Richard Ford passed through here a century and a half ago, describing these mountain villages as "coalitions of pigsties", adding that it was the duty of every good pig to "get fat as soon as he can and then to die for the good of his country".

Sought out by classical writers such as Strabo for its distinctive flavour, and produced since long before by the peoples of the Iberian peninsula, **jamón serrano** (mountain ham from white pigs) is a *bocadillo* standard throughout Spain – the English words "ham" and "gammon" are both derived from the Spanish. Some of the best ham of all, *jamón ibérico* or *pata negra* (both acorn-fed ham), comes from the Sierra Morena, where herds of sleek black pigs grazing beneath the trees are a constant feature. In October the acorns drop or are beaten down by their keepers and the pigs, waiting patiently below, gorge themselves, become fat and are promptly whisked off to the factory to be slaughtered and then cured in the dry mountain air. The meat of these black pigs is exceptionally fatty when eaten as pork but the same fat that marbles the meat adds to the tenderness during the curing process. This entails first of all covering the hams in coarse rock or sea salt to "sweat", after which they are removed to cool cellars to mature for up to two years. *Jamón serrano* from mass-produced white pigs is matured for only a few weeks, hence the incomparable difference in taste. At Jabugo the best of the best is then further graded from one to five *jotas* (the letter "J", for Jabugo) depending on its quality – a whole leg of *cinco jotas jamón* will set you back anything from €250 to €350.

The king of hams also demands an etiquette all of its own: in bars and restaurants everywhere it has its own apparatus (*la jamonera*) to hold it steady, and carving is performed religiously with a long, thin-bladed knife. The slices must not be wafer-thin nor bacon rashers, and once on the plate *jamón ibérico* becomes the classic partner for a glass of *fino*.

just a short walk from the focal Plaza del Álamo. Run by an expat British family who are enthusiastic hikers and have made very helpful booklets of walking routes in the zone, which you're welcome to take out with you for the day. The en-suite rooms are comfortable and overlook a peaceful garden. Breakfast is included. €

EATING AND DRINKING

Bar La Bodeguita Pza del Álamo; ☎ 666 636 587. On the compact main square, this is a friendly old place with a wide selection of liqueurs, and photos on the walls from bygone days. They also serve decent tapas. €

Bar-Restaurant El Roble C/Arias Montaño 8; ☎ 959 465 514. Welcoming place close to the main square with a wood fire in winter and an outdoor terrace in summer. The pork dishes – try the *presa ibérica* (pork steak) – are outstanding and the desserts aren't bad either, including a tasty *flan de turrón* (crème caramel with nougat). Also serves tapas and *raciones* in the bar. €€

Galaroza and around

The N433 east from Jabugo rolls along through country filled with dense oak woods surrounded by dry-stone walls, where you may catch a fleeting glimpse of a herd of *cerdos ibéricos*, the celebrated black pigs of the sierra. The enlongated village of **GALAROZA**, encircled by chestnut and fruit orchards, seems awash with water which for much of the year splashes and bubbles in its fountains and along the culverts lining the narrow streets. This may explain its annual **Fiesta de los Jarritos** during which everyone – including visitors – gets soaked as the town goes water-mad. September 6 is the date to avoid if you want to stay dry – and if you do turn up take note that the crazy crowds are no respecters of visitors or their cameras when the *cubos de agua* (buckets) start flying.

A **water sculpture** in the Plaza los Álamos celebrates the Fiesta de los Jarritos, although the fiesta's focal point is the nearby **Fuente del Carmen** – colloquially known as Fuente de los Doce Caños (twelve spouts) – a nineteenth-century fountain with evocative washing stones once used by the village women before the age of washing machines.

At the eastern end of Plaza los Álamos stands the seventeenth-century church of **Nuestro Señora del Carmen** (open service times, Mon–Sat autumn & winter 3pm, spring & summer 5pm, Sun 12pm; free) – not especially interesting inside excepting a unique seventeenth-century image of a pregnant *Virgin* by La Roldana. Possibly because of the wealth of pork here, Galaroza's 1600 inhabitants are known to their regional neighbours as *cachetonas* (chubby people).

ACCOMMODATION

GALAROZA AND AROUND

Hostal Toribio C/Primo de Rivera 2; ⌨ hostaltoribio. com. At the village's western end, this comfortable *hostal* has pleasant en-suite a/c rooms with heating and TV. Breakfast is included. €

Hotel Galaroza Sierra Just west of the village on the Jabugo road; ⌨ hotelgalaroza.com. Attractive, upmarket country hotel with pool and restaurant in its own grounds. Rooms are light and well equipped and come with TV, and the hotel also rents out fully equipped bungalows with fireplace sleeping up to four. Free parking. €€

EATING AND DRINKING

Bar Andaluz Pza los Álamos 3, the main square; ☎ 610 980 160. Good tapas and *raciones* bar serving up *pescaito frito* and *cerdo ibérico* meats on a pleasant terrace. €

El Encinar Hotel Galaroza Sierra. The hotel (see page 340) boasts perhaps the village's best restaurant, serving up typical dishes of the sierra – any of the game and *cerdo ibérico* dishes are worth trying – which also has a *menú* for a reasonable price. €€

La Taberna C/Fernando Marquez Tirado (on the left-hand side as you approach the village from the south); ☎ 663 998 227. Perfect pre-dinner stop for *tinto blanco de Huelva* and a plate of local, cured *morcillo* (black pudding) with locals. €

Fuenteheridos

Some 5km east of Galaroza, a right turn brings you almost immediately to **FUENTEHERIDOS**, one of the most picturesque of the Sierra Moreno *pueblos* – a huddle of whitewashed dwellings with contrasting red pantiled roofs. The typically tiled spire of its fine eighteenth-century Neoclassical **Iglesia del Espíritu Santo** hovers above the rooftops.

The village's interesting **Jardín Botánico** (botanical garden; daily 10am–dusk; free) is planted with specimens from all over the globe. It lies to the west of the village and north of the main road, close to the *Molino de Fuenteheridos* (see page 341).

ACCOMMODATION FUENTEHERIDOS

Bar-Restaurante Biarritz C/Virgen de la Fuente s/n; ⓦ biarritzrural.com. This bar-restaurant also lets a number of charming and well-equipped cottages and apartments in and around the village, sleeping up to four. €€

Camping El Madroñal 1km out of Fuenteheridos, along the HU-8114 towards Castaño Robledo; ⓦ campingelmadronal.com. Welcoming campsite with mature trees providing plenty of shade and decent facilities, including a large pool and restaurant. €

Finca La Media Legua Ctra N433 km91 (3km towards Aracena near the village of Los Marines); ⓦ fincalamedialegua.es. Inviting rural retreat in the midst of dense chestnut woods, offering stylishly decorated two- to six-person apartments with kitchenette, plus a pool. The complex has its own bar and restaurant. €€

Hostal Carballo C/La Fuente 16; ⓦ hostalcarballo.com. Welcoming *hostal* with a variety of light and spacious en-suite rooms, plus a pleasant roof terrace with views and easy parking nearby. You pay slightly extra for a balcony. €

Molino de Fuenteheridos Ctra N433 km97 (down a side road off the north side of the main road signed "Villa Onuba"); ⓦ molinosdefuenteheridos.com. This luxury option comprises a series of adobe-style chalets in wonderfully verdant woodland surrounding the main building, a former *cortijo* with many original features. Most chalets have terraces and all come with jacuzzis and are tastefully furnished with artworks. The public areas include a lounge with enormous fireplace and a garden pool. Breakfast is included. €€

EATING AND DRINKING

Bar-Restaurante Biarritz C/Virgen de la Fuente s/n. Good restaurant, just off the main square, with tasty *raciones* and a weekday *menú* (which you may need to ask for). €€

La Caldera C/Charneca s/n; ☎ 600 002 864. Pleasant *asador* (charcoal-grill restaurant) uphill from the main square, with an elegant dining room and patio terrace for warmer days. Food comprises a variety of well-prepared

sierra dishes – anything with *cerdo ibérico* is recommended by spritely staff. €€€

Rincón de Rafa Pza Mayor s/n; ☎ 690 918 186. The biggest of a clutch of bars on the main square, with a delightful shady terrace under a spreading chestnut tree – just the place for breakfast. Lunchtime and evenings are for tapas or *raciones*: try the *carrillada ibérica en salsa* (pork cheek) or a refreshing glass of gazpacho. €

Zufre

ZUFRE, about 25km southeast of Aracena, must be one of the most spectacular villages in Spain, hanging like a miniature Ronda on a high palisade at the edge of a ridge. Below the crumbling Moorish walls, the cliff falls away hundreds of metres, terraced into deep green gardens of orange trees and vegetables.

In town, and sharing a charming and leafy plazuela, the arcaded **Ayuntamiento** and parish church of **Purísima Concepción** – built of brick and pink stone – are both interesting sixteenth-century examples of the Mudéjar style, the latter built on the foundations of a mosque. In the basement of the Ayuntamiento is a gloomy line of stone seats, said to have been used by the Inquisition. For access, enquire at the Ayuntamiento during working hours for the key.

Zufre's real centre, however, is the **Paseo**, a little park with rose gardens, balcony and a bar at one end and a *casino* at the other, with spectacular views over the sierra from its open southern flank. The villagers gather round here for much of the day – there's little work either in Zufre or the surrounding countryside, and even the local bullring, cleverly squeezed on to a rock ledge above the Paseo, only sees use twice a year: at the beginning of the season in March, and at the town's September *feria*.

ARRIVAL AND INFORMATION ZUFRE

By bus Buses from Aracena (1 daily; Mon–Sat 5.30pm; 45min) connect with the bus from Seville. Return buses leave Zurfre for Aracena at 6.15am.

On foot You can walk from Aracena to Zufre (a day-long, 25km hike); the free map (available from the Turismo in Aracena), *Senderos de la Sierra de Aracena y Picos de Aroche*, details the route and shorter alternatives. The 1:25,000 IGN

maps, *hojas* (sheets) 917 and 918, are also useful.

Information Staff at the Ayuntamiento, Pza de la Iglesia (Mon–Fri 8am–2pm; ☎ 959 198 009), can provide information.

ACCOMMODATION AND EATING

Casa Pepa C/Portales 1, just off Pza La Quebrada; ☎ 959 198 128. Pleasant little country restaurant serving up tasty sierra standards such as *solomillo* (pork loin) and *rabo de toro*. €€

Casa Vesta Huerta Santa Zita (on the hillside northeast of the village, close to the Ermita de Santa Zita church);

ⓦ casa-vesta.com. Luxury guesthouse with infinity pool and a glorious view over the mountain range and turquoise reservoir. En-suite rooms come with four-poster beds and balconies. There's a fitness area, library and traditional Andalucían restaurant. No under 16s. €€€

Parque Natural de la Sierra Norte

East of Aracena there's more good – if slightly less wooded – hiking country along the northern frontier of Seville province, which – beyond the curiously elevated village of Zufre – traverses the **Parque Natural de la Sierra Norte**, a wildlife and nature zone stretching across the north of Seville province to the border with Córdoba. Places to head for, and which provide a base for further explorations, include the park's main town, **Cázalla de la Sierra**, with its numerous bodegas and, further east, the more tranquil **Constantina**, topped by a medieval castle. The park's website (ⓦ sierranortedesevilla.es) has information on most of the towns and villages in the sierra, including accommodation and lots of useful links.

INFORMATION   PARQUE NATURAL DE LA SIERRA NORTE

El Robledo Centro de Visitantes Two kilometres out of the Constantina on the El Pedroso road is the visitor centre (see website for opening hours; ☎ 955 889 593; ⓦ bit.ly/ElRobledo) for the Sierra Norte natural park.

Maps, guidebooks and information on activities such as horseriding and hiking in the park is available, there's also a botanical garden (same hours; free) displaying a wide variety of the park's flora.

Cázalla de la Sierra

The next place of any size east of Zufre, **CAZALLA DE LA SIERRA** lies some 50km further on, the latter stages of the journey following a mountainous and lonely route, stunning to drive, but a real test on foot.

When you finally reach it, Cázalla de la Sierra feels like a veritable metropolis: a charming country town with a number of sights and an ideal base for exploring the surrounding park. An ancient Iberian settlement, Cázalla became the Roman Callentum and later the Moorish Kazalla ("fortified city") from which the modern name derives. Its importance in post-*Reconquista* days was as a staging post along the route to Extremadura and the north. The place was noted in Roman times for its vines and wines, a tradition which survives today in the production of *aguardiente* and *anis* (aniseed liqueur), sold in bodegas around the town. The Turismo can advise on where to find them if you're interested.

Nuestra Señora de la Consolación

Pza Mayor • Tues–Sat 11am–1pm (also service times: Mon–Sat 7.30pm, Sun noon & 7pm) • Free

Cazalla's main attraction is the huge, fortress-like church of **Nuestra Señora de la Consolación** at the southern end of town, an outstanding example of *andaluz* mix-and-match architecture begun in the fourteenth century in Gothic-Mudéjar style, with some later Renaissance touches, and finally completed in the eighteenth century. The interior has a fine sixteenth-century retablo and an image of San Bruno by Juan Hernández.

Fronting the church's northern door, Calle Virgen del Monte – lined with some elegant *casas señoriales* – leads to the **market area**, a colourful and bustling place on weekdays.

La Cartuja

Sat–Sun 10am–3pm • Charge • ⓦ cartujadecazalla.com • Take the A455 for 3km towards Constantina, turning off along a signposted side road

A little out of town, Cazalla's fifteenth-century **Cartuja**, or Carthusian monastery, was until a couple of decades ago a near ruin; it's now being gradually and privately restored as an upmarket hotel and arts centre. What remains, particularly a beautiful portal and the cupola of a church with Mudéjar frescoes, is set in picturesque surroundings. The proprietors have now added an art gallery and there are frequent artistic and musical events held here.

ARRIVAL AND INFORMATION   CAZALLA DE LA SIERRA

By train Cazalla is served by trains on the Seville–Mérida line three times daily, but as the station lies 7km east of town and buses are infrequent, you'll need to take a taxi if you don't fancy the walk.

By bus Cazalla is one of the few places in the sierra with regular buses, serving Seville (2 daily; 1hr 40min).

Turismo On Plaza Mayor, next to the church of Nuestra Señora de la Consolación (Tues–Sat 10am–2pm plus Thurs 4–6pm, Sun 11am–1pm; ☎ 954 883 562; ⓦ cazalladelasierra.es). Staff can provide a town map and have copious information on the town and Parque Natural de Sierra Norte.

ACCOMMODATION

Hospedería La Cartuja ⓦ lacartujadecazalla.com. Out of town and surrounded by rolling hill country, the enchanting La Cartuja monastery (see page 343) has its own atmospheric inn with pool and eight elegantly styled rooms in what was formerly the monastery's gatehouse; also has its own restaurant and *cafetería*. Breakfast is included. €€

★ **Las Navezuelas** 3km out of town along the A432 road to El Pedroso (signed on the left); ⓦ lasnavezuelas. com. An inviting option, offering delightful rooms and studios in a white-walled sixteenth-century *cortijo* and mill set among woods and olive groves; it also has a pool and its own reasonably priced restaurant, and the owners can arrange horseriding excursions and advise on trekking routes. €€

★ **Palacio de San Benito** Paseo del Moro; ☎ 954 883 336. A few doors down from the Agustina restaurant, the walls of this grand hotel date back to the fifteenth century. Its famously romantic, en-suite bedrooms and breakfast with homemade specialities has made this place one of the most popular in the park. €€

EATING AND DRINKING

★ **Agustina** Pza del Consejo s/n, off the top end of the Paseo del Moro; ☎ 954 883 255. Stylish little restaurant serving tapas (try the *queso de cabra con miel*) in the bar below and full meals – *carillada ibérica* (pork cheeks) is a house special – in a restaurant above. Has a pleasant terrace fronting the old fountain. €€€

Bar El Torero C/Virgen del Monte 56; ☎ 954 884 883. This central bar, near the former Convento de San Francisco (now a bodega), serves good food with a smile. All breakfast standards available as well as tapas and *raciones* later in the day. €

Cafetería-Restaurante Manolo Paseo del Moro s/n; ☎ 955 217 015. Close to the *Posada del Moro* this is a decent restaurant specializing in sierra cuisine, particularly *carnes a la brasa* (charcoal-grilled meat), and also does barbecues on its sprawling terrace in summer. €€

Restaurante Posada del Moro C/Paseo del Moro s/n (follow signs for 'Julia & Lucia's'); ⓦ laposadadelmoro. com. This Michelin-recommended hotel restaurant is a serious venture and has won many critical plaudits. Julia and Lucia, the English chefs, use the riches of the sierra to embellish their traditional dishes with a creative edge. *Setas a la plancha* (sierra mushrooms) and *cola de toro* (stewed bull's tail) are two signature dishes, while there's a *menú* plus a more elaborate *menú de degustación* for double the price. €€€€

Constantina and around

Eighteen kilometres southeast of Cazalla lies **CONSTANTINA**, an important and beautiful mountain town and the main administrative centre for Seville's section of the Sierra Morena. For hikers this is as good a place as any to cut back to Seville if you're not counting on continuing across the provincial border into Córdoba. Founded in the fourth century by the Romans during the reign of the emperor Constantine, and named after his son, this was an important centre of wine-production that sent a vintage named *cocolubis* to the imperial capital. The town is a delightful place to wander around, particularly the old quarter, which is dotted with a number of notable eighteenth-century mansions. Constantina's *feria* (last week in Aug) is a rumbustious affair, with horseriding contests plus drinking, dancing and singing galore.

With transport you can make a trip to **La Pantalla** lake for swimming and fishing. It is reached by heading east for 3km along the A452 road to El Pedroso.

Castillo de la Armada

Topping the hill flanking the western edge of town and high above the streets below, the ruined **Castillo de la Armada** is what remains of a once impressive medieval fortress surrounded by shady gardens descending in terraces to the old quarter.

La Encarnación

Pza Llano del Sol 8 • Daily 7–8pm • Free

At the foot of the hill below the castle you'll find the sixteenth-century parish church of **La Encarnación**, which has a Mudéjar tower – Moorish influence having died hard in these parts – and a splendid, if crumbling, Plateresque portal by Hernán Ruíz, the architect of the cathedral inside the Mezquita at Córdoba and the belfry added to the Giralda in Seville. The church's *altar mayor*, a magnificent gilded work by Juan de Oviedo, is also worth a look.

ARRIVAL AND INFORMATION
CONSTANTINA AND AROUND

By bus There are daily buses from and to Seville (2 daily; 2hr).

By train The nearest train station is at Cazalla de la Sierra, 12km away (see page 343) with daily trains to Seville. There is no bus service to the station, but the Turismo can help with booking a taxi.

Turismo There's a Turismo cabin (Mon–Sat 9am–2pm, Sun 10am–2pm, plus Fri & Sat 6–9pm; ☎ 955 881 297; ⓦ constantina.es) on Avda Andalucía, near the entry to the town from El Pedroso; staff here can provide a useful town map. When closed, you can also pick up the map from the Ayuntamiento, C/Eduardo Dato 7, near La Encarnación church.

ACCOMMODATION

★ **La Casa Grande** Ctra Constantina–Cazalla km1; ⓦ casagrandeconstantina.es. A "*petit paradis*" created by its charming French-Spanish proprietors 1.5km from the village. This is a wonderful "gîte-style" country hotel with individually styled a/c rooms next to a large garden pool. Public areas include a bar and barbecue zone and there are mountain bikes for use by guests. They can also advise on trekking in the natural park. €̄

La Casa Mari Pepa C/José de la Bastida 25; ⓦ hostalrural-lacasa.webnode.es. The town's only *hostal*, occupying a *casa señorial* that has been lovingly transformed into a delightful series of distinctively decorated en-suite rooms. Breakfast is included. €̄

EATING AND DRINKING

There are numerous good **tapas bars** along and around C/Mesones, the pedestrianized main street, plus, a few minutes' walk away. There are also a number of excellent **wineries** in and around Constantina, including the *Bodegas de Fuente Reina* and *Bodegas de Fuente Fría*, who make dry reds and chestnut liqueur, and the *Anías la Violetra*, famous for their *aguardiente*.

Bar Bullhy Junior C/Mesones 30; ☎ 652 205 563. One of the town's top-notch tapas bars, serving up a range of sierra specialities including *solomillo al whisky* (pork loin in whisky). €̄

Bar Gregorio C/Alférez Cabrera 11; ☎ 955 881 043. Well worth seeking out, this central and popular bar does a good range of tapas and *raciones* and house specials include *lengua en salsa* (ox tongue). €̄

Cambio de Tercio C/Virgen del Robledo 53; ⓦ cambiodetercioconstantina.webnode.es. Arguably the town's best restaurant, taking its name from the stages of a *corrida* and continuing the theme with an amusing entrance imitating a bullring. There's a lively bar for tapas and *platos combinados* in the front and a pleasant room at the back for more formal dining. All is reasonably priced and the *solomillo de cerdo* (pork loin) is excellent. €€

Marisquería El León Padre Felix 4, off the Paseo de la Alameda; ☎ 955 881 071. An excellent *cervecería-marisquería* with a spacious bar and lively terrace. Among a wide tapas range (both fish and meat) the *jamón ibérico* and *chocos fritos* (fried cuttlefish) are very tasty. Conveniently placed next to *Bar La Rebotica*, which locals spill into for a post-dinner cocktail. €

Los Navarro Paseo de la Alameda 39; ☎ 954 496 361. Atmospheric and friendly bar-restaurant for tapas and *raciones* with a shady terrace on the Alameda. Reasonably priced *carnes a la brasa* (charcoal-grilled meats) – try the *solomillo* (pork loin) – are the speciality here, and they also offer a range of salads. €€

3

Córdoba
and Jaén

ZUHEROS VILLAGE

Córdoba and Jaén

Andalucía's most northerly province, Córdoba is bisected by the fertile valley of the Río Guadalquivir that meanders across it from east to west. On the river's northern bank, the provincial capital is a handsome city whose outstanding attraction is its 1200-year-old Moorish Mezquita, one of the world's great buildings. In the tangled lanes of the Judería, the old Jewish quarter that partially surrounds it, the sense of Córdoba's history as the centre of a vast empire is overwhelming. After the brilliance of the Mezquita, the rest of the city, particularly modern Córdoba, can seem like an anticlimax, but persist and you'll discover a host of striking post-*Reconquista* churches, elegant convents and mansions. Despite a reputation among its neighbours for sobriety, Córdoba has some of the most distinctive old bars in Andalucía, where taking a drink and a *tapa* is a particularly unique experience.

A few kilometres from the city there's more Moorish splendour at the ruins of **Medina Azahara**, a once-fabulous palace of the caliphs being painstakingly restored, while south of the river lies Córdoba's **Campiña**, a rolling landscape of grainfields, olive groves and vineyards, where Montilla, the province's rival to the wines of Jerez, is made. Little visited, the more elevated southern reaches of this area are particularly delightful, with towns and villages such as **Baena**, **Cabra** and **Zuheros** ringed by excellent hiking country. The equally unsung town of **Priego de Córdoba**, further south still, has a clutch of spectacular Baroque churches that are worth a trip in themselves.

The **province of Jaén** has been regarded since Moorish times as Andalucía's gateway – through the **Despeñaperros Pass** – to Castile and the cities of Toledo and Madrid to the north. Although often used as this gateway's doormat and something of a forgotten entity, the region's poorest province has some surprisingly worthy sights. The **city of Jaén** has a fine **Renaissance cathedral** as well as impressive **Moorish baths,** but is more often used as a stop on the way to the magnificent twin Renaissance towns of **Baeza** and **Úbeda**. Sharing a similar history, the noble families of these two conurbations competed in using their sixteenth-century wealth to employ some of the best architects and builders around. These craftsmen, such as the great architect **Andrés de Vandelvira** – whose imprint is everywhere – have left behind a monumental treasure in golden sandstone, one of the marvels not only of Andalucía, but of Spain and Europe as well. The province's mountainous eastern flank forms the heart of the **Cazorla Natural Park** and cradles the source of the Guadalquivir. Extending northeast from the town of **Cazorla**, the park's vast expanse of dense woodlands, lakes and spectacular crags are crowned by eagles' and vultures' nests and patrolled by the agile ibex. Its northerly reaches are guarded by many ruined Moorish castles, the most astonishing of which sits on the hill above the village of **Segura de la Sierra**. The rest is mainly **olive groves**, which cover a vast area of Jaén, and whose exclusive cultivation is the cause of much seasonal unemployment. But there is a beauty in the orderly files of trees, stretching across the red and creamy white hills to the horizon, which seem "to open and close like a fan", as Lorca poetically put it, as you pass.

Córdoba

CÓRDOBA stands upstream from Seville beside a loop of the Guadalquivir, which was once navigable as far as here. It is today a minor provincial capital, prosperous in a modest sort of way, but a mere shadow of its past greatness. The city's name – a

Highlights

❶ Córdoba The city of Córdoba is a veritable cultural feast of excellent museums and pretty palaces, with an old Jewish quarter and some excellent tapas bars and restaurants to boot. See page 348

❷ Mezquita, Córdoba This beautiful 1200-year-old mosque is one of the world's greatest Moorish architectural masterpieces. See page 353

❸ Medina Azahara The ruins of this sumptuous tenth-century Moorish palace evoke the dazzling grandeur of the Córdoba caliphate. See page 369

❹ Zuheros A delightful white village perched on a ridge in the midst of stunningly picturesque walking country. See page 383

❺ Priego de Córdoba The Baroque showpiece of Córdoba province, this charming town is crammed with fine churches and monuments. See page 384

❻ Baños Arabes, Jaén One of the largest and best-preserved Moorish bath complexes in Spain. See page 399

❼ Baeza and Úbeda The twin Renaissance jewels of Jaén province are filled with a wealth of magnificent monuments in honey-tinted stone. See pages 402 & 407

HIGHLIGHTS ARE MARKED ON THE MAP ON PAGE 350

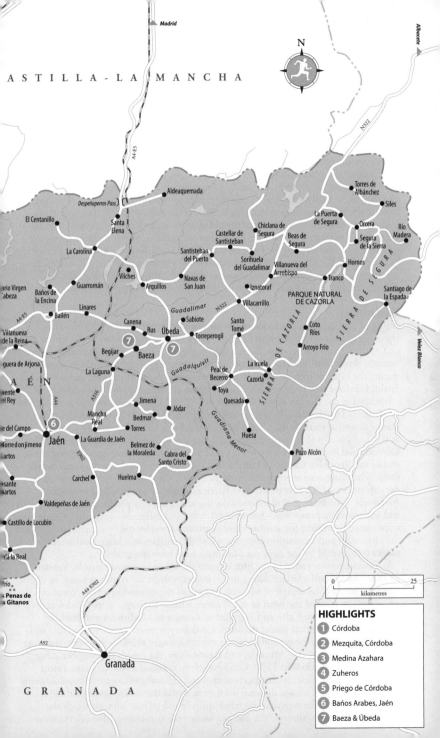

CASTILLA-LA MANCHA

Madrid

Albacete

N

Torres de Albánchez
Siles
El Centanillo
Despeñaperros Pass
Aldeaquemada
La Puerta de Segura
Orcera
Río Madera
Santa Elena
Chiclana de Segura
Beas de Segura
Segura de la Sierra
La Carolina
Castellar de Santisteban
Santisteban del Puerto
Sorihuela del Guadalimar
Villanueva del Arzobispo
Hornos
Vilches
Guarromán
Navas de San Juan
Tranco
Santuario Virgen de la Cabeza
Baños de la Encina
Arquillos
Iznatoraf
Villacarrillo
PARQUE NATURAL DE CAZORLA
Santiago de la Espada
Linares
Canena
Guadalimar
N322
Bailén
Rus
Sabiote
Santo Tomé
Coto Ríos
Villanueva de la Reina
Begíjar
Úbeda
Torreperogil
Velez Blanco
⑦
Baeza
⑦
Arroyo Frío
guera de Arjona
La Laguna
Guadalquivir
Peal de Becerro
La Iruela
SIERRA DE CAZORLA
JAÉN
A44
A316
Jimena
Jódar
Toya
Cazorla
SIERRA DE SEGURA
ente el Rey
Mancha Real
Bedmar
Guadiana Menor
Quesada
del Campo
⑥
Jaén
Torres
orre don jimeno
La Guardia de Jaén
Belmez de la Moraleda
Huesa
artos
Cabra del Santo Cristo
Pozo Alcón
sante artos
Carchel
Huelma
Valdepeñas de Jaén
Castillo de Locubin
A44 E902
alá la Real
rio
s Peñas de s Gitanos
A92
Granada

0   25
kilometres

GRANADA

HIGHLIGHTS

① Córdoba
② Mezquita, Córdoba
③ Medina Azahara
④ Zuheros
⑤ Priego de Córdoba
⑥ Baños Arabes, Jaén
⑦ Baeza & Úbeda

possible corruption of the Syrian *coteba* or "oil press" – is believed to be of Phoenician origin, dating from the time when merchant venturers sailed up the river to carry away the region's much-prized olive oil.

Córdoba is now principally famous for a single building, the **Mezquita** – the grandest and most beautiful mosque ever constructed by the Moors. It stands right in the centre of the city, surrounded by the **Judería**, the old Jewish and Moorish quarters, and is a building of extraordinary mystical and aesthetic power. Head for it on arrival and keep returning as long as you stay; its beauty and power increase with each visit.

The Mezquita apart, Córdoba is a city of considerable charm. It has few grand squares or mansions, tending instead to introverted architecture, calling your attention to the tremendous and often wildly extravagant **patios**, yet another Moorish legacy. Filled with pot plants, decorative tiles, tinkling fountains and a profusion of flowers in summer, these shady oases can usually be glimpsed beyond a forged iron *verja* (gate), and are the best to be seen in Andalucía. Besides the city's Moorish treasures, there is another Córdoba, to the **north of the old quarter**; an area rarely touched upon by visitors, but with its own rewarding churches and palaces, not to mention bars.

Córdoba's major fiesta is the **Feria de Mayo**, held in the final week in May. Earlier in the month, the **Cruces de Mayo** celebrations fill the town with lavishly decorated crosses, and a festival devoted to Córdoba's delightful patios, which were declared Unesco Intangible Cultural Heritage in 2012, follows immediately behind.

Brief history

Although archeological finds document an antiquity stretching back to Neolithic times, Córdoba's verifiable history begins with a Bronze Age **Iberian** settlement at the end of the second millennium BC trading on the mineral wealth – silver and copper – brought down from the Sierra Morena to the north. Apparently of little importance during the next millennium, and largely bypassed by the Carthaginian expansion into Spain, Córdoba rose to prominence under **Rome** at the end of the third century BC.

Founded as the Roman city of **Corduba** in 152 BC, Córdoba flourished as the capital of Hispania Ulterior and, foreshadowing its later brilliance, became famous for its poetry as well as its olive oil. Cicero once cracked that Cordoban poetry sounded as if it had got mixed up with the oil due to its guttural style of delivery. Later, after Córdoba had backed the wrong horse in the wars between Caesar and Pompey at the end of the Republic, Caesar sacked the city and an estimated thirty thousand people died. When Augustus reorganized Spain in 27 BC, Córdoba's fortunes improved as the capital city of the new province of Baetica, roughly corresponding to modern Andalucía. A brilliant period followed during which the city produced the poets **Lucan** and **Seneca** while prosperity – based on oil, wool and minerals – increased. Córdoba's importance continued for another three centuries, as evidenced by excavations opposite the city's train and bus station complex where the remains of a huge fourth-century **palace** constructed by the emperor Maximian have been unearthed.

As Roman power waned in the fifth century the area was overrun first by **Vandals** and then by **Visigoths** before falling to the **Moors** early in the eighth century. In 756 Córdoba became the capital of Moorish Spain and the succeeding three centuries – when the city formed the heart of the Western Islamic Empire – were Córdoba's golden age, as it grew to rival Cairo and Baghdad as a centre of Muslim art and learning. Though later its political power declined, Córdoba remained a centre of culture and scholarship and was the birthplace of the twelfth-century thinkers **Averroës**, the great Muslim commentator on Aristotle, and **Maimónides**, the Jewish philosopher. After conquest by **Fernando III** in 1236, Córdoba's glory vanished as the city sank into a long and steady decline. Such aspects of civilized life as the elaborate Moorish systems of water supply and sewage disposal fell into ruin and the mosques were turned into churches. Little of the wealth of imperial Spain found its way here, although the city's leatherworkers, silversmiths and *parfumeurs* (all continuing Moorish traditions) achieved some renown in the sixteenth century. Plagues in the next century decimated the population and when the English travel writer Richard Ford arrived in the 1830s he found "a poor and servile city". Córdoba suffered terrible repression during the wars against the **French** as it did again in the twentieth century when, during the Civil War, it was captured by the **Nationalists** who carried out brutal atrocities. Local voters took belated revenge for this in the first post-Franco elections of 1979 when they elected a **communist** council – the only major city in Spain to do so. Today, Córdoba boasts a progressive air and is an important city of learning. The university is renowned as a centre for agricultural studies and veterinary science.

Mezquita

C/Cardinal Herrero 1 • Mosque/cathedral Usually daily 10am–7pm, except Sun 8.30–11am, 3–7pm, but check the website • Charge • Belfry Daily 9.30am–6.30pm, until 5pm on Sun • Charge • ⓦ mezquita-catedraldecordoba.es

As in Moorish times, the **Mezquita** is approached through the **Patio de los Naranjos**, a classic Islamic ablutions court with fountains for ritual purification before prayer, which still preserves its orange trees. None of the original ablutions fountains survive, the present ones being purely decorative later additions. Originally, when in use for the Friday prayers, all nineteen naves of the mosque were open to this court, allowing the rows of interior columns to appear as an extension of the trees. Today, with all but one of the entrance gates locked, the image is still there, though subdued by the loss of those brilliant shafts of sunlight filtering through. The mood of the building has been distorted a little, from the open and vigorous simplicity of the mosque to the mysterious half-light of a cathedral.

Mihrab

The mosque's overall uniformity was broken only by the culminating point of al-Hakam II's tenth-century extension – the domed cluster of pillars surrounding the mosque's great jewel, the sacred **Mihrab**. Even here, although he lengthened the prayer hall by a third, al-Hakam carefully aligned the new *mihrab* at the end of the same central aisle that had led to the previous two. The *mihrab* had two functions in Islamic worship: it indicated the direction of Mecca and it amplified the words of the *imam*, or prayer leader.

DESIGNING THE MEZQUITA

Inside the Mezquita, a forest of supporting pillars stretches away into the distance. This was an early and sophisticated architectural improvisation to gain height. The original architect, **Sidi ben Ayub**, working under the instruction of Abd ar-Rahman I, had at his disposal columns in marble, porphyry and jasper from the old Visigothic cathedral and from numerous Roman buildings, as well as many more shipped in from all parts of the former Roman Empire. This ready-made building material could bear great weight, but the architect was faced with the problem of the pillars' varying sizes: many were much too tall but the vast majority would not be tall enough, even when arched, to reach the intended height of the ceiling. The long pillars he sank in the floor, while his solution for the short pillars (which may have been inspired by Roman aqueduct designs) was to place a second row of square columns on the apex, serving as a base for the semicircular arches that support the roof. For extra strength and stability (and perhaps also deliberately to echo the shape of a date palm, much revered by the early Spanish Arabs), he introduced another, horseshoe-shaped arch above the lower pillars.

A second and purely aesthetic innovation was to alternate brick and stone in the arches, creating the **red-and-white striped pattern** that gives a unity and distinctive character to the whole design. This architectural *tour de force* was unprecedented in the Arab world and set the tone for all future enlargements – excepting the Christian cathedral – of the building. Most impressively, it was completed within a year of its commencement in 785.

CÓRDOBA

EATING

El Abanico	14
Almudaina	21
Amaltea	28
Bar La Cavea	12
Bar Santos	18
La Bicicleta	24
Bodega Guzmán	6
Bodega Sociedad de Plateros	19
Bodegas Campos	20
El Caballo Rojo	15
Casa El Juramento	11
Casa Mazal	13
El Choco	16
El Choto	8
El Churrasco	9
El Gallo	4
Mesón San Basilio	23
Noor	17
La Regadera	27
Salón de Té	7
Sociedad Plateros	3
Taberna la Viuda	25
Taberna Salinas	5
Taberna San Miguel	1
Taberna Séneca	10
La Tata	22
El Tercio Viejo	2
La Tinaja	26

SHOPPING

Almacen Rafael	5
El Corte Inglés	1
Espaliu	6
Librería Luque	2
Meryan	4
Zoco (market)	3

Hotel Mezquita	13
Hotel NH Córdoba Guadalquivir	21
Hotel Plateros	7
Hotel Viento 10	20

La Llave de la Judería	6
Parador de Córdoba	1
Pensión El Portillo	12

FLAMENCO

La Bulería	2
Peña Flamenca "Fosforito"	1
Tablao Cardenal	3

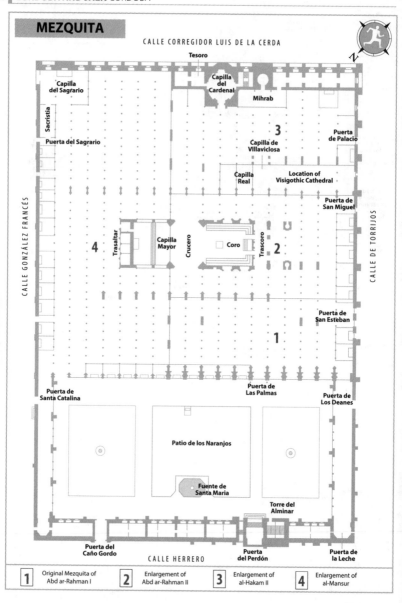

4

The paired pillars that flank the *mihrab* and support its arch were taken from the earlier *mihrab* of Abd ar-Rahman I, their prominent position no doubt a mark of respect by al-Hakam to his great predecessor. The inner vestibule of the niche (which is frustratingly fenced off) is quite simple in comparison, with a shell-shaped ceiling carved from a single block of marble. The chambers to either side, as well as the dome above the *mihrab*, are decorated with exquisite **mosaics** of gold, rust-red, turquoise and green, the work of Byzantine craftsmen supplied by the emperor Nicephorus II at al-

Hakam's request. These constitute the *maksura*, where the caliph and his retinue would pray, a fitting monument to this scholarly and sensitive ruler.

Cathedral Coro

Originally the whole design of the mosque would have directed worshippers naturally towards the *mihrab*. Today, though, you almost stumble upon it, as in the centre of the mosque squats a Renaissance **cathedral coro**. This was built in 1523, nearly three centuries of enlightened restraint after the Christian conquest, and in spite of fierce opposition from the town council. The erection of a *coro* and *capilla mayor*, however, had long been the "Christianizing" dream of the cathedral chapter and at last they had found a monarch, predictably Carlos V, who was willing to sanction the work. Carlos, to his credit, realized the mistake (though it did not stop him from destroying parts of the Alhambra and Seville's Alcázar); on seeing the work completed he told the chapter, "You have built what you or others might have built anywhere, but you have destroyed something that was unique in the world." Some details are worth noting, though, particularly the beautifully carved Churrigueresque **choir stalls** by Pedro Duque Cornejo, created with mahogany brought from the New World.

Other additions

To the left of the *coro* stands an earlier and happier Christian addition, the Mudéjar **Capilla de Villaviciosa**, built by Moorish craftsmen in 1371. Beside it are the dome and pillars of the **earlier mihrab**, constructed under Abd ar-Rahman II. The mosque's original and finely decorated timber-coffered ceiling was replaced in the eighteenth century by the present Baroque cupolas. Further post-Reconquista additions include the **Capilla Real**, installed by Alfonso X in the thirteenth century, with *azulejo* panels and lobed niches in Mudéjar style, and the early eighteenth-century **Capilla del Cardinal** (Chapterhouse – now housing the cathedral's treasury), the *tesoro* (treasury) and *sacristía*, none of which detracts from the building's imposing majesty.

The evocative belfry, the **Torre del Alminar**, at the corner of the Patio de los Naranjos, is built on the site of the original minaret and contemporaneous with the cathedral addition. The belfry was designed by Hernán Ruíz, who used the earlier tower as a core to support two additional sections, more than doubling its height. The climb to the top is a dizzying experience and the **views** over the Guadalquivir, town and Mezquita itself are tremendous. Close by, the **Puerta del Perdón**, the main entrance to the patio, was rebuilt in Moorish style in 1377. It's worth making a tour of the Mezquita's **outer walls** before leaving; parts of the original "caliphal" decoration (in particular some exquisite latticework) surrounding the portals are stunning. The west wall along Calle Torrijos is the most striking, where the **Puerta de San Esteban** was an important side entrance into the original mosque and is the oldest of the doorways, dated by an inscription above it to 855. The **Puerta de San Miguel** is sited in the oldest stretch of wall, and dates from the earlier Visigothic cathedral.

Alcázar

Pza Campo Santo de los Mártires s/n • Mid-June to mid-Sep Tues–Sun 8.15am–2.45pm; mid-Sept to mid-June Tues–Fri 8.30am–8.45pm, Sat & Sun 8.30am–2.30pm • Charge • ☎ 957 420 151

Dating from the time of the *Reconquista*, the **Alcázar de Los Reyes Cristianos**, a palace fortress, was completed in the fourteenth century and now houses a small municipal museum. The original Moorish *alcázar* stood beside the Mezquita, on the site presently occupied by the Palacio Episcopal. After the Christian conquest it was rebuilt a little to the west and used by monarchs – including Fernando and Isabel who were visited here by Columbus in 1486 – when staying in the city. That the buildings retain little of their original opulence today is due to their use as the residence of the **Inquisition** for three centuries prior to 1821, and later as a prison until as recently as 1951.

MOORISH CÓRDOBA AND THE BUILDING OF THE MEZQUITA

Córdoba's domination of **Moorish Spain** began thirty years after the conquest – in 756, when the city was placed under the control of **Abd ar-Rahman I**, the sole survivor of the Umayyad dynasty that had been bloodily expelled from the eastern caliphate of Damascus. He commenced the building of the **Great Mosque** (La Mezquita), purchasing the site of the former Visigothic Cathedral of Saint Vincent from the Christians. This building which, divided by a partition wall, had previously served both communities had itself been constructed on top of an earlier Roman temple dedicated to the god Janus. Demolishing the church as they built, Abd ar-Rahman's architects, for reasons of speed and economy, incorporated one of the cathedral's original walls – that facing west – into the new structure and this is the reason why the *mihrab*'s prayer wall is not precisely aligned towards Mecca. This original mosque was completed by his son **Hisham** in 786 and comprises about one-fifth of the present building, the first dozen aisles adjacent to the Patio de los Naranjos.

ABD AR-RAHMAN II

The Cordoban emirate soon began to rival Damascus both in power and in the brilliance of its civilization. **Abd ar-Rahman II** (822–52) initiated sophisticated irrigation programmes, minted his own coinage and received embassies from Byzantium. He in turn substantially enlarged the mosque. A focal point within the culture of al-Andalus, this was by now being consciously directed and enriched as an alternative to Mecca; it possessed an original script of the Koran and a bone from the arm of Muhammad, and, for the Spanish Muslim who could not go to Mecca, it became the most sacred place of **pilgrimage**. In the broader Islamic world it ranked fourth in sanctity after the Kaaba of Mecca, the city of Medina in Saudi Arabia, and the Al Aksa mosque of Jerusalem.

ABD AR-RAHMAN III

In the tenth century Córdoba reached its zenith under **Abd ar-Rahman III** (912–61), one of the great rulers of Islamic history. He assumed power at the age of 23 after his grandfather had killed his father during a period of internal strife. During his reign, according to a contemporary historian, he "subdued rebels, built palaces, gave impetus to agriculture, immortalized ancient deeds and monuments, and inflicted great damage on infidels to a point where no opponent or contender remained in al-Andalus. People obeyed en masse and wished to live with him in peace." In 929, with Muslim Spain and a substantial part of North Africa firmly under his control, Abd ar-Rahman III adopted the title of "caliph", or successor of the Prophet. It was a supremely confident gesture and was reflected in the growing splendour of Córdoba itself which, with a population approaching 500,000, had become the largest, most prosperous city of Europe, and outshone both Byzantium and Baghdad (the new capital of the eastern caliphate) in science, culture and scholarship. At the turn of the tenth century it could boast some 27 schools, 50 hospitals (with the first separate clinics for the leprous and insane), 600 public baths, 60,300 noble mansions, 213,077 houses and 80,455 shops. One of Córdoba's most magnificent buildings during this and later periods would have been the Umayyad palace of the caliphs, of which little except a bath complex remains (see page 361). Extending to the west of the Mezquita from Calle Torrijos to the city walls and southwards to the river, the palace was connected to the Mezquita by a secret passage. Built in the ninth century to allow the caliph privileged access to the mosque at all times, traces of this tunnel

The palace underwent extensive Mudéjar rebuilding during the fifteenth century, when the attractive **Moorish-style gardens** were added. One of the glories of Córdoba today, with lots of arbours and shady corners, the gardens are dotted with hefty chunks of Roman columns and other masonry testifying to the city's importance in the Roman era. From the tower's belvedere there are great **views** over the town and river, while the **interior** of the Alcázar features fifteenth-century royal (not on view) have been found in the building's southwest corner. The construction of a glorious new palace at **Medina Azahara** in the 930s as well as further development of the Great Mosque paralleled these new heights of confidence and splendour. Abd ar-Rahman III provided the Mezquita with a new minaret 80m high, topped by three pomegranate-shaped spheres, two of silver and one of gold and each weighing a ton. The minaret was badly damaged in a storm in 1589 and was later used as the core of the sixteenth-century Torre del Alminar that replaced it.

AL-HAKAM II

The caliph's successor **al-Hakam II** (961–76) was a man from another mould than that of his warrior father, best epitomized by his advice to his own son:

Do not make wars unnecessarily. Keep the peace, for your own wellbeing and that of your people. Never unsheathe your sword except against those who commit injustice. What pleasure is there in invading and destroying nations, in taking pillage and destruction to the ends of the earth? Do not let yourself be dazzled by vanity; let your justice always be like a tranquil lake.

In tune with these sentiments, al-Hakam was a poet, historian and the builder of one of the great libraries of the Middle Ages. This cultured ruler was also responsible for the mosque's most brilliant expansion, virtually doubling its extent. After demolishing the south wall to add fourteen extra rows of columns, he employed Byzantine craftsmen to construct a new *mihrab* or prayer niche. This has survived due to having been bricked up following the Christian Reconquista. Only rediscovered in the nineteenth century, it remains complete and is perhaps the most beautiful example of all Moorish religious architecture.

AL-MANSUR

Under the vizier-usurper **al-Mansur** (977–1002), who used his position as regent to push al-Hakam's child successor, Hisham II, into the background, repeated attacks were carried out on the Christians in the north, including the daring expedition to Santiago de Compostela in 997, when the pilgrimage cathedral's bells were seized. This military might was built on the incorporation of thousands of Berbers from North Africa into al-Mansur's army – a policy that was to have devastating implications for the future when the same Berbers turned on their paymasters and sacked and plundered the city, destroying al-Hakam's treasured library in the process. Within less than thirty years the brilliant caliphate of Córdoba had collapsed in a bloody turmoil as short-lived puppet caliphs attempted to stave off the inevitable.

When he was not away on his military campaigns, al-Mansur gave his attention to further embellishing the Great Mosque. As al-Hakam had extended the building as far to the south as was possible, al-Mansur completed the final enlargement by adding seven rows of columns to the whole east side. This spoiled the symmetry of the mosque, depriving the *mihrab* of its central position, but Arab historians observed that it meant there were now "as many bays as there are days of the year". They also delighted in describing the rich interior, with its 1293 marble columns, 280 chandeliers and 1445 lamps. Hanging inverted among the lamps were the bells of the cathedral of Santiago de Compostela. Al-Mansur had made his Christian captives carry them on their shoulders from Galicia – a process that was to be observed in reverse after Córdoba was captured by Fernando el Santo (the Saint) in 1236.

baths and some fine **Roman mosaics** that were discovered in the city. The second-century depiction of *Polyphemus and Galatea* is outstanding and the monochrome mosaic beside it is one of the largest complete mosaics in existence anywhere in the world. A fine third-century carved sarcophagus is also worth an appreciative look; a half-ajar portal on the sarcophagus's side indicates that access is open to the person within.

CÓRDOBA MONUMENT PASS

Tourist offices in Córdoba sell a combined **entry pass** to the Alcázar, Baños Califales, Museo Taurino and Museo de Julio Romero de Torres. Note that Córdoba changes its monument **opening hours** more than any other town in Andalucía; check in advance with any tourist office (see page 365).

Baños Califales

Pza Campo Santo de los Mártires s/n • Mid-June to mid-Sept Tues–Sun 8.30am–2.30pm; mid-Sept to mid-June Tues–Fri 8.30am–8.15pm, Sat 8.30am–4pm, Sun 8.30am–2.30pm • Charge • ☎ 608 158 893

The Alcázar gardens contain the impressive remains of a tenth-century Moorish *hammam*, or bathhouse, the **Baños Califales**, constructed in the reign of al-Hakam II. As their name implies, the baths were possibly attached to the Umayyad palace that once covered most of this area. Inside you can see various bathing rooms, which would have had gradated temperatures, lit by star-shaped windows set in barrel-vaulted ceilings; the western rooms date from the post-califal Taifa, Almoravid and Almohad periods. The baths would originally have been surrounded by plant-filled gardens and arbours where bathers could relax and chat; in the afternoon they normally passed into female hands, when a towel would be hung outside to warn absent-minded males of the change of use. Travellers to Moorish Córdoba record between three and six hundred bathhouses similar to these throughout the city, which would probably not be excessive for a population of half a million inhabitants. Today you can enjoy a modern reconstruction of the Moorish bathing experience (see page 361).

Jardín Botánico

Avda de Linneo s/n • Opening times for the gardens and museums vary, see the website • Charge • ⓦ jardinbotanicodecordoba.com

Some 300m downriver of the Alcázar, Córdoba's extensive **Jardín Botánico** features hothouses with exotic species of succulents, ferns and prickly plants, as well as a rose garden. At the garden's northern end a paleobotanical museum – housed inside a medieval watermill – displays 150,000 specimens of fossil plant life. The nearby arboretum exhibits trees and shrubs from all over the world including samples of Andalucía's own arboreal rarity, the **pinsapo** Spanish fir, transplanted from its only European habitat in the Sierra de Grazalema and Sierra de las Nieves. Other features include a garden for the visually impaired with a collection of plants recognizable by their aroma and texture, and a **cafetería**.

Puente Romano and around

The pedestrianized **Puente Romano** is an impressive 250m-long Roman bridge across the Río Guadalquivir probably built during the first or second centuries AD. Inscriptions record repairs to it carried out in Moorish times by the *wali* or governor al-Samh in the eighth century, and by al-Hakam II in the tenth, but the structure still retains much Roman stonework. A controversial refurbishment of the bridge in 2007, which replaced its former cobblestones with a redstone pavement, added modern lighting and remodelled the support walls, outraged many architectural experts and archeologists.

Torre de la Calahorra

Puento Romano s/n • Daily 10am–2pm & 4.30–8.30pm • Charge • ☎ 957 293 929

Guarding the southeastern end of the Puente Romano is the **Torre de la Calahorra**, a medieval tower that now houses a **museum** full of hi-tech gimmicks including weird tableaux, an illuminated Alhambra, a model of the Mezquita prior to its

Christian alterations and, improbably, a multimedia presentation on the history of man. From the tower you get a wonderful panoramic **view** towards the Mezquita and city beyond.

Albolafia waterwheel

Just west of the Puente Romano at its northern end, the reconstructed **Albolafia** is the sole survivor of a number of ancient **Moorish waterwheels** that once crossed the river here and which, besides grinding flour, pumped water to the Alcázar's gardens. So noisy were this wheel's rumblings that Queen Isabel – resident at the Alcázar during a royal visit – had it dismantled when it disturbed her sleep.

Hammam Baños Arabes

C/Corregidor Luis de la Cerda 51 • Daily, but reserve in advance; 2hr sessions 10am–midnight • Charge • ⓦ hammamalandalus.com

Slightly southwest of the Plaza del Potro, back towards the Mezquita, the **Hammam Baños Arabes** is a full-scale Moorish bath complex that re-creates the architecture and atmosphere of a medieval *hammam*. You'll need a bathing suit.

La Judería

Between the Mezquita and the beginning of the Avenida del Gran Capitán lies **La Judería**, Córdoba's old Jewish quarter. A fascinating network of lanes, it's just as atmospheric as Seville's *barrio* Santa Cruz (see page 256), although here too tasteless souvenir shops have gained ground.

4

Sinagoga

C/Maimónides 18 • Mid-June to mid-Sept Tues–Sun 9am–3pm; mid-Sept to mid-June Tues–Sat 9am–8pm, Sun 9am–3pm • Free • ☎ 957 749 015

Near the heart of the Judería is the **Sinagoga** (synagogue), one of only three in Spain that survived the Jewish expulsion of 1492 – the other two are in Toledo. This one, built in 1315, is minute, particularly in comparison to the great Santa María in Toledo, but it has some fine stuccowork elaborating on a Solomon's-seal motif together with Hebrew texts in the Mudéjar style, and it also retains its women's gallery.

Capilla de San Bartolomé

Pza del Cardenal Salazar s/n • Tues–Sun: mid-June to mid-Sept 10.30am–1.30pm; mid-Sept to mid-June 10.30am–1.30pm & 3.30–6.30pm • Charge

The **Capilla de San Bartolomé** is a superb Gothic-Mudéjar chapel built in the fifteenth century. Restored in 2010, the chapel's exquisite vaulting, original brick floor, glazed tiles and *yesería* (plasterwork) are well worth a look.

La Casa Andalusí

C/Judíos 12 • Daily 10am–7.30pm • Charge • ☎ 957 290 642

Near the synagogue there's a well restored twelfth-century mansion, **La Casa Andalusí**, with a fine patio and several Moorish wall panels. The museum attempts to re-create the atmosphere of the Moorish period with furniture and a variety of exhibits including a coin collection and implements from the paper factory.

Museo Taurino

Pza de Maimónides s/n • See website for complex opening hours • Charge • ⓦ museotaurinodecordoba.es

The small **Museo Taurino** (Bullfighting Museum) warrants a look, if only for the kitschy nature of its exhibits: among a number of mounted bulls' heads (some dating from the nineteenth century), two of them were given this "honour" for having killed matadors. Beside a copy of the tomb of Manolete, most famous of the city's fighters, is exhibited the hide of his taurine nemesis, Islero; you can also see the bloodstained vest from his ill-fated bullfight in 1947. Other displays include eighteenth-century bullfight posters and a series of photos from 1914 depicting a bullfighter being gored and killed.

Callejón de las Flores

The **Callejón de las Flores**, which lies close to the Mezquita's northeast corner, is the most famous street in town, a white-walled alley from whose balconies and hanging pots cascades a riot of geraniums in spring and summer. When viewed from its northern end, the *callejón* neatly frames the Mezquita's belfry – the picture that decorates every postcard rack in town.

Museo Arqueológico

Pza de Jerónimo Páez 7 • Mid-June to mid-Sept Tues–Sun 9am–3pm; mid-Sept to mid-June Tues–Sat 9am–8pm, Sun 9am–3pm • Charge • ☎ 957 355 525

To the northeast of the Mezquita lies the excellent **Museo Arqueológico**, rated among the best in Spain. The collection here is essential to gaining an understanding of Córdoba's importance as a Roman city in particular, as so little from this period survives above ground today. Housed in a building that incorporates the **Casa Páez**, a stunning sixteenth-century mansion next door, the museum visit starts on the first floor where the **prehistoric section** has a selection of Iberian sculptures unearthed throughout the province. Among sculptures in the **Roman section**, a first-century head of Drusus (son of the Emperor Tiberius) and a marble Aphrodite bending down are outstanding, as is the collection of Roman sculptures, mosaics and sarcophagi. The **Moorish period** is represented by a number of exhibits including some fine Caliphal ceramics and *azulejos* (tiles).

The lower floor is themed around the daily life of Córdoba's Roman and Moorish civilizations. Look out for the famous second-century **sculpture of Mithras** slaying the bull from a mithraeum excavated at Cabra in the south of the province (see page 376). This conventional image, which was placed in the retablo position in the small mithraic cult temples, shows Mithras plunging his dagger into the bull whose blood, initiates believed, gave birth to all living things, hence the dog and the snake trying to get their share. Nearby is a fine fourth-century relief of Daniel in the lions' den and a reconstruction of the tenth century *alminar* or minaret of the Mezquita that was replaced by the current bell tower in the sixteenth century.

The basement incorporates elements of a **Roman theatre** that can be seen from the entry foyer. Not much remains of the theatre, built in the first century and heavily plundered since it was abandoned in the fourth century, but you get a good idea of the seating area and crypt.

Plaza del Potro

The fine old **Plaza del Potro**, one of Córdoba's more historic landmarks, is named after the colt (*potro*) that adorns its sixteenth-century fountain. Originally a livestock market dealing in horses and mules, the area once had a villainous reputation, as did the remarkable inn opposite, the **Posada del Potro**, which Cervantes mentions in *Don Quijote*, and where he almost certainly stayed. Sensitively restored, the building, with an atmospheric cattle yard, is now a centre for the study of the art of flamenco and stages exhibitions and occasional concerts.

Museo de Bellas Artes

On the eastern side of Pza del Potro • Mid-June to mid-Sept Tues–Sun 9am–3pm; mid-Sept to mid-June Tues–Sat 9am–8pm, Sun 9am–3pm • Charge • ☎ 957 015 858

The former Hospital de la Caridad, founded in the sixteenth century, now contains the **Museo de Bellas Artes**. Among a fairly unremarkable collection is an *Immaculate Conception* by Murillo as well as works by Valdés Leal and other minor *andaluz* painters.

The ground floor has a small archeological collection, as well as a collection of modern sculpture and paintings. Look out for the Dalí-esque work *Mujeres Vela* (women sailing) by noted Montoro painter Antonio Rodríguez de Luna (see page 392).

Museo Julio Romero de Torres

Pza del Potro 1 • See website for opening hours • Charge • ⓦ museojulioromero.cordoba.es

Across the courtyard from the Museo de Bellas Artes is the small **Museo Julio Romero de Torres** devoted to the eponymous Cordoban artist (1874–1930), painter of some sublimely dreadful canvases, most of which depict reclining female nudes with furtive male guitar players. Though he's attacked by feminists and dubbed "the king of kitsch" by critics, the *cordobeses* won't have a word said against him. Depending on your tastes, you might find a trip to *Bodegas Campos*, just east of here at C/Lineros 32 (see page 368), rather more rewarding.

Plaza de la Corredera

To the north of Plaza del Potro, in an area that was once the *plateros* or silversmiths' quarter, you'll find **Plaza de la Corredera**, a wonderfully refurbished colonnaded square, much resembling Madrid's or Salamanca's Plaza Mayor. Unique in Andalucía, the square was completely enclosed in the seventeenth century, creating a suitable space for all kinds of spectacles. These have included burnings by the Inquisition as well as bullfights, from which event the tiny **Callejón Toril** (Bull Pen) on the eastern side takes its name. Today, bars and restaurants fill the square, their terraces popular places to sit out on summer evenings.

North of the monumental quarter

Many visitors to Córdoba make a stopover at the Mezquita and then leave without ever discovering the other Córdoba, to the north of the monumental quarter and the Judería, where the city's everyday life is carried on. Here, interspersed among the modern streets – many still built on the ancient grid – are **Gothic churches**, **convents** and **Renaissance palaces** that are little visited but well worth an hour or two. Note that churches are usually locked outside service times: early mornings or evenings (about 7–9pm) are the most promising times to catch them open, perhaps visiting a few of the area's excellent tapas bars en route if you opt for the latter.

Plaza Tendillas and around

Plaza Tendillas is the vibrant centre of modern Córdoba, as it was in Roman times. Dominated by the bronze equestrian statue of El Gran Capitán, a Cordoban general whose Italian campaigns in the late fifteenth century helped to project post-*Reconquista* Spain onto the world stage, it also features fountains – spurting water 2m into the air from the pedestrianized pavement – that are a big hit with tourists, children and dogs.

Off the east side of the plaza, along Calle Claudio Marcelo, lies the **Templo Romano**, the tortuously reconstructed remains (mostly pillars) of a first-century Roman temple thought to have been of a similar form to the Maison Carrée at Nîmes. Just northeast of here, the **Iglesia de San Pablo**, a fine Romanesque-Gothic church dating from the period following the *Reconquista*, has undergone numerous later modifications including a Baroque facade. Its interior retains a fine Mudéjar dome and coffered ceiling as well as a seventeenth-century sculpture of the Virgin, *Nuestra Señora de las Angustias* (*Our Lady of the Sorrows*), a masterpiece by Juan de Mesa, himself a native of Córdoba.

Northwest from here, at C/Alfonso XIII 14, is the striking **Círculo de la Amistad**, a casino founded in 1842 and set inside a former convent. Ask the porter to let you see the marvellous Renaissance **patio**, originally the convent's cloister.

Iglesia de San Miguel

Pza de San Miguel s/n

The imposing **Iglesia de San Miguel** is yet another *Reconquista* church founded in the thirteenth century by Fernando III, with a magnificent rose window above the early Gothic entrance. Built on the foundations of a former mosque (one of the original horseshoe-arched entrances to this survives) the triple-naved interior has some elegant vaulting and a Baroque retablo in pink marble. Tucked behind the church lies one of Córdoba's most atmospheric taverns, the *Taberna San Miguel* (see page 368).

San Lorenzo and around

East towards the *barrio* of San Lorenzo lies **San Andrés**, another post-*Reconquista* church and, further on, at the end of Calle Santa María de la Gracia, is the Gothic **San Lorenzo**, whose converted Moorish minaret tower, outstanding rose window and triple-arched portico combine to make it the best-looking church in the city. Inside, the apse has some fine fifteenth-century frescoes depicting scenes from the Passion.

Turning north along Calle Roelas, passing the nineteenth-century Neoclassical Iglesia de San Rafael, you'll come to another *Reconquista* church, **San Agustín**, in the plaza of the same name. Originally a Gothic church, it was substantially altered in the sixteenth century; inside it has frescoes and another sculpture of the Virgin by Juan de Mesa.

Palacio del Marqués de Viana

Pza de Don Gome 2 • Obligatory 45min guided tours July & Aug Tues–Sun 9am–2pm & 5–10pm; Sept–June Tues–Sat 10am–7pm, Sun 10am–3pm • Charge • ☎ 957 496 741

The **Palacio del Marqués de Viana**, one of Córdoba's finest palaces, was the seat of the marquises of Viana until the family sold up to a bank in 1981, after which it was opened – apparently just as the family left it – to the public. Started in the fourteenth century, the building has had numerous later additions, including most of the twelve outstanding **patios**, filled with flowers, the main attraction for many visitors today.

The compulsory tour (in Spanish only) shunts you around a bewildering number of drawing rooms, gaudy bedrooms (one with a Franco portrait), kitchens and galleries, linked by creaking staircases, while the Spanish commentary (foreign-language room descriptions are available) points out a wealth of furniture, paintings and weapons.

Iglesia de Santa Marina

Pza de Santa Marina s/n • Access most likely in early mornings or evenings (around 7–9pm)

North of the Palacio de Viana, the fortress-like **Iglesia de Santa Marina** dates from the thirteenth century (with Baroque modifications) and is one of the city's oldest churches, built shortly after the city was taken from the Moors. It shares the charming plaza of the same name with a monument to the celebrated Cordoban *torero* **Manolete**, who was born in the Santa Marina *barrio* and died in the ring in 1947.

Cristo de los Faroles

Pza de los Capuchinos

The simple white-walled Plaza de los Capuchinos is the site of **Cristo de los Faroles** (Christ of the Lanterns), an eighteenth-century sculpture of the Crucifixion that is the centre of much religious fervour. At night, when the lanterns flanking the cross are illuminated, the place has an unearthly, mystical ambience.

Torre de la Malmuerta

Pza de Colón s/n

Close to the northeast corner of the garden square of Plaza de Colón, the **Torre de la Malmuerta** (Tower of Bad Death) is an early fifteenth-century battlemented tower that was once part of the city walls. It takes its name from a crime of passion when a guard posted here is supposed to have killed his adulterous spouse.

Convento de la Merced

Pza de Colón s/n • Patio daily 9am–2pm & 5–9pm • Free

The west side of the Plaza de Colón is dominated by the lavishly ornate facade – adorned with barley-sugar pillars and twin belfries – of the eighteenth-century former **Convento de la Merced**, now the seat of the provincial government, and the biggest and best example of full-blown Baroque in town. Inside is an exquisite Renaissance patio with paired columns, elegant staircases and a central fountain.

ARRIVAL AND DEPARTURE CÓRDOBA

By train Córdoba's impressive train station is on Pza de las Tres Culturas, off Avda de America to the northwest of the old town. To reach the centre, pick up Avda de los Mozárabes, then veer east onto the broad Avda del Gran Capitán, which will lead you to the old town and the Mezquita, a 15min walk to the south. Bus #3 from outside the bus station will take you to the focal Pza Tendillas and C/San Fernando on the old quarter's eastern flank.

Destinations Algeciras (2 daily; 3hr 9min); Granada (6 daily; 2hr 5min); Jaén (4 daily; 1hr 40min); Málaga (12 daily; 55min); Ronda (2 daily; 1hr 50min); Seville (8 daily; 1hr 20min; AVE 18 daily; 45min).

By bus The bus station is in the same complex as the train station. Each bus company has its own *ventanilla* (sales window).

Destinations Almería (daily; 5hr 45min); Almodóvar del Río (10 daily Mon–Fri, 3 daily Sat & Sun; 30min); Cádiz (daily; 3hr 50min); Écija (6 daily; 55min); Granada (6 daily; 2hr 45min); Jaén (4 daily; 2hr); Madrid (8 daily; 4hr 45min); Málaga (6 daily; 2hr 40min); Seville (3 daily; 2hr).

By car Arriving by car can be a pain, especially during rush hour in the narrow streets around the Mezquita. Parking is also a major headache, so the best solution is to park your vehicle for the duration of your stay in a hotel garage or (emptied of any valuables) on a street out of the centre and get around the city on foot, which is both easy and enjoyable. On-street parking spaces are often to be found on Avda de la República Argentina on the western edge of the old quarter and across the river in the streets either side of the *Hotel NH Córdoba Guadalquivir*.

INFORMATION

Turismo Palacio de Congresos y Exposiciones, C/Torrijos 10 (Mon–Fri 9am–7.30pm, Sat & Sun 9.30am–2.30pm; ☎957 355 179). The city's main tourist office faces the Mezquita's west wall, and has a detailed town plan.

Tourist kiosks Turismo Consorcio, Córdoba's municipal tourist office (☎902 201 774; ⓦturismodecordoba. org) provides tourist information in Pza de las Tendillas in the centre of the modern town (daily 10am–2pm & 5–7.30pm), and on the main concourse of the train station (daily 9am–2pm). Both hand out useful guide maps, up-to-

date opening times and information on events.

Newspapers Córdoba's daily paper, *El Diario Córdoba* (ⓦdiariocordoba.com), is good for local and provincial news, events and entertainment.

Online information ⓦcordoba.es, ⓦinfocordoba.com.

City guided walks Several companies, including Córdoba Visión and Konexión Tours, offer guided walks around the old city (English spoken; 2–3hr); tickets available at any of the tourist offices.

ACCOMMODATION SEE MAP PAGE 354

Places to **stay** can be found all over Córdoba, but the majority are concentrated in the narrow maze of streets around the Mezquita. If you can resist the urge to lodge on the Mezquita's doorstep, a 5min walk in any direction leads to some real bargains. Finding a room at any time of the year – except during **Semana Santa** and the **May festivals** (the city's high season, and the rates we quote here) – isn't usually a problem. Upmarket places often drop their prices considerably in July and Aug, so it's always worth checking their websites for offers. Where listings below have a garage, unless otherwise stated you will be charged a daily rate for parking (around €10–20).

HOTELS AND HOSTALES

Casa de los Azulejos C/Fernando Colón 5; ⓦcasadelosazulejos.com. Charming small hotel with

distinctive, individually styled rooms, featuring iron bedsteads and artworks, arranged around a leafy patio that's used for art shows. More expensive rooms come with their own terraces. Pool open in summer. Can arrange garage parking. Breakfast is included. €€

Casa de los Naranjos C/Isabel Losa 8; ⓦcasadelosnaranjos.com. In the north of the town near the Pza de Colón, this is a small two-star hotel in a nineteenth-century townhouse with lots of charm and rooms overlooking a leafy patio. Own garage parking. Breakfast is included. €€€

★ **Hostal & Hotel Maestre** C/Romero Barros 4 & 16; ⓦhotelmaestre.com. Excellent *hostal* between C/San Fernando and the Pza del Potro, and neighbouring hotel, with attractive a/c en-suite rooms with TV. Also has some good-value two-person apartments. €

4

★**Hostal Alcázar** C/San Basilio 2; ⊛hostalalcazar. com. Comfortable and welcoming family-run *hostal* with a nice patio and range of a/c, en-suite rooms with TV. Also some good-value fully equipped apartments (sleeping up to four). Own garage nearby. Ten percent discount for direct phone bookings. Breakfast is included. €

Hostal Almanzor C/Cardenal González 10; ⊛hostal-almanzor.es. Attractive central *hostal* near the Pza del Potro where the light and airy soundproofed en-suite rooms come with TV, a/c and balcony. Free use of their car park. €

Hostal La Fuente C/San Fernando 51; ⊛hostallafuente. com. Welcoming *hostal* in a refurbished townhouse with a delightful patio and pristine en-suite rooms with safe, TV and a/c. Also rents out some nearby apartments for two. Wi-fi zone, and parking nearby. €

Hostal La Milagrosa C/Rey Heredia 12; ⊛lamilagrosahostal.es. Attractive and welcoming *hostal* with a beautiful patio and lots of plants, and attractive marble-floored, en-suite, a/c rooms. Quiet roof terrace with views of the Mezquita and beyond to the hills. Own garage. €

Hostal Lineros 38 C/Lineros 38; ⊛hostallineros38. com. This Moorish extravaganza of a *hostal* has been lovingly created by its friendly proprietors inside an ancient Mudéjar mansion. The comfortable rooms continue the theme and Moorish-inspired arabesques and horseshoe arches are everywhere. Own parking. €

Hostal Luís de Góngora C/Horno de la Trinidad 7; ⊛hgongora.com. Attractive a/c en-suite rooms in a friendly *hostal* with a pleasant location on the northern edge of the Judería. A couple of rooms are dark and gloomy, so check what you're offered. €

Hotel Amistad Córdoba Pza de Maimónides 3; ⊛nh-hoteles.com. Four-star hotel (part of the NH chain) incorporating three eighteenth-century mansions with Mudéjar patio and staircase, and located in the same square as the Museo Taurino. Car park available. €€€

★**Hotel Balcón de Córdoba** C/Encarnación 8; ⊛balcondecordoba.com. Luxurious boutique hotel in restored seventeenth-century convent. Lots of original features, plus a patio restaurant, rooftop terrace with close-up views of the Mezquita and comfy, spacious rooms. Parking can be arranged nearby. Breakfast is included. €€€€

Hotel Hacienda Posada de Vallina C/Corregidor Luis de la Cerda 83; ⊛hhposadadevallina.es. A historic *posada* where the Mezquita builders lodged and Columbus stayed (Room 204) on a visit to Isabel and Ferdinand. Opposite the Mezquita; the quiet en-suite rooms have a/c

and many have original features. €€

Hotel Las Casas de la Judería C/Tomás Conde 10; ⊛casasypalacios.com. Four-star hotel in an exquisitely charming restoration of an ancient *casa palacio* with elegant rooms arranged around patios with tinkling fountains and fragrant flowers. Rooms are decorated with period furnishings and artworks. Spa, restaurant and garage. €€€€

Hotel Mezquita Pza Santa Catalina 1; ⊛hotelmezquita. com. Atmospheric, central hotel in a converted sixteenth-century mansion facing the Mezquita's eastern wall. Attractive rooms equipped with satellite TV. €€€

Hotel NH Córdoba Guadalquivir Avda Fray Albino 1; ⊛nh-hoteles.es. Luxurious four-star with great views across the river towards the Mezquita and city from the front rooms. Facilities include restaurant, *cafetería*, pool and rooftop bar, and there's easy access to the town across the pedestrianized Puente Romano. Own garage and easy street parking nearby. €€€

★**Hotel Plateros** Pza Seneca 4; ⊛hotelplateros.com. Small, friendly hotel belonging to the *Plateros* chain of tapas bars and housed in an elegant refurbished old mansion on a charming plazuela. The a/c rooms are pleasant and the tapas bar below incorporates the ancient house's bodega whose walls were once part of the ancient Roman theatre. The hotel encourages cyclists and can store bikes. €€

Hotel Viento 10 C/Ronquillo Briceño 10; ⊛hotelviento10.es. Boutique hotel, near the river in the quieter east of the city, set in a restored seventeenth-century hospital. The light and airy en-suite a/c rooms are around a stunning patio. Luxury extras include a pillow menu, jacuzzi and sauna. €€

La Llave de la Judería C/Romero 38; ⊛lallavedelajuderia.es. Elegant, welcoming nine-room hotel in the Judería, belonging to the restaurant of the same name. The chintzy rooms are classically furnished; some have sit-out terraces. Facilities include minibar, computer with internet in all rooms (free) and rooftop terrace/ solarium. Own garage. Breakfast is included. €€€

Parador de Córdoba Avda de la Arruzafa s/n, 5km north of town in El Brillante suburb; ⊛parador.es. Attractive, modern *parador* with elegant, spacious rooms. Worth a trip for a drink in its gardens or a good-value meal in its terrace restaurant. €€€€

Pensión El Portillo C/Cabezas 2; ⊛pensionelportillo. com. Beautiful old *pensión* in an early nineteenth-century mansion with elegant tiled patio and friendly management. Pleasant, airy rooms – many with balconies – come with showers and include a few singles. €

EATING

SEE MAP PAGE 354

If you've come from Seville or the coast, the nightlife in Córdoba will seem rather tame by comparison. Places start closing at around 11pm, and by midnight the empty streets around the Mezquita, lit by lanterns, have a melancholy air.

When they are open, however, many of the city's **bars and restaurants** are among the best in Andalucía. Córdoba's restaurants are on the whole reasonably priced – and quite a few of the upmarket establishments are really excellent.

Be sure to try Córdoba's two specialities, *rabo de toro* (slow-stewed bull's tail) and *salmorejo* (a chunky gazpacho with pieces of ham and egg), available all over town. The *cordobeses* are proud of their **tabernas** – and with good reason, for few places anywhere can match them for sheer character and variety, not to mention tapas. Remember, too, when ordering *fino* that the equivalent brew here is **Montilla** and the best way to get up a barman's nose is to ask for any of the wines of Jerez, the product of the upstart province downriver. If you're new to Montilla-Moriles, to give it its full title, or have been unimpressed with the insipid concoctions sold abroad under the Montilla name, prepare for a pleasant surprise. Montilla, which vaguely resembles a mellow, dry sherry, is a giant on its native soil, and is considered a healthier tipple by the *cordobeses*; whereas Jerez sherry is fortified with alcohol, the process is totally natural, leading (they insist) to fewer hangovers (see box, page 375).

RESTAURANTS

Almudaina Pza Campo Santo de los Mártires 1; ⓦ restaurantealmudaina.com. Top-notch restaurant in an atmospheric sixteenth-century mansion. Among many fine dishes, the *rabo de toro a la cordobesa* is a house special, as are the artichoke dishes. €€€

★ **Amaltea** C/Ronda de Isasa 10; ⓦ amaltea.es. Excellent organic restaurant with separate veggie and coeliac menus. Specialities include couscous and chicken and mango curry. There are plenty of organic wines and occasional art exhibitions. €€€

El Caballo Rojo C/Cardenal Herrero 28; ⓦ elcaballorojo.com. Beneath the Mezquita's belfry, this is one of Córdoba's long-established and best traditional restaurants. The Moorish-influenced menu offers such specialities as *cordero a la miel* (lamb in honey). Expensive, but offers a *menú del día*. €€€

Casa Mazal C/Tomás Conde 3; ⓦ casamazal.es. *Sefardí* restaurant and cultural centre with a cuisine based on the Sephardic dishes of Spanish Jews such as *bacalao confitado a la naranja, limón y canela* (cod in orange, lemon and cinnamon) and *costillas de cordero con pasas al aroma de la miel* (lamb chops with raisins and honey). Musical events are staged at weekends. €€€

El Choco C/Compositor Serrano Lucena 14; ⓦ restaurantechoco.es. Kisko García regularly renews his Michelin star and offers innovative cuisine at his restaurant in the east of the city with two tasting menus. The menus, which change regularly with the seasons, may include *guiso con choco en amarillo* (cuttlefish stew) and *pato asado lentamente* (slow-cooked duck). Expect creative cooking with some surprises. €€€€

El Choto C/Almanzor 10; ⓦ restauranteelchotocordoba.es. Attractive, small and serious restaurant with a little outdoor terrace offering a range of well-prepared rice, fish and meat dishes including its signature dish *choto asado* (roast kid). €€€

★ **El Churrasco** C/Romero 16; ⓦ elchurrasco.com. One of the best of Córdoba's restaurants, with sumptuously decorated dining rooms and patio in a traditional *cordobés* townhouse. It has a long-standing reputation for its *churrasco ibérico*, a kind of grilled black-pig pork steak, served with pepper sauces. €€€

Mesón San Basilio C/San Basilio 19; ☎ 957 297 007. Excellent little neighbourhood restaurant with a nice patio, friendly service and weekday lunch *menú*. House specials include *presa ibérica* (pork steak) and *berenjenas fritas* (fried aubergine). €€

Noor C/Pablo Ruiz Picasso 8; ⓦ noorrestaurant.es. Córdoba's Michelin starred chef Paco Morales received his accolade for his unique take on Andalucian cuisine, served in his restaurant to the east of the city centre. The three tasting menus take you on a journey to the city's gastronomic past. Morales creates his own versions of thirteenth-century recipes such as *pichón asado con foie* (roast pigeon with foie gras) and *karim de piñones con melón* (a pine nut "soup" with melon). €€€€

La Regadera C/Ronda de Isasa 10; ☎ 957 101 400. Fresh, local produce takes centre stage in this restaurant, with its wall gardens, watering-can decorations and fresh herb garden. Signature dishes include *slow-cooked lamb* and *tartar de atún rojo* (tuna tartare). €€

La Tinaja Paseo de la Ribera 12; ☎ 957 047 998. Located by the river with a pleasant pavement terrace offering a range of tapas and *raciones*, including *mazamorra con atún rojo ahumado* (traditional almond soup with smoked tuna) and *cardos con gambas y almejas* (cardoons with shrimp and clams). €€

TABERNAS, TEAHOUSES AND TAPAS BARS

AROUND THE MEZQUITA AND JUDERÍA

El Abanico C/Velázquez Bosco 7, on the corner of Callejón de las Flores; ☎ 957 113 274. Despite being in the midst of tourist zone and decked in red and white flamenco dots, this is a good spot for tapas and a decent, well-priced lunchtime *menú*. Try the *croquetas de rabo de toro* (oxtail croquettes). €

Bar La Cavea Pza Jerónimo Páez, near the archeological museum; ☎ 957 484 532. Pleasant little bar with nice terrace where you can knock back a *jarrón* of beer with meat and fish tapas, and *raciones*. €

Bar Santos C/Magistral González Francés 3. On the Mezquita's doorstep, this small, busy bar decked in bullfighting memorabilia is famous throughout Andalucía for its football-sized *tortillas*, cooked to perfection. If you're not a Spanish omelette fan, other tapas and *bocadillos* are available. €

La Bicicleta C/Cardenal González 1; ☎ 666 544 690. Small café/bar with bike-themed decor serving salads,

FLAMENCO IN CÓRDOBA

As in many of Córdoba's provincial capitals, plenty of **flamenco** is on offer – but much of it is dire and tourist oriented. The places below can be depended upon for some reasonably authentic stuff. Free flamenco performances are also mounted by the local council and various other concerts are staged at the Gran Teatro, Avda Gran Capitán 3, and in the Alcázar gardens (details from the turismos and ⓦ cordobaflamenca.com).

La Bulería C/Pedro López 3, near Pza de la Corredera; ☎ 957 483 839. Nightly flamenco performances with *cantante* El Calli and his family forming the core of the show. They are serious and it gets near enough to the real thing. Food also served. Cover includes a free drink. Performances Tues–Sat 10.30pm.

Peña Flamenca "Fosforito" Pza Beatillas 1 in Taberna las Beatillas; ⓦ fosforitocordoba.es. This bar hosts authentic flamenco arranged by the Peña Fosforito, one of the oldest flamenco associations in the city. Check the website for details of performances and get there early to be sure of a seat. There are usually several performances a month, at 10pm.

Tablao Cardenal C/Buen Pastor 2, in the Judería; ⓦ tablaocardenal.es. Córdoba's best non-membership flamenco *tablao*, where you can catch performances by established artists in a pleasant open-air patio. It's reserving in advance for a front-line table. Cover includes first drink. Performances Mon–Thurs 10pm, Fri & Sat 10.30pm.

---

snacks, cheese boards, juices and yoghurts, plus some delicious homemade cakes. €

★ **Bodega Guzmán** C/Judíos 7; ☎ 957 290 960. Cavernous old bar frequented by bullfight aficionados, with a small *taurino* "museum" in its inner sanctum and outstanding Montilla served from a butt behind the bar. A very tasty *salmorejo* and *albóndigas* (pork meatballs) are house specials here. €

Salón de Té C/Buen Pastor 13; ⓦ lacasaandalusi. com. To the northwest of the Mezquita's belfry is this very attractive Moroccan tea salon with a charming patio offering over fifty varieties, including a special *hierba buena* (mint tea), as well as snacks. €

Taberna la Viuda C/San Basilio 52; ⓦ tabernalaviuda. com. Traditional tapas and *raciones* restaurant with a variety of dishes including *flamenquín con queso viejo* (deep-fried meat roll with cured cheese) and *revuelto de calabacín y ahumados* (courgette with scrambled eggs and smoked fish). Art exhibitions and live music on Tuesdays. €€

La Tata C/Zapatería Vieja 13; ☎ 628 806 648. Blink and you'll miss this tiny venue tucked off C/Cardenal González, but the generous *raciones* and daily *menú* are worth seeking out. The menu often changes. but expect hearty local fare. €€

AROUND THE PLAZA DEL POTRO

★ **Bodega Sociedad de Plateros** C/San Francisco 6; ☎ 957 470 042. Headquarters of the Plateros chain (with three bars in the city), and in a converted former convent. This bar serves a wide range of tapas including *rabo de toro* or tasty *berenjenas a la miel* (fried aubergines with honey), perfect partners for any of their own brands of Montilla. €€

Bodegas Campos C/Lineros 32; ⓦ bodegascampos. com. A wonderful, rambling old bodega where you can see the giant barrel-stocked cellars, signed by famous visitors including members of the Spanish royal family and ex-

British premier Tony Blair. The bar at the entrance sells their own excellent Montilla, where there are also excellent (if pricey) tapas. €€

AROUND AND NORTH OF PLAZA TENDILLAS

★ **Taberna San Miguel** Pza San Miguel 1; ⓦ casaelpisto.com. Known as *El Pisto* (ratatouille) and virtually unchanged for over a century, this is one of the city's legendary bars. Wonderful Montilla and tapas such as *rabo de toro*, *callos en salsa picante* (tripe) and the eponymous house *pisto*. €€

Taberna Séneca Pza Séneca 4; ⓦ hotelplateros.com. In the same building as the *Hotel Plateros* (see page 366) this is another bar in the Plateros chain serving the same great tapas and Montilla. House specials include *puntas de solomillo* (pork loin). They also serve a good *menú del día*. €€

AROUND PLAZA CORREDERA AND BEYOND

Casa El Juramento C/Juramento 6; ☎ 957 485 477. Atmospheric old bar with a charming patio and a good tapas selection. House specials include *croquetas de espinacas* (spinach croquettes) and *pimientos rellenos* (stuffed peppers). €

★ **El Gallo** C/María Cristina 6; ☎ 957 471 780. Fine old *cordobés* drinking hole that has changed little since it opened in 1936. Good tapas selection includes *calamares* and *gambas rebozadas* (fried prawns). The outstanding *amargoso* Montilla comes from their own bodega and is also sold by the bottle. €€

Sociedad Plateros C/María Auxiliadora 25; ⓦ sociedadplateros.com. Aficionados of the Plateros chain will enjoy this cavernous old mini-Mezquita serving up excellent *raciones* and *medias*. Some way from the centre, it's definitely worth the walk. House specials include *venado en salsa* (venison), and *bacalao al pil-pil* (cod in garlic). €€

★ **Taberna Salinas** C/Tundidores 3; ⓦ tabernasalinas. com. Reasonably priced *taberna* established in 1879, with dining rooms around a charming patio. Good *raciones* place – try their *naranjas con bacalao* (cod with oranges) – and serves a great *salmorejo*. €€

El Tercio Viejo C/Enrique Redel 17; ☎ 957 004 441. Handy for the Palacio de Viana, this popular local bar serves traditional tapas and *raciones* such as *rabo de toro* and *callos con chorizo* (tripe with chorizo) and the Córdoba delicacy *caracoles* (snails, served in spicy broth in a large cup). €

SHOPPING

SEE MAP PAGE 354

Córdoba is known for **silver** jewellery and embossed **leather** goods, both on offer at many workshops in the streets around the Mezquita.

Almacen Rafael C/Dr Barraquer 5, to the northeast of the Alcázar; ☎ 957 203 183. A well-stocked bodega selling most of Córdoba's Montilla wines.

El Corte Inglés Avda del Gran Capitán, at the junction with Avda Ronda de los Tejares; ⓦ elcorteingles.es. Córdoba's branch of the nationally famous department store.

Espaliu Ronda de Isaac 12; ⓦ joaquinespaliu.com. Stylish silver jewellery on sale at a riverside shop near the

Mezquita; they create their own designs.

Librería Luque C/Jesús y María 6 (slightly south of Pza Tendillas); ⓦ librerialuque.es. A good selection of books and walking maps.

Meryan Callejón de las Flores 2 (entry also via C/ Encarnación); ⓦ meryancor.com. This is one of the best places to buy authentic "Made in Córdoba" leather goods.

Zoco (market) C/Judíos, close to the synagogue. Spain's first designated handicraft market opened in the 1950s in a restored Mudéjar building with lovely patio. Shops sell a range of handcrafted goods including filigree silver jewellery and you can watch the artisans at work.

DIRECTORY

Banks Numerous banks with ATMs are located along Ronda de los Tejares and Avda del Gran Capitán. In the Judería there are ATMs in C/Torrijos on the northwest corner of the Mezquita and C/Corregidor Luis de la Cerda on the south side of the monument.

Hospital Hospital Reina Sofía, Avda Menéndez Pidal s/n (☎ 957 010 000), southwest of the centre. Cruz Roja, Paseo de la Victoria s/n (☎ 957 420 666); for emergencies dial ☎ 061.

Laundry Seco y Agua, C/Dr Marañon 3, slightly northwest of the Alcázar (Mon–Fri 9.30am–1.30pm & 5.30–8.30pm, Sat 9.30am–1.30pm), is an efficient *tintorería*; they will wash, dry and fold 5kg of clothes the same day.

Police A local police station is located in Pza Judá Levi, near the Mezquita (☎ 957 290 760). For emergencies dial ☎ 092 (local police), ☎ 091 (national).

Post office The main office is at C/Cruz Conde 15, just north of Pza Tendillas (Mon–Fri 8.30am–8.30pm, Sat 9am–2pm).

4

West of Córdoba

Just a few kilometres from the city is the historic site of **Medina Azahara**, a must for those on the Moorish trail, and with a fascinating eighteenth-century hermitage nearby. As you continue west along the southern fringes of the Sierra Morena, following the course of the Rio Guadalquivir, you will come to **Almodóvar del Río**, which has a remarkable castle, and can stop off at a string of charming rural towns. This area also features Córdoba province's largest natural park, the **Parque Natural de la Sierra de Hornachuelos**, a wonderful spot for birdwatching.

Medina Azahara

Mid-June to mid-Sept daily 9am–3.30pm; mid-Sept to March Tues–Sat 9am–6.30pm, Sun 9am–3.30pm; April to mid-June Tues–Sat 9am–8.30pm, Sun 9am–3.30pm • Charge • ☎ 957 103 637• There are a number of transport options (see page 372)

Some 7km to the west of Córdoba lie the vast and rambling ruins of **Medina Azahara**, a palace and administrative complex built on a dream scale by **Caliph Abd ar-Rahman III**. Naming it after a favourite wife, az-Zahra (the Radiant), he spent one third of the annual state budget on its construction each year from 936 until his death in 961. Since the first archeological excavations were carried out in 1911, work has been going on more or less continuously to piece together the fragments of this once fabulous creation, which is the reason it is currently only possible to visit a fraction of the excavated site. Over a century later, archeologists have excavated a mere ten percent of the site (including two thirds of the palace and the entire medina) and only five percent is currently open to the public. Note also that the same archeological and restoration work is ongoing and the route described below may have to be altered to allow for this.

Dar al-Wuzara and Plaza de Armas

The **site** is entered by the **Puerta Norte**, the typically Moorish "twisted gate" that forced would-be invaders to double back on themselves, thus making them easy targets. Behind you at this point lies the Dar al-Mulk or royal palace (currently not open to visitors), which is thought to have been the residence of Abd ar-Rahman III. The signed route leads to **Dar al-Wuzara** (House of the Viziers, aka Edificio Basilical), believed to have been the bureaucratic heart of the complex with administrative rooms, archives and a grand salon (with reconstructed horseshoe arches), originally fronted by a patio, now a garden. To the east of here, the route leads to the elegant arched **portico** and the **Plaza de Armas** – formerly a grand parade ground – beyond, still awaiting excavation. The portico is thought to have supported a balcony terrace from where the caliph reviewed his troops. Turning south, you can see the **Aljama mosque** below, one of the first buildings to be constructed on the site, oriented towards the southeast and Mecca. Its ground plan allows you to make out the main entrance, flanked by the base of a minaret (*alminar*), with patio, prayer hall – the floor of which was covered with esparto mats found in the excavations – and *mihrab*. The route now veers west passing the princely baths to the right, with washing fountains and marble surfaces, beyond which lay the royal apartments.

Royal House

For centuries, the site was looted for building materials; parts, for instance, were used in the Seville Alcázar (see page 251) and much of the surrounding town served as a quarry for the fifteenth-century construction of the monastery of San Jerónimo (now privately owned) at the end of the track that climbs above the ruins. In 1944, however, excavations unearthed the buried materials from a crucial part of the palace, the **Royal House**, where guests were received and meetings of ministers held. This has been meticulously reconstructed and, though still fragmentary, its main hall, the **Salón Rico de Abd al-Rahman III** – now restored to its formal glory – decorated with exquisite

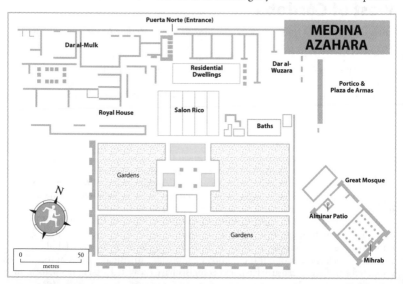

THE RISE AND FALL OF MEDINA AZAHARA

Ten thousand workers and 1500 mules and camels were employed in the construction of **Medina Azahara** in the early tenth century, and the site, almost 2000m long by 900m wide, stretched over three descending terraces above the Guadalquivir valley. Roman masonry was taken from sites throughout Andalucía and reused, while vast quantities of marble were shipped in from North Africa. In addition to the palace buildings, the complex contained a zoo, an aviary, four huge fish ponds, three hundred baths, four hundred houses, weapons factories, two barracks for the royal guard as well as markets, workshops and mosques. Visitors, so the chronicles record, were stunned by its wealth and brilliance: one conference room contained a pile of pure crystals, creating a rainbow when lit by the sun; another was built round a huge shallow bowl of mercury which, when the sun's rays fell on it, would be rocked by a slave, sending sunbeams reflected from its surface flashing and whizzing around the room, apparently alarming guests but greatly amusing the caliph.

Medina Azahara was a perfect symbol of the western caliphate's dominance and greatness, but it was to last for less than a century. Al-Hakam II, who succeeded Abd ar-Rahman, lived in the palace, continued to endow it, and enjoyed a stable reign. However, distanced from the city, he delegated more and more authority, particularly to his vizier Ibn Abi Amir, later known as al-Mansur (the Victor). In 976 al-Hakam was succeeded by his 11-year-old son Hisham II but after a series of sharp moves al-Mansur assumed the full powers of government, keeping Hisham virtually imprisoned at Medina Azahara, to the extent of blocking up connecting passageways between the palace buildings.

Al-Mansur was equally skilful and manipulative in his wider dealings as a dictator, and Córdoba rose to new heights of prosperity, retaking large tracts of central Spain and raiding as far afield as Galicia and Catalunya. But with his death in 1002 came swift decline as his role and function were assumed in turn by his two sons. The first died in 1008; the second, Sanchol, showed open disrespect for the caliphate by forcing Hisham to appoint him as his successor. At this, a popular revolt broke out and the caliphate disintegrated into civil war and a series of feudal kingdoms. Medina Azahara was looted by a mob at the outset and in 1010 was plundered and burned by retreating Berber mercenaries – splashes of molten metal from this conflagration are still to be seen in the Salon Rico. The ruins slowly disappeared under the earth until archeologists arrived at the site in the early twentieth century. But it was never secure and as late as the 1930s a visiting Gerald Brenan saw stones being carted off to service other buildings. In the 1960s academic study, excavation and reconstruction of the complex began in earnest, and this is set to continue for many decades to come.

marble carvings and mosaics, must rank among the greatest of all Moorish rooms. Modelled on the Roman basilica, it has a different kind of artistic representation from that found in the palaces at Granada or Seville – closer to natural and animal forms in its intricate Syrian Hom (Tree of Life) motifs. Unlike the later Spanish Arab dynasties, the Berber Almoravids and the Almohads of Seville, the caliphal Andalucians were little worried by Islamic strictures on the portrayal of nature, animals or even men – the beautiful stag in the site museum is a good example (see page 372) – and it may well have been this aspect of the palace's artistic decor that led to such zealous destruction during the civil war (see box, page 371). The reconstructed palace gives a scale and focus to the site, while elsewhere work continues in restoring and rebuilding more ruined structures. Beyond these there are little more than foundations, gardens and the odd horseshoe arch to fuel your imaginings, amid an awesome area of ruins, hidden beneath bougainvillea and rustling with cicadas.

Gardens

Over a decade ago biologists from Córdoba University carried out a study of soil samples from the site to gain an understanding of exactly which plants and flowers the Moors had cultivated in the extensive **gardens**. When the study was completed, planting began in an attempt to reconstruct the gardens of Medina Azahara as accurately as possible. The planted trees, shrubs, plants and herbs have now matured into a delightful and aromatic garden the caliphs would recognize.

Museum

Among the exhibits at the **museum** inside the Centro de Interpretación are outstanding examples of ceramics, glassware and carved stone and marble unearthed in the excavations. One superb work transferred from Córdoba's archeological museum is an exquisite tenth-century **bronze stag** – a gift of the Byzantine emperor Constantine VII to Abd ar-Rahman III – and found at the Moorish palace where it was used as the spout of a fountain.

ARRIVAL AND DEPARTURE   MEDINA AZAHARA

All visitors must arrive at the **Centro de Interpretación**, a state-of-the-art complex incorporating a museum, shop and *cafetería* as well as research facilities for scholars and archeologists. Here you are required to park any vehicle and pick up your entry tickets. Once you have your ticket you are free to walk the 2km to the site, but it is all uphill; best to take a bus (every 10–20min; charge) from the car park outside the Centro.

By bus A dedicated bus service links Córdoba with the site (April–Sept Tues–Sat 10.15am & 5pm, Sun 9.30am & 10.15am; Oct–March Tues–Sun 9.30am & 10.15am, which includes the bus to the site itself). The bus departs from a signed stop on the Glorieta (roundabout) Cruz Roja at the southern end of Paseo de la Victoria (confirm this at the tourist office); note that tickets must be bought in advance from any municipal tourist office kiosko. You could also take bus #01 or #02 from Avda de la República Argentina (at the northern end, near a petrol station); this will drop you off at

the intersection (cross with extreme care as the road is busy and there's no pedestrian crossing), from where it's a 1km walk to the Centro de Interpretación. Ask the driver for "El Cruce de Medina Azahara".

By car To drive to Medina Azahara Centro de Interpretación from Córdoba, follow Avda de Medina Azahara west out of town onto the road to Villarubia and Posadas. About 4km down this road, make a right turn (signed for the site), after which it's another 1km to the Centro de Interpretación.

By taxi A taxi from Córdoba will cost you at least €50 return for up to four people (including an hour wait) at the site while you visit. A convenient taxi rank is located outside the Turismo on the west side of the Mezquita.

Guided tours Córdoba Vision runs guided trips to the site (Tues–Sat 10.15am, 11am & 5pm, Sun 10.15am & 11am; ☎ 902 201 774; English spoken); buses leave from the same stop as the dedicated bus service, at the Glorieta (roundabout) Cruz Roja (see page 372).

EATING AND DRINKING

Los Almendros Ctra de Trassiera km8; ⓦ restaurantelosalmendros.com. A kilometre along the road beyond the *El Cruce* restaurant, this is a good *venta* serving typical *cordobés* cuisine including *rabo de toro* and *salmorejo* as well as lamb and venison. There's also a *menú cordobés*. €€

Restaurante El Candil C/Académico Menéndez Pidal,

Trassierra, 4km from Los Almendro on the CO-3402; ☎ 957 730 044. This is a popular place with locals who flock here for the *carnes a la brasa* (grilled meats) and game, with a pleasant eating area inside and leafy terrace outside. Try the *alcachofas a la Montillana* (artichokes in Montilla sauce) or the *arroz con setas y jabalí* (rice with wild mushrooms and boar). €€€

Las Ermitas

Tues–Sun: June to mid-Sept 10am–1.30pm; mid-Sept–May 10am–1.30pm & 4.30–6.30pm • Charge

A scenic signed road climbs for 3km beyond the *Los Almendros* (see page 372) to **Las Ermitas**, a beautiful jasmine-scented hermitage filled with cypresses, olives and cacti. Here you can see twelve cells dating from the eighteenth century – spaced out around a central shrine – where hermit monks once flagellated themselves in splendid isolation. These hills were inhabited by hermits from the earliest days of Christianity through the Visigothic and Muslim periods and solitaries occupied the hermitage until as recently as 1957. There are dramatic **views** over the valley of the Guadalquivir and Córdoba from the *mirador* of the giant cross, La Cruz del Humilladero.

Almodóvar del Río

Buses run from Córdoba to **ALMODÓVAR DEL RÍO**, where an impressive multi-turreted **castle** (April–Sept Mon–Fri 11am–2.30pm & 4–8pm, Sat & Sun 11am–8pm; Oct–March Mon–Fri 11am–2.30pm & 4–8pm, Sat & Sun 11am–7pm; charge; ⍵castillodealmodovar.com) sits on a hill high above the town dominating the landscape. Dating originally from the eighth century, and significantly expanded by Abd al-Rahman II in the ninth, the fortress underwent many later additions and restorations, most of them following its fall to the Christian army of Fernando III in 1240. Today the castle is owned by the Marqués de Motilla. It's a pleasant walk up from the town, and though there's little to see in the over-restored interior – now filled with rather tedious "historical" tableaux –there are fine **views** over the valley of the Guadalquivir from the battlements and patio where you can quaff some refreshment at the castle tavern.

Parque Natural de la Sierra de Hornachuelos

Some 20km west of Almodóvar del Río along the A431, a turn on the right (the A2212) leads after 8km to **HORNACHUELOS**, the gateway village to the extensive **Parque Natural de la Sierra de Hornachuelos**, a heavily wooded area on the lower slopes of the Sierra Morena. The park, rich in birdlife, is home to one of Andalucía's largest colonies of black vultures and Griffon vultures, along with a wide range of wildlife including the threatened Iberian lynx, deer, wild boar and, in the river valleys, otters.

ARRIVAL AND INFORMATION   PARQUE NATURAL DE LA SIERRA DE HORNACHUELOS

The park is best reached with your own transport.
Turismo Recinto Ferial s/n (Tues & Wed 9am–3pm, Thurs–Sun 10am–2pm; ⍵turismohornachuelos.es). This helpful office, signed on the right as you by-pass Hornachuelos, has information and maps.
Centro de Visitantes Huerta del Rey This is the park's main information centre, 2km beyond Hornachuelos as

you head into the park, and signed on the left (July–Sept Fri–Sun 9am–2pm; Oct–June Wed–Fri 10am–2pm, Sat & Sun 10am–2pm & 4–6pm, 6–8pm May & June; ☎957 579 656). It has informative displays on the park's flora and fauna and can provide maps and information on numerous waymarked walking routes.

ACCOMMODATION AND EATING

El Álamo Ctra Comarcal 141; ⍵complejoelalamo.com. A relatively upmarket motel-style option, with a/c en-suite rooms located in tasteful *cortijo* surroundings. The main building also has its own bar-restaurant. €
Cañada Verde Ctra Palma del Río s/n, to the west of

the village; ☎696 375 768. Large country house with stunning views of the woods and mountains. Clean, basic en-suite rooms with a/c and TV. Complex includes a pool, adventure park and wildlife park. Own restaurant. €€

The Campiña

To the south of Córdoba, and stretching to the mountains of the province's southern border, lies the **Campiña Cordobesa**. A fertile, undulating region of wheatfields, olive groves and productive vineyards, it has been renowned since Roman times when the eminent Roman writers Pliny and Martial praised its artichokes, fruit, wool and the excellence of its olive oil. The town of **Baena** keeps up the tradition with an oil so good that it carries an official *denominación de origen* label. Each of the villages of the Campiña has its own interesting castle, church, palace or Roman villa and sometimes a bodega – and there are towns such as **Priego de Córdoba**, a Baroque architectural feast and well off the tourist trail, that are undiscovered jewels. Even the smallest villages usually have a *hostal* or hotel, which opens up the possibility of **walks** exploring some of the Campiña's delightful countryside including – in its lower reaches – the **Parque Natural de las Sierras Subbéticas**, replete with wooded hills and river valleys. Many of the tourist offices in this zone stock a free bilingual booklet, *Guía de Senderismo*, which details eighteen walks in the park.

The towns and some of the larger villages are accessible by bus from Córdoba, but in many cases buses run few and far between. Your best bet for exploring the area is with your own transport.

Ruta del Vino

Leaving Córdoba by the A45 and then forking left along the N331 brings you to **Fernán Núñez**, a pleasant hill village. Among a number of interesting places further along this route are **Montilla**, the centre of Córdoba's wine production, **Rute**, where *anís*, a far stronger brew, is concocted, and the beautiful lakeside village of **Iznájar**, in the midst of some good trekking country.

Montemayor

Just beyond the village of Fernán Núñez is **MONTEMAYOR**, a charming and typical *campiña* village with a fourteenth-century **castle**. Off its neat little central plaza is the sixteenth-century church of **Nuestra Señora de la Asunción** (open during services Mon–Fri 9am, Sat & Sun 9am & noon; free) with a beautifully painted stucco sagrario and a sixteenth-century carved baptismal font, still used to initiate the newborn of the parish. The huge, famous **archeological collection** belonging to the priest (Padre Pablo Moyano) and the village was moved in 2013 from the church to the **Museo Arqueológico de Vlia** (as Montemayor was called in Roman times; Tues–Sat 10am–2pm, plus second and last Thursday of the month 11am–2pm; free; ☎957 384 582) where you can view the enormous accumulation of artefacts including coins, agricultural implements, grindstones, jewellery and sculpture, collected on the priest's walks in the surrounding fields over the years.

Hotel Castillo de Montemayor Ctra Córdoba–Málaga km35; ⓦhotelcastillodemontemayor.com. This is the best of a clutch of accommodation options around this road junction. The rooms are comfortable (get one at the back overlooking their garden pool for a better view) and below there's a decent-value restaurant with an outdoor terrace. €

Montilla

Beyond Montemayor the A45 highway presses on into the Sierra de Montilla and endless rows of vines begin to creep across the landscape as you enter Córdoba's **wine-producing region**. The tough Pedro-Ximénez vines planted here have to withstand searing summer temperatures, and send their roots deep down into the whitish-grey *albariza* soil searching for moisture. Eleven kilometres beyond Montemayor, **MONTILLA**, the capital of Córdoba's wine country, comes into view. Hardly the region's prettiest town, it does however boast one of its leading **bodegas**, a picturesque place founded in the eighteenth century.

Hostal Bellido C/Enfermería 57 ⓦhostalbellido.com. A welcoming and good-value *hostal* housed in an elegantly refurbished mansion right in the centre of town. The en-suite rooms are comfortable and come with TV, a/c and heating. €
Restaurante Las Camachas Avda de Europa 3, on the main road at the entrance to the town; ☎957 650 004. A very good, long-established restaurant renowned for its traditional *cordobés* cuisine such as *rabo de toro* (braised oxtail) and *alcachofas al Montilla* (artichokes in Montilla sauce). All washed down with Montilla from their wine cellar. €€€

Aguilar de la Frontera

AGUILAR DE LA FRONTERA, 7km south of Montilla, perched on top of a hill with a ruined ninth-century castle, is worth a visit to see its wonderful eighteenth-century octagonal plaza of **San José**, probably inspired by the better-maintained one at Archidona in Málaga. The rest of the town is equally charming, its sloping streets lined

MONTILLA-MORILES: NO HANGOVER GUARANTEED

The Romans and later the Moors (in spite of the Prophet's prohibition) developed the Campiña as a wine region. The great wine of Córdoba, **Montilla** (often called Montilla-Moriles, the latter village being its partner in production to the south) has suffered over the years from comparison with the wines of Jerez, with which it shares similar characteristics. The reasons for this are largely historical as, prior to the 1940s, much of Córdoba's vintage was sold to the great fino houses of Jerez and eventually marketed as sherry. In 1944 this was made illegal, after which Montilla was granted its own *denominación*, but the notion that the wines of this region are merely a less expensive alternative to sherry has been a tag that the industry here has found hard to shake off.

The most visual difference in the production of Montilla is the great *tinajas* – huge, earthenware urns in which the wine undergoes its fermentation. These Ali-Baba jars, direct descendants of the Roman dolium, have pointed ends that are buried in the earth inside the bodegas and are believed to impart a unique character to the wine. As in Jerez, the wine in these great vats also develops a flor (a thick layer of yeast) that covers the narrow neck of the urns. Later, the solera system (see box, page 172), during which the wine is aged and blended in oak butts for two years, is used to finish the process. If you happen to compare Montilla with the finos of Jerez, locals will tell you that Montilla doesn't need its alcohol added. The Pedro-Ximénez grape used for Montilla is baked in the furnace heat of the Campiña sun and produces wines of sixteen percent proof which, the bodegas here like to claim – unlike that synthetic *jerezano* – never give you a hangover.

Alvear SA Avda María Auxiliadora 1; ⊚ alvear.es. Founded in 1729 by Diego Alvear and still in the hands of the same family, this major producer of Montilla wines offers visits and tastings. (Book in advance for English visits.)

with white-walled houses, their windows protected by *rejas*, or iron grilles. From the **Torre del Reloj** (open only at Christmas and February 28 or for pre-booked visits; ☎ 957 688 203), a Baroque clock tower and local landmark, there are excellent views over the Campiña. At the top of the Cuesta de Jesús, the sixteenth-century **Santa María del Soterraño** (open service times; try 7.30–8.30pm), with an *artesonado* Mudéjar ceiling, Plateresque doorway and an impressive sagrario with a sculpture of Christ in a *camarín* by Donaire Trexo, is Aguilar's best church.

Centro de Interpretación del Paisaje y de la Historia (CIPHAF)

Cerro del Castillo • Tues 9.30am–1.30pm, Wed–Sun 9.30am–1.30pm & 5–7pm • Free • ☎ 957 661 771

At the entrance to the castle, the new visitors' centre is based around the Neolithic archeological remains found in the middle of the castle walls. Displays detail the finds and there's a video reconstruction of the castle, as well as fine views of the Campiña.

INFORMATION AND EATING
AGUILAR

Turismo Cerro del Castillo (Tues 9.30am–1.30pm, Wed–Sun 9.30am–1.30pm & 5–7pm; ☎ 957 661 771). The office based at the CIPHAF (see page 375) in the castle can provide you with information both on the town as well as the Sierra Subbética.

★ **La Casona** Avda Puente de Genil 6; ☎ 957 660 439.

Aguilar's best place to eat lies on the edge of town along the Puente Genil road. The restaurant offers well-prepared *venta*-style food – *solomillo* (pork loin), *salmorejo* and *rabo de toro* are specials – though the weekday *menú* is uninspiring. €€

Laguna de Zóñar

Some 4km southwest of Aguilar along the A309 and easily walkable, the **Laguna de Zóñar** is the largest of a group of little-known inland salt lakes. Visited in winter by large numbers of **migrating waterfowl**, this time of the year is best for spotting white-headed duck, a species that once almost disappeared but is now on the increase. Other

THE ERMITA DE LA VIRGEN

On the road leading east out of Cabra towards Priego de Córdoba, there's a wooded picnic and swimming area, **La Fuente del Río**, centred around a natural spring that is the source of the Río Cabra. Seven kilometres beyond this, a road on the left climbs 6km to the **Ermita de la Virgen de la Sierra**, a hermitage sited at an altitude of over 1200m from where there are stupendous **views** west towards the valley of the Guadalquivir, and east to the mountains of the Sierra Nevada. This is also the starting point for a hike to Zuheros (see page 383) via the Polje de la Nava, a marshy Karst basin, and the Chorreras waterfall, spectacular after rain.

★ **Venta Los Pelaos** C/Priego km5, at the start of the road to the Ermita de la Virgen; ☎ 957 724 655. This outstanding restaurant is a great place for a meal, with economically priced dishes and a terrace, though you'll struggle to get a table on Sun lunchtimes. €€

species that can be seen here include red-crested pochard, mallard, great-crested grebe, tufted duck and marsh harrier. In summer there's less to see, although sometimes flamingos fly in from the Fuente de Piedra in nearby Málaga, for a change of scene. Note that you can still gain access to routes around the lake and the lakeside hides when the visitor centre is closed. Other lakes in this group include the Laguna del Rincón, north of Moriles, and the Laguna de Tiscar, north of Puente Genil, both of which, unlike this one, tend to dry up in summer.

INFORMATION   LAGUNA DE ZÓNAR

Laguna de Zóñar Centro de Información Displays relating to the lagoon's flora and fauna, particularly birdlife (April & May Wed–Fri 9am–2pm, Sat & Sun 9am–2pm & 4–6pm; June, July & Sept Fri–Sun 9am–1pm; Oct–March Wed–Sun 9am–1pm; ☎ 957 335 252).

Cabra

22km from Aguilar, along the A45 and A342, is the pleasant Campiña town of **CABRA**. Possessing an old quarter with steep, winding streets lined with *rejas* – many holding pots sprouting colourful geraniums in summer – and a number of Baroque mansions, it's a lovely place to wander for an hour or so, or even stop over.

At the end of the town, near the medieval castle, the Baroque **Iglesia de la Asunción** (access only 30min before mass; ask at the Turismo, see page 377) was built over a mosque and is surrounded by palms and cypresses. It has a fine portal with twisted marble Solomonic pillars, and inside, an altar of red and black jasper together with fine choir stalls. The church of **San Juan Bautista** (access restricted to 30min before mass; ask at the

THE VÍA VERDE

The decline of the railway in the area south of Córdoba has had a beneficial knock-on effect for walkers and cyclists. The old line of the Tren de Aceite (olive oil train), which was closed in the 1980s, has now been transformed into the **Vía Verde** (❿ viasverdes.com), a rambling and biking route linking the towns and villages of Puente Genil, Lucena, Cabra, Doña Mencía, Zuheros and Luque, with a further extension planned to the east. Some of the stations along the route have been transformed into bars, restaurants and information centres. There are two outdoor activity centres and at its eastern end the route passes La Laguna del Conde (aka Laguna Salobral), the largest lagoon in the Subbética with a wealth of birdlife and its own information centre.

Vía Verde Centro de Interpretación Near the Fuente del Río, in Cabra's former railway station, signed on the left along the Avda de Góngora 500m before the Fuente itself. Opening times vary, call the Turismo for details (see page 377). Information for all the Vía Verde with details on walking and cycling (mountain bikes can be rented) along the route. Also has a *cafetería* and museum – complete with an original steam engine from the Tren de Aceite (oil train) – documenting the history of the line.

Turismo) in the old quarter – Visigothic in origin but much altered since – is reckoned to be one of Spain's oldest, with Moorish and Baroque features added. The Casa de Cultura, C/Martín Belda 27, holds a modest **archeological museum** (Tues & Sat 5–8pm, Wed–Fri & Sun 11am–2pm & 5–8pm; free) with local finds from the prehistoric, Visigothic, Roman and Moorish periods. On the same street to the west is the Círculo de la Amistad, Cabra's fine Casino with a lovely patio (daily 10am–2pm, 5–8pm). Just to the north of the central Parque Alcántara Romero, the town's ancient **Plaza de Toros**, built in 1857, is also worth a look (its gate is usually left open and you're free to wander around).

INFORMATION CABRA

Turismo C/Mayor 1, close to the Asunción church (July & Aug Mon–Sat 9.30am–2pm, Sun 11am–2pm; Sept–June Mon–Sat 9.30am–2pm & 4–8pm, Sun 11am–2pm; ☎ 957 523 493; ⓦ turismodecabra.es).

ACCOMMODATION

Hotel Villa María C/Antonio Povedano 23; ⓦ villamariacabra.com. An upmarket option near the Santo Domingo church in a well-refurbished townhouse with attractive a/c en-suite rooms with TV. Rates are around twenty percent cheaper Mon–Thurs. €€

Pensión Guerrero C/Pepita Jiménez 7, close to the Parque Alcántara Romero; ⓦ pensionguerrero.com. A very friendly budget *hostal* with a/c en-suite rooms with TV. Also some singles and accessible accommodation, plus bike storage. *Rough Guide* readers carrying this guide can claim a ten percent discount. €

EATING AND DRINKING

La Beltrana C/Antonio Povedano 23; ☎ 857 894 040. Part of the *Hotel Villa María*, with specials including *boquerones en vinagre* (anchovies) and *carillada de carne* (grilled meat). There's a pleasant summer terrace and a good weekday *menú*. €€

★ **Mesón La Casilla** C/Martín Belda 14; ⓦ mesonlacasilla.com. One of Cabra's top restaurants, with excellent service and superb *cordobés* specialities such as *alcachofas al hierbabuena* (artichokes with mint) and *medallones de frito de solomillo* (fried pork steak). There's also a weekday *menú*. €€

Mesón San Martín Pza de España 6; ⓦ mesonsanmartin.com. Very pleasant Michelin-recommended restaurant on an attractive square and with a small pavement terrace. A range of local specialities include *flamenquines* and black-pig cold cuts. €€

Lucena

Surrounded by hills covered with vines and olives, **LUCENA**, 11km down the N331 from Monturque, is a large industrial town that makes its money from furniture production and the manufacture of the great *tinajas*, or earthenware urns, used in the making of Montilla (see box, page 375). Once you've penetrated the rather drab outskirts, Lucena's revamped town centre is not without charm and there are a handful of sights well worth a look. A centre of learning in Moorish times, Lucena fell into Christian hands in 1240 when it was besieged by the armies of Fernando III El Santo, following which event most of its churches and other monuments were erected.

Castillo del Moral

Pza de España s/n • Daily 10am–6pm • Charge • ☎ 957 503 662

The focal **Plaza del Coso** (aka Plaza de España) is overlooked by the **Castillo del Moral** whose tower, the Torre del Moral, is the surviving remnant of an earlier castle where Boabdil, the last sultan of Granada, was briefly imprisoned by Isabel la Católica in 1483. The castle has an interesting **archeological museum** that focuses on Lucena's role in Roman times as a centre of *alfarería* (pottery).

Palacio de los Condes de Santa Ana

C/San Pedro 42 • Tues–Sat 10.30am–2pm & 5–8pm, Sun 10.30am–2pm • Free • ☎ 957 509 990

The stunning eighteenth-century Baroque Palacio de los Condes de Santa Ana houses the tourist office (on the ground floor next to a fine patio) and the town's museum on the first floor, reached via a lovely tiled staircase crowned by a spectacular octagonal dome.

San Mateo

Pza Nueva s/n • Daily 7.30am–1.30pm & 6.30–9pm • Free • ☏ 957 500 775

The church of **San Mateo** on the Plaza Nueva, a short walk northwest of the castle, houses some of the Baroque glories of the province. The church was started in the fifteenth century over a former mosque and has a superb Mannerist retablo and a beautiful eighteenth-century Baroque sagrario, with painted stucco cherubs and a feast of decorative detail topped off by a remarkable cupola, all the work of local artist Antonio de Castro.

Santuario de Nuestra Señora de Araceli

Mon–Fri 8.30am–2.30pm & 4.30–9.30pm, Sat & Sun 8.30am–3pm & 6–10.30pm • Free • ☏ 957 334 837

At the town's southern end, a road (CP 157) climbs to the **Santuario de Nuestra Señora de Araceli**, Lucena's much-venerated 900m-high hilltop shrine to the Virgin. The 6km trip is only really worth doing if you've got your own transport, though note that at weekends and in fine weather the car park and small café at the summit are often full to bursting point. The eighteenth-century Baroque shrine has plenty of over-the-top polychrome decor and an image of the Virgin in a *camarín*. Perhaps the best reason for a trip here is the stunning **vista** which, weather permitting, allows you to look out over five of Andalucía's eight provinces.

INFORMATION   **LUCENA**

Turismo C/San Pedro 42 (Mon–Sat 10.30am–2pm & 5–8pm, Sun 10.30am–2pm; ⓦ turlucena.com). A very   helpful office with lots of information on the town and surrounding area.

ACCOMMODATION AND EATING

Hotel Al-Yussana C/Veracruz 1; ☏ 957 500 300. Located a couple of blocks north of the Turismo, right in the centre of town, this modern hotel is friendly and offers decent value   and functional a/c rooms with TV. €

Las Tres Culturas C/Herrerías 2; ⓦ tresculturasrestaurante.com. This modern restaurant

SAVE THE DONKEY

Founded by local draper Pasqual Rovira in 1989, ADEBO (Association for the Defence of the Donkey) is Spain's oldest **donkey refuge**, and well worth a visit. The country's donkey population has shrunk dramatically from over one million fifty years ago to around 100,000 nowadays – most of which are crossbreeds. Only a few hundred remain of the five breeds of pure Spanish *burro* that have existed on the peninsula since pre-Roman times. One of these, the *raza córdobes*, was so renowned in the eighteenth century for its strength that George Washington asked the Spanish king, Carlos III, to send him some for his farm.

Used for centuries as beasts of burden, the donkeys often receive brutal treatment at the hands of uncaring owners. Working with scarce resources, and using the meagre profits from the family drapery business, Pasqual and his wife Quica have devoted their lives to ending this cruelty and saving the Spanish breeds – including the *cordobés* – from extinction. They were greatly helped in this when Queen Sofía rang Pasqual some years ago after reading about his work and offered her support, and suddenly, previously sceptical politicians in Córdoba and Madrid became enthusiastic about the venture.

The work of the sanctuary continues with the aid of voluntary contributions, and both the queen and her husband King Juan Carlos have sponsored donkeys, as have the late writer Camilo José Cela, Bill Clinton (remarking that the donkey is the mascot of the Democratic Party) and Fidel Castro. Tenor Plácido Domingo also donated royalties from his recorded version of the popular Christmas carol *Arre, Borriquito* ("Gee up, donkey") to the centre.

Lack of public funding in 2013 led to the closure of the sanctuary for visits, but you can still get a close-up view of the donkeys in their enclosures from paths round the outside.

To get to the donkey sanctuary, continue uphill from the Museo del Anís on the Paseo del Fresno, Rute, following the road for the campsite.

combines Córdoba's three distinct cultures in dishes such as *atún rojo con miel y frutos secos* (tuna with honey and dried fruit) and *cordero con ciruelas* (lamb with cherries). Pairing menus regularly available. €€€

El Valle C/Federico García Lorca 14; ☎957 501 512. This is an excellent restaurant for *cocina andaluza* with recommendable pork and game dishes. Its tapas bar has a weekday *menú*, and there's an attractive street terrace. €€

Rute

The scenic A45 Málaga road continues south from Lucena to **Benamejí**, 20km away, a pleasant agricultural village with a couple of *fondas*, close to the provincial border. However, the more interesting route lies along the road (CP167) that turns off left off the A45 8km out of Lucena, heading towards the small town of **RUTE**. Twelve kilometres from the turning, the whitewashed town, sited picturesquely on a hill overlooked by the hazy Sierra de Rute behind, comes into view. Beyond a ruined Moorish castle and a Baroque church, it has few monuments. Rute's fame throughout Andalucía is based on a far more potent allure: the manufacture of a lethal **anís** (aniseed apéritif) with springwater from the sierra. It comes in varying strengths and can be tasted at the twenty or so small bodegas scattered around the town; *Bodega Machaquito*, Paseo del Fresno 7 (⊕machaquito.com), is regarded as one of the best.

Museo del Anís

Paseo del Fresno 2 • Obligatory guided tours Mon–Fri 10am–2pm & 4–7pm, Sat 9am–2pm, Sun by appointment only; Oct–Dec daily 10am–2pm & 4–7pm • Free • ⊕ museodelanis.com

A guided tour at the **Museo del Anís** on the Paseo del Fresno in the upper town will tell you all you need to know about the making of *anís* and its history, with a chance to taste and buy at the end.

4

INFORMATION   **RUTE**

Turismo Municipal Parque Nuestra Señora del Carmen (Jan–Sept Mon–Fri 9am–3pm; Oct–Dec Mon–Fri 9am–3pm, Sat & Sun 10am–2pm & 4–7pm; ☎957 532 929). Near the main road through the town and close to the landmark *anís* monument, this office can provide a useful town map.

ACCOMMODATION AND EATING

Hotel María Luisa Ctra Lucena–Loja 22; ☎957 538 096. Comfortable three-star hotel with light and airy rooms overlooking a garden and excellent pool. The restaurant specializes in local, organic produce, and has a daily *menú*. Breakfast is included. €

Taberna Los Claveles Paseo del Fresno; ☎957 538 388. A busy bar with a large outside terrace, slightly west of the *Museo del Anís*, specialising in breakfasts, tapas and *raciones*. Try the fried fish or typical local dishes such as *flamenquín* and artichokes cooked in a number of ways. €€

Iznájar

Reached by following the scenic A331 road for 13km from Rute, **IZNÁJAR** is a picturesque, whitewashed farming village, with a spectacular location overlooking a reservoir. Despite the beauty, this is a place of long-standing poverty; it was here in 1861 that peasants, or *braceros*, revolted against the injustices of the landowning class – an uprising that was viciously suppressed.

Of Moorish origin (from the Arabic *hizn*, fort, and *achar*, refuge), Iznájar's ruined **Castillo** was constructed in the eighth century (guided tours July & Aug Mon–Sat 10am, 11.30am & 1pm; Sept–June Tues–Sun 11am, 12.30pm & 5pm; charge; tickets from the Turismo), and the church of **Santiago** was added to its interior in the sixteenth.

INFORMATION   **IZNÁJAR**

Turismo Municipal At the top of the village close to the arch leading to the church (July & Aug Mon–Sat 9am–3pm; Sept–June Tues–Sun 9am–2pm & 4–6pm; ☎957 534 479; ⊕turismodeiznajar.es).

ACCOMMODATION AND EATING

Bar Los Marcianos C/Cruz del Postigo 8, 3 blocks south of the Turismo; ☎957 534 424. Great views of the lake and countryside from the terrace (some 50m down the street from the bar entrance – let the staff know you've taken a seat) at this friendly bar. Breakfasts, tapas (over twenty on the list) and *raciones*. €

Camping Valdearenas Valdearenas Beach, just beyond the Hotel Caserío de Iznájar; ⓦ campingvaldearenas. es. Well-equipped campsite right on the beach with good facilities. Organizes a range of activities including canoeing, boat trips and mountain biking. €

Cortijo La Haza C/Adelantado 19; ⓦ cortijolahaza.com. Pretty farmhouse in olive groves 7km out of the village, with rustically furnished, beamed rooms arranged around a pool. It also has its own very good restaurant with vegetarian options and a *menú*. Ring for directions (English spoken). €€

Finca La Bobadilla Ctra Iznájar–Salinas; ⓦ barcelo. com. One of the most exclusive hotels in Spain and surrounded by vast tracts of woodland, which has appealed to guests as diverse as Tom Cruise and King Juan Carlos. No two rooms have the same shape or size; those numbered in the early 20s have the best mountain views. Call in for a drink at the bar if you're curious. Good online offers. €€€€

Hotel Caserío de Iznájar Ctra de Valdearenas s/n; ⓦ hoteliznajar.com. Overlooking the water with gardens and a fine pool, this charming hotel has light, spacious rooms with a/c, plus a restaurant and bar. Breakfast is included. €€

Ruta del Aceite

The **Ruta del Aceite** (Olive Oil Route), follows the N432 southeast out of Córdoba towards Priego de Córdoba. It takes in the olive-oil producing region centred on **Baena** before visiting some of the province's most picturesque villages, including **Luque** and **Zuheros**.

Espejo

At **ESPEJO**, 31km south of Córdoba, an impressive Moorish castle looms above the white-walled village, vineyards and olive groves spread out below. The fourteenth-century Gothic-Mudéjar **castillo** is the property of the dukes of Osuna, the great ruling family based to the southwest (see page 296), which once owned an enormous tract of Andalucía. The nearby, restored Gothic-Renaissance church of **San Bartolomé** (Mon–Fri call to arrange a viewing, Sat 10.30am–noon & 6.30–8pm; April–Oct 7.30–9pm, Sun 10.30am–noon; free; ☎ 667 996 761), dating from the fifteenth and sixteenth centuries, is also worth seeking out for its superb retablo *mayor* by Pedro Romana and a fine *artesonado* ceiling.

Castro del Río

Sited on a low hill on the north bank of the Río Guadajoz, **CASTRO DEL RÍO**, 9km on from Espejo, has a **Roman bridge** spanning the river and a ruined Moorish **castle** built on the foundations of a Roman fort. The village also claims a footnote in Roman history as this is believed to be the place where Pompey's troops rested up prior to their showdown battle with Caesar in 45 BC at nearby Montilla (Munda) that ended the civil war and, briefly, gave Caesar control of the whole Roman world. The **Iglesia de la Asunción**, founded in the thirteenth century with later additions, has a fine if somewhat eroded Plateresque portal, and the **Ayuntamiento** preserves the prison in which Cervantes was locked up for a week in 1568 when, working as a tax collector, he was falsely accused of fiddling the books. A modern sculpture of Don Quijote, honouring the great writer's literary creation, now adorns the exterior.

THE FALLING SOLDIER

Just outside the village of Espejo (see page 380) is the Haza del Reloj hillock, identified in 2009 as the location of legendary photojournalist **Robert Capa**'s **The Falling Soldier**, a symbol of the Spanish Civil War and one of the world's most famous, if controversial, war photos. The trenches have been restored, although there's no memorial plaque; ask in the village for directions.

BAENA'S OIL FOR CONNOISSEURS

Spain produces, and probably consumes, more **olive oil** than any other country in the world. However, this wasn't always so, and when the Greeks introduced the olive to the peninsula in the first millennium BC, it was regarded with suspicion by the native Iberians who went on using their traditional lard. Only with the arrival of the Roman legions did they begin to acquire a taste for it, and under Roman supervision Hispanic oil became the finest and most expensive in the empire. Later, sophisticated Moorish invaders taught the Iberians better cultivation techniques, as well as culinary and medicinal possibilities. The Moorish, and now Spanish, names for oil and the olive, *aceite* and *aceituna*, are a legacy of this time.

Today, Spaniards are great connoisseurs of quality oil and **Baena** has its own official **denominación de origen**, backed by an official regulatory body, the *Consejo Regulador*, guaranteeing the standards attained by strict methods of production. Baena's finest oil stands comparison with the best in Europe, and *almazaras* (oil mills), such as that operated for several generations by the Núñez de Prado family in the town, take a great amount of care at every stage in the production process. The olives cultivated on the estate are all harvested by hand prior to being ground to a paste on ancient granite stone mills. The "free run" oil – with no further pressure applied – that results from this process is regarded as the *grand cru* of the oil trade and it takes 11kg of olives to yield just one litre of such oil. With a markedly low acid content and an unfatty, concentrated flavour, this oil is far too good (and expensive) for cooking and is sparingly used to flavour gazpacho – in Córdoba province, *salmorejo* – or tasted on a morsel of bread as a *tapa*.

Núñez de Prado mill Avda de Cervantes 15, close to Pza de España; ☎ 957 670 141. With parts dating from the eighteenth century, this mill can be freely visited all year, although most of the action takes place between Nov and Feb when the harvested olives are pressed. Their shop sells a range of oils, including the purest oil, the celebrated *flor de aceite*, at bargain prices.

Baena

Beyond Castro del Río the N432 climbs gently through hills covered with olive groves until it reaches Andalucía's most celebrated oil production centre, **BAENA**, famous for centuries for the high quality of its olive oil. Baena was an important and populous place in the Moorish period, but the town shrank as a result of emigration in the twentieth century. Of late it has made a comeback based upon its oil and agricultural wealth and today exudes a busy and prosperous air, with huge metal tanks for storing the oil lining the roads on the outskirts of town. Most of Baena's sights lie in the upper town, reached by following Calle Juan Rabadán from the focal Plaza de España to the Plaza de la Constitución. The eighteenth-century arcaded **almacén** (warehouse) here houses a cultural centre and *Mesón Casa del Monte*, a good tapas bar and restaurant (see page 382).

Besides oil, Baena is also famous for its **Semana Santa** rituals, which include a drum-rolling contest when the streets are filled with the deafening sound of up to two thousand drums. Wednesday to Friday during Holy Week is the time to avoid, unless you have earplugs.

Museo Histórico de la Tercia

Casa de la Tercia, C/Henares s/n • Mid-April to Sept Tues & Wed 10.30am–2pm, Thurs–Sat 10.30am–2pm & 5–8pm, Sun 10.30am–2pm; Oct to mid-April Tues & Wed 9am–2pm, Thurs–Sat 10.30am–2pm & 5–7pm, Sun 9am–2pm • Charge

The Casa de la Tercia is an elegant eighteenth-century *casa señorial* that houses the town's interesting **Museo** Histórico de la Tercia. Spread over three floors, the museum has interesting exhibits from prehistory and Roman Baena (with a section dealing with ancient olive oil production), as well as the Moorish and medieval periods.

Santa María

Pza del Angel s/n • Enquire at the Turismo for opening hours • Free

At the top of Calle Henares, veering to the left brings you to the early sixteenth-century Gothic church of **Santa María** with a fine portal and a Moorish tower, probably the minaret of a former mosque. Ruined and roofless for many years after being put to the torch during the Civil War, this beautiful church has undergone a substantial restoration, and features a magnificent new wooden vaulted roof. The fine iron *reja* (altar screen) survives, while an image of what was lost, including a precious retablo, is preserved in a faded photograph in the sacristy (the Turismo also displays a copy in its lobby).

Madre de Dios

Pza Palacio s/n • Enquire at the Turismo for opening hours • Free

Behind the church of Santa María is the sixteenth-century Mudéjar convent of **Madre de Dios** with a fine late Gothic porch, and equally fine retablo, *coro* and *artesonados* in its church.

Museo del Aceite y del Olivar

C/Cañada 7 • Mid-April to Sept Mon 10.30am–2pm, Wed 10.30am–1.30pm, Thurs–Sat 10.30am–1.30pm & 5–8pm; Oct to mid-April Wed–Sun 10.30am–1.30pm • Charge • ⓦ museoaceite.com

A little way northwest of the Plaza de España, the **Museo del Aceite y del Olivar** pays tribute to the history and development of olive oil production in the area, including a section on the modern uses of oil and its by-products – Baena has a power station fuelled by olive waste. You can also sample and buy the famed oils.

INFORMATION   BAENA

Turismo C/Virrey del Pino 5, slightly east of the Pza de España (mid-April to Sept Mon–Wed 8am–2.30pm, Thurs– Sat 8am–2.30pm & 6–8pm; Oct to mid-April Mon–Fri 9am–2pm, Sat & Sun 10.30am–1.30pm; ☎ 957 671 757).

ACCOMMODATION AND EATING

Hostal Los Claveles C/Juan Valera 15; ☎ 957 670 174. This central and friendly *hostal* has squeaky-clean en-suite a/c rooms with TV and balcony. Can advise on parking nearby. €

Mesón Casa del Monte Pza de la Constitución; ☎ 957 665 169. This restaurant is a cut above the rest. Olive oil reigns supreme at all meals including breakfast. Try the house specials such as *berenjenas con salmorejo* and *bacalao confitado en aceite de oliva* (glazed cod in olive oil). €€

Picoteo Avda Padre Villoslada 29, 10min walk from Casa Grande; ☎ 957 945 465. A good place for breakfast, and for tapas and mains later in the day. Choose from giant flamenquines or more sophisticated dishes such as *codillo de cerdo asado* (roast ham shank). €€

Restaurante Casa Grande Avda Cervantes 35; ☎ 957 671 905. In the hotel of the same name, this is a reliable restaurant where house specials include local dishes such as *salmorejo* and *bolo molinero* (traditional mince dish), plus an excellent-value weekday lunch *menú*. Very pleasant summer terrace. €€

Luque

Seven kilometres beyond Baena is the attractive village of **LUQUE**, spread out below a daunting rocky outcrop topped by the almost obligatory castle. Dating from the thirteenth century, the ruins of the Moorish **castillo** are worth a look, and beside them is the golden limestone facade of the Gothic-Renaissance **church of La Asunción** with a retablo whose central image of San Juan is attributed to Martínez Montañés.

EATING AND DRINKING   LUQUE

Casa Frasco C/Padrón 6 ☎ 957 667 731. A worthwhile stop, with stunning views from the terrace, specializing in local meat – try the *chivo en salsa de almendra* (goat in almond sauce) – and in autumn, game such as hare, venison and partridge. The goat's cheese dishes are also good. €€€

Restaurante El Olivo C/Cronista Vicente Estrada, in the west of the village; ☎ 655 975 525. Popular spot for tapas in the busy bar and main meals in the more formal dining room. House specials include *alcachofas con foie* (artichokes with foie gras) and *ensalada de ciervo* (venison salad), plus grilled meats and *raciones*. €€

Zuheros and around

Nestling in a gorge backed by steep rock cliffs, **ZUHEROS** is a stunningly beautiful Subbética village. A cluster of white houses tumbles down the hill below a romantic Moorish **castle** built on and into the rock. Later Christian additions were made after it fell to Fernando III (El Santo) in 1240 and became a frontier bastion against the kingdom of Granada. The nearby early seventeenth-century **Iglesia de los Remedios** (open service times 6.30–8.30pm) has a fine retablo as well as a tower built on the remains of a minaret from an earlier mosque, while on the neighbouring small square a **mirador** gives a great view over the surrounding countryside.

Museo Arqueológico and castillo

On the edge of a small square facing C/Llana • Obligatory guided tours daily on the hour Tues–Sun 10am–2pm & 4–6pm (5–7pm April–Sept); outside these times ask at the Hotel Zuhayra • Charge • ☎ 957 694 545

The village's **Museo Arqueológico** displays fascinating finds from the Cueva de los Murciélagos (see page 383) as well as exhibits from the Roman and Moorish periods. The visit concludes with a visit to the **castillo**, which offers great **views** from its tower.

Cueva de los Murciélagos

Obligatory guided tours Tues–Fri 12.30pm & 4.30pm (also 5.30pm in summer), Sat & Sun 11am, 12.30pm, 2pm, 4pm & 5.30pm (5pm & 6.30pm in summer); tours must be prebooked • Charge • ☎ 957 694 545

In the hills above the village, reached by a paved, 4km road, the spectacular **Cueva de los Murciélagos**, first explored in 1938, is well worth a visit. Its name means "cave of the bats" and the hour-long tour (bring a sweater) takes in impressive stalagmites, stalactites and awesome rock formations while the guide relates the fascinating story of the remarkable **Neolithic cave paintings** and human remains found here.

4

INFORMATION
ZUHEROS

Turismo Municipal In the museum, opposite the castle entrance (Tues–Fri 10am–1.30pm; ☎ 957 694 545); has information about renting *casas rurales* in the area.

ACCOMMODATION AND EATING

★ **Hotel Zuhayra** C/Mirador 10; ⓦ zercahoteles.com. This charming place makes a perfect base to explore the surrounding natural park. They have handy route maps and stock copies of Clive Jarman's book *Walking in the Subbética Natural Park*. There's a swimming pool and guests get free use of the village swimming pool as well. Ten percent discount for *Rough Guide* readers with this guide if you book directly. Breakfast is included. The hotel also has a good restaurant with a summer terrace, serving homemade dishes such as *paté de perdiz* (partridge paté) and Zuhayra salad with goat's cheese, almonds and roast vegetables, plus a good-value *menú*. The downstairs bar offers tapas, *raciones* and homemade pizzas. €€

Mesón Atalaya C/Santo 58; ☎ 957 138 477. A good bar for tapas and *raciones*, with a restaurant at the back. A variety of local dishes include *rabo de toro* (stewed bull's tail) and *chivo de la sierra* (roast goat) plus a choice of vegetarian dishes and local goat's cheeses (which the village is noted for). €€

Doña Mencía

Not quite as pretty as some of its neighbours, **DOÑA MENCÍA**, 5km west of Zuheros, is a sizeable oil and wine centre lying at the foot of a slope covered with silver-leaved olives and interrupted by the occasional vineyard. On the town's western flank there are the walls and bastions of a fifteenth-century **castle** next to which there's an elegant carved stone **portal**, all that remains of an eighteenth-century Dominican monastery destroyed in the Civil War and now incorporated into a municipal open-air theatre.

Museo Histórico-Arqueológico

C/Juan Ramón Jiménez 5 • Mon–Fri 8am–3pm; weekends by appointment • ☎ 957 695 075

Off the main square at the end of Calle Juan Valera is a small **Museo Histórico-Arqueológico**, with exhibits from the prehistoric, Roman and Moorish periods found in the surrounding area. The museum occupies the site of the house of the nineteenth-century novelist Juan Valera who was born here, and whose best-known work, *Pepita Jiménez*, was set in nearby Cabra.

ACCOMMODATION AND EATING

DOÑA MENCÍA

★ **Casa Morejón** C/Obispo Cubero 3, just off Pza Andalucía; ☎ 957 676 169. Excellent, welcoming small *hostal* offering perhaps the best value en-suite rooms in Andalucía. They're functional, with no heating, but spotless and arranged around a charming tiled interior patio. There's also an excellent restaurant where specials include *gambas rebozadas* (deep-fried prawns), *tomates guisados* (baked tomatoes) and *gachas* (creamy dessert with fried bread and almonds), plus a bargain *menú*. €

Priego de Córdoba and around

The tranquil town of **PRIEGO DE CÓRDOBA**, 20km southeast of Luque, is capital of the Subbética and one of Andalucía's little-known Baroque wonders, with a feast of superb churches and a remarkable fountain. It's situated beneath the province's highest mountain, the 1600m **La Tiñosa**; the northern approach presents a dramatic view of the whitewashed buildings of its old quarter, laid out along the edge of a picturesque escarpment known as the Adarve.

Plaza de la Constitución, an elegant square fronted by the **Ayuntamiento**, forms the town's core; all the monuments are within easy walking distance from here. It should be possible to see most of the main **churches** on the same day; though note that some of them close on Sunday and Monday. Priego is also in the centre of a major **olive oil** zone, which produces some of Spain's finest oils. Several *almazaras* (oil mills) are open for visits and tastings; details are available from the Turismo (see page 388).

The towns and villages around Priego generally lack anything compelling in the way of sights, but two outstanding exceptions are the village of **Almedinilla**, where a remarkable Roman villa was discovered in the early 1990s, and, a little further afield, the picturesque town of **Montefrío** and its nearby prehistoric site. Note that opening times change frequently in Priego – check with Turismo (see page 388) before you visit.

Brief history

Despite evidence of long prehistoric habitation in nearby caves and a later Roman settlement, it was under the Moors that Medina Bahiga, as Priego was then known, flourished as part of the kingdom of Granada. Following a tug of war between the Moors and Christians during the fourteenth century, in which the town changed hands three times, it finally fell to the Christians in 1341. Recovery from the aftermath of this turbulent era came only in the eighteenth century when, in 1711, Priego became a dependency of the dukes of Medinaceli. An economic resurgence based on the production of silk and textiles poured great wealth into the town and it was during this time that most of the **Baroque churches**, Priego's outstanding attraction today, were constructed or remodelled. In the nineteenth century, though, the industry found it hard to compete with cheap cotton textiles produced in Catalunya and Britain, and a slow decline set in. The Europe-wide slump in textiles in the 1950s and 1960s caused by imports from Asia accelerated the problems and, as factories closed, many people emigrated to seek work elsewhere. Today the remnants of the textile industry, along with farming, are the town's main employers.

Castillo

Pza del Abad Palomino • Tues–Sat 11.30am–1.30pm & 4.30–6.30pm, Sun 11.30am–1.30pm • Charge

From the Plaza de la Constitución, head northeast towards the **Barrio de la Villa**, the old quarter, which contains most of Priego's principal monuments. A good place to begin is with the austere Moorish **Castillo**, whose impressive keep, the Torre del Homenaje, dominates the small Plaza del Abad Palomino. There are spectacular views from the other towers.

Carnicerías Reales

C/San Pedro de Alcantara s/n • Mon–Sat 11.30am–1.30pm & 5–9pm, Sun 11.30am–1.30pm • Charge

Near the castillo, to the rear of the church of San Pedro, the **Carnicerías Reales** is a sixteenth-century abattoir and meat market with a fine cobbled patio.

Iglesia de la Asunción

Pza del Abad Palomino • Mon & Wed–Sat 11.30am–1.30pm, Sun 10am–noon • Charge

The most important of the town's Baroque churches is the **Iglesia de la Asunción**, its modest whitewashed exterior dating from the sixteenth century. The original Gothic building was remodelled in the Baroque style in the eighteenth century by Jerónimo Sánchez de Rueda, an architect who did a similar job on many of Priego's other churches.

It is inside, however, that the surprises begin: an ornate white stucco Baroque interior leads towards a stunningly beautiful carved Mannerist **retablo** with images attributed to Juan Bautista Vázquez. The greatest surprise of all, though, lies through a portal on the left aisle where you enter the breathtaking **sagrario**, one of the masterpieces of Spanish Baroque. Here, a dazzling symphony of wedding-cake white stuccowork and statuary, punctuated by scrolls and cornices, climbs upwards beyond a balcony into a fabulous cupola illuminated by eight windows. The frothy depth of the stucco plaster was achieved by the use of esparto grass to lend it additional strength – a material

that has played a remarkable part in the craft history of Andalucía, even found in hats, baskets and sandals discovered in the Neolithic caves of Granada. This restored octagonal chapel is the work of Francisco Javier Pedrajas, a native of Priego and one of a number of leading sculptors, carvers and gilders working in the town at this time. The altar *mayor* and the *sagrario* have been declared national monuments.

Barrio de la Villa

Before taking in more Baroque mastery, take a look at the nearby and delightful **Barrio de la Villa**, which provides a welcome opportunity for a stroll. The ancient Moorish part of the town, a maze of sinuous whitewashed alleys with balconies and walls loaded with colourful pot plants, leads to a number of typical plazuelas. You should eventually stumble on one of the most charming, the **Plazuela de San Antonio**, replete with palms and wrought-iron *rejas*. Behind the Iglesia de la Asunción, Calle Bajondillo leads to the **Paseo de Adarve**, a superb, and originally Moorish, promenade with a spectacular **view** over the valley.

Iglesia San Pedro

Pza de San Pedro s/n • Daily 11am–2pm • Free

Just to the west of the castillo, the **Iglesia de San Pedro** is another Baroque treat with more stucco and a wonderful **altar mayor** in painted wood and stucco with a delightful domed *camarín* (shrine) behind, which holds a stirring image of the *Inmaculada*. The side chapel of the **Virgen de la Soledad**, with another *camarín*, has an image of the Virgin at the centre of its retablo by Pablo de Rojas.

Iglesia de San Juan de Dios

C/San Juan de Dios s/n • Sometimes open in the morning; check with Turismo • Free

A short distance west of Iglesia San Pedro, **Iglesia de San Juan de Dios** is an early example of Priego Baroque, completed in 1717. Beyond a stone portal designed by Santaella (see page 387), the triple-naved interior has a finely crafted cupola, and – in the Capilla de la Virgen de la Soledad – a *camarín* and retablo by Pedrajas.

Iglesia de la Aurora

C/Álvarez s/n • Mon, Wed & Fri–Sun 10.30am–1.30pm • Charge

To the south of the Barrio de la Villa stands the **Iglesia de la Aurora**, yet another Baroque gem remodelled from a former *ermita* (hermitage), whose exuberant facade, with Corinthian and Solomonic pillars topped by a Virgin and flanked by exquisite stone and marble decoration, is only a prelude to the interior. This, now restored to its full glory, is a single-naved Baroque explosion in painted wood and stucco descending from the grey and white cornices, with polychrome figures on its ceiling, dome and walls, to an animated and sumptuously theatrical **retablo**. The latter is a glittering amalgam of vegetal and geometrical forms, and the crowning achievement of Juan de Dios Santaella, another native Priego talent, born here in 1716. The church is also home to the **Cofradía de la Aurora**, a brotherhood whose sixteenth-century articles of foundation stipulate that they must proceed through the streets in musical procession every Saturday at midnight. Thus, whatever the weather, this band of men, hatted and cloaked, gather behind their banner and a huge lantern to proceed through the streets singing hymns to *La Aurora* (Our Lady of the Dawn), accompanied by guitars, accordions and tambourines.

Iglesia de San Francisco

C/San Francisco s/n • Mon–Fri 10am–1pm & 7–9pm, Sat & Sun 10am–12.45pm • Free

Just south of the church of La Aurora on an elegant old square, the **Iglesia de San Francisco** is another late-Gothic church that Santaella had a hand in remodelling and which has been restored to its former splendour. Once you've admired the facade and portal (both by Santaella), employing contrasting tones of marble, look inside: the retablo *mayor* is a splendid gilded work by Santaella again. The **chapel of Jesús Nazareno** has a sumptuous gilded and polychrome wood and stucco retablo by Pedrajas, the creator of the sagrario in the Asunción, and is topped off by another extravagant cupola by Santaella. The altarpiece's central image of *Jesús Nazareno* (Christ bearing the Cross) is a fine work, attributed to Pedro de Mena.

Fuente del Rey and around

At the southwestern end of the town, and easily reached by following Calle Río – a street dotted with many fine Baroque portals – to its end, lies the **Fuente del Rey**, a spectacular sixteenth-century 180-jet fountain (with many later additions) that pours water into a number of basins. The highest of these has a sculpture of a lion struggling with a serpent, while the second contains a larger late eighteenth-century depiction of Neptune and Amphitrite, the king and queen of the sea. Amphitrite is clutching the dolphin that returned her to Neptune after her attempted escape, incidentally emphasizing the power of the king, the work's intended ideological message, given that over the border in France monarchs were losing their heads. There are in fact two fountains here, the second being the **Fuente de la Salud**, to the rear of the plaza, a sixteenth-century Italianate work built on the spot, according to legend, where the conquering Alfonso XI pitched his camp in 1341. One of the most tranquil squares in Andalucía, this leafy area is a wonderful place to relax and get away from it all, which is why there are so many seats.

From just beyond the square you can **walk** to the Ermita del Calvario, from where there are fine **views** over the town. Take the steps to the left of the Fuente de la Salud.

Iglesia del Carmen

C/Rio s/n • Mon, Tues & Thurs–Sat 7.15–8pm, Sun 11.15am–noon & 7.15–8pm • Free

The **Iglesia del Carmen** is another church remodelled in the eighteenth century by Santaella. A brilliant white interior and cupola has a fine gilded retablo with a *camarín* also by Santaella.

Museo Niceto Alcalá Zamora

C/Río 46 • Mon–Sat 10am–2pm & 5–7pm, Sun 10am–2pm • Charge • ☏ 957 006 224

One of the historic buildings on Calle Río is the birthplace of, and now **museum** dedicated to, **Niceto Alcalá Zamora**, first president of the ill-fated Spanish republic from 1931 to 1936. On a visit to Scandinavia when the Civil War broke out, he never returned to Spain but spent the rest of his life in France and then Argentina where he died in 1949, unwilling to recognize the Franco regime. Much of the original furniture of this middle-class nineteenth-century family mansion survives intact.

Iglesia de las Angustias

C/Río s/n • Open only just before mass; ask at the Turismo • Free

Just off the Plaza de la Constitución at the start of Calle Río, the **Iglesia de las Angustias** is a charming small church and another work by Santaella. The interior has a fine cupola with typically exuberant polychrome stucco decoration.

Iglesia de las Mercedes

C/Carrera de las Monjas s/n • Wed 7.15–8pm, Fri–Sun 10am–1.30pm • Free

East of the Plaza de la Constitución, the **Iglesia de las Mercedes** was an ancient hermitage prior to its remodelling in the latter part of the eighteenth century when its interior was decorated in Rococo style by Pedrajas, highlighted by the four winged archangels at the scalloped corners. Another stunningly ornate snow-white cupola (which is almost Pedrajas's trademark), is balanced by an elegant retablo below. The exterior is an incomplete later addition.

Museo Histórico

C/Carrera de las Monjas 9 • Mon–Sat 10am–2pm & 6–8pm, Sun 10am–2pm • Charge • ☎ 957 540 947

Almost opposite the Iglesia de las Mercedes, Priego's **Museo Histórico** is housed in an elegant *señorial* mansion with a fine patio. The interesting collection displays finds from the surrounding area dating from the Paleolithic down to the Roman and Moorish periods.

ARRIVAL AND INFORMATION   PRIEGO DE CÓRDOBA

By bus Buses drop you in the central Pza de la Constitución, although the actual bus station is a 5min walk to the west of the centre on C/Nuestra Señora de los Remedios. There are easy connections with Córdoba (7 daily Mon–Fri, 3 daily Sat & Sun; 2h 30min) and Granada (4 daily Mon–Fri, 3 daily Sat,

2 daily Sun; 1h 30min).

Turismo Pza de la Constitución 3 (Mon–Sat 10am–2pm & 4.30–6.30pm, Sun 10am–2pm; ☎ 957 700 625; ⟨w⟩ turismodepriego.com).

ACCOMMODATION   SEE MAP PAGE 385

Casa Rosa Los Rios 28, Almedinilla, 2km beyond the Almedinilla exit; ☎ 957 720 802. Spotlessly clean, spacious en-suite rooms in quiet village house. Owner Mark can offer local advice. Dinner (€15 for three courses) available if pre-booked. Breakfast is included. **€**

Hostería de Rafi C/Isabel la Católica 4; ⟨w⟩ hostalrafi.es. This welcoming *hostal*, housed in a refurbished mansion, is an excellent deal. Comfortable a/c en-suite rooms come with satellite TV; own car park and a reasonably priced restaurant. **€**

Hotel Huerta de las Palomas Ctra Priego–Zagrilla km3; ⟨w⟩ zercahoteles.com. On the way to Zagrilla, this is a stylish four-star hotel in rolling countryside with well-equipped and spacious rooms; facilities include gym, pool

and restaurant. It also offers mountain biking, tennis and hiking. Breakfast is included. **€€**

La Patria Chica Carrera de las Monjas 47; ⟨w⟩ hotelpatriachica.com. Opened in 2017, this 19th century mansion offers charming rooms furnished with antiques and memorabilia. There's also an excellent restaurant, an original patio and quiet gardens. Breakfast is included. **€€**

La Posada Real C/Real 14; ☎ 957 541 910. Another possibility in the Barrio de la Villa, this is an attractive, flower-bedecked little place with cosy, a/c, en-suite balcony rooms with TV, and a friendly owner. Also rents three apartments nearby. Breakfast is included. Doubles **€**, apartments **€€**

EATING   SEE MAP PAGE 385

La Patria Chica Carrera de las Monjas 47, in hotel of same name; ☎ 957 058 383. Traditional cuisine with a modern touch such as *bolitas de flamenquín* (croquette-type deep-fried meat rolls). All dishes are all cooked with extra virgin olive oil. **€€€**

El Virrey C/Solana 16, off Pza San Pedro; ☎ 957 052 248. A good neighbourhood restaurant preparing a wide range of dishes such as *lomo ibérico* (pork loin) and *revuelto Minerva* (eggs with octopus and prawns). There's also a good weekday *menú*. **€€**

Carcabuey

Seven kilometres west of Priego, **CARCABUEY** is a charming place laid out on a hill topped by a ruined castle. The Gothic-Renaissance church of **La Asunción** lower down has a handsome Renaissance portal flanked with marble pillars, and inside an elegant **retablo** with the central figure of Christ attributed to Pedro de Mena and Alonso Cano. It is usually locked, so you'll need to ask at the nearby houses for the key.

ACCOMMODATION   CARCABUEY

La Zamora Ctra Cabra–Priego, A339 km14; ⟨w⟩ hostal-lazamora.com. This motel-style *hostal* on the nearby main highway, 3km towards Cabra, is the only place to stay. The en-

suite rooms are simple but clean and the welcome is warm; the restaurant below serves tapas, *raciones* and full meals and has a cheap *menú* (more at weekends). Free parking. **€**

Almedinilla

ALMEDINILLA, 9km east of Priego on the Jaén border, is a characteristic Subbética village squatting along the valley of the Río Caicena. From the road it might seem hardly worth a second glance, but the village is home to a remarkable **Roman villa** with unique features as well as a fine **museum**.

Villa Romana de El Ruedo

At the northern edge of Amedinilla, close to the main A340 highway • See website for opening times • Charge • ⓦ almedinillaturismo.es

Discovered in the early 1990s, the **Villa Romana de El Ruedo** is now recognized as one of the most important Roman villas in Andalucía. Once inside the entrance you will pass to the left the remains of an ancient **pottery kiln**. This would have provided the numerous ceramic containers necessary for the substantial oil and grain farming centred on the villa. Beyond this and beneath a canopy lies the villa proper, constructed and inhabited between the first and fifth centuries AD. Laid out around a central patio or **atrium**, with remains of walls well over 1m high, the bedrooms and living rooms – many bearing vestiges of frescoes and laid with mosaic floors – are adjoined by a bathing area and kitchen as well as bodegas for storing wine, the ruins of an oil mill and warehouses for holding grain. But it is on the north side of the patio in the dining room, or **triclinium**, where the most sensational finds were discovered. In the centre of this room is a well-preserved **podium** upon which diners would have reclined while eating. Behind this and set into the wall are the remains of a spectacular artificial **cascade** fed by a diverted nearby stream, unique in Spain and added when the villa was substantially remodelled in the third century AD, providing an aural backdrop to the diners' meals. Also unearthed here were a number of outstanding sculptures; the major work, a bronze figure of Hypnos, in Greek mythology the god of sleep, is now displayed in the Museo Histórico (see page 389).

To the north and east of the villa lie the remains of a **necropolis** that would have served the Roman settlement here, as well as the remnants of numerous other Roman dwellings. It is planned to excavate these too, eventually transforming the whole area into an archeological park. At the moment a **museum-information centre** (same hours), with reconstructions and exhibits discovered during the excavations, stands opposite the entrance to the villa.

Museo Histórico

On the east side of the village • See website for timings • Charge • ⓦ almedinillaturismo.es

Almedinilla's **Museo Histórico** is housed in a former oil and flour mill, El Molino de Fuente Ribera, whose grindstones were powered by the adjacent Río Caicena. The exhibits are distributed across three floors with the ground floor displaying the mill's grindstones, once used for making olive oil. Taking its theme from this machinery, the rest of the room charts the development of olive oil production from Iberian and Roman times to the present day – not losing an opportunity to remind visitors that the oil produced here today is as highly prized as it was in Roman times, carrying its own *denominación de origen*. The second floor is devoted to the **Iberian period**, particularly finds from Cerro de la Cruz, a hill settlement discovered on the crag behind the village by archeologists early in the last century. The remains displayed – pottery, burial goods, weapons and tools – detail a well-planned urban development existing between the fourth century BC and the first century AD. The museum can provide information about guided visits to the Cerro de la Cruz site.

The third floor houses the **Roman collection**, with the finds from the Roman villa of El Ruedo. Pride of place goes to the sculptures, particularly the fine and superbly restored bronze of the Greek god of sleep, **Hypnos**, discovered in the villa's dining room, and a work of exceptional quality. For the Greeks (and the Romans who knew him as Somnus), Hypnos was the personification of sleep and his mission was to lead the soul to a peaceful death, as in a dream. Made from individual casts of bronze later welded together, in his left hand he would have held an opium poppy to induce sleep, and in his right a horn from which he cast the night as he flew across the sky with the aid of wings protruding from his temples. Almost as fine is a bronze **hermaphrodite** depicting the dancing figure staring into a mirror held in their right hand (now lost) that would have reflected the feminine parts thus exciting the masculine side of their androgynous nature. This ancient fascination with dualism – as in life and death, darkness and light, male and female – is undoubtedly the work's underlying message.

Other sculptures in stone include a genius of the house, perhaps depicting spring, a partially damaged image of Perseus and Andromeda, and a head of Dionysos. A **maquette** of the Roman villa gives you an idea how it would have looked when in use.

ARRIVAL AND INFORMATION ALMEDINILLA

Arrival There are no buses to Almedinilla so you need your own transport to get there or you can get a taxi from Priego de Córdoba (around €15 one-way).

Turismo Should you have any problems gaining access to the Roman villa or museum, call at the Turismo (Pza de España s/n; ☎ 957 703 317; ⊚almedinillaturismo.es), who should be able to help. Guided tours include the Roman villa and museum, and can be booked by phone or online.

ACCOMMODATION AND EATING

Bar-Restaurante La Bodega Pza de España; ☎ 957 703 066. The village's main bar-restaurant serves tapas in its bar and a range of *cordobés* cuisine – including *salmorejo* and *rabo de toro* – and pizzas in its restaurant. There's also a midday *menú*. €€

Hospedería La Era Pza La Era 1; ⊚hospederialaera. com. Excellent and well-equipped en-suite a/c rooms in the heart of the village at this cunningly re-created copy of an ancient townhouse that, despite appearances, is completely modern. Breakfast is included. €€

Alcalá La Real

ALCALÁ LA REAL, 27km east of Priego, is a pleasant country town at the foot of a hill dominated by one of the most impressive Moorish forts in eastern Andalucía. Later reconstructed as the **Castillo de la Mota** (daily: April to mid-Oct 10.30am–7.30pm; mid-Oct to March 10.30am–5.30pm; charge), it preserves among its earlier gates the Moorish **Puerta de la Imagen**. After the fort had been taken during the *Reconquista*, Alfonso XI built – and this became the custom – the Renaissance church of **Santa María la Mayor** inside the walls. Designed by the leading architect of the sixteenth century, Diego de Siloé, and now magnificently restored, its interior floor conserves scores of Visigothic burial niches from an earlier building on the site. Displays in the church's small museum reveal activity on this hill going back to prehistoric times. The fort's imposing **Torre de la Homenaje** also has an interesting small **museum** with great views from the top of the tower.

INFORMATION AND ACCOMMODATION ALCALÁ LA REAL

Turismo The castle's ticket office doubles as the Turismo (daily: April to mid-Oct 10.30am–7.30pm; mid-Oct to March 10.30am–5.30pm; ☎ 953 102 717).

Hotel Torrepalma C/Conde de Torrepalma 2; ⊚hoteltorrepalma.com. This three-star hotel lies just off the town's main street, Avda de Andalucía, and has comfortable and well-equipped a/c rooms, plus its own bar-restaurant serving hearty local dishes. €

Montefrío

MONTEFRÍO, 24km southeast of Priego (or 32km by road), and just over the Granada border, is one of the more spectacularly sited towns in this part of the region. Its fame has grown considerably since its inclusion in National Geographic's *10 Villages with the Best Views In the World* in late 2015. Cradled between two rocky outcrops, each topped by a church that can be visited, the town has the even bigger Neoclassical **Iglesia de la Encarnación** (daily 9.30am–2pm; free) at its heart, with an enormous dome and bizarre acoustics. The most interesting of the hilltop churches is the sixteenth-century **Iglesia de la Villa** (Mon–Fri 11am–2pm, Sat & Sun 11am–2pm & 4.30–6.30pm; charge), a superb building designed by Diego de Siloé, and now a themed museum based on the reconquest of this part of Andalucía from the Moors. The interior has some exquisite **vaulting** and is surrounded by the ruins of the Moorish *alcazaba*; there are fine **views** over the town and beyond from its tower. The church is reached by a bracing climb along the road that ascends beyond the Turismo (see page 391).

ARRIVAL & INFORMATION MONTEFRÍO

By bus Montefrío is served by bus (3 daily Mon–Fri, 1 Sat; 1hr 30min) from Granada, run by Alsa (⊚alsa.es).

Turismo Pza de España 1, just uphill on the left from the Encarnación church (daily 10am–2pm, plus Sat 4.30–6.30pm; ⓦ montefrio.org). This office can supply information on Las Peñas de los Gitanos (see page 391).

ACCOMMODATION AND EATING

★ **Flor de Olivo** Avda de la Paz 23; ☎ 617 781 200. This French-Mediterranean restaurant has at the helm Jean Paul Vinay – who previously worked with Ferrán Adriá in El Bulli. The menu changes often but expect to find *tarrina de foie* (foie gras terrine) and ba*calao gratinado al alioli de miel* (cod with honey aioli). There's also a weekday lunch *menú*, and a *menú de degustación* that includes wine. €€€

Las Navillas m&m Cortijo Las Navillas, Ctra de Íllora km 16, to the south of town; ⓦ lasnavillasmm.es.

Comfortable rooms (some en suite) with large beds in a restored farmhouse. The owners can provide lots of information on walking and biking in the local area and organise walking holidays. Breakfast is included. €€

Restaurante El Pregonero Pza de España 3; ☎ 958 336 117. This atmospheric place serves tapas (in the bar) and specials such as *cochinillo* (suckling pig) and *jamón asado* (roast ham) in the restaurant, which has a pleasant outdoor terrace. €€

Las Peñas de los Gitanos

Signposted some 8km east of Montefrío along the GR3410 towards Illora

Six kilometres long and demarcated by limestone outcrops, the remarkable Neolithic site of **Las Peñas de los Gitanos** was occupied by Stone Age people in the third millennium BC. The overhanging rocks and caves were used as shelters by bulls, goats, sheep and other ancient beasts and this food source attracted early humans who would have hunted these animals in groups. These ancient hunters left behind paintings inside the caves (currently not on view), various **stone tombs** – some with carvings of animals and horns – and the remains of later stone and clay dwellings when they became Chalcolithic (copper age) village dwellers. Make sure to see Dolmen 23 (fronted by an information board), which is the best preserved of the group, with a finely worked entrance still intact. A detailed leaflet (in Spanish) is available from the Turismo in Montefrío (see page 391), but many of the dolmens and other remains are hard to find, so a **guided visit** is recommended.

ARRIVAL AND INFORMATION   LAS PEÑAS DE LOS GITANOS

To visit the site, which is on private land, you will need to contact Las Peñas de Los Gitanos S.L. (☎ 628 305 337; English spoken). Having arranged a visit and arrived at the site, park at the signed entry road (with locked gate barring vehicles) on the left where Señora Paqui Sánchez will normally meet you.

Guided visits Guided tours (five people minimum; 2 daily,

morning and late afternoon; 2hr) must be booked at least 24hr in advance through Paqui Sánchez. The meeting point is normally at the site entrance.

Auto-guided visits You can visit the site independently (charge) with the aid of a map, but will still need to contact Señora Sánchez to book and be allowed access.

Northeast of Córdoba

The A4 highway, which heads northeast out of Córdoba along the valley of the Guadalquivir, is the main road to Madrid and one of the great historical highways of Andalucía. Not only was this the bullion route between Madrid and its imperial seaports of Seville and Cádiz, but over a millennium and a half earlier, as the Vía Augusta, it formed the vital overland link joining Roman Spain with Gaul, Italy and Rome itself. Transport is easy, with buses linking Córdoba to most places, and trains to Andújar. The route has a number of delightful stopovers including the handsome small town of **Montoro**, an outstanding Moorish castle at **Baños de la Encina** and the historic **Despeñaperros Pass**.

Montoro

MONTORO lies 43km from Córdoba, beyond the villages of El Carpio and Pedro Abad, and just off the A4. Dramatically sited on an escarpment above a horseshoe bend in the Guadalquivir, the town is a centre of olive oil production obtained from extensive groves planted in the foothills of the Sierra Morena to the north. A labyrinth of narrow, white-walled streets surrounds the main square, the Plaza de España, dominated by the lofty tower of its Gothic-Mudéjar church, **San Bartolomé** (daily 11am–1pm & 7–7.30pm; free). The interior, behind the red sandstone facade, has a fine *artesonado* ceiling inlaid with mother-of-pearl recovered from under layers of whitewash. On the same square is the sixteenth-century **Ayuntamiento**, an old ducal mansion with a fine Plateresque frontage. The narrow main street (C/Corredera) connects Plaza de España with **Plaza del Charco** (aka Plaza Caridad), which contains the town's main **bars** and two *casinos*, the larger Casino de los Ricos (Rich) and the Casino de los Pobres (Poor), reflecting the bitter class divisions that once existed here and to some extent persist.

Santa María de la Mota archeological museum

Pza Santa María s/n · Sat, Sun & hols 11am–1pm, outside these times contact the Turismo on ☎ 957 160 089 · Free

A narrow street uphill out of the north side of the square leads into an atmospheric old quarter whose main feature is the thirteenth-century church of **Santa María de la Mota**, with some interesting Romanesque capitals, now converted into a small **archeological museum**.

Casa de las Conchas

C/Grajas 17 (signed from Pza de España)

One curiosity that shouldn't be missed is the **Casa de las Conchas**. Here the owners have covered both the exterior and interior with tens of thousands of seashells; the proprietor or his wife will proudly show you around and relate the story behind their lifelong obsession.

Museo Antonio Rodríguez de Luna

Pza del Charco 18 · Sun & hols 11am–1pm, or contact the Turismo on ☎ 957 160 089 · Free

Slightly uphill from the Plaza del Charco and set in the eighteenth-century Capilla de San Jacinto, the **Museo Antonio Rodríguez de Luna** houses some powerful abstract works by the eponymous Montoro-born artist who spent part of his life in Paris and Mexico and died in 1985.

Puente de Las Donadas

The elegant sixteenth-century bridge of **Las Donadas** over the Guadalquivir was paid for by local women who, tradition holds, sold their jewellery to place the town on a more direct, and lucrative, route to the north. Across the bridge, the Cardeña road leading up into the hills offers superb **views** back over the town.

ARRIVAL AND INFORMATION
MONTORO

By bus Montoro is served by bus (9 daily Mon–Fri, 2–3 daily Sat & Sun; 50min) from Córdoba, run by Autocares Ramírez.

Turismo C/Corredera 23 (Mon–Fri 9.30am–3pm, Sat 10am–1pm, Sun 10am–2pm; ☎ 957 160 089).

EATING

Casa José Pza de España 13; ☎ 670 285 314. Dine on the terrace on the square or inside with views of the river and Puente de las Donadas. There's a long list of tapas and raciones (many served as half-portions), plus good-value specials that include *lomo de ciervo con frutos rojos* (venison steak with red fruits) and a selection of *flamenquines*. €€

Andújar

Lying some 32km beyond Montoro, **ANDÚJAR** is a sizeable if simple country town that claims to be the world's biggest centre of sunflower-oil bottling. There's also a thriving commercial ceramics industry, as well as a couple of churches worth a visit for their artworks. The road into the town crosses a fifteen-arched Roman **bridge** spanning the Guadalquivir, which has been considerably restored from Moorish times onwards.

There are also a number of elegant **Renaissance palaces** within walking distance of the centre; the Turismo (see page 393) can provide a map detailing their locations.

Plaza de España

The central **Plaza de España**, a baking furnace in the heat of high summer, is overlooked by the impressive Gothic church of **San Miguel** (mid-June to mid-Sept Mon–Sat 7.30–9pm, Sun 11am–1.30pm; mid-Sept to mid-June Mon–Sat 6.30–8pm, Sun 11am–1.30pm) with a fine stone tower and Plateresque features. It is flanked by an equally striking late-Baroque **Ayuntamiento** – now restored to its full glory – with elegant portals.

Iglesia de Santa María

Pza de Santa María • Open lunchtime and evenings • Free • ☎ 953 500 139

The most interesting church in town is the **Iglesia de Santa María** on the plaza of the same name, reached by following Calle La Feria from Plaza de España. Built on the site of a former mosque, the freestanding bell tower probably replaced the mosque's minaret and now houses a small tourist office (see page 393). Inside, a chapel on the left has a fine *Christ in the Garden of Olives* by El Greco, a startling surprise in a nondescript country church. The superb **reja** that stands before the El Greco is the work of Master Bartolomé of Jaén, who also created the more famous one in the Capilla Real at Granada (see page 446).

Museo Arqueológico

C/Don Gome • Contact the turismo for opening times • Free • ☎ 953 513 178

The town's **archeological museum** is housed in the striking seventeenth-century Palacio de los Niños de Don Gome, decorated with moustached figures of feathered warriors inspired by the burgeoning Spanish American empire. The small collection consists of mainly Roman ceramics.

ARRIVAL AND INFORMATION ANDÚJAR

By train Andújar is served by train from Córdoba (5 daily; 50min) and Jaén (4 daily; 42min). The station lies a 20min walk south-west of the centre.

Turismo Torre del Reloj, Pza de Santa María s/n (mid-June to mid-Sept Tues–Sat 8am–2.30pm; mid-Sept–mid-June Tues–Fri 9am–2pm & 4.30–7pm, Sat 9am–2pm; ⓦ turismodeandujar.com).

ACCOMMODATION AND EATING

The most attractive **accommodation** options in the area are in the Parque Natural (see page 393).

Hotel Logasasanti C/Dr Fleming s/n; ⓦ logasasanti. com. The only hotel in town, with functional a/c rooms and a bar-restaurant with a cheap *menú*. €

Mesón Lourdes Corredera Capuchinos 10; ☎ 620 332 761. Popular bar and restaurant on the main high street serving fish, seafood and rice dishes (the paella is particularly tasty). Lengthy wine list and excellent-value daily *menú*. €€€

Palacio Sirvente de Mieres Altozano Serrano Palto 4; ⓦ palaciosirventedemieres.com. Studio and apartment accommodation (sleeping up to six) in a historic palace complete with sixteenth-century patio. Accommodation comes with a/c, TV and kitchenette. Studios €, apartments €€

Los Pincelinos C/Alcalá Venceslada 36; ☎ 953 511 154. Slightly more up-market restaurant in the south of town specialising in meat dishes (especially game). The house *paté de perdiz* is good as is the *leche frita* dessert (milk). €€€

Parque Natural Sierra de Andújar

A wonderful 30km drive into the **Parque Natural Sierra de Andújar**, to the north of Andújar along the A6177, leads to the thirteenth-century hermitage of **Nuestra Virgen de la Cabeza**, one of the most revered of Andalucía's shrines.

Once you arrive at the shrine, there's not much left of the ancient building, which was destroyed in the Civil War when two hundred Guardia Civil officers seized it, declaring their support for Franco's rebellion. Bombarded for eight months by Republican forces, the sanctuary was eventually set alight and the guards captured on May 1, 1937. The distasteful rebuild flanked by equally bleak Guardia Civil monuments was carried out during the Franco period, but the famous **romería** – in which brotherhoods and pilgrims converge on the shrine from all over Andalucía and Spain on the last Sunday in April – carries on undaunted. In a crypt to the side of the church is a display of hundreds of crutches, Zimmer frames and all kinds of surgical supports and braces left behind by "healed" pilgrims – a bizarre testament to the Virgin's curative powers.

INFORMATION

PARQUE NATURAL SIERRA DE ANDÚJAR

Centro de Visitantes As you drive up into the park, at the 13km point (July & Aug Fri–Sun 10am–2pm; Sept–June Thurs 10am–2pm, Fri–Sun 10am–2pm & 3–6pm; ☎953 539 628). The centre has displays on the natural park's flora and fauna including the threatened *lince ibérico* (pardel lynx); they can also provide a map of the park and have leaflets detailing hiking routes.

ACCOMMODATION

La Mirada Virgen de la Cabeza; ⊛hotelenandujar.com. A large complex close to the shrine, with hotel, campsite, wood cabins (for four), pool and small minimarket. Hotel rooms are en suite with a/c. Camping €, doubles/cabins €€

Los Pinos Crta del Santuario km14.2; ⊛lospinos.es. Tourist complex with cosy en-suite rooms, *apartamentos rurales* and cottages (sleeping up to four) in a pleasant woodland setting with a pool and good restaurant (see page 394). Doubles €, apartments €€, cottages €€€

Villa Matilde 3km down a track heading east from Los Pinos (signed "La Jandula"); ⊛villamatilde.org. A pleasant rural retreat offering (mostly) en-suite rooms in a converted villa with a pool and a restaurant that also caters for vegetarians. €

EATING

El Parral Crta del Santuario km2.5; ☎953 505 127. Busy *venta* on the route into the park where specials include grilled meats, roast lamb and kid, and rice dishes (must be preordered). They also offer several *menús*. €€

Los Pinos Crta del Santuario km14.2 ⊛lospinos.es. Part of the tourist complex of the same name (see page 394), this busy restaurant specializes in game – try the *chorizo de ciervo* (venison chorizo) and *perdiz en escabeche* (partridge in brine) – as well as rice and egg dishes, and the weekday lunchtime *menú*. There's a shady outside terrace. €€€

Baños de la Encina

The sizeable village of **BAÑOS DE LA ENCINA** has one of the most impressive Moorish castles in Andalucía. Crowning a low hill above the village, the tenth-century **Alcázar** is a magnificent sight with its fourteen square towers and enormous keep spaced out along a crenellated curtain wall.

Alcázar

C/Santa María s/n • Obligatory guided tours from the tourist office, check with the turismo for the complex opening hours • Charge (buy your ticket from the tourist office first)

Baños de la Encina's **Alcázar** was built by al-Hakam II of Córdoba in 967, in an attempt to control the rugged and mountainous territory to the north, the domain of various unruly Iberian clans, as well as the entry to Andalucía through the Despeñaperros Pass and along the nearby valley of the Guadalquivir. During the *Reconquista* the castle changed hands twice in the twelfth century and it was only in 1225 that it finally fell to Fernando III (El Santo) to be incorporated into the dominion of Castile. Entered through a double-horseshoe arch, where a plaque in Arabic script dates the edifice to year 357 of the *hegira* (967 AD), the fort has an oval ground plan and from the battlements there are **fine views** over the village and towards the Sierra de Cazorla to the east.

San Mateo

Pza de la Constitución s/n • Open some mornings and service times (check Turismo website for times: ⊛bdelaencina.com) • Donation requested

The splendid fifteenth-century red stone Gothic-Renaissance church of **San Mateo** dominates the main square. The most striking exterior feature is an elegant octagonal tower, while the interior has some wonderful vaulting and an exquisite sagrario (sanctuary) constructed in ebony and adorned with silver, marble and tortoiseshell.

Ermita del Cristo del Llano

Pza Ermita s/n • Daily 1–2pm by prior appointment only • ☎ 953 613 338 • Donation requested

It is worth heading out to the **Ermita del Cristo del Llano**, an eighteenth-century hermitage in the upper village that's less than a ten-minute walk from the tourist office. You'll need to book ahead to view the remarkable church and its startlingly beautiful **Baroque camarín** with stellar decoration and stucco polychrome angels and saints climbing to the roof.

ARRIVAL AND INFORMATION

By bus The town is served by buses from Jaén (3 daily; 1hr).

Turismo Municipal Avda José Luis Messía 2, two blocks north of the Alcázar (June to mid-Sept Mon, Wed & Thurs 10am–1.30pm, Fri–Sun 10am–1.30pm & 6.30–8.30pm;

BAÑOS DE LA ENCINA

hours differ slightly rest of the year; ☎ 953 613 338; ⓦ bdelaencina.com).They offer a 2hr 15min guided tour of the castle and monuments (daily except Tues: June to mid-Sept 11.15am; mid-Sept to May 11.15am & 4.30pm; charge).

ACCOMMODATION AND EATING

Hotel-Restaurante Baños Cerro de la Llaná s/n; ⓦ hotelbanos.com. Pleasant hotel on a hill behind the castle, with good-value balcony rooms, many with stunning Alcázar views (room 101 has the best). The restaurant offers tempting regional meat and game dishes, with a cheap lunchtime weekday *menú*. €

El Olivar de Guzmanes C/Trinidad 4; ⓦ elolivardeguzmanes.com. A restaurant with simple inside dining and an outside terrace with stunning mountain views. Specializes in *carne de monte* (game), *espárragos* (asparagus) and *alcachofas* (artichokes), plus paella (pre-order only). Weekday lunch *menú* and *menú de degustación* available. €€€

La Carolina

LA CAROLINA, 20km northeast of Baños de la Encina, is the most important of the new towns set up by Carlos III in the eighteenth century to protect the bullion route from Cádiz to Madrid. As with the other settlements it was named after a member of the royal family (in this case the king himself), settled with foreign immigrants and laid out on a regular grid-pattern street plan that still survives today. The town's central square, Plaza del Ayuntamiento, has the imposing, honey-coloured sandstone **Palacio de Pablo de Olavide**, built for Carlos III's radical minister, the force behind the Nuevas Poblaciones idea. De Olavide did not long enjoy the fruits of his labours, however, for the clergy, who were denied access to these new towns, wreaked their vengeance by denouncing him to the Inquisition. Arrested in 1776, he was divested of his property and confined to a convent in La Mancha subject to whatever penances the monks thought appropriate; he subsequently escaped to France. Flanking the *palacio*, the parish church of **La Concepción** contains a fine Baroque image of the *Virgen de las Angustias* in alabaster. The square is linked by a thoroughfare to an impressive tree-lined avenue entered via a gateway bearing images of Carlos III, at the far end of which lies the municipal **swimming pool**.

ARRIVAL AND DEPARTURE

LA CAROLINA

By bus La Carolina is served by frequent buses (around hourly) from Jaén (1hr 10 min).

ACCOMMODATION AND EATING

Del Arco Pza de las Delicias 6, on the attractive roundabout at the end of C/Madrid; ☎ 661 923 770. Popular restaurant serving traditional dishes with a modern twist, and a reputation as one of the best in the area. Try the *carpaccio de venado* (venison carpaccio), the *lomito de corzo* (roebuck steak) or the *tartar de pez espada* (swordfish tartare). €€€

Hotel La Perdiz On the main A4 highway, km268, at the edge of town; ⓦ hotellaperdiz.es. Lovely hotel with well-equipped rooms and stunning gardens with pool. Good restaurant with daily *menú*. €

DON QUIJOTE AND THE DESPEÑAPERROS PASS

Cervantes would have been familiar with the route through the Despeñaperros Pass, connecting La Mancha with Seville and Córdoba, where he lived both as a child and in later life. The brooding and threatening nature of the pass – probably greater before it was blasted to make room for road widening and the railway line – appealed to him, for he used it in two of the most memorable scenes in the adventures of **Don Quijote** and Sancho Panza. The centre of the pass is where Don Quijote ran mad and played "the desperate, the raving, the furious lover", in order that Sancho could convey news of this penance to his fantasized Lady Dulcinea del Toboso, in reality a slatternly country lass named Alonza Lorenzo. About 1km further on, the **Venta de Cardenas** was the inn that the deluded knight errant imagined to be a castle. When the morning after a night's hospitality the innkeeper demanded payment, Quijote refused with the explanation that knights never paid for their accommodation and made his exit. Sancho, however, was not so lucky and was given a violent tossing in a blanket to teach him a lesson. The old *venta* apparently survived until the nineteenth century, when it was seen by Borrow. However, it was subsequently demolished and a characterless hotel now stands on the site. It's still a stopover on this major transportation route and the lines of lorries parked outside belong to the truck drivers who use this inn today, the successors of the muleteers, drovers and carriers of Cervantes's time.

Despeñaperros Pass

Two kilometres beyond La Carolina, slightly before the village of Navas de Tolosa, a huge roadside **monument** marks the site of the important battle that took place in 1212 between the Christian armies under Alfonso VIII and the Almohad forces. The Moors suffered a crippling defeat, opening the way for the *Reconquista* of Andalucía. The monument depicts the Christian monarchs as well as the shepherd, an apparition of St Isidore in disguise, who, according to Christian belief, guided them through the well-defended Sierra Morena, thus enabling a surprise attack on the Moorish army who fled after defeat through the Despeñaperros Pass. This event, in fact, gave the pass its name – meaning the "overthrow of the dogs" (or Moors).

The **Despeñaperros Pass**, 14km further on, is the dramatic gateway between Andalucía and La Mancha and the only natural breach in the 500km length of the Sierra Morena. This narrow defile, flanked by daunting crags and slopes covered with dense pinewoods, was for centuries the main point of entry into Andalucía from the north and many travellers have left vivid accounts of arriving in the lush promised land of the south after traversing the dry and arid plains of La Mancha (from the Moorish *manxa*, or parched earth). George Borrow, however, also related the sense of foreboding due to the pass's evil reputation "on account of the robberies which are continually being perpetrated in its recesses". Richard Ford, when going the other way, described the land beyond the pass as where "commences the *paño pardo*, the brown cloth, and the *alpargata*, or the hempen sandal of the poverty-stricken Manchegos". The whole area surrounding the Despeñaperros Pass is a **Parque Natural**.

INFORMATION

DESPEÑAPERROS PASS

Centro de Visitantes Just off the A4 at Santa Elena (Jan–May Thurs–Sun 10am–2pm & 4–6pm; June–Sept Thurs–Sun 10am–2pm & 6–8pm; Oct–Dec Tues & Wed 10am–2pm, Thurs–Sun 10am–2pm & 4–6pm; ☎ 953 609 706). The visitor centre for the natural park has exhibitions of flora and fauna and lots of information on activities and accommodation.

Jaén

Surrounded by olive groves and huddled beneath the fortress of Santa Catalina on the heights above, **JAÉN**, the provincial capital and by far the largest town in the province, is an uneventful sort of place. Its name derived from the Arabic *Geen*, meaning a stop on the caravan route, the modern town is more northerly than Andalucian in its appearance and character, doubtless stemming from its resettlement with emigrants from the north following the *Reconquista,* and the subsequent long centuries spent as the front-line bulwark of Christian Spain against Moorish Granada. The city sits at the centre of an area impoverished by lack of economic development and chronic unemployment; while you would hardly want to go out of your way to get here, it makes an easy stopover en route to destinations such as Baeza, Úbeda and Cazorla to the northeast. And, given a chance, it has a surprising number of worthwhile sights, including an outstanding **cathedral**, the largest **Moorish baths** in Spain, some elegant old churches and mansions and an important museum. To the northeast of Jaén along the Baeza road lies the **La Laguna** complex, with a comprehensive museum dedicated to explaining the history and development of olive oil production.

Most of Jaén's sights lie within a few minutes' walk of the rather characterless main thoroughfare, the **Paseo de la Estación**. This cuts through the heart of the city from north to south linking the train station with the Plaza de la Constitución, the major hub of activity. The *paseo* is interrupted only by the Plaza de las Batalles, a square dominated by a grotesque sculpture commemorating the battles of Nava de Tolosa (against the Moors) and Bailén (against the French).

Brief history

Although the area around the city is liberally dotted with Iberian settlements, it was probably as the Roman settlement of Auringis that Jaén was born. A centre noted for its **silver mines** and settled by the Moors shortly after the conquest of 711, it must have been a thriving place, judging by the number of mosques. The Moors also made use of the **hot springs** that had been known to the Romans and utilized by them in the construction of several baths. Fernando III's Christian forces captured the city – then part of the newly founded Nasrid kingdom of Granada – in 1246 and made its ruler Ibn al-Ahmar (aka Muhammad ibn Yusuf ibn Nasr) into a vassal, obliged to pay annual tribute. It was from Jaén, two and a half centuries later, that the final assault on Boabdil's Granada was launched. The city then entered into a slow decline that gathered pace in the seventeenth and eighteenth centuries and led many of its citizens to emigrate to the imperial colonies, evidenced by towns with the same name in countries as far apart as Peru and the Philippines. Although Jaén's strategic importance played a part in the War of Independence, the economic disruption caused brought further decline in its wake, from which the city never really recovered. The province and city continually register some of the lowest income levels in the region, with well over fifty percent of the population describing themselves as living in poverty.

Jaén cathedral

Pza Santa Maria • Mon–Sat 10am–3pm & 5–8.30pm, Sun 10–11.30am & 4–8.30pm; ritual display of the Lienzo del Santo Rostro Fri 10.30am–noon & 6–7pm • Charge • ⓦ catedraldejaen.org

Jaén's massive and magnificent **cathedral** dwarfs the city. Begun in 1492 after the demolition of the great mosque that had previously occupied the site, the cathedral was not completed until 1802. A number of architects turned their hand to the project during this period, including the great Andrés de Vandelvira, whose work had the most influence over the building as it looks today. The spectacular **west facade**, flanked by twin 60m-high towers framing Corinthian pillars and statuary by the seventeenth-century master, Pedro Roldán, is one of the masterpieces of Andalucian Renaissance architecture. Inside, the overall mood of the building is more sombre, with bundles of great Corinthian columns surging towards the roof of the nave. Fine sixteenth-century **choir stalls** have richly carved images from the Old Testament as well as a number of grisly martyrdoms. The dim side chapels also have some interesting artworks, among them an eighteenth-century *Virgen de las Angustias* (Our Lady of the Sorrows) by José de Mora in the fifth

ACCOMMODATION

Albergue Inturjoven	2
Hotel Europa	4
Hotel Xauen	3
Inhouse Apartamentos	5
Parador Castillo de Santa Catalina	1

● EATING

Almacenes del Pósito	6
Bar 82	5
Bar El Gorrión	3
Casa Antonio	7
Mesón Río Chico	8
Parador Castillo de Santa Catalina	1
Restaurante Támesis	2
El Tostón	4

Ancient Walls

Castillo de Santa Catalina & Centro de Interpretación

Ancient Walls

Córdoba

Iglesia De La Magdalena

Palacio de Los Uribes (250m)

Train Station (700m); Museo Provincial (250m)

Granada & Madrid

STA. BÁRBARA
HOSPITALICO
STMA. TRINIDAD
CONCEPCIÓN VIEJA
PEÑUELAS
LLAMA DE S. JUAN
PLATICANTE
JUANITOS
REVENTÓN
Santo Domingo
SORIA DE S. JUAN
PZA. DE STA. LUISA DE MARILLAC
San Juan
PZA. DE S. JUAN
LA CUMBRES
EL CLAVEL
LA ALEGRÍA
POSTIGO
S. MÁCIAS
SANTIAGO
AGUILAR
Palacio de Villardompardo
SAN ANDRÉS
San Andrés
Baños Árabes, Museo de Artes y Costumbres Populares and Museo Internacional de Arte Naïf

C. PALACIOS
LA PAZ
ALTA DE STA. ANA
MERCED ALTA
La Merced
BAZO
DUQUE
CAPITAN ARANDA ALTA
SAN LORENZO
PARRILLA
LOS MÁCIAS
SANTIAGO
ALMENDROS
SANTA CRUZ
MARTÍNEZ MOLINA
Santa Clara
SAN PEDRO
ARROYO DE SAN PEDRO
LOS HUÉRFANOS
SANTA CRUZ
PLAZA DE LA MERCED
PLAZA DE CRUZ RUEDA
CARRERA DE JESÚS
ARCO DE S. LORENZO
Escuela de Artes y Oficios
ARROYO SELLADA
CONDE OBISPO
MONTERO MOYA
COMPAÑÍA
PLAZA DE LA AUDIENCIA
SAN BARTOLOMÉ
GRACIA
LAS HIGUERAS
HUERTAS
Monasterio de Santa Teresa
Palacio Arzobispal
Ayuntamiento
Turismo
MAESTRA
CAMP ANAS
BERNARDO LÓPEZ
CERÓN
PLAZA DE CERVANTES
DOCTOR ARROYO
PLAZA DE SAN BARTOLOMÉ
San Bartolomé
PLAZA DE JACINTO HIGUERAS
MILLÁN DE PRIEGO

GARCÍA REQUENA
JIMÉNEZ SERRANO
COELLO
JULIO ÁNGEL
ALCANT ARILLA
Catedral
ÁLAMOS
PLAZA DE S. FRANCISCO
Diputación
SALIDO
CAP. OVIEDO
PLAZA DE LOS JARDINILLOS
TORRES ACOSTA
CASTILLA
MARTÍNEZ MONTAÑÉS
ARQ. BERGES

Jabalcuz

FUENTE DE DON DIEGO
JOSEF A SEGOVIA
RAMÓN Y CAJAL
HURTADO
BERNABÉ SORIANO
PLAZA DEL PÓSITO
CARNICERÍAS
Palacio de Vilches
SAN CLEMENTE
MADRE SOLEDAD
SAN BARTOLOMÉ

San Félix

JORGE MORALES
MESSIA
MUÑOGRANADA
PESCADERÍA
Hacienda
ROLDÁN Y MARÍN
PASEO DE LA ESTACIÓN
CID CAMPEADOR
PLAZA COCA DE LA PIÑERA

ADARVES BATERÍA
OBISPO AGUILAR
S. FERNANDO
LOS ROMERO
IGNACIO FIGUEROA
PLAZA DE LA CONSTITUCIÓN
C. NUEVA
CORREA WEGLISON
NAVAS DE TOLOSA
AVENIDA DE MADRID
PIO XII
Bus Station

TORO
SALINEROS
VICENTE MONTUNO
PEDRO DÍAZ
R. DE LA CAPILLA
CUA TRO TORRES
V. DE LA CAPILLA
Rastro
CUESTA DE BELÉN

CARRETAS
ADARVES BAJOS
San Ildefonso
TEODORO CALVACHE
COBO MEDINA
DOCTORES AGAZ ZUBELZU
VERGARA
AVDA. DE GRANADA
SANTA CATALINA
ARTESANOS
GUADALQUIVIR

El Recinto
AGUSTINA DE ARAGÓN
AZULEJOS
LAS BERNARDAS
PTA. DEL ÁNGEL
Convento de las Bernardas
GENERAL CAST AÑOS

AGUSTINA DE ARAGÓN
CAMPO DE HÍPICA
Alameda de Calvo Sotelo
SIXTO CÁMARA
Plaza de Toros

N

0 — 200
metres

JAÉN

side chapel to the right. The church fills up on Friday mornings when the **lienzo del Santo Rostro** is ritually removed from its coffer behind the high altar. This Byzantine cloth icon bearing a likeness of Christ is believed locally to be the napkin with which St Veronica wiped Christ's face en route to Calvary. Long queues form to kiss the icon (preserved behind glass) and the attending priest wipes it with a handkerchief after each devotee.

The sacristy **museum** displays works by artists of the region as well as the *tenebrario*, a fifteen-armed candlestick by Master Bartolomé de Jaén who also made the magnificent *reja* in the Capilla Real at Granada (see page 446). Two fine seventeenth-century sculptures by Martínéz Montáñés, *San Lorenzo* and *Cristo Nazareno*, are also on display.

San Bartolomé

Pza San Bartolomé; entry through the sacristy • Mon 9.30–10.30am, Tues–Sat 9.30–10.30am & 6.30–8pm, Sun 9.30–10.30am & noon–1.15pm • Free

Between the cathedral zone and the Baños Árabes area, the sixteenth-century **San Bartolomé** is worth a look. A handsome church with a stone facade and triple belfry, it boasts an interior with a fine Mudéjar *artesonado* ceiling, an equally fine retablo by Sebastián de Solís, a fifteenth-century Gothic ceramic font and an outstanding *Expiration of Christ* by José de Medina.

Baños Árabes

Palacio de Villardompardo, Pza de María Luisa de Marillac s/n • Tues–Sat 9am–10pm, Sun 9am–3pm • Free

The **Baños Árabes**, a remarkable Moorish *hammam*, is the largest to survive in Spain. Originally part of an eleventh-century Moorish palace, the baths fell into disuse after the *Reconquista* and were used as a tannery. In the sixteenth century the Palacio de Villardompardo, whose restoration finished in 2014 and houses the **Museo de Artes y Costumbres Populares**, was built over them. They were rediscovered early last century and in the 1980s were painstakingly restored. 21st-century modifications now lead you into the baths over a glass floor allowing views of the Roman and Moorish remains that surround the complex. The various rooms (cold, tepid and hot) have wonderful brickwork ceilings with typical star-shaped windows, and pillars supporting elegant horseshoe arches. An underground passage (now closed) connected the baths with the centre of the Moorish palace, on top of which was built the Monastery of Santo Domingo (see page 400).

Museo de Artes y Costumbres Populares

Tues–Sat 9am–10pm, Sun 9am–3pm • Free

The **Museo de Artes y Costumbres Populares** contains a fascinating and well-presented folk history of the province on three floors using artefacts, clothing, toys, ceramics, photos and audiovisual aids.

Museo Internacional de Arte Naïf

Tues–Sat 9am–10pm, Sun 9am–3pm • Free

Also in the Baños Árabes complex is the **Museo Internacional de Arte Naïf**, the only museum of its kind in Spain. The museum displays works by (mainly) Spanish and international artists with the star attraction being the thirty paintings by Navarran artist María Victoria Otano Lecumberri.

South of the Baños Árabes

Just to the east of the Baños Árabes on Calle San Andrés stands the **church of San Andrés** (visits Mon–Sat by appointment only; free; ☎634 861 999) which, in the sixteenth-century Santa Capilla, contains a fabulous *reja* (altar screen) depicting the

Holy Family and the *Tree of Jesse* by Maestro Bartolomé of Jaén, creator of the *reja* in the Capilla Real in Granada (see page 446).

A block west of the Baños Árabes on Plaza de San Juan lies the ancient post-*Reconquista* church of **San Juan** (Mon–Sat 6.30–8.30pm, Sun 11.30am–noon; free), which has an elegant Romanesque tower and, inside, a fine sixteenth-century sculpture of the Crucifixion by Sebastián de Solís. A couple of streets north, Calle Santísima Trinidad leads to a **path** that climbs, ruggedly in parts, to the castle of Santa Catalina (see page 401), a much shorter route than the 3km-plus road.

North of the Baños Árabes

Standing to the north of the Baños Árabes on Calle Santo Domingo, the **Monastery of Santo Domingo** (ring the bell to see the patio Mon–Fri 9am–2pm; free), erected over a Moorish palace, was originally a fourteenth-century Dominican monastery and later became Jaén's university. Later still it was a seat of the Inquisition, before being transformed in more recent times into the office of the provincial historical archive (Archivo Histórico). From its earlier incarnations a fine sixteenth-century **portal** by Vandelvira and a beautiful **patio** with elegant twinned Tuscan columns survive.

Iglesia de la Magdalena

Pza de la Magdalena • Tues–Fri 11am–1pm & 5.30–8.30pm, Sat 11am–1pm & 6–8pm, Sun 9.30am–1pm • Free

The oldest church in Jaén was built over a mosque, the minaret of which is now its bell tower, and a patio at the rear preserves a pool used in Moorish times for ritual ablutions. In the cloister you can still see a few Roman tombstones used in the construction of the original Moorish building; this quarter was also the centre of the ancient Roman town. Inside, the church has a superb **retablo** by Jacobo Florentino depicting scenes from the Passion.

Museo Provincial

Paseo de la Estación 27 • Mid-June to mid-Sept Tues–Sun 9am–3pm; mid-Sept to mid-June Tues–Sat 9am–8pm, Sun 9am–3pm • Free

Five minutes' walk northeast of the centre, the excellent **Museo Provincial** has a remarkable collection of Iberian stone **sculptures**, among the most important in Spain.

Iberian collection

Housed in a separate building to the side of the museum, the museum's **Iberian sculptures** were found near the town of Porcuna, close to the province's western border, and date from the fifth century BC. One is of a magnificent bull, while another is a strange fragment – titled *grifomaquia* – depicting a struggle between a man and a griffon. All the works betray the artistic influence of the classical Greek world on the fertile Iberian imagination. The strange fact revealed by the archeological excavations when these works came to light is that they had been deliberately broken a short time after their execution and then laid in a long trench. No satisfactory explanation for this has yet been put forward. More sculptures are being put on show each year as they are uncovered by archeologists.

Main building

Items on display in the main building include Phoenician jewellery and ointment phials, Greek vases, and Roman mosaics and sculpture, among them an outstanding fourth-century **sarcophagus** found near Martós depicting seven miracles of Christ including the transformation of water into wine. A 21st-century addition here is a complete full-scale walk-in reconstruction of the remarkable fourth-century BC Iberian necropolis **tomb** at Toya near Cazorla. Room 11 deals with Jaén's significant **Moorish period** and has lamps and stoneware as well as a whole jugful of money that someone buried and never came back to collect. This room also has some fine **ceramics** that verify the Moorish origin of the green glazed plates and vases, still the hallmark of the pottery of Jaén province. A Visigothic section has examples of jewellery, vases and metalwork from this hazy period in Spanish history.

Upstairs, the **Museo de Bellas Artes** starts out with some interesting medieval wood sculpture before quickly degenerating into a hotchpotch of fairly awful stuff from the nineteenth and twentieth centuries, although there are a few laughs, not to mention a large number of steamy nudes. The tedium is somewhat relieved by a work by Huelvan artist Daniel Vasquéz Díaz, an engraving by Picasso and some interesting drawings and paintings by Manuel Angeles Ortiz, a native of Jaén who was a great friend of both Picasso and García Lorca.

Castillo de Santa Catalina

Ctra del Castillo s/n • July–Sept Mon–Sat 10am–2pm & 5–9pm, Sun 10am–3pm; Oct–June Mon–Sat 10am–6pm, Sun 10am–3pm • Charge • Taxis leave from Pza de la Libertad by the bus station; you can also walk to the castle on a 3km, near-vertical hike from the Baños Árabes, or take a much shorter (but still pretty taxing) path up from C/Santísima Trinidad, to the east of Santo Domingo

The **Castillo de Santa Catalina**, dominating the crag that rises behind the city, was originally a Moorish fortress constructed in the thirteenth century by Ibn al-Ahmar. After the Reconquista, the castle was much altered and today part of it has been stylishly converted into a modern *parador* (see page 402); little of the Moorish edifice now survives. What does remain has been reconstructed as a **Centro de Interpretación** housing – in the fort's five towers – a series of hi-tech interactive audiovisual gadgets explaining the building's history. A number of secret passageways connected the Moorish fortress with the town below and a few of these have been discovered.

A path from the *parador* car park leads to the older and ruined part of the edifice at the castle's southern tip, where a *mirador* beneath a huge, whitewashed cross gives a **spectacular view** of the city laid out below your feet and dominated by the massive cathedral. Beyond, Jaén's wealth and misery, the endless lines of olive groves, disappear over the hills into the haze. Non-guests are welcome to use the *parador's* bar and restaurant.

ARRIVAL AND INFORMATION

By train The train station is at the end of Paseo de la Estación, a good 10min walk (or an easier ride on bus #4 or #8) from the centre.

Destinations Andújar (4 daily; 45min); Córdoba (4 daily; 1hr 40min); Madrid (4 daily Mon–Sat, 3 on Sun; 3hr 45min); Seville (4 daily; 3hr).

By bus Jaén's bus station (⟨ᴡ⟩epassa.es for details of all Jaén's provincial services) is on Pza Coca de la Pinera, just off the Paseo de la Estación.

Destinations Almería (2 daily; 4hr); Almuñecar (daily; 3hr 45min); Baeza/Úbeda (16 daily; 1hr 25min); Cazorla

(3 daily; 2hr 30min); Córdoba (9 daily Mon–Fri, 6 on Sat & Sun; 2hr); Granada (14 daily Mon–Fri, 11 on Sat & Sun; 1hr 15min); La Guardia (4 daily Mon–Fri, 3 on Sat; 20min); Málaga (3 daily; 3hr 30min); Seville (5 daily; 4hr).

By car Arriving by car, either use the signed pay car parks around the centre or ask your lodging to advise.

Turismo C/Maestra 8 (Mon–Fri 9am–7.30pm, Sat 9.30am–3pm & 5–7pm, Sun 10am–3pm; ☎ 953 190 455; ⟨ᴡ⟩turjaen.org).

Provincial tourist office Diputación Provincial building, Pza de San Francisco (Mon–Fri 8am–3pm; ☎ 953 248 000).

ACCOMMODATION

SEE MAP PAGE 398

Jaén's **accommodation** is limited, and with the exception of the youth hostel, relatively expensive. However, there's usually no difficulty in finding a place to stay at any time of the year, and there are no seasonal rate changes.

★ **Albergue Inturjoven** C/Borja s/n; ⟨ᴡ⟩inturjoven. com. This youth hostel, with the imposing facade of a former eighteenth-century hospital, has excellent rooms – modern, minimalist, en-suite a/c doubles. There's also a pool, and, somewhat incongruously, a full-blown spa where

the variety of treatments cost far more than the rooms. €

Hotel Europa Pza de Belén 1; ⟨ᴡ⟩hoteleuropajaen.es. Perhaps the best of the more upmarket places in the centre, where attractive a/c rooms come with safe and satellite TV. The hotel also offers paid parking. €

Hotel Xauen Pza Deán Mazas 3; ⟨ᴡ⟩hotelxauenjaen. com. A modern option in the centre with decent a/c rooms with TV, plus a roof terrace with views of the castle. Breakfast is included. €€

Inhouse Apartamentos C/Lope de Sosa 20 ☎ 953 049 567. In a quiet residential area (with street parking), modern, comfortable a/c apartments for two or four with satellite TV and fully equipped kitchen. €€–€€€

★ **Parador Castillo de Santa Catalina** Castillo, 3km above the town; ⓦ parador.es. For a truly memorable experience you could stay at Spain's most spectacularly sited hotel. The very comfortable and elegantly furnished rooms have fine views with a sheer drop to the valley below; facilities include a pool, restaurant (see page 402), bar and ample parking. €€€

EATING

SEE MAP PAGE 398

Jaén tends to shut down after dark and in the absence of much nightlife you'll probably compensate by eating and drinking. In the centre, the best place to find food is on the east side of Plaza de la Constitución. Here, the tiny **Calle Nueva** has a whole crowd of tapas bars and places to eat. Another good tapas hunting ground lies near the cathedral.

RESTAURANTS

Casa Antonio C/Fermín Palma 3, north of the bus station; ⓦ casantonio.es. This top culinary choice offers innovative *jiennense* and Basque-inspired dishes; house specials include *cochinillo* (suckling pig) and *paletilla de cabrito asada* (stewed goat). €€€

Mesón Río Chico C/Nueva 12; ☎ 953 240 802. Atmospheric bar-restaurant with the dining room upstairs. Reasonably priced fish and meat dishes include *bacalao estilo mesón* (cod house style) and *rabo de toro* (oxtail). Good weekday *menú* for a few euros. €€

Parador Castillo de Santa Catalina Castillo, 3km above the town; ⓦ parador.es. To feast in baronial splendour you'll need to climb – or take a taxi – to this spectacularly located restaurant inside the *parador* (see page 402). In a re-created medieval banqueting room, dine on superb cooking, including a good-value *menú*. €€€

Restaurante Támesis C/Maestro Sapena 9; ⓦ restaurantetamesis.es. One of the best fine dining options in this part of Andalucía. Choose from tapas, sharing plates – some with a Mediterranean-Japanese twist – or the tasting menu that includes five extra virgin olive oils to try. Steak tartare is a house special, as is the *revuelto de habas con bacalao* (scrambled eggs with broad beans and cod). €€€

TAPAS BARS

Almacenes del Pósito Pza del Pósito 1, above the west side of Pza de la Constitución. A popular tapas, *raciones* and *copas* venue with a separate bar and lounge that are warm in winter and cool in summer. €

Bar 82 C/Arcos del Consuelo. If you can, squeeze yourself into this small, busy bar with an impressive list of tapas. Locals rate the *embutidos* (sausages) and *calamares* (fried squid). €

Bar El Gorrión C/Arcos del Consuelo. One of the city's most vibrant and atmospheric bars, noted for its *morcilla* and *salchichón* (salami); they also offer a range of cooked tapas such as *judías con perdiz* (beans with partridge). €

El Tostón C/Bernardo López 11. A reliable choice for tapas and *raciones*. Serves a good *revuelto de bacalao y gambas* (scrambled eggs with cod and prawns). €€

Baeza and around

Campo de Baeza, soñaré contigo cuando no te vea.
Fields of Baeza, I will dream of you when I can no longer see you.

Antonio Machado (1875–1939)

Fifty kilometres from Jaén along the winding A316, **BAEZA** is a tiny, compact and provincial country town with a perpetual Sunday air about it. Sited on the escarpment of the Loma de Úbeda, both Baeza and the neighbouring town of Úbeda (see page 407) have an extraordinary density of exuberant **Renaissance palaces**, richly endowed churches and magnificent public squares that are among the finest in Spain. Most of Baeza's main attractions lie within a few minutes' walk of the pleasant central joined squares of **Plaza de España** and the larger **Paseo de la Constitución**. Most monuments have no entry fee, but you may offer the guardian a small *propina* (tip).

Baeza's lively annual *feria* takes place during the second and third weeks in August and is a wonderfully rural affair with processions of *gigantones* (carnival giants), fireworks and an enormous funfair on the edge of town.

Brief history

Important in Roman times as Beatia, Baeza was later a Visigothic bishopric and then a prosperous commercial and agricultural centre under the Moors. After a prolonged and bitter struggle the town fell to the Christian forces in 1227, and *hidalgos* or nobles were granted estates in the surrounding countryside with orders to defend this frontier zone. The power of these noble houses was so untrammelled that they were soon warring among themselves for control of the town (a favoured place of battle being Baeza's Alcázar – until Isabel had it demolished). It was later, in the sixteenth century, however, that Baeza embarked on its most prosperous period. The nobility, made rich by farming and textile production, endowed the town with numerous Renaissance buildings.

Paseo de la Constitución

On the eastern side of the bar-lined **Paseo de la Constitución** is **La Alhóndiga**, an elegant porticoed sixteenth-century corn exchange and, almost opposite across the gardens, the arcaded eighteenth-century **Casa Consistorial**, or old town hall, which once fronted the old market square. At the southern end of the *paseo*, you'll find the **Plaza de los Leones** (also called the Plaza del Populo), a delightful cobbled square enclosed by Renaissance buildings. A central fountain incorporates Roman lions and a statue – which locals believe is Imilce, the Iberian wife of the Carthaginian general, Hannibal. The fountain is overlooked by some remarkable buildings including the **Antigua Carnicería** (old slaughterhouse), bearing

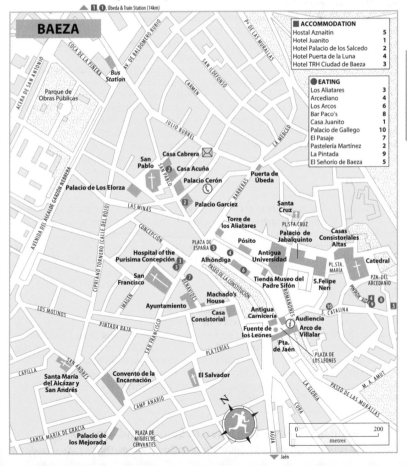

4

the arms of Carlos V, and beside the arch at the far end, the Audiencia housing the Turismo (see page 406). Also here, on a rounded balcony flanking the double arch of the Arco de Villalar and the Puerta de Jaén, the first Mass of the *Reconquista* is reputed to have been celebrated. The Puerta de Jaén was a memento (or rebuke) left by Carlos V to the town that had opposed him, and commemorated the Germanic ruler's procession through here in 1526 en route to marry Isabel of Portugal.

Palacio de Jabalquinto

Pza de Santa Cruz • **Patio** Mon–Fri 9am–2pm • Free

The stepped street behind the Plaza de los Leones ascends (via C/Romanones and C/Juan de Ávila) to a cluster of monuments that includes the finest of Baeza's palaces, the **Palacio de Jabalquinto** – now a seminary – with an elaborate Isabelline front showing marked Moorish influence in its stalactite decoration. Built in the fifteenth century by the Benavides family, the tranquil interior patio has a double tier of arcades around a central fountain and a superb Baroque **staircase** with fine carving.

Antigua Universidad

C/Beato Juan de Ávila s/n • **Patio & Aula Machado** Mon–Sun 10am–2pm & 4–7pm • Free

Next to the Palacio de Jabalquinto, the **Antigua Universidad** (old university) was founded in 1538. After functioning for nearly three centuries as a centre of study and debate, its charter was revoked in 1824 during the tyrannical reign of Fernando VII. From 1875 it was used as a school until, in 1979, the building once again became a centre of higher learning – as a summer school for the University of Granada. The interior has an elegant patio and, next to a sixteenth-century lecture hall (the Aula Machado), the preserved **classroom** used by the great *sevillano* poet and writer Antonio Machado when he served as a teacher here from 1912 to 1919. This experience must have provided much of the material for his most famous prose work, *Juan de Mairena*, the observations on life and culture of a fictional schoolmaster.

Santa Cruz

Pza de Santa Cruz s/n • Mon–Sat 11am–1pm • Free

The remarkable church of **Santa Cruz** is Baeza's oldest, built shortly after the *Reconquista* in the thirteenth century, although later much restored. Converted from an earlier mosque, the church betrays a combination of late Romanesque and early Gothic architectural styles. The austere, white-walled interior has slender stone columns as well as some fourteenth- and fifteenth-century frescoes, and (in the east aisle) the preserved arch of the *mihrab*.

Tienda Museo del Padre Sifón

C/Arco de las Escuelas 2 • Usually open at weekends only, with no fixed hours • Free

On Calle Arcos de las Escuelas you will find one of Baeza's quirkier attractions – a shop ostensibly selling local ceramics. Passing beyond the shelves of pots and a bottling plant for mineral water (thus the sculptor's nickname, "Father Siphon"), you'll enter a studio with a series of remarkable **marble replicas** of Baeza's famous buildings, including the Ayuntamiento, cathedral and the Palacio de Jabalquinto, all created in eye-straining detail by the shop's late, self-taught proprietor and local character, Diego Lozano, whose heirs now only open the shop at weekends.

Catedral de la Natividad de Nuestra Señora and around

Pza de Santa María s/n • Mon–Fri 10.30am–2pm & 4–7pm, Sat 10.30am–7pm, Sun 10.30am–6pm • Charge

---

BAEZA'S RENAISSANCE PALACES

Heading north from the Plaza de España, pedestrianized Calle San Pablo has a number of interesting Renaissance palaces, many with impressive facades, dating from the sixteenth century. In addition to the Gothic **Palacio Garcíez** (or Salcedo), now an upmarket hotel with a fine patio (see page 406), and the **Casa Acuña**, the following are well worth a look.

Casa Cabrera C/San Pablo. A *palacio* that's especially notable for its elegant Plateresque facade, which incorporates a double window and frieze over the entrance.

Palacio Cerón C/San Pablo. This palace played an important role in the cultural life of the town as Baeza's Casino; ask to be shown the wonderfully evocative salon upstairs with elegant mirrors and velvet curtains.

Former member Antonio Machado gave poetry readings here, and you can see the piano once played by a visiting Federico García Lorca.

Palacio de los Elorza C/Intendente P. Olavide. The remains of what must have been a fine sixteenth-century mansion, featuring a wonderfully exuberant Renaissance portal.

The **Plaza de Santa María** is another of Baeza's glorious squares, with a few welcome, shade-providing trees, fronted by a nucleus of fine Renaissance buildings. The rather squat sixteenth-century **Catedral de la Natividad de Nuestra Señora** dominates the square and inside has a fine nave by Andrés de Vandelvira that is, in many ways, a scaled-down version of his cathedral at Jaén. Like several of Baeza's and Úbeda's churches, the cathedral also has painted *rejas* by Maestro Bartolomé, a local craftsman who was responsible for some of the finest examples of this uniquely Spanish contribution to Renaissance art. His work enclosing the choir, with its depictions of a Virgin and Child accompanied by angels and cherubs, is stunning. In the Gothic **cloister**, part of the old mosque – which the church replaced – has been uncovered, but the cathedral's real novelty is a huge silver *custodia* cunningly hidden behind a painting of St Peter thats whirls aside on the insertion of a coin. To the east of the cathedral, and beyond Plaza del Arcediano, a narrow street leads to a *mirador* with a fine **view** over the olive groves in the valley of the Guadalquivir towards the distant Cazorla mountain range beyond.

Adjoining the cathedral on the north side is the old Renaissance **Casas Consistoriales Altas** (town hall) with Plateresque features, formerly the palace of the Cabrera family who have another mansion in the town. In the centre of the **Plaza de Santa María** is a sixteenth-century fountain erected by the same family, with pilasters and crude caryatids supporting the arms of Felipe II. Beyond this are the graffiti-covered walls of the sixteenth-century seminary of **San Felipe Neri** where students record their names and dates in bull's blood – a traditional way of celebrating graduation. The building now houses the International University of Andalucía.

Ayuntamiento and around

C/Benavides

West of the Paseo de la Constitución, the magnificent **Ayuntamiento** was originally the Palace of Justice and prison. Completed in 1559, its richly ornamented facade is exuberantly Plateresque with elegant balconies, coats of arms and, above, a phalanx of gargoyles decorating the cornice. At the end of the street and facing the same edifice is the charming (now privately owned) little **house of Antonio Machado**, marked with a plaque, where the poet lived for most of his time in Baeza.

Hospital of the Purísima Concepción

Calle San Francisco passes the exterior of the **Hospital of the Purísima Concepción**, with its elegant Renaissance facade. Adjoining it is the ruined convent of **San Francisco**, designed by Vandelvira and badly damaged during the War of Independence.

Sections of both buildings have now been converted into a hotel, banqueting hall and restaurant.

ARRIVAL AND INFORMATION

By train The nearest train station is Estación Linares-Baeza, 14km away and served by frequent trains from Seville, Córdoba and Granada. Infrequent buses connect with the town; a €15 taxi ride the best option.

By bus The bus station is at the end of C/San Pablo and along C/Julio Burell.

Destinations Cazorla (3 daily; 1hr 30min); Granada (7 daily;

BAEZA

2hr); Jaén (14 daily; 1hr); Úbeda (20 daily; 15min).

Turismo Pza del Populo s/n (Mon–Fri 9am–7.30pm, Sat & Sun 9.30am–3pm; ☎ 953 779 982). Housed in the splendid sixteenth-century former *Audiencia* (appeal court), this office can supply maps and information as well as details of guided city tours.

ACCOMMODATION

SEE MAP PAGE 403

Baeza has a decent range of places to stay, some of which are architectural gems. There's usually no problem finding rooms except during the *feria* in mid-Aug, and even then you should have no trouble if you ring ahead. **Prices** are often far lower if you don't stay on Fri or Sat.

★ **Hostal Aznaitin** C/Cabreros 2; ⓦ hostalaznaitin. com. Splendid modern *hostal* in the old quarter with well-equipped, pristine and stylish en-suite a/c rooms. Facilities include a pool and library. Breakfast is included. €

Hotel Juanito Avda Alcalde Puche Pardo 57; ⓦ juanitobaeza.com. Reasonably priced hotel for pleasant rooms with a/c and TV above the top-notch restaurant of the same name. Ask for a west-facing room at the back or a high room on the front (both with views) to avoid odours from the *gasolinera* next door. €€

Hotel Palacio de los Salcedo C/San Pablo 18; ⓦ palaciodelossalcedo.com. Lovely converted sixteenth-century palace with slightly over-the-top Louis XV-style rooms with a/c, TV, minibar and safe. Interior rooms are gloomy, but come with jacuzzi. Breakfast is included. €€

★ **Hotel Puerta de la Luna** C/Pintada Alta s/n; ⓦ hotelpuertadelaluna.com. Beautiful four-star hotel in a refurbished seventeenth-century *casa palacio*. The comfortably furnished tile-floored rooms are airy and well equipped. Facilities include two delightful patios, restaurant, library, small pool and a car park. €€€

Hotel TRH Ciudad de Baeza C/Concepción 3; ⓦ trhhoteles.com. Four-star hotel with attractive a/c rooms, partly housed in a converted Renaissance monastery with a stunning glassed-in patio. Breakfast is included. €€€

EATING

SEE MAP PAGE 403

RESTAURANTS

Casa Juanito Avda Alcalde Puche Pardo 57; ⓦ juanitobaeza.com. Opened in 1952, Baeza's most celebrated restaurant is lined with photos of the great and the good who have dined here. Traditional dishes such as *ensalada de perdiz* (partridge salad) and *cabrito al horno* (roast kid) star, and often feature on the *menú de degustación*. €€€

Palacio de Gallego C/Santa Catalina; ☎ 667 760 184. Specializing in *asados* (roasted dishes) including meat, tuna and *almejas* (clams) on the barbecue, this is one of the best restaurants in town. Situated near the Catedral, it's divided into a tapas bar and formal restaurant with pleasant terrace. €€€

El Pasaje C/Benavides 3; ☎ 953 741 729. A reliable place with a terrace offering a variety of fish and meat dishes – *ensalada de perdiz* (partridge salad) and *chuletillas de cordero lechal* (lamb chops) are specials, and there's a decently priced *menú*. €€

La Pintada C/Pintada Alta s/n; ☎ 953 74 70 19. Part of the *Hotel Puerta de la Luna* (see page 406), the restaurant has formal dining inside as well as patio tables. Traditional dishes feature on the menu, such as *espinacas baezanas*

(Baeza-style spinach) and *solomillo de jabalí* (wild boar steak). Good tasting *menú*. €€€

El Señorío de Baeza C/Concepción 3; ⓦ trhhoteles. com. The restaurant of the *Hotel TRH Ciudad de Baeza* (see page 406) is popular with locals; its good-value *menú* includes local dishes such as *pipirrana* (*jamón* and vegetable salad). €€€

CAFÉ

Pastelería Martínez C/San Pablo, next to the Palacio Cabrera; ☎ 953 748 219. Enjoy teatime treats at this café, which serves delicious pastries made on the premises. €

TAPAS BARS

Los Aliatares Pza de España s/n; ☎ 953 740 193. This modern bar is a great place to kick off your day with a lazy breakfast on the town's best terrace. Later on it serves good *tapas de autor* (signature tapas) such as *tortilla de gula* (eel omelette), as well as *raciones* and *tostas* – try the partidge pâté with anchovies. €

Arcediano C/Barbacana s/n; ☎ 953 748 184. An excellent tapas bar off the east side of Pza de España. They specialize in local cheeses and *salchichón* (salami), and offer a wide selection of wines. €

Los Arcos Portales Alhóndiga 11; ☎669 769 336. Reliable bar serving up a range of tapas, *raciones* and house specials including *patatas baezanas* (potatoes with mushrooms) and *bacalao a la baezana* (Baeza-style cod). There's also a decent *menú*. €€

Bar Paco's C/Pintada Alta s/n; ☎953 747 019. Part of the *Hotel Puerta de la Luna* (see page 406), this small, intimate bar has a great reputation for sophisticated tapas such as *mejillones al curry* (curried mussels). Choose one complimentary *tapa* with your drink from the long list and, if you're hungry, order further tapas or *raciones*. €

La Laguna

9km southwest of Baeza; 2km down a signed right turn off the A316 just beyond the village of Puente del Obispo • **Museo de la Cultura del Olivo** Open daily; see website for times • Charge • ⓦ museodelaculturadelolivo.com

La Laguna, a former hacienda or olive-oil estate and mill bought in 1992 by the Junta de Andalucía, now houses the impressive **Museo de la Cultura del Olivo**, outlining the history of the olive and production methods used since Roman times. The patio garden has examples of olive species from all over the world. La Laguna also possesses its own farm and lake (*laguna*).

Úbeda

Some 9km east of Baeza and built on the same escarpment overlooking the valley of the Guadalquivir, **ÚBEDA** looks less promising when you reach it. Don't be put off, though, for hidden away in the old quarter is one of the finest **Renaissance** architectural jewels in the whole of Spain, and perhaps even in Europe. During May and June Úbeda's annual **International Festival of Music and Dance** attracts big names from flamenco, rock, opera, jazz, blues and ballet. **Día de San Miguel**, on September 29, is when carnival giants, fireworks and a flamenco festival honour the town's patron saint.

4

Brief history

Little is known of Úbeda's previous incarnation as the Roman town of Betula, and it was only in the **Moorish** period that Obdah, as it became, grew into a prosperous and important centre endowed with walls and a castle. Following the Christian victory over the Moors at Navas de Tolosa in 1212, the Moors from Baeza moved into the city, feeling it provided a more secure refuge against the Christian forces. Despite this, Úbeda was taken a week later and, although an interlude of further freedom for the Muslim occupants was purchased from the Christian armies with massive donations, the town fell conclusively to Fernando III (El Santo) in 1234. As happened in Baeza, numerous noble families were then established by the king and built their mansions in the town. These haughty "**lions of Úbeda**", as they styled themselves, were soon warring among each other, the Arandas fighting the Traperas, and the Molinas against the Cuevas. The fighting got so bad at one point that in 1503 Fernando and Isabel ordered the destruction of the town's walls and towers, to enable the unruly aristocrats to be kept in check. Twelve of these noble families are represented by the twelve lions on the town's coat of arms.

In common with Baeza, it was in the sixteenth century, as a producer of textiles traded across Europe, that Úbeda's fortunes reached their zenith and members of the same noble families came to hold prominent positions in the imperial Spanish court. This was the age of the houses of **Cobos** and **Molinos**, two families who, linked by marriage, dominated the town's affairs. They were also responsible for employing **Andrés de Vandelvira** as their principal architect, whose buildings are the glory of Úbeda today. This prosperity, however, was short lived and the town declined in the seventeenth century as sharply as it had flourished in the sixteenth, which explains its architectural unity and lack of any significant Baroque edifices. Today, Úbeda is a moderately prosperous provincial town.

ÚBEDA

ACCOMMODATION

Las Casas del Consul	6
Hostal Santa María de Úbeda	4
Hotel La Paz	2
El Losal	1
Palacio de la Rambla	5
Parador Condestable Dávalos	3

● EATING

Asador Al-Andalus	5
Cantina La Estación	1
El Marqués	4
Parador Condestable Dávalos	3
Taberna Misa de 12	2

POTTERS' QUARTER

Alfarería Almarza
Alfarería Paco Tito
Alfarería Pablo Tito
San Millán
Alfarería Góngora
Puerta del Losal
Alfarería Melchor Tito

Mirador

Hospital de los Honrados Viejos del Salvador
Capilla del Salvador
Palacio de Mancera
Santa María de los Reales Alcázares
Antiguo Pósito
Palacio de D. Francisco de los Cobos
Oratorio de San Juan de la Cruz
Puerta del Losal
Casa de los Manueles
Casa de los Salvajes
Palacio del Condestable Dávalos
Palacio de las Cadenas
Alfarería Tito
Casa Montiel
Museo Arqueológico
Sinagoga del Agua
San Pablo
Ayuntamiento Viejo
Palacio Vela de los Cobos
Convento de Santa Clara
Museo Arte Andalusí
Iglesia de San Lorenzo
Pal. Guadiana
San Pedro
Torre del Reloj
El Marqués
Casa de las Torres
Puerta de Granada
San Nicolás
Casa del Caballerizo Ortega
Iglesia de la Trinidad
Palacio de los Bussianos
Palacio de la Rambla
Hospital de Santiago
Parque de Vandelvira
Plaza de Toros
Bus Station

Plaza de Vázquez de Molina and around

Follow the signs for the "Zona Monumental" and you'll eventually reach the **Plaza de Vázquez de Molina**, a magnificent Renaissance square at the heart of the old town. Most of the buildings around this square are the late sixteenth-century work of **Andrés de Vandelvira**, the architect of Baeza's cathedral and of numerous churches both in that town and here.

Palacio de las Cadenas

Pza Vázquez de Molina • Patio Mon–Fri 9am–2pm • Free

At the western end of the plaza, the **Palacio de las Cadenas** (or "chains", which once decorated the facade) was built by Vandelvira for the secretary of Felipe II, Juan Vázquez de Molina, whose family arms crown the doorway of a beautiful classical facade. The interior, these days occupied by the Ayuntamiento, features a superb double-tier arcaded patio, which you can visit.

Santa María de los Reales Alcázares

Pza Vázquez de Molina • Daily 10am–2pm & 5–8pm • Charge

Opposite the Palacio de las Cadenas, and between the lions marking the edge of the mansion's domain, lies the church of **Santa María de los Reales Alcázares**, built on the site of a former mosque and extensively restored in 2012. Behind the facade, topped by a double belfry, an elegant Gothic cloister encloses what was once the ablutions patio of the mosque. The church contains a fine *reja* by Maestro Bartolomé of Jaén depicting the Tree of Jesse.

Palacio del Condestable Dávalos

Pza Vázquez de Molina

The **Palacio del Condestable Dávalos**, which Vandelvira had a hand in designing, is the former dwelling of the chaplain of the church of El Salvador. This elegant building now houses what must be the most impressive *parador* in Andalucía (see page 412). A stunning arcaded interior patio now serves as the hotel's bar, and is best contemplated over a cool drink.

Capilla del Salvador and around

Pza Vázquez de Molina • Mon–Sat 9.30am–2pm & 4.30–6.30pm, Sun 11.30am–3pm & 4.30–7.30pm • Charge

At the eastern end of the Plaza Vázquez de Molina, Vandelvira erected the **Capilla del Salvador**, Úbeda's finest church and one of the masterpieces of Spanish Renaissance architecture. Vandelvira was in fact working to a design created in 1536 by Diego de Siloé (architect of Málaga's and Granada's cathedrals) but typically added his own flourishes. The church was originally the chapel of the mansion – which later burned down – of Francisco de Cobos y Molina, secretary of state to Carlos V and one of the most powerful men of his time. This remarkable building is almost unique in Spain for being built within a very short period (1540–1556) with hardly any later alterations. It also preserves many of its interior furnishings. The exterior **facade** has a carving of the Transfiguration of Christ flanked by statues of San Pedro and San Andrés with a wealth of Plateresque detail. Above the north door around the corner, Vandelvira has placed an image in the tympanum that is almost his trademark – Santiago the Moor slayer, used in Baeza and on the hospital of Santiago in the north of the town.

Entry to the church is via the doorway on the south side. The single naved interior with a beautiful cupola has a brilliantly animated retablo on the high altar representing the Transfiguration with a sensitively rendered image of Christ by Alonso de Berruguete who studied under Michelangelo; this is the only part of the altarpiece that completely survived the Civil War. The **reja** fronting the altar is yet another fine work by Maestro Bartolomé de Jaén. In the **sacristy** (all Vandelvira's work) there's a photograph of a statue by Michelangelo given to Francisco de Cobos by the state of Venice, which alas was another Civil War casualty.

Behind El Salvador, and beyond the sixteenth-century **Hospital de los Honorados Viejos del Salvador** (another Vandelvira work), Úbeda comes to a sudden halt at a **mirador** with fine views over a sea of olive groves backed by the Sierra de Cazorla.

Palacio Vela de los Cobos

C/Juan Montilla s/n • Viewing of interior by private tour only, details at the Turismo

Just behind Plaza Vázquez de Molina, the Plaza del Ayuntamiento has the **Palacio Vela de los Cobos**, another impressive building by Vandelvira dating from the middle of the sixteenth century, with an interesting corner balcony and an elegant facade topped off by a delightful, arcaded gallery.

Oratorio de San Juan de la Cruz and around

C/Carmen 13 • **Museum** Tues–Sun 11am–1pm & 5–7pm • Charge

To the north of Plaza Vázquez de Molina (easily reached along C/Francisco de los Cobos), the **Oratorio de San Juan de la Cruz** is where San Juan (St John of the Cross), an accomplished poet and mystic, died of gangrene in 1591. The original monastery was damaged in the Civil War and little of it survives, although a small **museum** preserves memorabilia from the saint's lifetime as well as his writing desk and the cell in which he died.

At the end of Calle San Juan de la Cruz, facing the monastery, the **Plaza del Primero de Mayo** (formerly the Plaza del Mercado) is a charming acacia-lined square with a bandstand at its centre marking the site of the fires of the *autos-da-fé* that were once carried out here on the orders of the Inquisition. The town council presided over these grisly events from the superb arcaded sixteenth-century **Ayuntamiento Viejo** on the square's western side.

Iglesia de San Pablo

Pza Primero de Mayo s/n • Tues–Sat 11am–1pm & 6–8pm, Sun 11am–1.30pm • Free

Dominating the northern flank of the Oratorio de San Juan de la Cruz is the idiosyncratic **Iglesia de San Pablo**, incorporating various Romanesque, Gothic and Renaissance additions and crowned by a Plateresque tower. It boasts a thirteenth-century balcony (a popular feature in Úbeda), and a superb portal. The interior has a fine *capilla* by Vandelvira (chapel of Camarero Vago) as well as some intricate carving in the Capilla de la Mercedes and superb *rejas* (altar screens).

Around Plaza del Primero de Mayo

Calle Horno Contado, which leaves **Plaza del Primero de Mayo** at the southeast corner, has two palaces you might want to see: a short way down on the right, the **Casa de los Manueles** has a fine facade and, a little further down on the left, the fifteenth-century **Casa de los Salvajes** (savages) is named after the two figures clothed in animal skins supporting the arms of its founder, Francisco de Vago. In reality they are probably indigenous people of the imperial colonies, from whose exploitation much of this conspicuous wealth was derived.

Calle Melchor Almagro, leaving the square on the north side of San Pablo, has another mansion, the wonderful Plateresque **Casa Montiel**, and, further along, a sixteenth-century Carmelite convent.

Museo Arqueológico

C/Cervantes 6 • Mid-June to mid-Sept Tues–Sun 9am–3pm; mid-Sept to mid-June Tues–Sat 9am–8pm, Sun 9am–3pm • Charge • ☎ 953 108 623

ÚBEDA'S POTTERS' QUARTER

Leaving the Plaza del Primero de Mayo by the Calle Losal in its northeast corner leads to the **Puerta del Losal**, a magnificent thirteenth-century Mudéjar gate with a double-horseshoe arch, which was formerly one of the main entrances to the old walled town. Through the arch you enter Calle Merced, soon arriving at Plaza Olleros (Potters' Square). Leading off this, Calle Valencia is the old **potters' street** where the workshops of Úbeda's main ceramic craftsmen are located. In addition to the workshop of Pablo Tito you can see those of other potters – including Juan and Antonio Almarza, and Góngora – all famous throughout Spain. Pablo Tito's equally well-known brother, Juan, also has a workshop on the west side of the Plaza del Ayuntamiento, near the Turismo.

Museo de Alfarería Pablo Tito C/Valencia 22; ⓦpablotito.com. One of the friendliest pottery workshops in town, where renowned ceramic artist Pablo Tito will usually give you a demonstration on the potter's wheel. Nearby in the yard is the kiln, where the system used to fire the pots – many glazed and tinted with Úbeda's traditional deep green – is inherited from the Moors; once the wood is burning, olive stones are introduced into the fire, which creates smoke and soaks up oxygen, producing a more even heat with superior results in both colour and glaze. There are only six of these traditional kilns left in the whole of Spain and three are in this street. The museum/gallery upstairs is devoted to Pablo's more ambitious works, including statuary, huge amphorae and a completely ceramic (and fully functioning) bathroom. He is famous also for his sculptures and has sculpted many eminent Spaniards including King Juan Carlos. Mon–Sat 8am–2pm & 4–8pm, Sun 10am–2pm.

Off the north side of Plaza del Primero de Mayo stands a fine fourteenth-century building whose elegant Mudéjar **patio** has pointed horseshoe arches. It also houses a small **Museo Arqueológico** displaying ceramics, sculpture and many other artefacts from the Roman, Moorish and medieval periods.

Sinagoga del Agua

C/Roque Rojas s/n • Daily 10.30am–1.30pm & 5.45–8pm • Charge • ☎ 953 758 150

To the west of Plaza del Primero de Mayo is one of Úbeda's most extraordinary finds – a thirteenth-century synagogue, known as the Sinagoga del Agua (Water Synagogue) because of its numerous wells and natural spring under the Mikveh purification area. The seven parts of the synagogue have been excavated and include the main area of worship, a Women's Gallery, the rabbi's quarters and the Mikveh, all unlit by natural light except at the summer solstice when the sun's rays light up the stairway.

Plaza San Pedro and around

On the Plaza San Pedro, the thirteenth-century **Convento de Santa Clara** contains a patio with a fine Gothic-Mudéjar multilobed portal. The convent also sells its own homemade *dulces* – tasty cakes, biscuits and pastries. Just south from here along Calle Narvaez at no. 11, the private **Museo Arte Andalusi** (to visit contact ☎619 076 132 or ⓦvandelviraturismo.com) is housed in a sixteenth-century mansion filled with period artefacts from other houses around the town. Heading west from Plaza San Pedro you come to another mansion, the **Palacio de la Rambla**, at the end of Calle Medina. The facade is another graceful work by Vandelvira; inside, there's an upmarket hotel (see page 412). Across from the plaza, the church of **San Pedro**, with a noteworthy portal, leads into Calle Pascua where, on the junction with Calle Real, stands the impressive tower of the **Palacio del Conde de Guadiana**, one of the most striking of all Úbeda's palaces. The tower is, in fact, a seventeenth-century work and the richly ornamented balconies are a delight.

Hospital de Santiago

C/Obispo Cobos • Mon–Fri 7am–2.30pm & 3.30–9.30pm, Sat & Sun 10am–2pm & 6–9.30pm • Free

Five minutes west of Plaza de Andalucía, along the pedestrianized Calle Obispo Cobos, is Vandelvira's huge **Hospital de Santiago**, commissioned by Bishop Cobos y Molina and begun in 1562. Perhaps the scale put Vandelvira off, for the exterior decoration is untypically restrained. You enter via a flight of steps flanked by a set of "lions of Úbeda" (see page 407), beyond which Vandelvira has inserted his trademark – Santiago the Moor slayer – above the arch. The equally restrained interior has a patio with columns of Genoa marble and a staircase with stunning vaulting, in addition to a striking chapel.

ARRIVAL AND INFORMATION ÚBEDA

By train Estación Linares-Baeza is the nearest train station, about 15km from Úbeda and served by frequent trains from Seville, Córdoba and Granada. There are infrequent connecting buses so a taxi (around €20) is the best option.

By bus The main bus station is on C/San José, west of the centre beyond the Hospital de Santiago.

Destinations Baeza (up to 20 daily; 15min); Cazorla (5 daily; 1hr); Córdoba (4 daily; 2hr 30min); Granada (10 daily;

2hr); Jáen (14 daily; 1hr 15min); Seville (4 daily; 4hr 30min).

By car On-street parking places are difficult to find. Most hotels have car parks or can advise. A central car park lies beneath the focal Plaza de Andalucía.

Turismo In the elegant eighteenth-century Palacio del Marqués del Contadero, C/Baja del Marqués 4 (Mon–Fri 9am–7pm, Sat & Sun 9.30am–3pm; ⊛ turismodeubeda. com).

ACCOMMODATION SEE MAP PAGE 408

The best area to stay is in the old quarter, which has a great choice of places, some in stunning ancient palaces and mansions. Úbeda's **high season** is in April and May and thus hotel rooms tend to be significantly cheaper in July and August. Many hotels apply a surcharge on Friday and Saturday.

Las Casas del Consul Pza del Marqués 5; ⊛ lascasasdelconsul.es. Attractive hotel in a beautifully refurbished seventeenth-century *casa palacio*. Rooms are elegant and well equipped, many with beams or exposed stone walls. There's also a wonderful patio and a rooftop pool. €

Hostal Santa María de Úbeda C/Prior Monteagudo 1; ⊛ santamariadeubeda.com. Welcoming hostal next to the *Santa María de los Reales Alcázares* church (with which it shares a wall), just south of the Ayuntamiento. Bright, en-suite rooms with a/c and TV. Breakfast is included. €

Hotel La Paz C/Andalucía 1; ⊛ hotel-lapaz.com. This decent two-star hotel has functional but spacious a/c balcony rooms with TV. Request a room on the fourth or

fifth floor to reduce traffic noise. €

El Losal Cuesta El Losal 6-8; ⊛ losaldeubeda.com. Comfortable, clean and well-equipped apartments in a restored sixteenth-century mansion, a 5min walk north of the Ayuntamiento. Guests have use of the lovely patio, gardens and pool. €

★ **Palacio de la Rambla** Pza del Marqués 1; ⊛ palaciodelarambla.com. In the old quarter, this upmarket *casa palacio* is owned by the Marquesa de la Rambla. The lavish interior – with eight palatial rooms set around a stunning Renaissance patio designed by Vandelvira – contains valuable furnishings and artworks. Price includes breakfast – brought to your room if you wish. Closed July and August. €€€

★ **Parador Condestable Dávalos** Pza de Vázquez de Molina 1; ⊛ parador.es. On arguably the most beautiful plaza in Andalucía, Úbeda's *parador* is housed in a fabulous sixteenth-century Renaissance mansion, with gorgeous patio and sumptuously furnished rooms and suites overlooking the square. Call in for a drink if you're not staying. €€€

EATING SEE MAP PAGE 408

Most reasonably priced restaurants are in the modern part of town, along **Avenida Ramón y Cajal**, but many of the town's more memorable places to eat are located in the **old quarter**.

Asador Al-Andalus C/Los Canos 28, north of the old quarter; ☎ 953 791 862. Just south of the *plaza de toros* (bull ring), this is a popular weekend venue serving local cuisine among Moorish decor. House specialities include *alcachofas salteadas* (braised artichokes) and *codillo de cerdo asado* (roast pork loin). €€€

Cantina La Estación Cuesta de la Rodadera 1;

⊛ cantinalaestacion.com. One of Úbeda's top restaurants and a big favourite with locals. Specialities served in the railway carriage interior include *presa ibérica en salsa de mostaza* (pork in mustard sauce) and *bacalao confitado* (glazed cod). There's an excellent *menú de degustación*. €€€

El Marqués Pza Marqués de la Rambla 2. Attractive restaurant serving a good-value *menú*, often featuring *lomo de orza* (pork) and *bacalao al pilpil* (spicy cod). In summer, the inviting terrace on the square allows you to contemplate the Palacio de la Rambla's elegant exterior. €€

Parador Condestable Dávalos Pza de Vázquez de

Molina 1; ⓦparador.es. A good choice if you want to dine in style in the old quarter. Superbly prepared regional dishes such as *andrajos de Úbeda* (stew of cod, prawns and pasta) and *cordero guisado* (braised lamb) are available on the *menú*. **€€€**

Taberna Misa de 12 Pza del 1ª de mayo 7; ⓦmisade12.com. Located in a square up from the Pza del Ayuntamiento, this small bar serves tapas and *raciones* inside and on its pleasant shady terrace. Charcoal-grilled meat is a speciality. **€€€**

Cazorla and around

From Úbeda, the next destination for most travellers is the spectacular **Cazorla Natural Park** (officially titled the Parque Natural de Cazorla, Segura y Las Villas), a wilderness area filled with deep ravines and wooded valleys and which, in its mountains, gives birth to the mighty Río Guadalquivir. The main route into the park from Úbeda, and the one also taken by the bus, is via the attractive small town of **CAZORLA**, the park's main gateway, located on its southern edge.

Some 50km southeast of Úbeda, at an elevation of 900m, Cazorla huddles towards the top of a valley that runs from the rugged limestone cliffs of the Peña de los Halcones. This rocky bluff, with its wheeling buzzards and occasional eagle, marks the southwestern edge of the park, containing the sierras of Cazorla and Segura, and the headwaters of the Río Guadalquivir.

On May 15, Cazorla honours its patron, **San Isicio**, with a vibrant *romería* preceded the night before by La Hoguera (bonfires). In July, Cazorla celebrates the **BluesCazorla** Festival (ⓦbluescazorla.com), in its twenty-third year in 2017 and recognized as the best of its kind by the Blue Music Awards.

4

Brief history

Little about the town today would lead you to believe that Cazorla has been around for over two thousand years. However, not only were there significant Iberian and Roman settlements here, this was also one of the first bishoprics of early Christian Spain. Under the Moors it was a strategic stronghold and one of dozens of fortresses and watchtowers guarding the Sierra. Taken after a bitter struggle in 1235 during the *Reconquista*, the town then acted as an outpost for Christian troops. Nowadays, the two castles that dominate the village testify to its turbulent past; both were originally Moorish, but later altered and restored by their Christian conquerors.

Plaza de la Corredera and around

A few minutes' walk south from Plaza de la Constitución along the main Calle Dr Muñoz leads to **Plaza de la Corredera** (or *del Huevo*, "of the Egg", because of its shape). This is the traditional meeting place for the *señoritos*, the class of landowners and their descendants who, through influence and privilege, still lay claim to the most important jobs and mould local destiny. The Ayuntamiento is here too – a fine Moorish-style palace off the far end of the plaza. The construction of the *Hotel Ciudad de Cazorla* (see page 415) on the square's east side caused a controversy in the town because of its jarring architectural style.

Plaza de Santa María and around

Beyond Plaza de la Corredera, Calle Gómez Calderón is one of a labyrinth of narrow, twisting streets descending to Cazorla's liveliest square, the **Plaza de Santa María**. This takes its name from the sixteenth-century cathedral church of **Santa María**, designed by Andrés de Vandelvira, which was damaged by floods in the seventeenth century and later torched by Napoleonic troops. Its impressive ruins, now preserved, and the fine open square with a Renaissance fountain form a natural amphitheatre for concerts and local events as well as being a popular meeting place. Just behind the church lies the

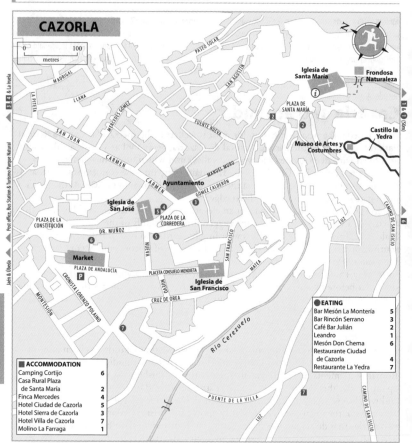

CAZORLA

■ ACCOMMODATION

Camping Cortijo	6
Casa Rural Plaza de Santa María	2
Finca Mercedes	4
Hotel Ciudad de Cazorla	5
Hotel Sierra de Cazorla	3
Hotel Villa de Cazorla	7
Molino La Farraga	1

● EATING

Bar Mesón La Montería	5
Bar Rincón Serrano	3
Café Bar Julián	2
Leandro	1
Mesón Don Chema	6
Restaurante Ciudad de Cazorla	4
Restaurante La Yedra	7

Frondosa Naturaleza (Wed–Sat 10am–2pm & 5–8pm, Sun 9am–2pm; free), a visitor centre for the Parque Natural with information and displays on the park's flora and fauna. The square itself is dominated by **Castillo la Yedra**, the austere, reconstructed tower of the lower of two Moorish castles. It also houses the **Museo de Artes y Costumbres** (mid-June to mid-Sept Tues–Sun 9am–3pm; mid-Sept to mid-June Tues–Sat 9am–8pm, Sun 9am–3pm; charge), a notable folklore museum.

La Iruela

Some 2km up the road heading into the park from Cazorla, the village of **LA IRUELA** has another ruined Moorish **fortress**, perched on a daunting but picturesque rocky peak – which must have been a wretched struggle for the Christian troops to subdue. It was later rebuilt by the Templars. There's also another ruined church here, Santo Domingo, attributed to Vandelvira. The village has a number of upmarket **places to stay**.

ARRIVAL AND INFORMATION

CAZORLA AND AROUND

By bus The terminus is on C/Hilario Marco, 300m downhill from the busy Plaza de la Constitución, the town's main square. Alsa (ⓦalsa.es) is the main bus operator.

Destinations Baeza (5 daily Mon–Fri, 4 daily Sat & Sun; 1hr 25min); Granada (3 daily; 3hr 45min); Jaén (4 daily; 2hr 10min); Úbeda (5 daily Mon–Fri, 4 daily Sat & Sun; 55min).

By car Arriving by car, once you reach the Pza de la Constitución you should head downhill to the car park; trying to find a place to park anywhere else can be futile, especially in high summer.

Turismo Paseo del Santo Cristo 19 (Tues–Sat 9.30am–1.30pm & 4–7/8pm; ☎ 953 710 102). The town's official tourist office lies 500m south of Pza de la Constitución, and can provide details on all aspects of the park and activities.

ACCOMMODATION

SEE MAP PAGE 414

Outside August, finding a **place to stay** is usually no problem, as most visitors are either en route to, or leaving, the Cazorla Natural Park. It's worth noting that outside high summer it can get quite chilly in the evenings and while all the hotel rooms have heating, not all the *hostales* do – check in advance if you think this may be a problem.

CAZORLA

Camping Cortijo Camino San Isicio s/n; ⓦ campingcortijo.com. Cazorla's campsite is located beyond the Castillo de la Yedra, 1km from the centre; to get there, follow the Camino San Isicio from the Pza de Santa María. The campsite has good facilities, plenty of shade and a pool. Wi-fi in the reception area only. Closed Dec–Feb. €̄

Casa Rural Plaza de Santa María Callejón de la Pza de Santa María; ⓦ plazadesantamaria.com. Restored seventeenth-century mansion offering pleasant doubles with en suite, a/c and heating. The house has several terraces with views of the castle and a garden courtyard with fountains. €̄

Hotel Ciudad de Cazorla Pza de la Corredera 8; ⓦ hotelciudaddecazorla.com. This hotel caused a ruckus when it was unveiled for its appearance (see page 413), but the comfortable, modern a/c rooms inside come with minibar and safe, and some have terraces. There's also a circular pool at the back and a garage. €̄

Hotel Villa Cazorla Ladera de San Isicio s/n; ⓦ villasdeandalucia.com/cazorla. One of the most attractive of the upmarket in-town places and set in leafy surroundings, it comprises a series of attractive, self-contained, a/c chalets with terraces, plus communal pool and restaurant. Own car park (free). Breakfast is included. €̄€̄

★ **Molino La Farraga** Camino de la Hoz s/n; ⓦ molinolafarraga.com. An enchanting *casa rural* with tastefully furnished, cosy en-suite rooms (many with terraces) in a densely wooded botanical garden location above the valley of the Río Cerezuelo, with a great pool and friendly proprietors. Breakfast is included. €̄

LA IRUELA

★ **Finca Mercedes** Ctra de la Sierra 1, La Iruela; ⓦ lafincamercedes.es. At the end of the village, this is a rustic, very friendly and excellent-value country inn. The en-suite rooms are cosy and those at the rear are the quietest with the best views. There's also a very good and economical restaurant plus pleasant garden with a superb pool. Free parking. €̄

Hotel Sierra de Cazorla 2km outside Cazorla, La Iruela; ⓦ hotelsierradecazorla.com. Modern complex comprising three- and four-star hotels, plus a spa. The three-star option is particularly good value with terrace balcony rooms, many (rooms A10–A17 particularly) having a spectacular view of the castle behind; there's also a restaurant, bar and great pool. They produce their own walks guide for guests. €̄€̄

EATING AND DRINKING

SEE MAP PAGE 414

RESTAURANTS

Leandro C/Hoz 3; ⓦ mesonleandro.com. Atmospheric and rustic restaurant offering mountain game such as venison and wild boar. The house specialities include venison grilled on a wood-fired range and a range of homemade burgers. €̄€̄€̄

Mesón Don Chema Escaleras del Mercado 2; ☎ 953 710 529. Down steps off focal C/Muñoz, this is an economical restaurant specializing in *carnes de monte* (mountain game). Other specialities include *jamón ibérico* and *queso curado* (cured cheese). €̄€̄

Restaurante Ciudad de Cazorla Pza de la Corredera 8; ⓦ hotelcuidaddecazorla.com. This restaurant is a popular spot, serving dishes of the region including *pierna de cabrito* (roast leg of goat). €̄€̄

★ **Restaurante La Yedra** C/Cruz de Orea 51; ☎ 953 710 292. One of the best restaurants in the town, serving local dishes with a modern twist. Specialities include *pulpo*

con patata al ajo (octopus with garlic potatoes) and the local dish *rin ran* (cream of vegetables with olives). €̄€̄€̄

TAPAS BARS

★ **Bar Mesón La Montería** Pza de la Corredera 20; ☎ 953 720 542. This place, one of the most popular of Cazorla's tapas bars, specializes in local game. *Pavías de bacalao* (deep-fried cod pieces) are a house special, or you could try their noted *venado en salsa* (venison stew). €̄€̄

Bar Rincón Serrano Pza de la Corredera 12; ☎ 953 721 004. Another good bar that is usually packed due to its custom of giving an excellent free *tapa* (which is chosen for you) with every drink. Try the *pavias de bacalao* (cod nuggets). €̄

Café Bar Julián Pza de Santa María 14; ☎ 615 680 475. Delicious *choto con ajos* (goat with garlic), *caracoles* (snails) and *alcachofas fritas* (fried artichokes) are just a few of the many dishes popular with locals who fill the terrace of this lively tapas bar all summer. €̄

Cazorla Natural Park

The **Cazorla Natural Park** – or **Parque Natural de Cazorla, Segura y Las Villas** to give its official name – is not as lofty as the Sierra Nevada (the highest peaks are 2000m), but outdoes it for beauty, slashed as it is by river gorges and largely covered in forest. The towering rock cliffs are the preserve of the acrobatic ibex, while the valleys and gorges swarm with birdlife and are home to unique pre-Ice Age plants. Covering an area of more than 2000 square kilometres, it is the largest protected area in Spain and the second largest in Europe. As the largest of Spain's natural parks, Cazorla also functions as an important **nature reserve**, with close to 1500 catalogued species. Judging from the number of *cabra hispánica* (Spanish mountain goat), *ciervo* (deer), *jabalí* (wild boar), *nutrias* (otters), birds and butterflies that even the casual visitor is likely to spot, the reserve appears to be fulfilling its role handsomely. Ironically, though, much of the best wildlife viewing will be at the periphery, or even outside the park, since the wildlife is most successfully stalked on foot and walking opportunities within the park itself are, surprisingly, somewhat limited, although things are slowly improving.

The best **times to visit** are late spring and early autumn. The winters can be uncomfortably wet and cold, and roads are often closed due to snow. In high summer, although walking is pleasant before noon, the climate tends to be hot and dry.

Arroyo Frío

The road into the park from Cazorla passes **Burunchel** and climbs over the Puerto de las Palomas with spectacular views before descending into the valley of the Guadalquivir. A little further on there's a turning for the scenically sited **parador** (25km from the turning) which, with your own transport, makes a nice stop-off for a drink or a meal (see page 420).

Back on the road into the heart of the park, beyond the turning, you will soon pass the hamlet of **ARROYO FRÍO**, which has a couple of accommodation options offering outdoor activities. **Horseriding** is available from a ranch, *Picadero El Campillo* (☎696 422 296), next door to the *Los Enebros* complex; they can provide tuition and hire out horses for guided half- and full-day treks.

Torre del Vinagre

The Río Borosa walk (see box, page 419) begins at **TORRE DEL VINAGRE**, 9km from Arroyo and 34km from Cazorla; there is also a **visitors' centre** here (see page 420), and, alongside it, a **botanical garden** (Tues–Sun: July & August 10am–2pm & 5–7pm; Sept–June 10am–2pm & 4–6pm; free) with living specimens of the park's flora. Following the road downhill from opposite the Torre del Vinagre building leads you to yet another information centre, **Río Borosa** (see page 420).

Coto Ríos

Some 5km beyond Torre del Vinagre, **COTO RÍOS** is a pleasant village with a river beach on the Guadalquivir; there's a campsite here, and lots of accommodation nearby (see page 421). It's not possible to reach the village from Cazorla to do the classic **walk along the Río Borosa** as a day-trek (see box, page 419) so you need your own transport.

Parque Cinegético

Eight kilometres northeast of Coto Ríos, keeping to the river's west bank, at the southern end of the Embalse del Tranco reservoir, is the **Parque Cinegético**, a wildlife park that includes specimens of all the park's fauna including ibex and mouflon, although it can

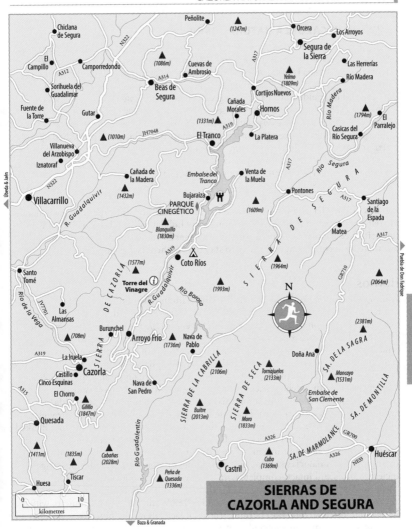

SIERRAS DE CAZORLA AND SEGURA

be difficult to see more than some rather bewildered deer and the odd wild boar from the viewing balcony (the views of the reservoir go some way to making up for the lack of wildlife). To reach the viewing areas, park at the entrance and walk a good kilometre through the woods to get to the first viewing hide. Early morning and evening are the best times to see the animals not struck down by midday torpor. It's worth noting that there are no further campsites or places to stay beyond here until you get to El Tranco.

El Tranco

Beyond the Parque Cinegético, the road continues along the west bank of the river, passing more picnic spots and *ventas* along the way, en route to **EL TRANCO**, 21km north, where the Guadalquivir is dammed to create the Embalse de Tranco reservoir. The island in the centre of the lake contains the ruined castle of **Bujaraiza**, all that

---

HIKING IN CAZORLA NATURAL PARK

Few hiking routes in the park are waymarked. Of these one leads from the Empalme de Valle to the Puente de las Herrerías via the Fuente del Oso (2km one way); another of about 1.7km curls round the Cerrada (Narrows) del Utrero near Vadillo-Castril village; the best-marked segment, through the lower Borosa gorge (see box, page 419), is also a mere 1.7km long.

Good **hiking guides** for the park include Guy Hunter-Watts' *Walking in Andalucía*, which covers six walks of between 5 and 19km (see page 556); it's also advisable to take a reliable map when doing any serious walking here. The Torre del Vinagre Centro de Interpretación (see page 420) should have copies of the 1:40,000 **map and guide pack, published by** Editorial Alpina. The map *Sierra de Cazorla* (covering the southern zone) includes a guide to walks and activities, and *Caminos Sierras de Cazorla y Segura* covers the central and northern sectors and details twenty *senderos* (footpaths) in the park.

---

remains of the village of the same name that disappeared beneath the waters when the dam was finished in 1944. Apart from a few holiday villas, a lakeside bar and a **campsite** (see page 421), 4km north of the village, El Tranco has little to detain you, but there are a couple of good places **to stay** beyond here (see page 421).

Hornos

From El Tranco, the road heads north and circles around the northern end of the reservoir before turning into the valley of the Río Hornos. Here you can glimpse the village of **HORNOS**, perched on a daunting rock pinnacle beneath the tower of its Moorish castle. The village has an isolated air with plenty of Moorish atmosphere; its narrow, white-walled streets are perfect for meandering. The castle is worth a look for the views and its planetarium (Jan–March, Nov & Dec Fri–Sun 11am–2pm & 4–6pm; April–June, Sept & Oct Thurs–Mon 11am–2pm & 4.30–7.30pm; July & Aug daily 11am–2pm & 6–9pm; charge; ⓦcosmolariumdehornos.com). Star-gazing activities take place regularly.

Plaza Mayor is overlooked by a solid sixteenth-century church, the **Iglesia de la Asunción**, with an early, if worn, Plateresque portal. Close by and reached through a small arch off the square lies a *mirador* with wonderful **views** over the reservoir, flanked by the heights of the Sierra de Segura. The waters reached a ten-year high in 2013 after a winter of heavy rain, but in general they have receded dramatically in recent years – a symptom of Andalucía's chronic and continuing drought. A stretch of the village's ancient walls is still intact, complete with a horseshoe-arched Moorish gateway.

You can **stay** in Hornos (see page 421), and a pleasant **walk** can be made along the reservoir's eastern banks to the hamlet of **LA PLATERA**, and the hill of Montero, with views along the reservoir, 4km beyond. The rock faces above the pine-covered slopes are home to a variety of plants, including yellow-flowered flax and throatwort. Common **bird** species in this area include azure-winged magpies, kestrels and sparrowhawks, but you will be extremely lucky to see the **Lammergeier** or bearded vulture in this, its only habitat in Spain outside the Pyrenees (see box, page 420).

Segura de la Sierra

Scenic though Hornos is, it is overshadowed in every sense by the Cazorla park's most spectacularly sited village, **SEGURA DE LA SIERRA**, 20km to the northeast. With a romantic castle crowning an almost conical 1100m-high hilltop, beneath which the tiered village streets seem in danger of collapsing into the olive groves far below, it's a landmark for far and wide. Segura's top-notch **olive oil** (including an organic variety) is famed throughout Spain, for which it has a coveted *denominación de origen* label (one of only 28 in the whole country); though the oil is not always easy to find in the

THE RÍO BOROSA WALK

The Río Borosa walk (probably the most popular walk inside the park, so expect crowds in high season), follows the Río Borosa upstream. From the visitors' centre at **Torre del Vinagre**, cross the road and take the path to the side of the Jardín Botánico. When you reach an electricity pylon turn left onto a downhill track. After passing a campsite and sports field on the left, cross a footbridge over the river and turn right, aiming for a white building peeping above the trees. Soon you'll pass a small campsite (with an open-air bar in summer) and about 1km from the footbridge you'll come to a car park at a *piscifactoría* (trout hatchery).

From here, follow the path as it crosses back and forth over the Borosa, swift and cold even in summer. After some 6km a signposted footpath diverges to the right; this also marks the beginning of the **Cerrada de Elías gorge**. Two or three wooden bridges now take the path back and forth across the river, which is increasingly confined by sheer rock walls. At the narrowest points the path is routed along planked catwalks secured to the limestone cliff. The walk from Torre del Vinagre to the end of the narrows takes about two hours.

Here the footpath rejoins the track; after another half-hour's walk you'll see a turbine and a long metal pipe bringing water from two **lakes** – one natural, one with a small dam – up the mountain. The road crosses one last bridge over the Borosa and stops at the turbine house. When you get to the gate, beyond which there's a steeply rising gully, count on another full hour up to the lakes. Cross a footbridge and start the steep climb up a narrow track over the rocks below the cliff (at one point the path passes close to the base of the palisade – beware falling stones). At the top of the path is a cavernous amphitheatre, with the Salto de los Órganos waterfall, one of the most spectacular in the park. The path ends about halfway up the cliff, where an artificial tunnel has been bored through the rock; walk through it to get to the lake.

Allow three and a half hours' walking time from Torre del Vinagre for the whole route and slightly less for the return journey – a full day's excursion. This walk is clearly detailed on the Editorial Alpina **map** (see box, page 418).

4

village itself, the tourist information at the castle (see page 419) has a small shop selling products of the sierra including olive oil and olives.

Once you've managed to climb the road that snakes up to it and passed through the medieval gate, you will find Segura to be a warren of narrow streets left behind by its former Moorish occupants. But its **history** goes back much further, perhaps as far as the Phoenicians who, local historians claim, called it Tavara. Greeks, Carthaginians, Romans and Visigoths came in their wake, until the last of these were prised out of this mountain eyrie by the invading Moors who constructed the castle they called Saqura. When it fell to the Christian forces under Alfonso VIII during the thirteenth century, the fort became a strategic outpost on the frontiers of the kingdom of Granada, whose borders were framed by the Guadalquivir and Segura river valleys.

Castillo

C/Regidor Juan de Isla 1 • Feb, March, Nov & Dec Sat & Sun 10.30am–2pm & 4–6.30pm; April–June, Sept & Oct Wed & Thurs 11am–2pm, Fri–Sun 10.30am–2pm & 4.30–7.45pm; July & Aug daily 10.30am–2pm & 5–8.45pm • Charge • ☎ 629 391 706 • Park at the bullring and walk up the steep 600m to the castle itself

Segura's **castillo** – now somewhat over-restored after being torched by French troops during the War of Independence – is open to visitors. Started in the eleventh century, it was much altered after the *Reconquista*. A Moorish bath survives from its earliest days, as well as the impressive *Torre de Homenaje* (keep) with spectacular **views** from its summit, and there is a vaulted chapel from the Christian period. You'll also see a crucial *aljibe* (well), without which the castle would have been vulnerable in times of siege.

On your way up, take in the views over the country for kilometres around, including the primitive rectangular **bullring**. The castle stages plays and concerts in July and August (for details and booking, ask at the castle or the Segura de la Sierra Turismo, see page 420).

Baños Árabes and around

C/Caballeros Santiaguistas s/n • Always open • Free

Segura's **Baños Árabes** is a splendid eleventh-century Moorish bathhouse off the central Plaza Mayor and behind the church. Inside, three well-preserved chambers are illuminated by overhead light vents and contain elegant horseshoe arches. To reach the baths, follow a descending street to the right-hand side of the parish church of Nuestra Señora Collado which brings you to a superb Moorish double arch in a preserved tower of the ancient walls. The baths are facing this.

Incidentally, a waymarked footpath, the GR147, leaves the double arch for Río Madera, a downhill, none-too-challenging, 15km hike.

ARRIVAL AND INFORMATION

CAZORLA NATURAL PARK

Public transport There is no public transport from Cazorla to the village of Coto Ríos.

Torre del Vinagre Centro de Interpretación Torre del Vinagre (April–June & Sept to mid-Oct Tues–Sat 10am–2.30pm & 4.30–7pm; July & Aug daily 10am–2pm & 6–8pm; mid-Oct to March Wed–Sat 10am–4pm, Sun 10am–2pm; ☎ 953 721 351). This visitors' centre, packed with motoring tourists in high summer, features a series of interactive sections detailing the park's flora and fauna, and has a shop and good café with a lunchtime *menú*.

Centro de Visitantes Río Borosa Following the road downhill and east for 1.4km from opposite the Torre del Vinagre Centro de Interpretación brings you to another *centro* (Thurs–Sun: June–Sept 10am–2pm & 6–8pm; Oct–May 10am–2pm & 4–6pm; ☎ 953 124 121), with information and displays relating to the park's fluvial wildlife.

Segura de la Sierra Turismo C/Regidor Juan de Isla 1, at the castle (see page 419) entrance (same opening hours as the castle; ☎ 627 877 919).

ACCOMMODATION AND EATING

There are a number of **campsites** – both *camping libre* (free camping) and official sites – dotted around the park; the Turismo at Cazorla (see page 415) will provide a complete list and map. In addition, there are hotels, apartments, villas and wood cabins – throughout the park, many of them very attractive indeed if you want to get away from it all. Note, however, that they tend to fill up in August, when ringing ahead is strongly advised. The **high-season prices** used for the codes here apply only to August. **Food** is available at many places inside the park and most hotels have their own restaurant and bar.

SIERRA DE CAZORLA

Parador de Cazorla Ctra JF-7094, in the park; ✪ parador. es. Some 25km from Cazorla and reached via a signed turn-off 12km south of Arroyo Frío, this somewhat featureless modern building is made attractive by its wonderful setting inside the park and its pleasant garden swimming pool. Rooms are comfortable and well equipped (make sure to ask for one with a view – rooms 4–11, 18–22 and all suites have the best). Also has a café-bar and very good, if pricey restaurant with a good-value set *menú* featuring sierra cuisine. **€€€**

THE RETURN OF THE BONE-BREAKER

The magnificent **Lammergeier** or **bearded vulture** was once a frequently spotted resident of the sierras of Segura and Cazorla as it soared and glided around the crags in search of prey. Then in the 1960s and 1970 the species declined dramatically, largely due to the drying up of the supply of carrion that these scavengers rely on to survive, and by the early 1980s, no more sightings were recorded. In 2006, the regional government started a programme of reintroduction of the species to Cazorla and neighbouring Sierra de Castil. Since then, 44 juveniles have been liberated in the park, the majority from a rearing centre in the park and the others from the mountains of the Pyrenees and Austria. All birds are fitted with radio transmitters enabling the park's naturalists to monitor their adaptation to their new environment. There are now over twenty birds, but as the Lammergeier takes eight years to reach breeding condition the growth of the colony will inevitably be slow. In 2017, however, the second lot of chicks were born in the park. The vultures are known as *quebrantahuesos* (bone-breakers) in Spanish, after their practice of hoisting the leg bones of victims high into the air and dropping them onto a rock below – nearly always the same one – splitting them open to allow the birds to extract the marrow.

MOVING ON FROM CAZORLA NATURAL PARK

With your own transport, you can avoid backtracking to Cazorla and take an alternative and attractive **route out of the park** heading south from Hornos along the A317 through the Sierra de Segura to Pontones and **Santiago de la Espada**, on the border with **Granada**. There are plenty more campsites signed along this route, and Santiago has several hotels. The same road continues to **Puebla de Don Fadrique**, where there is another recommended hotel-restaurant. From here you have a choice between the routes to Granada and Almería.

The Granada route via the cattle town of **Huéscar**, following the A330, takes in the interesting towns of Baza and Guadix and provides an opportunity en route to see the remarkable prehistoric discoveries at Orce (see page 518); otherwise the A317 heads across the deserted but picturesque wheatfields of Granada province's eastern panhandle towards **Vélez Blanco** (see page 517) with an impressive castle and prehistoric caves, and eventually hits the coast near the Almerian resort of Mojácar (see page 513).

ARROYO FRÍO

El Capricho del Valle Avda del Campillo 27, at the heart of the village; ⓦ caprichodelvalle.com. Small, pleasant hotel with pool offering en-suite rooms with TV, a/c, minibar and safe. The restaurant (*El Mesón*) specialises in *carnes a la brasa* (grilled meat) and local trout. €̄
Hotel Montaña In the centre of the village; ⓦ hmontana.com. A modern, comfortable hotel with spacious rooms with a/c and TV. Has its own restaurant, bar, lovely pool and car park. Can organize activities such as hiking, horseriding and canoeing. Breakfast is included. €̄€̄

TORRE DEL VINAGRE

Hotel Noguera de la Sierpe Ctra del Tranco km44.5; ⓦ lfhoteles.com. One of a string of relatively upmarket hotels close to the road, with views over its own private lake and the Guadalquivir valley. It's frequented in winter by hunters (the *patrón* is one). Largely self-catering *casas rurales* (sleeping up to four) overlooking the lake are available and there's a lovely pool. Breakfast is included in both rooms and *casas rurales*. Doubles €̄€̄, *casas rurales* €̄€̄€̄

COTO RÍOS

Camping Chopera de Coto-Ríos Coto Ríos; ⓦ campingchopera.es. One of the three good campsites in these parts, well shaded, and with a restaurant and pool. €̄
★ **Hotel La Hortizuela** A couple of kilometres south of Coto Ríos; ☎ 953 713 150. Good-value accommodation in a delightfully serene hideaway with garden pool and restaurant serving specialities of the sierra. €̄
El Hoyazo 7km further along the Tranco road from Coto Ríos; ⓦ bit.ly/ElHoyazo. Well-equipped apartments and bungalows sleeping up to four, with a fine pool. €̄€̄
Llanos de Arance Campsite On the opposite bank of the river to the A319, 1km north of Coto Ríos; ⓦ llanosdearance.com. Shady spot, with wood cabins, a pool, restaurant and excellent facilities. Limited wi-fi. Camping €̄, cabins €̄€̄

EL TRANCO

★ **Casa Rural Los Parrales** 3km beyond El Tranco; ☎ 953 107 540. Friendly hotel in a woodland setting with excellent en-suite rooms with a/c and TV. Lovely terrace overlooking the lake, large pool and organic veg garden. €̄
Montillana Campsite 4km north of El Tranco ☎ 953 126 194. A well-run campsite with plenty of shade, and good facilities including a supermarket, bar-restaurant and pool. Five wooden cabins sleeping up to six also available. Camping €̄, cabins €̄€̄

HORNOS

Hostal El Cruce C/Puerta Nueva s/n; ☎ 953 495 035. Pleasant *hostal-restaurante* whose prominent garden terrace is hard to miss as you enter the village. Offers good-value a/c en-suite rooms with TV. €̄
Raisa Apartamentos C/Puerta Nueva 35; ⓦ apartamentosraisa.es. On the right (and just before Hostal El Cruce) as you enter from Cazorla, this place offers pleasant, en-suite, a/c rooms and apartments with a restaurant below. €̄
Restaurante El Cruce C/Puerta Nueva s/n; ☎ 953 495 035. The leafy terrace of the *hostal*'s restaurant is arguably the best place to eat in Hornos. Specializes in hearty sierra cuisine and there's a weekday *menú*. €̄€̄

SEGURA DE LA SIERRA

Camping El Robledo 4km east of Cortijos Nuevos, on the road from Hornos; ⓦ campingelrobledo.es. This is the nearest campsite to Segura, with decent facilities including wooden cabins and a rustic bar-restaurant, plus plenty of shade. Organizes activities such as hiking, parapente and mountain biking. Wi-fi in cabins only. €̄
★ **Los Huertos de Segura** C/Castillo 11, in the upper village; ⓦ loshuertosdesegura.com. Comfortable studios and apartments with kitchenettes and terrace or balcony, with fine views. The friendly English-speaking proprietor has walking leaflets and can provide maps and advice. €̄

4

Granada and Almería

ALHAMBRA AND GRANADA

5 Granada and Almería

There is no more convincing proof of Andalucía's diversity than its eastern provinces: Granada, dominated by the Spanish peninsula's highest mountains, the snowcapped Mulhacén and Veleta peaks of the Sierra Nevada; and Almería, a waterless and, in part, semi-desert landscape. For most visitors, the city of Granada is one of the great destinations of Spain, home to Andalucía's most precious monument, the exquisite Moorish Alhambra palace and gardens. The city preserves, too, the old Moorish quarter of Albaicín and gypsy *barrio* of Sacromonte – places filled with the lingering atmosphere of this last outpost of Muslim Spain – as well as a host of Christian monuments. Granada is also an atmospheric place to be during Semana Santa, and a place of literary pilgrimage through its associations with Spain's greatest modern poet, Federico García Lorca.

South of Granada rear the peaks of the **Sierra Nevada** and its lower slopes, **Las Alpujarras**, a series of wooded valleys sprinkled with attractive whitewashed villages. This is wonderful country for walks and wildlife, with ancient cobbled paths connecting many of the villages, among them **Yegen**, one-time base of author Gerald Brenan, and **Trevélez**, Spain's highest village, famed for its snow-cured *jamón serrano*. The province's boast that you can ski in the Sierra Nevada's snowcapped peaks (at Pradollano) in the morning and swim on the coast in the afternoon is true: the resorts of **Almuñécar**, **Salobreña** and **Castell de Ferro**, along the **Costa Tropical**, all have reasonable beaches and less development than the Costa del Sol.

There's less of interest west and east of Granada. To the west, **Alhama de Granada** is a delightful spa on a scenic back road to Málaga. To the east, amid a landscape of dusty hills covered with clumps of esparto grass, lies **Guadix**, famous for its cave dwellings hacked out of the soft tufa rock, and the red stone Renaissance castle of **La Calahorra**. Beyond here, Granada's panhandle extends past the ancient country town of **Baza** to a lonely landscape of rolling sierras where small farms and isolated villages watch over fields of wheat, fruit orchards and pasture.

The **province of Almería** is a strange corner of Spain. Inland it has an almost lunar landscape of desert, sandstone cones and dried-up riverbeds; on the coast, with a few exceptions, it's relatively unspoilt, with development thwarted by sparse water supplies. The beach resorts are worth considering during what would be "off season" elsewhere; Almería is Spain's hottest province, and summers start well before Easter and last into November. In midsummer it's incredibly hot – often touching 35°C in the shade – while year-round there's an intense, almost luminous, sunlight.

The provincial capital and port, **Almería**, enjoyed a brief period of prosperity under the Moors but has been something of a backwater ever since, overlooked by the largest castle the Moors built in Andalucía, the **Alcazaba**, below the walls of which is a cave quarter, still populated by gypsies. East of the capital lie the province's best **beaches** and **resorts**, the least developed of the Spanish Mediterranean. One of the nicest, the small resort of **San José**, lies inside the **Parque Natural de Cabo de Gata**, a wildlife and wetland area that is home to some interesting desert plants as well as a breeding ground for enormous flocks of **flamingos** in summer. As you head north, you'll find **Los Escullos**, **Las Negras** and **Agua Amarga**, all attractively low-key places fronting a crystal-clear blue sea and sandy strands that see few visitors. North again, things liven up at **Mojácar**, Almería's most fashionable resort, an ancient hilltop village with an enjoyable seafront quarter. To the west of Almería city a dismal ocean of plastic

MOJACAR VILLAGE

Highlights

❶ The Alhambra, Granada One of the world's great monuments and the pinnacle of Moorish architectural splendour in Spain. See page 432

❷ The Albaicín, Granada Granada's ancient, atmospheric Moorish quarter. See page 441

❸ Capilla Real, Granada Stunning Gothic chapel built to house the remains of Isabel and Fernando, conquerors of Moorish Granada. See page 446

❹ Las Alpujarras A wildly picturesque mountain region dotted with traditional villages and many other vestiges of a Moorish past. See page 466

❺ Los Millares This third millennium BC settlement is one of the most important prehistoric sites in Europe. See page 483

❻ Alcazaba, Almería One of Andalucía's finest Moorish forts dominates the provincial capital. See page 494

❼ Cabo de Gata Natural Park Desert plants and volcanic hills are the features of this natural park, edged with coastal resorts where the beaches are often deserted. See page 506

❽ Mojácar Attractive "sugar cube" village on a rocky hill with a lively beach resort below. See page 513

❾ Mini Hollywood The Almería deserts have provided the backdrop for many Westerns and some of the movie sets can still be visited. See page 520

HIGHLIGHTS ARE MARKED ON THE MAP ON PAGE 426

Cordoba

JAÉN

CÓRDOBA

Jaén

N323

A44

Alamedilla

Villnuev
de las
Torres

Montejicar

Torre
Cardela

Pedro
Martínez

Benalúa de
las Villas

Piñar

Fonelas

Colomera

Iznalloz

Benalúa de
Guadix

Algarinejo

Montefrío

Illora

Moclin

Diezma

Purullena

Guadix

Fuente Vaqueros

Viznar

Jerez del Marquesado

La Calaho

GRANADA

① ② ③

Granada

Balcón de Canales

Loja

Salar

Moraleda
de Zafayona

Gabia
la Grande

SIERRA NEVADA

A92

Chimeneas

Monachil

A395

Ventas de
Huelma

A338

La Malahá

Alhendín

Pradollano

▲ *Cerro de Mulhacén*

Puerto de la Ragua

A397

Picacho de Veleta

*Veleta
(3394m)*

▲ *Mulhacén (3483m)*

Antequera & Málaga

Alhama de
Granada

Poblado de
Embalse

Padul

Dúrcal

Trévelez

Mecina
Bombaron

Yegen

A402

*Pantano de
los Bermejales*

A44

N323

Busquistar

④

Ugíjar

Zaffaraya Pass

Arenas del Rey

Albuñuelas

Lanjarón

Órgiva

Cádiar

Jorairátar

MÁLAGA

Otivar

Vélez de
Benaudalla

Torvizcón

Haza del
Lino

Turón

Albondón

*L
A
S
A
L
P
U
J
A
R
R
A*

Málaga

A7

Almuñecar

La Herradura

Salobreña

Puerto Motril

Motril

Castell de
Ferro

Calahonda

Albuñol

Adra

La Rábita

A7

A7-E15

COSTA TROPICAL

N

HIGHLIGHTS

1. The Alhambra, Granada
2. The Albaicín, Granada
3. Capilla Real, Granada
4. Las Alpujarras
5. Los Millares
6. Alcazaba, Almería
7. Cabo de Gata Natural Park
8. Mojácar
9. Mini Hollywood

MURCIA

PARQUE NATURAL
SIERRA DE MARÍA

Puebla de
Don Fadrique

Castril

Huéscar

Galera

Venta
Micena

Orce

Castilléjar

Cortes
de Baza

Fuente
Nueva

María

Cueva de
los Letreros

Vélez Blanco

Vélez
Rubio

A92N

Cuevas del
Campo

Cúllar
Baza

Las
Vertientes

A92N

SIERRA DE LAS ESTANCIAS

Baza

Caniles

Oria

Albox

Huércal-Overa

San Juan de
los Terreros

Tíjola

Purchena

Cantoria

Serón

Macael

ALMERÍA

Cóbdar

Albánchez

Cuevas del
Almanzora

Vera

Palomares

Lubria

A7

Garrucha

IERRA DE LOS FILABRES

Huéneja

Fiñana

Gérgal

A349

A8200

Uleila del
Campo

PARAJE NATURAL
KARST EN YESOS

Sorbas

Mojácar

8

SIERRA CABRERA

Tabernas

N340

Lucainena
de las Torres

Laujar de
Andarax

A348

Canjáyar

Fondón

Los Millares

5

Mini
Hollywood

9

Níjar

Carboneras

SIERRA DE GÁDOR

Alhama
de Almería

Gádor

Pechina

SIERRA DE ALHAMILLA

Fernán
Perez

Agua Amarga

Huercal de Almería

Viátor

Las Negras

Berja

Dalías

Almería

6

Rodalquilar

PARQUE
NATURAL DE
CABO DE GATA

Los Escullos

El Ejido

A7

Aguadulce

El Cabo de Gata

San José

COSTA DE ALMERÍA

Roquetas de Mar

7

Cabo de Gata

Almerimar

MEDITERRANEAN SEA

0   25
kilometres

5

tents – *invernaderos* – covers the plain of **Campo de Dalías** from the hills to the coast: a bonanza of drip-irrigation agriculture where salad vegetables are grown all year round to supply northern European markets.

Inland, northeast of the provincial capital, begins the most remarkable **desert landscape** in Europe: badlands of twisted gulches, dry riverbeds and eroded hills that have long attracted film producers. Much of *Lawrence of Arabia* was shot here, along with scores of spaghetti westerns, whose sets have been preserved at **Mini Hollywood**, near Tabernas: a fun visit, especially if you have kids to entertain. This weird scenery also shelters some interesting villages such as **Níjar**, a long-established ceramics centre, and the clifftop **Sorbas**.

The province of Almería also maintains relics of a rich **prehistoric** past, when the rains were regular and the landscape verdant. In the northeast, near the village of **Vélez Rubio**, is the **Cueva de los Letreros**, whose prehistoric cave paintings are among the most important in Spain, while north of the provincial capital, in the Almerían reaches of Las Alpujarras, is the exceptional archeological site of **Los Millares**.

Granada and around

Los dos ríos de Granada
Bajan de la nieve al trigo…

Granada's twin rivers
Tumble down from the snow to the wheat…   *Federico García Lorca*

The city of **GRANADA** has one of the most dramatic locations in Spain, poised below a magnificent backdrop of the snowcapped peaks of the Sierra Nevada. It's the perfect setting for a near-perfect edifice, the extraordinary **Alhambra** – the most exciting, sensual and romantic of all European monuments. It was the palace-fortress of the Nasrid kings, rulers of the last Spanish Muslim realm, and in its construction Moorish art reached a spectacular yet serene climax. The building, however, seems to go further than this, revealing something of the whole brilliance and spirit of Moorish life and culture. It should on no account be missed – and neither should the city itself.

If you're spending just a couple of days in Granada it's hard to resist spending both of them in the Alhambra. There are, however, a handful of minor Moorish sites in and around the run-down medieval streets of the **Albaicín**, the largest and most characteristic such quarter to survive in Spain. After the delights of Moorish Granada it takes a distinct readjustment and effort of will to appreciate the city's later Christian monuments – although the **Capilla Real**, at least, demands a visit, and Baroque enthusiasts are in for a treat at the **Cartuja**.

Practically everything of interest in Granada, including the hills of **Alhambra** (to the east) and the **Albaicín** and **Sacromonte** (to the northeast), is within easy walking distance of the centre. The only times you'll need a local bus or taxi are if you're arriving or leaving on public transport, since both the bus and train stations are some way out. **Gran Vía (de Colón)** is the city's main street, cutting its way through the centre along a roughly north–south axis between the Jardines del Triunfo and **Plaza Isabel la Católica**. It forms a T-junction at its southern end with C/Reyes Católicos, which runs east to the **Plaza Nueva** and west to the **Puerta Real**, Granada's two focal squares.

Brief history

Before the arrival of the Moors, Granada's mark on history was slight. An early Iberian settlement here, Elibyrge, was adapted by the **Romans** as Illiberis, but although its fertility was prized, it was greatly overshadowed by the empire's provincial capital at Córdoba. Later, after the region had come under **Visigothic** control in the sixth century, the old Roman town, centred on the modern-day Albaicín, grew a **Jewish suburb**, Garnatha, on the south slope of the Alhambra hill. Popular tradition has it that friction between this Jewish settlement and the Christian town led to the Jews assisting the **Moors** to take the city shortly after the invasion of 711.

The Moors adapted the name to Karnattah, and for three centuries it was an important city under the control of the Cordoban caliphate and, when this fell in 1031, under the Almoravid and Almohad Berber dynasties of Seville. When, however, Almohad power crumbled in the thirteenth century as the Christian *Reconquista* gathered momentum, an astute Arab prince of the **Nasrid** tribe, which had been driven south from Zaragoza, saw his opportunity to create an independent state. The kingdom, established in the 1240s by **Ibn al-Ahmar** (aka Muhammad ibn Yusuf ibn Nasr), was to outlast the vanished al-Andalus by a further two and a half centuries.

Nasrid Granada

Nasrid Granada was always a precarious state. Ibn al-Ahmar proved a just and capable ruler but all over Spain the Christian kingdoms were in the ascendant. The Moors of Granada survived only through paying tribute and allegiance to Fernando III of Castile – whom they were forced to assist in the conquest of Muslim Seville – and by the time of Ibn al-Ahmar's death in 1273 Granada was the only surviving Spanish Muslim kingdom. It had, however, consolidated its territory, which stretched from just north of the city down to a coastal strip between Tarifa and Almería, and, stimulated by Muslim refugees, developed a flourishing commerce, industry and culture. Over the next two centuries, Granada maintained its autonomy by a series of shrewd manoeuvres, its rulers turning for protection, as it suited them, to the Christian kingdoms of Aragón and Castile and the Merinid sultans of Morocco. The city-state enjoyed its most confident and prosperous period under **Yusuf I** (1334–54) and **Muhammad V** (1354–91), the rulers responsible for much of the existing Alhambra palace.

But by the mid-fifteenth century a pattern of coups and internal strife became established and a rapid succession of rulers did little to stem Christian inroads. In 1479 the kingdoms of Aragón and Castile were united by the marriage of Fernando and Isabel and within ten years had conquered Ronda, Málaga and Almería. The city of Granada now stood completely alone, tragically preoccupied in a **civil war** between supporters of the sultan's two favourite wives. The Reyes Católicos made escalating and finally untenable demands upon it, and in 1490 war broke out. **Boabdil**, the last Moorish king, appealed in vain for help from his fellow Muslims in Morocco, Egypt and Ottoman Turkey, and in the following year Fernando and Isabel marched on Granada with an army said to total 150,000 troops. For seven months, through the winter of 1491, they laid siege to the city. On January 2, 1492, Boabdil formally surrendered its keys. The Christian reconquest of Spain was complete.

Christian Granada

There followed a century of repression for Granada, during which Jews and then Muslims were treated harshly and finally expelled by the **Christian state and Church**, both of which grew rich on the confiscated property. The loss of Muslim and Jewish artisans and traders led to gradual economic decline, which was reversed only temporarily in the seventeenth century, the period when the city's Baroque monuments – La Cartuja monastery and San Juan de Dios hospital – were built. The city suffered heavily under **Napoleonic occupation**, when even the Alhambra was used as a barracks, causing much damage, and, although the nineteenth-century Romantic movement saw to it that the Alhambra suffered few more such violations, the sober *granadino* middle class have been accused repeatedly since of caring little for the rest of their city's artistic legacy. Over the last century and a half, they have covered over the Río Darro – which now flows beneath the town centre – and demolished an untold number of historic buildings to build avenues through the centre of the city.

5

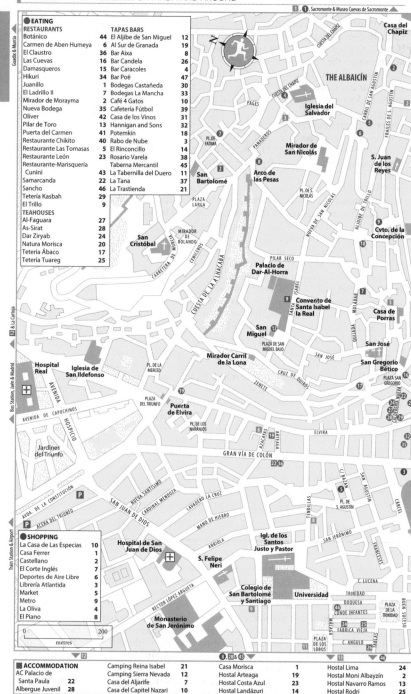

● EATING

RESTAURANTS
Botánico	44
Carmen de Aben Humeya	6
El Claustro	36
Las Cuevas	16
Damasqueros	15
Hikuri	34
Juanillo	1
El Ladrillo II	7
Mirador de Morayma	2
Nueva Bodega	35
Oliver	42
Pilar de Toro	13
Puerta del Carmen	41
Restaurante Chikito	40
Restaurante Las Tomasas	5
Restaurante León	23
Restaurante-Marisquería Cunini	43
Samarcanda	22
Sancho	46
Tetería Kasbah	29
El Trillo	9

TEAHOUSES
Al-Faguara	27
As-Sirat	28
Dar Ziryab	24
Natura Morisca	20
Tetería Ábaco	17
Tetería Tuareg	25

TAPAS BARS
El Aljibe de San Miguel	12
Al Sur de Granada	19
Bar Aixa	8
Bar Candela	26
Bar Caracoles	4
Bar Poë	47
Bodegas Castañeda	30
Bodegas La Mancha	33
Café 4 Gatos	10
Cafetería Fútbol	39
Casa de los Vinos	31
Hannigan and Sons	32
Potemkin	18
Rabo de Nube	3
El Rinconcillo	14
Rosario Varela	38
Taberna Mercantil	45
La Tabernilla del Duero	11
La Tana	37
La Trastienda	21

● SHOPPING
La Casa de Las Especias	10
Casa Ferrer	1
Castellano	2
El Corte Inglés	7
Deportes de Aire Libre	6
Librería Atlantida	3
Market	5
Metro	9
La Oliva	4
El Piano	8

■ ACCOMMODATION
AC Palacio de Santa Paula	22	Camping Reina Isabel	21	Casa Morisca	1	Hostal Lima	24
Albergue Juvenil	28	Camping Sierra Nevada	12	Hostal Arteaga	19	Hostal Moni Albayzín	2
		Casa del Aljarife	7	Hostal Costa Azul	23	Hostal Navarro Ramos	13
		Casa del Capitel Nazari	10	Hostal Landázuri	14	Hostal Rodri	25

5

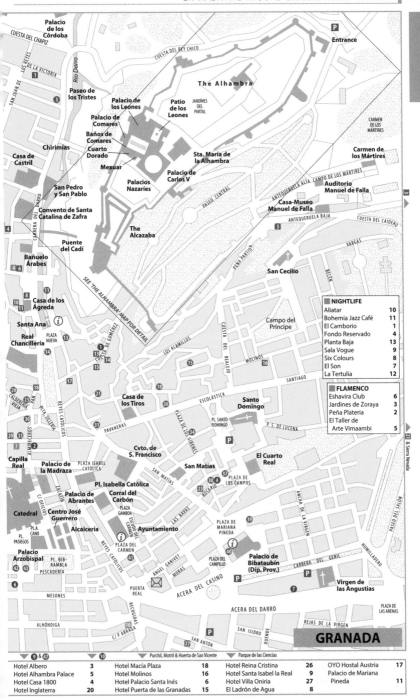

The Alhambra

Palacio de los Córdoba
CUESTA DEL CHAPIZ
CUESTA DE LA VICTORIA
Rio Darro
SAN JUAN DE LOS REYES
Paseo de los Tristes
Palacio de los Leones
Patio de los Leones
JARDINES DEL PARTAL
CARMEN DE LOS MÁRTIRES
Palacio de Comarés
Baños de Comarés
Cuarto Dorado
Chirimias
Casa de Castril
Mexuar
Sta. María de la Alhambra
Carmen de los Mártires
San Pedro y San Pablo
Palacios Nazaríes
Palacio de Carlos V
CAMPO DE LOS MÁRTIRES
ANTEQUERUELA ALTA
Auditorio Manuel de Falla
Convento de Santa Catalina de Zafra
CARRERA DEL DARRO
PASEO CENTRAL
Casa-Museo Manuel de Falla
Puente del Cadí
The Alcazaba
PEÑA PARTIDA
ANTEQUERUELA BAJA
CUESTA DEL CAIDERO
Bañuelo Árabes
SEE THE ALHAMBRA MAP FOR DETAIL
VARGAS
Casa de los Ágreda
San Cecilio
BELÉN
Santa Ana
Real Chancillería
PLAZA NUEVA
Campo del Príncipe
CUESTA DE GOMÉREZ
LOS ALAMILLOS
CUESTA DEL REALEJO
MOLINOS
SANTIAGO
Casa de los Tiros
ESCOLÁSTICA
Santo Domingo
REYES CATÓLICOS
CALDERERÍA VIEJA
CUESTA SIERRA
PLAZA DE LOS GIRONES
PL. SANTO DOMINGO
P. S. DE LUCENA
PAVANERAS
Capilla Real
Palacio de la Madraza
PLAZA ISABEL CATÓLICA
Cvto. de S. Francisco
San Matías
El Cuarto Real
PLAZA DE LOS CAMPOS
ANCHA DE LA VIRGEN
PASEO DEL SALÓN
Pl. Isabella Católica
SAN MATÍAS
BOSARIO
Palacio de Abrantes
Corral del Carbón
PLAZA GAMBOA
LAS NAVAS
Catedral
Centro José Guerrero
PLAZA DE MARIANA PINEDA
ESCUDO DEL CARMEN
Alcaicería
Ayuntamiento
PLAZA DEL CARMEN
PLAZA DEL CAMPILLO
Palacio de Bibataubín (Dip. Prov.)
CARRERA DEL GENIL
HUMILLADERO
PL. CANO
PL. PASIEGOS
Palacio Arzobispal
PL. BIB-RAMBLA
ÁNGEL GANIVET
MORAS
Virgen de las Angustias
PESCADERÍA
PUERTA REAL
ACERA DEL CASINO
PLAZA DE LAS ARENAS
MESONES
ACERA DEL DARRO
REJAS DE LA VIRGEN
ALHÓNDIGA
C/ P ARRAGA
SAN ISIDRO
DUENDE
GRANADA
RECOGIDAS
SAN ANTÓN
Entrance

NIGHTLIFE	
Aliatar	10
Bohemia Jazz Café	11
El Camborio	1
Fondo Reservado	4
Planta Baja	13
Sala Vogue	9
Six Colours	8
El Son	7
La Tertulia	12

FLAMENCO	
Eshavira Club	6
Jardines de Zoraya	3
Peña Platería	2
El Taller de Arte Vimaambi	5

▼ 9 & 47   ▼ 10   Purchil, Motril & Huerta de San Vicente   ▼ Parque de las Ciencias

Hotel Albero	3	Hotel Macía Plaza	18	Hotel Reina Cristina	26	OYO Hostal Austria	17
Hotel Alhambra Palace	5	Hotel Molinos	16	Hotel Santa Isabel la Real	9	Palacio de Mariana
Hotel Casa 1800	4	Hotel Palacio Santa Inés	6	Hotel Villa Oniria	27	Pineda	11
Hotel Inglaterra	20	Hotel Puerta de las Granadas	15	El Ladrón de Agua	8	

5

Modern Granada

Lorca described the *granadinos* as "the worst bourgeoisie in Spain", and they are regarded by many other Andalucíans as conservative, bad-tempered and cool. A strong small-shopkeeper economy – which discouraged industrial development – and a society where military and clerics were dominant inhibited innovation and liberal ideas through the early part of the twentieth century. This introverted outlook perhaps contributed also to the events of the **Civil War**, one of the greatest stains on the city's name. In 1936, following Franco's coup, a fascist bloodbath was unleashed during which an estimated seven thousand of the city's liberals and Republicans were assassinated, among them poet and playwright **Federico García Lorca**. The poet deserved better from his native city, of which he had written, "The hours are longer and sweeter here than in any other Spanish town … Granada has any amount of good ideas but is incapable of acting on them. Only in such a town, with its inertia and tranquillity, can there exist those exquisite contemplators of water, temperatures and sunsets."

Twenty-first century Granada remains strongly tied to the Alhambra, often the only part of the city visited by tourists. Despite attempts at modernization, the city appears to move little with the times. A tram system connecting the south of the city with outlying towns opened in September 2017 after years of delay and the city was only recently connected to the high-speed AVE train service.

The Alhambra

The Sabika hill sits like a garland on Granada's brow,
In which the stars would be entwined
And the Alhambra (Allah preserve it)
Is the ruby set above that garland.   *Ibn Zamrak, vizier to Muhammad V (1362–91)*

One of the most sensual architectural creations in the world and the greatest treasure of Moorish Spain, the **Alhambra** sits on a hill overlooking the city it has captivated for seven centuries. There are three distinct groups of buildings on the Alhambra hill (known as Sabika to the Moors): the **Palacios Nazaríes** (Royal Palaces or Casa Real), the palace gardens of the **Generalife**, and the **Alcazaba**.

Brief history

The Alcazaba, the fortress of the eleventh-century Ziridian rulers, was all that existed when the Nasrids made Granada their capital, but from its reddish walls the hilltop had already taken its name: Al Qal'a al-Hamra in Arabic means literally "the red fort". The first Nasrid king, **Ibn al-Ahmar**, rebuilt the Alcazaba and added to it the huge circuit of walls and towers that forms your first view of the castle. Within the walls he began a palace, which was supplied with running water by diverting the Río Darro nearly 8km to the foot of the hill; water is an integral part of the Alhambra and this engineering feat was Ibn al-Ahmar's greatest contribution. The Casa Real was essentially the product of his fourteenth-century successors, particularly **Muhammad V**, who built and decorated many of its rooms in celebration of his accession to the throne (in 1354) and conquest of Algeciras (in 1369). Also within the citadel stood a complete "government city" of mansions, smaller houses, baths, schools, mosques, barracks and gardens.

After their conquest of Granada, **Fernando and Isabel** lived for a while in the Alhambra. They restored some rooms and converted the mosque, but left the palace structure unaltered. As at Córdoba and Seville, it was their grandson **Emperor Carlos V** who wreaked the most insensitive destruction. He demolished a whole wing of rooms in order to build yet another grandiose Renaissance palace. This and the Alhambra itself were simply ignored by his successors and by the eighteenth century the Royal Palace was in use as a prison. In 1812 it was taken and occupied by **Napoleon's forces**, who looted and damaged whole sections of the building, and on their retreat from

5

A WALK TO THE ALHAMBRA

The standard approach to the Alhambra is along the **Cuesta de Gomérez**, a narrow, semi-pedestrianized road that climbs uphill from Plaza Nueva. The only traffic allowed to use this road are taxis and residents' vehicles. Should you decide to walk up (a pleasant 20min stroll from Plaza Nueva), after a few hundred metres you reach the **Puerta de las Granadas**, a massive Renaissance gateway, topped by three pomegranates, which became the city's symbol (*granada* is the fruit's Spanish name). Beyond the gate the path on the right climbs up towards a group of fortified towers, the **Torres Bermejas**, parts of which may date from as early as the eighth century, along with some other interesting sights. The left-hand path heads through woods of closely planted elms and past a huge terrace-fountain (courtesy of Carlos V), eventually reaching the main gateway of the Alhambra in Moorish times, the **Puerta de la Justicia**. A magnificent tower that forced three changes of direction, making intruders hopelessly vulnerable, it was built by Yusuf I in 1348 and preserves above its inner arch the Koranic symbol of a key (for Allah, the opener of the gates of Paradise) and, over the outer arch, an outstretched hand whose five fingers represent the five Islamic precepts: prayer, fasting, alms-giving, pilgrimage to Mecca and the oneness of God. A Moorish legend stated that the gate would never be breached by the Christians until the hand reached down to grasp the key. To reach the ticket office, continue uphill for 400m. Leaving the Alhambra, a lovely alternative route down to the city is the **Cuesta de los Chinos**, and its continuation the Cuesta del Rey Chico, which descends beneath two arches to the right of the *La Mimbre* restaurant near the Alhambra's ticket office. It winds gradually down, passing beneath the Alhambra's northern walls, to the Río Darro and a terrace of riverside cafés.

the city tried to blow up the entire complex. Their attempt was thwarted only by the action of a crippled soldier (José García) who remained behind and removed the fuses; a plaque honouring his valour has been placed in the Plaza de los Aljibes.

Two decades later the Alhambra's "rediscovery" began, given impetus by the American writer **Washington Irving**, who set up his study in the empty palace rooms and began to write his marvellously romantic *Tales of the Alhambra* (on sale all over Granada – and good reading amid the gardens and courts). Shortly after its publication the Spaniards made the Alhambra a **national monument** and set aside funds for its restoration. This continues to the present day and is now a highly sophisticated project, scientifically removing the accretions of later ages in order to expose and meticulously restore the Moorish creations.

Alcazaba

Having made your way from the ticket office (see page 438), go through the **Puerta del Vino** – named from its use in the sixteenth century as a wine cellar – and across the Plaza de los Aljibes you are confronted by the walls of the **Alcazaba**, the earliest, though most ruined, part of the fortress. Quite apart from filling in time before your ticket admits you to the Palacios Nazaríes, this is an interesting part of the complex and one where you can get a grip on the whole site.

Once inside, thread your way through remnants of the barracks to the Alcazaba's summit, the **Torre de la Vela**, named after a huge bell on its turret which until recent years was rung to mark the irrigation hours for workers on the *vega*, Granada's vast and fertile plain. The views from here are spectacular: west over the plunging ravine of the Darro with the city and the *vega* beyond, and north towards the Albaicín and Sacromonte hills, with the Alhambra itself behind and the snowcapped peaks of the Sierra Nevada forming a backdrop. It was on this same parapet at 3pm on January 2, 1492, that the Cross was first displayed above the city, alongside the royal standards of Aragón and Castile and the banner of St James. Boabdil, leaving Granada for exile in the Alpujarras, turned and wept at the sight, earning from his mother Aisha the famous rebuke: "Do not weep like a woman for what you could not defend like a man." The prescribed route continues via the **Jardín de los Ardaves**, a delightful seventeenth-century garden laid out along the fort's southern parapets with creepers, fountains and sweet-scented bushes.

To gain access to the palace you need to recross the **Plaza de los Aljibes** (where there are very welcome drinks kiosks). In Nasrid times this area was a ravine dividing the hill between the Royal Palace on one side and the Alcazaba on the other. Following the *Reconquista*, the ravine was filled in to hold two rainwater cisterns (*aljibes*) and the surface above laid out with fortifications. During the construction of Carlos V's palace in the sixteenth century, the area was cleared of these structures to create a parade ground, the rather desolate form it retains today. The underground **cisterns** can now be seen only as part of a guided visit (see page 438). Follow the arrows indicating the Palacios Nazaríes (Nasrid Palaces) to reach the royal palace. Fronting the entrance to the palace, a **Sala de Presentación** has a small exhibition – with some informative maquettes – detailing the development of the Alhambra.

Palacios Nazaríes

It is amazing that the **Palacios Nazaríes** has survived, for it stands in utter contrast to the strength of the Alcazaba and the encircling walls and towers. It was built lightly and often crudely from wood, brick and adobe, and was designed not to last, but to be renewed and redecorated by succeeding rulers. Its buildings show a superb use of light and space but they are principally a vehicle for ornamental stucco decoration. This, as Titus Burckhardt explains in *Moorish Culture in Spain*, was both an intricate science and a philosophy of abstract art in direct contrast to pictorial representation:

With its rhythmic repetition, [it] does not seek to capture the eye to lead it into an imagined world, but, on the contrary, liberates it from all pre-occupations of the mind. It does not transmit any specific ideas, but a state of being, which is at once repose and inner rhythm.

Burckhardt adds that the way in which patterns are woven from a single band, or radiate from many identical centres, served as a pure simile for Islamic belief in the oneness of God, manifested at the centre of every form and being.

Arabic inscriptions feature prominently in the ornamentation. Some are poetic eulogies of the buildings and builders, others of various sultans – notably Muhammad V. Most, however, are taken from the Koran, and among them the phrase "Wa-la ghaliba illa-Llah" (There is no Conqueror but God) is tirelessly repeated. It's said that this became the battle cry of the Nasrids upon Ibn al-Ahmar's return from aiding the Castilian war against Muslim Seville; it was his reply to the customary, though bitterly ironic, greetings of *Mansur* (Victor).

The palace is structured in three parts, each arrayed round an interior court and with a specific function. The sultans used the **Mexuar**, the first series of rooms, for business and judicial purposes. In the **Serallo**, beyond, they would receive embassies and distinguished guests. The last section, the **Harem**, formed their private living quarters and would have been entered by no one but their family and servants.

Mexuar

The council chamber, the main reception hall of the **Mexuar**, is the first room you enter. It was completed in 1365 and hailed (perhaps obsequiously) by the court poet and vizier Ibn Zamrak as a "haven of counsel, mercy and favour". Here the sultan heard the pleas and petitions of the people and held meetings with his ministers. At the room's far end is a small **oratory**, one of a number of prayer niches scattered round the palace and immediately identifiable by their angular alignment to face Mecca.

This "public" section of the palace, beyond which few would have penetrated, is completed by the Mudéjar **Cuarto Dorado** (Golden Room), redecorated under Carlos V, whose Plus Ultra motif appears throughout the palace, and the **Patio del Cuarto**

Dorado. The latter has perhaps the grandest facade of the whole palace, for it admits you to the formal splendour of the Serallo.

Serallo

The **Serallo** was built largely to the design of Yusuf I (1333–54), a romantic and enlightened sultan who was stabbed to death by a madman while worshipping in the Alhambra mosque. Its rooms open out from delicate marble-columned arcades at each end of the long **Patio de los Arrayanes** (Myrtles) with its serene fountain and pool flanked by clipped myrtle bushes. At the court's northern end is the **Sala de la Barca**, with a fine copy of its original cedar ceiling (destroyed by fire in the nineteenth century), and beyond this the fortified **Torre de Comares**, two floors of which are occupied by the royal throne room.

This room, known as the **Salón de Embajadores** (Hall of the Ambassadors), is the palace's largest and most majestic chamber. It was where the delicate diplomacy with the Christian emissaries would have been transacted – the means by which the Nasrid dynasty preserved itself – and as the sultan could only be approached indirectly it stands at an angle to the entrance from the Mexuar. It is perfectly square, with a stunning wooden dome, a superb example of *lacería*, the rigidly geometric "carpentry of knots" domed roof, and with a complex symbolism representing the seven heavens of the Muslim cosmos. The walls are completely covered in tile and stucco decoration and inscriptions, one of which states simply "I am the Heart of the Palace". It was here, symbolically, that Boabdil signed the terms of his city's surrender to the Reyes Católicos, whose motifs (the arms of Aragón and Castile) were later worked into the dome. Here, too, so it is said, Fernando met with Columbus to discuss his planned voyage to find a new sea route to India – the trip that led to the "discovery" of the Americas.

Carlos V tore down the rooms at the southern end of the Patio de los Arrayanes. From the arcade there is access (usually closed) to the gloomy **chapel crypt** (*cripta*) of his palace; it has a curious "whispering gallery" effect, whereby words whispered on one side of the crypt can be heard quite clearly on the opposite side.

Harem

The visit route continues to the **Patio de los Leones** (Court of the Lions), which has become the archetypal image of Granada, and constitutes the heart of the **harem** section of the palace. It was this area that moved Washington Irving to write in his *Tales of the Alhambra*:

It is impossible to contemplate this scene, so perfectly Oriental, without feeling the early associations of Arabian romance, and almost expecting to see the white arm of some mysterious princess beckoning from the gallery, or some dark eye sparkling through the lattice. The abode of beauty is here as if it had been inhabited but yesterday.

The stylized and archaic-looking lions beneath its fountain probably date, like the court itself, from the reign of Muhammad V, Yusuf's successor; a poem inscribed on the bowl tells how much fiercer the beasts would look if they weren't so restrained by respect for the sultan. Restoration of the lions was completed in 2013 and all twelve originals are now in place. The court was designed as an interior garden and planted with shrubs and aromatic herbs; it opens onto three of the finest rooms in the palace, each of which looks directly onto the fountain.

The most sophisticated rooms in this part of the complex, apparently designed to give a sense of the rotary movement of the stars, are the two facing each other across the court. The largest of these, the **Sala de los Abencerrajes**, has the most fabulous ceiling in the whole Alhambra complex: sixteen-sided, supported by niches of astonishing stalactite vaulting and lit by windows in the dome. Based on Pythagoras's theorem, the whole stupendous design – with a final and deft artistic flourish – is reflected in a fountain on the floor. Its light and airy quality stands at odds with its name and

5

history, for it was here that Abu al-Hassan, Boabdil's father, murdered sixteen princes of the Abencerraj family, whose chief had fallen in love with his favourite, Zoraya. The stains in the fountain are popularly supposed to be indelible traces of blood from the severed heads thrown into it – but are more likely to be from rust.

At the far end of the court is the **Sala de los Reyes** (Hall of the Kings), recently restored, whose dormitory alcoves preserve a series of unique paintings on leather. These, in defiance of Koranic law, represent human scenes. They were probably painted by a Christian artist in the last decades of Moorish rule and were once thought to portray images of the Nasrid rulers – hence the room's name.

The second of the two facing chambers on the court's north side, the **Sala de las Dos Hermanas** (Hall of the Two Sisters), is more mundanely named – from two huge slabs of white marble in its floor – but just as spectacularly decorated, with a dome of over five thousand honeycomb cells. It was the principal room of the sultan's favourite, opening onto an inner apartment and balcony (with surviving fragments of Moorish tinted glass in the dome), the **Mirador de la Daraxa** (Eyes of the Sultana); the romantic garden patio below was added after the Reconquista.

Beyond, you are directed along a circuitous route through **apartments** redecorated by Carlos V (as at Seville, the northern-reared emperor installed fireplaces) and later used by Washington Irving. Eventually you emerge at the **Peinador de la Reina** (Queen's Pavilion), which served as an oratory for the sultanas and as a dressing room for the wife of Carlos V; perfumes were burned beneath its floor and wafted up through a marble slab in one corner.

From here, passing the **Patio de la Lindaraja** added in the sixteenth century (though the basin of its marble fountain was taken from outside the Mexuar), you come to the **Baños Reales** (Royal Baths), wonderfully decorated in rich tile mosaics and lit by pierced stars and rosettes once covered by coloured glass. The central chamber was used for reclining and retains the balconies where singers and musicians – reputedly blind to keep the royal women from being seen – would entertain the bathers. Entry is not permitted to the baths, though you can make out most of the features through the doorways.

You exit via the exquisite **Portico del Partal**, with a tower and elegant portico overlooking a serene pool. What appears no more than a garden pavilion today is in fact the surviving remnant of the early fourteenth-century Palace of the Partal, a four-winged structure originally surrounding the pool, the Alhambra's largest expanse of water. The **Jardines del Partal** lie beyond this, and the nearby gate brings you out close to the entrance to the Palacio de Carlos V.

Palacio de Carlos V

Entering the **Palacio de Carlos V** strikes a totally different mood to what has gone before. The architecture of the palace with its rigid symmetries and dour exterior could not be more different from that of the Nasrid palaces. The building is dominated by its interior circular courtyard, where bullfights were once held. The palace itself was begun in 1526 but never finished – the coffered ceilings of the colonnade were added only in the 1960s before which the Ionic columns had projected into open sky – as shortly after commissioning it, Carlos V left Granada never to return, his plan to turn the city into the seat of the Spanish monarchy forgotten. Despite seeming totally out of place, however, the edifice is a distinguished piece of Renaissance design in its own right – the only surviving work of Pedro Machuca, a former pupil of Michelangelo. Lorca once referred to the stylistic clash between the two palaces as symbolic of "the fatal duel that throbs in the heart of each of Granada's citizens".

Museo de la Alhambra

Tues & Sun 8.30am–2.30pm, Wed–Sat 8.30am–8pm (till 6pm mid-Oct to mid-March) • Free

The lower floor of the Palacio de Carlos V houses the **Museo de la Alhambra**, a wonderful collection of artefacts that visitors are often too jaded to take in after the marvels of the Moorish palace outside. As well as fragments of sculptured plaster arabesques, wood carving and tilework saved from the Alhambra and a splendid ceramic collection, look out for some outstanding fourteenth- and fifteenth-century Nasrid paintings and equally stunning carved wood panels and screens. The rare and beautiful fifteenth-century **Alhambra Vase** (Jarrón de las Gacelas) is the museum's centrepiece. Almost 1.5m high, and made for the Nasrid palace from local red clay enamelled in blue and gold with leaping *gacelas* (gazelles), it is the ceramic equal of the artistic splendours in the palace. The museum regularly hosts interesting exhibitions, usually including pieces from the Alhambra storerooms and archives.

Museo de Bellas Artes

Tues & Sun mid-Oct to March 9am–6pm; April to mid-June & mid-Sept to mid-Oct 9am–8pm; mid-June to mid-Sept 9am–3pm • Charge

On the upper floors of the Palacio de Carlos V is the **Museo de Bellas Artes**, a cavernous gallery whose paintings and sculpture might command more attention elsewhere. In Room 1 there's a fine sixteenth-century woodcarving of the *Virgin and Child* by Diego de Siloé. Room 2 is dedicated to the works of Alonso Cano, the seventeenth-century *granadino* painter and sculptor. His powerful portrayals of *San Diego de Alcalá* and *San Antonio* stand out, as does a head of *San Juan de Dios*, the latter made with some assistance from Granada's other great sculptor, Pedro de Mena. Room 3 has more examples of the Andalucían sculptural tradition, including an *Ecce Homo* and a *Dolorosa* by José de Mora. Room 4 displays some minor Flemish works from the Golden Age, while the later rooms, devoted to paintings from the nineteenth and twentieth centuries, are fairly forgettable. Exceptions here are a typical work by Mariano Fortuny of Granada's *Ayuntamiento Viejo* and a handful of vibrantly coloured abstract works by Granada-born José Guerrero (see page 447). The final rooms are devoted to temporary exhibitions.

Baño de la Mezquita

Behind Carlos V's palace are the remnants of the town (with a population of forty thousand during the Nasrid period) that once existed within the Alhambra's walls. The main street, Calle Real, today lined with tedious tourist shops, guides you east towards the Generalife; on the way, it's worth looking into the well-preserved **Baño de la Mezquita**, where ablutions were performed prior to entering the Alhambra's main mosque. The mosque itself was demolished to make way for the undistinguished sixteenth-century church of Santa María de la Alhambra.

Convento de San Francisco

At the southern end of Calle Real the fifteenth-century **Convento de San Francisco** is also worth a visit. Built by Fernando and Isabel on the site of another Moorish palace, this is now a *parador* (see page 453) whose marvellous plant-filled patio, dominated by a soaring cypress projecting above the roof, preserves part of the chapel where the Catholic monarchs were buried – commemorated by a marble slab – before being removed to the cathedral. It's tricky to find, and you'll need to ask for directions at the hotel's reception. At the rear of the *parador*, there's a restaurant and a very pleasant terrace bar, both open to non-guests.

Generalife

Paradise is described in the Koran as a shaded, leafy garden refreshed by running water where the "fortunate ones" may take their rest under tall canopies. It is an image that perfectly describes the **Generalife**, the gardens and summer palace of the Nasrid rulers. Its name means literally "garden of the architect" and the grounds consist of a luxuriantly imaginative series of patios, enclosed gardens and walkways.

By chance, an account of the gardens during Moorish times, written rather fancifully by fourteenth-century Moorish historian, poet and palace vizier Ibn Zamrak, survives.

5

The descriptions that he gives aren't all entirely believable but they are a wonderful basis for musing as you lounge around by the patios and fountains. There were, he wrote, celebrations with horses darting about in the dusk at speeds that made the spectators rub their eyes (a form of festival still indulged in at Moroccan *fantasías*); rockets shot into the air to be attacked by the stars for their audacity; tightrope walkers flying through the air like birds; and men bowled along in a great wooden hoop shaped like an astronomical sphere.

Today, even devoid of such amusements, the gardens remain deeply evocative, above all, perhaps, the **Patio de la Sultana** (aka Patio de los Cipreses), a dark and secretive walled garden of sculpted junipers where the sultana Zoraya was suspected of meeting her lover Hamet, chief of the unfortunate Abencerrajes. The trunk of the 700-year-old **cypress tree** (marked by a plaque) is where legend says their trysts took place and where the grisly fate of the Abencerraj clan was sealed. Nearby is the inspired flight of fantasy of the **Escalera del Agua** (aka Camino de las Cascadas), a staircase with water flowing down its stone balustrades. At its base is a wonderful little **Summer Palace**, with various decorated belvederes.

ARRIVAL AND DEPARTURE
THE ALHAMBRA

By bus A dedicated minibus service, the Alhambrabus (#C3; daily 7am–10pm, every 5–10min; charge), links Pza Isabel La Católica in the centre with the Alhambra palace.

By car To approach the Alhambra by car, use the signed route heading from Puerta Real along the Paseo del Salón and the Paseo de la Bomba to the Alhambra's car park on the eastern edge of the complex.

On foot The standard approach to the Alhambra is along the Cuesta de Gomérez (see page 442).

INFORMATION

Opening hours The Alhambra is open daily (April to mid-Oct 8.30am–8pm, mid-Oct to March 8.30am–6pm; last admission 1hr before closing time; charge; ⓦalhambra-patronato.es).

Admission To protect the complex, only 6600 daily admissions are allowed. All tickets will state whether they are for morning (8.30am–2pm) or afternoon (2–8pm; mid-Oct to mid-March 2–6pm) sessions. You must enter between the stated times; once inside you may stay as long as you wish, but note that you will not be allowed to enter the complex (even with prebooked tickets) less than 1hr before closing time. To alleviate overcrowding, tickets are coded with a 30min time slot during which you must enter the Palacios Nazaríes. You will not be allowed to enter before or after this time, but again, once inside the palace you can stay as long as you like. Note also that the Museo de la Alhambra (see page 436) and the Museo de las Bellas Artes (see page 437), both in the palace of Carlos V, have different hours and admission fees to those of the Alhambra. If you're planning to spend the day at the Alhambra, book a slot for the Palacios Nazaríes between 11.30am and 1.30pm. This allows you entry to the Alcazaba and Generalife at any time afterwards. An earlier or later time slot limits your access to the Alcazaba and Generalife to before 2pm or after 2pm respectively.

BUYING TICKETS

Buying tickets in advance To guarantee entry on a specific day, you'll need to book in advance, either online (ⓦalhambra-patronato.es) or by phone (❶858 953 616; 24hr; English spoken). Note that you must provide your passport number (you may be asked to show this at the Alhambra as proof of purchase). After purchasing tickets, you can show them on your phone or print them before going. There are also ticket machines you can print from at the Alhambra (at least 1hr before your allocated time slot). For the latter, you will need your credit card for identification. If you've bought concessionary tickets, they can only be collected from the Alhambra ticket office.

Buying tickets on the day If you're buying tickets in person, you have three options: you can buy them at the Alhambra shop in town (C/Reyes Católicos 40; daily 9.30am–8.30pm), at the entrance (ticket office daily 8am–8pm; till 6pm mid-Oct to mid-March), where queues can be long, or by credit card from any ServiCaixa machine (several are located in a small building signed off the car park near the ticket office); insert your card into the machine and request a day and time. However, you should bear in mind that tickets allocated by these methods are only what remain after prebooked ticket sales, and this could well mean that no tickets are on sale at the entrance.

Night visits The Palacios Nazaríes is also open for floodlit night visits (mid-March to mid-Oct Tues–Sat 10–11.30pm; mid-Oct to mid-March Fri & Sat 8–9.30pm). Ticket offices are open from 15min before to 15min after each opening time and the availability of tickets (which can be prebooked) is subject to the same terms as for daytime visits.

Guided visits Themed guided tours with five different

routes (in English; year-round) allow visitors to view parts of the complex (many in the process of restoration) not normally open to the public. A schedule, *La Alhambra Otra Mirada*, and tickets, are available from the Alhambra ticket offices or can be bought online at ⓦ alhambra-patronato. es.

ESSENTIALS

Planning a route The ticket office entrance to the Alhambra brings you into the complex at the eastern end, near to the Generalife gardens. However, your time slot for entering the Palacios Nazaríes (usually up to 1hr ahead) means that it makes sense to start your visit with the Alcazaba, the oldest part of the complex, at the Alhambra's opposite (western) end. To get here from the entrance, walk up the short avenue lined with cypresses to a three-way fork, taking the signed path to the Alhambra. Cross the bridge over the "moat" (actually the Cuesta de los Chinos) following signs to the Alcazaba and Palacios Nazaríes. You will eventually pass the gates of the *Parador de San Francisco* (right) and the *Hotel América* to enter the C/ Real. Continue alongside the palace of Carlos V to reach the Puerta del Vino.

Bookshops On the lower floor of the Palacio de Carlos V is one of the three official Alhambra bookshops (*Librería de la Alhambra*) with a wide variety of texts and postcards relating to the monument; the others are next to the ticket office at the entrance and along the C/Real.

Eating and drinking If you're looking for a place to eat lunch or have a refreshing drink between palaces and museums, the shady terrace of *Restaurante La Mimbre* (see page 456) is one of the best-value places on the hill.

Alhambra Hill: other sights

After taking in the delights of the Alhambra and Generalife, most visitors are too tired to even think of more sightseeing – which is a pity, for there are a number of other sights on the hill worthy of a visit. These are not connected with the Alhambra but are very much part of Granada's more recent past and, in the case of the **Carmen de los Martires**, make a wonderful place to while away an hour before returning to the city.

Casa-Museo Manuel de Falla

C/Antequerela s/n • Obligatory guided tours Tues–Sat 10am–5pm, Sun 10am–3pm • Charge • ⓦ museomanueldefalla.com

From the Puerta de las Granadas, taking the right-hand path uphill leads, in its higher reaches, to the **Casa-Museo Manuel de Falla**, the former home of the great Cádiz composer. The tiny house has been re-created to appear just as he left it in 1939 – with piano, domestic clutter, medicine bottles by his bed (he was a lifelong hypochondriac), and stacks of books – before quitting fascist Spain for an exile spent in Argentina where he died in 1946. The walls and surfaces are dotted with mementoes and gifts from friends – including a series of sketches by Picasso – and the pretty garden with its bench and vista is where the composer relaxed ("I have the most beautiful panoramic view in the world", he wrote to friends). A summer café (April–Sept 8.30pm–1am) serves *pasteles* (cakes) and drinks. Occasional concerts of de Falla's works are performed in the nearby **Auditorio Manuel de Falla**, Paseo de los Mártires s/n, on Saturday evenings and Sunday mornings throughout the year (details from the Turismo).

Carmen de los Mártires

Paseo de los Mártires s/n • April to mid-Oct Mon–Fri 10am–2pm & 6–8pm, Sat & Sun 10am–8pm; mid-Oct to March Mon–Fri 10am–2pm & 4–6pm, Sat & Sun 10am–6pm • Free • ☎ 958 849 103

The enchanting **Carmen de los Mártires** is a turn-of-the-twentieth-century house set in a delightfully tranquil garden filled with palms, cypresses and tinkling fountains. Throughout the garden you'll come across grottoes, statues and follies as well as peacocks and black swans paddling around an artificial lake. After a visit to the Alhambra this makes a wonderfully tranquil oasis.

Hotel Alhambra Palace

Peña Partida 2–4 • ⓦ h-alhambrapalace.es

Just opposite the de Falla museum, the terrace of the exclusive neo-Moorish **Hotel Alhambra Palace** (open to the public providing you're decently dressed), with fine

5

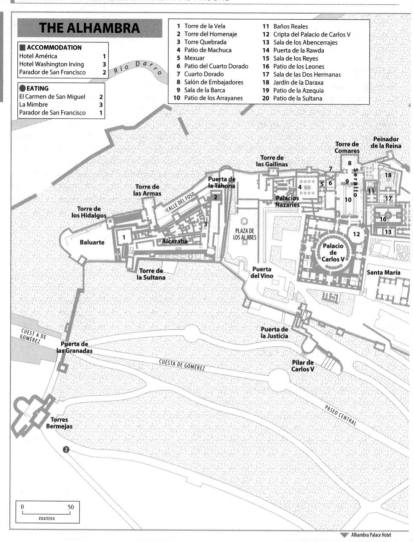

THE ALHAMBRA

ACCOMMODATION

Hotel América	1
Hotel Washington Irving	3
Parador de San Francisco	2

EATING

El Carmen de San Miguel	2
La Mimbre	3
Parador de San Francisco	1

1	Torre de la Vela	11	Baños Reales
2	Torre del Homenaje	12	Cripta del Palacio de Carlos V
3	Torre Quebrada	13	Sala de los Abencerrajes
4	Patio de Machuca	14	Puerta de la Rawda
5	Mexuar	15	Sala de los Reyes
6	Patio del Cuarto Dorado	16	Patio de los Leones
7	Cuarto Dorado	17	Sala de las Dos Hermanas
8	Salón de Embajadores	18	Jardín de la Daraxa
9	Sala de la Barca	19	Patio de la Azequia
10	Patio de los Arrayanes	20	Patio de la Sultana

▼ Alhambra Palace Hotel

views over the city, is a great place for a drink. Ask at reception to see the hotel's charming **theatre**, also in pseudo-Moorish style and where on June 7, 1922, an evening of poetry and song launched the career of a youthful Federico García Lorca (the guitarist Segovia appeared on the same bill). It is, of course, also possible to stay at the hotel (see page 453).

Hotel Washington Irving

Paseo del Generalife 2

Just north of the *Hotel Alhambra Palace*, the nineteenth-century **Hotel Washington Irving** is another of Granada's hotels with many historical associations. Opened in 1820, it played host to many of the nineteenth century's Romantic travellers including Irving himself. Seriously in need of attention for many years, the hotel reopened in late

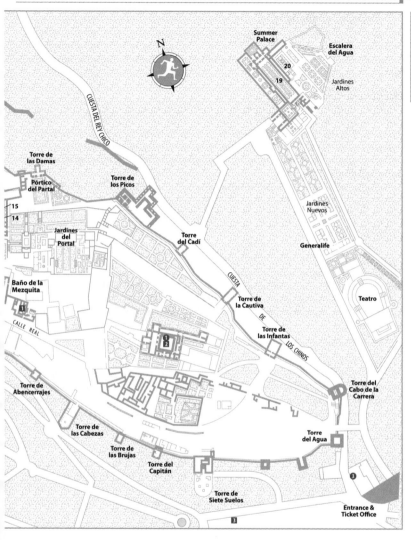

2016 after extensive restoration (see page 453). In 1928, *New York Times* journalist Mildred Adams met Federico García Lorca here for the first time and quickly fell under his spell. The poet sat down at the hotel's battered, out-of-tune piano in the lobby and sang her a Lorca about the arrest and death of a local flamenco singer. "In gesture, tone of voice, expression of face and body, Lorca himself was the ballad", she wrote later.

The Albaicín

Bus #C1 from Pza Nueva goes to Pza del Salvador in the heart of the barrio, and Pza San Nicolás, near the famous mirador; bus #C2 (roughly every 20min) deviates from this route to take in the adjoining barrio of Sacromonte

Declared a World Heritage Site by UNESCO in 1994, the **Albaicín** stretches across a fist-shaped area bordered by the Río Darro, Sacromonte hill, the old town walls

5

and the winding Calle de Elvira (which runs parallel to the Gran Vía). From the centre, the best approach is from the Plaza Nueva and along the Carrera del Darro, beside the river. Coming from the Alhambra, you can make your way along the Cuesta de los Chinos – a beautiful path and a nice little short cut back down to town.

Plaza Nueva and around

Before starting a tour of the Albaicín from the **Plaza Nueva**, take a look at the square itself. It was constructed just after the *Reconquista* as a new focus for the city, and soon served as the site of an act of stunning Christian barbarity: a bonfire of eighty thousand books from the former Muslim university. The square's elegant sixteenth-century fountain, the **Pilar del Toro**, is the last known work by the eminent Renaissance architect Diego de Siloé.

Flanking the plaza's north side is the austerely impressive **Real Chancillería** (Royal Chancery), built at the same time as the square, and what serves now as the law courts. Beyond its monumental entrance lies an elegant two-storeyed **patio** designed by Diego de Siloé with elaborate marble Doric columns and a staircase with stalactite ceiling.

Cuesta de Gomérez

The **Cuesta de Gomérez** leads up from south of Plaza Nueva to the Alhambra. It's here that many of Granada's renowned **guitar** manufacturers are gathered. Behind the windows of these places you may catch sight of a major concert or flamenco musician trying out a new instrument; they are not averse to giving the shop's customers a free concert or two.

Santa Ana

Pza Nueva • Open service times daily: June–Sept 7.30pm; Oct–May 6pm • Free

Perched over the Río Darro at the Plaza Nueva's eastern end is the sixteenth-century church of **Santa Ana**, whose elegant bell tower is the converted minaret of the mosque it replaced. The church's interior has flamboyantly decorated Baroque side chapels and a fine *artesonado* ceiling.

Hammam

C/Santa Ana 16 • Daily 10am–midnight • Charge; reservations plus swimsuit required • ⓦ granada.hammamalandalus.com

To get an idea of what a functioning **Moorish bathhouse** would have been like, head for the re-created **hammam** just behind the church of Santa Ana. Here you can wallow in the graded temperatures (cold, tepid and hot) of the traditional bath, surrounded by marble pavements, mosaic wall decor and plaster arabesques. There's also a nice *tetería* (tearoom) upstairs.

PERSONAL SAFETY IN THE ALBAICÍN

Thefts from tourists in the Albaicín are not unknown. The preferred method is bag snatching, and is rarely accompanied by violence. However, don't let the threat put you off visiting one of the city's most atmospheric quarters; applying a few common-sense measures should ensure that you come to no harm. Firstly, do not take any valuables (including airline tickets and passports) or large amounts of cash with you when visiting the Albaicín and keep what you have on your person, not in a bag. If your bag is snatched don't resist – the thief will be concerned only with making a speedy getaway. Finally, try not to look like an obvious tourist (map/guidebook in hand is a dead giveaway) or flaunt expensive-looking photographic equipment, and keep to streets where there are other people around, especially at night.

5

Carrera del Darro

Following the river's northern bank from the Plaza Nueva along the **Carrera del Darro**, glance back to where the river disappears from sight under the city and "moans as it loses itself in the absurd tunnel" as the young Lorca put it.

El Bañuelo

Carrera del Darro 31 • Daily 10am–8pm • Charge, Sun free • ☎ 958 027 900

A little way up the Carrera at no. 31 are the remains of the **El Bañuelo**, a marvellous and little-visited Moorish public bath complex. Built in the eleventh century, the sensitively restored structure consists of a series of brick-vaulted rooms with typical star-shaped skylights (originally glazed) and columns incorporating Roman and Visigothic capitals. When Richard Ford was here in the 1830s he found it being used as a wash house by the local women because "one of the first laws after the conquest of the Catholic sovereigns was to prohibit bathing by fine and punishment".

Convento de Santa Catalina de Zafra

Carrera del Darro 39 • Daily Jan–July & Sept–Dec 10am–12.30pm & 4.30–6.45pm

The nuns at the **Convento de Santa Catalina de Zafra**, housed in a sixteenth-century Mudéjar palace, are renowned for their convent *dulces* and will gladly supply you (through a *turno*) with their speciality, *glorias* (almond cakes).

Casa de Castril: the Museo Arqueológico

Carrera del Darro 43

A hundred metres beyond El Bañuelo lies **Casa de Castril**, a Renaissance mansion with a fine Plateresque facade and doorway, which houses the city's **Museo Arqueológico** with its interesting exhibits of finds from throughout the province.

Rooms 1 and 2 cover the Paleolithic and Neolithic periods, among which are some remarkable artefacts from the **Cueva de los Murciélagos** near Albuñol. In this fourth-millennium BC Neolithic cave, alongside a dozen cadavers arranged in a semicircle around that of a woman, were found some modern-looking esparto grass sandals and baskets, as well as a **golden diadem**. Room 3 has some interesting reconstructions of social life and culture in the Bronze Age and one exhibit shows how copper weapons and tools were manufactured using primitive moulds. Room 4 contains the Iberian and pre-Roman collection, with some fine examples of early lapidary work including a hefty carved stone bull, stone vases and outstanding alabaster vessels. The finds from the necropolis at **Punté Noye** near Almuñécar (the Phoenician Sexi) suggest a large colony here trading as far afield as Egypt and Greece from where the vases (some bearing pharaonic titles) were imported. The Roman section in Room 5 has a striking third-century bronze statue of a man in a toga as well as some interesting **early Christian lamps** from the fourth century.

Pride of place in the **Moorish section** (Room 7) is a fourteenth-century **bronze astrolabe**, demonstrating the superior scientific competence of the Arabic world at this time. The instrument was adopted by the Arabs from ancient Greece and used for charting the position of the stars in astrology, precisely orienting the *mihrab* of the mosques towards Mecca, determining geographical coordinates as well as trigonometry and converting Muslim dates into Christian ones. Its transmission from the Arab to the Christian world made possible the voyages of discovery to both east and west. More Moorish symmetry is evident in the designs on the vases, wooden chests and amphorae also displayed here.

Paseo de los Tristes and around

Continuing along the Río Darro from the Casa de Castril you'll eventually come to **Paseo de los Tristes** (aka Paseo del Padre Manjón), a delightful esplanade beside the river overlooked by the battlements of the Alhambra high on the hill above. It's a great

5

SACROMONTE: GRANADA'S GITANO QUARTER

Granada has an ancient and still considerable **gitano** (gypsy) population, from whose clans many of Spain's best flamenco guitarists, dancers and singers have emerged. Traditionally the gypsies inhabited cave homes on **Sacromonte hill**, and many still do, giving lively displays of dancing and music in their *zambras* (shindigs). These were once spontaneous, but are now blatantly contrived for tourists, and are often shameless rip-offs: you're hauled into a cave, leered at if you're female, and systematically extorted of all the money you've brought along (for dance, the music, the castanets, the watered-down sherry…). Which is not to say that you shouldn't visit – just take only as much money as you want to part with. Turn up mid-evening; the lines of caves begin off the Camino de Sacromonte, just above the Casa del Chapiz. When the university is in session, a few cave dwellings are turned into **discotecas** and packed with students at weekends.

You might also want to visit the **Museo Cuevas del Sacromonte** (Barranco de los Negros s/n; daily 10am–6pm, till 8pm May–mid-Oct; charge; ☎958 215 120), an intriguing museum depicting the life and times of the *barrio*. In this area – and Sacromonte generally – it would also be wise to heed our warnings on personal security (see box, page 442).

spot for a drink and especially so at night when the Alhambra is floodlit; there are several terrace bars fronting the river.

Two streets off here also contain **Moorish houses**: Calle del Horno de Oro (no. 14) and, two streets further along, Cuesta de la Victoria (no. 9). The street after this, the **Cuesta del Chapiz**, climbs left into the heart of the Albaicín, passing first, on the right, the **Casa del Chapiz**, in origin a Moorish mansion – with a charming patio – and today reclaimed as a school of Arabic studies. The **Camino del Sacromonte**, just beyond it, heads east towards the *barrio* of **Sacromonte**'s celebrated caves where, after sundown, the *gitanos* (gypsies) will attempt to entice you in for some raucous but often dubious flamenco (see box, page 444).

Iglesia del Salvador
Pza Salvador s/n • Open during services • Free

The **Iglesia del Salvador** is built on the site of a mosque of which the **courtyard** – with whitewashed arches and Moorish cisterns – is beautifully preserved. Diego de Siloé, the architect of the sixteenth-century church, which was badly damaged in the Civil War, converted the mosque's original **minaret** into its tower.

Plaza Larga
From the Iglesia del Salvador, Calle Panaderos leads into **Plaza Larga**, the busy heart of the Albaicín, with a concentration of restaurants and bars. The nearby Calle Agua has more **Moorish dwellings**: take a look at nos. 1, 37, 28 and 19. A busy little **market** is held in Plaza Larga (Mon–Sat mornings) selling the usual fruit and vegetables as well as potted plants and bootleg CDs and DVDs.

Mirador de San Nicolás
The **Mirador de San Nicolás** is justly famous for its panoramic **view** of the Sierra Nevada, the Alhambra and Granada spread out below. To get here from Plaza Larga, go through the Arco de las Pesas, an old arch in the west corner, and turn sharply left up Callejón de San Cecilio. When you reach it, the fifteenth-century church of San Nicolás is of little note, although the climb up the tower gives excellent views (daily 10am–2pm & 5–9pm; charge). The nearby **aljibe** (fountain) is a Moorish original, one of many in the Albaicín to survive from the time when every mosque – there were more than thirty of them – had its own. If you fancy quieter contemplation of the views, pop next door to the **Mezquita Nueva** (mosque) gardens (daily 11am–2pm & 6–8pm; free).

Convento de Santa Isabel la Real
C/Santa Isabel la Real • Obligatory guided tours Mon–Sat 6.30–7pm • Free

Below the Mirador de San Nicolás, Calle Nueva de San Nicolás descends into Calle Santa Isabel la Real, passing, on the right, the early sixteenth-century **Convento de Santa Isabel la Real** with a pretty patio. The **convent church** has a superb Plateresque doorway and, inside, a fine Mudéjar ceiling, and holds sculptures by Pedro de Mena and José Mora.

Palacio de Dar-al-Horra
C/Santa Isabel la Real • Daily: May to mid-Sept 9.30am–2.30pm & 5–8.30pm; mid-Sept to April 9.30am–5pm • Charge • ☎ 671 563 553

The Santa Isabella convent was partly constructed within a fifteenth-century Nasrid palace – part of which was the adjoining **Palacio de Dar-al-Horra**, of which only the patios and some arches survive. This renovated palacio was the residence of Aisha, the mother of the last king of Granada, Boabdil.

Plaza de San Miguel Bajo and around
Calle Santa Isabel drops into one of the Albaicín's most delightful squares, **Plaza de San Miguel Bajo**, lined with acacia and chestnut trees. The church of **San Miguel** on its eastern side is a sixteenth-century work by Diego de Siloé, built over yet another mosque, and preserves its original thirteenth-century *aljibe* (fountain) where the ritual ablutions would have been performed before entering. The square also has a clutch of good bars, whose terraces are extremely popular at night. The opposite end of the plaza leads to the **Mirador del Carril de la Lona** with its views over the western side of the city. You could also detour north from here – climbing uphill beyond the walls – to the church of **San Cristóbal**, which has another fine **view** of the Alhambra from its own *mirador*.

A pleasant walk back to the centre from Plaza de San Miguel is to head roughly south along calles San Miguel and San José, eventually meeting up with calles Calderería Nueva and Calderería Vieja, a vibrant and busy "Little Morocco" with food shops, restaurants and excellent teahouses (see box, page 455).

Palacio de la Madraza
C/Oficios s/n • Hours vary • Charge • Wlamadraza.ugr.es

Outside the Albaicín is a further group of Moorish buildings. The most interesting of them, and oddly one of the least known, is the so-called **Palacio de la Madraza**, a vividly painted building opposite the Capilla Real. Built in the early fourteenth century at the behest of Yusuf I – though much altered since – this is a former Islamic college (*medressa* in Arabic) and retains part of its old prayer hall, including a magnificently decorated **mihrab**. It now serves as a cultural centre where regular art exhibitions take place.

Corral del Carbón
Off C/de los Reyes Católicos • Daily 9am–8pm

Slightly south of the Palacio de la Madraza lies the **Corral del Carbón**, a fourteenth-century caravanserai (an inn where merchants would lodge and, on the upper floors, store their goods) that is unique in Spain. A wonderful horseshoe arch leads into a courtyard with a marble water trough. Remarkably, the building survived intact through a stint as a sixteenth-century theatre – with the spectators watching from the upper galleries – and later as a charcoal burners' factory, the origin of its present name. The building is a little tricky to find: it lies down an alleyway off the Calle de los Reyes Católicos, opposite the **Alcaicería**, the old Arab silk bazaar, burned down in the nineteenth century and poorly restored as an arcade of souvenir shops.

5

Casa de los Tiros

Pza de los Campos 6 • Mid-June to mid-Sept Tues–Sun 9am–3pm; mid-Sept to mid-June Tues–Sat 9am–8pm, Sun 9am–3pm • Charge • ☎ 600 143 175

East of the Corral del Carbón, an impressive Mudéjar mansion, the **Casa de los Tiros**, stands just behind Plaza de Isabel Católica. This was built just after the *Reconquista* ended and has a curious facade adorned with various Greek deities and heroes as well as a number of *tiros* (muskets) projecting from the upper windows. Above the door is a representation of the sword of Boabdil that the family who lived here claimed they held in custody. The interior – which is worth a look – now houses the mildly interesting **Museo Casa de los Tiros** exhibiting documents, furniture, engravings and photos from the city's past.

El Cuarto Real

C/Pavaneras 19 • Daily: April–Oct 10am–2pm & 5–9pm; Nov–March 10am–7pm • Free • ☎ 958 849 111

Southeast of the Casa de los Tiros lies the restored **El Cuarto Real**, a thirteenth-century Nasrid palace, of which only the fortified tower remains. Inside the *qubba* (reception room), the stunning architectural and decorative motifs on the walls, ceiling and evoke those in the **Serallo** at the Alhambra (see page 435), which they predate by some thirty years. Temporary exhibitions are held in the large modern hall that leads to the *qubba* and quiet, pleasant gardens surround the complex.

Capilla Real

Mon–Sat 10am–6.30pm, Sun 11am–6.30pm • Charge • ⓦ capillarealgranada.com

The **Capilla Real** (Royal Chapel) is Granada's most impressive Christian building, flamboyant late Gothic in style and built ad hoc in the first decades of Christian rule as a mausoleum for los Reyes Católicos, the city's "liberators". Before entering, note the stone frieze above the entrance that romantically alternates the initials of the two monarchs. Isabel, in accordance with her will, was originally buried on the Alhambra hill (in the church of the San Francisco convent, now part of the *parador*) but her wealth and power couldn't safeguard her wishes; both her remains and those of her spouse Fernando, who died eleven years later in 1516, were placed here in 1522. Isabel's final indignity occurred in the 1980s, when the candle that she asked should perpetually illuminate her tomb was replaced by an electric bulb – after many protests the candle was restored. But, as with Columbus's tomb in Seville, there is considerable doubt as to whether any of the remains in these lead coffins – so reverentially regarded by visiting Spaniards – are those of the monarchs at all. The chapel and tombs were desecrated by Napoleon's troops in 1812 and the coffins opened and defiled.

Tombs

The monarchs' **tombs** in a plain underground crypt below are as simple as could be imagined: Fernando and Isabel, flanked by their daughter Juana ("the Mad") and her husband Felipe ("the Handsome"), rest in lead coffins placed in a plain crypt (a not easily spotted "F" marking that of the king on the left of the central pair). The smaller coffin to the right is that of the infant Príncipe de Asturias who died before reaching the age of 2. Above them, however, is an elaborate Renaissance monument, with sculpted effigies of all four monarchs – the response of their grandson Carlos V to what he found "too small a room for so great a glory". The figures of Fernando and Isabel are easily identified by the rather puny-looking lion and lioness at their feet. Popular legend has it that Isabel's head sinks deeper into the pillow due to the weight of her intelligence compared with that of her husband. This is not without some truth; Fernando was never much more than a consort. Carved in Carrera marble by the Florentine Domenico Fancelli in 1517, the tomb's **side panels** depict the Apostles and scenes from the life of Christ and are especially fine. The Latin inscription at the monarchs' feet is brutally triumphalist in tone: "Overthrowers of the Mahometan sect and repressors of heretical stubbornness". The tomb of Juana and Felipe, a far inferior work, is by Ordóñez.

Reja
Near the tombs, and dating from the same period, is an equally magnificent **reja**, or gilded grille. The work of Maestro Bartolomé of Jaén, it is considered one of the finest in Spain. Its outstanding upper tier features scenes from the life of Christ and the Crucifixion.

Retablo
The altar's striking **retablo** is by Felipe Vigarny, dated 1522, depicting in one scene San Juan being boiled in oil; beneath the kneeling figures of Fernando and Isabel – sculptures possibly by Diego de Siloé – are images depicting events close to both their hearts, Boabdil surrendering the keys of Granada for him, the enforced baptism of the defeated Moors for her.

Sacristy
In the capilla's **Sacristy** are displayed the **sword of Fernando**, the **crown of Isabel**, and the banners used at the conquest of Granada. Also here is Isabel's outstanding personal collection of **medieval Flemish paintings** – including a magnificent **El Descendimiento** (Descent from the Cross) triptych by Dirk Bouts. Here too, are important works by Memling and van der Weyden – as well as various Italian and Spanish paintings, including panels by Botticelli, Perugino and Pedro Berruguete.

Granada Catedral
Gran Vía s/n • Mon–Sat 10am–6.15pm, Sun 3–6.15pm • Charge • ☎ 958 222 959

For all its stark Renaissance bulk, Granada's **Catedral**, adjoining the Capilla Real and entered from a door on Gran Vía, is a disappointment. It was raised on the site of the Great Mosque, with work commencing in 1521 – just as the royal chapel was finished – but was then left uncompleted until well into the eighteenth century. However, the main west facade by Diego de Siloé and Alonso Cano is worth a look. It still carries a provocative inscription honouring Primo de Rivera, founder of the fascist Falange Party, added in the Franco period, and, significantly for Granada today, never removed.

Inside, the church is delightfully light and airy due to its painted stonework and twenty giant pillars which push the central dome to a height of more than 30m. The Capilla Mayor has figures by Pedro de Mena of Fernando and Isabel at prayer, with, above them, oversized busts of Adam and Eve by *granadino* Alonso Cano, who also left quite a bit of work in the other chapels and is buried in the crypt – a marble and bronze plaque next to the main door honours him.

In the eighteenth-century **sagrario** there are more works by Cano as well as a fine *Crucifixión* by Martínez Montañés. In the side chapels are a triumphant sculpture of *Santiago* (St James) in the saddle, by Pedro de Mena (Capilla de Santiago) and an **El Greco** *St Francis* (Capilla de Jesús Nazareno).

Centro José Guerrero
C/Oficios 8 • Tues–Sat 10.30am–2pm & 4.30–9pm, Sun 10.30am–2pm • Free • ⓦ centroguerrero.org

Just south of the cathedral stands the **Centro José Guerrero**, a museum dedicated to the city's most famous modern artist and brilliant colourist José Guerrero (1914–91).

5

Influenced early on by Cubism and later by Miró, in 1950 Guerrero moved to New York, where he became a leading exponent of American Expressionism before returning to Spain in 1965. The museum displays arresting works from all his major periods of artistic development.

Hospital de San Juan de Dios

C/San Juan de Dios s/n • Mon–Sat 10am–1.30pm & 4–6.30pm, Sun 4–6.30pm • Charge • ☎ 958 275 700

North of the cathedral, and ten minutes' walk along Calle San Jerónimo, the Renaissance **Hospital de San Juan de Dios** is well worth a visit. It was founded in 1552 by Juan de Robles (Juan de Dios) as a hospital for the sick and a refuge for foundlings, and its elaborate facade has a statue by José de Mora depicting the saint on his knees holding a cross, which popular legend says is how he died. The hospital itself still functions and you'll have to pass the entrance hall to reach two marvellous **patios**. The outer and larger one is a beautiful double-tiered Renaissance work with a palm at each of its four corners and a fountain in the centre; the inner patio – with orange trees in the corners here – has delightful but deteriorating frescoes depicting the saint's miracles. Next door, the impressive church, a Baroque addition, has a Churrigueresque retablo – a glittering, gold extravaganza by Guerrero.

LORCA'S GRANADA

One of the ghosts that walks Granada's streets and plazas is that of Andalucía's greatest poet and dramatist **Federico García Lorca**. Born in 1898 at Fuente Vaqueros, a village in the *vega*, the fertile plain to the west of the city, he moved to Granada eleven years later. But it was his childhood spent growing up on the family farm, where he soaked up both the countryside and the folklore of its people, that was to have an enduring influence on his work.

Lorca published his first book of essays and poems while still at university in Granada, in 1918. It was in 1928, however, that he came to national prominence with *El Romancero Gitano*, an anthology of gypsy ballads. This success led to a trip to New York in 1929 where he spent a year at Columbia University ostensibly learning English, but actually gathering material for the collection of poems, *Poeta in Nueva York*, published after his death.

He returned to Spain in 1931 at the advent of the Spanish Republic and was given a government grant to run a travelling theatre group, La Barraca (the cabin). From this period the poet's major works for the stage – *Bodas de Sangre* (Blood Wedding) and *Yerma* – emerged.

In July 1936, on the eve of the Civil War, Lorca went back to Granada for the summer. This visit coincided with Franco's coup and control of the city was wrested by the Falangists, who initiated a reign of terror. Lorca, as a Republican sympathizer and declared homosexual, was hunted down by fascist thugs at the house of a friend – now the *Hotel Reina Cristina* (see page 452). Two days later he was murdered in an olive grove near the village of Viznar. His body was never found despite costly excavations carried out by the regional government a decade ago.

Anyone with an interest in tracing the **key locations** in Lorca's life should check out the places listed below; it's also possible to visit his death site in **Viznar** (see page 459). More avid followers should get hold of the excellent *Lorca's Granada* by Ian Gibson, his biographer.

HUERTA DE SAN VICENTE

Obligatory guided tours every 45min: April to mid-Sept Tues–Sun 9am–3pm; mid-Sept to April Tues–Sun 9.30am–5pm • Charge, Wed free • ⦿ huertadesanvicente.com • Take the southbound bus #C5 from Pza Isabel la Católica or Pza del Carmen (direction Palacio de Deportes), or a taxi

West of the centre is the **Huerta de San Vicente**, an orchard where the poet's family used to spend the summer months. It spreads back from C/de la Virgen Blanca, behind *Los Jardines Neptuno Flamenco* nightclub. The house – now restored and opened as a museum – is set in the centre of what is now the largest rose garden in Europe, the Parque Federico García

Monasterio de San Jerónimo

C/Rector López Argüeta 9 • Daily 10am–1pm & 4–7pm (till 6pm Oct–March) • Charge • ☎ 958 215 909

One block south of San Juan de Dios lies a little-known jewel: the sixteenth-century **Monasterio de San Jerónimo**, founded by the Catholic monarchs, though built after their death. This has an exquisite pair of Renaissance **patios** (or cloisters in this context), the largest an elegant work by Diego de Siloé with two tiers of 36 arches. The **church**, also by Siloé, has been wonderfully restored after use as cavalry barracks and has fabulous eighteenth-century frescoes, another monumental carved and painted retablo and, on either side of the altar, monuments to "El Gran Capitán" Gonzalo de Córdoba and his wife Doña María. The remains of this general, responsible for many of the Catholic monarchs' victories, may lie in the vault beneath, but the Napoleonic French were here too and, as Ford noted not much later, had "insulted the dead lion's ashes before whom, when alive, their ancestors had always fled". The church is little visited, and in late afternoon you may hear the nuns singing their offices in the railed-off choir loft above. A small shop at the entrance sells the convent's marmalade and *dulces*.

Hospital Real

Avda del Hospicio s/n • Mon–Fri 9am–2pm • Free

Lorca, the city's belated tribute. When the Lorcas had it, the five-acre holding was planted with vegetables and fruit trees. Then a tranquil rural plot on the city's edge, it has since been enveloped by ugly urban sprawl and it's hard to square the scene today with the poet's description of a "paradise of trees and water and so much jasmine and nightshade in the garden that we all wake up with lyrical headaches". The light and airy rooms contain some of their original furniture including, in Lorca's bedroom, his work desk, bed, a poster of the Barraca theatre company and the balcony (from outside, the furthest left of the three) looking towards the Sierra Nevada, which inspired one of his best-known poems, *Despedida* (Farewell). In a *hornacina*, or wall niche, outside is the tiny image of San Vicente placed there by Lorca's father; he bought the house in 1925 and changed its name to that of the saint.

LORCA MUSEUM

C/Poeta García Lorca, Fuente Vaqueros, 17km west of Granada • Obligatory guided tours on the hour: Daily: April & May 10am–1pm, 5pm & 6pm; June–Sept 10am–2pm; Oct–March 10am–1pm, 4pm & 5pm • Charge • ⓦ patronatogarcialorca.org • Take one of the services operated by Ureña (hourly from 9am; last bus returns to Granada at 9pm; 40min), which leave from Granada's Avda de Andaluces in front of the train station

Lorca's birthplace, in the tranquil farming village of Fuente Vaqueros, is now a house **museum**, lying just off the village's main square. A charming shrine to the poet's memory, the museum is stuffed with Lorca memorabilia, manuscripts and personal effects. The tour also includes a DVD with footage of Lorca and his engaging smile. After you've seen the house, you could also pay a visit to the parish church (open service times, 7–9pm) at the end of the street opposite, where Lorca's mother took him regularly as a child. The old stone font where Lorca – or "Federico" as he is known to all the world here – was baptized is still there.

CASA-MUSEO DE FEDERICO GARCÍA LORCA

C/Iglesia 20, signed from the main road into Valderrubio, 4km northwest of Fuente Vaqueros • Tues–Sat: mid-Sept to May 10am–5pm; June to mid-Sept 9am–3pm • Charge • ⓦ huertadesanvicente.com • Buses to Fuente Vaqueros (see above) continue to Valderrubio (20min)

The Lorca family had a house 4km to the northwest of Fuente Vaqueros in the pleasant village of Valderrubio, which is now open as a **museum**. Each year the family moved here at harvest time (Lorca's father was a wealthy landowner) and the infant Lorca spent many summers playing in surrounding fields. The house remained in the family until 1986.

The **Hospital Real** is a magnificent Renaissance building designed by Enrique Egas. Formerly known as the Hospital de los Locos, it was founded by the Catholic monarchs and finished by Carlos V. As its former name implies, it was one of the first lunatic asylums in Europe, though it now houses the main library of the University of Granada. Inside, a beautiful, arcaded patio and some fine *artesonado* ceilings are worth a look.

La Cartuja

Paseo de Cartuja s/n • Sun–Fri 10am–5.30pm, Sat 10am–12.15pm & 3–5.30pm • Charge • ⓦ cartujadegranada.com• From Pza Isabel La Católica get bus #C6 along Gran Vía then #N7, or it's a 10–15min walk beyond the Hospital Real

Granada's **La Cartuja**, on the northern outskirts of town, is the grandest and most outrageously decorated of all the country's lavish Carthusian monasteries. The monastery was founded in 1516 on land provided by "El Gran Capitán", Gonzalo de Córdoba (see page 449), though the building is noted today for its heights of Churrigueresque-inspired Baroque extravagance – added, some say, to rival the Alhambra. The **church** is of staggering wealth, surmounted by an altar of twisted and coloured marble described by one Spanish writer as "a motionless architectural earthquake". There are Bocanegra paintings and a seventeenth-century sculpture of the *Assumption* by José de Mora.

The **sagrario** drips with more marble, jasper and porphyry and has a breathtakingly beautiful gilded and frescoed **cupola** by Antonio Palomino, while the **sacristía** pulls out yet more stops with another stunning painted cupola and fascinating sculptural features influenced by the art of the Aztec and Maya civilizations encountered in the New World. Here also are fine sculptures of *San Bruno* by José de Mora in a side niche, and an *Inmaculada* by Alonso Cano.

Parque de las Ciencias

Avda de las Ciencias s/n • Tues–Sat 10am–7pm, Sun 10am–3pm • Charge • ⓦ parqueciencias.com• Bus #LAC, going south along Gran Vía, will drop you nearby

The last thing you might think of visiting in Granada is a science park, but the mammoth **Parque de las Ciencias** is a genuinely fun visit and especially good if you've got kids to entertain. Filled with interactive gizmos and gadgets, it features a number of themed pavilions – one is dedicated to a journey through the human body, another deals with the history of science in Andalucía, with plenty on the Moorish contribution, and the "natural spaces" pavilion has a stunning walk-in tropical butterfly garden featuring max exotic species. They also host big-name special exhibitions: dinosaurs, the *Titanic* and M.C. Escher's "infinite universes" have featured in the past decade. The showstopper is a planetarium that gives you a breathtaking ride through the universe, passing seven thousand stars along the way.

ARRIVAL AND DEPARTURE   GRANADA AND AROUND

BY PLANE

Granada airport (ⓦ aena.es), 17km west of the city on the A92 *autovía*, handles domestic flights to Madrid and Barcelona as well as international and budget flights. Buses (11 daily, 5.50am–8pm; 40min) take you into town. You can also get out to the airport from a stop on the east side of Gran Vía opposite the cathedral; check ⓦ siu.ctagr.es), or the tourist offices for the latest timetable. A taxi from the airport will cost about €25–30 into town.

BY TRAIN

The train station lies 1km or so northwest of the centre

on Avda de Andaluces, off Avda de la Constitución; to get into town take bus #LAC (at least every 7min, 6.45am–11.45pm) which runs between the station and the Palacio de Congresos. Bus #SN1 (at least every 15min, 6.30am–11.30pm) runs between the station and Camino de Ronda. Destinations Algeciras (3 daily; 4hr 30min); Almería (4 daily; 2hr 25min); Guadix (4 daily; 1hr 10min); Ronda (3 daily; 2hr 50min); Seville (4 daily; 3hr 20min).

BY BUS

Bus stations The city's main bus station, on Ctra de Jaén s/n, is some way out of the centre in the northern suburbs, and handles all services, including those to the Sierra Nevada but not to Viznar. To get to the centre, take city bus #SN1 (see page 450) to Caleta (near the train station) and change to the #LAC bus (see page 450) for Gran Vía Colón near the cathedral (15min).

Services and timetables For information on bus services and timetables check with the companies, which are all – except for the service to Viznar – based at the bus station. Alsa (@alsa.es) serves Almería, Alpujarras (high and low), Baza, Córdoba, Guadix, Jaén, Madrid, Málaga, Motril, Úbeda, Seville and the coast. Autocares Bonal (☏958 465 022) goes to Veleta and the north side of Sierra Nevada.

Destinations Almería (7 daily; 2hr 15min); Almuñécar (14 daily; 1hr 15min); Baeza/Úbeda (9 daily; 2hr 30min); Baza (9 daily; 1hr 30min); Cádiz (4 daily; 5hr); Cazorla (2 daily; 4hr); Córdoba (8 daily; 2hr 30min); Guadix (12 daily; 1hr); Jaén (15 daily; 1hr 15min); La Herradura (7 daily; 1hr 30min); Madrid (16 daily; 5hr); Málaga (15 daily; 1hr 45min); Mojácar (2 daily; 4hr 15min); Montefrío (3 daily; 1hr 30min); Motril (16 daily; 1hr 15min); Nerja (7 daily; 1hr

45min); Salobreña (12 daily; 1hr); Seville (9 daily; 3hr). For the Sierra Nevada/Alpujarras, the following buses all pass Lanjarón and Órgiva; current departure times are 8.30am, 2.30pm & 5pm to Ugíjar (also passing Albondón, Cádiar and Yegen); noon & 4.30pm to Bérchules (also passing Pampaneira, Bubión, Capileira, Busquístar and Trevélez); and 1.30pm to Berja (via Motril or Órgiva).

BY CAR

Central Granada is often choked with more traffic than its streets are able to bear, and finding on-street parking can be close to impossible. If you do arrive by car, you're best off leaving it in a car park or garage for the duration of your stay. Note that the city's main arteries, Gran Vía, C/Reyes Católicos and C/Recogidas, are part of a city-centre traffic exclusion zone. You may enter the zone only if your hotel is actually *on* one of its streets. Carefully read all signs in the central zone and check with your hotel beforehand to avoid a hefty fine.

INFORMATION

Turismo Municipal The city's best and most efficient tourist office is the municipal tourist office at Pza del Carmen s/n inside the Ayuntamiento (mid-March to mid-Oct Mon–Sat 10am–8pm, Sun 10am–2pm; mid-Oct to mid-March Mon–Sat 10am–7pm, Sun 10am–2pm; ☏958 248 280; @granadatur.com). They also have a sub-office in the Alhambra's ticket office (open same hours as the monument).

Turismo Regional The city's rather lethargic (but less busy) Junta de Andalucía Turismo (C/Santa Ana 2; Mon–Fri 9am–7.30pm, Sat & Sun 9.30am–3pm; ☏958 575 202), is up the steps to the right of the church of Santa Ana, off Pza Nueva.

Granada Card The Granada Card, valid for between 24 and 72 hours, gives access to seven of the city's monuments including the Alhambra, Capilla Real, Catedral, La Cartuja and Parque de Ciencias. You may enter each monument once only, and when buying it can choose a time for visiting the Alhambra's Palacios Nazaríes (subject to availability). It also includes nine bus journeys and a ride on the Granada sightseeing train. The card doesn't save you a great deal unless you intend to visit all the monuments, but it does guarantee you entry to the Alhambra, which is a benefit – even when the Alhambra is sold out, this scheme has a guaranteed 250 places per day. The card can be bought at the Turismo Municipal, El Corte Inglés department store, Parque de Ciencias, from the Audioguías: This is Granada kiosk in Pza Nueva or the Caja Granada bank at Pza Isabel La Católica 6 (during business hours). However, it's easiest to simply buy it online (@granadatur.com).

Granada City Tour A hop-on, hop-off electric train (daily

every 15-20 mins; charge; @granadacitytour.com) takes in the main sights from the city. The green route runs during the day and includes the Alhambra and Albaícin, while the red nocturnal route excludes the Alhambra.

Walking tours Daily city tours and guided Alhambra visits by officially approved guides (in English and Spanish) are run by Cicerone Granada (booking recommended in high season; @ciceronegranada.com). The walks take place in all weather, and leave from the green-and-white kiosk in the northeast corner of the Pza de Bib-Rambla.

Useful websites @granadatur.com, @turgranada. es, @granadainfo.com, @andalucia.org and @albaicin-granada.com.

Newspapers and listings The monthly *Go* (@laguiago. com) *and Yuzin* (@yuzin.com) are available from newspaper kiosks or free from the Tourismo Municipal, and have cultural and entertainment listings (the online versions are more up to date). The city's rather staid daily paper, *Ideal*, has a reliable entertainment guide, particularly in its weekend editions. Foreign press is sold by the kiosks in Pza Nueva and Puerta Real.

Hiking maps Maps of the Sierra Nevada and Las Alpujarras can be obtained from the Turismo, though for a more specialist selection try Cartográfica del Sur (@cartograficadelsur.com), which sells a wide range, including military maps. The CNIG (National Geographic Institute), C/Divina Pastora 7, by the Jardines del Triunfo (Sept–July Mon–Fri 9am–2pm) also sells 1:50,000 and 1:25,000 maps. The Metro bookshop (see page 459) is also a good source.

5

ACCOMMODATION

SEE MAPS PAGES 430 AND 440

Finding a **place to stay** in Granada usually isn't a problem, except during Semana Santa (Easter week) and very occasionally during Aug. Note that spring and early autumn are the high seasons here. In addition to the central zone, the atmospheric **Albaicín** quarter also makes a wonderful place to stay and while most of its addresses are upmarket, a few also cater for budget travellers. **Self-catering accommodation** (minimum stay two nights) is also an option: we've listed a couple below, but for a wider choice visit ⑩ granadadirect.com. With your own transport, staying in one of the **villages** to the south of the city is also an option.

HOTELS AND HOSTALES

Unless stated otherwise, where hotels or *hostales* have a garage, expect to pay around €10–25 per vehicle per day.

AROUND PLAZA NUEVA AND TOWARDS THE ALHAMBRA

Hostal Landázuri Cuesta de Gomérez 24; ⑩ hostallandazuri.com. Good-value rooms, some en suite, plus its own bar and a roof terrace with a view of the Alhambra. Some single rooms. Garage. €

Hostal Navarro Ramos Cuesta de Gomérez 21; ⑩ pensionnavarroramos.com. Appealing small *hostal* en route to the Alhambra; neat and tidy rooms, with and without bath, and some singles. No TV or a/c, but has fans in summer. €

Hotel Macía Plaza Pza Nueva 4; ⑩ maciahoteles.com. Centrally located modern hotel, offering stylishly furnished, well-equipped a/c rooms, many overlooking the square. *Rough Guide* readers with this guide can claim a ten-percent discount on direct bookings. €€€

Hotel Puerta de las Granadas Cuesta de Gomérez 14; ⑩ hotelpuertadelasgranadas.com. Small, modern hotel on the way to the Alhambra with a/c en-suite rooms; the top one has Alhambra views. €

OYO Hostal Austria Cuesta de Gomérez 4; ⑩ pensionaustria.com. Efficient, friendly, Austrian-run *hostal* in a quiet street. The compact en-suite rooms come with a/c, and it has its own garage. €

CATHEDRAL AREA

AC Palacio de Santa Paula Gran Vía de Colón 31; ⑩ marriott.com. Five-star hotel in three buildings including a fourteenth century Moorish mansion and sixteenth century convent. Some rooms include original stones, columns or Arabic inscriptions. Excellent restaurant and lovely patio that's part of the hotel bar. Sauna and all the trimmings you'd expect. €€€

Hostal Arteaga C/Arteaga 3; ⑩ hostalarteaga.es. Central and economical *hostal*, just off the Gran Vía, offering simple, small but brightly decorated en-suite a/c rooms

with TV on a quiet street. Helpful reception staff. €

★**Hostal Costa Azul** C/Virgen del Rosario 5; ⑩ hostalcostaazul.com. Friendly, small *hostal* with good en-suite rooms with heating and a/c. Also has its own restaurant next door and rents out luxurious apartments nearby. Doubles €, apartments €€

Hotel Inglaterra C/Cetti Meriem 6; ⑩ hotelinglaterragranada.com. Three-star hotel offering comfortable, sober, a/c rooms with satellite TV and minibar in a stylishly modernized building. €€

Hotel Villa Oniria C/San Antón 28; ⑩ villaoniria.com. Stylish hotel in restored nineteenth-century palace with original gardens, spa and roaring fire in the sitting room in the cooler months. A/c rooms with satellite TV and lots of luxury touches. Parking available. €€€

PLAZA DE LA TRINIDAD AND AROUND THE UNIVERSITY

Hostal Lima C/Laurel de las Tablas 17; ⑩ hostallimagranada.eu. Recently renovated *hostal*, two blocks from the cathedral, furnished in tiles and antiques, with en-suite a/c rooms with TV. The street can be noisy so book an interior room. Friendly owners. €

Hostal Rodri C/Laurel de las Tablas 9; ⑩ hostalrodri. com. Very comfortable, spotlessly clean and quiet *hostal*, just off Pza de la Trinidad near the cathedral. Some rooms are small, but all are comfortable with modern bathrooms. Very helpful staff. €

Hotel Reina Cristina C/Tablas 4; ⑩ hotelreinacristina. com. Modern and welcoming hotel inside an older building – with a fine patio – where Lorca spent his last days before being seized by the fascists. Twin-bedded rooms tend to be larger. Friendly staff; they also have a good restaurant and garage. €€€

ALBAICÍN, SACROMONTE AND NORTH OF THE CENTRE

★**Casa del Aljarife** Placeta de la Cruz Verde 2; ⑩ casadelaljarife.com. Delightful, small, upmarket *hostal* in a restored sixteenth-century house, near the heart of the Albaicín; four beautiful en-suite rooms (two with Alhambra views) and patio. €€

★**Casa del Capitel Nazari** Cuesta de Aceituneros 6; ⑩ hotelcasacapitel.com. Beautiful sixteenth-century *palacio* transformed into an enchanting small hotel with elegantly furnished beamed or *artesonado* (coffered ceilinged) rooms overlooking a triple-tiered patio; some rooms have an Alhambra view. Welcoming staff and *cafetería* make this rather special. Special offers from Nov–Feb and prices can be cut significantly in July and Aug. Parking nearby. €€€

★**Casa Morisca** Cuesta de la Victoria 9; ⑩ hotelcasamorisca.com. Stunningly romantic small hotel inside an immaculately renovated (for which it won an award) fifteenth-century Moorish mansion with an exquisite patio below the walls of the Alhambra in the Albaicín. Rooms are sumptuously equipped and there are re-created Moorish furnishings throughout (the splendid Mudéjar wooden ceilings are original). Room 15, with Alhambra views, is one to go for. Exterior rooms cost more. Designated street parking outside. €€€

★ **Hostal Moni Albayzín** Pza San Bartolomé 5; ☎ 958 285 284. The Albaicín's first budget *hostal* – and it's a cracker. The proprietors provide a hearty welcome and the en-suite rooms – with TV and a/c – are spotless. The roof terrace has views of the Alhambra and Sierra Nevada, and guests have use of fridge and washing machine. Street parking. Breakfast is included. €

Hotel Casa 1800 C/Benalúa 11; ⓦ hotelcasa1800granada.com. A stone's throw from the Paseo de los Tristes, this sixteenth-century restored mansion has a fine tiered patio. Romantic spacious rooms; the suite deluxe has a balcony with exceptional views of the Alhambra. Complimentary afternoon tea. €€€

★ **Hotel Palacio Santa Inés** Cuesta de Santa Inés 9; ⓦ palaciosantaines.es. Sumptuous eleven-room hotel in a beautiful, restored sixteenth-century Mudéjar mansion on the south side of the Albaicín with Alhambra views – especially from rooms 32–36. The nearby, similarly priced and equally delightful *Carmen de Santa Inés*, Placeta de Porras 7, off C/San Juan de los Reyes, is owned by the same proprietors and occupies an equally attractive restored Moorish *carmen*. €€€

Hotel Santa Isabel la Real C/Santa Isabel la Real 19; ⓦ hotelsantaisabellareal.com. Enchanting and welcoming small hotel housed in a wonderfully restored sixteenth-century Albaicín mansion close to the church of San Nicolás. Elegantly furnished, beamed rooms (some with Alhambra views) are equipped with minibar. Own car park. Breakfast is included. €€

El Ladrón de Agua Carrera del Darro 13; ⓦ ladrondeagua.com. Beautiful hotel inside a restored sixteenth-century Mudéjar *palacio* with lots of exposed brick, cool marble, understated decor and a charming patio. Some of the exquisitely furnished beamed rooms come with Alhambra views. €€€

★ **Palacio de Mariana Pineda** Carrera del Darro 9; ⓦ palaciomarianapineda.com. Fabulous five-room boutique hotel in a stunning seventeenth-century mansion, birthplace of the eponymous *granadina* heroine about whom Lorca wrote a play. Above a delightful patio, the beamed rooms are opulently furnished and decorated, and some have four-poster beds and Alhambra views. €€€

INSIDE AND AROUND THE ALHAMBRA

Hotel Albero Avda Santa María de La Alhambra 6; ⓦ hotelalbero.com. This excellent-value, attractive and friendly small hotel lies on the access road to the Alhambra to the south of the centre. Sparkling a/c rooms come with TV and balcony, and there's easy street parking. Ring if you have problems finding them and they will advise. €

Hotel Alhambra Palace Peña Partida 2–4; ⓦ h-alhambrapalace.es. On the Alhambra hill and a 5min walk from the palace entrance, this opulent four-star *belle époque* hotel in neo-Moorish style offers every service you would expect for the price, except a pool. Many of the classically furnished rooms have spectacular balcony views over the city and the same views can be enjoyed from the bar's terrace (open to the public). Car park available. Big discounts in July and Aug. €€€€

Hotel América Real de la Alhambra 53; ⓦ hotelamericagranada.com. Charming small hotel in the Alhambra grounds, bang opposite the *parador*, so you can get an early march on the queues. You pay for the location rather than creature comforts; while you do get a/c rooms, room prices are (unjustifiably) high. €€€

Hotel Molinos C/Molinos 12; ⓦ hotelmolinos.es. In the heart of the vibrant Realejo *barrio* and little over 4m wide, this place is listed in the *Guinness Book of Records* as the narrowest hotel in the world. Pleasant a/c en-suite rooms (some with balcony), and friendly proprietors. Own garage. €€

Hotel Washington Irving Paseo del Generalife 10; ⓦ eurostarshotels.com. One of the city's most historic hotels reopened in late 2016 after extensive restoration. Not much remains of the original fittings, though the five-star hotel retains its hallowed atmosphere and the library is dedicated to Washington Irving, with first editions of his books. The comfortable rooms come with everything you'd expect from a hotel of this calibre, with some having views of the Alhambra walls (extra), and there's a rooftop pool. €€€€

★ **Parador de San Francisco** Real de la Alhambra; ⓦ parador.es. Without doubt the best hotel in Granada – a converted fifteenth-century monastery (itself created from a Nasrid palace) in the Alhambra grounds. Unsurprisingly, this top-of-the-range *parador* is also the most expensive hotel in the city; rooms are elegantly furnished and well equipped, and all superior rooms and suites have Alhambra or Generalife views. Booking is advised at least four months ahead in summer or over Easter. Own car park. Non-guests can call in for a drink in the terrace bar or use the restaurant (see page 456). Standard room €€€€

YOUTH HOSTEL

Albergue Juvenil Avda Ramón y Cajal 2, off the Camino de Ronda; ⓦ inturjoven.com. With lots of facilities, Granada's hostel is handy for the train station: from there, turn left onto Avda de la Constitución and left again onto the Camino de Ronda – it's the large white building by a sports stadium (Estadio de la Juventud); from the bus station take

5

bus #SN2 and get off at the stop after the railway bridge. All rooms are en-suite doubles and staff are friendly, though the food is institutional. An excellent alternative is the hostel at Viznar, in the hills above the city (see page 459). €

CAMPSITES
Camping Reina Isabel 4km along the Zubia road to the southwest of the city ⓦcampingreinaisabel.com.

With a pool, less noise and more shade than *Camping Sierra Nevada*, this makes a pleasant rural alternative and – with your own transport – the city is within easy reach. €
Camping Sierra Nevada Avda de Madrid 107, northwest of the centre and 200m south of the bus station; ⓦcampingsierranevada.com. Easiest reached from the centre on bus #SN1, this is the most convenient city site, and – with a pool – probably the best. €

EATING

SEE MAPS PAGES 430 AND 440

Granada is quite a sedate place, at least compared to Seville or Málaga, and if it weren't for the university, you sense the city would go unnaturally early to bed. However, there's more than enough to entertain you on a brief stay, with some decent restaurants and plenty of animated bars, especially in the zone between **Plaza Nueva** and **Grand Vía**; the plazas of the **Albaicín** quarter, whose streets make for enjoyable (if confusing) evening wanderings; around the **Campo del Príncipe**, a spacious square with outdoor eating and drinking; at the foot of the west slopes of the Alhambra hill; and along the **Carrera del Darro**.

RESTAURANTS
With the arrival of more four- and five-star hotels, the quality, service and standards of Granada's restaurants has improved. Eating out is generally good value all over town, and there are a number of places worth paying a bit more for. Beware, of course, the inevitable tourist traps, particularly around the Plaza Nueva and C/Elvira. Note that you can also get substantial meals at many of the city's bars (see page 456).

PLAZA NUEVA AND CATHEDRAL AREA
El Claustro Gran Vía 31; ☎958 058 038. Part of the *AC Palacio de Santa Paula* hotel, this restaurant sits in the original sixteenth century cloisters, with outdoor dining in the courtyard as well. The cuisine gives a modern twist to local dishes; try the *pulpo seco con setas* (dried octupus with wild mushroom) or the *lomo de ciervo* (venison fillet). Booking essential. €€€
Las Cuevas C/Calderería Nueva. Crêpes, couscous, tagines, pizzas cooked in a wood-burning oven and a cheap *menú* make this a popular place with locals. There's a small terrace facing San Gregorio church. €€
Nueva Bodega C/Cetti Meriem 9; ☎958 225 938. Good-value local bodega with small outside terrace and extra dining space upstairs. Serves up basic tapas, *bocadillos* and *platos combinados*. €
Pilar de Toro C/Hospital de Santa Ana 12; ⓦpilardeltoro.es. Stylish, medium-priced bar-restaurant inside a former seventeenth-century *casa señorial* with exterior *terraza*, elegant patio bar (serving tapas) and, upstairs, a mid-priced restaurant with its own leafy and secluded patio. €€€

Restaurante León C/Pan 3; ☎958 225 143. Long-established economical restaurant serving many *carne de monte* (game) dishes and *flamenquines* (deep-fried meat roll). €€
Samarcanda C/Calderería Vieja 3; ☎958 210 004. This excellent Lebanese restaurant (with plenty of vegetarian options) is the best of the few places in "Little Morocco" where it's worth having a full meal. You could try their *menú de la casa* for two including Lebanese wine. €€
Tetería Kasbah C/Calderería Nueva 4; ⓦkasbahgranada.es. Styled as a "teahouse" serving delicious *pasteles árabes* (cakes) and crêpes, this little Moroccan place also offers more elaborate dishes including couscous and tagines, and has a vegetarian *menú*. €

ALBAICÍN
Carmen de Aben Humeya C/Cuesta de las Tomasas 12; ⓦabenhumeya.com. Superb Alhambra views from the terrace of this *bar-cafetería* serving salads, meat and fish dishes plus cocktails. €€€
Juanillo Camino del Monte 81. Well-known restaurant in Sacromonte with great views of the Alhambra, serving typical no-nonsense but well-prepared *raciones*, paella and *tortilla de Sacromonte* (lamb brain omelette). Take the bus from Pza Nueva if you can't face the hike. €€€
El Ladrillo II Plazoleta de Fatima; ⓦel-ladrillo-ii. negocio.site. This place specializes in *barcos* (large plates) of fried fish and paella, served at economical prices on tables beneath the stars – all of which make the climb here worthwhile. €€
Mirador de Morayma C/Pianista García Carrillo 2; ⓦmiradordemorayma.com. Situated in a gorgeous Albaicín *carmen* with a fine view of the Alhambra, this place offers traditional food and many *granadino* specialities: *conchinillo al horno* (baked suckling pig) is a signature dish, and the desserts are made by the sisters at the Convento de Santa Catalina. Insist on a terrace table (fine weather) or a ground-floor or first-floor table (but refuse the cellar). €€€€
Paprika Cuesta de Abarqueros 5; ⓦpaprikagranada. com. Stylish vegan restaurant popular with a younger international crowd. They serve world cuisine-inspired tapas and *raciones* as well as risottos, rice dishes, hummus and *curry Thai* accompanied by laidback sounds including jazz. There's a summer street terrace. €€

★ **Restaurante Las Tomasas** Carril de San Agustín 4, just below the Mirador de San Nicolás; ⓦlastomasas. com. Mid-priced restaurant in a huge and beautiful *carmen* serving *cocina andaluza* as well as an international menu, with a stunning terrace view of the Alhambra; *rabo de toro* (oxtail) is a speciality. You can also nurse a drink and (pricey) *pintxo* here if you don't want to dine formally. €€€

★ **El Trillo** Callejón del Aljibe del Trillo 3; ⓦrestaurante-eltrillo.com. Enchanting little mid-priced restaurant in an Albaicín *carmen* (villa and garden) offering Basque-influenced cuisine: *arroz con jabalí y setas* (rice with wild boar and mushroom) is a signature dish. It has outdoor tables on a delightful garden patio shaded by pear and quince trees, and a roof terrace. €€€

PLAZAS BIB-RAMBLA AND TRINIDAD

Botánico C/Málaga 3; ⓦbotanicocafe.es. A fusion restaurant with a healthy eating slant and a menu influenced by Asian, Mexican and North African cuisines. Its Scandinavian-style dining room is open from breakfast till late, so it also serves a variety of healthy snacks, juices and infusions. They have a small street terrace. €€

Oliver Pza Pescadería 12, slightly northwest of Pza de la Trinidad; ⓦrestauranteoliver.com. Good *raciones* bar and upmarket restaurant with cosy interior rooms and a popular (with the *granadino* smart set) outdoor terrace. Traditional cuisine. €€€

★ **Restaurante-Marisquería Cunini** Pza Pescadería 14; ☎958 250 777. A gleaming, marble-topped bar serves standing customers with high-quality fish tapas and *raciones*, plus there's a pricier and equally excellent seafood restaurant to the side (for which reservations are advised). Specialities include *caldereta de marisco* (fish casserole) and *pescado cocinado en barro* (fish cooked in an earthenware pot). €€€

Sancho C/Tablas 16; ☎958 254 654. A reliable spot off Pza de la Trinidad for fortifying breakfasts, healthy salads and siesta-inducing lunches. The house special is *carne a la brasa* (grilled meat). €€

PLAZA MARIANA PINEDA AND THE SOUTH CENTRAL AREA

Puerta del Carmen Pza del Carmen 1, same square as the Ayuntamiento; ⓦpuertadelcarmenrestaurante. com. Popular with *granadinos* working nearby, this *mesón* used to host Círculo Taurino (bullfighting society) meetings. *Carnes a la brasa* (charcoal-grilled meats) are house specials, as is the shoulder of pork. €€€

Restaurante Chikito Pza del Campillo 9; ⓦrestaurantechikito.com. Fronted by seven towering plane trees, and formerly the *Café Alameda* where Lorca, de Falla and the *Rinconcillo* group met. Literary lights from abroad such as Kipling and H.G. Wells all visited the bar's corner table (*mesa del rincón*). *Bacalao con bresa de pimientos* (cod in pepper sauce) is a house special, and their *sopa sevillana* (fish and rice soup) is mouthwatering. Decent tapas in the bar. €€€

ALHAMBRA AND CAMPO DEL PRÍNCIPE

El Carmen de San Miguel Pza Torres Bermejas 3; ⓦcarmensanmiguel.com. One of Granada's top places to eat, with a fabulous terrace looking out over the city. An innovative approach (occasionally overdone) to *andaluz* cuisine is illustrated by a signature dish, *cochinillo confitado a la vainilla con pure de manzana y ciruelas* (confit of suckling pig with vanilla, and apple and plum purée). €€€€

★ **Damasqueros** C/Damasqueros 3; ⓦdamasqueros. com. Tucked away to the north of Pza del Realejo is one of Granada's culinary secrets. Run by local chef Lola Marín who trained with Berasategui, this small venue serves a

---

TEAHOUSES IN GRANADA

The **teterías** (teahouses) in the "Little Morocco" district (see map page 430) on and around the *calles* Calderería Nueva and Calderería Vieja are a colourful part of Granada's social scene and well worth a visit.

Al-Faguara C/Calderería Nueva 7. A classic for teas (try their "té Pakistani"), juices and crêpes.

As-Sirat C/Calderería Nueva 5. The friendly, Moroccan-run "bridge between earth and paradise" is one of the oldest of Granada's teahouses and offers traditional Moroccan dishes, pastries and teas in its Moorish-inspired interior.

Dar Ziryab C/Calderería Nueva 11. Frequent live concerts of Middle Eastern and North African music; its cultural centre offers classes in guitar and Maghrebi music.

Natura Morisca C/Calderería Vieja 12. A bakery

selling Moroccan cakes, pastries and pies – try their *pastela*, a delicious spicy chicken- and egg-filled filo pastry.

Tetería Ábaco C/Álamo del Marqués 5. Worth the steep climb off Pza San Gregorio to admire the Alhambra views from the terrace as you sip your choice of tea from the over fifty different types.

Tetería Tuareg C/Corpus Cristi 5, just off the foot of C/Calderería Vieja. A popular, atmospheric teahouse with a candlelit, cave-like interior. Come here to sip teas with crêpes in the summer, or with *pasteles* in the winter.

weekly tasting menu based on a fusion of Arabic, Jewish and Christian recipes using seasonal produce. The wine list runs to over 120, but allow the *sumiller* to advise you. €€€€

Hicuri Pza de los Gironés 4, to the west of Campo del Príncipe; ⓦrestaurantehicuriartvegan.com. One of Granada's few vegan restaurants, with a brightly coloured interior and shady outside terrace. House specials include vegetable lasagne and tofu with teriyaki sauce. There's a daily *menú* and you can buy organic produce from the small shop. €€

La Mimbre Paseo del Generalife s/n, near the Alhambra's entrance; ⓦrestaurantelamimbre.es. With a delightful terrace shaded by willows (*mimbres*) this is one of the best restaurants on the Alhambra hill and just the place for a lunch between monuments. The food is well prepared, but they are sometimes overwhelmed in high season. Specials include *habas con jamón* (broad beans with ham) and braised oxtail. €€€

Parador de San Francisco Alhambra; ☎958 221 440. The *parador's* restaurant is one of the best in an upmarket chain often noted for its blandness. It boasts fine views and offers a varied and not-too-bank-breaking *menú*. À la carte includes *granadino* specialities such as *sopa de espárragos de la vega* (asparagus soup) and *pulpo asado sobre risotto de algas* (roast octopus with seaweed risotto). €€€€

TAPAS BARS

Granada's proximity to the Sierra Nevada brings a coolness to the city that means you're just as likely to find locals ordering a glass of rioja as the beloved fino preferred in the rest of Andalucía. One local wine worth trying is *vino de la costa* (coast wine – ironically made in the mountains of the Alpujarras); amber in colour, fairly potent, but relatively easy on hangovers, it's the ideal partner for a *tapa*. The bars recommended below are mainly for drinking, though most serve tapas and *raciones* and you could happily fill up and forget about going to a restaurant. The city has quite a reputation for its tapas, which are more elaborate than is usual in Andalucía and in most bars one comes free with each drink – a laudable trait in a city generally regarded as penny-pinching by most *andaluces*.

PLAZA NUEVA AND CATHEDRAL AREA

★ **Bodegas Castañeda** C/Almireceros 1, at the corner of C/Elvira; ☎958 215 464. A *granadino* institution and one of the city's oldest bars, though much refurbished and prettified; it's still an attractive first stop of an evening. Good tapas include generous pâté and cheese boards (*tablas*), *montaditos* (small open sandwiches), baked potatoes and gazpacho. €€

Bodegas La Mancha C/Joaquín Costa 10. Monumental spit-and-sawdust establishment (slightly more refined since refurbishment) hung with hams, and with great wine vats stationed behind the bar like rockets on a launch pad.

Tasty tapas on offer include *jamón de Trevélez* and *tortilla española*; they also sell excellent hot and cold *bocadillos* to eat in or take away. €

Casa de los Vinos C/Monjas del Carmen 2; ⓦcasadevinosgranada.es. Aka *La Brujidera*, this atmospheric place just off Pza Nueva is perhaps *the* place in Granada to sample Spanish wine. Take your pick from over 150 varieties including vermouths on tap and sparkling cavas. Food is limited to cold cuts, cheese and pâté as tapas or *raciones*. €€

★ **Hannigan and Sons** C/Cetti Merriem s/n; ☎958 224 826. Independent Irish house whose owner *is* named Hannigan. The usual range of beers and stouts are on offer and the place has an airy feel to it with a snug, some decorative stained glass and the only wooden floor in town. House specials include burgers, nachos and chicken wings. On Sat and Sun they do a slap-up Irish breakfast brunch (starting at 1pm) popular with late risers in to watch live football games on TV. €€

El Rinconcillo C/Hospital de Santa Ana 7, on south side of Pza Nueva. Friendly and compact bar with lively summer *terraza* serving good tapas and *raciones*. Try the *morcilla ibérica* (blood sausage) or the *ensaladilla rusa* (potato salad). €

La Trastienda C/Cuchilleros 11, on a small plaza just off C/Reyes Católicos; ☎958 226 965. Plush little drinking den hidden behind a shop selling wine, cheese and ham. Once you've negotiated your way around the counter it's surprisingly cosy in the back. Best tapas to go for are the *jamón ibérico* and *salchichón*. €

ALBAICÍN

El Aljibe de San Miguel Pza de San Miguel Bajo 6; ⓦaljibesanmiguelgranada.com. Small but attractive terrace on the square. House specials include *pollo al aljibe* (chicken with onion and cream) and *papas piquantonas* (spicy potatoes). €€

★ **Al Sur de Granada** C/Elvira 150, near the Moorish Puerta de Elvira arch; ⓦalsurdegranada.net. Great modern little bar-shop serving delicious cheeses, ham, salads and healthy breakfasts. They stock organic produce and over fifty Granada wines to try and buy. Often stages exhibitions of work by local artists on its walls. €

Bar Aixa Pza Larga; ☎958 255 042. Welcoming bar with terrace tables serving well-prepared tapas and *raciones*. Try their *migas* (breadcrumbs) stir-fried with crispy pork fat and green peppers or fresh anchovies. €

Bar Caracoles Pza Aliatar, slightly northeast of the Iglesia del Salvador; ☎650 877 353. Popular and atmospheric tapas place on this attractive square. It's famous for its *caracoles* (snails) as well as *callos* (tripe) and *rabo de toro* (oxtail). €

Café 4 Gatos Placeta de la Cruz Verde 6; ⓦcafe4gatos. com. Tucked in a tiny square on the Cuesta de San Gregorio,

5

this café-bar is small in size but big on breakfasts and sandwiches, and boasts Granada's best carrot cake. €

CAMPO DEL PRÍNCIPE AND CARRERA DEL DARRO

Bar Candela C/Santa Escolástica 9; ☎958 227 010. A mixture of students and neighbourhood artists fill this atmospheric Basque bar every night. They serve a long list of *montaditos* (small filled bread rolls) and *bocatas* (large filled rolls). €

Cafétería Fútbol Pza de Mariana Pineda 6; ⓦcafefutbol.com. A Granada classic since 1903 with a large, busy terrace on the leafy square. Serves breakfasts, *churros con chocolate* and ice-cream sundaes, as well as a long list of drinks. €

★ **Potemkin** Pza Hospicio Viejo s/n; ⓦpotemkinbar. es. Great pint-sized bar with cool sounds (mainly early twentieth-century jazz), which also stages art exhibitions. Japanese chef Miyuki's tapas are excellent, and he also makes mouthwatering sushi and maki rolls. Breakfasts and homemade cakes and desserts served in the morning. €

Rabo de Nube Paseo de los Tristes 5; ☎958 220 421. One of many terrace bars on this plaza – at the far end of the Carrera del Darro – and a wonderful place to sit out at night with a drink while gazing up at the Alhambra's illuminated battlements. They serve *tablas* (pâté and cheese boards) and house specials include *habas con jamón* (broad beans with ham) and fried fish. €€

Rosario Varela C/Varela 10, Realejo; ⓦrosariovarela. es. Lively bar with a varied selection of *raciones* and *tablas* (cheese/cold cuts boards). Tuna is a speciality – try the *tartar de atún con aguacate* (tuna tartare with avocado).

Long list of vermouths and gins, although they can mix any cocktail you fancy. €€

La Tabernilla del Darro Puente Espinosa 15; ⓦlatabernilladeldarro.com. Across one of the Darro bridges, this atmospheric little bar sits in part of the tunnels leading to the Alhambra. There's also a very pleasant terrace. Good list of tapas and wines. €

★ **La Tana** Placeta del Agua, Realejo; ⓦtabernalatana. com. *La Tana* has over four hundred Spanish wines on its list. Enjoy them over the good tapas – try the *calabaza frita* (fried squash) or the *anchoas con salmorejo* (anchovies with tomato soup). It's tiny, so be prepared for a squeeze. €

UNIVERSITY ZONE

Bar Poë C/Verónica de la Magdalena 40; ⓦbarpoe. com. Highly original bar frequented by foreigners and Erasmus students, and run by an Angolan-Brit couple, Ana and Matt, who serve an exotic free *tapa* with every drink. "Not any old *tapa*", as their publicity says, but all kinds of delights ranging from Portuguese *piri-piri* and Thai chicken to *feijoada* (Brazilian bean stew) and Italian vegetable bake. Wide range of drinks, *chupitos* (shots) and cocktails, including an electrifying *absintio* (absinthe). €

Taberna Mercantil C/Rector García Duarte 8, near the Hospital de San Juan de Dios. Basement bar popular with students who flock here to sup the owner's own (potent) sweet wine to the accompaniment of flamenco music and dancing, sometimes live. Tapas are on the basic side – olives with cold cuts on bread or a kebab – but the lively atmosphere more than makes up for them. €

NIGHTLIFE   SEE MAP PAGE 430

Granada's *discotecas* – mostly dismal teenage hangouts – are mainly concentrated along **C/Pedro Antonio de Alarcón** to the west of the centre, which turns into one big clubbing zone at weekends. For serious drinking into the early hours head out to the bars along the same street, as well as *calles* Gran Capitán and San Juan de Dios, both in the university area. There are, as everywhere in Spain, a fair scattering of **discobares** – drinking bars with loud sound systems, trendy decor and a fashion-conscious clientele. Granada also has a lively **LGBTQ+** scene, with some good bars.

Aliatar C/Recogidas 2. Located in an old cinema, this is a huge dance venue where you can watch yourself on the giant screens while the DJs play the latest hits. Occasional live concerts and cocktail evenings on Fri and Sat.

Bohemia Jazz Café Pza de los Lobos, 11. Atmospheric jazz bar complete with upright piano and walls lined with photos and jazz and film memorabilia. Occasional live bands.

Booga Club C/Santa Bárbara 3, near Hospital San Juan de Dios. Nightclub playing jazz, funk and African sounds

with jam sessions on Sun (not July and August).

El Camborio Camino del Sacromonte 47, Sacromonte. Fashionable *discobar* housed in a series of caves; it's especially lively at weekends from about 4am when Erasmus students crowd the dance floor. Be alert for bag snatchers in this area.

El Son C/Joaquín Costa 3, slightly west of Pza Nueva. Ultracool two-level bar with older salsa scene upstairs – where mojitos are a house speciality – and a cavernous, smoky (not tobacco smoke) dance bar.

Fondo Reservado C/Santa Ines 4, northeast of Pza Nueva. Funky gay and straight bar with a hilarious drag show and party nights every weekend. Occasional house sessions too.

La Tertulia C/Pintor López Mezquita 3, one block west of Pza Gran Capitán; ⓦtertuliagranada.com. Argentinian-run café-bar with regular live music, tango (usually on Tues) and jam sessions of music, poetry and acting. See website for monthly programme.

Planta Baja Horno de Abad, off Carril del Picón and slightly northwest of Pza de la Trinidad; ⓦplantabaja.

5

net. Long-established *discobar* – garage is big here – with plenty of live gigs.

La Sal C/Santa Paula 11, off the west side of Gran Vía. The city's oldest lesbian bar. Originally a lipstick lesbian dance bar, but now attracts gay men too.

Sala Vogue C/Duquesa 37, near the Hospital de San Juan de Dios. Popular *discoteca* with two dance floors, one indie pop-rock and the other techno. Sometimes stages live music.

Six Colours C/Tendillas de Santa Paula 11. This is the hottest LGBTQ+ place in town. The exotically decorated café-pub opens in late afternoon and goes on until the small hours. The main action begins after midnight.

FLAMENCO

Like many cities in Andalucía, Granada lays claim to the roots of **flamenco**, though you'd hardly believe it from the travesties dished up these days in the gypsy quarter of Sacromonte (see box, page 444). The bus-'em-in "flamenco shows" on offer in the city aren't much better either, being geared firmly to the tourist trade. However, up in the Albaicín there is one genuine *peña* (club), with consistently good artists and an audience of aficionados, and we also review here a number of other places that are reasonably authentic. Generally more rewarding are the **festivals** held throughout the year (see box, page 458). It's worth watching out for street posters, as well as checking listings

in the local daily paper, *Ideal*, or the monthly listings magazines/websites, *Yuzin* (ⓦyuzin.com), available at tourist offices, and *La Guía* (ⓦlaguiago.com).

Eshavira Club C/Postigo de la Cuna 2, off Calle Elvira near Puerta de Elvira; ⓦbit.ly/Eshavira. Small bar showcasing some of the best local flamenco, including the young talents from the Morente/Habichuela families. Jazz fusion bands also play. Flamenco takes place twice-weekly (Fri & Sat 11pm).

Jardines de Zoraya C/de los Panaderos 32; ⓦjardinesdezoraya.com. Pretty good Albaicín café-restaurant that offers nightly flamenco shows, often featuring big names. For the evening shows they offer a flamenco *cena* that includes a three-course meal. Their terrace garden is also very attractive.

Peña Platería Plazoleta de Toqueros 7; Albaicín; ⓦlaplateria.org.es. Private club devoted to the celebration of Andalucía's great folk art. There are frequent flamenco performances and visitors are generally welcomed so long as they show a genuine interest. You'll need to speak some Spanish and use a bit of charm.

El Taller de Arte Vimaambi Cuesta de San Gregorio 30, Albaicín; ⓦbit.ly/Vimaambi. A cultural and craft centre with frequent presentations of flamenco and *raíces* (roots) music from North Africa and South America, though not all concerts are open to non-members. Ring or check their Facebook page for the current programme.

SHOPPING

SEE MAP PAGE 430

Granada has a substantial **Maghrebi** community; for a wide range of Moroccan/traditional Spanish fruits and groceries try C/Calderería Nueva and neighbouring C/Calderería Vieja.

La Casa de Las Especias C/Puentezuelas 26; ☎607 262 429. Established in 1941, this family shop sells herbs and spices, incense, exotic teas and much more.

Casa Ferrer Cuesta de Gomérez 26; ☎958 221 832. Granada's oldest guitar-maker, who has made instruments for many famous names including Paco de Lucía.

Castellano C/Almireceros 6, between C/Elvira and Gran Vía; ☎958 221 225. One of the city's best places to buy *jamón serrano*, including the province's famed Trevélez hams. They also stock regional wines and brandies.

El Corte Inglés Carrera del Genil 22; ⓦelcorteingles.

es. Granada's branch of Spain's major department store is on the Acera del Darro, to the south of Puerta Real. The basement supermarket is great, with a wide range of Spanish and international food and wines.

Deportes de Aire Libre C/Paz 20, just southeast of Pza de la Trinidad; ☎958 523 361. This is a good outdoor pursuits shop selling climbing, camping and trekking gear.

Librería Atlantida Gran Vía 9; ☎958 224 403. A good bookshop with a wide selection, including lots on different aspects of Granada.

Market Pza San Agustín. The city's main food market is an ultramodern affair just north of the cathedral. Feast your eyes on fresh fruit (look out for mangos and avocados from the nearby Costa Tropical), vegetables, fish and meat, and the herbs and spices stalls.

GRANADA FESTIVALS

Granada has a number of good festivals, including the **Theatre Festival** at the end of May, and the **International Music and Dance Festival** at the end of June (ⓦgranadafestival. org), during which you may just be lucky enough to see a performance under the stars in the Alhambra. There's also an annual **jazz festival** in November. Information is available from any tourist office and tickets are sold at a kiosko on Acero del Casino, near the post office on Puerta Real.

5

Metro C/Gracia 31, off C/Alhóndiga, southwest of Pza de la Trinidad; ☎ 958 261 565. The city's best international bookshop, with a good range of titles on Granada and Lorca, plus some useful walking maps.

La Oliva C/Virgen del Rosario 9, close to Pza Mariana Pineda; ⓦ laoliva.eu. Wonderful shop specializing in the *gastronomía* of the province as well as the rest of Andalucía

(olive oil, wines, cheeses, honey). You can sample before you buy.

El Piano C/Gran Capitán 7, near the Hospital San Juan de Dios; ☎ 958 565 097. Interesting little shop selling international foods as well as doubling up as a vegan deli restaurant and takeaway – ideal for picnics.

DIRECTORY

Banks There are banks and ATMs along C/Reyes Católicos and Gran Vía.

Hospital Cruz Roja (Red Cross), C/Escoriaza 8 (☎ 958 222 222), or Hospital Clínico San Cecilio, Avda del Doctor Olóriz, near the Pza de Toros (☎ 958 023 000). For advice on emergency treatment phone ☎ 061.

Left luggage There are lockers at the train and bus stations as well as a *consigna* (left luggage office) at the latter. You can also leave luggage at Consigna Granada

(Placeta de las Descalzas 3, behind Pza Isabel La Católica; ⓦ consignagranada.es).

Police For emergencies dial ☎ 091 (national) or ☎ 092 (local). The Policía Local station is at Pza de Campos 3 (☎ 958 808 502). There is also a property lost-and-found section in the Ayuntamiento building on Pza del Carmen (☎ 958 248 103).

Post office Puerta Real (Mon–Fri 8.30am–8.30pm, Sat 9.30am–1pm).

Viznar

The village of **VIZNAR**, 10km northeast of Granada, will always be linked with the **assassination of Federico García Lorca** (see box, page 448) in August 1936. After his arrest in Granada, he was held for two days at a farmhouse called La Colonia before being taken to a bleak gully (*barranco*) nearby and shot. A poem of Lorca's seemed eerily prescient about his own end:

I realized I had been murdered.
They searched cafés and cemeteries and churches,
they opened barrels and cupboards,
they plundered three skeletons to remove their gold teeth.
They did not find me.
They never found me?
No. They never found me.

From the centre of the village the road towards La Fuente Grande passes the site of **La Colonia** (later demolished), near a white-walled cottage. From here, the road curves around the valley to the **Parque Federico García Lorca**, a sombre monumental garden marking the *barranco* and honouring all the Civil War dead. Climb the steps to the garden and veer left up more steps: the site of Lorca's murder was here, beneath a solitary olive tree. After the killing – he was shot with three others, including the liberal teacher Dióscoro García – a young gravedigger threw the bodies into a narrow trench. The supposed site is marked by a granite memorial. Between 2009 and 2013, an **archeological excavation** here attempted to discover Lorca's remains, but despite extensive digging nothing was found. Lorca experts and García's relatives were stunned by this revelation and it is now possible that the poet's body will never be found.

ARRIVAL AND ACCOMMODATION   VIZNAR

By bus Viznar is served by Fernandez de la Torre buses from Granada's Arco de Elvira bus stop on the Pza del Triunfo at the northern end of Gran Vía (Granada to Viznar Mon–Fri 9 daily, 8.30am–9.30pm; Viznar to Granada Mon–Fri 9 daily, 7.35am–9.50pm; 25min).

Albergue Juvenil Camino Fuente Grande;

ⓦ inturjoven.com. This excellent hostel sits at the top end of Viznar with sweeping views of the village and Granada's vast *vega* (fertile plain). Offering en-suite accommodation (mainly doubles but also rooms sleeping up to six), the hostel has a swimming pool, gym and basketball court. **€**

5 # West towards Málaga

Travelling from Granada to Málaga by bus will take you along the fast but dull A92 *autovía*, which crosses the *vega* to the west of the city. With your own transport and time to spare, you could take a more interesting and scenic route, stopping off at the delightful but little-visited town of **Alhama de Granada** and traversing the dramatic **Zafarraya Pass**, descending into Málaga by way of the ruggedly beautiful **Axarquía** region.

To do this, leave Granada by the route for Motril and the coast, along the A44 *autovía*. Four kilometres southwest of the city, take the exit signed Armilla and, from here, follow the A338 heading west towards the village of **La Malahá** (which has a fine roadside *venta*), and, 10km beyond, **Ventas de Huelma** where *Luciano* is another excellent *venta* stop. From here the road twists and climbs into the Sierra de la Pera and, after descending to the lakeside village of **Poblado del Embalse** – where there's a good **campsite**, *Los Bermejales* (see page 463) – continues through a rich landscape of bubbling streams and rocky gulches overlooked by hills planted with olives, to Alhama de Granada, 14km further.

Alhama de Granada

Scenically sited along a ledge overlooking a broad gorge, or Tajo, created by the Río Alhama, the spa town of **ALHAMA DE GRANADA** is one of the unsung gems of Granada province and makes a wonderful overnight stop or a base for exploring the surrounding hill country. It has a couple of striking churches in a well-preserved old quarter, and its baths, dating back to Roman and Moorish times (Al Hamma in Arabic means "hot springs"), still draw in numerous visitors to take the waters. They were greatly treasured during Moorish times, and the Spanish expression of regret "¡Ay de mi Alhama!" was the cry of sorrow attributed to Abu al-Hacen (the Mulhacen after whom the Sierra Nevada peak is named) when he lost the town in a crucial battle here against the Christian forces in 1482. It was this loss that severed the vital link between Granada and Málaga (and hence North Africa), foreshadowing the end of eight centuries of Moorish rule. Settlement started here much earlier, however, and the ancient Iberian town on the site was referred to by the Romans as Artigi.

Most of Alhama's sights are within a short walk of **Plaza de la Constitución**, the main square fronted by bars and restaurants. To see the interior of some of them, however, you will need to take a **guided tour** organized by the Turismo (see page 462).

El Castillo
Pza de la Constitución

At the northern end of Plaza de la Constitución stands El Castillo, the Alhama's **castle**, now privately owned. Although constructed in Moorish times, the castle suffered serious damage in sixteenth- and seventeenth-century confrontations and today only fragments of its original walls remain; these can be seen on Calle Adarve Remedios, on the building's northwest flank. The castle was substantially rebuilt and remodelled in the early twentieth century, when it suffered the unfortunate addition of crenellated battlements.

Iglesia del Carmen and around
Cuesta del Carmen s/n • Open service times (7.30pm winter, 8.30pm summer) or on a Turismo tour (see page 462)

Close to the castle's eastern flank, the sixteenth- to eighteenth-century **Iglesia del Carmen** is Alhama's prettiest church, overlooking the **Tajo** and fronted by a twin-basined ancient fountain where farmers water their donkeys on sultry summer evenings. The simple stone and white-walled interior focuses on a main altar featuring a Virgin in a *camarín*. Just off to the right here, with its back to the Tajo, is Artesanía Los Tajos, Calle Peñas 34 (may not be open – call the number on the door and if the owner is nearby, she'll

RICHARD FORD AND THE HANDBOOK FOR SPAIN

Very few books have been written about Spain that do not draw on **Richard Ford** and his 1845 *Murray's Handbook for Spain* – arguably the best, the funniest and the most encyclopedic guidebook ever written on any country. Born in 1796 into a family of means, Ford studied law but never practised, and in 1824 married Harriet Capel, the daughter of the Earl of Essex. When she received medical advice to seek a warmer climate for her health, Ford – inspired by Irving's recent publication of the *Conquest of Granada* – took his family off to Spain where they lived for three years, wintering in Seville and spending the summers living in part of the Alhambra in Granada.

Ford spent most of his time traversing the length and breadth of the country – but particularly Andalucía – on horseback, making notes and sketches. It's hard to believe that all this was not meant for some literary purpose, but it was only back in England – and six years after his return – when publisher John Murray asked him to recommend someone to write a Spanish travel guide, that Ford suggested himself. His marriage now broken, he settled in a Devon village in a house to which he added many Spanish features (including some souvenirs from the Alhambra) to work solidly for nearly five years on what became the *Handbook for Spain*. When Murray and others took exception to the final manuscript's often caustic invective, Ford was advised to tone it down and a revised – but still gloriously outspoken – edition finally appeared in 1845 to great acclaim. Curiously, although he became *the* resident expert on Spain, he never returned to the country that had put him on the literary map.

Ford's blind spots, such as his typically British prejudice against Baroque architecture (the more extravagant styles of which he dismissed as "vile Churrigueresque"), are often irritating, and the High Tory attitudes, sometimes verging on jingoism, added to a splenetic Francophobia, often threaten to tip over into the worst kind of churlishness. However, the author's enduring fascination with Spain and all things Spanish – he personally introduced amontillado sherry and Extremaduran *jamón serrano* into England – allied to a crisp writing style and a dry wit, invariably save him, and some of his passages, related with a wry irony, are still hilariously funny. His description of the hostelry at Alhama is typical:

The posada at Alhama, albeit called La Grande, is truly iniquitous; diminutive indeed are the accommodations, colossal the inconveniences; but this is a common misnomer, en las cosas de España. Thus Philip IV was called El Grande, under whose fatal rule Spain crumbled into nothing; like a ditch he became greater in proportion as more land was taken away. All who are wise will bring from Málaga a good hamper of eatables, a bota of wine, and some cigars, for however devoid of creature comforts this grand hotel, there is a grand supply of creeping creatures, and the traveller runs risk of bidding adieu to sleep, and passing the night exclaiming, Ay! de mi, Alhama.

open the shop for you), selling local **ceramics** as well as some remarkable traditional clay water-whistles called *canarios*. Once used by local shepherds and goatherds, they make an ear-splitting racket, as the proprietor will eagerly demonstrate. You can also view local handicrafts in the **Centro de Exposición Artesanal**, Hospital de la Reina (daily 11.30am– 1.30pm; free). About 50m east of the Iglesia del Carmen on Calle Baja Iglesia lies the so-called **Casa de la Inquisición**, which may have nothing to do with the Inquisition at all, but is noted for its fine Isabelline Gothic facade. Beyond here Calle Baja Iglesia ascends to Plaza de los Presos and the church of La Encarnación.

Iglesia Mayor de Santa María de la Encarnación and around

Pza de los Presos s/n • Daily 10am–2pm or on a Turismo tour (see page 462)

The town's main church, always referred to as **La Encarnación**, dominates the Plaza de los Presos, an agreeable little square with a central fountain. Donated by Fernando and Isabel after the conquest of the town from the Moors, the church was completed in the first half of the sixteenth century by some of the major architects of the time – among them Enrique Egas and Diego de Siloé, the designers of the Capilla Real and cathedral at Granada. Siloé was responsible for the striking and massive Renaissance belfry that towers above the town. The restrained single-naved interior displays some elegant vaulting and the *sacristía* has Andalucía's finest collection of vestments, including one from the fifteenth century with embroidery attributed to Isabel herself.

Opposite the church, on Plaza de los Presos, is an ancient **pósito** (granary) dating from the thirteenth century but incorporating parts of an earlier synagogue. Just downhill from here the sixteenth-century **Hospital de la Reina**, Calle Vendederas s/n (now a centre for local handicrafts), was the first building of this kind to be built in the kingdom of Granada. Leaving the square to the right of the church along Calle Alta Iglesia takes you past the misleadingly named **Casa Romana** on the right, an eighteenth-century mansion believed to have been constructed on the site of a Roman villa. The same street returns to the Plaza Mayor.

Balneario and around

Balneario July–Sept daily 2–4pm; April–June & Oct Sat–Mon 2–4pm • Charge

Alhama's only other site of note is a well-preserved first-century BC Roman **bridge** at the edge of the town, close to the A402 to Granada, a short distance along the road to the **Balneario** (baths). Beyond here, a (signed) twisting road leads 1km to the hot springs that gave Alhama its name. Although little remains of the Roman baths seen by Ford in the nineteenth century, elements of the Moorish *hammam* survive and can be seen by enquiring at the *Balneario de Granada*, a member of whose staff will conduct you into the depths to see some astonishing Moorish arches and the odd stone inscribed in Latin.

ARRIVAL AND INFORMATION   ALHAMA DE GRANADA

By bus Alhama is served by three buses in both directions (1 on Sat & Sun) from Granada and one daily bus from Velez Málaga (see page 91) in Málaga province. Full details are available from the bus company Alsa (ⓦ alsa.es). The bus stop is on Pza del Duque de Mandas in the lower town.

Turismo Carrera de Francisco de Toledo 10 (daily: April to mid-June & mid-Sept to Oct 9.30am–2.30pm & 5–7pm;

mid-June to mid-Sept 9.30am–2pm & 5–7.30pm; Nov–March 9.30am–2.30pm & 4–6pm; ☎ 958 360 686, ⓦ alhamadegranada.info). This helpful office close to the Pza de la Constitución can provide maps and information on walking in the area. They run guided tours of the town and its monuments, which depart from in front of the tourist office (Tues, Thurs & Sat noon; charge).

ACTIVITIES

Aranzada Bodega Camino Torresolana, to the north of the town; ⓦ aranzada.es. The only bodega in the west of the province, Aranzada produces five wines, including two made with the Rome grape, which is native to Alhama. Book in advance, stating if you require a tour in English.

Tours and wine tastings Sat & Sun noon–2pm (charge).

Bike Cycling Country, C/Salmerones Bajo 18 (ⓦ cyclingcountry.com), offer guided or self-guided bike tours around the spectacular countryside (from one day to two weeks), with top-quality bikes and equipment.

ACCOMMODATION

Things have improved immeasurably on the **accommodation** front since Ford was here (see box, page 461) and the dreaded *La Grande* is no more. Except in August (when it's wise to reserve in advance), there's usually no problem finding a room at any of the places listed below.

Balneario de Granada Ctra del Balneario s/n, 1km off the road into town from Granada; ⓦ balnearioalhamadegranada.com. The *Balneario*'s three-star spa hotel is pleasant enough and the comfortable parquet-floored rooms come with a/c and TV. However, despite being situated in dense pinewood, when it's full with visitors taking the waters it has the ambience of a

sanatorium. Rates include use of the thermal pool. €€

Hostal Ana Ctra de Granada 8; ⓦ hostalana.com. In the town centre, 300m north of the main square, this is a simple but clean and comfortable *hostal* offering en-suite rooms with TV and fridge. €

Hotel El Ventorro 3km out of town on the Málaga road (take the turn-off for Játar); ⓦ elventorro.net. An attractive rural alternative, fronting a lake and with its own decent restaurant (which, in recognition of the fact that there has been a *venta* on this site since the eighteenth century, offers a few eighteenth-century dishes). You can choose between delightfully decorated and furnished cave rooms or conventional rooms, all en suite. There is also a full-blown cave spa and a public swimming pool next door. Breakfast is included. Two-night minimum stay in August. €

★ **La Seguiriya** C/Las Peñas 12; ⊛ laseguiriya.com. This charming *hospedería rural* and restaurant (see page 463) lies 50m uphill off the main square, in an eighteenth-century house with fine views over the Tajo from its back terrace. The friendly proprietor is the daughter of a retired flamenco *cantante*, and the comfortably furnished en-suite

rooms are appropriately named after flamenco styles. They also offer outdoor activities including hiking, canoeing, horse riding and mountain biking. Breakfast is included. €

CAMPSITE

Camping Los Bermejales Arenas del Rey, Poblado de Embalse; ⊛ campinglosbermejales.com. Attractive lakeside campsite 14km outside town, with plenty of shade plus good facilities, pool and restaurant. Limited wi-fi. €

EATING AND DRINKING

Bar El Andaluz Pza de Andalucía 10; ☎ 628 414 215. A friendly tapas and *raciones* place serving up a range of tasty tapas including *home-made chorizo and morcilla* (blood sausage) and local cheeses. The lamb chops, desserts and local wines are also good. €€

★ **Los Caños de Alcaicería** Ctra Alhama–Vélez km10; ☎ 958 350 325. Ten kilometres out of Alhama in the direction of the Zafarraya Pass, this excellent, rustically decorated *venta* specializes in *carnes de monte* (meat and game). Recommended dishes include *churrasco de cerdo* (pork steak) and *solomillo* (pork loin), and there's an economical weekday *menú*. Also sells its own honey, *jamón* and *salchichón* (salami), produced on the premises. €€€

Mesón Diego Pza de la Constitución 12; ⊛ mesondediego.com. Excellent restaurant with a terrace on the square serving the usual meat dishes, generous *raciones* plus a good choice for vegetarians including a paella and delicious homemade desserts. €€

★ **La Seguiriya** C/Las Peñas 12; ⊛ laseguiriya.com. The attractive restaurant of the *hospedería rural* (see page 463) is the town's best place to eat. Chef Ámala Maiztegui hails from the Basque country and the small menu has a mixture of dishes from northern and southern Spain. House specials include *sopa de espárragos con almendras* (asparagus and almond soup), *lomo con ciruelas pasas* (pork with prunes) and *bacalao al horno* (baked cod). The menu also features a range of salads and in summer you can dine on the terrace with a spectacular Tajo view. €€

El Tigre Pza de la Constitución 1; ☎ 958 350 445. Small and busy bar on the main square specializing in *jamón* and *salchichón* (salami) *ibérico*, both from the Spanish black pig. They also offer *tostadas* (toast) with various toppings (tomato and anchovy are good) and the mother's "famous" *berenjenas* (aubergines), all washed down with house wine. For more room but less local colour, move upstairs to the cosy dining room. €€

From Alhama to the Zafarraya Pass

South of Alhama, the A402 climbs towards Ventas de Zafarraya passing, 10km out, a great-value *venta*, *Los Caños de Alcaicería* (see page 463). The road then toils on, cutting through a rich agricultural area to the isolated hamlet of Ventas de Zafarraya, 6km after the *venta*. Just beyond here the spectacular **Zafarraya Pass**, which slips through a cleft in the Sierra de Tejeda and was part of the old coach route, provides a dramatic entrance into the Axarquía region of Málaga province, with superb **views** to the distant Mediterranean. Roughly 6km beyond the pass lies the deserted medieval village of **Zalía**, after which the road continues to Vélez-Málaga (see page 91) and the coast.

Sierra Nevada National Park

Southeast from Granada rise the mountains of the **SIERRA NEVADA**, designated Andalucía's second **national park** in 1999, and a startling backdrop to the city, snowcapped for most of the year and offering skiing from November until late April. The ski slopes are at **Pradollano**, an unimaginative, developed resort just 28km away (40min by bus). Here, the direct car route across the range stops, but from this point walkers can make the relatively easy two- to three-hour trek up to **Veleta** (3394m), the second highest peak of the sierra and the third-highest summit on the Iberian peninsula (see page 464).

The main A395 access road from Granada to the national park has been a mixed blessing for the delicate ecosystem of the sierra, and the expanding horrors of the Pradollano ski centre, which regularly hosts big winter sports events, has only made things worse.

5

Monachil

Before the road was constructed in the 1920s few *granadinos* ever came up to the sierra, but one group who had worn out a trail since the times of the Moors were the *neveros*, or icemen, who used mules to bring down blocks of ice from the mountains, which they then sold in the streets. Their route to Veleta can still be followed beyond **MONACHIL**, a village on the Río Monachil southeast of Granada. It's worth stopping off here; there are places to stay (see page 465) and a number of companies offering adventure activities in the park (see page 465).

Pradollano

The route to Pradollano leaves Granada via the Paseo del Salón (where the bus picks up and drops off); two wagons stand as a memory to the tram service which, from the 1920s until 1970, used to ascend as far as Güejar Sierra. Beyond Pinos de Genil the road begins to climb seriously, passing a number of alpine-style roadside **ventas** that do good business in season. After some 17km, with your own transport you could make a stop at the **Balcón de Canales**; it offers fine **views** over the Río Genil and its dam. At the 23km point you will pass the "El Dornajo" Sierra Nevada National Park Visitors' Centre (see page 465), and a further 5km on, the ski resort of **PRADOLLANO** (aka Solynieve, "Sun and Snow") appears.

Pradollano is a hideous-looking resort and regarded by serious alpine skiers as something of a joke. But with snow lingering so late in the year (Granada's Turismo should be able to advise on the state of this, or contact Sierra Nevada Club on ☎902 708 090 or ⊛sierranevada.es) it has obvious attractions for anyone determined to ski in southern Spain. From the middle of the resort a lift takes you straight up to the main ski lifts, which provide access to most of the higher **slopes**, and when the snow is right you can ski a few kilometres back down to the *zona hotelera* (the lifts run only when there's skiing). There are plenty of places to rent gear. If you intend to ski (or walk) here be sure to double your **skin protection**; this is the most southerly ski centre in Europe, with intense sun at high altitudes.

Ascending Veleta

The ascent of **Veleta** is a none-too-challenging hike rather than a climb, but should only be attempted between May and September unless you're properly geared up; even then you'll need warm and waterproof clothing. From the *Albergue Universitario* (see page 466) the **Capileira-bound road** – permanently closed to motor traffic to protect the sierra's delicate environment – actually runs past the peak of Veleta. Asphalted – somewhat removing the sense of adventure from the trek – it is perfectly, and tediously, walkable; bikes are allowed, and while it's a fierce climb, the long, fast descent on the

---

THE SIERRA NEVADA'S FLORA AND FAUNA

The Sierra Nevada is particularly rich in **wild flowers**. Some fifty varieties are unique to these mountains, among them five gentians, including *Gentiana bory*, the pansy *Viola nevadensis*, a shrubby mallow *Lavatera oblongifolia* and a spectacular honeysuckle, the 7- to 10m-high *Lonicera arborea*.

Wildlife, too, abounds away from the roads. One of the most exciting sights is the *Cabra hispanica*, a wild horned goat that you'll see standing on pinnacles, silhouetted against the sky. They roam the mountains in flocks and jump up the steepest slopes with amazing agility when they catch the scent of a walker on the wind. The higher slopes are also home to a rich assortment of **butterflies**, among them the rare Nevada Blue as well as varieties of Fritillary. **Birdwatching** is also superb, with the colourful hoopoe – a bird with a stark, haunting cry – a common sight.

5

RUTA INTEGRAL DE LOS TRES MIL

The classic **Ruta Integral de los Tres Mil**, a complete traverse of all the sierra's peaks over 3000m high, starts in Jeres del Marquesado on the north side of the Sierra Nevada (due south of Guadix) and finishes in Lanjarón, in the Alpujarras. It's an exhausting three- to four-day itinerary described in detail in Andy Walmsley's book *Walking in the Sierra Nevada* (see page 556). For any serious exploration of the Sierra Nevada, essential equipment includes a tent, proper gear and ample food. It's serious mountain country where lives are regularly lost, so come prepared for the eventuality of not being able to reach (or find) the refuge huts, or the weather turning nasty.

other side makes it very much worth your while. Most hikers follow the well-worn short cuts between the hairpins the road is forced to make. With your own transport it's possible to shave a couple of kilometres off the total by ignoring the no-entry signs at the car park near to the *Albergue Universitario* and continuing on to a second car park further up the mountain from which point the road is then barred. Although the peak of the mountain looks deceptively close from here, you should allow two to three hours to reach the summit and ninety minutes to get back down. Make sure to bring **food and water** as there's neither en route and a picnic at the summit is one of the best meals to be had in Spain, weather permitting.

With a great deal of energy you could conceivably walk (or mountain bike) from Veleta to Capileira (see page 473) – but bear in mind that it's a good 30km distant, there are no facilities along the way and temperatures drop pretty low by late afternoon. En route, an hour beyond Veleta, you pass just under **Mulhacén** – the tallest peak on the Iberian peninsula at 3483m. Should you decide to detour from the Capileira route and climb it, be aware that an ascent involves two hours of exposed and windy ridge-crawling from the road, and a sudden, sheer drop on its northwest face. There is a gentler slope down to the Siete Lagunas valley to the east. The easiest way of scaling Mulhacén, though, is from Capileira (see box, page 474).

ARRIVAL AND DEPARTURE
SIERRA NEVADA NATIONAL PARK

By bus Monachil is connected by frequent buses to Granada, running from the terminal at the Paseo del Salón. Throughout the year Autocares Bonal runs daily buses from Granada to Pradollano and, just above this, to the *Albergue Universitario* (see page 466). From April to September services leave Granada bus station at 10am and 5pm, returning from the *Albergue Universitario* at 4pm and 6pm (and passing Pradollano 10min later). For the winter service (Oct–March) check with the bus company (see page 450) or with any Turismo. Tickets to Pradollano should be bought in advance at the bus station, although you can pay on board if the bus is not full.

INFORMATION AND TOURS

"El Dornajo" Sierra Nevada National Park Visitors' Centre Ctra de Sierra Nevada km23 (Wed–Sun 10am–5pm; ☎ 958 950 246). Signposted just off the A395, this is the national park's main information centre. Its shop sells guidebooks, maps and hats (sun protection is vital), has a permanent exhibition on the park's flora and fauna, and provides hiking information (English spoken). The centre also has a *cafetería* with a stunning terrace view beyond the ancient tram parked in a garden behind.

Monachil Turismo Municipal Pza Baja 1, Monachil (Mon–Fri 9am–2pm, Sat & Sun 10am–2pm; ☎ 673 366 028).

Pradollano Turismo Pza Pradollano (Dec–April Tues–Sun 10am–6pm; ☎ 673 366 334).

Spanish Highs ⓦ spanishhighs.co.uk. Organizes walking, hiking, mountaineering and skiing trips, and activities in the mountains ranging from one-day excursions to week-long holidays.

ACCOMMODATION

MONACHIL

Hotel Boutique Alicia Carolina C/Granada 1; ⓦ aliciacarolina.com. Friendly and homely accommodation in comfortable en-suite rooms with mountain views. The lovely roof terrace also has panoramic views. Opposite the Granada bus stop. Free parking. **€€**

5

PRADOLLANO

The Granada Turismo and the Sierra Nevada Club (☏ 902 708 090, ⓦ sierranevada.es) can advise on places to stay at the ski resort (many hotels open only during the ski season). We review some of the resort's budget options below, but other places can be very expensive in season, when you should expect to pay at least €80–100 per night for a double room.

Albergue Juvenil C/Peñones 22; ⓦ inturjoven.com. The resort's cheapest accommodation is the modern and comfortable youth hostel, on the edge of the ski resort, where you can get good-value doubles and four-bed studios and apartments, all en suite. They also rent out skis and equipment in season (Dec–Feb) when room prices include half-board. Open late Nov–early May. €

Albergue Universitario Peñones de San Francisco, 3km above the ski resort; ⓦ nevadensis.com. At an altitude of 2500m and often snowed in during winter, this isolated mountain hostel is an attractive option if seclusion

is what you're seeking. Sited just off the main road where the bus drops you, it offers bunk rooms and doubles sharing bathrooms and there's also a bar-restaurant with a daily *menú*. It's a stunning location for exploring the national park (the hostel can advise on walking routes) but without transport you'll be extremely isolated. The Granada bus (which only runs beyond the ski resort in summer) turns around at the *Albergue* and this marks the start of the Veleta ascent (see page 464). Price includes half-board in winter high season. €

Camping Ruta del Purche Ctra de Sierra Nevada km16; ⓦ campingrutadelpurche.es. Signed down a turn-off 16km out of Granada (the site is a further 3km from here) this is a well-run campsite with plenty of shade. Facilities include a bar-restaurant, pool and free wi-fi zone. It also rents out en-suite wood cabins (some with kitchen), sleeping up to four. €

DIRECTORY

Emergencies Inside the park, to report any emergencies, including forest fires, stranded hikers or personal injuries, there's a coordinated emergency service contactable on ☏ 112; the park's Guardia Civil unit can be reached on ☏ 062. **Maps** The best general map of the Sierra Nevada and of the lower slopes of the Alpujarras is co-produced by the Instituto Geográfico Nacional and the Federación Española

de Montañismo (1:50,000). Not far behind is the Editorial Alpina's *Sierra Nevada y La Alpujarra* (1:40,000) map, which has the bonus of a booklet (with an English edition) describing fourteen hikes in the sierra as well as useful background information on the zone. The CNIG's 1:25,000 sheets are more detailed for trekking purposes, and all three can be obtained from the El Dornajo visitor centre (see page 465).

Las Alpujarras

The A44 road south from Granada to Motril crosses the fertile *vega* after leaving the city and then climbs steeply until, at 850m above sea level, it reaches the **Puerto del Suspiro del Moro** – the Pass of the Sigh of the Moor. Boabdil, last Moorish king of Granada, came this way, having just handed over the keys of his city to the Reyes Católicos in exchange for a fiefdom over the Alpujarras. From the pass you catch your last glimpse of the city and the Alhambra. The road then descends and beyond Padul crosses the valley of Lecrín, planted with groves of orange, lemon and almond trees, the latter a riot of pink and white blossom in late winter. To the east, through a narrow defile close to Béznar, lie the great valleys of **Las Alpujarras**, first settled in the twelfth century by Berber refugees from Seville, and later the Moors' last stronghold.

The so-called **High Alpujarras** – the villages of **Pampaneira**, **Bubión** and **Capileira** – have all been scrubbed and whitewashed and are now firmly on the tourist circuit, as popular with Spanish as foreign visitors. Lower down, in the **Órgiva area**, are the main concentration of expatriates – mainly British, Dutch and Germans, seeking new Mediterranean lives. Many have moved here permanently, rather than establishing second homes (though there are houses for rent in abundance), and there's a vaguely alternative aspect to the community, which sets it apart from the coastal expats. In addition to property owners, the area has also attracted groups of New Age travellers. The locals, to their credit, seem remarkably tolerant of the whole scene.

Brief history

The valleys are bounded to the north by the Sierra Nevada, and to the south by the lesser sierras of Lujar, La Contraviesa and Gador. The eternal snows of the high sierras

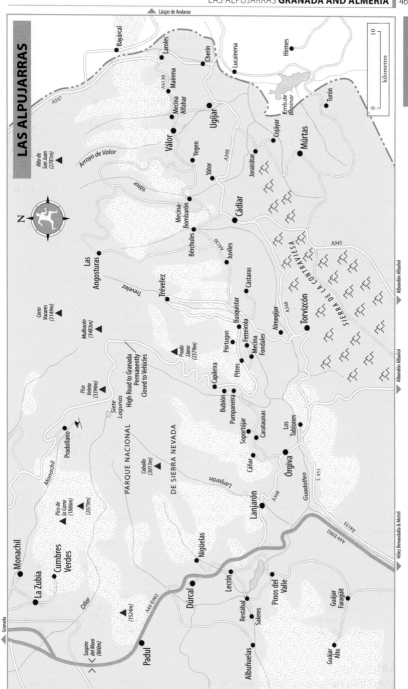

LAS ALPUJARRAS

keep the valleys and their seventy or so villages well watered all summer long. Rivers have cut deep gorges in the soft mica and shale of the upper mountains, and over the centuries have deposited silt and fertile soil on the lower hills and in the valleys; here the villages have grown, for the soil is rich and easily worked. The intricate terracing that today preserves these deposits was begun perhaps as long as two thousand years ago by **Visigoths** or **Ibero-Celts**, whose remains have been found at Capileira.

The **Moors** carried on the tradition, and modified the terracing and irrigation in their inimitable way. They transformed the Alpujarras into an earthly paradise, and there they retired to bewail the loss of their beloved lands in al-Andalus. After the fall of Granada, many of the city's Muslim population settled in the villages, and there resisted a series of royal edicts demanding their forced conversion to **Christianity**. In 1568 they rose up in a final, short-lived revolt, which led to the expulsion of all Spanish Moors. Even then, however, two Moorish families were required to stay in each village to show the new Christian peasants, who had been marched down from Galicia and Asturias to repopulate the valleys, how to operate the intricate irrigation systems.

Through the following centuries, the villages fell into poverty, with the land owned by a few wealthy families and worked by peasants. It was one of the most remote parts of Spain in the **1920s**, when the author Gerald Brenan settled in one of the eastern villages, Yegen, and described the life in his book *South from Granada*, and things changed little over the next forty-odd years. During the **Civil War**, the occasional truckload of Nationalist youth trundled in from Granada, rounded up a few bewildered locals, and shot them for "crimes" of which they were wholly ignorant; Republican youths came up in their trucks from Almería and did the same thing. In the aftermath, under Franco, there was real hardship and suffering, and in the **1980s** the region had one of the lowest per capita incomes in Spain, with – as an official report put it – "a level of literacy bordering on that of the Third World, alarming problems of desertification, poor communications and high under-employment".

Ironically, the land itself is still very fertile – oranges, chestnuts, bananas, apples and avocados grow here, while the southern villages produce a well-known dry rosé wine, *costa*. However, it is largely the influx of **tourism** and foreign purchase of houses and farms that has turned the area's fortunes around, bringing pockets of wealth and an influx of new life to the region.

ARRIVAL AND INFORMATION   LAS ALPUJARRAS

By bus There are several buses a day from both Granada and Motril, and one a day from Almería, to Lanjarón and Órgiva. One operated by Alsa (ⓦalsa.es) direct to the High Alpujarras, via Trevélez as far as Bérchules, leaves the main Granada bus station (daily noon & 4.30pm): in the other direction it leaves Bérchules at 5.50am and 5.05pm, passing Trevélez 25min later, to arrive in Granada at 9.35am and 8.50pm respectively. There's also a thrice daily service from Granada to Ugíjar in the Low Alpujarras, via Lanjarón, Órgiva, Torvizcón, Cádiar, Yegen and Valor (currently 8.30am, 2.30pm & 5pm; 3hr 30min to the end of the line). The return journey from Ugíjar currently runs at 5.45am, 7am and 3pm. There are also frequent daily buses between Granada and Órgiva (three via Lanjarón) and vice versa, and three daily buses link with Pampaneira, Bubión, Capileira and Pitres.

By car From Granada, the most straightforward approach to the Alpujarras is to take the Lanjarón turning – the A348 – off the Motril road (A44). Coming from the south, you can bear right from the road at Vélez de Benaudalla and continue straight along the A346 to Órgiva, the market town of the western Alpujarras.

Guidebooks There are many walkers' guides to the Alpujarras. Useful publications (see page 556) include Charles Davis's *34 Alpujarras Walks*, Jeremy Rabjohns' *Holiday Walks in the Alpujarras* and *GR142: Senda de la Alpujarra* (in Spanish) by Francisco Jiménez Richarte; there are also half a dozen Alpujarras treks featured in *Andalucía and the Costa del Sol* by John and Christine Oldfield and an equal number in Guy Hunter-Watts' *Walking in Andalucía*. You should also invest in a good map (see page 54).

Lanjarón

LANJARÓN has known tourism and the influence of the outside world for longer than anywhere else in the Alpujarras due to the curative powers of its **spa waters**. These gush from seven natural springs and are sold in bottled form as mineral water throughout Spain. Between March and December, when the spa baths are open, the town fills with the aged and infirm and the streets are lined with racks of herbal remedies, all of which imparts a rather melancholy air. This might seem good reason for passing straight on to the higher villages, though to do so would be to miss out on some beautiful local walks, and a pedestrianized town centre that is likely to grow on you.

Like so many spa towns, Lanjarón is Roman in origin, though today the place is largely modern, with a ribbon of buildings flanking its attractive, tree-lined main thoroughfare, split into three sections running west to east: Avenida de Andalucía, Avenida de La Alpujarra and Calle Real.

Lanjarón puts on a stirring **Semana Santa** – one of the best in the province, and worth going out of your way to see if you're in the area. Its other great shindig is the water festival on the eve of San Juan (June 24) when the unaware get drenched by cascades falling from balconies and "water bombs" are thrown around with abandon.

Lanjarón castle

Open access • Free

Below the main street, and beyond the town's new bypass, marking Lanjarón's medieval status as gateway to the Alpujarras, is a **Moorish castle**, refurbished and permanently open for visits. It was here on March 8, 1500, that the Moorish population made its final heroic stand against the Christian troops under the command of Fernando. Pounded by artillery, hundreds died as the town was taken. A ten-minute stroll reveals its dramatic setting – follow the signs downhill from the main street and out onto the terraces and meadows below the town.

Balneario de Lanjarón

Western end of the village • March–Dec • Charge • ⓦ balneariodelanjaron.com

It's fun to take the waters at Lanjarón's **Balneario** – go for a basic soak, or opt for one of the add-ons, such as massage, mud baths, pressure showers and all kinds of other alarming-sounding treatments such as *drenajes linfáticos* and *pulverizaciones faríngeas*.

ARRIVAL AND INFORMATION

LANJARÓN

By bus Buses stop at the roundabouts at either end of the town. Buy tickets on board or online from Alsa (ⓦ alsa.es). Destinations Almería (2 daily; 4hr 20min); Granada (7 daily; 1hr 15min); Órgiva (11 daily; 20min); Ugíjar (3 daily; 2hr).

Turismo Municipal Avda de Andalucía s/n (Mon–Sat 10am–2pm & 4.30–8.30pm, Sun 10am–2pm; ☏ 958 770 462). Located opposite the Balneario at the village's western end.

ACCOMMODATION

Thanks to the Balneario, there's no shortage of **places to stay** in town, most sited along the main street. In high summer it's essential to book ahead, while many places close in Jan and Feb. The nearest campsite is in Órgiva (see page 471).

★ **Hotel Alcadima** C/Francisco Tarrega 3, down a signed turn-off from the main street; ⓦ alcadima. com. A good-value hotel with the best pool and prettiest restaurant terrace in town. Many of the comfortable rooms

WALKS FROM LANJARÓN

The countryside and **mountains around Lanjarón** are spectacularly beautiful. Wander up through the backstreets behind the town and you'll come across a track that takes you steeply up to the vast spaces bordering on the Reserva Nacional de la Sierra Nevada national Park.

For a somewhat easier day's **walk**, go to the bridge over the river just east of town and take the sharply climbing, cobbled track that parallels the river. After a walk of 2hr–2hr 30min, through small farms with magnificent views and scenery, a downturn to a small stone bridge lets you return to Lanjarón on the opposite bank. Allow a minimum of 6hr for a leisurely expedition.

have stunning balcony views towards the castle and guests may use the spa. The hotel provides a free digital guide to the area. €€

Hotel Balcón de Lorca Avda de La Alpujarra 42, near the Balneario; ⓦhotelespanalanjaron.es. This great-value hotel, with an air of faded grandeur, has hosted such luminaries as García Lorca (Room 107) and Manuel de Falla

in its time. It comes with friendly staff, comfortable tile-floored rooms, its own bar-restaurant and a pool. €

Hotel Paris Avda de La Alpujarra 23 ⓦ hotelparislanjaron. com. A charming and very good-value main street hotel. Marble-floored rooms come with TV and many have fine views. Facilities include a good-value restaurant (guests only), pool and garage. Breakfast is included. €

EATING AND DRINKING

A selection of **bars** and **restaurants** line the Avda de Andalucía and many of the hotels and *hostales* have good-value meals and tapas, too – especially the hotels *España* and *El Sol*. On the Avda de Andalucía's "main square", midway between the Balneario and the church, lies Lanjarón's celebrated *churrería*, claimed by some to sell the best home-made potato crisps in Andalucía, and where there also are a couple of good ice-cream parlours.

Arca de Noe Avda de Andalucía 38, a ten-minute walk down the main street; ☏ 958 770 027. One of the most popular bars, where you can try the wines, cheeses, *jamones* and other products of the region and then buy from them from the well-stocked shop. €€

Asador Parque Avda Alpujarra 44; ⓦ asadorparque. com. Modern restaurant with pleasant terrace next to *Hotel España*, set in the gardens of the ruined Palacete de

la Duquesa de Santoña. Specials include *habas con jamón* (broad beans with ham) and fried aubergines, as well as salads and rice dishes. €€

Balcón de Lorca Avda de La Alpujarra 42; ☏ 958 771 386. Attached to the hotel of the same name, with atmospheric surroundings for dining on generous *raciones* and local dishes, including *solomillo de cerdo a la miel de romero* (pork fillet in rosemary honey). €€€

Hotel Alcadima C/Francisco Tarrega 3, down a signed turn-off from the main street; ⓦ alcadima.com. Probably the most romantic choice for dining out is the terrace restaurant of the *Hotel Alcadima* – pretty much the perfect place to while away a summer evening with a superb view of the castle. House specials include *pierna de cordero* (lamb with rosemary and citrus). €€€

Órgiva (Órjiva)

Heading east out of Lanjarón brings you after 7km to a turn-off for Las Barreras. Three kilometres further lies **ÓRGIVA**, the market centre of the western Alpujarras. It's a lively little town, with a number of good bars and hotels, and an animated and entertaining **Thursday market**. The contrast between the timeworn *campesinos* and their pack-mules, and some of the foreign New Age travellers who seek their indulgence and charity, is as bizarre as anything this side of Madrid. Many of the New Agers here inhabit a **tepee village**, *Beneficio*, above the town, where a polyglot community of over 250 mainly northern Europeans and their offspring endure freezing winters under canvas. In 2017, Órgiva introduced its own currency, known as a güevín (also the name for locals); one güevín is equal to one euro. Güevines, used in some local businesses, are designed to promote the town and the purchase of local (particularly organic) produce. Euros are, nevertheless, still accepted everywhere.

Another local resident is writer and farmer **Chris Stewart** who moved with his wife to an isolated *cortijo* (farmhouse) on the outskirts of Órgiva over twenty years ago. His

---

ÓRGIVA FESTIVALS

Órgiva comes to life with its annual fiesta on the days each side of September 29, the feast day of **San Miguel**, when the population doubles as prodigal sons and daughters all return to join in the fun. A more eccentric festival is the **Día del Señor** on the second Friday before Easter. This opens with a terrifying salvo of rockets on the Thursday before, when the town's womenfolk attack the church until they are able to make off with the effigies of El Señor (Christ) and the Virgin. On the Friday evening both Christ and his mother are paraded around town before re-entering the church in the early hours accompanied by great displays of emotion – not to mention more deafening rocketry. The town also holds a flamenco festival in early August.

quartet of books (see page 552) wittily describing life among the peasants, shepherds, New Age travellers and expats of the western Alpujarras proved highly popular and helped to place this area of Andalucía on the map.

Órgiva's other sights line the main street, Calle González Robles: the sixteenth-century Baroque **church** of Nuestra Señora de la Expectación, whose towers add a touch of fancy to the townscape, and a once crumbling but now over-restored Moorish **palace** that today houses the Ayuntamiento.

ARRIVAL AND INFORMATION

By bus Three buses a day from the Alsa stop, on Avda González Robles, serve the Low Alpujarras to Ugíjar as well as the High Alpujarran villages.

Destinations Almería (2 daily; 4hr 25min); Granada (9 daily; 1hr 15min); Lanjarón (11 daily; 20min); Ugíjar (3 daily; 1hr 45min).

ÓRGIVA (ÓRJIVA)

Turismo Municipal Pza Alpujarra s/n (April–Oct Tues–Sat 10am–2pm & 6–8pm, Sun 10am–2pm; Oct–March Tues–Sat 9am–2pm & 5–7pm, Sun 10am–2pm; ☎ 958 784 266, ⌨ orgivaturismo.wordpress.com). Located in the central square, this friendly office offers advice on events, accommodation and walking in the area.

ACCOMMODATION

Camping Órgiva Ctra A348 km19; ⌨ campingorgiva. com. The town's campsite lies 2km south of the centre beyond the *Hotel Taray* and has plenty of shade plus clean facilities and a restaurant and pool. It can also advise on walking routes and renting horses in the nearby Sierra de Lújar. €

Hotel Puerta Nazarí Ctra A348, km15.9; ⌨ hotelpuertanazari.com. A five-minute walk west of the town centre, this friendly hotel offers spotlessly clean en-suite rooms decorated in a Moorish style (some have rather lurid murals) with terrace or balcony. There's also a restaurant terrace with stunning views. €

EATING AND DRINKING

Many of the hotels and *hostals* have decent **restaurants** – Hotel Puerta Nazarí is worth trying – and there are a few tapas bars gathered around the square in C/García Moreno, fronting the church.

La Almazara C/González Robles 53; ☎ 958 784 628. A very good restaurant with a cosy wood-tabled interior room and a leafy garden terrace for warmer days. It offers a range of dishes such as *carrillada gratinada* (pork cheek *au gratin*) and grilled meats, and also does excellent burgers. €€

Baraka C/Estación 12, in the upper village near the

market. A very nice small Moroccan café and *tetería* offering falafel, couscous and tagines along with Hispanic dishes including guacamole and gazpacho. They make their own ices in summer and also offer a variety of international teas. There's an outdoor terrace. €€

Flor de Limonero Taray Botánico, Ctra A348 km18; ☎ 958 998 260. Órgiva's best restaurant serves fusion food with the emphasis on local produce, particularly *carne a la brasa* (chargrilled meat), plus an excellent range of vegetarian and vegan options. €€

The High Alpujarras

From Órgiva, you can reach the villages of the **High Alpujarras** by car or bus, or you could walk – the best way to experience the region. There is a network of paths in this area, though to avoid getting lost it's wise to equip yourself with a compass and the Instituto Geográfico Nacional/Federación Española de Montañismo 1:50,000 map, which covers all the territory from Órgiva up to Berja. A reasonable knowledge of Spanish is also invaluable.

At their best, Alpujarran **footpaths** are remnants of the old Camino Real, the mule routes that crossed Spain, and are engineered with cobblestones, and beautifully contoured, alongside mountain streams, through woods of oak, chestnut and poplar, or across flower-spangled meadows. In their bad moments they deteriorate to incredibly dusty firebreaks, forestry roads or tractor tracks, or (worse) dead-end in impenetrable thickets of bramble and nettle. Progress is slow, gradients are sharp and the heat (between mid-June and September) is taxing. Part of the path network through the High Alpujarras has been upgraded as the final section of the **European long-distance footpath** that begins in Athens and ends in Algeciras. Designated as footpaths E4 or GR7 in Spain, the full route is waymarked (in theory – you'll still need a good map where the posts are missing or misplaced) with red and white ringed posts.

Note that many establishments close between mid-June and the first week of July.

Soportújar and around

Following the high road from Órgiva, the first settlements you reach, almost directly above the town, are the isolated but pretty **CAÑAR** – at the end of a sinuous 5km drive off the main road – and **SOPORTÚJAR**, a maze of picturesque white-walled alleys bridged by numerous *tinaos* (see box, page 473). Like many of the High Alpujarran villages, they congregate on the neatly terraced mountainside, planted with poplars and laced with irrigation channels. Both have **bars** where you can get a meal, and Soportújar can provide accommodation. Perched precariously on the steep hillside, both villages share a rather sombre view of Órgiva in the valley below, and on a clear day the mountains of North Africa over the ranges to the south. Each village has a sixteenth-century church, both of which fell into a terrible state of disrepair at the end of the last century, and both of which, thankfully, have now been refurbished and saved.

Carataunas

Just below Soportújar, the tiny hamlet of **CARATAUNAS** is particularly attractive, with a labyrinth of narrow, white-walled streets overlooked by the elegant tower of its sixteenth-century church of Nuestra Señora de la Paz. The village is famous for its *embutidos* (sausages) as well as a rousing start to its Semana Santa on Palm Sunday, when an effigy of Judas is tossed on a bonfire.

Barranco de Poqueira

Shortly beyond Carataunas the road swings to the north after passing the turn-off to the Buddhist monastery of O Sel Ling (see page 473), and you have your first view of the **Gorge of the Poqueira**, a huge gash into the heights of the Sierra Nevada. Trickling deep in the cleft is the Río Poqueira, which has its source near the peak of Mulhacén. The steep walls of the gorge are terraced and wooded from top to bottom, and dotted with little stone farmhouses. Much of the surrounding country looks barren from a distance, but close up you'll find that it's rich with flowers, woods, springs and streams. A trio of spectacular villages – **Pampaneira**, **Bubión** and **Capileira** – teeter on the steep edge of the gorge among their terraces. They are, justifiably, the most touristy villages in the region and a bit over-prettified, with craft shops and the like, but nonetheless well worth it, as is some walking on the local mule paths. A number of fine **walking routes** are detailed with maps in *Landscapes of Andalucía and the Costa del Sol* (see page 556).

Pampaneira

PAMPANEIRA, the first of the Poqueira villages, is a neat, prosperous place, and a bit less developed and spoilt than its neighbours. Around its main square, Plaza de la Libertad,

---

HIGH ALPUJARRAS HIKES: THE HIGHLIGHTS

Rewarding **hikes** in the High Alpujarras include:

Pitres to Mecina Fondales A short (20min) hike to Mecina Fondales, and then a good hour-plus from neighbouring Ferreirola to Busquístar.

Busquístar to Trevélez One hour's hike, and then two-plus hours of road walking.

Pórtugos to Trevélez Two hours, meeting the tarmac a little beyond the end of the Busquistar route.

Trevélez to Bérchules Four hours, with the middle section on a dirt track.

Trevélez to Juviles Three hours, including some sections of firebreak.

ALPUJARRAN ARCHITECTURE

Alpujarran **village houses** are unlike any others in Spain – though they are almost identical to Berber houses across the straits in the Rif mountains of Morocco, where many of the Moorish refugees settled. They are built of grey stone, flat-roofed and low; traditionally they are unpainted, though these days *cal* (whitewash) – a luxury until recent times – is increasingly common. The coarse walls are about 75cm thick, for summer coolness and protection from winter storms. Stout beams of chestnut, or ash in the lower valleys, are laid from wall to wall; on top of these is a mat of canes, ilex or split chestnut; upon this, flat stones are piled, and on the stones is spread a layer of **launa**, the crumbly grey mica clay found throughout the area, which is made waterproof when pressed down.

The *launa* must – and this maxim is still observed today – be laid during the waning of the moon (though not, of course, on a Friday) in order for it to settle properly and thus keep rain out. Gerald Brenan wrote in *South from Granada* of a particularly ferocious storm: "As I peered through the darkness of the stormy night, I could make out a dark figure on every roof in the village, dimly lit by an esparto torch, stamping clay into the holes in the roof."

Another feature peculiar to the Alpujarras are the **tinaos**, a kind of portico or bridge that enables access from a dwelling in one row to another in an upper or lower row. In summer, time is passed on the roof terrace or *terrao*, especially once the sun has cooled in early evening. Bubión, Capileira and Pitres all have good examples of the traditional architectural style.

fronting the sixteenth-century Gothic-Mudéjar church of Santa Cruz are a number of bars, restaurants, *hostales* and craft shops, one of which, just down the hill, is a weaving workshop that specializes in traditional *alpujarreño* designs.

Monastery of O Sel Ling

Daily: June to mid-Oct 5–7.30pm; mid-Oct to May 4–6pm • Free • ⓦ oseling.com • The monastery is reached by a track on the left – signed "camino forestal" – 1km east of the turning to Soportújar

Above Pampaneira, on the very peak of the western flank of the Poqueira gorge in a stunning location, is the small Tibetan Buddhist **Monastery of O Sel Ling** (Place of Clear Light) founded in 1982 by a Tibetan monk on land donated by the communities of Pampaneira and Bubión. The simple stone-built monastery, complete with stupas and stunning **views** across the Alpujarras, welcomes visitors; lectures and courses on Buddhism are held regularly and there are simple cabins dotted around the site for those who wish to retreat. Should you have trouble finding it, ask at Nevadensis or Rustic Blue (see page 477).

Bubión

BUBIÓN, backed for much of the year by snowcapped peaks, lacks the focus of a proper main square and is probably the least attractive of the high villages, but – perhaps because of this – it certainly seems the most peaceful. There are no sights other than a municipal **museum**, the Casa Alpujarreña (Wed–Mon 11am–2pm, Fri– Sun 11am– 2pm & 5–7pm; charge), just off Plaza de la Iglesia near the church, which displays aspects of the folklore, daily life and architecture of the Alpujarras in a traditional house. Towards the end of August, Bubión celebrates its **Fiestas Patronales** with music, dance, fireworks and copious drinking.

Capileira

CAPILEIRA is the highest of the villages of the Lower Poqueira Gorge, and the terminus of Europe's highest road across the heart of the Sierra Nevada from Granada. This is closed to traffic except for a summer bus service (see page 477). A picturesque and tranquil place, except in high summer when it is deluged with visitors and coach tours, Capileira makes a fine base from which to explore the Poqueira Gorge, or you could

SCALING MULHACÉN – THE EASY WAY

In season (Easter to early December depending on the snow) the Parque Nacional authority runs a daily minibus service along the closed road from Capileira to the **Mirador de Trevélez** (with spectacular **views** on clearer days) and on to the **Alto del Chorrillo**, some 20km above the village. The 75-minute trip (with on-board guide) is great to do in itself, but why not add in the conquest of the highest peak in mainland Spain as well?

From the Alto del Chorillo bus stop it's a roughly 4hr hike to make the ascent and descent of Mulhacén – clearly described in Charles Davis's *34 Alpujarras Walks* (see page 556). The information centre next to the village bus stop can provide a simple map, but you'd be wise to take the Editorial Alpina map along, too (see page 54). Outward-bound morning buses currently leave from Capileira at 8.30am, 11am, 3pm and 5.30pm with the return from Alto del Chorillo at 9.45am, 12.15pm, 4.15pm and 6.45pm (confirm the timetable at the kiosko or when booking). Seats on the bus should be booked **in advance** – from the kiosko from where the buses depart, or by phone on ☎ 958 763 090 or ☎ 671 564 406. As you'll be in the high mountains you should come prepared for sudden changes in weather conditions and equip yourself accordingly. Take warm clothing, since the temperature at the summit will only be a few degrees, even in high summer.

even strike out for Trevélez about five hours to the northeast. Capileira's **museum** (Sat & Sun 11am–2pm; charge), just downhill from the kiosko, contains displays of regional dress and handicrafts as well as various bits and pieces belonging to, or produced by, Pedro Alarcón, the nineteenth-century Spanish writer, born in Guadix, who made a trip through the Alpujarras and wrote a (not very good) book about it.

On the Sunday prior to August 5, Capileira embarks on its annual **romería** to the summit of Mulhacén and the *ermita* of the Virgen de las Nieves.

The Tahá villages

PITRES is far less picturesque and less developed than the trio of high villages to its west and, like its equally unpolished neighbour, **PÓRTUGOS**, offers more chance of a room during high season. All around, too, spreads some of the best Alpujarran walking country.

Down below the main road are a trio of villages – **MECINA FONDALES**, **FERREIROLA** and **BUSQUÍSTAR** – which along with Pitres and Pórtugos and a couple of smaller settlements formed a league of seven villages known as the **Tahá** (from the Arabic "Tá" meaning obedience) under the Moors. These are among the most unspoilt of the Alpujarra *pueblos*, where you can find plenty of examples of typical regional architecture (see box, page 473). Ferreirola and Busquístar – the latter a huddle of grey *launa* roofs – are especially attractive, as is the path between the two, clinging to the north side of the valley of the Río Trevélez. You're out of tourist country here and the villages display their genuine characteristics to better effect.

Trevélez

The cut into the mountain made by the Río Trevélez is similar to the Poqueira, but grander and more austere. **TREVÉLEZ** village stands on a flank at the end of the ravine and its altitude – this is mainland Spain's highest conurbation – makes it a cool place even in high summer, when many of the inhabitants continue to don sweaters and coats. It's built in traditional Alpujarran style, with a lower and two upper (and much prettier) *barrios* overlooking a grassy, poplar-lined valley where the river starts its long descent. The upper *barrios* (*alto* and *medio*) are the best places to stay; the lower (*barrio bajo*) is more touristy, filled with stalls and shops selling the village's famed *jamones dulces*, crystals, earrings and herbal remedies and attracting streams of visitors, especially at weekends. There are fine walks in the valley and you can swim, too, in a makeshift pool by the bridge. The village is well provided with **places to stay** (see page 478) in both the lower and upper squares; if you are susceptible to low temperatures, outside July and August you may want a place with efficient heating.

Trevélez is traditionally the jump-off point for the high **Sierra Nevada** peaks (to which there is a bona fide path) and for treks across the range (on a lower, more conspicuous track). The latter begins down by the bridge on the eastern side of the village. After skirting the bleak Horcajo de Trevélez (3182m), and negotiating the Puerto de Trevélez (2800m), up to which it's a very distinct route, it drops down along the north flank of the Sierra Nevada to Jerez del Marquesado.

Juviles

Heading east from Trevélez, either by vehicle or on foot, you come to **JUVILES**, a great centre of silk production in Moorish times, and today an attractive village straddling the road. At its centre is an unwhitewashed, peanut-brittle-finish church with a clock that's usually running slightly slow (like most things around here). The villagers don't appear to have taken to their renovated plaza with its jarring ornamental fountains, lamp-standards and trees in brick boxes, and in the evening people still promenade in the road, knowing that there will be no traffic. Juviles also takes its share of the **jamón** business; a large attractive building on the main road as you exit towards Ugíjar houses **Jamones de Juviles S.A.** (ⓦjamonesdejuviles.com), a curing factory for this *alpujarreño* delicacy. Ring the doorbell and you will be invited inside to taste their fine hams, which can be bought whole or in smaller cuts.

Bérchules

BÉRCHULES, a high village of grassy streams and chestnut woods, lies just 6km beyond Juviles, but a greater contrast can hardly be imagined. It is a large, abruptly demarcated settlement, three streets wide, on a sharp slope overlooking yet another canyon.

WALKS IN THE HIGHER POQUEIRA GORGE

Capileira is a handy base for easy day walks in and around the higher part of the **Poqueira Gorge**. For a not-too-strenuous ramble, take the northernmost of the three paths below the village, each of which spans bridges across the river. This one sets off from alongside the Pueblo Alpujarreño villa complex and winds through the huts and terraced fields of the river valley above Capileira, ending after about ninety minutes at a dirt track within sight of a power plant at the head of the valley. From here, you can either retrace your steps or cross the stream over a bridge to follow a dirt track back to the village. In May and June, the fields are laboriously tended by hand, as the steep slopes dictate.

A number of reasonably clear paths or tracks also lead to **Pampaneira** (2–3hr; follow the lower path to the bridge below Capileira), continuing to **Carataunas** (a further 1hr, mostly road) and **Órgiva** (another 45min on an easy path) from where – if you time it right – you can get a bus back.

In the other direction, taking the Sierra Nevada road and then the first major track to the right, by a ruined stone house, you can reach **Pitres** (2hr), **Pórtugos** (30min more) and **Busquístar** (45min more). Going in the same direction but taking the second decent-sized track (by a sign encouraging you to "conserve and respect nature"), **Trevélez** is some five hours away. Rather than doing Mulhacén the "easy way" (see box, page 474), more skilled, equipped and ambitious climbers may wish to attempt the whole circuit, starting from Capileira. The summit of **Mulhacén**, the Spanish peninsula's highest peak at 3483m, is achievable in a day from here, but is perhaps more sensibly done over two days with an overnight stop at the *Refugio Poqueira*.

Refugio Poqueira At the head of the Poqueira valley; ⓦrefugiopoqueira.com. Marked on the Editorial Alpina map (see page 54), this *refugio* is open all year; advance booking required. €

5

Cádiar

CÁDIAR, just below Bérchules and the central town – or "navel" as Gerald Brenan termed it – of the Alpujarras, is in fact a fairly humdrum market town whose life centres on its main square, fronted by a sixteenth-century stone church, where a colourful produce market takes place on the 3rd and 18th of every month, sometimes including livestock.

A WALK AROUND THE TAHÁ

A circuit of the Tahá villages – with many fine stopping places for a picnic – is a good introduction to the Alpujarras, offering opportunities to appreciate both typical architecture and landscape within a compact area. The following walk around the **Southern Tahá** is an easy two-hour hike, although you'll probably want to take the diversion down to the picturesque Trevélez Gorge which adds another half-hour or so; allow three hours for the full circuit. There's little shade on parts of the route, so avoid the afternoon sun in summer. Remember that the second (uphill) part of the walk is the most strenuous.

The route starts in **Pitres**. Follow the narrow path, which begins as a concrete driveway curving behind *Restaurante La Carretera* (on the main road to the right as you enter the village) and descends southwards – veering left – to **Mecinilla**, which is soon visible below; you should be aiming for the left of the church tower. Ignoring turnings, after fifteen minutes or so you emerge in the upper part of the village (Mecilla). Cross the main Pitres–Ferreirola road into the lower village (Mecinilla), following the road past the *Hotel Albergue de Mecina* (with a decent tapas bar and restaurant) and the church on the left. Just after the *Bar El Aljibe* (on the left), go through a gap and take an immediate right. After a drinking fountain (marked "1964"), turn left; continue downwards through the narrow streets, eventually leaving the village beneath a *tinao* (see box, page 473). Initially following the edge of a ravine, the path continues downwards through orchards (crossing the road once but continuing clearly a little to the right) until reaching the maze of narrow, white streets that make up **Mecina Fondales** – this should take another half-hour or so. Take your time here, partly as it's one of the most peaceful and least spoilt villages, but also as the maze of streets makes it easy to get lost and the vociferous dogs zealously guarding their patches can be off-putting; ask for directions if you can.

From here, for the **shorter route**, take the Camino Real towards Ferreirola, a well-maintained mule track leaving the centre of the village heading east. For the **longer route**, head to the wash area known as "La Fuente" in the village's southeast corner – veer downhill to the left from the road to pass beneath an elaborate *tinao* topped by a vine trellis – to reach the five-basined wash place. From here take the track descending towards the river, bearing left where there's any confusion. After a while the gushing waters become audible below, and the path emerges high above the gorge with the Trevélez bridge visible ahead. Immediately before the bridge, turn left up a small path that crosses the Río Bermejo, before climbing steeply over rocks (ignore the right-hand fork) and continuing uphill to **Ferreirola**.

In Ferreirola, head for the church square; close by is another wash place. Take the path rising north alongside it, which, after another steepish climb, leads to **Atalbéitar**. The path actually emerges on the road below the village from where you turn left to continue the walk, but first you should visit Atalbéitar, another unspoilt hamlet, well off the usual tourist trail. Leaving the village, passing a lifeless oak tree and rubbish container on the right, turn left as the road bends to the right and follow this track in the direction of Pitres (now visible above) past a few houses. The path twice briefly joins the "road" (more of a dirt track); each time, take the path to the left where the road bends right. Leaving the track the second time, just before it joins the "main road", the path first skirts the Bermejo Gorge but then drops sharply to cross the river – some welcome greenery here hides the bridge until you're close to it. Across the river, the path climbs to an *acequia* (irrigation channel); turn right here and continue along the wooded path, past the *Albergue*, until you emerge on the main road slightly to the east of **Pitres**.

ON HORSEBACK TO LAS SIETE LAGUNAS

In late spring and summer (when the mountain snows have retreated) you might want to try a trip on horseback from Trevélez to **Las Siete Lagunas**, a spectacular collection of mountain lakes in a valley on the upper slopes of the mighty Monte Mulhacén. It's a five-hour journey each way and you spend a night on the mountain at an altitude of 3000m; you'll need your own sleeping bag and it's possible to pitch a tent at Siete Lagunas, although this is not essential. The highpoint of the trip is the sun rising above the Sierra de Gador in the east.

The route can also be done **on foot**, and although the ascent is signed ("Siete Lagunas") in its early stages you'd be much better off following the trekking route clearly described in Jeremy Rabjohns' book *Holiday Walks in the Alpujarras* (see page 556). If you don't plan to sleep out at the lakes you should allow at least ten hours' walking time to get up and down the same day. To ride up and down to Las Siete Lagunas, contact one of the horseriding companies in the area (see page 477).

ARRIVAL AND INFORMATION

By bus From Granada's main bus station, buses operated by Alsa (ⓦalsa.es) run direct to the High Alpujarras, stopping at Pampaneira, Bubión, Capileira and Pitres, Trevélez and Bérchules. In the other direction. they leave Bérchules and pass through Trevélez on the way to Granada. Cádiar is served by a thrice daily service from Granada via Lanjarón and Órgiva. There are also frequent daily buses between Granada and Órgiva and Lanjarón and vice versa.

PAMPANEIRA

Nevadensis Pza de la Libertad (Jan & Feb Fri–Sun 10am–2pm; March–June & Sept–Dec Tues–Sun 10am–2pm & 4–6pm; July & Aug Tues–Sun 10am–2pm; ⓦnevadensis.com; English spoken). A private, efficiently run information centre for the National Park of the Sierra Nevada. As well as providing information, they sell large-scale topographical maps of the area, walking guidebooks and outdoor clothing. They also organize themed guided walks in all seasons and offer activities and excursions including mountain biking, climbing, canyoning, hiking and cross-country skiing, as well as information on weather conditions.

THE HIGH ALPUJARRAS

BUBIÓN

Rustic Blue Barrio La Ermita s/n (Mon–Fri 10am–6pm; ⓦrusticblue.com; English spoken). This private information office, at the entrance to the village on the right, is a useful source of local knowledge and stocks walking guides to the area, as well as organizing week-long guided treks and horseriding tours. It can also provide information on renting apartments and houses in the village and throughout the Alpujarras.

Horseriding For horseriding trips of five to seven days, the friendly Rancho Rafael Belmonte (ⓦridingandalucia.com), at the bottom of the village near Rustic Blue, or Sierra Trails (ⓦspain-horse-riding.com), are the places to contact.

CAPILEIRA

Information The national park kiosko (daily 10am–2pm & 5–8pm) at the centre of the village, near where the bus stops, sells large-scale walking maps, hands out a free village map and acts as an information office.

ACCOMMODATION

PAMPANEIRA

Hostal Pampaneira C/José Antonio 1, near the bus stop at the entrance to the village; ⓦhostalpampaneira.com. Friendly place offering functional en-suite rooms above a popular bar-restaurant. Breakfast is included. €̄

Hotel Estrella de las Nieves C/Huertos 21, 200m up the road from the bus stop; ⓦestrelladelasnieves.com. The village's best option, with surprisingly modern and attractive rooms behind a traditional exterior. All are well equipped and many come with a terrace balcony (worth requesting this) and fine views. There's also a garden pool. Breakfast is included. €̄

BUBIÓN

Hotel Villa de Bubión Barrio Alto s/n, above the main road; ⓦvillasdeandalucia.com. The village's three-star luxury option consists of chalet-style villas in a rustic setting. Classically furnished interiors come with terrace balconies and fine views and there's also a restaurant and pool. €̄€̄

Las Terrazas de la Alpujarra Pza del Sol 7; ⓦterrazasalpujarra.com. Comfortable en-suite rooms and apartments with TV, close to the main road at the top of the village. Many rooms have great views. €̄

Los Tinaos C/Parras s/n, downhill from the main road; ⓦlostinaos.com. Pristine white apartments with flower-

5

filled terraces. The comfortable accommodation comes with heating (including open fire in the living room), galley kitchen and wonderful views. €

CAPILEIRA

Cortijo Catifalarga Ctra de Sierra Nevada s/n; ⓦcatifalarga.com. Some 500m beyond the *Ruta de Las Nieves* and signed up a track on the left, this is a delightful hideaway with charming rooms and two apartments inside a traditional *alpujarreño cortijo*, along with fabulous views and a pool. Also has its own bar-restaurant. Doubles €, apartments €€€

Cortijo Prado Toro 3km up the mountain from Cortijo Catifalarga; ⓦpradotoro.com. For those seeking even more solitude. At an altitude of 1500m, this delightful stone-built aparthotel has beamed rooms with tiled floors and stylishly rustic furnishings. There's also a great pool and garden plus spectacular views. €€

Finca Los Llanos Uphill from the bus stop; ⓦhotelfincaloslllanos.com. Rather luxurious possibility with apartment-style rooms with terraces. There's also a pool and a good restaurant. Breakfast is included. €€

Hostal Atalaya To the right as you enter the village; ⓦhostalatalaya.com. A nice little place with en-suite rooms and terrific views from those at the front (costing a few euros more). €

Mesón-Hostal Poqueira Near the bus stop; ⓦhotelpoqueira.com. En-suite heated rooms, some with terraces and views, at this welcoming option; there's a pool and good restaurant with an inexpensive *menú*. It also has some attractive apartments sleeping up to four for longer stays. Doubles €, apartments €€

PITRES

Balcón de Pitres Ctra Órgiva–Ugíjar km51; ⓦbalcondepitres.com. Pitres's campsite occupies a stunning position on the village's western edge, and has plenty of shade, a swimming pool, restaurant and great views. Closed Jan and Feb. €

Cortijo Opazo Carretera Altarbéitar, Pórtugos; ⓦcortijoopazo.com. 1.5k from Pitres on the road to Pórtugos, this traditional farmhouse has two cosy apartments named after the mountain peaks opposite. Guests have use of the large gardens and terrace, and owners can offer advice on walks and activities in the area. Dinner is available if booked 24 hours in advance. Minimum three nights' stay. €€

THE TAHÁ

Hotel Albergue de Mecina C/La Fuente 2, Mecina Fondales; ⓦhoteldemecina.com. Excellent two-star hotel with attractive rooms, many with terrace balcony and views. Has its own bar and there's also an wonderfully set garden pool. Information on the area is also available, and on hiring horses and mountain bikes. €€

L'Atelier C/Alberca 21, Mecina Fondales; ⓦatelier-mecina.com. The French vegetarian restaurant of the same name (see page 480) lets a few comfortable en-suite rooms above its restaurant in the heart of the village. Breakfast is included. €

TREVÉLEZ

Camping Trevélez Ctra Trevélez–Órgiva km1; ⓦcampingtrevelez.net. The village's campsite has decent facilities and good shade. Although it's officially open all year, you can expect arctic conditions in midwinter. It also rents out some heated cabins. €

Hostal Fernando C/Pista del Barrio Medio s/n; ☏958 858 565. A welcoming option in the *barrio medio*, offering en-suite rooms with great terrace views (from some); it also

---

BIRDWATCHING IN THE HIGH ALPUJARRAS

The High Alpujarras is an excellent place for **birdwatching**, particularly in late spring. Quiet roads and an abundance of footpaths and dirt tracks make access easy. At this time of the year, most of the species associated with the upland areas of southern Spain can be found in the **Poqueira Gorge** and the Trevélez River valley. Above the village of **Capileira**, a walk from the end of the metalled road in areas clear of pinewoods can turn up sightings of southern grey shrike, rock thrush, black-eared wheatear and the striking black-eyed race of northern wheatear, as well as ortolan bunting. Higher up, in autumn, honey buzzards can occasionally be seen heading for the Straits of Gibraltar and winter quarters in Africa. Higher still, the alpine accentor is to be spotted around mountain huts.

The more wooded parts of the **Trevélez valley** have booted eagle, buzzard, raven and the short-toed treecreeper, while lower down, near **Pitres**, scops owl and red-necked nightjar can be heard at dusk, and in late summer bee eaters congregate for their migration south. Throughout these areas golden eagle, crag martin, black redstart and rock bunting are also to be seen and, with a little more persistence and patience, the members of the warbler family – Dartford, spectacled, selodius and Bonelli's – can be turned up in suitable habitats.

lets out a couple of excellent-value apartments with kitchen and terrace. All come with heating and there's easy parking. €

Hostal Mulhacén Ctra Ugíjar s/n; ☎ 958 858 587. In the lower *barrio* and 100m along the Juviles road from Pza Francisco Abellán, this is another good possibility for en-suite rooms with TV, and offers great views down the valley. €

★ **Hotel La Fragua I & II** C/San Antonio 4; ⓦ hotellafragua.com. Next to the Ayuntamiento in the *barrio alto*, this is the most attractive of the village places with pine-furnished, en-suite, heated rooms with fine views. Their second hotel at the end of the same street is also good and has a pool. As this is a popular place with walking groups, it may be worth booking ahead. €

JUVILES

Pensión Tino C/Altillo Bajo 38; ⓦ juviles.net. At the western end of the main road running through the village, this small *hostal* offers clean and tidy en-suite rooms. Some rooms have views and there's a pretty, flower-filled roof terrace for taking breakfast. €

BÉRCHULES

Hotel Bérchules Ctra de Bérchules 20; ⓦ hotelberchules.com. On the main road into the village from Juviles, this is an agreeable two-star hotel with comfortable rooms above its own restaurant. There's also a pool. €€

El Mirador de Bérchules Pza de Zapata 1, in the barrio alto; ⓦ miradordeberchules.net. Welcoming place with fully equipped studios and apartments with terraces and views. It also has its own good restaurant (with a good value *menú*), tapas bar and pool. €€

CÁDIAR

Alquería de Morayma Ctra A348 km50; ⓦ alqueriamorayma.com. Upmarket aparthotel in a converted Alpujarran *cortijo* in 86 acres of farmland; there are charming and traditionally styled rustic rooms and apartments (almost the same price), many with terraces, plus a pool and good restaurant (open to non-guests). It offers guests mountain biking and horseriding and there are plenty of hiking trails. €€

EATING AND DRINKING

PAMPANEIRA

Bar Belezmín Pza de la Libertad 11; ☎ 958 763 102. On the leafy main square, this is a good bet for well-prepared regional dishes. They specialize in *carnes asados* (charcoal-grilled meats) and there's a pleasant terrace on the square and upstairs. €€

★ **Bodega La Moralea** C/Veronica 12, down the street with the stream off Pza de la Libertad; ☎ 958 763 225. Wonderfully atmospheric and entertaining little bar/shop selling fine *alpujarreño jamones* (from Juviles and Pampaneira) which hang from the ceiling. You'll usually get a sample cut from one of these as a free *tapa* when you order a drink. Also sells the oils, wines and cheeses of the region as well as other local products. €

Casa Julio Avda de la Alpujarra 9, up some steps near the bus halt; ☎ 958 763 322. This is perhaps the village's best restaurant, with a delightful terrace. The kitchen produces hearty mountain food such as *choto en salsa de almendras* (kid in almond sauce), *patatas a lo pobre* (potatoes with garlic) and a selection of salads. €

Chocolates Sierra Nevada Avda de la Alpujarra 3, up some steps just before you reach Casa Julio; ⓦ chocolatesierranevada.com. Friendly shop/café where you can try delicious handmade chocolates – try the chocolate figs – and buy local produce such as jam, honey and cakes. €

Ruta del Mulhacén Avda Alpujarra 6; ⓦ rutadelmulhacen.es. At the entrance to the village, this restaurant has a marked Moorish theme with its Alhambra murals, plus a terrace with exceptional views. *Potaje de hinojos* (fennel stew) and *gachas pimentonas* (spicy "porridge") are house specials, as is the *choto en salsa de almendra* (kid in almond sauce). €€

BUBIÓN

Casa Ángel C/Carretera 41, on the main road above the village; ☎ 649 155 001. Good and reliable village restaurant serving *carne a la brasa* (grilled meat) and homemade pizzas. Pleasant terrace with views and cosy open fire in the cooler months. €€

Estacion 4 C/Estación 4; ☎ 651 831 363. In the heart of the village, this is perhaps the most ambitious of the eating options. The dining room is bright and appealing, and the kitchen produces a variety of Arab-influenced dishes including kofta, falafel and aubergine croquettes. €€

Teide C/Carretera s/n; ☎ 958 763 037. Down from *Casa Ángel* on the main road, and probably the better of the two restaurants; the kitchen turns out hearty soups as well as a variety of *alpujarreño* favourites – *pierna de cordero al horno* (baked lamb) is a speciality – and there's a good-value *menú*. Sit in the leafy garden terrace on warmer days. €€

CAPILEIRA

La Casa de Paco y Pilar Ctra de la Sierra 16; ☎ 958 763 142. Uphill from the *Finca Los Llanos*, serving well-prepared mountain dishes such as *choto al ajillo* (roast kid with garlic) and *migas* (fried breadcrumbs with chorizo and garlic), along with some vegetarian dishes; it's also a good place to

5

sample the local *jamones* and cheeses. There's a nice garden terrace. €€

El Corral del Castaño Pza Calvario 16; ☎958 763 414. One of the more sophisticated restaurants in the village, with a nice shady terrace. The menu changes regularly and features dishes such as *borcheta de pollo con cítricos y jengibre* (chicken with citrus and ginger) and *bacalao confitado con timbal de verduras* (glazed cod with vegetable timbal). €€

PITRES

Bar Paco C/Carretera s/n, Busquístar. Just below the main road as you pass through the village, this is a reliable option for tapas and *raciones* and serves a good value weekday *menú*. €

Hotel San Roque C/Cruz 1 on the main road at the east side of the village; ☎958 857 528. The hotel restaurant is the only other place to eat, serving up traditional local dishes including *plato alpujarreño* with cured ham and *chuletas de cordero* (lamb chops). €€

THE TAHÁ VILLAGES

★**L'Atelier** C/Alberca 21, Mecina Fondales; ⊕atelier-mecina.com. Mecina's best place for food: a French-run restaurant specializing in vegetarian/vegan cuisine with an international slant, located in the old village bakery. The menu changes often, but it's all good. €€€

TREVÉLEZ

Casa Julio Pza de la Iglesia s/n ☎958 858 708. Popular *barrio* bar-restaurant serving *carnes a la brasa* (charcoal-grilled meats) as well as pizzas. They also have tapas in the bar and an outdoor terrace. €€

Mesón del Jamón C/Cárcel 13; ☎958 858 679. Head here to sample Trevélez's celebrated *jamones* – the restaurant also serves up regional specials such as *choto al ajillo* (roast kid with garlic) and *trucha* (trout). The panoramic terrace has great views. €€

Mesón Haraicel C/Real s/n, just above the main square in the lower barrio; ☎958 308 530. Good-value place, offering traditional local dishes and the house speciality *solomillo cortijero* (pork stuffed with ham), plus tapas and *raciones* in its bar. €€

Mesón Joaquín At the entrance to the village in the barrio bajo; ⊕jamonestrevelez.com. One of the village's *jamón* specialists, its ceiling hung with hams. Regional specialities include *habas con jamón* (beans with ham), *plato alpujarreño* (mixed fry-up with blood pudding, *jamón* and egg), *trucha con jamón* (river trout) and hearty mountain soups. €€

★**Mesón La Fragua** C/San Antonio s/n; ⊕hotellafragua.com. The hotel restaurant is Trevélez's best place to eat, serving well-prepared dishes in a rustic two-storey bar-restaurant. *Venao en salsa* (stewed venison) and *cordero a la moruna* (Moorish-style lamb) feature among a wide range of specialities, and there is a range of salads and vegetarian dishes, too. €€

BÉRCHULES

★**Abrasador** Ctra A-4130, on the way to Mecina Bombarón; ⊕elcercadoalpujarra.com. Part of the *El Cercado* apartment complex, this restaurant is one of the best places to eat in this part of the Alpujarras. The extensive menu features local specialities as well as grilled meats such as suckling pig. There's a good-value tasting menu and the weekday lunch *menú del día*. €€€

The eastern and southern Alpujarras

Cádiar and Bérchules mark the end of the western Alpujarras, and a striking change in the landscape; the dramatic, severe, but relatively green terrain of the Guadalfeo and Cádiar valleys gives way to open, rolling and much more arid land. The villages of the **eastern Alpujarras** display many of the characteristics of those to the west but as a rule they are poorer and less visited by tourists. There are attractive places nonetheless, among them **Yegen**, which Gerald Brenan wrote about, and the market centre of **Ugíjar**.

Yegen

YEGEN, some 7km northeast of Cádiar, is where author and historian **Gerald Brenan** lived during his ten or so years of Alpujarran residence (see box, page 481). Brenan connections aside, Yegen is an appealing and quiet place, with its two distinct quarters (*alto* and *bajo*), cobbled paths and cold-water springs.

Mecina Bombarón

From Yegen there's an easy 4km **walk** up to the hamlet of **MECINA BOMBARÓN**, along one of the old cobbled mule paths. This starts out from the old bridge across the gorge and is easy to follow from there, with Mecina clearly visible on the hill above. Mecina is also reachable by road.

5

Válor

Six kilometres beyond Yegen, and sited between deep ravines, **VÁLOR** is a charming and sleepy hamlet, a fact that belies its history as a centre of stubborn resistance in the sixteenth-century revolt by the Moors against the "insults and outrages" of the Christian ascendancy. These events are "celebrated" in the annual **Fiestas Patronales** in mid-September when the whole story – including battles between Moors and Christians – is colourfully re-enacted in the main square.

Ugíjar

UGÍJAR, 6km beyond Válor, is the largest community in these parts, and an unassuming, quiet market town. There are easy and enjoyable walks to the nearest villages – up the valley to Mecina Alfahar, for example – and a handful of **places to stay**.

Centro de Patrimonio Cultural de la Alpujarra

Pza de los Caños s/n • Mon–Fri 10am–1.30pm, Sat & Sun 11am–1.30pm • Free

In the centre of town, the **Centro de Patrimonio Cultural de la Alpujarra** sits behind the traditional facade of a restored mansion. Inside the starkly contrasting modern interior you can view farm implements and tools, wine making utensils and traditional handicrafts as well as information panels on daily life and culture in the Alpujarras. Most of what's on display was donated by a local family. There's also a small shop selling local produce and an information desk.

ARRIVAL AND DEPARTURE THE EASTERN AND SOUTHERN ALPUJARRAS

Buses run from and between Ugíjar, Yegen and Valor to Almería (8.30am & 2.30pm; 3hr) and Granada (5.45am, 7am & 3pm; 3hr 30min).

ACCOMMODATION

YEGEN
Alojamientos Las Eras C/Carretera 39; ⓦ alojamientoslaseras.com. A reliable option for modern, fully equipped apartments decorated in typical local style. All have an open fire in the living area, a TV and a terrace. €
Bar Pensión La Fuente C/Real 46, opposite the

GERALD BRENAN: SOUTH FROM GRANADA

Gerald Brenan's autobiography of his years in the Alpujarras, **South from Granada**, is the best account of rural life in Spain between the wars, and also describes the visits made here by Bloomsburyites Virginia Woolf, Bertrand Russell and the arch-complainer Lytton Strachey who attributed his Iberian ailments to "crude olive oil, greasy *tortillas* and a surfeit of *bacalao*" and proclaimed when he got home that "Spain is absolute death". Disillusioned with the strictures of middle-class life in England after World War I, Brenan rented a house in Yegen and shipped out a library of two thousand books, from which he was to spend the next eight years educating himself. Since only a handful of the inhabitants of Yegen were literate, the reserved, lanky stranger was regarded as an exotic curiosity by the villagers. With glazed windows in only two dwellings, no doctor, electricity or telephone and no road to the outside world, Yegen's rustic isolation together with its characters, traditions, superstitions and celebrations provided the raw material for his great work.

Towards the end of his stay he became involved in a number of scandals and, after getting a young teenage girl pregnant, moved to the small village of Churriana between Málaga and Torremolinos, with his wife, US writer and poet Gamel Woolsey. Here he died in 1987, a writer better known and respected in Spain (he made an important study of St John of the Cross) than in his native England. The contribution he made to informing the world about the Alpujarras, its history and culture, is recorded on a plaque fixed to his former home, now the **Casa de Brenan**, just along from the fountain in Yegen's main square.

5

fountain in the square; ☎958 851 067. The *barrio alto's* main bar rents out en-suite rooms and apartments (for four), and serves tapas and *raciones* in a room dotted with Brenan memorabilia and photos. The proprietor can provide a leaflet of walks (in Spanish; one route is named after Brenan) around the village. Doubles €, apartments €€
El Tinao La Carretera s/n; ☎958 851 212. Bright and airy en-suite rooms are offered at this bar-*hostal* on the main road through; they also let fully equipped village houses (prices on request) and serve meals. €

MECINA BOMBARÓN
Casas Blancas C/Casas Blancas 14; ⓦcasasblancas.es. These apartments are a pleasant and comfortable place to stay with sun balcony, TV and small kitchen. Some have jacuzzis. €€

VALOR
Balcón de Válor Ctra de Trevélez s/n, on the main road; ⓦbalcondevalor.com. On the village's eastern edge, this option has attractive, fully equipped apartments with terraces and a shared pool. Three nights' minimum stay in July & Aug. €€
Hostal Las Perdices Ctra de Trevélez s/n, on the main road; ⓦhlasperdices.com. Comfortable *hostal*, owned by the same proprietors as *Balcón de Válor*, offering en-suite rooms with TV. €€

UGÍJAR
Hostal-Mesón Vidaña Ctra de Almería s/n; ☎958 854 961. Decent *hostal* with en-suite, heated rooms with TV above an excellent restaurant. It's on the Almería road out of town. €

EATING AND DRINKING

YEGEN
Bar Pensión La Fuente Pza Fuente s/n; ☎958 851 067. A good breakfast option and later in the day also serves tapas and *raciones* as well as *platos combinados* and a daily *menú*. €€
El Tinao La Carretera s/n; ☎958 851 212. Irish-born Loranne can cook whatever you fancy, but she specializes in local dishes, steaks with all the trimmings and international dishes such as curries. €€

MECINA BOMBARÓN
Casa Joaquín Avda José Antonio Bravo 66, just below the church; ☎638 190 390. Popular village bar-restaurant serving a range of tapas and *raciones* in the bar and good hearty dishes in its restaurant – *chuletas de cordero* (lamb chops) and *costillas* (spare ribs) are house specials; there's

also a *menú*. €€

VALOR
Café Bar La Azahara C/Pradera s/n; ☎692 324 038. Excellent-value bar-restaurant just off the main street. As well as the usual local dishes, they also serve delicious homemade pizzas, paella and courgette quiche. €€

UGÍJAR
Pepe Aguado Trasera de la Iglesia 8, behind the church; ☎958 854 065. Perhaps the town's best place to eat, specializing in *carnes a la brasa* (charcoal-grilled meats). Specials include *perdiz en escabeche* (partridge in brine) and *rabo de buey* (stewed oxtail). They also serve tapas and *raciones* in their cosy bar. €€€

The Almerían Alpujarras

From Ugíjar the A348 toils eastwards and, once across the Río de Alcolea, enters the province of Almería where the starker – but no less impressive – terrain gradually takes on the harsh and desiccated character of the deserts that lie ahead. There are still the odd oases to be found, however, in **Laujar de Andarax** and the spa of **Alhama de Almería** and, just beyond the latter, a remarkable prehistoric site, **Los Millares**.

Laroles

If you're in no hurry to reach Laujar, take a scenic detour along the A337 and AL5402 through the hamlets of **LAROLES** and Bayárcal for a chance to see some of the national park's magnificent upland terrain or, in summer, to experience the Me Vuelves Lorca festival (see box, page 483). You could also consider overnighting to explore an area rich in trekking possibilities; it's on the route of the E4 (marked GR7 on Spanish maps) pan-European footpath.

Laujar de Andarax

It was at **LAUJAR DE ANDARAX**, 16km east of Ugíjar, at the source of the Río Andarax, that Boabdil, the deposed Moorish king of Granada, settled in 1492 and from where

ME VUELVES LORCA

Laroles plays host every summer to a **festival** called *Me Vuelves Lorca* – a nod to Lorca's La Barraca theatre company and a play on the Spanish *me vuelves loca* ("you drive me crazy"). Works by Lorca and plays and performances inspired by his influences (eg. flamenco and jazz) take place in an open-air theatre that was hand-built by locals around an ancient wheat-threshing circle. The theatre, the brain-child of Briton Anna Kemp, is modelled on the Minack Theatre in Cornwall. The crowd-funding initiative to kick-start the project gained the support of international and Spanish stars such as Leonard Cohen, Russell Crowe, Javier Cámara and Aitana Sánchez-Gijón, whose names are on the seats; the theatre is open for visits year-round. More information about the festival and its programme is available on ⓦ mevuelveslorca.com.

he intended to rule the Alpujarras fiefdom granted to him by the Catholic monarchs. But Christian paranoia about a Moorish resurgence led them to tear up the treaty and within a year Boabdil had been shipped off to Africa, an event that set in motion a series of uprisings by the Alpujarran Moors, ending in their suppression and eventual deportation, to be replaced by Christian settlers from the north.

The **Río Andarax's source**, at the town's eastern edge – signposted "*nacimiento*"– is a shady spot beside the falls. If you're here on a Sunday you'll find the falls a hive of activity as families pour in to make barbecues under the trees. In Laujar's centre the **Plaza Mayor** has a seventeenth-century four-spouted fountain – one of many dotted around the town – and an elegant late eighteenth-century **Ayuntamiento**, where you can pick up a street map. This will enable you to find four crumbling seventeenth-century **palacios** as well as the impressive Mudéjar-style seventeenth-century church of **La Encarnación**, which contains a sculpture of the Virgin by Alonso Cano.

Laujar is the centre of a burgeoning **wine industry** and home to the highest vineyards in the country. Although smoother and slightly less potent than the *costa* wines further west, the brew is just as palatable. The **Bodegas Valle de Laujar** (ⓦ bodegasvallelaujar. com), on the main road 2km west of town, was founded in 1992 and sells these wines both within Spain and abroad. At their small shop (daily 9am–2pm & 3.30–7pm) you can taste and buy their four good reds as well as four whites, two rosés and the only *cava* produced in Andalucía, plus cheeses and other local produce.

East of Laujar de Andarax

The road **east of Laujar de Andarax** passes a series of unremarkable villages, surrounded by slopes covered with vine trellises, little changed since Moorish times and little visited today. Among them is **FONDÓN**, whose church tower was the minaret of the former mosque, and **PADULES**, 11km beyond Laujar, where the municipal swimming pool might prove a greater lure in the baking heat of high summer. The prettier village of **CANJÁYAR**, 4km further on, also has a swimming pool, and becomes a centre of frenetic activity during the autumn *vendimia*, when the grapes are gathered in. The road then trails the course of the Andarax river valley through an arid and eroded landscape, skirting the Sierra de Gádor before climbing slightly to **ALHAMA DE ALMERÍA**, 16km further on. This is an appealing spa town, dating back to Moorish times, and most of its visitors are here to take the waters – hence the rather incongruous three-star hotel sited on the location of the original baths.

Los Millares

Wed–Sun 10am–2pm, but call to confirm; allow 2–3hr for your visit • Free • ☎ 677 903 404 • The bus between Alhama de Almería and Almería (Mon–Fri only) stops at Los Millares, but you need to adapt your visit to the morning bus service; the 5km distance is just about walkable (with fierce temperatures in summer) at a push, or you could take a taxi (about €15 one way); for more details on the limited transport to Los Millares, contact the Alhama Turismo (see page 462)

5

Leaving Alhama, after 5km the Almería road passes a signed turn-off leading to the remarkable pre-Bronze Age settlement of **LOS MILLARES**, one of the most important of its kind in Europe. Situated on a low triangular spur between two dried-up riverbeds, it was exposed in 1891 during the construction of the Almería-to-Linares railway line that passes below the site today. Two Belgian mining engineers, Henri and Louis Siret, who were also enthusiastic amateur archeologists, took on the excavations at the beginning of the twentieth century, funding them from their modest salaries. What they revealed is a Chalcolithic or Copper Age (the period between the Neolithic and the Bronze Age) **fortified settlement**. It dates from c.2700 BC and was occupied until c.1800 BC, when both stone and copper but not bronze were used for weapons and tools. While it is not entirely clear who the occupants were – possibly emigrants from the eastern Mediterranean or perhaps an indigenous group – the settlement they left behind is exceptional. Spread over twelve acres it consists of four sets of defensive walls, with a number of advanced fortlets beyond these, as well as an extraordinary cemetery with more than one hundred **tombs** that are without equal in Europe.

Looking over the barren landscape that surrounds the site today, it's hard to believe that five thousand years ago this was a fertile area of pine and ilex forests, inhabited by deer and wild boar. The nearby Río Andarax was then navigable and the inhabitants used it to bring copper down from mines in the Sierra de Gádor to the west. The population – perhaps as many as two thousand – not only hunted for their food but bred sheep, goats and pigs, grew vegetables and cereals, made cheese and were highly skilled in the manufacture of pottery, basketwork and jewellery, as is evidenced by the finds now in museums in Almería (see page 491) and Madrid.

Excavations are continuing at the site and information boards (in English and Spanish) have been set up at various points; a map on the wall of the entrance office shows **walking routes** outside the site that take in dolmens and ten forts related to the Los Millares settlement that were discovered in the surrounding hills. The most impressive of the forts (with fine **views** over the Los Millares site), Fortin Uno (Fort One), lies up a track on the opposite side of the road from the site entrance; the site guardians will advise how to reach it.

The site

A tour of the **site** begins with the outermost of four exterior **walls** that were constructed successively further west as the settlement expanded across the escarpment in the latter part of the third millennium BC. An impressive structure, 4m high when built, the fourth (and last) wall was lined with outward-facing bastions or towers, and at 310m is the longest wall known in Europe from this period. Its layout bears a striking similarity to a wall of the same epoch at the early Cycladic site of Halandriani on the island of Síros in Greece, suggesting a possible link with the Aegean. The **main gate**, towards the centre, is flanked by watchtowers, beyond which a walled passage gave access to the settlement.

A little way north of here are the remains of a primitive **aqueduct** which cut through the wall to carry water from a spring near to the village of Alhama into the populated area. Fifty metres east of the main gate, remains can be seen from the third wall. Close to here also are the remains of a number of circular **huts** – one of which has been partially reconstructed – in which the inhabitants of the site lived. Six to seven metres in diameter with pounded earth floors, they consisted of cavity stone walls filled with mud and pebbles, with a roof probably made from straw. Inside the huts the excavators found remains of hearths as well as grindstones, pottery and a variety of utensils.

The remains of the first wall, enclosing what may have been the citadel, lie further back still and excavations here recovered many of the patterned, bell-shaped vases to be seen in the museum at Almería (see page 491).

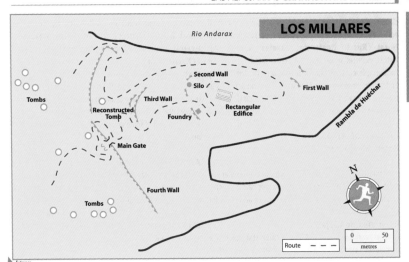

The necropolis

Retracing your steps to the outer (or fourth) wall will bring you to one of the reconstructed tombs, part of the ancient **necropolis**. This "beehive" tomb, originally sited outside the third wall, was encompassed by the later fourth wall. It is one of more than a hundred tombs (the rest lie west of this wall), and the typical structure of a low corridor punctuated by perforated slate slabs leading to a domed burial chamber bears a striking resemblance to tholos tombs of a similar date from the Aegean, particularly southern Crete. It has been suggested that early Cretans (for whom the bull was religiously significant) may have found their way here and that the importance of bulls and bullfighting on the Iberian peninsula may owe something to this link. Present academic thinking, however, tends towards the idea that the civilization here was of local origin.

More tombs, most in a collapsed state, in which clan members were buried together with their possessions such as arms, tools and what appear to be ceramic idols (suggesting the existence of a cult), lie beyond the outer wall. Originally, and again as in the Aegean, the tombs were covered with an earth mound or tumulus. Resist climbing over them; many are in a fragile condition and it's hard to overstate the importance of this site for posterity.

ARRIVAL AND INFORMATION

THE ALMERIAN ALPUJARRAS

LAUJAR DE ANDARAX
National Park information office On the edge of the town as you come in from Ugíjar (April–Sept Thurs & Sun 9.30am–2.30pm, Fri & Sat 9.30am–2.30pm & 5–8pm; Oct–March Thurs & Sun 10am–2.30pm, Fri & Sat 10am–2.30pm & 4–6pm; ☎ 958 515 535). The eastern panhandle of the Sierra Nevada National Park lies 15km to the north of Laujar.

ALHAMA DE ALMERÍA
By bus Alhama de Almería is served by bus from Almería (Mon–Fri 5 daily, Sat 2 daily, Sun 1 daily; 45min) – but note that transport to Los Millares from here is more difficult than you might imagine (see page 483).
Turismo C/Médicos 13 (Mon–Fri: April–Oct 6–8pm; Nov–March 5–7pm; ☎ 950 640 469). Offers information on transport to Los Millares.

ACCOMMODATION AND EATING

LAROLES
Alpujarras Camping ⓦ campingalpujarras.es. Campsite

is on the village's western edge, with good facilities, plenty of shade and a pool. Well-equipped wooden cabins,

5

sleeping up to four, are also available. Organizes plenty of activities including walking and cross-country skiing. €

Hotel Rural Real de Laroles C/Real 46; ⓦturismorurallaroles.com. A very good option for comfortable en-suite heated rooms with TV. The friendly and helpful proprietor can help with advice on activities in the area. The café/bar dishes up good, tasty food (for guests who have pre-booked only). €

LAUJAR DE ANDARAX

Hotel Almirez Ctra Laujar–Órgiva km1.6, at the western edge of town; ⓦhotelalmirez.es. With your own transport (or a 15min walk from the centre) you can reach this comfortable hotel, with spacious balcony rooms in a leafy setting. Owners can provide advice and maps for local walks. €

Hotel Villa de Laujar Paraje Cortijo de la Villa s/n; ⓦvillasdeandalucia.com. A lovely three-star hotel in a park down a side road at the town's eastern end. Attractive

studios and apartments are set in a rural landscape, and there's a bar-restaurant and two garden pools. Good weekday special offers. Breakfast is included. €€

El Nacimiento C/Paraje del Nacimiento km1.3, a short walk north of the centre along the road next to the Río Andarax; ☎950 513 692. The terrace next to the waterfall makes for very pleasant dining here. Specials include *conejo al ajillo* (rabbit in garlic) and *calamar a la brasa en salsa verde* (chargrilled squid with green sauce) as well as grilled meats. €€

ALHAMA DE ALMERÍA

Hotel San Nicolás C/Baños s/n; ⓦbalneariosannicolas. es. Situated over the baths with a slightly institutional ambience, this is the place where people taking the waters tend to stay. The rooms are three-star standard and there is also a restaurant serving a buffet menu and bar. Breakfast is included. €€

From Guadix to Almería

An alternative route from Granada to Almería – via the A92 and covered by Alsa buses (ⓦalsa.es) from the main bus station – goes via **Guadix**, a fine old Moorish town with a vast and extraordinary cave district. For those with transport, the route also offers the opportunity for a detour to the impressive Renaissance castle of **La Calahorra**.

To the northeast, the A92N *autovía* speeds traffic from Guadix towards Lorca and Murcia. There is a possible stop at the market town of **Baza**, beyond which the road pushes on through a sparsely populated landscape for the 70km between here and the towns of Vélez Rubio and Vélez Blanco with its fine castle (see page 517).

Guadix

Sited on the banks of the Río Guadix, in the midst of a fertile plain, **GUADIX** is a windblown sort of town, often coated in the red dust that gusts in from the surrounding hills. It's not a particularly attractive place and were it not for its remarkable cave district there would be little reason to stop. However, Guadix's old quarter is still largely walled, and the circuit includes an imposing Moorish gateway, the Puerta San Turcuato, plus some promising excavations.

Brief history

An ancient settlement, dating back to Paleolithic times, became the Roman town of Julia Gemella Acci in 45 BC, established by Julius Caesar as a base for exploiting seams of silver in the surrounding hills. Following a period of decline during the Visigothic era, the conquering Moors revived its fortunes, renaming the town Guadh-Haix ("River of Life"), and it rapidly grew in size, soon becoming a rival for Granada. It was renowned for its poetry, and bards such as Ibn Tofayl sang the praises of Guadix's beauty and its valley. It was also during the Moorish period that the town developed an important silk industry; mulberry trees can still be seen along the river. Industrial development was based upon the production of esparto grass products and cutlery. Guadix endured terrifying atrocities during the Civil War, which Gerald Brenan vividly described in *South from Granada*.

Catedral de Guadix

Pza de la Catedral s/n • Hours vary • Charge • ☎ 958 665 108

Inside the ancient city walls, the *barrio antiguo* is dominated by the imposing red sandstone towers of its sixteenth-century **Catedral**, built on the site of a former mosque and circled on Saturdays by a lively **market**. The edifice has been much hacked around and embellished over the years and the exterior is eighteenth-century Corinthian, the work of Vincente Acero. The sombre, late-Gothic interior was designed by Diego de Siloé, based on that of the cathedral at Málaga. Its best feature is the superb Churrigueresque choir stalls by Ruíz del Peral. Civil War reminders from both sides of the conflict include the defaced and destroyed heads of the saints on the carved marble pulpit and, near to the entrance, two plaques recording the names of local priests "killed by Marxism".

Plaza Mayor and around

Just across from the cathedral entrance, beneath an arch, stands the elegant **Plaza Mayor** (aka Plaza de la Constitución), an arcaded Renaissance square that was reconstructed after severe damage in the Civil War. Impressive sections of both Roman (second century) and Moorish walls (thirteenth century) lie to the north (best viewed when you enter the *Turismo*). A right turn in the stepped street (Calle Santisteban) at the far end of the square leads up to the Renaissance **Palacio de Peñaflor** with a twin towered brick facade featuring an interesting *balconada* (corner balcony). After a prolonged programme of refurbishment is completed, visitors will be able to see the stunning columned interior patio. Nearby, in the Placeta de Santiago, the whitewashed church of **Santiago** (daily April–Oct 7.30–8pm; Nov–March 6.30–7pm; free; ☎ 958 661 097), another work by Siloé, has an imposing Plateresque entrance and, inside, a beautiful *artesonado* ceiling.

Next to the Peñaflor mansion, a former theological seminary alongside the sixteenth-century church of **San Agustín** gives access to the conclusively ruined ninth-century Moorish **alcazaba**. In 2010, the commencement of a major programme of excavation unearthed a palace and the original gateway, but public funds have now dried up and at the time of writing, there was no date for reopening; contact the Turismo for more details. From the *alcazaba*'s battlements there are **views** over the cave district of Santiago and beyond towards the Sierra Nevada.

Roman Theatre

Avda Mariana Pineda • Mon–Fri 8am–1pm; Sat 10am guided tours (enquire at the tourist office) • Free

To the west of the cathedral lies the **Roman theatre**, discovered in 2008, but only under excavation since 2014. Built in 25AD, the theatre housed four thousand spectators and accounted for around one-tenth of the Roman city. Its 49.5m-wide stage is one of the largest in Andalucía and gives an idea of the importance of Roman Guadix. Excavations are currently centred on revealing the theatre gardens, buried under 4m of mud after the Río Guadix burst its banks at the end of the first century. The best view of the theatre is from the Paseo Torreón de Ferro, but it's worth entering the precinct to see the latest excavations close-up.

Barrio de las Cuevas

South of the *alcazaba* and sited in a weird landscape of pyramidal red hills, the **Barrio de las Cuevas**, or cave district, still houses some ten thousand people (most of whom, and contrary to popular belief, are not *gitanos* or gypsies), and to take a look around it is the main reason for most visits to Guadix.

The quarter extends across some 2.5 square kilometres, and the lower caves, on the outskirts, are really proper cottages sprouting television aerials, with upper storeys, electricity and running water. But as you walk deeper into the district, the design quickly becomes simpler – just a whitewashed front, a door, a tiny window and a chimney – and the experience increasingly voyeuristic. Penetrating right to the back you'll come upon a few caves which are no longer used: too squalid, too unhealthy

5

to live in, their whitewash faded to a dull brown. Yet right next door there may be a similar, occupied cave, with a family sitting outside, and other figures following dirt tracks still deeper into the hills.

Be aware that offers to show you around the interior of a cave will often be followed by a demand for substantial sums of money when you emerge.

Centro de Interpretación Cuevas de Guadix

Pza Padre Poveda, opposite the church of San Miguel, and signed along C/San Miguel heading south from the centre • Mon–Fri 10am–2pm & 4–6pm, Sat 10am–2pm • Charge • ⓦ mcicuevasdeguadix.blogspot.com

The easiest way to get an understanding of cave culture is to visit the **Centro de Interpretación Cuevas de Guadix**, or cave museum. Sited in a series of rehabilitated cave dwellings, it documents the history and reality of cave living with audiovisual aids and reconstructed rooms.

ARRIVAL AND INFORMATION
GUADIX

By bus The bus station, located to the southeast of the centre off Avda Medina Olmos, is a 5min walk from the walls and cathedral.

Destinations Almería (4 daily; 2hr); Granada (12 daily; 1hr); La Calahorra (3 daily; 50min).

By train Guadix station is on the northeast side of town, 1.5km out along Avda de Buenos Aires (the Murcia road). Destinations Almería (6 daily; 1hr 15min); Granada (4 daily; 1hr 10min).

Turismo Pza de la Constitución 15, close to the cathedral (Mon–Fri 9am–2pm & 4–pm; June–Sept 5–7pm; ☎958 662 804).

ACCOMMODATION

Cuevas de María C/Ermita Nueva 52; ⓦ cuevasdemaria.com. Comfortable and good-value self-catering caves, fully equipped with TV, salon, kitchen and washing machine, but no wi-fi. It's near the cave museum; to find it, make your way there and give the proprietors a ring for directions (English spoken). €̅

★**Hotel Abentofail** C/Abentofail s/n; ⓦ hotelabentofail.com. Stunning boutique hotel in a refurbished Mudéjar medieval building 70m south of the Plaza de la Constitución. All the rooms are beautifully presented and most have beams and exposed brickwork; the slightly pricier options have more space. Two delightful rooftop suites come with their own jacuzzi and panoramic views of the town. €̅€̅

Hotel Mulhacén Avda Buenos Aires 41; ⓦ hotelmulhacen.com. This modern option, about a 10min walk from the cathedral on the way to Guadix station, has functional, en-suite rooms with a/c and TV, plus its own parking. The restaurant serves good local dishes. €̅€̅

Hotel Palacio Oñate C/Mira de Amezcua 3; ⓦ palaciodeonate.com. Just south of the Plaza de la Constitución, this is an elegant turn-of-the-twentieth-century hotel with a spa complex. Stylish rooms come with a/c, minibar, room safe and TV, and there's also an excellent restaurant. Free session in the spa and sauna for guests. €̅€̅

Pedro Antonio Alarcón A couple of kilometres north of the centre along Avda de Buenos Aires; ⓦ cuevaspedroantonio.es. A cave hotel on the other side of town beyond the train station, with a luxurious complex of 23 caves with pool, gardens and restaurant. €̅€̅

FIESTA DE CASCAMORRAS

Guadix and Baza are linked by old rivalries that are kept alive in the annual **Fiesta de Cascamorras** from September 6 to 9. At the outset of this festival, a man dressed as a jester and carrying a sceptre travels from Guadix to Baza in an attempt to retrieve an ancient image of the Virgin, over which the two towns have disputed ownership since the sixteenth century. However, to retrieve the sacred image from the church, he must remain unblemished and so, as he nears Baza, a huge reception committee awaits him armed with drums of used engine oil at the ready.

Needless to say, he is coated from head to toe in the stuff within seconds of crossing the city limits – as are a whole crowd of the Virgin's protectors – and the oily mass then squelches its way to the Plaza Mayor where, amid the tolling of church bells, the mayor (from the safety of a balcony) proclaims that Guadix has blown it yet again, after which the town lets rip on a three-day binge of celebration.

EATING AND DRINKING

★ **Boabdil** C/Manuel de Falla 3, 200m northwest of the cathedral; ⓦrestauranteboabdil.es. Rated by many locals as the best option in town, with *carnes a la brasa* (charcoal-grilled meat) and seafood (especially squid) the house specialities. €€

La Bodeguilla C/Doctor Pulido 4, 300m northeast of the cathedral. A wonderfully atmospheric old bodega-bar with a nice range of tapas and *raciones*. Try the *jamón* or *pimentón con sardinas*. €

Baza

BAZA, 44km northeast of Guadix along the A92N, is another old Moorish town, only worth a detour if you have time and transport. Approached through an ochre landscape dotted with weird conical hillocks covered with esparto grass, the town is slightly smaller than Guadix, with a web of streets encircling its ancient central plaza. As with many towns in these parts, it has a history dating back well into prehistoric times. A prosperous Iberian settlement here named Basti produced the remarkable *Dama de Baza* sculpture (see page 489) and the town remained a considerable centre under the Romans, and later, like Guadix, a focus of silk production under the Moors; it was especially renowned for its silk prayer mats. Also like Guadix, Baza also has a **cave quarter**, albeit less touristic, on the northern side of town, close to the bullring.

As you head on from Baza, possible destinations include the Cazorla Natural Park (see page 416), to the north, or the Almería coast via the A92N *autovía* with the option of a detour to Orce (see page 518), the site of sensational finds concerning early humans in Spain, and the prehistoric cave paintings at Vélez Rubio (see page 516).

Iglesia Santa María

Pza Mayor • Fri & Sun 10am–noon • Free

The impressive Renaissance collegiate church of **Santa María** and its eighteenth-century brick tower – added when the previous one collapsed during an earthquake – leads you to the pedestrianized Plaza Mayor. Built over an earlier mosque, the church's elegant **Plateresque main door** – attributed to Diego de Siloé – is worth a look and inside there's an interesting marble pulpit and elegant vaulting.

Museo Arqueológico

Pza Mayor s/n (entry to museum is on C/Alhóndiga) • Tues, Wed & Sun 11am–2pm, Thurs–Sat 11am–2pm & 6–7.30pm • Charge • ☎958 861 947

The town's small **Museo Arqueológico** preserves finds from Baza's ancient past, including a copy of the *Dama de Baza*, a magnificent life-size fourth-century BC Iberian painted sculpture unearthed in 1971 in a necropolis on the outskirts of the town. The original is now in Madrid.

Baños Árabes

C/Caniles 19 • Wed–Sun 11am–1pm & 6–8pm • Free • ☎958 861 325

A few minutes' walk east of Plaza Mayor, following Calle Cabeza then turning left along Calle del Agua, and then right into Calle Caniles, leads to the **Baños Árabes**, an impressive tenth-century Moorish bath complex – one of the oldest and most complete surviving in Spain. The building has been sensitively restored – winning it a national architectural prize – and the cold, lukewarm and hot rooms are wonderfully preserved, as are the stunning brickwork walls, *bóvedas* (vaults) and star-shaped ceiling windows. Excavations have also revealed the heating furnace and wood store.

Iglesia de Santiago

Pza de Santiago • Mon–Fri 7.30pm • Free

5

Close to the Baños Árabes, the **Iglesia de Santiago** is a fine sixteenth-century church built over a former mosque. Inside there is a magnificent Mudéjar *artesonado* coffered and painted ceiling in the nave and apse.

ARRIVAL AND INFORMATION

By bus The bus station is on Avda Reyes Católicos to the west of the centre, and an easy 5min walk to the Pza Mayor. Destinations Guadix (8 daily; 45min); Granada (14 daily; 1hr 45min).

Turismo Municipal C/Alhóndigas 1 (Tues, Wed & Sun 11am–2pm, Thurs–Sat 11am–2pm & 6–7.30pm; ☎ 958 861 325).

ACCOMMODATION

Hostal Casa Grande Ctra de Ronda 28, a 10min walk south of the centre; ⓦ hostalcasagrande.es. A welcoming and excellent-value *hostal* with immaculate non-smoking en-suite rooms with a/c, heating and TV. It also has its own very good restaurant next door, with a superb value *menú*. €̄

Hotel Anabel C/María de Luna 3, four blocks east of the Pza Mayor; ⓦ hotelanabelbaza.com. This quiet, central hotel offers very comfortable and modern rooms with a/c, heating and TV. There's also a good bar-restaurant. €̄

EATING AND DRINKING

Bar La Dama Pza de las Eras, 100m south of the Pza Mayor. Pleasant terrace on the square near the Parque de la Alameda and a reliable option for breakfast, tapas and *raciones* including *pinchos morunos* (spicy kebabs) and *fried fish*. €̄

Casino Bastetano Pza Mayor s/n; ☎ 637 050 428. The town's Casino has a nice terrace on the south side of the Plaza Mayor – a great place for watching the world go by as you have a coffee or breakfast. They also serve up tapas and cocktails later in the day. €̄

Mesón Los Moriscos C/Cava Alta 3, 100m southwest of the Pza Mayor; ☎ 958 703 632. A little restaurant that lives up to its name and dishes up fine tapas and *platos combinados* in a mini-Alhambra-inspired dining room. €̄€̄

La Calahorra

The spectacular domed Renaissance **castle** of La Calahorra is most easily visited by car – continue southeast of Guadix along the A92 to Almería and the castle heaves into view at the 16km point. A turn-off to the right takes you the 4km to the village of **LA CALAHORRA**, where, on a hill above it, this brooding red stone monster dominates the landscape.

Castillo La Calahorra

Pza del Castillo • Wed only, 10am–1pm & 4–6pm; outside these times access is possible by visiting C/de los Claveles 2 in the village (☎ 958 677 098; avoid siesta time), home of the guardian, Antonino Tribáldoz, who (for a donation) will open it for you • Charge • Four daily buses from Gaudix (45min)

Constructed between 1509 and 1512, **Castillo La Calahorra** was owned by one Rodrigo de Mendoza, the bastard son of the powerful Cardinal Mendoza, who did much to establish Isabel on the throne. Rodrigo, created marquis of Zenete by Isabel, acquired a taste for the Renaissance during an Italian sojourn, and ordered the castle to be designed by an Italian architect as a wedding gift for his wife, María de Fonseca. The bleak location proved unattractive both to them and to their descendants, however, and it was rarely used.

Once inside, you'll be able to view an exquisite Renaissance **patio** – the last thing you'd expect behind such a dour exterior. The doorways, arches and stairway of this two-storey courtyard are beautifully carved from Carrara marble. Some of the palace's rooms have finely crafted *artesonado* ceilings and there's also a curious women's prison. Leave any vehicle at the bottom of the boulder-strewn track leading up to the castle and walk up to avoid severe damage to the underside of your car.

ACCOMMODATION AND EATING

Hospedería del Zenete Ctra La Ragua 1; ⓦ hospederiadelzenete.com. This four-star hotel on the northern outskirts is the village's luxury option and has great views of the castle from most rooms (make sure to request this). If you ring at least 24hr ahead they will arrange a guided visit to the castle for you. The restaurant has good *raciones* and more formal dishes such as *confit de pato a la miel de romero* (duck breast in rosemary honey) and *conejo a la brasa con alioli* (grilled rabbit with aioli). €€

Hostal-Restaurante La Bella Ctra de Aldeire 1; ⓦ hostallabella.com. A budget option in the village proper, with comfortable a/c rooms with TV; a couple on the front also have castle views. The restaurant below is pretty good too, and offers a cheap weekday *menú*. €̄

Puerto de la Ragua

From La Calahorra, a lonely but scenic mountain road – the A337 – toils south to the **Puerto de la Ragua**, at 1993m Andalucía's highest all-weather pass. The hairpin climb offers spectacular views back over the plain of the Hoya de Guadix and the rose-tinted La Calahorra castle. The pass itself can be chilly even in high summer.

INFORMATION   PUERTO DE LA RAGUA

National park information centre In the *refugio* at the top of the pass (open by phone appointment only, ☏ 958 980 246); they can provide maps of the area.

Towards Almería

East beyond La Calahorra, the A92 crosses the border into Almería and passes by **FIÑANA**, with another **castle**, this time Moorish and in a more ruinous state, and a well-preserved Moorish **mezquita**. Some 25km further on there's a turn-off for **GÉRGAL**, with another well-preserved fortress and, on the highest summit of the Sierra de los Filabres behind, an **observatory** housing one of the largest telescopes in Europe, sited here by a German-Spanish venture to take advantage of the almost constantly clear skies (see page 520). The A92 gradually descends into the valley of the Río Andarax – where you could detour to the prehistoric site of Los Millares (see page 483) – which it follows for the final 15km to Almería.

Almería

Cuando Almería era Almería
Granada era su alquería

When Almería was Almería
Granada was but its farm.   *Traditional Almerían couplet*

ALMERÍA is a pleasant and largely modern city, spread at the foot of a stark grey hill dominated by a magnificent Moorish fort. Founded by the Phoenicians and developed by the Romans, who named it Portus Magnus, it was as a Moorish city – renamed al-Mariyat (The Mirror of the Sea) – that Almería grew to prominence. The sultan Abd ar-Rahman I began the building programme soon after the conquest, in 713, with an arsenal beside the port, and the great **Alcazaba**, still the town's dominant feature, was added in the tenth century by Abd ar-Rahman III when the city formed part of the Cordoban caliphate.

The city's other sights pale by comparison, though it is worth taking time to look over the **cathedral** and, nearby, Andalucía's regional **photographic museum**. More sights surround the focal **Puerta de Purchena** where some remarkable **air-raid shelters** from the Civil War are open for visits; to the east lies the city's striking **archeological museum**, which should not be missed.

The city **beach**, southeast of the centre beyond the railway lines, is long but crammed for most of the summer. For a day-trip, the best options are Cabo de Gata or San José, both easily accessible by bus.

5

Brief history

The splendours created here by the **Moors** – most of which have been lost – inspired the popular rhyme at the beginning of this section, contrasting this early prosperity with the much later glories of Nasrid Granada. After the collapse of Moorish Córdoba, Almería's prosperity was hardly affected and, as a principality or *taifa* state, it became the country's major port, famed for its exports of silk, as well as a pirates' nest feared

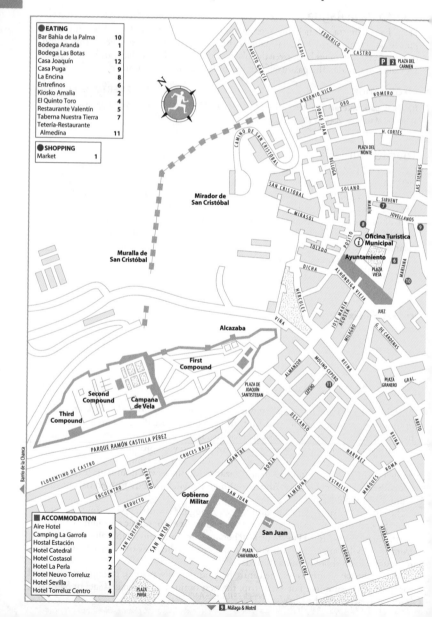

● **EATING**

Bar Bahía de la Palma	10
Bodega Aranda	1
Bodega Las Botas	3
Casa Joaquín	12
Casa Puga	9
La Encina	8
Entrefinos	6
Kiosko Amalia	2
El Quinto Toro	4
Restaurante Valentín	5
Taberna Nuestra Tierra	7
Tetería-Restaurante Almedína	11

● **SHOPPING**

Market	1

■ **ACCOMMODATION**

Aire Hotel	6
Camping La Garrofa	9
Hostal Estación	3
Hotel Catedral	8
Hotel Costasol	7
Hotel La Perla	2
Hotel Neuvo Torreluz	5
Hotel Sevilla	1
Hotel Torreluz Centro	4

around the adjacent coasts. This period ended when the city fell to the forces of Fernando in 1490 and the Moors were expelled. Their possessions and lands were doled out to the officers of the conquering army, forming the basis for the *señoritismo* that has plagued Almería and Andalucía throughout modern times. Predictably, there followed a prolonged decline over the next three hundred years, reversed only by the introduction of the railway and the building of a new harbour in the nineteenth

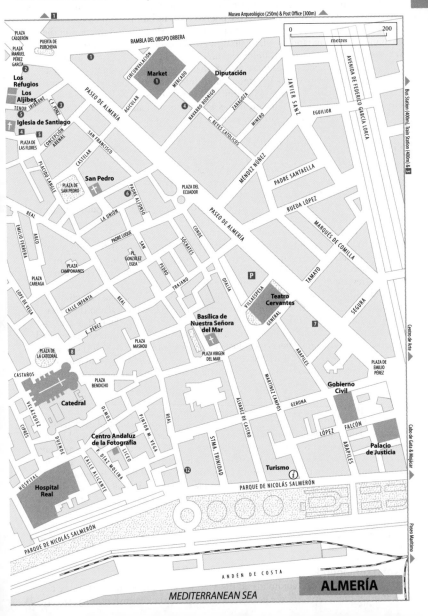

ALMERÍA

5

century, as well as the opening up to exploitation of the province's vast mineral wealth, particularly iron, lead and gold.

The **Civil War** interrupted this progress. The city's communist dockworkers gave staunch backing to the Republic, at one point in 1937 causing that the city be subjected to aerial bombardment and shelled from offshore by the German fleet (see page 497). It was one of the last cities to fall to Franco's forces in 1939, after which many suicides took place to avoid the fate planned for the most bitter enemies of the new order.

Although still the centre of one of the poorest areas in Europe, Almería today has found a more prosperous future based upon intensive vegetable production in the surrounding *vega*, in tandem with gaining a greater share of Spain's tourist economy. While even its most devoted admirers wouldn't describe it as a beautiful place, the provincial capital deserves more visitors than it gets. Enjoying something of a renaissance, the city has sunk enormous funds into smartening up the town centre, which has areas with considerable charm. Add to this a handful of fascinating sights and a friendly welcome in some great bars and restaurants, and you may be induced to give it a bit longer than the customary one-night transit.

Alcazaba

C/Almanzor s/n • April to mid-June Tues–Sat 9am–8.30pm, Sun 9am–3.30pm; mid-June to mid-Sept Tues–Sat 9am–3pm & 7–10pm, Sun 9am–3pm; mid-Sept to March Tues–Sat 9am–6pm, Sun 9am–3pm • Charge • ☎ 950 801 008

The **Alcazaba**, begun by Abd ar-Rahman III of Córdoba in 955, was just one part of a massive building programme that included a great mosque and city walls. During the eleventh century, when the city enjoyed a period of prosperous independence between the fall of the Cordoban caliphate and its capture by the Almoravids, the medina (walled city) here contained immense gardens and palaces and housed some twenty thousand people. It was adapted after the *Reconquista* by the Catholic monarchs but severely damaged during a great earthquake in 1522. A programme of restoration has begun to reverse the centuries of crumbling decay.

The Alcazaba can be reached by following any of the narrow streets that climb the hill west of the cathedral, aiming for the entrance below the walls in the Plaza Joaquín Santisteban, at the end of Calle Almanzor. Through the **Puerta Exterior**, a zigzagged entrance ramp – a traditional Moorish architectural feature to make attack precarious – leads to the **Puerta de la Justicia**, the gateway to the first of the Alcazaba's three great compounds. Halfway up the ramp to the right is the **Tower of Mirrors**, a fifteenth-century addition, where mirrors were employed to communicate with ships approaching the port below.

First compound

The **first compound** is the largest of the three. Now filled with delightful gardens and aromatic plants, it was originally designed as a military camp and an area in which the populace could seek protection when under siege. A **well** in the centre of this area raised water from a depth of 70m to supply the site. At the eastern end of the enclosure, the **Saliente Bastión** was a lookout point over the town below, and the sea beyond.

Below the north side of the compound, the **eleventh-century wall** (Muralla de San Cristóbal) descends the hill; it originally formed part of a great complex of walls, not only surrounding the city but also dividing it internally. Above the wall, which divides the first and second compounds, is the **Campana de Vela**, a bell erected during the eighteenth century to announce ships sighted nearing the port, or to summon soldiers to their battle stations.

Second compound

The **second compound** accommodated the Moorish kings, when resident in the city, and at other times served as the governor's quarters. In the eleventh century, when

Almería was the wealthiest, most commercially active city of Spain, the buildings here were of unparalleled brilliance. Their grandeur was even reputed to rival the later court of Granada, but the ruins that remain today make a valid comparison impossible.

What you can see, however, are the remains of **cisterns**, the old **mosque** – converted into a chapel by the Reyes Católicos – and once palatial dwellings, but sadly no sign of the magnificent stuccowork said to equal that of the Alhambra, the last remnants of which were sold off by the locals in the eighteenth century. The **Ventana de Odalisca**, a *mirador* window in the compound's northern wall, is a poignant reminder of lost glory. A legend attached to this concerns an eleventh-century Moorish slave-girl, Galiana, the king's favourite, who fell in love with a prisoner and arranged to help him escape. But the guards discovered them in the attempt and the prisoner threw himself from this window into the valley below, while Galiana died of a broken heart a few days later. Archeological excavations here have uncovered Moorish bath houses and other structures.

Third compound

The **third** and **highest compound** demonstrates the starkly contrasting style of the conquering Christians. When they took the city, the Catholic monarchs found the fortress substantially damaged due to an earthquake a couple of years before. They therefore built walls much stronger than the original Moorish structure, to cope with both potential future earthquakes and the innovation of artillery. Triangular in form, this upper fort is guarded by three semicircular towers built of ashlar masonry, both features at odds with the earlier Moorish design.

To the right, the **Torre del Homenaje** (Tower of Homage) bears the crumbling escutcheon of the Catholic monarchs and looks out over the **Patio de Armas** (Courtyard of Arms) where the guard would be assembled. From the **Torre de Pólvora** (Gunpowder Tower) and the battlements (take care as there are few handrails) fine views are to be had of the coast and of Almería's *gitano* cave quarter – the Barrio de la Chanca (see page 497) – on a low hill to the west.

Catedral de la Almería

Pza de la Catedral • s/n Mon–Fri 10am–7pm, Sat 10am–7pm, Sun 3–6pm • Charge • ☎ 605 429 979

Like the Alcazaba, the **Catedral**, in the heart of the old quarter, also has a fortress look about it. Begun in 1524 on the site of the great mosque – conveniently destroyed by the 1522 earthquake – it was designed in the late-Gothic style by Diego de Siloé, the architect of the cathedral at Granada (see page 447). Because of the danger of attack in this period from Barbarossa and other Turkish and North African pirate forces, the corner towers once held cannons. The threat was real and not long after its construction the cathedral chapter is recorded purchasing guns, muskets and gunpowder.

Like many of Andalucía's cathedrals, it was never completely finished and it may be that the city's inhabitants had no great affection for this austere giant, preferring instead their more intimate parish churches. The **exterior** is of little interest apart from a curious, pagan-looking relief of a garlanded radiant sun on the eastern wall – that is, facing the rising sun. Echoing the Roman Sol Invictus, or unconquerable sun, its appearance on the church has been put down to a sixteenth-century bishop with masonic leanings, but its true significance will probably never be known. Appropriately, as the province with the highest sun-hours statistic in Spain, Almería now uses the image as its official logo.

The interior

The cathedral is entered through the Puerta Principal, an elegant Renaissance doorway flanked by buttresses. Within, the sober Gothic **interior** is distinguished by some

5

superb sixteenth-century choir stalls carved in walnut by Juan de Orea. Just behind this, the **retrochoir** is a stunning eighteenth-century altar in contrasting red and black jasper. Behind the Capilla Mayor (or high altar) with some elegant and sinuous vaulting, the Capilla de la Piedad has a painting of the *Annunciation* by Alonso Cano and *Immaculate Conception* by Murillo, while the Capilla de Santo Cristo – next door to the right – contains the sixteenth-century sculptured tomb of Bishop Villalán, the cathedral's founder, complete with faithful hound at his feet. Further along again, a door (often closed) leads to the sacristy and a rather uninspiring Renaissance cloister – relieved by a small garden with palms and orange trees. The church also contains a number of fine **pasos** of the Passion carried in the Semana Santa processions at Easter; among these, *El Prendimiento* (the Arrest of Christ) is outstanding.

Centro Andaluz de la Fotografía

C/Pintor Diaz Molina s/n • Daily 11am–2pm & 5.30–9.30pm • Free • ⓦ centroandaluzdelafotografia.es

Housed in a converted nineteenth-century theatre, the **Centro Andaluz de la Fotografía** is Andalucía's first photo museum, often staging interesting exhibitions of work by *andaluz* and international photographers.

San Juan

C/General Luque s/n • Open for services only, usually 8pm April–Sept, 7pm Oct–March • Free

The seventeenth-century church of **San Juan** was built over the Moorish city's tenth-century main mosque. As with the Alcazaba, this was raised at the behest of Abd ar-Rahman III in 965 with three naves and a capacity for nine thousand worshippers. Inside, the church's southern wall survives from the original mosque and preserves the *mihrab* (prayer niche) of the original building. Now largely bare stone, this was once decorated with the finest *yesería* (plasterwork), tantalizing fragments of which survive. Next to this, there's another niche that would have contained the *minbar* or wooden pulpit used for readings from the Koran.

Plaza Vieja

To the north of the cathedral, the **Plaza Vieja** (officially Plaza de la Constitución) is a wonderful pedestrian square which – because of its restricted entrance – you would hardly know was there. It contains the **Ayuntamiento**, a flamboyant early twentieth-century building with a brown-and-cream facade and a monument to citizens put to the firing squad in 1824 for opposing the tyrannical reign of Fernando VII.

Around the Puerta de Purchena

Further sights, including the city **market** (see page 500), are located within a couple of minutes' walk of the **Puerta de Purchena**, the city's major traffic intersection, taking its name from a Moorish gate – long gone – where al-Zagal, the city's last Moorish ruler, surrendered to the Catholic monarchs in 1490.

Los Aljibes

C/Tenor Iribarne s/n • Tues–Thurs & Sun 10.30m–1.30pm, Fri & Sat 10.30am–1.30pm & 6–9pm • Free • ☏ 950 273 039

On the west side of the Puerta de Purchena junction are some well-preserved eleventh-century Moorish water cisterns – known as **Los Aljibes**. Constructed at the command of Jairán, the then *taifa* (independent) ruler of Almería, the *aljibes* were supplied by underground conduits channelling water obtained from springs in the surrounding hills. They were capable of holding more than six thousand litres of water, sufficient to supply thirty thousand inhabitants, the size of the city's population at that time. Inside, you can see the cistern's three brick-constructed naves and caliphal arches as well as the odd recycled Roman pillar.

Los Refugios

Pza Manuel Pérez García s/n • Obligatory guided tours; book in advance online • Charge • ⓦ almeriacultura.com

Off the southwest side of the Puerta de Purchena is the remarkable **Los Refugios**, a series of underground air-raid shelters used by the city's population during the Civil War bombardments by Nazi and Italian aircraft and naval forces. Between February 1937 and the spring of 1938 city engineers (using experience gained in the province's mining industry) constructed no less than 4.5km of tunnels beneath the city with 67 access points to shelter 35,000 citizens. Much of the rest of the then fifty thousand population took cover in the caves of the La Chanca district, now inhabited by the city's *gitano* community, or in private shelters. Open to the public as a museum, the tunnels are superbly constructed with ventilation pipes and shields to prevent fifth columnists throwing in hand grenades, and there is also an operating theatre. Visible too throughout the tunnels are the poignant graffiti and children's sketches scratched into the walls by those who sheltered here.

Calle de las Tiendas and around

Just west of the Puerta de Purchena **Calle de las Tiendas** – the oldest street in the city – was formerly called Calle Lencerías (Drapers' Street) and in the nineteenth century was Almería's most fashionable shopping thoroughfare. Some of the street lamps survive from this period.

Iglesia de Santiago

C/de las Tiendas • Mon–Fri 9.30am–noon & 7–8pm • Free

The **Iglesia de Santiago** dates from the same period as the cathedral, and is built with stone from the same quarry. A fine Plateresque portal incorporates a statue of Santiago slaying the Moors as well as scallop shells associated with the saint's shrine in Galicia, plus the coat of arms of the all-powerful Bishop Villalán, the cathedral's founder.

East of the centre

Some 300m east of the market, the **Avenida de Federico García Lorca**, formerly an unsightly dry riverbed bisecting the city from north to south, has been dramatically transformed into a stately avenue with palms, fountains and newsstands. It's a great place for a stroll, perhaps taking a coffee or a beer on a terrace of one of its numerous cafés.

Museo Arqueológico

Ctra de Ronda 91 • Tues–Sun 9am–9pm, Weds–Sat 9am–3pm; Sun & holidays 9am–3pm • Charge • ☏ 950 016 256

Almería's **Museo Arqueológico**, an impressive hi-tech museum to the east of the city centre, is well worth a visit. The main attraction for most is the first-floor display of finds from the remarkable Chalcolithic site at **Los Millares** (see page 483), which are superbly displayed. There is also an informative maquette depicting how the site would have looked at its zenith in the third millennium BC. The second floor displays more finds from Los Millares plus other prehistoric sites in the province, and has sections dealing with funerary rites and burial customs. The third floor is devoted to Almería province's Roman and Moorish past, with some particularly outstanding ceramics from the latter.

Barrio de la Chanca

To the west of the centre lies the **Barrio de la Chanca**, an area of grinding poverty occupied by *gitanos* and hard-pressed fisherfolk that has hardly changed since Brenan

5

ALMERÍA FESTIVALS

In August the city holds its annual **music and arts festival**, the Fiesta de los Pueblos Ibéricos y del Mediterráneo, with concerts and dance events, many of them free, taking place in the squares and various other locations throughout the city (details from either tourist office). The **Festival de Flamenco** with big-name artists performing on a stage set up in the atmospheric Plaza de la Constitución takes place in July. During the last week of the month, the city's main annual fiesta, the Romería de Augusto, also takes place with lots of street parties and spectacular processions with carnival giants.

vividly described it in his *South from Granada*; there are some occupied cave dwellings here, too, but it's not a place to visit alone after dusk.

ARRIVAL AND DEPARTURE   ALMERÍA

By plane Almería's airport (⟨w⟩ aena.es), 8km east of the city along the coast, handles scheduled budget services from the UK and other parts of Europe. Local buses make the journey from the centre; take line #22 (roughly every 1hr 10min, 6.45am–9.45pm) labelled "El Alquián", from the junction of Avda de Federico García Lorca and C/Gregorio Marañón.

By train and bus Almería's bus and train stations have been combined into a striking Estación Intermodal, Ctra de Ronda s/n, a couple of blocks east of Avda de Federico García Lorca. Train tickets are available at the station and any travel agent in town.

Destinations (train) Granada (4 daily; 2hr 30min); Guadix (6 daily; 1hr 20min); Seville (4 daily; 5hr 40min).

Destinations (bus) Agua Amarga (3 daily; 1hr 30min); Aguadulce (every 15min; 20min); Almerimar (3 daily; 1hr 30min); Cabo de Gato, via Retamar (6 daily; 55min); Carboneras (3 daily Mon–Fri, 1 daily Sat & Sun; 1hr 15min);

Córdoba (1 daily; 5hr); Garrucha (5 daily; 1hr 45min); Granada (7 daily; 2hr); Guadix (4 daily; 2hr); Jaén (3 daily; 4hr); Laujar de Andarax (3 daily; 2hr 15min); Las Negras (1 daily; 1hr 15min); Málaga (5 daily; 3hr); María (1 daily; 3hr 15min); Mojácar (3 daily; 1hr 10min); Níjar (4 daily; 1hr 15min); Rodalquilar (1 daily; 1hr 30min); Roquetas de Mar (every 30min; 30min); San José (3 daily; 45min); Seville (4 daily; 5hr 30min); Sorbas (2 daily; 1hr); Tabernas (6 daily; 40min); Úbeda (1 daily; 6hr 35min); Vélez Blanco (1 daily; 3hr 5min); Vélez Rubio (1 daily; 2hr 50min).

By boat There is a daily boat to Melilla on the Moroccan coast throughout the summer (less often out of season). It's a 6–8 hour journey, but one that cuts out the haul to Málaga or the usual port for Morocco, Algeciras. Check Wdirectferries.co.uk for details of sailings. There's also a daily 5–6 hour route to Nador (south of Melilla). For information and tickets contact Trasmediterránea (⟨w⟩ trasmediterranea. es), Parque Nicolás Salmerón 19, near the port.

INFORMATION

Turismo Parque Nicolas Salmerón s/n, at the junction with C/Martínez Campos (Mon–Fri 9am–7.30pm, Sat & Sun 9.30am–3pm; ☎ 950 175 220).

Oficina Turística Municipal Pza de la Constitución s/n (July & Aug daily 10am–2pm & 6–8pm; Sept–June Mon–Fri 9am–3pm, Sat & Sun 10am–2pm; ☎ 950 210 538). This helpful office has lots of information on the town and

province and gives out a free tapas bar guide. They also offer a guided tour in Spanish of the town, departing from their office (charge).

Useful websites ⟨w⟩ turismoalmeria.com, ⟨w⟩ almeriaturismo.es, ⟨w⟩ almeriacultura.com and ⟨w⟩ andalucia.org.

ACCOMMODATION   SEE MAP PAGE 492

Aire Hotel Pza de la Constitución 4; ⟨w⟩ airehotelalmeria. com. Stylish boutique hotel on this delightful square where rooms come with cutting-edge designer furnishings and decor, and lots of luxuries such as bathrobes and minibar. Public areas include *baños árabes* (Moorish-style baths). €€

Camping La Garrofa Ctra 340-A km435; ⟨w⟩ lagarrofa. com. Almería's nearest campsite lies 5km west of town on the coast at La Garrofa, and is easily reached by the buses to Aguadulce and Roquetas de Mar (where there's another giant site). There's plenty of shade and facilities include a

bar-restaurant and supermarket. €

Hostal Estación C/Calzada de Castro 37; ⟨w⟩ hostalestacion.com. Close to the train and bus stations, this *hostal* offers bright and cheery accommodation in decently furnished en-suite rooms with TV and a/c. Garage parking (extra) is available. €

Hotel Catedral Pza de la Catedral 8; ⟨w⟩ hotelcatedral. net. Elegant hotel in a nineteenth-century *casa señorial*, 20m from the cathedral's doorstep. Rooms are bright and stylishly furnished and the hotel has its own bar-restaurant.

€€€
Hotel Costasol Paseo de Almería 58; ⓦhotelcostasol. com. Central, comfortable hotel with spacious rooms; some on the front have terrace balcony. High-season rates drop considerably outside August. **€€**
Hotel La Perla Pza del Carmen 7; ⓦhotellaperla.es. The city's oldest hotel, refurbished from top to bottom in 2017, has played host to John Lennon, Clint Eastwood and various spaghetti western stars in its time. It has a/c rooms with satellite TV – some at the rear can be cramped, so check what you're offered. Can advise on parking. Rates fall outside Aug. **€€**

Hotel Sevilla C/Granada 25; ⓦhotelsevillaalmeria.net. Welcoming, modern, small hotel offering en-suite rooms equipped with a/c and TV. Public car park nearby. **€€**
Hotel Torreluz Centro & Hotel Nuevo Torreluz Pza Flores 8 & 10, ⓦtorreluz.com. One of the town's leading hotels, with outstanding-value two-star and four-star options in the same square. It's aimed at the corporate sector, which is reflected in the rather staid rooms. Garage. **€€**

EATING

SEE MAP PAGE 492

Almería has a surprising number of interesting and good-value places to **eat and drink**. Most of the best are around the Puerta de Purchena and in the web of narrow streets lying between the Paseo de Almería and the cathedral. The best place for early-evening **tapas** is around the Puerta de Purchena, where – especially at weekends – the whole town turns out during the evening *paseo* to see and be seen. Places around the cathedral and old town are more lively at lunchtime. As in Granada and Jaén, you get a free *tapa* with your drink, although here you can choose from an extensive list.

AROUND THE PUERTA DE PURCHENA

Bodega Aranda Rambla del Obispo Orbera 8, near the Puerta de Purchena; ☎950 237 597. This great tapas bar hums with life at lunch when local professionals come to grab a bite. In former days it was the "sordid" *pensión* where a penurious Gerald Brenan put up in 1921 (sleeping six to a room) while waiting for a letter with money from England – which never came. **€€**
Bodega Las Botas C/Fructuoso Pérez 3, just south of the Puerta de Purchena; ☎950 234 239. Very good tapas place with hanging *jamón serrano* shanks and upturned sherry butt tables; the excellent fino and manzanilla (served with a free *tapa*) go well with the *paella* and *gambas al pil-pil*. **€€€**
La Encina C/Marín 16; ☎950 273 429. This excellent mid-priced restaurant serves outstanding tapas in the bar at the front and creative and innovative rice, fish and meat dishes in a cosy restaurant at the rear (where you can see a Moorish well found during the restaurant's refurbishment). **€€€**
Entrefinos C/Padre Alfonso Torres 8, to the west of the market; ⓦentrefinos.es. Bodega and restaurant serving some of the best tapas in town and generous *raciones* including the *taco de salmón* (salmon) and the *solomillo estilo mozárabe* (Moorish-style beef fillet). **€€€**
Kiosko Amalia Pza Manuel Pérez García, off the Puerta de Purchena and next to the Refugios. A favourite terrace with locals for breakfasts, as well as churros, ice cream, snacks and their famous Americano coffee with Kola Cortals. **€**

★ **El Quinto Toro** C/Reyes Católicos 6; ☎950 239 135. Top-notch atmospheric tapas bar taking its name from the fifth bull in the *corrida* (reputed to always be the best). Friendly service and their legendary and mouthwatering *patatas a lo pobre con huevo* (potatoes with fried egg) are reason enough for a visit. **€€**
Restaurante Valentín C/Tenor Iribarne 19; ⓦrestaurantevalentin.es. This is a stylish upmarket restaurant and tapas bar noted for its fish, seafood and rice dishes. House specials include *cazuela de rape en salsa de almendras* (monkfish stew with almonds) and *bacalao al pil-pil* (spicy cod). **€€€**

AROUND THE CATHEDRAL

Bar Bahía de la Palma Pza Administración Vieja 1, next to Pza Vieja; ☎661 205 959. Great old bar and a good lunchtime tapas stop; they also serve *platos combinados* and a decent *menú*. Recorded flamenco music is often the accompaniment to the drinking here and some evenings they even put on live sessions. **€€**
Casa Joaquín C/Real 111, near the port. Fine, popular tapas bar that buzzes with contented drinkers most evenings. All tapas and *raciones* are excellent, especially the *seafood* and the prawns. No fixed menu prices, so ask for the price before you order. **€**
★ **Casa Puga** Corner of C/Lope de Vega and C/Jovellanos. With hams hanging from the ceiling and marble-topped tables and walls covered with *azulejos*, this is an outstanding tapas bar – founded in 1870 – with a great atmosphere and loyal clientele; try the *atún en escabeche* (marinated tuna) or *pinchitos* (pork skewers). If you can beat the rush you may be able to corner a table and make a meal of it. They also have one of the best wine cellars in Andalucía. **€€**
Taberna Nuestra Tierra C/Jovellanos 1, just north of Pza de la Constitución; ⓦtabernanuestratierra.com. Great tapas and *raciones* made with local ingredients only; specials are *tartar de arenque sobre sorbete de manzana* (herring tartare with apple sorbet) and *presa ibérica con ajos negros* (pork with black garlic). **€€**
★ **Restaurante Al Medína** C/Paz 2;

ⓦ restaurantealmedina.com. Very friendly little Moroccan-run *tetería* (tearoom), which serves full meals later in the day including tasty couscous and chicken and lamb tagines, with many vegetarian possibilities. They often stage live concerts of flamenco and North African music on Sat. €€

SHOPPING
SEE MAP PAGE 492

Market C/Aguilar de Campo. Located across the Paseo de Almería, the main street that leaves the Puerta de Purchena from its southern side, the colourful market is well worth a look.

DIRECTORY

Banks The major banks, most with ATMs, are along the Paseo de Almería; there's also an ATM at the airport.
Hospital The main infirmary is Hospital Torrecárdenas (ⓣ 950 016 000) in the northeastern suburbs.
Left luggage There are coin-operated lockers at the Estación Intermodal (train-bus) station.
Police Contact the Policia Municipal, Ctra de Níjar 68, off the north end of the Ctra de Ronda, to report thefts or lost property (ⓣ 950 621 206). In case of emergency dial ⓣ 092 (local police) or ⓣ 091 (national).
Post office C/San Juan Bosco 35 (Mon–Fri 8.30am–8.30pm, Sat 9.30am–1pm), to the right of the north end of Avda Federico García Lorca.

Costa Tropical

Almería's best beach resorts lie on its eastern coast, the Costa de Almería, between the city and Mojácar. To the west of the city, the nearest beaches such as **Aguadulce**, **Roquetas de Mar** and **Almerimar** are overdeveloped and the landscape is dismal, backed by an ever-expanding plastic sea of *invernaderos*, hothouses for cultivation of fruit and vegetables for the export market (see box, page 500). The plastic sea has now expanded west to cover most of the 30km-long Campo de Dalías plain and well beyond, and there's little to detain you until, beyond the large and ugly industrial town of Motril, you reach the **Costa Tropical**, the name given to Granada province's 60km of coastline. Here, along a coast of rugged cliffs peppered with inviting coves, lie the appealing resorts of **Salobreña**, **Almuñécar** and the more laidback **La Herradura**, all worth a visit.

Salobreña

Beyond Motril, the N340 road passes slopes dotted with almond and custard apple trees until, after some 10km, a spectacular vista opens up to reveal **SALOBREÑA**, a

---

PLASTICULTURA: ALMERÍA'S EL DORADO

West of Almería, and stretching from beneath the hills of the Sierra de Gador to the sea, lies the **Campo de Dalías**, a vast plain of salt flats and sand dunes that has become a shining sea of *plasticultura* – the intensive production of millions of tons of tomatoes, peppers, cucumbers, strawberries and exotic flowers. This industry has wrought quite a revolution in impoverished Almería, covering a once-barren wilderness with a shimmering sea of 64,000 acres of polythene canopies (producing twenty thousand tons of plastic waste annually) propped up by eucalyptus supports.

The boom is all due to the invention of **drip-feed irrigation** and it has led to phenomenal increases in the year-round production of crops, allowing cheap tropical fruit and flowers to fill the supermarket shelves of northern Europe throughout the year. The future of this miracle, however, may be precarious. Scientists have serious worries about the draining of the province's meagre water resources through the tapping of countless artesian wells – many as deep as 100m. For the moment, however, the Almerían farmers can count on the giant **seawater desalination plant** in El Ejido, one of the largest in Europe and capable of producing 30 cubic hectometres a year.

5

White Town tumbling down a hill topped by the shell of its Moorish castle and surrounded by a sea of sugar-cane fields. Comparatively undeveloped, the town is set back a 2km hike from the sea (#1 bus runs roughly every hour), and is thus less marketable for mass tourism, making it a far more relaxed destination than Almuñécar, its neighbour to the west. Beginning life as a Phoenician city dedicated to Salambo (the Syrian goddess of love), the town retained some importance in Moorish times – as the much-restored **Alcázar** reveals – but then languished in poverty until rescued by more recent prosperity, generated, in part, by its new trickles of tourism.

Below the Alcázar, down at the foot of the hill, the sixteenth-century church of **Nuestra Señora del Rosario** (open service times) stands on the site previously occupied by a Moorish mosque. There's also an animated **market** each Tuesday and Friday morning in the central Plaza del Mercado, but that's about as far as sightseeing goes.

Alcázar

C/Andrés Segovia s/n • Daily: 10am–1.30pm & 5.30–8pm (4–6pm Nov–March) • Charge • ☎ 958 610 011

On the eastern side of town, the **Alcázar** is worth a look, not least for the fine **views** from its crenellated towers. The hill topped by the fortress has long served a defensive role, and the first bastion here was built by the Phoenicians. This was expanded and added to by the later Romans, but it was in the Moorish period that the form it now has was finalized. The Nazarí rulers from Granada used it first as a prison before turning it into a summer palace.

ARRIVAL AND INFORMATION

By bus Buses arrive and depart from the Plaza de Goya at the entrance to the town, just off the N340.

Turismo Pza de Goya s/n (Mon–Fri 9.30am–1.30pm; ⓦ ayto-salobrena.org). They sell their own bilingual (Spanish and English) book of coastal and hill walks, *Rutas y Senderos de Salobreña*. A kiosko opens in summer (June–Sept Wed–Sun 5–8.45pm) on the Paseo Marítimo near El Peñón, the seafront promontory.

SALOBREÑA

ACCOMMODATION

Casas Faldas del Castillo C/Faldas del Castillo 16; ⓦ faldasdelcastillo.com. These two apartments (sleeping two) sit just under the castle. Sparklingly clean, they boast stunning views over the coast. Double rooms also available. €€

Hostal Mary Tere C/Fábrica Nueva 7, 300m southwest of the Turismo; ⓦ hostalmarytere.com. Attractive, pristine white *hostal* with en-suite balcony rooms with TV, a/c and heating above its own bar-restaurant. Guests can also benefit from discount beach loungers. €

★ **Hostal San Juan** C/Jardines 1; ⓦ hostalsanjuan. com. Perhaps the best deal in town is this friendly *hostal*, a couple of minutes' walk southeast from the Turismo. Situated in a beautifully restored townhouse with elegant patio, the en-suite rooms come with a/c and TV. Also has two nearby apartments. €€

Hotel Avenida Tropical Avda del Mediterráneo 35; ⓦ hotelavenidatropical.com. In town on the main avenue to the beach, this mid-range hotel has comfortable rooms with a/c, TV, safe, jacuzzi and sea or mountain views. €€

EATING AND DRINKING

La Bahía Playa del Peñón s/n. Slightly further back from the sea, but still with excellent views from its beach terrace, this has a better reputation then the adjacent *El Peñón*. House specialities include *fritura de pescado* (fried fish) and octopus. €€

La Bodega Avda de Motril s/n, effectively the Pza de Goya; ☎ 958 828 739. Reliable bar-restaurant offering well-prepared *granadino* cuisine – both fish and meat – in a rustic dining room. Octopus and seafood are signature dishes and there's a good wine list plus a reasonably priced lunchtime *menú del día*. €€€

Mesón de la Villa Pza F. Ramirez de Madrid, 200m south of the Turismo; ☎ 958 610 184. Inviting small restaurant with a terrace on this palm-fringed plaza. Serves a range of fish and meat dishes – *bacalao a la Villa* (cod with ratatouille) is a special – plus good tapas in its bar, and there's a reasonably priced wine list. €€

El Molino Paseo Marítimo s/n, 750m to the east of El Peñón; ☎ 647 701 056. A very good *beach restaurant* with a sea-view terrace, and a great place for fish and seafood. *Almejas al ajillo* (clams in garlic) and paella are house specials. €€

El Peñón Paseo Marítimo 1; ☎ 958 610 538. Sited on the seafront promontory (*peñón*) from which it takes its name, this is an extremely popular seafood restaurant with close-up views of the sea from its indoor and beach terraces.

5

Arroz con bogavante (lobster rice) is a signature dish. €€
La Portería C/Fábrica Nueva 1, 50m southwest of the
Turismo; ☎ 624 017 031. Perhaps the best of the economy
options in town, it's an excellent place for breakfast and,
later in the day, tapas, *raciones* and full meals. As well as
meat and fish they also offer decent salads and there's
a lunchtime *menú*. €€

Almuñécar

Fifteen kilometres west of Salobreña, **ALMUÑÉCAR** is Granada's flagship seaside
resort and, although marred by a number of towering holiday apartments, has
made admirable attempts to preserve its *andaluz* character. Founded early in the
first millennium BC by the Phoenicians as the wonderfully named Sexi, it possesses
ruins both from this and its later Roman and Moorish periods. The town's pebble
beaches, it has to be said, are rather cramped and not improved by the greyish sand,
but the esplanade, **Paseo Puerta del Mar** (aka Paseo del Altillo), behind them, with
palm-roofed bars (many offering free tapas) and restaurants, is fun. Almost hidden
among the plants, and in a rather dilapidated state, at the western end is the Laurie
Lee monument, erected in 1988 by the town in homage to the writer who lived
and worked in Almuñécar from 1935 to 1936. In *As I walked out one Midsummer
Morning,* he calls the town "Castillo". The *casco antiguo*, or old town, is atmospherically
attractive. There's an annual **jazz festival** – one of the most important in Spain, and
often attracting big names – held in July (🌐 jazzgranada.es).

Castillo de San Miguel

Barrio de San Miguel • April–Sept Tues–Sat 10am–1.30pm & 6.30–9pm, Sun 10am–1pm; Oct–March Tues–Sat 10am–1.30pm &
5–7.30pm, Sun 10.30am–1pm • Charge • ☎ 650 027 584

Almuñécar's impressive sixteenth-century **Castillo de San Miguel**, sitting atop a
headland – the Peñon del Santo – which bisects the resort's two bays, replaced
the Moorish Alcazaba, itself built on top of an earlier Roman fort, in the time of
Carlos V. Distinctive for its massive tower known as **La Mazmorra** ("the dungeon"),
this is where, in the Nasrid period, Granada's rulers imprisoned out-of-favour
ministers or overweening military commanders whom they saw as a threat. During
the *Reconquista* it was taken by Fernando and Isabel in 1489, three years before
the fall of Granada itself, and given the name of Almuñécar's patron saint. Held by
the French in the War of Independence, in 1808 it was bombarded by the British
navy and largely ruined, after which it served as the town's graveyard. The remains
have been dug up – bones, coffins and all – and relocated to a new cemetery
on the outskirts of town, and the castle restored. The interior now houses the
town's **museum**, containing artefacts and information documenting Almuñécar's
distinguished three-thousand-year history.

Museo Arqueológico

Pza Eras Castillo • April–Sept Tues–Sat 10am–1.30pm & 6.30–9pm, Sun 10am–1pm; Oct–March Tues–Sat 10am–1.30pm & 5–7.30pm,
Sun 10.30am–1pm • Charge, or same ticket as Castillo de San Miguel • ☎ 650 027 584

It's well worth stopping off at the small **Museo Arqueológico**, on the hill south of
the elegant Plaza Ayuntamiento (officially the Plaza de la Constitución, a name
nobody uses) in the Cueva de los Siete Palacios ("Cave of the Seven Palaces"), an
ancient structure that may well have been a water reservoir. The exhibits – mostly
discovered locally – are from the Phoenician, Roman and Moorish periods, including
an inscribed seventeenth-century BC **Egyptian vase** that carries not only the oldest
piece of written text discovered on the Iberian peninsula, but also the only known
reference to the early sixteenth-century BC pharaoh Apophis I, a ruler during the
hazy Hyksos period when foreign usurpers grasped the throne. If archeology is your
thing, ask at the Turismo for directions to remains of a first-century two-level **Roman
aqueduct** to the north of town.

Factoría de Salazones

Parque Botánico El Majuelo, Avda de Europa • Daily 8am–10pm • Free

In the Parque Botánico El Majuelo, a remarkable **Factoría de Salazones** or Roman fish-curing factory has been excavated. The tanks in which the **garum** was prepared are well preserved, and the quality of the famous fish sauce is recorded in the writings of Pliny the Elder. The surrounding botanical garden (open site) is extremely peaceful, with fine views towards the castle and walls.

Parque Ornitológico

Pza Abderraman • Daily: April–Sept 11am–2pm & 5–8pm; Oct–March 11am–2pm & 5–7pm • Charge • ☎ 958 882 735

To the south of the Castillo de San Miguel, the **Parque Ornitológico** is an aviary filled with a squawking collection of 1500 birds representing 120 international species including macaws, peacocks, owls, toucans and ducks.

Acuario Almuñécar

Pza Kuwait s/n • Daily: June–Sept 10am–2pm & 4–8pm; Oct–May 10am–2pm & 5–9pm • Charge • ☎ 958 882 735

Almuñécar's **aquarium** is a fun experience, especially if you've got kids in tow to entertain. Alongside the various tanks containing fish and crustaceans from around the world, the real highlight here is the water tunnel where sharks, stingrays, turtles and multitudes of other fish glide effortlessly through the water just a few centimetres above your head.

5

Ship House

Avda El Mediterráneo 34, near the N340 *autovía*

One remarkable but little-known sight is the astonishing **ship house** built by an ex-merchant sea captain, José-María Pérez Ruiz, in the northeastern suburb of the town close to the N340 road. After captaining his ship for thirty years, upon retirement Señor Pérez Ruiz decided to re-create his vessel on dry land – in concrete. When you approach the house you see nothing less than a 50m-long hull towering above the road complete with a bridge (now the captain's lounge and bedroom) sporting radar masts, radio antennae and all flags flying. The "deck" has all the paraphernalia of a real ship, and a swimming pool as well. Unfortunately, it's not open to visitors, but you should get a reasonable view from outside.

ARRIVAL AND INFORMATION
ALMUÑÉCAR

By bus The bus station is at the junction of Avda Juan Carlos I and Avda Fenicia, northeast of the centre.

Destinations Granada (9 daily; 1hr 30min); Málaga (9 daily; 1hr 30min).

Turismo Avda de Europa s/n (daily: July & Aug 10am–1.30pm & 6–9pm; Sept–June 10am–1.30pm & 5–8pm; ☎ 958 631 125). Located in a striking nineteenth-century neo-Moorish garden mansion, Almuñécar's provincial tourist office can provide copious information on the town and the Costa Tropical. The Turismo Municipal is located in a small kiosk on the seafront, at Paseo del Altillo s/n (Wed–Mon: July & Aug 10am–1.30pm & 5.30–8pm; Sept–June 10am–1.30pm & 4.30–7pm; ☎ 673 369 768, ⓦ almunecarinfo.com), providing information on Almuñécar and La Herradura.

ACCOMMODATION
SEE MAP PAGE 503

The pressure on **accommodation** in Almuñécar is not as acute as on the Costa del Sol and there are more than enough hotels to cope with the summer crush. Good-value *hostales* encircle the central Plaza de la Rosa in the old town and there are more to be found just east of here, in the streets off Avda de Andalucía. The nearest campsites lie 10km west at La Herradura (see page 505). The prices quoted here are for July and Aug; outside those months they can fall by up to fifty percent. In high season, some hotels require a minimum booking of two nights.

Almuñécar Playa SPA Hotel Paseo San Cristóbal s/n; ⓦ playasenator.com. The glaring terracotta exterior of this 225-room luxury hotel conceals a spectacular atrium lobby with waterfall and plants dangling from the glass roof. Not to everyone's taste, but you get four-star hotel facilities, including minibar and a pool. €€€€

Hostal San Sebastián C/Ingenio Real 18; ⓦ hostal-sansebastian.com. Clean, friendly *hostal* to the north of the town and with views of the *vega* (plain), offering colourful en-suite rooms with TV and ceiling fans. Can assist with parking. €

Hotel California Ctra de Málaga km313, northwest of the town on the main road; ⓦ hotelcaliforniaspain.com. Inviting, Moorish-style hotel with balcony rooms and bar offering evening meals with plenty of veggie options. Owners are keen paragliders and can also organize diving and skiing. €€

★ **Hotel Casablanca** Pza San Cristóbal 4 (aka Pza Abderramán); ⓦ hotelcasablancaalmunecar.com. With a wonderfully flamboyant neo-Moorish facade and interior, this family-run establishment is a gem. The service is friendly and the rooms, most with sea-facing terrace balconies, are well equipped. Own garage. €€

Hotel Helios Paseo San Cristóbal s/n; ⓦ heliosalmunecar.com. Long Almuñécar's leading hotel, the *Helios* offers tastefully furnished terrace balcony a/c rooms (mostly) with sea views, plus a pool and rooftop solarium. Breakfast is included. €€€€

Hotel Toboso C/Larache 2; ⓦ hoteltobosoalmunecar.com. Comfortable hotel a block south of the N340 offering a/c rooms with mountain or sea views plus garden and parking. Breakfast is included. €€

EATING
SEE MAP PAGE 503

There are countless **places to eat** lined along the Paseo Puerta del Mar, many of them offering cheap if unspectacular *menús*. The town's more interesting possibilities lie away from the seafront hurly-burly in the *casco antiguo* and beyond: Almuñécar has become something of a gastronomic hotspot and has a number of good restaurants. Nightlife centres around the focal Plaza Kelibia and the seafront Paseo del Altillo where a line of music clubs and **bars** – many with outdoor terraces – fill up on summer nights.

Bodega Francisco C/Real 15, north of Pza Rosa; ☎ 958 630 168. Wonderful old bar with barrels stacked up to the ceiling and walls covered with ageing *corrida* posters and mounted boars' heads. The fino and Montilla are both excellent, and the bar offers a wide range of tapas and *platos combinados*. Impromptu flamenco sometimes adds to the fun. €€

★ **El Chaleco** Avda Costa del Sol 37; ⓦ elchaleco.com. Slightly out of the way, this is a stunningly good-value Belgian-French restaurant with an outstanding kitchen. Among their signature dishes are *croquetas de pescado y mariscos* (fish and seafood croquettes) and *conejo a la flamenca* (rabbit cooked in beer with prunes). Add in very reasonable wine prices and you have one of the best dining-out bargains in Andalucía (which is why it's advisable to book). €€€

Mesón Antonio C/Manila 9; ☎ 667 391 947. One of the lively bars in the street and usually packed with locals, this *mesón* specializes in *carne a la brasa* (charcoal-grilled meat) and octopus. €€

★ **Mesón Gala** Pza Damasco 4; ⓦ restaurantegala.es. Slightly higher-end option, popular with locals and one of

several in an attractive square that's particularly lively on summer nights. Specials include *garbanzos con bogavante* (chickpeas with lobster) and *presa ibérica con salmorejo* (Iberian pork with thick tomato). Tapas available at the bar and on part of the terrace. €€€

Salitre Lute y Jesús Paseo Puerto del Mar; ☎ 602 418 694. One of a chain of three, this busy seafront fish restaurant reputedly serves the best *pulpo a la brasa* in town (charcoal-grilled octopus) as well as plates of tasty fried fish. €€

La Última Ola Paseo Puerto del Mar 4–5; ⓦ laultimaola. com. Excellent restaurant serving fish and seafood dishes, plus paellas (order in advance). Specials include salt-baked whole fish (bream, turbot, etc), depending on the catch of the day. Eat in the rather formal dining room or outside on the seafront. €€€

La Herradura

Beyond Almuñécar, the N340 passes tracks leading down to inviting coves with quiet **beaches**, a few of which have welcoming bars. After 8km the road descends into **LA HERRADURA**, a fishing village-resort with a long, sandy beach (pebbly in parts) making it a good place to stop off for a swim.

ARRIVAL AND INFORMATION   LA HERRADURA

By bus A daily bus service connects La Herradura with Almuñécar and there are stops along the seafront Paseo Andrés Segovia.

Turismo Municipal Paseo Andrés Segovia s/n, which is located at the extreme eastern end of the seafront (Tues–

Sat 10am–2pm; ☎ 629 069 467).

Windsurfing Windsurf La Herradura (Paseo Marítimo 34; ⓦ windsurflaherradura.com). Friendly and efficient windsurf, catamaran, kayak and dinghy sailing outfit that rents out gear and gives courses.

ACCOMMODATION

Hotel Almijara C/Acera del Pilar 6; ⓦ hotelalmijara. com. Just a short walk from the sea down the main street, this is a good, comfortable three-star hotel with light, well-equipped rooms with minibar and TV. Roof terrace with lovely sea views, but no pool. €€€

Nuevo Camping Paseo Andrés Segovia s/n, at the extreme western end of the seafront; ⓦ nuevocamping.

es. There are a couple of summer campsites with confusingly similar names; this is the best, with plenty of shade and good facilities. €

Pensión La Herradura C/Real 5; ☎ 958 827 644. This friendly *hostal* at the entrance to the town offers cheerful en-suite a/c rooms with TV, some with balcony. Own bar with tapas. Breakfast is included. €€

EATING AND DRINKING

La Barraca Playa de Cantarriján; ⓦ labarracacantarrijan.com. A popular bar and restaurant on the nudist Cantarriján beach west of La Herradura on the N340 road to Nerja (turn right at the roundabout after the tunnel, park and walk down to the beach), specializing in seafood and fish dishes. Live music several nights a week (check Facebook page for details). €€€

Mesón El Tinao Paseo Marítimo s/n, set back slightly from the seafront, 200m east of the market; ☎ 958 827 488. Atmospheric little bar-restaurant serving good tapas, *raciones* and full meals. They offer a great-value *menú de degustación* for two (including wine) and a fish and meat paella for two. Live music on Mon. €€€

Costa de Almería

The **Costa de Almería**, east of Almería, has a somewhat wild air, with developments constrained by lack of water and roads, and by the confines of the **Parque Natural de**

5

Cabo de Gata, a protected zone since 1987. If you have transport, it's still possible to find deserted beaches without too much difficulty, while small inlets shelter relatively low-key resorts such as **San José**, **Los Escullos**, **Las Negras** and **Agua Amarga**.

Further north is **Mojácar**, a picturesque hill village, which has become a beach resort of quite some size over the past decade. It is most easily – and most speedily – approached on the inland routes via Níjar (the A7-E15) or the "desert" road (N340A) through Tabernas and Sorbas.

Almería to Mojácar

The coast between Almería and Mojácar is backed by the **Sierra del Cabo de Gata**, which gives it a bit of character and wilderness. **Buses** run from Almería to all the main resorts, though to do much exploring, or seek out deserted strands, transport of your own is invaluable. The heat is blistering here throughout the summer, and you should bear in mind that during July and particularly August accommodation in the park is at a premium – try and book ahead if possible.

El Cabo de Gata and around

Heading east from Almería along the main AL12, and following a turn-off to the right, 3km beyond the airport, will take you south to **EL CABO DE GATA** (aka El Cabo). This is the closest resort to the city with any appeal: a lovely expanse of coarse sand, best in the mornings before the sun and wind get up. In the village itself there are plentiful bars, cafés and shops, plus a fish market.

Arriving at El Cabo, you pass a lake, the **Laguna de Rosa**, a protected locale that is home to flamingos and other waders. Four kilometres south of El Cabo, just beyond Las Salinas, is **ALMADRABA DE MONTELVA**, more a continuation than a separate destination, but an altogether more appealing place to hang around.

CABO DE GATA NATURAL PARK

Protected since 1987, the 71,500 acres of the **Cabo de Gata Natural Park** stretch from Retamar to the east of Almería across the cape to the Barranco del Honda, just north of Agua Amarga. The Sierra de Gata is volcanic in origin and its adjacent dunes and saltings are some of the most important wetland areas in Spain for **breeding birds** and **migrants**. At Las Salinas alone more than eighty species can be sighted throughout the year, including the magnificent pink flamingos as well as avocet, storks and egrets during their migrations. And there have been rarer sightings of Andouin's gull, as well as Bonelli's eagle and eagle owls around the crags.

Other **fauna** includes the rare Italian wall lizard (its only habitat in Spain), with its distinctive green back with three rows of black spots, as well as the more common fox (sporting its Iberian white tail tip), hare and grass snake. Among the **flora**, the stunted dwarf fan palm is mainland Europe's only native palm and the salt marshes are home to a strange parasitic plant, the striking yellow-flowering *Cistanche phelypaea*, which feeds on goosefoot.

The best times for sighting the fauna here are at **dawn and dusk** as, with temperatures among the highest in Europe and rainfall at 10cm a year the lowest, energy has to be conserved. There are seven official **Puntos de Información** in the park: at the Cabo de Gata lighthouse (see page 508), two near Isleta del Moro (see page 510), Pozo de los Frailes, near San José (see page 509), Playa de los Muertos, near Agua Amarga (see page 512) and the main centre at Rodalquilar (see page 510). There is also a private information office in the resort of San José (see page 509). The official offices should have free copies of *Cuaderno de Senderos* (in Spanish) detailing fourteen walks in the park of between 2 and 12km. Any hiking in the park is greatly assisted by using the Editorial Alpina 1:50.000 *Cabo de Gata-Níjar* map, which accurately marks trekking routes, tracks and campsites.

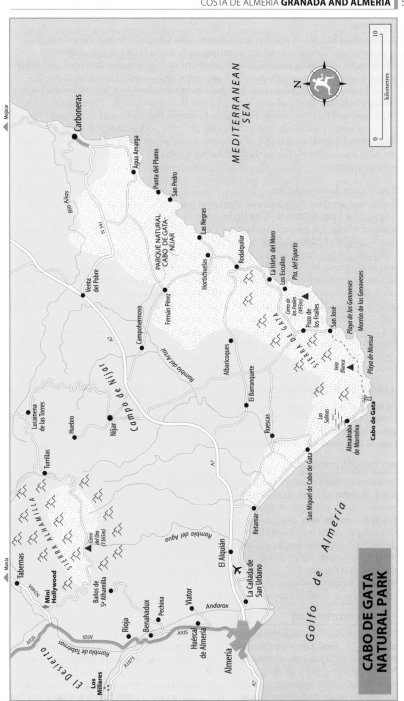

CABO DE GATA
NATURAL PARK

5

Las Salinas

Just south of El Cabo is another area known as **las Salinas** – the Salt Pans – and it is exactly that. The hills of salt are a striking sight in the bright sun, and there's a commercial salt-drying enterprise at its southern end. In summer **flamingos** and other migrants are a common sight here (see box, page 506), so take binoculars if you can – just before dusk is a good time. The park authorities have now installed **hides** (signed off the road). The local industry has a pedigree dating back to the Phoenicians, who began controlling the seawater that entered through the marshes to create pools for the extraction of salt in the first millennium BC. The park authorities like to cite the modern industry as an example of resource extraction and environmental conservation working hand in hand. Certainly the flamingos seem perfectly happy with the arrangement.

Beaches near El Cabo de Gata

Some 4km south of **Almadraba de Montelva**, past a hill known as the Pico de San Miguel, the **Faro de Cabo de Gata** (lighthouse) marks the cape's southern tip. There's a *mirador* here, from where you can get a great view of the rock cliffs and – on clearer days – a sight of Morocco's Rif mountains.

Beyond the lighthouse a track leads to two of the finest **beaches** in the province, and to the resort of San José beyond. This track is closed to cars, which is all to your advantage for it makes for a fine walk through the natural park. Starting out as a paved road, climbing up from the lighthouse, this soon degenerates into a dirt track, passing prickly pear cactus plantations grown for their fruit, and access tracks to the wonderful fine sand beaches of **Monsul** (6km out) – with freshwater springs and a track west to the even more secluded Media Luna cove – and further east, **Los Genoveses** (10km from the lighthouse). A couple of kilometres further, and beyond another spur, you'll sight the sea and the resort of San José. To reach San José **by car**, you'll need to double back to El Cabo de Gata and follow the signed road further inland.

ARRIVAL AND INFORMATION   EL CABO DE GATA AND AROUND

By bus Six buses a day run between Almería and El Cabo (55min), making an intermediate stop at Retamar, a pleasant holiday development.

Cabo de Gata Natural Park information In the Cabo de Gata lighthouse car park, 8km from the village (Easter week Mon–Sat 10am–2pm & 4–6pm; June Fri–Sun 10am–2pm & 4–6pm; July to mid-Sept daily 10am–2pm & 6–8pm) has maps and information on the natural park.

ACCOMMODATION

The seafront at El Cabo has a rather listless air and no places to stay; for **rooms** you'll need to head slightly inland. It's also possible to stay in Almadraba de Montelva.

Camping Cabo de Gata Ctra Cabo de Gata s/n; ⓦ campingcabodegata.com. Around 2km northwest of the resort and 800m inland from the sea, this is not the shadiest place to camp. But the facilities are good and there's a pool and restaurant. €

Hostal Las Dunas C/Barrionuevo 58, San Miguel de Cabo de Gata; ⓦ hostallasdunas.com. Set 100m back from the beach, this is a pleasant enough place where the functional rooms are en-suite with a/c, heating and TV. Parking. €€

Hotel Blanca Brisa C/Las Joricas, San Miguel de Cabo de Gata 49; ⓦ blancabrisa.com. Good-value and welcoming modern two-star hotel on the edge of town with comfortable a/c rooms with terrace balcony and TV. Also has its own bar-restaurant and parking. Four-night minimum stay in Aug. Breakfast is included. €€

EATING AND DRINKING

La Goleta Paseo Marítimo, San Miguel de Cabo de Gata; ☎ 633 877 878. About halfway down the seafront with frontline views of the sunset, this restaurant specializes in fresh fish and seafood, with *pulpo* (octopus) at the top of menu. The rice dishes – try the *arroz con bogavante* (rice with lobster) – are also good, and there's a *menú del día* on weekdays. €€€

Restaurante Bar El Faro On the road to the lighthouse; ☎ 950 160 054. Established in 1965, this friendly restaurant has stunning sea and lighthouse views from the terrace. Serves locally caught fish and seafood, and tasty *arroces* (rice dishes); the *arroz de la abuela* with meat and fish, and the *arroz negro* (black rice) are particularly good. Leave room for the home-made desserts. €€€

San José

The attractive little resort of **SAN JOSÉ** has a sandy beach in a small cove, with shallow water, while more fine beaches lie within walking distance. Two decades ago it was almost completely undeveloped, though things have changed, with a rash of apartments and a yacht harbour.

If you've followed the walk from the lighthouse to San José (see page 508) and want to continue along the coast there's another **track**, running 12km north to Los Escullos and La Isleta del Moro. To start the walk take the road north out of San José, along which you'll shortly come to a turn-off along a dirt track on the right that heads around a hill – Cerro del Enmedio – towards the coast. The track branches at various points and you'll have to decide whether to follow the coastal tracks (which can be impassable) or the surer inland route. The first track off to the coast provides access to a beautiful and secluded cove. Further on, the route skirts the 500m-high Cerro de los Frailes, beyond which lie the inlets of Los Escullos and La Isleta.

ARRIVAL AND INFORMATION   SAN JOSÉ

By bus San José is served by three daily buses from Almería (55min).

Natural Park information There's a privately run information centre for the natural park on Avda de San José, near the centre of the village (Mon–Sat 10am–2pm & 5.30–8.30pm, Sun 10am–2pm; ☎ 950 380 299, ⓦ cabodegata-nijar.com). They have lots of information on activities such as guided walks and horse treks in the area, plus a complete list of accommodation, including apartments to

rent. At Pozo de los Frailes, 4km from San José, you'll find a Punto de Información kiosko (check website for opening times; ☎ 670 944 951; ⓦ bit.ly/PozoFrailes), which also has information on the natural park.

Activities Horses can be hired for exploring the park from the *Hotel Cortijo El Sotillo* (see page 509). Alpha (ⓦ alphabuceo.com) is a PADI-certificated diving centre located in the Puerto Deportivo (marina), offering courses in snorkelling and scuba diving.

ACCOMMODATION

The only time it's difficult to find a room is during **high season** (July and August), when some places require minimum stays of at least four days (applying a surcharge for shorter durations). It's essential to book ahead in high season and advisable at other times of the year, too. As with other seaside destinations, rates fall by up to fifty percent outside July and August (we quote the high-season rates for the price codes below).

Camping Tau Camino de Cala Higuera s/n; ⓦ campingtau.com. San José's good campsite has modern facilities and plenty of shade. It's reached via a signed road on the left as you enter the village. Closed Oct–March. €

Cortijo El Sotillo Ctra San José s/n; ⓦ cortijoelsotillo. es. To the left on the main road in, and 1km from the centre, this is a refurbished eighteenth-century ranch house converted into a four-star country hotel with elegant, rustically furnished rooms, decent mid-priced restaurant, bar, pool, tennis courts and stables with horses for hire. Free parking. €€€

Hostal Brisa Mar C/Ancla s/n; ⓦ hostalbrisamar.com. Just south of the roundabout into the resort, this hostal has

bright and airy a/c en-suite balcony rooms with TV and a pretty garden. €€

Hostal Sol Bahía C/Correo 5; ⓦ solbahiasanjose.es. Near the main junction in the centre of the village, this is one of the better-value central places, offering spacious, a/c, en-suite balcony rooms with TV. €€

Hotel Doña Pakyta C/Correo s/n; ⓦ hotelpakyta.es. One of the swishest places in town, at the western end of the bay, offering light and airy terrace balcony rooms with four-star frills, stunning sea views and direct beach access. €€€

Hotel La Posada de Paco C/Correo s/n; ⓦ laposadadepaco.com. On the main street and slightly east of the main junction, this is a stylish small hotel with pool, spa and a/c terrace rooms with satellite TV. Breakfast is included. €€

Pensión Aloha C/Cala Higuera s/n; ⓦ pensionaloha. com. Good *hostal* with excellent a/c en-suite balcony rooms and the bonus of a fine palm-fringed pool at the rear; they also have a very good tapas bar below. €€

EATING AND DRINKING

There are numerous **bars** and **restaurants** on the central Plaza de Génova and facing the nearby beach on C/del

Puerto Deportivo, offering everything from fast food and pizzas to excellent fresh local fish.

5

4 Nudos Puerto Deportivo; ☎620 938 160. This is a harbourside restaurant where rice dishes (such as *arroz con pulpo y almejas* – rice with octopus and clams) and fresh fish are house specials. It also does a few meat dishes and has a pleasant terrace. €€€

Bar El Octopus C/Ancla 36, about 100m north of the seafront; ☎660 248 335. As you would expect, this small modern bar-restaurant serves octopus dishes – the octopus risotto is a house special – as well as tuna dishes and locally-caught fish. There's a small street terrace and weekly live music and jam sessions. €€

La Gallineta Pozo de los Frailes, 4km from San José on the AL-3108; ☎646 515 868. Set inside an elegantly furnished traditional house beside a restored Moorish waterwheel, this is the area's only place with any pretensions, serving up sophisticated Mediterranean meat and fish dishes. The very attractive dining room is complemented by some very good cooking and *cerdo ibérico* (black-pig pork), *arroces* (rice dishes) and paellas all feature, along with a "fish of the day" dish, too. €€€

La Pita Flamenca C/Correo s/n; ☎950 380 307. Near the roundabout at the entrance to the village, this friendly French-run place combines local dishes with Normandy cuisine. House specials include baked camembert and a homemade burger with three kinds of meat and vegetables. Serves healthy and hearty breakfasts, too. Live music on Sat July–Sept, jam sessions on Fri Oct–June. €€

Los Escullos

The village beyond San José along the rugged coastline is the isolated and peaceful hamlet of **LOS ESCULLOS**, 8km north by road. There's a good if rather pebbly beach and a formidable once-ruined – but now refurbished – fort, the eighteenth-century **Castillo de San Felipe**, one of the many built along the Almería coast as defences against pirates (only six remain). Cultural events and art exhibitions are occasionally held in the patio, itself free to wander around.

ACCOMMODATION AND EATING **LOS ESCULLOS**

Camping Los Escullos Paraje Los Escullos s/n; ⓦlosescullossanjose.com. The village campsite is set back from the sea with limited shade, but has decent facilities including pool, restaurant and shop. Comfortable wooden cabins also available. Five-night minimum stay in Aug. Camping €, cabins €€

Casa Emilio Paseo Marítimo s/n; ⓦhostalcasaemilio. es. This beachfront *hostal-restaurante*, offering a/c en-suite rooms with sea-view terrace balcony, is the best of a couple of options here, with a good bar and restaurant below. Breakfast is included. €€

La Isleta del Moro

LA ISLETA DEL MORO, 2km beyond Los Escullos, is a small fishing village that still manages to retain a sleepy atmosphere and has a rather scruffy pebble beach, although there's a better one – Playa la Ola – in the east of the village, backed by a car park.

INFORMATION **LA ISLETA DEL MORO**

Punto de Información kioskos One on the viewing point to the west of the village (June & Sept Fri–Sun 10am–2pm; July & Aug Tues–Sun 10am–2pm & 6–8pm) and at La Amatista, at the viewing point 1km out of village en route to Rodalquilar (June & Sept Fri–Sun 10am–2pm; July & Aug Tues–Sun 10am–2pm & 6–8pm), with information on the natural park.

ACCOMMODATION AND EATING

★ **Bar-Restaurante La Ola** Off the village's main square and set back from the beach; ⓦlaolarestaurante. es. The best tapas bar-restaurant in these parts, with a shady terrace. Wonderfully atmospheric, it serves up seafood tapas and *raciones*, plus great fish and *mariscos*. House favourites here include a mouthwatering *paella* and *cuajadera* (seafood stew). €€€

Pensión Isleta del Moro ☎950 389 713. This welcoming *hostal*-restaurante, overlooking the harbour, has reasonably priced en-suite sea-view balcony rooms, plus a decent bar-restaurant serving tapas and seafood. €€

Rodalquilar

The road north of La Isleta climbs over the cliffs above the village and heads inland before descending to a pleasant valley, passing after 4km the desert hamlet of **RODALQUILAR**, which is surrounded by scrub, palms and cactuses and was once a centre of gold and silver mining initiated by the Romans. Its nineteenth-century workings scar the crags behind the village, where a daunting edifice still bears the inscription in English "Guard Block B." You will also pass the lines of ruined miners' dwellings from this era along the entry road leading to a natural park information office (see page 511). Today the village has a vaguely "alternative" air about it and its desert location has attracted many artists and creative types who have houses in the village and around.

Jardín Botánico El Albardinal

C/La Fundición, next to the information office • June–Aug Tues–Sun 10am–1pm & 6–8.30pm; Sept–June Tues–Fri 9am–2pm, Sat & Sun 10am–2pm & 4–6pm • Free

This large **botanical garden**, divided into over thirty spaces, has been planted with plants and trees, some of which are endangered, native to the park or which have adapted to its semi-desert conditions. Named after the *albardo* plant, similar to the esparto grass, the gardens offer a unique insight into the area's flora, which is quite unlike any other in Andalucía. Allow an hour for your visit.

ARRIVAL AND INFORMATION   RODALQUILAR

By bus Rodalquilar is served by a single daily bus from Almería (1hr 30min).

Natural Park information office C/Fundición s/n, opposite the church in the centre (Thurs & Fri 9am–3pm, Sat & Sun 10am–2pm & 4–6pm; ☎ 671 594 419). Next to the office, the *Casa de los Volcanes* has an interesting exhibition on volcanic activity in the Natural Park (Thurs–Sat 10am–2pm; free).

ACCOMMODATION AND EATING

Bar Fidel C/Gorriones 4; ☎ 950 389 832. At the east end of the village, this friendly bar serves tapas (the choice changes daily), home-made burgers, and fresh fish and seafood. €€

Hotel Rodalquilar Paraje de los Albacetes; ⓦ hotelrodalquilar.com. An attractive desert inn on the village's eastern edge, with comfortable tile-floored rooms arranged around a sunken courtyard. Facilities on offer include a restaurant, pool, spa, sauna and gym. €€€

Las Negras

LAS NEGRAS, a pretty beach settlement 5km further along the coast beyond Rodalquilar, is situated in the folds of a beautiful cove, with an *atalaya* (watchtower) sited on the edge of the village as you approach. There's a pebbly beach backed by a few **bars** and eating places and that's about it. On the seafront, the PADI-certificated Buceo de Las Negras (ⓦ buceolasnegras.com) offers **scuba-diving** courses (beginners and advanced) and also rents out kayaks and boats.

ACCOMMODATION AND EATING   LAS NEGRAS

La Bodeguiya C/Bahía de las Negras 21; ☎ 950 388 142. Right on the seafront, this tiny bar with perhaps the lowest ceiling in the area has just a few seats inside and out, and very small tapas menu. However, the cocktails, sea views, atmosphere and nightly live music (jam sessions and concerts) make it well worth a visit.

Camping La Caleta La Playa s/n; ⓦ campinglacaleta. com. The village campsite, set in a tranquil location with its own bay, has some shade and good facilities including a pool, supermarket and restaurant. It's reached via a 1km-

long road signed on the right just outside the village on the way in. €

Hostal Arrecife C/Bahía 6; ☎ 654 619 816. A friendly and very good-value *hostal* just a stone's throw from the beach. The attractive en-suite rooms are spotlessly clean and come with a/c, TV and – the highlight – sea-view balconies. €

El Manteca Playa s/n; ☎ 950 388 077. Appealing seafront restaurant with a great terrace fronting the beach and where paella, fresh fish and *calamares fritos (fried squid)* are the main attractions. €€

San Pedro

If you fancy a change of beach scene, Buceo de Las Negras (see page 511) offers boat trips along the coast and to the ruined village of **SAN PEDRO**. If a boat isn't available, you'll have to walk – an attractive hike when it's cool – to visit the village with its

5

caves and ruined castle; it lies 4km north of Las Negras on a poor track. The place was inhabited until the 1990s when the mainly elderly residents upped sticks to Las Negras, which had acquired a road, leaving their houses – now occupied by northern European pseudo-hippies – to crumble. If you are feeling really energetic, you could walk 7km on from here along the coast to Agua Amarga, via two pleasant beaches at **Cala del Plomo** and **Cala d'En Medio**. If you attempt these walks, remember to wear a sunhat and take along drinking water as the only supply is at San Pedro and this dries up in drought years.

Agua Amarga

AGUA AMARGA, just short of the Cabo de Gata Natural Park's northern boundary, is a delightful little fishing village cut off from the surrounding world by a long road and limited accommodation. To reach it from Las Negras (a route not served by public transport) you'll need to head inland to the village of **Fernan Pérez**, from where a narrow road heads east for 11km to reach the small resort.

Many of the summer visitors here are Italians who rent a tasteful crop of villas. The excellent, fine sand **beach**, backed by a number of bars and restaurants, has outlets renting windsurf boards and canoes.

ARRIVAL AND INFORMATION   AGUA AMARGA

By bus Aqua Amarga is served by one bus daily on Mon, Wed & Fri–Sat from Almería (1h 30min).

Punto de Información kiosko En route to Carboneras (see page 512) at the entrance to the walk down to the

lonely Playa de los Muertos beach (June & Sept Fri–Sun 10am–2pm; July & Aug Wed–Mon 10am–2pm & 6–8pm), so-called because dead bodies from shipwrecks frequently washed up here.

ACCOMMODATION

Apartamentos Caparrós C/Aguada 13; ☎950 138 246. For longer stays (two nights-plus) this reliable agency has four fully equipped sea-view apartments with terrace, some fronting the beach. Minimum seven nights in July and August. €€

Family Agua Amarga C/La Lomilla; ⓦ familyaguaamarga.com. Friendly and charming French-run *hostal* set back from the south end of the beach, where attractive en-suite rooms (some with sea view) are complemented by a small garden pool and a very good restaurant. Breakfast is included. €€

Hostal-Restaurante La Palmera C/Aguada 4;

ⓦ hostalrestaurantelapalmera.com. Right on the beach, this friendly hotel has bright and cool en-suite rooms with a/c and TV. All have sea-view terrace balconies above a bar-restaurant serving tapas and *raciones*. Minimum two-night stay in August. Breakfast is included. €€

Hotel El Tío Kiko C/Embarque 12 ⓦ eltiokiko.com. On a rise behind *Family Agua Amarga* (see opposite), this luxury boutique hotel (adult-only mid-June to mid-Sept) has stylishly furnished terrace sea-view rooms arranged around a pool. Discounts on room rates outside July and Aug. Breakfast included. €€€

EATING AND DRINKING

Hotel las Calas C/Desagüe 1a; ☎950 138 016. The restaurant of this hotel offers pleasant dining on the beachfront terrace with a selection of reasonably priced fish and rice-based dishes such as *arroz con bogovante* (lobster).

€€

Los Tarahis C/Desagüe s/n; ☎950 138 235. With a sea-view terrace, this is a decent place serving fish and *arroces* (such as paella), as well as salads. €€

Mojácar and around

Beyond the Cabo de Gata Natural Park, **CARBONERAS**, 11km north of Agua Amarga, is a large but easy-going fishing port with an average beach slightly marred by the shadow of a massive cement factory around the bay. North of here lies a succession of small, isolated coves, backed by a characteristically arid Almerían landscape of scrub-covered hills and dried up *arroyos*, or watercourses. The **Carboneras–Mojácar road** itself winds perilously – and scenically – through the hills and offers access to some deserted grey sand beaches before ascending to the Punta del Santo with fine views along the coast. The descent from here brings you to the **Playa de Macenas**, another attractive beach before the urban sprawl of Mojácar takes over. If you turn right in Macenas and take the coastal track past the fine *torreón* (watchtower) for a few kilometres, you reach a couple of remote beaches, Bordenares and Playa **del** Sombrerico, the latter with a beach *chiringuito* (bar).

Mojácar

MOJÁCAR, Almería's main resort, is split between the ancient hilltop village – **Mojácar Pueblo** – sited a couple of kilometres back from the sea, a striking town of white cubist houses wrapped round a harsh outcrop of rock, and the resort area of **Mojácar Playa**, which ribbons for a couple of miles along the seafront.

In the 1960s, when the main Spanish *costas* were being developed, this was virtually a ghost town, its inhabitants having long since taken the only logical step, and emigrated. The town's fortunes revived, however, when the local mayor, using the popularity of other equally barren spots on the Spanish islands and mainland as an example, offered free land to anyone willing to build within a year. The bid was a modest success, attracting one of the decade's multifarious "artist colonies", now long supplanted by package holiday companies and second-homers. These days something of a tourist trap, the hill village has a plush 150-room hotel as well as a *parador* in the beach resort below, both symbolic of the changing times.

Mojácar Pueblo

The hilltop settlement of **MOJÁCAR PUEBLO** goes back at least to prehistoric times, and became prominent during the Roman period when Pliny described it as one of the most important towns of Baetica – as the Roman province was called. Coins found from this era give the Roman name as Murgis, which the later Moors adapted to Muxacra. The village's **main fountain** (the Fuente Mora) – signed to the right off the road climbing towards the centre – has been newly restored with lots of marble and geraniums and was where forty years ago veiled women still used to do the family washing. A plaque nearby relates how keen the Moors were to hang on to their hilltop eyrie when challenged by the *Reconquista*. First declaring loyalty to the Reyes Católicos, the Moorish mayor, Alabez, then stated that if the Catholic monarchs wouldn't accede to the request to be left in peace, "rather than live like a coward I shall die like a Spaniard. May Allah protect you!" The monarchs were impressed and, for a time at least, prudently granted Alabez's wish.

An ancient custom, no longer practised but parodied on every bangle and trinket sold in the tourist shops, was to paint an **indalo** on the doorways of the village to ward off evil. This symbol – a matchstick figure with arms outstretched, holding an arc – comes from the 6000-year-old Neolithic drawings in the caves at Vélez Blanco to the north, and anthropologists believe that it is a unique case of a prehistoric symbol being passed down in one location for numerous millennia.

Indalos apart, sights in the upper village are limited to strolling around the sinuous, white-walled streets, looking at the heavily restored fifteenth-century church of **Santa María**, and savouring the view over the strangely formed, arid surrounding hills and coast to the north from the **mirador** in the main square, Plaza Nueva.

Mojácar Playa

Down below on the seafront, **Mojácar Playa** is refreshingly brash: an excellent beach with warm and brilliantly clear waters, flanked by lots of fine beach bars and *discotecas*, rooms for rent, several hotels and *hostales*, and a good campsite. The beach resort's focal point is an ugly Centro Comercial, at the intersection – known locally as El Cruce – of the seafront highway with the road climbing inland to Mojácar Pueblo.

5

By bus Three daily buses run from Almería to Mojácar (1h 10min). Half-hourly buses run between the beach and Mojácar Pueblo; you can pick them up from a stop (known as "El Cruce") outside the Centro Comercial on Mojácar Playa, or at various stops along the seafront.

Turismo Pza Frontón s/n, in the square to east side of the church (Mon–Sat 9.15am–2pm & 4.30–7pm, Sun 9.15am–

2pm; ☎ 902 575 130; ⓦ mojacar.es). You'll need their free map to negotiate the maze of narrow streets here. It also covers the coastal strip and is a useful aid to getting your bearings.

Punto de información Small tourist office on the beach at El Cruce (Mon–Sat 10am–2pm; June–Sept also 4.30–7pm; Sun 10am–2pm; ☎ 902 575 130; ⓦ mojacar.es).

ACCOMMODATION

MOJÁCAR PUEBLO

Hostal Arco Pza Nueva, beneath the arch on the north side; ⓦ hostalarcoplaza.es. Just off the main square, this is a reliable option for a/c en-suite rooms with TV. **€**

Hostal El Olivar C/Estación Nueva 11; ⓦ hostalelolivar. es. Clean and comfortable *hostal* just around the corner from the Turismo offering en-suite rooms with a/c and TV. Friendly, helpful owners. Breakfast is included. **€€**

MOJÁCAR PLAYA

Camping El Cantal de Mojácar Ctra Garrucha–Carboneras; ☎ 950 478 204. A couple of kilometres south of El Cruce, the Mojácar Playa campsite has decent facilities, good shade, a restaurant and a supermarket. **€**

Hotel Apartamentos Marazul Paseo del Mediterráneo 279, 1km south of El Cruce; ⓦ mojacarmarazul.com. Fully equipped sea-view apartments, sleeping up to eight,

with a pool. Meals available at nearby *Hotel El Puntazo* (see below). Prices are almost halved outside high summer. **€€€**

Hotel El Puntazo Paseo del Mediterráneo s/n, 1km south of El Cruce; ⓦ hotelelpuntazo.com. This sprawling seafront hotel is one of the resort's top addresses and an obvious landmark. Attractive and well-equipped rooms come with sea views and lots of frills, including a pool. **€€€**

Hotel Sal Marina Paseo del Mediterráneo 261, close to the Hotel El Puntazo; ⓦ hotelsalmarina.com. Attractive and well-equipped a/c balcony rooms with sea views. Rates fall by thirty percent outside August. **€€**

Parador de Mojácar Paseo del Mediterráneo 339, just south of El Cruce; ⓦ parador.es. Mojácar's modern seafront *parador* is none too exciting, but offers classically furnished rooms with safe, TV and minibar, and many have a sea view. Public areas include a garden pool, restaurant and gym. **€€€€**

EATING AND DRINKING

MOJÁCAR PUEBLO

Casa Minguito Pza Ayuntamiento s/n, on the west side of the church, next to the town hall; ☎ 950 478 614. A good mid-priced restaurant for carefully prepared Spanish standards. Specials include fish and *mariscos*, and they do a two-person paella. There's also a *menú* and a terrace on the leafy square. **€€**

La Ermita Pza Nueva 1; ☎ 642 981 958. With a terrace and restaurant overlooking the village, this is a friendly spot for salads, fresh fish (the Garrucha prawns are particularly good) and grilled meats including lamb chops and home-made burgers. **€€**

MOJÁCAR PLAYA

Food along the seafront is generally dismal and overpriced,

with standards falling markedly in high season; we've selected a few of the safer places to try below. Most of the reasonable options lie to the south of El Cruce.

Casa Egea Paseo del Mediterráneo 127, 2km south of El Cruce on the seafront; ⓦ casaegea.com. On the seafront, this is a long-established and reliable restaurant specializing in fresh fish, seafood and local specialities such as stews. **€€**

Parador de Mojácar Paseo del Mediterráneo 339, just south of El Cruce; ⓦ parador.es. The *parador's* restaurant is perhaps the best place to eat on the seafront, with a bright and modern main room with panoramic sea views and an outdoor terrace. The kitchen serves a variety of regional dishes including fresh fish from Garrucha and there's a good-value *menú*. **€€€**

NIGHTLIFE

After dark you'll find plenty of **nightlife** in the throbbing beach bars and seafront *discotecas* of Mojácar Playa. Most of the action takes place along the coastal strip covering the 3km to the south of El Cruce, and there's little nightlife in the hill village.

Chiringuito El Cid Avda del Mediterráneo 34, Mojácar

Playa; ⓦ facebook.com/chiringuitoelCiD. South of El Cruce, this *chiringuito* has been on the beach since 1978. It serves food all day and cocktails at night when flamenco and jazz concerts take place (see Facebook page for details).

Mandala Beach Paseo de Mediterráneo 391, Mojácar Playa; ⓦ mandalabeachmojacar.com. About 650m north of El Cruce, this is one of Mojácar's most popular beach club. Lounge by the pool to chill-out music by day and/or party to concerts and DJ sessions by night.

North of Mojácar

North of Mojácar, there's a clutch of resorts – none of them much to write home about – and a few last sights of interest, before the road crosses Andalucía's border into Murcia.

Garrucha

A couple of kilometres north of Mojácar, **GARRUCHA** is a lively, if undistinguished, town and fishing harbour with a sizeable fleet. When this comes home to port with its catch in mid-afternoon, the ensuing auction at the port-side market is wonderfully entertaining. The fleet also lands a good supply of the seafood – the *gamba roja* (red prawns) are renowned, though pricey – served at the numerous **fish restaurants** lining the seafront harbour promenade, El Malecón.

PALOMARES AND THE H-BOMBS

Palomares was once at the centre of one of the world's biggest nuclear scares. Here, on January 17, 1966, an American B-52 bomber collided with a tanker aircraft during a mid-air refuelling operation. Following the collision in which many of the crew of both aircraft perished, three ten-megaton **H-bombs** (each one hundred times more powerful than that used at Hiroshima) fell on land and a fourth into the sea, just off the village. Those that fell in the fields were recovered quickly, though one had been damaged, causing radioactive contamination nearby. Fifteen US warships and two submarines searched for many weeks before the fourth bomb was recovered. On March 19, thousands of barrels of plutonium-contaminated soil were transported by the USAF for disposal in South Carolina. Nobody has ever convincingly explained how the incident happened, nor is it known why the bombs didn't explode, for the damaged bomb had actually lost its safety catch.

The fourth bomb made a fortune for local fisherman Francisco Simó Orts (known ever after as "**Paco, él de la Bomba**") who saw where the missile fell into the sea and aided the search to locate it. With the assistance of a lawyer he also – as the finder – claimed salvage rights under maritime law calculated at one or two percent of the value of the object salvaged. As each bomb was worth two billion dollars according to the Pentagon the sum claimed was twenty million dollars and Paco appeared at the New York Federal Court to make his case. The Pentagon duly settled out of court for an undisclosed sum. Palomares' world-famous fisherman died in 2003.

The story, however, is far from over. In 2004 when tests on plots designated for housing construction revealed significant **radioactive contamination**, the land was immediately expropriated by the Spanish government. In 2006 the Spanish and US governments agreed to share the cost of a further decontamination programme, and a survey of the area to determine how this should be done revealed abnormal levels of radiation in snails and other wildlife indicating dangerous amounts of radioactive material still in the subsoil. In 2008 it was revealed that scientists had located two highly radioactive trenches – near where one of the bombs had fallen – used by the US Army to bury contaminated earth following the incident in 1966. Further tests by US scientists revealed that **significant contamination remains** and in 2011, the US proposed to remove the contaminated soil but left the decision on where to take it up to the politicians. In early 2017, under pressure from the US, the Spanish government reduced the area to be cleaned from 55,000 cubic metres to 28,000, a move that ecologists have contested in Spanish and European courts. To date, the contaminated area remains fenced off and, until someone decides where to take the contaminated waste and who's paying for it (estimated costs range from €30 to €600 million), Palomares' radioactive soil is staying put.

5

Cuevas del Almanzora

From Garrucha, the road heads 9km inland, skirting the estuary of the Río Almanzora and the small farming town of Vera, to **CUEVAS DEL ALMANZORA**, 6km farther north. A town with a distinguished past, it has a number of sights, including a well-preserved sixteenth-century Gothic castle built to defend the settlement from piracy, and a handful of Guadix-style cave dwellings where evidence of habitation by Neanderthal and Cro-Magnon man was found. The castle – the splendidly restored **Castillo del Marqués de Los Vélez** – now houses an interesting archeological museum and the **Museo Campoy** displaying artworks by Goya, Picasso, Miró, Toral and Vásquez Díaz among others (opening times vary: charge).

Palomares

From Cuevas del Almanzora there's a road to the coast and the village of **PALOMARES**, of nuclear notoriety (see box, page 515). The rather curious feature of this otherwise dull hamlet is a church tower that resembles – with its rounded cone – an atom bomb. Near where you rejoin the coast, Vera's **Parque Aquático** (mid-May to mid-Sept daily 11am–6pm; till 7.30pm July & Aug; charge; ⓦaquavera.com) is a fun place to kill a couple of hours, especially if you're towing kids; it's got all the usual water features, and they allow you to take your own picnic inside.

Vélez Rubio to Orce

In the north of Almería province, two small towns are worth an excursion: at **Vélez Rubio**, there's a cave with important **prehistoric paintings** depicting the *indalo* (see page 513), while at neighbouring **Vélez Blanco** there's a fine Renaissance **castle**. Although both are served by two daily **buses** from Almería, transport of your own will make these detours much more rewarding.

Vélez Rubio

Inland from Cuevas del Almanzora, a rambling 60km drive along the A7 and A327 will bring you out at the town of **VÉLEZ RUBIO**, surrounded by sierras, olive groves and fields of cereals. It's no great shakes as towns go (Vélez Blanco is a better proposition for an overnight stop), but has some diversions.

A small town **museum**, inside the eighteenth-century Hospital Real, contains an interesting collection of artefacts and ceramics from prehistoric to Moorish times, with a section on the ancient cave paintings in this area (C/Carrera del Carmen 19; April–Oct Tues & Sun 10am–2pm, Wed–Sat 10am–2pm & 5–8pm; Nov–March Tues & Sun 10am–2pm, Wed–Sat 10am–2pm & 4–7pm; charge).

La Encarnación

Pza La Encarnación • Tues–Sun 11am–1pm & 5.30–7.30pm (6–8.30pm June–Aug) • Free

The magnificent Baroque church (Almería province's biggest) of **La Encarnación**, constructed in the eighteenth century, has an imposing carved facade that includes, above the entrance, the arms of the marquises of Villafranca y Vélez, who built it. Inside, the main altar has a superbly detailed, 20m-high carved wood **retablo**, and there's a splendid Baroque organ constructed in 1796.

ARRIVAL & INFORMATION   **VÉLEZ RUBIO**

By bus 1 daily from Almería (2h 50min) and 3 daily from Granada (1h 45min–3h 15min) to the bus station on Paseo de la Libertad in the town centre.

Turismo In the town museum, C/Carrera del Carmen 19

(April–Oct Tues & Sun 10am–2pm, Wed–Sat 10am–2pm & 5–8pm; Nov–March Tues & Sun 10am–2pm, Wed–Sat 10am–2pm & 4–7pm; ☎950 412 560; ⓦvelezrubio.org).

Vélez Blanco

5

Nestling at the foot of a rocky outcrop, the whitewashed village of **VÉLEZ BLANCO**, 6km north of Vélez Rubio, is a smaller and more attractive conurbation. Its main attraction is its **castle**, which looms over the town from the top of the hill.

Castle

Wed–Sun: April–Sept 10am–2pm & 5–8pm; Oct–March 10am–2pm & 4–6pm; guided tour weekends 10.30am • Free, small charge for tour • ☎ 607 415 055

Atop the hill is an outstanding Renaissance **castle** – an extension of the original Moorish *Alcazaba* – built by the marquises of Vélez Blanco in the early years of the sixteenth century. It is today something of a trompe l'oeil, with an empty shell behind the crenellated battlements: a gutting that took place as recently as 1904, after the castle was sold off by the impecunious marquis for 80,000ptas (€500) to an American millionaire, George Blumenthal. Blumenthal tore out the whole interior including the **Patio de Honor** – a fabulous courtyard carved in white marble by Italian craftsmen – and shipped it off to the United States. After service as this plutocrat's Xanadu, it has since been reconstructed inside the Metropolitan Museum of Art in New York. The castle's interior, much of it now supported by steel girders, has fragments of the original decoration. Given the Met's reluctance to return its dubiously acquired prize exhibit, a complete and exact reconstruction of the original using marble from the nearby quarries of Macael has begun. A book on sale in the small shop at the entrance – *El Castillo de Vélez Blanco* by Alfonso Ruiz García – has an image of the reconstituted patio in the New York Met, plus a watercolour of what it looked like in situ. Make sure to take in the fine **views** from the tower, the Torre del Homenaje, if it's open.

Cueva de los Letreros

4km north of Vélez Rubio • Obligatory guided tours, contact tourist office for details • Charge • ☎ 694 467 136

The main point of a trip to Vélez Blanco is to see the prehistoric cave paintings of the **Cueva de los Letreros**. The cave or *abrigo* (rock shelter) is beyond a secure fence on the side of the hill behind the petrol station, a good kilometre's walk. Once through the gate of the compound you will be able to see remarkably fresh-looking red and brown sketches of human figures, birds, animals, astronomical signs and not very well-preserved *indalos* (see page 513) that have been dated to around 4000 BC and are among the oldest representations of people and animals together. Unfortunately, the local practice of touching the *indalos* and throwing water on the paintings in order to make them clearer has not helped their preservation, but what remains is still stunning.

ARRIVAL & INFORMATION

VÉLEZ BLANCO

By bus 1 daily from Almería (3h 15min).

Information office The Almacén del Trigo information office (Thurs, Fri & Sun 10am–2pm, Sat 10am–2pm & 6–8pm; Oct–March afternoons are 4–6pm; ☎ 950 415 354) at the far end of the town (follow the signs), has information on Vélez and the surrounding Parque Natural de la Sierra de María (see page 518).

ACCOMMODATION AND EATING

Bar Alfonso C/Federico de Motos 7, on the north side of the town; ☎ 626 665 483. Busy bar with giant picture window with views of the village and valley, serving tapas and *raciones*. *Pulpo al horno* (baked octopus) and *plato egetano* (pork loin, red pepper and cheese) are house specials. Slightly up the street is the bar's lovely summer terrace, with even better views. €̄

Bar Sociedad C/Corredera 14; ☎ 950 415 027. The busiest bar in town serves up good tapas and *raciones* inside or, in better weather, on a lively pavement terrace.

There's also a hearty daily *menú*. €̄

Hostal La Sociedad C/Corredera 14; ☎ 950 415 027. The *hostal* adjoining the popular bar *Bar Sociedad* (see above) has plain but functional budget en-suite rooms with heating and TV. Breakfast is included. €̄

Hotel Rural Velad C/Balsa Parra 28, on the road into the town from Vélez Rubio; ⌨ hotelvelad.com. Large rustic-style hotel with commanding views over the valley (ask for a room at the front when you book). The comfortable en-suite rooms have both heating and a/c.

5

Bar downstairs serves tapas and snacks. Street parking at the front. €€
Restaurante El Molino C/Curtidores s/n; ☎ 950 415 070. The town's best restaurant lies a short distance from the *Bar Sociedad*, up some steps opposite a tiled fountain.

With three rooms and a small terrace, it offers very good fish and meat dishes – house specialities include *paletilla de cabrito* (kid goat) and *gambas al ajillo* (spicy prawns) as well as fresh trout. €€€

Sierra de María

Walkers – and those in need of greenery after endless desert landscapes – may be tempted to continue northwest from Vélez Blanco along the A317 to **María**, a small town set among pinewoods and, incidentally, the highest settlement in Almería. It is also the jumping-off point for the **SIERRA DE MARÍA**, a natural park.

Beyond María the AL9101 soon enters an extensive plain covered with wheat fields and stretches arrow-straight and apparently endlessly to the distant mountains. In high summer this plain is a cauldron beneath vast cloudless skies and you'll be lucky to meet another vehicle. Apart from a couple of godforsaken hamlets and the occasional wheeling eagle overhead, there are few features to punctuate this desolate but beautiful panorama. The landscape takes on a doubly dramatic aspect when you realize that one and a half million years ago this plain was a great lake visited by elephants, hippos, rhinos, water buffaloes, musk oxen, giant bears and ferocious hyenas as well as lions, leopards and lynxes. Early humans were known to have been in the area as early as 500,000 years ago but finds in 2003 seem to have pushed this back by an astonishing additional one million years which, if scientifically confirmed, would make it the earliest appearance of primitive humans on the continent of Europe by a long way. These Stone Age arrivals probably came from Africa and lived on a diet of wild plants and carrion supplemented by fracturing the craniums and bones of the dead beasts to extract the brains and marrow – they had not yet developed the technology to take on and hunt big game.

INFORMATION   SIERRA DE MARÍA

Visitor centre Information about the nine walking trails, and on the park in general, is available from a visitor centre (Thurs, Fri & Sun 10am–2pm, Sat 10am–2pm & 6–8pm: Oct–March afternoons are 4–6pm; ☎ 950 415 354), at the Almacén de Trigo (granary), Avda Marqués de los Vélez in Vélez Blanco.

Orce

When you finally reach it, the dusty and impoverished little settlement of **ORCE** hardly lives up to the self-styled billing, proclaimed on all its literature, as the *Cuna de la Humanidad Europea* (Cradle of European Man). The heart of the village is a tree-lined main square, **Plaza Nueva**, with an eighteenth-century fountain fronted by the Ayuntamiento and, in one corner the village's main bar, *Cervecería La Plaza*.

Other than the **prehistoric museum**, Orce's only other sights of note lie just off the main square. The first is the eleventh-century **Moorish Alcazaba** (pre-booked visits with the Turismo only) with an impressive tower, and the other, opposite across a square, is the eighteenth-century **Iglesia de Santa María** (open service times or pre-book with Turismo) with a fine retablo.

Along the Galera road, 1km out of Orce, the green valley of the Río Galera contains the Manantial de Fuen Caliente, a beautiful natural pond filled with fish, which has become the local **swimming pool**, complete with *cafetería*.

Centro de Interpretación Arqueológico

Camino de San Simón, at the north end of the village • Tues–Sun: 11am–2pm • Charge • ☎ 958 746 171

A large modern structure houses the Orce discoveries and explains (in a rather simplified fashion) the life of the settlement's prehistoric inhabitants. As well as impressive animal remains from the periods of the finds there are displays (in Spanish) reconstructing the lifestyle of these early humans. The star exhibit is a copy (the original is under lock and key in the Ayuntamiento) of the small million-and-a-half-year-old **fragment of human skull** that has brought worldwide celebrity to the town. While the theory is not accepted conclusively by many experts (a point made in the museum presentation), its discoverers claim it belonged to a child of unknown gender who is thought to have been devoured by a great hyena. Most archeologists and paleontologists working in the area are now fairly sure that the skull fragment is not human but believed that the dating would eventually be confirmed due to remarkable **lithic artefacts** (stone tools; displayed in the museum) found in 1998–99 and around 1.4 million years old.

Their belief was confirmed in 2013 when a **child's milk tooth** (excavated in 2002 but subjected to a rigorous ten-year dating process) was conclusively dated to 1.4 million years ago. The tooth, thought to be from the *Homo erectus* era, became the oldest human remain found on the continent of Europe. During excavation and restoration periods (one month during the period June–Sept), the Turismo organizes free guided tours of the three Paleolithic settlements located on the outskirts of the village. Check for exact dates and times.

ARRIVAL & INFORMATION ORCE

By bus 3 daily Mon–Fri, 1 daily Sat & Sun from Granada (2h 20min); the stop is at the west entrance to the village.
Turismo In the sixteenth-century Casa Palacio de los Segura, C/Tiendas 18 (Tues–Sun: 11am–2pm; ☎ 858 997 877; ⓦ orce.es).

ACCOMMODATION AND EATING

Cervecería La Plaza Pza Nueva s/n; ☎ 618 771 148. The village's main bar serves up good tapas, *raciones* and even pizzas, which can be eaten inside or on their terrace on the leafy square. €
Mesón La Mimbrera C/Mimbrera s/n; ⓦ lamimbreraorce.com. Just off the main square, this is the village's best place to eat, serving tasty game and regional dishes – *cordero segureño* (roast lamb) is a speciality. €€
El Mirador de Galera C/Cervantes 3, Galera; ⓦ elmiradordegalera.com. Eight self-catering caves (sleeping two to eight) in Orce and Galera (7km west) with fully equipped kitchens, open fire, TV, terrace and fine views. €€

Inland Almería

One way of reaching the coast to the east of Almería is to take a trip through the weird lunar landscape of the province's distinctive desert scenery. There are two possible routes: via **Níjar** along the A7 *autovía* to Carboneras, or via the more interesting **Tabernas** and **Sorbas** route (along the N340) to Mojácar. The latter more northerly route passes by Almería's old western film set, **Mini Hollywood**, and a detour off this road can also be made to the pottery centre of **Níjar**. A visit to the underground caves of **Sorbas** is also a great adventure.

The road to Tabernas

The main road to Tabernas heads north out of Almería along the valley of the Río Andarax and forks right at Benhadux – along the A340 – passing the village of **Rioja** before it enters a dramatic brown-tinged-with-purple eroded landscape that looks as if it should be the backdrop for a Hollywood western. Some 10km past Rioja, in a particularly gulch-riven landscape, at **Mini Hollywood** you discover that someone else had the same idea first.

As well as the landscape and cheap labour costs, the film-makers were also drawn to the same unpolluted crystalline air that has lured astronomers here; to the north of

5

Tabernas, at Calar Alto in the Sierra de Filabres, a series of high-powered telescopes enables the **Hispano-German observatory** to study the heavens.

Mini Hollywood

Check website for opening times · Charge · ⓦ oasysparquetematico.com · The Almería–Tabernas bus stops on the outward journey, but doesn't stop on the return; a taxi to Tabernas then an onward bus to Almería from there, is your only alternative

A visit to **MINI HOLLYWOOD** (aka Oasys Parque Temático) is hard to resist – especially if you're travelling with kids – although better value if timed with one of the daily shows. The old film set's most famous production was *A Fistful of Dollars*, a connection that its publicity flyers never tire of repeating. Once inside, you'll see a main street overlooked by a water tower, which you may just recognize from the 1960s classic, or from *The Good, the Bad and the Ugly*, another film made here along with countless other spaghetti and paella westerns. You can wander into the *Tombstone Gulch* saloon for a drink, and in summer there are daily shows when actors in full cowboy rig and blasting off six guns stage such epics as the capture, escape and final shooting of Jesse James. Meanwhile, in between performances the saloon stages shows of cancan girls flaunting their frillies. There's also a somewhat incongruous **zoo** – with birds, reptiles and big cats – plus a **pool** and numerous **fast food** outlets.

Fort Bravo

April–Oct daily 9am–7.30pm; two shows daily · Charge · ⓦ fortbravooficial.com

Beyond Mini Hollywood and towards Tabernas, on the left, is **Fort Bravo**, the location for *Once Upon a Time in the West*, among other productions. Here you can see a couple of less commercialized film sets in a much more spectacular setting, including an Indian village complete with wigwams, a Mexican town and a US cavalry frontier fort, as well as camels and buffalo.

Tabernas

Some 8km along the N340 beyond Fort Bravo, and surrounded by torrid desert scrubland, **TABERNAS** lies at the foot of a hill dominated by an impressive-looking **Moorish castle** where Fernando and Isabel ensconced themselves during the siege of Almería. Unfortunately, the castle is mainly ruined and there's little to hang around for – though you might want to stop for a drink in the searing summer heat. Just beyond the village a road on the left – followed after 1km by a right turn towards the hamlet of Senés – leads to the **Plataforma Solar de Almería** (Mon–Fri 8.30am–4.30pm, guided tours by appointment only; charge; ⓦ psa.es) the largest solar research and development centre in Europe, where row upon row of mirrors reflect the powerful sunlight and generate energy. Current projects are investigating solar thermal systems, desalination via solar power and solar water treatment.

ACCOMMODATION AND EATING

TABERNAS

Los Albardinales Ctra N340 km474, to the north of the village en route from Sorbas; ⓦ losalbardinales. com. The producer of the organic *oro del desierto* (desert gold) olive oil also runs a restaurant where the oil and other local, organic produce star in dishes like *chuletillas de cabrito lechal* (goat chops) and *pipirrana del desierto* (pepper and tomato salad). Be sure to visit the olive oil museum and mill before you leave. €€€

Jardín del Desierto C/San Sebastián 2 in the village centre, off the main Avda de Andalucía; ⓦ jardindeldesierto.com. A welcoming oasis of clean, comfortable en-suite rooms as bright as the flowers they're named after. All have a/c and TV, and some include a jacuzzi. You can also cool off in the pool. €

Across the Sierra Alhamilla

Beyond Tabernas there are more dramatic landscapes – badlands with naked ridges of pitted sandstone, cut through by twisted and dried-up riverbeds, all of which vary in colour from yellow to red and from green to lavender-blue depending on the time of day and the nature of the stone. After 9km a road on the right opens up the possibility of a wonderfully scenic trip south to Níjar **across the Sierra Alhamilla**. This road climbs through more Arizona-type landscape, first to the hamlet of **Turrillas**, and then turns east to **Lucainena de las Torres**, a cluster of white boxes surrounding its red-roofed church. Beyond Lucainena the road snakes over the rugged Sierra Alhamilla to descend into Níjar, 16km to the south.

Níjar

NÍJAR is a neat, white and typically Almerían little town, with – in its upper Moorish *barrio* – narrow streets designed to give maximum shade. Little remains of the Moorish fort here but a strong **pottery** tradition – dating back to when the Moors held sway and including attractive traditional patterns created with mineral dyes – lives on. The town is also known for its **jarapas**: bed-covers, curtains and rugs made from rags.

Firmly on the tourist trail, due to the inexpensive handmade pottery manufactured in **workshops** around the town (especially along Avda García Lorca – the broad main street – and the parallel C/Real), Níjar still retains a relaxed and tranquil air.

ARRIVAL & INFORMATION   NÍJAR

By buses Buses stop at the north end of the village. Destinations: Almería (Mon–Fri 5 daily, Sat–Sun 1 daily; 1hr 15min).

Turismo C/Real 1, at junction of C/Real with Avda García Lorca (Mon–Sat 10am–2pm & 6–8pm; Oct–May afternoons 4–6pm; ⓦturismonijar.es). They can provide information on the town and the region as well as the Parque Natural de Cabo de Gata (see box, page 506).

ACCOMMODATION AND EATING

Accommodation is in short supply, but there are several **bars** and **restaurants** along the main street, Avda García Lorca. Don't miss out on the **tapas bars** on the very appealing square, Plaza de la Glorieta, beyond the church in the *barrio alto*.

Bar La Glorieta Pza de la Glorieta s/n; ☏ 676 202 852.

> ## BLOOD WEDDING
>
> An event at Níjar in 1928 inspired one of Lorca's most powerful plays, **Bodas de Sangre** (*Blood Wedding*). A young woman named Francisca was about to marry a man named Casimiro at a farmhouse near Níjar. She was a reluctant bride, an heiress with a modest dowry, he a labourer pressured by his scheming brother and sister-in-law to make this match and thus bring money into the family. A few hours prior to the wedding, Francisca eloped with her cousin, with whom she had been in love since childhood, but who had only realized his feelings when confronted with the reality of losing her. They were swiftly intercepted by Casimiro's brother, who shot her cousin dead. His brother was convicted of the murder, while Casimiro, the groom, was unable to overcome his humiliation and, it is said, never looked upon Francisca or even her photograph again. Francisca never married and lived as a recluse until her death in 1978.
>
> Lorca avidly followed the story in the newspapers and had a knowledge of the area from time spent in Almería as a child. An interesting afterword is told by the writer **Nina Epton**, who, on a visit to San José in the 1960s, was dining at the house of a wealthy Spanish *señorón*, or landowner, while a group of farm labourers waited outside on a long bench, no doubt for payment. In her book *Andalusia* she describes what happened when eventually she accompanied Don José, her host, to speak to the men:
>
> *Among them was a wizened old man called Casimiro whom I would not have looked at twice before I was told that a dramatic incident in his youth had inspired Federico García Lorca to take Casimiro for his model of the novio in "Blood Wedding".*

5

BUYING NÍJAR POTTERY

For **traditional Níjar pottery** head to the shops along Avda García Lorca – the broad main street – or, for more authentic work, the *barrio alfarero*, along Calle Real running parallel to García Lorca, where the *talleres* (workshops; 10am–2pm & 4–7pm) of Granados, El Oficio and the friendly Angel y Loli (at no. 54, where you can also see an old kiln) are located. Also here, off the bottom of the street in a studio-shop called La Tienda de los Milagros (☏ 950 360 359), is resident English ceramic artist Matthew Weir who has a more modernist approach. His *almeriense* wife Isabel produces hand-dyed and woven *jarapas* and textiles in wool and silk.

Friendly little bar with an elevated terrace that offers decent tapas and generous *raciones* – paella is often on the menu here – as well as being a good place for a nightcap. €€
Cortijo La Alberca Camino del Huebro; ☏ 619 665 931. Around 1km outside of town, to the north, this restored farmhouse offers homely en-suite rooms with mountain views. The surrounding estate is surprisingly verdant with fruit trees and fountains. Breakfast is included. €€
La Mandila On the bend to the upper square at no. 17; ☏ 678 841 248. A good stop for breakfast, lunch, tapas and *raciones*. Try the *ajo blanco* (garlic and almond soup) and the *caracoles en salsa* (snails). €

Sorbas

As you head east along the N340 from Tabernas, 18km beyond the turn-off to Lucainena de las Torres, you will come to the extraordinary small town of **SORBAS**. Surrounded by moonscapes, its clifftop houses overhanging an ashen gorge, it's best seen from the main road. Like Níjar, it is reputed for its **pottery**, although Alfarería Juan Simón (C/San Roque 21, in the western part of the town) is the only workshop still in operation. This tidy little town is also on the tourist trail, especially on Thursdays when tourists flock in from Mojácar for the weekly **market** in the same plaza.

Paraje Natural de Karst en Yesos

Just south of Sorbas, signed from the main N340 • Obligatory guided tours (English & Spanish) June–Aug 10am–7pm, Sept–May 10am–6pm; check the website for details of more challenging explorations lasting up to 4hr 30min • Charge • ⓦ cuevasdesorbas.com

The main pull for visitors to Sorbas is the astonishing scenery in the surrounding **Paraje Natural de Karst en Yesos**, where around six million years ago water erosion carved out subterranean chasms full of stalagmites and stalactites. There are three guided visits to the caves (booking essential) of varying difficulty – the easiest lasts two hours – with helmets and flashlights and not a little scrambling and squeezing. Above ground, the water's action has created flat-topped, volcano-like protrusions and deep gorges. These are visible from the main N340, but for a closer look take the minor A1102 towards Los Molinos del Río Aguas east of Sorbas. At the crest of a hill, a track to the left leads to a peak above the gorge, where sweeping circular views extend over the lunar landscape as far as the snowcapped peaks of the Sierra Nevada; it's a great place to watch the sunset. Alternatively, you could follow the track descending through the tumbledown but picturesque hamlet of **Los Molinos** to follow the course of the dried-up river gorge.

ARRIVAL & INFORMATION

SORBAS

By bus There are daily bus from Almería (1 daily Sat, 2 daily Sun–Fri; 1hr).
Centro de Visitantes Fifty metres downhill from the Turismo (Feb, March, Nov & Dec Thurs–Sun 10am–2.30pm; April–June, Sept & Oct Tues–Sat 10am–2pm & 4–7pm, Sun 10am–2.30pm; July & Aug Mon–Sat 10am–2pm & 4–7pm, Sun 10am–2.30pm; ☏ 950 364 563). An interesting and informative information centre for the Karst en Yesos caves.

ACCOMMODATION

Hostal La Escapada C/Martín Salinas, Uleila del Campo 1; ⓦ laescapada.es. At the southern end of the nearby village of Uleila del Campo (14km northwest), this friendly small *hostal* with en-suite, a/c rooms. Has a bar downstairs. €̄

Hostal Sorbas Ctra 340 s/n, on the right as you come in from Tabernas; ☎950 364 160. Good *hostal* on the main road at the entrance to the town, offering comfortable a/c rooms with TV. Breakfast is included. €̄

EATING AND DRINKING

Cafe Bar El Almendro La Mela, 10km north of Sorbas on the A1101; ⓦel-almendro.com. English-run bar-restaurant in the small village of La Mela, favoured by locals, both Spanish and expat. They're famous for their signature slow-roasted lamb (served as part of the traditional Sunday roast). €€

El Fogón Ctra N340 km496, on the main road and part of Hostal Sorbas; ☎950 364 160. Reliable bar and restaurant serving *raciones* and local dishes such as *gorullos* (rabbit stew) and *potaje de trigo* (meat and wheat stew). €€

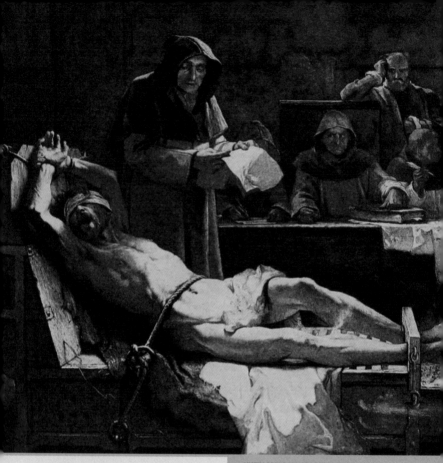

VICTIM OF THE SPANISH INQUISITION

Contexts

History

As the southernmost region of the Iberian peninsula, Andalucía has manifested throughout its history a character essentially different from the rest of Spain. Due to the variety of peoples who settled here, the region has always had an enriching influence on the territories further north. This meeting place of seas and cultures, with Africa just 14km off the coast of its southern tip, brought Andalucía into early contact with the sophisticated civilizations of the eastern Mediterranean and a long period as part of the North African Moorish empire. The situation was later reversed when Andalucía sent out explorers to the New World and became the gateway to the Spanish American empire.

Prehistory

The first Europeans of whom we have knowledge lived in Andalucía. Over the last twenty years a series of spectacular discoveries at **Orce**, 113km northeast of Granada, rocked the archeological world as the date for the **arrival of early humans in Europe** was pushed back from c.700,000 years ago to perhaps a million years before this, making Orce – the findings were scientifically confirmed in 2013 – the earliest known site of human occupation in Europe by a long way. Arriving from Africa and crossing the straits by swimming or on rafts these Stone Age people colonized an area of now vanished lakeland near Orce. Here they hunted hippos, hyenas, mammoths and vultures and made tools from flint. The find that confirmed the new dating was a human milk tooth, from a child aged around 10, at least 1.4 million years old. Evidence of occupation by Stone Age societies stretching back some 400,000 years was already known about from discoveries at nearby **Venta Micena** where early inhabitants hunted elephant and rhino and left behind tools and camp fires. Some of the earliest **human fossils** found on the Iberian peninsula were unearthed inside the **Gibraltar** caves with evidence of **Neanderthals** dating from around 100,000 BC. In the Paleolithic period, the first **Homo sapiens** arrived on the Iberian peninsula from southern France, settling around the Bay of Biscay as well as in the south. They were cave dwellers and hunter-gatherers and at the Pileta and Nerja caves in Málaga have left behind remarkable **cave paintings** depicting the animals that they hunted. During the later Neolithic phase, a sophisticated material culture developed in southern Spain attested to by the finds of esparto sandals and baskets as well as jewellery in the **Cueva de los Murciélagos** in Granada.

Subsequent prehistory is more complex and confused. There does not appear to have been any great development in the cave cultures of the north. Instead the focus shifts south – where **Neolithic colonists** had arrived from North Africa – to Valencia and **Almería**. Cave paintings have been found in rock shelters such as those at **Vélez Blanco** dating from around 4000 BC. Here also, not long afterwards, **metalworking** began

1.5 million years ago	25,000 BC	12,000 BC	c.4000 BC
Early humans active at Orce, in today's Granada province, after arriving from Africa.	Cave dwellers occupying caves in Málaga province.	Dolmens constructed in Málaga and Catalunya.	Neolithic colonists arrive from north Africa. Esparto baskets and jewellery found in Cueva de Murciélagos, Granada.

and the debate continues as to what led to this dramatic leap forward: a development by the indigenous inhabitants, or the arrival of "technicians" – evidenced by many trading artefacts such as ivory and turquoise – from the eastern Mediterranean. The fortified site of **Los Millares** (c.2700 BC), in the centre of a rich mining area in Almería, with its Aegean-style "beehive" tombs is one of the most important remains from this era. In the same period, **dolmens** were being constructed such as those at **Antequera**, a building style that spread from here throughout the peninsula and into the rest of Europe. This dolmenic culture also influenced a ceramic style, typified by bell-shaped artefacts and giving rise to the name **Beaker folk**. More developments occurred in the same area of Almería about 1700 BC when the **El Argar** civilization started to produce bronze and worked silver and gold, trading across the Mediterranean. This culture fanned out across the south between 1700 and 1000 BC and, during the first millennium BC, the **Iberian civilization** fully established itself.

Tartessus and the Iberians

The **kingdom of Tartessus** appeared early in the first millennium BC and typifies the great strides forward being made by the Iberians of the south. Both the Bible (which names it Tarshish) and Greek and Latin texts refer to this important kingdom and trading centre. It was probably sited on the estuary of the Río Guadalquivir on the border of Huelva and Seville provinces; its precise location has yet to be identified, although its prowess as a producer and exporter of bronze, gold and silver as well as a creator of sophisticated **jewellery** is apparent from the finds displayed in Seville's archeological museum. The Tartessians were also a literate people, but nothing of their literature survives apart from scattered inscriptions that have thus far defied translation. In the mid-sixth century BC Tartessus incurred the wrath of the rising power of Carthage through its friendship with the Greeks and not long after that appears to have been destroyed by them.

The Iberians at other centres in the south also developed sophisticated cultures based upon agriculture, stockbreeding, fishing, mining and iron production. When the Romans came into contact with them in the third century BC they found a literate people with written laws, and a vibrant culture that included music and dance. Their skills in the plastic arts – an enduring flair throughout the peninsula's history – are displayed in artefacts such as the splendid **Dama de Baza**, a dramatic fourth-century BC painted terracotta statue of a woman, discovered at Baza in Granada. The Iberian skill with masonry and stone sculpture can be seen at the necropolis at **Toya** in Jaén province, and other remarkable works from the fifth century BC are in the museum at Jaén itself.

The first colonists

The southern coast attracted colonists from different regions of the Mediterranean. The **Phoenicians** – founders of a powerful trading empire based in modern Lebanon – established the port of Gadir (Cádiz) about 1100 BC. This was obviously connected with their intensive **trading operations** in the metals of the Guadalquivir valley carried from Tartessus where they may even have had a factory. Their wealth and

2500 BC	c.1100 BC	9th–4th century BC	5th century BC
Chalcolithic (Copper Age) sites flourish in Almería.	Phoenicians found Cádiz.	Kingdom of Tartessus flourishes around Guadalquivir estuary. Greeks establish trading posts along east coast.	Carthage colonizes southern Spain. Celto-Iberian culture develops, with Greek influence.

success gave rise to a Spanish "Atlantis" myth, based around Huelva. Besides metals, the Phoenicians also came for the rich fishing along the southern coast, which stimulated industries for salting and preserving the catch. The salt itself was gained from beds such as those at the **Cabo de Gata** – still commercially operating today – in Almería. Other operations, such as the **purple dyeing industry**, for which the Phoenicians were famous, exploited the large stocks of murex shellfish in coastal waters. The coastline of Andalucía is dotted with Phoenician **settlements** from this time such as those at Malaka (Málaga), Sexi (Almuñécar) and Abdera (Adra). Market rivalry also brought the **Greeks**, who established their trading colonies along the northeastern coast – the modern Costa Brava – before penetrating southwards into the Phoenician zone. They were encouraged by the Tartessians, no doubt in an attempt to break the Phoenician economic stranglehold on the region.

When the Phoenicians were incorporated into the Persian Empire in the sixth century BC, however, a former colony, **Carthage**, moved into the power vacuum, destroyed Tartessus and ejected the Greeks from the south. Carthage then turned the western Mediterranean into a jealously guarded trading monopoly, sinking ships of other states who attempted to trade there. This she tenaciously held on to, as the rising power of Rome forced her out of the central Mediterranean. In the course of the third century BC, Carthage built up Spain into a new base for her empire, from which to regain strength and strike back at her great rival. Although making little impact inland, the Carthaginians occupied most of Andalucía and expanded along the Mediterranean seaboard to establish a new capital at Cartagena ("New Carthage") in Murcia. The mineral wealth of Andalucía, particularly **silver**, was used to finance the military build-up as well as to recruit an enormous army of Iberian mercenaries. Under Hannibal they prepared to invade Italy and in 219 BC attacked Saguntum (modern Sagunto), a strategic ally of the growing Roman Empire. This precipitated the **Second Punic War**, bringing Roman legions to the Spanish peninsula for the first time. Heading south from modern Catalunya, they successively conquered the coastal towns; the **end of Carthaginian domination** of Spain was sealed in 206 BC at the battle of Ilipa (Alcalá del Río), just north of Seville. When Cádiz fell the following year, Rome became master of the southern peninsula and **Itálica** (near Seville) was founded as the first Roman city in Spain. A new and very different age had begun.

The Romans and Visigoths

The **Roman colonization** of the peninsula was far more intense than anything previously experienced and met with great resistance from the Celtiberian tribes of the north and centre, although much less so in Andalucía where the Turditanian people, tired of Carthaginian oppression, welcomed the invaders. In the final years of the Roman republic many of the crucial battles for control of the Roman state were fought out in Spain, ending with Julius Caesar's victory at Munda, south of Córdoba, in 45 BC. After Caesar's assassination, his successor Augustus reorganized Spain into three provinces, the southernmost of which became **Hispania Baetica**, roughly modern Andalucía, with **Corduba** (Córdoba) as its capital.

In this period Spain became one of the most important and wealthiest centres of the Roman Empire and Andalucía was its most urbane heartland. Unlike the rugged and

214 BC	210 BC	27 BC	c.409–415 AD
Second Punic War with Rome.	Roman colonization begins. Important Roman cities at Itálica, Córdoba, Cádiz, Carmona and Málaga.	Octavian-Augustus becomes first Roman Emperor and divides Spain into three parts: Lusitania, Baetica and Tarraconensis.	Vandals invade southern Spain.

ALMOHAD ARCHITECTURE

In the eleventh century, Andalucía fragmented into rival kingdoms or *taifas*, allowing successive waves of Moorish invaders to move into the power vacuum. One of these, the ultra-fundamentalist **Almohads**, left behind a number of remarkable buildings of which the foremost is the magnificent **Giralda** tower in Seville (see page 248), the surviving minaret of the Friday mosque demolished to construct the Gothic cathedral. At 100m high with elaborate *sebka* brickwork panels adorning its exterior walls, it was started in 1184 under architect Ahmed ibn Baso and completed twelve years later.

fractious Celtiberians further north, the sophisticated Iberians of the south had their own municipal traditions and took easily to Roman ideas of government. Indeed, their native languages and dialects had disappeared early in the first century AD as Latinization became complete. For four centuries Andalucía enjoyed a "**Golden Age**" with unprecedented prosperity based on the production of olive oil, wool, grain, wine and the highly prized *garum* fish sauce made at centres such as **Baelo Claudia** near Tarifa. Another important development was a massive expansion of mining at **Río Tinto** in Huelva. During this period, Baetica supplied **two Roman emperors**, Trajan (one of the greatest) and his adopted son Hadrian, along with the outstanding writers Seneca and Lucan. The finest monuments of the period were built in the provincial capital at Córdoba, and cities such as Cádiz, Itálica, Málaga and Carmona, linked by a network of superb roads and adorned with temples, baths, amphitheatres and aqueducts, were the equal of any in the empire. In the fourth and fifth centuries, however, the Roman political framework began to show signs of **decadence and corruption**. Although the actual structure didn't totally collapse until the Muslim invasions of the early eighth century, it became increasingly vulnerable to **barbarian invasions** from northern Europe. Early in the fifth century AD, the Suevi (Swabians), Alans and Vandals swept across the Pyrenees leaving much devastation in their wake. The Romans, preoccupied with attempts to stave off Gothic attacks on Italy, bought off the invaders by allowing them to settle within the imperial borders. The Suevi settled in Galicia, the Alans in Portugal and Murcia, while the **Vandals** put down roots in Baetica, providing the origin of Andalucía's name. The resulting wars between the invaders only served to further weaken Rome's grip on the peninsula as a burgeoning Christian Church – its first Spanish council was held at Iliberis (Granada) – gained more influence over the population.

The Visigoths

Internal strife was heightened by the arrival of the **Visigoths** from Gaul, allies of Rome and already Romanized to a large degree. The triumph of Visigothic strength in the fifth century resulted in a period of spurious unity, based upon an exclusive military rule from their capital at Toledo, but their numbers were never great and their order was often fragmentary and nominal, with the bulk of the subject people kept in a state of disconsolate servility and held ransom for their services in times of war. Above them in the ranks of the military elite there were constant plots and factions – exacerbated by the Visigothic system of elected monarchy and by their adherence to the heretical Arian

5th–7th century	711	722	756
Visigoths take control of most of Spain.	Moors under Tariq invade and defeat Visigothic King Roderic near Jerez. Peninsula conquered in seven years.	Pelayo defeats Moors at Covadonga in Asturias in northern Spain; the *Reconquista* begins.	Abd ar-Rahman I proclaims Emirate of Córdoba. Great mosque of Córdoba (Mezquita) begun.

philosophy. When **King Leovigild** attempted to impose this creed on Andalucía in the mid-sixth century, the region revolted with the king's son Hermenegild at its head, but the insurrection was brutally crushed. In 589 **King Recared** converted to Catholicism, which for a time stiffened Visigothic control, but religious strife was only multiplied: forced conversions, especially within the Jewish enclaves, maintained a constant simmering of discontent. The Visigoths precariously held on to their domain for a further century as plots and counterplots surrounded the throne. This infighting led indirectly to the Moorish invasions of Andalucía when **King Witiza**, who died in 710, was thwarted by a usurper, Roderic, duke of Baetica, from handing over the throne to his son, Achila. Once **King Roderic** had installed himself on the throne the embittered family of Witiza appealed to the Muslims in North Africa for assistance to overthrow him. The North Africans, who had long eyed the riches of Andalucía with envy, now saw their opportunity.

The Moorish conquest

In contrast to the long-drawn-out Roman campaigns, the **Moorish conquest** of the peninsula was effected with extraordinary speed. This was a characteristic phenomenon of the spread of Islam – Muhammad left Mecca in 622 and by 705 his followers had established control over all of North Africa. Spain, with its political instability, wealth and fertile climate, was an inevitable extension of their aims. In 711 **Tariq**, governor of Tangier, led a force of seven thousand Berbers across the straits and routed the Visigoth army of King Roderic on the banks of the Río Guadalete close to Jerez. Two years later the Visigoths made a last desperate stand at Mérida and within a decade the Moors had conquered all but the wild mountains of Asturias. The land under their authority was dubbed **al-Andalus**, a fluid term which expanded and shrank with the intermittent gains and losses of the Reconquista. It was Andalucía, however, that was destined to become the heartland of the Moorish ascendancy and where the Moors were to remain in control for most of the next eight centuries.

The Moorish incursion was not simply a military conquest. The Moors (a collective term for the numerous waves of Arab, Syrian and Berber settlers from North Africa) were often content to grant a limited autonomy in exchange for payment of tribute; their administrative system was tolerant and easily absorbed both Spanish Jews and Christians, those who retained their religion being known as "Mozarabs". This **tolerant attitude** was illustrated when the Moorish army reached Córdoba where they found the large Visigothic church of St Vincent, now the fabulous Mezquita. Unlike previous invaders, they did not sack or burn the heathen temple but purchased half of it to use as a mosque while the Christians continued to use the other half for their own services. Al-Andalus was a distinctly Spanish state of Islam. Though at first politically subject to the eastern caliphate (or empire) of Baghdad, it was soon virtually independent. In the tenth century, at the peak of its power and expansion, Abd ar-Rahman III asserted total independence, proclaiming himself caliph of a new **western Islamic empire**. Its capital was **Córdoba** – the largest, most prosperous and most civilized city in Europe. This was the great age of Muslim Spain: its scholarship, philosophy, architecture and craftsmanship were without rival and there was an unparalleled growth in urban life, trade and agriculture, aided by magnificent irrigation projects. These and other

928	967	1013	1037
Abd ar-Rahman III constructs the palace of Medina Azahara near Córdoba and extends the Mezquita.	Al-Mansur usurps the caliphal powers of Córdoba caliphate and forces Christians back into Asturias.	Caliphate disintegrates into *taifas*, or petty kingdoms.	Fernando I unites kingdoms of Castile and León-Asturias.

engineering feats were not, on the whole, instigated by the Moors who instead took the basic Roman models and adapted them to a new level of sophistication. In **architecture** and the **decorative arts**, however, their contribution was original and unique – as may be seen in the astonishingly beautiful monuments of Seville, Córdoba and Granada.

The Cordoban caliphate (and the emirate that preceded it) created a remarkable degree of unity, despite a serious challenge to their authority by the rebel leader **Ibn Hafsun** from his Bobastro fortress (north of Málaga) in the latter years of the ninth century. But its rulers were to become decadent and out of touch, prompting the brilliant but dictatorial **al-Mansur** to usurp control. Under this extraordinary ruler Moorish power reached new heights, using a professional Berber army to push the Christian kingdom of Asturias-León back into the Cantabrian mountains and sacking its most holy shrine, Santiago de Compostela, in 997. However, after al-Mansur's death the caliphate quickly lost its authority and in 1031 disintegrated into a series of small independent kingdoms or **taifas**, the strongest of which was Seville.

Internal divisions meant that the *taifas* offered less resistance to the Christian kingdoms that were rallying in the north, and twice North Africa had to be called upon for reinforcement. This resulted in two distinct new waves of Moorish invasion – first by the fanatically Islamic **Almoravids** (1086) and later by the **Almohads** (1147), who restored effective Muslim authority and left behind one of Moorish Spain's most elegant monuments, the **Giralda** tower in Seville. However, their crushing defeat by the Christian forces under Alfonso VIII in 1212, at the battle of **Las Navas de Tolosa** in Jaén, marked the beginning of the end for Moorish Spain.

The Christian Reconquest

The **Reconquest** of land and influence from the Moors – the *Reconquista* – was a slow and intermittent process. It began with a symbolic victory by a small force of Christians at Covadonga in the region of Asturias (722) in northern Spain and was not completed until 1492 with the conquest of Granada by Fernando and Isabel.

Covadonga resulted in the formation of the tiny Christian **kingdom of Asturias**. Initially just 25km by 19km in area, it had by 914 reclaimed León and most of Galicia and northern Portugal. At this point, progress was temporarily halted by the devastating campaigns of al-Mansur. However, with the fall of the Cordoban caliphate and the divine aid of Spain's Moor-slaying patron saint, the avenging Santiago (St James the Apostle), the *Reconquista* moved into a new and powerful phase. The frontier castles built against Arab attack gave name to **Castile**, founded in the tenth century as a county of León-Asturias. Under Fernando I (1037–65) it achieved the status of a kingdom and became the main thrust and focus of the *Reconquista*. In 1085 this period of confident Christian expansion reached its zenith with the capture of the great Moorish city of Toledo. The following year, however, the Almoravids arrived by invitation from Seville, and military activity was effectively frozen – except, that is, for the exploits of the legendary **El Cid**, a Castilian nobleman who won considerable lands around Valencia in 1095, thus checking Muslim expansion up the eastern coast.

The next concerted phase of the *Reconquista* began as a response to the threat imposed by the Almohads. The kings of León, Castile, Aragón and Navarra united in a crusade that resulted in the great victory at Las Navas de Tolosa. Thereafter Muslim power was

1085	1086	1147	1212
Christians capture Toledo.	Almoravids invade Spain from North Africa.	Invasion by Almohads from Morocco; Seville becomes Moorish capital in Spain.	Almohad advance halted by Christian victory at Las Navas de Tolosa (Jaén).

paralyzed and the **Christian armies** moved on to take most of al-Andalus. Fernando III ("El Santo", the saint) led Castilian soldiers into Córdoba in 1236 and twelve years later into Seville. By the end of the thirteenth century only the Nasrid **kingdom of Granada** remained under Muslim authority and this was to provide a brilliant sunset to Moorish rule in Andalucía. Its survival for a further two centuries while surrounded by its Christian enemies was due as much to skilful diplomacy as to payment of tribute to the monarchs of Castile.

Two factors should be stressed regarding the *Reconquista*. First, its unifying religious nature – the **spirit of crusade**, intensified by the religious zeal of the Almoravids and Almohads, and by the wider European climate (which in 1085 gave rise to the First Crusade). At the same time the *Reconquista* was a movement of **recolonization**. The fact that the country had been under arms for so long meant that the nobility had a major and clearly visible social role, a trend perpetuated by the redistribution of captured land in huge packages, or **latifundia**. Heirs to this tradition still remain as landlords of the great estates, most conspicuously in Andalucía where it has produced wretched conditions for the workers on the land ever since. Men from the ranks were also awarded land, forming a lower, larger stratum of nobility, the **hidalgos**. It was their particular social code that provided the material for Cervantes in *Don Quijote*.

Any spirit of mutual cooperation that had temporarily united the Christian kingdoms disintegrated during the fourteenth century, and independent lines of development were once again pursued. **Castile** emerged as the strongest over this period: self-sufficiency in agriculture and a flourishing wool trade with the Netherlands enabled the state to build upon the prominent military role under Fernando III.

Los Reyes Católicos

Los Reyes Católicos – the Catholic Monarchs – was the joint title given to **Fernando V of Aragón** and **Isabel I of Castile**, whose marriage in 1469 united the two largest kingdoms in Spain. Unity was in practice more symbolic than real: Castile had underlined its rights in the marriage vows and Aragón retained its old administrative structure. So, in the beginning at least, the growth of any national unity or Spanish – as opposed to local – sentiment was very much dependent on the head of state. Nevertheless, from this time on it begins to be realistic to consider Spain as a single political entity.

At the heart of Fernando and Isabel's popular appeal lay a **religious bigotry** that they shared with most of their Christian subjects. The **Inquisition** was instituted in Castile in 1480 and in Aragón seven years later. Aiming to establish the purity of the Catholic faith by rooting out heresy, it was directed mainly at Jews (despite Fernando's half-Jewish parentage) – resented for their enterprise in commerce and influence in high places, as well as for their faith. Expression had already been given to these feelings in a pogrom in 1391; it was reinforced by an edict issued in 1492 that forced up to 400,000 Jews to flee the country. A similar spirit was embodied in the reconquest of the Nasrid **kingdom of Granada**, also in 1492. During this long campaign Gonzalo Fernández de Córdoba, "El Gran Capitán", developed the Spanish army into a formidable force that was set to dominate the battlefields of Europe for the next century and a half. As Granada was the last stronghold of Muslim authority, the

1236–48	1238	1262–92	1469
Fernando III conquers Córdoba and Seville.	Ibn al-Ahmar founds the Nasrid dynasty and starts the construction of the Alhambra palace.	Cádiz falls to Alfonso X; Sancho IV takes Tarifa.	Castile and Aragón united by the marriage of Isabel and Fernando, los Reyes Católicos (the Catholic Monarchs).

COLUMBUS AND THE CATHOLIC MONARCHS

After many frustrating years trying to find backers for his plan **to reach the Indies by sailing west**, Columbus's luck turned in 1491 when he spent a period at the Franciscan monastery of **La Rábida** in the province of Huelva. The abbot of La Rábida, Juan Pérez, a former confessor to Queen Isabel, was moved to write to her on Columbus's behalf. It was a timely moment as Granada had just fallen, the treasury was empty, and the promise of gold and glory for a resurgent Spain now attracted Isabel and her husband King Fernando. On August 3, 1492, Columbus set out from Palos, a port in Huelva, with three small vessels and 120 men. On October 12, he made landfall on Watling Island (aka San Salvador) in the Bahamas. After leaving a colony of men on Hispaniola (modern Haiti) he returned to Palos on March 15, 1493, to enormous acclaim. The Spanish conquest of the Americas had begun.

religious rights of its citizens were guaranteed under the treaty of surrender. Then the policy was reversed and forced mass conversions were introduced. The subsequent and predictable rebellions – particularly violent in **Las Alpujarras** – were brutally put down and within a decade those Muslims under Christian rule had been given the choice between conversion or expulsion.

The New World

The year 1492 was symbolic of a fresh start in another way: it was in this year that **Columbus** sailed from Huelva to make the **"discovery" of America**. The papal bull that followed, entrusting Spain with the conversion of the Native Americans, further entrenched Spain's sense of a mission to bring the world to the "True Faith". The next ten years saw the systematic conquest, colonization and exploitation of the **New World**, with new territory stretching from Labrador in modern Canada to Brazil, and new-found wealth pouring into the royal coffers. The control of trade with the New World was carried on through **Seville** where the Casa de Contratación (House of Trade) was established in 1503. The city rapidly grew into one of the great cities of Europe during which it enjoyed two centuries of commercial monopoly. Paradoxically, Andalucía as a whole benefited little from this wealth, which was appropriated by the crown for its foreign campaigns and by absentee landlords. Over the succeeding two centuries the region languished as a backwater and the poverty of the peasants led many to emigrate to the New World in order to better themselves, turning much of the region into a vast, unpopulated desert.

The Habsburg Age

Carlos I, a Habsburg, came to the throne in 1516 as a beneficiary of the marriage alliances of the Catholic monarchs. Four years later, he was elected emperor of the Holy Roman Empire as Carlos V (**Charles V**), inheriting not only Castile and Aragón, but also Flanders, the Netherlands, Artois, the Franche-Comté and all the American colonies to boot. With such responsibilities it was inevitable that attention would be diverted from Spain, whose chief function became to sustain the Holy Roman Empire with gold and silver from the Americas. It was only with the accession of

1479	1492	1502
The Spanish Inquisition begins in Seville.	Fall of Granada, the last Moorish kingdom. "Discovery" of America by Cristóbal Colón (Columbus).	Great Moorish rebellion. Inquisition offers Moors baptism or expulsion.

Felipe II in 1556 that Spanish politics became more centralized and that the notion of an absentee king was reversed.

This was a period of unusual religious intensity: the **Inquisition** was enforced with renewed vigour, and a "final solution" to the problem of the Moriscos (subject Moors), who continued to adhere to their ancient traditions and practise Muslim worship in secret, resulted in a decree banning Arabic dress, books and speech. The result was another rising of Moriscos in Las Alpujarras that was fiercely suppressed, with Muslims being forcibly deported to other parts of the country. Felipe III later ordered the expulsion of half the total number of Moriscos in Spain – allowing only two families to remain in each Alpujarran village in order to maintain irrigation techniques. The **exodus** of both Muslim and Jews created a large gulf in the labour force and in the higher echelons of commercial life – and in trying to uphold the Catholic cause, an enormous strain was put upon resources without any clear-cut victory. Despite being a golden literary and artistic age, politically and economically the seventeenth century was a disaster for Spain. Lurching progressively deeper into debt, she suffered heavy defeats on the battlefield as her possessions in the Netherlands and France were lost, and recurring financial crises and economic stagnation engendered a deepening mood of disillusionment. **Andalucía** shared in this decline, exacerbated by the tendency of the mercantile classes to involve themselves only in entrepôt trade which left most of the profits in the hands of other countries. There was also no stimulus given to industrial production by the custom of merchants retiring from commerce and investing their profits in land, which created a landed gentry weighed down by honours and titles whose lifestyle came to be looked upon as being incompatible with commerce.

The Bourbons

The **Bourbon dynasty** succeeded to the Spanish throne in the person of Felipe V (1700); with him began the **War of the Spanish Succession** against the rival claim of Archduke Charles of Austria, assisted by British forces. As a result of the Treaty of Utrecht that ended the war (1713), Spain was stripped of all territory in Belgium, Luxembourg, Italy and Sardinia, but Felipe V was recognized as king. **Gibraltar** was seized by the British in the course of the war. For the rest of the century Spain fell very much under the French sphere of influence, an influence that was given political definition by an alliance with the French Bourbons in 1762. This Gallic connection brought the ideas of Enlightenment Europe into the peninsula and during the reign of Carlos III (1759–88) a number of radically minded ministers attempted to deal with the nation's chronic problems. Along with a more tolerant attitude towards the **gitanos** (gypsies) who had become victims of racial abuse and hostility, the king's minister, Pablo de Olavide, began an imaginative, if ultimately unsuccessful, scheme to **repopulate the Sierra Morena** in Andalucía with foreign immigrants.

Contact with France also made involvement in the **Napoleonic Wars** inevitable and led eventually to the defeat of the Spanish and French fleet at the **Battle of Trafalgar** off the coast of Cádiz in 1805. Popular outrage was such that the powerful prime minister, Godoy, was overthrown and King Carlos IV forced to abdicate (1808). Napoleon seized the opportunity to install his brother, Joseph, on the throne, while French armies and generals ransacked and stole much of the country's artistic heritage.

1516	1519	1556	1587
Carlos I succeeds to the throne and (1520) becomes the Holy Roman Emperor, inaugurating the Golden Age.	Magellan starts global voyage from Sanlúcar de Barrameda; Cortés lands in Mexico.	Accession of Felipe II (d.1598).	Sir Francis Drake carries out raid on Cádiz.

Fierce local resistance in the form of guerrilla warfare was accompanied by armies raised by the various local administrations. Thus it was that a militia put in the field by the junta of Seville inflicted a resounding defeat on a French army at **Bailén** in Jaén in 1808, which forced Joseph, the "intruder king", to flee back across the border. This resistance was eventually backed by the muscle of a British army, first under Sir John Moore, later under the Duke of Wellington, and the French were at last driven out in the course of the **War of Independence** (Peninsular War). Meanwhile, the **American colonies** had been successfully asserting their independence from a preoccupied centre and with them went Spain's last real claim to significance on the world stage. The entire nineteenth century was dominated by the struggle between an often reactionary monarchy and the aspirations of liberal constitutional reformers.

The nineteenth century

Between 1810 and 1813, while the war raged on across the peninsula, an ad hoc Cortes (parliament) meeting in **Cádiz** had set up a **liberal constitution** which stipulated a strict curtailment of the powers of the crown with ministers responsible to a democratically elected chamber. The first act of the despotic Fernando VII on being returned to the throne was to abolish this, and until his death in 1833 he continued to stamp out the least hint of liberalism. But the Constitution of 1812 was to remain a "sacred text" for a future democratic Spain, besides introducing the word "liberal" to Europe's political vocabulary. On Fernando's death, the right of succession was contested between his brother, Don Carlos, backed by the Church, conservatives and Basques, and his infant daughter, Isabel, who looked to the Liberals and the army for support.

So began the **First Carlist War**, a civil war that divided Spanish emotions for six years. Isabel II was eventually declared of age in 1843, her reign a long record of scandal, political crisis and constitutional compromise. Liberal army generals under the leadership of General Prim effected a coup in 1868 and the queen was forced to abdicate, but attempts to maintain a Republican government foundered. The Cortes was again dissolved and the throne returned to Isabel's son, Alfonso XII. The military began increasingly to move into the power vacuum left by the weakened monarchy. The **pronunciamiento** – whereby an officer backed by military force "pronounced" what was in the best interests of a city or region – was born in this period and was to plague the country into modern times.

The **nineteenth century** in Andalucía mirrored Spain's national decline. The loss of the American colonies had badly hit the region's trade, and this was compounded by the phylloxera plague from the 1870s onwards which wiped out most of the vineyards, brought the sherry industry to its knees, and fuelled the growth of strikes in the cities and popular uprisings on the land as the economy deteriorated. Parodoxically, this century also did more than any other to bestow on Andalucía the image it has held ever since. Writers, artists and travellers of the **Romantic Age** saw in its bullfights, flamenco, bandits and beguiling women a world of gaiety and colour, epitomized in the operas *Carmen* and *The Barber of Seville*, both works from this period. The years preceding World War I merely heightened the discontent, which found expression in the growing **political movements** of the working class. The Socialist Workers' Party was

1588	1609	1649
The British defeat the Spanish Armada; Spain's demise as a sea power begins.	Expulsion of Moriscos, last remaining Spanish Muslims.	Great plague in Seville wipes out one third of the population.

founded in Madrid after the restoration of Alfonso XII, and spawned its own trade union, the UGT (1888). Its anarchist counterpart, the CNT (Confederación Nacional de Trabajo), was founded in 1911, gaining substantial support among the oppressed peasantry of Andalucía. The loss of **Cuba** in 1898 emphasized the growing isolation of Spain in international affairs and added to economic problems with the return of soldiers seeking employment where there was none. In Andalucía a regionalist movement known as **Andalucismo** was born demanding land reform and greater Andalucían autonomy.

Into the twentieth century

A call-up for army reserves to fight in **Morocco** in 1909 provoked a general strike and the "Tragic Week" of rioting in Barcelona. Between 1914 and 1918, Spain was outwardly neutral but inwardly turbulent; inflated prices made the postwar recession harder to bear. The general disillusionment with parliamentary government, together with the fears of employers and businessmen for their own security, gave **General Primo de Rivera** sufficient support for a military coup in 1923. Coming himself from Jerez de la Frontera, the paternalistic general backed the great **Ibero-American Exhibition of 1929** at Seville which, it was hoped, would calm the agitation for radical change by promoting a "rose-coloured" image for the troubled region; its most immediate effect was to bankrupt the city. Dictatorship did result in an increase in material prosperity, heavily assisted by a massive public works policy, but serious political misjudgements and the collapse of the peseta in 1929 made de Rivera's voluntary resignation and departure into exile inevitable. The legacy of this dictatorship was to reinforce a belief on the right that only a firm military hand would be capable of holding society together, and many of those who served in Primo de Rivera's administration were to back the Franco regime in the next decade. The victory of antimonarchist parties in the 1931 municipal elections forced the abdication of the hopelessly out of touch King Alfonso XIII, and the **Second Republic** was declared.

The Second Republic

The **Second Republic**, which lasted from 1931 to 1936, was ushered in on a wave of optimism that finally some of the nation's fundamental ills and injustices would be rectified. But the government – a coalition of radicals, socialists and leftist republicans struggling to curb the power of vested interests such as the army, the Church and the landowning class – was soon failing to satisfy even the least of the expectations that it had raised. Moreover it lost support when it got involved in activities identified with earlier repressive regimes, as happened at the village of **Casas Viejas** (modern Benalup-Casas Viejas) in Cádiz, when it ordered the troops to open fire on a group of starving workers who had been the victims of a lockout by the local landowner and who were attempting to raise the area in an anarchist revolt.

Anarchism was gaining strength among the frustrated middle classes as well as among workers and peasantry. The **Communist Party** and left-wing **socialists**, driven into alliance by their mutual distrust of the "moderate" Socialists in government, were also

1700	1759–88	1808	1812
War of Spanish Succession brings Bourbon Felipe V to the throne. The British seize Gibraltar.	Enlightenment ideas enter Spain; colonies of Germans, French and Swiss settle in the Sierra Morena.	French occupy Spain.	Liberal constitution declared in Cádiz.

THE LAW OF HISTORICAL MEMORY

In Spain as well as abroad the **legacy of Franco** remains controversial. In the years following the restoration of democracy there was no national debate about the dictator's 35-year rule and unlike other countries, such as Germany and Argentina, Spain has never fully come to terms with its former dictatorship. Instead politicians on both sides of the divide tacitly agreed not to mention the legacy of the Franco regime and no war crimes trials were held. But many others were angry at a pact that meant that crimes committed in the Franco years not only went unpunished, but weren't even recognized as having taken place. In 2007 the Spanish PSOE government – led by José Luís Rodrigo Zapatero, whose own grandfather was executed by Franco's forces – decided to address this issue and passed into law **La Ley de Memoria Histórica** (The Law of Historical Memory). This rules that sentences handed down by kangaroo courts during the regime – that led to the imprisonment or execution of thousands of Franco's opponents – were "illegitimate". It also decrees that local governments must locate, exhume from mass graves and identify the victims of the Franco regime. Historians claim that the remains of tens of thousands of Franco's opponents are buried in unmarked graves throughout the country.

The law also stipulates that all statues, plaques, street name plates and symbols relating to the regime must be removed from public buildings (however, church property was excluded). It deals, too, with the dictatorship's monumental legacy – the vast basilica of the **Valle de los Caídos** near Madrid, where the remains of Franco and the founder of the fascist Falange party, José Antonio Prima de Rivera, are interred. The law prohibits all political events at the site, thus preventing the traditional "mass for the Caudillo" formerly celebrated every November 20 (the anniversary of Franco's death), and its celebration of the fascist cause.

forming a growing bloc. There was little real unity of purpose on either left or right, but their fear of each other and their own exaggerated boasts made each seem an imminent threat. On the right the **Falangists**, basically a youth party founded in 1923 by **José Antonio Primo de Rivera** (son of the dictator), made uneasy bedfellows with conservative traditionalists and dissident elements in the army upset by modernizing reforms.

In an atmosphere of growing confusion, with mobs fighting on the streets and churches and monasteries being torched while landed estates were taken over by those impatient for agrarian reform, the left-wing Popular Front alliance won the general election of **February 1936** by a narrow margin. Normal life, though, became increasingly impossible: the economy was crippled by strikes, the universities became hotbeds for battles between Marxists and Falangists, and the government failed to exert its authority over anyone. Finally, on July 17, 1936, the military garrison in Morocco rebelled under **General Franco**'s leadership, to be followed by risings at military garrisons throughout the country. It was the culmination of years of scheming in the army, but in the event far from the overnight success its leaders almost certainly expected. Airlifting his troops into Seville by means of German transport planes, Franco ensured that the south and west quickly fell into Nationalist hands, but Madrid and the industrialized north and east remained loyal to the Republican government.

1830–70	1835	1898	1923–30
Romantic Age. Richard Ford's *A Handbook for Travellers in Spain* (1845) puts Andalucía on the visitors' map.	First Carlist War. Peasant risings throughout Andalucía.	Loss of Cuba, Spain's last American colony.	Primo de Rivera dictatorship. De Rivera resigns due to ill health and popular agitation urges a republic.

The Civil War

The ensuing **Civil War** was undoubtedly one of the most bitter and bloody the world has seen. Violent reprisals were taken on their enemies by both sides – the Republicans shooting priests and local landowners wholesale, the Nationalists carrying out mass slaughter of the population of almost every town they took. Contradictions were legion in the way the Spanish populations found themselves divided from each other. Perhaps the greatest irony was that Franco's troops, on their "holy" mission against a godless "anti-Spain", comprised a core of Moroccan troops from Spain's North African colony.

It was, too, the first **modern war** – Franco's German allies demonstrated their ability to wipe out entire civilian populations with their bombing raids on Gernika and Durango in the Basque country, and radio proved an important weapon, as Nationalist propagandists offered the starving Republicans "the white bread of Franco". Despite sporadic help from Russia and thousands of volunteers in the International Brigades, the Republic could never compete with the professional armies and the massive assistance from Fascist Italy and Nazi Germany enjoyed by the Nationalists. As hundreds of thousands of refugees flooded into France, **General Francisco Franco**, who had long before proclaimed himself head of state, took up the reins of power.

Franco's Spain

The early reprisals taken by the victors were on a massive and terrifying scale. Executions were commonplace in towns and villages, typified by the summary killing of **Blas Infante Pérez de Vargas**, "the father of Andalucían nationalism", by Falangist hoodlums at his home near Seville. Infante was a prominent regional autonomist and a libertarian socialist, both anathema to the new regime. His legacy today is the design of Andalucía's green and white flag. Other victims in Andalucía included playwright Federico García Lorca, while artists and writers such as Nobel-prizewinner Juan Rámon Jiménez, Antonio Machado and Rafael Alberti fled the country to escape the same fate. The "White Terror", as the Francoist repression is now termed, imprisoned upwards of two million people in concentration camps until "order" had been established by authoritarian means. Only one party was permitted and censorship was rigidly enforced. By the end of World War II, during which Spain was too weak to be anything but neutral, **Franco** was the only fascist head of state left in Europe, and responsible for sanctioning more deaths than any other in Spanish history. Spain was economically and politically isolated and, bereft of markets, suffering – almost half the population were still tilling the soil for little or no return. The misery of the peasantry was particularly acute in Andalucía and forced mass emigrations to Madrid, Barcelona and Europe beyond.

When General Eisenhower visited Madrid in 1953 with the offer of huge loans, it came as water to the desert, and the price, the **establishment of American nuclear bases** such as those at Rota near Cádiz and Morón de la Frontera, was one Franco was more than willing to pay. Once firmly in the US camp the Franco regime (administered by the so-called *tecnocratas* group of ministers) rapidly transformed Spain into a market economy and in the late Fifties the country joined the International Monetary Fund, the International Bank for Reconstruction and Development and the OECD in quick succession. However belated, economic development was incredibly rapid, with Spain

1931	1936	1936
King Alfonso XIII is forced out; Second Republic is declared.	Spanish Civil War begins when army officers in Spanish Morocco under generals Mola and Francisco Franco lead a revolt.	Blas Infante, "father of Andalucían nationalism", executed by Franco's forces in Seville.

enjoying a growth rate second only to that of Japan for much of the 1960s, a boom fuelled by the tourist industry, the remittances of Spanish workers abroad and the illegality of strikes and industrial action at home. Increased **prosperity**, however, only underlined the political bankruptcy of Franco's regime and its inability to cope with popular demands. Higher incomes, the need for better education, and a creeping invasion of Western culture made the anachronism of Franco ever clearer. His only reaction was to attempt to withdraw what few signs of increased liberalism had crept through, and his last years mirrored the repression of the postwar period. Franco finally died in November 1975, nominating **King Juan Carlos** as his successor.

The new Spain

On October 28, 1982, *sevillano* Felipe González's Socialist Workers' Party – the PSOE – was elected with massive support to rule a country that had been firmly in the hands of the right for 43 years. The **Socialists** captured the imagination and the votes of nearly ten million Spaniards with the simplest of appeals: "for change". It was a telling comment on just how far Spain had moved since Franco's death, for in the intervening years change seemed the one factor that could still threaten the new-found democracy.

Certainly, in the Spain of 1976 the thought of a freely elected left-wing government would have been incredible. **King Juan Carlos** was the hand-picked successor of Franco, groomed for the job and very much in with the army – of which he remained official commander-in-chief. His initial moves were cautious in the extreme, appointing a government dominated by loyal Francoists who had little sympathy for the growing opposition demands for "democracy without adjectives".

To his credit, however, Juan Carlos recognized that some real break with the past was now urgent and inevitable, and set in motion the process of **democratization**. He legitimized the Socialist Party and, controversially, the Communists. When elections were held in June 1977, the centre-right **UCD** Christian-Democrat party gained a 34 percent share of the vote, the **PSOE** (Spanish Socialist Workers' Party) coming in second with 28 percent, and the Communists and Francoist Alianza Popular both marginalized at nine percent and eight percent.

It was almost certainly a vote for democratic stability rather than for ideology. The king, perhaps recognizing that his own future depended on the maintenance of the new democracy, lent it his support – most notably in February 1981 when a tragicomic Civil Guard colonel named Tejero stormed the Cortes brandishing a revolver and, with other officers loyal to Franco's memory, attempted to institute an **army coup**. But the crisis, for a while, was real. Tanks were brought out onto the streets of Valencia, and only three of the army's ten regional commanders remained unreservedly loyal to the government. But as it became clear that the king would not support the plotters, most of the rest affirmed their support. Juan Carlos had taken the decision of his life and emerged with immensely enhanced prestige in the eyes of most Spaniards.

The new political system had successfully dealt with the first real challenge to its authority and following these events Spanish democracy – even in army circles where most of the old guard were gradually pensioned off – now became firmly institutionalized. And in the fourteen-year rule of the charismatic **Felipe González** (always known as "Felipe") and the PSOE the system found, at least until the

1939	1953	1962	1975	1980
Civil War ends; Franco dictatorship begins.	US makes economic deal with Franco in return for military bases.	Development of Costa del Sol tourism begins.	Death of Franco. Spain reverts to a constitutional monarchy.	Andalucía votes to become an autonomous region.

Nineties' slide into the political mire and defeat, a party of enduring **stability** and to the left of exasperating **moderation**.

The swing to the right

The final years of González's and the PSOE's period in power were dogged by a series of **scandals**. The most serious of all, however, was the **GAL affair** (Grupo Antiterrorista de Liberación) when it was discovered that a state-sponsored antiterrorist unit had been fighting a dirty war against ETA that included kidnappings and even assassinations of suspected terrorists. The press – and a later judicial investigation – exposed police participation in these crimes and a clear chain of command reaching up to the highest echelons of the PSOE government. González narrowly avoided being hauled before the courts, and the nation's progressive disillusion with his government saw the rise to prominence of **José-María Aznar** as leader of the **Partido Popular** conservatives (a merger of the UCD and Alianza Popular).

A former tax inspector with little charisma, Aznar offered dogged criticism of the PSOE government's incompetence and corruption that finally won the PP a narrow **victory** in the 1996 elections. Unable to make any significant impact on changing public opinion and with the PSOE in turmoil, early in 1998 González finally **resigned** from the leadership of the party he had led in government and opposition for 23 years.

A desperate PSOE then formed an alliance with the ex-Communist Izquierda Unida party, believing that their combined votes could still prevent a likely Aznar victory in the forthcoming general election. However, the voters turned out to support the government and the outcome of the March 2000 **general election** was a stunning **triumph for Aznar** and the PP, and for the first time since the death of Franco the right was in power with an overall majority.

The result was disaster for the left, and the PSOE then elected **José Luis Rodríguez Zapatero**, a relatively unknown young politician as leader. A moderate, Zapatero admitted the PSOE's past mistakes, stating emphatically that any government led by him would be radically different. This seemed to go down well with the electorate, and the opinion polls started to move in the PSOE's favour.

The return of the PSOE

In 2001, José María Aznar announced that he would lead the PP up to the next general election but would then resign, and that it must seek a new leader. As leader designate (to take over following the election), the party chose Aznar's nominee, the less prickly, cigar-puffing **Mariano Rajoy**, minister for the interior and deputy prime minister. Early in 2004 all the indicators suggested the following March general election would deliver a comfortable victory for the ruling PP and its new leader. Then on March 11, and three days before polling day, a series of **bombs exploded on rush-hour commuter trains** travelling into Madrid, killing 191 people and injuring almost two thousand others. The nation was thrown into shock by the most savage attack seen in Spain since the Civil War. Despite the discovery by police within hours of a van connected to the bombings containing detonators and a Koranic audiotape, the PP leadership decided that the Basque terrorist group ETA had to be the culprits. This was a high-risk

1981	1982	1985
Attempted military coup fails; members of parliament are held hostage in the Spanish Parliament.	Sevillano and PSOE leader Felipe González elected prime minister. Elections for first Andalucían parliament.	Spain–Gibraltar frontier opens after being closed by Franco in 1969 protesting the British presence.

tactic for the government but it seemed convinced that by pinning the responsibility on ETA it would deflect attention away from its support for the Iraq war (ninety percent of Spaniards had been against it) just long enough for the votes to be counted. No mention was to be made of any possible link with Islamic militant groups and at the same time the blaming of ETA would conveniently vindicate Aznar's hardline stance against Basque terrorism and separatism.

The scheme failed. Many voters saw through the government's "blame ETA" smokescreen and correctly believed that the attack to be the work of Islamic terrorists as a retaliation for Spain's participation in the Iraq war. The result was an unexpected victory for Zapatero and the PSOE, whose first act was to announce the immediate withdrawal of Spanish troops from Iraq, an election promise. This aligned him firmly with the German and French governments in Europe to whom Aznar had been hostile, but incurred the displeasure of US president George W. Bush, who shunned Zapatero for the rest of his presidency.

Zapatero's initial record was competent if unspectacular. He enjoyed the benefit of a favourable economic climate with consistently high growth figures and an economy producing more jobs than any other euro-zone member. But in the latter part of 2007, the impact of the **world economic downturn** became desperately felt in Spain, as one of the major drivers of the Spanish economy, the huge construction industry, went into meltdown. The general election of March 2008 took place against a backdrop of economic uncertainty, and although the result was another PSOE victory the reality was that they had scraped home seven seats short of an overall parliamentary majority.

The PSOE government's second term was dominated by fallout from the post-2008 world financial and economic crisis. Unemployment rose to above twenty percent, while austerity programmes saw civil service and teachers' salaries cut, benefits and pensions frozen and welfare programmes cancelled. Appearing weary and indecisive, Zapatero announced that he would not lead the party into the next general election, and the party chose "safe pair of hands" veteran minister, Alfredo Pérez Rubalcaba, to succeed him. The subsequent 2011 election delivered the predicted landslide victory for the PP and the PSOE suffered its most crushing defeat since the return of democracy. In his victory speech the PP leader, and now prime minister, Mariano Rajoy, gravely announced that "Difficult times are coming" as the financial crisis continued to wreak havoc across world markets.

Difficult times

On taking power the Rajoy government first blamed the socialists for the economic mess in which they had left the country, and then set about imposing even harsher **austerity measures** than the outgoing administration, dictated by the EU in Brussels and the German government in Berlin. Having been promised, that cutting government debt would eventually lead to prosperity, the reality for vast numbers of Spaniards has been unemployment, which soared to 27 percent in 2014, the highest in the EU. The major victims of this tragedy have been the under-30 age group, close to 50 percent of whom are out of work.

Other headaches for Rajoy's ministers included a **banking crisis** and **endemic corruption**, which has left the country with unfinished airports, tramways and metro systems – all constructed during the boom years at eye-watering cost – that are

1986	1992	1996
Spain joins the European Union.	Expo '92 World Fair in Seville celebrates 500th anniversary of Columbus's discovery of America.	Felipe González and PSOE lose general election after fourteen years in power.

unlikely ever to see a plane, tram or train. Embarrassingly for Rajoy, one of the biggest corruption scandals involved the PP's party treasurer who not only stashed away tens of millions of party funds in Swiss bank accounts, but claimed that the party's senior politicians (including Rajoy) had all received regular and illegal cash payments in brown envelopes (ie tax free).

The perennial stone in the shoe of Madrid administrations, the **autonomous region of Catalunya**, also caused unwelcome waves by announcing its intention to hold a referendum on independence in November 2014. In response, Madrid flatly stated that this would be unconstitutional and therefore illegal. When the Tribunal Constitucional (Constitutional Court) backed the government view and declared the referendum illegal the Catalan government rebranded the poll as a "participation exercise" carrying only a symbolic function. It thus went ahead and when the votes were counted there was an eighty-percent majority in favour of independence. However, the turnout was low and the poll was widely boycotted by those opposed to independence. The Constitutional Court later decided that the poll had nevertheless been illegal and the Catalan president Artur Mas and other ministers who had organised the ballot were suspended from office and given heavy fines.

A new political landscape

In the spring of 2014 further convulsions were taking place in the PSOE opposition party, after a series of opinion polls ranked the party in second place to a highly unpopular PP government. Blame for their poor showing fell on leader Alfredo Pérez Rubalcaba and, following a disastrous performance by the party in the European Elections, he offered his resignation. At a special congress the party chose Pedro Sánchez, a telegenic university economics lecturer, as its new leader. Sanchez adopted an uncompromising abrasive style in dealing with the PP government which did not go down well with many of the party's *barones* ("barons") such as Felipe Gónzalez and José Luís Rodríguez Zapatero who favoured a more consensual approach. Leading the party into the December 2015 general election he lost to the PP who, despite winning the most seats, fell well short of a majority. The PSOE performance was hampered by the arrival of a new radical party, **Podemos** (We Can), which captured a large number of votes from younger Spaniards, tired of the traditional two-party "charade". Podemos's leader, the 39-year-old bearded and pony-tailed **Pablo Iglesias**, attracted large crowds to his hustings, declaring that he was determined to undermine the corrupt regime – including all the major parties – that has governed Spain since the death of Franco.

The governing PP was stricken by almost constant media stories of corruption at national and local levels which had led to a loss of its core supporters. Many of these had been attracted by a new centre-right party, **Ciudadanos** (Citizens), led by a charismatic 37-year-old lawyer, Albert Rivera. A Catalan opposed to the secession of Catalunya from Spain, he has received death threats from Catalan nationalists.

In an attempt to resolve the stalemate following the 2015 election the PP government announced a new election for June 2016. Now a four-party race, the result was once more inconclusive with the PP again finishing as the largest party but forty seats short of an overall majority. The result was even worse for the PSOE, whose 85-seat haul was the lowest in its 140-year history. Despite having had to face a new challenge from Podemos, Sanchez was blamed by the *barones* and the party hierarchy for the terrible

2000	2002	2003	2004
Partido Popular election victory gives the right an overall majority for first time since Franco dictatorship.	Spain adopts the euro currency.	Picasso museum opens in Málaga, the artist's birthplace.	Madrid train bombings kill 191 and injure thousands, influencing the outcome of the general election held three days later.

result and a civil war in the party led to Sanchez resigning from his position as leader and as a member of the Congress. He declared that he would go out on the road to convince the PSOE membership that his policies were the only ones that could win power again. A new election for the leadership was held in May 2017 with Sanchez again as a candidate facing the *barones'* preferred choice of Susana Díez, president of the region of Andalucía. Against most expectations, the rank and file supported him and Sanchez won a remarkable victory.

The 2016 election result produced the most fragmented parliament since the return of democracy in 1977. The negotiations between the four major parties failed to produce a stable coalition and Rajoy and the PP are currently in power as a minority government, dependent upon smaller parties and abstentions to get them through key votes.

But the wider picture is worrying. Spain is only now starting to recover from the worst recession in decades, which saw a property crash and unemployment peaking at 27 per cent, with over 50 per cent unemployment for adults under 25. While the jobs market is improving, unemployment is still at 18 per cent – more than double the pre-crisis rate of 8.5 per cent, and the second highest in Europe behind Greece. Rather than resolving Spain's political problems, the elections have only added to the political uncertainty and instability leaving Spain with a government unlikely to last a full parliamentary term – with all the implicit damaging consequences for the Spanish economy.

Modern Andalucía

Andalucía shared in the progressive decentralization of power in Spain throughout the post-Franco period and in 1980 became an **Autonomous Region** with a regional government (Junta de Andalucía) based in Seville. Largely because of its enduring social problems, Andalucía remained a socialist bulwark for the PSOE throughout the Eighties – the so-called *sartenilla* (frying pan) of the south that traditionally "fries" the right-wing votes further north. During the 1990s this support enabled the discredited PSOE government of Felipe González to remain in power while denying Aznar's PP its longed-for majority when it finally did become the largest party.

Despite a more fickle attitude to voting (or abstaining) in general elections, which allowed the PP to eventually win a majority in the national parliament, in regional elections to Andalucía's **autonomous parliament** *andaluzes* have voted solidly and consistently to maintain this in the hands of the PSOE. The PSOE's victory in 2015 (albeit with a junior coalition partner) was the tenth in a row for a socialist party that has held the reins of power for the whole of the period since regional elections were inaugurated in 1982.

Among a number of corruption scandals which threatened to end the PSOE's monopoly of power in Andalucía, by far the biggest was the so-called **EREs corruption case** – the second largest of its kind in Spanish history – in which as much as €1.2 billion euros of public funds and EU grants were siphoned off into the hands of politicians and administrators. Almost 250 politicians and public officials have been arrested to face trial. The money, which was used to buy cars, houses and luxury goods, as well as prostitutes and cocaine, was intended to aid the embattled Andalucían

2007–8	2014	2017
World economic downturn hits Andalucía; unemployment rises steeply.	Following scandals involving the royal family, King Juan Carlos I abdicates in favour of his son who becomes Felipe VI with his consort Queen Letizia.	After sixty years Basque militant group ETA ends its armed campaign and surrenders its arms caches.

economy, stimulate employment and keep ailing companies afloat. But many members of the regional government saw it merely as a means to feather their own nests. EREs (Expedientes de Regulación de Empleo) are grants made to overstaffed companies to enable them to reduce their workforces with redundancy payments and thus improve their competitiveness. But many "employees" who received these payments had never worked for the companies that issued them. Other payments were channelled into fake companies set up merely to receive the illegal monies. The ensuing and interminable court case (which opened in 2011, is still ongoing and due to restart in 2018) revealed a breathtaking lapse of any apparent control over the use of these funds by the Andalucían government or the EU authorities in Brussels. When the scandal hit the headlines, Andalucía's PSOE leader and president **Antonio Griñan** resigned. He has now been formally charged along with his predecessor Manuel Chaves and twenty other ministers and senior civil servants in the regional government.

His successor as PSOE leader, **Susana Díaz**, in an attempt to distance the party from the scandal, set up an Anti-Fraud and Corruption Office in the Junta de Andalucía and declared that every last eurocent spent by the regional government in the last twenty years will be investigated and where fraud has taken place those responsible will answer to the courts.

Times of crisis

For the ordinary people of Andalucía the combined effects of the prolonged **economic crisis** and a stagnant economy have been a devastating blow. Contradicting the sunny image presented to most of its visitors, chronic economic and social problems continue to plague the region, and not for nothing is Andalucía known as the "workhouse of Spain". The regional **unemployment** level is among the European Union's highest at an alarming 28 percent (compared with 18 percent for Spain as a whole), although this spikes to over 30 percent in provinces such as Cádiz and Jaén, the region's poorest. Earnings per head are also a third lower than the national average. The region has also been severely affected by Spain's **economic recession**. The collapse of the building sector led to construction companies going bust, estate agents filing for bankruptcy and tens of thousands of unemployed building workers swelling the dole queues. As a result, poverty is real and food banks are common features in towns and cities across the region.

On **the land** ancient problems remain. Jaén province has been called the world capital of olive oil. It accounts for thirty percent of world production and over forty percent of Spain's. The olive oil industry is the province's greatest employer with ninety percent of the workforce reliant on it. But the harvesting season – which provides the majority of jobs – only runs from October to April, and then the workers are once again laid off. There is little other work available and it is a hard struggle for most agricultural workers to provide a decent living for their families. Another major problem that remains from the nineteenth century is the **vast inequality in land ownership**. In Andalucía some two percent of the population still owns more than sixty percent of the land. In Jaén this means a small number of big landowners and very few smallholders. Creating jobs has never been a priority for the big concerns and now they are using EU grants to mechanize the olive harvest, similar to what has happened with grapes, thus reducing the number of jobs even further.

2018	**2020**
Pedro Sánchez of the Spanish Socialist Workers' Party (PSOE) becomes Prime Minister.	Pedro Sánchez starts a second term, overseeing Spain's first coalition government since the 1930s. Spain suffers one of the worst Covid-19 crises in the world, with the health service essentially overwhelmed, with over 114,000 deaths.

The resulting hard times are pushing *andaluzes* towards the time-honoured solution – **emigration**. In the 1950s and 1960s, 1.7 million people left the region for other parts of Spain or jobs in the factories of Germany or France. Their grandchildren are now following in their footsteps to Germany, France, the UK and other parts of Europe. The difference from earlier migrations is that many of those emigrating this time are highly educated or trained workers between the age of 25 and 35, including researchers, biologists, architects, physicians, engineers and information technologists, many of whom have lost their jobs in the recession. As these are precisely the kind of workers that the region cannot afford to lose if it wishes to take advantage of any economic upturn, the implications are disturbing.

Andalucía's **education** system, which should be the hope for the future, has suffered grievous cuts in expenditure in addition to a new package of reforms – the eighth in recent decades – as the central government endeavours to impose its ideas in the absence of any political consensus. But as demotivated teachers – victims of pay cuts and wage freezes – attempt to implement the latest round of changes, the students vote with their feet: over 35 percent of the region's 18–24 age group dropped out of school at 16. The unsurprising result is that Andalucía comes near the bottom of tables measuring Spanish academic performance, while in international comparisons Spain itself falls well below the world average for a developed country.

2021	2022
After challenging times for the tourism industry, Spain fully reopens for visitors.	The Madrid Summit took place with NATO leaders from around the world, the first in Spain for 25 years.

Flamenco

Flamenco is undoubtedly the most important musical-cultural phenomenon in Spain. Over the past couple of decades it has experienced a huge resurgence in popularity, and a profile that has reached out far beyond its Andalucían homeland. The sanitized kitsch flamenco, all frills and castanets, exploited as an image of tourist Spain during the Franco period, has been left far behind by a new age expressing the vitality and attitudes of a younger generation of flamenco clans. In line with this trend, in 2010 UNESCO added flamenco to its intangible cultural heritage list, as a world-class art form to be encouraged, protected and supported.

In Andalucía, the fact that the public are so knowledgeable and demanding about flamenco means that musicians, singers and dancers found even at the most humble local club or festival are usually very good indeed.

Origins

The **roots of flamenco** evolved in southern Spain from many sources: Morocco, Egypt, India, Pakistan, Greece and other parts of the Near and Far East. How exactly they came together as flamenco is a source of great debate and obscurity, though most authorities believe the roots of the music were brought by **gypsies** arriving in the fifteenth century. In the following century, it fused with elements of Arab and Jewish music in the Andalucían mountains, where Jews, Muslims and "pagan" gypsies had taken refuge from the forced conversions and clearances effected by the Catholic monarchs and the Church. The main flamenco centres and families are to be found today in quarters and towns of gypsy and refugee origin, such as Alcalá del Río, Utrera, Jerez, Cádiz and the Triana *barrio* of Seville.

There are two theories about the origins of the name flamenco. One contends that Spanish Jews migrated through trade to Flanders, where they were allowed to sing their religious chants unmolested, and that these chants became referred to as flamenco by the Jews who stayed in Spain. The other is that the word is a mispronunciation of the Arabic words *felag* (fugitive) and *mengu* (peasant), a plausible idea, as Arabic was a common language in Spain at the time.

The gypsy inheritance

Flamenco aficionados enjoy heated debate about the purity of their art and whether it is more validly performed by a **gitano** (gypsy) or a **payo** (non-gypsy). Certainly, flamenco seems to have thrived enclosed, preserved and protected by the oral tradition of the gypsy clans. Its power, and the despair which its creation overcomes, has emerged from the precarious and vulnerable lives of a people surviving for centuries at the margins of society. Flamenco reflects a passionate need to preserve their self-esteem. These days, there are as many acclaimed *payo* as *gitano* flamenco artists. However, the concept of an **active inheritance** is crucial. The veteran singer **Fernanda de Utrera**, one of the great voices of "pure flamenco", was born in 1923 into a gypsy family in Utrera, one of the *cantaora* centres. She was the granddaughter of the legendary singer "Pinini", who had created her own individual flamenco forms, and with her younger sister Bernarda, also a notable singer, inherited their flamenco with their genes. Even the members of **Ketama**, the ground-breaking Madrid-based flamenco-rock group who split up in 2004, came from two gypsy clans – the Sotos and the Carmonas.

The Golden Age

Although flamenco's exact origins are obscure, it is generally agreed that its "laws" were established in the nineteenth century. Indeed, from the mid-nineteenth century into the early twentieth, flamenco enjoyed a legendary "**Golden Age**", the tail end of which is preserved on some of the earliest 1930s recordings. The original musicians found a home in the *cafés cantantes*, traditional taverns which had their own group of performers (*cuadros*). One of the most famous was the *Café de Chinitas* in Málaga (see page 71), immortalized by the Granada-born poet García Lorca. In his poem *A las cinco de la tarde* (*At five in the Afternoon*), Lorca claimed that flamenco is deeply related to bullfighting, not only sharing root emotions and passions, and flashes of erratic genius, but because both are possible ways to break out of social and economic marginality. Just such a transformation happened in 1922 when the composer Manuel de Falla, the guitarist Andrés Segovia and the poet García Lorca were present for a legendary *Concurso de Cante Jondo*. A gypsy boy singer, **Manolo Caracol**, reportedly walked all the way from Jerez and won the competition with the voice and flamboyant personality that were to make him a legend throughout Spain and South America. The other key figure of this period, who can be heard on a few recently remastered recordings, was **Pastora Pavón**, known as *La Niña de Los Peines*, and popularly acclaimed as the greatest female flamenco voice of the twentieth century. In addition to *cafés cantantes*, flamenco surfaced – as it does today – at fiestas, in bars or *tablaos* and at *juergas*, informal, private parties.

The art of flamenco

It is essential for an artist to invoke a response, to know they are reaching deep into the emotional psyche of their audience. They may achieve the rare quality of **duende** – total emotional communication with their audience, and the mark of great flamenco of whatever style or generation. *Duende* is an ethereal quality: moving, profound even when expressing happiness, mysterious but nevertheless felt, a quality that stops listeners in their tracks. And many of those listeners are intensely involved, for flamenco is not just a music – for many it is a way of life, a **philosophy** that influences daily activities. A flamenco is not only a performer but anyone who is actively and emotionally involved in the unique philosophy.

The music

For the musicians, this fullness of expression is integral to their art, which is why, for as many famous names as one can list, there are many, many other lesser-known musicians whose work is startlingly good. Not every superb flamenco musician gets to be famous, or even to record, for flamenco thrives most in **live performance**. Exhilarating, challenging and physically stimulating, it is an art form that allows its exponents huge scope to improvise while obeying certain rules. Flamenco guitarist Juan Martín has remarked that "in microcosm it imitates Spanish society – traditional on the outside but, within, incredible anarchy".

There is a **classical repertoire** of more than sixty flamenco songs (*cantes*) and dances (*danzas*) – some solos, some group numbers, some with instrumental accompaniment, others *a cappella*. These different forms of flamenco are grouped in "families" according to more or less common melodic themes. The most common beat cycle is twelve – as in the blues. Each piece is executed by juxtaposing a number of complete musical units called *coplas*. Their number varies depending on the atmosphere the *cantaor* wishes to establish and the emotional tone they wish to convey. A song such as a *cante por solea* may take a familiar 3/4 rhythm, divide phrases into 4/8 measures, and then fragmentally subdivide again with voice ornamentation on top of that. The resulting complexity and the variations between similar phrases constantly undermine repetition, contributing greatly to the climactic and cathartic structure of each song.

FLAMENCO DANCE

Most popular images of flamenco dance – twirling bodies in frilled dresses, rounded arms complete with castanets – are **sevillanas**, the folk dances performed at fiestas, and, in recent years, on the nightclub floor. "Real" flamenco dance is something rather different and, like the music, can reduce the onlooker to tears in an unexpected flash, a cathartic point after which the dance dissolves. What is so visually devastating about flamenco dance is the physical and emotional control the dancer has over the body: the way the head is held, the tension of the torso and the way it allows the shoulders to move, the shapes and angles of seemingly elongated arms, and the feet, which move from toe to heel, heel to toe, creating rhythms. These rhythms have a basic set of moves and timings but they are improvised as the piece develops and through interaction with the guitarist.

Flamenco dance dates back to about 1750 and, along with the music, moved from the streets and private parties into the *cafés cantantes* at the end of the nineteenth century. This was a great boost for the dancers' art, providing a home for professional performers, where they could inspire each other. It was here that legendary dancers like **El Raspao** and **El Estampio** began to develop the spellbinding footwork and extraordinary moves that characterize modern flamenco dance, while women adopted for the first time the flamboyant **hata de cola** – the glorious long-trained dresses, cut high at the front to expose their fast moving ankles and feet.

Around 1910, flamenco dance had moved into Spanish theatres, and dancers like **La Niña de los Peines** (see page 546) and **La Argentina** were major stars. They mixed flamenco into programmes with other dances and also made dramatic appearances at the end of comic plays and silent movie programmes. **Flamenco opera** was established, interlinking singing, dancing and guitar solos in comedies with a local flamenco flavour.

In 1915 the composer Manuel de Falla composed the first flamenco ballet, **El Amor Brujo** (*Love, the Magician*), for the dancer Pastora Imperio. The celebrated dancer, **La Argentina**, who had established the first Spanish dance company, took her version of the ballet abroad in the 1920s, and with her choreographic innovations, flamenco dance came of age, working as a narrative in its own right. Another key figure in flamenco history was **Carmen Amaya**, who from the 1930s to the 1960s took flamenco dance on tour around the world, and into the movies. In the 1950s the dance found a new home in the **tablaos**, the aficionados' bars, which became enormously important as places to serve out a public apprenticeship. More recently the demanding audiences at local and national fiestas have played a part.

Artistic developments were forged in the 1960s by **Matilde Coral**, who updated the classic dance style, and in the 1970s by **Manuela Carrasco**, who had such impact with her fiery feet movement, continuing a rhythm for an intense and seemingly impossible period, that this new style was named after her (*manuelas*). Manuela Carrasco set the tone for the highly individual dancers of the 1980s and 1990s, such as **Mario Maya** and **Antonio Gades**. These two dancers and choreographers have provided a theatrically inspired staging for the dance, most significantly by extending the role of a dance dialogue and story – often reflecting on the potency of love and passion, their dangers and destructiveness.

Gades has led his own company on world tours but it is his influence on film that has been most important. He had appeared with Carmen Amaya in *Los Araños* in 1963 but in the 1980s began his own trilogy with film-maker Carlos Saura: *Boda de Sangre* (Lorca's play, *Blood Wedding*), *Carmen* (a reinterpretation of the opera) and *El Amor Brujo* (a film version of de Falla's work). The films featured Paco de Lucía and his band, and the dancers **Laura del Sol** and **Christina Hoyos** – the latter one of the great contemporary dancers. Hoyos herself created a superb ballet, *Sueños Flamencos* (*Flamenco Dreams*) and was also a force behind the founding of Seville's Museo del Baile Flamenco (see page 267).

Songs and singer

Flamenco **songs** often express pain, and with a fierceness that turns that emotion inside out. Generally, the voice closely interacts with improvising guitar (*toque*), the two inspiring each other, aided by the **jaleo**: the hand-clapping *palmas*, finger-snapping *palillos* and shouts from participants at certain points in the song. This *jaleo* sets the tone by creating the right atmosphere for the singer or dancer to begin, and bolsters and appreciates the talent of the artist as they develop the piece.

Aficionados will shout encouragement, most commonly "*¡Olé!*" – when an artist is getting deep into a song – but also a variety of stranger-sounding phrases. A stunning piece of dancing may, for example, be greeted with "*¡Viva la máquina escribir!*" (long live the typewriter), as the heels of the dancer move so fast they sound like a machine; or the cry may be "*¡Agua!*" (water), as the scarcity of water in Andalucía has given the word a kind of glory. An essential characteristic of flamenco is the singer or dancer taking certain risks, by putting into their performance feelings and emotions that arise directly from their own life experience, exposing their own **vulnerabilities**. Aficionados tend to acclaim more a voice that gains effect from surprise and startling moves than one governed by recognized musical logic. Vocal prowess or virtuosity can be deepened by sobs, gesticulation and an intensity of expression that can have a shattering effect on an audience. Thus pauses, breaths, body and facial gestures of anger and pain transform performance into **cathartic events**. *Siguiriyas*, which date from the Golden Age, and whose theme is usually death, have been described as cries of despair in the form of a funeral psalm. In contrast there are many songs and dances such as *tangos*, *sevillanas* and *fandangos* that capture great **joy**.

The **sevillana** originated in medieval Seville as a spring country dance, with verses improvised and sung to the accompaniment of guitar and castanets (which are rarely used in other forms of flamenco). **El Pali** (Francisco Palacios), who died in 1988, was the most well-known and prolific *sevillana* musician, his unusually gentle voice and accompanying strummed guitar combining an enviable musical pace with a talent for composing popular poetic lyrics. In the last few years dancing *sevillanas* has become popular in bars and clubs throughout Spain, but their great natural habitats are **Seville's April Feria** and the annual pilgrimage to **El Rocío**. It is during the Seville *feria* that most new recordings of *sevillanas* emerge.

Among the best contemporary singers are the aforementioned **Fernanda** and **Bernarda de Utrera**, **Enrique Morente**, **El Cabrero**, **Juan Peña El Lebrijano**, the **Sorderas**, **Fosforito**, **José Menese** and **Carmen Linares**. However, one of the most popular and commercially successful singers of modern flamenco was the extraordinary **El Camarón de la Isla** (the "Shrimp of the Isle" of León, near his Cádiz home), who died in 1992. Collaborating with the guitarists Paco and Pepe de Lucía, and latterly Tomatito, Camarón raised **cante jondo**, the virtuoso "deep song", to a new art. His high-toned voice had a corrosive, rough-timbred edge, cracking at certain points to release a ravaged core sound. His incisive sense of rhythm, coupled with almost violent emotional intensity, made him the quintessential singer of the times.

Flamenco guitar

The flamenco performance is filled with pauses. The singer is free to insert phrases seemingly on the spur of the moment. The **guitar accompaniment**, while spontaneous, is precise and serves one single purpose – to mark the *compas* (measures) of a song and organize rhythmical lines. Instrumental interludes which are arranged to meet the needs of the *cantaor* (as the creative singer is called) not only catch the mood and intention of the song and mirror it, but allow the guitarist to extemporize what are called *falsetas* (short variations) at will. When singer and guitarist are in true rapport the intensity of a song develops rapidly, the one charging the other, until the effect can be overwhelming.

The flamenco **guitar** weighs less than most acoustic guitars and often has a pine table and pegs made of wood rather than machine heads. This is to produce the preferred bright responsive sound that does not sustain too long (as opposed to the mellow and longer sustaining sound of classical guitar). If the sound did sustain, particularly in fast pieces, chords would carry over into each other.

NUEVO FLAMENCO: AN EVOLVING ART FORM

In the 1980s, the Spanish press hailed **Ketama** (named after a Moroccan village famed for its hashish) as creators of the music of the "New Spain" after the release of their eponymous first album, which fused flamenco with rock and latin salsa. Later they pushed the frontiers of flamenco further still by recording *Songhai*, an album collaborating with Malian *kora* player Toumani Diabate and British bassist Danny Thompson, followed by *De Aki A Ketama* developing more rock-fusion themes. *Blues de la Frontera* (Frontier Blues), the first disc of **Pata Negra** ("black leg" – the highest quality of cured ham – and an everyday term used for anything good), caused an equal sensation. This flamenco revival of the 1980s and 1990s is no longer confined to the purists who kept old-time flamenco alive in their *peñas* or clubs. On radio and on CD-players blaring from market stalls right across the country you hear the typical high-pitched treble tones of commercial flamenco singers such as **Tijeritas**. The European success of the flamenco-rumba of the **Gipsy Kings**, a high-profile gypsy group from southern France, has further opened and prepared the ear of European popular audiences for something more powerful. Rumba, a Latin form, has come back to Spain from Latin America, and so is known as a music of *ida y vuelta* ("go and return"), one of the many fusions of the Spanish music taken to the New World with the *conquistadores* and their descendants, where it has mixed with African and other elements, before making its way back again. The impetus began at the end of the 1970s, with the innovations of guitarist **Paco de Lucía** and, especially, the late great singer **El Camarón de la Isla**. These were musicians who had grown up learning from their flamenco families but whose own musical tastes have embraced international rock, jazz and blues. Paco de Lucía blended jazz and salsa with the flamenco sound. Camarón, simply, was an inspiration – and one whose own idols (and fans) included Chick Corea and Miles Davis, as well as flamenco artists. Latterly flamenco musicians are to be found playing in many different contexts, including rock and folk genres – the result is an exciting and dynamic scene.

The guitar used to be simply an accompanying instrument – originally the singers themselves played – but at the end of the nineteenth century and in the early decades of the twentieth century it began developing as a **solo** form, absorbing influences from classical and Latin American traditions. The greatest of these early guitarists was **Ramón Montoya**, who revolutionized flamenco guitar with his harmonies and introduced tremolo and a whole variety of arpeggios – techniques of right-hand playing. After him the revolution was continued by Sabicas and Niño Ricardo and Carlos Montoya. The classical guitarist **Andrés Segovia** was another influential figure; he began his career playing flamenco in Granada. Then in the 1960s came the two major guitarists of modern times, the late **Paco de Lucía** (see below) and **Manolo Sanlúcar**. These days, solo guitarists have immediately identifiable sounds and rhythms: the highly emotive **Pepe Habichuela** and **Tomatito**, for example, or the unusual rhythms of younger players like **Ramón el Portugués**, **Enrique de Melchor** and **Rafael Riqueni**. Flamenco guitar has now consolidated its position on the world's great stages as one of the most successful forms of instrumental music.

Nuevo flamenco

One of flamenco's great achievements has been to sustain itself while providing much of the foundation and inspiration for new music emerging in Spain today. In the 1950s and 1960s, rock'n'roll displaced traditional Spanish music, as it did indigenous music in many parts of the world. In the 1980s, however, flamenco reinvented itself, gaining new meaning and a new public through the music of Paco de Lucía, who mixed in **jazz**, **blues** and **salsa**, and, later, groups like Pata Negra and Ketama, who brought in more **rock** influences. Purists hated these innovations but, as José "El Sordo" (Deaf One) Soto, Ketama's main singer, explained, they were based on "the classic flamenco that we'd been singing and listening to since birth. We just found new forms in jazz and salsa: there are basic similarities in the rhythms, the constantly changing harmonies and improvisations. Blacks and gypsies have suffered similar segregation so our music has a lot in common."

Paco de Lucía, who made the first moves was, until his untimely death in 2014, the best known of all contemporary flamenco guitarists, and reached new audiences through his performance in Carlos Saura's films *Blood Wedding* and *Carmen*, along with the great flamenco dancers, Cristina Hoyos and Antonio Gades. Paco, who was a non-gypsy, won his first flamenco prize at the age of 14, and went on to accompany many of the great traditional singers, including a long partnership with Camarón de la Isla, one of the greatest collaborations of modern flamenco. He introduced new harmonies, chord structures, scales, open tunings and syncopation that initiated the most vital renaissance of *toque* since Ramón Montoya, a remarkable achievement considering the rigid and stylized nature of this most traditional of forms. He started forging new sounds and rhythms for flamenco following a trip to Brazil, where he fell in love with bossa nova, and in the 1970s he established a sextet with electric bass, Latin percussion, and, perhaps most shocking, flute and saxophone from Jorge Pardo. Paco also introduced into Spanish flamenco the Peruvian **cajón**, a half-box resembling an empty drawer played by sitting straddled across the top; this reintroduced the sound of the foot of the dancer. Over the latter period of his career he worked with jazz-rock guitarists such as John McLaughlin and Chick Corea, while his own regular band, featuring singer Ramón de Algeciras, was one of the most original and distinctive sounds on the flamenco scene.

Other artists experimented, too, throughout the 1980s. **Lolé y Manuel** updated the flamenco sound with original songs and huge success; **Jorge Pardo** followed Paco's jazz direction; **Salvador Tavora** and **Mario Maya** staged flamenco-based spectacles; and **Enrique Morente** and **Juan Peña El Lebrijano** both worked with Andalucían orchestras from Morocco, while **Amalgama** worked with southern Indian percussionists, revealing surprising stylistic unities. Another interesting crossover came with **Paco Peña**'s 1991 *Misa Flamenca* recording, a setting of the Catholic Mass to flamenco forms with the participation of established singers such as Rafael Montilla "El Chaparro" from Peña's native Córdoba, and a classical academy chorus. The more commercially successful crossover with rock and blues, pioneered by **Ketama** and **Pata Negra**, became known, in the 1990s, as **nuevo flamenco** (see box, page 547). This "movement" is associated particularly with the label Nuevos Medios, and in Andalucía, and also Madrid, where many of the bands are based, is a challenging, versatile and musically incestuous new scene, with musicians guesting at each other's gigs and on one another's records. The music is now a regular sound at nightclubs, too, through the appeal of singers like **Aurora**, one of the first to crack the pop charts, and **Martirio** (Isabel Quiñones Gutiérrez), a flamboyant personality who appears dressed in lace mantilla and shades, like a cameo from a Pedro Almodóvar film, and sings songs with ironic, contemporary lyrics about life in the cities.

In general, the new songs are more sensual and erotic than the traditional material, expressing a pain, suffering and love worth dying for. Martirio's producer, **Kiko Veneno**, who wrote Camarón's most popular song, *Volando voy*, is another artist who has brought a flamenco sensitivity to Spanish rock music, as has Rosario, one of Spain's top female singers. Other contemporary bands and singers to look out for on the scene include **La Barbería del Sur** (who add a dash of salsa), **Wili Giménez**, **Raimundo Amador** and **José El Francés**. In the mid-1990s **Radio Tarifa** emerged as an exciting group who started out as a trio, expanded to include African musicians, and whose output mixes Arabic and traditional sounds onto a flamenco base.

Flamenco continues to attract legions of new *aficionados* in the twenty-first century and with the addition of the new *Bienal de Flamenco* in Málaga – a six-month festival spread across the province – and the *Bienal de Sevilla*, which has been running for almost forty years, both demonstrate that flamenco is as popular now as it has ever been.

Jan Fairley

Books

The listings below represent a selective reading list on Andalucía and matters Spanish, especially in the sections on history. Most titles are in print, although we've included a few older classics. We have also included websites below for some publishers whose publications are not widely distributed and where it is possible to order from their website. Where the publisher has more than one entry the website appears in the details of the first publication listed.

A reliable **specialist source** in the UK for out-of-print books on all aspects of Spain is Paul Orssich, 2 St Stephens Terrace, London (⊚orssich.com). The ★ symbol indicates titles that are especially recommended.

GENERAL ACCOUNTS

INTRODUCTIONS

David Baird *Inside Andalusia; Back Roads of Southern Spain; East of Málaga* (Santana, Málaga; ⊚santanabooks.com). *Inside* is a book that grew out of the author's series of articles published in the now defunct *Lookout* magazine, giving an anecdotal, yet perceptive, overview of the region with plenty of interesting and offbeat observations and glossy illustrations. *Back Roads* is a drivers' guide to Andalucía, displaying the same erudition, while *East of Málaga* is an in-depth guide to the Axarquía and its coastline.

★ **John Hooper** *Spaniards: A Portrait of the New Spain.* This excellent, authoritative portrait of post-Franco Spain was originally written (by the *Guardian's* then Spain correspondent) in the 1980s. The revised second edition (2006) has already become somewhat dated, but despite only passing references to Andalucía, along with Giles Tremlett's book (see page 551), this is still one of the best possible introductions to contemporary Spain.

★ **Michael Jacobs** *Andalusia.* Well-crafted, opinionated and wide-ranging introduction to Andalucía. It covers everything from prehistory to the Civil War and manages to cram in perceptive pieces on flamenco, gypsies and food and drink. A gazeteer at the back details major sights. One of the best introductions to the region.

★ **Giles Tremlett** *Ghosts of Spain.* Tremlett (the Madrid correspondent of the *Guardian*) digs into the untold story of Spain's Civil War dead and the collective conspiracy of silence surrounding the war's terrors, and goes on to peel away the layers of the post-Franco era to present an enthralling and often disturbing study of contemporary Spain.

RECENT TRAVELS AND ACCOUNTS

Alastair Boyd *The Sierras of the South: Travels in the Mountains of Andalusia.* A sensitively worked portrait of the Serranía de Ronda which describes one Englishman's continuing love affair with a region he knew as home for twenty years. His earlier *The Road from Ronda* is a Sixties' view of the same landscape – the *campesinos* are still struggling.

Adam Hopkins *Spanish Journeys: A Portrait of Spain.* Although researched a couple of decades ago, this is still an enjoyable and highly stimulating exploration of Spanish history and culture, weaving its considerable scholarship in an accessible and unforced travelogue form, and full of illuminating anecdotes.

Elizabeth Nash *Seville, Córdoba and Granada: a cultural and literary history.* An eloquent, themed and multilayered exploration of the literary and cultural history of Andalucía's three major cities by *The Independent's* Madrid correspondent.

MERCURIO LITERARY REVIEW

Spanish-speakers should look out for **Mercurio** (⊚revistamercurio.es), an excellent monthly literary review carrying articles on Andalucía's literary figures past and present as well as reviews of many new books (fiction and nonfiction) dealing with *andaluz* and broader Spanish themes. Best of all, it's free and available from most good bookshops in the region's major towns and provincial capitals. If you can't locate a copy, email them from their website for a list of stockists.

★ **Chris Stewart** *Driving Over Lemons – An Optimist in Andalucía*. Author and musician Stewart describes – often hilariously – his move with family to an Alpujarran farmhouse (El Valero) and the numerous adventures involved in setting up house there. The sequel, *A Parrot in the Pepper Tree*, has more stories from El Valero interspersed with accounts of some of the author's earlier adventures as a sheep shearer in Sweden, drummer with rock band Genesis, and greenhorn flamenco guitarist in Seville. *The Almond Blossom Appreciation Society* delivered another cocktail of humorous, improbable and poignant tales. The "fourth book" in the trilogy, *The Last Days of the Bus Club*, was published in 2014 and ladles out another enjoyable helping of El Valero bonhomie.

EARLIER TWENTIETH-CENTURY WRITERS

★ **Gerald Brenan** *South From Granada; The Face of Spain*. *South From Granada* is an enduring classic. Brenan lived in a small village in Las Alpujarras in the 1920s, and records this and the visits of his Bloomsbury contemporaries Virginia Woolf, Lytton Strachey and Bertrand Russell. *The Face of Spain* is a later collection of highly readable travel writings gathered on a trip through Franco's Spain in 1949 with a substantial chunk devoted to Andalucía.

★ **Laurie Lee** *As I Walked Out One Midsummer Morning; A Rose For Winter; A Moment of War*. *Midsummer Morning* is the irresistibly romantic account of Lee's walk through Spain – from Vigo to Málaga – and his gradual awareness of the forces moving the country towards Civil War. As an autobiographical account, of living rough and busking his way from the Cotswolds with a violin, it's a delight; as a piece of social observation, painfully sharp. In *A Rose For Winter* Lee describes his return, twenty years later, to a very different Andalucía, while in *A Moment of War* he looks back again to describe a winter fighting with the International Brigade in the Civil War – an account by turns moving, comic and tragic.

James A. Michener *Iberia*. A bestselling, idiosyncratic and encyclopedic compendium of fascinating interviews and impressions of Spain in 1968 on the brink of the post-Franco years.

Jan Morris *Spain*. Morris wrote this in six months in 1960, on her (or, at the time, his) first visit to the country. It is an impressionistic account – good in its sweeping control of place and history, though prone to see everything as symbolic. The updated edition is plain bizarre in its ideas on Franco and dictatorship – a condition towards which Morris seems to believe Spaniards were naturally inclined.

Walter Starkie *Don Gypsy*. The tales of a Dublin professor who set out to walk the roads of Spain and Andalucía in the 1930s with only a fiddle for company. The pre-Civil War world

CUSTOMS AND CULTURE

★ **Edward Lewine** *Death and the Sun: A matador's season in the heart of Spain*. Bullfight aficionado Lewine takes on the perilous task of trying to make this Spanish

– good and bad – is astutely observed and his adventures are frequently amusing. Like Borrow earlier (see page 552), he fell for the gypsies and became an expert on their culture.

OLDER CLASSICS

George Borrow *The Bible in Spain; The Zincali*. On first publication in 1842, *The Bible in Spain* was subtitled by Borrow *Journeys, Adventures and Imprisonments of an English-man*; it is one of the most famous books on Spain – slow in places but with some very amusing stories. *Zincali* is an account of the Spanish gypsies, whom Borrow got to know pretty well and for whom he translated the Bible into *gitano*.

★ **Richard Ford** *A Handbook for Travellers in Spain; Gatherings from Spain*. The *Handbook*, first published in 1845, must be the best guide ever written to any country and stayed in print as a Murray's Handbook (one of the earliest series of guides) well into the twentieth century. Massively opinionated, it is an extremely witty book and in its British, nineteenth-century manner, incredibly knowledgeable and worth flicking through for the proverbs alone. *Gatherings* is a filleted – but no less entertaining – abridgement of the *Handbook* produced "for the ladies" who were not expected to be able to digest the original. Also recommended is the biography *Richard Ford, Hispanophile, Connoisseur and Critic* by Ian Robertson: a fascinating read, it illuminates the creation of Ford's great work and places him in the context of the Victorian world of arts and letters.

★ **Washington Irving** *Tales of the Alhambra* (originally published 1832; abridged editions are on sale in Granada). Half of Irving's book consists of Oriental stories, set in the Alhambra; the rest of accounts of his own residence there and the local characters of his time. Irving also wrote *The Conquest of Granada* (1829; o/p), a description of the fall of the Nasrids.

ANTHOLOGIES

Jimmy Burns (ed) *Spain: A Literary Companion*. A good anthology, including worthwhile nuggets of most authors recommended in this bibliography, amid a whole host of others.

Lucy McCauley *Travellers' Tales: Spain*. A wide-ranging anthology slanted towards more recent writing on Spain; includes strong pieces on Andalucía by many of the authors mentioned in this bibliography.

David Mitchell *Travellers in Spain: an Illustrated Anthology*. A well-told story of how four centuries of travellers – and most often travel writers – saw Spain. It's interesting to see Ford, Brenan, Laurie Lee and the rest set in context.

bloodsport comprehensible to nonbelievers. He spends a year on the road in the company of top matador Francisco Rivera Ordoñez – whose great-grandfather was revered by

Hemingway – and provides a fascinating insight into the gruelling routine of long road journeys between towns, often dingy hotels and the bitter recriminations when the "boss" has had a disastrous day in the ring.

Timothy Mitchell *Flamenco Deep Song*. Diametrically opposed to Woodall's work (see page 553), the author sets out to debunk the mystagogy of flamenco purists by arguing that they are shackling the form's development and ends up with an improbable defence of the Gipsy Kings. A

well-researched and entertaining read whether or not you accept its iconoclastic premise.

Paul Richardson *Our Lady of the Sewers*. An articulate and kaleidoscopic series of insights into rural Spain's customs and cultures, which are fast disappearing.

★ **James Woodall** *In Search of the Firedance: Spain through Flamenco*. This is a terrific history and exploration of flamenco, and as the subtitle suggests it goes way beyond the music alone to get to the heart of the culture.

HISTORY

GENERAL HISTORY

Juan Lalaguna *A Traveller's History of Spain*. A lucid – and pocketable – background history to the country, which spans the Phoenicians to Franco, Felipe González and the emergence of democratic Spain.

M. Vincent & R.A. Stradling *Cultural Atlas of Spain and Portugal*. The deceptive, coffee-table format belies a formidable historical, artistic and social survey of the Iberian peninsula from ancient times to the present; excellent colour maps and well-chosen photos amplify the text.

PREHISTORIC AND ROMAN PERIODS

James M. Anderson *Spain: 1001 Archaeological Sites*. A good guide and gazetteer of Spain's archeological sites with detailed instructions on how to get to them.

Henri Breuil *Rock Paintings of Southern Andalucía*. Published in 1929, this is still the definitive guide to the subject.

Roger Collins *Spain: An Archeological Guide*. Covering around 140 sites, temples, mosques and palaces dating from prehistory to the twelfth century, this book devotes more space per entry to maps, plans and data, making it a more useful *vade mecum* to the major sites than Anderson's work (see above).

Maria Cruz Fernández Castro *Iberia in Prehistory*. A major study of the Iberian peninsula prior to the arrival of the Romans, which includes extensive coverage of early Andalucían sites such as Los Millares as well as the later Iberian settlements encountered by the Phoenicians and Greeks. This is the first volume of the publisher's (Blackwells) important series on the history of Spain from the prehistoric era through to the Civil War.

S.J. Keay *Roman Spain* (British Museum Publications/ California UP). Definitive survey of a neglected subject, well illustrated and highly readable.

John S. Richardson *The Romans in Spain*. A new look at how Spain came to be a part of the Roman world, which also examines the influences that flowed from Spain to Rome – and vice versa.

Chris Stringer & Robin McKie *African Exodus*. If you want to understand Spain's role in the Neanderthal story, this lively and accessible account by an expert in the field

(aided by the science editor of *The Observer*) is the book. The story of the last of the Neanderthals hanging on in a cave above the Zaffaraya Pass in northern Málaga only adds to the drama of the landscape itself.

VISIGOTHIC SPAIN TO THE NINETEENTH CENTURY

J.M. Cohen *The Four Voyages of Christopher Columbus*. The man behind the myth; Columbus's astonishing voyages as described by the man himself in his log are interwoven with opinions of contemporaries on the great explorer, including his biographer son Hernando. A fascinating collection, superbly translated.

Roger Collins *The Arab Conquest of Spain 710–97*. Cogently argued and controversial study which documents the Moorish invasion and the significant influence that the conquered Visigoths had on the formative phase of Muslim rule by a scholar uniquely expert in both fields. Collins's *Visigothic Spain* is a significant companion volume, while his earlier *Early Medieval Spain 400–1000* takes a broader overview of the same subject.

★ **J.H. Elliott** *Imperial Spain 1469–1716*. Best introduction to the "Golden Age" – academically respected and a gripping tale.

★ **Richard Fletcher** *Moorish Spain*. A fascinating, provocative and highly readable narrative with a suitably iconoclastic conclusion to the history of Moorish Spain. The best introduction to the subject.

L.P. Harvey *Islamic Spain 1250–1500*. Comprehensive account of its period – both the Islamic kingdoms and the Muslims living beyond their protection.

Henry Kamen *The Spanish Inquisition: An Historical Revision; Philip of Spain; Spain's Road to Empire*. Kamen's 1965 *Inquisition* was a highly respected examination of the Inquisition and the long shadow it cast across Spanish history and development. *The Spanish Inquisition: An Historical Revision* returns to the subject in the light of more recent evidence, while *Philip of Spain* is the first full biography of Felipe II, the ruler most closely associated with the Inquisition. In *Empire*, Kamen skilfully dissects the conquest of the Americas and Philippines and concludes that the Spanish were ill-suited to the imperial role, displaying both organizational incompetence and little interest in the peoples they subjugated.

Elie Kedourie *Spain and the Jews: the Sephardi Experience, 1492 and after*. A collection of essays on the three-million-strong Spanish Jews of the Middle Ages and their expulsion by the Catholic monarchs.

John Lynch *Spain 1516–1598*. New interpretation of Spain's rise to empire with plenty of interesting detail on Andalucía's trading role – especially the cities of Seville and Cádiz – in the exploitation of the Americas. The same author's *Hispanic World in Crisis and Change 1598–1700* and *Bourbon Spain 1700–1808* carry the story forward to the critical crossroads that determined Spain's future for the ensuing century and a half.

Bernard F. Reilly *The Contest of Christian and Muslim Spain*. A fascinating and detailed study of the stresses and strains of the crucial tenth and eleventh centuries when Christians, Muslims and Jews were locked in a struggle for supremacy on one hand and survival on the other, by an acknowledged expert on the subject.

James Reston Jr *Dogs of God*. An alternative take on the Inquisition to Kamen's (see page 553) connecting it with the epic year 1492 and linking religious intolerance to the final defeat of the Moors in Spain and Columbus's sudden widening of the Spanish crown's sphere of influence.

THE TWENTIETH CENTURY

★ **Gerald Brenan** *The Spanish Labyrinth*. First published in 1943, Brenan's study of the social and political background to the Civil War is tinged by personal experience, yet still an impressively rounded account.

★ **Raymond Carr** *Modern Spain 1875–1980; The Spanish Tragedy: the Civil War in Perspective*. Two of the best books available on modern Spanish history – concise and well-told narratives.

★ **Ronald Fraser** *Blood of Spain; In Hiding; The Pueblo*. Subtitled *An Oral History of the Spanish Civil War. Blood of Spain* is an impressive – and brilliantly unorthodox – piece of research, constructed entirely of oral accounts. *In Hiding*

is a fascinating individual account of a Republican mayor of Mijas (in Málaga) hidden by his family for thirty years until the Civil War amnesty of 1969. *Pueblo* is a penetrating and compelling study of the trials and tribulations of one Costa del Sol mountain village seen through the eyes of its inhabitants which speaks for much of Andalucía today.

★ **Ian Gibson** *Federico García Lorca; The Assassination of Federico García Lorca; Lorca's Granada*. The biography is a gripping book and *The Assassination* a brilliant reconstruction of the events at the end of his life, with an examination of fascist corruption and of the shaping influences on Lorca, twentieth-century Spain and the Civil War. *Granada* explores Lorca's city by way of a collection of fascinating walks around the town.

★ **Paul Preston** *Concise History of the Spanish Civil War; Franco; The Spanish Holocaust*. A formidable expert on the period, Preston has succeeded in his attempt to provide a manageable guide to the Civil War labyrinth – with powerful illustrations. *Franco* is a penetrating – and monumental – biography of the dictator and his regime, which provides as clear a picture as any yet published of how he won the Civil War, survived in power so long, and what, to this day, was his significance. *Holocaust* relates the grisly story of the tens of thousands executed in the 1930s and 1940s during Franco's reign of terror, as well as the abuse of women and children.

★ **Hugh Thomas** *The Spanish Civil War*. This exhaustive thousand-page study is regarded (both in Spain and abroad) as the definitive history of the Civil War, but is not as accessible for the general reader as Preston's account (see page 554).

★ **Gamel Woolsey** *Málaga Burning* (Pythia Press, US); original title *Death's Other Kingdom* (Eland, UK). A long-ignored minor classic written in the late 1930s and reprinted (and retitled) by a US publisher in which the American poet and wife of Gerald Brenan vividly describes the horrors of the descent of their part of Andalucía into civil war. The Eland edition includes an interesting biographical afterword by Michael Jacobs.

ART AND ARCHITECTURE

Marianne Barrucand & Achim Bednoz *Moorish Architecture*. A beautifully illustrated guide to the major Moorish monuments.

Bernard Bevan *History of Spanish Architecture*. Classic study of Iberian and Ibero-American architecture which includes extensive coverage of the Mudéjar, Plateresque and Baroque periods.

★ **Titus Burckhardt** *Moorish Culture in Spain* (o/p). An outstanding book which opens up ways of looking at Spain's Islamic monuments, explaining their patterns and significance and the social environment in which, and for which, they were produced.

Godfrey Goodwin *Islamic Spain*. Architectural guide with

descriptions of virtually every significant Islamic building in Spain, and a fair amount of background.

★ **Michael Jacobs** *Alhambra*. If you've fallen under the Alhambra's spell then this sumptuously produced volume with outstanding photographs and expert commentary is the perfect book. It authoritatively guides you through the history and architecture of Andalucía's emblematic monument, placing it in its Islamic context, and concludes with a fascinating essay on the hold that the palace has had on later artists, travellers and writers from Irving and Ford to de Falla and Lorca.

David Talbot Rice *Islamic Art*. A classic introduction to the whole subject.

FICTION AND POETRY

SPANISH FICTION

Pedro de Alarcón *The Three-Cornered Hat and Other Stories* (o/p). Ironic nineteenth-century tales of the previous century's corruption, bureaucracy and absolutism by a writer born in Guadix. He also wrote *Alpujarra* (o/p), a not very well-observed tour through the Sierra Nevada.

Arturo Barea *The Forging of a Rebel.* Superb autobiographical trilogy, taking in the Spanish war in Morocco in the 1920s and Barea's own part in the Civil War in Andalucía and elsewhere. The books were published under the individual titles *The Forge*, *The Track* and *The Clash*.

★ **Miguel de Cervantes** *Don Quijote. Quijote* (or *Quixote*) is of course the classic of Spanish literature and remains an excellent and witty read, especially in J.M. Cohen's classic Penguin translation or a later version by Edith Grossman.

Juan Ramón Jiménez *Platero and I.* Andalucía's Nobel Prize-winning poet and writer from Moguer in Huelva paints a lyrically evocative picture of Andalucía and its people in conversations with his donkey, Platero.

Antonio Machado *Eighty Poems; Juan de Mairena* (o/p). The best-known works in English of this eminent *sevillano* poet and writer. The novel *Juan de Mairena* draws on his experience as a schoolteacher in Baeza.

★ **Arturo Pérez Reverte** *The Seville Communion.* An entertaining crime yarn by one of Spain's leading writers, involving a hacker in the Pope's computer, a stubborn old local priest up against rapacious bankers eager to bulldoze his church, a number of corpses, and an investigator dispatched by the Vatican. All is played out against the colourfully described backdrop of Seville. *The Dumas Club*, an engrossing tale about a bibliophile's search for a book on black magic, *The Fencing Master*, a political thriller set in nineteenth-century Spain, and *The Nautical Chart*, a search for treasure in a galleon sunk off the coast of Andalucía, are other translated works by Pérez Reverte. His most recent novel in translation, *The Siege*, is a murder mystery set in the city of Cádiz in 1811, during the Napoleonic siege.

SPANISH PLAYS AND POETRY

A.J. Arberry (trans.) *Moorish Poetry.* Excellent collection of Hispano-Arab verse.

Cola Franzen (trans.) *Poems of Arab Andalusia.* Sensitively rendered collection of verse by some of the best poets of Moorish al-Andalus.

Federico García Lorca *Five Plays: Comedies and Tragicomedies; Selected Poems; Poem of the Deep Song; Poet in New York.* Andalucía's great pre-Civil War playwright and poet. The first two volumes have his major theatrical works and poems, while *Deep Song* is a moving poetic paean to *cante jondo*, flamenco's blues, inspired by García Lorca's contact with *gitano* culture. Published posthumously, *Poet in New York* is a formidable collection of poems composed during a year studying at Columbia University. Arturo Barea's *Lorca: the Poet and his People* is also of interest.

San Juan de la Cruz *The Poetry of Saint John of the Cross.* Excellent translation by South African poet Roy Campbell of the poems of this mystical confessor to Teresa of Ávila who died at Úbeda.

FOREIGN FICTION

★ **Douglas Day** *Journey of the Wolf.* Outstanding first novel by an American writer, given the seal of approval by Graham Greene ("gripping and poignant"). The subject is a Civil War fighter, "El Lobo," who returns as a fugitive to Poqueira, his village in the Alpujarras, forty years on.

Ernest Hemingway *Fiesta/The Sun Also Rises; For Whom the Bell Tolls.* Hemingway remains a major element in the American myth of Spain. *Fiesta* contains some lyrically beautiful writing while *For Whom the Bell Tolls* – set in Civil War Andalucía – is considerably more laboured. He also published an enthusiastic and not very good account of bullfighting, *Death in the Afternoon.*

Amin Maalouf *Leo the African.* A wonderful historical novel, re-creating the life of Leo Africanus, the fifteenth-century Moorish geographer, in the last years of the kingdom of Granada, and on his subsequent exile in Morocco and world travels.

SPECIALIST GUIDES

★ **Phil Ball** *Morbo – The Story of Spanish Football.* Excellent account of Spanish football from its nineteenth-century beginnings with the British workers at the mines of Río Tinto to the golden years of Real Madrid and the dark days of Franco, with the ever-present backdrop of the ferocious *morbo* – political, historical, regional and linguistic rivalry – that has driven it since.

Christopher Turner *The Penguin Guide to Seville.* A set of interesting guided walks around Andalucía's capital city.

★ **Sandy Walker** *Campo – A Guide to the Spanish Countryside.* On one level a how-to book on planting and cultivating trees, on another a guide to almost every kind of fruit tree grown in Andalucía (where the author has her farm). All kinds of trees from almonds and olives to carobs and pomegranates are covered and there's fascinating detail on the history, local background, and the medicinal potential of each species – she even throws in the odd recipe.

HIKING, CLIMBING AND CYCLING

David & Ros Brawn *Sierra de Aracena* (Discovery, UK; ⓦ walking.demon.co.uk). Excellent walking guide to this magnificent Sierra by two experienced walkers. Covers 27 walks (from 3–14km) with an accompanying map (sold separately) and all routes are GPS waypointed.

Matt Butler *Holiday Walks from the Costa del Sol* (Sigma, UK; ⓦ sigmapress.co.uk). Holiday walks within reach of a Costa del Sol base, covering the coast from Cádiz province in the west to Granada province in the east. Free internet updates available.

Chris Craggs *Andalusian Rock Climbs*. Introductory guide to one of Andalucía's fastest-growing sports. Has descriptions of all the major climbs plus details of how to get there.

Charles Davis *Costa del Sol Walks* (Santana, Málaga). Well-written guide to 34 walks – between 4km and 8km – along the Costa del Sol between Nerja and Estepona; each walk has its own map. The same author's *Walk! The Axarquía* (Discovery, UK) is a reliable guide to this picturesque region, describing thirty walks between 5km and 22km, all GPS-waypointed. Davis has also published *34 Alpujarras Walks* (Discovery, UK) with a similar format detailing 34 GPS-waypointed treks between 4km and 25km. In both, each walk has its own map; there are also waterproof 1:40,000 *Axarquía/Alpujarras Tour and Trail* maps (sold separately) with all walks (and GPS points) marked.

Harry Dowdell *Cycle Touring in Spain*. Well-researched cycle touring guide which describes eight touring routes of varying difficulty in the north and south of Spain. Plenty of practical information on preparing your bike for the trip, transporting it and what to take.

★**Guy Hunter-Watts** *Walking in Andalucía*; *Coastal Walks in Andalucía*. Walking is a first-rate hiking guide to the natural parks of Grazalema, Cazorla, Los Alcornocales, Aracena and La Axarquía, as well as the Alpujarras and the Sierra Nevada, with 36 walks between 8km and 17km each with a colour map. *Coastal Walks* details forty hikes along the coast and its hinterland between Vejer and Almería. A new publisher has improved the maps and presentation of both books and the routes can be downloaded as a GPX file to a GPS device or smartphone.

★**John & Christine Oldfield** *Andalucía and the Costa del Sol*. This addition to the popular *Landscapes* walking guide series has 23 clearly described walks (with maps) ranging from 5km to 22km in Las Alpujarras, Sierra Nevada, Axarquía and Grazalema, as well as the areas bordering the Costa del Sol.

Jeremy Rabjohns *Holiday Walks in the Alpujarra* (Sigma, UK). Excellent walking guide by Alpujarras resident Rabjohns describing 24 walks between 3km and 22km in length with clear maps (including many village street maps) and background information. Free updates and corrections available online.

Kirstie Shirra & Michelle Lowe *Walking the GR7 in Andalucía*. A well-described guide to hiking the 450km-long GR7 from Tarifa to the fringes of the Cazorla Natural

Park in Jaén. Both the northern (via Cazorla) and southern (via Las Alpujarras) routes are covered, and there's plenty of background detail. The route can easily be broken up into shorter walks of a day's duration, taking a bus or taxi back to the start point.

Andy Walmsley *Walking in the Sierra Nevada* (Cicerone, UK). Forty-five walks of varying distance and difficulty from 3hr strolls to the seriously arduous *Tres Mils* (3000m-plus) peaks.

WILDLIFE

John R. Butler *Birdwatching on Spain's Southern Coast* (Santana, Málaga). A guide to the major – and many minor – birdwatching sites of Andalucía including the Costa de Almería, Costa de la Luz and the Doñana National Park. The author – who lives in Málaga and leads birdwatching tours – includes maps and the usual bird calendars as well as the highly unusual (and laudable) information concerning sites accessible (the vast majority are) to wheelchair-using and disabled birdwatchers.

Teresa Farino & Mike Lockwood *Travellers' Nature Guides: Spain*. Excellent illustrated wildlife guide to the peninsula by two Spanish-based experts; conveniently divided into regional groupings with detailed maps, it covers many of Andalucía's major habitats for spotting flora and fauna.

Ernest García & Andrew Paterson *Where to Watch Birds in Southern Spain*. A well-planned guide to birdwatching sites throughout Andalucía with location maps and reports detailing species to be seen according to season.

Frederic Grunfeld and Teresa Farino *Wild Spain*. A knowledgeable and practical guide to Spain's national parks, ecology and wildlife, with a section on Andalucía.

Oleg Polunin & Anthony Huxley *Flowers of the Mediterranean*. Useful if by no means exhaustive field guide.

Oleg Polunin & B.E. Smythies *Flowers of South-West Europe*. Covers all of Spain, Portugal and southwest France; the taxonomy is old, but still unsurpassed for its plates, line drawings and keys.

★**Svensson, Grant, Mullarney & Zetterstrom** *The Collins Bird Guide*. The best bird field guide yet published covers (and illustrates) the birds of Europe including almost everything you're likely to encounter in Spain.

FOOD AND WINE

★**Vicky Benninson** *A Taste of Place: Andalucía*. A cornucopia of a book covering all aspects of food and drink in Andalucía: what to buy, where to buy it, and what to do with it in the kitchen; plus – if you prefer to dine out – where to eat *andaluz* cuisine at its very best throughout the region.

Penelope Casas *The Foods and Wines of Spain*; *Tapas: the little dishes of Spain*. An excellent overview of classic Spanish and Andalucían cuisine, plus the same author's guide to the tapas labyrinth.

Marion Trutter *Culinaria Spain*. Part of the encyclopedic Culinaria series, this is a great book for winter evenings in front of the fire, with plenty of stunning photos of Spanish locations and loads of useful information on Iberian food and drink. There's a chapter devoted to Andalucía giving you the lowdown on everything from salmorejo and olive oil to tuna and jamón serrano.

★ **Alan Davidson** *The Tío Pepe Guide to the Seafood of Spain and Portugal*. An indispensable book that details and illustrates every fish and crustacean you're likely to meet in Andalucía. His *Mediterranean Seafood* is another classic.

★ **Julian Jeffs** *Sherry*. The story of sherry – history, production, blending and brands. Rightly a classic, and the best introduction to Andalucía's great wine now in a fully revised and updated sixth edition (older editions are still available for a song). The same author's *Wines of Spain* is an erudite guide to traditional and up-and-coming wine regions, with details of vineyards, grape varieties and vintages.

Jean Claude Juston *The New Spain – Vegan and Vegetarian Restaurants* (o/p). Useful guide to vegetarian and vegan restaurants throughout Spain by the ex-owner/ chef of a vegetarian restaurant in the Alpujarras. Each

listing has its own review and there's lots of background information on Spanish veggie websites and magazines plus details of animal-friendly organizations.

Elisabeth Luard *The La Ina Book of Tapas*; *Flavours of Andalucía*. The first is the bible for all classic tapas recipes, while the *Flavours of Andalucía* parades the major dishes of the region province by province.

Simone Ortega *Spain: The Cookbook*. English translation of the Spanish Cookery classic 1080 Recetas. Covering the whole gamut of Spanish regional cooking in over a thousand clear, concise recipes, this is a Spanish Mrs Beeton without the starchy, Victorian prose style.

John Radford *The New Spain*; *The Wines of Rioja*. The lavish coffee-table format disguises *New Spain*'s serious content: a detailed region-by-region guide to Spanish wine with colour maps, bodega and vintage evaluations and fine illustrations. *Wines of Rioja* is a comprehensive survey of the wines and producers in this emblematic Spanish wine region.

★ **Paul Richardson** *Late Dinner*. A joyous dissection of the food of Spain, region by region, season by season, nibble of ham by shoot of asparagus. A celebration of culture and cuisine, this is the best general introduction to what Spanish food – and life – is really all about.

LEARNING SPANISH

Assimil Spanish (🌐 bit.ly/AssimilSpanish). An ingenious language learning method developed by Assimil almost 90 years ago. The books are now up-to-date and use dialogues and exercises to help you learn by "intuitive assimilation" (hence the name). It uses a two-wave system (the first passive the second active) to get you to intermediate level. If you're new to the language you'll probably need the CDs or MP3 CD as well, to assist with pronunciation and accent.

★ **Collins Spanish Dictionary** Recognized as the best single-volume bookshelf dictionary. It's regularly revised and updated, so make sure you get the latest edition.

Duolingo This app for smart phone or computer is the best free way to learn a language, and ranks right up there with paid for methods as well. Spanish is well covered, with extra content, but is best used alongside some traditional grammar study as well.

Hugo's Spanish in Three Months One of the best of the

CD- and book-linked home-study courses, which aims to give you reasonable fluency within three months. The same series also has an advanced course.

Untza Otaola Alday *Colloquial Spanish*. Excellent book-based beginner's course (supporting CDs are sold separately) with well-structured lessons and exercises. *Colloquial Spanish 2* takes you to the next level.

Rough Guide Spanish Dictionary Good pocket-sized dictionary that should help with most travel situations.

Michel Thomas Method *Foundation Course and Advanced Spanish*. The revolutionary "100 percent audio" CD-based learning system devised by the late polyglot Thomas has been praised by many learners (including Woody Allen and Emma Thompson) who have struggled with the more traditional "grammar grind" methods. It also has an advanced course.

LIVING IN SPAIN

David Hampshire *Living and Working in Spain* (Survival Books, UK; 🌐 survivalbooks.net). An information-packed comprehensive guide to moving to, and setting up home or working in, Spain. It's now in need of an update, but much information is still valid.

Guy Hobbs & Heleina Postings *Live and Work in Spain and Portugal* (Vacation Work, UK). Well-researched handbook full of useful information on moving to the peninsula, buying property, seeking work, starting a

business, finding schools and lots more.

David Searl *You and the Law in Spain*. Invaluable, lucid and comprehensive guide to the Spanish legal and tax system and an essential read if you are thinking of buying property, working or setting up a business in Spain. Sadly, it has ceased publication and the 24th updated edition (2015) was the last in the series. However, it's still worth getting hold of to help you traverse the minefield of the Spanish legal system.

Spanish

Once you get started, Spanish is among the easiest languages to get a grip on. English is spoken, but only in the main tourist areas to any extent, and wherever you are you'll get a far better reception if you at least try communicating with Spaniards in their own tongue. Being understood, of course, is only half the problem – getting the gist of the reply, often rattled out at a furious pace, may prove far more difficult.

The list of essential words and phrases that follows should be enough to get you started. If you're using a dictionary, bear in mind that in Spanish CH, LL, and Ñ count as separate letters and are listed after C, L, and N respectively. There is a list of recommended books and CDs on learning Spanish in the "Books" section of this Guide (see page 551).

PRONUNCIATION

The rules of *pronunciation* are pretty straightforward and, once you get to know them, strictly observed. Unless there's an accent, words ending in d, l, r, and z are stressed on the last syllable, all others on the second last. All *vowels* are pure and short; combinations have predictable results.

A somewhere between the A sound of back and that of father

E as in get

I as in police

O as in hot

U as in rule

C in Castilian (standard Spanish) is lisped before E and I, hard otherwise: *cerca* is pronounced "thairka". However, many parts of Andalucía pronounce as an "s" – "sairka" or even "Andalusia".

G works the same way, a guttural H sound (like the ch in loch) before E or I, a hard G elsewhere – *gigante* becomes "higante".

H is always silent

J the same sound as a guttural G: *jamón* is pronounced "hamon".

LL sounds like an English Y or LY: *tortilla* is pronounced "torteeya/torteelya".

N is as in English unless it has a tilde (accent) over it, when it becomes NY: *mañana* sounds like "manyana".

QU is pronounced like an English K.

R is rolled, RR doubly so.

V sounds more like B, *vino* becoming "beano".

X has an S sound before consonants, normal X before vowels.

Z (in *castellano*) is the same as a soft C, so *cerveza* becomes "thairvaitha", but again much of Andalucía prefers the "s" sound – "sairvaisa".

USEFUL WORDS AND PHRASES

BASICS

Yes, No, OK Sí, No, Vale
Please, Thank you Por favor, Gracias
Where, When? ¿Dónde, Cuando?
What, How much? ¿Qué, Cuánto?
Here, There Aquí, Allí
This, That Esto, Eso
Now, Later Ahora, Más tarde
Open, Closed Abierto/a, Cerrado/a
With, Without Con, Sin
Good, Bad Buen(o)/a, Mal(o)/a
Big, Small Gran(de), Pequeño/a
Cheap, Expensive Barato, Caro
Hot, Cold Caliente, Frío
More, Less Más, Menos
Today, Tomorrow Hoy, Mañana
Yesterday Ayer

GREETINGS AND RESPONSES

Hello, Goodbye Hola, Adiós
Good morning Buenos días
Good afternoon/night Buenas tardes/noches
See you later Hasta luego
Sorry Lo siento/discúlpeme
Excuse me Con permiso/perdón
How are you? ¿Como está (usted)?
I (don't) understand (No) Entiendo
Not at all/You're welcome De nada

Do you speak English? ¿Habla (usted) inglés?
I don't speak Spanish No hablo español
My name is ... Me llamo ...
What's your name? ¿Como se llama (usted)?
I am English Soy inglés(a)
...Australian australiano(a)
...Canadian canadiense(a)
...American americano(a)
...Irish irlandés(a)

HOTELS AND TRANSPORT

I want Quiero
I'd like Quisiera
Do you know ...? ¿Sabe ...?
I don't know No sé
There is (is there)? (¿)Hay(?)
Give me ... (one like that) Deme ...(uno así)
Do you have ...? ¿Tiene ...?
the time la hora
a room una habitación
... with two beds/double bed ... con dos camas/cama matrimonial
... with shower/bath ... con ducha/baño
It's for one person/two people Es para una persona/ dos personas
It's for one night/one week Es para una noche/una semana
It's fine, how much is it? ¿Está bien, cuánto es?
It's too expensive Es demasiado caro
Don't you have anything cheaper? ¿No tiene algo más barato?
Can one ...?...camp (near) here? ¿Se puede ...?...¿acampar aquí (cerca)?
Is there a hostel nearby? ¿Hay un hostal aquí cerca?
How do I get to ...? ¿Por dónde se va a ...?
Left, right, straight on Izquierda, derecha, todo recto
Where is ...? ¿Dónde está ...?
... the bus station ... la estación de autobuses
... the train station ... la estación de tren
... the nearest bank ... el banco más cercano
... the post office ...the toilet ... el correos/ la oficina de correos...el baño/aseo/servicios
Where does the bus to ... leave from? ¿De dónde sale el autobús para ...?
Is this the train for Seville? ¿Es este el tren para Sevilla?
I'd like a (return) ticket to ... Quisiera un billete (de ida y vuelta) para ...
What time does it leave (arrive in ...)? ¿A qué hora sale (llega a ...)?
What is there to eat? ¿Qué hay para comer?
What's that? ¿Qué es eso?

What's this called in Spanish? ¿Como se llama éste en español?

NUMBERS AND DAYS

one un/uno/una
two dos
three tres
four cuatro
five cinco
six seis
seven siete
eight ocho
nine nueve
ten diez
eleven once
twelve doce
thirteen trece
fourteen catorce
fifteen quince
sixteen diez y seis
twenty veinte
twenty-one veintiuno
thirty treinta
forty cuarenta
fifty cincuenta
sixty sesenta
seventy setenta
eighty ochenta
ninety noventa
one hundred cien(to)
one hundred and one ciento uno
two hundred doscientos
two hundred and one doscientos uno
five hundred quinientos
one thousand mil
two thousand dos mil
two thousand and one dos mil uno
two thousand and two dos mil dos
first primero/a
second segundo/a
third tercero/a
fifth quinto/a
tenth décimo/a
Monday lunes
Tuesday martes
Wednesday miércoles
Thursday jueves
Friday viernes
Saturday sábado
Sunday domingo

FOOD AND DRINK

"Quisiera uno así" ("I'd like one like that") can be an amazingly useful phrase.

BASICS

Aceite Oil
Ajo Garlic
Arroz Rice
Azúcar Sugar
Fruta Fruit
Huevos Eggs
Mantequilla Butter
Pan Bread
Pimienta Pepper
Queso Cheese
Sal Salt
Verduras/Legumbres Vegetables
Vinagre Vinegar

RESTAURANT TERMS

Almuerzo Lunch
Botella Bottle
Menú Set meal
La carta Menu
Cena Dinner
Cubierto Set of cutlery
Cuchara Spoon
Cuchillo Knife
La cuenta The bill
Desayuno Breakfast
Mesa Table
Tenedor Fork
Vaso Glass

MENU TERMS

a la brasa (charcoal-) grilled
a la gallego/a Galician style
a la navarra stuffed with ham
a la parilla/plancha grilled
a la romana fried in batter
a la rondeña Ronda style
a la sal baked in a salt crust
al ajillo in garlic
al horno baked
alioli with mayonnaise
asado roast
cazuela, cocido stew
cocina casera home-made
en salsa in (usually tomato) sauce
escabeche/escabechado pickled or marinated
frito fried
guisado casserole
ibérico superior meat from Spanish black pigs
rehogado baked

SOUPS (*SOPAS*) AND STARTERS (*ENTREMESES*)

Ajo blanco Creamy tomato-free "gazpacho" with garlic and almonds
Caldillo Clear fish soup
Caldo verde/gallego Thick, cabbage-based broth
Gazpacho Chilled tomato, peppers and garlic soup
Migas Fried breadcrumbs
Sopa de cocido Meat soup
Sopa de gallina Chicken soup
Sopa de mariscos Seafood soup
Sopa de pasta Noodle soup (*fideos*)
Sopa de pescado Fish soup
Sopa de picadillo Chicken and vegetable broth garnished with egg

SALAD (*ENSALADA*)

Ensalada (mixta/verde) (Mixed/green) salad
Pimientos rellenos Stuffed peppers
Verduras con patatas Boiled potatoes with greens

FISH (*PESCADOS*)

Anchoas Anchovies (tinned)
Anguila Eel
Angulas Elvers (baby eel)
Atún Tuna
Bacalao Cod (often salt)
Besugo/Pargo Red bream
Bonito Tuna
Boquerones Anchovies (fresh)
Chanquetes Whitebait
Dorada Gilthead bream
Lenguado Sole
Lubina Sea bass
Merluza Hake
Mero Grouper
Mojama Salted blue-fin tuna
Pescadilla Small whiting
Pez espada Swordfish
Pulpo Octopus
Rape Monkfish
Rodaballo Turbot
Salmón Salmon
Salmonete Mullet
Sardinas Sardines
Trucha Trout
Urta Member of the bream family

SHELLFISH (*MARISCOS*)

Almejas Clams
Calamares Squid
Cangrejo Crab
Centollo Spider crab
Chipirones Small squid

Cigalas King prawns
Conchas finas Large scallops
Erizo de mar Sea urchin
Gambas Prawns/shrimps
Langosta Lobster
Langostinos Giant king prawns
Mejillones Mussels
Ostras Oysters
Percebes Goose barnacles
Puntillitas Baby squid
Sepia Cuttlefish
Vieiras/Conchas Scallops
Zamburiñas Baby clams

MEAT (*CARNE*) AND POULTRY (*AVES*)

Albóndigas Meatballs
Cabra Goat
Callos Tripe
Carne de vaca Beef
Cerdo Pork
Cerdo Ibérico Black pig pork
Chorizo Spicy sausage
Choto/Cabrito Kid
Chuletas Chops
Ciervo/Venado Deer/venison
Cochinillo Suckling pig
Codorniz Quail
Conejo Rabbit
Cordero Lamb
Criadillas Testicles
Escalopa Escalope
Faisán Pheasant
Hamburguesa Hamburger
Hígado Liver
Jabalí Wild boar
Lengua Tongue
Lomo Loin (of pork)
Mollejas Sweetbreads
Morcilla Blood sausage
Pato Duck
Pavo Turkey
Perdiz Partridge
Pollo Chicken
Rabo de toro Stewed bull's tail
Riñones Kidneys
Salchicha Sausage
Salchichón Cured salami-type sausage
Sesos Brains
Solomillo Pork tenderloin
Ternera Veal

VEGETABLES (*LEGUMBRES*)

Aguacate Avocado
Ajo Garlic

Alcachofas Artichokes
Berenjena Aubergine/eggplant
Calabaza Pumpkin
Cebollas Onions
Champiñones/Setas Mushrooms
Coliflor Cauliflower
Espárragos Asparagus
Espinacas Spinach
Garbanzos Chickpeas
Guisantes Peas
Habas Broad beans
Judías blancas Haricot beans
Judías verdes/negras rojas/ Green, red, black beans
Lechuga Lettuce
Lentejas Lentils
Nabos Turnips
Palmitos Palm hearts
Patatas (fritas) Potatoes (chips/ french fries)
Pepino Cucumber
Pimientos Peppers
Puerros Leeks
Repollo Cabbage
Setas Mushrooms
Tomate Tomato
Zanahoria Carrot

RICE DISHES

Arroz a banda Rice with seafood, the rice served
  separately
Arroz a la cubana Rice with fried egg and home-made
  tomato sauce
Arroz a la marinera Paella: rice with seafood and
  saffron
Arroz negro "Black rice", cooked with squid ink
Paella a la catalana Mixed meat and/or seafood rice
  dish; sometimes distinguished from a seafood paella
  by being called *paella a la valenciana*

DESSERTS (*POSTRES*)

Alfajores Honey and almond pastries
Arroz con leche Rice pudding
Crema catalana Crème brûlée
Dulces Tarts or cakes
Flan Crème caramel
Helado Ice cream
Melocotón en almíbar Peaches in syrup
Miel Honey
Nata Whipped cream (topping)
Natillas Custard
Pastel Cake or pudding
Peras al vino Pears cooked in wine
Pestiños Anís or wine fritters
Polvorones Almond cakes
Pudín Pudding

Tarta de Santiago Pastry tart with almond filling
Tocino de cielo Andalucía's rich crème caramel
Yemas Egg-yolk cakes
Yogur Yogurt

FRUIT (*FRUTAS*)

Albaricoques Apricots
Almendras Almonds
Castañas Chestnuts
Cerezas Cherries
Chirimoyas Custard apples
Chumbo Prickly pear
Ciruelas Plums, prunes
Dátiles Dates
Fresas Strawberries
Granada Pomegranate
Higos Figs
Limón Lemon
Manzanas Apples
Melocotón Peach
Melón Melon
Membrillo Quince
Naranjas Oranges
Nectarinas Nectarines
Pera Pear
Piña Pineapple
Plátanos Bananas
Pomelo Grapefruit
Sandía Watermelon
Uvas Grapes

TAPAS AND SNACKS

Aceitunas Olives
Albóndigas Meatballs, usually in sauce
Anchoas Anchovies (canned)
Banderilla *Tapa* on a cocktail stick
Berberechos Cockles
Boquerones Fresh anchovies
Calamares a la romana Squid, deep fried in rings
Calamares en su tinta Squid in ink
Callos Tripe
Caracoles Snails, often served in a spicy/curry sauce
Caracolas Whelks
Carne en salsa Meat in tomato sauce
Cazón en adobo Marinated and deep-fried dogfish
Champiñones Mushrooms, usually fried in garlic
Chipirones Whole baby squid
Chorizo Spicy sausage
Cocido Stew
Costillas Spare ribs
Croqueta Croquette filled with fish, meat or vegetables
Empanadilla Fish/meat pasty
Ensalada malagueña Málaga salad with salt-cod,
  oranges and potato

Ensaladilla Russian salad (diced vegetables in
  mayonnaise)
Escalibada Aubergine (eggplant) and pepper salad
Espinacas con garbanzos Spinach with chickpeas
Flamenquines Ham or veal in breadcrumbs, deep fried
Gambas (al ajillo) Shrimps (fried with garlic)
Habas con jamón Broad beans with ham
Hígado Liver
Huevo cocido Hard-boiled egg
Jamón ibérico Top-quality black pig mountain-cured
  ham
Jamón serrano Mountain- (or factory-) cured ham from
  white pigs
Jamón York Regular ham
Judías Beans
Mejillones Mussels (either steamed, or served with
  diced tomatoes and onion)
Montadito *Tapa* served on bread
Morcilla Blood sausage (black pudding)
Navajas Razor clams
Pan con tomate Bread, rubbed with tomato and oil
Patatas alioli Potatoes in garlic mayonnaise
Patatas/Papas a lo pobre Potatoes cooked with
  onions, garlic and parsley
Patatas bravas Fried potato cubes topped with spicy
  sauce and mayonnaise
Pimientos Peppers
Pincho moruno Kebab
Pulpo Octopus
Puntillitas Deep-fried baby squid
Revuelto Scrambled eggs
Riñones al Jerez Kidneys in sherry
Salchichón Cured sausage
Sardinas Sardines
Sepia Cuttlefish
Tabla *Tapa* served on a wooden board
Tortilla de camarones Fritters with small prawns
Tortilla española Potato omelette
Tortilla francesa Plain omelette

DRINKS

Café Coffee
Café solo Espresso coffee
Café con leche White coffee
Descafeinado Decaff
Té Tea
Chocolate Drinking chocolate
Agua Water
Agua mineral Mineral water
... (con gas) ... (sparkling)
...(sin gas) ... (still)
Leche Milk
Limonada Lemonade
Zumo Juice

Horchata Tiger-nut drink

ALCOHOL
Anís Aniseed liqueur
Brandy Coñac/brandy
Cerveza Beer

Champán Champagne
Fino (de Jerez) Sherry
Manzanilla Fino from Sanlúcar
Pacháran Sloes-based liqueur
Ron Rum
Vino Wine

GLOSSARY

Acequia irrigation channel.

Alameda park or tree-lined promenade.

Albariza type of soil in wine-growing zones with high chalk content enabling retention of moisture.

Alcalde mayor of town or village.

Alcazaba Moorish castle.

Alcázar Moorish fortified palace.

Almohads Muslims originally of Berber stock, who toppled the Almoravids and ruled Spain in the late twelfth and early thirteenth centuries.

Almoravids fanatical Berber dynasty from the Sahara who ruled much of Spain in the eleventh and twelfth centuries.

Artesonado wooden coffered ceiling of Moorish origin or inspiration.

Atalaya watchtower.

Autovía/autopista dual carriageway, highway, motorway or expressway.

Ayuntamiento town hall (also Casa Consistorial).

Azulejos glazed ceramic tiles (originally blue – hence the name).

Balneario spa.

Barrio suburb or quarter.

Bodega cellar, wine bar or warehouse.

Bracero landless agricultural worker.

Calle street.

Camarín shrine (located inside a church) with a venerated image.

Campiña flat stretch of farmland or countryside.

Cante jondo deeply felt flamenco song.

Capilla mayor chapel containing the high altar.

Capilla real royal chapel.

Carmen Granada villa with garden.

Carretera highway or main road.

Cartuja Carthusian monastery.

Casa forestal woodland hunters' house/hotel.

Casa rural rural guesthouse or villa for rent.

Casa señorial/palacio aristocratic mansion.

Casco antiguo the old part of a town or city.

Casino social and gaming club.

Castillo castle.

Centro comercial shopping centre/mall.

Chiringuito beachfront restaurant.

Churrigueresque extreme form of Baroque art named after José Churriguera (1665–1725) and his extended family, its main exponents.

Ciudad town or city.

Ciudadela citadel.

Colegiata collegiate (large parish) church.

POLITICAL PARTIES AND ACRONYMS

Ciudadanos (Citizens) National centre-right party led by Albert Rivera, currently supporting the minority PSOE regional government in Andalucía.

ETA Basque militant group.

Falange Franco's old Fascist party; now officially defunct although a number of minor political groupings still use the name for their internet ravings.

Fuerza Nueva Descendants of the above, also on the way out but also with a presence on the internet.

IU Izquierda Unida Broad-left alliance of Communists and others.

OTAN NATO.

PA Partido Andalucista The Andalucían Nationalist Party.

PCE Partido Comunista de España (Spanish Communist Party). Now defunct.

Podemos New left-wing political party founded by Pablo Iglesias in 2014 which won 45 seats in the 2016 national election to the Cortes.

PP Partido Popular Right-wing party, previously led by former Prime Minister, Mariano Rajoy.

PSOE Partido Socialista Obrero Español The Spanish Socialist Workers' Party. Led by Pedro Sánchez and currently the main opposition party in the Cortes.

UGT Unión General de Trabajadores Spain's most powerful trade union.

Comunidad autónoma autonomous region with significant powers of self-government.

Convento monastery or convent.

Converso Jew who converted to Christianity.

Copa/copas alcoholic drink(s).

Coro central part of church built for the choir.

Coro alto raised choir, often above west door of a church.

Corral type of patio or yard.

Correos post office.

Corrida de toros bullfight.

Cortes Spanish parliament in Madrid.

Cortijo rural farmhouse in Andalucía.

Coto de caza hunting reserve.

Cuesta slope/hill.

Cueva cave.

Custodia large receptacle or monstrance for Eucharist wafers.

Desamortización (disentailment) nineteenth-century expropriation of church buildings and lands.

Duende to have soul (in flamenco).

Embalse artificial lake, reservoir or dam.

Ermita hermitage.

Esparto grass used for mats, window blinds and olive presses.

Feria annual fair.

Finca farm.

Fogón stove.

Gitano gypsy.

Huerta vegetable garden.

Isabelline ornamental form of late Gothic developed during the reign of Isabel and Fernando.

Jarra wine jug or pitcher.

Jornalero landless agricultural day-labourer.

Judería Jewish quarter.

Juerga (gypsy) shindig.

Junta de Andalucía government of the Autonomous Region of Andalucía.

Latifundio large estate.

Locutorio telephone office.

Lonja stock exchange building.

Marismas marshes.

Matanza pig slaughter.

Medina Moorish town.

Mercado market.

Mesón traditional restaurant or inn.

Mezquita mosque.

Mihrab prayer niche of Moorish mosque facing towards Mecca.

Mirador viewing point.

Monasterio monastery or convent.

Morisco Muslim Spaniard subject to medieval Christian rule – and nominally baptized.

Movida the (nightlife) scene; where the action is.

Mozárabe Christian subject to medieval Moorish rule; normally allowed freedom of worship.

Mozarabic the architectural style evolved by Christians under Arab domination.

Mudéjar Muslim Spaniard subject to medieval Christian rule, but retaining Islamic worship; most commonly a term applied to architecture which includes buildings built by Moorish craftsmen for the Christian rulers and later designs influenced by the Moors. The 1890s–1930s saw a Mudéjar revival, blended with Art Nouveau and Art Deco forms.

Palacio aristocratic mansion.

Panadería bakery.

Pantano reservoir held by a dam.

Parador luxury state-run hotel, often converted from minor monument.

Parroquia parish church.

Paseo promenade; also the evening stroll thereon.

Paso float bearing tableau that is carried in Semana Santa processions.

Patio inner courtyard.

Piscina swimming pool.

Plateresco/Plateresque elaborately decorative Renaissance style. The sixteenth-century successor of Isabelline forms named for its resemblance to silversmiths' work (*platería*).

Playa beach.

Plaza square.

Plaza de toros bullring.

Plaza mayor a town or city's main square regardless of its name.

Posada old name for an inn.

Pueblo village or town.

Puerta gateway, also mountain pass.

Puerto port.

Rambla dry riverbed.

Reconquista the Christian reconquest of Moorish Spain.

Reja iron screen or grille, often fronting a window or guarding a chapel.

Retablo carved or painted altarpiece.

Río river.

Rociero adhering to the traditions of the El Rocío pilgrimage.

Rococo late-Baroque style with a profusion of rock-like forms, scrolls and crimped shells. From the French *rocaille* – "rockwork".

Romería religious procession to a rural shrine.

Sacristía, sagrario sacristy or sanctuary of a church.

Sacristía (ii) wine cellar in sherry bodega.

Saeta passionate flamenco song in praise of the Virgin and Christ.

Sagrario tabernacle or side chapel.

Sebka decorative brickwork developed by the Almohads (eg, Giralda).

Semana Santa Holy Week, celebrated throughout Andalucía (and Spain) with elaborate processions.

Señoritismo behaving in a condescending manner; generally applied to rich landowners.

Sevillana rhythmic flamenco dance.

Sierra mountain range.

Sillería choir stall.

Solar aristocratic town mansion.

Solera blending system for sherry and brandy.

Tablao flamenco show.

Taifa small Moorish kingdom, many of which emerged after the disintegration of the Córdoba caliphate.

Tajo gorge.

Tetería Arabic tearoom.

Torno dumbwaiter used by convents to sell their cakes and pastries.

Trascoro end-wall of the choir.

Urbanización residential housing estate.

Vega cultivated fertile plain.

Venta roadside inn.

Yeso/yesería plaster/plasterwork.

Small print and index

A ROUGH GUIDE TO ROUGH GUIDES

Published in 1982, the first Rough Guide – to Greece – was a student scheme that became a publishing phenomenon. Mark Ellingham, a recent graduate in English from Bristol University, had been travelling in Greece the previous summer and couldn't find the right guidebook. With a small group of friends he wrote his own guide, combining a contemporary, journalistic style with a thoroughly practical approach to travellers' needs.

The immediate success of the book spawned a series that rapidly covered dozens of destinations. And, in addition to impecunious backpackers, Rough Guides soon acquired a much broader readership that relished the guides' wit and inquisitiveness as much as their enthusiastic, critical approach and value-for-money ethos. These days, Rough Guides include recommendations from budget to luxury and cover more than 120 destinations around the globe, from Amsterdam to Zanzibar, all regularly updated by our team of roaming writers.

Browse all our latest guides, read inspirational features and book your trip at **roughguides.com**.

Rough Guide credits

Editors: Tim Binks, Kate Drynan
Cartography: Carte
Picture editor: Piotr Kala

Layout: Pradeep Thapliyal
Head of DTP and Pre-Press: Katie Bennett
Head of Publishing: Kate Drynan

Publishing information

Tenth Edition 2023

Distribution

UK, Ireland and Europe
Apa Publications (UK) Ltd; sales@roughguides.com
United States and Canada
Ingram Publisher Services; ips@ingramcontent.com
Australia and New Zealand
Booktopia; retailer@ booktopia.com.au
Worldwide
Apa Publications (UK) Ltd; sales@roughguides.com

Special Sales, Content Licensing and CoPublishing
Rough Guides can be purchased in bulk quantities
at discounted prices. We can create special editions,
personalised jackets and corporate imprints tailored to
your needs. sales@roughguides.com.
roughguides.com

Printed in Turkey
All rights reserved
© Geoff Garvey, 2023

Maps © 2023 Apa Digital AG
License edition © Apa Publications Ltd UK

This book was produced using **Typefi** automated
publishing software.

Help us update

We've gone to a lot of effort to ensure that this edition of
The Rough Guide to Andalucía is accurate and up-to-
date. However, things change – places get "discovered",
opening hours are notoriously fickle, restaurants and
rooms raise prices or lower standards. If you feel we've got
it wrong or left something out, we'd like to know, and if
you can remember the address, the price, the hours, the
phone number, so much the better.

Please send your comments with the subject
line "**Rough Guide Andalucía Update**" to mail@
uk.roughguides.com. We'll credit all contributions and
send a copy of the next edition (or any other Rough Guide
if you prefer) for the very best emails.

Acknowledgements

A big thank you to all the wonderful hotels, guest houses restaurants and establishments that are featured in this guide
and all the knowledgeable and helpful people we have met on our travels that have helped make this guide, we wouldn't
be able to do it without you.

ABOUT THE AUTHORS

Marc Di Duca has been a full time travel author for the last two decades, covering regions as
diverse as the Caribbean and Siberia for all major travel publishers. When not on the road, he
lives near Mariánské Lázně in the Czech Republic with his wife and two sons.

Tim Hannigan Spain was the first foreign country that Tim Hannigan visited, at the age of
16, and it made a lasting impression. He has travelled widely since then, and has worked on
guidebooks for Rough Guides, Insight Guides, DK Eyewitness and Tuttle, covering diverse
destinations ranging from China to Cornwall. But he is still drawn back repeatedly to southern
Spain. He also studies travel writing as an academic, and is the author of *The Travel Writing Tribe*
and several narrative history books.

Photo credits

(Key: T-top; C-centre; B-bottom; L-left; R-right)

All images **Shutterstock**

Cover: Frigiliana town, Málaga **Botond Horvath/Shutterstock**

Index

Map symbols

The symbols below are used on maps throughout the book

▬▬ ▪	International boundary	✈	Airport	⊤	Fountain	▲	Mountain peak
▬▬ ▪	Province boundary	Ⓜ	Metro stop	☀	Lighthouse	◠	Cave
▬▬	Motorway	Ⓣ	Tram stop	☼	Viewpont	⚲	Skiing
═══	Road	Ⓟ	Parking	♙	Castle	> <	Pass
═══	Pedestrian road	✉	Post office	⌂	Mosque	☽	Sand dunes
— —	Ferry	ⓘ	Information office	♁	Monastery	▨	Building
- - - -	Footpath	⊞	Hospital	✡	Synagogue	⊣	Church
▬▬	Wall	©	Telephone office	∴	Ruins	▦	Park
▬▬▪	Rail line	@	Internet access	⊠	Entrance gate	▭	Beach
- - - -	Cable car	♦	Place of interest	⌂	Mountain range	⌐	Cemetery

Listings key

- ■ Accommodation
- ● Eating
- ■ Drinking/nightlife
- ● Shopping